The HUTCHINSON

ENCYCLOPEDIA OF

MODERN

POLITICAL

BIOGRAPHY

The HUTCHINSON
ENCYCLOPEDIA OF
MODERN
POLITICAL
BIOGRAPHY

Westview Press
A Member of the Perseus Books Group

Britain in 1999 by

Printed and bound by
De Agostini, Novara, Italy

No part of this publication may be reproduced or transmitted in any
form or by any means, electronic or mechanical, including photocopy,
recording, or any information storage and retrieval system, without
permission in writing from the publisher.

Published in 1999 in the United States of America by Westview Press,
5500 Central Avenue, Boulder, Colorado 80301-2877, and in the United
Kingdom by Westview Press, 12 Hid's Copse Road, Cumnor Hill, Oxford
OX2 9JJ

A CIP catalog record is available from the Library of Congress.
ISBN 0-8133-3741-0

The paper used in this publication meets the requirements of the
American National Standard for Permanence of Paper for Printed
Library Materials Z39.48-1984.

10 9 8 7 6 5 4 3 2 1

Contents

Preface

The domain of what we regard as political tended to broaden in the 20th century, as the franchise itself broadened in those countries with representative political systems. The right to vote was complemented by the right to be heard, to know, to inquire, to question, to hold to increasingly close account – until at the end of the century, the politicians in wealthy democracies were spending huge amounts of time and money trying to find out what their electorates wanted, then seeking to give it to them in some form.

As we have broadened our conception of the political space, so we have broadened our definition of political actors. Outside of the ranks of parliamentarians and local councillors, few people in public life are seen as outside of the political process – even if they are not necessarily counted within the party political arena. Trade unionists and business people, environmentalists and feminists, civil servants and human-rights activists, farmers and fishermen, professionals, and even the 'underclass', or the poor, now pursue their public agendas in a way designed to influence the political process – usually by making a mark on the media. Journalists and TV producers themselves are thus inevitably part of that process – even where they strictly observe the vows of political neutrality.

And as the political space has widened, so also has geographical space. Even before we entered the era in which globalization became the most widely debated issue in world affairs, we became conscious that no country could wall itself off from world economic and political developments and that our worlds were constructed increasingly by international, rather than national, forces. Thus a biographical encyclopedia of the 20th century must go very wide indeed, if it is to be comprehensive; it must include in its coverage monarchs other than our own (including some who rule as well as reign, such as the ruling houses of some Arab states); dictators of states whose leadership is not settled by election; presidents and prime ministers of nations where they are; military leaders in those countries where the armed forces provide the leadership; as well as the main characters in that unique institution of increasing importance to us, the European Union.

We confine ourselves to the 20th century; though the confines of that for a political encyclopedia are very wide. More people have involved themselves in politics, defining that as broadly as we do, than in all the centuries before ours put together. The 20th century has been called the century of the common man and woman; and though it excludes many millions because of poverty and lack of political power, it is also the first century in which we can treat the world as a political unit in embryo, and see the need to include larger and larger numbers into a global polity so that we may contain the pressures of demography and dwindling resources.

The Encyclopedia has been designed to be as up-to-date and accurate as possible, so that it truly is a snapshot of the leading men and women in the world at the end of the millennium. All of the contributors are experts in their fields – but all welcome comments, corrections, and additions from our readers.

Three features mark out this Encyclopedia from other similar works in the field:

- first, we provide lists of further reading for those readers who want to take a closer interest in any of the subjects listed here;
- second, we provide a unique country-by-country index, so that the biographical subjects are identified by state as well as by name;
- third, we include a chronological index by year of birth, so that you easily see the entry of famous men and women onto the field of history.

The Encyclopedia is written with care for information and enjoyment – and to help you chart a way through the complexities and storms of the 20th century.

JOHN LLOYD
Fellow, St Antony's College, Oxford,
and Senior Writer at the Financial Times

Contributors and Advisers

Ahmed Aghrout, *University of Salford*

Dr Lawrence Black, *London Guildhall University*

Dr Andrew Colquhoun, *Freelance Writer*

Professor John Crump, *University of Stirling*

Rachel Cutler, *University College, London*

Dr J Denis Derbyshire, *Consultant in Political Science*

Dr Ian Derbyshire, *Consultant in Political Science*

Professor Lord Desai, *London School of Economics*

Dr Martin Doherty, *University of Westminster*

Dr Nina Fishman, *University of Westminster*

Dr Elizabeth Hallett, *Freelance Writer*

Professor Rick Halpern, *University College, London*

Dr Chris Holdsworth, *Freelance Writer*

Dr Stuart Jones, *University of Manchester*

Professor Tony Kirk-Greene, *St Antony's College, Oxford*

John Lloyd, *Fellow, St Antony's College, Oxford, and Senior Writer at the Financial Times*

Dr Jill Lovecy, *University of Manchester*

Dr Małgorzata Nawrocka-Colquhoun, *Freelance Writer*

Dr Anna Prazmowska, *London School of Economics*

Dr Conor Smyth, *Queen's University, Belfast*

Ruth Watson, *St Anthony's College, Oxford*

Editorial Director
Hilary McGlynn

Managing Editor
Katie Emblen

Project Editor
Shereen Karmali

Editors
Clare Collinson
Anna Farkas
Tessa Hanford
Małgorzata Nawrocka-Colquhoun
Susan Purkis
Edith Summerhayes
Catherine Thompson
Karen Young

Technical Project Editor
Tracey Auden

Production
Tony Ballsdon

Art and Design
Terence Caven

Picture Research
Elizabeth Loving

Abacha, Sani (1943–1998)

Nigerian army officer, head of state 1993–98. In 1983 he took part in the coup that ended the Second Republic. In 1985 President ◊Babangida appointed him chief of staff. He retained his position during the purges of army leadership in 1989. By 1992 he was a full general as well as defence minister and chair of the joint chiefs of staff. In 1993 he seized power following presidential elections in which Chief Moshood ◊Abiola appeared to be the winner. He arrested Abiola and suppressed a strike by oil workers. The Abacha regime received international condemnation for the hanging of the environmentalist and human-rights campaigner Ken Saro-Wiwa in 1995. Abacha died of illness in 1998.

Born in Kano state, Abacha belonged to the Kanuri ethnic group. He joined the army in 1962 and trained at the School of Infantry, Warminster, UK, 1966–71.

Abbas, Ferhat (1899–1985)

Algerian nationalist leader and politician. He was the first president of the exile-based Gouvernement Provisoire de la République Algérienne (GPRA) 1958–61, and was elected president of the national assembly after independence.

French-educated, Abbas had been until the outbreak of the war in 1954 a fervent advocate of assimilation and federation with France. However, in 1955 he joined the Front de Libération Nationale (FLN), which was the main resistance organization. His political career ended one year after independence because of his disagreement with what he viewed as the consolidation of a one-man regime. Placed under house arrest then released, he went into exile and wrote his last book, *L'Indépendance confisquée/The Confiscation of Independence*, in which he denounced the usurpation of power.

Abbās II or *Abbās Hilmī Pasha* (1874–1944)

Last khedive (viceroy) of Egypt, 1892–1914. On the outbreak of war between Britain and Turkey in 1914, he sided with Turkey and was deposed following the establishment of a British protectorate over Egypt.

Abbās II succeeded his father, Tewfik. At first he tried to overthrow British rule; he abolished and reduced taxes, and disagreed with Cromer and Kitchener

before throwing in his lot with Turkey in 1914. He was deposed on 19 December 1914, and the khedivate passed, with the title of sultan, to Hussein Kamil Pasha, his uncle (reigned 1914–17).

Abbey, Joseph Leo Seko (1940–)

Ghanaian economist and diplomat. He was educated at the London School of Economics, Iowa State University, USA, and the University of Western Ontario, Canada. He was high commissioner to Canada 1984–86, to the UK 1986–90, and ambassador to the USA from 1990.

Abboud, Ibrahim (1900–1983)

Sudanese general and politician. After an army coup in 1958, Abboud became president of the supreme council of the armed forces, and subsequently premier and president. His power was severely limited after a civilian coup in October 1964; he resigned from the presidency a month later.

He was educated at Gordon College and the Military College, Khartoum. He served in Eritrea, Ethiopia, and North Africa during World War II, was deputy commander in chief of the Sudanese army 1954–56, and commander in chief in 1956.

Abd al-Hamid II (1842–1918)

Last sultan of Turkey 1876–1909. In 1908 the Young Turks under Enver Pasha forced Abd al-Hamid to restore the constitution of 1876 and in 1909 insisted on his deposition. He died in confinement. For his part in the Armenian massacres suppressing the revolt of 1894–96 he was known as the 'Great Assassin'; his actions still motivate Armenian violence against the Turks.

He succeeded on the deposition of his brother Murad V. His reign included wars with Serbia in 1876, Russia 1877–78, and Greece in 1897.

Abdel Meguid, Ahmed Esmat (1923–)

Egyptian politician and diplomat. After the return of the League of Arab States to Cairo he was appointed its secretary general in May 1991.

Educated in law, he represented his country as permanent delegate to the United Nations 1972–82, and was minister of foreign affairs 1984–91 and deputy prime minister 1985–91.

Abdullah, ibn Abdul Aziz al-Saud (1924–   )

Saudi Arabian prince, first deputy prime minister from 1982. On the assassination, in 1975, of King ◊Faisal, he became second deputy prime minister and he was designated Crown Prince and first deputy prime minister on the death of his half-brother King ◊Khalid in 1982. After his half-brother King ◊Fahd suffered a stroke, power was temporarily ceded to Abdullah, his legal successor, in January 1996.

Born in Riyadh, he was the 13th son of King Abdul Aziz ◊Ibn Saud, the founder of the Saudi dynasty. He is viewed as the leader of the traditionalists within the Saudi royal family. He was educated in private by selected religious scholars and intellectuals and spent much of his early life in the desert, where he developed close links with Bedouin tribal leaders. He later became governor of Mecca and, since 1963, has commanded the 400,000-strong Saudi National Guard, which is recruited from leading Saudi tribes and acts as a counterbalance to the army.

Abdullah, Sheik Muhammad (1905–1982)

Indian politician, known as the 'Lion of Kashmir'. He headed the struggle for constitutional government against the Maharajah of Kashmir, and in 1948, following a coup, became prime minister. He agreed to the accession of the state to India, but was dismissed and imprisoned from 1953 (with brief intervals of freedom) until 1966, when he called for Kashmiri self-determination. He became chief minister of Jammu and Kashmir in 1975, accepting the sovereignty of India.

Abdullah ibn Hussein (1882–1951)

King of Jordan 1946–51. In 1921, after the collapse of the Ottoman empire, he became emir of the British mandate of Transjordan, covering present-day Jordan, and became king when the mandate ended in May 1946. In May 1948 King Abdullah attacked the newly established state of Israel, capturing large areas. He retained the area called the West Bank (Arab Palestine) after a cease-fire in 1949 and renamed the country the Hashemite Kingdom of Jordan. He was assassinated in July 1951 by a Palestinian Arab fanatic.

The son of ◊Hussein ibn Ali, King of the Hejaz, and the brother of ◊Faisal I of Iraq, he was born in Mecca and educated in Constantinople (Istanbul), Turkey. From 1912 to 1914, Abdullah sat in the Ottoman legislature, representing Mecca, but sided with Britain during World War I. Between 1916 and 1918, working with the British guerrilla leader T E ◊Lawrence, he played a key role in the Arab revolt against Ottoman rule, leading guerrilla raids on Turkish garrisons.

FURTHER READING
Wilson, M E *King Abdullah, Britain, and the Making of Jordan* 1988

Aberhart, William (1878–1943)

Canadian politician, premier of Alberta 1935–43. He tried to establish a currency system on social-credit principles, but the necessary legislation was rejected by the Supreme Court of Canada. Aberhart subsequently reverted to more orthodox financial methods.

Born in Ontario and educated at Queen's University, he was principal of the high school in Calgary, Alberta, and founder of the Calgary Prophetic Bible Institute. He organized a social credit movement, which won the provincial election 1935.

The Alberta legislature passed the necessary legislation (for his currency system), including the Bank Taxation Bill, the Credit Regulation Bill, and Press Control Bill, but all these measures were declared ultra vires (beyond the legislature's legal powers) by the Supreme Court of Canada, and their decision was upheld by the Judicial Committee of the Privy Council.

Abernathy, Ralph D (1926–1990)

US Baptist clergyman and civil-rights activist. Martin Luther ◊King Jr's chosen successor as head of the Southern Christian Leadership Conference (SCLC), Abernathy went on to devote his attention to religious ministry and the issues of worldwide peace.

Abernathy was an early civil-rights organizer and leading confidante of Martin Luther King Jr. As well as pursuing a career in civil rights, he was pastor of the West Hunter Street Baptist Church in Atlanta, Georgia, from 1961 until his death. Although Abernathy was a competent leader of the SCLC, the organization did not regain its previous influence. He resigned the SCLC leadership in 1977 to run unsuccessfully for Andrew Young's congressional seat. Abernathy consequently turned his attention away from the civil-rights movement.

Abiola, Moshood Kastumawo (1937–1998)

Nigerian politician, president in 1993. First elected to parliament as a National Party member in 1979, he won the 1993 presidential elections as the Social Democratic Party candidate, but was arrested and charged with treason following a military coup. After spending a year in prison his detention was declared illegal but the election result remained invalid. He died as his release was being negotiated.

Abiola was born at Abeokuta in Ogun state, and educated at the local Baptist Boys High School and at the University of Glasgow. He initially pursued a career in accountancy, mainly in public and private publishing companies, and he continued his interests in publishing and telecommunications after entering politics.

Abubakar, Siddiq (1903–1988)

Nigerian leader and sultan of Sokoto 1938–88. As spiritual leader of Nigeria's Muslims he had the title of Sarkin Musulmi ('Commander of the Faithful'). He was a highly influential figure in the political structure of the emirates of northern Nigeria, introducing such reforms as the extension of education and voting rights to women. Before independence he played a dominant part in the Northern House of Chiefs and was minister without portfolio in the regional government. After independence he refused to participate in party politics. He was known for his political and religious tolerance and his work to promote Nigeria's unity and territorial integrity.

Abubakar was born in Sokoto on the day British forces entered the city to crush resistance to colonial rule. In 1938 he succeeded his uncle Hassan as sultan.

Abu Nidal or *al-Banna, Sabri Khalil* (1934–   )

Palestinian-Arab terrorist. During the late 1950s he joined Yassir ◊Arafat's Fatah guerrilla group, which was linked to the Palestinian Liberation Organization (PLO). However, he was critical of what he saw as its moderate stance and, when expelled in 1973, set up his own, more extreme Palestinian Arab terrorist organization, the Al-Fatah Revolutionary Command, also known as Black June. This clandestine body was responsible for a series of ruthless assassinations, hijackings, and kidnappings of Israeli, Western, and 'moderate Palestinian' targets. The Abu Nidal group's activities have been condemned by the PLO, which sentenced Abu Nidal to death in 1974.

The Abu Nidal group's attempted assassination, in June 1982, of the Israeli ambassador in London, Shlomo Argov, gave Israel the pretext to launch an invasion of Lebanon, while its December 1985 attacks on passengers at Rome and Vienna airports led to US bombing reprisals against Libya. Abu Nidal received backing initially from Iraq and then, in the early 1980s, from Syria and Libya. Iraqi assistance was resumed in 1990.

Abzug, Bella Savitsky (1920–1998)

US feminist, lawyer, and politician. A powerful speaker and legislator who pressed for women's rights, peace, and civil rights, Abzug became known as 'Battling Bella' or 'Hurricane Bella'. She was elected to Congress as a Democrat to represent a Manhattan district 1970–76. She wrote numerous articles for magazines and anthologies on the women's movement, and in 1972 published *Bella! Ms Abzug Goes to Washington*. Throughout the 1980s she remained politically active, and wrote *Gender Gap: Bella Abzug's Guide to Political Power for American Women* (1984).

Born in the Bronx, New York, Abzug practised law in New York City 1944–70, and represented individuals named by Senator Joseph McCarthy as suspected communists in the 1950s. She also represented the American Civil Liberties Union, was a founder of the Women's Strike for Peace and the National Women's Political Caucus in the 1960s, and opposed US military intervention in Vietnam. She was a spokeswoman for a variety of issues, including welfare reform, openness in government, equal rights, aid to cities, and consumer and environmental protection.

While in Congress she served on numerous government committees and presidential commissions, and was co-author of the Freedom of Information and Privacy Acts. In 1976 she gave up her seat in Congress to run for the US Senate, but was unsuccessful. However, she continued to be politically active and attended the Earth Summit in Rio de Janeiro, the Global Forum of Women conference in Dublin in 1992, and the UN World Conference on Women in Beijing in 1995.

Achad Haam or *Ahad ha-Am* pseudonym of Asher Ginzberg (1858–1927)

Jewish writer, philosopher, and Zionist leader. He founded the periodical *Ha-Shiloa* (1897), and stressed the necessity for a renewal of the Hebrew spirit. In 1907 he moved to London and in 1922 to Palestine, where he settled. He was a close adviser of the Zionist leader Chaim ◊Weizmann.

Born in the Ukraine, he went to Palestine in 1891 and 1893 and became convinced that Zionism needed to emphasize its cultural and spiritual nature, thus disagreeing with the political aims of many other Zionists. He also warned, in 1891, that the Arabs of Palestine were opposed to Jewish political designs on their territory.

Acheampong, Ignatius Kutu (1931–1979)

Ghanaian army officer and politician, military ruler of Ghana 1972–78. He led the coup of January 1972 that overthrew the president, Dr Busia, and was himself replaced by his deputy, Frederick Akuffo, in a bloodless coup in 1978.

On seizing power, Acheampong became president of the National Redemption Council and formed a new government. His programme of 'self-reliance' included the government's nationwide food-production programme 'Operation Feed Yourself', which gave Ghana an abundance of maize and rice. However, his subsequent mismanagement of the economy prompted a series of plots to overthrow his regime. He and Akuffo were executed in June 1979 after a coup led by young officers, whose Armed Forces Revolutionary Council returned Ghana to civilian rule in September 1979.

He was born in Kumasi and educated at the Central College of Commerce, Agona Swedru. His early career was as a schoolteacher, and he became vice principal of Agona Swedru College of Commerce, then a tutor at Kumasi Commercial College. His military career began in 1959, and he received his instruction in the UK, at the Mons Officer Cadet School, and in the USA, at the military academy at Fort Leavenworth in Kansas. He advanced rapidly in the Ghanaian army and by 1971 was commander of the First Infantry Battalion.

Achebe, Chinua (Albert Chinualumogo) (1930–   )

Nigerian novelist. His themes include the social and political impact of European colonialism on African people, and the problems of newly independent African nations. Among his works are the seminal *Things Fall Apart* (1958), one of the first African novels to achieve a global reputation, and *Anthills of the Savannah* (1987).

Achebe was born in Ogidi, East Central State, and graduated in English literature from University College, Ibadan, in 1953. In 1954 he was appointed talks producer for the Nigerian Broadcasting Company, and served as director of external broadcasting 1961–66. During the Nigerian civil war he wrote and lectured throughout the world as a spokesperson for the Biafran cause.

During Nigeria's second republic he joined the People's Redemption Party and became its deputy national president in 1983. The same year he wrote and published a political tract entitled 'The Trouble with Nigeria', criticizing the lack of political leadership in the country. Achebe has received honorary doctorate degrees from 12 universities around the world, the Nigerian Natural Merit Award, and the Order of the Federal Republic of Nigeria. He was professor of English at the University of Nigeria, Nsukka, from 1976 until his retirement in 1981.

Acheson, Dean (Gooderham) (1893–1971)

US politician. As undersecretary of state 1945–47 in Harry Truman's Democratic administration, he was associated with George C Marshall in preparing the Marshall Plan, and succeeded him as secretary of state 1949–53.

Acheson's foreign policy was widely criticized by Republican members of Congress, especially Senator Joe ◊McCarthy, for an alleged weak response to communist advances in Southeast Asia, especially after the outbreak of the Korean War. Acheson advocated containment of the USSR. He survived a vote calling for his resignation, but left the State Department in 1952 following the election to the presidency of the Republican Dwight D

The first requirement of a statesman is that he be dull. This is not always easy to achieve.
DEAN ACHESON
Observer 21 June 1970

Eisenhower. Acheson was highly critical of the UK's foreign-policy aims, notably of the claim to a 'special relationship' with the USA.

His books include *Power and Diplomacy* (1958) and *Present at the Creation* (1969), which won the Pulitzer Prize for History.

Achour, Habib (1913–   )

Tunisian trade union leader and politician. He joined the nationalist Néo-Destour party in 1934 and with Farhat ◊Hachad formed the Union Générale des Travailleurs Tunisiens (UGTT) in 1946. A veteran militant of the party, he, however, strongly opposed the participation of the UGTT in politics in the early years of independence. Co-opted onto the Néo-Destour political bureau, he became afterwards the union's secretary general 1963–66 and 1970–78. Accused of having instigated the anti-government riots in 1978, he was put to trial and sentenced to ten years' hard labour. Pardoned and released in 1981, he was reinstated as president of the UGTT.

Adamkus, Valdas (1926–   )

Lithuanian-US politician and administrator, president of Lithuania from 1998. He emigrated to the USA in 1944, after fighting the Nazi German and Soviet occupations of his homeland. On his retirement as

Gerry Adams. *Rex*

head of the Scientific Research Center of the US Environmental Protection Agency (EPA), he returned to Lithuania and was narrowly elected president in a run-off contest in January 1998.

In the second round of the presidential election in January 1998, he unexpectedly defeated Arturas Palauskas, by 49.9% to 49.3%, having trailed well behind in the first round. As president, he pledged continuing rapprochement with Russia, whilst seeking to deepen Lithuania's links with Western Europe and the USA.

Adams, Grantley Herbert (1898–1971)

Barbadian centre-left politician, prime minister 1954–58, and West Indies' Federation prime minister 1958–62. In 1938 he formed the Barbados Labour Party (BLP), the country's first political party. As prime minister of Barbados he promoted social reforms, including improvements in health provision and old-age pensions, but his move towards the centre ground led to a split in the BLP in 1955, with the formation of the left-wing Democratic Labour Party (DLP) by Errol ◊Barrow; the DLP took power in 1961 after full internal self-government had been achieved.

Strongly committed to Caribbean integration, Adams was prime minister of the Federation of the West Indies from its formation in 1958 until its dissolution in 1962. After his party's defeat in December 1961, he remained as BLP leader until 1970, rebuilding its strength and enabling his son, Tom ◊Adams, to become prime minister in 1976.

Adams studied classics at Oxford University and trained as a barrister in England, before returning to the Caribbean to practise from the mid-1920s. After riots swept across Barbados in 1938, he formed the BLP the following year, and later became president of the Barbados Workers' Union (BWU) in 1944, winning for the union the right of collective bargaining.

FURTHER READING
Hoyos, F A *Grantley Adams and the Social Revolution* 1974

Adams, Henry Brooks (1838–1918)

US historian and novelist, a grandson of President John Quincy Adams. He published the nine-volume *History of the United States During the Administrations of Jefferson and Madison* (1889–91), a study of the evolution of democracy in the USA.

◆ ADAMS, GERRY (GERARD) (1948–) ◆

Northern Ireland politician, president of Sinn Féin (the political wing of the Irish Republican Army, IRA) from 1978. He was elected member of Parliament for Belfast West in 1983 but declined to take up his Westminster seat, as he refused to take an oath of allegiance to the Queen; he lost his seat in 1992 but regained it in 1997, still refusing to sit in the Westminster Parliament. Despite doubts about his ability to influence the IRA, he has been a key figure in Irish peace negotiations. He was the main architect of the IRA cease-fire in 1994 and in 1997 he entered into multiparty talks with the British government which, on Good Friday, 10 April 1998, resulted in an agreement accepted by all parties and subsequently endorsed in referenda held simultaneously in Northern Ireland and in the Irish Republic. However, Sinn Féin lost support to the moderate republican Social Democratic Labour Party (SDLP) in the June 1998 elections to the new Northern Ireland Assembly.

Adams was interned 1972–77 on suspicion of involvement in terrorist activity. In 1993 it was revealed that he had held talks about a possible political solution with the leader of the SDLP, John ◊Hume, and with representatives of the British government. In August 1994, when Adams announced an IRA cease-fire, the British government removed all restrictions on his public

appearances and freedom to travel to mainland Britain (in force since 1988). The unwillingness of the IRA to decommission its arms prior to full British troop withdrawal from Northern Ireland led to a delay in the start of all-party peace talks in 1995, and the resumption of IRA violence in February 1996 damaged his credibility and cast doubt over the peace process.

Adams was criticized for failing to denounce the violence, whether it was the work of the main body of the IRA or a more militant section of it. Nevertheless, in September 1998, he met the Unionist leader, David Trimble, at Stormont, Belfast, in a historic meeting, the first of its kind for several generations.

Adams was born in Belfast, the son of an IRA activist who was sentenced to eight years' imprisonment for attempted murder, and became active in Northern Ireland politics at an early age. In 1971 he was given his first IRA command, the 2nd Battalion, Belfast brigade, which murdered 48 people in 10 months. From 1994 he travelled widely, particularly to the USA, to promote the cause of Sinn Féin and all-Ireland integration. His autobiography *Cage Eleven* (1990) drew heavily on his experience as an internee and prisoner. A biography, *Gerry Adams: Before the Dawn*, appeared in 1996.

He also published the classic autobiography *The Education of Henry Adams* (1907). *Democracy, an American Novel* (1880) reflects his disillusionment with the US political system.

Politics, as a practice, whatever its professions, has always been the systematic organization of hatreds.

HENRY ADAMS *Education of Henry Adams* chap 1

Adams, Tom (John Michael) (1931–1985)

Barbadian centre-left politician, prime minister 1976–85. He led the Barbados Labour Party (BLP) to victory in 1976 after 15 years in opposition. As prime minister and finance minister, he promoted modernization of the infrastructure and legal system, and market-centred economic reforms, including the development of 'offshore' financial services. He also developed close ties with the USA, supplying troops to assist the US-led invasion of Grenada in 1983, although initially denying any threat from its left-wing regime. He was the son of Grantley◊Adams, founder of the BLP.

After Adams died suddenly in March 1985, he was succeeded as BLP leader and prime minister by Bernard St John.

Adams followed in his father's footsteps by winning the Barbados Island Scholarship to study politics, philosophy, and economics at Oxford University and later becoming a barrister. He remained in England until 1963, working with the BBC and becoming active in the UK Labour Party. On his return to Barbados, he worked with his father to rebuild the fortunes of the BLP and was elected to the Barbadian parliament in 1966. He took over as parliamentary leader of the BLP in 1971, and became its chair in 1973.

Addams, Jane (1860–1935)

US social reformer, feminist, and pacifist. In 1889 she founded and led the social settlement of Hull House in the slums of Chicago, one of the earliest community welfare centres. She was vice president of the National American Woman Suffrage Alliance 1911–14, and in 1915 led the Women's Peace Party and the first Women's Peace Congress. She shared the Nobel Peace Prize in 1931.

◆ ADENAUER, KONRAD (1876–1967) ◆

German Christian Democrat politician, chancellor of West Germany 1949–63. With the French president Charles de Gaulle, he achieved the postwar reconciliation of France and Germany and strongly supported all measures designed to strengthen the Western bloc in Europe.

Adenauer was mayor of his native city of Cologne from 1917 until his imprisonment by Hitler in 1933 for opposition to the Nazi regime. After the war he headed the Christian Democratic Union (CDU) and became chancellor, combining the office with that of foreign minister. He was re-elected chancellor in 1953 and retained the post of foreign minister until 1955.

His visit to Moscow in 1955 resulted in the establishment of diplomatic relations between West Germany and the USSR and several thousand German prisoners, still held in the Soviet Union, were sent home. He was a staunch advocate of West Germany's participation in the defence of Western Europe, and in 1955 the republic joined both NATO and the Western Union. From 1958 onwards Adenauer strove to make his country a dominant force in the European Economic Community, and after de Gaulle was restored to power in France, he worked with him to obtain closer links between both countries, an effort culminating in the reconciliation treaty signed in Paris in January 1963.

In October 1962, following allegations from Adenauer's government, five members of the editorial staff at the weekly news magazine *Der Spiegel* were arrested in a federal police raid, for allegedly publishing military information of a secret nature. Many irregularities surrounded the government's action against the magazine, and the following month five cabinet ministers resigned.

Adenauer was criticized in some quarters for allowing Germany to be France's junior partner in Europe. In home affairs, his authoritarianism, coupled with incidents such as the *Der Spiegel* affair and his generally cool relations with Willy Brandt, the mayor of West Berlin, tarnished both his own and his party's image. He retired from the chancellorship in October 1963, being succeeded by Ludwig Erhard, but remained chair of the CDU until 1966.

FURTHER READING

Adenauer, Konrad *Memoirs* 1966
Heidenheimer, Arnold J *Adenauer and the CDU* 1960
Hiscocks, R *The Adenauer Era* 1966
Prittie, T *Adenauer* 1972
Schwarz, H-P *Konrad Adenauer: A German Politician in a Period of War, Revolution and Reconstruction* 2 vols 1995 and 1997

Hull House served as a model for others throughout the USA, and provided innovative services such as day care. Addams was a US leader in attempts to reform child-labour laws and was president of the Women's International League for Peace and Freedom in 1919. Her publications include *Democracy and Social Ethics* (1902), *Newer Ideals of Peace* (1907), and *Twenty Years at Hull House* (1910).

Adler, Cyrus (1863–1940)

US educator and public figure. In 1892 he was appointed curator at the Smithsonian Institution and later served as its librarian and assistant secretary. From 1908 until his death, he was president of Dropsie College and a leader of the American Jewish Committee. His appeal for protection of the rights of religious ethnic minorities was adopted in the final text of the Treaty of Versailles after World War I.

Born in Van Buren, Arkansas, Adler studied Semitic languages at the University of Pennsylvania and at Johns Hopkins University, where he received a PhD in 1887.

Adorno, Theodor Wiesengrund (1903–1969)

German social theorist and cultural critic. A member of the Frankfurt School (Institute for Social Research),

Konrad Adenauer in Berlin, 1954. *AKG London*

he emigrated to the USA in 1933 and returned to Germany in 1949. With Max ◊Horkheimer he published the *Dialectic of Enlightenment* (1947), which argued that rationality had not been an emancipatory force, but that modern science had been an instrument of dehumanization. He was also the main contributor to *The Authoritarian Personality* (1950), which analysed the psychological origins of fascism within a broadly Freudian framework.

Aehrenthal, Count Aloys von (1854–1912)

Austro-Hungarian diplomat and politician. He was foreign minister during the Bosnian Crisis of 1908.

He studied at the universities of Prague and Bonn and entered the diplomatic service in 1877, serving as ambassador in St Petersburg 1898–1906. He succeeded Agenor Goluchowski (1849–1921) as foreign minister in 1906 and directed the foreign policy of the Dual Monarchy until his death. Aehrenthal was generally identified with the peace party in Austria–Hungary.

'Aflaq, Michel (1910–1989)

Syrian political philosopher, founder of the Ba'ath (Arab Resistance) Party in the early 1940s. During 1949 'Aflaq was briefly education minister, under President Hashem al-◊Atassi. He failed twice in bids to be elected to the Syrian parliament, in 1947 and 1949, but remained influential as secretary general of the Ba'ath Party. After Ba'ath came to power, in a March 1963 coup, he became marginalized as the party's military wing gained the ascendancy. After the military wing's coup in 1966, 'Aflaq left Syria and became based mainly in Baghdad, Iraq, where the Iraqi Ba'ath Party seized power in 1968.

'Aflaq formed the Ba'ath Party along with Salah al-Din al-Bitar and other intellectuals. Its basic tenet was 'One Arab Nation with an Eternal Mission', as expressed in the slogan 'Unity, Freedom, and Socialism'. 'Aflaq believed that there existed a single Arab nation, which had been divided artificially by the Ottomans, European and US imperialism, and Zionism.

Born in Damascus, into a Greek-Orthodox Christian family, during studies in Paris he became influenced by communist thinking. From this base, he developed, during the late 1930s, a unique brand of revolutionary-socialist Arab nationalism. It linked together religion and nationalist politics since, as 'Aflaq wrote, both 'spring from the heart and are issued by the will of God'.

FURTHER READING
'Aflaq, Michel *In the Ways of the Ba'ath* 1959

Afrifa, Okatakyie Akwasi Amankwa (1936–1979)

Ghanaian army officer, former head of state from April

to September 1969, and a principal leader of the coup of 1966 that overthrew Kwame ◊Nkrumah. In 1969 he became chair of the National Liberation Council, the ruling military group, and subsequently head of state. The same year he returned Ghana to civilian rule. He retired from the army in 1970 and later that year joined the council of state, remaining in office until 1972 when the Busia government was ousted by General ◊Acheampong. He was arrested for supporting Busia and detained until 1973. Acheampong was overthrown in 1978, and Afrifa was elected to parliament in 1979. The same year, following the Rawlings coup, he was arrested on corruption charges and executed.

Aga Khan III or *Aga Sultan Sir Mohammed* (1877–1957)

Spiritual head (*imam*) of the Ismaili Muslim sect, born in Karachi, India (now Pakistan). He succeeded to the title in 1885.

He founded Aligarh University in 1910. He worked for the British cause in both world wars, and in 1937 was president of the League of Nations assembly. He welcomed the creation of Pakistan in 1947, and hoped for a blending of European and Ismaili culture. A keen racecourse enthusiast, he owned several Derby winners.

Aga Khan IV, (Karim) (1936–)

Spiritual head (*imam*) of the Ismaili Muslim sect. He succeeded his grandfather in 1957.

Agnew, Spiro (Theodore) (1918–1996)

US vice president 1969–73, a Republican. He was governor of Maryland 1966–69, and vice president under Richard ◊Nixon. Agnew took the lead in a campaign against the press and opponents of the Vietnam War. Although he was one of the few administration officials not to be implicated in the Watergate affair, he resigned in 1973, shortly before pleading 'no contest' to a charge of income-tax evasion.

Aguinaldo, Emilio (1869–1964)

Filipino revolutionary leader. He became a militant nationalist on Luzon island during the 1890s and led a year-long insurrection against the Philippines' Spanish colonial rulers in 1896, which ended with his exile to Hong Kong in 1897. After the outbreak of the Spanish-American War in April 1898, Aguinaldo, with assistance from the USA, returned to Luzon to lead an anti-Spanish insurrection, at the same time as US attacks. He established a 'Visayan Republic', with its capital at Malolos and himself as president. He opposed the peace treaty that concluded the Spanish-American War in 1899 and led a two-year-long rebellion against US occupying forces, which claimed 4,000 US and 10,000 Filipino lives. In July 1901

Aguinaldo made an oath of allegiance to the USA, in return for an amnesty. In 1935 he ran unsuccessfully for president, being defeated by Manuel Quezon.

Aguinaldo was born near Cavitte, on Luzon island. After 1901 he retired to private life, but continued to call for full independence and became dubbed the 'Filipino Garibaldi'. During World War II he was charged with cooperating with the Japanese occupying the Philippines, but was subsequently exonerated.

FURTHER READING
Aguinaldo, E, and Pacis, V A *A Second Look at America* 1957

Aguiyi-Ironsi, Johnson (1925–1966)

Nigerian politician and soldier, head of state in 1966. He commanded the Nigerian contingent during the UN involvement in the Congo from 1960, and was appointed commander in chief in 1965. He assumed power following the officers' coup of January 1966, but was killed in the counter-coup led by Yakuba ◊Gowon in July 1966.

Aguiyi-Ironsi joined the colonial army in 1942 and was trained in the UK.

Ahern, Bertie (1951–)

Irish politician, Taoiseach (prime minister) from 1997, leader of Fianna Fáil from 1994. After the May 1997 election he formed a minority government as Ireland's youngest Taoiseach. His promotion of peace negotiations culminated in the 1998 Good Friday Agreement between Northern Ireland's contending parties, which received 94% backing in a referendum in the Irish Republic in May 1998.

He was elected to parliament (Dáil) in 1977 and was minister of state in the Department of Taoiseach and Defence in 1982, in Charles Haughey's short-lived minority government. When Fianna Fáil returned to power, he was minister for labour 1987–91 and minister for finance 1991–94. Meanwhile Albert Reynolds had taken over the Fianna Fáil leadership and formed successive coalitions with the Progressive Democrats and Labour. In 1994 Reynolds lost Labour support and was forced to resign. He also surrendered the Fianna Fáil leadership and Ahern was elected as his successor.

Born in Dublin, Ireland, and educated at the College of Commerce and University College, Dublin, Ahern qualified and practised as an accountant before becoming active in politics. In 1979 he started serving on Dublin City Council, becoming Lord Mayor 1986–97.

Ahidjo, Ahmadou (1924–1989)

Cameroonian politician, president 1960–82. He became president following the amalgamation of most of the British Cameroons with the French Cameroons in 1960, and was re-elected to that post in 1972, 1975, and 1980. After his resignation in 1982, he went into voluntary exile in France. His one-party state, although severe on the rival, but outlawed, Union des Populations Camerounaises (UPC), was relatively successful economically and less repressive than many West African states.

Ahidjo was first elected to the territorial assembly in 1947. He represented Cameroon in the Assembly of French Union from 1953 to 1957, and held various senior positions in the territorial assembly of Cameroon between 1957 and 1960.

He was born in Garoua, and educated at the Ecole Supérieure d'Administration, Yaoundé. Before entering politics he worked as a radio operator in the post office.

Ahtisaari, Maarti (1939–)

Finnish diplomat and politician, president from 1994. Prior to being chosen as the Social Democratic Party presidential candidate, he was undersecretary general of the United Nations, representing it in Namibia 1989–90 and in Yugoslavia in 1993. He strongly supported Finland's membership of the European Union and pledged himself to work for better relations with Russia.

Aidid, Muhammad Farah (1936–1996)

Somali soldier and politician. A one-time colleague of the Somali president Siad Barre, in 1990 he established an anti-Barre paramilitary organization, the United Somali Congress (USC), which eventually drove the president from office in 1991. Rivalry subsequently developed within the ruling coalition and Somalia was again plunged into civil war. During 1993 United Nations peacekeeping forces (principally US Marines) targeted Aidid as the principal villain in the conflict and conducted an abortive mission to capture him. He was killed in faction fighting in August 1996.

Aidid was made head of intelligence by President Siad Barre but fell from favour and was imprisoned for six years on charges of sedition. Released in 1984, he was appointed ambassador to Turkey and later India. Despite his return to favour, he joined opposition to the president, becoming chair of the United Somali Congress, which, from a base in Ethiopia, ousted the Barre regime in 1991.

Rivalry developed between Aidid and Ali Mahdi Muhammad, a former ally and Somalia's self-proclaimed president, and the country was subsequently ravaged by a bitter struggle between them. After two years of civil war, Aidid and Mahdi signed a peace agreement in March 1994, but Aidid was ousted as factional leader in June 1995.

Aidit, D N (1923–1965)

Indonesian politician, leader of the Indonesian Communist Party (PKI) 1951–65. Under Aidit's leadership the PKI became one of the largest political parties in Indonesia. With an estimated 20 million members at its peak in 1965, it was the largest Stalinist party in the world outside China and the USSR. In 1963 Aidit and the PKI began a unilateral action of land reforms in which villagers seized land belonging to upper classes. This led to a failed coup attempt on 30 September 1965 after which the army began the wholesale massacre of communists and which brought ◊ Suharto to power.

Ait Ahmed, Hocine (1926–)

Algerian nationalist and politician. He was a member of the Front de Libération Nationale (FLN) and the Conseil National de la Révolution Algérienne (CNRA) during the liberation war. Arrested in 1956 by the colonial authorities, he remained in prison until 1962. Deputy in the national assembly at independence, he withdrew from it in 1963 and organized his own opposition party, the Front des Forces Socialistes (FFS). Having attempted to mount a war from his homeland Kabylia against the Ben Bella regime, he was arrested and sentenced to death. He escaped from prison in 1966 and fled the country.

The legalization of multiparty politics in Algeria ended his exile in 1989, but did not prevent him from being outspoken in his criticism of the way the democratic process is conducted.

Akaka, Daniel Kahikina (1924–)

US Democratic politician, senator for Hawaii from 1990. He was elected to the US House of Representatives, as a Democrat for Hawaii, in 1976 and became senator for Hawaii in 1990. He was the first native Hawaiian to serve in both chambers of the US Congress.

Born in Honolulu, he served in the Army Corps of Engineers during World War II and then, after a university education, worked as a school teacher and administrator.

Akayev, Askar (1944–)

Kyrgyz politician, president from 1990. A reform-communist politician, he joined the Communist Party of the Soviet Union (CPSU) in 1981 and became executive president in Kyrgyzstan in November 1990, after hundreds died in Kyrgyz–Uzbek ethnic riots in the Fergana Valley. He promoted economic restructuring, privatization of land, price liberalization, secular values, and independence within the Commonwealth of Independent States (CIS) from December 1991.

A former professor of radiophysics, he became an ally of the reforming Soviet communist leader Mikhail Gorbachev, who offered Akayev the post of Soviet vice president in August 1991 in the wake of the failed anti-Gorbachev coup in Moscow. He declined, and was directly elected, unchallenged, as Kyrgyzstan's president in October 1991. A constitutional amendment in 1996 increased his presidential powers.

Akhmatova, Anna, pen name of Anna Andreevna Gorenko (1889–1966)

Russian poet. She was a leading member of the Acmeist movement. Among her works are the cycle *Requiem* (1963), written in the 1930s and dealing with the Stalinist terror, and *Poem Without a Hero* (1962, begun 1940).

In the 1920s she published several collections of poetry in the realist style of Osip Mandelshtam, but her lack of sympathy with the post-revolutionary regimes inhibited her writing, and her work was banned 1922–40 and again from 1946. From the mid-1950s her work was gradually rehabilitated in the USSR. In 1989 an Akhmatova Museum was opened in Leningrad (now St Petersburg).

FURTHER READING

Driver, S *Anna Akhmatova* 1972
Haight, Amanda *Anna Akhmatova: A Poetic Pilgrimage* 1976
Reeder, Roberta *Akhmatova: Poet and Prophet* 1995

Akintola, Samuel Ladoke (1910–1966)

Nigerian political leader and journalist. He obtained a degree in law from a UK university, returning to Nigeria in 1949 to become a major political figure of the Yoruba ethnic group. In 1955 he became deputy leader of the Action Group under Chief Obafemi ◊Awolowo. He succeeded Owolowo to become premier of the Western Region in 1959. In 1962 a rift between the two leaders led, in 1964, to Akintola forming a new party, the Nigerian National Democratic Party, which formed an alliance with the ruling party, the Northern People's Congress. He was re-elected to power in 1965 amidst accusations of ballot-rigging and major unrest, and assassinated in 1966 in Nigeria's first military coup.

Alain, pen name of Emile-Auguste Chartier (1868–1951)

French philosopher. He was an influential exponent of the ideas of French radicalism, through his books and, from 1906, his daily newspaper column in which he extolled the role of individual citizens and their rights against the state. A graduate of the Ecole Normale Supérieure and a philosophy teacher, Alain volunteered for service in World War I in 1914, although a pacifist. From 1927 he also contributed regularly to the *Nouvelle Revue Française* and co-founded the Committee of Anti-Fascist Intellectuals in 1934.

Al-Bakr, Ahmed Hassan (1914–1982)

Iraqi soldier and politician, prime minister of Iraq

in 1963 and 1964, and prime minister and president 1968–79. A member of the socialist Ba'ath Party, during his term of office as head of government and head of state, as well as chair of the Revolutionary Command Council (RCC), Al-Bakr wielded absolute power. However, he gradually ceded control to Saddam ◊Hussein, who replaced him as president in 1979.

Al-Bakr's regime modernized industry in Iraq and developed irrigation schemes to aid agriculture. Conflict also arose during his presidency with the Kurds in the north of the country.

Al-Bakr was educated at the Military Academy, Baghdad, and took part in the coup that ousted the Iraqi monarchy in 1958.

Albizu Campos, Pedro (1891–1964)

Puerto-Rican revolutionary. A member of the Nationalist Party, he was the most prominent *independentista* of his time. He masterminded a nationalist uprising in Puerto Rico in 1950 and was accused of being behind an attempt to assassinate President Harry S Truman. Sentenced to a 53-year prison term for this, he was offered a conditional pardon that was revoked in the wake of further nationalist attacks.

Born in Ponce, Puerto Rico, and educated at Harvard, Albizu Campos joined the Nationalist Party in 1924. He was jailed from 1936 to 1947 for advocating the violent overthrow of the US administration of Puerto Rico. He died in prison.

Albright, Madeleine (1937–)

US diplomat and Democrat politician, secretary of state from 1997. An adviser to leading Democrat politicians from the early 1970s, she was appointed US ambassador to the United Nations by President Bill Clinton in 1993.

Albright was born in Prague, the daughter of a Czech diplomat. After spending World War II in exile in London, her family secured asylum in the USA following the communist takeover of Czechoslovakia in 1948. She was a university professor and adviser on international affairs before becoming the country's first female secretary of state in 1997.

Alcalá Zamora y Torres, Niceto (1877–1949)

Spanish politician, first president of Spain 1931–36. In April 1936 a Socialist motion in the Cortes (national assembly) censuring the president was carried and he resigned.

Alebua, Ezekiel (1947–)

Solomon Islands right-of-centre politician, prime minister 1986–89. He rose from the ranks of the right-of-centre Solomon Islands United Party (SIUPA) to become deputy prime minister in the 1984–86 government led by Peter ◊Kenilorea. After Kenilorea's resignation in December 1986, he was narrowly elected by the national parliament to take over as prime minister and held this position until SIUPA was defeated in the general election of 1989. Under his premiership, the Solomon Islands joined Papua New Guinea and Vanuatu to form the 'Spearhead Group' in 1988, dedicated to preserving Melanesian cultural traditions. In 1997 Alebua stepped down as leader of the National Party, which had been formed in 1996 as the successor to SIUPA, and was replaced by Edward Hunuehu.

Alemán Lacayo, (José Arnoldo) (1946–)

Nicaraguan right-wing politician, president from 1997. Standing as the candidate of the right-wing Liberal Alliance, he defeated Daniel ◊Ortega in the October 1996 presidential contest. He assumed office in January 1997 and declared as his administration's priorities a fight against corruption and the resolution of legal problems arising from the Sandinista Liberation Front (FSLN)'s confiscation of land during the 1980s.

A graduate of Léon University, during the 1960s he was a leader of the pro-Somoza Liberal Student Youth Organization. He worked as an attorney and university lecturer during the 1970s, but, following the overthrow of the Somoza regime, was imprisoned in 1980 for alleged counter-revolutionary activity. He was placed under house arrest again in 1989, by the left-wing Sandinista (FSLN) government of Daniel Ortega before, in 1990, being elected mayor of the capital, Managua.

Alemán Valdés, Miguel (1902–1983)

Mexican right-wing politician, president 1946–52. Standing as candidate of the ruling National Revolutionary Party (NRP), he was elected in 1946 as the first civilian president of Mexico since Francisco ◊Madero between 1911 and 1913. He changed the NRP's name to the Institutional Revolutionary Party (PRI), to indicate the permanence of the revolution.

The son of a revolutionary general, Alemán was educated at the National University of Mexico City and became a successful lawyer who defended the rights of workers. A deputy for Veracruz state 1930–35 and a senator from 1935, he served as state governor 1936–40. He directed the successful 1940 presidential campaign of Manuel ◊Ávila Camacho, under whom he served as interior minister 1940–45.

As president, Alemán promoted communications improvements and industrialization and, for the first time since the Mexican revolution, industrialists were brought into the government. In addition, labour unions were purged of left-wing leaders and the pace of land distribution slowed down, with the Alemán presidency marking a decisive shift towards the path of capitalist development and closer Mexican relations with the USA. Alemán and his family profited from his political activities, and used the amassed fortune to develop Acapulco as a luxury tourist centre.

Alessandri Palma, Arturo (1868–1950)

Chilean president 1920–25 and 1932–37. Social and political reforms proposed in his first presidential term were blocked by an opposition-controlled congress. Forced into exile, he returned to achieve a measure of economic recovery at the expense of the repression of opponents, a policy that made him a controversial figure in Chilean history. During his second term, he established a central bank and introduced monetary reform to stabilize the national currency.

Alessandri was born in Linares and educated at the University of Chile, becoming a radical lawyer with a gift for oratory, and emerging as a national anti-government figure in 1915. He held several government posts including industry and public works, finance, and the interior, before labour and middle-class voters elected him president. In 1946 he was elected senator.

FURTHER READING
Alexander, Robert J *Arturo Allessandri: A Biography* 1977

Alexander I, Karageorgevich (1888–1934)

Regent of Serbia 1912–21 and king of Yugoslavia 1921–34, as dictator from 1929. The second son of ◊Peter I, King of Serbia, he was declared regent for his father in 1912 and on his father's death became king of the state of South Slavs – Yugoslavia – that had come into being 1918.

Rivalries with neighbouring powers and among the Croats, Serbs, and Slovenes within the country led Alexander to establish a personal dictatorship. He was assassinated on a state visit to France, and Mussolini's government was later declared to have instigated the crime.

As regent, Alexander distinguished himself in the Balkan Wars of 1912 and 1913 and during World War I he was commander in chief of the Serbian army. He accompanied the army in its retreat before the Central Powers, then headed the Serbian government in exile at Corfu, and visited the Western Allies' capitals. In 1922 he married Marie, daughter of Ferdinand of Romania. He was succeeded by his son, Peter II.

Alexander of Hillsborough, Albert Victor Alexander, Viscount Hillsborough (1885–1965)

British politician. He was First Lord of the Admiralty on three occasions, 1929–31, 1940, and 1945, and minister of defence 1947–50. In 1950 he was made a viscount. He was chancellor of the Duchy of Lancaster 1950–51 and Labour leader in the House of Lords 1955–64.

Alfaro, Eloy (1842–1912)

Ecuadorian general and politician, president 1895–

1901 and 1907–11. He was involved in various revolts before overthrowing President Luis Cordero in 1895, backed by the military. However, he was unable to avoid political conflict or run an orderly government.

At 22, Alfaro kidnapped the governor of Manabí and was a revolutionary leader for the next 25 years. During his first term in office he promoted religious freedom, instituted civil marriage, and encouraged state education. After his second period as president he was forced into exile and later lynched by opponents in Quito.

Alfonsín Foulkes, Raúl Ricardo (1927–   )

Argentine politician and president 1983–89. Becoming president at the time of the country's return to civilian government, he set up an investigation of the army's human-rights violations, with the subsequent trial and detention of many former military and political leaders. Economic problems caused him to seek help from the International Monetary Fund and introduce austerity measures, leading to debt restructuring and fiscal reform.

Educated at a military academy and a university law school, Alfonsín joined the Radical Union Party (UCR) at the age of 18 and eventually went on to lead it, until he was replaced in November 1995. He was active in local politics 1951–62, being imprisoned in 1953 by the right-wing Perón regime, and was a member of the national congress 1963–66. With the return to civilian government in 1983 and the legalization of political activity, Alfonsín and the UCR won convincing victories and he became president. Failures in economic policy and hyperinflation made him step down in 1989, several months before the end of his term. His successor, the Perónist Carlos Menem, instituted emergency economic measures on taking office.

FURTHER READING
Institute of Latin American Studies, London *Argentina in the Crisis Years (1983–1990): From Alfonsín to Menem* 1993

Algren, Nelson Abraham (1909–1981)

US novelist and social historian. Although known primarily as a novelist and as the lover of Simone de ◊Beauvoir, Algren's research led him to become a champion of the poor and disenfranchised. In the late 1930s Algren joined such writers as Saul Bellow and Arna Bontemps in the Illinois Writers Project, a branch of the federal Works Progress Administration. He conducted interviews and collected information for the national 'America Eats' programme, a pioneering enterprise researching immigration, settlement, and customs as they related to food.

FURTHER READING
Algren, Nelson, et al *America Eats* 1992
Drew, Bettina *Nelson Algren: A Life on the Wild Side* 1989

Ali, Muhammad, adopted name of Cassius Marcellus Clay, Jr (1942–   )

US boxer. Olympic light-heavyweight champion in 1960 at the age of 18, he went on to become world professional heavyweight champion in 1964, and was the only man to regain the title twice. He was known for his fast footwork and extrovert nature. Ali courted controversy with his outspoken opinions throughout his career. After converting to Islam in the 1960s, he became a prominent supporter of the civil-rights movement. Following the death of ◊Malcolm X in 1965, Ali and his family received death threats and were assigned body guards. He refused induction into the United States Army during the Vietnam War, arguing that he was entitled to draft exemption as a Muslim minister. He was arrested, his boxing licence was suspended, and he was stripped of his heavyweight title.

Ali, (Chaudri) Muhammad (1905–1980)

Pakistani politician, prime minister 1955–56. In 1932 he was made accountant general of Bahawalpur state and re-established its finances. In 1936 he became private secretary to the Indian finance minister and in 1945 was the first Indian to be appointed financial adviser of war and supply. In 1947, on the partition of India, he became the first secretary general of the Pakistan government, in 1951 finance minister, and in 1955 prime minister. He resigned in 1956 because of lack of support from members of his own party, the Muslim League.

Born in Jullundur, India, he was educated at Punjab University. In 1928 he left a chemistry lectureship at Islamia College, Lahore, for the Indian Civil Service. A man of powerful intellect, he was often described in Pakistan as the 'brains trust' of the post-partition governments.

Ali, Ibn Hussein (1879–1935)

Ruler of the Hejaz 1924–25. Born in Mecca, he was the eldest son of King ◊Hussein ibn Ali of the Hejaz, whom he succeeded in 1924 when his father was forced off the throne in the Wahabi Rebellion, but himself had to abdicate in 1925. For the rest of his life he lived in exile in Baghdad, Iraq, where his brother, ◊Faisal I, was king.

Ali, Maulana Muhammad (1878–1931)

Muslim Indian political activist. Following a period of imprisonment 1915–19, with his brother, Maulana Shaukat ◊Ali, he joined the Khilafat movement to protest against British policy towards the sultan of Turkey, who was also caliph of Islam. Muhammad became its leader and allied with the Indian National Congress, adopting Mahatma ◊Gandhi's *satyagraha*, a strategy of nonviolent resistance to British rule. He was elected president of the Congress in 1923.

The Khilafat movement was undermined by the abolition of the caliphate by Mustafa Kemal ◊Atatürk, President of Turkey, but it continued with dwindling support and influence. During the late 1920s both brothers broke with Congress and afterwards concentrated on affairs concerning the Muslim community, although they remained highly influential political leaders.

With his brother, Muhammad was closely associated with the internal politics of Aligarh College prior to World War I. In 1911 he founded *Comrade*, an English-language weekly paper espousing pan-Islamic views. Shortly afterwards he moved the paper to Delhi and also bought an Urdu paper, *Hamdard*, which he used to set forth his political views.

Ali, Maulana Shaukat (1873–1938)

Muslim Indian political activist. The brother of Maulana Muhammad ◊Ali, he organized *Anjuman-i-Khuddam-i-Kaaba* in 1913 to provide support for Muslim causes in the Middle East. He later joined the Khilafat movement and allied with the Indian National Congress.

After the outbreak of World War I, the continued activities of *Anjuman-i-Khuddam-i-Kaaba* led to the detention of both brothers 1915–19.

Ali, Salim Rubayi (1934–1978)

President of South Yemen 1969–78. A leading member of the Marxist National Liberation Front, he succeeded Qahtan Muhammad al-Shaabi as president in June 1969, after a power struggle. He was executed after his deposition in 1978.

Ali presided over an Eastern-European-style socialist regime, which developed close links with the USSR, but whose repression caused the departure of large numbers of its people to North Yemen. From 1977, as a result of taking the Soviet and Ethiopian side against the West Somali and Eritrean liberation movements, South Yemen became isolated within the Arab world. Ali responded by seeking rapprochement with the conservative regime in North Yemen. However, this was sabotaged by left-wing extremists, who placed a bomb in a suitcase carried by an envoy in June 1989, resulting in the assassination of the North's president, Ahmed bin Hussein al-Ghashmi. Ali was then swiftly deposed and, after 12 hours of heavy fighting in Aden, executed by a firing squad.

Ali, Tariq (1943–)

British political activist and writer. He was born in Lahore (then part of British India, now in Pakistan) and came to the UK in 1963 to study at Oxford University. A prominent revolutionary in the 1960s, Ali was particularly associated with the Vietnam Solidarity Campaign and student radicalism. He was a member of the (Trotskyist) International Marxist Group, editor of the radical publications *Black Dwarf* and *Red Mole*, and later joined the editorial board of *New Left Review*. His application for membership of the Labour Party was rejected in 1983.

His many publications include *The Coming British Revolution* (1972), *Can Pakistan Survive?* (1983), *The Nehrus and the Gandhis* (1985), and *Street Fighting Years: An Autobiography of the Sixties* (1987). Ali has also published novels and worked as a television producer, notably on Channel Four's *Bandung File*. In 1998 he wrote (and co-produced) *Ugly Rumours*, a play satirizing the Blair government.

Alia, Ramiz (1925–)

Albanian communist politician, head of state 1982–92. He gradually relaxed the isolationist policies of his predecessor, Enver Hoxha, and following public unrest introduced political and economic reforms, including free elections in 1991, when he was elected executive president. In September 1994 Alia was convicted of abuse of power while in office and sentenced to eight years' imprisonment, but was released in July 1995 following an appeal court ruling. In October 1997 the Albanian prosecutor general dropped genocide charges against Alia.

Born in Shkodër in northwestern Albania, the son of poor Muslim peasants, Alia joined the National Liberation Army in 1944, actively opposing Nazi control. After a period in charge of agitation and propaganda, he was inducted into the secretariat and politburo of the ruling Party of Labour of Albania (PLA) 1960–61. On 22 November 1982 he succeeded Haxhi Lleshi as president of the Presidium of the newly elected People's Assembly. On the death of Hoxha in April 1985 he became party leader, soon earning the description of the 'Albanian Gorbachev'. In April 1991 he was elected executive president of the Republic of Albania, following the PLA's victory in multiparty elections. A month later, in conformity with the provisions of the new interim constitution, which debarred the Republic's president from holding party office, he resigned as PLA first secretary and from its politburo and central committee. Sali ◊Berisha replaced Alia as president in March 1992.

Ali Aref Bourhan (1934–)

Djibouti politician, president of the French Territory of the Afars and the Issas (French Somaliland prior to 1967; Djibouti from 1977) 1967–77. His political philosophy had to encompass the prospect of eventual independence for the territory, but Bourhan held that this would only be effective and practical if the new republic remained firmly within the French community.

Bourhan entered the political arena in 1957, when he became a member of French Somaliland's territorial assembly. In 1958 he became vice president of the assembly, and by 1967 his political career had led him to become vice president and then president of the council of government.

In 1967 a referendum for an 'enlarged autonomy' was held and the territory was renamed the French Territory of the Afars and the Issas (TFAI). In the new government, dominated by the Afar party L'Union Nationale pour l'Indépendence (UNI), led by Alī Arif, Bourhan retained the presidency under the slogan 'Unity and progress within the French community'.

The issue of the country's independence came before the UN General Assembly in 1975, when a resolution of immediate granting of independence to the TFAI was adopted. Following elections held in March 1977 he was succeeded as president by Hassan Gouled. The territory became fully independent, as Djibouti, in June 1977.

Ali Mahdi, Mohammed (1934–)

Somali politician, president 1991–97. He became a member of parliament shortly before the October 1969 coup that brought Mohammed Siad ◊Barre to power. Following the change of government he left politics to go into business. He joined the opposition United Somali Congress (USC), the party that took control when Barre's government collapsed in 1991. He became president of an interim government but the appointment was opposed by other organizations, particularly the Somali National Movement (SNM), which led the secession of the northern part of the country. A conference held in 1991 partially helped to restore order and Ali Mahdi was confirmed as interim president for another two years. However hostilities continued and in 1994 he took part in peace talks in Nairobi aimed at forming a government of national reconciliation. These and subsequent efforts failed to bring peace to Somalia.

Ali Mahdi was born in Jowa and comes from the Hawiye ethnic group.

Aliyev, Geidar Alirza (1923–)

Azerbaijani politician, president from 1993. An Azeri Muslim veteran of the Communist Party of the Soviet Union (CPSU), of which he was a full Politburo member 1982–87, he returned to politics in his newly independent homeland in 1991. He became president in June 1993, after Albufaz Elchibey was overthrown in a military coup, and was elected in October 1993 in a contest boycotted by the opposition. His authoritarian regime has developed closer ties with Russia, while gradually promoting market-centred economic reforms. He was re-elected in 1995 and 1998.

Born in Nakhichevan and educated at the Azerbaijan State University, he became a member of the CPSU in 1945. Aliyev worked in the KGB in Azerbaijan, where he was communist party leader 1969–82. A pragmatist, who had made his reputation purging party corruption

in Azerbaijan, he survived the initial period of reforms promoted by the Soviet leader Mikhail Gorbachev from 1985, before being retired from the CPSU Politburo in October 1987. In 1991 he became leader of the Nakhichevan autonomous region (situated in Armenia), and in 1992 founded the New Azerbaijan Party.

In October 1998 Aliyev was re-elected with 75% of the vote but the opposition and some foreign observers maintained that the poll was marred by fraud.

Allende (Gossens), Salvador (1908–1973)

Chilean left-wing politician. Elected president in 1970 as the candidate of the Popular Front alliance, Allende never succeeded in keeping the electoral alliance together in government. His failure to solve the country's economic problems or to deal with political subversion allowed the army, backed by the US Central Intelligence Agency (CIA), to stage the 1973 coup that brought about the death of Allende and many of his supporters.

Allende became a Marxist activist in the 1930s and was elected to congress in 1937 and the senate in 1945. He rose to prominence as a presidential candidate in 1952, 1958, and 1964. In each election he had the support of the socialist and communist movements but was defeated by the Christian Democrats and Nationalists. As president, his socialism and nationalization of US-owned copper mines led the CIA to regard him as a communist and to its involvement in the coup that replaced him by General Pinochet.

He was the first Marxist head of state to be democratically elected and his appointment marked a swing to the left in Chilean politics.

FURTHER READING
Debray, Régis *Conversations with Allende: Socialism in Chile* 1971
Evans, Les *Disaster in Chile: Allende's Strategy and Why it Failed* 1974
IDOC International: no 58 *Chile: The Allende Years, the Coup under the Junta: Documents and Analysis* 1973

Alvear, Marcelo Torcuato de (1868–1942)

Argentine statesman, diplomat, and president 1922–28. He was a co-founding member of the Radical Civic Union (UCR) party and an activist in the struggle to establish a liberal democracy in the country. During his presidency he instituted some reforms and established a breakaway party, the Anti-personalist party, which aligned itself with the UCR-opposed conservatives.

On losing the 1928 elections to Hipólito ◊Irigoyen, Alvear once again realigned his allegiances to the UCR party when, in 1930, Irigoyen's government was ousted following a conservative-led military coup. His attempts at re-election in 1931 and 1937 failed.

Alvear was born in Buenos Aires and educated at the Universidad de Buenos Aires. He served as minister of public works in 1911, as a member of parliament

1912–17, and as a diplomat to France under President Irigoyen 1917–22, whom he succeeded in 1922. Alvear has also published widely on democracy and the public arena.

Amado, Jorge (1912–1998)

Brazilian novelist. His first novel, *O país do carnaval/The Country of the Carnival* (1932), follows a youthful member of the intelligentsia seeking political answers in the wake of the revolution of 1930. Amado's next few novels outlined his personal manifesto and highlighted the cause of various exploited groups in society. *Gabriela, cravo e canela/Gabriela, Clove and Cinnamon* (1952) marked a change in style and emphasis and focused on sociopolitical change.

He was imprisoned for his leftist political beliefs in 1935 and spent several years in exile, though he briefly represented the Communist party of Brazil as federal deputy of the Brazilian parliament 1946–47.

FURTHER READING
Amado, Jorge and de Onis, Harriet (translator) *Dona Flor and Her Two Husbands: A Moral and Amorous Tale* 1998
Amado, Jorge et al *Gabriela, Clove and Cinnamon* 1998
Amado, Jorge and Rabassa, Gregory (translator) *The War of Saints* 1995

Amery, Leo(pold Charles Maurice Stennett) (1873–1955)

British Conservative politician. He was First Lord of the Admiralty 1922–24, secretary for the colonies 1924–29, secretary for the dominions 1925–29, and secretary of state for India and Burma (now Myanmar) 1940–45.

Amery was born in India and educated at Harrow

Idi Amin, 1976. *Rex*

and Oxford, England. He was chief correspondent for *The Times* during the South African War 1899–1902 and subsequently edited *The Times History of the South African War* (seven volumes, 1900–09). He entered Parliament in 1911 as Unionist member for South

---

◆ AMIN (DADA), IDI (1925–) ◆

Ugandan politician, president 1971–79. He led the coup that deposed Milton Obote in 1971, expelled the Asian community in 1972, and exercised a reign of terror over his people during which an estimated 300,000 people were killed. After he invaded Tanzania in 1978, the Tanzanian army combined with dissident Ugandans to counter-attack. Despite assistance from Libya, Amin's forces collapsed and he fled in 1979. He now lives in Saudi Arabia.

Amin was commissioned into the new Ugandan army in 1962 and an alliance with President Obote led to rapid promotion; by 1966 he was commander of the armed forces. Mounting evidence of Amin's corruption and brutality had convinced Obote to replace him at the end of 1970, but Amin seized power before he could do

so. He suspended the constitution and all political activity and took legislative and executive powers into his own hands. During his brutal regime a large proportion of the educated elite were killed or fled into exile, as well as significant numbers of the Acholi and Langi peoples and Christians. His so-called 'economic war' against foreign domination resulted in the mass expulsion of the Asian population in 1972, appropriation of their assets promoting further collapse in the economy.

Amin was born into the marginal Kakwa ethnic group in the northern pastoral periphery of Uganda, and received no formal schooling. He joined the colonial army in 1946, originally as a cook, and later fought the Mau Mau in Kenya. Between 1951 and 1960 he was the heavyweight boxing champion of Uganda.

Birmingham (later known as Sparkbrook), a seat he retained until 1945. He served as an intelligence officer during World War I, and supported the introduction of imperial tariffs. Amery strongly criticized Prime Min-

---

You have sat too long here for any good you have been doing – In the name of God, go.

LEO AMERY Speech by Amery repeating Oliver Cromwell's words, addressed to Neville Chamberlain, House of Commons
7 May 1940

---

ister Neville Chamberlain for signing the Munich Agreement in 1938, and was influential in bringing about the fall of Chamberlain's government in 1940.

Amin, Mustafa (1914–1997)

Egyptian journalist and writer, considered one of the pioneers of Arab journalism. His criticism of Gamal ◊Nasser's regime led to his arrest in 1965 and he was sentenced to life imprisonment in 1966, to be pardoned by Anwar ◊Sadat in 1974.

He started his career by writing for magazines and later founded a weekly newspaper and publishing house *Dar Akhbar al Yom* in 1944. He wrote 'First Class Prison' and 'Second Class Prison' as accounts of his imprisonment for his political activities.

Anami, Korechika (1897–1945)

Japanese general. He held several commands in China and Manchuria 1938–43, before being sent to New Guinea to take charge of operations there. He became director general of army aviation in 1944, and was appointed minister of war in April 1945. He committed suicide on 15 August 1945.

Anderson, John (1922–)

US Independent politician. Anderson ran, unsuccessfully, against Ronald ◊Reagan in the 1980 presidential elections. Formerly a moderate Republican, he was unable to accept Reagan's conservative agenda and left the party to challenge him as an Independent. Reagan, however, achieved a landslide victory with 51% of the vote; Anderson received 7%.

Anderson, Marian (1902–1993)

US contralto who was one of the most important nonpolitical figures in the civil-rights movement and the fight against racism in the USA. She toured Europe in 1930, but in 1939 was barred from singing at Constitution Hall, Washington, DC, because she was black. Following this, the first lady Eleanor Roosevelt arranged for her to sing at the Lincoln Memorial in Washington, DC, before an audience of 75,000, marking a historic occasion in the struggle for equal rights. In 1955 she sang at the Metropolitan Opera, the first black singer to appear there. In 1958 she was appointed

an alternate (deputizing) delegate to the United Nations.

Andrade, Mario Pinto de (1928–1990)

Angolan politician and poet, founder member in 1956 of the People's Movement for the Liberation of Angola (MPLA), and its president 1960–62. He was succeeded as president by Agostinho ◊Neto, but, despite clashes with Neto, remained general secretary until 1973. In 1974 he split from Neto and joined the 'Activa Revolta' opposition. Following Portugal's withdrawal from Angola in 1975 and the subsequent civil war, Andrade remained in exile in Guinea-Bissau, Cape Verde, and Mozambique. He died in London after a long illness.

In 1954 he studied sociology at the Sorbonne University in Paris, and it was here that he became active in his opposition to Portuguese colonial rule.

Andreotti, Giulio (1919–)

Italian Christian Democrat politician, a fervent European. He headed seven postwar governments: 1972–73, 1976–79 (four successive terms), and 1989–92 (two terms). In addition he was defence minister eight times, and foreign minister five times. In 1993 Andreotti was among several high-ranking politicians accused of possible involvement in Italy's corruption network; he went on trial in September 1995 charged with using his influence to protect Mafia leaders in exchange for political support.

In November 1995 Andreotti and four others were charged with the murder in 1979 of journalist Carmine Pecorelli, who was alleged to have been blackmailing Andreotti, and in February 1996, with other prominent former ministers, he was arraigned on further corruption charges.

Andropov, Yuri (1914–1984)

Soviet communist politician, president of the USSR 1983–84. As chief of the KGB 1967–82, he established a reputation for efficiently suppressing dissent.

Andropov was politically active from the 1930s. His part in quelling the Hungarian national uprising of 1956, when he was Soviet ambassador, brought him into the Communist Party secretariat in 1962 as a specialist on East European affairs. He became a member of the Politburo in 1973 and succeeded Brezhnev as party general secretary in 1982. Elected president in 1983, he instituted economic reforms.

Angelou, Maya, born Marguerite Annie Johnson (1928–)

US writer and black activist. She became noted for her powerful autobiographical works *I Know Why the Caged Bird Sings* (1970) and its four sequels up to *All God's Children Need Traveling Shoes* (1986). Based on her traumatic childhood, they tell of the struggles towards physical and spiritual liberation of a black woman from growing up in the South to emigrating to Ghana.

FURTHER READING
Angelou, Maya *I Know Why the Caged Bird Sings* 1970, *Gather Together in My Name* 1974, *Singin' and Swingin' and Gettin' Merry Like Christmas* 1976, *The Heart of a Woman* 1981, *All God's Children Need Traveling Shoes* 1986

The sadness of the women's movement is that they don't allow the necessity of love. See, I don't personally trust any revolution where love isn't allowed.

MAYA ANGELOU *California Living* 14 May 1975

Annan, Kofi (1938–)
Ghanaian diplomat, secretary general of the United Nations (UN) from 1997. Heading the peacekeeping department of the UN from 1993, he oversaw its peacekeeping operations in Somalia from 1993 and in Bosnia-Herzegovina from 1995. In February 1998 he negotiated an agreement with Iraq to allow UN inspectors unrestricted access to supposed chemical and biological weapon sites.

I am a cheerleader, I am a promoter, I am a salesman, I am a debt collector, I am a father confessor, and there are aspects I still have to discover.

KOFI ANNAN On his first 13 months in the job; *Time*, 9 March 1998

Annan was the son of a Fante tribal chief. He gained a management degree from the Massachusetts Institute of Technology (MIT), USA, and went on to become a diplomat after joining the World Health Organization (WHO) in 1962. He was elected secretary general of the UN after the USA vetoed the re-election of Boutros Boutros-Ghali.

Antall, József (1932–1993)
Hungarian politician, prime minister 1990–93. He led the centre-right Hungarian Democratic Forum (MDF) to electoral victory in April 1990, becoming Hungary's first post-communist prime minister. He promoted gradual, and successful, privatization and encouraged inward foreign investment.

He founded the MDF, a Christian–nationalist coalition, in 1988, when political pluralism was sanctioned by Hungary's ruling reform communists, and led the most stable and longest-serving administration of post-communist Eastern Europe.

The son of a former minister who was arrested by the German Gestapo in 1945 for helping to save the lives of hundreds of Jews fleeing the Third Reich, he trained as a historian and worked as a teacher, archivist, and museum director in Budapest. His support for the 1956 reform movement, crushed by Soviet tanks, led to his being taken briefly into police custody and banned from teaching and publishing until 1963.

As chairman of the MDF he showed skill as a negotiator in the round-table talks that led to the free elections of 1990. As prime minister, heading Hungary's first democratically elected government for more than 40 years, he oversaw the establishment of a legal system to promote a market economy and attract foreign investment. Relations with Western Europe, particularly Germany and Austria, were also greatly improved. Despite being diagnosed as having lymphatic cancer in 1991, Antall's deeply instilled devotion to public service persuaded him to continue with his duties until his death.

FURTHER READING
Révész, Sándor *Antall József távolról, 1932–93* 1995

Anthony, Kenny (1951–)
St Lucian centre-left politician, prime minister from 1997. Appointed leader of the St Lucia Labour Party (SLP) in 1996, he quickly revived the SLP's flagging fortunes and led it to a crushing victory in May 1997, when it won all but one of the House of Assembly seats to end a period of 15 years in opposition. Anthony became prime minister, and also held the finance, planning, home affairs, and development portfolios.

His government's declared priorities were diversification of the economy, a reduction in the level of unemployment, and a crackdown against corruption.

Antonescu, Ion (1886–1946)
Romanian general and politician. He headed a pro-German government during World War II, which enforced the Nazis' anti-Semitic policies, and was executed for war crimes in 1946.

Antonescu became prime minister in 1940 and seized power, forcing King Carol to abdicate and installing Carol's son Michael as monarch. He established a fascist-style dictatorship and allied Romania with Germany against the USSR. King Michael had him arrested in August 1944; he was tried in 1945 and shot in 1946.

Following the fall of communism in Romania in 1989, many nationalists called for a re-evaluation of Antonescu's regime on the grounds that he had been vilified by communist propaganda.

FURTHER READING
Braham, Randolph *Destruction of Romanian and Ukrainian Jews during the Antonescu Era* 1997

Craca, Ioana (ed) *Procesul lui Ion Antonescu* 1995
Maniu, Iuliu *Pinii si confruntari politice 1940–44* 1994
Watts, Larry L *Romanian Cassandra: Ion Antonescu and the Struggle for Reform, 1916–41* 1993

Anwar, Ibrahim (Anwar bin Dato' Ibrahim Abdul Rahman) (1947–)

Malaysian politician, minister of finance 1991–98, and deputy prime minister 1993–98. A charismatic and outspoken critic on issues such as rural poverty, wealth distribution, and political corruption, he was presumed to be Malaysia's next prime minister, but was sacked from his various positions in September 1998 and put on trial charged with homosexual acts and corruption.

Educated at the University of Malaya, and a student Islamic activist in the 1960s and 1970s, he founded the Malaysian Muslim Youth Movement (ABIM) in 1971 and led mass anti-government demonstrations in 1971 and 1974, for the latter of which he was arrested. After his release in 1976 he continued to lead the ABIM until 1982 when the prime minister, Mahathir Mohamad, invited him to join UMNO (Malaysia's ruling party). He rose rapidly in the government holding several senior cabinet posts, including the ministries of agriculture 1984–86 and education 1986–91.

Anyaoku, Eleazar Chukwuemeka (Emeka) (1933–)

Nigerian diplomat and secretary general of the Commonwealth from 1990. He joined the Commonwealth Development Corporation in 1959 and the Nigerian diplomatic service in 1962. In 1963 he was Nigeria's representative to the United Nations (UN) in New York. In 1971 he joined the Commonwealth Secretariat in London. He was appointed assistant secretary general in 1975, and in 1977 deputy secretary general in charge of international affairs. In 1983 he was made Nigeria's foreign minister under President ◊Shagari, but when Shagari was almost immediately overthrown in a coup, he returned to his old post in the Commonwealth. He is the first African to hold the post of Commonwealth secretary general.

Anyaoku holds a chieftancy title as the Ichie Adazie of Obosi.

Aoun, Michel (1935–)

Lebanese soldier and Maronite Christian politician, president 1988–90. As commander of the Lebanese army, he was made president without Muslim support, his appointment precipitating a civil war between Christians and Muslims. His unwillingness to accept a 1989 Arab League-sponsored peace agreement increased his isolation until the following year when he surrendered to military pressure. He left the country in 1991 and was pardoned by the new government the same year.

Born in Beirut, Aoun joined the Lebanese army and rose to become, in 1984, its youngest commander. When, in 1988, the Christian and Muslim communities failed to agree on a Maronite successor to the outgoing president Amin Gemayel (as required by the constitution), Gemayel unilaterally appointed Aoun. This precipitated the creation of a rival Muslim government, and, eventually, a civil war. Aoun, dedicated to freeing his country from Syrian domination, became isolated in the presidential palace and staunchly opposed the 1989 peace plan worked out by parliamentarians under the auspices of the Arab League. After defying the government led by Prime Minister Selim al-Hoss in the face of strong military opposition, in October 1990 Aoun sought asylum in the French embassy, but the Lebanese refused to fly him to Paris until he had repaid monies allegedy fraudulently appropriated. Eventually, in August 1991, he left Lebanon for exile in France. He was pardoned by the Lebanese government in the same year.

Aquino, (Maria) Corazon ('Cory'), born Cojuangco (1933–)

Filipino centrist politician, president 1986–92. She was instrumental in the nonviolent overthrow of President Ferdinand ◊Marcos in 1986. As president, she sought to rule in a conciliatory manner, but encountered opposition from the left (communist guerrillas) and right (army coup attempts), and her land reforms were seen as inadequate.

The daughter of a Tarlac province sugar baron, she studied law in the Philippines and the USA and in 1956 married Benigno Simeon Aquino (1932–1983), a Liberal Party politician who was the country's youngest-ever mayor, governor, and senator. The chief political opponent of the right-wing president Marcos, Benigno Aquino was imprisoned in 1972 for alleged subversion. A death sentence imposed in 1977 was commuted and from 1980, with Benigno requiring heart surgery, the Aquinos were allowed to live in exile in the USA. On Benigno's return, in August 1983, he was assassinated by a military guard at Manila airport. Corazon Aquino, who had stayed in the Philippines to campaign for the opposition in the 1984 legislative elections, was drafted by the opposition to contest the February 1986 presidential election. She claimed victory over Marcos and, accusing the government of voting fraud, led a nonviolent 'people's power' campaign that succeeded in overthrowing Marcos on 25 February 1986.

A devout Roman Catholic, Aquino enjoyed strong church backing in her 1986 campaign. The USA provided strong support as well and was instrumental in turning back a 1989 coup attempt. She introduced a new pluralist constitution in 1987 and survived a further six attempted coups. She was debarred by the new constitution from contesting the 1992 presidential elections, which was won by her loyal defence secretary Fidel ◊Ramos.

FURTHER READING
Buss, C A *Cory Aquino and the People of the Philippines* 1987
Criosostomo, I *Cory: Profile of a President* 1986

Arafat, Yassir, born Mohammed Abed Ar'ouf Arafat (1929–   )

Palestinian nationalist politician, cofounder of al-Fatah in 1957, president of the Palestinian Authority, and leader of the Palestine Liberation Organization (PLO) from 1969. His support for Saddam ◊Hussein after Iraq's invasion of Kuwait in 1990 weakened his international standing, but he was subsequently influential in the Middle East peace talks and in 1993 reached a historic peace accord of mutual recognition with Israel, under which the Gaza Strip and Jericho were transferred to PLO control. He returned to the former occupied territories in 1994 as head of an embryonic Palestinian state, and in 1995 reached agreement on further Israeli troop withdrawals from areas in the West Bank. He took the unprecedented step in October 1995 of inviting the terrorist organization Hamas to talks on Palestinian self-rule.

In November 1995 the Israeli prime minister, Yitzhak ◊Rabin, was assassinated by an Israeli extremist and the peace process appeared to be threatened. Rabin was suceeded by the moderate Shimon ◊Peres but he lost the 1996 general election and was replaced by the hard-line Likud leader Binjamin ◊Netanyahu. Despite this, Arafat continued his efforts for a lasting peace. He was elected president, with almost 90% of the popular vote, of the self-governing Palestinian National Council in 1996.

In 1994 Arafat was awarded the Nobel Prize for Peace jointly with Rabin and Israeli foreign minister Shimon Peres.

In the 1970s Arafat's activities in pursuit of an independent homeland for Palestinians made him a prominent figure in world politics, but in the 1980s the growth of factions within the PLO effectively reduced his power. He was forced to evacuate Lebanon in 1983, but remained leader of most of the PLO and in 1990 persuaded it to recognize formally the state of Israel.

FURTHER READING
Hart, Alan *Arafat* 1994
Mishal, S *The PLO under Arafat* 1986
Wallach, John and Janet *Arafat: In the Eyes of the Beholder* 1991

Aragon, Louis Marie (1897–1982)

French communist poet and novelist, a politically committed writer prominent in anti-fascist campaigns of the 1930s and in the Resistance during World War II. Aragon had been drawn to the surrealist Dada movement after World War I, along with André Breton, but went on to join the French Communist Party (PCF) in 1927. He adopted a socialist realist style in his novels of this period and made several visits to Russia with Elsa Triolet, the Russian-born communist writer whom he married. A frequent contributor to the PCF daily paper, *L'Humanité*, Aragon organized on behalf of the Resistance amongst intellectuals and writers, producing some of his finest poetry in this period.

He was unusual amongst the major literary and intellectual figures associated with the PCF in both taking on formal responsibilities within the PCF and remaining loyal to it through the trauma of destalinisation and the crushing of the Hungarian uprising. He edited the party's literary journal *Les Lettres Françaises* and was elected to the party's Central Committee in 1954.

Araña Osorio, Carlos (1918–   )

Guatemalan soldier and right-wing politician, president 1970–74. He was elected president on a programme of law and order and social reform. However, although a five-year development plan was introduced, reforms were shelved and, in November 1970, a one-year state of siege was declared. Strict curfew and press censorship laws were imposed, while the armed forces launched a concerted campaign against communist guerrillas, terrorists, and 'habitual criminals' (those with more than ten recorded arrests). The crackdown continued after 1971 and a 'police state' was effectively established, with detentions without trial and intimidation of political opponents.

A tough right-wing army colonel, Araña rose to prominence between 1966 and 1968 when he directed a war against guerrillas, but was dismissed by President ◊Méndez Montenegro, after claims that he had links to the *Mano Blanca* (White Hand) rightist paramilitaries who had abducted the archbishop of Guatemala.

Arbenz Guzmán, Jácobo (1913–1971)

Guatemalan social democratic politician and president from 1951 until his overthrow in 1954 by army rebels led by Carlos Castillo Armas, operating with the help of the US Central Intelligence Agency (CIA).

Guzmán brought in policies to redistribute land, much of it owned by overseas companies, to landless peasants; he also encouraged labour organization and brought in communist administrators. However, increasing repression, after an attempted coup in 1952, lost him popular support. His last years were spent in exile in Mexico, Uruguay, and Cuba.

As a young army officer, he married the daughter of a wealthy El Salvador family and was subsequently driven by hostility to the established order. He helped lead the October 1944 popular revolution against the dictatorial regime of Jorge Ubico, and became defence minister in the democratically elected government of Juan José Arévalo 1945–50. He was elected president in 1950 and took office in March 1951.

Archer, Jeffrey Howard, Baron Archer of Weston-super-Mare (1940–)

English writer and politician. He was a Conservative member of Parliament 1969–74, and lost a fortune in a disastrous investment, but recouped it as a best-selling novelist and dramatist. His books, which often concern the rise of insignificant characters to high political office or great business success, include *Not a Penny More, Not a Penny Less* (1975), *Kane and Abel* (1979), *First Among Equals* (1984), and *The Fourth Estate* (1997).

In 1985 he became deputy chair of the Conservative Party, but resigned in November 1986 after a scandal; he subsequently cleared his name in a successful libel action against the *Daily Star*. Baron 1992.

Arendt, Hannah (1906–1975)

German-born US political philosopher. Her concerns included totalitarianism, the nature of evil, and the erosion of public participation in the political process. A pupil of the philosophers Edmund Husserl and Karl Jaspers at Heidelberg University, she left for France when the Nazis came to power and emigrated to the USA in 1940. She was the author notably of *The Origins of Modern Totalitarianism* (1951), in which she pointed out the similarities between Nazism and Soviet communism, both of which fed on the atomization and alienation that characterized modern life. In *The Human Condition* (1958) she expounded an ideal of public life, based on active citizenship, which looked back to the classical Greek polity as its model. Her critique of modernity was also evident in *Eichmann in Jerusalem* (1963), where she coined the phrase 'the banality of evil' to describe how bureaucratic efficiency can facilitate the acceptance of the worst atrocities.

FURTHER READING
Young-Bruehl, Elisabeth *Hannah Arendt, for Love of the World* 1982

Arens, Moshe (1925–)

Israeli politician and engineer, deputy leader of the Likud Party from 1992. He was elected to the Knesset (Israeli Parliament) in 1974. In 1982 he was appointed ambassador to the USA and in 1986 he was given responsibility for Israeli–Arab affairs. Although instinctively right-wing in his views, he was also a pragmatist and, although initially opposed to dealings with the Palestine Liberation Organization (PLO), accepted the need for compromise.

Born in Poland, he was brought to the USA as a child and completed his education there, qualifying as an aeronautical engineer. In 1948 he emigrated to Israel and became active in an underground movement opposed to British rule in Palestine. At the same time he taught in Haifa and from 1962 led a team developing military aircraft. For this work he was awarded the Israeli Defence Prize in 1971. He then directed his energies to politics.

Arevalo Bermejo, Juan José (1904–1990)

Guatemalan president 1945–51, elected to head a civilian government after a popular revolt in 1944 ended a 14-year period of military rule. During his years in power, there were more than 20 attempts to oust him. He sought to promote social justice, with labour law and educational reforms, and health projects. He also renewed the dispute with the UK over Belize. However, many of his reforms were later undone by subsequent military rulers.

Arias Madrid, Arnulfo (1901–1988)

Panamanian authoritarian political leader, president 1940–41, 1949–51, and October 1968. He was elected president in 1940 by a large majority and, influenced by European fascism, pursued controversial racist policies, disenfranchising the non-Spanish-speaking population, declaring support for the Axis powers during World War II, and imprisoning dissidents. He was ousted in October 1941 in a US-supported coup and was exiled until 1945. Arias was re-elected president in 1949, but was deposed in May 1951, after suspending the constitution and establishing his own secret police; he lost his political rights until 1960. After an unsuccessful presidential bid in 1964, he was re-elected in 1968, but was ousted by the National Guard after only 11 days. He failed in a final presidential bid, made in 1984.

Born into a prominent Panamanian family, he studied medicine at Harvard University and in 1931 led the US-based Communal Action coup that deposed President Florencio Harmodio Arosemena. Too young to become president himself, he served as agriculture and public works minister under his brother, Harmodio Arias (1886–1962), who was president 1932–36 and held diplomatic posts in Europe.

Arias Navarro, Carlos (1908–1989)

Spanish politician. As a state prosecutor in the Spanish Civil War, he gained notoriety as the 'Butcher of Málaga' during the nationalists' savage repression of the province. He became prime minister after the assassination of Luis Carrero Blanco in December 1973, and was confirmed as the first prime minister of the monarchy following Franco's death in 1975. He resigned in 1976 under Juan Carlos I, having proved too hardline to effect the transition to democracy.

During his political career he also served as director general of security 1957–65, mayor of Madrid 1965–73, and minister of the interior in June 1973.

Arias Sanchez, Oscar (1940–)

Costa Rican politician, president 1986–90, and secretary general of the left-wing National Liberation

Party (PLN) from 1979. He advocated a neutralist policy and in 1987 was the leading promoter of the Central American Peace Plan, which brought peace to neighbouring Nicaragua. He lost the presidency to Rafael Angel Calderón Fournier in 1990. He was awarded the Nobel Prize for Peace in 1987.

Educated at universitites in Costa Rica, the USA, and the UK, he taught political science at the University of Costa Rica 1969–72 before holding ministerial posts under President José ◊Figueres Ferrer and serving congress 1978–82. From 1990 he led the Arias Foundation for Peace and Human Progress.

Aristide, Jean-Bertrand (1953–)

President of Haiti 1990–91 and 1994–95. A left-wing Catholic priest opposed to the right-wing regime of the Duvalier family, he relinquished his priesthood to concentrate on the presidency. He campaigned for the National Front for Change and Democracy, representing a loose coalition of peasants, trade unionists, and clerics, and won 70% of the vote. He was deposed by the military in September 1991 and took refuge in the USA. In September 1994, under an agreement brokered by former US president Jimmy Carter, the military stepped down and allowed Aristide to return. Constitutionally barred from seeking a second term in December 1995, he was succeeded by his preferred candidate René Préval.

A United Nations arms and oil embargo was imposed on Haiti 1993–94 in an attempt to force Aristide's return.

FURTHER READING
Aristide, Jean-Bertrand *An Autobiography* 1993

Armstrong, Robert Temple, Baron Armstrong of Ilminster (1927–)

English civil servant, cabinet secretary in Margaret ◊Thatcher's government. He achieved notoriety as a key witness in the *Spycatcher* trial in Australia 1987. Defending the British government's attempts to prevent Peter Wright's book alleging 'dirty tricks' from being published, he admitted to having sometimes been 'economical with the truth'. He retired in 1988 and was made a life peer.

After Oxford University he joined the civil service and rose rapidly to deputy-secretary rank. In 1970 he became Prime Minister Edward Heath's principal private secretary; Thatcher later made him cabinet secretary and head of the home civil service.

Arnold, Eve (c. 1925–)

US photographer and photojournalist. In the 1950s, the heyday of US magazine photojournalism, Arnold joined the prestigious picture agency Magnum (1954), becoming its first US woman member. She photo-graphed many memorable events and people of the era, including the US civil-rights movement, Senator Joseph McCarthy, and Malcolm X. In the early 1960s, Arnold moved to London to work on *The Sunday Times*. While she continued to create picture stories featuring entertainers, politicians, and heads of state, she also chronicled in photographs the status of women around the world.

Arriaga, Manuel José de (1842–1917)

Portuguese president 1911–15. He was elected deputy for Funchal as a Republican in the parliament of 1882–84 and for Lisbon 1890–92. He took part in the revolution that drove King Manuel II from the country and was elected the first president of the republic in 1911.

Arriaga was born at Horta, Azores, of a distinguished family that was descended from Alfonso III of Castile. He studied law at the University of Coimbra, and, while there, was disinherited by his father for his republican sympathies. He wrote essays on jurisprudence and political economy.

Arthur, Owen S (1949–)

Barbadian centre-left politician, prime minister from 1994. In 1993 he succeeded Henry Forde as leader of the Barbados Labour Party (BLP) and led the party to a landslide victory in September 1994, at a time of economic difficulties. With his appointment as prime minister, he also received the finance, economic affairs, and civil service portfolios.

Arthur studied economics at the University of the West Indies, and worked in Jamaica as an economic planner. In the early 1980s he held junior positions in the BLP government of Tom ◊Adams.

Arzú, Irigoyen Alvaro (1947–)

Guatemalan politician, president from 1996. He served briefly as minister of foreign affairs in 1991, before resigning to become secretary general of the National Advancement Party (PAN). As the country's president, he concluded a peace agreement with the left-wing Guatemalan National Unity (URNG) guerrilla movement, ending 36 years of civil war, and granted amnesty for all human rights violations during the conflict.

A successful businessman, Arzu was mayor of Guatemala City 1985–90. In 1990 he stood (unsuccessfully) as presidential candidate for the right-of-centre PAN.

Arzu won the presidency in January 1996 in the second round run-off elections, defeating his Republican Front opponent.

Asanuma, Inejiro (1898–1960)

Japanese politician, leader of the Japan Socialist Party. In 1946 he was elected to the lower house of the Diet

Herbert Asquith. *Mary Evans Picture Library*

(parliament) in the first post-war election and repeatedly thereafter. He was stabbed to death by a 17-year-old right-wing assassin as he made a public speech in 1960.

Ashdown, Paddy (Jeremy John Durham) (1941–)

British politician, leader of the merged Social and Liberal Democrats from 1988 (Liberal Democrat Party from 1989). His party significantly increased its seat holding in the 1997 general election, winning more seats than it had had since the 1920s, and cooperated in areas such as constitutional reform with the new Labour government of Tony Blair. From 1997 Ashdown sat with Blair on a joint cabinet committee, whose scope was extended from constitutional issues in November 1998 to cover areas such as health, education, and Europe.

Ashdown served in the Royal Marines as a commando, leading a Special Boat Section in Borneo, and was a member of the Diplomatic Service 1971–76. He became a Liberal member of Parliament for Yeovil, Somerset, in 1983. In January 1999 he announced his intention to resign as leader of the Liberal Democrats in the summer of that year.

Ashe, Arthur (Robert, Jr) (1943–1993)

US tennis player and coach. He was the first black American man to win the US Open in 1968, the Australian Open in 1970, and Wimbledon in 1975. In the late 1960s he became active in human-rights issues, particularly opposing racial discrimination. Pursuing his conviction that sport could help overcome injustice, as an established champion Ashe made a point of visiting South Africa despite the opposition of many black South Africans. His involvement in anti-apartheid protests led to his being arrested on two occasions. He was cofounder of the Black Tennis Association and wrote *A Hard Road to Glory* (1988), a history of blacks in sports. After his contraction of

◆ ASQUITH, HERBERT HENRY, 1ST EARL OF OXFORD AND ASQUITH (1852–1928) ◆

British Liberal politician, prime minister 1908–16.

Asquith was born in Yorkshire, and on completing his education at Oxford became a barrister, achieving prominence in 1889 as junior counsel in a case involving the Irish nationalist politician Charles Parnell. He was first elected Liberal member of Parliament for East Fife in 1886 and held the seat until 1918. In William Gladstone's 1892–95 government, he was home secretary, and as early as 1898 he was touted as a potential successor to Gladstone as party leader.

He enhanced his position with powerful defences of the Liberal doctrine of free trade against Joseph Chamberlain's advocacy of tariff reform. When Henry Campbell-Bannerman formed his Liberal government in 1905, Asquith was made chancellor of the Exchequer, introducing differential tax rates and means-

> *One to mislead the public, another to mislead the Cabinet, and the third to mislead itself.*
>
> HERBERT ASQUITH Remark quoted in Alistair Horne
> *Price of Glory* on the War Office's
> sets of figures.

tested old-age pensions for those aged 70 or more in his 1908 budget. He became prime minister on

AIDS – from a blood transfusion following a multiple bypass operation – became known in 1992, Ashe campaigned for AIDS-related causes until his death. The Arthur Ashe Foundation for the Defeat of AIDS was launched on the eve of the 1992 US Open.

FURTHER READING

Ashe, Arthur, and Rampersad, Arnold (contributor) *Days of Grace: A Memoir* 1994

Evensen Lazo, Catherine *Arthur Ashe* 1998

Weissberg, Ted, et al *Arthur Ashe* 1992

Ashley, Jack, Lord Ashley (1922–)

British Labour politician. Profoundly deaf since 1967, Ashley campaigned inside and outside Parliament for the deaf and other disability groups. He sat as member of Parliament for Stoke-on-Trent 1966–92, when he was raised to the peerage.

Ashley's autobiography *Journey into Silence* (1973) describes his long struggle to come to terms with his disability and resume his political career after an operation and viral infection had permanently deprived him of all hearing.

Ashrawi, Hanan (1946–)

Palestinian political leader. She was chief spokesperson of the Palestinian Liberation Organization delegation at the Madrid peace conference in 1991, but refused to join Yassir ◊Arafat's Palestinian Authority. In 1994 she launched the Palestinian Independent Commission for Citizens' Rights to defend the rights of citizens in the Palestinian self-rule areas of Gaza and Jericho. In January 1996 she was elected to the newly formed Palestinian Council.

Born in Ramallah, in the British mandate for Palestine (now the West Bank), she opposed the Israeli occupation of the West Bank and Gaza. She became professor of English literature at Bir Zeit University in the West Bank in 1981. She is a Christian.

Askin, Robert (Robin William) (1907–1981)

Australian Liberal politician, premier of New South Wales 1965–75. When he led his party to electoral victory in 1965 he ended 24 years of Labor government in New South Wales. He was noted for political shrewdness and conservative policies, strongly opposing the Whitlam Labor federal government and curbing public demonstrations against the Vietnam War. His reputation has been tarnished by allegations that he allowed corruption and organized crime to flourish during his term of office.

A tram driver's son, he worked as a bank clerk before being elected to the New South Wales assembly in 1950, after war-time military service.

Assad, Hafez al (1930–)

Syrian Ba'athist politician, president from 1971. He became prime minister after a bloodless military coup in 1970, and the following year was the first president to be elected by popular vote. Having suppressed dissent, he was re-elected in 1978, 1985, and 1991. He is a Shia (Alawite) Muslim. In February 1997 he was reported to be seriously ill.

He ruthlessly suppressed domestic opposition, and was Iran's only major Arab ally in its war against Iraq. He steadfastly pursued military parity with Israel, and made himself a key player in any settlement of the Lebanese civil war or Middle East conflict generally. His support for United Nations action against Iraq

---

Campbell-Bannerman's resignation in 1908.

Forcing through the radical budget of his chancellor David Lloyd George led Asquith into two elections during 1910 and resulted in the Parliament Act of 1911, limiting the right of the Lords to veto legislation. After 1911 Asquith was dependent upon the Irish nationalists for his majority in the Commons and his endeavours to pass the Home Rule for Ireland Bill (very much a Gladstonian legacy) were troublesome. Including Ulster in its provisions led to the Curragh 'Mutiny' and incipient civil war. Unity was re-established by the outbreak of World War I. Asquith then led the country to war in 1914 but there were stories of shell shortages at the front and he faced criticism for his reluctance to expand the machinery of government and in general for his 'wait and see' attitude. A coalition government was formed in May 1915, but even this was

divided over the question of conscription. By December 1916 he was driven to resign and was replaced by Lloyd George.

This caused a fatal split in the Liberal Party, which divided into Lloyd George and Asquithian wings, briefly re-uniting in 1923 (when Baldwin declared for tariff reform) on the Liberal touchstone of free trade. Asquith remained its official leader until 1926, but lost his own seat in the 1918 election and lost Paisley (which he had won in a 1920 by-election) in 1924. Whatever his talents as a parliamentarian, debater, and proponent of Liberalism, Asquith presided over the demise of the Liberal Party as a major player in British politics.

Hanan Ashrawi, 1991. *Rex*

following its invasion of Kuwait in 1990 raised his international standing. In 1995, following intense US diplomatic pressure, he was close to reaching a mutual peace agreement with Israel. However, the assassination of Yitzhak ◊Rabin in November 1995 and the return of a Likud-led government in Israel seriously threatened the peace process.

FURTHER READING
Ma'oz, M *Assad: The Sphinx of Damascus* 1988
Seale, P *Assad of Syria* 1988

Astor, Nancy, born Nancy Witcher Langhorne (1879–1964)

US-born viscountess and politician. She married the 2nd Viscount Astor in 1906, to whose seat she succeeded in 1919. The first woman to sit in the British House of Commons, she promoted temperance and women's rights and wrote an early biography *My Two Countries* (1923).

Asturias, Miguel Ángel (1899–1974)

Guatemalan author and diplomat. His novels, such as *El señor presidente/The President* (1946), *Men of Corn* (1949), and *Strong Wind* (1950), attacked Latin-American dictatorships and 'Yankee imperialism'. He was awarded the Nobel Prize for Literature in 1967.

In 1942 he was elected to the Guatemalan Congress and held diplomatic posts in Central and South America 1946–54, before being temporarily exiled. He was ambassador to France 1966–70.

Atassi, Hashem al- (1874–1960)

Syrian politician, president 1936–39, 1949–51, and 1954–55.

Educated in Istanbul, Turkey, he served as a district governor in Ottoman administration before World War I. In 1920 he was briefly prime minister in a nationalist government set up by ◊Faisal (later Faisal I of Iraq). Thereafter, during the 1920s and 1930s period of French Mandate rule, al-Atassi established himself as leader of the National Bloc, which fought for Syrian independence, and served as president of Syria 1936–39. He did not actively participate in the final phase of the struggle for independence, achieved in 1946. However, in 1949, following a military coup by Muhammad Sami al-Hinnawi, he became prime minister. After another coup, by Adib al-Shishakli in December 1949, al-Atassi was made president. However, frustrated by the restrictions placed on his powers, he resigned in 1951 and campaigned to overthrow al-Shishakli. He returned as president in 1954, before retiring from politics in September 1955.

Atatürk, Mustafa Kemal, name (Turkish 'Father of the Turks') assumed in 1934 by Mustafa Kemal Pasha (1881–1938)

Turkish politician and general, first president of Turkey from 1923. After World War I he established a provisional rebel government and in 1921–22 the Turkish armies under his leadership expelled the Greeks who were occupying Turkey. He was the founder of the modern republic, which he ruled as a virtual dictator, with a policy of consistent and radical Westernization.

Kemal, born in Thessaloniki, was banished in 1904 for joining a revolutionary society. Later he was pardoned and promoted in the army and was largely responsible for the successful defence of the Dardanelles against the British in 1915. In 1918, after Turkey had been defeated, he was sent into Anatolia to implement the demobilization of the Turkish forces in accordance with the armistice terms, but instead he established a provisional government opposed to that of Constantinople (modern Istanbul, then under Allied control) and in 1921 led the Turkish armies against the Greeks, who had occupied a large part of Anatolia. He checked them at the Battle of the Sakaria, 23 August–13 September 1921, for which he was granted the title of Ghazi ('the Victorious'), and within a year had expelled the Greeks from Turkish soil. War with the British was averted by his diplomacy, and Turkey in Europe passed under Kemal's control. On 29 October 1923 Turkey was proclaimed a republic with Kemal as first president.

FURTHER READING
Kazoncigil, Ali, and Özbudun, Ergun *Atatürk: Father of a Modern State* 1981
Kinross, J P D *Atatürk: The Rebirth of a Nation* 1964
Macfie, A L *Atatürk* 1994
Renda, Gunsel, and Kortpeter, C M (eds) *The Transformation of Turkish Culture: The Atatürk Legacy* 1986

Atwood, Margaret Eleanor (1939–   )

Canadian novelist, short-story writer, and poet. Her novels, which often treat feminist themes with wit and irony, include *The Edible Woman* (1969), *Life Before Man* (1979), *Bodily Harm* (1981), *The Handmaid's Tale* (1986), *Cat's Eye* (1989), and *The Robber Bride* (1993).

Collections of poetry include *Power Politics* (1971), *You are Happy* (1974), and *Interlunar* (1984).

FURTHER READING

Davidson, Arnold and Cathy *The Art of Margaret Atwood* 1981
Grace, S E *Violent Duality: A Study of Margaret Atwood* 1980
Ingersoll, E E (ed) *Atwood: Conversations* 1990
Rigney, B H *Margaret Atwood* 1987

Auden, W(ystan) H(ugh) (1907–1973)

English-born US poet. He wrote some of his most original poetry, such as *Look, Stranger!* (1936), in the 1930s when he led the influential left-wing literary group that included Louis MacNeice, Stephen Spender, and C Day-Lewis. He moved to the USA in 1939, became a US citizen in 1946, and adopted a more conservative and Christian viewpoint, for example in *The Age of Anxiety* (1947).

When he laughed, respectable senators burst with laughter, / And when he cried the little children died in the streets.

W H AUDEN 'Epitaph on a Tyrant'

His openly political work of the 1930s cast him as a leader of the left-wing poets of that decade. Among his works from the period, *Look, Stranger!* and *Spain* (1937) are characterized not only by their commitment to a cause but by their relatively simple style, an attempt to reach a wider audience.

In the early 1940s Auden reconverted to Christianity, and in three long poems – *The Sea and the Mirror* (1944), *For the Time Being* (1945), and *The Age of Anxiety* – he inaugurated the religious, aesthetic, and socio-psychological themes that dominated his verse in the later 1940s and 1950s. He became more conservative in his political and social beliefs, and while editing *Collected Shorter Poems* (1927–57 and 1967) and *Collected Longer Poems* (1968), he expunged many of his earlier radical poems.

FURTHER READING

Callan, E *Auden: A Carnival of Intellect* 1983
Carpenter, H *Auden: A Biography* 1981
Gingerich, M E *Auden: A Reference Guide* 1978
Mendelson, E *Early Auden* 1981
Rodway, A *Preface to Auden* 1984
Rowse, A L *The Poet Auden* 1988
Spender, S (ed) *W H Auden: A Tribute* 1975

Aung San (1916–1947)

Burmese (Myanmar) politician. He was a founder and leader of the Anti-Fascist People's Freedom League, which led Burma's fight for independence from the UK. During World War II he collaborated first with Japan and then with the UK. In 1947 he became head of Burma's provisional government but was assassinated the same year by political opponents. His daughter ◊Suu Kyi spearheaded a nonviolent pro-democracy movement in Myanmar from 1988.

Imprisoned for his nationalist activities while a student in Rangoon, Aung escaped to Japan in 1940. He returned to lead the Burma Independence Army, which assisted the Japanese invasion in 1942, and became defence minister in the puppet government set up by the Japanese. Before long, however, he secretly contacted the Resistance movement, and from March 1945 openly cooperated with the British in the expulsion of the Japanese. Burma became independent in 1948, after his death.

Aurobindo Ghose, known as *Shri Aurobindo* (1872–1950)

Indian religious writer and leader, founder of Aurobindo Ashram (a centre for religious study) at Pondicherry, southern India. He wrote extensively on Hindu theology and philosophy, proposing a system called integral yoga to bring together body and soul, individual and community. Through his widespread influence on the Hindu intelligentsia he strengthened the modern Hindu movement in the 1930s and 1940s. After his death his followers developed the city of Auroville at his ashram.

Ávila Camacho, Manuel (1897–1955)

Mexican politician, president 1940–46. In 1938 he was made minister of national defence and was elected president in 1940, as candidate of the Mexican Revolutionary Army. As president he pursued a less radical programme of agricultural, industrial, and educational reforms than his predecessor, Lázaro ◊Cárdenas. During World War II his government developed close ties with the USA and, in 1945, after oil tankers were sunk by German submarines, Mexican fighter planes were sent to the Pacific.

A self-educated farmer's son, Ávila Camacho joined the revolutionary army of Victoriano ◊Huerta in 1914, becoming a brigadier general. In 1920 he was chief of general staff to Lázaro Cárdenas, and during the 1930s secured a reputation as a conciliatory negotiator with rebel forces. He retired from politics in 1946.

Avksent'yev, Nicolai Dmitriyevich (1878–1943)

Russian politician, leader of the right wing of the Socialist Revolutionary Party. After the February Revolution of 1917, he became chair of the peasants'

Clement Atlee, c. 1935. *AKG London*

deputies at the All-Russian Congress of Soviets, then minister of the Interior in the Provisional Government and chair of the pre-parliament. He worked for a time under the Bolsheviks after they had seized power in the October Revolution, but later emigrated.

Awolowo, Obafemi, Chief Awolowo (1909– 1987)

Nigerian politician, premier of the Western Region 1954–59. He was co-founder of the Action Group, a party based on the Yoruba of western Nigeria, which he led from 1951 until the party was banned in 1966. Having lost the premiership in 1959, he became leader of the opposition in the federal parliament from 1960 and was imprisoned in 1962. Released after the 1966 coup, he was appointed federal commissioner for finance and vice president of the federal executive council of Nigeria 1967–71.

By profession a lawyer, Awolowo was a solicitor and advocate of the Nigerian supreme court, and returned to private practice after 1971. His bid for the presidency in 1979 as the Unity Party of Nigeria candidate was unsuccessful.

Awolowo was educated in Protestant schools, and worked as a teacher, trader, trade-union organizer, and journalist, before becoming an external student of law at London University.

◆ ATTLEE, CLEMENT (RICHARD), 1ST EARL ATTLEE (1883–1967) ◆

British Labour politician, prime minister 1945–51.

Attlee was born in London, educated at Oxford, and practised as a barrister 1906–09. Social work in London's East End and cooperation in poor-law reform led him to become a socialist; he joined the Fabian Society in 1907 and the Independent Labour Party in 1908. He lectured in social science at the London School of Economics in 1913. After service at Gallipoli and on the western front in World War I (he achieved the rank of major), Attlee was mayor of Stepney in East London 1919–20 and was Labour member of Parliament for Limehouse 1922–50 and for West Walthamstow 1950–55.

In the first Labour government he was undersecretary for war. From 1927 he served on a government inquiry into the government of India; he was chancellor of the Duchy of Lancaster 1930–31, and postmaster general from March 1931. Having retained his seat in the 1931 election, Attlee was catapulted upwards in the Labour hierarchy. In 1935 he succeeded George Lansbury as leader and defended his position in a ballot against Herbert Morrison after the 1935

election. Attlee was party leader until 1955. His startling rise from what all acknowledged to be a competent but colourless minister to party leader owed much to Labour's weak position after 1931, but also to the perceived weaknesses of Ramsay Macdonald's character, to which Attlee's taciturnity could not have stood in greater contrast.

Democracy means government by discussion, but it is only effective if you can stop people talking.

CLEMENT ATTLEE Speech at Oxford
14 June 1957

In the coalition government during World War II he was Lord Privy Seal 1940–42, dominions secretary 1942–43, and Lord President of the Council 1943–45, as well as deputy prime minister to Winston Churchill from 1942. Though famously described by Churchill as 'a sheep in wolf's clothing', Attlee balanced a variety of difficult and sometimes competing roles with

Aylwin, (Azòcar) Patricio (1919–)

Chilean lawyer and politician who, as leader of the opposition coalition, triggered the national plebiscite of October 1989 that brought down General ◊ Pinochet in the 1988 elections. Power was formally transferred from the military regime to Aylwin in 1990, but his inability to secure the two-thirds majority in Congress necessary to amend the 1980 constitution allowed the outgoing junta to nominate almost one-fifth of the Senate's membership and thus to thwart Aylwin's efforts to lift press censorship and abolish the death penalty.

Continuing revelations about the previous regime's record on human rights triggered violent demonstrations, but Pinochet still resisted attempts to remove him as military commander in chief.

Aylwin was born in Santiago. After a successful legal career, he was elected president of the Christian Democratic Party in 1973.

Ayub Khan, Muhammad (1907–1974)

Pakistani soldier and president 1958–69. He served in the Burma Campaign 1942–45, and was commander in chief of the Pakistan army in 1951. In 1958 Ayub Khan assumed power after a bloodless army coup. He won the presidential elections in 1960 and 1965, and established a stable economy and achieved limited land reforms. His militaristic form of government was

---

characteristic calmness. In July 1945 he became prime minister after a Labour landslide in the general election. His was the first Labour government to enjoy an absolute majority and it introduced a sweeping programme of nationalization and welfare reform, bringing the National Health service to life in 1948. The government also saw the end of the British Raj in India. Faced with severe economic problems after the war and with the considerable international strains of the Cold War, the government was returned to power with a much reduced majority in 1950 and finally defeated in 1951. Attlee remained party leader, at least in part to thwart his great rival Herbert Morrison. He was created 1st Earl in 1955 on his retirement from the Commons.

Attlee was an unlikely political great. But his celebrated understatedness, as epitomized by the title of his 1954 memoirs, *As It Happened*, enabled him effectively to unite the quarrelsome Labour Party and to coordinate the efforts of his government ministers, ensuring their all-round success.

FURTHER READING
Burridge, Trevor *Clement Attlee* 1985
Harris, Kenneth *Attlee* 1982

---

unpopular, particularly with the Bengalis. He resigned in 1969 after widespread opposition and civil disorder, notably in Kashmir.

Azad, Maulana Abul Kalam (1888–1958)

Indian Muslim scholar, author, journalist, and politician. During World War I he advocated a programme of non-cooperation with the British, which influenced Mahatma ◊ Gandhi and for which he was imprisoned. He was elected president of the Indian National Congress in 1940 and was also president of the Congress Party during negotiations for India's independence. After independence he was in charge of the ministry of education.

Azad is also well known as a Muslim scholar and developed new principles of interpretation of the Koran arguing that it must be interpreted in the light of the historical circumstances under which it was written. He also emphasized that religion revealed by God is the same for all humanity and that real religion is the direct worship of one God without any mediating agency.

Azaña, Manuel (1880–1940)

Spanish politician, prime minister 1931–33 and 1936. He was the first prime minister of the second Spanish republic, and the last president of the republic during the Civil War 1936–39, before the establishment of a dictatorship under General Francisco Franco.

Azcona del Hoyo, José Simon (1927–)

Honduran politician, president 1986–90. A moderate conservative, he signed the American Peace Accord of 1987 despite his government's quiet acceptance of the presence in Honduras of Nicaraguan contras backed by the USA. He was barred by law from seeking a second term.

He served in the governments of Roberto Suazo and Walter López 1982–86, which were ostensibly civilian administrations but, in reality, remained in control of the army commander in chief, General Gustavo Alvarez. The latter was removed by junior officers in 1984, and in 1986 Azcona narrowly won the presidential election.

Born in La Ceiba, he trained as a civil engineer in Honduras and Mexico, developing a particular interest in urban development and low-cost housing. As a student he became interested in politics and fought the 1963 general election as a candidate for the Liberal Party of Honduras (PLH), but his career was interrupted by a series of military coups.

Azhari, Ismail (1902–1969)

Sudanese politician, first prime minister of Sudan 1954–56 and president 1964–69. Imprisoned by the British for nationalist agitation, he was elected head of the National Unionist Party in 1952, and led the country in the two years preceding full independence.

Azhari was born at Omdurman and educated at Gordon College, Khartoum, and the American University of Beirut, Lebanon. Following the army coup led by Ibrahim ◊Abboud in 1958, he was politically inactive but assumed the presidency when the Abboud regime fell. He was toppled by General Nimeri's coup in 1969, and died a few months later.

Azikiwe, Nnamdi (1904–1996)

Nigerian politician and president 1963–66. A leading nationalist in the 1940s, he advocated self-government for Nigeria. He was prime minister of Eastern Nigeria 1954–59 and on independence became governor general of the Federation of Nigeria 1960–63. During the civil war triggered by the secession of Biafra 1967–70 he initially backed his own ethnic group, the Ibo, but switched his support to the federal government in 1969.

Leader of the Nigeria People's Party from 1978 until political parties were banned in 1984, he retired from politics in 1986.

Azikiwe was born in Zungeru, Niger state, and educated in the USA. He worked as a newspaper editor in the Gold Coast (now Ghana) from 1934, returning to Nigeria in 1937 to start the *West African Pilot* in Lagos, where he built up a chain of newspapers. In 1946 he was a founder of the National Council of Nigeria and the Cameroons and acted as its president 1946–60. He was accused of using government funds to save the African Continental Bank in which he held shares in 1956, and was censured by a tribunal. His books, mainly on African nationalism, include *Renascent Africa* (1937), *The African in Ancient and Medieval History* (1938), *Political Blueprint of Nigeria* (1943), and *Military Revolution in Nigeria* (1972).

Aziz, Tariq, born Mikhail Yuhanna (1936–)

Iraqi politician, deputy prime minister from 1979, and foreign minister 1983–91. Saddam ◊Hussein's right-hand man, Aziz was a loyalist who remained staunchly faithful to the Iraqi leader. After 1983, and especially during the Gulf War, Aziz was the chief international spokesman for Iraqi policy. He visited Egypt in 1983 in the first formal contact between the two nations since 1978. In the summer of 1990 he led Iraq's intimidation of its erstwhile Arab allies, culminating in the invasion of Kuwait in August of that year. Throughout his tenure, Aziz was credited with bringing Iraqi diplomacy more into the mainstream.

Aziz held various journalistic posts and rose to prominence in Iraqi politics after Hussein's Ba'ath Party seized power in 1969, becoming one of the party's leading ideologists and being assigned to serve as minister of information in 1974. He became a member of the Arab Ba'ath Party regional leadership in 1977, deputy prime minister in 1979, and foreign minister 1983–91. Aziz was poised for such high-level posts because of his underground activism on behalf of the Arab Ba'ath Socialist Party before the revolution, where he met Hussein, then a member of the Ba'ath's military unit, in the 1950s.

Aziz was born near the northern Iraqi city of Mosul into a Christian family. His birth name was Mikhail Yuhanna, which he later changed to Tariq Aziz. His family moved to Baghdad when he was a young boy and he studied English literature at the Baghdad College of Fine Arts.

Aznar, José Maria (1953–)

Spanish politician, prime minister from 1996. He became premier of the Castile-León region in 1987. Elected leader of the right-of-centre Popular Party (PP) in 1989, Aznar and the PP lost to the ruling Social Workers' Party (PSOE) in the elections of 1989 and 1993. A minority PP government headed by Aznar was installed in 1996.

When the PSOE lost its parliamentary majority in March 1996, the ensuing general election produced an inconclusive result. After months of abortive negotiations with other parties, Aznar formed a minority PP government, pledging to restore Spain as a credible European power.

B

Baader, Andreas (1943–1977)

German radical left-wing political activist. With Ulrike Meinhof (1934–1976) and Gudrun Ensslin (1940–1977), he formed the Rote Armee Fraktion/Red Army Faction (RAF), also known as the Baader–Meinhof gang, urban guerrillas who aimed to bring down the West German state through acts of violence and political assassination. Sentenced to life imprisonment in 1977, he and Ensslin both died in prison, allegedly by suicide.

Baader was born in Munich. He studied under the Palestinian revolutionary group al-Fatah in Jordan, before returning to Germany to join the 1960s student protest movement. He was imprisoned in 1968 for setting fire to shops in Frankfurt, but escaped in 1970. His death followed the failure of the RAF to secure the release of its three leaders by holding a Lufthansa plane hostage at Mogadishu, Somalia.

Babangida, Ibrahim (1941–)

Nigerian politician and soldier, president 1985–93. He became head of the Nigerian army in 1983, and in 1985 led a coup against President Muhammadu Buhari, assuming the presidency himself. From 1992 he promised a return to civilian rule but resigned in 1993, his commitment to democracy increasingly in doubt.

Babangida was born in Minna, Niger state, and trained at military schools in Nigeria and the UK. He became an instructor in the Nigerian Defence Academy and by 1983 had reached the rank of major general. In 1983, after taking part in the overthrow of President Shehu Shagari, he was made army commander in chief. Responding to public pressure in 1989, he allowed the formation of competing political parties and promised a return to a democratic civilian government in 1992.

In an attempt to end corruption, he banned anyone who had ever held elective office from being a candidate in the new civilian government. Similarly, applications for recognition from former political parties were also rejected. Having twice blocked the release of presidential election results (once in 1992 and once in 1993) after allegations of fraud, Babangida stepped down in 1993, nominating Ernest Shonekan as his successor.

Badinter, Robert (1928–)

French lawyer and socialist politician. He was appointed by President François Mitterrand as president of the French Constitutional Council 1986–95.

A reforming lawyer and close political associate of Mitterrand, Badinter served as his first minister of justice 1981–86 and was responsible for abolishing capital punishment in October 1981, handing France's two remaining guillotines over to a museum. His other modernizing and liberal reforms of this period included incorporating Article 25 of the European Convention of Human Rights into French law, enabling French citizens to take an appeal, in cases involving a claimed violation of human rights, to the European Court in Strasbourg.

Badoglio, Pietro (1871–1956)

Italian soldier and Fascist politician who served as a general in World War I and later commanded the Italian forces in the conquest of Abyssinia (Ethiopia). He succeeded Mussolini as prime minister of Italy from July 1943 to June 1944 and negotiated the armistice with the Allies.

Baez, Joan (1941–)

US folk singer and pacifist activist. Her pure soprano in the early 1960s popularized traditional English and US folk songs such as 'Silver Dagger' and 'We Shall Overcome' (an anthem of the civil-rights movement). She helped Bob Dylan at the start of his career and has recorded many of his songs. She founded the Institute for the Study of Non-Violence in Carmel, California, in 1965.

> I've never had a humble opinion. If you've got an opinion, why be humble about it?
>
> JOAN BAEZ Remark

Bailey, Liberty Hyde (1858–1954)

US horticulturist and botanist who advised the US President Franklin D Roosevelt on his agricultural policy and ran Roosevelt's Country Life Commission 1908, which aimed to improve the standard of life and living conditions of rural communities.

Baker, Howard Henry (1925–1994)

US Republican politician. He was senator for Tennessee 1967–85, Senate minority leader 1977–81, and majority leader 1981–85. As White House chief of staff 1987–88, he helped the administration deal with the revelation of the Irangate scandal (the illegal sale of arms to Iran by members of the US government in order to fund the rebels in Nicaragua).

After serving in the US Navy during World War II, Baker joined the family law firm in Knoxville, Tennessee. He was a member of the Senate select committee to investigate the Watergate scandal in 1973, which brought down President Richard Nixon. After poor results in the New Hampshire primary, he withdrew from the contest for the Republican nomination for president in 1980.

Baker, James Addison III (1930–)

US Republican politician. Under President Ronald Reagan, he was White House chief of staff 1981–85 and treasury secretary 1985–88. After managing George Bush's successful presidential campaign, Baker was appointed secretary of state in 1989 and played a prominent role in the 1990–91 Gulf crisis and the subsequent search for a lasting Middle East peace settlement. In 1992 he left the state department to become White House chief of staff and to oversee Bush's unsuccessful re-election campaign. In 1997 he

served as a UN special envoy to try and broker a peace settlement for the disrupted territory of Western Sahara.

A lawyer from Houston, Texas, Baker entered politics in 1970 as one of the managers of his friend George Bush's unsuccessful campaign for the Senate. He served as undersecretary of commerce 1975–76 in the Gerald Ford administration and was deputy manager of the 1976 and 1980 Ford and Bush presidential campaigns. Baker joined the Reagan administration in 1981 and in 1988 masterminded the campaign that won Bush the presidency. The most powerful member of the Bush team, he was described as an effective 'prime minister'.

Baker, Kenneth Wilfrid (1934–)

British Conservative politician, home secretary 1990–92. He was environment secretary 1985–86, education secretary 1986–89, and chair of the Conservative Party 1989–90, retaining his cabinet seat, before becoming home secretary in John ◊Major's government. After his dismissal in 1992, he became a frequent government critic. He retired from Parliament in 1997.

Baker, Newton Diehl (1871–1937)

US Democrat politician. He was secretary of war under Woodrow Wilson 1915–21 and a US member of the Court of International Justice at The Hague in 1928.

Baker was born in Martinsburg, West Virginia, and

◆ BALDWIN, STANLEY, 1ST EARL BALDWIN OF BEWDLEY (1867–1947) ◆

British Conservative politician, prime minister 1923–24, 1924–29, and 1935–37, and leader of the Conservative Party 1923–37.

Baldwin was born in Bewdley, Worcestershire, the son of an iron and steel magnate, and he was educated at Harrow and Cambridge. In 1908 he became Unionist member of Parliament for Bewdley, which he represented until 1937. In 1916 he was made parliamentary private secretary to Andrew Bonar Law. Baldwin was financial secretary to the Treasury 1917–21, and then appointed to the presidency of the Board of Trade. In 1919 he anonymously gave the Treasury £50,000 of war loan for cancellation, representing about 20% of his personal fortune. He spoke briefly but persuasively about the threat Lloyd George posed to the Conservative Party during the Carlton Club meeting of October 1922 that put paid to the coalition government. Opposition to Lloyd George (notably his preparedness to sell honours, which Baldwin found ethically dubious) defined Baldwin's political trajectory in the period when Labour and the Conservatives came to dominate British party politics. He was made

chancellor under Bonar Law, achieving a settlement of war debts with the USA.

As prime minister 1923–24 and again 1924–29, Baldwin pursued a policy of moderation, healing rifts in the party by bringing back ex-coalitionists and even Winston Churchill, after 20 years in the Liberal Party. Other policy initiatives granted widows' and orphans' pensions, and equal voting

---

When we speak of Empire it is in no spirit of flag-wagging. We feel that in this great inheritance of ours, separated as it is by the seas, we have yet one home and one people.

STANLEY BALDWIN Speech 5 December 1924

---

rights for women in 1928. His political qualities were backed up by a vision of England espoused in *On England and Other Speeches* (1926). After the 1926 General Strike, however, in which Baldwin appealed to middle-class opinion and constitutional rights (rather than adopting

educated at Johns Hopkins and Lee universities. He was major of Cleveland 1911–15. In 1928 he was elected president of the Woodrow Wilson Foundation.

Bakhtiar, Shahpur (1914–1991)

Iranian politician, the last prime minister under Shah ◊Pahlavi, in 1979. He was a supporter of the political leader Muhammad Mossadeq in the 1950s, and was active in the National Front opposition to the shah from 1960. He lived in exile after the 1979 Islamic revolution, until his assassination by Islamic zealots at his home in Paris.

Bakhtiar was born and educated in France, and served in the French army during World War II. He returned to Iran in the 1940s to find that his father had been executed for treason by the Pahlavi regime headed by Reza Shah. Nevertheless, Bakhtiar became a civil servant and eventually director of the department of labour in the oil-rich province of Khuzistan. A social democrat, he had already joined the Iran Party, which subsequently affiliated with the National Front led by Muhammad ◊Mossadeq. When Mossadeq became prime minister in 1951, Bakhtiar seemed likely to benefit, but the coup against Mossadeq in 1953 temporarily ended Bakhtiar's political career and he spent some time in prison.

By 1960 the National Front had been revived as a result of the unpopularity of the shah's government, and Bakhtiar became the Front's spokesperson on

Churchill's more confrontational tone), the Trades Disputes Act was passed, which punished the unions. And with rising unemployment the 'safety first' strategy adopted for the 1929 election failed.

In opposition, Baldwin's leadership was under pressure from press barons like Lord Rothermere and the Empire lobby in his own party to adopt a tariff policy. This he was reluctant to do, having lost the 1923 election on the issue, and he challenged the press on the constitutional grounds of enjoying 'power without responsibility'. He joined the national government of Ramsay MacDonald in 1931 as Lord President of the Council, guiding the Government of India Bill onto the legislative books in 1935. His third premiership, 1935–37, was again dominated by a constitutional crisis, the abdication of Edward VIII, which Baldwin handled with characteristic skill. After moving to the Lords in 1937, Baldwin was increasingly criticized for endeavouring to seek appeasement with the dictators Hitler and Mussolini, and for the failure to rearm more effectively. Nonetheless, his skill at managing the Conservative Party and adapting it to the much enlarged franchise after 1918 and his quiet and moral authority, were undoubted. See picture on page 32.

student affairs. As opposition to the Pahlavi regime increased, the shah looked for support from the Front, and in 1979 Bakhtiar, as a member of the executive willing to do a deal with the shah, was made prime minister in spite of having publicly criticized him. Soon afterwards, Ayatollah ◊Khomeini came to power; Bakhtiar fled to France, where many attempts were made on his life, in spite of French government protection.

Balaguer Ricardo, Joaquín Videla (1906–)

Dominican Republic centre-right politician, president 1960–62, 1966–78, and 1986–96. The country's figurehead president in 1960 under the dictator Rafael ◊Trujillo Molina, he formed the Christian Social Reform Party (PRSC) in 1965, and was elected president in 1966. He established a more democratic regime and closer links with the USA, but faced coup attempts, right-wing terrorism, and left-wing guerrilla incursions. He retired in 1978, but failure of the economic policies of the left-of-centre Dominican Revolutionary Party (PRD) brought him back to power in 1986.

After re-election in 1990 and 1994, accusations of electoral malpractice led to new elections in 1996, which he did not contest, although his influence continued through his support for the successful candidate Leonel ◊Fernández.

With a doctorate in law from Santo Domingo University and the Sorbonne, Paris, Balaguer first practised as a law professor. During the 1940s he was ambassador to Colombia and Mexico, before entering politics. He was foreign secretary 1954–56 under Trujillo, and fled to the USA soon after the dictator's assassination in 1961, returning to the Dominican Republic in 1965.

Balbo, Count Italo (1896–1940)

Italian aviator and politician. He was one of the main figures in Mussolini's 'March on Rome' but later quarrelled with him over the alliance with Germany.

A well-known aviator, famed for his long-distance flights to demonstrate Italian aviation, he served as minister of aviation in the 1930s. His popularity irked Mussolini, and he was despatched as governor to Libya in 1936. This did not stop him voicing his objections to Mussolini's growing friendship with Hitler and he tried to persuade Mussolini to stay out of the war. Shortly after Italy's entry into the war, Balbo was flying back to Libya from Italy when his aircraft was shot down over Tobruk by Italian anti-aircraft guns and he was killed.

Baldwin, James Arthur (1924–1987)

US writer and civil-rights activist. He portrayed with vivid intensity the suffering and despair of African-Americans in contemporary society. After his first novel, *Go Tell it on the Mountain* (1953), set in Harlem, and *Giovanni's Room* (1956), about a homosexual

Stanley Baldwin, 1935. *AKG London*

relationship in Paris, his writing became more politically indignant with *Another Country* (1962) and *The Fire Next Time* (1963), a collection of essays.

Anyone who has ever struggled with poverty knows how extremely expensive it is to be poor.
JAMES BALDWIN *Nobody Knows My Name*, 'Fifth Avenue, Uptown: A letter from Harlem'

FURTHER READING
Macebush, S *James Baldwin* 1973
O'Daniel, T B *James Baldwin: A Critical Evaluation* 1977
Pratt, L H *James Baldwin* 1978
Sylvander, C W *James Baldwin* 1981

Balfour, Arthur James, 1st Earl of Balfour and Viscount Traprain (1848–1930)

British Conservative politician, prime minister 1902–05, foreign secretary 1916–19, and leader of the Conservative Party 1902–1911.

Balfour was the son of a Scottish landowner, and was educated at Eton and Cambridge. He was Conservative member of Parliament for Hertford 1874–1885, East Manchester 1885–1906, and the City of London 1906–1922. In Lord Salisbury's ministry he was secretary for Ireland in 1887, and for his ruthless vigour was called 'Bloody Balfour' by Irish nationalists. In 1891 and again in 1895 he became First Lord of the Treasury and leader of the Commons, and in 1902 he succeeded Salisbury (his uncle) as prime minister. He introduced the 1902 Education Act, which outraged non-conformists by funding Anglican schools. His cabinet was divided over Joseph Chamberlain's tariff-reform proposals, and in the 1906 elections suffered a crushing defeat.

Balfour retired from the party leadership in 1911. In 1915 he joined the Asquith coalition as First Lord of the Admiralty. As foreign secretary 1916–19 he issued the Balfour Declaration in favour of a national home in Palestine for the Jews and was involved in peace negotiations after World War I, signing the Treaty of Versailles. He was Lord President of the Council 1919–22 and 1925–29. An intellectual in demeanour (often described by contemporaries as 'languid'), Balfour had a troubled political career, but enjoyed a lengthy period as an elder statesman of British politics and as an aristocratic figure of stability in British Conservatism in the era between Salisbury and Baldwin. His *Chapters in Autobiography* (edited by Blanche Dugdale) was published in the year he died.

FURTHER READING
Egremont, Max *Balfour: A Life of Arthur James Balfour* 1980
Jenkins, Roy *Asquith* 1964
Koss, Stephen *Asquith* 1976
Levine, Naomi *Asquith* 1991
Mackay, Ruddock *Balfour: Intellectual Statesman* 1985
Ramsden, John *The Age of Balfour and Baldwin* 1978
Young, Kenneth *Arthur James Balfour* 1963

Balladur, Edouard (1929–)

French Gaullist politician, prime minister 1993–95, during President François ◊Mitterrand's second period of 'co-habitation' with a government of the right, having masterminded France's first wave of privatizations as minister of finance under Jacques ◊Chirac's premiership, 1986–88.

Balladur was a policy advisor to Georges ◊Pompidou as prime minister and president. After a period in private sector management, he worked closely with Chirac in the early 1980s, helping to engineer the Gaullist party's conversion to neo-liberalism. A supporter of the European Union and advocate of organizational unity on the French right, Balladur was initially a popular prime minister, but controversial initiatives such as state funding for private (Catholic) schools and lowering the minimum wage for young workers left him poorly placed for the 1995 presidential elections, when he was eliminated by Chirac on the first ballot.

Ballance, John (1839–1893)

New Zealand Liberal politician, born in Northern Ireland; prime minister 1891–93. He emigrated to New Zealand, founded and edited the *Wanganui Herald*, and held many cabinet posts. He passed social legislation and opposed federation with Australia.

Banda, Hastings Kamuzu (1905–1997)

Malawi politician, president 1966–94. He led his country's independence movement and was prime minister of Nyasaland (the former name of Malawi) from 1964. He became Malawi's first president in 1966 and was named president for life in 1971; his rule was authoritarian. Having bowed to opposition pressure and opened the way for a pluralist system, Banda stood in the first free presidential elections for 30 years in 1994, but was defeated by Bakili Muluzi. In January 1996 he and his former aide, John Tembo, were acquitted of the murders of three senior politicians and a lawyer in 1983.

Banda studied in the USA, and was a doctor in the UK until 1953. In October 1993 he underwent brain surgery, temporarily handing power to a presidential council. He announced his retirement from active politics in August 1994.

Bandaranaike, Sirimavo born Ratwatte (1916–)

Sri Lankan politician, prime minister from 1994. She succeeded her husband Solomon ◊Bandaranaike to become the world's first female prime minister,

> *She carried on her husband's policies of socialism, neutrality in international relations, and ... active encouragement of the Buddhist religion and ... Sinhalese language and culture.*
> ENCYCLOPAEDIA BRITANNICA 1990

1960–65 and 1970–77, but was expelled from parliament in 1980 for abuse of her powers while in office. Her daughter Chandrika Bandaranaike ◊Kumaratunga was elected president in 1994.

Bandaranaike, Solomon West Ridgeway Dias (1899–1959)

Sri Lankan nationalist politician. In 1952 he founded the Sri Lanka Freedom Party and in 1956 became

> *Oxford ... revealed to me my life's mission and ... was the dearer to me because she had taught me to love my country better.*
> SOLOMON BANDARANAIKE On Magdalen Bridge on his last afternoon at Oxford University, contrasting the mellowness of the scene with the disease and poverty of his own country.

prime minister, pledged to a socialist programme and a neutral foreign policy. He failed to satisfy extremists and was assassinated by a Buddhist monk.

Bandera, Stepan (1909–1959)

Ukrainian nationalist politician, leader of the extreme Ukrainian National League that opposed Polish rule in Galicia (western Ukraine) before World War II. After the Galician capital, Lviv, was occupied by Nazi forces in 1941, Bandera's followers proclaimed an independent Ukrainian state and set up a government, but were arrested by the Germans and sent to concentration camps.

After the war, the term 'Banderovites' was applied to all militant Ukrainian nationalists who engaged in guerrilla warfare against the occupying Soviet authorities.

Bang, Nina Henriette Wendeline (1866–1927)

Danish Social Democrat politician. In 1918 she was elected to the upper house of the Danish parliament. In

1924 she became education minister, and was the first woman to hold cabinet rank in Denmark.

Bani-Sadr, Abu'l-Hassan (1933–)

Iranian politician, first president of Iran, 1980–81, after the Islamic Revolution of 1979. He was an important figure in the Iranian Revolution of 1978–79, serving as a bridge between the political intelligentsia and the Islamic clergy opposition to the shah's regime. After the revolution, Bani-Sadr became foreign and economics minister in November 1979 and was elected the first president of the Islamic Republic in January 1980, and chair of the defence council. After his dismissal by Ayatollah ◊Khomeini, he fled to France.

After taking office as president, Bani-Sadr was criticized by Islamic fundamentalists within the ruling Islamic Republican Party for his conciliatory stance in the US hostage crisis. He was dismissed in mid-1980 by Ayatollah Khomeini for failing to establish a 'truly Islamic country' and a committee of inquiry found him guilty of disobeying Khomeini's orders as Imam (religious leader). He fled to France, where he was granted asylum and where he founded a National Resistance Council. In his extensive writings he has remained committed to a form of Islamic socialism, viewing a belief in equality as an essential feature of Islam.

The son of a preacher and landowner, Bani-Sadr studied theology, economics, and sociology at Tehran University. He supported Muhammad ◊Mossadeq in his opposition to the shah of Iran, Muhammad ◊Reza Pahlavi, and, after a brief imprisonment for underground activities, was exiled from 1964. Settling in Paris, he earned a doctorate in economics and sociology at the Sorbonne University and became an advisor to Ayatollah Khomeini, when the latter moved to Paris in 1978.

FURTHER READING
Bani-Sadr, Abu'l-Hassan *My Turn to Speak* 1981

Banks, Dennis (1932–)

Ojibwa activist. He co-founded the American Indian Movement in (1968) and was a leader in such protest actions as the Trail of Broken Treaties (1972) and the occupation of Wounded Knee (1973). In 1992 he appeared in the film *The Last of the Mohicans*.

Banzer Suárez, Hugo (1926–)

Bolivian military leader and president 1971–78 and from 1997. His second term of presidency marked the fifth successive peaceful transition of government in Bolivia.

A member of the centre-right party Acción Democrática Nacionalista (AND; Nationalist Democratic Action), Banzer was minister for education 1964–66, and president elect 1971–78. During the period

1985–93 he pursued a diplomatic position as ambassador to Argentina. In 1989 he became an AND candidate for the forthcoming elections. In 1992 he was elected head of the AND party, and re-elected in 1995.

Baraka, (Imamu) Amiri born LeRoi Jones (1934–)

US poet, dramatist, and militant black activist. One of the major black voices of his generation, he began his literary career with personal and romantic poetry as in *Preface to a Twenty Volume Suicide Note* (1961), before turning to the theatre as a revolutionary force for black separatism in such plays as *Dutchman* and *The Slave* (both 1964).

A rich man told me recently that a liberal is a man who tells other people what to do with their money.

AMIRI BARAKA *Kulchur* Spring 1962 'Tokenism'

In 1965 he converted to Islam and changed his name, as part of his campaign for African-American consciousness. His ideological focus shifted in the 1970s, attacking capitalism as much as racism.

Barayi, Elijah (1930–1994)

South African trade unionist and the first president of the Congress of South African Trade Unions (COSATU). As a teenager he was one of the organizers of the Youth League of the African National Congress and was arrested and detained on several occasions. He became a mineworker in the 1970s, becoming involved in trade-union affairs. He helped establish the National Union of Miners in 1982 and became its vice president. COSATU was founded as a multiracial organization in 1985.

Barber, Anthony Perrinott Lysberg, Baron Barber of Wentbridge (1920–)

British Conservative politician. He was chair of the Conservative Party 1967–70 and in 1970 was appointed chancellor of the Duchy of Lancaster in Edward Heath's new cabinet. Shortly afterwards he became chancellor of the Exchequer on the death of Iain Macleod, a post he held until the Conservative defeat in February 1974. In October 1974 he retired from Parliament and was made a life peer in December 1974.

He was educated at Retford Grammar School and Oriel College, Oxford. After war service, during which he took a law degree while prisoner of war, he became a barrister and was elected Conservative MP for Doncaster in 1951. Between 1955 and 1964 he was successively a government whip, parliamentary private secretary to the prime minister, Harold Macmillan, economic secretary to the Treasury, and financial secretary to the Treasury, entering the cabinet in 1963 as minister of health.

Barbie, Klaus (1913–1991)

German Nazi, a member of the SS paramilitary organization from 1936. During World War II he was involved in the deportation of Jews from the occupied Netherlands 1940–42 and in tracking down Jews and Resistance workers in France 1942–45. He was arrested in 1983 and convicted of crimes against humanity in France in 1987.

His work as SS commander, based in Lyon, included the rounding-up of Jewish children from an orphanage at Izieu and the torture of the Resistance leader Jean ◊Moulin. His ruthlessness during this time earned him the epithet 'the Butcher of Lyon'. Having escaped capture in 1945, Barbie was employed by the US intelligence services in Germany before moving to Bolivia in 1951. Expelled from there in 1983, he was returned to France, where he was tried by a court in Lyon. He died in prison.

Barco Vargas, Virgilio (1921–)

Colombian liberal politician and president 1986–90. His administration succeeded in signing an agreement with the guerrilla group Movimento 19 de abril (M-19), enabling it to form itself into a political party on the condition that decommissioning was realized and insurgency activity was concluded. Economic stagnation was a major problem during his administration.

Ironically, against this climate, the guerrilla groups Fuerzas Armadas Revolucionarias de Colombia (FARC; Revolutionary Armed Forces of Columbia) and the Ejército de Liberación Nacional (ELN; National Liberation Army) increased their insurgency activities. This caused major problems for the Barco administration with many regions of the country under paramilitary control.

Barnes, George Nicoll (1859–1940)

British politician, active in Labour and trade-union politics. He was a cabinet minister 1917–20, and a member of the Versailles peace conference after World War I. He prepared the draft proposals for the Commission on World Labour, which subsequently developed into the International Labour Office.

Barnes was born in Dundee, entered Parliament in 1906, and represented a Glasgow constituency until 1922.

Barre, Raymond Octave Joseph (1924–)

French centre-right politician, prime minister 1976–81 under President Valéry ◊Giscard d'Estaing, when he gained a reputation as a tough and determined budget-cutter.

Born in Réunion, Barre was a successful academic economist, holding a chair at the Sorbonne before serving on the European Commission 1967–72. When appointed to the premiership, replacing Jacques ◊Chirac, his only previous governmental experience was as minister of foreign trade 1974–76. An early advocate of neo-liberal ideas in France and a strong defender of the Fifth Republic's institutions, he represented Lyon in the National Assembly from 1978, as a member of Giscard's Union pour la Démocratie Française, and was elected mayor in 1995. He stood unsuccessfully in the 1988 presidential elections.

Barrientos Ortuño, René (1919–1969)

Bolivian military leader and president 1966–69. He launched a moderate (albeit military) administration, maintaining the conservative reforms instituted by his predecessors.

While a commander in the Bolivian air force, he actively supported the National Revolutionary Movement (MNR) – the majority political party. In 1964 he was elected vice president, under Victor Paz Estenssoro. Later in 1964, Paz Estenssoro was overthrown by Barrientos, as head of a military junta, thus initiating another period of military rule and political instability. In May 1965, Alfredo Ovando Candia joined him as co-president, but Barrientos became sole president after winning the 1966 elections. He was killed in a helicopter crash and was succeeded by his vice president, Luis Adolfo Siles Salinas.

Barrios de Chamorro, Violeta (c. 1939–)

Nicaraguan newspaper publisher and politician, president 1990–96. With strong US support, she was elected to be the candidate for the National Opposition Union (UNO) in 1989, winning the presidency from David ◊Ortega Saavedra in February 1990 and thus ending the period of Sandinista rule and the decade-long Contra war. She did not contest the 1996 presidential election.

Chamorro's political career began in 1978 with the assassination by the right-wing dictatorship of her husband, Pedro Joaquín Chamorro (1924–1978), the crusading editor of the anti-Somoza newspaper *La Prensa*. A devout and conservative Catholic, Violeta took over the management of the newspaper, which helped to overthrow the Somoza regime in 1979. She was a member of the new Sandinista-led Government of the National Reconstruction 1979–80 but then faced repression from the Marxist regime. She was chosen as presidential candidate for UNO, a 14-party coalition, in September 1989. In the 1990 elections UNO won 51 of the 92 seats in the National Assembly. The Sandinista Liberation Front (FSLN), however, remained the largest party, and together with reactionary elements within Chamorro's own coalition, obstructed the implementation of her policies. Her early presidency was marked by rising unemployment, strikes, and continuing skirmishes between Contra rebels and Sandinista militants in the mountains (despite official disbanding of the Contras in June 1990). A peace accord was reached with the rebels in 1994 and the military was reformed.

Barrow, Errol Walton (1920–1987)

Barbadian left-of-centre politician, prime minister 1961–76 and 1986–87. He co-founded the Democratic Labour Party (DLP) in 1955, becoming its chair in 1958, and leading the DLP to victory following independence in 1961. Defeated in 1976 by the BLP, led by Tom ◊Adams, he returned to power with a decisive majority in 1986. A critic of the US intervention in Grenada in 1983, Barrow oversaw a review of Barbadian participation in the US-backed regional security system.

After his death he was succeeded as DLP leader and prime minister by Erskine Lloyd ◊Sandiford. Barrow's sister, Nita Barrow (1916–), served as governor general of Barbados 1990–96.

Barrow was born in Barbados. After flying in the RAF between 1940 and 1947, he studied at London University and Lincoln's Inn. Returning to Barbados, he became active in the Barbados Labour Party (BLP), led by Grantley ◊Adams, and was elected to the House of Assembly in 1951.

Barry, Marion Jr (1936–)

US Democrat politician, mayor of Washington, DC, 1978–90 and from 1995. He was active in the black civil-rights movement from 1960 as cofounder and chair until 1967 of the Student Nonviolent Coordinating Committee (SNCC).

As a student at the University of Tennessee, Barry became involved in the campaign for civil rights and organized the first lunch-counter sit-ins in Nashville, Tennessee, in 1960. He met Martin Luther King that year and helped to establish the SNCC, based in Atlanta, Georgia, which advocated direct action through protests, sit-ins, and boycotts. In 1967 Barry set up the Youth Pride programme to help poor, unemployed blacks in Washington, DC, which became a nationwide model. He was elected to the Washington city council in 1974, elected mayor in 1978, and re-elected in 1982 and 1986 despite a deterioration in schools and public services, and a rise in violent crime and drug abuse. Convicted of cocaine possession in 1990, he was imprisoned for six months. Emerging a born-again Christian, he revived his political career, winning a city council seat in 1992, and was re-elected mayor in November 1994. He has retained strong support in the 70% African-American city, and has become more radical, allying himself with Louis ◊Farrakhan and marrying Cora Masters, his fourth wife, a long-time black activist academic. In August 1997 Barry was stripped of control of nine major city agencies by Congress under the terms of a financial rescue package for the troubled city.

Barton, Edmund (1849–1920)

Australian politician. He was leader of the Federation Movement from 1896 and first prime minister of Australia 1901–03.

Educated at Sidney University, he worked as a barrister before entering the New South Wales assembly in 1879. As prime minister and foreign minister 1901–03 he secured passage of the 'white Australia' Immigration Restriction Act. He resigned in 1903 to become a High Court judge

FURTHER READING
Reynolds, John *Edmund Barton* 1948

Baruch, Bernard Mannes (1870–1965)

US financier. He was a friend of the British prime minister Winston Churchill and a self-appointed, unpaid adviser to US presidents Woodrow Wilson, Franklin D Roosevelt, and Harry Truman. He strongly advocated international control of nuclear energy.

> *Let us not be deceived – we are today in the midst of a cold war.*
> BERNARD BARUCH Speech to South Carolina Legislature 16 April 1947

Barudi, Mahmud Sami al- (1839–1904)

Egyptian nationalist activist and poet. He was a leading figure of the modern Arabic literary renaissance. Much of his work was modelled on classical Abbasid poetry, of which he compiled an important anthology.

Barudi was a fervent nationalist; his participation in an unsuccessful revolt in 1882 against British rule in Egypt led to 17 years' exile in Ceylon (now Sri Lanka).

Bashir, Omar Hassan Ahmad al- (1944–)

Sudanese president and prime minister. An army officer, he came to power after overthrowing the democratically elected government of Sadiq al-Mahdi in 1989 and initiating what had been described as an Islamic revolution. In 1989 he became prime minister, commander in chief and minister of defence, and chair of the Revolutionary Command Council (RCC). He abolished all existing institutions, political parties, and trade unions, with the justification of reducing regional and religious tensions. Political opposition was ruthlessly crushed. He survived a coup in 1990. In 1992 a temporary parliament appointed al-Bashir as head of state before voting itself out of existence in 1993. Al-Bashir is a keen Pan-Islamicist and Pan-Arabist.

After leaving school Bashir trained as a paratrooper. Before he seized power in 1989 he was serving as a brigadier in the El Muglad area of southern Kordofan.

Basu, Jyoti (1914–)

Indian politician, chief minister of West Bengal from 1977. He is the longest-serving chief minister of any

Indian state and also the leader of the longest-running, democratically elected Communist government in the world.

Basu was educated in Calcutta, Cambridge, and London where he met British Communist Party leaders and formed the Indian Communist Group at London. After obtaining his law degree in 1940 he returned to India and joined the Communist Party of India (CPI). Basu was elected to the Bengal legislative council in 1946 and remained a member of the legislature when the state was partitioned the following year. When the CPI split in 1964 he became a founding member of the Communist Party of India-Marxists (CPM) and held various positions in the party.

Batista, Fulgencio, Colonel Batista y Zaldívar (1901–1973)

Cuban right-wing dictator, dictator-president 1934–44 and 1952–59. Having led the September 1933 coup to install Ramón ◊Grau San Martín in power, he forced Grau's resignation in 1934 to become Cuba's effective ruler, as formal president from 1940. Exiled in the USA 1944–49, he ousted President Carlos Prío Socarrás in a military coup in 1952. His authoritarian methods enabled him to jail his opponents and amass a large personal fortune. He was overthrown by rebel forces led by Fidel ◊Castro in 1959. Batista fled to the Dominican Republic and later to Portugal. He died in Spain.

During his first presidency Batista sponsored economic and social reforms, influenced by European fascist-corporatism, but at the 1944 presidential elections his preferred candidate was defeated by Grau and he went into exile. After deposing Socarrás, whose regime was tainted with corruption, Batista suspended the constitution and held a rigged election in 1954. His increasing authoritarianism provoked uprisings and, after a derided sham election in 1958, he was overthrown on 1 January 1959 by Castro, whose rebel forces had waged a three-year-long insurgency.

Batista was born in Banes, in eastern Cuba. He was a career soldier from 1921 and, as an army sergeant, participated in the August 1933 overthrow of the dictator Gerardo ◊Machado y Morales. A month later, he led the military coup that ousted Manuel de ◊Céspedes and installed Grau in power. Batista, by now a colonel, was made army chief of staff and took power the following year.

Batlle y Ordóñez, José (1856–1929)

Uruguayan statesman, political reformer, and president 1903–07 and 1911–15. Many industries were nationalized by the state during his administration and significant improvements were made in the areas of working hours, pensions, and unemployment benefits. He also gave women the vote. Proposals made during his presidency subsequently influenced changes to the nation's constitution in 1917, with the creation of national socialist governance.

Batlle was leader of the Asociación Nacional Republicana (ANR; Colorado Party) and instituted major legislative changes during his second term in office, particularly in relation to social and governmental reform. The welfare state, however, funded by taxation on the livestock sector, was particularly fragile, as fluctuations in the market had major repercussions on the state finances.

His first term in office was less productive, having to contend with the 1904 civil war between Colorado and right-of-centre Blanco party factions.

Batt, Philip (1927–)

US politician and governor of Idaho from 1995. A strong fiscal conservative, Batt is an outspoken critic of high taxation and regulation. His special interests are in agriculture and he is a member of a number of farming and growers' organizations.

Born in Wilder, Idaho, Batt graduated from Wilder High School and attended the University of Idaho 1944–48. His college studies were interrupted for two years when he volunteered for service with the Army Air Force. He was elected to the Idaho state legislature in 1965 and served two years in the Idaho house of representatives. He later served 14 years in the Idaho state senate with six years as the senate majority leader. He held the office of Lieutenant Governor 1978–82, where he positioned himself as an ombudsman.

Bavadra, Timoci (1934–1989)

Fijian centre-left politician, prime minister in 1987. A Melanesian chief from the main island of Viti Levu, Bavadra formed the left-of-centre Fijian Labour Party (FLP) in 1985, which advocated a neutralist, non-nuclear foreign policy and racially bipartisan and socialist domestic policies. After the April 1987 general election he was able to form a coalition government with the Indian community-oriented National Federation Party (NFP) to end 17 years of rule by the conservative Alliance Party of Kamisese ◊Mara. However, after only 32 days as prime minister, Bavadra was ousted in a military coup, led by Major General Sitiveni ◊Rabuka, who was concerned that the FLP–NFP government would favour ethnic Indians at the expense of the ethnic Fijian community.

On Bavadra's death from cancer in November 1989, his widow, Adi Kuini Bavadra (1949–), took over as FLP president until 1991, and became president of the All National Congress (ANC) in 1995. She opposed constitutional changes by the Rabuka regime, which sought to entrench ethnic Fijian control. Unlike her husband, who was a commoner, Adi Bavadra is of noble birth and related to Kamisese ◊Mara and Penaia ◊Ganilau.

Bayer, Mahmud Jelâl (1884–1986)

Turkish politician, president 1950–60. With Adnan ◊Menderes, he founded the Democrat Party in 1945 and, following the party's victory in the 1950 election, was elected as Turkey's first civilian president. His open partisanship in what was by convention a politically neutral office eroded his popularity, and he was deposed by a military coup in 1960. A death sentence was commuted to life imprisonment, from which he was released in 1964.

Bayer was a member of the Young Turk movement from 1907, and served under Mustafa Kemal ◊Atatürk, the first president of Turkey, notably as a successful minister of economy 1932–37.

Bazargan, Mehdi (1907–)

Iranian politician, prime minister in 1979. In 1977 he cofounded the Human Rights Association and in February 1979, following the overthrow of the government of Shapour ◊Bakhtiar, he became Iran's first post-revolutionary prime minister, heading the Provisional Government. The moderate Bazargan faced opposition from leftists and fundamental Islamists and in November 1979 he resigned, following the hostage-taking of US diplomats in Tehran by radical Islamic students.

A devout Muslim, he had served as a deputy minister 1951–53 under Muhammad ◊Mossadeq and in 1961 cofounded the Freedom Movement of Iran. During the regime of Shah Reza Pahlavi, from 1953, Bazargan became a leader of the opposition to the shah's authoritarian rule and was imprisoned several times.

Following his resignation, he became a critic of the Islamic Revolution's excesses and of corruption, founding, in 1987, the Association for Defence of the Freedom and Sovereignty of the Iranian Nation. Bazargan opposed the 1980–88 war with Iraq and faced harassment from militants within the regime, but escaped arrest.

Beatrix, (Wilhelmina Armgard) (1938–)

Queen of the Netherlands. The eldest daughter of Queen Juliana, she succeeded to the throne on her mother's abdication in 1980. In 1966 she married West German diplomat Claus von Amsberg (1926–), who was created Prince of the Netherlands. Her heir is Prince Willem Alexander (1967–).

Beauvoir, Simone de (1908–1986)

French writer and feminist, author of the major feminist text Le Deuxième Sexe/The Second Sex (1949) and cofounder, with Jean-Paul ◊Sartre, of the left-wing review Les Temps Modernes/Modern Times (1946). Her novel Les Mandarins/The Mandarins (1954), portraying the left-wing intelligentsia in which she herself figured so prominently, won the Prix Goncourt. Her extraordinarily rich and original study of the feminine condition drew on literature, myth, and history to show how women have been denied their independence, identity, and sexuality in male-dominated societies.

As a politically committed writer in the period of Cold War confrontations and decolonization, de Beauvoir lent her name to left-wing petitions and campaigns, opposing France's resort to censorship and torture during the Algerian war. From the late 1960s she found a new audience within the women's liberation movement. As president of the campaigning group Choisir and lead signatory to the 1971 Manifeste des 343 'salopes' (in which women from many public walks of life acknowledged having terminated a pregnancy), de Beauvoir contributed to the changed climate of opinion in France on abortion which finally allowed its de-criminalization under Simone Veil's 1975 legislation. Themes of choice and identity had been explored in her early novel L'Invitée/She Came to Stay (1943) and reappeared in her extended autobiography, a frank and vivid account not only of one woman's life from birth to old age, but also of intellectual life in the 20th century, starting with the Mémoires d'une jeune fille rangée/Memoirs of a Dutiful Daughter (1958).

Beaverbrook, (William) Max(well) Aitken, 1st Baron Beaverbrook (1879–1964)

Canadian-born British financier, newspaper proprietor, and politician. He bought a majority interest in the Daily Express in 1919, founded the Sunday Express in 1921, and bought the London Evening Standard in 1923. He served in David Lloyd George's World War I cabinet and Winston Churchill's World War II cabinet.

> The Daily Express declares that Great Britain will not be involved in a European war this year or next year either.
> MAX BEAVERBROOK Daily Express 19 September 1938

Having made a fortune in cement in Canada, he entered British politics, first in support of Andrew Bonar Law, then of Lloyd George, becoming minister of information 1918–19. In World War II he was minister of supply 1940–41.

> Beaverbrook is so pleased to be in the Government that he is like the town tart who has finally married the Mayor!
> BEVERLEY BAXTER On Lord Beaverbrook, quoted in Harold Nicolson, Diary, June 1940

Between the wars he used his newspapers, in particular the Daily Express, to campaign for empire free trade, against Prime Minister Stanley Baldwin. Later he opposed British entry to the European Economic Community.

FURTHER READING

Chisholm, Anne, and Davie, Michael *Beaverbrook: A Life* 1992

Driberg, Tom *Beaverbrook* 1956

Gourlay, Logan (ed) *The Beaverbrook I Knew* 1994

Taylor, A J P *Beaverbrook* 1972

Bebel, (Ferdinand) August (1840–1913)

German socialist. In 1869, with Wilhelm Liebknecht, he was a founding member of the Verband deutsche Arbeitervereine (League of German Workers' Clubs), and became its leading speaker in the Reichstag (German parliament). Also known as the Eisenach Party, it was based in Saxony and southwestern Germany before being incorporated into the SPD (Sozial-demokratische Partei Deutschlands/German Social Democratic Party) in 1875.

Beckett, Margaret, born Jackson (1943–)

British Labour politician, president of the board of trade 1997–98, president of the Council and leader of the Commons in 1998. On John ◊Smith's death in 1994, Beckett took over as acting party leader, but was defeated by Tony ◊Blair in the 1994 leadership election. She also lost in the concurrent deputy leadership contest to John ◊Prescott. Beckett became president of the board of trade when the new Labour government was formed in 1997, but in the July 1998 cabinet reshuffle was moved sideways to become leader of the Commons.

Drawn from the party's Bennite left wing, Beckett was first elected to Parliament in 1974 and served as a party whip, until being defeated at the 1979 general election. She returned to Parliament in 1983, representing Derby South, and, having moderated her policy approach yet still attracting strong trade-union support, she was elected deputy leader in 1992 and worked loyally alongside John Smith.

Bedjaoui, Mohamed (1929–)

Algerian lawyer and diplomat. He chaired and co-chaired several United Nations commissions (co-president of the UN Commission of Enquiry to Iran in 1980, vice president of the UN Council for Namibia 1979–82, and chair of the Group of 77, 1981–82) and was involved in many international law organizations. In February 1994 he was appointed president of the International Court of Justice.

He acted as legal adviser to the Gouvernement Provisoire de la République Algérienne (GPRA) 1958–61, and was minister of justice 1964–70. He represented Algeria both as ambassador and permanent representative to the UN until 1982.

Begin, Menachem (1913–1992)

Israeli politician. He was leader of the extremist Irgun Zvai Leumi organization in Palestine from 1942 and prime minister of Israel 1977–83, as head of the right-wing Likud party. Following strong encouragement from US president Jimmy ◊Carter, he entered into negotiations with President Anwar ◊Sadat of Egypt, which resulted in the Camp David Agreements. In 1978 he and Sadat were jointly awarded the Nobel Peace Prize. In 1981 Begin won a new term of office but his health was failing. The death of his wife in 1992 was a grave blow, resulting in his retirement in September 1983. For the rest of his life he was a virtual recluse.

Begin was born in Brest-Litovsk, Russia (now Brest, in Belarus), studied law in Warsaw, and fled to the USSR in 1939. As leader of the Irgun group, he was responsible in 1946 for a bomb attack at the King David Hotel, Jerusalem, which killed over 100 people.

FURTHER READING

Sofar, Sasson *Begin: An Anatomy of Leadership* 1988

Belafonte, Harry (Harold George) (1927–)

US singer, actor, producer, and human-rights activist. One of the most successful black American performers in history, Belafonte's 'Banana Boat (Day-O)' kick-started a national craze for calypso music. His films, including *Island in the Sun* and *Odds Against Tomorrow*, frequently featured controversial storylines. Belafonte spent the vast majority of the 1970s and 1980s as a tireless humanitarian. Most famously, he was a central figure of the USA for Africa effort, singing on the 1986 single 'We Are the World'. A year later, he replaced Danny Kaye as UNICEF's Goodwill Ambassador.

FURTHER READING

Fopelson, Genia *Harry Belafonte* 1991

Belafrej, Ahmed (1908–1990)

Moroccan nationalist and politician, prime minister in 1958. Minister in charge of foreign affairs 1955–58, he became prime minister May–December 1958; his government was brought down because of pressures from progressive factions of his party and the spreading countryside revolts.

A founding member of the Parti de l'Istiqlal in 1944, Balafrej was the second most prominent figure of the Moroccan nationalist movement after Allal al-Fassi. He authored with early nationalist leaders what was the first manifesto calling for the independence of Morocco and the end of the protectorate. His political career ended in 1972 after he served as the king's personal representative 1963–72.

Belaid, Abdessalem (1928–)

Algerian politician, prime minister 1992–93, he Appointed minister of industry and energy 1966–77, he opposed the self-management system and almost single-handedly chose and carried out a state-centralized programme of industrialization. Removed in 1984 after being in charge of the ministry of light industry since 1977, he returned eight years later to assume the premiership 1992–93. His handling of the economic situation, and particularly his attempt to reverse the process of economic liberalization, faced fierce opposition leading to his dismissal.

He was a political advisor to the Gouvernement Provisoire de la République Algérienne (GPRA) in 1961 and president director-general of the state-owned oil company Sonatrach 1964–66.

Belaúnde Terry, Fernando (1913–)

Peruvian politician and president 1963–68 and 1980–85. He championed land reform and the construction of roads to open up the Amazon valley. He fled to the USA in 1968 after being deposed by a military junta. After his return, his second term in office was marked by rampant inflation, a devaluation of the currency in 1967, enormous foreign debts, terrorism, mass killings, and human-rights violations by the armed forces.

Further Reading

Kuczynski, Pedro-Pablo *Peruvian Democracy under Economic Stress: An Account of the Belaunde Administration, 1963–1968* 1977

Belkacem, Krim (1922–1970)

Algerian nationalist and politician. He was vice president of the Gouvernement Provisoire de la République Algérienne (GPRA) until independence. He participated as a member of the delegation that negotiated with the French administration the Evian accords on the independence of Algeria. His opposition to Mohammed ◊Ben Bella's regime led to his exile, where he formed an opposition party, the Mouvement Démocratique du Renouveau Algérien (MDRA) in Paris in 1967.

He was sentenced to death *in absentia* for allegedly conspiring with his followers in Algeria to murder Kaid Ahmed, head of the party. He was assassinated in Frankfurt, Germany, in 1970.

Bell, Francis Henry Dillon (1851–1936)

New Zealand Reform Party centre-right politician, prime minister in 1925.

Bell was attorney general 1918–26 and minister for external affairs 1923–26, being best known in the international sphere as New Zealand delegate to League of Nations conferences and to the Imperial Conference in 1928. He was a caretaker prime minister for 16 days in 1925 – the shortest tenure this century – following the death in office of William Ferguson ◊Massey. Bell was succeeded as prime minister by Joseph ◊Coates, of the Reform Party.

Belloc, (Joseph) Hilaire (René Pierre) (1870–1953)

French-born British writer. He wrote nonsense verse for children, including *The Bad Child's Book of Beasts* (1896) and *Cautionary Tales for Children* (1907). Belloc also wrote historical, biographical, travel, and religious books (he was a devout Catholic). With G K ◊Chesterton, he advocated a return to the late medieval guild system of commercial association in place of capitalism or socialism.

Belloc was born in St-Cloud on the outskirts of Paris, and educated at Oxford University. He became a British subject in 1902. In 1906 he was elected Liberal member of Parliament for South Salford, but he became disillusioned with English politics and retired from Parliament in 1910.

Among his writings on contemporary politics are *The Party System* (1911), with Cecil Chesterton (1879–1918), and *The Servile State* (1912), opposing the growing size and influence of the British state in the wake of 'new liberalism'.

Further Reading

Corrin, J P *G K Chesterton and Hilaire Belloc: The Battle Against Modernity* 1981

Speaight, R *Life of Hilaire Belloc* 1957

Ben Ali, Zine el Abidine (1936–)

Tunisian politician, president from 1987. After training in France and the USA, he returned to Tunisia and became director general of national security. He was made minister of the interior and then prime minister under the ageing president for life Habib ◊Bourguiba, whom he deposed in 1987 in a bloodless coup with the aid of ministerial colleagues. He ended the personality cult established by Bourguiba and moved towards a pluralist political system. He was re-elected in 1994, with 99% of the popular vote.

His hardline stance against Islamic militancy provoked criticism from human-rights organizations.

Ben Barka, Mehdi (1920–1965)

Moroccan politician. He became president of the National Consultative Assembly in 1956 on the country's independence from France. He was assassinated by Moroccan agents with the aid of the French secret service.

Ben Barka had been tutor to King Hassan. As a major opposition leader after independence, he became increasingly leftist in his views, and in 1964 was twice sentenced to death in his absence following allegations of his involvement in an attempt on the king's life and for backing Algeria in border disputes. Lured to Paris to discuss an anticolonial film in 1965, he was kidnapped, tortured, and shot by Moroccan agents with the support of the French secret services. The case put a strain on France's diplomatic relations with Morocco until after former President Charles de Gaulle's death in 1970.

Ben Bella, Mohammed Ahmed (1916–)

Algerian politician. He was among the leaders of the Front de Libération Nationale (FLN), the first prime minister of independent Algeria 1962–63, and its first president 1963–65. His centralization of power and systematic purges were among the reasons behind his overthrow in 1965 by Houari ◊Boumédienne. He was detained until 1979. In 1985 he founded a new party, Mouvement pour la Démocratie en Algérie (MDA), and returned to Algeria in 1990 after nine years in exile. The cancellation of the 1991 legislative elections led to his exile for the second time, and his party was banned in 1997.

Beneš, Edvard (1884–1948)

Czechoslovak politician. He worked with Tomáš ◊Masaryk towards Czechoslovak nationalism from 1918 and was foreign minister and representative at the League of Nations. He was president of the republic from 1935 until forced to resign by the Germans and headed a government in exile in London during World War II. He personally gave the order for the assassination of Reinhard ◊Heydrich in Prague in 1942. Having signed an agreement with Joseph Stalin, he returned home as president in 1945 but resigned again after the communist coup in 1948.

FURTHER READING

Beneš, Edvard *Democracy Today and Tomorrow* 1940

Lukes, Igor *Czechoslovakia Between Stalin and Hitler: The Diplomacy of Edward Beneš in the 1930s* 1996

Taborsky, Edward *President Edward Beneš: Between East and West* 1981

Zemen, Zbynek, and Klimek, Antoni *The Life of Edvard Beneš, 1884–1948: Czechoslovakia in Peace and War* 1997

Ben-Gurion, David, adopted name of David Gruen (1886–1973)

Israeli statesman and socialist politician. He was one of the founders of the state of Israel, the country's first prime minister 1948–53, and again 1955–63. He retired from politics in 1970, but remained a lasting symbol of the Israeli state.

He was born in Poland and went to Palestine in 1906 to farm. He was a leader of the Zionist movement, and as defence minister he presided over the development of Israel's armed forces into one of the strongest armies in the Middle East.

FURTHER READING

Bar Zohar, M *The Armed Prophet* 1967

Teveth, B *Ben Gurion: The Burning Ground 1886–1948* 1987

Benn, Tony (Anthony Neil Wedgwood) (1925–)

British Labour politician, formerly the leading figure on the party's left wing. He was minister of technology 1966–70 and secretary of state for industry 1974–75, but his campaign against entry to the European Community (EC; now the European Union) led to his transfer to the Department of Energy 1975–79. A skilled parliamentary orator, he twice unsuccessfully contested the Labour Party leadership.

Born the son of the 1st Viscount Stansgate, a Labour peer, Benn was educated at Oxford. He was member of Parliament for Bristol Southeast 1950–60, when he succeeded to his father's title. Despite refusing to accept the title and being re-elected in Bristol in 1961, he was debarred from sitting in the House of Commons by a judgement of the Electoral Court. His subsequent campaign to enable those inheriting titles to disclaim them led to the passing of the Peerage Act in 1963; Benn was the first person to disclaim a title under this act.

We are not here just to manage capitalism but to change society and to define its finer values.

TONY BENN Speech, Labour Party Conference 1975

He was again MP for Bristol Southeast 1963–83 and was postmaster general in the 1964 Labour government, becoming a member of the cabinet in 1966 as minister of technology. After Labour's defeat in 1970, he was the opposition spokesperson on trade and industry 1970–74 and a leading campaigner against Britain's entry into the EC. He was chair of the Labour Party 1971–72. In March 1974 he became secretary of state for industry. At the time of the 1975 referendum he campaigned against the renegotiated terms of British membership of the EC, and in June 1975 was appointed secretary of state for energy.

He unsuccessfully contested the Labour Party leadership in 1976, defeated by James Callaghan. In 1981 he challenged Denis Healey for the deputy leadership of the party and was so narrowly defeated that he established himself as the acknowledged leader of the left. In 1984 he became MP for Chesterfield and in 1988 he made another unsuccessful bid for the Labour leadership against Neil Kinnock. Though marginalized on the party's left wing, he remained an outspoken backbench critic of the centralization of party control that has been exercised under the leadership of Tony Blair.

His diaries *Out of the Wilderness* (1987), *Office Without Power* (1988), *Against the Tide* (1989), *Conflicts of Interest* (1990), *Future for Socialism* (1991), *The End of an Era* (1992), *Years of Hope* (1994), and *The Benn*

Diaries, 1940–90 (1995) cover in enormous detail the events of the period.

FURTHER READING
Adams, Jad *Tony Benn* 1992

Bennett, Richard Bedford, 1st Viscount Bennett (1870–1947)

Canadian Conservative politician, prime minister 1930–35. He was minister of finance in 1926. In the election of 1935 he was heavily defeated because of his failure to cope with the effects of the economic depression. He was succeeded as premier by Mackenzie ◊King.

Bennett graduated in law from Dalhousie University, and practised in New Brunswick. Later he worked in Calgary and entered the legislature of the Northwest Territories. His opposition to the provisions for separate Catholic schools in the proposed constitutions of Alberta and Saskatchewan won him the leadership of the small band of Conservatives in Alberta's first legislature in 1905. At the 'reciprocity' elections in 1911 he was returned by Calgary with a large majority. His opposition to the railway policy of the Robert Laird Borden government enhanced his reputation. He opposed ministerial policy during World War I and withdrew from politics in 1917, but was returned again for Calgary in 1925, and was selected in 1927 to replace Arthur ◊Meighen as leader of the party in opposition. Bennett was chiefly responsible for the Conservative election victory in 1930.

An ardent champion of protective tariffs, Bennett came to London in 1930 as head of the Canadian delegation to the Imperial Conference, and presided over the Ottawa (Imperial Economic) Conference in 1932. In 1938 he took up permanent residence in England, and was created a viscount in 1941.

Ben Salah, Ahmed (1926–)

Tunisian trade unionist and politician. He succeeded Farhat Hachad as secretary general of the Union Générale des Travailleurs Tunisiens (UGTT) in 1952 and sided with Habib ◊Bourguiba during the 'Youssefist' crisis in 1955.

Socialist-oriented and a fervent partisan of collectivism, he marked Tunisia's economic policy in the 1960s as minister of economics. The failure of his agricultural cooperative system led to his dismissal by Bourguiba in 1969 and he was arrested and sentenced to ten years' hard labour. He escaped from prison in 1973 and stayed in exile until he was pardoned by President Zine ◊Ben Ali in 1988.

Bentsen, Lloyd Millard (1921–)

US Democrat politician. Elected to the House of Representatives in 1948, he served three terms. He was a senator from Texas 1971–93, chairing the Senate Finance Committee 1986–92. He was chosen by Michael ◊Dukakis as the vice-presidential nominee in the 1988 election. Bentsen was secretary to the Treasury 1993–94.

Ben Youssef, Salah (1910–1961)

Tunisian nationalist and politician. Habib ◊Bourguiba's chief assistant and secretary general of the Néo-Destour party from the mid-1930s, he was to represent the most serious and strongest challenge to the former's leadership. Exiled in Egypt from 1952 and influenced by pan-Arabism and pan-Islamism ideals, he bitterly opposed the deal between Bourguiba and the French authorities to grant Tunisia home rule and called for full independence. He was expelled from the party, and the widespread revolt that followed his expulsion nearly caused a civil war.

Defeated, he sought refuge first in Tripoli and later in Cairo, and was assassinated in Frankfurt in 1961.

Ben Zvi, Izhak (1884–1963)

Israeli politician, president 1952–63. He was born in Poltava, Russia, and became active in the Zionist movement in Ukraine. In 1907 he went to Palestine but was deported in 1915 with David ◊Ben-Gurion. They served in the Jewish Legion under Field Marshal Allenby, who commanded the British forces in the Middle East. In 1952 he succeeded Chaim ◊Weizmann as the second president of the newly formed state.

Bérégovoy, Pierre (Eugène) (1925–1993)

French Socialist politician, prime minister 1992–93. A close ally of François ◊Mitterrand, he was named chief of staff in 1981 after managing the successful presidential campaign. He was social affairs minister 1982–84 and finance minister 1984–86 and 1988–92. He resigned as premier after the Socialists' defeat in the March 1993 general election, and shortly afterwards committed suicide.

Bérégovoy's working-class background contrasted sharply with that of the other Socialist Party leaders. As finance minister, he was widely respected by France's financial community. He replaced the unpopular Edith ◊Cresson as prime minister in April 1992. He pledged to reduce unemployment and cut taxes to stimulate economic growth.

Born in Deville-les-Rouen, the son of a Ukrainian immigrant, Bérégovoy had a limited formal education and was largely self-taught. Leaving school at 15, he worked in a textile factory and then on the railways, where he supplemented his education by attending a school organized by the Communist Party. Moving to Gaz de France, Bérégovoy climbed swiftly up the managerial ladder, until in 1981 François Mitterrand recognized his talents and made him secretary general of his personal office. He was also mayor of Nevers 1983–93.

Bérégovoy masterminded Mitterrand's successful 1988 election campaign and expected to be made prime minister but did not attain this office until 1992, when President Mitterrand, concerned about the Socialist Party's poor performance in the March 1992 elections, replaced Edith Cresson with Bérégovoy, hoping he would revive the party's fortunes. To do this within a year was an impossible task; in March 1993, when he realized the extent of the Socialist Party's defeat in the national assembly elections, he became deeply depressed. He blamed himself for the defeat; the now distant attitude of his mentor Mitterrand increased his depression. On 1 May 1993 he took his own life.

Berezovsky, Boris Abramovich (1958–)

Russian entrepreneur and associate of Boris ◊Yeltsin, deputy secretary of the Commonwealth of Independent States from 1998.

In the latter stages of Boris Yeltsin's presidency, the government came to be seen as dominated by 'oligarchs' – financier industrialists who had rapidly amassed large fortunes since the collapse of the USSR. First among these was Boris Berezovsky, who, in the late 1980s, saw the wealth that could be made by selling cars to a market in constant and chronic deficit – making deals with factory managers and cutting them into the huge premium charged. On the fortune built up by his company Logovaz he extended his empire into media, airlines, oil, and banking. His closeness to Yeltsin through his powerful daughter, Tatyana Dyachenko, was such that most believed him, in the mid-1990s, to be more powerful than any minister or adviser. He survived an assassination attempt in 1994 and was persistently rumoured to be connected with the murder of Vladimir Listiev, head of the state TV service ORT; but his power remained such that Yeltsin appointed him deputy head of the National Security Council and then, in 1998, deputy secretary of the Commonwealth of Independent States, a role that allowed him to deepen his links with the leaders of the post-Soviet republics and to further his business interests.

Chief among those who pumped some $150 million into Yeltsin's re-election campaign in 1996, he then swung away from the ailing president to back the governor of Krasnoyarsk, Alexander ◊Lebed.

Beria, Lavrenti Pavlovich (1899–1953)

Soviet politician. In 1938 he became minister of the interior and head of the Soviet police force that imprisoned, liquidated, and transported millions of Soviet citizens. On Stalin's death in 1953, he attempted to seize power but was foiled and shot after a secret trial. Apologists for Stalin have blamed Beria for the atrocities committed by Soviet police during Stalin's dictatorship.

Berisha, Sali (1941–)

Albanian political leader, president 1992–97. He cofounded the Democratic Party (DP), the country's first opposition party, which swept to power in the March 1992 general election. A month later, Berisha became Albania's first noncommunist president since the end of World War II.

Berisha's presidency oversaw gradual, market-centred economic reform and entry into the Council of Europe. However, he was criticized for endorsing state control of the media and for thwarting the efforts of his socialist opponents, who boycotted the May–June 1996 general election. In 1997 Berisha faced mounting unrest and the effective rebellion of southern Albania in the wake of the collapse of bogus pyramid 'investment' schemes in which half the population had participated. He resigned as president after his party was trounced in the June–July 1997 legislature elections, but was re-elected as leader of the DP in October 1997. His support base in northern Albania remained barely under government control, and, in March 1998, he called to the West to intervene in neighbouring Kosovo province where Serbs were accused of genocide against the Albanian population.

Born in Tropoja, Berisha was educated at the University of Tirana and was a low-ranking member of the ruling communist Albanian Workers' Party (SPA). He was elected a deputy to the People's Assembly in 1981. Following a career as a teacher and physician at the Clinic of Cardiology at a hospital in Tirana, he was elected a member of the European Committee on Medical Scientific Research in 1986.

Beriya, Lavrenti Pavlovich (1899–1953)

Georgian Communist. He was USSR commissar (minister) for internal affairs 1938–45 and deputy prime minister under Stalin, in charge of security matters, 1941–53. In 1945 he was made a marshal of the Soviet Union. Beriya ended the Great Purge by liquidating his predecessor Yezhov and many NKVD (Soviet secret police) officials, and organized the deportation of hundreds of thousands from eastern Poland, the Baltic States, and areas formerly occupied by the Germans. He was also in charge of the security police in the satellite states of Eastern Europe.

In the struggle for power after Stalin's death Beriya was defeated, arrested, and shot as an 'imperialist agent'.

As a young man, Beriya joined the Bolshevik party in 1917. From 1921 to 1931 he worked in leading positions in the Cheka and GPU (secret police) organs of Transcaucasia. From 1932 to 1938 he was first secretary of the Transcaucasian committee of the Communist Party and virtual dictator of Transcaucasia.

Berlin, Isaiah (1909–1997)

Latvian-born British philosopher and historian of ideas. In *The Hedgehog and the Fox* (1953), he wrote about Leo Tolstoy's theory of irresistible historical forces; and in *Historical Inevitability* (1954) and *Four Essays on Liberty* (1969), he attacked all forms of historical determinism.

Berlin emigrated with his family to the UK in 1920, and was professor of social and political theory at Oxford 1957–67. He was president of the British Academy 1974–78. A pluralist, he was a believer in individual freedom and was a lifelong supporter of Zionism. He was knighted in 1957.

His other works include *Karl Marx* (1939) and *Vico and Herder* (1976).

FURTHER READING
Ignatieff, M *Isaiah Berlin* 1998

Berlinguer, Enrico (1922–1984)

Italian Communist who freed the party from Soviet influence. Secretary general of the Italian Communist Party from 1972, by 1976 he was near to the premiership, but the murder in 1978 of former prime minister Aldo Moro by Red Brigade guerrillas prompted a shift in popular support towards the socialists.

A leading spokesperson for 'national communism', he sought to adapt Marxism to local requirements and to steer away from slavish obedience to Moscow. The rift between the Italian Communist Party and the Soviet Union widened during the late 1970s and early 1980s, when Berlinguer heavily criticized the Soviet Union's policies of intervention in Afghanistan and Poland.

Berlusconi, Silvio (1936–)

Italian entrepreneur and right-of-centre politician, prime minister March–December 1994. After building up an extremely profitable business empire, Fininvest, he turned his Milan-based pressure group, Forza Italia, into a political party to fight the March 1994 general election and, with the federalist Northern League and right-wing National Alliance, won a clear parliamentary majority. He resigned following allegations of corruption in his business dealings, and received a 16-month prison sentence for bribery in December 1995. In April 1996 Berlusconi led (unsuccessfully) the centre-right Freedom Pole coalition in the general election, and stood trial on further charges of company bribery and tax evasion. He was cleared of tax-evasion charges in February 1998. In April he was formally elected leader of Forza Italia.

Berlusconi rapidly established himself as one of Italy's leading entrepreneurs, moving from housing development into radio and television, films, and cinemas. He acquired one of the country's greatest football teams, AC Milan, in 1986 and Italy's largest department store, La Standa, in 1988. His initial political success depended on cooperation with the Northern League, whose aspirations included the separation of the rich north from the impoverished south, and the Rome-based National Alliance (AN), successors to the Fascist party of Benito Mussolini. His administration soon ran into difficulties over an alleged conflict of interest between his business concerns and political responsibilities, and it was this that led to his resignation.

Bernadotte, Count Folke (1895–1948)

Swedish diplomat and president of the Swedish Red Cross. In 1945 he conveyed Nazi commander Heinrich Himmler's offer of capitulation to the British and US governments, and in 1948 was United Nations mediator in Palestine, where he was assassinated by Israeli Stern Gang guerrillas. He was a nephew of Gustaf VI of Sweden.

Bernstein, Carl (1944–)

US journalist. With fellow *Washington Post* reporter Bob ◊Woodward, he unmasked the Watergate scandal and cover-up, and co-authored the best seller *All the President's Men* (1974).

Bernstein, Eduard (1850–1932)

German socialist thinker, journalist, and politician. He propounded a reformist as opposed to a revolutionary socialism, notably in his *Die Voraussetzung des Sozialismus/The Preconditions of Socialism* (1899). He contested the 'immiseration' thesis of classical Marxism, and argued that the gradual improvement in working-class living standards in a modern capitalist economy demanded a revision of traditional socialist methods. As a member of the Reichstag (German parliament) 1902–06, 1912–18, and 1920–28 he played a leading role in converting his party to a reformist strategy.

Bernstein, Herman (1876–1935)

Russian-born US writer and diplomat. He became a correspondent for the *New York Herald* with the American Expeditionary Force in Siberia. His sensational *Willy–Nicky Correspondence* (1918) printed secret telegrams exchanged between the ex-Kaiser Wilhelm II and Tsar Nicholas II.

Berri, Nabih (1939–)

Lebanese politician and soldier, leader of Amal ('Hope'), the Syrian-backed Shi'ite nationalist movement. He became minister of justice in the government of President Amin ◊Gemayel in 1984. In 1988 Amal was disbanded after defeat by the Iranian-backed Hezbollah ('Party of God') during the Lebanese civil wars, and Berri joined the cabinet of Selim Hoss in 1989. In December 1990 Berri was made minister of state in the newly formed Karami cabinet, and in 1992 retained the same post in the cabinet of Rashid al-Sohl. He subsequently became president of the national assembly.

Berrios Martínez, Rubén (1930–1993)

Puerto Rican politician and public official. An accomplished orator, he was the head of the Puerto Rican Independence Party 1970–93, and a member of the Puerto Rican Senate 1972–73. In 1971 he was jailed for three months for a sit-in on the island of Culebra protesting against the US military presence there.

Besant, Annie, born Wood (1847–1933)

English socialist and feminist activist, born in India. She was associated with the radical atheist Charles Bradlaugh (1833–1891) and the socialist Fabian Society. In 1889 she became a disciple of the Russian spiritualist and mystic Madame Blavatsky (1831–1891). Thereafter she went to India where she founded the Central Hindu College in 1898 and became president of the Theosophical Society in 1907, a post she held until her death. She also became involved in the Indian independence movement, established the Indian Home Rule League in 1916, and became the only British woman to serve as president of the Indian National Congress in 1917.

The sister-in-law of the English writer Walter Besant (1836–1901), she was separated from her clerical husband in 1873 because of her freethinking views. She and Bradlaugh published a treatise advocating birth control and were prosecuted; as a result she lost custody of her daughter.

Her *Theosophy and the New Psychology* was published in 1904.

FURTHER READING
Nethercott, A H *The First Five Lives of Annie Besant* 1961, *The Last Five Lives of Annie Besant* 1963

Bessmertnykh, Aleksandr (1934–)

Soviet politician, foreign minister January–August 1991. He began as a diplomat and worked mostly in the USA, at the United Nations headquarters in New York and the Soviet embassy in Washington, DC. He succeeded Eduard ◊Shevardnadze as foreign minister in January 1991, but was dismissed in August of the same year for exhibiting 'passivity' during the abortive anti-Gorbachev coup attempt.

Betancourt, Rómulo (1908–1981)

Venezuelan president 1959–64 whose rule was plagued by guerrilla violence and economic and political division. He expanded welfare programmes, increased expenditure on education, encouraged foreign investment, and tried to diversify the Venezuelan economy to decrease its dependence on oil exports.

While a law student, Betancourt opposed the dictatorship (1908–35) of Juan Vicente ◊Gómez. He helped found the social democratic party Acción Democrática in 1941, and was president of the junta that ruled 1945–47. Betancourt was exiled for a decade after the military rebellion led by Marcos ◊Pérez Jiménez in 1948. Returning in December 1958, he was elected president in February 1959.

FURTHER READING
Alexander, Robert J *The Venezuelan Democratic Revolution: A Profile of the Regime of Rómulo Betancourt* 1964

Betancur Cuartas, Belisario (1923–)

Colombian conservative politician and president 1982–86. He was the first president to have open and direct negotiations with insurgent guerrilla groups with the aim of incorporating them into political life. The talks failed, leading to violent attacks.

Betancur negotiated with guerrilla groups such as the Fuerzas Armadas Revolucionarias de Colombia (FARC; Revolutionary Armed Forces), Ejército de Liberación Nacional (ELN; National Liberation Army), and the Movimento 19 de abril (M-19). The violent consequences included the M-19 bloody takeover of the Palacio de Justicia in Bogotá in 1985.

Bethe, Hans Albrecht (1906–)

German-born US physicist who in 1938 worked out the details of how nuclear mechanisms power stars. He also worked on the first atom bomb but later became a peace campaigner. He was awarded the Nobel Prize for Physics in 1967.

He has been a leading voice in emphasizing the social responsibility of the scientist and opposed the US government's Strategic Defense Initiative (Star Wars) programme.

Bethmann Hollweg, Theobald Theodor Friedrich Alfred von (1856–1921)

German politician, imperial chancellor 1909–17. He was largely responsible for engineering popular support for World War I in Germany, but his power was overthrown by a military dictatorship under Erich von ◊Ludendorff and Paul von ◊Hindenburg.

Beveridge, William Henry, 1st Baron Beveridge (1879–1963)

British economist and politician. He was born in India, the son of a civil servant, and was educated at Oxford. In 1903 he became subwarden at Toynbee Hall in East London, and in 1906 took a post on the *Morning Post* newspaper before entering the civil service in 1908. Here he was responsible for the introduction of national insurance in 1911 and held various positions, notably at the Board of Trade, until taking up Sidney Webb's offer to work at the London School of Econ-

Aneurin Bevan, British Labour politician who introduced the National Health Service. *Grace Robertson/Mary Evans Picture Library*

ber of Parliament for Berwick-upon-Tweed in 1944 to push for his reforms and was made a Liberal peer in 1946.

A prolific writer on social and economic policy, Beveridge tied together voluntarist and collectivist strands and also stressed the responsibility of the individual in resolving social problems. While he was a firm believer in the potential of bureaucratic state planning, he was disappointed that the legislation passed by the post-war Labour government denuded the role of voluntary organizations. Prominent among over a thousand publications were *Unemployment: A Problem of Industry* (1909) and *Full Employment in a Free Society* (1944). His autobiography, *Power and Influence*, was published in 1957.

FURTHER READING
Harris, Jose *William Beveridge: A Biography* 1977

Bevin, Ernest (1881–1951)
See page 48.

Bhattari, Krishna Prasad (1925–   )
Nepalese politician, prime minister 1990–91. As an

omics (of which he was director 1919–37). In 1942, working with a government committee on social insurance and allied services, he produced the Beveridge Report which formed the basis of the welfare state in post-war Britain. It promised comprehensive support 'from cradle to grave', identifying disease, want, squalor, idleness, and ignorance as the 'five giants' to which social policy should attend. The report was popular in the country, but less so with the Conservative Party. Beveridge became Liberal mem-

---

◆ BEVAN, ANEURIN (NYE) (1897–1960) ◆

British Labour politician, minister of health 1945–51. Born in Tredegar, the son of a Welsh miner, Bevan was himself a miner at 13. He became member of Parliament for Ebbw Vale in 1929, retaining the seat until his death. The experience of Ramsey Macdonald's capitulation in 1931 and the unemployment and European fascism of the 1930s gave force to Bevan's left-wing socialism. Bevan never doubted Labour's role as the central agent of socialism, although he was briefly expelled (with Stafford Cripps) from the party in 1939 for advocating a popular front. In 1934 he married left-wing member of Parliament Jennie Lee.

During the war, whilst supporting Labour's participation in the coalition, Bevan was a stern critic of Winston Churchill. Bevan's appointment by Clement Attlee as minister of health 1945–51 was then slightly surprising. In fact Bevan, suspected by critics to be little more than a dissenting voice, proved to be an effective administrator. In 1948 he inaugurated the

National Health Service (NHS), unifying local and voluntary hospitals and combating the resistance of the British Medical Association. He was also successful in getting a large-scale housing and building programme

This island is made mainly of coal and surrounded by fish. Only an organizing genius could produce a shortage of coal and fish at the same time.
ANEURIN BEVAN Speech at Blackpool 18 May 1945

underway, supporting council rather than private schemes. Bevan was minister of labour from January to April 1951, but resigned (with Harold Wilson and John Freeman) when Hugh Gaitskell's 1951 budget, raising capital for the Korean War, introduced charges into the NHS.

Thereafter Bevan led left-wing criticism of the Labour leadership through the 1950s. In 1952 he

opponent of absolute monarchy, he was in hiding for 12 years until 1990, when, as leader of the centrist Nepali Congress Party, he became prime minister in the wake of the revolution that year, which ended the uncontested rule of King ◊Birendra. However, in 1991, in Nepal's first multiparty elections in three decades, he offered his resignation to the king after losing his own seat in the 205-member House of Representatives to the Marxist leader of the United Communist Party, Madan Bhandari.

Bhindranwale, Sant Jarnail Singh (1947–1984)

Indian Sikh fundamentalist leader who campaigned for the creation of a separate state of Khalistan during the early 1980s, precipitating a bloody Hindu–Sikh conflict in the Punjab. Having taken refuge in the Golden Temple complex in Amritsar and built up an arms cache for guerrilla activities, Bhindranwale, along with around 500 followers, died at the hands of Indian security forces who stormed the temple in 'Operation Blue Star' in June 1984.

Bhumibol Adulyadej (1927–)

King of Thailand from 1946. Born in the USA and educated in Bangkok and Switzerland, he succeeded to the throne on the assassination of his brother. In 1973 he was active, with popular support, in overthrowing the military government of Marshal Thanom Kitti-

---

published 'In Place of Fear', a statement of his socialist vision drawing on personal experience. The Bevanites, such as Bevan's close friend (and later biographer) Michael Foot, were largely organized around the journal *Tribune*. In 1955 Bevan stood and lost the election for the party leadership. In 1956, a partial reconciliation with the new leader Hugh Gaitskell led to Bevan's appointment as shadow foreign secretary. In 1957, at the party conference, he turned against the left, rejecting the argument for unilateral nuclear disarmament by declaring a Labour foreign secretary should not be sent 'naked into the conference chamber'. Bevan died of cancer in July 1960.

With an instinctive socialism and outstanding oratorical talent (despite a stammer), Bevan could fire the Labour Party like no other. He remains an idol of the Labour Party to this day.

FURTHER READING
Campbell, John *Nye Bevan A Biography* 1987
Foot, Michael *Aneurin Bevan, 1897–1945* 1962, *Aneurin Bevan, 1945–1960* 1973
Lee, Jenny *My Life with Nye* 1960

kachorn and thus ended a sequence of army-dominated regimes in power from 1932.

Bhutto, Zulfikar Ali (1928–1979)

Pakistani politician, president 1971–73, and prime minister from 1973 until the 1977 military coup led by General ◊Zia ul-Haq. In 1978 Bhutto was sentenced to death for conspiring to murder a political opponent and was hanged the following year. He was the father of Benazir Bhutto.

Bhutto, Benazir (1953–)

See page 50.

Bidault, Georges Augustin (1899–1983)

French Christian Democrat politician, cofounder of the Mouvement Républicain Populaire (MRP) and prime minister 1946 and 1949–50.

A history teacher active in inter-war Catholic movements, Bidault was elected president of the National Resistance Council 1943–44 and served in several Fourth Republican governments as foreign minister. A supporter of Charles ◊de Gaulle in 1958, his commitment to retaining France's presence in Algeria led him into General Salan's pro-settler terrorist Organisation de l'Armée Secrète (OAS) from 1961 and then into exile from 1963. In the aftermath of the May 1968 events, President de Gaulle authorized his return to France and immunity from prosecution.

Biffen, (William) John (1930–)

British Conservative politician. In 1971 he was elected to Parliament for the Wrekin seat, in Shropshire. Despite being to the left of Margaret ◊Thatcher, he held key positions in government from 1979, including leader of the House of Commons from 1982, but was dropped after the general election of 1987. He subsequently became a greatly respected backbencher before retiring from Parliament in 1997.

His publications include *Inside the House of Commons* (1989) and *Inside Westminster* (1996). He was created a baron in 1997.

Biko, Steve (Stephen) (1946–1977)

South African civil-rights leader. An active opponent of apartheid, he was arrested in September 1977; he died in detention six days later. Following his death in the custody of South African police, he became a symbol of the anti-apartheid movement. An inquest in the late 1980s found no-one was to blame for Biko's death.

Five former security policemen confessed to being involved in Biko's murder in January 1997. They applied for an amnesty to the Truth and Reconciliation Commission (TRC), the body charged with healing South Africa by exposing its past and laying foundations for a more peaceful future. The amnesty application angered Biko's family, and his widow challenged the legitimacy of the TRC in the Constitutional Court.

Biko founded the South African Students Organization (SASO) in 1968 and was cofounder in 1972 of the

---

The power of a movement lies in the fact that it can indeed change the habits of people. This change is not the result of force but of dedication, of moral persuasion.

Steve Biko Interview, July 1976

Black People's Convention, also called the Black Consciousness movement, a radical association of South African students that aimed to develop black pride.

Bildt, Carl (1949–)

Swedish politician, prime minister 1991–94. Leader of the Moderate Party (MS) from 1986, he pledged an end to the 'age of collectivism' and in 1991 formed a right-of-centre coalition after decades of social democratic politics. A year later, after battling unsuccessfully with Sweden's worst economic crisis since the 1920s, he persuaded his former political opponents to join him in a fight for economic recovery, heading what

was, in effect, a government of national unity. In 1995 he succeeded David Owen as European Union negotiator in the former Yugoslavia, and in 1996 was appointed 'High Representative' for Bosnia-Herzegovina, overseeing the reconstruction side of the Dayton peace agreement until June 1997.

Bildt was elected to the Riksdag (parliament) in 1979. He became leader of the Moderate Party in 1986 and when the ruling Social Democratic Labour Party lost its parliamentary majority after the 1991 general election, he formed with other right-of-centre parties what became known as the 'bourgeois coalition'. He won widespread support for Swedish membership of the European Community (now the European Union) before he and his party were defeated in the 1994 elections.

Bingham, Hiram (1875–1956)

US explorer and politician who from 1907 visited Latin America, discovering Machu Picchu, Vitcos, and other Inca settlements in Peru. He later entered politics, becoming a senator.

Bird, Lester B (1938–)

Antiguan politician, prime minister from 1994. He succeeded his father Vere ◊Bird as prime minister and

---

◆ Bevin, Ernest (1881–1951) ◆

British Labour politician.

He was born in rural Somerset into a poor family and his mother was a devout Methodist, but, orphaned at the age of six, he lived with his sister, left school at eleven, and worked as a farm labourer. In 1894 he went to Bristol and had a succession of jobs including van boy and van driver. He became involved in a Baptist Sunday-school class for young adults whose teacher was also interested in socialism. Bevin himself joined the Social Democratic Federation and led unemployed agitation.

Bevin was drawn into trade-union activity in the Bristol docks in 1910. His outstanding leadership qualities were recognized by the dockers' union leaders in London, notably Ben Tillett, and he was appointed a full-time official in 1911. During World War I Bevin took a prominent part in organizing the wartime docks around the country. Again his leadership qualities were recognized, this time by civil servants and politicians.

In 1920 Bevin seized the opportunity presented by an enquiry into dockers' wages to expose their working conditions, casual labour, and low wages. He won his case and earned the title 'the Dockers' KC'. In 1921 he took the initiative in bringing

together 14 unions to form the Transport and General Workers' Union (TGWU). He became its first general secretary.

Bevin guided the TGWU to becoming a large, powerful union. He became a member of the Trades Union Congress General Council and played a leading role in the 1926 General Strike. He worked closely with the TUC general secretary, Walter Citrine, to ensure that the trade-union movement played a constructive part in British political life. He remained a committed socialist, and with Citrine took up a strong anti-fascist position from 1933.

My [foreign] policy is to be able to take a ticket at Victoria Station and go anywhere I damn well please.

Ernest Bevin *The Spectator* April 1951

In 1940 he accepted Winston Churchill's invitation to join the wartime coalition government and war cabinet as minister of labour. He made the ministry the most powerful

leader of the Antigua Labour Party (ALP) when the latter retired from politics in 1993, and led the ALP to victory in 1994. He had served as a deputy prime minister in his father's governments, and in various ministerial posts, including economic development 1976–81 and foreign affairs 1981–94. As prime minister, he retained the foreign and social affairs portfolios.

Bird entered national politics in 1971 as chair of the ALP, and became opposition leader in the Senate 1976–81. He was first elected to the House of Representatives in 1976.

Initially he trained as a barrister at Grays Inn in London, after studying in the USA at the University of Michigan, and he later pursued a private career as a lawyer and volunteer dentist. Although the second son of Vere Bird, he succeeded his father because his elder brother, Vere Bird, Jr, had been barred from holding public office in November 1990, after an inquiry into arms shipments via Antigua to Colombian drugs barons.

Bird, Vere Cornwall (1910–)

Antiguan politician, chief minister 1960–67, and prime minister 1967–71 and 1976–94. He formed the centre-left Antigua Labour Party (ALP) in 1968, but lost power to George ◊Walter, leader of the Progressive Labour Movement (PLM), in 1971. Having regained control in 1976, he earned the title 'father of the nation' by negotiating Antigua's independence from British colonial rule in 1981. A political conservative, Bird pursued a policy of political non-alignment, although in 1983 Antigua assisted the USA in its invasion of Grenada.

In September 1993 he announced his retirement as ALP leader and prime minister, and was succeeded in both positions by his second son, Lester ◊Bird.

Initially Vere Bird trained with the Salvation Army, before moving into trade unionism, and founding the Antigua Trade and Labour Union (ATLU) in 1939. The political committee of the ATLU later became the nucleus of the ALP. Before independence in 1981, Bird served in the Legislative Council.

Birendra, Bir Bikram Shah Dev (1945–)

King of Nepal from 1972, when he succeeded his father Mahendra; he was formally crowned in 1975. King Birendra oversaw Nepal's return to multiparty politics and introduced a new constitution in 1990.

Birkenhead, F(rederick) E(dwin) Smith, 1st Earl of Birkenhead (1872–1930)

British lawyer and Conservative politician. He was a flamboyant and ambitious character, and played a

home department, and made manpower planning the most effective method of directing the war economy.

Clement Attlee made Bevin foreign secretary in the 1945 Labour government. He remained in office until March 1951. A highly successful foreign secretary, he was revered by his staff and noted for his ability to take decisions quickly. He proved an excellent negotiatior in the protracted meetings with the USSR. He is credited with the initiatives that resulted in the Marshall Plan and also the North Atlantic Treaty Organization (NATO).

Bevin was the outstanding British union leader of the 20th century. He was a creative administator who combined great vision with the determination to see his projects through to fruition. Trusted and valued by Churchill and Attlee, he played critical roles firstly in Britain's victory in World War II and then in securing Britain's and western Europe's successful recovery after the war.

Further Reading

Bullock, Alan *The Life and Times of Ernest Bevin, Volume 1, 1991–1940* 1960, *Volume 2, 1940–1945* 1967; *Ernest Bevin, Foreign Secretary, 1945–51* 1983

Ernest Bevin. *AKG London*

Benazir Bhutto. *Rex*

local estate agent. Inheriting his father's political and legal ambitions, in 1895 he received a law degree at Wadham College, Oxford. In 1899 he became a barrister, ending three years of teaching law at Oxford. He began to practise in Liverpool, and enlarged his reputation through involvement with a number of causes célèbres. In 1906 he was elected Conservative member of Parliament for the Walton division of Liverpool.

Smith's first speech in the House of Commons in 1906, an outright attack on the government and free trade, lifted the depression from which the Conservative Party was suffering after its crushing defeat at the polls, and established Smith as a brilliant speaker. His prominence grew, and in 1911 he became a privy councillor. On the formation of the first wartime coalition ministry in May 1915, he became solicitor general, and six months later Attorney General with a seat in the cabinet. The latter office he held again in the second coalition of December 1916.

In January 1919 Smith became Lord Chancellor. His originality and strong personality were felt throughout the House of Lords, and he showed a generosity and breadth of view that compelled those who had thought of him merely as a combatant lawyer to change their views. He took a prominent part in the negotiations that led to the signing of the Anglo-Irish Treaty,

major role in securing the Anglo-Irish Treaty in 1921 which created the Irish Free State (now the Republic of Ireland). As a lawyer, his greatest achievement was the Law of Property Act of 1922, which forms the basis of current English land law.

Although characterized by the press and politicians as a swashbuckling orator, Smith proved himself a tireless, responsible, and far-sighted statesman. He also wrote a number of popularist literary works.

Smith was born in Birkenhead, the eldest son of a

◆ BHUTTO, BENAZIR (1953–) ◆

Pakistani politician, leader of the Pakistan People's Party (PPP) from 1984 (in exile until 1986), prime minister of Pakistan 1988–90 (when the opposition manoeuvred her from office and charged her with corruption) and again 1993–96, when she was removed from office under suspicion of corruption.

Born into a wealthy, feudal, land-owning family, Benazir Bhutto was educated at Harvard and Oxford universities. She returned to Pakistan in 1977 but was placed under house arrest after General ◊Zia ul-Haq seized power from her father, Prime Minister Zulfikar Ali Bhutto, who was hanged in 1979. On her release she moved to the UK and became, with her mother Nusrat (1934–), the joint leader in exile of the opposition PPP.

When martial law had been lifted, she returned to Pakistan in April 1986 to launch a campaign for open elections. She became the first female leader of a Muslim state in November 1988. In her first

year in office she struck an uneasy balance with the military establishment, improved Pakistan's relations with India, and led her country back into the Commonwealth in 1989.

In August 1990 she was removed from office by presidential decree, and a caretaker government was installed. Charges of corruption and abuse of power were levelled against her and her husband Asif Ali Zardari (who was also accused of mass murder, kidnapping, and extortion), and her party was defeated in the subsequent general election. Bhutto and her husband claimed that the charges were fabrications, the government's intention being to strike a deal whereby they would receive pardons on condition that they leave the country and effectively abandon politics.

Bhutto increased her political standing during 1993 as two of her erstwhile opponents, President Ghulam Ishaq Khan and Prime Minister Nawaz Sharif, sought to win her support in their on-going power struggle. Both resigned in July, and

earning the respect of the Irish delegates and overcoming the animosity he thus aroused among his former Conservative associates. During Stanley Baldwin's second government, Smith became secretary of state for India in 1924, but his position became controversial and he resigned in October 1928.

FURTHER READING
Campbell, John *F E Smith: First Earl of Birkenhead* 1983

Bishop, Maurice (1944–1983)
Grenadian socialist politician, president 1979–83. Founder of the New Jewel Movement (NJM) in 1973, a mass anti-colonial Marxist–Leninist organization, he became prime minister of a provisional revolutionary government in 1979, after Eric ◊Gairy was ousted in a coup. Radical elements within the NJM embarked on a socialist economic programme, aligning the country with communist Cuba and the USSR, and in October 1983 Bishop, who had tried to improve relations with a concerned USA, was deposed. He was killed by the military under General Hudson Austin, who had seized power as a Revolutionary Military Council. These events precipitated armed intervention on 25 October 1983 by a US–Caribbean 'liberation force'.

Heavily influenced by US-inspired Black Power ideology in the late 1960s, Bishop suffered permanent physical injury from repression by government henchmen for his political activity, and his father was killed by police in 1974.

Bishop was born in Aruba, in the Netherlands Antilles, into a middle-class family. He first became

---

in October Bhutto was sworn in as prime minister for a second time, following her party's success in parliamentary elections. She compromised during this second term, supporting a large military budget while trying to foster greater social reform. However, she was removed from office by President Farooq Leghari in November 1996 amidst increasing concern over government corruption. She had faced a great deal of criticism from opposition parties for not curbing ethnic and religious violence. The PPP endured a crushing defeat in the February 1997 general election. In September 1997 the government, headed by Nawaz Sharif, secured the freezing of four Swiss bank accounts belonging to Benazir Bhutto's family members with funds reputedly exceeding $50 million. In January 1998, a further 12 charges were filed against the Bhutto family by the government. In August a Swiss judge asked for Bhutto to be indicted on money-laundering charges.

In 1996 *The Times* rated her as the world's most powerful woman.

---

acquainted with Black Power while studying law in London and, on his return to the West Indies, witnessed the April 1970 Black Power disturbances in Trinidad. Following his election to the Legislative Council in 1976, Bishop became leader of the opposition to Gairy's government. The largely bloodless coup that placed him in power in March 1976 took place while Gairy was attending a UN meeting in New York, and was triggered by his alleged plans to 'liquidate' the NJM. When Bishop was deposed in a power struggle within the NJM on 13 October 1983 he was initially placed under house arrest; he was released by his supporters after six days, but swiftly shot.

Bitar, Salah Eddin (1912–1980)
Syrian politician, prime minister several times between 1963 and 1964 and in 1966. He was, with Michel ◊'Aflaq, a cofounder of the pan-Arab socialist doctrine of Ba'athism, which was particularly influential in Syria and Iraq. When the Ba'ath Party split into several factions in 1966 he left Syria for exile in Beirut, Lebanon.

Bitat, Rabah (1926–)
Algerian nationalist and politician. A founding member of the Comité Révolutionnaire d'Unité et d'Action (CRUA) and the Front de Libération Nationale (FLN), he was arrested in 1955 by the colonial authorities and detained in France until 1962.

The struggle for power at independence and his marginalization, by being given the honorific post of third vice president, led to his disapproval of Mohammed ◊Ben Bella's regime and exile to France in 1963. After returning to Algeria in 1965, he was appointed minister of transport 1966–77 and became president of the national assembly 1977–90.

Biya, Paul (1933–)
Cameroonian politician, prime minister 1975–82 and president from 1982. He entered politics under the aegis of President Ahmadou ◊Ahidjo, becoming prime minister in 1975. When Ahidjo retired unexpectedly in 1982, he became president and reconstituted the government with his own supporters. He survived a coup attempt in 1984, reputedly instigated by Ahidjo, and was re-elected president in 1988 with more than 98% of the vote.

Biya first became politically prominent as a junior minister in Ahidjo's administration in 1962, and was appointed a minister of state in 1968.

He was born in Muomeka'a, and studied at Paris University, graduating with a law degree.

Bjelke-Petersen, Joh(annes) (1911–)
Australian right-wing politician, leader of the Queens-

land National Party (QNP) and premier of Queensland 1968–87.

Bjelke-Petersen was born in New Zealand, the son of a Danish Lutheran minister. He worked as a peanut farmer before entering the Queensland parliament in 1947. His Queensland state chauvinism and extremely conservative policies, such as lack of support for Aboriginal land rights or for conservation issues and attacks on the trade-union movement, made him a controversial figure outside as well as within Queensland, and he was accused more than once of electoral gerrymandering. In 1987 he broke the coalition of the QNP with the Australian Liberal Party to run for prime minister, but his action, by splitting the opposition, merely strengthened the hand of the Labor prime minister Bob Hawke. Amid reports of corruption in his government, Bjelke-Petersen was forced to resign the premiership in 1987.

His wife, Florence, was a senator 1981–92.

FURTHER READING
Bjelke-Petersen, Joh *Don't You Worry About That: Joh Bjelke-Petersen's Memoirs* 1990

Black, Hugo LaFayette (1886–1971)

US jurist. He was elected to the US Senate in 1926 and, despite his earlier association with the Ku Klux Klan,

distinguished himself as a progressive populist. He was appointed to the US Supreme Court by Franklin D Roosevelt in 1937, resigning shortly before his death.

Black was born in Harlan, Alabama, and was educated at the University of Alabama. He became a barrister in 1906. He served as judge and prosecuting attorney in Birmingham, Alabama, before entering the Senate. His majority opinion of 1952 held invalid the seizure of the steel companies by President Harry S Truman.

Black Elk (1863–1950)

Native American religious leader, born into the Oglala Lakota people. He tried to find ways of reconciling indigenous traditions with Christianity and the new reality of white dominance. Although he continued his calling as a shaman, he converted to Christianity in 1886.

At the age of 17, Black Elk had a vision of the Lakota people rising up and freeing their lands from the white settlers. In order to understand more about this invading culture, he joined Buffalo Bill's Wild West Show and toured the USA and Europe. When he returned home, he witnessed the disaster of the Ghost Dance movement, which swept through American Indian communities in the late 1800s and taught that they

---

◆ BLAIR, TONY (ANTHONY CHARLES LYNTON) (1953–) ◆

British politician, born in Edinburgh, Scotland, leader of the Labour Party from 1994, prime minister from 1997. A centrist in the manner of his predecessor John ◊Smith, he became Labour's youngest leader by a large majority in the first fully democratic elections to the post in July 1994. In 1995 he won approval of a new Labour Party charter, intended to distance the party from its traditional socialist base and promote 'social market' values. He and his party secured a landslide victory in the 1997 general election with a 179-seat majority. He retained a high public approval rating of 60% in February 1998.

Blair retained a remarkably high level of public approval throughout his first year as prime minister, which included the key initiatives of Scottish and Welsh devolution and a peace agreement in Northern Ireland. Along with the creation of an elected mayor for London, they were approved in 1997–98 referenda. The economic strategy of the Blair government differed little from that of the preceding Conservative administrations, involving tight control over public expenditure and the promotion, in the Private Finance Initiative, of 'public/private partnerships'.

As prime minister, Blair governed in

presidential style, delegating much to individual ministers, but intervening in key areas, such as welfare reform, in an effort to build up public support. He was supported by a large team of political advisers and media 'spin doctors'.

We are not the masters. The people are the masters. We are the people's servants.

TONY BLAIR Addressing new Labour members of Parliament at the House of Commons, May 1997

Blair was educated at Fettes College and Oxford University. He became a barrister in 1976 and practised as a lawyer before entering the House of Commons in 1983 as member for the Durham constituency of Sedgefield. He was elected to Labour's shadow cabinet in 1988 and given the energy portfolio; he shadowed employment from 1991 and home affairs from 1992. Like John Smith, he did not ally himself with any particular faction and, in drawing a distinction between 'academic and ethical socialism', succeeded in winning over most sections of his party, apart from the extreme left. His publications include *New Britain: My Vision of a Young Country* (1996).

would be made invincible and throw out the white settlers. The movement was crushed at Wounded Knee in 1890. This seems to have led Black Elk to question his calling and he converted to Catholicism in 1904.

Blaize, Herbert Augustus (1918–1989)

Grenadian centrist politician, prime minister in 1967 and 1984–89. Cofounder of the centrist Grenada National Party (GNP), he led the official opposition after full independence in 1974. In hiding from 1979, following the left-wing coup by Maurice ◊Bishop, he returned after the US invasion of 1983, and led a reconstituted New National party (NNP) to power in 1984. Suffering from terminal cancer, he relinquished the NNP leadership to Keith ◊Mitchell early in 1989, and was succeeded as prime minister by Ben Jones.

Before entering politics, Blaize qualified and practised as a solicitor. He was elected to parliament in 1957, having helped to establish the centrist GNP, and held various ministerial posts before becoming prime minister briefly in 1967.

Blake, George (1922–1994)

British double agent who worked for MI6 and also for the USSR. Blake was unmasked by a Polish defector in 1961 and imprisoned, but escaped to the Eastern bloc in 1966. He is said to have betrayed at least 42 British agents to the Soviet side.

Blanco, (Salvador) Jorge (1926–)

Dominican Republic left-wing politician, president 1982–86. A lawyer–politician noted for defending victims of political persecution, he joined the Senate as a member of the left-wing Dominican Revolutionary Party (PRD). As president he steered a restrained course overseas, maintaining good relations with the USA and avoiding close association with communist Cuba, but the implementation of harsh austerity measures at home, necessitated by a collapse in the world sugar market, forfeited his government's popular support. The divided PRD was defeated in 1986 by the Christian Social Reform Party (PRSC), led by Joaquín ◊Balaguer. In 1991 Blanco was sentenced to 20 years' imprisonment for misappropriation of public funds.

Despite the leftist credentials of his administration, the deteriorating economy had made it unable to keep its pledge to improve welfare services; instead, currency devaluation in April 1984 led to bloody price riots in Santo Domingo, claiming 60 lives. Corruption scandals and the adoption of stringent economic policies from 1985 in return for IMF loans further damaged his government's credibility.

Blanco first rose to prominence as attorney general in 1965 when the socialist Juan ◊Bosch was attempting to force his way back to power. After the restoration of order, he was a member of the commission that

negotiated the withdrawal of US troops from the country.

Blanco-Fombona, Rufino (1874–1944)

Venezuelan diplomat and writer. He was born in Caracas and lived there until his opposition to the dictatorship of Juan Vicente ◊Gómez forced him into exile in Europe. He also campaigned against US influence in Latin America. Blanco-Fombona published influential literary essays on modernism. His novel *Hombre de oro/Man of Gold* (1916) bitterly attacked the corrupt state of Spanish-American politics.

Bliss, Tasker Howard (1853–1930)

US general and diplomat. He served in the Puerto Rican campaign of the Spanish–American War in 1898. Afterwards, he proved himself an able administrator in Cuban affairs, and in 1902 negotiated the treaty of reciprocity with Cuba. Towards the end of World War I he was chief of general staff in Washington 1917–18, represented the USA on the Supreme War Council in 1918, and was chosen as one of the five US delegates to the Inter-Allied Peace Conference in Paris in 1919.

Blum, Léon (1872–1950)

French socialist politician, parliamentary leader of the Section Française de l'Internationale Ouvrière (SFIO) in the inter-war period and the first socialist prime minister of France 1936–37, when his Popular Front government introduced paid holidays and the 40-hour working week in France. He was prime minister again in 1938 and 1946.

As prime minister leading a Socialist–Radical coalition supported in parliament by the Communists, Blum negotiated the Matignon agreements on pay and conditions with employers and unions, which ended the spontaneous wave of factory occupations triggered by the Left's electoral victory in June 1936. He brought the Bank of France under state control, and nationalized the armaments industry. Controversially, he also pursued a policy of non-intervention in the Spanish Civil War. As France's first Jewish prime minister, Blum was subjected to vitriolic anti-Semitic attacks from France's extreme right. Arrested and imprisoned by the Vichy authorities in September 1940, and deported to Buchenwald following the adjournment of his trial at Riom in 1942, Blum was only released, by the Allies, in 1945.

Born into a middle-class Jewish family, a law graduate and member of the Conseil d'Etat, Blum was converted to socialism by Jean Jaurès during the Dreyfus affair in the late 1890s. At the party's 1920 Tours Congress he led the minority opposed to joining the Third International. Elected as an SFIO deputy 1919–40, Blum argued that socialists should distinguish between their 'exercise of power' (with a limited programme of reforms at a time of national crisis) and their 'conquest of power' (having won a clear mandate to reorganize society on socialist lines).

Blunkett, David (1947–)

British Labour politician, secretary of state for education and employment from 1997. He was leader of Sheffield city council from 1980 before becoming member of Parliament for Sheffield Brightside in 1987. He was shadow spokesperson on local government 1988–92, shadow health secretary 1992–94, and shadow education and employment secretary 1994–97. Blunkett overcame the disability of blindness to rise through the ranks of the trade union movement and local government to the forefront of national politics.

Blunkett was born in Sheffield, England, and educated initially in specialist establishments for the blind. He took part-time and evening courses before studying at Sheffield University and Huddersfield College of Education, eventually becoming a lecturer himself. He was chair of the social services committee of Sheffield city council 1976–80.

Blunt, Anthony Frederick (1907–1983)

English art historian and double agent. As a Cambridge lecturer, he recruited for the Soviet secret service and, as a member of the British Secret Service 1940–45, passed information to the USSR. In 1951 he assisted the defection to the USSR of the British agents Guy ◊Burgess and Donald Maclean (1913–1983). He was the author of many respected works on Italian and French art, including a study of Poussin 1966–67. Unmasked in 1964, he was given immunity after his confession.

Born in Bournemouth, England, Blunt was educated at Marlborough School and Cambridge University, where he became a fellow in 1932. He was director of the Courtauld Institute of Art 1947–74 and Surveyor of the Queen's Pictures 1945–1972. He was stripped of his knighthood in 1979 when the affair became public.

Bly, Robert Elwood (1926–)

US writer. His book *Iron John: A Book About Men* (1990), in which he argued that men needed to rediscover the warrior side of their natures, started the 'men's movement'. His *Light Around the Body* (1967) won the National Book Award for poetry.

Bly helped to organize American Writers Against the Vietnam War in 1966, denouncing the war in his own poetry. Becoming interested in matriarchal religions, Bly conducted seminars on the Great Mother, a pre-Christian deity, in the 1960s and 1970s. In *Iron John* he argued that men had moved away from the traditional male values as a result of the feminist movement, and needed to distance themselves from their mothers and learn from older men. This was seen as a backlash against the feminist movement.

Boateng, Paul Yaw (1951–)

British Labour politician and broadcaster. Elected member of Parliament for Brent South in 1987, he was appointed to Labour's shadow Treasury team in 1989, the first black appointee to a front-bench post. He served on numerous committees on crime and race relations. In May 1997 he was appointed parliamentary undersecretary for health in the new Labour government.

Educated in Ghana and the UK, Boateng qualified as a solicitor in 1976. He was at the Paddington Law 1976–79 and then in private practice. He became a barrister in 1987. He was Labour member for Walthamstow on the Greater London Council 1981–86, and a governor of the Police Staff College 1981–84.

Boganda, Barthélemy (1910–1959)

Central African Republic politician and founder of the republic. In 1949 he formed the Mouvement d'Evolution Sociale de l'Afrique Noire (MESAN) as a popular mass movement, and 1950–51 began a campaign to cause unrest in the territory. The Central African Republic (consisting of Ubangi-Shari) gained partial independence in 1958 with Boganda as head of the new government. He was killed in a mysterious air crash shortly before elections.

Born in Ubangi-Shari (part of French Equatorial Africa), he was adopted by Catholic missionaries and in 1938 ordained as a priest. Entering politics in 1946 he unsuccessfully attempted to set up rural cotton and transport cooperatives to break the expatriate monopoly.

Bogart, Humphrey (DeForest) (1899–1957)

US actor. On 24 October 1947 he led a group of Hollywood's writers, producers, and actors to Washington, DC, to express their displeasure with the House Un-American Activities Committee (HUAC) investigation in Hollywood. Calling themselves 'The Committee for the First Amendment', the 50 representatives included such people as Lauren Bacall, Groucho Marx, Frank Sinatra, John Huston, Ronald ◊Reagan, and Danny Kaye. The committee attempted to protect the rights of the 'Hollywood Ten', but also to protest the violation of their constitutional rights, holding press conferences in Kansas City, St Louis, Chicago, and finally in Washington, DC, outside the doors of HUAC. The committee brought trouble for some of its members. As a result, Bogart, who was at the peak of his popularity before the trip, found his heroic image damaged by his high profile defence of the 'impertinent subversives'.

FURTHER READING
Barbour, A D *Humphrey Bogart* 1973
Bogart, Stephen *Bogart: In Search of My Father* 1995

Eyles, Allen *Humphrey Bogart* 1990
Lax, Eric and Sperber, A M *Bogart: The Life of a
Hollywood Legend, the History of a Hollywood Era* 1997
Meyers, Jeffrey *Bogart: A Life in Hollywood* 1997
Pettigrew, Terrence *Bogart* 1983

Boggs, Thomas Hale, Sr (1914–1973)
US Democrat representative for Louisiana 1941–43
and 1947–73. He chaired the Special Committee on
Campaign Expenditures in 1951 and became majority
whip in 1961. He was majority leader of the Democrats
when his plane disappeared over Alaska.

Bohlen, Charles 'Chip' (1904–1974)
US diplomat. Educated at Harvard, he entered the
foreign service in 1929. An interpreter and adviser to
presidents Franklin D Roosevelt at Tehran and Yalta,
and Harry S Truman at Potsdam, he served as
ambassador to the USSR 1953–57.

Bokassa, Jean-Bédel (1921–1996)
Central African Republic president 1966–79 and self-
proclaimed emperor 1977–79. Commander in chief
from 1963, in December 1965 he led the military coup
that gave him the presidency. On 4 December 1976 he
proclaimed the Central African Empire and one year
later crowned himself emperor for life.

His regime was characterized by arbitrary state
violence and cruelty. Overthrown in 1979, Bokassa was
in exile in the Côte d'Ivoire until 1986. Upon his return
he was sentenced to death, but this was commuted to
life imprisonment in 1988.

Bokassa, born at Bobangui, joined the French army
in 1939 and was awarded the Croix de Guerre for his
service with the French colonial forces in Indochina.
When the Central African Republic achieved independence in 1960, he was invited to establish an army.
After seizing power, he annulled the constitution and
made himself president for life in 1972, and marshal of
the republic in 1974. In 1976 he called in former
president David Dacko (1930–), whom he had overthrown, as his adviser, and proclaimed the Central
African Republic. In 1977 he made himself emperor for
life. Backed by France, Dacko deposed him in a coup
while Bokassa was visiting Libya during 1979.

Bolger, Jim (James Brendan) (1935–)
New Zealand National Party centre-right politician,
prime minister 1990–97. His government improved
relations with the USA, which had deteriorated sharply
when the preceding Labour governments had banned
nuclear-powered and nuclear-armed ships from entering New Zealand's harbours. It also oversaw an upturn
in the economy. However, the failure to honour election pledges, particularly in the welfare area, where
there were cuts in provision, meant that National Party

support slipped in the November 1993 general election
and the government was only re-elected with a majority of one. The October 1996 general election, held for
the first time under a mixed-member system of proportional representation, was inconclusive and Bolger
was forced to form a coalition government, with the
New Zealand First Party leader, Winston ◊Peters, as
his deputy. In November 1997 he resigned and was
replaced as prime minister by his transport minister,
Jenny ◊Shipley, who had led a right-wing revolt against
his leadership.

A successful farmer, Bolger joined the conservative
National Party in the 1960s and was elected to parliament in 1972, representing King Country. He held a
variety of cabinet posts under Robert ◊Muldoon's
leadership 1977–84, including fisheries, labour, and
immigration, and was an effective, if uncharismatic,
leader of the opposition from March 1986, taking the
National Party to a landslide record electoral victory
over the Labour Party, led by Michael ◊Moore, in
October 1990.

Bolkiah, Hassanal (1946–)
Sultan of Brunei from 1967, following the abdication
of his father, Omar Ali Saifuddin (1916–1986). As
absolute ruler, Bolkiah also assumed the posts of
prime minister and defence minister on independence
in 1984.

As head of an oil- and gas-rich microstate, the sultan
is reputedly the world's richest individual, with an
estimated total wealth of $22 billion, which includes
the Dorchester and Beverly Hills hotels in London and
Los Angeles and, at a cost of $40 million, the world's
largest palace. He was educated at a British military
academy.

Bondevik, Kjell Magne (1947–)
Norwegian politician, prime minister from 1997, chair
of the Christian People's Party (KrF) 1983–95. He
became politically active as a theology student, and
was elected to parliament (the Storting) in 1973. He
entered the coalition led by Kare Willoch in 1983 and
was deputy prime minister 1985–86. When the Labour
prime minister Gro Harlem Brundtland resigned in
October 1997, Bondevik accepted the monarch's invitation to form a KrF-led government. His coalition
relied on the support of 42 members in the 165-
member parliament.

Born in Molde, he was educated at the Free Faculty
of Theology, University of Oslo, and was ordained a
minister in 1979.

Bondfield, Margaret Grace (1873–1953)
British Labour politician and trade unionist. She
became a trade-union organizer to improve working
conditions for women. She helped to found the

National Federation of Women Workers in 1906 and was active in the Cooperative Women's Guild. She became chair of the Trades Union Congress in 1923 and was a Labour member of Parliament 1923–24 and 1926–31. As Minister for Labour 1929–31 she was the first woman to be a British cabinet minister.

Bondfield was born in Somerset, became a shop assistant, and began her political career in the National Union of Shop Assistants, of which she was assistant secretary 1898–1908. She was the only woman delegate to the Trades Union Congress in 1899.

Bongo, Omar, adopted name of Albert-Bernard Bongo (1935–   )

Gabonese politician, president from 1968. Minister of national defence 1964–65 and vice president in 1967 under President Léon M'ba, he succeeded as president, prime minister, and secretary general after M'ba's death in 1967, and established the Gabonese Democratic Party (PDG) as the only legal party in 1968. He converted to Islam in 1973, and presided over the exploitation of Gabon's rich mineral resources without notably diminishing inequalities. In 1993 he was re-elected for the fourth time and from 1995 remained in power as president only.

Gabon's reserves of uranium, manganese, and iron give it the highest per-capita income of any African country, and Bongo successfully utilized these resources, gaining control of part-foreign-owned ventures, concluding economic and technical agreements with China, and maintaining ties with France. Although his regime was authoritarian, Gabon's prosperity diluted serious opposition, and he was re-elected in 1979 and 1986. An attempted coup in 1989 was defeated by loyal troops.

In 1990 the first multiparty elections since 1964 were won by the PDG, despite claims of widespread fraud. Bongo was re-elected in 1993, having faced opposition candidates for the first time.

He was born in Lewai, Franceville, and educated in Brazzaville. From 1957 he pursued a career in the French civil service, becoming head of the ministry of information and tourism in 1963.

Bonham-Carter, (Helen) Violet, Baroness Asquith of Yarnbury (1887–1969)

British president of the Liberal party 1945–47. A close supporter of Winston Churchill, she published *Winston Churchill as I Knew Him* in 1965. She was the daughter of the Liberal politician H H ◊Asquith. She was created a DBE in 1953 and Baroness in 1964.

Bonner, Yelena (1923–   )

Soviet human-rights campaigner. Disillusioned by the Soviet invasion of Czechoslovakia in 1968, she resigned from the Communist Party (CPSU) after marrying her second husband, Andrei ◊Sakharov, in 1971, and became active in the dissident movement.

Bonomi, Ivanoe (1873–1952)

Italian socialist politician, prime minister 1921–22 and 1944–45. An opponent of Mussolini's seizure of power, he left politics in 1924, but after 1942 was a leading figure in the anti-Fascist struggle. He replaced Pietro ◊Badoglio as prime minister in 1944 and established a broad, anti-Fascist coalition government. In 1945 he was forced to resign in favour of the more radical Ferruccio Parri. He became president of the senate in 1948.

Bonomi was first elected to parliament in 1909, following an earlier career in journalism. After his expulsion from the Italian Socialist Party in 1912, he founded a reformist socialist movement, and between 1916 and 1921 accepted various ministerial appointments under Vittorio ◊Orlando, Francesco ◊Nitti, and Giovanni ◊Giolitti.

Originally a graduate in natural sciences and law, Bonomi took up journalism in 1898, writing for *Avanti!* and *Critica socialista*.

Boothby, Robert John Graham, Baron Boothby (1900–1986)

British politician, born in Scotland. He became Unionist member of Parliament for East Aberdeenshire in 1924 and was parliamentary private secretary to Winston ◊Churchill 1926–29. He advocated the UK's entry into the European Community (now the European Union).

He was parliamentary secretary to the ministry of food 1940–41, and in 1948 became an original member of the Council of United Europe. He was a prominent commentator on public affairs on radio and television. He was created a KBE in 1958 and Baron in 1958.

Boothroyd, Betty (1929–   )

British Labour politician, Speaker of the House of Commons from 1992. A Yorkshire-born daughter of a textile worker and weaver, and a former West End dancer, she was elected member of Parliament for West Bromwich in the West Midlands in 1973 and was a member of the European Parliament 1975–77. The first woman to hold the office of Speaker, she controlled parliamentary proceedings with a mixture of firmness and good humour.

Borah, William Edgar (1865–1940)

US Republican politician. He was a senator for Idaho 1907–40. An arch-isolationist 'irreconcilable', he campaigned successfully against US entry into the League of Nations after World War I.

Borah was born in Fairfield, Illinois, and educated at the University of Kansas. He called the arms-limitation conference that took place 1921–22, chaired the Senate committee on foreign relations 1924–33, and endorsed the Kellogg–Briand pact to renounce war in 1927; he also fought against the repeal of the Neutrality Act in 1939, and resisted US participation in the International Court of Justice.

Borden, Robert Laird (1854–1937)

Canadian Conservative politician, prime minister 1911–20. Throughout World War I he represented Canada at meetings of the Imperial War Cabinet, and he was the chief Canadian delegate at the Paris Peace Conference in 1919. He played an important role in transforming Canada from a colony to a nation, notably by insisting on separate membership of the League of Nations in 1919.

Borden was born in Grand Pré, Nova Scotia. He practised law in Halifax, and was a member of the House of Commons 1896–1921, representing Halifax for most of that time. From 1910 he led the Conservative opposition. He succeeded Wilfred ◊Laurier as prime minister after the latter's defeat on the Reciprocity Bill at the general election of 1911. After his retirement from politics he published two volumes of lectures, *Canadian Constitutional Studies* (1922) and *Canada in the Commonwealth* (1929). His *Memoirs* were published posthumously in 1938.

Boris III (1894–1943)

Tsar of Bulgaria from 1918, when he succeeded his father, Ferdinand I. From 1934 he was a virtual dictator until his sudden and mysterious death following a visit to Hitler. His son Simeon II was tsar until deposed in 1946.

FURTHER READING

Dermendzhiev, Khristo *Tsar Boris III: zhivot i delo v dati i dokumenti* 1990

Dimitroff, P *Boris III of Bulgaria* 1988

Kamtchiyski, Nicolaï P *Boris III, roi de Bulgarie et son pays* 1936

Borja Cevallos, Rodrigo (1937–)

Ecuadorian politician and president 1988–92. He was a social democrat and his election as president marked a major change in governmental control to the left. Borja Cevallos's administration inherited a problematic economic situation following the failures of successive previous governments to halt national economic decline and inflationary pressures.

Bormann, Martin (1900–1945)

German Nazi leader. He took part in the abortive Munich beer-hall putsch (uprising) in 1923 and rose to high positions in the Nazi Party, becoming deputy party leader in May 1941 following the flight of Rudolf Hess to Britain.

In 1943 Hitler made him his personal secretary, a position in which he controlled access to Hitler, preventing bad news from reaching him and exercising enormous influence over Hitler's decisions. Bormann was believed to have escaped the fall of Berlin in May 1945 and was tried in his absence and sentenced to death at the Nürnberg trials of 1945–46. A skeleton uncovered by a mechanical excavator in Berlin in 1972 was officially recognized as his by forensic experts in 1973, though there continued to be frequent reports of his being seen in various parts of the world, usually South America.

Bornó, (Joseph) Louis (1865–1942)

Haitian politician, president 1922–30. Elected prime minister during the US occupation of Haiti, Bornó replaced the National Assembly with a docile legislative Council of State, which re-elected him in 1926. With violence mounting against his regime, the USA appointed an investigating commission in 1930, which recommended the appointment of a neutral president and the election of an assembly in preparation for the withdrawal of US forces in 1934. Reluctantly, Bornó stepped down in May 1930, being replaced by Eugene Roy.

Drawn from an elite mulatto (mixed ethnic) background, Bornó initially studied law in Paris and later became a prominent diplomat, serving as envoy to the Dominican Republic and as a foreign minister.

Boross, Peter (1928–)

Hungarian politician, prime minister 1993–94. Brought into Joszef ◊Antall's government as a nonpolitical technocrat, he became deputy chair of the ruling Hungarian Democratic Forum in 1991 and acting prime minister during Antall's recurring bouts of illness. When Antall died in December 1993, Boross succeeded him, but lost office to Gyula Horn, of the ex-communist Hungarian Socialist Party, in the July 1994 elections.

His introduction to politics and his subsequent rapid rise in government was almost entirely due to Antall's influence.

Bosch, (Gavino) Juan Domingo (1909–)

Dominican Republic writer and socialist politician, president in 1963. His left-wing Partido Revolucionario Dominicano (PRD; Dominican Revolutionary Party) won a landslide victory in the 1962 elections. In office, he attempted agrarian reform and labour legislation, but was opposed by the USA as a 'communist sympathiser', overthrown by the army, and forced into exile. Attempts to restore Bosch to power in 1965 led to civil war and intervention by US Marines. After his return in 1970, he formed the Dominican Liberation

Party (PLD) in 1973, but his bids for the presidency in 1982, 1986, and 1990 were unsuccessful. His achievement was to establish a democratic political party after three decades of dictatorship.

Bosch was educated at the University of Santo Domingo. In exile from 1937 as a result of his opposition to the dictatorial regime of Rafael ◊Trujillo Molina, he worked as a teacher and writer. He helped form the anti-Trujillo, left-wing PRD in Cuba in 1939, and returned to the Dominican Republic after the assassination of Trujillo in 1961. Standing as the PRD's candidate, Bosch was elected president in December 1962, in the country's first free elections for 38 years. He attracted strong support from workers and peasants but, after seven months in power, was overthrown by a military coup led by Colonel Elías Wessin y Wessin. His supporters failed to restore him to power in 1965, and he lost the 1966 presidential election to Joaquín ◊Balaguer, remaining in exile in Europe until 1970.

Bose, Subhas Chandra (1897–1945)

Indian nationalist politician, president of the Indian Congress Party 1938–39. During World War II, he recruited Indian prisoners of war to fight the British in his Indian National Army (INA).

He left India in 1941 to go to Germany in an attempt to recruit prisoners of war to the INA. A similar drive in Japan in 1943 gained only a small number of recruits and the INA was ineffectual as a fighting force, most of its members defecting to the British as soon as the opportunity occurred. Bose was killed while flying to Japan for a further recruiting drive in 1945.

Bossi, Umberto (1941–)

Italian politician, founder of the Lombard Autonomy League in 1982, and leader of the conservative-populist Northern League (LN), based in Milan, from 1984. A committed federalist, blaming Italy's lack of economic progress on the southern regions, Bossi declared an independent 'Republic of Padania' in September 1996, embracing the whole of northern Italy.

Born in Varese and educated at Pavia University, Bossi was elected to the senate in 1987. His proposed Republic of Padania, which would include the cities of Milan, Florence, and Venice, was dismissed by other party leaders as unconstitutional and impracticable, but Bossi persisted in his mission.

Botha, Louis (1862–1919)

South African soldier and politician. He was a commander in the Second South African War (Boer War). In 1907 he became premier of the Transvaal and in 1910 of the first Union South African government. On the outbreak of World War I in 1914 he rallied South Africa to the Commonwealth, suppressed a Boer revolt, and conquered German South West Africa.

Botha was born in Natal. Elected a member of the Volksraad (parliament) in 1897, he supported the more moderate Piet Joubert (1834–1900) against Paul Kruger (1825–1904). On the outbreak of the Second South African War he commanded the Boers besieging Ladysmith, and in 1900 succeeded Joubert in command of the Transvaal forces. When the Union of South Africa was formed in 1910, Botha became prime minister, and at the Versailles peace conference in 1919 he represented South Africa.

Botha, P(ieter) W(illem) (1916–)

South African politician, prime minister 1978–89. He initiated a modification of apartheid, which later slowed down in the face of Afrikaner (Boer) opposition, and made use of force both inside and outside South Africa to stifle African National Congress (ANC) party activity. In 1984 he became the first executive state president. After suffering a stroke in 1989, he unwillingly resigned both the party leadership and presidency and was succeeded by F W de Klerk.

> *After all, Moses had a mixed marriage.*
> P W BOTHA Speech 4 Sept 1980

Bottai, Giuseppe (1895–1959)

Italian politician. One of the founders of the Fascist Party, Bottai took an active part in the March on Rome in October 1922. He was among the Fascist Grand Council members who demanded Mussolini's resignation in July 1943. Sentenced to death by the Republic of Salò and to life imprisonment by the Italian authorities after World War II, he escaped and joined the French Foreign Legion. He returned to Italy on being offered amnesty.

Bottai served the Fascist regime as minister of corporations 1929–32, governor of Rome 1935–36, and minister of national education 1936–43.

Bottomley, Virginia Hilda Brunette Maxwell (1948–)

British Conservative politician, national heritage secretary 1995–97. In a cabinet reshuffle in July 1995 she was moved from the high-profile health secretary post to the department of national heritage. As health secretary 1992–95 she oversaw a radical restructuring of, and cutbacks in, the National Health Service in the name of increased efficiency and competitiveness.

Before entering Parliament she was a magistrate and psychiatric social worker. She became a member of Parliament for Surrey Southwest in 1984. As an MP she became parliamentary private secretary to Chris Patten, then to Geoffrey Howe, and was made a junior environment minister in 1988. Her husband, Peter Bottomley (1944–), is Conservative MP for Worthing West.

Boucetta, M'Hamed (1925–)

Moroccan nationalist and politician. He was minister of foreign affairs 1977–84 and of cooperation 1977–81.

He joined the Parti de l'Istiqlal (PI) when it was formed in 1944 and became its secretary general from 1974 following the death of Allal al-Fassi. He remained attached to the conservative line of the party when it split in 1959 leading to the formation of the Union Nationale des Forces Populaires by Mehdi Ben Barka. His moderate stance within the opposition facilitated dialogue and cooperation with the monarchy.

Boudiaf, Mohamed (1919–1992)

Algerian nationalist leader and politician. He was one of the nine leaders who created the Comité Révolutionnaire d'Unité et d'Action (CRUA) in 1954 as a prelude to the armed struggle. Arrested during the war, he was released in 1962. He formed the Parti de la Révolution Socialiste in opposition to Mohammed ◊Ben Bella's single-party regime.

Imprisoned then freed in 1963, he went into exile to Europe and later to Morocco. He returned to Algeria in January 1992 to preside over the designated Haut Comité d'Etat after Benjedid's resignation. He waged a campaign against corruption and made a commitment to relaunch the democratic process. He was assassinated six months later in Annaba.

Boumaza, Bachir (1927–)

Algerian nationalist and politician. After his early involvement in the party of Messali Hadj, he joined the Front de Libération Nationale (FLN) and was instrumental in setting up its federation in France. He was supportive of, and close to, Mohammed ◊Ben Bella during the struggle for power in 1962 and became minister of labour and social affairs 1962–63, national economy 1963–64, and industry and energy 1964–65. His disagreement with Houari ◊Boumédienne led to his exile in 1966.

After a long retirement, he returned to public life and was appointed president of the council of the nation (upper chamber of the parliament) in 1997.

Boumédienne, Houari, adopted name of Mohammed Boukharouba (1925–1978)

Algerian politician who brought the nationalist leader Mohammed ◊Ben Bella to power by a revolt in 1962 and superseded him as president in 1965 by a further coup. During his 13 years in office, he presided over an ambitious programme of economic development and promoted Algeria as an active champion of the Third World cause. In late 1978 he died of a rare blood disease.

Bourassa, Henri (1868–1952)

Canadian politician and journalist. Elected in 1896 to the Dominion House of Commons as a Liberal, he resigned in 1899 as a protest against Canadian participation in the Boer War and was triumphantly re-elected as a Nationalist. He left the Dominion Parliament in 1907 and was a member of the Québec legislature 1908–12. In 1910 he established the Montréal nationalist newspaper *Le Devoir*.

His Québec Nationalist following joined forces with Ontario Conservatives to defeat the Liberal prime minister Wilfrid Laurier in 1911, but Bourassa bitterly opposed the Conservative policy of conscription in World War I. He sat again in the House of Commons 1925–35.

Bourgeois, Léon Victor Auguste (1851–1925)

French politician. Entering politics as a Radical, he was prime minister in 1895, and later served in many cabinets. One of the pioneer advocates of the League of Nations, he was awarded the Nobel Peace Prize in 1920.

Bourguiba, Habib ben Ali (1903–)

Tunisian politician, first president of Tunisia 1957–87. He became prime minister in 1956 and president (for life from 1975) and prime minister of the Tunisian republic in 1957; he was overthrown in a bloodless coup in 1987.

Bourguiba was the youngest of seven children and was educated at the University of Paris. He became a journalist and leader of the nationalist Néo-Destour party. Due to his nationalist aspirations, he was imprisoned by the French protectorate of Tunisia 1934–36, 1938–43, and 1952–55. Although he was an autocrat, his rule as president was both moderate and progressive.

Bouteflika, Abdelaziz (1937–)

Algerian politician and diplomat. He joined the Armée de Liberation Nationale (ALN) in 1956 and became minister of sports and tourism in 1962, and of foreign affairs 1963–79. A close ally of Houari ◊Boumédienne, he was one of the small group of politicians and officers that masterminded the coup against Mohammed ◊Ben Bella in 1965.

A dynamic and ambitious diplomat, Bouteflika played a major role in the shaping and conduct of Algeria's foreign policy. He represented his country in several regional and international meetings and conferences, one of which was his assumption of the presidency of the special session of the UN General Assembly on the New International Economic Order in 1975. He retired from political life in 1980.

Bouterse, Désiré

Surinamese military leader and president 1980–87. He ruled dictatorially during his presidency, and set about suppressing all forms of democratic opposition.

Bouterse, a commander in chief of the armed forces, was responsible for the military coup that removed former president Henck Arron from power in 1980.

His influence and support from the military enabled him to ward off several coup attempts in 1980 and 1981. A guerrilla war in the mid-eighties caused severe economic difficulties for his administration and in 1987 his rule came to an end with democratic constitutional elections in which a civilian government was once again put back into power.

Boutros-Ghali, Boutros (1922–)

Egyptian diplomat and politician, deputy prime minister 1991–92, secretary general of the United Nations (UN) 1992–96. He worked towards peace in the Middle East in the foreign ministry posts he held 1977–91. After taking office at the UN he encountered a succession of challenges regarding the organization's role in conflict areas such as Bosnia-Herzegovina, Somalia, Haiti, and Rwanda, with which he dealt with varying degrees of success. In June 1996 the US government signified its intention to veto his re-election for a second term, and in December 1996 he was replaced by Kofi Annan.

A professor at Cairo University 1949–77, Boutros-Ghali specialized in African affairs. In 1977 he accompanied President Anwar Sadat of Egypt to Jerusalem on the diplomatic mission that led to the Camp David Agreements and was appointed minister of state for foreign affairs that year. Boutros-Ghali was elected head of La Francophonie, the French-speaking nations, in November 1997.

Braddock, Elizabeth Margaret (Bessie) (1899–1970)

British union activist and Labour politician. Born in Liverpool, she was a city councillor in Liverpool from 1930 until 1961. She was Liverpool's first Labour and first female member of Parliament, winning the Exchange division in 1945 and holding this until 1970. A right-winger, she was a powerful and caustic platform speaker and a stout defender of working people's rights to better health and education services. She turned down the offer of a post in the 1964 Labour government.

Braddock's early activism was in the Cooperative movement and the Union of Distributive and Allied Workers. She left the Independent Labour Party in 1920 to join the Communist Party and then Labour in 1924. She married John Braddock in 1922 and together they dominated the divisive world of Liverpool Labour politics. They also wrote *The Braddocks* (1962).

Bradshaw, Robert Llewellyn (1916–1978)

St Kitts and Nevis politician, prime minister 1967–78. After universal adult suffrage had been granted by the British colonial rulers in 1952, Bradshaw led the St Kitts Labour Party (SKLP) to electoral victory and became trade minister in 1956. He became chief minister of the three-island colony of St Kitts–Nevis–Anguilla in 1966, and in 1967, after associate statehood was secured, his position was designated 'prime minister'.

However, within two months, an uprising led to the effective secession of Anguilla. Bradshaw's concentration of attention on his St Kitts powerbase led to a worsening of relations with Nevis island, where support for the SKLP was limited and where, in 1970, the secessionist Nevis Reformation Party (NRP) was formed. Bradshaw fought and won the 1975 general election on the platform of immediate independence from British control, but this was not achieved until 1983, five years after his death.

Bradshaw, as a sugar factory worker, was a founding member in 1932 of the St Kitts Workers' League, which was formed by black sugar-field and factory workers to act as a trade union and incipient political organization. He served as vice president of the league until 1945, when it became the St Kitts Labour Party and he became its leader. He was elected to the islands' legislative council in 1946, but continued to campaign, through strikes and political demonstrations, for more representative government.

When the West Indies Federation was formed in 1958, he served as finance minister in Grantley Adams's federal government, until the federation's collapse in 1962.

Braine, John (Gerard) (1922–1986)

English novelist. His novel *Room at the Top* (1957) cast Braine as one of the leading Angry Young Men of the period. It created the character of Joe Lampton, one of the first of the northern working-class antiheroes, who reappears in *Life at the Top* (1962).

In *Room at the Top* Joe Lampton fights a crippling 'wrong' class background to achieve success, but finds there is no room in a corrupt middle-class world for anyone who tries to be honest. In *Life at the Top* Lampton, disenchanted with worldly success, eventually resolves his inner struggles by accepting the responsibilities of marriage and children. Other novels include *The Jealous God* (1964), a study of the Catholic priesthood; *One and Last Love* (1981), a celebration of true love; and two spy stories.

Braithwaite, Nicholas (1929–)

Grenadian centrist politician, prime minister 1991–95. Following the US-led invasion of Grenada, which ousted the left-wing military government of General Hudson Austin, Braithwaite served as chair of the non-political interim council appointed by the governor general, which held power 1983–84. He became leader of the centrist National Democratic

Congress (NDC) in 1988, and as prime minister pursued a free-market economic programme, which brought down inflation at the expense of high unemployment levels.

Braithwaite stepped down as NDC leader in 1994 and resigned as prime minister in 1995, being replaced by George Brizan, the new NDC leader.

Brandeis, Louis Dembitz (1856–1941)

US jurist. As a crusader for progressive causes, he helped draft social-welfare and labour legislation. In 1916, with his appointment to the US Supreme Court by President Woodrow Wilson, he became the first Jewish justice and maintained his support of individual rights in his opposition to the 1917 Espionage Act and in his dissenting opinion in the first wiretap case, *Olmstead v US*, in 1928.

Brătianu, Ion (1864–1927)

Romanian premier and virtual dictator during World War I and almost until his death. He concluded with the Entente powers (Britain, France, and Russia) a treaty on the basis of which Romania declared war on Germany and Austria in August 1916. He was in opposition from 1919 to 1921. He was the son of Ioan Constantin Brătianu.

Brennan, William J(oseph), Jr (1906–1997)

US judge and associate justice of the US Supreme

Willy Brandt, 1955. *AKG London*

◆ BRANDT, WILLY, ADOPTED NAME OF KARL HERBERT FRAHM (1913–1992) ◆

German socialist politician, federal chancellor (premier) of West Germany 1969–74. He played a key role in the remoulding of the Social Democratic Party (SPD) as a moderate socialist force (leader 1964–87). As mayor of West Berlin 1957–66, Brandt became internationally known during the Berlin Wall crisis of 1961. He was awarded the Nobel Peace Prize in 1971.

In the 'grand coalition' 1966–69, Brandt served as foreign minister and introduced Ostpolitik, a policy of reconciliation between East and West Europe, which was continued when he became federal chancellor in 1969 and culminated in the 1972 signing of the Basic Treaty with East Germany. He chaired the Brandt Commission on Third World problems 1977–83 and was a member of the European Parliament 1979–83.

Brandt was born in Lübeck, and joined the SPD at 17. A fervent anti-Nazi, he changed his name when he fled to Norway in 1933, where he took Norwegian citizenship, attended Oslo University, and worked as a journalist. On the German occupation of Norway in 1940 he went to Sweden,

where he continued as a journalist, supporting the anti-Nazi resistance movement. He returned to West Germany in 1945 and entered the Bundestag (federal parliament) in 1949. He resigned from the chancellorship in 1974, following the discovery that a close aide, Gunther Guillaume, had been an East German spy.

Brandt continued to wield considerable influence in the SPD, particularly over the party's radical left wing. The Brandt Commission on Third World problems produced the notable report 'North–South: A Programme for Survival' (1980), which advocated urgent action by the rich North to improve conditions in the poorer southern hemisphere.

He had not expected his Ostpolitik to bring about the reunion of Germany so speedily but fortunately lived to see it happen. From 1976 he was president of the Socialist International (SI) but was too ill to attend its 1992 meeting in Berlin, where he was buried after his death later that year.

Court 1956–90. A liberal, he wrote many important Supreme Court majority decisions that assured the freedoms set forth in the First Amendment and established the rights of minority groups. He was especially noted for writing the majority opinion in *Baker v Carr* of 1962, in which state voting reapportionment ensured 'one person, one vote', and in *US v Eichman* of 1990, which ruled that the law banning desecration of the flag was a violation of the right to free speech as provided for in the First Amendment.

Brenton, Howard (1942–)

English dramatist. His political theatre, deliberately provocative, includes *The Churchill Play* (1974) and *The Romans in Britain* (1980).

Bloody Poetry (1984) is an examination of the poet Shelley, and he co-wrote *Pravda* (1985) with David Hare and *Moscow Gold* (1990) with activist/writer Tariq Ali.

Brezhnev, Leonid Ilyich (1906–1982)

Soviet leader. A protégé of Stalin and Nikita Khrushchev, he came to power (after he and Alexei ◊Kosygin forced Khrushchev to resign) as general secretary of the Communist Party of the Soviet Union (CPSU) 1964–82 and was president 1977–82. Domestically he was conservative; abroad the USSR was established as a military and political superpower during the Brezhnev era, extending its influence in Africa and Asia.

Brezhnev, born in the Ukraine, joined the CPSU in the 1920s. In 1938 he was made head of propaganda by the new Ukrainian party chief Khrushchev and ascended in the local party hierarchy. After World War II he caught the attention of the CPSU leader Stalin, who inducted Brezhnev into the secretariat and Politburo in 1952. Brezhnev was removed from these posts after Stalin's death in 1953, but returned in 1956 with Khrushchev's patronage. In 1960, as criticism of Khrushchev mounted, Brezhnev was moved to the ceremonial post of state president and began to criticize Khrushchev's policies openly.

Brezhnev stepped down as president in 1963 and returned to the Politburo and secretariat. He was elected CPSU general secretary in 1964, when Khrushchev was ousted, and gradually came to dominate the conservative and consensual coalition. In 1977 he regained the additional title of state president under the new constitution.

He suffered an illness (thought to have been a stroke or heart attack) March–April 1976 that was believed to have affected his thought and speech so severely that he was not able to make decisions. These were made by his entourage, for example, committing troops to Afghanistan to prop up the government. Within the USSR, economic difficulties mounted; the Brezhnev era was a period of caution and stagnation, although outwardly imperialist. See photograph on page 82.

FURTHER READING
Kelley, D R (ed) *Soviet Politics in the Brezhnev Era* 1980
McCauley, M (ed) *The Soviet Union under Brezhnev* 1983
Navazelskis, Ina *Leonid Brezhnev* 1988

Briand, Aristide (1862–1932)

French republican politician, 11 times prime minister 1909–29. A skilful parliamentary tactician and orator, he was seldom out of ministerial office 1906–32. As foreign minister 1925–32, he was the architect, with the German chancellor Gustav ◊Stresemann, of the 1925 Locarno Pact (settling Germany's western frontier) and the 1928 Kellogg–Briand Pact (renouncing war). In 1930 he outlined an early scheme for the political and economic unification of Europe.

A law graduate, initially attracted to the syndicalism of Ferdinand Pelloutier and then to Jean ◊Jaurès's socialism, Briand's subsequent nationalism gave way to pacifist convictions in the 1920s.

Bridges, Harry (Alfred Renton) (1901–1990)

Australian-born US labour leader. In 1931 he formed a trade union of clockworkers and in 1934, after police opened fire on a picket line and killed two strikers, he organized a successful general strike. He was head of the International Longshoremen's and Warehousemen's Union for many years.

Born in Melbourne, Australia, he ran away to sea and settled in San Francisco, USA. Accusations by the Federal Bureau of Investigation that he had concealed membership in the Communist Party on his immigration papers were later proved false.

Brink, André (Philippus) (1935–)

South African novelist, dramatist, and critic. One of the most talented, committed, and controversial of modern Afrikaans writers, he used his novels to reveal the moral corrosiveness of the apartheid system; for example, *'n Droë wit seisoen/A Dry White Season* (1979, filmed 1989), about a white liberal investigating the death of a black political activist.

In 1961 Brink became a lecturer in modern literature and drama at Rhodes University. He was a leading figure in the literary movement known as the Sestigers ('people of the sixties'), a small group of authors of Boer extraction who sought to challenge their own tradition and explore such subjects as religion and sex. Brink's first works were largely apolitical, but the novel *Kennis van die Aand/Looking on Darkness* (1973), which treated the theme of interracial sexual relations, incurred the wrath of the Afrikaner establishment and was banned in South Africa.

Brittain, Vera (Mary) (1893–1970)

English socialist writer. She was a nurse to the troops

overseas 1915–19, as told in her book *Testament of Youth* (1933).

During the 1920s she was active in the feminist 'Six Point' group. She married political scientist George Catlin (1896–1979); their daughter is the politician Shirley ◊Williams, aspects of whose childhood are recorded in her mother's *Testament of Experience* (1957).

FURTHER READING
Bailey, H *Vera Brittain* 1987

Brittan, Leon (1939–)

British Conservative politician and lawyer. He was chief secretary to the Treasury 1981–83, home secretary 1983–85, secretary for trade and industry 1985–86 (resigning over his part in the Westland affair), and senior European commissioner from 1988. Appointed commissioner for external trade from 1993, he was at the forefront of the negotiating team that concluded the Uruguay round of GATT trade talks, leading to greater trade liberalization. He became vice president of the European Commission in 1989.

Brooke, Peter Leonard (1934–)

British Conservative politician, a member of Parliament from 1977. Appointed chair of the Conservative Party by Margaret Thatcher in 1987, he was Northern Ireland secretary 1989–92 and national heritage secretary 1992–94.

As Northern Ireland secretary, he aroused criticism (and praise) for observing that at some future time negotiations with the IRA might take place. In 1991 his efforts to institute all-party and all-Ireland talks on reconciliation proved abortive but he continued to be held in high regard on both sides of the border.

Brooke was born in London, educated at Oxford University, and worked as a management consultant in New York and Brussels. The son of a former home secretary, Lord Brooke of Cumnor, he became an MP in 1977 and entered Thatcher's government in 1979. Following a number of junior appointments, he succeeded Norman Tebbit as chair of the Conservative Party in 1987. As national heritage secretary, he argued for regulatory measures to protect against invasions of privacy by the press.

Brookeborough, Basil Stanlake Brooke, Viscount Brookeborough (1888–1973)

Northern Ireland Unionist politician. He entered Parliament in 1929, held ministerial posts 1933–45, and was prime minister of Northern Ireland 1943–63. He was a staunch advocate of strong links with Britain.

FURTHER READING
Barton, B *Brookeborough: The Making of a Prime Minister* 1988

Browder, Earl Russell (1871–1973)

US politician. Born in Wichita, Kansas, Browder was a member of the US Communist Party from 1921, becoming its secretary general from 1936. He was also a nominee for US president in 1940, advocating reconciliation between socialism and capitalism, a stance that caused his expulsion by the Communists in 1946.

FURTHER READING
Ryan, James G *Earl Browder: The Failure of American Communism* 1997

Brown, (James) Gordon (1951–)

British Labour politician, born in Scotland, chancellor of the Exchequer from 1997. He entered Parliament in 1983, rising quickly to the opposition front bench, with a reputation as an outstanding debater. He took over from John ◊Smith as shadow chancellor in 1992. After Smith's death in May 1994, he declined to challenge his close ally Tony Blair for the leadership, retaining his post as shadow chancellor, and assuming the chancellorship after the 1997 general election.

On becoming chancellor in 1997, he ceded to the Bank of England full control of interest rates. He used his position as chancellor to promote key initiatives, notably the 'welfare to work' programme directed against unemployment and funded by a windfall tax imposed on privatized utilities. He gained the reputation of being an 'iron chancellor', maintaining firm control over public expenditure. This led to criticisms within his party from those seeking more funds for welfare reform and the National Health Service.

Brown was born in Kirkcaldy, Fife, the son of a Church of Scotland minister. He won a first in history at Edinburgh University before he was 20. After four years as a college lecturer and three as a television journalist, he entered the House of Commons as MP for Dunfermline East in 1983.

Brown, (Ronald Harmon) Ron (1941–)

US cabinet officer and lawyer. For several years he made his name as a corporate lobbyist. In 1988 he served as a strategist to Jesse Jackson's presidential campaign. Successful handling of Bill Clinton's campaign in 1992 led to Brown being appointed secretary of commerce in 1993.

Born in Washington, DC, the son of Howard University graduates, he grew up in Harlem. After graduating from Middlebury College in 1962 and serving with the US Army 1962–66, he earned his law degree at St John's University School of Law in 1970. While working for the National Urban League (NUL) in New York, he was elected district leader of the Democratic Party in Mount Vernon, New York, in 1971. He was with the Washington, DC, office of the NUL from 1973–79, and he then held a series of positions under Senator Edward Kennedy; he worked for the Democratic National Committee 1981–85. In 1981 he had joined the Washington, DC, law firm of Patton, Boggs & Blow, thereby becoming its first black American partner. His role as a unifier at the Democratic Convention led to his being chosen in 1989 to head the Democratic National Committee.

Brown, George Alfred, Baron George-Brown (1914–1985)

British Labour politician. He entered Parliament in 1945, was briefly minister of works in 1951, and contested the leadership of the party on the death of Hugh Gaitskell, but was defeated by Harold Wilson.

He was secretary for economic affairs 1964–66 and foreign secretary 1966–68. He was created a life peer in 1970.

Brown, Jim (James Nathaniel) (1936–)

US American footballer. As a running back for the Cleveland Browns between 1957 and 1965, he became the first NFL (US National Football League) player to reach the 10,000-yard career mark in rushing. His career total of 126 touchdowns was one of several other NFL records that he set. When he retired in 1965 he had taken his career total to 12,312 yards at 5.2 yards a carry, an average which has never been surpassed. He subsequently embarked on a film career, but attracted more publicity as an outspoken campaigner for black rights.

Bruce, David K E (Kirkpatrick Este) (1898–1977)

US statesman and diplomat. Between 1948 and 1949 he administered the Marshall Plan in France. He was ambassador to France 1949–52, to West Germany 1957–59, and to Great Britain 1961–69. He was a representative to the Vietnam Peace Talks in Paris 1970–71 and liaison officer to Communist China 1973–74. He was ambassador to NATO 1974–76.

Bruce was born in Baltimore, Maryland, served in the field artillery in World War I, and was admitted to the Maryland bar in 1921. He was with the Foreign Service 1925–27, subsequently turning his attention to business and farming 1928–40. He helped to organize the Office of Strategic Services in 1941.

Bruce, Lenny (1925–1966)

US comedian and satirist. Bruce became famous for his on-stage monologues on racism, homophobia, drug-taking, nuclear testing, and the death penalty. Arrested over 15 times in two years, Bruce's satirical attention turned to the legal system. He died in 1966 of a drugs overdose.

FURTHER READING
Bruce, Lenny, and Bogosian, Eric (designer) *How to Talk Dirty and Influence People: An Autobiography* 1992

Bruce, Stanley Melbourne, 1st Viscount Bruce of Melbourne (1883–1967)

Australian National Party politician, prime minister 1923–29. He introduced a number of social welfare measures and sought closer economic ties with the UK, campaigning for 'Imperial Preference'. With the economy worsening, he lost the 1929 general election and also his seat, but emerged as an energetic diplomat, serving as Australia's high commissioner to London 1933–45.

Born into a wealthy Victorian family, he studied at Cambridge University, England, practised as a barrister in the UK, and was wounded fighting in World War I. On his return to Australia, he was elected to the federal parliament in 1918 and served as treasurer in Billy ◊Hughes's National Government 1921–22. He was made a viscount in 1947 and worked in the United Nations Food and Agricultural Organization 1946–51.

FURTHER READING
Edwards, Cecil *Bruce of Melbourne: Man of Two Worlds* 1965

Brundtland, Gro Harlem (1939–)

Norwegian Labour politician, head of the World Health Organization (WHO) from 1998. Environment minister 1974–76, she briefly took over as prime minister in 1981, a post to which she was re-elected in 1986, 1990, and again held 1993–96, when she resigned. Leader of the Norwegian Labour Party from 1981, she resigned the post in 1992 but continued as prime minister. Retaining her seat count in the 1993 general election, she led a minority Labour government committed to European Union membership, but failed to secure backing for the membership application in a 1994 national referendum. She was chosen as the new leader of the WHO in 1998.

She trained as a physician, but concentrated on politics from 1974. She chaired the World Commission on Environment and Development, which produced the Brundtland Report, published as *Our Common Future* in 1987.

Brüning, Heinrich (1885–1970)

German politician. Elected to the Reichstag (parliament) in 1924, he led the Catholic Centre Party from 1929 and was federal chancellor 1930–32 when political and economic crisis forced his resignation.

Bruton, John (1947–)

Irish politician, leader of Fine Gael (United Ireland Party) from 1990 and prime minister 1994–97. The collapse of Albert ◊Reynolds's Fianna Fáil–Labour government in November 1994 thrust Bruton, as a leader of a new coalition with Labour, into the prime ministerial vacancy. He pledged himself to the continuation of the Anglo-Irish peace process as pursued by his predecessor; in 1995 he pressed for greater urgency in negotiations for a permanent peace agreement. However, his alleged over-willingness to support the British government's cautious approach to the peace process produced strong criticism in April 1995 from the Sinn Féin leader, Gerry Adams.

A Dublin-trained lawyer and working farmer, Bruton entered parliament in 1969 and, as party spokesperson, made steady progress through the departments of agriculture, industry and commerce, and education. He served in the government of Garret ◊FitzGerald 1982–87 before succeeding him as party leader.

Bryan, William Jennings (1860–1925)

US politician who campaigned unsuccessfully for the presidency three times: as the Populist and Democratic nominee in 1896, as an anti-imperialist Democrat in 1900, and as a Democratic tariff reformer in 1908. He served as President Woodrow Wilson's secretary of state 1913–15. In the early 1920s he was a leading fundamentalist and opponent of Clarence ◊Darrow in the Scopes monkey trial.

Bryan was born in Salem, Illinois, and educated at Illinois College and Union College of Law, Chicago. In 1891 he was elected to Congress from the First District of Nebraska, which had previously been Republican, but the Democrat Bryan carried it with his demands for banking and tariff reform and his call for 'free silver'. He served two terms in Congress, and took a leading part in the debates on the questions of bimetallism and free trade.

When the presidential convention of the Democratic party met in Chicago in 1896, it was known that the issue would be joined between the gold-standard Democrats of the east and the free-silver forces of the west and south. Bryan delivered a stirring speech for free silver in which he used the phrase 'You shall not crucify mankind on a cross of gold'. Bryan was nominated on a free-silver plank. The Republicans promptly nominated William McKinley on a gold-standard ticket. An exciting campaign ensued, but Bryan was unsuccessful.

You shall not press down upon the brow of labor this crown of thorns, you shall not crucify mankind upon a cross of gold.
WILLIAM BRYAN Speech at the National Democratic Convention, Chicago, 1896

Undismayed by the defeat of 1896, the Democrats renominated Bryan for president against McKinley in 1900. This time his campaign included not only the free-silver issue, but a bitter crusade against imperialism growing out of the US annexation of the Philip-

pines, Guam, and Puerto Rico as a result of the victories in the Spanish–American War. Bryan once more went down to crushing defeat. Again in 1908 the Democrats nominated Bryan and again Bryan lost. Bryan held office as Woodrow Wilson's secretary of state until June 1915, when he resigned because of President Wilson's attitude over the sinking of the *Lusitania*.

Brzezinski, Zbigniew (1928–)

US academic and Democratic politician, born in Poland; he taught at Harvard University, USA, and became a US citizen in 1949. He was national security adviser to President Jimmy Carter 1977–81 and chief architect of Carter's human-rights policy.

FURTHER READING
Brzezinski, Zbigniew *The Grand Chessboard: American Primacy and its Geostrategic Imperatives* 1997

Bucaram, Ortiz Abdalá (1952–)

Ecuadorian politician and president 1996–97. He founded the Ecuadorian Roldosista Party (PRE) in 1982 and was elected mayor of Guayaquil 1984. In 1996 he succeeded in his bid for the presidency, defeating his opponent from the Social Christian Party (PSC). In February 1997 he was removed from office by Congress.

Bucaram trained as a lawyer and was a keen sportsman, representing his country as an Olympic hurdler. During the presidential election campaign he appealed to Ecuador's poorer classes, promising to focus on the country's social welfare programmes.

Buchan, John, 1st Baron Tweedsmuir (1875–1940)

Scottish writer and politician. His popular adventure stories, today sometimes criticized for their alleged snobbery, sexism, and anti-Semitism, include *The Thirty-Nine Steps*, a tale of espionage published in 1915, *Greenmantle* (1916), and *The Three Hostages* (1924).

He was Conservative member of Parliament for the Scottish universities 1927–35, and governor general of Canada 1935–40.

Buckley, William F(rank) (1925–)

US conservative political writer, novelist, and founder-editor of the *National Review* (1955). In such books as *Up from Liberalism* (1959), and in a weekly television debate *Firing Line*, he represented the 'intellectual' right-wing, antiliberal stance in US political thought.

Buhari, Muhammadu (1942–)

Nigerian politician and soldier, president 1983–85. He led the military coup that ousted Shehu ◊Shagari in 1983. Having assumed the presidency himself, he imposed an authoritarian regime of austerity measures, and was deposed in a coup led by Ibrahim ◊Babangida in 1985. He was detained until 1988.

Buhari was trained at military academies in Nigeria, the UK, and India, and became military governor of North-Eastern State 1975–76 and of Bornu State in 1976. From 1976 to 1978 he was appointed federal commissioner for petroleum resources and he became chair of the Nigerian National Petroleum Corporation 1976–79, before returning to army duties.

Bukharin, Nikolai Ivanovich (1888–1938)

Soviet politician and theorist. A moderate, he was the chief Bolshevik thinker after Lenin. Executed on Stalin's orders for treason in 1938, he was posthumously rehabilitated in 1988.

He wrote the main defence of war communism in his *Economics of the Transition Period* (1920). He drafted the Soviet constitution of 1936, but in 1938 was imprisoned and tried for treason in one of Stalin's show trials. He pleaded guilty to treason, but defended his moderate policies and denied criminal charges. Nevertheless, he was executed, as were all other former members of Lenin's Politburo except Trotsky, who was murdered, and Stalin himself.

We might have a two-party system, but one of the two parties would be in office and the other in prison.

NIKOLAI IVANOVICH BUKHARIN Attributed remark

Bulatović, Momir (1928–)

Montenegrin politician, president of Montenegro 1990–97. He was a founder member of the League of Communists of Yugoslavia, and went on to become leader of the Republican League of Communists. He became chair of the Democratic Party of Socialists (DPS) in 1990, and fought the presidential election in the same year.

He was educated at Titograd University (since 1992 known as Podgorica).

Bulganin, Nikolai Aleksandrovich (1895–1975)

Soviet politician and military leader. His career began in 1918 when he joined the Cheka, the Soviet secret police. He helped to organize Moscow's defences in World War II, became a marshal of the USSR in 1947, and was minister of defence 1947–49 and 1953–55. On the fall of Georgi Malenkov he became prime minister (chair of the council of ministers) 1955–58 until ousted by Nikita Khrushchev.

Bülow, Bernhard Heinrich Martin Karl, Prince von Bülow (1849–1929)

German diplomat and politician. He was chancellor of the German Empire 1900–09 under Kaiser Wilhelm II and, holding that self-interest was the only rule for any state, adopted attitudes to France and Russia that unintentionally reinforced the trend towards opposing European power groups: the Triple Entente (Britain, France, Russia) and the Triple Alliance (Germany, Austria–Hungary, Italy).

Bunche, Ralph Johnson (1904–1971)

US diplomat. He was principal director of the United Nations Department of Trusteeship 1948–54 and UN undersecretary 1955–67, acting as mediator in Palestine 1948–49 and as special representative in the Congo 1960. He became UN undersecretary general in 1968. In 1950 he was awarded the Nobel Peace Prize.

◆ BUCHANAN, PAT(RICK JOSEPH) (1938–) ◆

US right-wing Republican activist and journalist. Although a TV and radio commentator, he often attacked the mass media. He was a candidate for the Republican nomination for president in 1992 and 1996.

Buchanan was special assistant and speechwriter to President Richard Nixon 1966–73, and was President Ronald Reagan's White House director of communications 1985–87. In 1993 he became chair of his own broadcasting company.

An advocate of 'America First' protectionism, the outlawing of abortion, an end to US participation in United Nations peacekeeping missions, and a moratorium on immigration, he became referred to by opponents as the USA's equivalent to the Russian extremist xenophobe Vladimir Zhirinovsky. From 1992 he was chair of the American Cause protectionist group.

Buchanan was born in Washington, DC, educated at Georgetown and Columbia universities, and worked as a journalist on the *St Louis Globe-Democrat* 1962–65 before taking a job in Nixon's law firm.

When Nixon became president in 1969, it was Buchanan who prepared his daily briefing. Buchanan attacked the television networks, which he believed were under the control of antigovernment liberals and were too influential. Appointed special consultant to the president in 1972, he stayed on under Gerald Ford.

In the book *Conservative Voters, Liberal Victories* (1975), Buchanan attacked the media for undermining public support for the Vietnam War. From 1975 to 1978 he wrote a syndicated political

Bunche was born in Detroit, the grandson of a slave, and educated at California and Harvard universities. He taught at Harvard and Howard universities and was involved in the planning of the UN. In 1950 he became professor of government at Harvard.

Bundy, McGeorge (1919–1996)

US public official and educator. He was special national security adviser to presidents John F Kennedy and Lyndon Johnson 1961–66 and played a prominent role in pursuing the Vietnam War.

Bundy was born in Boston, Massachusetts. He taught and served as a dean at Harvard University. He went on to become Ford Foundation president 1966–79, and history professor at New York University.

Bunker, Ellsworth (1894–1984)

US diplomat and executive. He was ambassador to South Vietnam during the crucial stages of the Vietnam War 1967–73, and the chief negotiator of the Panama Canal treaties 1973–78, which became controversial during the 1976 presidential campaign.

He was born in Yonkers, New York. He was an executive in the sugar industry 1927–66, and became a diplomat in 1951. He was ambassador to Argentina, Italy, India, and Nepal 1951–61.

Burger, Warren Earl (1907–1995)

US jurist, chief justice of the US Supreme Court 1969–86. Appointed to the court by President Richard Nixon because of his conservative views, Burger showed himself to be pragmatic and liberal on some social issues, including abortion and desegregation. It was Burger's ruling against presidential executive privilege in 1974, at the height of the Watergate scandal, that forced the release of damning tapes and documents that were to prompt the resignation of Nixon.

Burger's early rulings on the Supreme Court were conservative, upholding judicial restraint, the use of non-unanimous jury verdicts, and the death penalty. However, in 1971 he backed court-ordered bussing so as to overcome state-imposed school segregation and, for the first time, applied to women the constitutional guarantee of equal protection under the law. The most controversial decision of the Burger-led Supreme Court was its ruling, in the 1973 Roe v Wade case, in favour of a woman's right to abortion. Later, Burger's views in this area changed.

Burger was born in St Paul, Minnesota, and became a partner in 1935 in a law firm there. An active Republican, he was made assistant attorney general in the Dwight Eisenhower administration in 1953, and a US Court of Appeals judge for the District of Columbia in 1955. Burger became a prominent critic of the liberal 'activist' rulings of the Supreme Court of Chief Justice Earl Warren 1953–69, arguing that the US legal system had become dangerously tilted in favour of criminals whose convictions were being reversed on legal and procedural technicalities. His writings in favour of a strict 'constructionist', or literal, interpretation of constitutional law attracted the attention of Richard Nixon, elected US president in 1968, and he was nominated to succeed the retiring Earl Warren in 1969.

Burgess, Guy Francis de Moncy (1911–1963)

British spy, a diplomat recruited in the 1930s by the USSR as an agent. He was linked with Kim ◊Philby, Donald Maclean (1913–1983), and Anthony ◊Blunt.

Burgess was born in Devon and educated at Eton and Cambridge University where he became a communist. He worked for the BBC from 1936 to 1939, as talks producer, and wrote war propaganda from 1939 to 1941. In 1951 he defected to the USSR with Donald Maclean.

Burnham, (Linden) Forbes (Sampson) (1923–1985)

Guyanese Marxist-Leninist politician. He was prime minister 1964–80 in a coalition government, leading the country to independence in 1966 and declaring it the world's first cooperative republic in 1970. He was executive president 1980–85. Resistance to the US landing in Grenada 1983 was said to be due to his forewarning the Grenadans of the attack.

---

column, and from 1978 to 1982 he introduced the commentary programme *Confrontation* on NBC radio. He was moderator of the TV show *Capital Gang* 1988–92 and editor of the newsletter *PJB – From the Right* 1990–91.

His controversial challenge for the Republican presidential nomination against the incumbent George Bush in 1992 was unsuccessful, despite winning 37% support in the opening New Hampshire primary. In the 1996 open contest for the Republican nomination, Buchanan ran a vigorous populist campaign which, railing against abortion, illegal immigration, and the big business elite, drew in support from the self-styled 'moral majority' religious right and disaffected blue-collar workers. In the New Hampshire primary he narrowly defeated the Senate leader Bob Dole, but his campaign subsequently never got more than 20–30% support, and Dole went on to gain the nomination.

In 1950 he cofounded the People's Progressive Party with Cheddi ◊Jagan, and in 1955 he founded the more moderate People's National Congress.

Burnham, Harry Lawson-Webster Levy-Lawson (1862–1933)

English politician and newspaper proprietor. He presided over the International Labour Conferences in Geneva, Switzerland (1921, 1922, and 1926). His name is perpetuated in the 'Burnham scale' by which schoolteachers' salaries are calculated, the result of a standing committee which he chaired. He became manager of the *Daily Telegraph* in 1903, and proprietor in 1916. He sold the newspaper in 1928.

Burns, John Elliot (1858–1943)

British labour leader, born in London of Scottish parentage. He was sentenced to six weeks' imprisonment for his part in the Trafalgar Square demonstration on 'Bloody Sunday', 13 November 1887, and was leader of the strike in 1889 securing the 'dockers' tanner' (wage of 6d per hour). An Independent Labour member of Parliament 1892–1918, he was the first working-class person to be a member of the cabinet, as president of the Local Government Board 1906–14.

Burroughs, William S(eward) (1914–1997)

US writer. One of the most culturally influential postwar writers, his work is noted for its experimental methods, black humour, explicit homo-eroticism, and apocalyptic vision. In 1944 he met Allen Ginsberg and Jack Kerouac, all three becoming leading members of the Beat Generation.

He settled in Tangier in 1954 and wrote his celebrated anti-novel *Naked Lunch* (1959). A landmark federal court case deemed *Naked Lunch* not obscene; this broke the ground for other books, helping to eliminate censorship of the printed word in the USA.

Bush, George W, Jr (1946–)

US politician. Governor of Texas from 1994 and son of former president George ◊Bush, he served on the boards of various charitable, business, and civic organizations and in the late 1990s was heavily tipped as a potential presidential candidate.

George W Bush grew up in Midland and Houston, Texas. He received a bachelor's degree from Yale University and an MBA from Harvard Business School. He founded an oil- and gas-exploration company in Midland and worked in the energy business from 1975–86, then moved to Washington, DC, to help in his father's presidential campaign. He assembled the group of partners that purchased the Texas Rangers baseball franchise in 1989 and later built the Ranger's new home, the Ballpark at Arlington, Texas. He also

◆ BUSH, GEORGE HERBERT WALKER (1924–) ◆

41st president of the USA 1989–93, a Republican. He was director of the Central Intelligence Agency (CIA) 1976–81 and US vice president 1981–89. As president, his response to the Soviet leader Mikhail Gorbachev's diplomatic initiatives were initially criticized as inadequate, but his sending of US troops to depose his former ally, General ◊Noriega of Panama, proved a popular move at home. Success in the 1991 Gulf War against Iraq further raised his standing. Domestic economic problems 1991–92 were followed by his defeat in the 1992 presidential elections by Democrat Bill Clinton.

Bush, the son of a Connecticut senator, moved to Texas in 1948 to build up an oil-drilling company. A congressman 1967–70, he was appointed US ambassador to the United Nations 1971–73 and Republican national chair 1973–74 by President Richard Nixon, and special envoy to China 1974–75 under President Gerald Ford.

During Bush's time as head of the CIA, General Noriega of Panama was on its payroll, and Panama was later used as a channel for the secret supply of arms to Iran and the Nicaraguan Contra guerrillas. Evidence came to light in 1987 linking Bush with the Irangate scandal. But Noriega

became uncontrollable and, in December 1989, Bush sent an invasion force to Panama and set up a puppet government.

Read my lips – no new taxes.
GEORGE BUSH Promise made during 1988 US presidential campaign

As president, Bush soon reneged on his election pledge of 'no new taxes', but not before he had introduced a cut in capital-gains tax that predominantly benefited the richest 3% of the population. In 1990, having proclaimed a 'new world order' as the Cold War was officially declared over and facing economic recession in the USA, he sent a large army to Saudi Arabia after Iraq's annexation of Kuwait, and ruled out negotiations. His response to Iraq's action contrasted sharply with his policy of support for Israel's refusal to honour various United Nations Security Council resolutions calling for its withdrawal from occupied territories, but the ousting of Iraqi forces from Kuwait was greeted as a great US victory.

served as a managing general partner of the Texas Rangers.

Busia, Kofi (1913–1978)

Ghanaian politician and academic, prime minister 1969–72. He became a leader of the National Liberation Movement 1954–59, in opposition to Kwame ◊Nkrumah, and went into exile in 1959. Following the 1966 coup, he returned as adviser to the National Liberation Council and then founded the Progress Party, leading it to electoral victory in 1969. He was ousted as prime minister in a military coup in 1972, and returned to exile in the same year.

Busia was educated in Kumasi and at Achimota College, and at the universities of London and Oxford. He was one of the first Africans to be appointed as an administrative officer in the Gold Coast (now Ghana). He resigned that position to become a lecturer, and later became professor of sociology at the University College of Ghana. During his first exile he took up the chair of sociology at Leiden University in the Netherlands, and after 1972 he held various academic posts. He died in Oxford, England.

Bustamante, (William) Alexander, born Clarke (1884–1977)

Jamaican centre-right politician, prime minister

Despite this success, the signing of the long-awaited Strategic Arms Reduction Treaty (START I) in July 1991, and Bush's unprecedented unilateral reduction in US nuclear weapons two months later, his popularity at home began to wane as criticism of his handling of domestic affairs mounted.

After his defeat at the polls in November 1992 and prior to handing over to his successor, Democrat Bill Clinton, on 20 January 1993, Bush initiated 'Operation Restore Hope' in Somalia, in which US Marines were drafted in as part of a multinational effort to deliver aid to famine-stricken areas, and signed the START II treaty with Russia, which bound both countries to cut long-range nuclear weapons by two-thirds by the year 2003. He also supported the more controversial bombing of strategic targets in Iraq after alleged infringements of the UN-imposed 'no-fly zone'. One of his sons, George W Bush, Jr, was elected as Republican governor of Texas in November 1994, and another, Jeb Bush, was narrowly defeated in the Florida governorship race. See photograph on page 392.

FURTHER READING

Campbell, Colin (ed) *The Bush Presidency* 1991
Green, F *George Bush* 1989
Sufrin, M *George Bush* 1989

1962–67. Founder of the Bustamante Industrial Trade Union for sugar plantation workers in 1938, he was imprisoned by the British colonial authorities 1941–42 for his union and political activities. In 1943 he established the Jamaica Labour Party (JLP) as the political wing of his union and served as chief minister 1953–55. As leader of the Labour Party, he became Jamaica's first prime minister on independence in 1962. He pursued a conservative policy programme and developed close ties with the USA. He was knighted in 1955.

Born in Blenheim, near Kingston, the son of an Irish planter, he was adopted at the age of 15 by a Spanish seaman called Bustamente. He spent his early life abroad, variously as a soldier in the Spanish army and working in numerous professions in Cuba, Panama, and New York. He returned to Jamaica in 1932 a rich man, but his social conscience led him to become active in trade-union affairs. In 1938 he faced charges of political sedition, but was successfully defended by his barrister cousin, Norman ◊Manley, founder of the People's National Party and later prime minister. From 1947 to 1948 he served as mayor of Kingston.

Buthelezi, Chief Mangosuthu Gatsha (1928–)

South African Zulu leader and politician, president of the Zulu-based Inkatha Freedom Party (IFP), which he founded as a paramilitary organization for attaining a nonracial democratic society in 1975. Buthelezi's threatened boycott of South Africa's first multiracial elections led to a dramatic escalation in politically motivated violence, but he eventually agreed to register his party and in May 1994 was appointed home affairs minister in the country's first post-apartheid government. In December 1995 there were unsubstantiated claims that he had colluded with the security service during the apartheid period.

Buthelezi, great-grandson of King Cetewayo, became chief minister of KwaZulu, then a black homeland in the Republic of South Africa, in 1970. Opposed to KwaZulu becoming a Black National State, he argued instead for a confederation of black areas, with eventual majority rule over all South Africa under a one-party socialist system. He was accused of complicity in the factional violence between Inkatha and African National Congress supporters that racked the townships during the early 1990s.

Butler, Richard Austen ('Rab'), Baron Butler of Saffron Walden (1902–1982)

British Conservative politician. As minister of education 1941–45, he was responsible for the 1944 Education Act that introduced the 11-plus examination for selection of grammar school pupils; he was chancellor of the Exchequer 1951–55, Lord Privy Seal 1955–59, and foreign minister 1963–64. As a candidate for the prime ministership, he was defeated by Harold Macmillan in 1957 (under whom he was home secretary 1957–62), and by Alec Douglas Home in 1963.

Butler was born in India, the son of an administrator, and he was educated at Marlborough and Cambridge University. He was elected Member of Parliament for Saffron Walden, Essex, in 1932.

> Politics is the art of the possible.
>
> RICHARD AUSTEN ('RAB') BUTLER
> Attributed remark

FURTHER READING
Howard, A *'Rab': The Life of R A Butler* 1987

Buyoya, Pierre (1949–   )

Burundian soldier and head of state 1987–93. In 1987 he led a military coup against his close colleague President Jean-Baptiste Bagaza. A member of the Tutsi ethnic group, Buyoya promised fairer treatment for the Hutu majority. However, only a few months later thousands of Hutus were killed by Tutsis, and in 1991 Buyoya was forced to move towards a multiparty democracy. A coup in 1992 led by the former foreign minister failed. Buyoya continued to press for greater democracy, and this led to the elections that brought to power Burundi's first Hutu president, Melchior Ndadaye.

Buzek, Jerzy Karol (1940–   )

Polish politician, prime minister of Poland from 1997. A chemical-engineering professor and a veteran trade-union activist, he was named prime minister of a new centre–right coalition in October 1997, after the Solidarity Electoral Action (AWS) emerged victorious in general elections. Outlining his new government's programme, he promised to push for rapid integration with the North Atlantic Treaty Organization (NATO) and the European Union (EU), to cut bureaucracy, decentralize finances, and expedite privatization plans.

Buzek joined Solidarity at its birth in 1980, chaired its first, fourth, fifth, and sixth national congresses and was an elected deputy to the Sejm (parliament). He participated in Solidarity's underground leadership after the movement was outlawed, and was an activist of the union's regional and national leadership. As co-author of the AWS economic programme, the mild-mannered Buzek emerged as the ideal candidate to lead the coalition government formed in 1997 by the AWS and the pro-business Freedom Union (UW).

Born in Silesia, Buzek, was a scientific researcher and professor at the Chemical Engineering Institute of the Polish Academy of Sciences in Geiwice.

Cabral, Amilcar (1924–1973)

Guinean nationalist leader. He founded the African Party for the Independence of Portuguese Guinea and Cape Verde (PAIGC) in 1956 and, after abortive constitutional discussions with the Portuguese government, initiated a revolutionary war in 1963. He was murdered in 1973 just as his aim was being achieved. His brother, Luiz ◊ Cabral, became the first president of an independent Guinea-Bissau in 1974.

Amilcar Cabral was noted for his commitment to politicizing the peasantry and establishing alternative institutions in liberated territories. He presided over a successful war that forced the Portuguese to concede independence.

Educated at Lisbon University, Portugal, he initially worked as an agronomist and agricultural engineer for the colonial authorities.

Cabral, Luiz (1931–)

Guinean nationalist leader and politician, first president of the republic of Guinea-Bissau 1974–80. As a member of the African Party for the Independence of Portuguese Guinea and Cape Verde (PAIGC), he went into exile in 1960 and took part in the guerrilla struggle to win independence. Success made him president of the new republic in 1974, but he was later overthrown in a coup. He was the brother of the nationalist leader Amilcar ◊ Cabral.

By 1972 in the revolutionary war the PAIGC claimed to have won over two-thirds of Portuguese Guinea, and in 1973 the 'liberated areas' were declared independent, a national people's assembly was set up, and Luiz Cabral was appointed president of a state council. A coup in Portugal ended the fighting and the PAIGC negotiated independence with the new government in Lisbon.

Luiz Cabral was educated in Portuguese Guinea, and became a clerk and a trade-union organizer before entering politics.

Caetano, Marcello José des Neves Alves (1906–1980)

Portuguese right-wing politician. Professor of administrative law at Lisbon from 1940, he succeeded the dictator António Salazar as prime minister from 1968 until his exile after the military coup of 1974. He was granted political asylum in Brazil.

Cairns, James Ford ('Jim') (1914–)

Australian Labor politician, regarded as the leader of Labor's left wing in the 1960s and early 1970s when he was heavily involved in the movement against the Vietnam War and conscription. He was treasurer and deputy prime minister in Gough ◊ Whitlam's government 1974–75 but was dismissed for his role in the 'loans affair', which centred on unorthodox loan negotiations by the minister for minerals and energy, Rex Connor.

Born in Melbourne, he served in the police force and military before securing a doctorate and lecturing at Melbourne University. He was selected to the federal parliament in 1955 and was narrowly defeated in 1967 by Whitlam in Labor's leadership contest.

Cai Yuanpei or Ts'ai Yüan-p'ei (1863–1940)

Chinese educator, scholar, and politician. In 1911 he became the first minister of education of the new Chinese Republic, presiding over the creation of a new school system. He resigned in 1912 but continued to be active in educational affairs, helping to promote a work-study programme for Chinese students in France. Appointed chancellor of Beijing (Peking) University in 1916, he encouraged free debate and scholarship at the university, transforming it into one of the country's foremost intellectual centres.

One of the youngest candidates ever to obtain the highest degree in the classical Civil Service examination system, he taught in various schools and colleges in his home province of Zhejiang (Chekiang) and in Shanghai, before joining ◊ Sun Yat-sen's anti-Manchu republican movement.

In his later years he became a member of the Guomindang (nationalist party), but became increasingly critical of the party's suppression of free speech. He died in Hong Kong.

Caldera Rodriguez, Rafael (1916–)

Venezuelan politician and president 1969–74 and 1994–98. A member of the political party Convergencia (National Convergence), he also had a prolific academic career. Caldera's first term as president was noted for significantly reducing guerrilla and terrorist activity. Economic crisis during his second term, however, was a major preoccupation resulting in new proposals to tackle oil dependence, rising inflation, falling standards of living, and a growing national deficit. The proposals brought about initial protests, but they were insufficient to cause a premature termination of his administration.

Caldera was born in January 1916, in San Felipe, Yaracuy state. He studied law and political sciences, before graduating with a doctorate in political sciences, in April 1939, from the Universidad Central de Venezuela. He was active during his university studies as secretary of the Central Council of Catholic Youth 1932–34, and a member of the board of the National Union of Students (UNE). Initially, he followed a university career 1943–68 as a professor specializing in sociology and employment law. He was also a prolific linguist, capable of speaking more than five languages.

Politically, Caldera worked actively in a number of posts, most notably as a national congress deputy in Yaracuy state 1941–94, national attorney general 1945–46, a representative of the federal district and national constituency assembly 1946–47, and a national congress deputy for the federal district in 1948 and 1959–64. He was also president of the house of deputies 1959–62.

Caldera was ·a renowned writer, who published extensively on employment law, politics, democratic issues, sociology, and development, with in excess of 50 publications of various types, many of which have been translated into other languages.

Calderón Guardia, Rafael Ángel (1900–1971)

Costa Rican politician, president 1940–44, who introduced social security reforms. His unwillingness to accept defeat in the 1948 presidential elections led to civil war.

Popularly elected president in 1940, he introduced a labour code and social security legislation, receiving support from both the right and the communist left, and brought Costa Rica into World War II on the Allies' side. He was succeeded as president, 1944–48, by his close associate Teodoro Picado. In the presidential election in 1948, Calderón was defeated by Otilio Ulate. Picado's attempts to annul the result caused a revolutionary civil war that forced Picado and Calderón into exile and brought José ◊Figueres to power.

Educated partly in Belgium, Calderón worked in Costa Rica as a physician, before entering politics in 1934, seeking to promote housing and health reform. He served successively as vice president and president of the congress between 1935 and 1939 and was also leader of the Republican, or Calderista, party.

Calderón Sol, Armando (1948–)

El Salvadorean right-wing politician, president from 1994. He was elected to serve as mayor of San Salvador 1988–94 and chair of the right-wing National Republican Alliance (ARENA) in 1990 and, as its candidate, won the May 1994 presidential election by a large margin in the run-off round.

Born in San Salvador, he studied law and social science at the University of El Salvador and, after working in an investment bank, became leader of ARENA in the Legislative Assembly from 1985. During his presidency, failure to combat the rising level of

---

◆ CALLAGHAN, (LEONARD) JAMES, BARON CALLAGHAN OF CARDIFF (1912–) ◆

British Labour politician. He was home secretary 1967–70 and prime minister 1976–79 in a period of increasing economic stress. As chancellor of the Exchequer 1964–67, he introduced corporation tax, capital-gains tax, and selective employment tax, and resigned following devaluation.

As foreign secretary in 1974, Callaghan renegotiated the UK's membership of the European Community (now the European Union). In 1976 he succeeded Harold Wilson as prime minister and in 1977 entered into a pact with the Liberals to maintain his government in office. Strikes in the so-called 'winter of discontent' 1978–79 led to the government losing a vote of no confidence in the Commons, forcing him to call an election in May 1979, when his party was defeated by the Conservatives.

Callaghan was born in Portsmouth, England, and educated at Portsmouth state schools. He became a tax officer in the Inland Revenue. After war service in the navy he entered Parliament as Labour MP for South (later Southeast) Cardiff in 1945, and held junior office from 1947 until 1951. Callaghan subsequently made a considerable reputation as chief opposition spokesperson on financial affairs.

A lie can be half-way round the world before the truth has got its boots on.

JAMES CALLAGHAN Speech 1 November 1976

Between 1970 and 1974 he was successively opposition spokesperson on home affairs, employment, and foreign and Commonwealth affairs. In March 1974 he became secretary of

crime and concern at the polarizing effect of his government's free-market economic policy led to a rise in support for the left-of-centre opposition, the National Liberation Front (FMLN), at ARENA's expense.

Callaghan, Daniel J (1890–1942)

US rear admiral. After serving as a naval aide to President Franklin D ◊Roosevelt, Callaghan was given command of a cruiser, and then became chief of staff to the naval commander, South Pacific. He returned to sea commanding a squadron of five cruisers and eight destroyers and was killed in the Battle of Guadalcanal in November 1942.

Callejas Romero, Rafael Leonardo (1943–)

Honduran right-wing politician, president 1990–94. He won the November 1989 presidential election, and his party, the right-wing National Party of Honduras (PNH), also won the concurrent assembly elections. However, Callejas was faced with a deteriorating economy which he failed to improve. Consequently, the opposition Liberal Party (PLH), led by Carlos Roberto ◊Reina Idiaquez, swept to power in elections four years later.

After studying at Mississippi University in the USA, Callejas worked as an agricultural planner for the government and served as a natural resources minister in the 1970s, before moving into banking. A member of the PNH, he became leader of his own faction and, as party president, stood unsuccessfully for the presidency in 1985.

James Callaghan, c. 1973. AKG London

state for foreign and Commonwealth affairs, holding that office until he succeeded Harold Wilson as leader of the Labour Party and prime minister in April 1976. Between 1967 and 1976 he was treasurer of the Labour Party and was chair of the party 1973–74.

Callaghan was the first prime minister since Ramsay ◊MacDonald to be forced into an election by the will of the Commons. In 1980 he resigned the party leadership under left-wing pressure, and in 1985 announced that he would not stand for Parliament in the next election. He was created a life peer in 1987.

FURTHER READING

Callaghan, James *Time and Chance* (memoirs) 1987

Donoughue, B *Prime Minister: The Conduct of Policy under Harold Wilson and James Callaghan* 1987

Morgan, Kenneth O *James Callaghan* 1997

Calles, Plutarco Elías (1877–1945)

Mexican political leader, president 1924–28. His administration saw the construction of new roads and irrigation works, as well as land reforms. In 1928 he retired to become a landowner and financier, but founded the National Revolutionary Party in 1929 through which he controlled succeeding presidents.

Known for his fanatical anticlericalism and his efforts to restrict foreign influence in the oil industry, he was defeated by Lázaro Cárdenas and exiled to the USA in 1936 as a result of his criticism. He was allowed to return in 1941.

Born in Guaymas, Sonora, he became a school teacher. He took part in the revolt against Porfirio ◊Díaz in 1911 as an ally of Venustiano ◊Carranza, and became governor of Sonora 1917–19 and secretary of the interior 1920–23.

Calvo, Carlos (1824–1906)

Argentine diplomat and writer. He wrote many seminal works on international law, the most well known being *Derecho internacional teórico y práctico de Europa y América/Theoretical and Practical International Law of Europe and America* (1868). This publication embodied the 'Calvo doctrine', which stipulated that diplomatic intervention should only be utilized once local solutions have been exhausted.

Calvo was also responsible for the creation of the

'Calvo clause', which embodies many national treaties, statutes, and constitutions. In essence, the clause states that a final jurisdiction upheld by a local court could preclude the necessity for an appeal for external diplomatic intervention. Calvo had a diverse and active career, most of which was spent abroad as a diplomat.

Calwell, Arthur Augustus (1896–1973)

Australian Labor politician. He campaigned against conscription during World War I as a Labor Party branch secretary and, after a career as a civil servant, entered federal parliament in 1940, representing Melbourne. He became minister for immigration in 1945, in which position he initiated a programme that was based for the first time on large-scale non-British immigration from Europe, coining the term 'New Australians'. He became deputy leader of the Labor Party in 1951 and leader when in opposition 1960–67, surviving an assassination attempt in 1966.

FURTHER READING
Kiernan, Colm *Calwell* 1978

Campbell, Kim (1947–)

Canadian Progressive Conservative politician, prime minister (briefly) in 1993. She was the country's first woman prime minister. She held the posts of minister for state affairs and northern development 1989–90, attorney general 1990–92, and defence in 1992. Four months after taking over as prime minister, she lost the October 1993 election to the Liberal Party's candidate, Jean Chrétien, and in December resigned as leader of the Progressive Conservative Party.

> *Don't mess with me, I got tanks.*
> KIM CAMPBELL Remark while defence minister

Campbell-Bannerman, Henry (1836–1908)

British Liberal politician, prime minister 1905–08, leader of the Liberal party 1898–1908. The Entente Cordiale was broadened to embrace Russia during his premiership, which also saw the granting of 'responsible government' to the Boer republics in southern Africa. He was succeeded as prime minister and Liberal leader by H H ◊Asquith, who had effectively led the House during Campbell-Bannermann's premiership, as the latter was dogged by ill health.

Campbell-Bannerman was born in Glasgow and educated at Glasgow High School, Glasgow University, and Trinity College, Cambridge. In 1868 he successfully contested Stirling Buroughs as a Liberal in the general election that followed the Reform Act of 1868. In 1871 he became financial secretary to the War Office. He was again financial secretary for war, 1880–82, secretary to the Admiralty, 1882–84, and was given cabinet rank in 1884, becoming chief secretary for Ireland.

In 1886 he announced his adherence to his leader, William Gladstone, when the latter declared himself in favour of Irish Home Rule, and was secretary for war in 1886, fulfilling the same office in the government of 1892–95. When Harcourt resigned the Liberal leadership in 1898, Campbell-Bannerman was selected for the vacant post. The outbreak of the Boer War, and the opposition of Campbell-Bannerman to the imperial policy of a section of the Liberal party, led to still graver differences, but in 1901 a meeting of the party unanimously confirmed him in his leadership.

In 1905 the Unionists resigned and King Edward VII sent for Campbell-Bannerman. At the election that followed, the political pendulum swung, the Liberals being returned with a large majority. The principal proposals of his government were an Education bill, an Irish Councils bill, and a Plural Voting Abolition bill, all of which were either rejected or previously altered by the House of Lords. Amongst the important measures that were passed were the Small Holdings Act, a Trades Dispute Act, the Patents Act, and the Merchant Shipping Act. Campbell-Bannerman was also a supporter of women's suffrage. Almost immediately after his acceptance of the premiership Campbell-Bannerman began to fail in health. The leadership of the House passed for all practical purposes into the hands of Asquith, and Campbell-Bannerman ultimately resigned less than three weeks before his death.

Campbell-Bannerman was the son of a strong Conservative who, as Lord Provost of Glasgow, was knighted in 1941. His elder brother, James Alexander Campbell, was a Conservative MP from 1880 to 1906. He assumed the name Bannerman in 1872 under the will of a maternal uncle.

Campíns, Luis Herrera (1925–)

Venezuelan politician and president 1979–83. During his presidency, Campíns sought to cool down the economy as the market for oil exports weakened and economic recession become more pronounced, after years of prosperity.

Campíns was cofounder, along with Rafael ◊Caldera, of the Comité Organizado Por Elecciónes Independientes (COPEI) in 1946. He was arrested in 1952 for participating in activist activities against the administration of President Peréz Jiménez. He was a member of congress from 1959, and selected by the COPEI party to stand as presidential candidate in 1978.

Cámpora, Héctor (1909–1980)

Argentine left-wing politician and president May–July 1973. His election came against a background of growing discontentment among supporters of Juan Péron concerned with increasing civil unrest and deepening economic turmoil. His presidency was immediately marred by violence, increased terrorist activity, deaths, and kidnappings. Cámpora resigned, to be succeeded by Perón.

In early 1973 Argentina was on the verge of a crisis resulting in an earlier-than-scheduled election. The failure of Juan Perón to return early enough from Spain to register as a presidential candidate resulted in Cámpora being nominated. He gained the 1973 elections and was inaugurated as president on 25 May 1973. Political divisions within the Peronist movement further worsened the already violent situation, precipitating his resignation.

Canaris, Wilhelm Franz (1887–1945)

German admiral and intelligence expert. A U-boat commander during World War I, he subsequently became an intelligence specialist, and served as head of military counterintelligence 1935–44. Right-wing but not a Nazi, he was active in the resistance to Hitler, especially 1938–41, and was arrested, almost certainly unjustly, for involvement in the July Plot against Hitler in 1944. He was executed in Flossenberg concentration camp on 9 April 1945.

Cárdenas, Lázaro (1895–1970)

Mexican centre-left politician and general, president 1934–40. A civil servant in early life, Cárdenas took part in the revolutionary campaigns 1913–28 that followed the fall of President Porfirio ◊ Díaz. As president of the republic, he attempted to achieve the goals of the revolution by building schools, distributing land to the peasants, developing workers' cooperatives, nationalizing foreign oil properties, and developing transport and industry. Although he was popular, the constitution restricted him to one term in office. He was minister of defence 1943–45.

Of humble *mestizo* (mixed Spanish and native American) peasant origin, he reached the rank of general before serving as governor of his home state of Michoacán 1928–38.

Cardoso, Fernando Enrique (1931–)

See page 76.

Cardoso, Benjamin Nathan (1870–1938)

US jurist and Supreme Court justice. He was appointed to the US Supreme Court by President Herbert Hoover in 1932. During the F D Roosevelt administration, he upheld the constitutionality of New Deal programmes to counter the depression of 1929 conveyed in such famous cases as *Ashwander* v *Tennessee Valley Authority* 1936.

Born in New York, USA, Cardozo was educated at Columbia University and became a barrister in 1891.

◆ CARABILLO, TONI (1926–1997) ◆

US writer, feminist, and historian. A pioneer of the modern-day women's movement, Carabillo was a founding member of the National Organization for Women (NOW). She led the successful fight in 1971 for NOW to adopt a lesbian and gay rights position and was a contributor to many of NOW's position papers. Carabillo's work on the development of the feminist struggle ensured that she became known as the 'historian' of the movement. She co-authored with Judith Meuli *The Feminisation of Power* and, with Meuli and June Bundy Csida, *The Feminist Chronicles, 1953–1993*. She cofounded the Feminist Majority and Feminist Majority Foundation with Eleanor Smeal, Peg Yorkin, Meuli, and Katherine Spillar in 1987. As a feminist advocate, Carabillo appeared on both national and local television and radio. She authored many op-ed articles, a number of which were nationally syndicated.

Carabillo served on NOW's National Board from 1968 to 1977 and as NOW's national vice president from 1971 to 1974. She chaired NOW's National Advisory Committee from 1975 to 1977, and led west-coast efforts for ratification of the Federal Equal Rights Amendment from 1980 to 1982. Carabillo used her design skills to good advantage also, designing many of the pins and buttons of the feminist movement, including the ERA 'Failure is Impossible' medallion, NOW's logo, NOW's commemorative medallion, and the Feminist Majority's women's symbol with Capitol dome pin and logo.

Carabillo died in 1997 at her home in Los Angeles, California, at the age of 71 after a seven-year battle with lymphoma and lung cancer. Beside her throughout the illness and at her death was her life partner of 30 years, Judith Meuli. At the time of her death she was completing a new book, *The Feminist Chronicles of the 20th Century*, which would be completed by her co-authors Meuli and Smeal. Carabillo left her library – arguably the most extensive collection on feminism in the 20th century – to the Feminist Majority Foundation.

FURTHER READING

Carabillo, Toni, et al *Feminist Chronicles: 1953–1993* 1993

Carabillo, Toni, and Meuli, Judith *Feminization of Power* 1988

After a brief career as a corporate counsel, he was elected to the New York Supreme Court in 1913 and was appointed associate justice of the court of appeals in 1917, becoming its chief judge in 1926.

Carey, James (Barron) (1911–1973)

US labour leader. He helped organize and was first president of the United Electrical, Radio and Machine Workers of America (UE) 1935–41. At odds with the UE's Communist leaders, he was elected president of the rival International Union of Electrical, Radio and Machine Workers (IUE) 1949–65.

He was born in Philadelphia.

Carías Andino, Tiburcio (1876–1969)

Honduran right-wing National Party politician, dictator-president 1933–49. During his presidency press and labour union freedoms were curtailed and his term was twice extended by the congress. He chose not to contest the 1948 presidential elections, which were won by Juan Manuel ◊Gálvez, the government candidate, but attempted, unsuccessfully, a comeback in the 1954 elections.

Active in the right-wing National Party from its inception in 1902, Carías spent parts of the following two decades in exile in El Salvador and Guatemala. He secured most votes in the 1924 presidential election, but fell short of a majority and his running mate, Miguel Paz Baraona, became president. After defeat in the 1928 presidential election, he finally had success in 1932, taking office in 1933. However, he assumed power at a time of political instability and economic depression, which he reacted to with political repression and retrenchment.

Carlos, John (1945–)

US athlete. Carlos was a 200-metre runner who finished third in the final at the 1968 Mexico Olympics. On the winners podium he and Tommie Smith (the gold medal winner), who were both members of the Olympic Project for Human Rights, barefoot and with a glove on one hand, gave the black power salute during the US national anthem. For his action Carlos was suspended by the International Olympic Committee and ordered to leave the Olympic village. On his return to the US he received death threats and his wife committed suicide soon afterwards.

Accused of bringing politics into sport, Carlos said that the Games were intrinsically political: 'Why do they play national anthems? Why do we have to beat the Russians?' In 1977 he founded the John Carlos Youth Development Program in Los Angeles, California, a project which assisted poor young black people with their education. Ironically, in 1982 Carlos was asked by the Los Angeles Olympic Organizing Committee to promote the Games and to help bridge the gap between the Games themselves and the members of the Los Angeles black community.

Carlot Korman, Maxime

Vanuatuan politician, prime minister 1991–95 and in 1996. In December 1998 Carlot supported President

---

◆ CARDOSO, FERNANDO HENRIQUE (1931–) ◆

Brazilian politician and president 1994–98 and again from 1998. He was selected as a candidate for the 1994 presidential elections by a three-party coalition led by his own party, the moderate centre-left Partido da Social Democracia Brasileira (PSDB; Brazilian Social Democratic Party), and was elected president with approximately 54% of the votes. His success was partly due to his active promotion of the economic policy during his campaign.

As finance minister under President Itamar Franco 1993–94, Cardoso had engineered an economic restructuring programme called the Plano Real, that involved the introduction of a new currency, the Real. The Real's introduction during his first term as president served to significantly stabilize the Brazilian economy and reduced the hyperinflation that the country had experienced for many years. Immediately on taking up office, Cardoso's administration set about on a programme of major social, economic, and legislative reforms that enabled his government to change conditions within the areas of agriculture, employment, health, education, and security. The reforms also brought about increasing privatization of state-owned enterprises.

Although his first term in office was relatively successful, the fragility of the global economic money markets and speculative investment flows caused particular problems for the Cardoso administration. Cardoso was also successful in passing through the National Congress, a constitutional amendment, enabling presidents to seek a second four-year term in office. His re-election as president in the 1998 elections until 2002 was expected to enable him to continue with his programme of socio-economic and political reforms. His task, however, was not easy, as economic crises in emerging developing world countries in 1998, such as in Asia, had major repercussions on the stability of the national currency and overall effectiveness of national economic policy.

Cardoso was born in Rio de Janeiro, graduated in social sciences from the Universidade de São Paulo (USP) in 1952, later progressing on to

Ati George ◊Sokomanu's ousting of the prime minister, Father Walter ◊Lini. These actions were ruled unconstitutional by the Supreme Court and Carlot was sentenced to five years' imprisonment in 1989. This decision was swiftly reversed by the Court of Appeal and, following the December 1991 general election, Carlot became prime minister, forming a coalition with Lini, who now led the Anglophone National United Party (NUP). Carlot's government restored diplomatic relations with France, which had been broken in 1987 over the issue of French support for the Union of Moderate Parties (UMP). The UMP lost power after the November 1995 general election, but, with a 'hung parliament' in which no party had an absolute majority, he was able to return briefly as prime minister between February and September 1996.

Drawn from the country's ethnic French and Roman Catholic community, he became leader of the UMP, a Francophone centrist party, in the 1980s, which was in opposition to the Vanuaaku Party (VP), led by Walter Lini.

In 1997 Carlot left the UMP, which was now dominated by his fierce rival Serge ◊Vohor, to form the Vanuatu Republican Party (VRP).

Carlsson, Ingvar (Gösta) (1934–)

Swedish socialist politician. Leader of the Social Democratic Labour Party (SDAP) from 1986, he was deputy prime minister 1982–86 and prime minister 1986–91 and 1994–96.

Henrique Cardoso. *Rex*

doctoral research in the social sciences at USP, graduating in 1961. He fulfilled a long, productive and distinguished post-doctorate academic career, researching and teaching in both Brazil and elsewhere. Between 1964 and 1981, he held academic positions in several universities in Chile, France, Mexico, England, and the USA, in addition to Brazil.

He initiated his political career in 1978 as a substitute senator within the former Movimento Democrático Brasileiro (MDB; Brazilian Democratic Movement), replacing Franco Montoro. In 1986, Cardoso was re-elected senator by the Partido do Movimento Democrático Brasileiro (PMDB; Brazilian Democratic Movement Party), a party that he left in 1988 to found the Partido da Social Democracia Brasileira (PSDB; Brazilian Social Democratic Party). In the national executive he was charged with the role of minister of state for foreign affairs 1992–93 and finance minister 1993–94 under President Franco.

FURTHER READING

Cardoso, F H *Dependency and Development in Latin America* 1979

After studying in Sweden and the USA, Carlsson became president of the Swedish Social Democratic Youth League in 1961. He was elected to the Riksdag (parliament) in 1964 and served in the governments of Olof Palme 1969–75 and 1982–86, becoming deputy prime minister in 1982. On Palme's assassination in February 1986, Carlsson replaced him as SDAP leader and prime minister. He lost his majority in September 1991 and resigned, but was returned in September 1994 at the head of a minority SDAP government. In 1995 he announced his intention to resign in March 1996, citing personal reasons.

Carlucci, Frank Charles (1930–)

US politician. A former diplomat and deputy director of the Central Intelligence Agency (CIA), he was national security adviser 1986–87 and defence secretary 1987–89 under President Ronald Reagan, supporting Soviet–US arms reduction.

Educated at Princeton and Harvard universities, Carlucci, after fighting in the Korean War, was a career diplomat during the later 1950s and 1960s. He returned to the USA in 1969 to work under presidents Richard Nixon, Gerald Ford, and Jimmy Carter, his posts including US ambassador to Portugal and deputy director of the CIA. An apolitical Atlanticist, Carlucci found himself out of step with the hawks (pro-war advisers) in the Reagan administration, and left to work in industry after barely a year as deputy secretary of defence. In December 1986, after the Irangate scandal, he replaced John ◊Poindexter as national security adviser.

Carmichael, Stokely, former name of Kwame Touré (1941–1998)

Trinidad-born US civil-rights activist. He coined the term 'Black Power'. As leader of the Black Panthers 1967–69, he demanded black liberation rather than integration, and called for armed revolution. He then moved to Guinea, changed his name, and worked for the Pan-African movement.

Although born in Port-of-Spain, Trinidad, Carmichael was educated in the USA. He took part in civil-rights demonstrations from 1961 and joined the Student Nonviolent Coordinating Committee (SNCC) in 1964, organizing volunteers to teach southern blacks to read and to help them to register for the vote. He was president 1966–67 of the SNCC when it became the radical wing of the civil-rights movement after the murder of ◊Malcolm X. He left the Black Panthers in 1969 when they decided to cooperate with white radicals.

Carmona, Antonio (1869–1951)

Portuguese politician and general. After a military coup in 1926 he was made prime minister and minister of war, with dictatorial powers. In 1928 he was elected president for life by plebiscite, and in 1932 he appointed António ◊Salazar as prime minister and virtual dictator.

Carpenter, Edward (1844–1929)

English socialist and writer. He campaigned for such causes as sexual reform, women's rights, and vegetarianism. He lived openly as a homosexual and made a plea for sexual toleration in *Love's Coming of Age* (1896).

Carpenter was inspired by the writings of Henry Thoreau, Walt Whitman, and William Morris. He campaigned against pollution and vivisection and tried to grow his own food. His liberal idealism influenced later writers, including E M Forster and D H Lawrence. Carpenter's books include *The Simplification of Life* (1884), *Civilization: Its Cause and Cure* (1889), the long poem *Towards Democracy* (1883–1902), and the reminiscences *My Days and Dreams* (1916).

Carranza, Venustiano (1859–1920)

Mexican revolutionary leader, president 1914–20. His presidency was marked by civil unrest and his reluctance to implement reforms set out in the 1917 constitution.

Carranza supported Francisco ◊Madero in the successful 1910–11 revolution against Porfírio ◊Díaz. In 1913, when Madero was overthrown as president by Victoriano ◊Huerta, Carranza, in combination with General Álvaro ◊Obregón, Francisco Villa, and Emiliano ◊Zapata, fought against Huerta and headed the Constitutionalist Army. In August 1914, after Huerta was ousted, Carranza took over as president. However, Villa and Zapata refused to recognize his leadership and the civil war continued.

Essentially cautious, Carranza had to be persuaded by his ally Obregón to promise to introduce social and

◆ Carter, Jimmy (James Earl) (1924–) ◆

39th president of the USA 1977–81, a Democrat. Jimmy Carter was born on 1 October 1924, in Plains, Georgia. During his formative years, his life revolved around peanut farming, talk of politics, and devotion to the Baptist faith. Upon graduation in 1946 from the Naval Academy in Annapolis, Maryland, Carter married Rosalynn Smith. After seven years' service as a naval officer, he returned to Plains. In 1962 he entered state politics, and in 1970 was elected governor of Georgia. He attracted attention by emphasizing ecology, efficiency in government, and the removal of racial barriers. Carter announced his candidacy for the US presidency in December 1974 and began a two-year campaign that gradually gained momentum. At the Democratic Convention, he was nominated on the first ballot. Carter campaigned hard against President Gerald Ford, debating with him three times and eventually winning the presidential election by

297 electoral votes to 241 for Ford. In office he pursued the policies that made him a popular governor of Georgia. He established a national energy policy to deal with the energy shortage and stimulated production by decontrolling domestic petroleum prices. He prompted government efficiency through civil service reform and

I've looked on a lot of women with lust. I've committed adultery in my heart many times. This is something God recognizes I will do – and I have done it – and God forgives me for it.
Jimmy Carter Interview in *Playboy* November 1976

proceeded with deregulation of the trucking and airline industries. He sought to improve the environment. His expansion of the national park system included protection of 103 million acres of

agrarian reforms, as set out in the constitution of 1917. However, Carranza worked to frustrate full implementation of the reforms and in 1920, when he sought to prevent Obregón succeeding him as president, Obregón led a popular rebellion. Carranza was forced to flee from Mexico City to the mountains of Puebla state, where he was ambushed and murdered in the village of Tlaxcalantongo.

Carrera Andrade, Jorge (1903–1978)

Ecuadorian poet and diplomat who helped to found the Ecuadorian Socialist Party in 1926. His first poetry collection, *Estanque inefable/Ineffable Pond* (1922), consisted of mostly rural poems. In the course of his diplomatic career he held positions in Europe, Japan, and South America. His travels influenced his writing as evidenced by his adaptation of the Japanese haiku verse form into Spanish. Translations of his poems include *Selected Poems* (1972).

Carrington, Peter Alexander Rupert, 6th Baron Carrington (1919–   )

British Conservative politician. He was defence secretary 1970–74, and led the opposition in the House of Lords 1964–70 and 1974–79. While foreign secretary 1979–82, he negotiated independence for Zimbabwe, but resigned after failing to anticipate the Falklands crisis. He was secretary general of NATO 1984–88 and chaired European Community-sponsored peace talks on Yugoslavia in 1991. He was knighted 1958; he succeeded as Baron in 1938.

Carroll, James (1858–1927)

New Zealand Maori politician and advocate of Maori

Jimmy Carter, 1983. *AKG London*

rights. He was minister for Maori affairs 1899–1912 and acting prime minister in 1909 and 1911. His main work was in arbitrating between the Maori and the

Alaskan lands. To increase human and social services, he created the Department of Education, bolstered the Social Security system, and appointed record numbers of women, blacks, and Hispanics to government jobs.

In foreign affairs, Carter campaigned consistently for human rights. In the Middle East, through the Camp David Agreement of 1978, he helped bring peace and reconciliation between Egypt and Israel. He succeeded in obtaining ratification of the Panama Canal treaties. Building upon the work of predecessors, he established full diplomatic relations with the People's Republic of China and completed negotiation of the SALT II nuclear limitation treaty with the USSR.

The Soviet invasion of Afghanistan caused the suspension of plans for ratification of the SALT II pact. The seizure as hostages of the US embassy staff in Iran dominated the news during the last 14 months of the Carter administration. The hostage crisis, and rising inflation at home, contributed to Carter's defeat in 1980. Even then, he continued the difficult negotiations over the

hostages. Iran finally released the 52 Americans the same day Carter left office. Carter returned to Georgia, where in 1982 he founded the non-profit Carter Centre in Atlanta to promote peace and human rights worldwide. The Centre has initiated projects in more than 65 countries to resolve conflicts, prevent human-rights abuses, build democracy, improve health, and revitalize urban areas. Carter takes an active part in the activities of the Centre to this day, acting as a peace ambassador around the world.

He and his wife still reside in Plains. They have three sons, John William (Jack), James Earl III (Chip), Donnel Jeffrey (Jeff), and a daughter, Amy Lynn.

FURTHER READING
Carter, Jimmy *Keeping Faith: Memoirs of a President* 1982
Hargrove, Erwin *Jimmy Carter as President* 1988
Meyer, P *James Earl Carter* 1978
Miller, W L *Yankee from Georgia* 1978

government over land settlements, adopting a policy of *taihoa* (marking time or delaying) rather than forcing the Maori to accept European ways.

Carson, Edward Henry, Baron Carson (1854–1935)

Anglo-Irish politician and lawyer who played a decisive part in the trial of the writer Oscar Wilde. In the years before World War I he led the movement in Ulster to resist Irish Home Rule by force of arms if need be.

Educated at Portarlington School and Trinity College Dublin, Carson was one of the leading legal and political figures of his day. He represented the Marquis of Queensbury in the 1895 case that ruined the career of Oscar Wilde, and was solicitor general 1900–06. Leader of the Irish Unionist Party from 1910, he mobilized the resistance of Protestant Ulster to Home Rule and, in threatening armed rebellion against the Liberal government, effectively wrecked the scheme by 1914. He became attorney general in 1915 and was a member of the war cabinet 1917–18. He resigned as Unionist leader in 1921 and served as a Lord of Appeal 1921–29, and was created a life peer as Baron Carson of Duncairn in 1921. Although Carson secured the exclusion of part of Ulster from control by a Dublin parliament, he failed in his goal of preventing self-government for any part of Ireland.

FURTHER READING
Jackson, Alvin *Sir Edward Carson* 1993

Casement, Roger David (1864–1916)

British diplomat and Irish revolutionary. While in the British consular service, he exposed the ruthless exploitation of the people of the Belgian Congo and Peru, for which he was knighted in 1911 (degraded 1916). He was hanged for treason by the British for his involvement in the Irish nationalist cause.

Born in County Dublin, Casement joined the British consular service in 1892. He gained an international reputation and was knighted for his reports on the exploitation of plantation workers by Europeans in the Congo and Peru. However, in 1904 he joined the Gaelic League and upon his retirement in 1913, joined the Irish Volunteers. In 1914 he made his way to Berlin in the hope of raising German support for Irish independence and tried to recruit for an Irish Brigade among British prisoners in Germany. In 1916 he was captured in Ireland, having returned there in a German submarine in the hope of postponing a rebellion. He was sentenced to death and executed as a traitor in August 1916 in spite of appeals for clemency from, among others, Sir Arthur Conan Doyle. British government agents circulated details of his diaries, which revealed an active homosexual private life, in the attempt to discredit him. His remains were returned to Ireland in 1965.

Casey, Richard Gardiner, Baron Casey (1890–1976)

Australian diplomat, Liberal politician, and governor general 1965–69. In 1924 he was involved in the formulation of the Statute of Westminster and from 1931 served in the House of Representatives as a United Australian (now Liberal) Party deputy and, from 1935, minister. In 1940 he was appointed minister plenipotentiary in Washington, DC, USA, beginning Australia's formal diplomatic representation overseas. He was a member of the British war cabinet in World War II and governor of Bengal, India, 1944–46. Re-elected to the Australian federal parliament in 1949, he was minister for external affairs 1951–60, working to build up Australia's relations with Asia and to foster the alliance with the USA. Unable to work harmoniously with Prime Minister Robert ◊Menzies, he retired in 1960 and was granted a life peerage.

The son of an affluent Brisbane pastoralist businessman, he was educated at Melbourne and Cambridge, England, and served in Gallipoli and on the Somme during World War I.

> *It is not necessary to be governor general to get to know a lot about Australia, but it helps.*
> RICHARD GARDINER CASEY 1966

Castelo Branco, Humberto de Alencar (1900–1967)

Brazilian politician and president 1964–67. His government succeeded in stabilizing the economy, reorganizing the financial system, and renegotiating foreign debt, but failed to alter traditional patterns of authority and prevent the emergence of hardline factions amongst the military, which established the 'tutelary regime' that survived until 1985. He was succeeded in office by his war minister Artur da Costa e Silva in 1967.

In the course of his army career Castelo Branco fought in Italy as commander in chief of the Brazilian army, and was responsible for coordinating the anti-Goulart military conspiracy of 1964. Linked to other veteran officers in the Escola Superior da Guerra, founded in the 1940s in Rio de Janeiro, his foreign policy was anticommunist, and he believed that short-term arbitrary technocratic measures should be taken to create the conditions for democracy.

He was educated at the Pôrto Alegre Military Academy in Rio Grande do Sul and at France's Ecole Supérieure de Guerre, and attended the General Command course at Fort Leavenworth, USA.

Castillo Armas, Carlos (1914–1957)

Guatemalan soldier and anti-communist political leader, coup leader, and ruler 1954–57.

Imprisoned after a failed coup attempt in 1950, he escaped and launched an invasion in June 1954 to 'liberate' Guatemala from the left-wing regime of Jácobo ◊Arbenz Guzmán, who was overthrown. Castillo Armas was installed as president through a plebiscite based on oral votes and, with other political parties banned, his National Democratic Movement won the December 1955 assembly elections. Arbenz Guzmán's land reforms were reversed and a crackdown was launched against communist and trade-union activity, before Castillo Armas was assassinated in July 1957.

Castle, Barbara Anne, Baroness Castle (born Betts) (1911–)

British Labour politician, a cabinet minister in the Labour governments of the 1960s and 1970s. She led the Labour group in the European Parliament 1979–89 and became a life peer in 1990.

Castle was minister of overseas development 1964–65, transport 1965–68, employment 1968–70 (when her White Paper *In Place of Strife*, on trade-union reform, was abandoned because it suggested state intervention in industrial relations), and social services 1974–76, when she was dropped from the cabinet by Prime Minister James Callaghan. She crit-

icized him in her *Diaries* (1980).

Castle was born in Bradford and educated at Bradford Girls' Grammar School and St Hugh's College, Oxford. She entered Parliament as Labour MP for Blackburn in 1945, and was chair of the Labour Party 1958–59.

Her proposals for the reform of industrial relations, *In Place of Strife*, encountered considerable opposition from the trade-union movement and within the Labour Party because they sought to create a legal framework for industrial relations, including a number of penal sanctions. The proposals were dropped in the face of this opposition, although she remained secretary of state until Labour's defeat in 1970.

She campaigned vigorously against Britain's entry into the European Economic Community between 1970 and the referendum of 1975. In March 1974 she became secretary of state for social services, but she was dropped from the government following its reconstruction on the appointment of James Callaghan as prime minister in 1976.

Her autobiography, *Fighting All the Way*, was published in 1993.

◆ CASTRO (RUZ), FIDEL (1927–) ◆

Cuban communist politician, prime minister 1959–76, and president from 1976. He led two unsuccessful coups against the right-wing regime of Fulgencio ◊Batista and led the revolution that overthrew the dictator in 1959. He raised the standard of living for most Cubans but dealt harshly with dissenters. From 1990, deprived of the support of the USSR and experiencing the long-term effects of a US trade embargo, Castro faced increasing pressure for reform; in September 1995 he moved towards greater economic flexibility by permitting foreign ownership in major areas of commerce and industry. In January 1996 the *rapprochement* between Cuba and the USA appeared to have progressed after a visit by Democratic members of the House of Representatives, although the US embargo was not lifted. In 1998 he invited the Pope to make an unprecedented visit to Cuba. In February 1998 Castro was elected president.

Of wealthy parentage, Castro was educated at Jesuit schools and, after studying law at the University of Havana, gained a reputation through his work for poor clients. He opposed the Batista dictatorship, and took part, with his brother Raúl, in an unsuccessful attack on the army barracks at Santiago de Cuba in 1953. After some time in exile in the USA and Mexico, Castro attempted a secret landing in Cuba in 1956 in which all but 11 of his supporters were killed. He eventually gathered an

army of over 5,000 which overthrew Batista on 1 January 1959 and he became prime minister a few months later. Raúl Castro was appointed minister of armed forces.

Castro's administration introduced a centrally planned economy based on the production for export of sugar, tobacco, and nickel. He nationalized the property of wealthy Cubans, Americans, and other foreigners in 1960, resulting in the severance of relations by the USA, an economic embargo, and US attempts to subvert Cuba's government (or invade and overthrow it). This enmity came to a head in the Cuban missile crisis of 1962. Aid for development was provided by the USSR, which replaced the USA as Cuba's main trading partner, and Castro espoused Marxism-Leninism until, in 1974, he rejected Marx's formula 'from each according to his ability and to each according to his need' and decreed that each Cuban should 'receive according to his work'. He improved education, housing, and health care for the majority of Cubans but lost the support of the middle class, hundreds of thousands of whom fled the country. After 1990 events in Eastern Europe and the disintegration of the USSR left Castro increasingly isolated, and by 1993 the US embargo had gravely weakened the country's economy, provoking increasing numbers of Cubans to flee the country. See photograph on page 82.

Fidel Castro with Nikita Khrushchev and Leonid Brezhnev in Moscow, 1963. *AKG London*

Castro, Cipriano (1858–1924)

Venezuelan military leader and dictator 1899–1908, known as 'the Lion of the Andes'. When he refused to pay off foreign debts in 1902, British, German, and Italian ships blockaded the country, leaving the nation almost bankrupt. He presided over a corrupt government and is renowned for being one of the most corrupt leaders in South American history. There were frequent rebellions during his rule, and opponents of his regime were exiled or murdered.

Cato, (Robert) Milton (1915–1997)

St Vincent and the Grenadines centrist politician, chief minister 1967–69, and prime minister 1969–72 and 1974–84. He helped to establish the St Vincent Labour Party (SVLP) in 1954, and from 1967 served as chief minister with a SVLP majority. Having negotiated Associate Statehood for St Vincent in 1969, he was redesignated prime minister. After 1974 he headed a coalition government that led the country to independence within the British Commonwealth in 1979. Beset by economic depression and allegations of corruption, the SVLP was defeated in 1984 by the New

Democratic Party (NDP), led by James Mitchell. A year later Cato announced his retirement from politics.

His governments oversaw improvements in the economic infrastructure, especially electricity and roads, and promoted closer regional links, including the establishment of the Organization of Eastern Caribbean States (OECS) in 1981. However, it also had to suppress an uprising on Union Island in November 1979 and faced a general strike in June 1981, which forced the withdrawal of controversial industrial relations legislation.

Born into relative poverty, Cato, after securing a scholarship to a grammar school, served in the Canadian Volunteer Army during World War II and later trained as a barrister in England. On his return to St Vincent in 1949, he set up a legal practice and entered local politics. In 1958, when St Vincent became part of the Federation of the West Indies, he went to Trinidad as one of the island's representatives. With the Federation's collapse in 1961, he was elected to the St Vincent parliament. Between 1972 and 1974, Cato lost the premiership to Mitchell.

Catt, Carrie Chapman (1859–1947)

US suffragist, born at Ripon, Wisconsin. She organized the Iowa Woman Suffrage Association in 1890, and then transferred her activities to the National American Woman Suffrage Alliance, serving as president 1900–04, and again in 1915. She later became the leader of the campaign to submit a woman suffrage amendment to the Federal Constitution. This was adopted by Congress in 1919 and ratified in 1920; it gave the franchise to every female aged 21 and over in the USA.

Catt was also president of the International Woman Suffrage Alliance 1904–23.

Cavaco Silva, Anibal (1939–)

Portuguese politician, finance minister 1980–81, and prime minister and Social Democratic Party (PSD) leader 1985–95. Under his leadership Portugal joined the European Community in 1985 and the Western European Union in 1988.

Cavaco Silva studied economics in the UK and the USA, and was a university teacher and research director in the Bank of Portugal. In 1978, with the return of constitutional government, he entered politics. His first government fell in 1987, but an election later that year gave him Portugal's first absolute majority since the restoration of democracy. He was re-elected in 1991 but became an increasingly divisive figure. He stepped down as leader of the PSD before the 1995 elections, which the party lost to the Socialists. In 1996 he was defeated in the presidential election contest.

Ceaușescu, Nicolae (1918–1989)

Romanian politician, leader of the Romanian Communist Party (RCP), in power 1965–89. He pursued a policy line independent of and critical of the USSR. He appointed family members, including his wife Elena Ceaușescu (1919–1989), to senior state and party posts, and governed in an increasingly repressive manner, zealously implementing schemes that impoverished the nation. The Ceaușescus were overthrown in a bloody revolutionary coup in December 1989 and executed on Christmas Day that year.

Ceaușescu joined the underground RCP in 1933 and was imprisoned for antifascist activities 1936–38 and 1940–44. After World War II he was elected to the Grand National Assembly and was soon given ministerial posts. He was inducted into the party secretariat and Politburo in 1954–55. In 1965 he

became leader of the RCP and from 1967 chair of the state council. He was elected president in 1974. As revolutionary changes rocked Eastern Europe in 1989, protests in Romania escalated until the Ceaușescu regime was toppled. After his execution, the full extent of his repressive rule and personal extravagance became public.

FURTHER READING

Almond, Mark *The Rise and Fall of Nicolae and Elena Ceaușescu* 1992

Banbury, Lance *In Memoriam Nicolae Ceaușescu (1918–89)* 1996

Ceaușescu, Nicolae *Nicolae Ceaușescu: Speeches and Writings* 1978, *The Nation and the Cohabiting Nationalities in the Contemporary Epoch* 1983, *Cardinal Problems of Our Time* 1980, *The Solving of the National Question in Romania* 1980

Fischer, Mary Ellen *Nicolae Ceaușescu: A Study in Political Leadership* 1989

Kligman, Gail *The Politics of Duplicity: Controlling Reproduction in Ceaușescu's Romania* 1998

Loring, Ulick, and Page, James *Yugoslavia's Royal Dynasty* 1976

Sweeney, John *The Life and Evil Times of Nicolae Ceaușescu* 1991

Cerezo Arévalo, Mario Vinicio (1942–)

Guatemalan politician, president 1986–91. He led the centre-left Guatemalan Christian Democratic Party (PDCG) to victory in congressional and presidential elections in 1985, to become the country's first civilian

Romanian president Nicolae Ceaușescu and Chinese leader Hua Guofeng review troops and civilians in Bucharest, Romania. *Rex*

president in two decades. He was criticized for failing to tackle economic problems and for being too accommodating to the military, but his period in office helped to consolidate military rule. He was debarred by the constitution from standing for a second term, and his PDCG successor, Alfonso Cabrera, was defeated by the right-wing Jorge ◊Serrano Elias in the 1990 presidential election.

Césaire, Aimé Fernand (1913–)

Martinique left-wing politician, poet, and playwright. He represented Martinique in the French National Assembly from 1946, was mayor of Fort-de-France 1945–83, and became president of the Martinique Regional Council in 1983. Originally a communist, he opposed the USSR's invasion of Hungary in 1956 and left the party to form the Martinique Progressive Party (PPM), which has advocated autonomy for the island. His works include the play *The Tragedy of King Christophe* (1963) and the poem 'Notebook of a Return to my Native Land' (1939).

In his writings Césaire emerged as a fierce critic of colonialism, developing the positive concept of négritude, which reflects awareness of black heritage, values, and culture and was used to rally decolonized Africans in the 1950s.

Césaire studied at the prestigious Ecole Normale Supérieure in Paris, and returned to Martinique in 1939 to become a college lecturer. Thereafter he pursued a dual career in literature and politics.

Céspedes, Carlos Manuel de (1871–1939)

Cuban revolutionary and politician, president in 1933. He participated in the revolution of 1895 and the Spanish–American War of 1898. Céspedes became provisional president in August 1933, following the overthrow of Gerardo ◊Machado after a coup directed by Fulgencio ◊Batista. However, he was forced to resign after a further coup in September 1933 by Batista and a student junta, which installed Ramón ◊Grau San Martín in his stead.

Born in New York City, he was the son of Carlos Manuel de Céspedes (1819–1874), a prosperous Cuban plantation owner who led a rebellion against Spanish rule from 1868 and was president of the Cuban 'Republic in Arms' from 1869 to 1873.

Chadli, Benjedid (1929–)

Algerian politician, president 1979–92. An army colonel, he supported Houari ◊Boumédienne in the overthrow of Mohammed ◊Ben Bella in 1965, and succeeded Boumédienne in 1979, pursuing more moderate policies. Following the victory of the Front Islamique du Salut (FIS) in the first round of legislative elections in 1991, Benjedid, under pressures from the army, resigned in January 1992.

Chamberlain, (Arthur) Neville (1869–1940)

British Conservative politician, son of Joseph ◊Chamberlain. He was prime minister 1937–40; his policy of appeasement toward the Italian fascist dictator Benito Mussolini and German Nazi Adolf Hitler (with whom he concluded the Munich Agreement in 1938) failed to prevent the outbreak of World War II. He resigned in 1940 following the defeat of the British forces in Norway.

The younger son of Joseph Chamberlain and half-brother of Austen Chamberlain, he was born in Birmingham, of which he was lord mayor in 1915. He was minister of health in 1923 and 1924–29, and his policies centred on slum clearance. In 1931 he was chancellor of the Exchequer in the national government, and in 1937 succeeded Stanley Baldwin as prime minister. Trying to close the old Anglo-Irish feud, he agreed to return to Ireland those ports that had been occupied by the navy.

> *Peace with honour. I believe it is peace for our time.*
> NEVILLE CHAMBERLAIN Speech from 10 Downing Street, 30 September 1938

He also attempted to appease the demands of the European dictators, particularly Mussolini. In 1938 he went to Munich and negotiated with Hitler the settlement of the Czechoslovak question. He was ecstatically received on his return, and claimed that the Munich Agreement brought 'peace in our time'. Within a year, however, the UK was at war with Germany.

FURTHER READING

Charmley, John *Chamberlain and the Lost Peace* 1989
Dilks, David *Neville Chamberlain, 1869–1929* 1985
Feiling, K *Neville Chamberlain* 1946
Fuchser, L W *Neville Chamberlain and Appeasement* 1982
Rock, William *Neville Chamberlain* 1969

Chamberlain, (Joseph) Austen (1863–1937)

British Conservative politician, elder son of Joseph ◊Chamberlain; as foreign secretary 1924–29 he negotiated and signed the Pact of Locarno, which fixed the boundaries of Germany; for this he won the Nobel Peace Prize in 1925. In 1928 he also signed the Kellogg–Briand pact to outlaw war and provide for peaceful settlement of disputes.

He was elected to Parliament in 1892 as a Liberal–Unionist, and after holding several minor posts was chancellor of the Exchequer 1903–06. During World War I he was secretary of state for India 1915–17 and member of the war cabinet in 1918. He was chancellor of the Exchequer 1919–21 and Lord Privy Seal 1921–22, but failed to secure the leadership of the party in 1922, as many Conservatives resented the part he had taken in the Irish settlement of 1921.

Chamberlain, Joseph (1836–1914)

British politician, reformist mayor of and member of

Parliament for Birmingham. In 1886 he resigned from the cabinet over William Gladstone's policy of home rule for Ireland, and led the revolt of the Liberal–Unionists.

By 1874 Chamberlain had made a sufficient fortune in the Birmingham screw-manufacturing business to devote himself entirely to politics. He adopted radical views, and took an active part in local affairs. Three times mayor of Birmingham, he carried through many schemes of municipal development. In 1876 he was elected to Parliament and joined the republican group led by Charles Dilke, the extreme left wing of the Liberal Party. In 1880 he entered Gladstone's cabinet as president of the Board of Trade. The climax of his radical period was reached with the unauthorized programme, advocating, among other things, free education, graduated taxation, and smallholdings of 'three acres and a cow'.

As colonial secretary in the Marquess of Salisbury's Conservative government, Chamberlain was responsible for relations with the Boer republics up to the outbreak of war in 1899. In 1903 he resigned to campaign for imperial preference or tariff reform as a

---

The day of small nations has long passed away. The day of Empires has come.
JOSEPH CHAMBERLAIN Speech in Birmingham 12 May 1904

---

means of consolidating the empire. From 1906 he was incapacitated by a stroke. Chamberlain was one of the most colourful figures of British politics, and his monocle and orchid made him a favourite subject for political cartoonists.

Chambers, George Michael (1930–)

Trinidad and Tobago centre-left politician, prime minister 1981–86. A member of the People's National Movement (PNM), he took over as PNM leader and prime minister after the sudden death of Eric ◊Williams in 1981. During the early 1980s, with oil prices falling and state overinvestment in infrastructural projects, Chambers had to adopt stringent measures to restore economic stability. He also attacked corruption, which had plagued the PNM government in the 1970s, and pursued an independent foreign policy, being one of the few Caribbean leaders who did not support US military intervention in Grenada in 1983.

The PNM was defeated by the National Alliance for Reconstruction (NAR), led by Arthur ◊Robinson, in 1986, and Chambers was subsequently replaced as PNM leader by Patrick ◊Manning.

Largely self-educated, Chambers worked as a legal clerk before entering politics as a member of the PNM. He entered parliament in 1966 with a huge majority and held a series of cabinet posts in the governments of

Williams. Immensely popular, he increased the PNM's majority in the 1981 general election after succeeding Williams as prime minister.

Chambers, Whittaker, born Jay Vivian Chambers (1910–1961)

US journalist, writer, and Soviet agent. An active US communist 1925–29 and 1931–38, he wrote for the *Daily Worker* and edited the *New Masses*. He became an agent of Soviet intelligence and passed classified government information to Moscow. Disillusioned by Stalin's purges, he became a virulent anticommunist and edited *Time* Magazine's foreign affairs section.

He was born in Philadelphia and studied at Columbia University. He gained a modest reputation as a writer, and later translated several works, notably *Bambi*, into English. In 1948 he testified that many executive branch officials were communist sympathizers and said that Alger ◊Hiss had given him classified materials; this brought about a libel suit by Hiss, who was found guilty; the Hiss–Chambers trial remains a symbol of the whole era that extended from the idealism of communism in the 1930s to the disillusionment of the late 1940s. Chambers was also an editor of the *National Review* 1957–60.

Chamorro Vargas, Emiliano (1871–1966)

Nicaraguan soldier and right-wing politician, president 1917–21 and in 1926. Following the withdrawal of US troops from Nicaragua in 1925, Chamorro seized power in a coup. However, US refusal of diplomatic recognition and its threat to send gunboats persuaded him to flee from office. In 1950, having failed to achieve political influence for the Conservatives, Chamorro signed a Pact of the Generals with his Liberal Party opponent, President Anastasio ◊Somoza García, under which the Conservatives were promised a share of government posts.

A conservative military leader, Chamorro joined the successful revolt, in 1909, against the Liberal dictator José Santos ◊Zelaya. He reluctantly accepted the country's occupation by the US Marines and, as minister in Washington 1913–16, signed the August 1914 Bryan–Chamorro Treaty that granted the USA, for $3 million, an option to construct an inter-oceanic canal through Nicaragua.

Chan, Julius (1939–)
See page 87.

Chandos, Oliver Lyttelton, 1st Viscount Chandos (1893–1972)

English industrialist and Conservative politician. He was president of the Board of Trade 1940–41, minister of state in the Middle East 1941–42, minister of production 1942–45, and secretary of state for the colonies 1951–54. He was created Viscount Chandos in 1954.

Lyttelton studied at Cambridge University, served in the Grenadier Guards during World War I, and had a successful career in industry until 1940 when he became Conservative member of Parliament for Aldershot, a seat he continued to hold until 1954. His period of office as secretary of state for the colonies coincided with the Mau Mau crisis in Kenya. In 1954 he retired from politics and returned to his substantial business interests.

Chaplin, Charlie (Charles Spencer) (1889–1977)

English film actor and director. One of cinema's most popular stars, he made his reputation as a tramp with a smudge moustache, bowler hat, and twirling cane in silent comedies, including *The Kid* (1921) and *The Gold Rush* (1925). His work combines buffoonery with pathos, as in *The Great Dictator* (1940) and *Limelight* (1952). When accused of communist sympathies during the Joe McCarthy witchhunt, he left the USA in 1952 and moved to Switzerland.

FURTHER READING

Chaplin, Charlie *My Autobiography* 1964, 1993, published as *My Early Years* 1982
Huff, Theodore *Charlie Chaplin* 1951
McCabe, John *Charlie Chaplin* 1978
Manvell, Roger *Chaplin* 1973
Robinson, David *Chaplin: His Life and Art* 1985, 1987

Charles, (Mary) Eugenia (1919–)

Dominican centre-right politician, prime minister 1980–95; cofounder and first leader of the centre-right Dominica Freedom Party (DFP). Two years after Dominica's independence the DFP won the 1980 general election and Charles became the Caribbean's first female prime minister. In 1993 she resigned the leadership of the DFP, but remained as prime minister until the 1995 elections, which were won by the opposition United Workers' Party (UNP). She then announced her retirement from politics.

As leader of the DFP, and as a member of parliament from 1975, she campaigned against the authoritarian government of Patrick ◊John. This culminated in the ousting of John in February 1980, after strikes and demonstrations, and a landslide victory for the DFP the following July. In 1981 she survived two coup plots by supporters of John. She embarked on a free-market economic strategy, promoted land reform, and supported the USA in its anti-communist Caribbean policy. She also, unusually for the leader of a Caribbean Commonwealth country, developed closer links with France.

Her DFP government was re-elected in 1985 and, by a narrow margin, in 1990. After her retirement as DFP leader in 1993, she was replaced by the foreign affairs minister Brian Alleyne, and, at the age of 76, did not contest the 1995 election, which was won by the UNP led by Edison ◊James.

◆ CHAMOUN, CAMILLE OR *KAMIL SHAM'UN* (1900–1987) ◆

Lebanese Maronite Christian politician, president 1952–58. As president, he pursued pro-Western policies, antagonizing leftist-Nasserists, and, after being accused of rigging the 1957 elections, became increasingly authoritarian. His refusal as president to support Lebanon's possible accession into Syria and Egypt's new United Arab Republic and rumours that he was seeking a second term led to civil war in June–July 1958, which was ended by the landing of US troops and by the election of army commander General Fuad Shihab (Chehab) as president. Chamoun responded by founding the National Liberal Party, but was to return only briefly to government, in 1975–76 and 1984.

During the 1960s and 1970s Chamoun remained a leading figure within the Christian camp, which attempted to preserve Lebanon's political pluralism under Christian Maronite leadership, and which resisted integration into Pan-Arab alignments. During the civil war of 1975–82 he headed a loose Lebanese Front of Christian-Maronite factions and his supporters set up armed militias, known as the Tigers. By 1980 the

Tigers had been eliminated as a fighting force by the Phalangists, led by Bechir Gemayel. Chamoun's son, Danny Chamoun (1934–1990), succeeded him as party leader in 1987, but was murdered, with his wife and two sons, by pro-Syria militias.

Born in Deir al-Qamar in the Shuf region of southern Lebanon, Chamoun studied at the French Law College of Beirut. He was first elected a member of the Lebanese parliament in 1934 and became finance minister in 1938 and interior minister in 1943, when he helped negotiate Lebanon's unwritten intercommunal National Pact that provided for power-sharing between a Maronite Christian president and a Sunni Muslim prime minister. Chamoun resigned from the government in 1948 after President Bishara al-Khuri had amended the constitution to enable him to serve a second term. In September 1952, with opposition growing to government corruption under al-Khuri, Chamoun staged a semi-coup, forcing al-Khuri to resign, and parliament elected Chamoun as his replacement.

She was born in Pointe Michel, Dominica, and educated in the UK, where she qualified as a barrister. She returned to practise in the Windward and Leeward Islands in the West Indies and did not begin her active political career until relatively late in life, in 1968. Her backing for US intervention in Grenada in 1983 earned her the sobriquet of 'the Iron Lady of the Caribbean'.

Chavez, Cesar Estrada (1927–1993)

US labour organizer who founded the National Farm Workers Association in 1962 and, with the support of the AFL-CIO (federation of North American trade unions) and other major unions, embarked on a successful campaign to unionize California grape workers. He led boycotts of citrus fruits, lettuce, and grapes in the early 1970s, but disagreement and exploitation of migrant farm labourers continued despite his successes.

Chávez Frías, Hugo

Venezuelan military officer and president from 1998. He was elected with 56% of the vote and it was expected that the new regime would usher in a radical restructuring of the Venezuelan political system. In 1992 he had initiated a coup against the government of the then president Carlos Andrés ◊Pérez, along with a group of other senior ranking officers. The coup, although unsuccessful, sparked off a wave of deaths and coup attempts.

The 1992 coup was preceded by a severe economic crisis and huge foreign debt repayments, with an austerity programme that lead to widespread civil strikes, rioting, and many deaths. The coup orchestrated by Chávez emphasized that, despite over three decades of democratic rule, the military were prepared to overrule any form of government.

Chavis, Benjamin Franklin (1948–)

US civil-rights campaigner. As executive director of the National Association for the Advancement of Colored People (NAACP) from 1993, he succeeded in putting the NAACP more in touch with the concerns of the black community, recruiting 160,000 new members, although he was criticized by conservative blacks for his friendly relations with Louis ◊Farrakhan of the Nation of Islam.

Chavis was a direct descendant of John Chavis (1763–1838), a former slave who graduated from Princeton University. He was sentenced to 34 years in prison in 1972 as leader of the Wilmington Ten, convicted of conspiracy and arson. While in prison he gained a master of divinity degree and taught a seminar on black church studies at Duke University, North Carolina. The convictions were overturned in 1980. He became executive director of the Commission for Racial Justice and commissioned a study, *Toxic Wastes and Race in the United States* (1987), which showed that a large number of hazardous-waste dumps were in black neighbourhoods.

◆ CHAN, JULIUS (1939–) ◆

Papua New Guinean right-of-centre politician, prime minister 1980–82 and 1994–97. He negotiated a cease-fire in the six-year-long separatist conflict on Bougainville island in 1994, but it failed to hold and fighting resumed. Chan also promoted privatization and reformed local government, abolishing the provincial tier, in 1995. He resigned as prime minister in March 1997, after riots in Port Moresby, which were triggered by his government's planned use of UK and South African mercenaries to combat Bougainville's guerrillas. He was reinstated in June 1997, after a commission of inquiry ruled that he was not guilty of misconduct. However, in the June 1997 general election his conservative, business-oriented People's Progress Party (PPP) lost much support and Chan failed to win his parliamentary seat.

Born on Tanga Island, New Ireland District, to the northeast of New Guinea, of mixed Melanesian and Chinese parentage, Chan studied agricultural science at the University of Queensland, Australia. He set up a shipping business and was first elected to the Papua New Guinea House of Assembly in 1968, forming, in 1970, the PPP. Between 1972 and 1977 Chan was finance minister, under Prime Minister Michael ◊Somare of the Pangu Pati (PP), and in 1977 to 1978 was deputy prime minister and industry minister. He then took the UMP into opposition, before becoming prime minister in March 1980, when Somare lost a no-confidence vote.

He returned to opposition after the 1982 general election, won by Somare, before serving as deputy prime minister and trade and industry minister 1987–88 and finance minister 1985–87 and 1992–94 under Prime Minister Paias ◊Wingti, of the People's Democratic Movement (PDM). When Wingti was forced to step down as prime minister in August 1994, after the Supreme Court ruled that recent elections had been invalid, Chan returned as prime minister, heading a broad coalition.

Chehab, Fuad (1901–1973)

Lebanese soldier and president. He was educated at the French military academies of Damascus and St Cyr. He served in the army under the French mandate, becoming commander in chief on independence in 1946. During a break in his military career he was prime minister for six days during an emergency in September 1952. As president 1958–64 he restored stability to Lebanon, which had been shaken by the 1958 civil war.

Chen Boda (1904–1989)

Chinese communist politician, political adviser to ◊Mao Zedong 1937–41 and director of the Cultural Revolution 1966–70. A radical leftist, he was brought into the Politburo in 1966 and served as head of the Cultural Revolution Group, the body charged with directing the Cultural Revolution, working alongside ◊Jiang Qing. However, in 1970 Chen was suddenly purged and dismissed from his party posts.

He was not seen in public again until the 1980–81 show trial of the ultra-leftist 'Gang of Four', when he was accused (and found guilty) of being a member of the 'Lin Biao Clique'. The clique was accused of having plotted to assassinate Mao Zedong in 1970, with the aim of installing in power his 'designated successor', ◊Lin Biao. Chen was sentenced to 18 years' imprisonment in January 1981, but was released in mid-1982 on health grounds.

Born in Huian county, in Fujian province, the son of a poor peasant, Chen joined the Chinese Communist Party (CCP) in 1924 and studied at the Sun Yat-sen University 1927–30.

A skilled communist propagandist, from 1937 to 1941 Chen worked as the political secretary, speech writer, and adviser to party leader Mao Zedong, who was then based in Yanan. In the new People's Republic of 1949, Chen worked as editor of *Hongqi/Red Flag*, the CCP's theoretical journal, from 1958.

Chen Duxiu (1879–1942)

Chinese communist politician, party leader 1921–27. A founder member of the Chinese Communist Party (CCP) and its leader from July 1921, Chen followed conventional Leninist thinking and sought to foment a socialist revolution in China through CCP-led workers' uprisings in the country's coastal cities. Discredited both by the failure of his efforts and by his association with Trotskyist groups, Chen was replaced as CCP leader by Li Lisan. He was expelled from the CCP in 1929 and died in Sichuan.

The failure of Chen's efforts was partly a result of the limited size of China's industrial proletariat, but also because of repression by the Kuomintang (Guomindang, nationalist) forces of Jiang Jie Shi (Chiang Kai-shek). In April 1927 Chiang staged a successful coup against the CCP in China to establish a new right-wing Kuomintang government, with its headquarters in Nanjing.

Born in Huaining in Anhui province, the son of a landlord, Chen had a classical education in Huangzhou, passing the first stage of the imperial civil service examination in 1896. However, influenced by reformers within the imperial administration who advocated modernization and 'learning from the West', he studied abroad in Tokyo and France 1902–10 and became an advocate of such liberal concepts as democracy and science. He set up the journal *New Youth* in 1915 and became a lecturer at Beijing University in 1918, participating in the May Fourth Movement (on 4 May 1919), in which Chinese nationalists protested against the Conference of Versailles decision not to require Japan to hand over to China recently occupied German concessions. Radicalized by the May Fourth Movement, Chen became a founding member of the Chinese Communist Party.

Chen Yi or *Ch'en I* (1901–1972)

Chinese communist military and political leader, foreign minister 1958–69.

Chen studied in France, and joined the Chinese Communist Party (CCP) on his return, in 1923. He worked in the Whampoa Military Academy and was involved in the joint military advance by CCP and Kuomintang (Guomindang) nationalist forces in the 'Northern Expedition' of 1926–27. Chen emerged as a supporter of ◊Mao Zedong in the struggle with the Kuomintang, but remained in Henan province in 1934 when the main CCP force set out on its 1934–35 'Long March' from Jiangxi, in the south-centre, to Shaanxi, in northern China. He rejoined Mao in 1937 and took a leading role in the military campaign against the Japanese occupying forces.

Chen formed the 4th Route Army in Kiangxi in 1940, and commanded the East China Liberation Army in 1946, restyled the 3rd (East China) Army in 1948. He prepared an amphibious operation against Taiwan, but failed to capture Quemoy island in 1949. Created marshal of the People's Republic in 1955, Chen served as mayor of Shanghai 1949–58 and became foreign minister in 1958. He was dropped from the CCP Politburo during the Cultural Revolution, in 1969, after being severely criticized by the young, ultra-leftist Red Guards.

Chen Yun, adopted name of Liao Chenyun (1905–1995)

Chinese communist economic planner. Born near Shanghai, as Liao Chenyun, he trained as a typesetter and joined the Chinese Communist Party (CCP) in 1925, just four years after it was founded. Chen helped organize an armed workers' uprising in Shanghai in 1927, before joining ◊Mao Zedong and the Red Army in their mountain base in Jiangxi province in 1933. He entered the CCP Politburo in 1934 and participated in the 1934–35 'Long March' northwards from Jiangxi. At the crucial Zunyi conference of May 1935, which established Mao's ascendancy within the party, Chen sided with Mao and became a close aide of the party leader. After the establishment of the People's Republic in 1949, he became a leading economic policymaker, but criticized Mao's disastrous experimental Great Leap Forward (1958–62) to communism, which was based on the establishment of large agricultural and industrial communes, and resulted in more than 20 million deaths from famine.

During the early 1960s Chen oversaw the reconstruction of the Chinese economy through the reintroduction of private farming plots and markets. He favoured a planned economy in which market forces would be allowed to operate in a controlled manner, 'like a bird in a cage'. Although Chen fell temporarily from power during the mid-1960s Cultural Revolution, unlike many other senior figures he retained his seat on the CCP's influential Central Committee.

In 1977–78 Chen supported ◊Deng Xiaoping's rise to power and Deng's early market-centred economic reforms. However, still convinced of the merits of a 'birdcage economy', he expressed concern from the late 1980s that market forces were being allowed to run out of control, with serious destabilizing social and political consequences. He retired from the CCP Central Committee and Politburo in 1987, after a record 53 years, due to ailing health, but remained influential behind the scenes, wielding significant patronage power as one of the 'Eight Immortals' who had ruled China since the communist victory in 1949. His death left only five 'Immortals', including Deng, alive.

Chernenko, Konstantin Ustinovich (1911–1985)

Soviet politician, leader of the Communist Party of the Soviet Union (CPSU) and president 1984–85. He was a protégé of Leonid Brezhnev and from 1978 a member of the Politburo.

Chernenko, born in central Siberia, joined the Komsomol (Communist Youth League) in 1929 and the CPSU in 1931. The future CPSU leader Brezhnev brought him to Moscow to work in the central apparatus in 1956 and later sought to establish Chernenko as his successor, but he was passed over in favour of the KGB chief Yuri Andropov. When Andropov died in February 1984 Chernenko was selected as the CPSU's stopgap leader by cautious party colleagues and was also elected president. From July 1984 he gradually retired from public life because of failing health.

Chernomyrdin, Viktor Stepanovich (1938–)

Russian politician, prime minister 1992–98. A former manager in the state gas industry and communist party apparatchik, he became prime minister in December 1992 after Russia's ex-communist-dominated parliament had ousted the market reformer Yegor Gaidar. He assumed temporary control over foreign and security policy after President Boris Yeltsin suffered a heart attack in November 1995, and again in November 1996 when Yeltsin underwent open-heart surgery. From March 1997 Chernomyrdin lost direct control over the economy to the promoted reformist ministers Anatoly Chubais and Boris Nemtsov. In March 1998 he was dismissed as prime minister, along with the entire government, by President Yeltsin.

Although lacking charisma, Chernomyrdin emerged as a respected and pragmatic reformer who, enjoying strong establishment support, brought a measure of stability to the country. He formed the Russia is Our Home party in May 1995 and was viewed as a leading challenger for the Russian presidency until Yeltsin stood for re-election in 1996. His negotiated settlement of a hostage crisis in southern Russia in June 1995, although controversial, won him popular support, leading to a temporary cease-fire in the civil war in Chechnya and peace talks between the two sides. After being dismissed in 1998, he announced that he would be a candidate in the next presidential elections, planned for 2000.

Chernov, Viktor Mikhailovich (1873–1952)

Russian politician. He was leader of the Socialist Revolutionaries, occupying a central position in the party. In 1917 he was minister of agriculture in Alexandr Kerensky's provisional government. In 1918 he was elected chair of the Constituent Assembly. He emigrated in 1920 and died in the USA.

Chesterton, G(ilbert) K(eith) (1874–1936)

English novelist, essayist, and poet. He wrote numerous short stories featuring a Catholic priest, Father Brown, who solves crimes by drawing on his knowledge of human nature. Other novels include the fantasy *The Napoleon of Notting Hill* (1904) and *The Man Who Was Thursday* (1908), a deeply emotional allegory about the problem of evil.

Smile at us, pay us, pass us; but do not quite forget. / For we are the people of England, that never have spoken yet.

G K CHESTERTON *The Secret People*

He was also active as a political essayist, and with the writer Hilaire ◊Belloc advocated a revolt against capitalism in the direction opposite to socialism by strengthening the 'small man' and discouraging big business. He was president of the 'Distributist League', of which the magazine *GK's Weekly* (1925) was (more or less) the organ.

FURTHER READING

Baker, Dudley *G K Chesterton* 1973

Coren, Michael *Gilbert: The Man Who was G K Chesterton* 1989

Sparkes, Russell *Prophet of Orthodoxy: The Wisdom of G K Chesterton* 1997

Sullivan, J (ed) *G K Chesterton: A Centenary Appraisal* 1974

Chiang Ching

Wade-Giles transliteration of ◊Jiang Qing.

Chiang Ching-kuo

Wade-Giles transliteration of ◊Jiang Qing-guo.

Chiang Kai-shek

Wade-Giles transliteration of ◊Jiang Jie Shi.

Chiari, Roberto Francisco (1905–)

Panamanian politician, member of the National Liberal Party, president 1960–64. Faced with the country in recession, he introduced tax reforms and borrowed from the international community to finance a $207 million development plan, targeted at both urban and rural areas. He also intervened personally to end a serious strike during 1960–61 by 10,000 banana workers.

Born in Panama City, into a wealthy family with extensive interests in sugar and dairying, his father, Rodolfo Chiari, was president 1924–28. Roberto Chiari, who had been a second vice president in 1949, was elected president in 1960 as the candidate of a four-party coalition, led by his National Liberal Party.

Chifley, Ben (Joseph Benedict) (1885–1951)

Australian Labor prime minister 1945–49. He united the party in fulfilling a welfare and nationalization programme 1945–49 (although he failed in an attempt to nationalize the banks in 1947) and initiated an immigration programme and the Snowy Mountains hydroelectric project.

Chifley was minister of postwar reconstruction 1942–45 under John ◊Curtin, when he succeeded him as prime minister. He crushed a communist-led coal miners' strike in 1949 by using troops as mine labour. He was leader of the opposition from 1949 until his death.

The son of a New South Wales blacksmith, he began work at 15 and was largely self-educated. He worked on the railways, cofounded the Locomotive Engineers Union in 1920, and was elected to the federal House of Representatives in 1928 but lost his seat in 1931.

Childers, (Robert) Erskine (1870–1922)

English civil servant and writer, Irish republican, author of the spy novel *The Riddle of the Sands* (1903).

A Londoner by birth and educated at Haileybury and Cambridge, Childers served as Clerk of the House of Commons 1895–1910. He converted to Irish Home Rule in 1908, and it was aboard his yacht the *Asgard* that arms were landed for the Irish Volunteers in 1914. He served with the Royal Navy Air Services 1914–19, yet his support for Home Rule hardened into a severe republi-

canism. He was appointed director of publicity for the IRA (Irish Republican Army) in 1919 and, elected to the Dáil (then the unofficial republican parliament) in 1921, became its minister for propaganda. Childers served as first secretary to the Irish delegation in negotiations with the British government in 1921, but opposed the treaty that his colleagues agreed with the British. He fought with the republicans in the 1922 civil war, and was captured, court-martialled, and executed by the Free State government.

Childers, Erskine H(amilton) (1905–1974)

Irish Fianna Fáil politician, president 1973–74. He sought the reunification of Ireland, but condemned the campaign of violence by the Irish Republican Army (IRA) to achieve that end. He was a strong advocate of Ireland's membership of the European Community (EC, now the European Union).

Although, after entering Irish politics in 1938, he held a number of ministerial posts and was elected deputy leader of the Fianna Fáil party in 1969, he was always in the shadow of his famous father, Robert Erskine ◊Childers, a leading figure in the struggle for Irish independence.

Childers was born in London and studied history at Trinity College, Cambridge. He moved to Ireland in 1932, when he became advertising manager of the *Irish Press*, the paper newly founded by the de Valera family, and was secretary of the Federation of Irish Manufacturers 1936–44. He entered politics as much out of duty as vocation. An idealist, he hoped to make the presidency a vehicle for moderate, intellectual debate, which would counter the extremism of people less patient in their search for a solution to the North–South divide.

Chiluba, Frederick (1943–)

Zambian politician and trade unionist, president from 1991. In 1993 he was forced to declare a state of emergency, following the discovery of documents suggesting an impending coup. He later carried out a major reorganization of his cabinet but failed to silence his critics. He secured re-election in November 1996.

A shop steward in his early twenties, he rose rapidly to become chairman general of the 300,000-member Zambian Congress of Trades Unions at the age of 31. After a series of strikes in 1981, he spent three months in prison, during which time he became a 'born-again' Christian. When one-party rule officially ended in 1990, Chiluba entered the political arena, becoming leader of the Movement for Multiparty Democracy (MMD). As MMD candidate in the 1991 presidential elections, he won 75% of the votes. He has been criticized for the harshness of his economic policies and accused of favouring particular ethnic groups in his cabinet and other appointments.

Chirac, Jacques René (1932–)

French Gaullist politician and head of state, president from 1995 and twice prime minister 1974–76 and 1986–88, 'co-habiting' on the second occasion with the socialist president François Mitterrand. Chirac led the Gaullist party 1974–95, refounding it in 1976 as the Rassemblement pour la République (RPR). He also served as the first elected mayor of Paris 1977–95.

After converting the RPR to neo-liberal economic policies and to further European integration, Chirac led the right to electoral victory in 1986. His second government brought in major privatizations prior to the 1987 stock-market crash, but ceded ground over proposed nationality and university reforms. In 1993 he declined the premiership (which went to his former finance minister Edouard ◊Balladur). In 1995, having twice stood unsuccessfully against Mitterrand for the presidency in 1981 and 1988, he was able to outdistance the socialist Lionel Jospin (and, on the first ballot, Balladur). Controversially, he decided temporarily to resume Pacific nuclear testing in late 1995. With his government increasingly unpopular over welfare cutbacks – linked to meeting the Maastricht criteria for European Monetary Union – Chirac miscalculated in calling early parliamentary elections in June 1997, the Left's victory leading him into 'co-habitation' with a government led by Lionel ◊Jospin.

From an affluent Parisian background, Chirac trained at France's elite Ecole Nationale d'Administration, was a policy adviser to Prime Minister Georges ◊Pompidou from 1962, and then held successive ministerial posts 1967–73, gaining the nickname 'the Bulldozer' . He supported Valéry ◊Giscard d'Estaing, the non-Gaullist centre-right presidential candidate, in 1974, but subsequent disagreements led to his resignation as Giscard's first prime minister in 1976.

Chisholm, Shirley Anita St Hill (1924–)

US Democrat politician. The first black American woman elected to Congress, in 1964, she served until 1983.

Although born in Brooklyn, New York City, the child of an immigrant from British Guiana (now Guyana), she spent her childhood in Barbados. A specialist in early-childhood education, she worked at the Mount Calvary Child Care Center 1946–52, before running her own nursery school. She later became director to the city of New York on day-care facilities. In Congress she campaigned successfully for the extension of employment protection to domestic workers, and fought to combat sexism and racism. Her autobiography, *Unbought and Unbossed*, was published in 1970. From

1983 she was a member of staff at Mount Holyoke College, Massachusetts.

Chissano, Joaquim (1939–)

Mozambique nationalist politician, president from 1986; foreign minister 1975–86. In October 1992 he signed a peace accord with the leader of the rebel Mozambique National Resistance (MNR) party, bringing to an end 16 years of civil war, and in 1994 won the first free presidential elections.

He was secretary to Samora ◊Machel, who led the National Front for the Liberation of Mozambique (Frelimo) during the campaign for independence in the early 1960s. When Mozambique achieved internal self-government in 1974, Chissano was appointed prime minister. After independence he served under Machel as foreign minister and on his death succeeded him as president.

Choibalsan (died 1952)

Mongolian revolutionary leader. In 1921 he helped to establish the Mongolian People's Revolutionary Party, and when in that year Soviet Red Army units entered Urga, the capital of Outer Mongolia, and sponsored the creation of a pro-Soviet government, Choibalsan became a deputy war minister. In succeeding years he became the dominant leader of the Mongolian People's Republic (formally established in 1924) and had eliminated all his rivals by 1940.

Originally trained as a lamaist monk, he went to Siberia, where he made contact with Russian revolutionaries. He founded his first revolutionary organization in 1919.

His policies were modelled on those of Stalin, including the cultivation of a personality cult and harsh treatment of landowners. He was also responsible for the execution of thousands of lamaist monks.

Chomsky, (Avram) Noam (1928–)

US professor of linguistics and political commentator. He proposed a theory of transformational generative grammar, which attracted widespread interest because of the claims it made about the relationship between language and the mind and the universality of an underlying language structure. He has been a leading critic of the imperialist tendencies of the US government. Chomsky was an active opponent of the US involvement in the Vietnam War, and continued to speak out against exploitive reactionary policies and the complicity of the media in presenting the official view of events and not questioning basic assumptions. His political works include *American Power and the New Mandarins* (1969) and *Deterring Democracy* (1991).

FURTHER READING

Barsky, Robert F *Noam Chomsky: A Life of Dissent* 1997
Chomsky, Noam, et al *The Chomsky Reader* 1987

Choonhavan, Chatichai (1922–1998)

Thai conservative politician, prime minister 1988–91. He promoted a peace settlement in neighbouring Cambodia as part of a vision of transforming Indochina into a thriving open-trade zone. Despite economic success, he was ousted in a bloodless military coup in 1991.

A field marshal's son, Choonhavan fought in World War II and the Korean War, rising to major general. After a career as a diplomat and entrepreneur, he moved into politics and became leader of the conservative Chart Thai (Thai Nation) party and, in 1988, prime minister. He was overthrown in February 1991 and was allowed, the following month, to leave the country for Switzerland. He later returned to found the Chart Pattana (National Development) party in 1992. It was a member of the governing coalition from 1994.

Chrétien, (Joseph Jacques) Jean (1934–)

French-Canadian politician, prime minister from 1993. He won the leadership of the Liberal Party in 1990 and defeated Kim ◊Campbell in the October 1993 election. He was a vigorous advocate of national unity and, although himself a Québecois, consistently opposed the province's separatist ambitions. His Liberal Party won the Canadian election in June 1997 to gain its first back-to-back win in 44 years.

Chrétien held ministerial posts in the cabinets of Lester ◊Pearson and Pierre ◊Trudeau. After unsuccessfully contesting the Liberal Party leadership in 1984, he resigned his parliamentary seat, returning in 1990 to win the leadership on his second attempt.

Christopher, Warren (1925–)

US Democrat politician, secretary of state 1993–96. Trained as a lawyer, he was deputy attorney general under President Jimmy Carter 1977–81 and led negotiations for the release of US hostages in Iran. In 1992 he masterminded the selection of President Bill Clinton's cabinet team; in September 1993 he secured the signing of a historic Israeli–PLO accord in Washington, DC; and in November 1995 he brokered a peace agreement for Bosnia-Herzegovina. Regarded as a skilled negotiator, unrestricted by strong political bias, he retired after President Clinton was re-elected for a second term.

Chuan Leekpai (1938–)

Thai politician, prime minister 1992–95 and from 1997. Representing the liberal Democrat Party (DP), he served in a succession of ministerial positions 1975–91 before becoming prime minister in September 1992, after a DP-sponsored pro-democracy campaign. This government collapsed in 1995, following a public land scandal, in which Chuan was not personally implicated. Chuan returned as prime minister in November 1997, at a time of economic crisis caused by a recent currency collapse, and headed an eight-party coalition.

As the economy contracted in 1998, he launched austerity measures, which involved the repatriation of many foreign workers.

Chuan studied for the bar before being elected to parliament for his native Trang Province in 1969. His 1992–95 administration sought to liberalize the financial system, promote rural development, decentralize government, and tackle corruption. However, although viewed as less corrupt than preceding administrations, it eventually collapsed over a scandal concerning the working of its land distribution programme.

Chubais, Anatoly Borisovich (1955–)

Russian politician and economist, head of the United Energy Corporation. The most politically agile and longest-lasting of the group of young economists who came into Boris ◊Yeltsin's first government in 1991, Chubais was the architect and the chief executive of the privatization of the Russian economy. Though formally dismissed from the government, he played a key role in the re-election of Yeltsin in 1996 and was rewarded with the title of chief of staff. Out of office again in 1997, he became head of the United Energy Corporation.

Having started the economic reform in 1992, he conducted it at breakneck speed, unloading everything from small shops to giant oil corporations onto a market primed by millions of privatization vouchers issued to every man, woman, and child. Chubais, a fierce anti-communist, presented his drive as a means of breaking the economic power of the Communist Party and creating a middle class; however, his programme, especially its second phase in which he disposed of the energy sector, was marked by increasing corruption and insider dealing.

Chulalongkorn or Rama V (1853–1910)

King of Siam (modern Thailand) from 1868. He studied Western administrative practices and launched an ambitious modernization programme after reaching his majority in 1873. He protected Siam from colonization by astutely playing off French and British interests.

Chulalongkorn was partly educated by English tutors and travelled to Europe in 1897. His wide-ranging reforms included the abolition of slavery, centralization of administration to check the power of local chiefs, and reorganization of court and educational systems.

Chun Doo-hwan (1931–)

South Korean military ruler who seized power in 1979, and was president 1981–88 as head of the newly formed Democratic Justice Party.

Chun, trained in Korea and the USA, served as an army commander from 1967 and was in charge of military intelligence in 1979 when President Park

Chung Hee was assassinated by the chief of the Korean Central Intelligence Agency (KCIA). General Chun took charge of the KCIA and, in a coup, assumed control of the army and the South Korean government. In 1981 Chun was appointed president, and oversaw a period of rapid economic growth, governing in an authoritarian manner, until 1988 when he retired to a Buddhist retreat.

In 1995 Chun was arrested on charges of staging the coup that had brought him to power in 1979.

Churchill, Lord Randolph Henry Spencer (1849–1895)

British Conservative politician, chancellor of the Exchequer and leader of the House of Commons in 1886; father of Winston Churchill.

Born at Blenheim Palace, Woodstock, Oxfordshire, son of the 7th Duke of Marlborough, he entered Parliament in 1874. In 1880 he formed a Conservative group known as the Fourth Party with Drummond Wolff (1830–1908), J E Gorst, and Arthur Balfour, and in 1885 his policy of Tory democracy was widely accepted by the party. In 1886 he became chancellor of the Exchequer, but resigned within six months because he did not agree with the demands made on the Treasury by the War Office and the Admiralty. In 1874 he married Jennie Jerome (1854–1921), daughter of a wealthy New Yorker.

Churchill, Winston (Leonard Spencer) (1874–1965)

See page 94.

We shall go on to the end. We shall fight in France, we shall fight on the seas and oceans, we shall fight with growing confidence and growing strength in the air, we shall defend our island, whatever the cost may be. We shall fight on the beaches, we shall fight on the landing grounds, we shall fight in the fields and in the streets, we shall fight in the hills; we shall never surrender.

WINSTON CHURCHILL *Hansard* 4 June 1940

Winston Churchill announces victory over Germany on the radio, 8 May 1945. *AKG London*

Ciano, Galeazzo, Count (1903–1944)

Italian Fascist politician. Son-in-law of the dictator Mussolini, he was foreign minister and member of the Fascist Supreme Council 1936–43. He voted against Mussolini at the meeting of the Grand Council in July 1943 that overthrew the dictator, but was later tried for treason and shot by the Fascists.

Ciller, Tansu (1946–)

Turkish politician, prime minister 1993–96 and a forthright exponent of free-market economic policies. She won the leadership of the centre-right True Path Party and the premiership on the election of Suleyman ◊Demirel as president. Her support for a military, as opposed to a diplomatic, approach to Kurdish insurgency provoked international criticism; in 1995 relations with her coalition partners deteriorated, and a general election was called for December. The result was inconclusive and, after prolonged attempts to form a new coalition, she agreed in 1996 to have a rotating premiership with the Motherland Party leader, Mesut Yilmaz. However, this arrangement foundered in June 1996 following allegations of corruption against Ciller. In October 1997 her husband was charged with changing figures on the balance sheet of an US firm owned by the family.

Trained as an economist, Ciller became economic adviser to Prime Minister Demirel in 1990. She joined the government in 1991 and, on assuming the premiership in May 1993, embarked on an extensive economic-reform programme, combining privatization with austerity measures, and securing a customs union agreement with the European Union. Nicknamed Turkey's 'iron lady with a smile', she made her husband take her maiden name.

Citrine, Walter McLennan Citrine, 1st Baron (1887–1983)

English trade-union leader and administrator. He was general secretary of the Trades Union Congress (TUC) 1926–46 and took a leading part in the struggle to secure the repeal of the Trades Dispute Act of 1927. He served on the National Coal Board until 1947 and was president of the Central Electricity Authority 1947–57. He was knighted in 1935 and created a peer in 1946.

Citrine was born in Liverpool and trained as an electrician. He was appointed district secretary of the Electrical Trades Union in 1914, and became president of the Federated Engineering and Shipbuilding Trades, Merseyside, in 1917.

Claes, Willy (1938–)

Belgian politician, secretary general of the North Atlantic Treaty Organization (NATO) 1994–95, with a proven reputation as a consensus-builder. He was a clear favourite for the post, but subsequent allegations about his involvement (while Belgian foreign minister)

◆ CHURCHILL, WINSTON (LEONARD SPENCER) (1874–1965) ◆

British politician, prime minister 1940–45 and 1951–55.

Churchill was born at Blenheim Palace, Woodstock, Oxfordshire, the eldest son of Lord Randolph Churchill. He was educated at Harrow and Sandhurst and joined the army in 1895. As both soldier and military correspondent he served in India, Egypt, and South Africa.

He entered politics in 1900 as Conservative member of Parliament for Oldham, and disagreeing with Joseph Chamberlain's tariff reform policy, in 1906 he joined the Liberals. He was colonial undersecretary in the Liberal government 1908–10, and in 1910 became president of the Board of Trade, and introduced legislation for the introduction of labour exchanges. As home secretary in 1910, he used the army against rioting miners in Tonypandy, South Wales, and also was involved in dealing with the Sidney Street siege in 1911. He became First Lord of the Admiralty in 1911, but was forced to resign in 1915, taking responsibility for the Dardanelles disaster. He joined the army and served in the trenches in France 1915–16. In 1917 he became minister of munitions in David Lloyd George's cabinet.

He served as secretary for war and air in the coalition government 1919–21. He rejoined the Conservatives as member of Parliament for Epping in 1924 and was chancellor of the Exchequer 1924–29, returning Britain to the gold standard. He edited the government newspaper, the *British Gazette*, during the General Strike in May 1926. He was out of office between 1929 and 1939, and was a severe critic of Neville Chamberlain's appeasement policy. On the outbreak of war, he returned to the Admiralty and in May 1940 he replaced Chamberlain as prime minister, leading a coalition government.

Churchill proved an inspirational wartime leader. His close relationship with the US president Franklin D Roosevelt and the signing of the 1941 Atlantic Treaty began Britain's 'special relationship' with the USA. The tripartite meeting with Roosevelt, Churchill, and Stalin in the Crimea at Yalta in 1945 planned the final defeat of Germany and its postwar occupation. In June 1945, Churchill attended the Potsdam Conference in the final stages of the war, but he was replaced by Clement Attlee in July, following the Conservative defeat in the general election.

in illegal dealings with Agusta, the Italian aircraft manufacturer, eventually forced his resignation in November 1995.

Prior to becoming secretary general, he was foreign affairs minister and deputy prime minister. A Flemish-speaking socialist, he had risen to high political office via the trade-union movement. In August 1998 he went on trial, charged with receiving illegal income in the late 1980s on purchases of French and Italian arms.

Clark, Joe (Charles Joseph) (1939–)

Canadian Progressive Conservative politician who became party leader in 1976, and in May 1979 defeated Pierre ◊Trudeau at the polls to become the youngest prime minister in Canada's history. Following the rejection of his government's budget, he was defeated in a second election in February 1980. He became secretary of state for external affairs (foreign minister) 1984 in the government of Brian ◊Mulroney.

Clarke, Kenneth Harry (1940–)

British Conservative politician. A cabinet minister 1985–97, he held the posts of education secretary 1990–92 and home secretary 1992–93. He succeeded Norman Lamont as chancellor of the Exchequer in May 1993, bringing to the office a more open and combative approach. Along with his colleagues Malcolm Rifkind, Tony Newton, and Patrick Mayhew, in 1996 he became the longest continuously serving

---

As opposition leader Churchill was concerned with the USSR's intentions in Eastern Europe and warned of 'the Iron Curtain' descending on Europe. He promoted the concept of a united Europe – a united Europe that Britain would be allied to but not a member of. In 1951 Churchill again became prime minister until his resignation in 1955. He remained member of Parliament for Woodford until 1964.

Churchill was a keen amateur painter and historian. His books include a six-volume history of World War II (1948–54) and a four-volume *History of the English Speaking Peoples* (1956–58). In 1995 the British government paid Winston Churchill's family £13.25 million for Churchill's pre-1945 writings, the ' Chartwell Papers', to prevent their sale abroad. In 1953 Churchill was made a Knight of the Garter. See photograph on page 93.

FURTHER READING

Brendan, P *Churchill: A Brief Life* 1987
Churchill, Winston *My Early Life* 1930
Gilbert, M *Churchill: A Life* 1991
Manchester, W *The Last Lion: Visions of Glory* 1983, *The Caged Lion* 1988
Taylor, A J P, and others *Churchill Revisited: A Critical Assessment* 1969

---

minister since Lord Palmerston in the early 19th century.

Clarke was politically active as a law student at Cambridge. He was elected to Parliament for Rushcliff, Nottinghamshire, in 1970. From 1965 to 1966, Clarke was secretary for the Birmingham Bow Group. A junior member of the first Thatcher government of May 1979, he became a minister of state in 1982, paymaster general in 1985, with special responsibility for employment, and chancellor of the Duchy of Lancaster in 1987. In 1988 he was made minister of health, in 1990 education secretary, in 1992 home secretary, and chancellor in 1993. He was a contestant for the leadership of the Conservative Party after its defeat in the 1997 general election. At odds over the new leader's anti-European policy, he declined to accept a position in the shadow cabinet of William Hague.

They are 18-year-olds in the saloon bar, trying every bottle on the shelf.
KENNETH CLARKE On the Labour Party's new Treasury team; *Independent*, 24 May 1997

Cleaver, (Leroy) Eldridge (1935–1998)

US political activist. He joined the Black Panthers in 1967, becoming minister of information, and stood for US president in 1968. After a fight with the police, he fled to Cuba in 1968 and Algeria in 1969. His political autobiography, *Soul on Ice*, was published in 1968.

So Elvis Presley came, strumming a weird guitar and wagging his tail across the continent ... and, like a latter-day Johnny Appleseed, sowing the seeds of a new rhythm and style in the white souls of the new white youth of America.
ELDRIDGE CLEAVER *Soul on Ice*

While in prison 1957–66, Cleaver became a Black Muslim minister. Later he became a born-again Christian in France, and toured the USA as an evangelist. His *Post-Prison Writings and Speeches* were published in 1969.

Clémenceau, Georges Eugène Benjamin (1841–1929)

French radical politician, prime minister 1906–09 and 1917–20 when he chaired the Versailles peace conference but failed to secure the Rhine as a frontier for France in the Treaty.

Elected mayor of Montmartre, Paris, in the war of 1870, and deputy for Montmartre 1876–93, Clémenceau's extreme radicalism and ferocious attacks on opponents earned him the nickname 'the Tiger'. He was a prominent defender of Alfred Dreyfus through the daily paper *La Justice*, which he founded after losing his seat in 1893. Elected senator for Var from 1902, as interior and prime minister from 1906 he adopted a moderating stance in settling church–state relations, saw his attempt to introduce income tax defeated, but acted decisively to crush a series of strike movements in industry and agriculture. In 1917 his intervention secured the appointment of Marshal Foch as supreme commander of allied forces.

Clerides, Glafkos John (1919–)

Greek Cypriot lawyer and politician, president of Cyprus from 1993. Leader of the right-of-centre Democratic Rally, he unsuccessfully contested the presidency in 1978, 1983, and 1988, and then won it by a narrow majority in 1993 at the age of 73. His personal ties with the Turkish leader Rauf Denktaş raised expectations that he might be more successful than his predecessors in resolving his country's divisions, and peace talks resumed in June 1996. He was narrowly re-elected in February 1998, and in March 1998 began talks with the European Union on the country's possible accession.

Clinton, Hillary Diane Rodham (1947–)

US lawyer and first lady. In 1993 President Bill Clinton appointed her to head his task force on the reform of the national health-care system, but her proposal of health insurance for all US citizens was blocked by Congress in 1994. In the same year the Justice Department appointed a special prosecutor to investigate the Whitewater affair relating to alleged irregularities in property deals made by the Clintons in Arkansas. A formidable, polarizing figure, Hillary Clinton became the first ever first lady to be subpoenaed to appear before a Federal Grand Jury.

Hillary Rodham was born in the suburbs of Chicago. She graduated from Yale law school in 1973 and married Bill Clinton in 1975. She was one of the team of lawyers appointed to work on the impeachment of President Richard Nixon in 1974. The Clintons moved to Arkansas in 1976, and she joined the Rose law firm. As head of the Arkansas Education Standards Committee from 1983, she succeeded in getting the state to pass a law in 1985 allowing the dismissal of teachers for incompetence. A longtime advocate of children's rights, she has published the book *It Takes a Village and Other Lessons Children Teach Us* (1996).

◆ CLINTON, BILL (WILLIAM JEFFERSON) (1946–) ◆

42nd president of the USA from 1993, a Democrat. He served as governor of Arkansas 1979–81 and 1983–93, establishing a liberal and progressive reputation. As president, he sought to implement a New Democrat programme, combining social reform with economic conservatism as a means of bringing the country out of recession. He introduced legislation to reduce the federal deficit and cut crime, but the loss of both houses of Congress to the Republicans in 1994 presented a serious obstacle to further social reform. However, he successfully repositioned himself on the centre-right to become, in November 1996, the first Democrat since F D Roosevelt to be elected for a second term.

Born in the railway town of Hope, Arkansas, Clinton graduated from Georgetown University in 1968, won a Rhodes scholarship to Oxford University 1968–70, and graduated from Yale University Law School in 1973. He was elected attorney general for Arkansas in 1975.

With his running mate Al ◊Gore, Clinton won the 1992 presidential campaign by focusing on domestic issues and the ailing economy. He became the first Democrat in the White House for 13 years. During his first year in office, Clinton secured the passage of an ambitious deficit-reduction plan, combining spending cuts with tax increases targeted against the rich, and won Congressional approval of the controversial North American Free Trade Agreement (NAFTA) and wide-ranging anticrime bills.

His alleged involvement in irregular financial dealings in the 1980s (the Whitewater affair) thereafter clouded his presidency and in the autumn of 1994 his much-championed health-care reform proposals were blocked by Congress. A subsequent diplomatic success in Haiti failed to prevent a devastating defeat for his party in the November 1994 midterm elections.

There is nothing wrong with America that cannot be cured by what is right with America.

BILL CLINTON Inaugural speech as US president 1993

In June 1995 Clinton issued the first veto of his presidency in an attempt to block proposed cuts in public-spending programmes that had earlier been approved by Congress. This was followed by further vetoes as he established himself as the further vetoes as he established himself as the conservative defender of the status quo against the 'New Right' Republican extremism. The

Clodumar, Kinza (1945–)

Nauruan politician, president 1997–98. He was elected executive president by parliament in February 1997, ending several months of political instability that had witnessed three changes of government. As well as president, Clodumar held the finance, public service, and foreign affairs portfolios. He embarked on a programme of wide-ranging economic reform, designed to restructure Nauru's economy following the depletion of its phosphate reserves. However, these measures provoked opposition in parliament and in June 1998 Clodumar was defeated in a no-confidence vote and replaced as president by Bernard ◊Dowiyogo.

Educated in Nauru and Australia, where he studied economics and politics at the Australian National University, Clodumar was first elected to the Nauru parliament in 1971. He remained an MP until 1979, serving as finance minister 1977–78 in Dowiyogo's government. Between 1979 to 1983 Clodumar worked as head of Nauru's development and industry department, but returned to politics as an MP 1984–92 and from 1995, when he became speaker of parliament.

Israeli–PLO accord on the West Bank, the Bosnia-Herzegovina peace agreements in the former Yugoslavia, and the Northern Ireland cease-fire were significant foreign policy successes for the Clinton administration and welfare reform was a domestic achievement. Clinton secured the Democratic presidential nomination in 1996 unopposed and comfortably defeated his Republican challenger, Bob Dole, in the November election, attracting 49% of the popular vote.

Clinton placed higher educational standards as the top priority of his second term. However, he faced a Congress controlled by the Republicans. A court case charging him with sexual harassment, raised by Paula Jones, a former Arkansas state employee, was thrown out by a federal judge in April 1998. However, he still faced a judicial investigation into his role in fund-raising for the 1996 election campaign and allegations, arising from the Jones's case, that he had had an improper relationship with a White House intern, Monica Lewinsky. Nevertheless, with the US economy booming, Clinton's public approval ratings remained high. In February 1999 the US Senate voted to acquit Clinton on two impeachment charges of lying under oath and obstructing justice in an effort to conceal a sexual relationship with Ms Lewinsky.

Clynes, John Robert (1869–1949)

British Labour politician. He was chair of the Parliamentary Labour Party 1921–22, Lord Privy Seal and deputy leader of the Commons in 1924, and home secretary 1929–31.

A textile worker by trade, he went on to play a prominent part in Lancashire trade-union and Labour Party affairs. He entered Parliament in 1906 and, except for the period 1931–35, retained his seat until 1945.

Coates, Joseph Gordon (1878–1943)

New Zealand Reform Party centre-right politician, prime minister 1925–28.

He first became a cabinet minister in 1919, in the Reform Party government of William Ferguson ◊Massey. During Coates's term as prime minister, highways and hydro-electric power were developed and race relations improved. He was subsequently a minister 1931–35 in the United Party government of George William ◊Forbes.

Cohn, Roy M (Marcus) (1927–1986)

US lawyer. As chief counsel to Joseph ◊McCarthy's Communist-hunting US Senate permanent investigations subcommittee 1953–54, he was an often celebrated, often denigrated US national figure. From 1954 to 1986 he became a political power broker and much-sought legal talent in New York City.

Cohn was born in New York City. He was admitted to the bar there at the age of 21. He became assistant US attorney for subversive activities and soon special assistant to the US attorney general. He performed energetically at the Julius and Ethel Rosenberg spy trial. Thrice tried and acquitted on federal charges of conspiracy, bribery, and fraud, he was disbarred two months before his death.

Cohn-Bendit, Daniel (1945–)

German student activist and politician. His 22nd March Movement was prominent amongst the leftist movements that took part in the students' and workers' demonstrations in France in May 1968. Expelled from France on the orders of the interior minister, Cohn-Bendit re-emerged in the 1980s as a prominent activist in the German Green Party, running an alternative bookshop in Frankfurt. In 1998 he was invited to head the French Green Party list for the European elections in June 1999.

Of German nationality, although born in France, Cohn-Bendit was, in 1968, a sociology student at Nanterre. Sharply critical of the French Communist Party (PCF) as a visionless bureaucracy, he was the target of a xenophobic personal attack in its daily paper, *L'Humanité*. This rebounded on the PCF, with street demonstrations chanting 'We are all German Jews'. Cohn-Bendit authored *Links radicalismus – Gewalter gegen die Krankheit des Communismus/Obsolete Communism – the Left-Wing Alternative* (1968).

Cole, G(eorge) D(ouglas) H(oward) (1889–1959)

English economist, historian, and detective-story writer. Chair of the Fabian Society 1939–46 and 1948–50 and its president from 1952, he wrote numerous books on socialism, including biographies of William Cobbett (1925) and Robert Owen (1925) and a history of the British working-class movements (1948), often in collaboration with his wife, Margaret Isabel Cole (1893–1980), and her brother, Raymond Postgate. The Coles also collaborated in writing detective fiction.

Born in London, G D H was educated at St Paul's School and Balliol College, Oxford, where he became a reader in economics in 1925 and Chichele Professor of Social and Political Theory in 1944.

FURTHER READING
Cole, M *The Life of G D H Cole* 1971

Collins, (Lewis) John (1905–1982)

English Christian social reformer, peace campaigner, and cleric. He joined the Labour Party in 1938 and formed Christian Action in 1946. Following his appointment as a canon of St Paul's Cathedral in 1948, he became a national figure campaigning for social reform, justice, and peace. He was a founding sponsor of the Campaign for Nuclear Disarmament (CND) in 1958 and served as its first chair 1958–60 in an uneasy relationship with its president, Bertrand Russell.

He was also active in campaigning against South African apartheid, being awarded a gold medal in 1978 by the United Nations Committee against Apartheid.

His autobiography, *Faith Under Fire*, was published in 1966. Collins remained at St Paul's until 1981.

He was educated at Cambridge, ordained at Canterbury Cathedral in 1928, and taught theology at King's College, London.

Collor de Mello, Fernando Affonso (1949–)

Brazilian politician, president 1990–92. He founded the right-wing Partido de Reconstrução Nacional (PRN; National Reconstruction Party) in 1989. As its candidate, he won the first public presidential election in 29 years to become the youngest ever Brazilian president, promising to root out government corruption and entrenched privileges. His administration was based on renewed economic stability and sustained development, although his attempts to reduce inflation were unsuccessful.

However, rumours of his own past wrongdoing led to his constitutional removal from office by a vote of impeachment in congress in October 1992.

Collor de Mello resigned in December at the start of his trial and was subsequently banned from public office for eight years, but in January 1998 he was acquitted on eight counts of illegal enrichment. He was succeeded by his vice president Itamar ◊Franco.

He was mayor of Maceió 1979–81, federal deputy 1982–85, and governor of the state of Alagoas 1986–89.

Compaoré, Blaise (1952–)

Burkinabè politician; president of Burkina Faso from 1987, and chair of the Popular Front of Burkina Faso. An army officer, Compaoré was second-in-command

---

◆ COLLINS, MICHAEL (1890–1922) ◆

Irish revolutionary and politician; chair of the Provisional Government in 1922 and founder of the Irish Free State.

Born in Clonakilty, County Cork, Collins moved to London in 1906 where he was employed by the Post Office. At the same time, however, he joined the secretive revolutionary organization known as the Irish Republican Brotherhood, and returned to Ireland in 1915, in time to take part in the abortive Easter Rising of 1916.

Released from internment in December 1916, Collins rapidly became a leading figure in the Irish Volunteers and Sinn Féin; he was elected to the Dáil (then the illegal republican parliament) in 1918 and served as minister for home affairs and minister for finance. His other role in the Anglo–Irish struggle was as director of organization and intelligence for the IRA (Irish Republican Army), and he was instrumental in the establishment of a crucial intelligence network and a ruthlessly efficient band of assassins known as 'the Squad'.

His courage, determination, and success earned him the unwavering devotion of many subordinates but the animosity of many rivals. His renowned ability to elude capture by the British served only to enhance his reputation.

Much against his own wishes, Collins was nominated by Éamon ◊de Valera to take part in the 1921 negotiations with the British, while his chief obdurately remained in Ireland. He accepted the resulting treaty, which recognized the partition of Ireland and granted dominion status to the Irish Free State, an outcome falling short of a 32-county republic. However, Collins regarded the settlement as a 'stepping stone' to full independence and for a time continued to support the IRA in its war on the new state of Northern Ireland.

He struggled to avoid armed conflict with his former colleagues who rejected the treaty, but took advantage of the standoff between pro- and anti-treaty factions to organize (with British

to President Thomas ◊Sankara, under whom he served as minister of state and as a member of the National Council for the Revolution (CDR). In 1987 Sankara was killed in the coup that brought Compaoré to power. Compaoré tolerated the development of mult-party politics and his government was not considered severely repressive. He was re-elected by popular vote in 1991.

Compton, John George Melvin (1926–   )

St Lucian centrist politician, prime minister 1964–79 and 1982–96. He left the St Lucia Labour Party (SLP) to form the breakaway United Workers' Party (UWP) in 1961, becoming chief minister in 1964. After St Lucia left the Windward Islands federation in 1967, he was redesignated prime minister, with the finance and planning portfolios, and guided the country to independence within the British Commonwealth in 1979. In opposition to SLP governments from 1979, he led the UWP to a decisive victory in 1982. He retired in 1996 and was knighted in 1997.

Politically active from the mid-1950s, Compton entered the St Lucia Legislative Council in 1957 as a member of the SLP and served as trade and industry minister 1958–61. On his retirement he was succeeded as UWP leader and prime minister by Vaughan Lewis.

Compton was born in Canouan island, in the Grenadines (part of St Vincent and the Grenadines). He studied economics and law at the London School of Economics and worked as a barrister.

---

assistance) the former into an efficient Free State army, of which he was commander in chief. The Civil War began in June 1922 when, under British pressure, government troops launched an attack on anti-treaty forces occupying the Four Courts building in Dublin. Collins himself was killed on 20 August 1922 at Beal na Blath in County Cork during an IRA attack on a government inspection tour. He was only 32 years old. Following his death, his successors crushed the IRA with a ruthlessness that outdid anything the British had attempted in the earlier phase of the independence struggle.

Collins has since been regarded as the only 'irreplaceable' member of the revolutionary leadership, and his death has engendered much speculation on the alternative course of independent Ireland, had he lived to lead it.

FURTHER READING
Coogan, Tim Pat *Michael Collins: A Biography* 1990
Mackey, James A *Michael Collins: A Life* 1996

Connerly, Ward(ell) (1939–   )

US civil servant and civil-rights campaigner. In 1996 Connerly served as chair of the California Civil Rights Initiative, which campaigned for the passage of Proposition 209 to eliminate racial preferences. He founded the American Civil Rights Institute (ACRI) in 1997 – a new, national civil-rights organization. As an advocate of equal opportunity and against preferences, set-asides, and quotas, Connerly's views have provoked much controversy and have been well documented by the international, national, and Californian press.

Connerly earned his bachelor's degree in political theory from California State University, Sacramento. He was chief deputy director of the California State Department of Housing and Community Development 1971–73 and prior to that worked for the Assembly Housing Committee. Connerly currently serves as chair of the ACRI, is on the board of the California Chamber of Commerce, and is chair of the California Governor's Foundation.

Connolly, James (1870–1916)

Irish socialist and revolutionary. He helped found the Irish Socialist Republican Party in 1896, organized a strike of transport workers in 1913 with the Irish Labour leader James Larkin (1876–1947), and took part in the Easter Rising against British rule in 1916, for which he was executed by the British.

Born in Edinburgh of Irish parents, Connolly combined a Marx-inspired socialism with a Fenian-inspired republicanism. In Dublin in 1896 he founded the Irish Socialist Republican Party, but disillusioned moved to the USA, where he was active in the International Workers of the World. Returning to Ireland in 1910, he was active in trade-union, industrial, and political affairs in Belfast and Dublin and played a key role in the establishment the Irish Labour Party.

Connolly the international socialist opposed World War I, but Connolly the Irish republican hoped to take advantage of it to begin an anti-British rebellion. Consequently he committed his small Irish Citizen Army to a joint operation with the Irish Republican Brotherhood that resulted in the 1916 Easter Rising. Connolly was a signatory of the declaration of the Irish Republic, and was responsible for its more socially radical sentiments. He was commandant general of the Dublin Division in the Rising and was wounded in the fighting. News of his execution while sitting propped up in a chair was said to have fuelled the indignation of Irish nationalists at the government's treatment of the rebels.

FURTHER READING
Greaves, C Desmond *The Life and Times of James Connolly* 1961
Morgan, A *James Connolly, A Political Biography* 1988

Conrad, Franz Xaver Josef, Count Conrad von Hötzendorf (1852–1925)

Austrian general, field marshal from 1916. Appointed chief of staff in 1906, he was largely responsible for modernizing and reorganizing the Austro-Hungarian army. Believing in an aggressive policy towards Italy and Serbia, he supported the diplomatic moves that set the war in motion. He was a good organizer and strategist but his performance in the field was poor and his successes were largely due to German support.

Constantine I (1868–1923)

King of the Hellenes (Greece) 1913–17 and 1920–22. He insisted on Greek neutrality in World War I and was forced by the rebel government of Eleuthérios Venizelos and the Allies to give up the throne. He was recalled in 1920 but after a military revolt he abdicated in favour of his son, George II. He married Sophia Dorothea, sister of Emperor William II of Germany, in 1889.

As a military leader Constantine was held responsible for the disastrous Greek campaign to regain Thessaly from the Turks in 1897, but in 1912–13 he was successful against the Turks and Bulgarians in the Balkan Wars and by the end of 1913 his dominions were double those of his father, George I, in area.

Constantinescu, Emil (1939–)

Romanian political leader, president from 1996. He unsuccessfully challenged Ion Iliescu for the presidency in 1992, but led the centre-right Democratic Convention of Romania (DCR) coalition to victory in the parliamentary and presidential elections in November 1996. The declared priorities of his new administration were to tackle corruption, increase the pace of privatization, and improve relations with neighbouring Hungary.

Constantinescu was born in Tighina, in modern-day Moldova, and brought up in the Carpathian Mountains, a stronghold of armed resistance against the communists after World War II. He was educated at the university of Bucharest where he later worked as a professor of geology. He was a low-ranking member of the communist party during the communist era, involved in propaganda work. Constantinescu's victory in 1996 was seen as a crucial stage in Romania's transition to democracy, which began with the 'partial revolution' of 1989.

Cook, Arthur James (1883–1931)

Welsh miners' leader. Born in Wookey, Somerset, he became a coal miner in the Rhondda and a leading figure in the South Wales branch of the Union of Mineworkers. A left-wing socialist, he became general secretary of the national union in 1924 and was one of the miners' leaders during the General Strike of 1926. A powerful orator, he fought successfully to hold the union together after the strike.

In 1928 Cook drew up the 'Cook–Maxton' manifesto with James Maxton of the Independent Labour Party, criticizing the Labour Party for abandoning the socialist principles of its pioneers.

FURTHER READING
Davies, Paul *A J Cook* 1987

Cook, Robin (Robert Finlayson) (1946–)

British Labour politician, foreign secretary from 1997, born in Scotland. A member of the moderate-left Tribune Group, he entered Parliament in 1974 and became a leading member of Labour's shadow cabinet, specializing in health matters. When John Smith assumed the party leadership in July 1992, Cook remained in the shadow cabinet as spokesperson for trade and industry. He became shadow foreign secretary under Smith's successor, Tony ◊Blair, in October 1994. As foreign secretary, he placed a new emphasis on human rights as part of an ethical foreign policy.

It's better to send middle-aged men abroad to bore each other than send young men abroad to kill each other.

ROBIN COOK On UN negotiations with Saddam Hussein, *Independent*, 14 February 1998

The son of a headmaster, Cook was born in Bellshill, Lanarkshire; he graduated in English literature at Edinburgh University and worked for the Workers' Educational Association before entering politics. He was MP for Edinburgh Central 1974–83 and for Livingston from 1983. He favoured the introduction of proportional representation.

Coolidge, (John) Calvin (1872–1933)

30th president of the USA 1923–29, a Republican. As governor of Massachusetts in 1919, he was responsible for crushing a Boston police strike. As Warren ◊Harding's vice president 1921–23, he succeeded to the presidency on Harding's death. He won the 1924 presidential election, and his period of office was marked by economic growth.

As president, Coolidge inherited two scandals from his predecessor: the maladministration of a bureau for war veterans, and an attempt to hand over public oil lands to private companies. Coolidge declined to run for re-election in 1928, supporting the candidacy of his secretary of the interior, Herbert ◊Hoover, who won the presidency. He was known as 'Silent Cal' because of his natural reticence.

Coolidge was born in Plymouth Notch, Vermont, the son of a farmer and storekeeper, graduated from

Amherst College in 1895, and became a barrister in 1897. He was a member of the Massachusetts House of Representatives 1907–08, mayor of Northampton 1910–11, member of the Massachusetts Senate 1912–15, and lieutenant governor of Massachusetts 1916–18.

I think the American people want a solemn ass as a President. And I think I'll go along with them.

CALVIN COOLIDGE On himself, quoted in *Time* magazine, May 1956

FURTHER READING
Coolidge, Calvin *The Autobiography of Calvin Coolidge* 1929, 1972

McCoy, Donald R *Calvin Coolidge: The Quiet President* 1967

White, William *Puritan in Babylon: The Story of Calvin Coolidge* 1938, 1973

Coombs, Herbert Cole ('Nugget') (1906–1997)
Australian economist. He was appointed governor of the Commonwealth Bank in 1949, and when the central and trading functions of the bank were separated in 1959, Coombs became governor of the Reserve Bank and chair of its board until 1968. He was also personal adviser to seven Australian prime ministers, from John ◊Curtin to Gough ◊Whitlam, chancellor of the Australian National University 1968–76, and was active in the area of Aboriginal welfare and land rights.

Born near Perth, he secured a doctorate on central banking at the London School of Economics in the 1930s and became influenced by the theories of the UK economist John Maynard Keynes. He returned to Australia in 1934 and, working for the Treasury from 1939, was in charge of postwar reconstruction 1943–49.

Cooper, (Alfred) Duff, 1st Viscount Norwich (1890–1954)
English Conservative politician. He was elected Conservative member of Parliament in 1924 and was secretary of war 1935–37, but resigned from the Admiralty in 1938 over Neville Chamberlain's appeasement policy. He served as minister for information 1940–42 under Winston Churchill and as ambassador to France 1944–47.

He was educated at Eton and Oxford and served with the Grenadier Guards in World War I. His publications include *Talleyrand* (1932), *Haig* (1935), and *King David* (1943).

Cooper, Whina Josephine (1895–1994)
New Zealand campaigner for Maori rights, and parti-

cularly for claims to traditionally-held land. Despite traditional prejudice about the role women should play, by the strength of her intellect and personality she became the leading voice of the Maori people from the 1930s and the best-known advocate of racial harmony in her country. She was founding president of the Maori Women's Welfare League in 1951, and in 1975 led a historic march to publicize Maori land claims.

Whina's potential was recognized at an early age by her father, who favoured her over her brothers, and later by the Maori minister for native affairs Sir James ◊Carroll, who financed her education. During her long life she founded many Maori pressure groups and, in addition to her campaigning, worked as a gum-digger, shopkeeper, teacher, farmer, and herbalist, was married twice and produced six children. Her success was such that she received successive honours, culminating in the DBE in 1981. Paradoxically, this international recognition, coupled with her refusal to accept a more passive female role, alienated her from some of her own people.

Copland, Douglas Berry (1894–1971)
New Zealand-born Australian economist and diplomat. He was financial adviser to the Australian government from the 1930s to the end of World War II. He spent two years as Australian minister to China 1946–48; and was the first vice chancellor of the Australian National University.

Cordero Rivadenara, León Febres
Ecuadorian politician and president 1984–88. He was an advocate of the free-market economy, but proved unable to reverse existing economic trends and widespread social inequalities and so became extremely unpopular with the electorate, the military, and members of the National Congress.

Cordero inherited a national economic crisis, with high inflation exacerbated by currency devaluation during the period of the world oil crisis when he replaced Osvaldo Hurtado Larrea as president.

Cosby, Bill (William Henry) (1937–)
US comedian and actor. His portrayal of the dashing, handsome secret agent in the television series *I Spy* (1965–68) revolutionized the way in which blacks were presented on screen. His sardonic humour, based on wry observations of domestic life and parenthood, found its widest audience in *The Cosby Show* (1984–92). He was awarded the Kennedy Center Honor in 1998.

He won three Emmy awards for the *I Spy* series and *The Cosby Show* consistently topped the national ratings and provided new role models for young black Americans. It also made him one of the richest performers in show business. Among his other TV series was *Fat Albert and the Cosby Kids* (1972–84).

He hosted the game show *You Bet Your Life* from 1992.

Cosgrave, Liam (1920–   )

Irish politician, Taoiseach (prime minister) 1973–77, leader of Fine Gael 1965–77. He signed the ill-fated Sunningdale agreement of December 1973 with the British government and representatives of the moderate Unionist and Nationalist parties in Northern Ireland. The agreement, which proposed a power-sharing executive in Northern Ireland, coupled with cross-border institutions to deal with security and common socio-economic matters, collapsed under extremist unionist pressure in 1974. At home, Cosgrave was prepared to make few concessions to reformist opinion on the Republic's social legislation, and even fewer towards traditional republicanism. He presided over severely repressive legislation to curb the Irish Republican Army (IRA) in the Republic, including the declaration of a state of emergency in September 1976.

The son of William ◊ Cosgrave, he was born in Dublin and educated at St Vincent's College, Castleknock, and King's Inns, Dublin. A member of the Dáil from 1943–81, Cosgrave was minister for external affairs 1954–57 and headed a Fine Gael–Labour coalition government from 1973, resigning as party leader when he badly lost the general election of 1977.

Cosgrave, William Thomas (1880–1965)

Irish revolutionary and politician; president of the executive council (prime minister) 1922–32, leader of Cumann na Gaedheal 1923–33, and leader of Fine Gael 1935–44.

Cosgrave was born in Dublin and educated by the Christian Brothers. He was a founding member of Sinn Féin and fought in the Easter Rising of 1916. He was sentenced to death, but his sentence was commuted, and he was elected a member of Parliament on a Sinn Féin ticket in 1917. He sat in the first Dáil (then the illegal republican parliament) in which he was minister for local government. Following the deaths of Michael Collins and Arthur Griffiths, Cosgrave succeeded them as chair of the provisional government and president of the Dáil government respectively. In September 1922 he became president of the executive council (prime minister) of the Irish Free State. He oversaw the ruthless crushing of the 'Irregular' forces during the Civil War in 1922–23, executing a great many more Irish Republican Army (IRA) men than had the British. Thereafter the Free State settled down under his leadership to a period of dull and conservative stability. Nevertheless this stability was crucial to the new state's democracy, illustrated by the peaceful transference of power to Cosgrave's old enemies in Fianna Fáil in 1932.

FURTHER READING

Collins, Stephen *The Cosgrave Legacy* 1996

Prager, Jeffrey *Building Democracy in Ireland: Political Order and Cultural Integration in a Newly Independent Nation* 1986

Costa e Silva, Artur da (1902–1969)

Brazilian military general and president 1967–69. He was renowned for his repressive government, resorting to press censorship and the initiation of emergency powers in 1968, following considerable public and congressional criticism.

Costa e Silva participated in the coup that removed President João Goulart from power in 1964. He was a former minister in the government of Castelo Branco 1964–66, and become his successor in 1967. He governed Brazil during an economically strong period, which enabled him effectively to silence the strong political opposition until 1969, when illness forced him to end his presidency.

Costello, John (1891–1976)

Irish politician, Taoiseach (prime minister) 1948–51 and 1954–57. Acts of terrorism by the Irish Republican Army (IRA) sharply increased during his second term of office. He oversaw the withdrawal of Eire from the Commonwealth and the formal change of name to the Republic of Ireland in 1949.

Born in Dublin and educated at University College Dublin, Costello was one of the senior legal advisers to the first Free State government. He was attorney general 1926–32, representing the Free State at imperial conferences and the League of Nations. He assisted in the drafting of the 1931 Statute of Westminster, which regularized relations between the British government and the dominions. Costello entered politics in 1933 as a Fine Gael TD (member of parliament) and, untainted by a civil war background, was the compromise candidate as Taoiseach in the formation of the first interparty government in 1948. He caused surprise by declaring Ireland a republic, and taking it out of the Commonwealth in 1949, while his handling of the 'Mother and Child' controversy of 1950–51 seemed to demonstrate the continuing domination of Irish life by the Roman Catholic Church. His second term of office was ended by the IRA's 'border campaign', which caused the break-up of his coalition. Thereupon Costello retired from politics and returned to legal practice.

Coty, René (1882–1962)

French centrist politician and head of state. As second president of the Fourth Republic 1954–59, Coty called on the National Assembly to invest General Charles ◊ de Gaulle as prime minister following the coup in Algiers in May 1958, and backed this with the threat of his own resignation.

A lawyer by training, his long parliamentary career from 1923 was based in his home town of Le Havre. Coty was a compromise candidate for the presidency, entering the election on the 11th ballot and elected on the 13th ballot in December 1953.

Cousins, Frank (1904–1986)

British trade unionist and politician. He was general secretary of the Transport and General Workers' Union (TGWU) 1956–69, and was minister of technology 1964–66 and Labour member of Parliament for Nuneaton 1965–66.

He resigned from the cabinet in disagreement over the government's prices and incomes policy and returned to the TGWU, also resigning his seat in Parliament. He was chair of the Community Relations Board 1968–70, a body designed to promote better race relations. He withdrew from public life in 1970.

FURTHER READING
Goodman, G *The Awkward Warrior, Frank Cousins: His Life and Times* 1979

Cowan, Edith Dircksey, born Edith Brown (1861–1932)

Australian social worker and politician. She became the first woman in Australia to be elected a member of parliament, when elected to the Western Australian Legislative Assembly in 1921, representing the National Party. As a private member, she introduced the Women's Legal Status Act in 1923, to allow women to become lawyers, but lost her seat in 1924.

The daughter of western Australia pastoralists, she helped found the Children's Protection Society in 1906.

Cox, Archibald (1912–)

US professor of law and solicitor general. He is best known as director of the office of the Watergate special prosecution force in 1973; he was fired when he demanded that President Richard Nixon turn over possibly incriminating tapes.

He was born in Plainfield, New Jersey. He served as solicitor general of the USA under presidents John F Kennedy and Lyndon Johnson 1961–65. A widely published expert on labour law, he was professor at Harvard 1946–61 and 1965–84.

Craig, James, 1st Viscount Craigavon (1871–1940)

Ulster Unionist politician, the first prime minister of Northern Ireland 1921–40. Craig became a member of Parliament in 1906, and was a highly effective organizer of Unionist resistance to Home Rule. As prime minister he carried out systematic discrimination against the Catholic minority, abolishing proportional representation in 1929 and redrawing constituency boundaries to ensure Protestant majorities. He was created Viscount in 1927.

Craxi, Bettino (Benedetto) (1934–)

Italian socialist politician, leader of the Italian Socialist Party (PSI) 1976–93, and prime minister 1983–87. In 1993 he was one of many politicians suspected of involvement in Italy's corruption network; in 1994 he was sentenced in absentia to eight and a half years in prison for accepting bribes, and in 1995 he received a further four-year sentence for corruption. In April 1996, with other former ministers, he was found guilty of further corruption charges, and received a prison sentence of eight years and three months.

The most recent charges related to a scandal over the building of Milan's underground railway in the 1980s. Craxi, living in self-imposed exile in Tunisia, rejected the charges as false.

Craxi was born in Milan, and became a member of the chamber of deputies in 1968 and general secretary of the PSI in 1976. In 1983 he became Italy's first socialist prime minister, successfully leading a broad coalition until 1987. In February 1993 he was forced to resign the PSI leadership in the face of mounting allegations of corruption.

Cresson, Edith (1934–) born Campion

French socialist politican, the first woman prime minister of France 1991–92. A longstanding supporter of François ◊Mitterrand, she served under his presidency as minister for agriculture 1981–83, tourism 1983–84, trade 1984–86, and European affairs 1988–90. Outspoken in promoting and protecting French trade, her government lacked clear direction and proved unpopular. Replaced as prime minister by former finance minister Pierre ◊Bérégovoy, Cresson was appointed to the European Commission in 1994.

Cripps, (Richard) Stafford (1889–1952)

British Labour politician, representing Bristol East 1931–52, and expelled from the Labour Party 1939–45 for supporting a 'Popular Front' against Neville Chamberlain's appeasement policy. Prominent in the Socialist League during the 1930s, he was solicitor general 1930–31, ambassador to the USSR 1940–42, minister of aircraft production 1942–45, and chancellor of the Exchequer 1947–50. He was knighted in 1930.

Inducements of a material kind can never replace the spiritual urge ... from our sense of devotion to a cause which transcends our own personal interests.

(RICHARD) STAFFORD CRIPPS Address in a Birmingham church, 11 May 1947

Born in London, Cripps was educated at Winchester and University College London. He was the son of the politician Charles Alfred Cripps (1852–1941) and of Theresa, the sister of the social reformer Beatrice Webb.

Cristiani Burkard, Alfredo (1947–)

El Salvadorean right-wing politician, president 1989–94. He negotiated, in December 1991, an end to the 12-year-long civil war with the Farabundo Martí National Liberation Front (FMNL) socialist guerrilla movement. In 1992 he settled a border dispute with Honduras.

Born in San Salvador, Cristiani studied at Georgetown University, USA. The head of the coffee producers' association, he was taken hostage by anti-government guerrillas in 1980 during the country's civil war. This spurred him into political activity, and he joined the right-wing National Republican Alliance (ARENA). He became ARENA's leader, after the defeat of Robert d'Aubuisson by José Napoleón ◊Duarte in the 1984 presidential ●lection, and led the party to success in assembly elections in 1988.

Croce, Benedetto (1866–1952)

Italian philosopher, historian, and literary critic; the personification of the intellectual opposition to fascism. A leading liberal, he served as minister of public instruction 1920–21 under Giovanni Giolitti, and his later *Storia d'Italia dal 1871 al 1915/History of Italy from 1871 to 1915* (1928) provided a sophisticated vindication of the liberal regime. His 'Manifesto of Anti-Fascist Intellectuals' (1925) marked him out as a prominent opponent of Mussolini. A monarchist, he again served as a minister under Pietro Badoglio and Ivanoe Bonomi 1943–44.

Croker, Richard (1841–1922)

Irish-born US Democratic politician. From 1886 to 1902 he was the 'boss' of Tammany Hall, the Democratic Party political machine in New York.

Croker was born in Clonakilty, County Cork, but his parents emigrated to New York when he was two years old. In 1868 he was elected alderman, and then held various municipal offices, and acquired great influence in Tammany Hall. He fought to oust 'Boss' Tweed in 1870, and after the death of Tweed's successor, John Kelly, Croker became Tammany 'boss'.

Cromer, Evelyn Baring, 1st Earl of Cromer (1841–1917)

English colonial administrator. In Egypt, he was controller general of finance 1879–80 and effective ruler as agent and consul general 1883–1907. He rescued the government from threatened bankruptcy, reorganized the administration, and laid the foundations of modern Egypt.

During his administration the Sudan was restored to Anglo-Egyptian rule, settled by the Battle of Omdurman in 1898.

Cromer was born in Norfolk, entered the Royal Artillery in 1858, was aide-de-camp to Henry Stokes in the Ionian Islands in 1861, and was appointed private secretary to the viceroy of India 1872–76. His first appointment in Egypt was as commissioner of the Egyptian public debt in 1877. He was made Baron Cromer in 1892, Viscount in 1898, and Earl in 1901.

Crosland, (Charles) Anthony (Raven) (1918–1977)

British Labour politician, president of the Board of Trade 1967–69, secretary of state for local government and regional planning 1969–70, secretary of state for the environment 1974–76, and foreign secretary 1976–77. He entered Harold Wilson's first government in 1964, and after holding junior office, he entered the cabinet as secretary of state for education.

Crosland was educated at Highgate School, London, and Trinity College, Oxford. From 1947 to 1950 he was a fellow and lecturer of Trinity College. He was Labour member of Parliament for South Gloucestershire 1950–55 and was MP for Grimsby from 1959 until his death. On the right wing of the Labour Party, he supported Hugh Gaitskell in the internal party debates over Clause Four and unilateral nuclear disarmament. He was opposition spokesperson on the environment 1970–74 and was appointed foreign secretary following the reconstruction of the government on James Callaghan's appointment as prime minister.

A man of outstanding natural gifts, he wrote a number of books and pamphlets, his main book being *The Future of Socialism* (1956), the theme of which was that Western capitalism had solved the problems both of stability and of steady progress, and also that there was no need for Labour to be identified with a 'thou shalt not' philosophy.

FURTHER READING
Crosland, Susan *Tony Crosland* 1987

Crossman, Richard Howard Stafford (1907–1974)

British Labour politician. He was minister of housing and local government 1964–66 and of health and social security 1968–70. His posthumous 'Crossman Papers' (1975) revealed confidential cabinet discussions.

By yesterday morning British troops were patrolling the streets of Belfast. I fear that once Catholics and Protestants get used to our presence they will hate us more than they hate each other.

RICHARD CROSSMAN *Diaries* 17 August 1969

Cubas Grau, Raúl (1943–)

Paraguayan politician and president 1998–99. He emphasized the urgency of his administration's aim of rejuvenating the economy and tackling the scourge of drug trafficking and poverty within the country. He also proposed the establishment of policies to reduce political corruption and increase the international image of his nation. He resigned as president and fled to Brazil after being accused of assassinating his longtime rival, Vice President Luis Maria Argaña in March 1999.

A former economy minister under Carlos ◊Wasmosy, he is a member of the dominant Asociación Nacional Republicana (ANR; Colorado Party), and was originally its vice-presidential candidate in the 1998 election campaign until the presidential candidate, Lino César ◊Oviedo, was removed in mid-campaign. He is an engineer by profession.

Cudlipp, Hugh, Baron of Aldingbourne (1913–1998)

Welsh publishing and newspaper magnate, a dynamic pioneer of British tabloid journalism. He was chair of Odhams Press, Daily Mirror Newspapers, and the International Publishing Corporation.

Cudlipp was managing editor of the *Sunday Express* 1950–52, and editorial director of the *Daily Mirror* and *Sunday Pictorial* 1959–63. His books include *Publish and Be Damned* (1955), *At Your Peril* (1965), and his autobiography, *Walking on the Water* (1976). He was made a life peer in 1974.

Cunningham, Evelyn

US writer and reporter, best known as the 'Lynching Editor' of the *Pittsburgh Courier* in the 1940s and 1950s, when it was the most influential newspaper in black America. She earned her name for stories on the fight for equal rights in the early 1960s, reporting on a variety of rights issues, including the school desegregation fight in Birmingham, Alabama, the Montgomery bus boycott, and the murders of black sharecroppers who exercised their right to vote. In 1975 she served on President Richard ◊Nixon's Committee on the Rights and Responsibilities of Women, helping to write the groundbreaking report 'A Matter of Simple Justice'. A founder of the Coalition of 100 Black Women, Cunningham helped forge coalitions of women of all ethnic and racial backgrounds.

As a special assistant to Governor Rockefeller and director of the Women's Unit, she organized a state woman's political conference and cooperated with the National Organization of Women (NOW) and other women's organizations to create a receptive climate for feminism. In the 1990s she was actively involved with several organizations, including the Citizen's Committee of New York, Resources for Midlife and Older Women, and Richard Allen's Center of Culture and Arts.

Cunningham, John A ('Jack') (1939–)

British Labour politician, secretary of state for agriculture 1997–98, minister for the cabinet office and chancellor of the Duchy of Lancaster from 1998. He was arguably the most experienced member of Tony Blair's first cabinet, having served as parliamentary private secretary to James Callaghan 1972–76 and as parliamentary undersecretary for energy 1976–79. He was elected to the Labour shadow cabinet in 1983 and afterwards shadowed environment 1983–89, the leader of the House of Commons 1989–92, foreign and Commonwealth affairs 1992–94, trade and industry 1994–95, and national heritage 1995–97.

Born in Jarrow, he studied at Bede College, Durham University. He was a research fellow at Durham 1966–68 before deciding to abandon an academic career to become a full-time officer for the General and Municipal Workers' Union (GMWU). This led him into politics. He represented Whitehaven 1970–83 and Copeland from 1983 in the House of Commons. He was promoted in the July 1998 cabinet reshuffle to minister of state for the cabinet office and chancellor of the Duchy of Lancaster, with the task of 'ensuring that the prime minister's objectives are delivered'.

Cunninghame-Graham, Robert Bontine (1852–1936)

Scottish writer, politician, and adventurer. He wrote many travel books based on his experiences in Texas and Argentina 1869–83 and in Spain and Morocco 1893–98. He became the first president of the Scottish Labour Party in 1888 and the first president of the Scottish National Party in 1928.

Cunninghame-Graham was born in London and educated at Harrow, but before he was 17 he set off to tour South America, and became a rancher. In 1884 he inherited the family estate of Ardoch in Dumbartonshire, settled there, and entered politics. From 1886 to 1892 he was member of Parliament for Northeast Lanarkshire, and with Keir ◊Hardie organized the Scottish Labour Party. In 1887 he was imprisoned as a ringleader in riots in Trafalgar Square, London. He died in Buenos Aires, Argentina.

Cuno, Wilhelm Carl Josef (1876–1933)

German industrialist and politician who was briefly chancellor of the Weimar Republic in 1923.

Cuomo, Mario Matthew (1932–)

US Democrat politician. He was governor of New York State 1983–95. One of his party's foremost thinkers, he was for many years seen as a future president. His key concern was that rich and poor America should unite.

Cuomo was born in New York and became a lawyer. Following the publication of *Forest Hills Diary: The Crisis of Law Income Housing* (1974), an account of his assessment of a proposed public housing project in a middle-class community, he became secretary of state of the state of New York, acting as the governor's negotiator in statewide crises. In 1994 he wrote *The New York Idea: An Experiment in Democracy*.

Curley, James Michael (1874–1958)

US Democratic politician. He was a member of the US House of Representatives 1912–14, and several times mayor of Boston between 1914 and 1934, when he was elected governor. He lost a bid for the US Senate in 1936 and did not hold political office again until elected to the House in 1942. His fourth and last mayoral term began in 1946, during which time he spent six months in federal prison on a mail-fraud conviction.

Born in Boston, Curley became active in the local Democratic party soon after leaving school. He served in the state legislature 1902–03, on the Boston Board of Aldermen 1904–09, and on the Boston City Council 1910–11. The flamboyant Curley's political career inspired Edwin O'Connor's *The Last Hurrah* (1956).

Curtin, John Joseph Ambrose (1885–1945)

Australian Labor politician, prime minister and minister of defence 1941–45. He was elected leader of the Labor Party in 1935. As prime minister, he organized the mobilization of Australia's resources to meet the danger of Japanese invasion during World War II. He died in office before the end of the war.

During the war he clashed with UK prime minister Winston Churchill over the latter's view that Australia was dispensable, withdrawing Australian troops from the Middle East in 1942 to help defend against the Japanese threat at home. At the same time, he reassessed the need for US support and invited General Douglas MacArthur to establish his headquarters in Australia.

The son of Irish Catholic immigrants, he left school in Melbourne at the age of 13. He was largely self-educated and was an active socialist and union organizer from an early age. He was elected to the federal parliament at the fourth attempt in 1928, lost his seat in 1931, but re-entered the house in 1934.

FURTHER READING
Lee, N E *John Curtin: Saviour of Australia* 1983

Curzon, George Nathaniel, 1st Marquess Curzon of Kedleston (1859–1925)

British Conservative politician, viceroy of India 1899–1905. During World War I, he was a member of the cabinet 1916–19. As foreign secretary 1919–24, he negotiated the Treaty of Lausanne with Turkey.

As viceroy of India, Curzon introduced various reforms, including the creation of the North-West Frontier Province, reorganization of Indian finance, and the establishment of the imperial cadet corps. He resigned this post in 1905, after a dispute with Horatio Kitchener, commander of the British forces in India.

The British Empire is under Providence the greatest instrument for good that the world has seen.

GEORGE CURZON Dedication of his book *Problems of the Far East*

The eldest son of the 4th Baron Scarsdale, Curzon was born in Kedleston, Derbyshire, and educated at Eton public school and at Oxford University. He became private secretary to the Marquess of Salisbury in 1885, and sat in Parliament as Conservative member for Southport 1886–98. On his return to England from India, Curzon became a prominent member of the opposition in the House of Lords. He was elected chancellor of Oxford University in 1907. When Andrew Bonar Law retired as prime minister in 1923, Curzon hoped to succeed him, but the post went to Stanley Baldwin. He was created Baron (Irish peerage) in 1898, Earl in 1911, and Marquess in 1921.

FURTHER READING
Dilks, David *Curzon of India* 1969
Gilmour, David *Curzon* 1994
Rose, Kenneth *Superior Person* 1969

D

D'Abernon, Edgar Vincent (1857–1941)

English financier and diplomat. He became ambassador to Berlin, Germany, in 1920, and was instrumental in achieving the stabilization of the Deutschmark after World War I, realizing the Dawes Plan (see Charles ◊Dawes), negotiating the Anglo-German commercial treaty of 1924, and initiating the Pact of Locarno. He was created a peer in 1914.

D'Abernon was born in Slinfold, Sussex, studied at Eton, and served in the Coldstream Guards for five years. In 1882 he was appointed president of the council of the Ottoman Public Department and in 1883 financial adviser to the Egyptian government. In 1889 he became governor of the Imperial Ottoman Bank. He was elected Conservative member of Parliament for Exeter in 1899 but was defeated in 1906 and again in 1910, when he contested Colchester as a Liberal.

Daladier, Edouard (1884–1970)

French Radical politician, prime minister in 1933, 1934, and 1938–40, when he signed the Munich Agreement in 1938 (ceding the Sudeten districts of Czechoslovakia to Germany). After declaring war on Germany in September 1939, his government failed to aid Poland and, at home, imprisoned pacifists and communists. After his government resigned in March 1940, Daladier was arrested by the Vichy authorities, tried with Léon Blum at Riom in 1942, then deported to Germany 1943–45. He was re-elected as a deputy 1946–58.

Son of a baker and an *aggrégé* in history and geography, Daladier came into politics after military service in World War I. Elected deputy for Vaucluse 1919–40, he was a minister in the centre-left coalitions of 1924–26 and 1932–33, and then brought his party into the Popular Front (with socialists and communists) from 1934, serving as minister of defence 1936–38. As prime minister, he shifted to a centre-right alliance.

Dalai Lama (1935–)

See page 108.

Daley, Richard Joseph (1902–1976)

US politician and controversial mayor of Chicago 1955–76. He built a formidable political machine and ensured a Democratic presidential victory in 1960 when J F Kennedy was elected. He hosted the turbulent national Democratic convention in 1968.

Born in Chicago, Daley became involved in local Democratic politics at an early age. He attended law school at DePaul University, gaining admission to the bar in 1933. He served in the Illinois legislature 1936–46. He was Cook County clerk 1935–55 before being elected mayor of Chicago, remaining in office until his death. His son, Richard M Daley, was appointed mayor of Chicago in 1989.

Dalton, (Edward) Hugh (John Neale), Baron Dalton (1887–1962)

British Labour politician and economist, born in Wales. Chancellor of the Exchequer from 1945, he oversaw nationalization of the Bank of England, but resigned in 1947 after making a disclosure to a lobby correspondent before a budget speech. He was created Baron in 1960.

FURTHER READING

Dalton, Hugh *High Tide and After* 1962, *Call Back Yesterday* 1973
Pimlott, B *Hugh Dalton* 1985
Pimlott, B (ed) *The Political Diary of Hugh Dalton* 1987

D'Annunzio, Gabriele (1863–1938)

Italian poet, novelist, and dramatist. Elected deputy in 1897, he associated himself with the right-wing nationalism of the pre-war years, and was a controversial advocate of interventionism 1914–15, turning public opinion to the side of the Allies in 1915. After serving in World War I, he led an expedition of volunteers in 1919 to capture the Dalmatian port of Fiume, which he held until 1921. His style of rule prefigured fascism, especially in its aestheticization of politics. He became a national hero, and was created Prince of Montenevoso in 1924. Influenced by the German philosopher Nietzsche's writings, he later became an ardent exponent of fascism.

FURTHER READING

Ledeen, Michael A *The First Duce* 1977

Danquah, Joseph Kwame Kyeretwi Boakye (1895–1965)

Ghanaian nationalist leader and leader of the opposition after independence. An outstanding scholar, he gained degrees in philosophy and law from English universities. Returning to Ghana in 1931 he founded the *West African Times* and became involved in nationalist politics. In 1947 he founded the United Gold Coast Convention (UGCC), the major party until Kwame ◊Nkrumah broke away from the UGCC to found the Convention People's Party in 1949. Following his election to parliament in 1951 he became a major opposition leader. He was opposition candidate in the 1960 elections but lost to Nkrumah. In 1961 he was detained for a year without charge. He was re-arrested in 1964 and died in prison in 1965.

Danquah was a member of the royal family of Akyem Abuakwa.

Darling, Alistair Maclean (1953–)

British Labour politician and lawyer, chief secretary to the Treasury 1997–98, and secretary of state for social security from 1998. He was chair of the Lothian Regional Transport Committee 1986–87 before being elected to the House of Commons in 1987, representing Edinburgh Central. He served as opposition spokesperson on home affairs 1988–92 and on the Treasury, economic affairs and the City 1992–96, and as shadow chief secretary to the Treasury 1996–97.

After graduating in law at the University of Aber-deen, he practised for a short period before becoming active in local politics. He was promoted to secretary of state for social security in the July 1998 cabinet reshuffle and had the difficult task of overseeing welfare reform.

Darnand, André Joseph Auguste (1897–1945)

French admiral and extreme right-wing activist, founder of the Service d'Ordre Légionnaire (SOL) in 1941 and its successor, the Milice Française in 1943, whose security police collaborated with the German army and Gestapo. Decorated for bravery in World War I, Darnand moved in the interwar period between the Action Française's leagues, Jacques Doriot's fascistic Parti Populaire Français, and the Cagoule. After the 1940 Armistice he supported Henri ◊Pétain and joined the Waffen SS as an officer in 1943, taking the oath of allegiance to Hitler before becoming the Vichy minister of interior in 1944. At the Liberation he fled to Germany, was captured in Italy and returned to France, where he was tried and executed by firing squad in October 1945.

Darrow, Clarence Seward (1857–1938)

US lawyer, born in Ohio, a champion of liberal causes and defender of the underdog. He defended many

---

◆ DALAI LAMA, TITLE OF TENZIN GYATSO (TIBETAN 'OCEANIC GURU') (1935–) ◆

Spiritual leader of Tibetan Buddhism and political ruler of Tibet from 1940 until 1959, when he went into exile in protest against Chinese annexation and oppression.

The Dalai Lama is the title of the second hierarch of the Gelugpa (Yellow Hat) monastic order. Tenzin Gyatso, who was born Bstan-Dzin Gyatso into a peasant family at Taktser, north of Lhasa, was identified by monks to be the Reincarnation of the Compassionate in 1937, becoming the 14th Dalai Lama. He was enthroned in Lhasa in 1940, but until 1950 his sovereign powers were exercised by a Chinese-dominated regency.

He temporarily fled 1950–51 when the Chinese communist Red Army overran Tibet, but in May 1951 negotiated a settlement with the Chinese communist government, under which Tibet was promised autonomy within the new People's Republic. He served as titular ruler of Tibet until March 1959, when, following brutal suppression of a local uprising against Chinese rule, he, along with thousands of Tibetan refugees, made a dramatic escape from Lhasa to India. He then settled at Dharmsala in the Punjab, India, where he set up a government-in-exile. China offered to lift the ban on his living in Tibet, providing that he refrained from calling for Tibet's independence. The Dalai Lama stated that he would never return to Tibet as a mere figurehead ruler and continued to press for self-government in internal affairs and the cessation of forcible Sinification in Tibet. He concerned himself closely with the welfare of the many Tibetans who have fled into exile.

He was awarded the Nobel Peace Prize in 1989 for his non-violent campaign for self-government. Tibetan Buddhists believe that each Dalai Lama is a reincarnation of his predecessor and also of Avalokitesvara, an emanation of Buddha. When he dies, his soul is believed to enter the body of a newborn boy, who is identified through traditional tests. His deputy is called the ◊Panchen Lama. The first to bear the title of Dalai Lama was Sonam Gyatso, in 1578.

FURTHER READING

Avedon, J *In Exile from the Land of Snows* 1984
Dalai Lama *Freedom in Exile* 1990, *Violence and Compassion* 1996
Goodman, M H *The Last Dalai Lama* 1986
Levenson, C B *The Dalai Lama: A Biography* 1988

trade-union leaders, including Eugene ◊Debs in 1894. He was counsel for the defence in the Nathan Leopold and Richard Loeb murder trial in Chicago in 1924, and in the Scopes monkey trial. Darrow matched wits in the latter trial with prosecution attorney William Jennings ◊Bryan. He was an opponent of capital punishment.

Das, Chitta Ranjan (1870–1925)

Bengali patriot and politician. He participated in the campaign against the partition of Bengal, and chaired the Bengal Provincial Congress in 1917 and the Indian National Congress in 1918. He joined Mahatma Gandhi's noncooperation movement in 1920 and helped form the Swarajiya Party in 1922. Opposed to Hindu communalism, he was popular with both Muslim and Hindu communities in Bengal. He was elected mayor of Calcutta City Corporation in 1924.

Imprisoned 1921–22, he emerged to help form the Swarajiya Party to contest district and provincial council elections (then boycotted by the Indian National Congress). As mayor of Calcutta City, he came to an agreement with Gandhi that allowed both Swarajists and Gandhians to campaign from the Congress platform.

Called to the bar in 1894, he soon acquired a reputation for skilfully representing nationalists, such as ◊Aurobindo Ghose (1908), accused of terrorism by the British colonial government in India.

Although he himself rejected violence, many of his followers were either involved in terrorism or openly advocated the use of violence in opposition to colonial rule. A strong supporter of the trade-union movement, he campaigned on behalf of railway workers and labourers on the Assam tea plantations. He and his followers were thus a powerful force for radicalism within the Indian nationalist movement, a radicalism that grew in the years following his death.

His achievements in forging unity between Hindus and Muslims in Bengal survived his death by only a few years: factionalism and violence led ultimately to the partition of the province on independence in 1947.

Daud Khan, Sardar Muhammad (1909–1978)

Afghan prime minister 1953–63 and president 1973–78. He was a cousin of King Muhammad Zahir Shah (ruled 1933–73). Opposition to his authoritarian rule forced his resignation from the premiership in 1963. With support from the Pathan tribes in the northwest and Soviet backing, he overthrew the monarchy in July 1973 and declared the country a republic. He was assassinated in a military coup.

Davies, Ron (1946–)

British Labour politician, born in Wales, secretary of state for Wales 1997–98. After serving as a local government councillor 1969–84 he was elected to the House of Commons in 1983, representing Caerphilly.

Dalai Lama. *Rex*

He was placed in the Whips Office 1985–87 and then made steady progress within the party. He was opposition spokesman on agriculture and rural affairs 1987–92, to which responsibility for food issues was added in 1989. Then, after a short period as shadow minister for agriculture, he served as shadow secretary of state for Wales 1992–97. In 1997 he oversaw the successful introduction of legislation to create an elected assembly with devolved powers in Wales, but in 1998, in controversial circumstances, he resigned as the Labour candidate for the leadership of the National Assembly for Wales and as secretary of state for Wales.

Born near Newport, south Wales, Davies was educated at Portsmouth Polytechnic and the University College of Wales, Cardiff. He was a school teacher 1968–70, and then a Workers' Educational Association tutor/organizer 1970–74, and Further Education Adviser to the Mid-Glamorgan Local Education Authority 1974–83.

Davis, Angela Yvonne (1944–)

US left-wing activist for black American rights, prominent in the student movement of the 1960s. In 1970 she went into hiding after being accused of supplying guns used in the murder of a judge, who had been seized as a hostage in an attempt to secure the release of three black convicts. She was captured, tried, and acquitted. At the University of California she studied under

Herbert ◊Marcuse, and was assistant professor of philosophy at the University of California at Los Angeles 1969–70. In 1980 she was the Communist vice-presidential candidate.

Davison, Emily Wilding (1872–1913)

English militant suffragette who died after throwing herself under the king's horse at the Derby at Epsom (she was trampled by the horse). She joined the Women's Social and Political Union in 1906 and served several prison sentences for militant action such as stone throwing, setting fire to pillar boxes, and bombing David Lloyd George's country house.

Her coffin was carried through London draped in the colours of the suffragette movement, purple, white, and green. It was escorted by 2,000 uniformed suffragettes. Davison was a teacher with degrees from Oxford and London universities.

Dawes, Charles Gates (1865–1951)

US Republican politician. In 1923 the Allied Reparations Commission appointed him president of the committee that produced the Dawes Plan, a loan of $200 million that enabled Germany to pay enormous war debts after World War I. It reduced tensions temporarily in Europe but was superseded by the Young Plan (which reduced the total reparations bill) in 1929. Dawes was made US vice president (under Calvin Coolidge) in 1924, received the Nobel Peace Prize in 1925, and was ambassador to the UK 1929–32.

Dawes was born in Marietta, Ohio. During World War I he became a major of engineers in France in 1917, a member of the Allied Purchasing Board, and brigadier general in 1918.

Dayan, Moshe (1915–1981)

Israeli general and politician. As minister of defence in 1967 and 1969–74, he was largely responsible for the victory over neighbouring Arab states in the 1967 Six-Day War, but he was criticized for Israel's alleged unpreparedness in the 1973 October War and resigned along with Prime Minister Golda ◊Meir.

He returned to office, as foreign minister in 1977, but resigned two years later in protest over the refusal of the government of Menachem Begin to negotiate with the Palestinians.

FURTHER READING
Dayan, M *Diary of the Sinai Campaign* 1966, *My Father, His Daughter* 1985
Slater, R *Warrior Statesman: The Life of Moshe Dayan* 1992

Deakin, Alfred (1856–1919)

Australian politician, prime minister 1903–04, 1905–08, and 1909–10. In his second administration, he enacted legislation on defence and pensions.

Educated at Melbourne University, he worked first as a barrister and then as a journalist before being elected to the Victorian parliament as a Liberal, in 1879. He held ministerial posts in the 1880s and entered the Commonwealth parliament in 1901, holding his seat until 1912.

Deakin, Arthur (1890–1955)

English trade-union leader. He became national secretary of the General Workers' Group of the Transport and General Workers' Union in 1932, and succeeded Ernest Bevin as general secretary of the union 1940–55.

He was a constant opponent of communism within his own union and the trade-union movement as a whole.

Deakin was born in Sutton Coldfield, West Midlands. He began work in a steel factory at 13 and became an active socialist and trade-union official from 1919.

FURTHER READING
Gabay, A C *The Mystic Life of Alfred Deakin* 1992

Dean, John (1926–)

US civil servant and counsel to US president Richard ◊Nixon. Dean testified before the Ervin Committee that President Nixon had been involved in the cover-up over the Watergate affair. Dean's frank and damaging testimony almost single-handedly forced Nixon's resignation.

De Bono, Emilio (1866–1944)

Italian general and Fascist politician. He took part in Mussolini's 'March on Rome' in 1922 and was later governor of Tripolitania 1925–28. As colonial minister 1929–35, he spent much of his time preparing for the conquest of Abyssinia (Ethiopia), and commanded the Italian forces in Abyssinia in 1935. He voted against Mussolini in 1943 and was shot as a traitor.

Debray, Régis (1941–)

French Marxist theorist. He was associated with Che ◊Guevara in the revolutionary movement in Latin America in the 1960s. In 1967 he was sentenced to 30 years' imprisonment in Bolivia but was released after three years. His writings on Latin American politics include *Strategy for Revolution* (1970). He became a specialist adviser to President Mitterrand of France on Latin American affairs.

Debré, Michel Jean-Pierre (1912–)

French Gaullist politician and prime minister. He was minister of justice in 1958, the chief author of the Fifth Republic's constitution and its first prime minister 1959–62. He accepted Charles ◊de Gaulle's negotiations for Algerian independence despite his own attachment to keeping Algeria French. He was later minister of finance and deputy premier 1966–68, minister for foreign affairs 1968–69, and minister of defence 1969–73 before standing for the presidency in 1981, when he was eliminated on the first ballot.

Born in Paris into a medical family, Debré graduated in law and public administration, then joined the Conseil d'Etat. Active in the Resistance and an advocate of constitutional and administrative reform, he established the Ecole Nationale d'Adminstration in 1945 to provide a unified and modernized training for a 'fast-track' civil service elite. Elected as a senator 1945–58, he was a vocal supporter of de Gaulle and became closely involved in preparing his return to government in 1958.

Debs, Eugene V(ictor) (1855–1926)

US labour leader and socialist who organized the Social Democratic Party in 1897. He was the founder and first president of the American Railway Union in 1893, and was imprisoned for six months in 1894 for defying a federal injunction to end the Pullman strike in Chicago. He was socialist candidate for the presidency in every election from 1900 to 1920, except that of 1916.

I said then, I say now, that while there is a lower class, I am in it; while there is a criminal element, I am of it; while there is a soul in prison, I am not free.

EUGENE DEBS Speech at his trial, 14 September 1918

Debs was born in Terre Haute, Indiana, and was elected to the Indiana state legislature in 1884. He opposed US intervention in World War I and was imprisoned in 1918 for allegedly advocating resistance to conscription, but was pardoned by President Warren Harding in 1921. In 1920 he polled nearly a million votes, the highest socialist vote ever in a US presidential election, despite having to conduct the campaign from a federal penitentiary in Atlanta, Georgia.

Deby, Idriss (1952–)

Chadian soldier and politician, president from 1990. As founder and leader of the Patriotic Salvation Movement (MPS), Deby seized power in an armed coup. His presidency was constitutionally endorsed when he won Chad's first democratic presidential election in July 1996.

Deby was born in eastern Chad, and joined the army at the age of 20, later training as a pilot in France. He returned to Chad in 1978 and supported Hissène Habré's opposition to President Goukouni Oueddi, enabling Habré to come to power in 1982. Deby then became commander in chief of the armed forces and military adviser to President Habré, but fled the country in 1989 after being accused of plotting a coup. He founded the MPS in 1990 and, from a base in

Sudan, ousted Habré at the end of the same year, making himself interim head of state. He promised an eventual return to civilian rule, and in 1994 signed a treaty of friendship with Col Khaddhafi of Libya. He was elected president in July 1996 under a new multiparty constitution, based on the French dual-executive model.

Defferre, Gaston Paul Charles (1910–1986)

French socialist politician. As interior minister 1981–86 he introduced a major decentralization and regionalization package (the 'Defferre Laws'), breaking with the French Left's Jacobin tradition of reliance on a strong, centralized state.

Based in Marseilles, its mayor and then deputy 1945–86, Defferre sought to modernize and adapt his party, the Section Française de l'Internationale Ouvrière (SFIO), to the Fifth Republic through an alliance with the centre against the Gaullists in the mid-1960s. This attempt failed. From 1971 he was eclipsed by François Mitterrand in the refounded Socialist Party (PS), following his very weak showing on the first ballot of the 1969 presidential elections.

De Gasperi, Alcide (1881–1954)

Italian politician. A founder of the Christian Democrat Party, he was prime minister 1945–53 and worked for European unification.

FURTHER READING
Carrillo, E *Alcide De Gasperi, the Long Apprenticeship* 1965

Dehaene, Jean-Luc (1940–)

Belgian politician, prime minister from 1992. He successfully negotiated constitutional changes to make Belgium a federal state. His centre-left coalition was re-elected in 1995.

Born in Montpellier, France, and educated at the University of Namur, he entered politics by joining the trade-union wing of the Flemish Christian Socialists (CVP). He was a government adviser 1972–81, establishing a reputation as a skilful mediator. In this role in 1988 he negotiated the formation of a five-party coalition, led by Wilfried ◊Martens, and became his deputy. When the coalition collapsed in 1992 he constructed another three-party government which he led.

Dehaene came to the notice of a wider public in 1994 when he was proposed by Germany and France as the successor to European Commission president Jacques Delors. Seeing Dehaene as a 'federalist', UK prime minister John Major vetoed his appointment, in contrast to the other 11 European Union heads of government.

de Klerk, F(rederik) W(illem) (1936–)

South African National Party politician, president 1989–94. Projecting himself as a pragmatic conserva-

F W de Klerk, 1990. *Rex*

tive who sought gradual reform of the apartheid system, he won the September 1989 elections for his party, but with a reduced majority. In February 1990 he ended the ban on the African National Congress (ANC) opposition movement and released its effective leader Nelson ◊ Mandela. By June 1991 he had repealed all racially discriminating laws. After a landslide victory for Mandela and the ANC in the first universal suffrage elections in April 1994, de Klerk became second executive deputy president.

He was awarded the Nobel Prize for Peace jointly with Mandela in 1993.

Trained as a lawyer, he entered the South African parliament in 1972. He served in the cabinets of B J Vorster and P W Botha 1978–89, replacing Botha as party leader in February 1989 and as state president in August 1989.

He entered into negotiations with the ANC in December 1991, and in March 1992 a nationwide whites-only referendum gave him a clear mandate to proceed with plans for major constitutional reform to end white minority rule. In February 1993 he and Mandela agreed to the formation of a government of national unity after multiracial elections in 1994, but

◆ DE GAULLE, CHARLES ANDRÉ JOSEPH MARIE (1890–1970) ◆

French general, wartime leader, and head of state. A professional soldier with a distinctive vision of France's 'grandeur', General de Gaulle led the Free French Forces and the Resistance movement in World War II and headed France's Provisional Government 1944–46. He returned to government in June 1958 to found the Fifth Republic, following a military rebellion in Algeria, and served as its first president 1958–69.

Born in Lille into the landed gentry, de Gaulle was severely wounded and taken prisoner in World War I. He had trained at the Saint-Cyr military college and returned to a lecturing post there in the 1920s, winning a reputation as a forceful critic of military orthodoxy and publishing a subtle analysis of the psychology of military leadership, *Le Fil de l'epee/The Edge of the Sword* (1932). On 18 June 1940 he made a historic radio broadcast from London, urging French patriots at home and abroad to defy any armistice with Germany, declaring 'France has lost a battle; she has not lost the war'. In Algiers in 1943, outmanoeuvring his US-backed rival, General Giraud, he formed a broad-based Provisional Government. He entered Paris in triumph on 26 August 1945.

His government, the first in France to include communist ministers, nationalized much of the energy, transport, banking, and insurance sectors; introduced indicative economic planning under Jean Monnet; and extended the franchise to French women. Frustrated by the inter-party bargaining within his government, de Gaulle resigned as prime minister in January 1946. The following year he founded the Rassemblement du Peuple Français (RPF) to mobilize opposition to the new Fourth Republic but disbanded this movement in 1953 and withdrew from politics.

Responding to calls from both President René Coty and the military rebels in Algiers, de Gaulle returned to power on 2 June 1958 as the Fourth Republic's last premier, determined to make the French presidency the powerhouse of his new Republic. This was only partially achieved by the 1958 constitution, drafted under the supervision of his justice minister, Michel Debré, and having reformed the presidential electoral system in 1962, he became the first French president directly elected by universal suffrage in 1965. He also sought to reassert France's voice in international affairs. In Algeria, he was able to conclude a negotiated independence, but only

Charles de Gaulle in Algiers after his election as French president, June 1958. *AKG London*

in May 1995 he withdrew the National Party from the governing coalition in order to develop a 'strong and vigilant opposition'.

Despite winning the Nobel Peace Prize, de Klerk's reputation was badly damaged by revelations to the Truth and Reconcilliation Commission, the body charged with exposing the truth about the apartheid years. In August 1997 de Klerk resigned as leader of the National Party, claiming that he was retiring to rid the Afrikaner-dominated party of the remains of apartheid. He was succeeded by Marthinus van Schalkwyk in September 1997.

De La Madrid Hurtado, Miguel (1934–)

Mexican politician, president 1982–88. As minister of planning and budget under José ◊López Portillo, he formulated an economic development plan that sought to use Mexico's oil wealth to promote economic growth. A conservative technocrat who

could be trusted to carry on the politics of his predecessor, he was chosen as the candidate of the ruling Institutional Revolutionary Party (PRI) in 1981.

Born in Colima, Mexico, he studied law in Mexico City and public administration at Harvard, USA. He became an adviser to the Bank of Mexico, then entered government service in the ministry of finance.

de León Carpio, Ramiro (1942–)

Guatemalan centrist politician, president 1993–96. Between 1984 and 1986 he was a deputy in the Constituent Assembly and secretary general of the centrist National Political Union of the Centre (UCN), and then, in June 1993, when serving as a human-rights ombudsman, was appointed president by the National Congress. This followed the military's ousting of President Jorge ◊Serrano Elias, who had attempted to impose an authoritarian regime. De Léon headed a national unity government, but became increasingly dependent on military support as guerrilla activity by the Guatemalan Revolutionary National Unity (URNG) movement increased. He was replaced by Alvaro ◊Arzú Irigoyen, who was popularly elected president in January 1996.

Born in Guatemala City, he studied law at Rafael Landirer Catholic University. He held a variety of legal, academic and bureaucratic positions, before helping to form UCN in 1983.

Deliyiannis, Theodoros (1826–1905)

Greek politician, five times prime minister 1885–86, 1890, 1895–97, 1902–03, and 1904–05. His political career was based on attempting to recover Greek provinces from Turkey. He was assassinated by opponents of his laws to restrict gambling.

after four more years of bloody war (and a further, unsuccessful, military rebellion led by General Salan in 1961). Hostile to the USA's dominance within the Atlantic Alliance and to 'Anglo-Saxon' influence in Europe, de Gaulle withdrew French forces from the North Atlantic Treaty Organization (NATO) in 1966, sustained an independent French nuclear capability, and unilaterally vetoed UK entry into the European Economic Community twice, in 1963 and 1967. He also successfully resisted the introduction of majority voting in the European Council of Ministers in 1965.

De Gaulle's authority was dramatically shaken when, in this period of rising national prosperity, violent confrontations between students and the forces of order on the streets of Paris sparked a massive strike movement in May 1968. His party nevertheless won a large parliamentary majority in the June parliamentary elections but de Gaulle resigned the following year when his proposals for senate and regional reform were defeated in a referendum. He retired once more to Colombey-les-Deux-Eglises and was succeeded as president by his former prime minister, Georges Pompidou. He published his three-volume *Mémoires de guerre/War Memoirs* (1954–59) and his two-volume *Mémoires d'espoir/Memoirs of Hope* (1970–71).

Dellinger, David (1915–   )

US pacifist, peace activist, editor, and author. He was jailed for draft resistance during World War II and was an outspoken opponent of US involvement in Vietnam. He published widely, promoting pacifism and nonviolence.

He was born in Wakefield, Massachusetts, and graduated from Yale University, prior to studying at Oxford University, Yale Divinity School, and Union Theological Seminary. His passionate pacifism would lead him to the forefront of militant, nonviolent activism. Upon his release from jail in 1945 he formed the Libertarian Press printing cooperative. In 1956 he became editor and publisher of *Liberation*, a major voice of radical pacifism. He was an important link to the North Vietnamese government and facilitated the release of US prisoners of war. He was jailed again for being the leader of an antiwar demonstration that erupted into a riot in Chicago, but his conviction was overturned. He became editor of *Seven Days* magazine (1975–80). In the 1980s he moved to Vermont to teach and write. His books include *Revolutionary Non violence* (1970), *More Power Than We Know* (1975), and *From Yale to Jail* (1993).

Delors, Jacques Lucien Jean (1925–   )

French socialist politician, economy and finance minister 1981–84 under François Mitterrand's presidency, and president of the European Commission 1985–94, when he oversaw significant budgetary reform, the introduction of the Single European Market, and the negotiation and ratification of the 1992 Maastricht Treaty on European Union.

Active in social Catholic movements influenced by Emmanuel Mounier, Delors worked for the Bank of France in 1944 and then as head of research for the French Catholic Labour Confederation (CFTC) in 1957, before joining the staff of Gaullist prime minister Jacques Chaban-Delmas as his social affairs adviser 1969–72. A member of the Socialist Party from 1974 and elected to the European Parliament in 1979, he was the architect of the early economic U-turn of the French Left, introducing an austerity programme ('*rigueur*') in June 1982 as well as three successive

---

◆ DENG XIAOPING OR TENG HSIAO-PING (1904–1997) ◆

Chinese communist politician, 'paramount leader' 1978–97.

A veteran of the 1934–35 Long March and a survivor of 'anti-rightist' purges during the Cultural Revolution 1966–69, Deng re-emerged after the death of ◊Mao Zedong in 1976 to become the country's 'paramount leader' from 1978. Twice named 'Man of the Year' by *Time* magazine, Deng mixed a consistent belief in the need for the Chinese Communist Party (CCP) to maintain firm centralized political control, to avert the threat of chaos, with pragmatic encouragement of market economic forces, with the aim of strengthening China. During the 'Deng era' 1978–97, Chinese living standards were transformed, with annual GDP growth exceeding 9%, enabling 200 million people to work their way out of absolute poverty. However, Deng also sanctioned, in June 1989, the brutal military crackdown on prodemocracy demonstrators in Tiananmen Square, Beijing, in which 2,000 unarmed students were massacred and which greatly tarnished his reputation in the West.

Born in Jiading, in the fertile and traditionally rebellious southwestern province of Sichuan, Deng was the son of an educated, middle-class minor landowner. He went to Paris in 1920 for six years as a worker-student and became a committed Marxist, changing his first name from Ziansheng to Xiaoping ('Little Peace') and forming in 1922, along with ◊Zhou Enlai, an overseas branch of the CCP. In 1926 Deng studied in Moscow and, after joining Mao at Jiangxi in 1930, participated in the 1934–35 Long March – the escape from Jiang Jie Shi's (Chiang Kai-shek's) nationalist forces – and served as a political commissar in the communist Red Army during the liberation struggle and civil war of 1937–49. A forceful and blunt-speaking figure, Deng's skills were administrative rather than military, and after the Communist takeover in 1949, he worked closely alongside the head of state Liu Shaoqi and Prime Minister Zhou Enlai. He was general secretary of the CCP 1956–66, heading the policy-framing secretariat.

At the outset of the Cultural Revolution 1966–69, Deng was denounced by Maoist ultra-leftists as a bourgeois 'capitalist roader'. He was subjected to a humiliating street trial, dismissed from the CCP Politburo (of which he had been a member since 1955) and, along with his third wife, Zhou Lin, was sent to remote Nanchang for 're-education through labour' in a tractor factory. During this period Deng also suffered a family tragedy, when his eldest son, Deng Pufang, facing interrogation from zealous Red Guards about his father's 'conspiracy' against Mao, fell out of a fourth floor window at Beijing University and was paralysed from the waist down for life. In 1973, with the help of his patron, Zhou Enlai, Deng Xiaoping was rehabilitated as vice premier. He became acting premier after Zhou suffered a heart attack in 1974. On Zhou's death, in January 1976, he went into hiding, but, with the assistance

devaluations. Having been passed over for the premiership in 1984, Delors accepted nomination to the European Commission. As its president, although criticized by some as being too federalist in outlook, he sustained a high-profile and pro-active role. He declined to stand as the Socialists' 1995 presidential candidate, even though polls suggested he would win.

de Maizière, Lothar (1940–)

German politician, leader 1989–90 of the conservative Christian Democratic Union (CDU) in East Germany. He became premier after East Germany's first democratic election in April 1990 and negotiated the country's reunion with West Germany. In December 1990 he resigned from Chancellor Helmut Kohl's cabinet and as deputy leader of the CDU, following allegations that he had been an informer to the Stasi (East German secret police). In September 1991 he resigned from the legislature, effectively leaving active politics.

Shortly after his resignation, the press published allegations that, for at least a year, the western CDU had been actively working to discredit de Maizière. Known as the 'CDU affair', the scandal threatened to embroil Chancellor Kohl.

Demirel, Süleyman (1924–)

Turkish politician, president from 1993. Leader from 1964 of the Justice Party, he was prime minister 1965–71, 1975–77, and 1979–80. He favoured links with the West, full membership of the European Union, and foreign investment in Turkish industry.

De Mita, Luigi Ciriaco (1928–)

Italian conservative politician, leader of the Christian Democratic Party (DC) from 1982, prime minister 1988–90. He entered the chamber of deputies in 1963 and held a number of ministerial posts in the 1970s before becoming DC secretary general. In 1993 he resigned as head of a commission on parliamentary reform, and was subsequently under investigation for extortion in connection with misuse of government aid, but possible charges against him were subsequently dropped.

---

of his southern ally Ye Jianying, he was reinstated in July 1977. This followed popular pro-Deng protests, soon after the death, in September 1976, of Chairman Mao Zedong.

Although only nominally the vice premier and deputy leader of the CCP, by December 1978 Deng had eclipsed Hua Guofeng and had established himself as the controlling force in China. His close links with key figures within the People's Liberation Army (PLA) was a key to his success. Working with his protégés ◊Hu Yaobang (to 1987), ◊Zhao Ziyang (to 1989), and ◊Jiang Zemin (from 1989), Deng proceeded to liberalize the economy and open up China to greater Western contact.

If you are a member of the Chinese Communist Party, you have to accept party orders.

DENG XIAOPING Remark attributed to Deng following his dismissal of protégé Hu Yaobang in January 1987 in the wake of student prodemocracy demonstrations.

A thorough pragmatist, Deng believed in 'crossing the river by feeling for the stones'. His approach to economic and political theory was summed up in his dictum: 'What does it matter whether the cat is black or white, as long as it catches mice ?' His policy of 'socialism with Chinese characteristics', misinterpreted in the West as a drift to capitalism, had particular success in rural areas. There, China's peasants, freed from state control over production practices

and marketing of their output, responded remarkably to the new Dengist slogan, 'to grow rich is glorious'.

Nevertheless, Deng was consistent in his opposition to what he termed the 'spiritual pollution' of Western liberal democratic values, overseeing crackdowns against intellectuals and students in 1957 (the Anti-Rightist Campaign), 1978 ('Democracy Wall'), and 1989 (Tiananmen Square). He retired from his last formal post, chair of the State Central Military Commission, in November 1989. Yet, despite deteriorating health, which eventually left him virtually blind, deaf, and immobile, he continued to press for economic reform and exert backroom influence. In 1992 he made a final return to centre-stage by calling, during a whistlestop tour of the booming southern seaboard provinces, for acceleration of his 'socialist market economy' reforms. A subsequent purge of military leaders was later claimed to have been carried out at Deng's instigation. His death, in February 1997, preceded by just four months China's recovery of sovereignty over Hong Kong, which he had helped negotiate in 1984, devising a typically innovative 'One Country, Two Systems' formula. See photograph on page 116.

FURTHER READING

Bonavia, D *Deng* 1989
Deng Xiaoping *Selected Works of Deng Xiaoping* 1984
Franz, U *Deng Xiaoping* 1988
Goodman, D *Deng Xiaoping* 1990
Lee, C H *Deng Xiaoping: The Marxist Road to the Forbidden City* 1985

Deng Xiaoping during an official visit to Paris in 1975. He studied in Paris in the early 1920s. *Rex*

Denktaş, Rauf R (1924–)

Turkish-Cypriot nationalist politician. In 1975 the Turkish Federated State of Cyprus (TFSC) was formed in the northern third of the island, with Denktaş as its head, and in 1983 he became president of the breakaway Turkish Republic of Northern Cyprus (TRNC). He was re-elected in 1995, and survived a heart attack in March 1996.

Denktaş held law-officer posts under the British crown before independence in 1960. Relations between the Greek and Turkish communities progressively deteriorated, leading to the formation of the TFSC. In 1983 the TRNC, with Denktaş as its president, was formally constituted, but recognized internationally only by Turkey.

The accession of the independent politician Georgios Vassilou to the Cyprus presidency offered hopes of reconciliation, but meetings between him and Denktaş during 1989, under UN auspices, failed to produce an agreement. The talks resumed in 1992 but failed to reach a successful conclusion. Direct talks with Vassilou's successor Glafkos Clerides began in July 1997.

Denning, Alfred Thompson, Baron Denning of Whitchurch (1899–1999)

British judge, Master of the Rolls 1962–82. In 1963 he conducted the inquiry into the Profumo scandal. A vigorous and highly innovative civil lawyer, he was controversial in his defence of the rights of the individual against the state, the unions, and big business. He was knighted in 1944 and created Baron in 1957.

FURTHER READING
Jowell, J L, and McAuslen, J P W B *Lord Denning, The Judge and the Law* 1984

Den Uyl, Joop (1919–1987)

Dutch politician, prime minister 1973–77. His ministry was beset with difficulties, notably the Arab oil embargo, caused by his government's support for Israel during the Yom Kippur War. He imposed economy measures to save energy. His Socialist Party (PvdA) was returned with an increased number of seats in the 1977 general election, but its coalition with the Christian Democrats collapsed. He was leader of the opposition 1977–86.

Den Uyl first achieved political prominence as a member of the Amsterdam city council, to which he was elected as a candidate for the PvdA. He was appointed minister for economic affairs in 1965, and became leader of the opposition 1967–73.

Derby, Edward George Villiers Stanley, 17th Earl of Derby (1865–1948)

British Conservative politician, member of Parliament 1892–1924. He was secretary of war 1916–18 and 1922–24, and ambassador to France 1918–20.

Derby became financial secretary to the War Office in 1900, and was appointed postmaster general in 1903. As director general of recruiting 1915–16, during World War I, he organized the 'Derby Scheme' of voluntary enlistment.

De Roburt, Hammer (1923–1992)

Nauruan politician, president 1968–76, 1978–83, and 1987–89.

Educated partly in Australia, De Roburt worked as a teacher in Nauru, but, during the country's occupation 1942–45, he was deported to Japan. He became head chief of Nauru in 1956 and was elected the country's first president on independence in 1968. He was re-elected in 1971 and 1973, but criticisms of his personal style of government led to his replacement, in December 1976, by Bernard ◊Dowiyogo.

Following a campaign of opposition to Dowiyogo's leadership orchestrated by De Roburt's supporters, De Roburt was recalled as prime minister in April 1978. He lost power briefly during 1986 and secured only a narrow majority in the 1987 elections. De Roburt was finally ousted, on a no-confidence motion, in 1989 and was replaced as prime minister by Kenas Aroi, his 'unacknowledged natural son'. After Aroi had resigned on health grounds, Dowiyogo was then elected by the Nauruan parliament as president in December 1989, defeating De Roburt by ten votes to six. This was De Roburt's final challenge for the presidency and on his death, in July 1992, he was given a state funeral.

Despard, Mrs Charlotte, born French (1844–1939)

English suffragette and social reformer. She was a poor law guardian, a socialist orator, and an extreme pacifist during World War I.

Afterwards she lived in Dublin, where she was a strong supporter of Éamon ◊ de Valera. She was a sister of John French, 1st Earl of Ypres.

Deutscher, Isaac (1907–1967)

Polish journalist and political commentator, active in the UK.

He came to London in 1939 and worked on the editorial staff of *The Economist* and *Observer*. His name was associated with the Marxist revisionist challenge to the Cold War tradition of analysis in the USSR. His *Stalin: A Political Biography* (1949) continues to be a definitive contribution to both historic and political writing on the subject. Between 1954 and 1963 Deutscher published a three-volume biography of Leon Trotsky.

Deutscher was born into a Hasidic Jewish community. By 1926 he broke with his background and joined the Polish Communist Party. He was expelled in 1934 when the Polish communists were accused of supporting Trotsky in his conflict with Stalin. Hence-

Moraji Desai. *Rex*

◆ DESAI, MORARJI RANCHHODJI (1896–1995) ◆

Indian politician. An early follower of Mahatma Gandhi, he was independent India's first non-Congress Party prime minister 1977–79, as leader of the Janata Party, after toppling Indira Gandhi. Party infighting led to his resignation of both the premiership and the party leadership.

Born in Gujarat, western India, Desai's early career was as a civil servant working for the British Raj. Strongly influenced by Mahatma Gandhi, Desai resigned from the civil service in 1930 and committed his life to the Indian freedom movement. Although jailed for his participation in the Civil Disobedience Campaign, he was elected to the Bombay legislature in 1935 and became the state's chief minister in 1951. A disciplined teetotaller, vegetarian and, from the age of 32, celibate, he imposed prohibition in the state.

Jawaharlal ◊ Nehru brought Desai into the federal administration of independent India in 1956 and appointed him finance minister in 1958. However, his relations with Nehru's daughter Indira Gandhi, who became prime minister in 1966, were strained – Desai having previously

derided her as a 'mere schoolgirl'. He resigned in 1969 in opposition to plans to nationalize India's banks. His departure caused a serious split in the ruling Congress Party; Desai went on to form the Janata Party, which gained power after the state of emergency 1975–77 imposed by Indira Gandhi when she was found guilty of electoral malpractice.

At the age of 81, Desai became the world's oldest prime minister and, as a true Gandhian, sought to encourage the revival of cottage industries, and delayed the manufacture of India's nuclear bomb. However, the fractious Janata coalition stayed together for only two years. Desai's frank, difficult, obdurate, and eccentric personality contributed to his demise as premier in July 1979, when he retired from politics. He remained in remarkable health and ascribed his longevity to his ascetic regimen and, in particular, the health-giving powers of his remarkable twice daily ritual of drinking his own urine, which he described as 'the water of life'.

Éamon de Valera, 1932. *AKG London*

forth Deutscher criticized the USSR and the communist movement from a left-wing position.

Dewar, Donald Campbell (1937–)

British Labour politician, born in Scotland, secretary of state for Scotland from 1997. He joined the Labour Party while at university and contested the Aberdeen South parliamentary seat at the age of 27, later winning it 1966–70. Following a period out of Parliament, he represented Glasgow Garscadden from 1978. He was opposition spokesperson on Scottish affairs 1981–92 and on social security 1992–95, and then opposition chief whip 1995–97. He successfully oversaw the passage of legislation in 1997 to create a devolved parliament for Scotland, and in 1998 was elected Labour leader for the Scottish parliament.

Born in Glasgow, he was educated at Glasgow Academy and then Glasgow University, where he was president of the Union 1961–62. After leaving university he devoted himself to politics within the Labour Party.

Dewey, John (1859–1952)

US philosopher who believed that the exigencies of a democratic and industrial society demanded new educational techniques. He expounded his ideas in numer-

---

◆ DE VALERA, ÉAMON (1882–1975) ◆

Irish revolutionary and politician; president of Sinn Féin 1917–26; leader of Fianna Fáil 1926–59; president of the executive council (prime minister) 1932–37; Taoiseach (prime minister) 1937–48, 1951–54, and 1957–59; president of the Republic of Ireland 1959–73.

De Valera was born in New York, of an Irish mother and Spanish father. Brought up in Limerick, he was educated at a Christian Brothers school, Blackrock College, and University College, Dublin. He joined the Gaelic League in 1908 and the Irish Volunteers in 1913. He fought in the 1916 Easter Rising, commanding the 3rd Battalion at Boland's Mill. He was the last commander to surrender and was sentenced to death by court-martial. His life was spared, partly on account of his US background and, released in 1917, he was elected member of Parliament for East Clare, and became president of both Sinn Féin and the Volunteers.

Along with the other Sinn Féin leaders, he was seized in the 'German plot' arrests of May 1918, but his escape from Lincoln prison was organized by Michael ◊ Collins. Thereupon de Valera went to the USA where, despite raising some $5 million for the republican cause, he failed to secure US recognition of the Republic. In his absence, control of the republican struggle in Ireland had effectively passed into the hands of Michael Collins.

Upon de Valera's return to Ireland in December 1920, his relationship with Collins remained a difficult one; the latter was running a ruthless guerrilla war over which de Valera, the public face of Irish republicanism, had little control. Their relationship worsened when de Valera refused to take any part in the formal negotiations with the British government for a final settlement, while ordering Collins to do so. His supporters claim he did so the better to maintain republican unity at home, or to intervene decisively in case of deadlock. His critics argue that he knew a compromise short of 'the Republic' was inevitable, and did not wish personally to be held responsible for it. De Valera in the event rejected the treaty, not on the grounds of special treatment for the unionist counties of Ulster, but on its requirement that Irish representatives would be oath-bound to the British crown. His rejectionist stance split the republican movement, and led to civil war in

ous writings, including *School and Society* (1899), and founded a progressive school in Chicago. A pragmatist thinker, influenced by the US philosopher William James, Dewey maintained that there is only the reality of experience and made 'inquiry' the essence of logic.

Dewey was born in Vermont and from 1904 was professor of philosophy at Columbia University, New York.

His other writings include *Experimental Logic* (1916), *Reconstruction in Philosophy* (1920), *Quest for Certainty* (1929), and *Problems of Men* (1946).

Dewey, Thomas Edmund (1902–1971)

US public official and governor of New York 1942–54. Dewey was twice the Republican presidential candidate, losing to Franklin D Roosevelt in 1944 and to Harry Truman in 1948, the latter race being one of the greatest electoral upsets in US history.

Although the clear favourite to win the 1948 election, Dewey lost because of divisive splits in the Democratic camp. In addition, Dewey ran a restrained campaign, whereas Truman embarked on a 'whistle stop' train tour of the country.

Dewey was born in Owosso, Michigan, and received a law degree from Columbia University 1925. He was appointed chief assistant to the US attorney in the Southern District of New York 1931. Having gained a reputation as a crime fighter while serving as special investigator of organized crime 1935–37, he was Manhattan district attorney 1937–38.

After his terms as governor, Dewey retained much influence in the Republican Party, and helped to promote the presidential candidature of Dwight D Eisenhower 1952 and 1956 and that of Richard Nixon 1960.

FURTHER READING
Stolberg, Mary M *Fighting Organised Crime: Politics, Justice, and the Legacy of Thomas E. Dewey* 1995

Diallo, Boubacar Telli (1929–1977)

Guinean politician and first secretary general of the Organization of African Unity (OAU). After independence he became Guinea's first permanent representative to the United Nations (UN). He was OAU secretary general 1964–72, and later became minister of justice. He was implicated in a coup plot, was imprisoned without trial, and died of starvation in 1977.

Díaz, (José de la Cruz) Porfirio (1830–1915)

Mexican soldier and politician, dictator-president (*caudillo*) of Mexico 1877–80 and 1884–1911. He seized power after losing the 1876 presidential election. He dominated the country for the next 34 years, although between 1880 and 1884 his ally Manuel Gonzáles was formally president. He centralized the state at the

---

Ireland. De Valera was arrested by Free State troops in August 1923 and held until July 1924, while the anti-Treaty Irish Republican Army (IRA) was crushed by the government.

In 1926 de Valera formed a new political party, Fianna Fáil, and entered the Free State parliament in 1927, taking the oath of allegiance as an 'empty formula'. He formed his first government in 1932 and began the process of breaking the remaining links with Britain under the 1921 settlement. His new constitution of 1937 removed all references to the crown and governor general, and turned the state into a republic in all but name. The constitution was strongly Roman Catholic in character, although it stopped short of establishing Catholicism as the state church. De Valera initiated an economic war with Britain, by suspending payment of annuities due under the pre-settlement Land Purchase Acts. Not until 1938 was agreement reached with the British to end the economic conflict.

During World War II, de Valera maintained a strict neutrality, and rejected an offer from Winston Churchill in 1940 to concede the principle of Irish unity in return for Irish entry into the war. He was equally forthright in resisting US pressure for outright Irish cooperation, although he was prepared to render quiet assistance to the Allies where he could. Fearful too that IRA activity would attract unwanted attention from either the British or the Germans, he cracked down severely on that organization, having six IRA men executed during the war, allowing three to die on hunger-strike, interning 500 and imprisoning 600 more. However, gestures aimed at demonstrating Ireland's independence of Britain, such as his signing of the book of condolences at the German embassy in Dublin on the occasion of Hitler's death, served only to worsen relations with the British and put back even further the remote day when Ulster unionists might consider a rapprochement with the rest of Ireland.

De Valera failed to show himself capable of adapting Ireland to the challenges of the postwar world. The economy stagnated while Irish cultural and artistic development was retarded. A great part of the youth of the country abandoned it through emigration. Throughout his long career, de Valera worked for the restoration of the Irish language and the ending of partition, and whatever may be said of his other achievements, he neither secured nor even approached his primary objectives.

expense of the peasants and Indians, and dismantled all local and regional leadership. Despite significant economic advance, Díaz faced mounting revolutionary opposition in his final years. His retraction of a promise not to seek re-election in 1910 triggered a rebellion, led by Francisco ◊Madero, which led to Díaz's overthrow in May 1911. Díaz fled to France, and died in exile in Paris.

He was supported by conservative landowners and foreign (especially US) capitalists, who invested in railways, mines, and the oil industry. Land, partly confiscated from Native Americans, became concentrated in the hands of a few, and opposition was suppressed, partly through Díaz's rural police force, the Guardias Rurales. His advisers, known as the *Científicos* ('scientists'), preached a positivist liberal philosophy of strong government to support economic development, under the slogan 'plenty of administration and no politics'.

A *mestizo* (of mixed Spanish and Native American ancestry), he was born into poverty in Oaxaca city, and was forced into work at an early age following the death of his father. He studied law with the help of a more affluent cousin, and joined the Liberal Army, becoming a successful general in the 1860s War of the Reform. He retired from the army and took up agriculture from the late 1860s, and unsuccessfully contested the presidency in 1871.

FURTHER READING
Beals, Carleton *Porfirio Díaz: Dictator of Mexico* 1932

Díaz Ordaz, Gustavo (1911–1979)

Mexican right-wing political leader, president 1964–70. He sought to continue the reform programme instituted by Adolfo ◊López Mateos and developed closer relations with the USA, but was criticized for the excessive force used in the crackdown against student demonstrators during the 1968 Olympics in Mexico City, when more than a hundred students were killed.

Educated at the University of Puebla, he became a lawyer, law professor, and judge who served in the Puebla state government before being elected as a deputy to the National Congress in 1943. He served as a senator 1946–52 and under President López Mateos he was interior minister 1958–63. A leading member of the right wing of the ruling Institutional Revolutionary Party (PRI), Díaz was elected president in 1964.

Diefenbaker, John George (1895–1979)

Canadian Progressive Conservative politician, prime minister 1957–63; he was defeated after criticism of the proposed manufacture of nuclear weapons in Canada.

Diefenbaker was born in Grey County, Ontario, and educated at Saskatchewan University. After graduation he served with the Canadian army in 1916, and was called to the Saskatchewan Bar in 1919. A brilliant defence counsel, he became known as the 'prairie lawyer'. He became a member of parliament in 1940, leader of his party in 1956, and prime minister in 1957. In 1958 he achieved the greatest landslide in Canadian history. A 'radical' Tory, he was also a strong supporter of Commonwealth unity. He resigned the party leadership in 1967, repudiating a 'two nations' policy for Canada. He was known as 'the Chief'.

Dies, Martin (1900–1972)

US Democratic politician. A Texas lawyer and rancher, he was a member of the House of Representatives 1931–45 and 1953–59. He was chair of the House Un-American Activities Committee ('Dies Committee') 1938–45.

Dilke, Charles Wentworth (1843–1911)

British Liberal politician, member of Parliament 1868–86 and 1892–1911. A Radical, he supported a minimum wage and legalization of trade unions. He succeeded to a baronetcy in 1869.

Dillon, James (1902–1986)

Irish politician. Born in Dublin, the son of John ◊Dillon, he studied business management in London and Chicago. He cofounded the National Centre Party in 1932, and was vice president of Fine Gael in 1933. He was the only member of the Dáil who was openly hostile to Irish neutrality in World War II. He served in the interparty governments of 1948–51 and 1954–57, and was a modernizing leader of Fine Gael 1959–65.

Dillon, John (1851–1927)

Irish nationalist politician. He was a vigorous supporter of Charles ◊Parnell until the O'Shea divorce affair, when he became the leader of the anti-Parnellite Irish National Federation. He supported John ◊Redmond as leader of the Irish Parliamentary Party and succeeded him in 1918, but was overwhelmingly defeated by Sinn Féin in the elections that year.

The son of John Blake Dillon, he qualified as a surgeon before entering Parliament in 1880. Dillon was a militant agrarian in the 1880s, and served a number of periods of imprisonment. He split with Parnell and led the main anti-Parnellite faction of Fine Gael, before stepping aside to allow the party to re-unite under Redmond in 1900. Thereafter he worked effectively if not closely with Redmond, the latter mostly in London, while Dillon tended the party machine at home. He took part in the main negotiations during the prolonged Home Rule crisis after 1910, and declined to lend active support to the British war effort after 1914. He bitterly denounced the government's policies towards the rebels in Ireland in 1916 and accurately predicted the shift in Irish national sentiment towards outright separatism. In

1918, he was defeated by Éamon ◊de Valera at East Mayo – the seat he had held since 1885 – and retired from public life.

Dimitrov, Georgi Mikhailovich (1882–1949)

Bulgarian communist, prime minister from 1946. He was elected a deputy in 1913 and from 1919 was a member of the executive of the Comintern, an international communist organization. In 1933 he was arrested in Berlin and tried with others in Leipzig for allegedly setting fire to the parliament building. Acquitted, he went to the USSR, where he became general secretary of the Comintern until its dissolution in 1943.

FURTHER READING

Dimitrov, Georgi *Georgi Dimitrov Speaking* 1976
Gunadaprasad, Mukherjee G *Georgi Dimitrov: A Leader of the Working Class* 1983
Moser, Charles A *Dimitrov of Bulgaria: A Political Biography of Dr Georgi M Dimitrov* 1979

Ding Ling, assumed name of Jiang Wei-Chih (1904–1986)

Chinese novelist. Her works include *Wei Hu* (1930) and *The Sun Shines over the Sanggan River* (1951).

She was imprisoned by the Kuomintang (Guomindang, the nationalists under Jiang Jie Shi (Chiang Kai-shek) in the 1930s, wrongly labelled as rightist and expelled from the Communist Party in 1957, imprisoned in the 1960s and intellectually ostracized for not keeping to Maoist literary rules; she was rehabilitated in 1979. Her husband was the writer Hu Yapin, executed by Jiang Jie Shi's police in 1931.

Dini, Lamberto (1932–)

Italian politician, prime minister 1995–96. Director general of the Bank of Italy from 1979, he was brought into government, as treasury minister, by premier Silvio ◊Berlusconi in 1994. On the latter's resignation, Dini was asked to form a non-political 'technocrat' government of 20 members. He declared three priorities: improving public finances, regulating political parties' access to the media, and reforming electoral procedures.

In the months following his appointment, Dini made real progress in achieving his objectives, but in November 1995 he faced a no-confidence motion from Berlusconi's party, Forza Italia, over his economic policy. He resigned, but agreed to remain as caretaker prime minister until the April 1996 general elections, when he was succeeded by Romano Prodi, who gave Dini the foreign-affairs portfolio.

Dinkins, David (1927–)

Mayor of New York City 1990–93, a Democrat. He won a reputation as a moderate and consensual community politician and was Manhattan borough president be-

fore succeeding Edward I Koch to become New York's first black American mayor. He lost his re-election bid in 1993.

Diop, Cheikh Anta (1922–1986)

Senegalese politician and historian. He studied at the Sorbonne University, Paris, 1946–60, where he became active in anti-colonial movements and published a controversial proposition that ancient Egypt had been a purely African civilization. Returning home he founded a radical opposition party, the Bloc des Masses Sénégalaises, which was dissolved in 1963 and regrouped in 1976 as the Rassemblement Nationale Démocratique (RND). In 1961 he founded the Front Nationale du Séné, which was banned in 1965. The RND was legalized by President Abdou ◊Diouf in 1981 and led by Diop until his death, but never enjoyed popular support. Diop was widely mourned as 'Senegal's most fertile and brilliant son, one of the fiercest fighters for Black Culture'.

Diouf, Abdou (1935–)

Senegalese left-wing politician, president from 1980. He became prime minister in 1970 under President Leopold Senghor and, on his retirement, succeeded him, being re-elected in 1983, 1988, and 1993. His presidency was characterized by authoritarianism.

Diouf was born in Louga in northwestern Senegal, studied at Paris University, and was a civil servant before entering politics. He was chair of the Organization of African Unity 1985–86. He leads the Senegalese Socialist Party.

Di Pietro, Antonio (1950–)

Italian judge. He was head of the *mani puliti* (clean hands) series of anti-corruption investigations that began in 1992. His investigations into allegations of corruption in Milan's local government proved instrumental in discrediting, and eventually bringing down, Italy's old political order, and opened the door for Silvio ◊Berlusconi's right-wing alliance to win the 1994 general election. In December 1994 Di Pietro resigned, claiming his work had been increasingly hampered by government interference. In February 1996 he was himself arraigned on corruption charges, which were viewed as having been designed by his opponents to dissuade him from entering politics in the forthcoming general elections. He was subsequently cleared.

Prior to entering the legal profession, Di Pietro was a police officer and computer expert. In 1992 he became the de facto leader of a team of seven Milan-based magistrates, who over a period of several years investigated more than 1,000 industrialists and politicians on charges of corruption. In September 1994 Di Pietro announced an end to his investigations and proposed a 14-point plan for preventing a recurrence of corruption. Prime Minister Berlusconi gave a cautious welcome to his proposals, but in December 1994 Di Pietro resigned, citing undue government interference in his work; within two weeks, the ruling coalition collapsed and Berlusconi (himself under investigation) resigned. In May 1996 Di Pietro accepted an offer to head the nation's public works ministry, in the new Italian government formed by the centre-left Olive Tree coalition. He resigned in November 1996.

In 1994 he was voted Italy's most popular man for his role in the *mani puliti*.

Djukanović, Milo (1962–)

Montenegrin politician, reformist president of Montenegro from 1997. He joined the League of Communists of Yugoslavia (LCY) in 1979, serving as a member of the Central Committee 1986–89. He served as prime minister of Montenegro 1991–97, when he succeeded Momir ◊Bulatović as president.

His anti-◊Milošević coalition won the Montenegro assembly elections in May 1998.

Born at Naksic, Montenegro, he was educated at Titograd University (since 1992 known as Podgorica).

Dobrynin, Anatoly Fedorovich (1919–)

Soviet diplomat, ambassador to the USA 1962–86, emerging during the 1970s as a warm supporter of détente.

Dobrynin joined the Soviet diplomatic service in 1941. He served as counsellor at the Soviet embassy in Washington, DC, 1952–55, assistant to the minister for foreign affairs 1955–57, undersecretary at the United Nations 1957–59, and head of the USSR's US department 1959–61, before being appointed Soviet ambassador to Washington in 1962. He remained in this post for 25 years. Brought back to Moscow by the new Soviet leader Mikhail Gorbachev, he was appointed to the Communist Party's Secretariat as head of its international department, before retiring in 1988.

Dobson, Frank (1940–)

British Labour politician, secretary of state for health from 1997. Sponsored by the National Union of Railwaymen, he represented the London constituency of Holborn and St Pancras from 1979. He was opposition

◆ DJILAS, MILOVAN (1911–1995) ◆

Yugoslav dissident and political writer. A close wartime colleague of Marshal ◊Tito, he was dismissed from high office in 1954 and twice imprisoned 1956–61 and 1962–66 because of his advocacy of greater political pluralism and condemnation of the communist bureaucracy. He was formally rehabilitated in 1989.

Djilas was born in Montenegro and was a partisan during World War II. He joined the illegal Yugoslav Communist Party (CPY) after studying philosophy and law in Belgrade and was imprisoned 1933–36 for protesting against the Yugoslav monarchy. He entered the CPY's controlling Politburo in 1940, during World War II, when he became a ruthless military leader of Tito's anti-Nazi partisan guerrillas.

In postwar Yugoslavia, Djilas held key positions, but as a romantic communist of principle he became disillusioned and critical of Soviet-style communism, where ends justified means and where a party elite had emerged as a privileged social stratum. This was the subject of his first book, *The New Class*, which was smuggled to the West and published in 1957. These criticisms led to his censure in 1954 and resignation from the CPY, and his imprisonment in 1956.

Released from prison in 1961, he was jailed within a year after castigating the former Soviet leader Josef Stalin as 'the greatest criminal in history' in *Conversations with Stalin* (1962), which

recounted Djilas's own meetings with Stalin 1944–45. Released in 1966, though still subject to surveillance, he wrote further works on communism and Yugoslav recent history, most notably *Memoir of a Revolutionary* (1973), which chronicles his own career.

Officially rehabilitated in 1989, Djilas predicted that Mikhail Gorbachev's *glasnost* (political openness) and *perestroika* (economic restructuring) reforms would lead to the collapse of Soviet communism and a dangerous resurgence of nationalism. He became reviled in his final years in what had become an increasingly nationalistic Yugoslavia for his humanistic criticisms of Serb aggression in Croatia and Bosnia.

FURTHER READING
Clissold, Stephen *Djilas: The Progress of a Revolutionary* 1983
Djilas, Milovan *Of Prisons and Ideas* 1986, *The Fall of the New Class: A History of Communism's Self-Destruction* 1998
Djilas, Milovan; Milenkovitch, Michael and Deborah (eds) *Parts of a Lifetime: Milovan Djilas* 1975
Reinhartz, Dennis *Milovan Djilas: A Revolutionary as a Writer* 1981
Sulzberger, Cyrus Leo *Paradise Regained: Memoir of a Rebel* 1989

spokesperson on education 1981–83, shadow health minister 1983–87, shadow leader of the Commons 1987–89, and opposition spokesperson on energy 1989–92. After John Smith became Labour leader, Dobson served as opposition spokesperson on employment 1992–93, transport and London 1993–94, and environment and London 1994–97, under the new Labour leader, Tony Blair. As health secretary, he fought with the Treasury for more funds to enable the rise in numbers of those on waiting lists to be reversed.

Born at Dunnington, near York, he was educated at the London School of Economics. Before entering Parliament he worked for the Central Electricity Generating Board 1962–70, the Electricity Council 1970–75, and then in the office of the local government ombudsman 1975–79. Before entering the House of Commons he served on Camden Borough Council 1971–76, and as its leader 1973–75.

Doe, Samuel Kanyon (1950–1990)

Liberian politician and soldier, head of state 1980–90. After seizing power in a coup, Doe made himself general and army commander in chief. As chair of the People's Redemption Council (PRC), he was the first Liberian ruler to come from an indigenous Liberian group, ending the political dominance of the US-Liberian elite. He lifted the ban on political parties in 1984 and was elected president in 1985, as leader of the newly formed National Democratic Party of Liberia. Despite alleged electoral fraud, he was sworn in during January 1986. Having successfully put down an uprising in April 1990, Doe was deposed and killed by rebel forces in September 1990. His regime was notable for incompetence and a poor human-rights record.

Doe was born into the Krahn ethnic group. He left secondary school in 1967 and joined the army in 1979, rising to the rank of master sergeant in 1989.

Doi, Takako (1929–)

Japanese socialist politician. She was elected Speaker of the House of Representatives in 1993, and led the Social Democratic Party of Japan (SDJP), formerly the Japan Socialist Party (JSP), 1986–91. The country's first female major party leader, she was largely responsible for the SDJP's revival in the late 1980s. Her resignation followed the party's crushing defeat in local elections in April 1991. In 1996 she was persuaded to lead the Social Democratic Party (SDP) again in the general election campaign, but could not prevent its support falling further.

Dolci, Danilo (1924–1997)

Italian writer and social reformer. He devoted himself to social work amongst the poor of Sicily, travelling widely to spread his message and raise funds for relief projects. His publications include *To Feed the Hungry* (1955) and *Waste* (1963).

Dole, Bob (Robert Joseph) (1923–)

US Republican politician, leader of his party in the Senate 1985–87 and 1995–96. He unsuccessfully stood as a candidate for the Republican presidential nomination in 1980 and 1988; in 1996 he captured the nomination, but lost the presidential election to Democrat Bill Clinton. Regarded initially as a hardline right-of-centre 'mainstreet' Republican, his views later moderated, particularly in the social sphere. He retired from politics in 1996 and became a special counsel to a Washington law firm.

Dole was born in Kansas, the son of a Methodist trader. He was severely wounded in Italy during World War II, permanently losing the use of his right arm. He went on to train as a lawyer and was elected to the House of Representatives in 1960 and to the Senate in 1968, representing his home state. He chaired the Republican Party's National Committee 1971–73 during Richard ◊Nixon's administration, and was chair of the Senate Finance Committee in 1981, responsible for getting President Ronald Reagan's tax bills through Congress.

As Gerald ◊Ford's running mate during the 1976 presidential campaign, he earned the reputation of being a ruthless manipulator. During the Irangate scandal (revelation of the illegal sale of arms to Iran by members of the US government in order to fund the rebels in Nicaragua) 1986–87, he was spokesperson for the Republican Party.

He is married to Elizabeth Hanford, who was transportation and labour secretary under presidents Ronald Reagan and George Bush.

Dole, Elizabeth Hanford (1936–)

US lawyer, Republican politician, and cabinet member. While President Ronald Reagan's secretary of transportation 1983–87, she promoted road safety. As President George ◊Bush's secretary of labour 1989–90, she ended the Pittsdown Coal Strike. She became president of the American Red Cross in 1991.

Elizabeth Dole was born in Salisbury, North Carolina, and is the wife of the Republican politician Bob ◊Dole. She was active in US politics from 1968, when she worked for the White House office of consumer affairs. Originally a Democrat, Dole was a Washington consumer protection lawyer in the 1970s. Her last political post was in 1990 as secretary of labour under President Bush.

Elizabeth Dole worked for five presidents. Under President Richard ◊Nixon she became deputy assistant to the president of consumer affairs and, in 1974, took up the post of federal trade commissioner. Between 1980 and 1981 she was director of president-elect Ronald ◊Reagan's human services group. With Reagan in the White House, she became head of public liaison and then secretary of transportation. After a year as the secretary of labour under George Bush, she left to take up her role for the American Red Cross and remained there – taking a year off in 1995 to campaign with her husband Bob Dole for the US presidential election.

FURTHER READING
Lucas, Eileen *Elizabeth Dole: A Leader in Washington* 1998

Dollfuss, Engelbert (1892–1934)

Austrian Christian Socialist politician. He was appointed chancellor in 1932, and in 1933 suppressed parliament and ruled by decree. In February 1934 he crushed a protest by the socialist workers by force, and in May Austria was declared a 'corporative' state. The Nazis attempted a coup on 25 July; the Chancellery was seized and Dollfuss murdered.

Dong Biwu (1886–1975)

Chinese communist politician, vice president 1959–67. After the communist victory in 1949, he became a vice premier and, before becoming vice president in 1959, was chief justice of the Supreme People's Court 1954–59. A member of the Chinese Communist Party (CCP) Politburo from 1938 until his death, Dong, unusually for a moderate within the CCP, escaped being purged during the 1966–69 Cultural Revolution.

A founding member of the CCP in 1921, he studied in Moscow 1927–31, and returned to China to work closely with Mao Zedong in the Jiangxi soviet (people's republic). Dong participated in the Long March from Jiangxi to northern China 1934–35 and during the 1937–45 war against Japan he liaised between the CCP and the Kuomintang (Guomindang, nationalist) government of Jiang Jie Shi (Chiang Kai-shek).

Born in Hubei province, into a landless gentry family, Dong received a classical education and studied in Japan 1913–18, after the Republican Revolution of 1911.

Dönitz, Karl (1891–1980)

German admiral, originator of the wolf-pack submarine technique, which sank Allied shipping in World War II. He succeeded Hitler in 1945, capitulated, and was imprisoned 1946–56.

He was in charge of Germany's U-boat force 1939–43 and his 'wolf-packs' sank 15 million tonnes of Allied shipping during the course of the war. He succeeded Erich ◊Raeder as commander in chief of the navy in January 1943 and devoted himself to trying to overcome Allied naval superiority. Hitler trusted him when he had lost faith in his army and Luftwaffe commanders, and so Dönitz was appointed to succeed him in May 1945. His sole deed as leader of the Reich was to negotiate its surrender. He was arrested on 23 May, tried at Nürnberg, and was sentenced to ten years' imprisonment.

Donovan, William Joseph (1883–1959)

US military leader and public official. Donovan served as US district attorney 1922–24 and as assistant to the US attorney general 1925–29. He was national security adviser to presidents Herbert Hoover and F D Roosevelt and founded the Office of Strategic Services (OSS) in 1942. As OSS director 1942–45, Donovan coordinated US intelligence during World War II.

Born in Buffalo, New York, USA, Donovan was educated at Columbia University and was admitted to the bar in 1907. He was decorated for bravery during World War I, gaining the nickname 'Wild Bill'. When the OSS became the Central Intelligence Agency (CIA) in 1947, President Harry Truman passed over Donovan as its first director. President Dwight D Eisenhower appointed Donovan ambassador to Thailand 1953–54, calling him America's 'last hero.'

Dos Santos, José Eduardo (1942–)

Angolan left-wing politician, president from 1979, a member of the People's Movement for the Liberation of Angola (MPLA). By 1989 he had negotiated the withdrawal of South African and Cuban forces, and in 1991 a peace agreement to end the civil war. In 1992 his victory in multiparty elections was disputed by Jonas Savimbi, leader of the rebel group National Union for the Total Independence of Angola (UNITA), and fighting resumed, escalating into full-scale civil war in 1993. Representatives of the two leaders signed a peace agreement in 1994. Dos Santos's proposal to make Savimbi vice president was declined by the latter in 1996.

Dos Santos was born into a poor family in Luanda, and was educated locally. He joined the youth wing of the MPLA in 1961, and became the party representative in Congo-Brazzaville. In 1963 he went to the USSR to complete university degrees in petrochemical engineering and in military telecommunications. He returned to Angola in 1970 and resumed the guerrilla war against Portugal 1970–73, which continued as a civil war between the MPLA and UNITA after independence in 1975. He held key positions under President Agostinho Neto, and succeeded him on his death. Despite the uncertainty of the cease-fire between the MPLA and UNITA in 1991, Dos Santos confirmed his pledge of substantial political reform. In June 1996, two years after the peace agreement, Dos Santos carried out a radical restructuring of his government.

Douglas, Clifford Hugh, known as Major Douglas (1879–1952)

English social reformer, founder of the economic theory of social credit, which held that interest should be abolished and credit should become a state monopoly. During a depression, the state should provide purchasing power by subsidizing manufacture and paying dividends to individuals; as long as there was spare capacity in the economy, this credit would not cause inflation.

Douglas, Denzil (1953–)

St Kitts' centre-left politician, prime minister of St Kitts and Nevis from 1995. He led the St Kitts Labour Party (SKLP) to victory in July 1995, ending the 15-year-old premiership of the centre-right People's Action Movement (PAM) under Kennedy ◊ Simmonds. Douglas faced calls for secession from the federation by the legislators of Nevis Island, who complained of the dominance of St Kitts. After a referendum on secession in 1998 fell narrowly short of the required two-thirds majority of Nevis voters, he pledged to negotiate a more autonomous constitutional framework.

Douglas, Marjory Stoneman (1890–1998)

US author and conservationist. Her book *The Everglades: River of Grass* (1947) warned of the environmental perils facing the region. She cofounded Friends of the Everglades and is widely credited with helping to slow the destruction of the swamp ecosystem.

She was born in Minneapolis, Minnesota. She graduated from Wellesley College in 1912 and worked as a journalist and educator in Miami. As well as her ecological works, she also wrote several books of children's literature.

Douglas-Home, Alec (Alexander Frederick), Baron Home of the Hirsel (1903–1995)

British Conservative politician. He was foreign secretary 1960–63, and succeeded Harold Macmillan as prime minister in 1963. He renounced his peerage (as 14th Earl of Home) and re-entered the Commons after successfully contesting a by-election, but failed to win the 1964 general election, and resigned as party leader in 1965. He was again foreign secretary 1970–74, when he received a life peerage. The playwright William Douglas-Home was his brother. He was knighted in 1962.

Dove, Mabel (1905–1984)

Ghanaian politician and journalist, the first woman to be elected to a national assembly in West Africa. She joined the Convention People's Party (CPP) in 1950 and wrote for the party newspaper, the *Accra Evening News*; Kwame Nkrumah appointed her editor for a brief period in 1951. She was nominated as the only CPP woman candidate in the 1954 election and won a resounding victory. However, she lost her nomination in the 1957 election.

Born in Accra, Dove came from a family of Sierra Leonean origin. She was educated in Freetown and in the UK, returning to Ghana in 1926 to pursue a career in journalism. In 1933 she married J B Danquah, editor of the *Times of West Africa* and later a nationalist politician; they divorced in the early 1940s.

Dowiyogo, Bernard (1946–)

Nauruan politician, president 1976–78, 1989–95, 1996, and from 1998. In 1973 he established himself as leader of a loose opposition group, the Nauru Party, in an assembly filled with independents and in December ousted and replaced Hammer ◊ De Roburt, who had been president since 1968. Opposition, orchestrated by De Roburt's supporters, forced Dowiyogo's resignation in April 1978 and De Roburt was re-installed. Dowiyogo then served as justice minister under De Roburt from 1983, before replacing him as president in December 1989, winning a parliamentary vote by a ten-to-six margin. As prime minister, Dowiyogo pressed for demilitarization of the South Pacific, suspending diplomatic relations with France in 1995 over the issue of nuclear testing. He was replaced as premier by Lagumot Harris in November 1995, but briefly won back power in November 1996 and, after serving as education minister, returned for a longer spell as prime minister in June 1998.

After training, in Australia, as a lawyer, Dowiyogo was first elected to the Nauru parliament in 1973.

Drago, Luis María (1859–1921)

Argentine politician. As minister of foreign affairs under Julio A Roca, he objected to the blockade of Venezuelan ports in 1902 conducted by the UK, Italy, and Germany as a punitive measure for nonpayment of debt. He formulated the Drago Doctrine, which stated that public debt could not be used as an excuse for armed intervention in, or territorial occupation of, a state by European power. Although never universally adopted, his doctrine was influential in international law.

Drees, Willem (1886–1988)

Dutch socialist politician, prime minister 1948–58. Chair of the Socialist Democratic Workers' Party from 1911 until the German invasion of 1940, he returned to politics in 1947, after being active in the resistance movement. In 1947, as the responsible minister, he introduced a state pension scheme.

Drnovšek, Janez (1950–)

Slovene politician, prime minister from 1992. A trained economist, he was elected to the Slovenian parliament in 1986 and became Yugoslavia's 'rotating president' in 1989–90. A founder-member of the centre-left Slovene Liberal Democrats (LDS) in 1990, he helped secure multiparty democracy and independence for Slovenia in 1991. Prime minister from April 1992, his government built a competitive market economy and commenced membership talks with the European Union.

Born in Celje and educated at the Faculty of Economic Sciences, University of Maribor, his early career was as a director of a construction company and bank chief executive. In 1991 he acted as Slovenia's main negotiator in the independence talks with the Yugoslav army.

Further Reading
Drnovšek, Janez *Moja resnica: Jugoslavija 1989 – Slovenija 1991* 1996

Duarte, José Napoleon (1925–1990)

El Salvadorean politician, president 1980–82 and 1984–88. He was mayor of San Salvador 1964–70, and was elected president in 1972, but was soon exiled by the army for seven years in Venezuela. He returned in 1980, after the assassination of Archbishop Oscar Romero had increased support for the Christian Democratic Party (PDC), and became president, with US backing. He lost the 1982 presidential election, but was successful in May 1984. On becoming president again, he sought a negotiated settlement with the left-wing guerrillas in 1986, but resigned in mid-1988, as he had terminal liver cancer.

Trained in the USA as a civil engineer, he became a lawyer and helped form the anti-imperialist PDC in 1960.

Du Bois, W(illiam) E(dward) B(urghardt) (1868–1963)

US educator and social critic. Du Bois was one of the early leaders of the National Association for the Advancement of Colored People (NAACP) and the editor of its journal *Crisis* 1909–32. As a staunch advocate of black American rights, he came into conflict with Booker T Washington, opposing the latter's policy of compromise on the issue of race relations.

In 1905 Du Bois founded the Niagara Movement, which was merged with the newly founded NAACP in 1909. His book *Souls of Black Folk* (1903) emphasized his revolt against the principles of Booker T Washington.

Du Bois was born in Great Barrington, Massachusetts. He earned a PhD from Harvard in 1895 and taught economics and history at Atlanta University 1897–1910, returning in 1932 to teach sociology. In 1944 he rejoined the NAACP as research director. Du Bois now began to shift from a nonideological radical position towards a Marxist and pro-Soviet viewpoint, and he joined the Communist Party in 1961. In 1962 he went to live in Accra, Ghana, where he died.

◆ Dubček, Alexander (1921–1992) ◆

Czechoslovak politician, chair of the federal assembly 1989–92. He was a member of the Slovak resistance movement during World War II, and became first secretary of the Communist Party 1967–69. He launched a liberalization campaign (called the Prague Spring) that was opposed by the USSR and led to the Soviet invasion of Czechoslovakia in 1968. He was arrested by Soviet troops and expelled from the party in 1970. In 1989 he gave speeches at pro-democracy rallies, and after the fall of the hardline regime, he was elected speaker of the National Assembly in Prague, a position to which he was re-elected in 1990. He was fatally injured in a car crash in September 1992.

The son of Slovak communists who had earlier emigrated briefly to the USA, Dubček grew up and was educated in the USSR. A committed socialist, he returned to Czechoslovakia in 1938 and fought as a Slovak patriot against the Nazis 1944–45. In 1939 he joined the Communist Party and gradually rose through its hierarchy, becoming chief secretary of the regional committee in 1953 and first secretary of the Slovak Communist Party's Central Committee in 1963. As Czechoslovakia's Communist Party leader from January 1968, he sought to popularize the system by introducing liberalizing economic, political and cultural reforms, dubbed 'socialism with a human face'. This reform movement was crushed in August 1968 when Warsaw Pact forces invaded Czechoslovakia.

Initially, Dubček cooperated with the post-invasion, Soviet-directed 'normalization' process, but in 1969 was replaced as party leader by the more conservative Gustáv ◊Husák. He served briefly as Czechoslovakia's ambassador to Turkey, but in 1970 was expelled from the Communist Party. Political banishment for two decades followed, with Dubček working as a clerk for the Slovakian forestry ministry. Though disenchanted with the cautious, stifling Husák regime, he retained his faith in the socialist dream and did not join the Charter 77 dissident movement formed by playwright Václav ◊Havel. He returned to prominence in November 1989, appearing with Havel on the balcony overlooking Prague's Wenceslas Square to acclaim the downfall of the communist regime.

Further Reading
Dubček, Alexander *Hope Dies Last* 1993
Dubček, Alexander, with Sugar, Andras *Dubček Speaks* 1990
Shawcross, William *Dubček and Czechoslovakia 1968–90* 1990

Alexander Dubček. *AKG London*

Du Cann, Edward Dillon Lot (1924–)

British Conservative politician, economic secretary to the Treasury 1962–63, minister of state at the Board of Trade 1963–64, chair of the Conservative Party 1965–67, and chair of the 1922 Committee (the backbench party organization of Conservative MPs) 1972–84.

He was educated at Woodbridge School and St John's College, Oxford. He served with the Royal Naval Volunteer Reserve 1943–46, and then became prominent in the unit trust movement in the City of London. He became MP for Taunton in 1956 and held posts in the government during the 1960s, but did not receive office when the Conservatives returned to power in 1970. He became the first chair of the Select Committee on Expenditure in 1971 and chair of the Public Accounts Committee in 1974.

Dukakis, Michael Stanley (1933–)

US Democrat politician, governor of Massachusetts 1974–78 and 1982–90, presiding over a high-tech economic boom, the 'Massachusetts miracle'. He was a presidential candidate in 1988.

Dukakis was born in Boston, Massachusetts, the son of Greek immigrants. After studying law at Harvard and serving in Korea 1955–57, he concentrated on a political career in his home state. Elected as a Democrat to the Massachusetts legislature in 1962, he became state governor in 1974. After an unsuccessful first term, marred by his unwillingness to compromise, he was defeated in 1978. He returned as governor in 1982, committed to working in a more consensual manner, was re-elected in 1986, and captured the Democratic Party's presidential nomination in 1988. After a poor campaign, Dukakis was defeated by the incumbent vice president George Bush. His standing in Massachusetts dropped and he announced that he would not seek a new term.

Duke, David (1950–)

US Republican politician. A fierce campaigner for white rights, Duke founded National Association for the Advancement of White People (NAAWP) and has been linked to far-right white supremacy groups. Duke worked for the US State Department during the Vietnam War as an instructor for Laotian military officers. As a Republican congressman 1989–93, he authored the conservative House Bill of 1990.

Dulles, John Foster (1888–1959)

US politician. Senior US adviser at the founding of the United Nations, he was largely responsible for drafting the Japanese peace treaty of 1951. As secretary of state 1952–59, he was an architect of US Cold War foreign policy and secured US intervention in South Vietnam after the expulsion of the French in 1954.

Dulles presided over the creation of the Central Treaty Organization (CENTO) alliance in the Middle East and the Southeast Asia Treaty Organization (SEATO). He was highly critical of the UK during the Suez Crisis in 1956.

Durán Bellén, Sixto (1922–)

Ecuadorian politician and president 1992–96. He took office during a deepening national economic crisis and was successful in reducing the inflation rate of 50% in the early 1990s to less than 10% by 1996. Social problems were still severe however, with over half the population living at subsistence levels.

The election of the conservative Durán Bellén marked yet again another change in Ecuadorian politics. Unlike the administration of President Borja Cevallos, his party, the Republican Unity Party, favoured free market reform and privatization. His administration immediately implemented new policies that would encourage privatization and increase foreign investment. He also aimed to reduce bureaucracy. Economic austerity measures were also instituted, particularly a reduction in state expenditure.

Duvalier, François (1907–1971)

Right-wing president of Haiti 1957–71. Known as 'Papa Doc', he ruled as a dictator, organizing the Tontons Macoutes ('bogeymen') as a private security force to intimidate and assassinate opponents of his regime. He rigged the 1961 elections in order to have his term of office extended until 1967, and in 1964 declared himself president for life. He was excommunicated by the Vatican for harassing the church, and was succeeded on his death by his son Jean-Claude ◊Duvalier.

FURTHER READING
Abbott, E *Haiti: The Duvaliers and their Legacy* 1988
Mougins, J F *Papa, Doc, Baby Doc: Haiti and the Duvaliers* 1987

Duvalier, Jean-Claude (1951–)

Right-wing president of Haiti 1971–86. Known as 'Baby Doc', he succeeded his father François Duvalier, becoming, at the age of 19, the youngest president in the world. He continued to receive support from the USA but was pressured into moderating some elements of his father's regime, yet still tolerated no opposition. In 1986, with Haiti's economy stagnating and with increasing civil disorder, Duvalier fled to France, taking much of the Haitian treasury with him.

Dworkin, Andrea (1946–)

US feminist writer. Arguing that pornography is a form of sexual discrimination, she worked with the lawyer Catharine MacKinnon (1946–) to draft legislation outlawing pornography. They published *Pornography and Civil Rights: A New Day for Women's Equality* (1988).

> *All feminist arguments, however radical in intent or consequence, are with or against premises implicit in the male system, which is made credible or authentic by the power of men to name.*
> ANDREA DWORKIN *Pornography* chap 1

Woman Hating (1974) is a history of the ways in which women have been subjugated by men, such as foot-binding in China and witch-hunting. She edited the anthology *Take Back the Night: Women on Pornography* (1982). In *Right Wing Women* (1983) she discussed the reasons why women join the Republican Party. Her novels include the semi-autobiographical *Mercy* (1990).

Dylan, Bob, adopted name of Robert Allen Zimmerman (1941–)

US singer and songwriter. His lyrics provided catch-phrases for a generation and influenced innumerable songwriters. He began in the folk-music tradition. His early songs, as on his albums *The Freewheelin' Bob*

> *I'm just as good a singer as Caruso ... I hit all those notes and I can hold my breath three times as long if I want to.*
> BOB DYLAN In the documentary film *Don't Look Back* 1967

Dylan (1963) and *The Times They Are A-Changin'* (1964), were associated with the US civil-rights movement and antiwar protest. From 1965 he worked in an individualistic rock style, as on the albums *Highway 61 Revisited* (1965) and *Blonde on Blonde* (1966).

FURTHER READING
Dylan, Bob *Bob Dylan, Self-Portrait* 1970
Rinzler, Alan *Bob Dylan* 1978
Shelton, Robert *No Direction Home* 1986
Shepard, Sam *Rolling Thunder Logbook* 1977
Spitz, Bob *Dylan* 1988

Dzerzhinsky, Feliks (1877–1926)

Russian revolutionary and first chair of the NKVD, the Soviet secret police. Dzerzhinsky was born in Minsk, in today's Belarus, then the Polish part of the Russian empire. Active in the Polish Social Democratic Movement, he was accused of being a political agitator and exiled to Siberia. Henceforth his main political involvement was one with the Russian revolutionary movement. In 1917 he was one of the organizers of the October Revolution. During the civil war that ensued he became responsible for counter-espionage and sabotage. His name is linked with the brutal activities of the NKVD during that period. After the civil war he became commissar for transport and in 1924 chair of the Supreme Economic Council, which tried to find a middle way between rapid industrialization and the 'New Economic Policy' attitude of conciliating the farmers.

Eanes, António dos Santos Ramalho (1935–)

Portuguese politician, president 1976–86. He helped plan the 1974 coup that ended the regime of Marcello Caetano, and as army chief of staff put down a left-wing revolt in November 1975.

Earle, Steve (Stephen Fain) (1955–)

US musician and prominent anti-death penalty campaigner. His song 'Ellis Unit One' features on the soundtrack of the film *Dead Man Walking* (1995). An accomplished song-writer and musician, Earle came to prominence in the 1980s with his album *Copperhead Road* (1988).

East, Catherine (1916–1996)

US federal worker and feminist. East was one of the foremost motivators in establishing the National Organization of Women (NOW). In particular, she helped build links between women active in the labour and feminist movements. East began her career in the US Civil Service Commission. She worked for the Department of Labor from 1963–75 and held senior positions on many presidential advisory committees from 1962–77.

Eban, Abba, originally Aubrey Solomon (1915–)

South African-born Israeli diplomat and politician. He was Israeli ambassador to the United Nations (UN) 1948–59 and, simultaneously, Israel's ambassador in Washington, DC, 1950–59. Returning to Israel, he was elected to the Knesset (parliament) and subsequently held several government posts, culminating in that of foreign minister 1966–74.

History teaches us that men and nations behave wisely once they have exhausted other alternatives.

ABBA EBAN Speech 16 December 1970

Eban was born in Cape Town, South Africa, and educated in the UK; he taught at Cambridge University before serving at Allied HQ during World War II. He subsequently settled in Israel.

Ebert, Friedrich (1871–1925)

German socialist politician. He was the first president of the German Republic, from February 1919 until his death. He became socialist leader of the Reichstag (parliament) in 1916 and succeeded Prince Max of Baden as chancellor in 1918.

Ebert was born in Heidelberg, trained as a saddler, and helped to found a saddlers' union. In 1894 he became editor of the *Bremen Burgerzeitung*, a socialist paper, then secretary of the Bremen branch of the Socialist Party.

Always a moderate, Ebert did much to hold together the Weimar system in its early years.

Ecevit, Bülent (1925–)

Turkish social democrat politician, prime minister in 1974, 1977, and 1978–79. He was born in Istanbul and educated there and at London and Harvard universities. A journalist and poet, he entered parliament as a representative of the Republican People's Party in 1957, and was labour minister 1961–65. During his first term as prime minister he ordered the military invasion of Cyprus. His final term was notable for the introduction of martial law to combat terrorism. He was later imprisoned by the military dictatorship in Turkey in the 1980s. From 1987 he has been chair of the Party of the Democratic Left.

Echandi Jiménez, Mario (1915–)

Costa Rican politician, president 1958–62. He won the 1958 presidential election as candidate of the conservative National Union, and pursued a cautious programme, encouraging trade and industry, but lacked support within the national assembly and faced declining coffee prices. In the 1970 presidential election he was defeated by José ◊Figueres Ferrer.

Educated at the University of Costa Rica, Echandi worked as a lawyer before serving as ambassador to the USA 1950–51 and foreign minister 1951–53, under President Otilio Ulate. Between 1953 and 1958, during the presidency of Figueres Ferrer, he was leader of the opposition in the national assembly. He was again ambassador to the USA 1966–68.

Echeverría Alvarez, Luis (1922–)

Mexican politician, president 1970–76. He espoused

reforms such as land redistribution and the expansion of social security, but his administration was troubled by runaway inflation, high unemployment, and a declining balance of trade.

With a background as a lawyer and law professor, he joined the Institutional Revolutionary Party (PRI) and held many government posts from the 1940s, including secretary of the interior 1964–69. In 1977 he became ambassador to UNESCO.

Ede, James Chuter, Baron Chuter-Ede (1882–1965)

British Labour politician. He was home secretary in the Labour government 1945–51 and introduced the Criminal Justice Act of 1948. In 1951 he became leader of the House of Commons until Labour's defeat in the October 1951 general election.

He entered Parliament as Labour member for Mitcham in 1923 and represented South Shields 1929–31 and 1935–64. He served on Surrey county council for many years and was deputy lieutenant for Surrey in 1931. He was parliamentary secretary to the Board of Education 1940–44 and his knowledge of local government was of great assistance to R A Butler in drafting the 1944 Education Act.

Ehrlichmann, John (1925–)

US politician and President Richard ◊Nixon's chief domestic adviser 1969–73. Ehrlichmann was arrested and imprisoned for his part in the Watergate cover-up. He became a regular on the lecture circuit, as well as a writer.

FURTHER READING
Ehrlichman, John *Witness to Power: The Nixon Years* 1982

Eichelberger, Robert L(awrence) (1886–1961)

US general, a commander of US forces in the Pacific 1942–45.

◆ EDEN, (ROBERT) ANTHONY, 1ST EARL OF AVON (1897–1977) ◆

British Conservative politician, prime minister 1955–57, member of Parliament for Warwick and Leamington 1923–57.

Eden was born at Windlestone Hall, Bishop Auckland, and educated at Eton and Christchurch College, Oxford. In 1926 he was appointed parliamentary private secretary to Austen Chamberlain, then foreign secretary.

We are not at war with Egypt. We are in armed conflict.

ANTHONY EDEN Referring to the Suez Crisis. Speech November 1956

Eden became undersecretary of state for foreign affairs in 1931, and in 1934 Lord Privy Seal, becoming minister for League of Nations affairs in 1935. Following the resignation of Samuel Hoare in 1935 over the Abyssynian question, Eden was appointed foreign secretary, at 39 the youngest foreign secretary for over a century. He resigned in 1938 over disagreements with Neville Chamberlain about policy towards Fascist Italy. In September 1939 he re-entered the Cabinet as dominions secretary.

Eden was the first secretary of state for war in Winston Churchill's wartime coalition government. He became foreign secretary later in 1940 succeeding Lord Halifax who went to Washington, DC, as British ambassador. He negotiated the alliance treaty with the USSR in 1942 and led the British delegation to the San Francisco conference in 1945 that drew up the United Nations Charter. From 1942 he was also leader of the House of Commons.

Eden was deputy leader of the opposition 1945–51 and became deputy prime minister and foreign secretary in Churchill's government in 1951. He negotiated the Korean and Vietnam settlements in 1954 and the withdrawal of British forces from the Suez Canal zone. His success as foreign secretary made him Churchill's natural successor and he became prime minister in April 1955. He led the Conservatives to victory in the general election of 26 May 1955, when they increased their majority from 17 to 59 seats.

In November 1956 British and French armed forces occupied the Suez Canal zone ahead of the invading Israeli army. The action was condemned by the United Nations and under pressure from the USA, Eden withdrew British troops. The controversy over the invasion at home and abroad and the adverse impact on the British economy precipitated Eden's resignation as prime minister, due to ill health, on 9 January 1957.

Eden's publications include *Place in the Sun, Foreign Affairs* (1939), *Freedom and Order* (1949), *Days for Decision* (1949), and three volumes of *Memoirs* (1960–65). He was created an Earl in 1961.

FURTHER READING
Carlton, David *Anthony Eden: A Biography* 1981
Eden, Anthony *The Eden Memoirs* 1960–65
Rhodes James, Robert *Anthony Eden* 1986

He was commandant of West Point Military Academy when the USA entered the war, and was sent to take command of US I Corps in the Pacific. He fought in New Guinea, defeating the Japanese at Buna in January 1943, and then took command of the US 8th Army for the assault on the Philippines in 1945.

Eichmann, (Karl) Adolf (1906–1962)

Austrian Nazi. As an SS official during Hitler's regime 1933–45, he was responsible for atrocities against Jews and others, including the implementation of genocide. He managed to escape at the fall of Germany in 1945, but was discovered in Argentina in 1960, abducted by Israeli agents, tried in Israel in 1961 for war crimes, and executed.

He was in charge of the Gestapo department controlling the Jewish population of all German-occupied territory. He organized the mass deportation of Jews from Germany and Bohemia to concentration camps in Poland in 1941. He was given the task of organizing the Final Solution to the 'Jewish problem' at the Wannsee Conference in 1942 and set up extermination camps, specifying the design of the gas chambers and crematoria.

Einaudi, Luigi (1874–1961)

Italian politician and economist; president of Italy 1948–55. As budget minister from 1947 he devised a rigorous deflationary policy of tight monetary control and high interest rates that continued until 1950. While this contributed to high unemployment and may have delayed Italy's postwar industrial recovery, it also helped to revive confidence in the lira and laid the foundation for growth in the post-1950 era.

Einaudi was professor of public finance in Turin 1902–49 and a senator 1915–45; the post of budget minister was specially created for him by Prime Minister Alcide ◊de Gasperi.

Eisenhower, Dwight David ('Ike') (1890–1969)

See page 132.

Eisner, Thomas (1929–)

German-born US entomologist and conservation activist. He is an authority on the role of chemicals in insect behaviour. A campaigner for the preservation of biodiversity, in order to prevent the extinction of species and the loss of potentially useful chemicals, he advocates 'chemical prospecting', whereby drug companies buy the rights to extract chemically rich organic matter from forests, leaving the forests themselves intact.

Thomas was born in Berlin but moved to New York with his family in 1947. His early entomological work concentrated on the bombardier beetle. He became professor of biology at Cornell University, New York, in 1976, and director of the Cornell Institute for

Anthony Eden, c. 1935. *AKG London*

Research in Chemical Ecology. Concerned at the environmental implications of the population explosion, he became a member of Zero Population Growth.

Eliécer Gaitán, Jorge (1902–1948)

Colombian politician who was a charismatic and populist liberal leader. He was assassinated in an urban riot in Bogotá.

Eliécer Gaitán held several influential political positions. In 1936 he served as the mayor of Bogotá and was minister of education in 1940.

His death occurred during the period, known as *La Violencia*, which provoked riots and civil unrest among Liberal and Conservative supporters, with a death toll of several hundred thousands, marking one of the bloodiest periods in the country's history.

Eliécer Gaitán was born in Bogotá and educated in law at the Universidad Nacional de Colombia, and also in Italy.

Elizabeth II (Elizabeth Alexandra Mary) (1926–)

Queen of Great Britain and Northern Ireland from 1952, the elder daughter of George VI. She married her third cousin, Philip, Duke of Edinburgh, in 1947. They have four children: Charles, Anne, Andrew, and Edward.

Princess Elizabeth was born in London on 21 April

1926; she was educated privately, and assumed official duties at 16.

During World War II she served in the Auxiliary Territorial Service, and by an amendment to the Regency Act she became a state counsellor on her 18th birthday. On the death of George VI in 1952 she succeeded to the throne while in Kenya with her husband and was crowned on 2 June 1953.

With an estimated wealth of £5 billion (1994), the Queen is the richest woman in Britain, and probably the world. In April 1993 she voluntarily began paying full rates of income tax and capital gains on her private income, which chiefly consists of the proceeds of a share portfolio and is estimated to be worth around £45 million.

Eman, 'Henny' (Jan Hendrik Albert) (1948–)

Aruban centre-right politician, prime minister 1986–89 and from 1994. In 1978 he succeeded his father as leader of the centre-right Aruban People's Party (AVP) and in the following year he was elected to the Netherlands Antilles parliament. Having secured separate status (but not independence from the Netherlands) for Aruba, in 1986 Eman became the country's first prime minister. He lost power to Nelson Oduber of the People's Electoral Movement (MEP) after the January 1989 general election, but returned to office in August 1994, heading a coalition government.

Born into a political family, his grandfather had founded the AVP, which campaigned for separate status for Aruba, the second largest of the six islands of the Netherlands Antilles. Educated in the Netherlands, where he studied law and wrote a masters degree, at the University of Leiden, on the subject of separate status, Eman returned to Aruba to begin a business career.

Enahoro, Anthony Eronsele (1923–)

Nigerian politician, journalist, and company director. A founder member of the Action Group in 1951, he became an active supporter of self-rule. After independence he was the chief opposition spokesperson on foreign affairs. Arrested in 1962, he fled to the UK from

---

◆ EISENHOWER, DWIGHT DAVID ('IKE') (1890–1969) ◆

34th president of the USA 1953–60, a Republican. A general in World War II, he commanded the Allied forces in Italy in 1943, then the Allied invasion of Europe, and from October 1944 all the Allied armies in the West. As president he promoted business interests at home and conducted the Cold War abroad. His vice president was Richard Nixon.

Every gun that is made, every warship launched, every rocket fired signifies, in the final sense, a theft from those who hunger and are not fed, those who are cold and are not clothed.

DWIGHT EISENHOWER Speech in Washington 16 April 1953

Eisenhower was born in Denison, Texas. A graduate of West Point military academy in 1915, he served in a variety of staff and command posts before World War II. He became commander in chief of the US and British forces for the invasion of North Africa in November 1942, commanded the Allied invasion of Sicily in July 1943, and announced the surrender of Italy on 8 September 1943. In December he became commander of the Allied Expeditionary Force for the invasion of Europe and was promoted to general of the army in December 1944. After the war he served as commander of the US Occupation Forces in Germany, then returned to the USA to become

Chief of Staff. He served as president of Columbia University and chair of the joint Chiefs of Staff between 1949 and 1950. Eisenhower became supreme commander of the Allied Powers in Europe in 1950, and organized the defence forces in the North Atlantic Treaty Organization (NATO). He resigned from the army in 1952 to campaign for the presidency; he was elected, and re-elected by a wide margin in 1956.

A popular politician, Eisenhower held office during a period of domestic and international tension, although the USA was experiencing an era of postwar prosperity and growth. Major problems during his administration included the ending of the Korean War, the growing civil-rights movement at home, and the Cold War. His proposals on disarmament and the control of nuclear weapons led to the first International Conference on the Peaceful Uses of Atomic Energy, held under the auspices of the United Nations in Geneva in 1955.

FURTHER READING

Ambrose, Stephen E *Eisenhower* 1983

Brendon, Piers *Ike* 1987

Eisenhower, David *Eisenhower: At War, 1943–1945* 1986

Kreig, J P *Dwight D Eisenhower: Soldier, President, Statesman* 1987

Miller, M *Ike the Soldier* 1987

Sixsmith, E K G *Eisenhower as Military Commander* 1973

where he was extradited, and he was sentenced in Nigeria to 15 years in prison for treason. He was released in 1966 by the new military government of Yokuba ◊Gowon. In 1978 he joined the National Party of Nigeria, which became the ruling party of the Second Republic, and was elected chair of the party in his home state. In 1993 he formed the Movement for National Reform, which joined with other groups to oppose the ◊Abacha regime. He was detained August–December 1994.

Enahoro was born in Uromi, Bendel state, and educated in Lagos. He became editor of several newspapers including the *Southern Nigerian Defender* in 1944 and the *Nigerian Star* 1950–52.

Ennals, David Hedley (1922–1995)

British Labour politician. After entering Parliament as MP for Dover in 1964, he held several posts in Harold Wilson's government. He lost his seat in 1970 and from 1970 to 1973 was campaign director of the National Association for Mental Health. In February 1974 he was elected MP for Norwich North and in March 1974 became minister of state at the Foreign Office. He entered the Cabinet in July 1976 as secretary of state for Social Services.

He was educated at Queen Mary's Grammar School, Walsall, and the Loomis Institute, Windsor, Connecticut. After war service he became secretary of the Council for Education in World Citizenship 1947–52, and secretary of the United Nations Association 1952–57. In 1957 he became overseas secretary of the Labour Party, a post he held until he entered Parliament in 1964. Between 1966 and 1970 he was successively parliamentary undersecretary for the Army, parliamentary undersecretary at the Home Office, and minister of state, Department of Health and Social Security.

Enver Pasha (1881–1922)

Turkish politician and soldier. He led the military revolt of 1908 that resulted in the Young Turks' revolution. He was killed fighting the Bolsheviks in Turkestan.

He entered the army in 1898, became active in the Young Turk movement in 1905, and following the 1908 revolution was appointed military attaché to Berlin. He returned to Salonika in 1909 when the Turkish counter-revolution began and assisted in the overthrow of Abdul Hamid. He was active in organizing the Arabs of Tripoli in the Tripoli War against Italy in 1911, and in the Second Balkan War he recaptured Adrianople from the Bulgarians in 1913. By that time he had been appointed minister of war, with the rank of Pasha, and married a princess.

His pro-German influence was a major factor in the Turkish decision to align with Germany against the Allies in World War I, although his attempts at military command during the war were invariably failures.

Dwight Eisenhower, c. 1955. *AKG London*

After the Turkish surrender he fled to the Caucasus, from where he urged resistance to the terms of the peace treaty. Having no success in returning to power in Turkey, he joined a group of anti-Bolsheviks in Uzbekistan and was killed leading them in a skirmish.

Erhard, Ludwig (1897–1977)

West German economist and Christian Democrat politician, chancellor of the Federal Republic 1963–66. He became known as the 'father of the German economic miracle'. As economics minister 1949–63 he instituted policies driven by his vision of a 'social market economy', in which a capitalist free market would be tempered by an active role for the state in providing a market-friendly social welfare system. His period as chancellor was less distinguished.

FURTHER READING
Nicholls, A J *Freedom with Responsibility: The German Social Market Economy in Germany, 1948–1963* 1994

Erlander, Tage Fritiof (1901–1985)

Swedish politician. Elected to parliament as a Social Democrat in 1933, he was minister without portfolio in the wartime coalition government from 1944, and was minister for ecclesiastical affairs when chosen to succeed Per Albin Hansson as party leader and prime minister in 1946. He made way for the younger Olof ◊Palme in 1969.

Erlander became active in the Social Democratic Party while studying at the University of Lund. He was a moderate, and his brand of consensual government was dubbed 'Harpsund democracy' after his country estate, where he consulted with leaders in all walks of society.

Ershad, Hussain Muhammad (1930–)

Military ruler of Bangladesh 1982–90. He became Chief of Staff of the Bangladeshi army in 1979 and assumed power in a military coup in 1982. As president from 1983, Ershad introduced a successful rural-oriented economic programme. He was re-elected in 1986 and lifted martial law, but faced continuing political opposition, which forced him to resign in December 1990.

In 1991 he was formally charged with the illegal possession of arms, convicted, and sentenced to ten years' imprisonment. He received a further sentence of three years' imprisonment in February 1992 after being convicted of corruption. In January 1997 he was released from prison on bail by the supreme court and resumed leadership of the Jatiya Dal party. The party withdrew from the governing national consensus coalition in March 1998.

Erzberger, Matthias (1875–1921)

German politician. Long a hate figure for the German right, he first attracted controversy as an advocate of peace without annexations in 1917. Subsequently, as a member of the armistice delegation, he supported acceptance of the terms of the Treaty of Versailles despite fierce German opposition. He resigned in 1921 after an unsuccessful libel action against a political opponent, and was assassinated in August 1921.

Erzberger was a centre party deputy from 1903. Appointed as finance minister and vice premier in 1919, he drastically reformed the tax system and nationalized the German railways. He was killed in the Black Forest by members of the extremist group Organisation Consul.

Escobar, Pablo Gaviria (1949–1993)

Colombian drug dealer, racketeer, and politician. From humble beginnings he became the leader of an international drugs cartel based in the city of Medellín. His activities, which included political assassination and terrorism, brought international condemnation.

As head of the Medellín cartel, Escobar transformed the law-abiding city of Medellín into the narcotics capital of South America. His political ambitions in the 1980s (in 1982 he was elected to congress) led to the assassination of opponents as well as indiscriminate acts of terrorism. After escaping from 'voluntary imprisonment' he was killed by police while resisting arrest.

The son of a small farmer and a teacher, he became involved in petty crime at an early age. Stealing cars and smuggling cigarettes led to dealing in marijuana and then cocaine in the 1970s, and he became a key player in the rapidly growing drugs trade. Incongruously, he achieved a different sort of fame with the unique zoological collection that he established on the Magdalena River. A determined campaign by the Colombian government, encouraged by the USA, eventually brought his voluntary surrender.

Eshkol, Levi (1895–1969)

Israeli politician, prime minister 1963–69. A member of the centre-left Mapai party, he served as finance minister 1952–63 and as prime minister and defence minister 1963–69, transferring the latter post to Moshe ◊Dayan during the Six-Day War of 1967. Eshkol established diplomatic relations with West Germany and was also the first Israeli leader to visit the USA. Despite internal political difficulties 1964–65, he remained prime minister until his death

Born in the Ukraine into a pious Jewish family, he settled in Palestine as an agricultural worker in 1914. After Israeli independence in 1948, he supervised the founding of several hundred new villages to absorb immigrants.

Esquivel, Manuel (1940–)

Belizean politician, prime minister 1984–89 and from 1993. During his terms in office he was responsible for negotiating the reduction of UK military forces in Belize.

Following a career in teaching, he helped to form the United Democratic Party (UOP) in 1973 and was appointed to the Senate in 1979. He became UDP leader in 1983 and built up enough support to win a landslide victory in the 1984, first post-independence elections.

Born in Belize city, he was educated at the Loyola University in the USA and at the University of Bristol in the UK.

Es-Sa'id, Nuri, officially *Nouri Said Pasha* (1888–1958)

Iraqi politician, prime minister 1930–58. In 1921 he became Iraq's first chief of general staff and a year later defence minister. From 1930 he filled the office of prime minister many times until he was assassinated in July 1958 after the coup of Brigadier Abdul Karim ◊Kassem.

Born in Kirkuk and educated at the Istanbul Staff College for the Turkish Army, he fled to Egypt when his pan-Arab activities became suspect. In World War I he fought against the Turks under King ◊Hussein of the Hejaz.

Estimé, Dumarsais (1900–1953)

Haitian populist politician, president 1946–50. Elected as president by the National Assembly after a military coup removed the dictatorial Elie ◊Lescot, he implemented a populist-nationalist programme, which included banning foreign ownership of land, expansion of education, legalization of trade unions, ress freedom, promotion of tourism, and encouragement of the practice of voodoo. In 1950 he was deposed in a coup by Major Paul Eugène Magloire, after declaring martial law and attempting to lift the ban on the re-election of presidents. He fled to the USA, where he died in exile.

His election as president represented a return to power for the country's black political elite, after 31 years of dominance by the mulatto (mixed ethnic) elite. In the 1960s he was declared a national hero posthumously by François Duvalier, in whose administration his widow and son served.

Orphaned at a young age, Estimé was raised by an uncle who was a member of the Haitian Senate. He became a mathematics teacher and taught Duvalier. In 1930 he was elected to the Chamber of Deputies and, as education secretary under President Sténio ◊Vincent, he initially made his mark in reforming higher education.

Estrada, Joseph Ejercito ('Erap') (1937–   )

Filipino right-of-centre populist politician, president from 1998. Despite opposition to his candidacy from the Roman Catholic Church and the business and political elite, Estrada, enjoying a power-base among the poor and with the backing of the right-of-centre Struggle of the Nationalist Filipino Masses (LMMP), secured a clear victory in the May 1998 presidential elections. He inherited a worsening economy, with a growing budget deficit and rising unemployment, but pledged to continue with the market-centred reform programme initiated by his predecessor Fidel ◊Ramos. During his campaign, Estrada had promised to alleviate poverty, combat corruption and crime and, ambitiously, establish peace and order across all the Philippines, including secessionist Mindanao, within six months.

After an early career as a filmstar and playboy, Estrada became a charismatic, populist politician. He served as mayor of San Juan 1969–86 and was elected to the Philippines Senate in 1987 and as vice president in 1992.

Estrada Cabrera, Manuel (1857–1923)

Guatemalan politician, liberal dictator-president 1898–1920. Immediately after taking over as president, he changed the constitution to end the restriction to single presidential terms, and was subsequently elected and re-elected on four occasions, in rigged contests. His administration became increasingly corrupt. A revolution in 1920, triggered by the murder of an anti-government legislator, attracted broad support from labour groups and the Unionist Party. It resulted in the Congress declaring Estrada 'mentally incompetent' and forcing him to resign. He fled the country and died in exile.

Born in Quetzaltenango, he was a lawyer and supreme court justice before election to the national assembly in 1885. He became interior minister under President José María Reina Barrios from 1892 and took over as president when Reina Barrios was assassinated in February 1898. After early sponsorship of public health, education, and agricultural and communications improvements, widespread corruption set in, although there was economic advance, leading to the emergence of a new elite of coffee planters. Estrada ruled increasingly as a tyrannical dictator, employing secret police informers, confiscating church property, and using the army to suppress a succession of revolutionary uprisings, strikes, and assassination attempts.

Estrada Palma, Tomás (1835–1908)

Cuban revolutionary, the country's first president 1902–06. During the 1890s, as head of the Cuban revolutionary junta in New York, he secured US financial and military support for the independence struggle and in 1901 was elected president of the Cuban Republic. He attracted US financial aid and inward economic investment and, standing as the Moderate Party candidate, was re-elected president in 1906. However, the defeated opposition Liberals refused to accept his victory and forced his resignation later in 1906, leading to a three-year period of US rule.

A Protestant in a largely Catholic country, Estrada was born near Bayamo, in eastern Cuba. During the Ten Years' War 1868–78 against Spanish colonial rule, he reached the rank of general and served briefly from 1877 as president of the provisional republic. He was imprisoned by the Spanish and, after his release, spent the 1880s in Honduras and the USA, where he was principal of a Quaker School for Latin American boys, in Central Valley, New York.

Evans, Gwynfor (1912–   )

Welsh Nationalist politician. Evans became vice president of Plaid Cymru in 1943, he was president of the party 1945–81, and was member of Parliament for Carmarthen 1966–70 and again 1974–79. His numerous publications on the question of Welsh independence include *Welsh Nation Builders* (1987).

He was educated at the universities of Wales and Oxford.

Evers, (James) Charles (1922–)

US civil-rights leader and mayor. He was field director of the National Association for the Advancement of Colored People (NAACP) in Mississippi and mayor of Fayette, Mississippi, in 1969, the first black mayor to be elected in a racially mixed southern town in the 20th century.

He was born in Decatur, Mississippi. After serving in the US Army during the Korean War, he moved to Chicago where he was a successful nightclub owner, real estate agent, and disc jockey. He returned to Mississippi to become NAACP field director in 1963. He published his autobiography in 1971 and was re-elected mayor in 1973 after an unsuccessful attempt for the governorship on an independent ticket in 1971. In 1978 he failed in his bid to become a US senator.

Ewing, Winnie (Winnifred Margaret) (1929–)

Scottish Nationalist politician. Her victory at the Hamilton by-election in 1967 established the Scottish National Party (SNP) as a major political force. Although ousted there in 1970, she won the Moray and Nairn seat in 1974. After losing this position in 1979 she was elected to the European Parliament in the same year, representing the Highlands and Islands, and was re-elected in 1984, 1989, and 1994. She became president of the SNP in 1988.

One of the best-known figures in the SNP, she became president of the SNP European Free Alliance in 1981, and is known as 'Madame Ecosse' because of her work in Europe.

Born in Glasgow, she was educated at Glasgow University, and became a lawyer and president of the Glasgow Bar Association.

Eyadema, Etienne Gnassingbé (1935–)

Togolese army officer and politician. In 1967, after serving in the French army, he overthrew President Nicolas Grunitzky to become Togo's unelected president. A 1972 national referendum confirmed his presidency. He won a hollow victory in the 1993 elections because all the main opposition parties refused to take part and their supporters boycotted the polls.

After Grunitzky was deposed, he set up the National Reconciliation Committee. For a time he shared the presidency with Col Kleber Dadjo, but he soon assumed full power and became Togo's first general. In 1969 he became founder–president of the Movement of the Togolese National Rally. Having secured the presidency, he established a one-party state, but had to concede some of his power in the face of public dissent.

Eyadema was born at Piya, in northern Togo. His military career involved spells in the Far East, Algeria, Niger, and Dahomey (now Benin), and he took part in the 1963 coup when President Sylvanus Olympio was assassinated. After this, he was commissioned and he proceeded through the ranks of lieutenant, captain, and commander, before becoming army chief of staff and then lieutenant colonel in 1965.

Fabius, Laurent (1946–)

French politician, leader of the Socialist Party (PS) 1992–93. As prime minister 1984–86, he introduced a liberal free-market economic programme, but his career was damaged by the 1985 Greenpeace sabotage scandal.

Fabius became economic adviser to PS leader François Mitterrand in 1976, entered the National Assembly in 1978, and was a member of the socialist government from 1981. In 1984, at a time of economic crisis, he was appointed prime minister. He resigned after his party's electoral defeat in March 1986, but remained influential as speaker of the National Assembly and as its president from 1988. In January 1992 he was elected PS first secretary (leader), replacing Pierre Mauroy. He was ousted as leader in April 1993, after the Socialists lost more than 200 seats in the March general election.

Fadden, Artie (Arthur William) (1895–1973)

Australian politician, leader of the Country Party 1941–58 and prime minister August–October 1941.

After working as a cane-cutter and an accountant, he was elected to the Queensland parliament, representing the rural-based Country Party. He entered the federal parliament in 1936. He was deputy prime minister and treasurer with the Liberal–Country Party coalition government of Robert ◊Menzies 1949–58, delivering a record 11 budgets. He was created a KCMG in 1951.

FURTHER READING
Fadden, Arthur *They Called Me Artie* 1969

Fadeev, Aleksandr Aleksandrovich,
pseudonym of Aleksandr Aleksandrovich Bulyga (1901–1956)

Russian novelist. He wrote *Razgrom/The Nineteen* (1927) about Siberian Red guerrillas during the Civil War, and *Molodaya Gvardiia/The Young Guard* (1945). As general secretary of the Soviet Writers' Union 1946–55, Fadeev took a prominent part in the campaign led by Communist Party secretary Andrey Zhdanov in the name of Socialist Realism against unorthodox trends in literature. However, his own work sometimes attracted official sanction for not stressing the central role of the party. Fadeev espoused

Stalinism; when this fell into disfavour after the dictator's death, he committed suicide.

Fahd (Ibn Abdul Aziz) (1923–)
See page 138.

Fairbairn, Joyce (1939–)

Canadian politician and literacy campaigner. She was appointed to the senate for Lethbridge, Alberta, in 1984 and, in 1993, was appointed to the cabinet as the first female leader of the government in the senate. Fairbairn launched a campaign for literacy in Canada in 1987 and was appointed minister with special responsibility for literacy in 1993. In 1997 she became the special advisor for literacy to the minister of human-resources development.

Fairbairn moved to Ottowa from her native Alberta, completing a degree in journalism at Carleton University in 1961. She worked originally as a journalist for the United Press International as part of the Parliamentary Press Gallery Bureau before entering politics. In 1970 she became legislative assistant to Prime Minister Pierre ◊Trudeau, later becoming his communications coordinator.

Faisal I (1885–1933)

King of Iraq 1921–33. During his reign, which included the achievement of full independence in 1932, he sought to foster pan-Arabism and astutely maintained a balance between Iraqi nationalists and British interests. He was succeded by his only son, Ghazi I, who was killed in an car accident in 1939.

Born in Ta'if, Hejaz, the third son of ◊Hussein ibn Ali, the king of Hejaz and founder of the Hashemite dynasty, he was brought up and educated in Constantinople (Istanbul), Turkey, where his father lived in exile, until 1908. During World War I, he joined his father and brothers in Hejaz to take an important role in a 1916–18 Arab nationalist revolt, which liberated the Middle East from Ottoman control. He commanded a 'Northern army', which harassed Turkish forces in guerrilla operations and took Damascus in October 1918. In March 1920 he was declared king of Syria by a nationalist congress, but was deposed by French military force in July 1920. Under the prompting of the British archaeologist Gertrude Bell, the

British mandate government in Iraq held a plebiscite in August 1921, which resulted in Faisal being overwhelmingly elected king. In 1923 he was made a constitutional monarch by the national assembly.

Throughout Faisal I's reign, the strongly pro-Western Nuri ◊ Es-Sa'id was an influential figure, serving as prime minister from 1930.

Faisal II (Faisal ibn Ghazi ibn Faisal of Hashim) (1935–1958)

King of Iraq 1939–58, with a regent until 1953. Although in 1956, in the aftermath of the Suez intervention, he formally declared that Iraq would continue to stand by Egypt, rivalry later grew between the two incipient Arab blocs. In February 1958 he therefore concluded, with his cousin King ◊ Hussein of Jordan, a federation of the two countries in opposition to the United Arab Republic of Egypt and Syria. In July 1958 he and his entire household were assassinated during a military coup and Iraq became a republic.

Born in Baghdad, Faisal was the great grandson, with King Hussein of Jordan, of ◊ Hussein ibn Ali. He succeeded his father, Ghazi I, the king of Iraq from 1933, who was killed in an car accident in 1939. After an education at Harrow public school in England, he was installed, on his 18th birthday, in May 1953 as the third king of modern Iraq, thus ending the 14-year regency of his uncle, Emir Abdul Illah.

Faisal (Ibn Abd al-Aziz) (1905–1975)

King of Saudi Arabia 1964–75. Ruling without a prime minister, he instituted a successful programme of economic modernization, using Saudi Arabia's vast annual oil revenues, which grew from $334 million in 1960 to $22.5 billion in 1974, after the quadrupling of world oil prices in 1973–74. A generous welfare system was established, including free medical care and education to postgraduate level, and subsidized food, water, fuel, electricity, and rents; slavery was outlawed; and financial support was given to other Arab states in their struggle with Israel. In March 1975 Faisal was assassinated by a mentally unstable nephew, Prince Museid, and his half-brother ◊ Khalid became king.

Born in Riyadh, Faisal was one of 43 sons of King Abdul Aziz ◊ Ibn Saud, the founder of the Saudi dynasty. Faisal fought alongside his father and, in 1925, led the army to victory over ◊ Hussein ibn Ali, in the Al Hijaz (the Hejaz) region of western Arabia. He became viceroy of Al Hijaz in 1932 and Saudi foreign minister from 1940. During the 'first oil boom' of 1947–52, he played a key role in shaping Saudi policies. In 1953, when his elder half-brother Saud became king, Faisal was declared Crown Prince and continued as foreign minister. He later served as prime minister from 1958–60 and from 1962. An advocate of gradual modernization and westernization, Faisal came into conflict with the more conservative King Saud from the 1960s and in November 1964 Saud was forced to abdicate in Faisal's favour.

FURTHER READING

Beling, W (ed) *King Faisal and the Modernization of Saudi Arabia* 1980

◆ FAHD (IBN ABDUL AZIZ) (1923–   ) ◆

King of Saudi Arabia from 1982. He encouraged the investment of the country's enormous oil wealth in infrastructure and new activities – such as petrochemical industries – in order to diversify the economy, and also built up the country's military forces. When Iraq invaded neighbouring Kuwait in August 1990, King Fahd joined with the USA and other international forces in 'Operation Desert Storm' in the course of the 1990–91 Gulf War, in which Saudi Arabia was used as the base from which Kuwait was liberated, in February 1991.

Falling oil prices from the 1980s led to a gradual reduction in the country's financial reserves and to some retrenchment and, in the 1990s, gradual privatization. From the early 1990s King Fahd's absolutist regime faced twin pressures from liberals, campaigning for democratic elections, and from fundamentalist Islamic groups, which opposed the monarchy and sought the full imposition of Islamic *sharia* law. In May 1993 a group of Islamic activists, led by Muhammad al-Masari, formed a Committee for the Defence of Legitimate Rights to monitor the regime's adherence to Islamic principles. In response to prodemocracy pressures, in August 1993 the king established an advisory Shura Council, comprising 60 members of the national elite, drawn from outside the royal family, and also established a system of regional government. In November 1995 King Fahd suffered a stroke, and in January 1996 he temporarily ceded power to Crown Prince Abdullah, his legal successor.

Born at Ta'if, the 11th son of King Abdul Aziz ◊ Ibn Saud, the founder of the Saudi dynasty, he was the eldest of seven sons borne by Ibn Saud's favourite wife, Hassa bint Ahmad al-Sudairi. He was educated at the royal court and at overseas universities. He served under King Saud as education minister from 1953 and interior minister from 1962 and, under King ◊ Faisal, who

Falkender, Marcia Matilda, Baroness Falkender (born Williams) (1932–)

English political worker, private and political secretary to Labour prime minister Harold Wilson from 1956. She was influential in the 'kitchen cabinet' of the 1964–70 government, as described in her book *Inside No 10* (1972).

Fall, Albert Bacon (1861–1944)

US civil servant who was involved in the Teapot Dome Scandal in the 1920s, which exposed US president Warren Harding's administration to allegations of corruption. As an official at the department of the interior, Fall was responsible for letting private companies exploit oil deposits on federal land, arguing that it was in the interest of the government. His own wealth grew through loans from oil executives, delivered in 'a little black bag'. Fall was tried and imprisoned in 1929.

FURTHER READING
Stratton, David H *Tempest over Teapot Dome: The Story of Albert B Fall* 1998

Fanfani, Amintore (1908–)

Italian right-wing politician. He was a Christian Democrat premier of Italy in 1954, 1958–59, and 1960–63. Subsequently he became foreign minister and was noted for his 'European' policy. He was again premier 1982–83 and in 1987.

Fanfani entered politics after World War II and held various offices under Alcide De Gasperi before becom-

was his full brother, he became second deputy prime minister from 1967. Fahd's influence increased further when ◊Khalid, his half-brother, became king in 1975. He became Crown Prince and first deputy prime minister, with effective charge of much of the day-to-day government. He became an influential negotiator of oil prices and promoter of peace in the Middle East, convening a summit conference at Fez in August 1981. On Khalid's death, in June 1982, Fahd became king and also head of government. He appointed his half-brother Abdullah ibn Abdul Aziz al-Saud, who was commander of the National Guard, as Crown Prince and first deputy prime minister, and his full brother, Sultan ibn Abdul Aziz al-Saud, the defence minister, as second deputy prime minister.

The Gulf War cost the Saudis $50 billion, and at its conclusion King Fahd pressed for reparations from Iraq, which he had formerly provided with up to $20 billion in financial assistance during the 1980–88 Iran–Iraq war.

FURTHER READING
Al-Kilani, K *Progress of a Nation: A Biography of King Fahd* 1985

King Fahd of Saudi Arabia, 1996. *Rex*

ing prime minister. After the failure of his 'opening to the left' in the 1960s, Fanfani became associated with the more conservative groups within the Christian Democrat Party. He played a leading role in the campaign for a referendum on the 1970 Divorce Bill, but was discredited by the negative vote. The communist gains in 1975 were seen as a further setback to his position.

Fang Lizhi (1936–)

Chinese political dissident and astrophysicist. Born in Guangzhou (Canton), he became a physics professor at the Hefei Institute of Science and Technology in Anhui province from 1978 and university vice president from 1984. In the mid-1980s he emerged as a fierce critic of the Chinese Communist Party (CCP)'s suppression of political pluralism, democracy, and human rights. As a consequence, he became dubbed 'China's Sakharov', after the Russian dissident Andrei ◊Sakharov.

In December 1986 Fang encouraged his students to campaign for genuine local elections. The prodemocracy crusade spread and got out of hand, leading to the dismissal, in 1987, of the reformist CCP leader Hu Yaobang and to Fang's dismissal from his university posts and from the CCP. However, he found a post as research fellow at the Beijing Astronomical Observatory. Along with his politically liberal wife, Li Shux ian, who was associate professor in Beijing University's physics department, Fang was accused by the CCP leadership of being the 'black hand' behind the 1989 student prodemocracy protest movement which shook the communist regime.

After the Red Army massacred the student demonstrators in Tiananmen Square, Beijing, in June 1989, Fang and his wife sought refuge in the US embassy in Beijing, where they remained until June 1990, when they were allowed to leave China. Fang took up a research post in Cambridge University, England, before moving to the USA.

Farinacci, Roberto (1892–1945)

Italian politician. Fascist Party Secretary from 1924 to 1926, he became a member of the Fascist Grand Council in 1935 and was appointed minister of state in 1938. An ardent racist and anti-Semite, notorious for his extremism and pro-Nazi tendencies, he edited the *Regime Fascista*, the party organ. He was shot while attempting to flee to Switzerland.

Farinaci was born in Isernia. He was ultimately captured and killed on the same day, and by the same band of partisans, as Mussolini.

Farmer, James Leonard (1920–)

US civil-rights activist. A founding member of the Congress of Racial Equality (CORE), he was its national director 1961–66. He was the executive director of the Coalition of American Public Employees and became a professor at Mary Washington College, Fredericksburg, Virginia. He was awarded the Presidential Medal of Freedom in 1998.

Farmer was born in Marshall, Texas. While connected with CORE, he led student sit-ins and Freedom Bus rides. In 1985 he published *Lay Bare the Heart: An Autobiography*.

Farouk (1920–1965)

King of Egypt 1936–52. He succeeded the throne on the death of his father ◊Fuad I. His early popularity was later overshadowed by his somewhat unsuccessful private life, and more importantly by the humiliating defeat of the Egyptian army by Israel in 1948. In 1952 a group called the 'Free Officers', led by Mohammed Neguib and Gamal Abdel Nasser, forced him to abdicate, and he was temporarily replaced by his son Ahmad Fuad II. Exiled for the remainder of his life, he died in Rome in 1965.

Farrakhan, Louis born Louis Eugene Walcott (1933–)

Black American religious and political figure. Leader of the Nation of Islam, Farrakhan preached strict adherence to Muslim values and black separatism. His outspoken views against Jews, homosexuals, and whites caused outrage. In 1995 he organized the 'Million Men March' of about 400,000 black men in Washington, DC.

In 1986 Farrakhan was banned from entering the UK for his anti-Semitic views. In one speech he referred to Judaism as a 'gutter religion'.

Born in the Bronx in New York, Farrakhan studied to be a teacher and worked as a singer before he was recruited to the Black Muslims by ◊Malcolm X. When the group was dissolved in 1985 he remained faithful to its original principles, forming a splinter group using its original name, the Nation of Islam. A powerful leader and impressive speaker, he increased the group's membership to over 15,000 in the 1990s.

FURTHER READING
Levinsohn, Florence Hamlish *Looking for Farrakhan* 1997

Fassi, Allal al- (1910–1974)

Moroccan nationalist leader. Arrested in 1937 by the colonial authorities, he was sent into exile in Gabon and his organization, the Parti National (PN), was dissolved. Upon his return in 1946, his party was already reconstituted as the Parti de l'Istiqlal (PI), advocating this time the cause of independence. He voluntarily decided to go to Egypt and worked there to rally support for Moroccan independence until his return in 1956. Becoming president of the PI in 1960, he joined the opposition and remained an ardent defender of his country's territorial claims.

Among the first prominent figures of the nationalist movement in Morocco, his early struggle was for greater political, civil, and educational rights for Moroccans.

Fateh Singh, Sant (1911–1972)

Sikh religious leader. Born in the Punjab, India, he was a campaigner for Sikh rights and was involved in religious and educational activity in Rajastan, founding many schools and colleges there. In 1942 he joined the Quit India Movement, and was imprisoned for his political activities. During the 1950s he agitated for a Punjabi-speaking state, which was achieved once Haryana was created as a separate state in 1966.

Faulkner, (Arthur) Brian (Deane), Baron Faulkner of Downpatrick (1921–1977)

Northern Ireland Unionist politician. He was the last prime minister of Northern Ireland 1971–72 before the Stormont parliament was suspended. He was created Baron in 1977.

Faure, Edgar (1908–1988)

French Radical politician, prime minister in 1952 and 1955–56, when he was the first prime minister since 1876 to dissolve the national assembly rather than resign after a no-confidence vote. As education minister after the student revolt of 1968, he reformed the curriculum and university management, giving institutions autonomy and introducing staff–student representation. He was president of the national assembly 1973–78.

A lawyer by training, Faure was France's assistant prosecutor at the Nuremberg trials in 1945. Elected deputy for the Jura *département* 1946–58 and rarely out of ministerial office 1949–58, he led his party's conservative wing against Pierre ◊Mendès-France. Appointed professor of law at Dijon University from 1962, he returned to government under President Charles ◊de Gaulle, as minister for agriculture 1966–68, for education 1968–69 and, under Georges ◊Pompidou, for social affairs 1972–73. Faure also published historical and political works and (under the pseudonym Edgar Sunday) detective novels.

Fawcett, Millicent, born Garrett (1847–1929)

English suffragette and social reformer, younger sister of Elizabeth Garrett Anderson. A non-militant, she rejected the violent acts of some of her contemporaries in the suffrage movement. She joined the first Women's Suffrage Committee in 1867 and became president of the Women's Unionist Association in 1889. She was president of the National Union of Women's Suffrage Societies 1897–1919.

She was also active in property reform and campaigned for the right of married women to own their own property, and the higher education and employment of women. She was made a DBE in 1925.

Fawcett was born in Aldeburgh, Suffolk. In 1867 she married Henry Fawcett, the politician. Her publications include *Some Eminent Women of our Time* (1889), *Women's Suffrage* (1912), *Women's Victory and After* (1920), and *What I Remember* (1925).

Federzoni, Luigi (1878–1967)

Italian Fascist politician. As minister of the interior 1924–26, he subjected the press to stringent controls, but also instructed prefects to curb Fascist violence. Distrusted by Fascist activists, he was moved away from key political positions, and served as senator 1928–39 and president of the senate 1929–39. He was sentenced to life imprisonment in 1945, but amnestied in 1947.

Federzoni began his political career in the Italian Nationalist Association and entered Fascism through the fusion of the two movements in 1923. He was appointed minister of colonies 1922–24 and 1926–28.

Feinstein, Dianne, born Goldman (1933–)

US Democrat politician. She was mayor of San Francisco 1978–88, the first woman in the post, and became senator from California in 1993.

She was born in San Francisco. An expert on criminal justice, she was appointed to the California Women's Board of Terms and Paroles in 1962, elected to the Board of Supervisors in 1969, and was its president 1970–72 and 1974–76. In December 1978, following the assassination of Mayor George Moscone

(1949–1978), she was elected to finish Moscone's term as mayor to the end of 1979, and then re-elected mayor. She achieved a reputation as a tough hands-on governor, with no detail too small for her attention.

She was defeated by Senator Pete Wilson (1933–) in the election for governor of California in 1991, and elected to the Senate in 1992 to fill the vacancy left by him. She was re-elected in 1994 after the most expensive race in Senate history.

Feng Guozhang or *Feng Kuo-chang* (1859–1919)

Chinese militarist. He served as a provincial military governor before becoming acting president of the Chinese Republic 1917–18. During his one year in office China declared war on Germany.

He trained at the Beiyang Military Acacemy, one of the military schools established during the last decades of the Qing (Ch'ing) Dynasty. On graduating, he entered the service of ◊Yuan Shikai, commander of the Beiyang Army, China's first modern army. After the creation of a republic in 1912, he became one of a number of influential militarists known as the 'Beiyang Clique'.

Feng Yuxiang or *Fung* or *Feng Yü-hsiang*, known as *the Christian General* (1882–1948)

Chinese warlord. He rose through the ranks to command an independent force and in 1924 took Beijing (Peking), and set up a government that included members of the Nationalist Party. He supported the Nationalist government in 1927, but became apprehensive of the growing personal power of ◊Jiang Jie Shi (Chiang Kai-shek), and joined in two successive revolts, both of which failed.

He left China in 1947 to visit the USA, and died in a ship fire on his return journey.

Ferdinand (1861–1948)

King of Bulgaria 1908–18. Son of Prince Augustus of Saxe-Coburg-Gotha, he was elected prince of Bulgaria in 1887 and in 1908 proclaimed Bulgaria's independence from Turkey and assumed the title of tsar. In 1915 he entered World War I as Germany's ally, and in 1918 he abdicated.

Fergusson, Honorable Muriel McQueen (1899–1997)

Canadian lawyer and politician who was the first woman speaker of the Senate of Canada. From her appointment to the Senate in 1953 to her appointment as speaker in 1972, Fergusson served on various Senate committees concerned with the rights of women. Previously, she was the first woman elected to the

Fredericton City Council in New Brunswick, and was the first woman deputy mayor of that city until she entered the Senate.

McQueen Fergusson was born in New Brunswick. She graduated from Mount Allison University in 1921, went on to study law at Dalhouise University and, against her mother's wishes, articled in her father's law office; she was admitted to the bar in 1925. After her husband's death in 1942, she took over the running of the firm. Her career in politics began with her application for regional director of the family allowance programme, which was rejected because she was a woman. However, she continued to challenge the status quo and later became the first director of the family allowance and old-age security programmes in New Brunsuck.

She retired from the Senate in 1975 at the age of 75 and died in Fredericton, New Brunswick, on 11 April 1997.

Fernández, Leonel (1953–)

Dominican Republic centre-left politician, president from 1996. Selected as presidential candidate of the centre-left Dominican Liberation Party (PLD) following the retirement of Juan ◊Bosch, Fernández was narrowly elected president in 1996, after receiving backing from the outgoing president Joaquín ◊Balaguer. Pledging to fight poverty and corruption, he also launched a shake-up of the top ranks of the military and police, but the lack of a PLD majority in Congress weakened his position.

Ferraro, Geraldine Anne (1935–)

US Democratic politician, vice-presidential candidate in the 1984 election.

Ferraro, a lawyer, was elected to Congress in 1981 and was selected in 1984 by Walter Mondale to be the USA's first female vice-presidential candidate from one of the major parties. The Democrats were defeated by the incumbent president Ronald Reagan, and Ferraro, damaged by investigations of her husband's business affairs, retired temporarily from politics. She was appointed in 1993 to the United Nations Human Rights Commission.

Field, Winston Joseph (1904–1969)

English-born Rhodesian politician. He went to Rhodesia in 1921 and entered politics in 1958, becoming prime minister in 1962. In 1964 he was succeeded by the more militant Ian ◊Smith.

He was educated at Bromsgrove School, England. Before going into politics, he was a successful tobacco farmer.

Figueiredo, João Baptista de Oliveiro (1918–)

Brazilian military leader, politician, and president

1979–85. His election to presidential office was significant in that he endeavoured to bring about the greater liberalization of military governmental control and his rule effectively enabled the country to move closer to democratic control. His administration was faced with severe economic problems, high inflation, and poor wealth distribution.

The initiation of a programme of economic measures to redistribute wealth was aimed specifically to assist those most affected by economic conditions – the poor, lower classes. He aligned salary increases to inflation, devalued the currency, and altered interest rates. In his quest for the greater democratization of politics, Figueiredo allowed the creation of new political parties early in his administration, which angered many on the extreme political right. In 1985 Brazil elected its first civilian president since the period of military rule commenced in 1964.

Figueiredo, a general and former head of the national intelligence service in 1974, was selected by the military as a presidential candidate in the 1979 elections to succeed President Ernesto Geisel (1908–1996).

Figueres Ferrer, José (1906–1990)

Costa Rican social-democrat politician, leader of the democratic revolution of 1948–49 and president 1953–58 and 1970–74. In 1948 he founded Democratic Action, from which the social-democratic National Liberation Party (PLN) emerged (in 1951), and led an armed revolution to ensure that President Rafael Ángel ◊Calderón Guardia, who had lost a presidential election to Otilio Ulate, did not return to power. Figueres headed a reformist junta for 18 months, which abolished the army, enfranchised women, and nationalized the banking, insurance, and power sectors, before handing over power in 1949 to Ulate. Figueres was popularly elected president in 1953, and introduced welfare and educational reforms. In his second term 1970–74, he established diplomatic relations with the USSR and promised a war against poverty, but social and economic reforms were more limited.

Figueres spent four years of his early adult life in the USA before returning to Costa Rica and becoming a successful planter. After a making a radio speech critical of President Calderón, he was forced into exile in Mexico 1942–44.

His son, José María ◊Figueres Olsen, was president 1994–98.

FURTHER READING
Ameringer, Charles D *Don Pepe: A Political Biography of José Figueres of Costa Rica* 1979

Figueres Olsen, José María (1954–)

Costa Rican politician, president 1994–98. Standing as the candidate of the centre-left National Liberation Party (PLN), he won the February 1994 presidential election, narrowly defeating Miguel Angel Rodríguez Echeverría of the Social Christian Unity Party (PUSC). Figueres held office at a time of economic difficulties and decided not to seek re-election in February 1998. He was succeeded as president by his 1994 rival, Rodríguez.

The son of José ◊Figueres Ferrer, he studied engineering at the Westpoint military academy and public affairs at Harvard University in the USA. After a career in business management, he served as minister of foreign trade and agriculture.

Fikes, Bettie Mae (1948–   )

US musician and civil-rights activist. Born in Selma, Alabama, Bettie Mae Fikes began singing at the age of four. After spending some time in California, she returned to Selma, where historical events drew her into the role of a music leader for the civil-rights movement – at which time she received a three-week jail sentence for singing during the Selma voting-rights struggle in 1963. In May 1998 she appeared at Carnegie Hall, and performed with folk singers Peter, Paul, and Mary at the Newport Folk Festival. In the 1990s she toured with the Freedom Singers – a group that emerged from the Student Nonviolent Coordinating Committee (SNCC) in the 1960s.

Firestone, Shulamith (1945–   )

Canadian feminist writer and editor. Her book *The Dialectic of Sex: The Case for Feminist Revolution* (1970), which analysed the limited future of feminism under Marxist and Freudian theories, exerted considerable influence on feminist thought.

She was one of the early organizers of the women's liberation movement in the USA. Her other works include *Notes from the Second Year* (1970).

First, Ruth (1925–1982)

South African journalist and opponent of apartheid. In her youth she joined the South African Communist Party and was secretary of the Progressive Youth Council. She worked as a journalist from 1947, the year she exposed the appalling conditions of black workers at Bethal Farm in South West Africa (modern Namibia). In 1956 she was arrested together with 156 others including Nelson ◊Mandela on treason charges. Following the publication of her book *South West Africa* in 1963 she was prohibited from publishing any more of her writings. Later that year she was arrested and held in solitary confinement for 117 days. In 1964 she went into political exile in the UK where she became a lecturer at Durham University. In 1978 she left for Mozambique to become research director at the Centre for African Studies at the Eduardo Mondlane University in Maputo. She was killed by a parcel bomb in 1982, an act widely attributed to the South African authorities.

She married the South African Communist Party leader Joe ◊Slovo in 1949.

Fisher, Andrew (1862–1928)

Australian Labor politician. Born in Scotland, he went to Australia in 1885. He entered the Australian parliament in 1901 and became Labor Party leader in 1907. He was prime minister 1908–09, 1910–13, and 1914–15, and Australian high commissioner to the UK 1916–21.

He left school at an early age and worked in the coalmines before migrating. A teetotal Presbyterian, he introduced welfare reforms, including invalidity pensions and maternity allowances, and began the transcontinental railway. An opponent to conscription to assist the imperial war effort, he resigned as party leader in 1915 in favour of Billy ◊Hughes.

Fitt, Gerry (Gerard), Baron Fitt (1926–   )

Northern Ireland politician. From 1962 to 1972 he represented the Dock Division of Belfast as a Republican Labour member of the Northern Ireland parliament, then founded and led the Social Democratic Labour Party (SDLP). He was an SDLP MP for nine years, resigning the leadership in 1979 to sit as an Independent socialist. He lost his Belfast seat in the 1983 general election.

He had earlier been a member of the Northern Ireland executive 1973–75, and was its deputy chief executive in 1974.

In the course of his career, Fitt, an opponent of violence, had to endure the animosity of both Republican and Loyalist extremists. He was created Baron in 1983.

FitzGerald, Garret Michael (1926–   )

See page 144.

Fleming, Ian Lancaster (1908–1964)

English author. His suspense novels feature the ruthless, laconic James Bond, British Secret Service agent 007. The first novel in the series was *Casino Royale* (1953); others include *From Russia with Love* (1957), *Goldfinger* (1959), and *The Man with the Golden Gun* (1965). Most of the novels were made into successful films.

During World War II he worked for British Intelligence where he had the opportunity to give full rein to his vivid imagination in disseminating false information and rumours.

Fleming was born in London, the son of an army officer who died in World War I. He was educated at Eton, Sandhurst, and Munich and Geneva universities. After a number of years with Reuters news agency, he worked successively with banking and stockbroking firms, and in World War II was personal assistant to the director of naval intelligence.

Flores Facussé, Carlos Roberto (1950–)

Honduran politician, president from 1998. A member of the centre-right Liberal Party of Honduras (PLH), he was a minister 1982–86 under President Roberto Suazo Córdova, and in 1989 an unsuccessful presidential candidate. He was president of the national assembly for four years before his election as head of state.

Educated in the USA, Flores was a co-owner of the independent *La Tribuna* daily newspaper and fought his presidential election campaign on a free-market platform.

Flosse, Gaston (1931–)

French Polynesian right-of-centre politician, head of government 1984–87 and from 1991. He founded the Tahoeraa Huiraatira (TH) as a regional offshoot of the right-wing Rally for the Republic (RPR) party in 1977 and served in the French National Assembly 1978–82 and 1993–97. President of the French Polynesia Territorial Assembly's council of ministers from 1984, he resigned in 1987 after criticisms of inappropriate use of public funds, but returned in 1991 and also served as minister for foreign affairs and tourism. Formerly a supporter of French nuclear tests in the South Pacific, he changed his stance in 1995 as opposition to renewed nuclear tests helped to strengthen the movement for independence from France, a policy which he firmly opposed.

Born at Rikitea, in the Gambier islands, Flosse became mayor of Pirae in 1965 and was first elected to the French Polynesia Territorial Assembly in 1967.

Flynn, Elizabeth Gurley (1890–1964)

US labour leader and social reformer. She became an organizer for the Industrial Workers of the World. She also worked for women's suffrage, peace, and other progressive causes, and was one of the founders of the American Civil Liberties Union.

She was born in Concord, New Hampshire. She worked for such causes as the release of civilians imprisoned during World War I on war-related charges, and then worked to free the controversially convicted murderers Nicola Sacco and Bartolomeo Vanzetti. She joined the Communist Party and became one of its most outspoken leaders in the USA. She served two years in prison, charged with advocating the overthrow of the US government. She chaired the Communist Party of America 1961–64. She died in Moscow where she had gone to work on her autobiography.

Foley, Thomas S(tephen) (1929–)

US Democrat politician. He was speaker of the House of Representatives 1989–94.

Foley was born in Spokane, Washington. A member of the House of Representatives from 1965, he was chair of the Democratic Study Group from 1974 and chair of the Congressional Agriculture Committee 1974–80. He became majority whip in 1980 and majority leader 1986. He was a reform-minded liberal who

◆ FITZGERALD, GARRET MICHAEL (1926–) ◆

Irish politician, leader of the Fine Gael party 1977–87. As Taoiseach (prime minister) 1981–82 and 1982–87, he attempted to solve the Northern Ireland dispute, ultimately by participating in the Anglo-Irish Agreement in 1985. He tried to remove some of the overtly Catholic features of the constitution to make the Republic more attractive to Northern Protestants.

Having entered the Seanad Éireann (Irish senate) in 1965, FitzGerald was minister for foreign affairs 1973–77, under Liam Cosgrave, and then became Taoiseach himself, leading a Fine Gael–Labour Party coalition. Always an internationalist in outlook, he recognized at an early stage the significance to Ireland of its membership of the European Community (EC; now the European Union) and, as part of that membership, the need to find a peaceful, lasting accommodation with its nearest neighbour, the UK.

In 1985 he signed the Anglo-Irish Agreement with the UK prime minister Margaret Thatcher. The agreement provided for regular consultation between the two governments and the exchange of information on political, legal, security, and cross-border matters, and, significantly, contained the provision that no change in the status of Northern Ireland would be made without the consent of the majority of its people.

FitzGerald was born in Dublin, the son of Desmond FitzGerald, a cabinet minister in the Irish Free State. He studied law at University College and King's Inns, Dublin, and became a barrister in 1947. Initially he worked for the Irish airline, Aer Lingus, but then decided to pursue an academic career. After a period as a Rockefeller research assistant at Trinity College, he lectured in politics at University College in Dublin 1959–87.

He also worked as a journalist – as Irish correspondent for the BBC, the *London Financial Times*, and *The Economist*, and economics correspondent for the *Irish Times*. His books include *Planning in Ireland* (1968), *Towards a New Ireland* (1972), and a well-received autobiography *All in a Life* (1991).

did not upset his opponents. He was the first incumbent speaker to be defeated in an election since 1960.

Foot, Dingle Mackintosh (1905–1978)

British lawyer and Labour politician, solicitor general 1964–67. He was the brother of Michael Foot. He was knighted in 1964.

Foot, Hugh Mackintosh, Baron Caradon (1907–1990)

British Labour politician. As governor of Cyprus 1957–60, he guided the independence negotiations, and he represented the UK at the United Nations 1964–70. He was the son of Isaac Foot and brother of Michael Foot. He was created a KCMG in 1951 and Baron in 1964.

Foot, Isaac (1880–1960)

British Liberal politician. A staunch Nonconformist, he was minister of mines 1931–32. He was the father of Dingle, Hugh, and Michael Foot.

Foot, Michael Mackintosh (1913–)

British Labour politician and writer. A leader of the left-wing Tribune Group, he was secretary of state for employment 1974–76, Lord President of the Council and leader of the House 1976–79, and succeeded James Callaghan as Labour Party leader 1980–83.

The son of Isaac ◊Foot, the Liberal politician, and brother of Hugh ◊Foot and Dingle ◊Foot, he was educated at Leighton Park School, Reading, and Wadham College, Oxford. A journalist, he was elected Labour member of Parliament for Plymouth (Devonport) in 1945, but was defeated in 1955 and elected for Ebbw Vale in 1960.

The members of our secret service have apparently spent so much time looking under the beds for Communists, they haven't had time to look in the bed.

MICHAEL FOOT Attributed remark, referring to the Profumo Affair
1963

For most of his career Foot was a leading member of the left wing of the Labour Party and a prominent member of the Tribune Group. Not only did he succeed Aneurin Bevan as MP for Ebbw Vale, he was widely regarded as the latter's successor as leader of the Left. There was no ministerial post for Foot in the Wilson government, but he became an opposition spokesperson between 1970 and 1974. Foot was runner-up to Callaghan in the Labour Party leadership contest of 1976.

His publications include: *Guilty Men* (1957), *The Pen and the Sword* (1957), *Aneurin Bevan* (two volumes published in 1962 and 1973), and *H G: The History of Mr Wells* (1995).

Garret FitzGerald. *Rex*

FURTHER READING
Hoggart, Simon, and Leigh, David *Michael Foot: A Portrait* 1981
Jones, Mervyn *Michael Foot* 1994

Forbes, George William (1869–1947)

New Zealand centre-right politician, prime minister 1930–35. He was Liberal Party whip from 1912 and leader between 1925–28. He became leader again, when it had become the United Party, in 1930, and also prime minister. A genial, uncomplicated politician, described as a 'plain man without frills', Forbes led the country through the difficulties of the Great Depression, heading a United Party–Reform Party coalition. However, his inflexibility as unemployment increased led to a crushing electoral defeat in 1935 and a first-ever victory for the Labour Party, led by Michael ◊Savage.

After winning a land ballot in 1893, Forbes became a farmer. He was first elected to the House of Representatives in 1908 and remained a member of Parliament until his retirement in 1943. During his long political career he switched between the Liberal, National, United, and Coalition parties.

Ford, Gerald R(udolph) (1913–)

38th president of the USA 1974–77, a Republican. He

was elected to the House of Representatives in 1948, was nominated to the vice presidency by Richard Nixon in 1973 on the resignation of Spiro ◊Agnew, and became president in 1974, when Nixon was forced to resign following the Watergate scandal. He granted Nixon a full pardon in September 1974.

Ford was appointed vice president in December 1973, at a time when Nixon's re-election campaign was already being investigated for 'dirty tricks', and became president the following August. Ford's visit to Vladivostok in 1974 resulted in agreement with the USSR on strategic arms limitation. He survived two assassination attempts in September 1975. He was defeated by Jimmy Carter in the 1976 election by a narrow margin. He is the only US president never to have been elected as vice president or president.

Ford was born in Omaha, Nebraska, was an All-American footballer at college, and graduated from Yale Law School. He served in the US navy 1942–46, and became a Republican representative from Michigan in 1948. In 1965 he became House minority leader, and permanent chair of the Republican national conventions in 1968 and 1972.

FURTHER READING
Fitzgerald, Carol (ed) *Gerald R Ford* 1988
Ford, Gerald *A Time to Heal* 1979
Osborne, John *The White House Watch: The Ford Years* 1977

Ford, Henry (1863–1947)

US car manufacturer. He built his first car in 1896 and founded the Ford Motor Company in 1903. His Model T (1908–27) was the first car to be constructed solely by assembly-line methods and to be mass-marketed; 15 million of these cars were sold.

Ford's innovative policies, such as a $5 daily minimum wage (at the time nearly double the average figure in Detroit) and a five-day working week, revolutionized employment practices, but he opposed the introduction of trade unions.

History is more or less bunk. The only history that is worth a tinker's damn is the history we make today.

HENRY FORD Interview with Charles N Wheeler *Chicago Tribune* 25 May 1916

Ford was politically active and a pacifist; he opposed US intervention in both world wars and promoted his own anti-Semitic views. In 1918 he ran unsuccessfully for the Senate, and in 1923 he considered running for the presidency, but later announced his refusal to stand against Calvin ◊Coolidge. In 1936 he founded, with his son Edsel Ford (1893–1943), the philanthropic Ford Foundation; he retired in 1945 from the Ford Motor Company, then valued at over $1 billion.

FURTHER READING
Herndon, B *Ford* 1969
Lacey, R *Ford: The Man and the Machine* 1986
Nye, D *Henry Ford: Ignorant Idealist* 1979
Rae, J B *Henry Ford* 1969

Forde, Frank (Francis Michael) (1890–1983)

Australian Labor politician, prime minister for six days in 1945. He was deputy prime minister and minister for the army under John ◊Curtin from 1941 and on Curtin's death was sworn in as caretaker prime minister 6–13 July. He was defeated by Ben ◊Chifley in the subsequent leadership contest and in 1946 was appointed high commissioner to Canada until 1953.

Born in Queensland, he worked as a school teacher and electrical engineer before being elected to the state assembly in 1917. He entered the federal parliament in 1922 and, hard-working and loyal, became Labor Party deputy leader in 1932.

Forrest, John, 1st Baron Forrest of Bunbury (1847–1918)

Australian explorer and politician. He crossed Western Australia from west to east in 1870, when he went along the south coast route, and in 1874, when he crossed much further north, exploring the Musgrave Ranges. He was born in Western Australia, and was its first premier 1890–1901, enfranchising women in 1899. He was knighted in 1891 and created Baron in 1918.

A trained surveyor, he was surveyor general 1883–90. He sat in the federal parliament 1901–18, being treasurer (finance minister) in five governments, and emerged as a staunch protectionist. In 1918 he was the first Australian-born person to become a peer, but died at sea, on his way to England, before taking up his seat in the House of Lords.

Forrestal, James Vincent (1892–1949)

US Democratic politician. As undersecretary from 1940 and secretary of the navy from 1944, he organized its war effort, accompanying the US landings on the Japanese island of Iwo Jima. He was the first secretary of the Department of Defense 1947–49, a post created to unify the three armed forces at the end of World War II.

Forrestal was born in Matteawan, New York, educated at Dartmouth College and Princeton, and became a stockbroker. In his position as undersecretary to the navy, he was responsible for all material provided for the navy, and was the driving force behind an immense production of ships, planes, guns, and other munitions of war. Exhaustion and illness forced him to resign in 1949, and he committed suicide. He wrote *The Forrestal Diaries*, published posthumously in 1951. The US Navy's 'Forrestal' class of aircraft carriers is named after him.

Foster, William Zebulon (1881–1961)

US Communist leader. Secretary of the American Communist Party, he was the party's presidential candidate three times. He was indicted with 11 others on charges of advocating the overthrow of the US government, but was excused trial because of illness.

He was born in Taunton, Massachusetts. An itinerant labourer in his youth, he joined the Socialist Party in 1901 and worked as a labour organizer for the next two decades, gaining fame for organizing the 1919 steel strike. He took over the chairmanship of the party and held the post until 1956. He died in Moscow shortly after going there for medical treatment. Although lacking formal education, he wrote many essays and books.

Foucault, Michel Paul (1926–1984)

French philosopher. A pioneering contributor to the development of postmodernist thought through his explorations of madness, sexuality, and crime, Foucault's subversion of conventional assumptions about 'social deviance' gained widespread currency from the late 1970s.

Born in Poitiers, the son of a well-to-do surgeon and a graduate of the Ecole Normale Supérieure, Foucault rejected phenomenology and existentialism, while his historicization of the self and of human knowledge also challenged the ideas of Marxism. He shared with theorists like Jacques Lacan, in the field of linguistic philosophy, and Claude Lévi-Strauss, in the field of social anthropolgy, an underlying concern with uncovering the intellectual archaeology of key concepts and ideas. In his work he applied this approach to unravelling the interplay of power and knowledge in the social construction of 'deviant behaviour'. His major publications include *Histoire de la folie/Madness and Civilization* (1961) and *Les Mots et les choses/The Order of Things* (1966).

Fowler, (Peter) Norman (1938–)

British Conservative politician, chair of the party 1992–94. He was a junior minister in Edward Heath's government, transport secretary in Margaret Thatcher's first administration in 1979, social services secretary in 1981, and employment secretary 1987–89.

Fowler was chair of the Cambridge University Conservative Association in 1960. He worked as correspondent for *The Times* until 1970, when he became a member of Parliament. In 1997 he became the environment secretary in William Hague's shadow cabinet. He was knighted in 1990.

Fowler, Gerald (Gerry) (1935–1993)

British politician and academic. A Labour member of parliament 1966–79, he campaigned for equal access for all to higher education.

The loss of his parliamentary seat in 1970 allowed him to experience as an academic the Open University and the new polytechnics – two of the innovations in which he had been involved politically. As rector of the Polytechnic of North London 1982–92, and as a combative chair of the Committee of Directors of Polytechnics, he was involved in the transfer of the polytechnics from local government control and their elevation to university status in 1992.

Franco, Francisco (Paulino Hermenegildo Teódulo Bahamonde) (1892–1975)

Spanish dictator from 1939. As a general, he led the insurgent Nationalists to victory in the Spanish Civil War 1936–39, supported by Fascist Italy and Nazi Germany, and established a dictatorship. In 1942 Franco reinstated a Cortes (Spanish parliament), which in 1947 passed an act by which he became head of state for life.

Franco was born in Galicia, northwestern Spain. He entered the army in 1910, served in Morocco 1920–26, and was appointed Chief of Staff in 1935, but demoted to governor of the Canary Islands in 1936. Dismissed from this post by the Popular Front (Republican) government, he plotted an uprising with German and Italian assistance, and on the outbreak of the Civil War organized the invasion of Spain by North African troops and foreign legionaries. After the death of General Sanjurjo, he took command of the Nationalists, proclaiming himself *caudillo* (leader) of Spain. The defeat of the Republic with the surrender of Madrid in 1939 brought all Spain under his government. On the outbreak of World War II, in spite of Spain's official attitude of 'strictest neutrality', his pro-Axis sympathies led him to send aid, later withdrawn, to the German side.

At home, he curbed the growing power of the Falange Española (the fascist party), and in later years slightly liberalized his regime. In 1969 he nominated ◊Juan Carlos as his successor and future king of Spain. He relinquished the premiership in 1973, but remained head of state until his death.

FURTHER READING
Crozier, Brian *Franco: A Biographical History* 1967
Ellwood, Sheelagh *Franco* 1994
Gallo, Max *Spain Under Franco: A History* translation 1974
Payne, Stanley *Franco's Spain* 1968
Preston, Paul *Franco: A Biography* 1993
Trythall, J W D *Il Caudillo: A Political Biography of Franco* 1970

Franco, Itamar (1931–)

Brazilian politician and president 1992–94, governor of Minas Gerais state from 1998. During his first months in office he attracted widespread criticism, both from friends (for his working methods and lack of clear policies) and opponents. Franco's greatest achievement was the introduction in 1994 of the Plano Real programme to stabilize the economy. He was defeated by Fernando Henrique Cardoso in the October 1994 presidential election but Cardoso saw the programme implemented.

He also introduced a rapid privatization programme and was bold enough to acknowledge the poverty that afflicted the nation, requesting the middle classes to organize themselves into groups to help the disadvantaged.

Although vice president 1990–92, he had a largely low-profile political career until his elevation to head of state. Replacing President Fernando Collor after his removal on charges of corruption, Franco came to the office with a clean record.

Franjiyeh, Suleiman or *Sulayman Franjiyya* (1910–   )

Lebanese Maronite Christian politician, president 1970–76. He emerged as a fierce rival of the conservative Maronite political clans of Camille Chamoun and Bechir Gemayel and from 1960 sat in the Lebanese parliament, serving as a minister 1960–61 and 1968–70. He was elected president, by the parliament, in August 1970, when he defeated Elias Sarkis by a single vote.

Although aware of the dangers posed to Lebanon's stability by the presence of Palestinian guerrillas, as president Franjiyeh took no action and in April 1975 civil war broke out. An opponent of cooperation with Israel, he became increasingly close to Syria during the final year of his presidential term, which ended in September 1976, and in early 1976 he invited Syrian armed intervention.

During the late 1970s the Franjiyeh clan's Marada militia became involved in clashes with the larger Phalangist militia of the Gemayels. The Phalangists had greater success and were responsible for the assassination in June 1978 of Suleiman Franjiyeh's son, Antoine, and daughter-in-law and grandaughter. This influenced his decision, during 1983–84, to join the Sunni Muslim militia of Rashid Karami and the Druze Muslim militia of Walid Jumblatt in an anti-Gemayel National Salvation Front. Franjiyeh backed the 1989 Taif Agreement for a Syrian-guided reformist regime. The agreement was similar to one he had devised in 1976, but which had been rejected by the Muslim-Palestinian camp.

Franjiyeh was born into a dominant Maronite Christian family in the Zagharta region of northern Mount Lebanon. His elder brother, Hamid Franjiyeh, was a candidate for the presidency in 1952 and a former foreign minister. Suleiman became organizer of the Franjiyehs' Marada militia and in 1957, after Hamid had suffered a stroke, entered politics as the Franjiyeh clan's leader.

Frank, Hans (1900–1946)

German bureaucrat and governor of Poland in World War II. Originally a lawyer and a member of the Nazi Party from its early years, he became Reichs Commissioner for Justice in 1933. After the German invasion of Poland in 1939 he was appointed governor general of the Generalgouvernement, that part of Poland not incorporated into the Reich. He was executed for war crimes.

He ran a brutal and repressive regime aimed at the total subjugation of the Poles and the extraction of every possible economic advantage from the territory using slave labour and Jewish extermination. As the Soviet army approached in August 1944 he resigned his post and fled. He was captured after the defeat of Germany, tried at Nürnberg, and hanged on 16 October 1946.

Frank, Karl Hermann (1898–1946)

Czech Nazi politician. Originally a leader of the Sudeten German Nazi Party, he became secretary of state for Bohemia and Moravia after their annexation by Germany in 1939. Among other atrocities, he was responsible for the destruction of Lidice and the murder of its inhabitants in June 1942 as a reprisal for the assassination of Reinhard ◊Heydrich. He was captured at the end of the war, tried, and publicly hanged near Prague in May 1946.

Franklin, (Stella Marian Sarah) Miles (1879–1954)

Australian novelist. Her first novel, *My Brilliant Career* (1901), autobiographical and feminist, drew on her experiences of rural Australian life. *My Career Goes Bung*, written as a sequel, was not published until 1946.

Miles Franklin was born at Talbingo, near Tumut, New South Wales. In 1906 she went to Chicago, USA, where for nine years, with fellow Australian Alice ◊Henry, she worked with suffragette and women's trade-union organizations. She then lived in London from 1915, before returning to Australia in 1927.

Fraser, (John) Malcolm (1930–   )

Australian Liberal politician, prime minister 1975–83. He was nicknamed 'the Prefect' because of a supposed disregard of subordinates.

Born in Melbourne, the grandson of an influential politician and businessman, Fraser was educated at Oxford University, and later became a millionaire sheep farmer, following his father's occupation. He entered the federal parliament in 1955 and began his ministerial career in 1966, holding the defence portfolio 1969–71 during the Vietnam War. His resignation from the Cabinet in 1971 was followed by John ◊Gorton's removal as prime minister after a no-confidence vote. In March 1975 he replaced Bill Snedden as

Eduardo Frei Montalva. *Rex*

Liberal Party leader. In November, following the Gough Whitlam government's economic difficulties, he blocked finance bills in the Senate, became prime minister of a caretaker government, and in the consequent general election won a large majority. He lost to Bob Hawke in the 1983 election. The period 1975–87 has been viewed as full of missed opportunities and lacking a clear direction, but Fraser took a firm stance against South African apartheid.

Fraser, Peter (1884–1950)

New Zealand Labour politician, prime minister 1940–49. A member of the New Zealand parliament from 1918, Fraser was minister of health and education 1935–40 and when Michael ◊Savage died in office, he became prime minister. During his period as prime minister he coordinated the New Zealand war effort. After 1945 he concentrated on problems of social legislation, encouraged state control over key industries, and, in 1949, promoted controversial legislation to bring in military conscription.

Born in Fearn, Ross and Cromarty, Scotland, he emigrated to New Zealand in 1910. He became a trade-union leader in Auckland and joined the Labour Party on its formation in 1916.

Frei Montalva, Eduardo (1911–1982)

Chilean president 1964–70. Elected as the only effective anti-Marxist candidate, he pursued a moderate programme of 'Chileanization' of US-owned copper interests. His regime, characterized by social reform, was plagued by inflation and labour unrest, but saw considerable economic development.

Frei split with the Conservatives in 1938 to help found the Falanga Nacional, an anti-fascist Social Christian party, which joined forces with the Social Christian Conservatives in 1957. He was elected to the Chilean senate in 1949 and again in 1957. He was a shrewd opposition leader, arguing for reform within a democratic framework.

He gained a place in the senate in 1973 and maintained his position as head of the New Christian Democratic Party until its suspension by the military in 1977.

He was born and educated in Santiago. As well as a politician, he was also a publicist and a writer.

FURTHER READING
Frei Montalva, Eduardo *Latin America, the Hopeful Option* 1978, *The Mandate of History and Chile's Future*

Frei Ruiz-Tagle, Eduardo (1942–)

See page 150.

French, Marilyn (1929–)

US feminist writer. Her first novel, *The Women's Room* (1977), the story of a generation of 1950s housewives who transform themselves into independent women in the 1970s, sold 4 million copies, and was made into a television film in 1980. In *The War against Women* (1992) she discussed the harm done to women for the sake of religion and cultural customs, such as female infanticide in China.

'I hate discussions of feminism that end up with who does the dishes', she said. So do I. But at the end, there are always the damned dishes.

MARILYN FRENCH *The Women's Room* chap 1, 21

Freud, Clement Raphael (1924–)

British journalist, television personality, and from 1972 to 1987 Liberal member of Parliament; a grandson of the pioneer of psychoanalysis, Sigmund Freud.

Freyberg, Bernard Cyril, 1st Baron Freyberg (1889–1963)

English-born New Zealand soldier and administrator, governor general 1946–52. During World War II he commanded the 2nd New Zealand Expeditionary Force in the Middle East; the Commonwealth forces in Greece, Crete, and North Africa in 1941; and the New Zealand Corps in Italy 1944–45.

Born in London, he emigrated with his parents to New Zealand in 1891 and was educated at Wellington

College. During World War I he served courageously with the Royal Naval Division in Gallipoli and France, winning the Victoria Cross, the highest decoration for valour in the British armed forces, and three Distinguished Service Orders (DSOs). He was made a brigadier general in 1916, at the age of 27. Between the wars he worked in the British War Office. He was created a KCB in 1942 and Baron in 1951.

Frick, Wilhelm (1877–1946)

German Nazi politician and governor of part of Czechoslovakia in World War II. As minister of the interior 1933–43 he was responsible for many of the laws and decrees that kept the Nazi party firmly in control of Germany. He became Reichs Protector for Bohemia and Moravia in 1943, although his secretary Karl ◊Frank actually wielded most of the power. Arrested after the war, he was tried at Nürnberg and hanged in October 1946.

Friedan, Betty (Elizabeth), born Goldstein (1921–)

US liberal feminist. Her book *The Feminine Mystique* (1963) started the contemporary women's movement in the USA and the UK. She was a founder of the National Organization for Women (NOW) in 1966 (and its president 1966–70), the National Women's Political Caucus in 1971, and the First Women's Bank in 1973.

Friedan also helped to organize the Women's Strike for Equality in 1970 and called the First International Feminist Congress in 1973.

Frondizi, Arturo (1908–1995)

Argentine politician and president 1958–62. He implemented a programme of economic reforms to stimulate the economy and succeeded in gaining aid from the International Monetary Fund (IMF) to finance economic reforms. His attempts at curbing inflation, however, brought negative effects – particularly in industry, and necessitated military intervention to maintain public order.

Frondizi was a staunch opponent of Juan Perón and rose in political importance after 1955. Ironically, in the 1958 elections, Frondizi received considerable support from Peronists in return for their re-admittance into political life. In 1962, with the participation of Peronists once again in national elections, Frondizi's military support was undermined when the Peronists gained massive victories. The military, however, invalidated the election results and selected José Guido to assume the presidency, which lasted for 18 months.

Fuad I (1868–1936)

King of Egypt from 1923. Son of the khedive Ismail, he

◆ FREI RUIZ-TAGLE, EDUARDO (1942–) ◆

Chilean politician and president from 1993. He was the son of the politician and former president Eduardo ◊Frei Montalva. The president of his party, the Partido Demócrata Cristiano (PDC; Christian Democrat Party), from 1991, he became its official presidential candidate in May 1993 and was elected in December of that year. He assumed the position as president in March 1994, for a six-year term. Frei's administration aimed to transform the country into a modern and equitable society by means of progressive policies to realize sustained economic growth, reducing poverty and improving labour relations. He also instituted programmes to assist in the construction of an equitable education and health system and attempted to provide the conditions necessary for prolonged political stability and increased international activity.

As the country had made some economic progress under former president Patricio ◊Aylwin, Frei's initial period in office was marked by relative economic stability. However, such national stability was rather fragile in that tensions emerged between the government and the military.

Born in Santiago, Frei obtained a civil engineering degree (specializing in hydraulics),

from the Instituto Luis Campino, Universidad de Chile. He later went to Getión, in Italy, to study business administration. From 1969 to 1988, he followed a career with a private engineering company, Sigdo Knoppers SA, although his political career had commenced as far back as 1958, when he became a member of the PDC.

His political interests were greatly influenced by his father. During the military regime, he was a cofounder and activist in the Comité Pro Elecciones Libres (Committee for Free Elections). A member of the committee, he travelled extensively throughout the country to gain support for a 'no' vote in the October 1988 plebiscite. Close to his father's death, in January 1982, he participated in the creation of the Fundacao Frei – a political and academic institution that existed until 1993.

In December 1989 he was elected senator for Santiago, and headed numerous commissions. In 1991 he was head of public security within the PDC party. In November 1991 he was elected president of the party, with 70% of the party votes.

succeeded his elder brother Hussein Kamel as sultan of Egypt in 1917. Egypt was declared independent in 1922 and the promulgation of the 1923 constitution enabled him to assume the title of king. His pretension to be king of Sudan as well was not realized. Opposed to the constitution, he favoured the restoration of the autocracy of the ruling family and was almost constantly in conflict with the nationalists, represented by the Wafd.

Fuchs, (Emil Julius) Klaus (1911–1988)

German spy who worked on atom-bomb research in the USA in World War II, and subsequently in the UK. He was imprisoned 1950–59 for passing information to the USSR and resettled in eastern Germany.

Fuentes, Carlos (1928–)

Mexican novelist, lawyer, and diplomat. More than any other Mexican novelist, he presents the frustrated social philosophy of the failed Mexican revolution. He received international attention for *The Death of Artemio Cruz* (1962), *Terra nostra* (1975), and *El gringo viejo/The Old Gringo* (1985).

Born in Panama City, Panama, the son of a diplomat, he studied law at the National Autonomous University of Mexico and worked as a diplomat for the Mexican government in the 1950s and 1975–77.

Fujimori, Alberto (1938–)

Peruvian politician, president from 1990. As leader of the newly formed Cambio 90 (Change 90) he campaigned on a promarket reformist ticket and defeated his more experienced Democratic Front opponent. Lacking an assembly majority and faced with increasing opposition to his policies, he closed congress and imposed military rule in early 1992, to fight the Sendero Luminoso (Shining Path) guerrillas and the left-wing Tupac Amaru Revolutionary Movement (MRTA). In 1993 a plebiscite narrowly approved his constitutional reform proposals, allowing him to seek, and achieve, re-election in 1995.

His successful handling of the hostage crisis at the Japanese embassy in Lima 1996–97, when over 80 people were held by MRTA guerrillas, did much to enhance his reputation. Fujimori gained the largest ever majority vote for a single candidate with 60% of the vote in the 1995 elections.

In August 1994 Fujimori dismissed his wife Susana Higuchi as first lady, claiming that she was 'disloyal' and opposed him politically. She denied the charges and unsuccessfully challenged his leadership; in November 1995 they divorced.

Fujimoro was born in Lima, the son of Japanese immigrants, and educated in agricultural engineering, graduating in 1961 from the Universidad Nacional Agraria de la Molina. He then studied at the University of Wisconsin, USA.

Fukuda, Takeo (1905–1995)

Japanese politician, prime minister 1976–78. First

◆ FULBRIGHT, (JAMES) WILLIAM (1905–1995) ◆

US Democratic politician. A US senator 1945–75, he was responsible for the Fulbright Act 1946, which provided grants for thousands of Americans to study abroad and for overseas students to study in the USA. Fulbright chaired the Senate Foreign Relations Committee 1959–74, and was a strong internationalist and supporter of the United Nations.

Fulbright was a member of the US House of Representatives 1942–45 before becoming senator for Arkansas. After World War II he anticipated the creation of the United Nations, calling for US membership in an international peacekeeping body. He was an advocate of military and economic aid to Western nations but a powerful critic of US involvement in the Vietnam War and other military ventures against small countries.

Fulbright was born in Sumner, Missouri. He studied in England at Oxford University on a Rhodes scholarship, and then at the George Washington University law school. He was a special attorney in the antitrust division of the Department of Justice 1934–35, and was president of the University of Arkansas 1939–41. Defeated in the 1974 congressional elections, Fulbright spent the rest of his career working in private law practice.

In 1954 Fulbright stood out publicly against the notorious campaign against left-wingers that was being orchestrated by Senator Joseph ◊McCarthy. However, he signed a declaration opposing desegregation, in order to safeguard his political base in conservative Arkansas. During the 1960s and 1970s, Fulbright advocated a more liberal US foreign policy. He led the congressional opposition to the use of presidential power to launch armed interventions overseas – notably the Bay of Pigs invasion of Cuba in 1961, the intervention in the Dominican Republic in 1965, and the escalation of the war in Vietnam – and chaired televised hearings on the Vietnam War. The future president Bill Clinton worked in Fulbright's Senate office as a college student.

His publications include *Old Myths and New Realities* (1964), *Arrogance of Power* (1966), and *The Pentagon Propaganda Machine* (1970).

elected to the Diet (parliament) in 1952, he became a powerful faction leader in the conservative Liberal Democratic Party and continued to wield great influence until he relinquished the leadership of his faction in 1986.

He entered politics in 1950 after he resigned from his post as a civil servant in the finance ministry.

Fulbright, (James) William (1905–1995)
See page 151.

Fuller, John Frederick Charles (1878–1966)
British major general and military theorist who propounded the concept of armoured warfare, which, when interpreted by the Germans, became Blitzkrieg in 1940.

G

Gaidar, Yegor Timurovich (1956–)
See page 154.

Gair, Vinc(ent) Clair (1902–1980)
Australian Labor, later Democratic Labor Party, politician. He was premier of Queensland 1952–57, when he was expelled from the Australian Labor Party as a consequence of the split in the party. Gair continued as premier and formed the Queensland Labor Party but lost the election later the same year to the Country–Liberal Party coalition. In 1962 the Queensland Labor Party became a state branch of the Democratic Labor Party (DLP) and Gair entered the federal parliament as a Queensland senator and leader of the DLP. He was appointed ambassador to Ireland in 1974 in an unsuccessful move by the Labor government to gain an extra Senate seat and was recalled by the new Fraser government in 1976.

Gair left school at the age of 14 and began his career as a railway clerk. He joined the Australian Labor Party in 1919 and was first elected to the Queensland parliament in 1932.

Gairy, Eric Matthew (1922–1997)
Grenadian centre-left politician, chief minister 1957–62 and prime minister 1967–79. Initially a champion of the rural poor, he founded the Grenada United Labour Party (GULP) in 1950. He became chief minister of the Federation of the West Indies in 1957. As prime minister he led Grenada to independence within the British Commonwealth in 1974, but his regime became increasingly autocratic and corrupt, imposing restrictions on the media and unions, and order through his 'Mongoose Gang' of thugs. In 1979 he was ousted in a left-wing coup and, unsuccessful in further elections, he retired as GULP leader in 1996.

Gairy came from a poor country background, and actively promoted the rights of the rural poor in his early political career, founding the Manual, Maritime, and Menial Workers' Union in the late 1940s, and the left-of-centre GULP, the island's first political party. Elected to Grenada's Legislative Council in 1951, he antagonized white planters by leading a campaign to increase workers' pay. As a result, he was exiled to the dependency of Carriacou, 48 km/30 mi away, for six years.

After succeeding Herbert ◊Blaize as prime minister, he held many ministerial portfolios himself. His idiosyncratic style of rule was compounded by his belief in voodoo and his conviction that he was under surveillance by UFOs. He was deposed while in New York addressing the United Nations by the left-wing opposition leader Maurice ◊Bishop, in a largely bloodless coup led by General Hudson Austin. Returning to Grenada, after Bishop had been removed, he unsuccessfully contested the 1984 elections. The GULP failed to win any seats at the 1995 general election and in 1996, after suffering a stroke, Gairy retired.

He was knighted in 1977.

Gaitskell, Hugh (Todd Naylor) (1906–1963)
British Labour Party leader from 1955. In 1950 he became minister of economic affairs, and then chancellor of the Exchequer until October 1951. As party leader, he tried to reconcile internal differences on nationalization and disarmament.

> *I became a Socialist because I hated poverty and squalor.*
> HUGH GAITSKELL Labour Party Conference 1955

Born in London, he was educated at Winchester public school and at Oxford, and later lectured on political economics at London University. He spent most of World War II working at the Ministry of Economic Warfare, and in 1945 became Labour member of Parliament for Leeds South, retaining this seat until his death. In 1955 he defeated Aneurin Bevan for the succession to Clement Attlee as Labour leader, and he was re-elected party leader in 1960. He died suddenly in office in 1963.

He led an attack on Clause 4 and against the unilateralism of the Campaign for Nuclear Disarmament (CND) 1959–61.

FURTHER READING
Brivati, Brian *Hugh Gaitskell* 1997
Williams, P M *Hugh Gaitskell* 1979

Galán, Luis Carlos (died 1990)
Colombian liberal politician and prospective presidential candidate in the 1990 elections. He was vehemently outspoken about the drug cartels and Mafia, and supported the government campaign,

initiated in 1983, against the drug trade. The campaign, however, turned into a bloody war. Galán was assassinated.

His death led the government to implement new extradition laws and the confiscation of many Mafia-owned properties.

Galbraith, John Kenneth (1908–)

Canadian-born US economist who criticized the neoclassical view that in the economy market forces were in a state approximating perfect competition. He suggested that the 'affluent society' develops an economic imbalance, devoting too many resources to the production of consumer goods and not enough to public services and infrastructure.

> *Politics is not the art of the possible. It consists in choosing between the disastrous and the unpalatable.*
>
> JOHN KENNETH GALBRAITH Letter to President J F Kennedy 2 March 1962

Galbraith was critical of the view put forward by the advocates of monetarism that state spending was unable to reduce unemployment. His commitment to the development of the public sector was in sympathy with Keynesian economics. In his book *The Affluent Society* (1958), he documents the tendency of free-market capitalism to create private splendour and public squalor.

Galbraith became a US in citizen 1937. He was a professor of economics at Harvard 1949–75, worked for the Office of Price Administration during World War II, and served as ambassador to India 1961–63. He was an adviser to President J F Kennedy and the Democratic presidential candidates Adlai Stevenson, Eugene McCarthy, and George McGovern, and believed strongly in a governmental role in economic planning.

Galbraith argued that the motivation of large corporations depended on the influence of the 'technostructure' or departmental management, and that such corporations were motivated more by the desire for security and expansion than the desire to maximize profits. Advertising was seen as a particularly important means of achieving market power and secure expansion. On the other hand, corporations were constrained by the 'countervailing power' of other firms, trade unions, consumer groups, and governments.

His works include *American Capitalism* (1952), *The New Industrial State* (1967), *Economics and the Public Purpose* (1973), and *The Culture of Containment* (1992). He has also written novels.

FURTHER READING
Galbraith, J K *A Life in Our Time* 1981
Gambs, John *John Kenneth Galbraith* 1975
Munro, C L *Galbraithian Vision: The Cultural Criticism of John Kenneth Galbraith* 1977

Galinski, Heinz (1912–1992)

German Jewish community leader. A survivor of the Auschwitz and Buchenwald concentration camps, he helped to re-establish a strong Jewish community in postwar Germany, and was chair of the Central Council of German Jews 1988–92. He devoted his life to the

---

◆ GAIDAR, YEGOR TIMUROVICH (1956–) ◆

Russian politician and economist. He served as first deputy prime minister in charge of the economy, then early in 1992 was made acting prime minister – a title that was never confirmed because of the opposition of an increasingly hostile Russian parliament. That opposition grew too strong for his continued tenure of office; President Boris ◊Yeltsin accepted his resignation in December 1992, and he was replaced by Viktor ◊Chernomyrdin. He later returned to the government, again as first deputy prime minister in charge of economic reform 1993–94.

The 'shock' Gaidar administered to the economy in January 1992 – liberalization of most prices, removal of barriers to trade, semi-convertibility of the rouble, deep cuts in public spending (especially in the military budget), slashing of subsidies to companies – was followed by a massive and rapid privatization programme, administered by Anatoly ◊Chubais. The pace was frantic, though he was forced to slow down and to restore some budget cuts owing to growing and increasingly militant opposition.

His 'shock therapy' has been held by most Russians and some outside observers as being a major contributory factor in the partially corrupt and unpopular reception of capitalism in Russia. It could, however, be argued that his reforms were stopped in their tracks, and that the corruption that increasingly marked political and economic life grew because of the lack of reform, not because of it. Yet his great weakness was the lack of a political base; he relied wholly on Yeltsin's support both as acting prime minister and when he later returned to the government. His party, 'Choice of Russia', did much less well than expected in the polls in 1993 and was all but eliminated from parliament in later elections. Gaidar remained, however, an influential figure outside government and parliament, frequently

preservation of the memory of the Holocaust as a warning against the revival of neo-Nazism.

Gallegos Freire, Rómulo (1884–1969)

Venezuelan politician and writer. He was Venezuela's first democratically elected president in 1948 before being overthrown and exiled by a military coup the same year. He was also a professor of philosophy and literature. His novels, focusing on Venezuelan life, include *La trepadora/The Climber* (1925) and *Doña Bárbara* (1929). He returned to Venezuela in 1958.

Galtieri, Leopoldo Fortunato (1926–)

Argentine general and president 1981–82. A leading member from 1979 of the ruling right-wing military junta and commander of the army, Galtieri became president in December 1981. Under his leadership the junta ordered the seizure in 1982 of the Falkland Islands (Malvinas), a British colony in the southwestern Atlantic claimed by Argentina. After the surrender of his forces he resigned as army commander and was replaced as president. He and his fellow junta members were tried for abuse of human rights and court-martialled for their conduct of the war; he was sentenced to 12 years in prison in 1986, but only served a small portion of his sentence.

Gálvez, Juan Manuel (1887–)

Honduran National Party politician, president 1949–54. A member of the right-wing National Party, he was elected in 1948 to succeed the dictator Tiburcio ◊Carías Andino as president, assuming office in 1949.

Gálvez promoted economic development and diver-

being consulted by Yeltsin as well as by foreign political leaders, bankers, and economists.

Yegor Gaidar was born into the Soviet elite; his father was *Pravda*'s military correspondent, and his grandfather, Igor, was both a hero of the Civil War and one of the best-known children's story writers of the Stalin period. From the early 1980s Gaidar studied Western economists and by the late 1980s was beginning to advance theories of increasingly radical liberalization in the pages of *Pravda* and the Communist Party's monthly journal, *Kommunist*.

The natural leader of a group of talented, young, and Western-oriented economists, Gaidar was recommended to Boris Yeltsin as the cabinet minister in charge of economic reform for the new Russian government that Yeltsin was forming in the latter part of 1991, after winning the election for the presidency of Russia – though Russia was still part of the USSR. Gaidar drafted the speech Yeltsin gave in October 1991 that set out a course for radical economic reform.

sification and road construction. His hostile attitude to labour organizations culminated in a violent general strike in 1954, spearheaded by banana workers.

Gambari, Ibrahim Agboola (1944–)

Nigerian diplomat and political scientist, the country's permanent representative to the United Nations (UN) from 1985. He was director general of the Nigerian Institute of International Affairs 1983–84, and minister of foreign affairs 1984–85. In 1988 he chaired the national seminar commemorating the 25th anniversary of the Organization of African Unity (OAU).

Gambari was born in Ilorin, Kwara state. He was educated at King's College, Lagos, the London School of Economics, and Columbia University, New York. He held a number of lectureships and research positions at universities in the USA, Italy, and China.

Gamsakhurdia, Zviad (1939–1993)

Georgian politician, president 1990–92. He was a fervent nationalist and an active anticommunist. After nationalist success in parliamentary elections when Georgia achieved independence in 1991, he was elected head of state by a huge margin. His increasingly dictatorial style of government and his hostile attitude to non-ethnic Georgians led to his forced removal and flight to neighbouring Armenia in 1992. He returned to western Georgia in 1993 to lead a rebellion against Edvard ◊Shevardnadze's presidency, but Shevardnadze, with Russian help, destroyed his ill-equipped supporters, and the deposed president was later reported dead, although uncertainty remained as to whether he had committed suicide or been killed by Russian troops.

Born in Tbilisi, the son of the Georgian novelist Konstantin Gamsakhurdia, he was a highly literate scholar who became a university lecturer in American studies, translated Shakespeare into Georgian, and spoke Russian, German, and French.

He became politically active in the 1950s but was not at ease in the bureaucratic communist state of the USSR. He founded the Initiative Group for the Defence of Human Rights in Georgia in 1974. With the arrival of Mikhail Gorbachev's concept of *perestroika*, he saw the future of Georgia entirely in nationalist terms and pressed for complete independence. When this was achieved in 1991 he became his country's first democratically elected president. However, his vision of a single-ethnic Georgia became an obsession, and his dictatorial methods brought him many enemies.

Gandhi, Indira Priyadarshani, born Nehru (1917–1984)

Indian politician, prime minister of India 1966–77 and 1980–84, and leader of the Congress Party 1966–77 and subsequently of the Congress (I) party. She was

Prime Minister Indira Gandhi with Congress Party members in her garden, 1984. *Rex*

interest in politics and became a pilot with Indian Airlines. But after the death in a plane crash of his brother Sanjay (1946–1980), he was elected to his brother's Amethi parliamentary seat in 1981. In the December 1984 parliamentary elections he won a record majority. His reputation was tarnished by a scandal concerning alleged kickbacks to senior officials from an arms deal with the Swedish munitions firm Bofors and, following his party's defeat in the general election of November 1989, Gandhi was forced to resign as premier. He was killed by a bomb on 21 May in the middle of the 1991 election campaign at a rally near Madras, while attempting to regain office.

assassinated in 1984 by members of her Sikh bodyguard, resentful of her use of troops to clear malcontents from the Sikh temple at Amritsar.

> *Politics is the art of acquiring, holding and wielding power.*
>
> INDIRA GANDHI Quoted in *Observer* 4 May 1975

Her father, Jawaharlal ◊Nehru, was India's first prime minister. She married Feroze Gandhi in 1942 (died 1960, not related to Mahatma Gandhi) and had two sons, Sanjay Gandhi (1946–1980), who died in an aeroplane crash, and Rajiv ◊Gandhi, who was assassinated in 1991. In 1975 the validity of her re-election to parliament was questioned, and she declared a state of emergency. During this time Sanjay Gandhi implemented a social and economic programme (including an unpopular family-planning policy) that led to his mother's defeat in 1977.

FURTHER READING
Ali, Tariq *Nehru and the Gandhis* 1985
Carras, M *Indira Gandhi* 1979
Moraes, D *Indira Gandhi* 1980

Gandhi, Rajiv (1944–1991)

Indian politician, prime minister from 1984 (following his mother Indira ◊Gandhi's assassination) to November 1989. As prime minister, he faced growing discontent with his party's elitism and lack of concern for social issues. He was assassinated at an election rally.

Elder son of Indira Gandhi and grandson of Jawaharlal ◊Nehru, Rajiv Gandhi was born into the Kashmiri Brahmin family that had governed India for all but four years since 1947. He initially displayed little

Ganilau, Ratu Penaia (1918–1993)

Fijian politician, governor general 1983–87 and president 1987–93. As governor general, he took the controversial decision to dissolve parliament in May 1987 after Major General Sitiveni ◊Rabuka launched a coup against the new pro-Indian centre-left government of Timoci ◊Bavadra. Ganilau briefly headed an interim administration, before Rabuka launched a second coup in September 1987. In December 1987, following Fiji's exclusion from the British Commonwealth, he assumed the title of president and died in office in December 1993.

Born into a noble family, Ganilau played international rugby before beginning his political career. He worked as a colonial administrator and as a minister in the Alliance party governments of Kamisese ◊Mara, before and after independence in 1970.

His son, Brigadier Epeli Ganilau was army chief of staff during the early 1990s.

Garang, John (1945–)

Sudanese guerrilla leader of the southern rebels in the country's civil war. He defected from the army in 1970 and joined the Anya Nya rebels. In 1983 he set up the Sudanese People's Liberation Army (SPLA), which raided government installations in southern Sudan. In 1984 he formed the Sudanese People's Liberation Movement (SPLM). In 1991 the SPLM formed a government in exile with Garang as leader. His position was weakened by opposition to his authoritarian style of leadership and the overthrow of his ally in Ethiopia ◊Mengistu Haile Mariam. In August 1997 South African president Nelson ◊Mandela invited Garang and Sudanese president Omar Hassan al-◊Bashir to take part in peace talks.

Born in Jonglei, Garang belongs to the Dinka ethnic group. He received a doctorate in agriculture from Iowa State University, USA.

Garbus, Martin (1930–)

US lawyer specializing in civil-liberty cases. His clients included Soviet dissident Andrei Sakharov, Nelson Mandela, and Václav Havel, for whom he drafted the section on civil liberties in the Czech constitution.

Garbus was born into a poor immigrant family in New York. A law professor at Yale and Colombia, he specialized in First Amendment rights and represented, amongst others, comedian Lenny Bruce (against obscenity charges in 1964), LSD apologist Timothy Leary, Viking Penguin in the Salman Rushdie case, and black people in Mississippi wanting to exercise their right to vote. His books include *Ready for the Defense* (1971, revised 1987) and *Traitors and Heroes* (1989).

García Perez, Alan (1949–)

Peruvian politician and president 1985–90; leader of the moderate reformist left-wing American Popular Revolutionary Alliance party (APRA; Aprista Party). He inherited an ailing economy and was forced to trim his socialist programme. His government was marked by scandals, economic crisis, and the failure to confront growing political violence caused by guerrillas and drugs traffickers. He lost to political novice Alberto Fujimori in the 1990 presidential elections.

He was born in Lima and educated in Peru, Guatemala, Spain, and France. He became APRA's secretary general in 1982. In 1985 he succeeded Fernando ◊Belaúnde Terry as president, becoming the first civilian president to be democratically elected.

FURTHER READING
Boland, Ray Charles *A Citizen of the World* 1994
Cameron, Maxwell A *Democracy and Authoritarianism in Peru: Political Coalitions and Social Change* 1994
Crabtree, John *Peru under García: An Opportunity Lost* 1992
Palmer, David Scott *The Shining Path of Peru* 1992
Poole, Deborah, and Rénique, Gerard *Peru: Time for Fear* 1992

Gardiner, Gerald Austin (1900–1990)

English lawyer. As Lord Chancellor in the 1964–70 Labour governments, Gardiner introduced the office of ombudsman to the UK, and played a major role in the movement for the abolition of capital punishment for murder (which became law in 1965).

Garner, John Nance (1868–1967)

US political leader and vice president of the USA 1933–41. He served in the US House of Representatives 1903–33. A Democratic leader in the House, he was chosen as Speaker in 1931. He later served as vice president during Franklin D Roosevelt's first two terms. Opposing Roosevelt's re-election in 1940, Garner retired from public life.

◆ GANDHI, MAHATMA (SANSKRIT 'GREAT SOUL'), HONORIFIC NAME OF MOHANDAS KARAMCHAND GANDHI (1869–1948) ◆

Indian nationalist leader. A pacifist, he led the struggle for Indian independence from the UK by advocating nonviolent noncooperation (*satyagraha*, defence of and by truth) from 1915.

The moment the slave resolves that he will no longer be a slave, his fetters fall. He frees himself and shows the way to others. Freedom and slavery are mental states.

MAHATMA GANDHI *Non-Violence in Peace and War* vol 2, chap 5

He was imprisoned several times by the British authorities and was influential in the nationalist Congress Party and in the independence negotiations in 1947. He was assassinated by a Hindu nationalist in the violence that followed the partition of British India into India and Pakistan.

Gandhi was born in Porbandar, Gujarat, and studied law in London, later practising as a barrister. He settled in South Africa where, until 1914, he led the Indian community in opposition to racial discrimination. Returning to India, he emerged as leader of the Indian National Congress. He organized hunger strikes and events of civil disobedience, and campaigned for social reform, including religious tolerance and an end to discrimination against the so-called untouchable caste. See photograph on page 158.

FURTHER READING
Brown, J M *Gandhi: Prisoner of Hope* 1990
Gandhi, Mahatma *Autobiography* 1948
Mehta, V *Mahatma Gandhi and his Apostles* 1977
Payne, R *The Life and Death of Mahatma Gandhi* 1969
Richards, G *The Philosophy of Gandhi: A Study of his Ideas* 1982

Mahatma Gandhi, c. 1945. *AKG London*

Garner was born in Red River County, Texas, and briefly attended Vanderbilt University. After privately studying law in Clarksville, Texas, he was admitted to the bar in 1890. He was appointed county judge in 1895 before embarking on a career in Democratic party politics and serving in the state legislature 1898–1902.

Garvey, Marcus (Moziah) (1887–1940)

Jamaican political thinker and activist, an early advocate of black nationalism. He led a Back to Africa movement for black Americans to establish a black-governed country in Africa. The Jamaican cult of Rastafarianism is based largely on his ideas.

Garvey founded the Universal Negro Improvement Association (UNIA) in 1914, and moved to the USA in 1916, where he established branches in New York and other northern cities. Aiming to achieve human rights and dignity for black people through pride and economic self-sufficiency, he was considered one of the first militant black nationalists.

Gates, Henry Louis (1950–)

US academic and social activist. A scholar of black American studies, he has republished such forgotten works as *Our Nig* (1859) by Harriet E Wilson, the earliest known novel by a black American. He pub-

lished *The Signifying Monkey: A Theory of African-American Literary Criticism* (1988).

Gates was born in Keyser, West Virginia. He was the first black American to be awarded a PhD from Cambridge University, England, for a thesis on attitudes to black American and African culture in the 18th century. He received the MacArthur Foundation 'genius' award for his work on literary theory in 1981. In 1991 he was made professor of humanities and chair of the department of Afro-American studies at Harvard University. He wants to increase the number of black-studies courses in colleges in the USA in order to raise public awareness of the cultural achievements of black Americans. Other publications include *Colored People: A Memoir* (1994).

Gaviria (Trujillo), César (1947–)

Colombian Liberal Party politician, president 1990–94. He was finance minister 1986–87 and minister of government 1987–89. He supported a constitutional amendment that prohibited the extradition of Colombian citizens wanted in the USA for drug-related crimes and sought more US aid in return for stepping up the drug war.

An economist, Gaviria began his career in local government at the age of 22 and became mayor of his home town, Pereira, at 27. He went on to the house of representatives and became a deputy minister at 31. As acting president in 1988, while President Virgilio Barco Vargas was out of the country, Gaviria negotiated the freedom of a kidnapped presidential candidate. In 1989 he left the government to manage the campaign of another presidential candidate, who was assassinated later the same year.

Geingob, Hage Gottfried (1941–)

Namibian politician, from 1990 the first prime minister of an independent Namibia. He played a major role in the South West Africa's People's Organization (SWAPO), as its representative in Botswana 1963–34, and as a petitioner to the United Nations (UN) 1964–71 to obtain international recognition for SWAPO. In 1975 he was the founding director of the UN Institute for Namibia in Lusaka, educating future administrators for an independent Namibia. In 1989 he returned to Namibia as the head of SWAPO's election campaign and played a leading role in drawing up the post-independence constitution.

Geingob qualified as a schoolteacher before gaining a Masters degree in political science in the USA.

Gemayel, Amin (1942–)

Lebanese politician, a Maronite Christian; president 1982–88. He succeeded his brother, president-elect Bechir ◊Gemayel, on his assassination on 14 September 1982. The Lebanese parliament was unable to agree on a successor when his term expired, so separate governments were formed under rival Christian and Muslim leaders. Following the end of his term of office as president, Gemayel was largely instrumental in ending Lebanon's civil war in 1989.

Gemayel, Bechir (1947–1982)

Lebanese Maronite Christian soldier and politician, assassinated in 1982 while president-elect. Through the systematic elimination of rival Maronite Christian militia, by 1980 he had uncontested control of a Maronite enclave in East Beirut. The evident distancing of his Phalangist party from Israeli support, and its wish to expel all foreign influence from Lebanese affairs, effected his election as president on 22 August 1982. Having twice escaped assassination, he was killed 22 days later in a car bomb explosion.

The son of Sheikh Pierre ◊Gemayel, he joined the militia of his father's Phalangist party at the age of 11. On his return after a brief period in the USA working in a Washington law office, he was appointed the party's political director in the Ashrefieh sector of East Beirut, and was an active leader of the Christian militia in the civil war of 1975–76 and thereafter.

Syrian or Israeli groups were suspected of being behind Gemayel's assassination and more than 1,000 civilians were killed in a subsequent 'anti-terrorist sweep' by the Maronite militia. His brother, Amin ◊Gemayel, replaced him as president.

Gemayel, Sheikh Pierre (1905–1984)

Lebanese Maronite Christian politician. In 1936 he founded the Kateb (Kataib), or Phalangist, party modelled on the Spanish and German Fascist organizations, and in 1937 became its leader. He was twice imprisoned, in 1937 and in 1943, the year in which he organized a general strike. He held various ministerial posts 1960–67 and led the Phalangist militia in the April 1975–October 1976 civil war, during which at least 30,000 were killed and there were controversial attacks on Palestinian refugee camps in East Beirut. He was the father of Amin and Bechir Gemayel.

Gemayel was educated at the University of St Joseph, Beirut, and Cochin Hospital, Paris, where he trained as a pharmacist.

Genscher, Hans-Dietrich (1927–)

German politician, chair of the West German Free Democratic Party (FDP) 1974–85, and foreign minister 1974–92. A skilled and pragmatic tactician, Genscher became the reunified Germany's most popular politician.

Born in Halle, East Germany, Genscher settled in West Germany in 1952. He served as interior minister 1969–74 and then as foreign minister, committed to Ostpolitik and European cooperation. As FDP leader, Genscher masterminded the party's switch of

allegiance from the Social Democratic Party to the Christian Democratic Union, which resulted in the downfall of Helmut ◊Schmidt's government in 1982.

Gentile, Giovanni (1875–1944)

Italian philosopher and politician, whose writings formed the basis of the Italian Fascist state under Mussolini. As minister of education from 1924, he reformed both the school and university systems. He edited the *Encyclopedia italiana* and wrote the entry in it for 'fascism'. He was assassinated by partisans.

Gentile's doctrine of 'actualism' was seized by the Fascists, to justify their authoritarian policies.

George, Eddie (Edward Alan John) (1938–)

British banker, governor of the Bank of England from 1993. A hard-line advocate of low inflation when appointed governor, George quickly showed his determination to expound his views on the UK economy. Despite setbacks in his dealings with the chancellor of the Exchequer, George was never deterred from his long-term aim of securing greater independence for the Bank of England. Response to his efforts came with the Bank of England Act of 1998, which strengthened the Bank's governance and accountability, as well as formalizing its responsibility for the conduct of monetary policy.

Unlike his predecessors, he was prepared to be forthright in public with regard to economic policy as well as his differences with the chancellor of the Exchequer 1993–97. Although he believed in the need to keep interest rates high in order to keep inflation down and sustain economic growth, by the end of 1995, with signs of an economic slowdown becoming clear, George acknowledged that Chancellor Kenneth Clarke had been right to overrule him and hold rates down. During 1998 the Bank of England remained in line with the USA and with European Union countries, lowering interest rates in order to avert global economic crisis.

George joined the Bank of England in 1962, working initially on Eastern European affairs. He was seconded to the Bank for International Settlements 1966–69, and worked for the International Monetary Fund 1972–74 on international monetary reform. He served at the Bank of England as adviser on international monetary questions 1974–77, as deputy chief cashier 1977–80, and as assistant director (gilt edged division) 1980–82. He was appointed executive director in 1982 and deputy governor in 1990. His appointment as governor in 1993 is due to expire in 2003.

George II (1890–1947)

King of Greece 1922–23 and 1935–47. He became king on the expulsion of his father Constantine I in 1922 but was himself overthrown in 1923. Restored by the military in 1935, he set up a dictatorship under Joannis

◊Metaxas, and went into exile during the German occupation 1941–45.

Gephardt, Richard Andrew (1941–)

US politician. A lawyer and Democratic alderman in his home town of St Louis, Missouri, he went to the US House of Representatives in 1977. Gephardt sought to protect US jobs by championing restrictions on imports. He ran for the Democratic nomination as president in 1986, losing to Michael ◊Dukakis, and served as house majority leader 1989–95.

Gestido, Oscar Daniel (1901–1967)

Uruguayan politician and president in 1966. He took over the presidential office at a time of major economic decline and political corruption. Gestido's untimely death shortly after his election as president led to his counterpart, Jorge ◊Pacheco Areco, becoming president.

Ghannouchi, Rachid (1941–)

Tunisian politician. He founded the Mouvement de la Tendance Islamiste in 1979 (renamed Ennahda in 1989), which was never legalized as a political party. Arrested and sentenced to life imprisonment on charges of violence and plotting with foreign powers to overthrow Habib ◊Bourguiba's government in 1987, he was pardoned and freed in 1988 after President Zine ◊Ben Ali's general amnesty. Denied recognition and participation in the multiparty elections, his movement went underground and was again accused of waging a war against Ben Ali's regime. Subjected to a major crackdown 1991–92, he fled the country and obtained political asylum in the UK.

Gheorgiu-Dej, Gheorghe (1901–1965)

Romanian communist politician. A member of the Romanian Communist Party from 1930, he played a leading part in establishing a communist regime in 1945. He was prime minister 1952–55 and state president 1961–65. Although retaining the support of Moscow, he adopted an increasingly independent line during his final years.

Giap, Vo Nguyen (1910–)

Vietnamese military leader and communist politician. When ◊Ho Chi Minh formed the Vietminh in 1941 in China, Giap organized the army that returned to Indochina in 1944 to fight the Japanese and liberated Hanoi on 19 August 1945. As commander in chief of a guerrilla force of 60,000, he led the struggle against the French colonial forces, conclusively defeating them at Dien Bien Phu on 7 May 1954. With the growth of US influence in South Vietnam, Giap sent North Viet-

namese troops to help the Vietcong (the National Liberation Front), and he took direct control of communist military operations in South Vietnam in 1967, launching the Tet Offensive in February 1968. He was responsible for the defeat of the US army in 1973.

Born in Quangbiln Province, then part of the French protectorate of Indochina, Giap joined the Communist Party in 1930. With a doctorate in law from the University of Hanoi (1938), he fled to China when the party was banned in 1939, and became military aide to Ho Chi Minh. When Vietnam was partitioned in 1954, he became commander in chief of the North Vietnam army. His training manual on guerrilla warfare was published in English as *People's War, People's Army* (1962). He was minister of national defence and deputy prime minister of Vietnam 1976–80.

Gibson, Althea (1927–)

US tennis player, the first black American woman to compete at the US Championships at Forest Hills in 1950 and at Wimbledon in 1951. In 1957 she took both the women's singles and doubles titles at Wimbledon and the singles at Forest Hills. In 1958 she successfully defended all three titles.

Born in Silver, South Carolina, and raised in New York, Gibson was hindered in her tennis career by racial discrimination and segregation. In 1943 she won the New York State Negro girls' singles title, and in 1948 the national Negro women's title. She later played professional golf.

FURTHER READING
Biracree, Tom *Althea Gibson* 1989

Gierek, Edward (1913–)

Polish communist politician. He entered the Politburo of the ruling Polish United Workers' Party (PUWP) in 1956 and was party leader 1970–80.

A miner's son, Gierek lived in France and Belgium for much of the period between 1923 and 1948, becoming a member of the Belgian Resistance. He joined the French Communist Party in 1931, and the Belgian Communist Party in 1939. In 1946 he became a member of the Polish Workers Party (PWP) in Belgium. In 1957 he became First Secretary of the Polish United Workers Party (PUWP) in Silesia. After replacing Władysław ◊Gomułka as PUWP leader in December 1970, he embarked on an ambitious programme of industrial modernization using Western investment. He aimed to reform the party and to liberalize cultural and social life. He also opposed the Soviet intervention in Afghanistan. The normalization of relations between Poland and the German Federal Republic was one of his notable successes. In September 1980, following waves of strikes spearheaded by the Solidarity free trade union, Gierek resigned.

FURTHER READING
Bromke, Adam *Gierek's Poland* 1973

Gilman, Charlotte Anna, born Perkins (1860–1935)

US feminist socialist poet, novelist, and historian, author of *Women and Economics* (1898), proposing the ending of the division between 'men's work' and 'women's work' by abolishing housework. Her best-known story, a classic of 19th-century feminist literature, is 'The Yellow Wall-Paper Story'.

There is no female mind. The brain is not an organ of sex. As well speak of a female liver.

CHARLOTTE GILMAN *Woman and Economics*

From 1909 to 1916 she wrote and published a magazine called *The Forerunner*, in which her feminist Utopian novel *Herland* (1915) was serialized.

Gimbutas, Marija (1921–1994)

Lithuanian-born US-based archaeologist whose feminist theories challenged traditional views of society in prehistoric Europe. She proposed that Stone Age Europe was a peaceful and harmonious place, where men and women were equals and worshipped life-giving goddesses, in particular the great Mother Goddess; the invading Indo-Europeans brought a male-dominated society and warlike gods.

Gimbutas's radical ideas are treated with considerable scepticism by most scholars in the field, but they have been adopted with enthusiasm by many feminists. Works include *The Language of the Goddess* (1989) and *The Civilization of the Goddess* (1991).

Gimbutas first established her reputation with solid works such as *The Prehistory of Eastern Europe* (1956) and the enormous *Bronze Age Cultures of Central and Eastern Europe* (1965). Appointed a professor at the University of California at Los Angeles, she organized and directed Neolithic excavations in Yugoslavia, Greece, and Italy, and developed her theories in the *Gods and Goddesses of Old Europe* (1974), theories which culminated in her last two works, on the supposed Mother Goddess cult.

Gingrich, Newt (Newton Leroy) (1943–)

US Republican politician, speaker of the House of Representatives from 1995. A radical-right admirer of Ronald Reagan, he was the driving force behind his party's victory in the 1994 congressional elections, when it gained a House majority for the first time since 1954. On taking office, he sought to implement a conservative populist manifesto – 'Contract with America' – designed to reduce federal powers, balance the budget, tackle crime, and limit congressional terms.

Gingrich was a professor of military history before entering Congress as House representative for Georgia in 1979. He established himself as a powerful and partisan speaker, and became House minority whip for

the Republican Party in 1989. He set about attacking the leadership of the incumbent Democratic Party with charges of sleaze and corruption and, after their defeat in the 1994 mid-term elections, was elected speaker. He fulfilled his party's pledge to put all measures in its manifesto to a House floor vote within the first 100 days of the new Congress. However, many were subsequently watered down by the Republican-controlled Senate, and Gingrich's personal popularity fell during 1995–96.

It was the first time a person saved an air-bag's life.

THOMAS HARKIN On Republican politician Bob Dole's $300,000 loan to speaker of the House of Representatives Newt Gingrich; *Time* 19 May 1997

In December 1995 Gingrich faced investigation by special committee following allegations that he had violated tax laws. He was reprimanded and fined $300,000 by the House's ethics committee in January 1997, but was nevertheless re-elected speaker. In 1998, after Republican losses in the House, he resigned his position as speaker.

Ginsberg, (Irwin) Allen (1926–1997)

US poet and political activist. His reputation as a visionary, overtly political poet was established by *Howl* (1956), which expressed and shaped the spirit of the Beat Generation and criticized the materialism of contemporary US society. His poetry drew heavily on Oriental philosophies and utilized mantric breath meditations.

What if someone gave a war & Nobody came?

ALLEN GINSBERG 'Graffiti'

Ginsberg travelled widely – to Cuba, India, and Czechoslovakia in the 1960s, and China and Nicaragua in the 1980s – spreading his Zen-socialist politics of radical but passive dissent.

Ginsburg, Ruth Joan Bader (1933–)

US judge. Appointed Supreme Court justice by President Bill Clinton in 1993, she was only the second woman to serve on the court. Ginsburg made her reputation as a civil liberties lawyer in the 1960s and 1970s, particularly with the six cases on gender equality she argued before the Supreme Court 1973–76. She won five, establishing a legal framework for women's rights.

In the late 1960s and early 1970s, Ginsburg acted as director of the Women's Rights Project of the American Civil Liberties Union before becoming a judge. She gained a reputation as a moderate, precise judge on the US Court of Appeals of the District of Columbia 1980–93.

Giolitti, Giovanni (1842–1928)

Italian liberal politician, born in Mondovi. He was prime minister 1892–93, 1903–05, 1906–09, 1911–14, and 1920–21. He opposed Italian intervention in World War I and pursued a policy of broad coalitions, which proved ineffective in controlling fascism after 1921.

FURTHER READING
Giolitti, G *Memories of My Life*
Salomone, A W *Italy in the Giolittian Era* 1960

Giscard d'Estaing, Valéry (1926–)

French centre-right politician and head of state, president of France 1974–81. At home he secured divorce and abortion law reforms early on, reduced the voting age to 18, and amended the constitution to enable the parliamentary opposition to refer legislation to the Constitutional Council. In Europe, he helped initiate the new Exchange Rate Mechanism in 1978 and direct elections to the European Parliament from 1979. Faced with increasingly difficult economic circumstances, he brought in Raymond ◊Barre as prime minister to manage a deflationary programme from 1976. Defeated by François ◊Mitterrand in 1981, he was re-elected to the National Assembly in 1984, resigning in 1989 in order to sit in the European Parliament.

Giscard had served as finance minister under the presidencies of Charles ◊de Gaulle 1962–66 and Georges ◊Pompidou 1969–74, but remained outside the Gaullist movement, projecting himself as leader of a 'new centre': European, Atlanticist, and committed to enhancing parliament's role. In 1978 he founded a broad-based confederation, the Union pour la Démocratie Française (UDF), and led it until 1996.

An early graduate of Michel ◊Debré's postwar Ecole Nationale d'Administration, Giscard was a member of the prestigious Finance Inspectorate until he entered the National Assembly as an Independent in 1956, inheriting his grandfather's seat for Puy-de-Dôme. After Pompidou's death in office, Giscard narrowly defeated the socialist François Mitterrand on a programme of social and political reform, appointing the Gaullist Jacques ◊Chirac as his prime minister.

Giuliani, Rudolph W (1944–)

US Republican politician, mayor of New York from 1993. A former federal prosecutor, he was elected mayor of the traditionally Democrat-dominated New York City, at the second attempt, in 1993. As a result of demographic shifts and his own non-partisan 'quality of life' programme, the crime rate fell dramatically and the economy expanded. In November 1997 he became the first Republican since Florio La Guardia in 1937 to be re-elected.

Born in Brooklyn, Giuliani worked in the US department of justice during the mid-1970s and was a mayoral candidate in 1989. He controversially endorsed the Democrat incumbent, Mario Cuomo, in the 1994 governorship race in New York and campaigned for re-election in 1997 on a joint Republican Party and Liberal Party ticket.

Glenn, John Herschel, Jr (1921–)

US astronaut and politician. On 20 February 1962 he became the first American to orbit the Earth, doing so three times in the Mercury spacecraft *Friendship* 7, in a flight lasting 4 hr 55 min. After retiring from NASA, he was elected to the US Senate as a Democrat from Ohio in 1974; he was subsequently re-elected in 1980 and 1986. Glenn became the oldest person in space when, at the age of 77, he embarked on a nine-day mission aboard the shuttle *Discovery* in October 1998.

As a senator, he advocated nuclear-arms-production limitations and increased aid to education and job-skills programmes. He unsuccessfully sought the Democratic presidential nomination in 1984.

Gligorov, Kiro (1917–)

Macedonian politician, president of Macedonia from 1991. He was a member of the presidency of the Socialist Federation of Republics of the Republic of Yugoslavia 1971–72 and the president of the parliament 1974–78. Following the break-up of the former Yugoslavia, he became the president of Macedonia.

Gligorov was educated at the Faculty of Law, Belgrade University. During World War II he was a member of the Presidium of the Antifascist Assembly of the People's Liberation of Macedonia, and the Antifascist Council of the People's Liberation of Yugoslavia. He rose steadily in the ranks of the communist administration, serving as the federal secretary for Finance 1962–67 and vice president of the Federal Executive Council 1967–69.

In October 1998 the right-wing nationalist VRMO–DPMNE opposition secured the largest share of seats in the first round of parliamentary elections.

Glubb, John Bagot, known as *Glubb Pasha* (1897–1986)

British military commander, founder of the Arab Legion (the Jordanian army), which he commanded 1939–56. Under his leadership the Legion grew in number from 1,000 to 9,000, becoming the most powerful Arab military force.

Glubb was a member of the Royal Engineers in World War I, and in 1920 volunteered for service in Iraq. On Iraqi independence in 1930, he went to Transjordan as second in command of the Arab Legion, taking over as commander from 1939. The Legion distinguished itself during World War II. Glubb was dismissed by King Hussein in 1956. He was knighted that year.

Goebbels, (Paul) Joseph (1897–1945)

German Nazi leader. As minister of propaganda from 1933, he brought all cultural and educational activities under Nazi control and built up sympathetic movements abroad to carry on the 'war of nerves' against Hitler's intended victims. On the capture of Berlin by the Allies, he committed suicide.

He was born in the Rhineland, became a journalist, joined the Nazi party in 1924 when it was still in its early days, and was given control of its propaganda in 1929. He was totally committed to Nazism and as minister of propaganda his organizational abilities and oratory were major factors in disseminating the party line throughout Germany and abroad. He was appointed special plenipotentiary for total war in August 1944 and was granted powers to draft any able-bodied person in the Reich into war work. In the final days of Berlin he moved into the Führerbunker, poisoned his six children, and then ordered an SS officer to shoot him and his wife.

His swift reaction to the 1944 July Plot was instrumental in preventing the anti-Nazi conspirators gaining any advantage. He instigated myths about resistance organizations, which gave many Allied leaders sleepless nights and led to complex military tactical dispositions to deal with threats that never actually existed.

FURTHER READING

Heiber, H *Goebbels* 1973

Reuth, R G *Goebbels* 1993

Semmler, R *Goebbels, the Man Next to Hitler* 1981

Trevor-Roper, H (ed) *The Goebbels Diaries: The Last Days* 1978

Goering, Hermann Wilhelm (1893–1946)

Nazi leader, German field marshal from 1938. He was part of Hitler's inner circle, and with Hitler's rise to power was appointed commissioner for aviation from 1933 and built up the Luftwaffe (airforce). He built a vast economic empire in occupied Europe, but later lost favour and was expelled from the party in 1945. Tried at Nürnberg for war crimes, he poisoned himself before he could be executed.

Goering was born in Bavaria. He was a renowned fighter pilot in World War I, and joined the Nazi party in 1922. He was elected to the Reichstag (parliament) in 1928 and became its president in 1932. He was appointed minister of the interior for Prussia in 1933. This position gave him full control of the police and security forces; he organized the Gestapo and had the first concentration camps built, then handed control to the SS to enable him to concentrate on developing the Luftwaffe. He supervised the four-year economic plan to ready the country for war 1935–39. The Luftwaffe's failure to break the British air defences was a serious blow to his reputation from which he never really recovered, and he retired to his country estate in 1942.

FURTHER READING

Lee, A *Goering, Air Leader* 1972

Mosley, L *The Reich Marshal: A Biography of Hermann Goering* 1974

Overy, R J *Goering: The 'Iron Man'* 1984

Goh Chok Tong (1941–)

Singaporean politician, prime minister from 1990. A trained economist, Goh became a member of parliament for the ruling People's Action Party in 1976. Rising steadily through the party ranks, he was appointed deputy prime minister in 1985, and was subsequently chosen by the cabinet as Lee Kuan Yew's successor, first as prime minister and from 1992 also as party leader.

Gokhale, Gopal Krishna (1866–1915)

Indian political adviser and friend of Mahatma Gandhi, leader of the Moderate group in the Indian National Congress before World War I.

Goldman, Emma (1869–1940)

US political organizer, feminist, and co-editor of the anarchist monthly magazine *Mother Earth* 1906–17. In 1908 her citizenship was revoked and in 1919 she was deported to Russia. Breaking with the Bolsheviks in 1921, she spent the rest of her life in exile. Her writings include *My Disillusionment in Russia* (1923) and *Living My Life* (1931).

The history of progress is written in the blood of men and women who have dared to espouse an unpopular cause, as, for instance, the black man's right to his body, or woman's right to her soul.

EMMA GOLDMAN 'What I Believe', *New York World* 1908; quoted in Shulman (ed) *Red Emma Speaks* part 1

Born in Lithuania and raised in Russia, Goldman emigrated to the USA in 1885 and worked in a clothing factory in Rochester, New York. There she became attracted to radical socialism and moved to New York City in 1889, where she became part of the anarchist movement. In 1893 she was jailed for inciting unemployed workers to riot; she was again imprisoned for opposing military conscription during World War I.

FURTHER READING

Drinnon, Richard *Rebel in Paradise: A Biography of Emma Goldman* 1961

Shulman, Alex *To the Barricades: The Anarchist Life of Emma Goldman* 1971

Goldstein, Vida Jane Mary (1869–1949)

Australian feminist and suffragette. In 1903 she stood as an independent female candidate for the Australian senate, becoming the first woman in the British

Empire to stand for election to a national parliament. Although unsuccessful, she polled more than 51,000 votes. She later campaigned in Victoria for women's suffrage, which was granted in 1908, and during World War I formed the pacifist Women's Peace Army.

The daughter of progressive parents, she joined anti-sweatshop and prison-reform campaigns in the 1890s, adopting a quasi-socialist stance. In her later years she devoted herself to Christian Science.

Goldwater, Barry (Morris) (1909–1998)

US Republican politician, presidential candidate in the 1964 election, when he was overwhelmingly defeated by Lyndon Johnson. As senator for Arizona 1953–65 and 1969–87, he voiced the views of his party's right-wing faction. Many of Goldwater's conservative ideas were later adopted by the Republican right, especially the administration of Ronald Reagan.

Goldwater was born in Phoenix, Arizona, and educated at Staunton Military Academy, Virginia, and Arizona University. He entered the family store business in 1929. He served in the Army Air Forces during World War II, and achieved the rank of major general in 1962 in the Air Force Reserve. After a stint in 1949 on the Phoenix city council, he ran successfully for the Senate.

After his defeat in the presidential elections, Goldwater was discredited for a time, but his stock rose as a consequence of the Vietnam War and of his position on the Watergate scandal that brought down the Republican president Richard Nixon. He wrote *The Conscience of a Conservative* (1960) and *Why Not Victory?* (1962).

Gollancz, Victor (1893–1967)

British left-wing writer and publisher, founder in 1936 of the Left Book Club. His own firm published plays by R C Sherriff and novels by Daphne Du Maurier, Elizabeth Bowen, and Dorothy L Sayers, among others.

In 1945 he formed the 'Save Europe Now' movement and became an active supporter of the Campaign for Nuclear Disarmament (CND) in the late 1950s. His memoirs *Reminiscences of Affection* were published posthumously in 1968.

Gollancz was born in London, the son of orthodox Jews, and was educated at Oxford. He was knighted in 1965.

Golwalkar, Madhavrao Sadashivrao, known as 'Guruji' ('the Teacher') (1906–1973)

Indian Hindu nationalist. Trained as a zoologist and a lawyer, Golwalkar became head of the Rashtriya Swayamsevak Sangh (RSS, National Volunteer Corps) in June 1940 and developed it into a powerful and fiercely anti-Muslim and anti-Christian youth movement. He crusaded for a united India and advocated a union of India and Pakistan but believed that non-Hindu peoples had to either adopt the Hindu culture

and religion or remain 'wholly subordinated to the Hindu nation'.

The most comprehensive statement of his ideas was made in his book *We or Our Nationhood Defined* (1938) in which he praised Hitler's theories of racial supremacy as 'a good lesson for us in Hindustan to learn and profit by'.

Gómez, Juan Vicente (1857–1935)

Venezuelan dictator 1908–35 and president. The discovery of oil during his rule attracted US, British, and Dutch oil interests and made Venezuela one of the wealthiest countries in Latin America. Gómez amassed a considerable personal fortune and used his well-equipped army to dominate the civilian population.

He failed to implement any social or educational policies, with the result that many Venezuelans suffered hardship under his rule. His domination lasted until his death, even though his presidency was interrupted for two intervening periods, 1915–22 and 1929–31.

Gómez was born in San Antonio de Táchira. He became vice president in 1902, under Cipriano Castro, becoming president when Castro was exiled in 1908. He became commander in chief of the army in 1915.

Gompers, Samuel (1850–1924)

English-born US labour leader. His early career in the Cigarmakers' Union led him to found and lead the American Federation of Labor in 1886. Gompers advocated nonpolitical activity within the existing capitalist system to secure improved wages and working conditions for members.

He helped to found the Federation of Organized Trades and Labor Unions in 1881, and spent three years as its president. When this organization merged with the American Federation of Labor in 1886, he was elected president of the new body and, with the exception of 1895, held this position for the remainder of his life.

Gompers was born in London but emigrated to the USA in 1863. In 1919 he was elected president of the International Commission on Labor Legislation of the Paris Peace Conference, and was later a member of the advisory committee to US delegates to the Disarmament Conference, Washington, DC. His autobiography, *Seventy Years of Life and Labor*, was published in 1925.

Gomułka, Władysław (1905–1982)

Polish communist politician, party leader 1943–48 and 1956–70. He introduced moderate reforms, including private farming and tolerance for Roman Catholicism.

Gomułka, born in Krosno in southeastern Poland, was involved in underground resistance to the Germans during World War II, taking part in the defence of Warsaw. Leader of the Communist Party in Poland from 1943, he was ousted by the Moscow-backed

Bolesław Bierut (1892–1956) in 1948, but was restored to the leadership in 1956, following riots in Poznań. Gomułka was forced to resign in December 1970 after sudden food-price rises induced a new wave of strikes and riots.

Göncz, Árpád (1922–)

Hungarian politician, president from 1990. He was an active opponent of the communist administration as a founder member of the Free Initiatives Network, the Free Democratic Federation, and the Historic Justice Committee. He became a member of parliament in 1990, and acting president of Hungary from May 1990 until August 1990 when he formally took office.

Born in Budapest, Göncz was educated at Pazmany Peter University, Budapest. His early career included working as a banking clerk for the Land Credit Institute. He was a member of the Industrial Smallholders Landworkers and Bourgeois Party and the Industrial Youth Organization. In 1957 he was sentenced to life imprisonment as a defendant in the political Bibo trial. He was released under an amnesty in 1963. As a writer, he won the Wheatland Prize and the Attila Jozsef Prize, and served as the president of the Hungarian Writers Federation 1989–90.

FURTHER READING
Göncz, Árpád *Homecoming and Other Stories* 1991
László György *Göncz, Árpád* 1994

González Márquez, Felipe (1942–)

Spanish socialist politician, leader of the Socialist Workers' Party (PSOE), and prime minister 1982–96. His party was re-elected in 1989 and 1993, but his popularity suffered as a result of economic upheaval and revelations of corruption within his administration. During 1995 he was himself briefly under investigation for alleged involvement with anti-terrorist death squads in the 1980s, and in March 1996, he and his party were narrowly defeated in the general elections.

After studying law in Spain and Belgium, in 1966 he opened the first labour-law office in his home city of Seville. In 1964 he joined the PSOE, and he rose rapidly to the position of leader. In 1982 the PSOE won a sweeping electoral victory and González became prime minister. Under his administration left-wing members of the PSOE, disenchanted with González's policies, formed a new party called Social Democracy in 1990. After his party's failure to retain an absolute majority in the 1989 parliamentary elections, González formed a coalition with Catalan and Basque nationalist parties, promising increased devolution to the country's regions.

The PSOE suffered during the early 1990s from a series of corruption scandals, and in 1995 González was accused of having been personally involved in the setting up of the Antiterrorist Liberation Group, a paramilitary group that had been responsible for the deaths of scores of Basque separatists in the 1980s. A preliminary probe into the allegations was abandoned as a result of insufficient evidence, but the scandal cost him the support of his Catalan coalition partner.

Gonzáles Víquez, Cleto (1858–1937)

Costa Rican liberal patriarchal politician, president 1906–10 and 1928–32. Along with Ricardo ◊Jiménez Oreamuno, he dominated the country's politics between 1906 and 1937. In his second term he dealt ably with the problems presented by economic depression from 1929.

A historian and jurist, 'Don Cleto' was one of Costa Rica's most respected politicians during the era between 1889 and 1940 when a democratic system was established and consolidated. Twice prime minister, he governed with probity and moderation, promoting gradual reforms.

Goodman, Arnold Abraham, Baron Goodman (1913–1995)

English lawyer and political adviser. Once described as the most powerful man in Britain, he was adviser to three prime ministers: Harold ◊Wilson, Edward ◊Heath, and John ◊Major. He had the unique distinction of having been made a peer by a Labour prime minister and a Companion of Honour by a Conservative one.

Goodman was born in London and studied law at University College London, and Downing College, Cambridge, where he obtained a double first. Although Goodman advised governments of all political persuasions, he is best remembered for his links with the Labour Party, and particularly Harold Wilson. Perhaps the key to his success as a lawyer and negotiator was that he carried very little ideological baggage, thereby winning the trust of people with widely differing backgrounds and persuasions.

A lifelong bachelor who considered women to be intellectually inferior, he held numerous offices, including chair of the Arts Council, master of an Oxford college, chair of the *Observer* newspaper, director of two national opera houses, cofounder of the National Theatre, government negotiator in dealings with Rhodesia (now Zimbabwe and Zambia), chair of the Newspaper Publishers' Association, chair of the Housing Association, and lawyer to trade unions and popular media stars. He credited his ability to fulfil so many roles to an absence of domestic distractions.

Gorbachev, Mikhail Sergeyevich (1931–)
See page 166.

Gore, Al(bert) (1948–)

US politician, vice president from 1993. A Democrat, he became a member of the House of Representatives 1977–79, and was senator for Tennessee 1985–92. He was on the conservative wing of the party, but held liberal views on such matters as women's rights, environmental issues, and abortion. As vice president he was unusually active in foreign affairs, and put forward proposals for 'reinventing government' by cutting red tape and improving efficiency.

Gore was born in Tennessee, where his father was senator, and worked as a journalist, a property developer, and a farmer before going into politics. He was known to have strong views on arms control, military, and foreign policy. An unsuccessful contestant for the Democrats' presidential nomination in 1988, he was thought to be the clear frontrunner for 2000, but his prospects were somewhat damaged by Justice Department's investigations into potentially illegal fundraising for the Democrats in 1996, to which Gore, through making fund-raising telephone calls from the White House, was found to be linked.

Goria, Giovanni (1943–1994)

Italian Christian Democrat politician, prime minister 1987–88. He entered the chamber of deputies in 1976 and held a number of posts, including treasury minister, until he was asked to form a coalition government in 1987. He resigned as finance minister in 1993 to fight allegations of corruption.

Gorman, Teresa (1931–)

British Conservative politician. She became Conservative member of Parliament for Billericay in 1987. An outspoken supporter of free-market principles (or Thatcherism) she was also chair of the Alliance of Small Firms and Self-Employed People from 1973 until 1987. A firm opponent of the bureaucracy of the European Community, she fought against British participation in it and had the Conservative whip removed through her opposition to the Maastricht bill in 1996.

Gorman was educated at London University and was a councillor in Westminster 1982–86.

Gorton, John Grey (1911–)

Australian Liberal politician, prime minister 1968–71. A member of the Senate, he was elected party leader and prime minister following the death of Harold ◊Holt in 1968. He then transferred to the lower house, winning Holt's vacant seat. His prime ministership was marred by conflicts with his colleagues over his style of leadership and lack of consultation, while divisions over the continuing involvement of Australia in the Vietnam War led to a drop in electoral support. In 1971, following the resignation of his defence minister Malcolm ◊Fraser, a party vote of confidence resulted in a tied ballot and Gorton resigned rather than use his casting vote to stay in power.

Gorton was born in Melbourne and educated at Oxford University, England. During World War II he was an air force pilot, receiving severe facial injuries

---

◆ GORBACHEV, MIKHAIL SERGEYEVICH (1931–) ◆

Soviet president, in power 1985–91. He was a member of the Politburo from 1980. As general secretary of the Communist Party of the Soviet Union (CPSU) 1985–91 and president of the Supreme Soviet 1988–91, he introduced liberal reforms at home (*perestroika* and *glasnost*), proposed the introduction of multiparty democracy, and attempted to halt the arms race abroad. He became head of state in 1989. He was awarded the Nobel Peace Prize in 1990.

No party has a monopoly over what is right.
MIKHAIL GORBACHEV Quoted in *Observer* 2 March 1986

Gorbachev radically changed the style of Soviet leadership, encountering opposition to the pace of change from both conservatives and radicals, but failed both to realize the depth of hostility this aroused against him in the CPSU and to distance himself from the party. His international reputation suffered in the light of harsh state repression of nationalist demonstrations in the Baltic states. Following an abortive coup attempt by hardliners in August 1991, international acceptance of independence for the Baltic states, and accelerated moves towards independence in other republics, Gorbachev's power base as Soviet president was greatly weakened and in December 1991 he resigned. He contested the Russian presidential elections in June 1996, but attracted a humiliating 0.5% of the vote.

Gorbachev, born in the northern Caucasus, studied law at Moscow University and joined the CPSU in 1952. From 1955 to 1962 he worked for the Komsomol (Communist Youth League) before being appointed regional agriculture secretary. As Stavropol party leader from 1970 he impressed Yuri Andropov, and was brought into the CPSU Secretariat in 1978.

Gorbachev was promoted into the Politburo and in 1983, when Andropov was general secretary, took broader charge of the Soviet economy. During the administration of Konstantin Chernenko 1984–85, he was chair of the Foreign Affairs Commission. On Chernenko's death in 1985 he was appointed party leader. He initiated wide-ranging reforms and broad economic restructuring, and introduced campaigns against

Mikhail Gorbachev and his wife Raisa, 1989. *Rex*

when shot down. He was elected to the Senate in 1949. He held various government posts, including minister for the navy 1958–63 and the first minister for education and science 1966–68. After his resignation from the prime ministership, he held the defence portfolio under William ◊McMahon until he was dismissed for his publication of a newspaper series *I Did It My Way*. He resigned from the Liberal Party in 1975 and stood unsuccessfully for the Senate as an independent. He was knighted in 1977.

Gottwald, Klement (1896–1953)

Czechoslovakian communist president 1948–53. He criticized the Munich capitulation in 1938 and went into exile in Moscow, where he remained until 1945, meeting Edvard Beneš, the head of the Czechoslovakian government in exile, in 1943. Vice premier in the Czechoslovakian coalition government of 1945, he became premier after the elections in the following year. He used this position to complete the communist seizure of power in 1948, and in 1948 he succeeded Beneš as president.

He was born in Dedice, Moravia. In 1921 he joined the newly formed Czechoslovakian Communist Party. He soon became a prominent figure and in 1930 was made general secretary of the party. His presidency

alcoholism, corruption, and inefficiency. In the 1988 presidential election by members of the Soviet parliament, he was the sole candidate.

In March 1990 he was elected to a five-year term as executive president with greater powers. At home his plans for economic reform failed to avert a food crisis in the winter of 1990–91 and his desire to preserve a single, centrally controlled USSR met with resistance from Soviet republics seeking more independence. Early in 1991

Sometimes ... when you stand face to face with someone, you cannot see his face.
MIKHAIL GORBACHEV After summit meeting with US president Ronald Reagan, Iceland, 12 October 1986

Gorbachev shifted to the right in order to placate the conservative wing of the party and appointed some of the hardliners to positions of power. In late spring he produced a plan for a new union treaty to satisfy the demands of reformers. This plan alarmed the hardliners, who, in late summer, temporarily removed him from office. He was saved from this attempted coup mainly by the efforts of Boris ◊Yeltsin and the ineptitude of the plotters.

Soon after his reinstatement, Gorbachev was obliged to relinquish his leadership of the party, renounce communism as a state doctrine, suspend all activities of the Communist Party (including its most powerful organs, the Politburo and the Secretariat), and surrender many of his central powers to the states. He continued to press for an agreement on his proposed union treaty in the hope of preventing a disintegration of the Soviet Union, but was unable to maintain control and on 25 December 1991 resigned as president, effectively yielding power to Yeltsin.

FURTHER READING
Aslund, Anders *Gorbachev's Struggle for Reform* 1989
Brown, Archie *The Gorbachev Factor* 1996
Lewin, Moshe *The Gorbachev Phenomenon* 1988
Medvedev, Zhores *Gorbachev* 1986
Sheehy, Gail *Gorbachev: The Making of the Man Who Shook the World* 1991

was characterized by a subservience of Czech affairs to Soviet interests, and by the sensational 'deviationist' trials in which several of his former associates were executed. He died in Moscow.

Goulart, João, Marquis of Belquior (1918–1976)

Brazilian politician and president 1961–64. A weak and vacillating leader, he alienated moderate opinion by flirting with nationalist and left-wing groups. His administration was plagued with economic problems and with the growing influence of communist party members. He was ejected by a coup in 1964, engineered by the army and supported by powerful conservative politicians in the Brazilian Democratic Union (UDN).

Goulart was linked with the Brazilian Labour Party (PTB) in the late 1940s and was the protégé of Getulio Vargas. He became minister of labour, industry, and commerce 1953–54 and vice president 1956–61. He became leader of the PTB in 1960 and, having been accused by the army of nurturing procommunist sympathies against military hostility, the army reluctantly agreed to allow him to become president of a parliamentary regime in 1961.

Gould, Bryan Charles (1939–)

New Zealand-born British left-of-centre Labour politician, an unsuccessful challenger for the party leadership in 1992.

Born in New Zealand, Gould, from a state school background, won a university scholarship at the unprecedented age of 15 and was later a Rhodes Scholar at Oxford University, England. He decided to settle in England in 1964, working as a diplomat and then as a lecturer at Oxford University. A fierce critic of the British class system, he joined the Labour Party and was elected a member of Parliament in 1974. He lost his Southampton seat in the Conservative electoral landslide of 1979, but returned in 1983, representing Dagenham, having spent the intervening four years as a television journalist. His rise in the Labour Party was rapid and in 1986 he became a member of the shadow cabinet and a director of its election campaigns. His communication skills soon made him a nationally known figure.

He favoured modernization of the Labour Party, but retained left-wing views in areas such as closer integration within the European Union (which he opposed as a 'Eurosceptic'), defence spending, and state intervention in the economy. Following his defeat in the 1992 Labour Party leadership contest by the more moderate John ◊Smith, he resigned from the shadow cabinet in September. In 1994 he announced his retirement from active politics, and returned to an academic career in New Zealand.

Gow, Ian Reginald Edward (1937–1990)

British Conservative politician. After qualifying as a solicitor, he was elected member of Parliament for Eastbourne in 1974. He became parliamentary private secretary to Margaret ◊Thatcher in 1979 and her close ally. He secured steady promotion but resigned his post as minister of state in 1985 in protest at the signing of the Anglo-Irish Agreement. A strong critic of terrorist acts, he was killed by an Irish Republican Army car bomb.

Gowda, H D Deve (1933–)

Indian political leader, prime minister 1996–97. Representing the centrist Janata Party, he became chief minister of the state of Karnataka in 1994. Chosen as prime minister in May 1996, he led a 13-party United Front coalition government, but was forced to step down in April 1997 when the Congress Party withdrew its support.

Gowda was persuaded by President Shankar Dayal Sharma to lead a United Front coalition government when the Hindu chauvinist Bharatiya Janata Party's (BJP) attempt to form a federal government failed after 13 days. The Gowda administration declared its priority as rural development and social welfare. Unable to speak Hindi, Gowda was dubbed India's first 'regional prime minister'.

Gowon, Yakubu (1934–)

Nigerian politician, head of state 1966–75. He became army chief of staff following a coup in January 1966, and five months later seized power in a further coup. Unsuccessful in his efforts to prevent the secession of the eastern region of Biafra, Nigeria was plunged into civil war 1967–70. After leading the federal army to victory, he reunited the country with his policy of 'no victor, no vanquished'. His later administration was plagued by allegations of corruption and Gowon's failure to timetable a return to civilian rule. Deposed by a bloodless coup in 1975, he went into exile in the UK, returning to Nigeria in 1983.

Gowon was born into a Christian family in northern Nigeria. He joined the army in 1954, and was educated at Sandhurst military college in the UK. Between 1961 and 1962 he served in the Congo as part of the United Nations peacekeeping force. During his exile in the UK he studied at the University of Warwick, gaining a doctorate in political science in 1984.

Gramm, Phil (1942–)

US senator. He was first elected to the House of Representatives as a Democrat, but had his House Budget Committee seat removed because he chose to co-author the economic programme of Ronald ◊Reagan. He set a precedent by resigning from Congress and winning re-election as a Republican. Gramm's legislative record reflects his right-wing beliefs and anti-welfare state stance. It includes the Gramm–Latta Budgets, which cut federal spending, and the Gramm–Rudman Act, which placed the first binding constraints on Federal spending. Gramm also fought the Clinton Health Care Bill, and pursued reforms to the welfare system, which included assessing the potential for investment-based social security.

Born in College Station, Texas, Gramm taught economics at Texas A&M University. He published numerous articles and books on monetary theory and policy, private property, and the economics of mineral extraction.

FURTHER READING
Gramm, Phil *The Role of Government in a Free Society*

Gramsci, Antonio (1891–1937)

Italian Marxist who attempted to unify social theory and political practice. He helped to found the Italian Communist Party in 1921 and was elected to parliament in 1924, but was imprisoned by the Fascist leader Mussolini from 1926; his *Quaderni di carcere/Prison Notebooks* were published posthumously in 1947.

Gramsci believed that politics and ideology were independent of the economic base, that no ruling class could dominate by economic factors alone, and that the working class could achieve liberation by political and intellectual struggle. His concept of hegemony argued that real class control in capitalist societies is ideological and cultural rather than physical, and that only the working class 'educated' by radical intellectuals could see through and overthrow such bourgeois propaganda.

His humane and gradualist approach to Marxism, specifically his emphasis on the need to overthrow bourgeois ideology, influenced European Marxists in their attempt to distance themselves from orthodox determinist Soviet communism.

FURTHER READING
Clark, M N *Antonio Gramsci and the Revolution that Failed* 1977
Davidson, A *Antonio Gramsci: Towards an Intellectual Biography* 1977
Joll, James *Antonio Gramsci* 1977
Sassoon, S *Gramsci's Politics* 1980

Grandi, Dino, Count (1895–1988)

Italian politician who challenged Mussolini for leadership of the Italian Fascist Party in 1921 and was subsequently largely responsible for Mussolini's downfall in July 1943.

Grandi, a leading figure in the Fascist Party during the 1920s, was Italian foreign minister 1929–32 and ambassador to the UK 1932–39. After Mussolini's rescue from prison in 1943, Grandi fled from Italy and lived for four years in Lisbon, Portugal.

Grau San Martín, Ramón (1887–1969)

Cuban politician, president 1933–34 and 1944–48. He helped overthrow the dictator Gerardo ◊Machado in 1933, and his successor Carlos Manuel de ◊Céspedes, to become provisional president himself. Viewed by the USA as too radical, he was ousted following a further coup by Fulgencio ◊Batista in 1934. As president from 1944, he moved to end press censorship and promoted improvements in education, health provision, and housing. He retained background influence from 1948 during the presidency of Carlos Prío Socarrás.

Endemic corruption and nepotism led to his loss of support, but Grau's economic success enabled Prío, his preferred candidate, to win the 1948 presidential election. Grau retired from politics after unsuccessfully running against Batista in the 1954 fraudulent presidential election.

He was born in Pinar de Rio, in western Cuba, and studied medicine at the University of Havana, where he later became a professor. Before winning the presidency in 1944, Grau challenged Batista in the presidential elections of 1940, but was defeated in a rigged contest.

Green, William (1873–1952)

US labour leader. He was president of the American Federation of Labor 1924–52, and helped shape the National Industrial Recovery Act in 1933 and the National Labor Relations Act in 1935. An opponent of industrial unionism, he forced out the unions that then formed the Congress of Industrial Organization (CIO); he would struggle with the CIO to the end of his life. He was the epitome of the respectable, responsible labour leader who chose to restrain the more radical approach to management and labour relations.

Green was born in Coshocton, Ohio. A coal miner from the age of 16, he rose in the union ranks and served in the Ohio senate 1911–15. He was secretary-treasurer of the United Mine Workers of America 1913–24. In 1949 he attended a conference in London, England, that formed the International Confederation of Free Trade Unions to promote noncommunist labour unions in Europe.

Greenwood, Arthur (1880–1954)

British Labour politican. A wartime member of David Lloyd George's secretariat, he was member of Parliament for Nelson and Colne 1922–31, and for Wakefield 1932–54. He became deputy leader of the parliamentary Labour Party in 1935, showing himself an outspoken critic of 'appeasement'. In 1945 he was minister without portfolio, and in 1945 became Lord Privy Seal, resigning from the government in 1947. He remained treasurer of the Labour Party and became chair of the Labour Party's national executive in 1953.

Born in Leeds and educated at the university there, he supported the Leeds Municipal Strike in 1913. His son, Anthony Greenwood (1911–1982) was also a Labour MP, entering Parliament in 1946.

Greer, Germaine (1939–)

Australian academic and feminist, author of *The Female Eunuch* (1970). The book is a polemical study of how patriarchy – through the nuclear family and capitalism – subordinates women by forcing them to conform to feminine stereotypes that effectively 'castrate' them. With its publication, Greer became identified as a leading figure of the women's movement.

Mother is the dead heart of the family, spending father's earnings on consumer goods to enhance the environment in which he eats, sleeps, and watches the television.

GERMAINE GREER *The Female Eunuch*, 'Obsession'

However, the book has been criticized by other feminists for placing too much emphasis on sexual liberation as the way forward. In *Sex and Destiny: The Politics of Human Fertility* (1984), a critique of the politics of fertility and contraception, Greer seemed to reverse this position. Her other works include *The Obstacle Race* (1979), a study of women and painting; and *The Change* (1991), a positive view of the menopause.

Born in Melbourne, she was educated at a Catholic,

Germaine Greer. *Penguin Books Ltd*

convent school and then at Melbourne and Sydney universities. She secured her doctorate at Cambridge, England. Based in the UK, she lectured at Warwick University from 1963 to 1964, and has also worked successfully as a television art critic and commentator.

FURTHER READING
Greer, Germaine *Daddy, We Hardly Knew You* (autobiography) 1989

Grey, Edward, 1st Viscount Grey of Fallodon (1862–1933)

British Liberal politician, member of parliament for Berwick on Tweed 1885–1916, nephew of Charles Grey. As foreign secretary 1905–16 he negotiated an entente with Russia in 1907, and backed France against Germany in the Agadir Incident of 1911. He published his memoirs, *Twenty-Five Years*, in 1925. He became Baronet in 1882 and was created Viscount in 1916.

Griffith, Arthur (1872–1922)

Irish journalist, propagandist, and politician. He was active in nationalist politics from 1898 and united various nationalist parties to form Sinn Féin in 1905. When the provisional Irish parliament declared a republic in 1919, he was elected vice president and signed the treaty that gave Eire its independence in 1921. He was elected the country's first president in 1922, dying in office later that year.

Born in Dublin, Griffith was educated at the Christian Brothers school, was a founder member of the Gaelic Literary Society in 1893, and was active in the Gaelic League and the Irish Republican Brotherhood. He left the latter organization in 1910. Although a leading figure in the revolutionary period of Irish politics, Griffith opposed the use of force, and took no part in the 1916 Easter Rising. Instead he advocated Irish independence under a dual monarchy on the Austro-Hungarian model, coupled with a protectionist scheme to encourage Irish economic self-sufficiency. These ideas formed the basis of the programme of the Sinn Féin movement, which Griffith established in 1905. The organization remained comparatively weak until the government (wrongly) concluded that it had inspired the 1916 Rising, whereupon Griffith was arrested. Meanwhile, his movement was taken over by the Volunteers and the Irish Republican Brotherhood, and Griffith found himself vice president of an avowedly republican organization. He headed the Irish delegation that negotiated the settlement with the British in December 1921, and was elected president of the Dáil in January 1922, following Éamon de Valera's resignation. Griffith died suddenly of a cerebral haemorrhage on 12 August 1922.

FURTHER READING
Younger, Carlton *Arthur Griffith* 1981

Griffiths, James (1890–1975)

Welsh miners' leader and politician. A strong believer in a measure of devolution for Wales, he argued for a separate Welsh Office, and became the first secretary of state for Wales 1964–66. Born in Bettws, Ammanford, Carmarthenshire, he became a leading official in the miners' union in South Wales, and was elected Labour member of Parliament for Llanelli 1936–70. He was deputy leader of the Labour Party 1955–58.

In the Labour governments of 1945 to 1951, he was minister of National Insurance and secretary of state for the colonies. He saw himself as a moderating influence in Labour Party politics during the tensions of the Gaitskell–Bevan disputes in the 1950s. His autobiography, *Pages from Memory*, was published in 1969.

Griffiths, Martha, born Wright (1912–)

US politician. A Democratic congresswoman from Michigan 1955–75, Griffiths was best known for her brilliant political manoeuvre in successfully adding sex discrimination as a prohibited act in the 1964 Civil Rights Act. She also successfully campaigned for equality in government pensions and secured social security benefit payments for women's heirs. She was widely acknowledged as having worked harder in Congress for women than anyone had done before. In 1983, sitting as the first woman elected as lieutenant governor, she was inducted into the National Woman's Hall of Fame.

FURTHER READING
George, Emily *Martha W Griffiths* 1982

Grimond, Jo(seph), Baron Grimond (1913–1993)

British Liberal politician, born in St Andrews, Scotland. As leader of the Liberal Party 1956–67, he aimed at making it 'a new radical party to take the place of the Socialist Party as an alternative to Conservatism'. An old-style Whig and a man of culture and personal charm, he had a considerable influence on postwar British politics, although he never held a major public position. During his term of office, the number of Liberal seats in Parliament doubled.

He studied law, but after wartime service began a political career. It was his ill luck to become leader of the Liberal Party at a time when the Labour Party, in its ascendancy, was, with the Conservatives, squeezing the Liberals almost out of existence. The party might well have ceased to survive without his inspiration. However, when he passed it to Jeremy Thorpe in 1967 it was in much better shape. After Thorpe's resignation in 1976, Grimond became leader again for three months before handing over to David Steel.

He married Laura Bonham Carter, of the great Liberal dynasty, who was also politically active. He represented the remote Orkney and Shetland constitu-ency for 33 years before entering the House of Lords in 1983.

Grivas, George (Georgios Theodoros) (1898–1974)

Greek Cypriot general who from 1955 led the underground group EOKA's attempts to secure the union (Greek *enosis*) of Cyprus with Greece.

Gromyko, Andrei Andreyevich (1909–1989)

Russian politician, president of the USSR 1985–88. As ambassador to the USA from 1943, he took part in the Tehran, Yalta, and Potsdam conferences; as United Nations representative 1946–49, he exercised the Soviet veto 26 times. He was foreign minister 1957–85. It was Gromyko who formally nominated Mikhail ◊Gorbachev as Communist Party leader in 1985.

Grosz, George (1893–1959)

German-born US Expressionist painter and graphic artist. He was a founder of the Berlin Dada group in 1918, and excelled in savage satirical drawings criticizing the government and the military establishment. After numerous prosecutions, he fled his native Berlin in 1932 and went to the USA.

His brilliant drawings make him a leader in the school of German Expressionism, but from 1933 he and his work disappeared into oblivion so far as the majority of Germans were concerned, since his paintings were among those condemned in the Nazi dictator Hitler's exhibition 'Degenerate Art'. Even in the late 1920s, long before Hitler had come to power, Grosz's *Ecce Homo*, showing Christ on the Cross wearing a gas mask and army boots, brought him to court on a charge of blasphemy. He is also associated with the Neue Sachlichkeit (New Objectivity) movement.

Grosz studied in Dresden and was deeply affected by the spirit of revolt among German artists after the World War I. With ruthless and acid cynicism, he satirized militarism, capitalism, the complacent middle classes, and the reactionary powers represented by the generals, the big industrialists, and the church. He became a naturalized US citizen in 1938, but his work in the USA, which was often more traditional in subject matter and style, had little of his former power. Increasingly depressed by his failure to be recognized as a serious painter, he returned to Berlin in 1959, dying just a few months later.

His autobiography, *A Little Yes and a Big No*, appeared in 1946.

Grotewohl, Otto (1894–1964)

German politician. In 1949 he became prime minister of the German Democratic Republic.

From 1925 to 1933 he was a Social Democratic member of the Reichstag (parliament) and was subsequently imprisoned in a concentration camp. After World War II he became a member of the Socialist

Unity party, a fusion of socialists and communists, in the Soviet zone of Germany.

Guevara, Che (Ernesto) (1928–1967)

Latin American revolutionary. He was born in Resario, Argentina, and trained there as a doctor, but left his homeland in 1953 because of his opposition to the right-wing president Juan Perón. In effecting the Cuban revolution of 1959 against the Cuban dictator Fulgencio ◊Batista, he was second only to Fidel ◊Castro and Castro's brother Raúl. Between 1961 and 1965 he served as Cuba's ministry of industry. In 1965 he went to the Congo to fight against white mercenaries, and then to Bolivia, where he was killed in an unsuccessful attempt to lead a peasant rising near Vallegrande. He was an orthodox Marxist and renowned for his guerrilla techniques.

In November 1995 the location of the mass grave in which Guevara's body was buried was revealed by a witness to the burial to be in the village of Valle Grande in Bolivia. The remains of Guevara were unearthed in 1997 and returned to Cuba for a hero's burial.

FURTHER READING
Anderson, Jon Lee *Che Guevara* 1997
Ebon, Martin *Che: The Making of a Legend* 1969
Harris, Richard *Death of a Revolutionary* 1970
Sauvage, Leo *Che Guevara: The Failure of a Revolutionary* 1974
Sinclair, A *Che Guevara* 1970

Gummer, John Selwyn (1939–)

British Conservative politician. He was minister of state for employment 1983–84, chair of the party 1983–85, paymaster general 1984–85, minister for agriculture 1985–89, secretary of state for agriculture 1989–93, and secretary of state for the environment 1993–97.

Gummer was born in Stockport and educated at Cambridge University. He was elected Conservative member of Parliament for Lewisham West in 1970, was defeated in the 1974 general election, and returned to Parliament in 1979 as Conservative MP for Eye, Suffolk (Suffolk Coastal since 1983). A prominent lay member of the Church of England, he left in 1994, after its decision to permit the ordination of women priests, and became a Roman Catholic.

Gursel, Cemal (1895–1966)

Turkish soldier and politician. He became commander-in-chief of the Turkish land forces in 1958. After leading an army coup in 1960 he became president of the Committee of National Unity, head of state, and prime minister 1960–61. He was elected president in October 1961 after the resumption of constitutional government. After illness he was replaced as president in March 1966.

He entered the army in 1915 and became general in command of the Third Army in 1957. He overthrew President Adrian Menderes in 1960. He was replaced as president by General Cevedet Sunay, the former chief of general staff.

Guthrie, Arlo (1947–)

US singer and songwriter. The son of folk singer Woody ◊Guthrie, Arlo Guthrie came to prominence in 1967 at the Newport Folk Festival with the song 'Alice's Restaurant'. An autobiographical tale with an anti-Vietnam War stance, satirizing both the police and the army, the song went on to become an anthem for the anti-Vietnam War movement.

Guthrie involved himself with environmental and peace causes, performing regularly with his father's contemporary, Pete Seeger. In 1992 he purchased the Old Trinity Church, where 'Alice's Restaurant' was set, and established the Guthrie Center – a non-profitmaking organization offering programmes for children recovering from abuse, support for HIV/AIDS, and other services for the local community.

FURTHER READING
Brock, Alice May *Mooses Come Walking* 1995
Guthrie, Arlo *Alice's Restaurant* 1968

Guthrie, Woody (Woodrow Wilson) (1912–1967)

US folk singer and songwriter. Guthrie provided inspiration for generations of radical folk musicians and over a thousand songs are testimony to his prolific genius. Guthrie took to the road at an early age, travelling on trains and composing songs based on his experiences, 'Dustbowl Ballads'. He later became a significant figure in the left-wing folk music movement, writing such classics as 'This Land is Your Land', 'Deportees', and 'Hard Travelin''. He teamed up with Pete ◊Seeger, recording for Folkways, amongst other labels. During this time he also worked in the trade-union movement and wrote for 'The People's World'. His autobiography, *Bound for Glory* (1943), is considered a seminal work and was made into a film in 1976.

Gysi, Gregor (1948–)

German politician, elected leader of the Communist Party in December 1989 following the resignation of Egon ◊Krenz. He continued to lead the party after it was renamed the Party of Democratic Socialism (PDS) and oversaw its electoral success in October 1994, when the PDS captured 30 Bundestag seats.

A lawyer, Gysi acted as defence counsel for dissidents during the 1970s.

H

Haakon VII (1872–1957)

King of Norway from 1905. Born Prince Charles, the second son of Frederick VIII of Denmark, he was elected king of Norway on the country's separation from Sweden, and in 1906 he took the name Haakon. On the German invasion in 1940 he refused to accept Vidkun ◊Quisling's collaborationist government, and instead escaped to London and acted as constitutional head of the government-in-exile. He served as a powerful personification of Norwegian nationhood.

Habermas, Jürgen (1929–)

German social theorist, a member of the Frankfurt school. His central concern is how a meaningful engagement in politics and society is possible in a society dominated by science and the technology and bureaucracy based on it.

In *Theorie und Praxis/Theory and Practice* (1963) and *Erkenntnis und Interesse/Knowledge and Human Interest* (1968), he argues that reason, formerly a weapon of intellectual and political freedom, has been appropriated by science. Far from being a disinterested pursuit of knowledge, it is an instrument for achieving a range of unquestioned social and political ends. In *Theory of Communicative Action* (1981) he describes how a 'communicative rationality' can be developed, reclaiming lost ground and allowing rational political commitment.

Habibie, Bacharuddin Jusuf (1936–)

Indonesian politician. Elected vice president of Indonesia in March 1998, he became president in May after President Thojib ◊Suharto resigned amid growing economic turmoil. Although he quickly promised wide-ranging economic and political reforms, many critics called for his resignation, seeing him as a puppet of Suharto tainted by the corruption of the old regime, and doubted whether he had the political support or abilities to lead a country in economic crisis.

Trained in Germany as an aeronautical engineer and head of research at Messerschmitt 1966–74, Habibie was minister of research and technology before he became vice president, and was known for expensive and ill-conceived projects. As a virtual appointee of Suharto he has little grass-roots support or senior-level administrative experience.

Habré, Hissène (c. 1930–)

Chadian nationalist and politician, prime minister in 1978 and president 1982–90. Formerly a leader of the Chadian National Liberation Front (Frolinat), he joined the Armed Forces of the North (FAN) in the early 1970s, but made peace with President Félix Malloum and was appointed prime minister in 1978. After Malloum was overthrown by the Frolinat leader Goukouni Oueddi in 1979, Habré became defence minister, and in 1982 he seized control, aided by the US Central Intelligence Agency (CIA). With French military assistance and support from African heads of state, he forced Libya to withdraw from northern Chad but was ousted in a coup led by his military commander Idriss Deby in 1990.

Throughout his presidency Habré maintained an uneasy control. In 1984 he dissolved the military arm of Frolinat and formed a new party, the National Union for Independence and Revolution (UNIR), but opposition to his regime grew. He was endorsed as president in 1989 for a further seven-year term under a revised constitution introduced in July 1990, but in December 1990 the government fell. Initially reported killed, and replaced by Deby, he went to live in Cameroon.

Habré was the son of a desert shepherd, and worked as a clerk for the French army before becoming an administrator.

Habte-wold, Tshafe Tezaz Aklilu (1912–1974)

Ethiopian prime minister 1961–74. He accompanied Emperor ◊Haile Selassie into exile following the Italian invasion. In 1941 he returned to Ethiopia and was appointed vice foreign minister and, two years later, foreign minister. He played an important role in the establishment of the Organization of African Unity (OAU) in Addis Ababa in 1963. He became deputy prime minister in 1957 and prime minister in 1961. He was forced to resign in 1974, following the unrest caused by the government's handling of the 1973 famine. Later the same year he was executed by the regime that ousted Haile Selassie.

Habte-wold was born in Addis Ababa and studied law at the Sorbonne, Paris.

Habyarimana, Juvenal (1937–1994)

Rwandan politician and soldier, president 1973–94. In 1973, as fighting between the Tutsi and Hutu tribes recommenced, he led a bloodless coup against President Grégoire Kayibanda and established a military regime. He founded the National Revolutionary Development Movement (MRND) as the only legally permitted political organization and promised an eventual return to constitutional government; civilian rule was adopted in 1980. In April 1994 Habyarimana and Burundian president Cyprien Ntaryamira were killed when their plane was shot down over Kigali, sparking an escalation in the civil war and a wave of atrocities against Tutsi civilians.

Habyarimana was born in Gasiza, in Gisenji prefecture. He joined the national guard and by 1973 had risen to the rank of major general and head of the guard.

Hacha, Emil (1872–1945)
Czech politician, president, and lawyer. He succeeded Eduard Beneš as president after the 1938 Munich Pact. As German forces entered the country on 14 March 1939, he was forced to sign a declaration in Berlin placing his country under German 'protection'. In 1945 he was arrested as a war criminal but died before he could come to trial.

Hacha was born at Trhove Suiny, Bohemia, in the modern-day Czech Republic. After practising as an advocate he became president of the Czechoslovak supreme administration court in 1925. After March 1939 Hacha was left nominally in office, but in reality he was only the 'State president' of the German-ruled 'Protectorate of Bohemia and Moravia'. He soon urged the Czechs to support the German occupation.

Hachad, Farhat (1904?–1952)
Tunisian trade-union leader. He founded the Union Générale des Travailleurs Tunisiens (UGTT) in 1946. He skilfully backed the nationalist movement's struggle for independence, and at the same time presided over the promotion and development of an autonomous labour union both organically and professionally from the Néo-Destour party. He was assassinated by a European terrorist group in 1952.

After Hachad, and particularly from independence onwards, the UGTT was to lose a great deal of its power and overall became an organization under the control of the party.

Haener, Dorothy
US rights activist. As a member of the United Auto Workers (UAW), Haener's union activity always involved the equal participation of women in the union, as well as in the workplace. In 1966 she attended the Status of Women Commissions conference in Washington, DC, where she planned to form a civil-rights organization for women with Betty ◊Friedan and others. Haener served on US president Richard Nixon's Task Force on Women's Rights and Responsibilities in 1969.

Hague, William Jefferson (1961–)
British Conservative politician, leader of the Conservative Party from 1997. He entered the House of Commons in 1989, representing the constituency of Richmond, Yorkshire, and was private secretary to the chancellor of the Exchequer 1990–93, parliamentary undersecretary of state for social security 1993–94, minister for social security and disabled people 1994–95, and secretary of state for Wales 1995–97. After the Conservative Party's defeat in the May 1997 general election, the then party leader John Major resigned and Hague was elected his successor. In 1998 he committed the party to oppose joining the European single currency for at least a decade and launched major reforms of the party's organization.

> It was inevitable that the *Titanic* would set sail, but that does not mean it was a good idea to be on it.
> WILLIAM HAGUE On the advent of the single European currency;
> *Daily Telegraph*, 7 January 1998

Born in Yorkshire, Hague came to public attention in 1977 when, at the age of 16, he addressed the party's annual conference. He was educated at Oxford University where he became president of the Union in 1981. After completing an MBA course he worked for a management consultancy company 1983–88 before entering full-time politics.

In the party-leadership election in May 1997, there were five candidates in the first ballot: Kenneth Clarke, Michael Howard, Peter Lilley, John Redwood, and Hague. In the final ballot there was a straightforward contest between the former chancellor, Clarke, and Hague, who won by a wide margin of 92 votes to 70. The new leader, the youngest for more than 200 years, promised to unite the party and included in his shadow cabinet three of his rivals, Howard, Lilley, and Redwood – Kenneth Clarke having earlier declined an invitation to join him.

FURTHER READING
Hague, W *A Fresh Future for the Conservative Party* 1997, *Britain and the Single Currency* 1997, *Speaking with Conviction: A Collection of Speeches* 1998

Haig, Alexander Meigs (1924–)
US general and Republican politician. He became

> This has been a pimple on the ass of progress festering for two hundred years, and I guess someone decided to lance it.
> ALEXANDER HAIG Referring to the Falklands conflict *Sunday Times*
> 1982

President Richard Nixon's White House Chief of Staff at the height of the Watergate scandal, was NATO commander 1974–79, and secretary of state to President Ronald Reagan 1981–82.

Haig, Douglas, 1st Earl Haig (1861–1928)

British army officer, commander in chief in World War I, born in Edinburgh, Scotland. His Somme offensive in France in the summer of 1916 made considerable advances only at enormous cost to human life, and his Passchendaele offensive in Belgium from July to November 1917 achieved little at a similar loss. He was created field marshal in 1917 and, after retiring, became first president of the British Legion in 1921.

A national hero at the time of his funeral, Haig's reputation began to fall after David Lloyd George's memoirs depicted him as treating soldiers' lives with disdain, while remaining far from battle himself.

Every position must be held to the last man: there must be no retirement. With our backs to the wall, and believing in the justice of our cause, each one must fight on to the end.

DOUGLAS HAIG Order given 12 April 1918

He served in the Omdurman and South African campaigns, and in World War I commanded the 1st Army Corps 1914–15, and the 1st Army in 1915 until he succeeded John French as commander in chief the same year. He then loyally supported the French marshal Ferdinand Foch in his appointment as supreme commander of the Allied armies and in his victorious 1918 offensive, and it was Haig's foresight that persuaded Foch to extend his attack north, so breaking the Hindenburg Line.

FURTHER READING

De Groot, G J *Douglas Haig 1861–1928* 1988
Travers, T *The Killing Ground* 1987

Haile Selassie, Ras (Prince) Tafari ('the Lion of Judah') (1892–1975)

Emperor of Ethiopia 1930–74. He pleaded unsuccessfully to the League of Nations against the Italian conquest of his country 1935–36, and was then deposed and fled to the UK. He went to Egypt in 1940 and raised an army, which he led into Ethiopia in January 1941 alongside British forces and was restored to the throne on 5 May. He was deposed by a military coup in 1974 and died in captivity the following year. Followers of the Rastafarian religion believe that he was the Messiah, the incarnation of God (Jah).

Born in Horror, he was educated by Jesuit missionaries and teachers at the imperial court. At the age of 14 he was appointed governor of Gora Muleta and four years later he took the governorship of Horror, previously held by his father. He was appointed heir to the empress Zauditu in 1916, and became her close

adviser, securing Ethiopia's admission into the League of Nations in 1923. After he became emperor in 1930 he worked to centralize power and achieve administrative reform. Following his restoration, he regained Ethiopian sovereignty in 1945 and played a leading role in the establishment of the Organization of African Unity in 1963. He incorporated Eritrea into Ethiopia in 1962, giving rise to a long-running civil war.

FURTHER READING

Clapham, C S *Haile-Selassie's Government* 1969
Kapuściński, R *The Emperor and Shah of Shahs* 1994
Lockot, H W *The Mission: The Life, Reign and Character of Haile Sellassie I* 1989

Hailsham, Douglas McGarel Hogg, 1st Viscount and Baron (1872–1950)

British lawyer and Conservative politician. He was Attorney General 1922–24 and 1924–28, and Lord Chancellor 1928–29 and again 1935–38.

He was Conservative member of Parliament for Marylebone 1922–28. He succeeded Lord Halifax as Lord President (a cabinet post) in 1938, but resigned in November that year. He was the father of the politician Quintin Hogg.

Hailsham, Quintin McGarel Hogg, Baron Hailsham of St Marylebone (1907–)

British lawyer and Conservative politician. Having succeeded as 2nd Viscount Hailsham in 1950, he renounced the title in 1963 to re-enter the House of Commons, and was then able to contest the Conservative Party leadership elections. He took a life peerage in 1970 on his appointment as Lord Chancellor 1970–74 and was Lord Chancellor again 1979–87.

The moment politics becomes dull democracy is in danger.

QUINTIN HOGG, BARON HAILSHAM Remark 1966

Born in London, the son of Douglas Hailsham, he was educated at Eton and Christ Church, Oxford. He was called to the bar in 1932 and became a QC in 1953. From 1938 to 1950 he was Conservative member of Parliament for Oxford. Having succeeded to his father's title, he went to the House of Lords under protest. In 1956 he became First Lord of the Admiralty, vigorously defending the government's Suez policy, and in 1957 was made minister of education. In September 1957 he became Lord President of the Council, and was Conservative Party chair from 1957 to 1959. He was Lord Privy Seal 1959–60, and leader of the House of Lords 1960–63, again holding the post of Lord President. From 1959 to 1964 Hailsham was minister for science and technology.

In 1963 he disclaimed his peerage, and was an unsuccessful contender for the Conservative leadership. He was MP for St Marylebone from 1963 to 1970 and secretary of state for education and science from

April to October 1964. In 1970 he was made a life peer on his appointment as Lord Chancellor in the Conservative government of 1970 to 1974.

He publications include *The Left was Never Right* (1945) and *The Case for Conservatism* (1947).

Haldane, Richard Burdon, 1st Viscount Haldane (1856–1928)

British Liberal politician, born in Scotland. As secretary for war 1905–12, he sponsored the army reforms that established an expeditionary force, backed by a territorial army and under the unified control of an imperial general staff. He was Lord Chancellor 1912–15 and in the Labour government of 1924. His writings on German philosophy led to accusations of his having pro-German sympathies. He was created Viscount in 1911.

His publications include *Human Experience* (1926).

Haldeman, H(arry) R(obbins) (1926–1993)

US presidential aide. He was chief of staff to Richard Nixon 1969–1973. Immensely protective and loyal towards his president, Haldeman was crucially involved in the Watergate cover-up and, after being convicted of obstructing justice and lying, served 18 months in a federal prison.

> *Once the toothpaste is out of the tube, it is awfully hard to get it back in.*
>
> H R HALDEMAN On the Watergate affair 1973

As a young man he began a career in advertising, rising to the vice-presidency of the prestigious agency J Walter Thompson, before being enlisted as an aide to the ambitious Republican politician Richard Nixon. He worked in Nixon's successful vice-presidential re-election campaign of 1956, his unsuccessful presidential campaign of 1960, and his campaign for the California governorship in 1962. When Nixon eventually won the presidency in 1968 he chose Haldeman as his Chief of Staff. With Henry Kissinger and John Ehrlichman, he formed part of the close-knit group of advisers dubbed by the press 'the Teutonic Trio'. In this capacity, Haldeman controlled the White House with military discipline, screening the president from unwanted visitors and sometimes even from his own colleagues. This unquestioning loyalty eventually led to his own demise. While the former president was granted a free pardon by his successor, Gerald Ford, Haldeman, with Ehrlichman, was left unprotected. After his release from prison he rebounded to a third successful career, in the hotel business.

Halifax, Edward Frederick Lindley Wood, 1st Earl of Halifax (2nd creation) (1881–1959)

British Conservative politician, viceroy of India 1926–31. As foreign secretary 1938–40 he was associated with Neville Chamberlain's 'appeasement' policy.

He received an earldom in 1944 for services to the Allied cause while ambassador to the USA 1941–46. He

> *I often think how much easier the world would have been to manage if Herr Hitler and Signor Mussolini had been at Oxford.*
>
> EDWARD HALIFAX Speech 4 November 1937

was created Baron in 1925 and succeeded as Viscount 1934.

Hallowes, Odette Marie Celine (1912–)

French-born war heroine. From 1942 she worked as a British agent in German-occupied France. She was captured, tortured, and sent to Ravensbruck concentration camp. In 1945 she escaped. Her outstanding courage and endurance won her the MBE (1945), the George Cross (1946), and the Légion d'Honneur (1950).

Her first marriage in 1931 was to an Englishman. In 1947 she married Capt Peter Churchill, who had served as a British agent with her in France. This marriage was dissolved in 1955. In 1956 she married Geoffrey McLeod Hallowes.

Hallstein, Walter (1901–)

German lawyer and politician. Educated at the universities of Bonn, Munich, and Berlin, he held academic posts before becoming chair of the German UNESCO Committee 1949–50. In 1950 he led the German delegation to the conference on the Schuman Plan. He was secretary of state at the German foreign office 1951–58 and president of the European Commission 1958–67. His publications include *United Europe: Challenge and Opportunity* (1962).

Hamaguchi, Osachi, also known as *Hamaguchi Yūko* (1870–1931)

Japanese politician, prime minister 1929–30. His policies created social unrest and alienated military interests. His acceptance of the terms of the London Naval Agreement in 1930 was also unpopular.

Shot by an assassin in November 1930, he died of his wounds nine months later.

Hamer, Fannie Lou, born Townsend (1918–1977)

US civil-rights leader. In 1962 she began work for the Student Nonviolent Coordinating Committee. Throughout the 1960s and 1970s she campaigned for voter registration and desegregation of schooling in the Mississippi Freedom Democratic Party. She was elected to the Central Committee of the National Women's Political Caucus when it was founded in 1971.

Born in Montgomery County, Mississippi, the granddaughter of a slave, Hamer worked on a plantation. Her growing commitment to the civil-rights movement was affected by her own experiences: in 1961, she was sterilized without her consent, and dismissed for attempting to register as a voter.

FURTHER READING

Mills, Kay *This Little Light of Mine: The Life of Fannie Lou Hamer* 1994

Rubel, David, and Young, Andrew *Fannie Lou Hamer: From Sharecropping to Politics* 1990

Hamilton, Alice (1869–1970)

US physician, social reformer, and antiwar campaigner who pioneered the study of industrial diseases and industrial toxicology.

Hamilton was born in New York State and educated at the University of Michigan, Johns Hopkins Medical School, and in Germany at Leipzig and Munich. As a member of the Illinois Commission on Occupational Diseases, in 1910 she supervised a survey of industrial poisons. She and her staff identified many hazardous procedures and consequently state legislature introduced safety measures in the workplace and medical examinations for workers at risk. The following year Hamilton was appointed special investigator for the US Bureau of Labor and rapidly became the leading authority on lead poisoning in particular and industrial diseases in general. She lectured at Harvard from 1919, almost 30 years before Harvard accepted women as medical students.

During and after World War I she attended International Congresses of Women and was a pacifist until 1940, when she urged US participation in World War II. During the 1940s and 1950s she spoke out on such subjects as contraception, civil liberties, and workers' rights. In the 1960s she was still considered worthy of attention by the Federal Bureau of Investigation when she protested against US military actions in Vietnam.

Hammarskjöld, Dag (Hjalmar Agne Carl) (1905–1961)

Swedish secretary general of the United Nations 1953–61. He opposed the UK over the Suez Crisis of 1956. His attempts to solve the problem of the Congo (now the Democratic Republic of Congo), where he was killed in a plane crash, were criticized by the USSR. He was awarded the Nobel Peace Prize in 1961.

FURTHER READING

Cordier, A W *The Quest for Peace: The Dag Hammerskjöld Memorial Lectures* 1965

Hammarskjöld, D *Markings* 1997

Jordan, R S *Dag Hammarskjöld Revisited: The UN Secretary-General as a Force in World Politics* 1983

Urquhart, B *Hammarskjöld* 1994

Hammett, (Samuel) Dashiell (1894–1961)

US crime novelist. He introduced the 'hard-boiled' detective character into fiction and attracted a host of imitators, with works including *The Maltese Falcon* (1930, filmed 1941), *The Glass Key* (1931, filmed 1942), and his most successful novel, the light-hearted *The Thin Man* (1932, filmed 1934). His Marxist politics were best expressed in *Red Harvest* (1929), which depicts the corruption of capitalism in 'Poisonville'.

Hammett was a former Pinkerton detective agent. In 1951 he was imprisoned for contempt of court for refusing to testify during the McCarthy era of anticommunist witch hunts. He lived with the dramatist Lillian ◊Hellman for the latter half of his life.

FURTHER READING

Layman, Richard *Shadow Man: The Life of Dashiell Hammett* 1981

Nolan, William *Hammett: A Life on the Edge* 1983

Wolfe, Peter *Beams Falling* 1979

Hand, Learned Billings (1872–1961)

US jurist. He became federal district judge under President William Taft in 1909 and was appointed to the Second Circuit Court of Appeals by President Calvin Coolidge in 1924. He served as chief judge of that court 1939–51, handing down opinions in landmark copyright, antitrust, and constitutional First Amendment cases.

Born in Albany, New York, and educated at Harvard University, Hand received his law degree in 1896. Although never appointed to the US Supreme Court, he was considered a leading jurist of his day. A collection of his essays, 'The Spirit of Liberty', was published in 1952.

Hani, Chris (Martin Thembisile) (1942–1993)

South African communist and anti-apartheid activist, leader of Umkhonto we Sizwe (the military wing of the African National Congress (ANC)) from 1987 and secretary general of the South African Communist Party (SACP) from 1991. One of the most popular black South African leaders, particularly among the radical young, he was seen as a potential successor to Nelson Mandela. He was assassinated by a right-wing extremist.

Hani joined Umkhonto we Sizwe in 1962, but fled the country later the same year after being sentenced to prison under the Suppression of Communism Act. While in exile he fought against white rule in Rhodesia (now Zimbabwe and Zambia) and subsequently ran an Umkhonto network in Lesotho, where he survived two assassination attempts. In 1987 he was made chief of staff of Umkhonto. His death in April 1993 came as a serious blow to the ANC, for whom he provided a vital and influential link with black militant groups.

Hani was born in the Transkei. He joined the SACP and Umkhonto we Sizwe after graduating as a classical scholar in Latin and English. Despite his military experience gained in Zimbabwe, upon his return to

South Africa in 1990, Hani threw himself whole-heartedly into seeking a peaceful solution to his country's problems. He was very popular among the mass of black South Africans and moderate whites. His acceptance of the SACP leadership in December 1991 seemed to reduce his chances of succeeding Mandela. Hani was, however, following a longer-term strategy, with the aim of mobilizing working-class blacks, and perhaps even showing that a practical form of communism could succeed in a single country where it had failed internationally.

FURTHER READING
Berger, M *Chris Hani* 1994
Mali, Th *Thami Mali Remembers Chris Hani: The Sun that Set Before Dawn* 1993

Hansen, Hans Christian (1906–1960)

Danish politician. He trained as a compositor and became prominent in the Social Democratic party. Hansen was party secretary 1939–41 and in 1945, and chair of the Socialist Youth International 1935–39. He was a member of the Danish parliament, the Folketing, in 1936; minister of finance in 1945 and 1947; minister of commerce in 1950; minister for foreign affairs 1953–55; and prime minister and minister for foreign affairs in 1955. Hansen was prime minister again from the election of 1957 until his death in 1960.

Haq, Fazlul (1873–1962)

Bengali politician, a leader of the Muslim peasantry. He was a member of the Viceroy's Defence Council, established in 1941, and was Bengal's first Indian prime minister 1937–43.

Hara, Kei or *Hara Takashi* (1856–1921)

Japanese politician, president 1918–21. As the head of the majority party in the Diet (parliament), he became prime minister in 1918 and presided over the first party cabinet since the establishment of the Meiji Constitution. He proved to be a conservative premier, moving cautiously on political and social reform. Although he expanded the electorate by lowering tax qualifications, he did not endorse the principle of universal manhood suffrage.

From a samurai family, he worked as a newspaper editor before joining the Ministry of Foreign Affairs in 1882. He resigned from government service to join the Seiyukai, a political party formed in 1900, and shortly afterwards gained a seat in the lower house of the Diet. As home minister in various non-party cabinets (1906–08, 1911–12, and 1913–14) and leader of the Seiyukai, he was able to advance the party's interests by appointing pro-Seiyukai provincial governors and promoting regional economic development. He was assassinated by an ultra-nationalistic fanatic.

Hardie, (James) Keir (1856–1915)

British socialist politician, born in Scotland, member of Parliament 1892–95 and 1900–15. He worked in the mines as a boy and in 1886 became secretary of the Scottish Miners' Federation. In 1888 he was the first Labour candidate to stand for Parliament; he entered Parliament independently as a Labour member in 1892, became chair of the Labour party 1906–08 and 1909–10, and in 1893 was a chief founder of the Independent Labour Party.

Hardie was born in Lanarkshire but represented the parliamentary constituencies of West Ham, London, 1892–95 and Merthyr Tydfil, Wales, from 1900. A pacifist, he strongly opposed the Boer War and World War I, and his idealism in his work for socialism and the unemployed made him a popular hero.

FURTHER READING
Benn, C *Keir Hardie* 1997
McLean, Ian *Keir Hardie* 1975
Morgan, K O *Keir Hardie: Radical and Socialist* 1975
Reid, F *Keir Hardie* 1978

Harding, Warren G(amaliel) (1865–1923)

29th president of the USA 1921–23, a Republican. He opposed US membership of the League of Nations. There was corruption among members of his cabinet (the Teapot Dome Scandal), with the secretary of the interior later convicted for taking bribes.

Harding was born in Ohio, and entered the US Senate in 1915. As president he concluded the peace treaties of 1921 with Germany, Austria, and Hungary, and in the same year called the Washington Naval Conference to resolve conflicting British, Japanese, and US ambitions in the Pacific.

America's present need is not heroics, but healing; not nostrums but normalcy; not revolution, but restoration.
WARREN G HARDING Speech in Boston 14 May 1920

Before entering politics, Harding was a newspaper editor and publisher. He was an Ohio state senator 1898–1904 and lieutenant governor 1904–05. The various treaties stemming from the Washington Conference, providing for naval disarmament, and ostensibly stabilizing international relations between the great power signatories, were considered at the time a diplomatic coup for the USA and Harding, which reinforced the traditional US position of neutrality. He died in office on 2 August 1923, shortly after undeniable evidence of corruption in his administration began to surface.

FURTHER READING
Harding, Warren *From Printer to President* 1922
Mee, Charles *The Ohio Gang* 1981
Russell, Francis *The Shadow of Blooming Grove* 1968

Sinclair, Andrew *The Available Man: The Life Behind the Masks of Warren Gamaliel Harding* 1965
Wade, L R *Warren G Harding* 1989

Hardy, Frank (Francis Joseph) (1917–1994)

Australian radical political writer and radio personality, a member of the Communist Party from 1939. He is best known for the novel *Power Without Glory* (1950), a semi-fictional account of the life of Melbourne millionaire sports promoter and financier John Wren, for which Hardy faced court proceedings for libel but was found not guilty.

Hardy was born in Victoria, left school at 13, and initially worked as a casual labourer and joined the army in 1942, where he founded a newspaper, *Troppo Tribune*. He was for many years a member of the Communist Party of Australia. In the late 1960s he was associated with the land rights struggle of the Gurindji Aboriginal people of central Australia.

FURTHER READING
Hardy, Frank *The Hard Way* 1961

Hare, David (1947–   )

English dramatist and screenwriter. He cofounded the theatre company Joint Stock in 1974. His plays satirize the decadence of postwar Britain, and include *Slag* (1970), *Teeth 'n' Smiles* (1975), *Fanshen* (1975) on revolutionary Chinese communism, *Plenty* (1978), and *Pravda* (1985) (with Howard ◊Brenton) on Fleet Street journalism.

In a trilogy of plays he looks critically at three aspects of the establishment in Britain: *Racing Demon* (1990) – at the Church of England, *Murmuring Judges* (1991) – at the legal system, and *The Absence of War* (1994).

Hariri, Rafik al- (1944–   )

Lebanese Muslim businessman and politician, prime minister 1992–98. He was active in pushing ahead with reconstruction of the country's shattered infrastructure and in improving education and international links, using his strong personal connections with Saudi Arabia and Syria. He was replaced as prime minister in December 1998 by Salim al-Hoss.

Born in Sidon, after studying in Beirut, al-Hariri became a successful, multi-millionaire businessman, with large interests in construction and banking. From the late 1970s he used his wealth to set up, in Sidon, the Islamic Establishment for Culture and Education, the Kfarfalous Educational and Medical Centre, and the Hariri Foundation, the latter providing educational scholarships. He also became involved in efforts to negotiate an end to the Lebanese civil war of 1975–89, helping to frame the Ta'if Agreement that eventually ended the war. A Sunni Muslim political moderate, he became prime minister – a position reserved in Lebanon for the Sunni Muslim community – in October 1992, after a general election.

Harman, Harriet (1950–   )

British Labour politician and lawyer, secretary of state for social security 1997–98. She entered the House of Commons in 1982 as member of Parliament for Peckham (Camberwell and Peckham since 1997) and joined the opposition front bench as shadow minister for social services 1984–87, later becoming shadow spokesperson on health 1987–92, shadow chief secretary to the Treasury 1992–94, shadow secretary of state for employment 1994–95, shadow health secretary 1995–96, and shadow social security secretary 1996–97.

After graduating with a law degree, she was a legal officer with the National Council for Civil Liberties 1978–82. She faced criticism in 1997 for announcing cuts in benefits for lone parents and was often seen to be at odds with her free-thinking deputy, Frank Field. Despite her close political links with Prime Minister Tony Blair, she was dismissed from the cabinet in the reshuffle of July 1998.

Harriman, (William) Averell (1891–1986)

US diplomat, administrator of lend-lease in World War II, Democratic secretary of commerce in Harry Truman's administration 1946–48, negotiator of the Nuclear Test Ban Treaty with the USSR 1963, and governor of New York 1955–58.

Harriman graduated from Yale University in 1913. A business executive and financier, he joined F D Roosevelt's National Recovery administration in 1934, and was closely associated with the New Deal. He was Roosevelt's special representative in Britain in 1941, and chair of the president's special mission to Russia in 1941. He was US ambassador to Britain in 1946, and later shared responsibility for the administration of the European Recovery Programme in its application to Britain. He was director of the Mutual Security Agency 1951–53. In the opening rounds of the Vietnam War peace talks 1968–69, he was chief negotiator, appointed by Lyndon Johnson; his successor was Henry Cabot Lodge II.

FURTHER READING
Abramson, R *Spanning the Century: The Life of W Averell Harriman, 1891–1986* 1992
Harriman, W A *Special Envoy to Churchill and Stalin, 1941–1946* 1976

Harrington, Michael (1928–1989)

US writer and activist. During Harrington's four decades as the USA's leading Socialist thinker, writer, and speaker, he contributed to every progressive movement. His book *The Other America* (1997) is credited with spurring the Great Society anti-poverty programmes. Throughout his involvement in the student and civil-rights movements in the 1950s and 1960s, and his leadership of the Democratic Socialist Organizing Committee (DSOC) and the Democratic

Socialists of America (DSA) in the 1970s and 1980s, he consistently urged Socialists to reach beyond isolation and build coalitions with labour and progressive groups in day-to-day struggles. As DSOC and DSA's representative to the Socialist International, he earned the respect, and the ear, of socialist leaders throughout the world.

FURTHER READING
Gorman, Robert A *Michael Harrington: Speaking American* 1995
Harrington, Michael, and Howe, Irving (introd) *The Other America: Poverty in the United States* 1997

Harris, Arthur Travers (1892–1984)

British marshal of the Royal Air Force in World War II. Known as 'Bomber Harris', he was commander in chief of Bomber Command 1942–45.

He was an autocratic and single-minded leader, and was criticized for his policy of civilian-bombing selected cities in Germany; he authorized the fire-bombing raids on Dresden, in which more than 100,000 died.

He never lost his conviction that area bombing could, by itself, bring the war to an end, and stretched his theories to the utmost with the devastating raids on Hamburg, Berlin, and Dresden. He also showed a flair for dramatic actions, such as the celebrated 'thousand bomber raid' on Cologne in May 1942. Although his policies were endorsed by the War Cabinet, Harris was the only senior British commander not to receive a peerage after the war, and no medal was ever struck for the men of Bomber Command. He was made a KCB, however, in 1942.

Hart, Gary, born Hartpence (1936–   )

US Democrat politician, senator for Colorado from 1974. In 1980 he contested the Democratic nomination for the presidency, and stepped down from his Senate seat in 1986 to run, again unsuccessfully, in the 1988 presidential campaign.

Hart, Judith Constance Mary, Baroness Hart (1924–1991)

British Labour politician and sociologist. She was minister of overseas development 1969–70 and 1977–79, and minister of state 1974–75.

She was born in Burnley, Lancashire, and was educated at Clitheroe Royal Grammar School and the London School of Economics, becoming Labour member of Parliament for Lanark in 1959. She was joint parliamentary undersecretary for state for Scotland 1964–66, minister of state for Commonwealth Affairs 1966–67, and minister of social security 1967–68. She entered the cabinet in 1968 as paymaster general and became minister of overseas development in 1969, but was no longer a member of the cabinet. In March 1974 she again became minister of overseas development.

Of strong left-wing views, she opposed Britain's entry to the European Economic Community (EEC;

now the European Union) and in July 1975 resigned out of dissatisfaction with government policies. Re-appointed overseas development minister in 1977, she was a member of the Labour Party's National Executive Committee from 1969 and chair of the party's Industrial Policy Sub-Committee. She received a DBE in 1979 and became a life peer in 1988.

Hasan, Mohammad ('Bob'), Chinese name *The Kian Seng*

Indonesian entrepreneur of Chinese descent and long-time friend and financial advisor of President Thojib ◊Suharto. During the Indonesian revolution for independence Hasan supplied the rebel army with provisions and introduced Suharto to senior officers. Suharto later rewarded him with trade concessions and Hasan came to dominate Indonesia's timber and plywood industries. In 1997 he took over Astra International, Indonesia's second biggest company, and in 1998 was made trade minister. He was replaced shortly after Suharto resigned in May 1998.

Hashimoto, Ryutaro (1937–   )

Japanese conservative politician, leader of the Liberal Democratic Party (LDP) and prime minister 1996–98. A former finance and trade minister, he succeeded the Social Democrat Tomiichi ◊Murayama as prime minister, advocating a wider international role for Japan and, domestically, gradual deregulation. Hashimoto resigned after the LDP did badly in the 1998 upper-house elections.

He rose to prominence under the tutelage of the former LDP prime minister and faction leader Kakuei ◊Tanaka, serving as health and welfare minister 1978–79, transport minister 1986–87, and finance minister from 1989. As trade minister during the 1994–96 Social Democrat–LDP coalition administration, he drew popular acclaim for the tough negotiating stance he adopted in trade talks with the USA. A forceful, charismatic figure, he was elected leader of the LDP in September 1995 in a contest in which rank-and-file party members were allowed to participate for the first time. Hashimoto called a snap election in October 1996, but it produced an inconclusive result with the LDP remaining short of an absolute majority.

The son of a bureaucrat-politician, Hashimoto studied law at university, then briefly worked as a manager in the textile industry before embarking, from the early 1960s, on a career in politics as an LDP member of the house of representatives.

FURTHER READING
Hashimoto, R *Vision of Japan: A Realistic Direction for the 21st Century* 1994

Hasina Wazed, Sheika (1947–   )

Bangladeshi political leader, prime minister and defence minister from 1996. She led the centrist

Awami League (AL) back to power in 1996 after an interval of 21 years.

The daughter of the country's first president, Sheik Mujibur ◊Rahman, who was assassinated in 1975, Hasina escaped death when her father and other family members were murdered. She returned from exile abroad in 1981 and assumed the leadership of the AL a year later. She led campaigns that ousted the military dictatorship of General Ershad in 1990 and the Bangladesh National Party (BNP) government of Begum Khaleda Zia in 1996. New investigations into the killings of August 1975 raised concerns about Hasina's political motives, prompting the BNP to boycott parliament.

Hassan II (1929–)

King of Morocco from 1961. He succeeded to the throne upon the death of his father, Mohamed V. Following riots in Casablanca in 1965, he established a royal dictatorship and survived two coup attempts. The occupation of the former Spanish Western Sahara in 1976 enabled him to rally strong popular support and consolidate his power. He returned to constitutional government in 1984, with a civilian prime minister leading a government of national unity.

It was not until February 1998 that the opposition accepted and participated in the formation of an elected government that was still controlled by the monarchy. In the late 1990s the king's poor health led to a debate about the succession and the likely survival of the monarchical system in Morocco.

Hatoyama, Ichiro (1883–1959)

Japanese conservative politician, prime minister 1954–56. In 1945 he organized the conservative Japan Liberal Party (Nihon Jiyuto), which gained a victory in the elections the following year. On the verge of becoming prime minister, he was purged from official life by the US occupation authorities for his role in supporting the military cabinets of the 1930s. Although he was rehabilitated in 1951, he found that leadership of the Liberal Party was now firmly in the hands of ◊Yoshida Shigeru. He formed a new conservative party, the Japan Democratic Party (Nihon Minshuto), which successfully ousted Yoshida from power in 1954, and became premier. During his premiership relations with the USSR were normalized, thus paving the way for Japan's entry into the United Nations in 1956, and the two conservative parties were merged in 1955 to form the Liberal Democratic Party (Jiyu Minshuto).

Hatoyama was first elected to the Diet (parliament) in 1915 and became a prominent leader of the Seiyukai party in the 1930s. As education minister 1931–34, he clamped down hard on liberal university teachers who questioned the nature of the Japanese state.

Hatta, Mohammad (1902–1980)

Indonesian politician and economist, prime minister 1948–50, vice president 1950–56. Hatta was arrested by the Dutch in 1934 for political activities and exiled to Bandanaira Island until 1942 when the Japanese invaded Indonesia. In August 1945 he and Achmed ◊Sukarno were kidnapped by militant students who persuaded them to declare Indonesia's independence. Hatta served as vice president of the revolutionary government and subsequently as prime minister and vice president of an independent Indonesia. He resigned as vice president in December 1956 over disagreement with Sukarno's anti-Western foreign policies.

Hattersley, Roy Sydney George (1932–)

British Labour politician and author. On the right wing of the Labour Party, he was prices secretary 1976–79 and deputy leader of the party 1983–1992. In 1994 he announced his retirement from active politics, and later expressed disagreement with some of the policies of the new party leadership, which he considered had swung too far to the right in its views on promoting income distribution through the taxation and welfare system.

Hattersley was born in Sheffield, Yorkshire, and became a Labour member of Parliament in 1964. During Labour's long period in opposition, he was shadow home secretary and shadow chancellor. He also developed a secondary career as a successful author and newspaper columnist writing for *Punch*, *The Listener*, and *The Guardian*. His publications include *Politics Apart* (1982), *Press Gang* (1983), *Economic Priorities for a Labour Government* (1987), and *50 Years On* (1997).

Hatton, Derek (1948–)

British left-wing politician, former deputy leader of Liverpool city council. A leading member of the Militant Tendency, Hatton was removed from office and expelled from the Labour Party in 1987.

He revealed in his autobiography (1988) how Militant acted as a subversive party-within-a-party. Subsequently he embarked on a career in advertising and public relations.

Haughey, Charles James (1925–)

Irish politician; Taoiseach (prime minister) 1979–81, 1982, and 1987–92; leader of Fianna Fáil 1979–92. He succeeded Jack Lynch as Fianna Fáil leader and Taoiseach in 1979, to be confronted with serious economic problems and an intensely difficult period in Anglo-Irish relations, as the UK's Thatcher government attempted to face down the Irish Republican Army (IRA) hunger strikes of 1980 and 1981. Haughey lost office in 1981 after an early general election and regained it for a short period in 1982. His final period of office, beginning in 1987, was mired in difficulty, and saw Haughey forced to accept coalition with the Progressive Democrats. In 1998 the Irish Director of Public Prosecutions elected to prosecute him for his alleged attempts to obstruct an earlier hearing into payments made to politicians in the 1980s.

Born in Dublin, Haughey studied law at King's Inns and University College, Dublin. He entered the Dáil (lower house of the Irish parliament) in 1957, becoming minister for justice in 1961. In 1970, along with Neil Blaney, he was dismissed from the government by Taoiseach Jack Lynch for alleged involvement in importing arms into the country, for use by nationalists in Northern Ireland. He was subsequently acquitted of all charges.

FURTHER READING

Arnold, B *Haughey: His Life and Unlucky Deeds* 1994
Dwyer, T R *Haughey's Thirty Years of Controversy* 1992
Kennedy, T *Charles J Haughey: Kinsaley* 1986

Havers, Robert Michael Oldfield, Baron Havers (1923–1992)

British lawyer, Lord Chancellor 1987–88. After a successful legal career he became Conservative member of Parliament for Wimbledon in 1970 and was solicitor general under Edward Heath and attorney general under Margaret Thatcher. He was made a life peer in 1987 and served briefly, and unhappily, as Lord Chancellor before retiring in 1988. He was knighted in 1972 and created Baron in 1987.

Havers was involved in a fraught period of legal history as attorney general, including his acceptance of a plea of diminished reponsibility from the 'Yorkshire Ripper' which the judge refused to accept, insisting on a trial for murder; his prosecution of Sarah Tisdall for the resignation of trade secretary Leon Brittan; his unsuccessful case against Clive Ponting for a similar offence; and his involvement in the *Spycatcher* case, when he attracted criticism for the way that the government pursued the book's author, Peter Wright, for revealing details of his work for the security services.

Hawke, Bob (Robert James Lee) (1929–)

Australian Labor politician, prime minister 1983–91, on the right wing of the party. He was president of the Australian Council of Trade Unions 1970–80. He announced his retirement from politics in 1992.

He retired after his former finance minister, Paul ◊Keating, defeated him in a December 1991 party leadership ballot, and became a television commentator. A 'man of the people', he was the first Labor prime minister to win more than two elections.

The son of a Congregational Church cleric, Hawke studied law at the University of West Australia and was Rhodes scholar at Oxford University, England. President of the Australian Labor Party from 1973, he was elected to the federal parliament in 1980. As prime minister from 1982 he oversaw economic deregulation

◆ HAVEL, VÁCLAV (1936–) ◆

Czech dramatist and politician, president of Czechoslovakia 1989–92 and of the Czech Republic from 1993.

Václav Havel was born on 5 October 1936 in Prague. He was educated at the Economics Faculty of the Czechoslovak Technical University in Prague from 1952 to 1957, and at the Academy of Performing Arts in Prague from 1962 to 1966. He went on to join first the ABC Theatre in Prague, and then the Theatre on the Balustrade, where he wrote *The Garden* (1963), *The Memorandum* (1965), and *The Increased Difficulty of Concentration* (1968).

Havel played an important role in the events leading to the Prague Spring of 1968. From 1965 he had been working for the non-Marxist monthly *Tvar*. He was also the chair of the Club of Independent Writers and a member of the Club of Engaged Non-Partisans. He was in favour of the humanization of communism under Alexander Dubček's leadership, the opening up of the state, and the relaxation of censorship. Frustrated at the rate of change, he expressed his thoughts in a paper published in the *Literarní Lísty* on 4 April

1968 entitled 'On the Subject of Opposition', in which he sought the institutionalization of an opposition party. He later called for the reinstatement of the Social Democratic Party.

His works were banned from libraries, theatres, and bookshops in 1971. In April 1975 he wrote an open letter to President Gustáv Husák, in which he complained about the effect of the communist policy of normalization on society. His political stand culminated in the publication in January 1977 of Charter 77; Havel became a founder member of the movement that took its name from the charter, and became one of its first three spokespersons. In April 1979 he became a cofounder of the Committee for the Defence of the Unjustly Oppressed (VONS).

Following the publication of Charter 77, he was imprisoned on three occasions, most notably in 1979, when he was arrested along with nine other VONS activists, and tried and sentenced to four years' imprisonment for sedition. It was during this period of imprisonment that a series of *Letters to Olga* (June 1979–September 1982) were published. During the late 1980s there was a

and with his open governing style remained popular until the economic recession of 1990.

FURTHER READING
Hurst, J *Hawke: The Definitive Biography* 1979, *Hawke PM* 1983

Haya de la Torre, Victor Raúl (1895–1979)

Peruvian politician, political thinker, and founder of the American Popular Revolutionary Alliance (APRA; Aprista Party) in 1924, the voice of radical nationalistic dissent in Peru.

He was imprisoned in 1931, after standing against Colonel Luis Sánchez Cerro, and was released on the latter's assassination in 1933 and went into hiding 1934–45.

The Aprista Party was outlawed 1931–34 and 1935–45, but in 1945 it supported the successful candidate José Luis Bustamante; control of the government, however, lay in Haya's hands. On Bustamante's overthrow in 1948, Haya sought refuge in the Colombian embassy in Lima and later left for Mexico in 1954. He returned to Peru when constitutional government was restored in 1957 and fought a bitter election campaign in 1962, which, after army intervention, he lost to Fernando ◊Belaúnde Terry. Haya was instrumental in drafting the constitution of 1979, restoring parliamentary democracy, but died before the Aprista Party finally gained power in 1985 under Perez Alan García

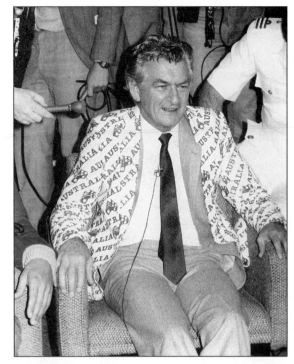

Bob Hawke. *Rex*

perceptible increase in open dissatisfaction with the government, especially amongst the young. Thousands signed the petition 'A Few Sentences', of which Havel was one of the authors. The political leadership had run out of ideas, and was seen as ideologically bankrupt. Following the rise to power of Mikhail Gorbachev in the USSR, the government could no longer rely on Soviet military assistance to crush opposition groups.

The period of social unrest came to a head on 17 November 1989, when a student protest in Narodní Trida was brutally suppressed by the police. At a meeting of the Drama Club on 19 November Havel became the leader of the Civic Forum, a new umbrella opposition group. On 29 November 1989 he was elected president by the Federal Assembly and promised free elections in his inaugural address. He was re-elected in 1990 and went on to become an outstanding and well-respected head of state. During his second term of office, despite his efforts Czech and Slovak political factions split irrevocably. He went on to become the first president of the new Czech Republic on 26 January 1993.

He has been honoured for his literary works and for his lifelong commitment to human rights and justice. See photograph on page 184.

FURTHER READING
Havel, Václav *Open Letters: Selected Prose 1965–90* 1991, *Disturbing the Peace: A Conversation with Karel Hvízdala* 1990, *The Anatomy of a Retinence: Eastern European Dissidents and the Peace Movement in the West* 1986, *Politics and Conscience* 1986, *Letters to Olga* translation 1988, *Art of the Impossible: Politics as Morality in Practice* 1997

Havel, Václav, Keane, John (ed) *The Power of the Powerless: Citizens against the State in Eastern Europe* 1990

Simmons, Michael *The Reluctant President: A Political Life of Václav Havel* 1991

Symynkywicz, Jeffrey B *Václav Havel and the Velvet Revolution* 1995

Vladislav, Jan (ed) *Living in Truth: 22 Essays* 1989

Whipple, Tim D (ed) *After the Velvet Revolution: Václav Havel and the New Leaders of Czechoslovakia Speak Out* 1991

Václav Havel pictured in Prague in November 1989 shortly before his election as president of the National Assembly. *Rex*

Hayden, Bill (William George) (1933–)

Australian Labor politician. He was leader of the Australian Labor Party and of the opposition 1977–83, minister of foreign affairs 1983–88, and governor general 1989–96.

As minister for social security 1972–75 and treasurer in 1975, he introduced much welfare legislation, including the universal health insurance scheme Medibank. He spoke openly in support of euthanasia and of marriage and adoption rights for homosexuals in 1995.

Hayden, Tom (1939–)

US radical activist, state legislator, and author. Hayden ran for the US Senate in California in 1976. He was founder of the Indochina Peace Campaign, founder and chair of the California Campaign for Economic Democracy in 1977, and chair of the California Solar-Cal Council 1978–82. He was elected to the California State Assembly in 1982 and was author of several books, including *The American Future* (1980).

Hayden was born in Royal Oak, Michigan. One of the best-known student radical leaders of the 1960s, he was a cofounder of the Students for a Democratic

◆ HEATH, EDWARD (RICHARD GEORGE) (1916–) ◆

British Conservative politician, prime minister 1970–1974, Conservative Party leader 1965–75.

Heath was born in Broadstairs, Kent, and educated at Chatham House Grammar School, Ramsgate, and Balliol College, Oxford. He was president of the Oxford Union in 1939. During World War II he was a commissioned officer in the Royal Artillery 1940–46.

In 1950 Heath was elected Conservative member of Parliament for Bexley. He was government chief whip 1955–59, minister of labour 1959–60, Lord Privy Seal 1960–63, and president of the Board of Trade 1963–64. He was firmly pro-European and led the British delegation to negotiate entry to the European Economic Community (EEC) 1963–64.

In 1965, after the Conservative Party defeat in the 1964 general election, Heath became leader of the Conservative Party when Alec Douglas Home resigned. The Conservatives were defeated by Labour in the snap general election of 1966. Heath became prime minister with the unexpected victory of the Conservative Party in the June 1970 general election.

He came to power pledged to a new industrial policy, reform of trade unions, and British

entry to the EEC. He achieved British entry to the EEC on 1 January 1973 after a series of close votes in Parliament.

Heath's industrial policy failed due to rising unemployment (over 1 million) and rising inflation, caused by unprecedented increase in world prices for imported foods and raw materials. He executed a 'U-turn' on industrial policy and provided government aid to 'lame duck' industries. He also instituted a de facto incomes policy, which provided for generous wage increases for the lower paid.

Before the 'U-turn', Heath's industrial policy and the Industrial Relations Act of 1971 brought conflict with the trade unions. Confrontation with the post office workers, the workers at the Upper Clyde Shipyard, and the miners weakened the government. In 1972 the government dealt with the first national coalminers' strike since 1926 by appointing the Wilberforce Commission, which recommended substantial wage concessions.

In the winter of 1973–74, the miners again went on strike in pursuit of a wage increase outside the government's incomes policy. In February 1974 Heath called a general election on the issue of 'Who governs Britain?'. This resulted in

Society (SDS) in 1961, president of SDS 1962–63, cofounder of the Economic Research and Action Project in 1964, and leader of the Newark Community Union Project 1964–67. He was married to actress Jane Fonda.

Hayek, Friedrich August von (1899–1992)

Austrian economist. Born in Vienna, he taught at the London School of Economics 1931–50, Chicago 1950–62, and Freiburg from 1962. His publication *The Road to Serfdom* (1944) set out to combat the wartime vogue for collectivism, and argued that economic freedom was the necessary precondition for political freedom and democracy. His ideas were enthusiastically devoured by the leaders of the resurgent free-market conservatism in the late-1970s and 1980s, although these disciples did not always share Hayek's commitment to liberal values. He won the 1974 Nobel Prize for Economics with Gunnar Myrdal.

Haywood, William Dudley (1869–1928)

US labour leader. One of the founders of the Industrial Workers of the World (IWW, 'Wobblies') in 1905, Haywood was arrested for conspiracy to murder an antiunion politician. His acquittal in 1907 made him a labour hero. Arrested again for sedition during World War I, he spent his later years in exile in the USSR.

---

a hung parliament and the election of a minority Labour government.

Heath remained leader of the Conservative Party through the October 1974 general election, but his leadership and policies came under attack

---

It is the unpleasant and unacceptable face of capitalism.

EDWARD HEATH On the Lonrho scandal
Hansard 15 May 1973

---

inside the parliamentary party. Margaret Thatcher successfully challenged Heath for the party leadership in February 1975.

Heath returned to the backbenches and was a consistent critic of the Thatcher government 1979–90, particularly on Europe, and he continued to be critical of the European policy of Thatcher's successors, John Major and William Hague. In 1998 Heath published his autobiography, *The Course of My Life*. See photograph on page 449

FURTHER READING

Campbell, John *Edward Heath: A Biography* 1994
Laing, Margaret *Edward Heath* 1973
Roth, Andrew *Heath and the Heathmen* 1972

Born in Salt Lake City, Utah, Haywood worked in the mines, joining the Western Federation of Miners (WFM) in 1896. By 1899 he had become a national leader of the WFM and, in his tireless tours of the country, won the nickname 'Big Bill'.

Healey, Denis Winston, Baron Healey (1917–   )

British Labour politician. While secretary of state for defence 1964–70 he was in charge of the reduction of British forces east of Suez. He was chancellor of the Exchequer 1974–79. In 1976 he contested the party leadership, losing to James Callaghan, and again in 1980, losing to Michael Foot, to whom he was deputy leader 1980–83. In 1987 he resigned from the shadow cabinet.

Born in Keighley, Yorkshire, he was educated at Bradford Grammar School and Balliol College, Oxford. He served in the army during World War II and became Labour member of Parliament for Southeast Leeds in 1952. From 1945 to 1952 he was secretary of the international department of the Labour Party and from 1952 took part in many international conferences. He was a British delegate to the Western Union and the Council of Europe 1963–64. From 1954 to 1961 he was a member of the Fabian Society executive.

He became secretary of state for defence in 1964, a post he held until Labour's defeat in 1970. He was opposition spokesperson on foreign affairs from 1970 to 1972 and on economic affairs from 1972 to 1974. He was made a life peer in 1992.

He published an autobiography, *The Time of My Life*, in 1989.

FURTHER READING

Reed, B, and Williams, G *Denis Healey and the Politics of Power* 1971

Healy, Timothy Michael (1855–1931)

Irish lawyer, politician, and first governor general of the Irish Free State. Healy supported the Irish nationalist Charles ◊Parnell until the split in the Irish Nationalist party occasioned by the O'Shea divorce case in 1890. Later he was in favour of reunion under the leadership of John Redmond, but in 1900 he was expelled from the party for his opposition to the United Irish League. He was readmitted in 1908, but was again expelled in 1910, in which year he formed, with William O'Brien, the Independent Nationalist party. Healy retired from politics in 1918. In 1922 he became the first governor general of the Irish Free State, a post he held for five years.

Healy was born in Bantry, Ireland. He was called to the Irish Bar in 1884, and became a Queen's Counsel in 1899. In 1903 he was called to the English Bar, and he was a Bencher of Gray's Inn and of King's Inn, Dublin. He was elected member of Parliament for Wexford in

1880, for Monaghan in 1833, for South Londonderry in 1885, for North Longford in 1887, for North Louth in 1892, and North East Cork in 1910, a seat he retained until 1918.

Hearst, William Randolph (1863–1951)

US newspaper publisher, celebrated for his introduction of banner headlines, lavish illustration, and the sensationalist approach known as 'yellow journalism'. A campaigner in numerous controversies, and a strong isolationist, he was said to be the model for Citizen Kane in the 1941 film of that name by Orson Welles.

FURTHER READING

Mugridge, I *The View from Xanadu: William Randolph Hearst and United States Foreign Policy* 1995

Procter, B H *William Randolph Hearst: The Early Years, 1863–1910* 1998

Swanberg, W A *Citizen Hearst: A Biography of William Randolph Hearst* 1962

Heffer, Eric Samuel (1922–1991)

British Labour politician, member of Parliament for Walton, Liverpool, 1964–91. He held a ministerial post 1974–75, joined Michael Foot's shadow cabinet in 1981, and was regularly elected to Labour's National Executive Committee, but found it difficult to follow the majority view.

Born in Liverpool, Heffer left school at 15 and entered an apprenticeship as a carpenter and joiner, becoming a member of the Amalgamated Society of Woodworkers. He soon joined the Labour Party, beginning a life-long association with socialism. After war service with the Royal Air Force, he returned to his trade, but became steadily more involved in party politics. In 1960 he was elected to Liverpool city council and in 1964 to Parliament. In 1974 Harold Wilson appointed him minister of state, in the department of industry, but he resigned in 1975 over a disagreement with the government's European policies. A practising Christian, Heffer won many admirers for his refusal to compromise his principles, but it blighted his ministerial career.

FURTHER READING

Heffer, E *Never a Yes Man: The Life and Politics of an Adopted Liverpudlian* 1991

Heinemann, Gustav (1899–1976)

German politician and lawyer. From 1946 he was lord mayor of Essen, Germany, until, in 1949, he became minister of the interior 1949–50. He was a founder member of the Christian Democratic party, but left in 1952, largely because of disagreement with Konrad Adenauer's foreign policy, and joined the Social Democrats in 1957. He was minister of justice in Kurt Kiesinger's coalition cabinet 1966–69. Between 1969 and 1974 he was president of the Federal Republic.

Heinemann was born in Schwelm, Westphalia, Germany.

Hekmatyar, Gulbuddin (1949–)

Afghani leader of the Mujaheddin (Islamic fundamentalist guerrillas), prime minister 1993–94 and in 1996. Strongly anticommunist and leading the Hezb-i-Islami (Islamic Party) faction, he resisted the takeover of Kabul by moderate Mujaheddin forces in April 1992 and refused to join the interim administration, continuing to bombard the city until being driven out. In June 1993, under a peace agreement with President Burhanuddin Rabbani, Hekmatyar was readmitted to the city as prime minister, but his forces renewed their attacks on Kabul during 1994. He was subsequently dismissed from the premiership, but returned to Kabul in June 1996, when he became combined prime minister, defence minister, and finance minister. However, in September he was driven out of Kabul by the Talibaan (fundamentalist student army) who had seized control of much of Afghanistan.

Hekmatyar became a Mujaheddin in the 1980s, leading the fundamentalist faction of the Hezb-i-Islami, dedicated to the overthrow of the Soviet-backed communist regime in Kabul. He refused to countenance participation in any interim 'national unity' government that was to include Afghan communists. Renewed bombardment of Kabul by Hezb-i-Islami forces in 1992 led to his faction being barred from government posts. His fierce fight for Kabul from 1995, with Ahmed Shah Mesood, the defence minister, led to chaos. In March 1998 he returned from exile in Iran and proposed a new peace settlement.

Hellman, Lillian Florence (1907–1984)

US dramatist. Her work is concerned with contemporary political and social issues. *The Children's Hour* (1934) on accusations of lesbianism, *The Little Foxes* (1939) on industrialists, and *Toys in the Attic* (1960) are all examples of a social critique cast in the form of the 'well-made play'. In the 1950s she was summoned to appear before the House Committee on Un-American Activities.

She lived 31 years with the writer Dashiell Hammett, and in her will set up a fund to promote Marxist doctrine. Since her death there has been dispute over the accuracy of her memoirs, for example *Pentimento* (1973).

Helms, Jesse (1921–)

US Republican senator. Born in Monroe, North Carolina, he attended Wingate College and Wake Forest College and served in the US navy 1942–45. He was administrative assistant to US senator Willis Smith 1951–53 and to US senator Alton Lennon in 1953. He was elected to the US Senate in 1972, and re-elected in 1978, 1984, 1990, and 1996.

FURTHER READING
Ferguson, Ernest B *Hard Right: The Rise of Jesse Helms* 1986
Helms, Jesse *When Free Men Shall Stand* 1977

Helms, Richard McGarrah (1913–)

US director of the Central Intelligence Agency (CIA) 1966–73, when he was dismissed by President Richard Nixon. In 1977 he was convicted of lying before a congressional committee because his oath as chief of intelligence compelled him to keep secrets from the public. He was originally with the Office of Strategic Services, before it developed into the CIA in 1947.

Hemingway, Ernest (Miller) (1899–1961)

US writer. In 1921 he settled in Paris, where he met the writers Gertrude Stein and Ezra Pound. His style was influenced by Stein, who also introduced him to bullfighting, a theme in his first novel, *Fiesta (The Sun Also Rises)* (1927), and the memoir *Death in the Afternoon* (1932). *A Farewell to Arms* deals with wartime experiences on the Italian front, and *For Whom the Bell Tolls* (1940) has a Spanish Civil War setting. He served as war correspondent both in that conflict and in Europe during World War II.

Born in Oak Park, Illinois, Hemingway developed a passion for hunting and adventure in his youth. Other works by Hemingway include *The Torrents of Spring* (1926), a burlesque of Sherwood Anderson, *The Green Hills of Africa* (1935), and *The Fifth Column*, a play about the Spanish Civil War. His last years were spent mainly in Cuba, where he committed suicide.

FURTHER READING
Baker, Carlos *Ernest Hemingway: A Life Story* 1969
Lynn, Kenneth *Hemingway* 1987
Meyers, J *Hemingway* 1986
Meyers, J (ed) *Hemingway: The Critical Heritage* 1982
Nagel, James (ed) *Ernest Hemingway: The Writer in Context* 1984

Henderson, Arthur (1863–1935)

British Labour politician and trade unionist, leader of the Labour Party 1914–1918, born in Scotland. He helped to transform the Labour Party from a pressure group into a party of government, and was home secretary 1924–29 in the first Labour government. As foreign secretary 1929–31 he accorded the Soviet government full recognition. He worked for international disarmament and was awarded the Nobel Peace Prize in 1934.

Henderson was born in Glasgow and brought up in Newcastle upon Tyne. In 1903 he was elected to Parliament as member for Rochdale. He worked closely with other Labour politicians, including Kier ◊Hardie and Ramsay ◊MacDonald. Henderson suc-

ceeded MacDonald as secretary of the Labour Party, a post he held until shortly before his death.

At the start of World War I, in August 1914, the parliamentary Labour Party split. MacDonald resigned as party leader and was succeeded by Henderson. He took Labour into the 1915 coalition, serving as the first Labour cabinet minister. Henderson later served in David ◊Lloyd George's war cabinet. He visited Russia in 1917, after the first revolution, and became convinced that the price of keeping Russia in the war was British attendance at a Stockholm conference of international socialists. This led to a breach with Lloyd George and Henderson's resignation from the cabinet. As a result of these experiences, he became an internationalist and converted Labour to the ideas of the League of Nations.

After 1918, when Henderson resigned the leadership in favour of MacDonald, he concentrated his efforts into turning Labour into a broad-based party. His success was such that MacDonald was able to form the first Labour government in 1924. After its collapse in 1931, Henderson once more took on the role of leader of the opposition, this time facing his former colleague MacDonald, who headed a coalition.

Henderson left school at the age of 12 and became an engineering apprentice. His interest in politics developed through his involvement in local trade-union activities, and he rose through the local and regional trade-union movement. He attended the 1899 meeting in London that led to the establishment of the Labour Representation Committee. In 1903 he became treasurer of that committee.

As foreign secretary, Henderson took a pro-active role in European affairs, forging links with several leading politicians in Europe and the self-governing divisions of the British Empire. During his parliamentary career, Henderson sat for various constituencies, finally as MP for Clay Cross 1933–35. Although he never held office again after 1931, he continued to work for the League of Nations, and in 1934 he was awarded the Nobel Peace Prize in recognition of his contribution to peace during the turbulent interwar years.

FURTHER READING
Leventhal, F M *Arthur Henderson* 1989

Heng Samrin (1934–)

Cambodian politician, national leader 1981–91. A Khmer Rouge commander 1976–78, he became disillusioned with its brutal tactics. He led an unsuccessful coup against ◊Pol Pot in 1978 and established the Kampuchean People's Revolutionary Party (KPRP) in Vietnam, before returning in 1979 to head the new Vietnamese-backed government, becoming KPRP leader in 1981. He was replaced as prime minister by the reformist Hun Sen in 1985 but retained control over the government until 1991 as KPRP leader.

Henlein, Konrad (1898–1945)

Sudeten-German leader of the Sudeten Nazi Party in Czechoslovakia, closely allied with Hitler's Nazis. He was partly responsible for the destabilization of the Czechoslovak state in 1938, which led to the Munich Agreement and secession of Sudeten to Germany.

Henry, Alice (1857–1943)

Australian journalist and women's suffragette. Her first articles appeared in 1884, and over the following two decades she covered a variety of social causes, including women's hospitals and care of the disabled. She was a pioneer of women's trade-union movements in Australia and later settled in the USA, where she became a powerful speaker and key figure in the National Women's Trade Union League of America.

Herbert, A(lan) P(atrick) (1890–1971)

English politician and writer. He was an Independent member of Parliament for Oxford University 1935–50 and the author of several novels, including *The Water Gipsies* (1930). His successful campaigns as an MP included an amendment to the divorce laws, which became law in 1937, and an attack on the proposal to subject books to purchase tax.

Herbert was born in London and educated at Oxford. He became a barrister in 1918, but never practised. His first novel, *The Secret Battle* (1919), dealing with an officer's breakdown on the western front during World War I, was reissued just before World War II and led to an improvement in court-martial procedure.

Hernández Colón, Rafael (1936–)

Puerto Rican centrist politician, governor 1973–77 and 1985–93. Active as a Popular Democratic Party (PDP) politician in the 1960s, he served as president of the senate 1969–72. A deteriorating economy led to his defeat as governor in 1976, but he was returned in 1985, defeating the incumbent Carlos ◊Romero Barceló, whose New Progressive Party (PNP) had advocated full US statehood for Puerto Rico (the PDP favoured enhancement of its existing Commonwealth status). After a 1991 referendum vote on the island's future status rejected his government's proposals, he decided not to seek another term as governor.

Hernández Colón studied law at the University of Puerto Rico, but also trained at a US military academy. During the early 1960s he worked as a law professor in Puerto Rico, and became active in the PDP.

Hernández Martínez, Maximiliano (1883–1966)

El Salvadorean dictator, president 1931–44 during the inter-war Depression. An admirer of fascist theories, he ruthlessly suppressed opposition, killing an estimated 45,000 peasants who had participated in a communist-organized uprising in 1932. He sharply reduced government spending during the Depression and financed road-building programmes from current revenues. A general strike, led by students, which erupted after a failed army uprising in protest against a further extension of his term in office, forced his resignation in March 1944 and exile to Honduras.

Trained at El Salvador's Military Polytechnic, Hernández was a professional soldier who rose to the rank of army commander in chief in 1931. He seized power from President Arturo Araújo in a palace revolt in December 1931, at a time of economic and social unrest, and was elected president in 1935. He subsequently remained in office through having constitutional conventions extend his term.

In 1944 revolt against him spread to Guatemala, where it led to the ousting of Jorge ◊Ubico Castañeda. Hernández was murdered in Honduras, in 1966, by his chauffeur, following a quarrel.

Herriot, Edouard (1872–1957)

French radical politician. A leading parliamentarian of the inter-war period, Herriot was president of his party 1919–26, 1931–35, and 1945–56, and prime minister 1924–25, 1926, and 1932. As president of the chamber of deputies 1936–40 and a staunch republican, he challenged the legality of the 1940 parliamentary vote establishing the Vichy regime.

A graduate of the Ecole Nationale Supérieure, Herriot taught philosophy before becoming mayor of Lyon 1905–40 and 1945–57, and representing the Rhône department in parliament 1912–40 and 1946–57. Herriot combined internationalism (opposing Raymond ◊Poincaré's 1923 occupation of the Ruhr) with social conservativism (distancing himself from Edouard ◊Daladier's participation in the Popular Front alongside socialists and communists). Arrested by the Vichy authorities in 1940 and deported to Germany in 1944, he served again as president of the National Assembly 1947–54.

Herter, Christian Archibald (1895–1967)

US Republican politician and diplomat. From 1943 he was a member of the House of Representatives, and he was governor of Massachusetts 1953–57. He was undersecretary of state 1957–59 and secretary of state 1959–61. His major contribution was to alleviate Soviet pressure on West Berlin.

Herter was born in France, of US parents, and educated at Harvard. He served as assistant secretary of commerce to Herbert Hoover 1919–24, and in 1931 began his party political career as a Republican representative in the Massachusetts legislature. As secretary of state he was the successor to John Foster Dulles.

Hertling, Count Georg Friedrich von (1843–1919)

German politician who was appointed imperial chancellor in November 1917. He maintained a degree of support in the Reichstag (parliament) but was powerless to control the military leadership under Erich von ◊Ludendorff.

Hertzog, James Barry Munnik (1866–1942)

South African politician, prime minister 1924–39, and founder of the Nationalist Party in 1913 (the United South African National Party from 1933). He opposed South Africa's entry into both world wars.

Hertzog was born in Cape Colony of Boer descent. In 1914 he opposed South African participation in World War I. After the 1924 elections he became prime minister, and in 1933 the Nationalist Party and General Jan Smuts's South African Party were merged as the United South African National Party. In September 1939 his motion against participation in World War II was rejected, and he resigned.

Herzl, Theodor (1860–1904)

Austrian founder of the Zionist movement. The Dreyfus case convinced him that the only solution to the problem of anti-Semitism was the resettlement of the Jews in a state of their own. His book *Jewish State* (1896) launched political Zionism, and he became the first president of the World Zionist Organization in 1897.

He was born in Budapest and became a successful playwright and journalist, mainly in Vienna.

FURTHER READING
Bein, A *Theodor Herzl* 1957
Gurko, M *Theodor Herzl* 1988
Pawel, Ernst *The Labyrinth of Exile* 1989
Stewart, D *Theodor Herzl* 1972

Herzog, Chaim (1918–)

Israeli politician and soldier, president 1983–93. In 1975 he was ambassador to the United Nations (UN). Returning to Israel, he joined the Labour Party and was elected to the Knesset (parliament) in 1981. His public standing made him an obvious choice for the presidency in 1983.

The son of Israel's chief rabbi, he studied law in Britain and Israel and in World War II served in the British army as a tank commander. He disagreed with British rule in Palestine and joined an underground movement opposing it. After Israel achieved independence in 1948 his military experience was put to use and he was appointed chief of military intelligence 1954–62.

Born in Belfast, Northern Ireland, he emigrated to Poland with his parents in his teens before returning to the UK for military service in World War II.

Heseltine, Michael (Ray Dibdin) (1933–)

British Conservative politician, deputy prime minister 1995–97. A member of Parliament from 1966 (for Tavistock 1966–74 and for Henley from 1974), he was secretary of state for the environment 1990–92 and for trade and industry 1992–95.

Heseltine was born in Swansea, south Wales, and was educated at Shrewsbury School and Oxford University. He was minister of the environment 1979–83, when he succeeded John Nott, and minister of defence from 1982 to January 1986, when he resigned over the Westland affair and was then seen as a major rival to Margaret Thatcher. In November 1990, Heseltine's challenge to Thatcher's leadership of the party brought about her resignation. After the Conservatives' defeat in 1997, he announced that he would not contest the party's vacant leadership because of heart problems but he has continued to make known his views on European issues.

The day before Heseltine announced his challenge for the party leadership, the deputy prime minister Geoffrey Howe had attacked Thatcher's stance on Europe during his vitriolic resignation speech in the House of Commons. Heseltine supported closer ties with Europe and asserted that he had a better chance of leading the Conservative Party to victory at the next election. He also promised a review of the poll tax. On the first ballot of the leadership contest Thatcher narrowly failed to gain the 15% majority required for re-election and two days later announced her resignation as party leader. Foreign secretary Douglas Hurd and chancellor of the Exchequer John Major then joined the contest against Heseltine. On election day, 27 November 1990, with Major two votes short of an absolute majority, both Hurd and Heseltine conceded defeat. On 28 November Heseltine rejoined the cabinet as secretary of state for the environment. In April 1991 he announced a replacement for the unpopular poll tax.

After the 1992 general election, Heseltine was made secretary for trade and industry. His announcement of a drastic pit-closure programme in October 1992 met with widespread opposition. Forced to bow to public pressure, he agreed, together with Prime Minister John Major, to instigate an inquiry into the country's future energy needs, which resulted in 12 of the 31 coal mines destined for closure being temporarily reprieved.

In 1994 his proposals for privatization of the Post Office were rejected. He was appointed deputy prime minister in the cabinet reshuffle that followed the July 1995 snap leadership election, which was called, but only narrowly won, by Prime Minister John Major.

FURTHER READING
Critchley, Julian *Heseltine* 1987

Hess, (Walter Richard) Rudolf (1894–1987)

German Nazi leader. Imprisoned with Adolf Hitler

1924–25, he became his private secretary, taking down *Mein Kampf* from Hitler's dictation. In 1933 he was appointed deputy *Führer* to Hitler, a post he held until replaced by Hermann Goering in September 1939. On 10 May 1941 he landed by air in the UK with his own compromise peace proposals and was held a prisoner of war until 1945, when he was tried at Nürnberg as a war criminal and sentenced to life imprisonment. He died in Spandau prison, Berlin.

Hess was effectively in charge of the Nazi party organization until his flight in 1941. For the last years of his life he was the only prisoner left in Spandau.

FURTHER READING
Douglas-Hamilton, James *Motive for a Mission* 1971
Padfield, Peter *Hess: Fight for the Führer* 1991
Schwarzwaller, Wulf *Rudolf Hess: The Last Nazi* 1988

Heuss, Theodor (1884–1963)

German politician and writer, first president of the Federal German Republic 1949–59. Educated in Berlin, he was influenced by the social liberal ideas of Friedrich ◊Naumann and joined the left liberals in 1903 and the German Democratic Party in 1918. He was a member of the Reichstag (parliament) 1924–28 and 1930–33. After World War II he became leader of the Free Democratic Party in West Germany and played an important role in the drafting of the Basic Law (constitution) of the Federal Republic.

He Xiangning or Ho Hsiang-ning (1880–1972)

Chinese revolutionary and feminist. She was one of the first Chinese women publicly to advocate nationalism, revolution, and female emancipation, and one of the first to cut her hair short. An active advocate of links with the communists and Russia, she went to Hong Kong in 1927 when ◊Jiang Jie Shi (Chiang Kai-shek) broke with the communists, and was an outspoken critic of his leadership. She returned to Beijing (Peking) in 1949 as head of the overseas commission.

Educated in Hong Kong and Japan, she married fellow revolutionary ◊Liao Zhongkai in 1905. Her husband was assassinated in 1925.

Heydrich, Reinhard Tristan Eugen (1904–1942)

German Nazi, head of the *Sicherheitsdienst* (SD), the party's security service, and Heinrich ◊Himmler's deputy. He was instrumental in organizing the 'final solution', the policy of genocide used against Jews and others. 'Protector' of Bohemia and Moravia from 1941, he was ambushed and killed the following year by three members of the Czechoslovak forces in Britain, who had landed by parachute. Reprisals followed, including several hundred executions and the massacre in Lidice.

Heydrich is believed to have had Jewish ancestry, although this was not widely known at the time and

seems, if anything, only to have made him a more fanatical Nazi. He was responsible for the fake attack on a German radio station at Gleiwicz in 1939 that provided the pretext for the German invasion of Poland, and went on to organize the Einsatzgruppen in 1941.

FURTHER READING
Brissaud, A *The Nazi Secret Service* 1974
Burgess, A *Seven Men at Daybreak* 1966
Deschner, G *Heydrich: The Pursuit of Total Power* 1981
Graber, G S *The Life and Times of Reinhard Heydrich* 1981
MacDonald, C A *The Killing of SS Obergruppenführer Reinhard Heydrich, 27 May 1942* 1990

Hill, Joe born Joel Emmanuel Hagglung (*c.* 1872–1915)

Swedish-born US labour organizer. A member of the Industrial Workers of the World (IWW, 'Wobblies'), he was convicted of murder on circumstantial evidence in Salt Lake City, Utah, in 1914. Despite calls by President Woodrow Wilson and the Swedish government for a retrial, Hill was executed in 1915, becoming a martyr for the labour movement.

Born in Sweden, Hill emigrated to the USA in 1901. His original name is sometimes given as Joseph Hillstrom. He frequently contributed to the IWW's *Solidarity* and *Industrial Worker* newspapers, and is remembered for his many popular pro-union songs.

FURTHER READING
Foner, Ph S *The Case of Joe Hill* 1965
Smith, G M *Joe Hill* 1969

Hill, Octavia (1838–1912)

English campaigner for housing reform and public open spaces. She cofounded the National Trust in 1894.

With encouragement and financial help from the art critic and social reformer John Ruskin, she pioneered a successful experiment in social housing. In 1864 she bought slum property in Marylebone, London which she rented to poor families. She served with Beatrice ◊Webb on the Poor Law Commission in 1889.

Hill was born in Wisbech, Cambridgeshire, and educated privately. In 1856 she became secretary of the classes for women at the Working Men's College. Her first housing project was so successful in increasing the self-respect and improving the material welfare of her tenants that the Countess Ducie gave her charge of a property in Drury Lane, London. Eventually she was at the head of a staff of assistants responsible for collecting the rents of 6,000 dwellings and tenements in London. Hydon Heath and Hydon's Ball, a tract of wooded land near Godalming, was purchased after her death and dedicated to her memory. Her publications include *Homes of the London Poor* (1875) and *Our Common Land* (1878).

Hillery, Patrick (John) (1923–)

Irish politician, president 1976–90. As minister of foreign affairs, he successfully negotiated Ireland's entry into the European Economic Community (EEC, now the European Union) in 1973. Thereupon he became Ireland's first EEC Commissioner. In 1976 Hillery was returned unopposed to the presidency, following the resignation of his predecessor.

Born in Miltown Malbay, County Clare, Hillery studied chemistry and medicine at University College Dublin. He entered the Dáil (lower house of the Irish parliament) for Fianna Fáil in 1951 and served various governments as minister for education, industry and commerce, labour, and foreign affairs.

Hillman, Sidney (1887–1946)

Lithuanian-born US labour leader. He was president of the Amalgamated Clothing Workers of America (ACWA) union, which by 1940 dominated the manufacture of men's clothing and had pioneered such reforms as the 40-hour week and industry-wide wage scales. A strong backer of the New Deal, he was appointed as a labour adviser to the National Recovery Administration in 1933, and to several war production boards during World War II. A founder of the Congress of Industrial Organizations (CIO), he was the first chair of the CIO's Political Action Committee 1943–46, and a vice chair of the newly founded World Federation of Trade Unions 1945–46. Hillman was an advocate of cooperation instead of confrontation between labour and management; he pioneered his union's policy of lending money to companies and providing research to improve efficiency.

Hillman was born in Zagare, Lithuania. A labour activist in Russia, he was imprisoned for participation in the abortive revolution of 1905. Upon his release, he emigrated in 1907 to the USA, settling in Chicago. A garment worker, he emerged in the 1910 Hart, Schaffner, and Marx strike in Chicago as one of the leaders of the United Garment Workers (UGW) and negotiated a new contract that was regarded as a model of labour-management relations. In 1914 he went to New York City where he led a split from the UGW that resulted in the formation of the ACWA; he was elected its first president in 1914, an office he held until his death.

Hilly, Francis Billy (1947–)

Solomon Islands politician, prime minister 1993–94. He replaced Solomon ◊Mamaloni as prime minister after the June 1993 general election, but his fractious coalition was soon weakened by the resignation of key ministers and in October 1994, having lost his parliamentary majority, Hilly was dismissed by Governor General Moses Pitakaka and Mamaloni returned as premier.

Educated at the University of the South Pacific, Hilly is from the Western Province, where his political career began. An independent member of the Solomon Islands parliament 1976–84 and since 1993, he worked in the pre-independence governments of the late 1970s and under Mamaloni.

Himes, Chester (Bomar) (1909–1984)

US novelist. After serving seven years in prison for armed robbery, he published his first novel, *If He Hollers Let Him Go* (1945), a powerful depiction of racist victimization set in a Californian shipyard. He later wrote in the crime thriller genre, most notably in *The Real Cool Killers* (1958), *Rage in Harlem* (1965), and *Cotton Comes to Harlem* (1965).

He also published two volumes of autobiography, *The Quality of Hurt* (1972) and *My Life of Absurdity* (1976).

FURTHER READING
Margolies, Erward, et al *The Several Lives of Chester Himes* 1997
Wilson, M L, et al *Chester Himes* 1988

Himmler, Heinrich (1900–1945)

German Nazi leader, head of the SS elite corps from 1929, the police and the Gestapo secret police from 1936, and supervisor of the extermination of the Jews in Eastern Europe. During World War II he replaced Hermann Goering as Hitler's second-in-command. He was captured in May 1945 and committed suicide.

Born in Munich, he joined the Nazi Party in 1925 and became chief of the Bavarian police in 1933. His accumulation of offices meant that he had command of all German police forces by 1936, which made him one of the most powerful people in Germany. He was appointed minister of the interior in 1943 in an attempt to stamp out defeatism and following the July Plot in 1944 became commander in chief of the home forces. In April 1945 he made a proposal to the Allies that Germany should surrender to the USA and Britain but not to the USSR, which was rejected.

FURTHER READING
Breitman, R *The Architect of Genocide: Himmler and the Final Solution* 1992

Hinden, Rita (1909–1971)

South African-born British socialist writer. She was born in Cape Town, South Africa, and her family emigrated to Palestine in 1927 (the first family from South Africa to do so). She continued her education in Liverpool and at the London School of Economics. A Zionist, Hinden joined the Independent Labour Party and in 1939 (having returned briefly to Palestine), the Labour Party. In 1940, with Arthur Creech-Jones, she founded the Fabian Colonial Bureau, which proved an influential research body through which Hinden published *Plan For Africa* (1941).

She married in Palestine in 1933 and she and her

husband returned to Britain the same year. In the 1950s she was active in the Socialist Union and as editor of the revisionist journal *Socialist Commentary*. An ethical socialist, whose beliefs owed much to R H ◊Tawney, in 1964 she edited a posthumous volume of his essays, *The Radical Tradition*.

Hindenburg, Paul Ludwig Hans Anton von Beneckendorf und von (1847–1934)

German field marshal and right-wing politician. During World War I he was supreme commander and, with Erich von Ludendorff, practically directed Germany's policy until the end of the war. He was president of Germany 1925–33.

Born in Posen of a Prussian Junker (aristocratic landowner) family, he was commissioned in 1866, served in the Austro-Prussian and Franco-German wars, and retired in 1911. Given the command in East Prussia in August 1914, he received the credit for the defeat of the Russians at Tannenberg and was promoted to supreme commander and field marshal. Re-elected president in 1932, he was compelled to invite Adolf Hitler to assume the chancellorship in January 1933.

FURTHER READING
Kitchen, M *The Silent Dictatorship: The Politics of the German High Command under Hindenburg and Ludendorff, 1916–19* 1976
Wheeler-Bennett, J *The Wooden Titan* 1936

Hiratsuka, Raicho (1886–1971)

Japanese pioneer of the women's movement. She was a founder of the Bluestocking Society (Seitosha) in 1911 and of the New Women's Association (Shin Fujin Kyokai) in 1920. After World War II she was president of the Federation of Japanese Women's Societies (Nihon Fujin Dantai Rengokai).

Hirohito, regnal era name *Shōwa* (1901–1989)

Emperor of Japan from 1926, when he succeeded his father Taishō (Yoshihito). After the defeat of Japan in World War II in 1945, he was made a figurehead monarch by the US-backed constitution of 1946. He is believed to have played a reluctant role in General ◊Tōjō's prewar expansion plans. He was succeeded by his son Akihito.

As the war turned against Japan from June 1942, Tōjō involved him more in national life, calling upon the people to make sacrifices in his name. He belatedly began to exert more influence over his government as defeat became imminent in 1945, but was too late to act before the atomic bombs were dropped on Hiroshima and Nagasaki. His speech on Japanese radio on 15 August 1945 announcing the previous day's surrender was the first time a Japanese emperor had directly addressed his people. The Shōwa emperor ruled Japan with dignity during and after the US occupation

following World War II. He was a scholar of botany and zoology and the author of books on marine biology.

Hiss, Alger (1904–1996)

US diplomat and liberal Democrat, a former State Department official, imprisoned in 1950 for perjury when he denied having been a Soviet spy. There are doubts about the justice of Hiss's conviction.

Hiss, president of the Carnegie Endowment for International Peace and one of President F D Roosevelt's advisers at the 1945 Yalta Conference, was accused in 1948 by a former Soviet agent, Whittaker ◊Chambers, of having passed information to the USSR during the period 1926–37. He was convicted of perjury for swearing before the House Un-American Activities Committee that he had not spied for the USSR (under the statute of limitations he could not be tried for the original crime). Richard ◊Nixon was a prominent member of the committee, which inspired the subsequent anticommunist witch-hunts of Senator Joseph ◊McCarthy. The official Soviet commission on KGB archives reported in 1992 that Hiss had never been a spy.

Hiss was born in Baltimore, Maryland, and graduated from Johns Hopkins University in 1926 and Harvard Law School in 1929. He was secretary to Justice Oliver Wendell Holmes 1929–30, and practised law in Boston and New York 1930–33. He entered the Department of State in 1936.

FURTHER READING
Gwynn, B *Whittaker Chambers: The Discrepancy in the Evidence of the Typewriter* 1993
Hiss, A *Alger Hiss: Recollections of a Life* 1988
Tanenhaus, S *Whittaker Chambers: A Biography* 1997
Worth, E J *Whittaker Chambers: The Secret Confession* 1993

Hitler, Adolf (1889–1945)

See page 194.

Ho Chi Minh (1890–1969) adopted name of Nguyen Tat Thanh

North Vietnamese communist politician, prime minister 1954–55, and president 1954–69. Having trained in Moscow shortly after the Russian Revolution, he headed the communist Vietminh from 1941 and fought against the French during the Indochina War 1946–54, becoming president and prime minister of the republic at the armistice. Aided by the communist bloc, he did much to develop industrial potential. He relinquished the premiership in 1955, but continued as president. In the years before his death, Ho successfully led his country's fight against US-aided South Vietnam in the Vietnam War 1954–75.

FURTHER READING
Fenn, Ch *Ho Chi Minh: A Biographical Introduction* 1973
Jenkins, Ch, et al (eds) *Reflections from Captivity* 1978

Warbey, W *Ho Chi Minh and the Struggle for an Independent Vietnam* 1972

Hodza, Milan (1878–1944)

Czechoslovak politician, prime minister 1936–38. He and President Edvard ◊Beneš were forced to agree to the secession of the Sudeten areas of Czechoslovakia to Germany before resigning on 22 September 1938.

FURTHER READING

Kollár, Karol *Milan Hodza: moderný teoretik, pragmatický politik* 1994

Hoffa, Jimmy (James Riddle) (1913–c. 1975)

US labour leader, president of the International Brotherhood of Teamsters (transport workers) from 1957. He was jailed 1967–71 for attempted bribery of a federal court jury after he was charged with corruption. He was released by President Richard Nixon with the stipulation that he did not engage in union activities, but was evidently attempting to reassert influence when he disappeared. He is generally believed to have been murdered.

An ego is just imagination. And if a man doesn't have imagination he'll be working for someone else for the rest of his life.

JIMMY HOFFA *Esquire*

Jimmy Hoffa succeeded in 1964 in bringing all lorry drivers into the same union. The possibility of his calling them all out on strike alarmed the government and industry. In addition, he was seeking to extend the Teamsters to airline, railway, and other transport workers.

FURTHER READING

Hoffa, James R *The Trials of Jimmy Hoffa* 1970

Sheridan, Walter *The Fall and Rise of Jimmy Hoffa* 1972

Hoffman, Abbie (Abbot) (1936–1989)

US left-wing political activist, founder of the Yippies (Youth International Party), a political offshoot of the hippies. He was a member of the Chicago Seven, a radical group tried for attempting to disrupt the 1968 Democratic Convention.

Hoffman was arrested 52 times and was a fugitive from justice 1973–80. He specialized in imaginative political gestures to gain media attention, for example throwing dollar bills to the floor of the New York Stock Exchange in 1967. His books include *Revolution for the Hell of It* (1969). He campaigned against the Vietnam War and, later, for the environment. He committed suicide.

Hofmeyr, Jan Hendrik (1894–1948)

South African statesman and historian. In the coalition government of 1933 he was minister for the interior, education, and public health. His sympathies for the Bantu people soon made him unpopular with many of the Afrikaners. In 1936 he strongly opposed the bill to destroy the Cape native franchise, and in 1938 he resigned. When World War II broke out Hofmeyr rejoined the government as minister of finance and in 1943 was appointed deputy prime minister. In the 1948 elections his liberal attitude towards the non-European races alienated many electors, but his party supported him and he remained in the forefront of the opposition to the Prime Minister Daniel Malan's policy of segregation.

He studied at Oxford University as a Rhodes scholar and became principal of the University of Witwatersrand at the age of 25. In 1929 he entered parliament as member for Johannesburg and took a leading part in the movement for the reconciliation of leading South African politicians Jan Smuts and James Hertzog and the reunion of South Africans of British and Boer (Afrikaner) stock, from which the United Party originated.

Hogg, Quintin

British politician; see ◊Hailsham.

Holbrooke, Richard (1941–)

US diplomat. He was appointed head of the US negotiating team in the Balkans in July 1994 and within seven months had persuaded Bosnian Muslim and Croat leaders to sign an accord, leading to the creation of a Bosnian Muslim–Croat federation. He went on to negotiate an overall peace agreement at Dayton, Ohio, in September 1995. However, despite strenuous efforts he failed to secure a peace agreement for the divided island of Cyprus in April 1998.

Holbrooke served as an aide to Henry Cabot Lodge II in the Vietnam War and returned to the state department in President Jimmy Carter's administration, becoming assistant secretary at the age of 35.

On Ronald Reagan's election, he left government to take up a financial career in Wall Street but returned to public service under President Bill Clinton, first as ambassador to Germany and then, from 1994, as assistant secretary of state for European and Canadian affairs. Disillusioned with the failure of the US administration to provide leadership in tackling the United Nations crisis in Bosnia-Herzegovina, Holbrooke was on the point of leaving his post when Clinton intervened personally, appointing him US special envoy in the former Yugoslavia. He resigned from the State Department in February 1996 to continue his business career.

Holkeri, Harri Hermanni (1937–)

Finnish politician, prime minister 1987–91. Joining the centrist National Coalition Party (KOK) at an early age, he eventually became its national secretary.

◆ HITLER, ADOLF (1889–1945) ◆

German Nazi dictator, born in Austria. He was *Führer* (leader) of the Nazi Party from 1921 and wrote *Mein Kampf/My Struggle* 1925–27. As chancellor of Germany from 1933 and head of state from 1934, he created a dictatorship by playing party and state institutions against each other and continually creating new offices and appointments. His position was not seriously challenged until the July Plot of 1944, which failed to assassinate him. In foreign affairs, he reoccupied the Rhineland and formed an alliance with the Italian Fascist Benito ◊Mussolini in 1936, annexed Austria in 1938, and occupied Sudeten under the Munich Agreement. The rest of Czechoslovakia was annexed in March 1939. The Ribbentrop–Molotov pact was followed in September by the invasion of Poland and the declaration of war by Britain and France. He committed suicide as Berlin fell.

Hitler was born in Braunau-am-Inn, and spent his early years in poverty in Vienna and Munich. After serving as a volunteer in the German army during World War I, he was employed as a spy by the military authorities in Munich and in 1919 joined, in this capacity, the German Workers' Party. By 1921 he had assumed its leadership, renamed it the National Socialist German Workers' Party (Nazi Party for short), and provided it with a programme that mixed nationalism with anti-Semitism. Having led an unsuccessful uprising in Munich in 1923, he served nine months in prison, during which he wrote his political testament, *Mein Kampf*.

The party did not achieve national importance until the elections of 1930; by 1932, although Field Marshal ◊Hindenburg defeated Hitler in the presidential elections, it formed the largest group in the Reichstag (parliament). As the result of an intrigue directed by Chancellor Franz von ◊Papen, Hitler became chancellor in a Nazi–Nationalist coalition on 30 January 1933. The opposition was rapidly suppressed, the Nationalists removed from the government, and the Nazis declared the only legal party. In 1934 Hitler succeeded Hindenburg as head of state. Meanwhile, the drive to war began; Germany left the League of Nations, conscription was reintroduced, and in 1936 the Rhineland was reoccupied.

Hitler and Mussolini, who were already both involved in the Spanish Civil War, formed an alliance (the Axis) in 1936, joined by Japan in 1940. Hitler conducted the war in a ruthless but idiosyncratic way, took and ruled most of the neighbouring countries with repressive occupation forces, and had millions of Slavs, Jews, Romanies, homosexuals, and political

enemies killed in concentration camps and massacres. He narrowly escaped death on 20 July 1944 from a bomb explosion at a staff meeting, prepared by high-ranking officers. On 29 April 1945, when Berlin was largely in Soviet hands, he married his mistress Eva Braun in his bunker under the chancellery building and on the following day committed suicide with her.

Hitler's father, originally called Schicklgruber until he changed his name late in life, was a minor customs officer in the Austrian service. Hitler was the only son of his third wife. Hitler's father died when he was 14, leaving no resources for his continued education. With his mother he went to Vienna hoping to become an architect, but had to earn his living as assistant to a house-painter and by selling indifferent sketches. After spending a few years in Vienna he left to settle in Munich in 1912. These years of penury were formative both of his philosophy of life and of his character and it was probably then that he first absorbed the anti-Semitic and pan-Germanic views current among extreme nationalists at the time.

Hitler joined a Bavarian reserve regiment at the start of World War I, serving in the trenches as a dispatch rider. He reached the rank of *Gefreiter* (lance corporal), was wounded in the Battle of the Somme in 1916, and gassed in 1918. He became convinced that Germany had been betrayed by Jewish and Marxist influences and returned from the war bitter at Germany's defeat. Back in Bavaria, he attended, and later conducted, courses designed to keep ex-soldiers away from Bolshevism, where he came under the influence of Gottfried Feder, the intellectual founder of the Nazi movement.

He then became the seventh member of an insignificant political group in Munich, the German Workers' Party, and soon distinguished himself with his almost hypnotic popular oratory. Through his friends Erich ◊Röhm, a staff officer at Munich, and von Epp, he maintained close contacts with the German army, the Reichswehr. He ousted Anton Drexler, the founder of the party, as leader in 1921. The party was now called the National Socialist German Workers' Party and adopted Hitler's nationalist and anti-Marxist creed. After an argument with Röhm over the role of the newly created SA (*Sturmabteilung*) troops (the Brownshirts), Hitler organized a special detachment to be his own disciplined political soldiers rather than the brawling street-fighters of Röhm's Brownshirts. This was formally established in 1926 as the SS (*Schutzstaffel*) in imitation of Mussolini's *fasces*.

Thinking that the Weimar Republic was on the

verge of collapse, Hitler launched an abortive coup in Munich in November 1923, in alliance with Röhm, the war hero Erich von ◊Ludendorff, and Hermann Goering, in an attempt to make Ludendorff dictator. The coup failed and Hitler was arrested and tried for treason. He was sentenced to five years' imprisonment and during his incarceration in the fortress of Landsberg he worked on the final draft of *Mein Kampf* with the aid of Rudolf Hess.

During his time in prison, the Nazi Party all but disintegrated and when he was released under an amnesty in 1924, he set to work immediately to rebuild the party organization. Although for some time the Strasser brothers, creators of the Nazi Party in northern Germany, were more influential than Hitler in the party ranks, he gradually recovered the ground he had lost and ousted the Strassers. By 1930 he was the undisputed head of a considerable party. Funds were increasingly flowing in from the big industrialists, who saw National Socialism as a safeguard against communism. 'Nationalism' gradually superseded 'Socialism' in the party programme, although its language still played lip service to its more revolutionary roots.

When the world economic crisis came in 1930, Hitler ably exploited the discontent of both the working class and the more solid middle-class elements, who saw their standard of living threatened by the crisis. His rhetoric won over many converts and in the next election in September 1930 the Nazis increased their representation in the Reichstag from 12 to 107 seats. He stood against Hindenburg in the presidential election of 1932 and although he was beaten in the second ballot, he had managed to poll some 13 million votes and was now a political power to be reckoned with. In a rapidly deteriorating political situation, Chancellor Heinrich Brüning felt compelled to govern by decree and, though liberal in outlook, his regime paved the way to dictatorship. He resigned as chancellor in June 1932 and was succeeded by von Papen. Hitler had regarded himself as heir to the chancellorship but was blocked by the covert resistance of the old right-wing regime, with its backing of industrialists and Junkers (aristocratic landowners). Von Papen dissolved the Reichstag and held fresh elections but the Nazi Party doubled its strength to 230 seats and Hitler was now head of the biggest single party. Eventually Hitler and von Papen reached an agreement: Hitler renounced the socialist section of his programme, and von Papen released the subsidies from the industrialists to Hitler's coffers, and induced Hindenburg to accept Hitler as chancellor in January 1933.

During 1933, the Weimar Republic gave way to the Third Reich and by the end of the year the one-man party had become the one-party state. Political opponents 'disappeared', either assassinated or sent to concentration camps. Having crushed opposition in Germany at large, Hitler turned his attention to stifling the last vestiges of dissent in his own party. In the 'Night of the Long Knives' of 30 June 1934, over a hundred leading Nazis were murdered, including Gregor Strasser, Röhm, and Kurt von Schleicher and his wife. All power now passed to the National Socialist executive, which, for all practical purposes, meant Hitler himself. When Hindenburg died in August 1934, Hitler was declared his successor but abjured the title of *Reichspräsident* in favour of *Führer* and *Kanzler* (chancellor).

From the moment Hitler came to power he instituted a reign of terror against Jews, homosexuals, Romanies, and political opponents. Anti-Semitic measures were introduced in stages, starting with boycotts of Jewish businesses in April 1933 and culminating in the full horror of the extermination camps and the 'final solution' in 1941. Official propaganda was directed against Jews, stoking up popular hatred as in the organized terror of the Kristallnacht when Jewish businesses and property were attacked by government-sponsored mobs on 9 November 1938. Jews were increasingly marginalized by a combination of vicious propaganda and anti-Jewish laws, such as forcing all Jews to wear yellow stars, making them visible targets for both official repression and private hostility. Once World War II started, these policies were carried into the countries Germany occupied and by 1941, there was a network of extermination camps, mainly in Poland. The Holocaust reached its height after the Wannsee Conference of 20 January 1942, a meeting of top Nazi officials who developed a systematic policy of efficient extermination. There are no definitively accurate figures for the number of people exterminated by the Nazis but it is reckoned that by the end of the war some 6 million Jews had been killed and over a million people belonging to other groups, such as Slavs and Romanies, designated as *Untermenschen* ('subhumans').

Having established his position in Germany, Hitler now began his long campaign to restore German power in Europe, heralding his advent to power by a series of increasingly grave breaches of treaty obligations and flouting European opinion. He began a massive programme of rearmament, secretly at first and then ever more flagrantly. For example, Germany was not supposed to have an air force but Goering built the Luftwaffe from scratch under the guise of a civilian airline, announcing its existence officially in April 1935.

Hitler then turned to the territorial clauses of the various treaties binding Germany, starting with the plebiscite in the Saar region in January 1935. The result, partly influenced by terrorism, was an overwhelming majority for retrocession to Germany and Hitler used this as a bolster to denounce the military clauses of the Treaty of Versailles in March 1935 and introduce conscription for the Reichswehr. A year later he boldly risked marching his forces into the demilitarized Rhineland zone, in defiance of the Pact of Locarno of 1925, which, he claimed, had been abrogated by a Franco-Soviet alliance. The remilitarization of the Rhineland was followed by two years of the most active German military preparations combined with a complete overhaul of the economy to make Germany self-sufficient.

When the Civil War broke out in Spain in July 1936, Hitler seized the opportunity to test his newly built army and air force on the side of the right-wing General Franco. Other events abroad during 1936–37, such as the League of Nations' failure to check Mussolini's Abyssinian adventure, increased the nervous tension in Europe, and went far to strengthen Hitler's position. Mussolini was a natural ally and the two countries allied in the Rome–Berlin Axis in October 1936.

From the end of 1937, Hitler pursued an aggressively expansionist foreign policy which for two years won spectacular successes. He annexed Austria in March 1938 by manipulating an abrupt crisis in Austro-German relations, then sending the German army across the frontier and declaring *Anschluss*, the incorporation of Austria within the Reich. He then moved on to the campaign to 'liberate' Sudeten, an ethnic German area within Czechoslovakia – this was an attack on a sovereign state bound by treaty with the Western powers and by ethnic ties with Russia. However, Hitler well understood the underlying realities of the immediate political situation and realized that the West was not prepared to fight. The Munich Agreement in August 1938 handed him Sudeten in return for assurances that he had no more territorial claims to make, the same claim he had made after the annexation of Austria. He then took the rest of Czechoslovakia piece by piece during early 1939 and at the same time announced his annexation of Memel in violation of the Versailles Treaty. Hitler now seemed, in the eyes of the average German, not only to be the preserver of peace but a consummate statesman, surpassing all his predecessors in extending the Reich frontiers. Within less than a year he had added 10 million Germans to the Third Reich, broken the one formidable bastion to German expansion to the southeast, and made himself the most powerful dictator in Europe since Napoleon.

In March 1939 Hitler renounced the nonaggression treaty with Poland of 1934 and demanded the return of Danzig and the 'Polish Corridor'. The UK and France guaranteed Polish independence and warned Hitler they would stand by Poland. Hitler was shaken by this development, particularly when the two Western powers began negotiations with Moscow. Rather than abandon his designs on Poland he forgot his hatred of communism and proposed a nonaggression pact with the USSR. Stalin agreed and the Ribbentrop–Molotov pact was signed on 23 August 1939. Without any danger of Soviet interference, Hitler launched his Blitzkrieg on Poland on 1 September 1939, and two days later the UK and France declared war.

After the invasion of Poland, Germany swept through the Netherlands, Belgium, and France in equally rapid succession and simultaneously launched invasions of Norway and Denmark. The spectacular events of spring and summer 1940, culminating in the armistice with France, only confirmed Hitler's genius in the eyes of the average German. In the spring of 1941 German forces invaded Yugoslavia and Greece, while the

Holland, Sidney George (1893–1961)

New Zealand National Party right-of-centre politician, prime minister 1949–57. He removed wartime controls, abolished the Legislative Council (the upper house of parliament), pursued a market-centred economic strategy, and participated in conferences on the Suez Crisis in 1956. He was knighted in 1957, but, with his health deteriorating, retired in September 1957 and was replaced as prime minister and party leader by Keith ◊Holyoake.

Born in Greendale, Canterbury, Holland trained as an engineer and was managing director of an engineering company, before being elected to parliament in 1935, as a member of the conservative National Party. He became leader of the National Party and the opposition in 1940, before succeeding Peter ◊Fraser as prime minister in December 1949. His government's attack on trade-union power provoked a 23-week-long dock workers' strike in 1951, after which Holland called and won a snap general election in July 1951.

Hollis, Roger Henry (1905–1973)

British civil servant, head of the secret intelligence service MI5 1956–65. He was alleged to have been a double agent together with Kim Philby, but this was denied by the KGB in 1991. He was knighted in 1960.

Holstein, Friedrich August von (1839–1909)

German diplomat and foreign-affairs expert. He

air force belaboured the UK with bomber raids and the navy struck at its seaborne supplies.

Hitler decided to weaken the British by attacking the empire in the east. However, this plan depended on the neutrality of the USSR and, not being sure of this, Hitler and his advisers decided to combine the attack on Egypt with an invasion of the USSR itself, Operation Barbarossa, in June 1941. This was a fatal decision which brought a powerful enemy into play against him and opened up an enormous second front. It revealed the essential weakness underlying all Hitler's foreign policy and it is possible that he took the decision against the advice of other Nazi leaders and the German general staff. From then on he strove to divide the USSR from the Western Allies by stressing Germany's anti-Bolshevik crusade.

The German campaigns in the Balkans and the Mediterranean were brilliant in conception and execution, but British intervention in Greece and British resistance in Crete and Libya delayed Hitler's timetable, and as the summer of 1941 wore on it became obvious that German optimism had outrun itself. The reverses in the Battle of Britain in July 1941 were a great blow to German morale and for some time Hitler was silent, but at a meeting of the Winter Help Campaign on 4 October, he announced a 'gigantic operation' which would bring about the defeat of the USSR. Following the failure of the German army before Moscow, Hitler sacked the commander in chief, Walther von Brauchitsch, in December 1941, and assumed direct control of all military operations. When the USA entered the war after the attack on Pearl Harbor in December 1941, four-fifths of the world was now ranged against Germany.

Hitler's New Year message for 1942 showed a marked decline in buoyancy, although the German armies were still a powerful force, and in the early half of 1942, the German armies in the USSR reached the Volga at Stalingrad while Erwin Rommel was threatening Cairo and Alexandria in North Africa. Yet before the autumn was past Rommel had been routed at El Alamein and the Soviets had destroyed von Paulus's 6th Army before Stalingrad. Hitler began to speak less of German victory than of the inability of the Allies to defeat Germany, and he soon faced new crises. Mussolini was deposed in July 1943 and Italy capitulated to the Allies.

After the German armies had been driven out of the USSR, and with the D-Day landings in Normandy in June 1944, it soon became clear that the Allies would not, as Hitler had promised, be 'driven into the sea'. The German 'opposition', led by army generals and supported by industrialists, liberals, and even elements of the left, attempted a coup d'état, the July Bomb Plot. The signal was to be the assassination of Hitler, but the bomb which was placed in his headquarters by a staff officer named von Stauffenberg did not kill him and the coup failed. It succeeded only in bringing about Hitler's most savage purge: thousands of men and women were executed who were not even necessarily implicated in the plot, but who might conceivably have led another rising. Himmler took command of the army inside Germany so as to tighten the Nazi grip on it. However, as the year wore on, the Allies steadily closed in from all sides.

As the Allies pressed into Germany in April 1945, Hitler married his mistress, Eva Braun, on 29 April and both then committed suicide in the air-raid shelter under the ruined chancellery in Berlin the following day. It is generally considered that their bodies were subsequently burned in the courtyard. See photograph on page 198.

FURTHER READING

Bullock, Alan *Hitler: A Study in Tyranny* 1952, *Hitler and Stalin: Parallel Lives* 1991
Fest, Joachim *Hitler* 1974
Kershaw, Ian *Hitler* 1991
Trevor-Roper, Hugh *The Last Days of Hitler* 1947

refused the post of foreign minister, but played a key role in German diplomacy from the 1880s until his death.

Holt, Harold Edward (1908–1967)

Australian Liberal politician, prime minister 1966–67. His brief prime ministership was dominated by the Vietnam War, to which he committed increased Australian troops.

Holt was born in Sydney and educated at Melbourne University. He worked as a solicitor and entered the federal parliament in 1935 for the United Australia (later Liberal) Party. He was minister of labour 1940–41 and 1949–58, and federal treasurer 1958–66, when he succeeded Robert Menzies as prime minister. He was also minister for immigration 1949–56, during which time he made the first modifications to the White Australia Policy, relaxing some restrictions on Asian immigration. He was drowned in a swimming accident.

Holyoake, Keith Jacka (1904–1983)

New Zealand National Party right-of-centre politician, prime minister in 1957 (for three months) and 1960–72, during which time he was also foreign minister. During his second period as prime minister he secured electoral victories for the National Party on three occasions, developed closer ties with Australia,

Adolf Hitler at a party rally, 1934. *Rex*

supported the USA in Vietnam, and negotiated special access for New Zealand dairy produce to the UK market, within the European Community. He was knighted (GCMG) on his retirement in 1972 and, between 1977 and 1980, became the first former prime minister to serve as governor general.

The son of a North Island farmer, Holyoake promoted farming interests throughout his political career and favoured a property-owning democracy. He served in parliament 1932–72 and was agriculture minister from 1949, before succeeding Sidney ◊Holland as prime minister in September 1957; however, he lost the general election 12 weeks later.

Further Reading

Clark, M (ed) *Sir Keith Holyoake: Towards a Political Biography* 1997

Homma, Masaharu (1888–1946)

Japanese general. He spent most of his military career in intelligence duties and had little experience of field command. He unwisely boasted he could complete the invasion of the Philippine Islands in 1941 within 45 days. General Douglas ◊MacArthur withdrew into the Bataan Peninsula, prolonging the defence consider-

ably, and Homma was reprimanded and replaced in all but name by General Yamashita. Homma was recalled to Japan and held administrative posts for the rest of the war. He was arrested by US troops in September 1945, tried for his part in the 'Bataan Death March', and executed in Manila in 1946.

Hoover, Herbert (Clark) (1874–1964)

31st president of the USA 1929–33, a Republican. He was secretary of commerce 1921–28. He lost public confidence after the stock-market crash of 1929, when he opposed direct government aid for the unemployed in the Depression that followed.

> *He is not a complicated personality, but rather a personality of monolithic simplicity ... an extremely plain man living in an extremely fancy age.*
>
> James M Cox On Herbert Hoover, quoted in the *Sun*, August 1949

Hoover was born in West Branch, Iowa. He became a mining engineer, and travelled widely before World

War I. After the war he organized relief work in occupied Europe. A talented administrator, he was subsequently associated with numerous international relief organizations, and became food administrator for the USA 1917–19. President Woodrow Wilson later made him a member of the War Trade Council, and as such he took part in Paris in the negotiation of the Versailles Treaty. In 1928 he defeated the Democratic candidate for the presidency, Al Smith (1873–1944), by a wide margin.

The shantytowns, or Hoovervilles, of the homeless that sprang up around large cities after the stock-market crash were evidence of his failure to cope with the effects of the Depression and prevent the decline of the economy. He was severely criticized for his adamant opposition to federal relief for the unemployed, even after the funds of states, cities, and charities were exhausted. In 1933 he was succeeded by F D Roosevelt.

FURTHER READING

Burner, D *Herbert Hoover: A Public Life* 1979
Nash, G H *The Life of Herbert Hoover* 1983–88
Smith, R *An Uncommon Man* 1984
Warren, H G *Hoover and the Great Depression* 1959
Wilson, Joan H *Herbert Hoover: Forgotten Progressive* 1975

Hoover, J(ohn) Edgar (1895–1972)

US director of the Federal Bureau of Investigation (FBI) from 1924 until his death. He built up a powerful network for the detection of organized crime. His drive against alleged communist activities after World War II and his opposition to the J F Kennedy administration brought much criticism for abuse of power.

He served under eight presidents, none of whom would dismiss him since he kept files on them and their associates. Hoover waged a personal campaign of harassment against leaders of the civil-rights movement, notably Martin Luther ◊King, Jr.

Hoover was born in Washington, DC. He entered the Department of Justice in 1917, and in 1921 became assistant director of the Bureau of Investigation.

FURTHER READING

Gentry, Curt *J Edgar Hoover: The Man and His Secrets* 1991
Nash, J R *Citizen Hoover* 1972
Theoharis, A G, and Cox, J S *The Boss* 1988

Hopkins, Harry Lloyd (1890–1946)

US government official. Originally a social worker, in 1935 he became head of the Works Progress Administration (WPA), which was concerned with Depression

---

◆ HONECKER, ERICH (1912–1994) ◆

German communist politician, in power in East Germany 1973–89, elected chair of the council of state (head of state) in 1976. He governed in an outwardly austere and efficient manner and, while favouring East–West détente, was a loyal ally of the USSR. In 1989, following a wave of prodemocracy demonstrations, he was replaced as leader of the Socialist Unity Party (SED) and head of state by Egon ◊Krenz, and expelled from the Communist Party. He died in exile in Chile.

Honecker, the son of a Saarland miner, was brought up as a communist and joined the socialist Young Spartacus Union at the age of ten. He joined the German Communist Party in 1929 and was a propagandist in the Saar until his imprisonment by the Nazis 1935–45 for 'subversive' antifascist activity. He directed the party's youth movement in East Germany after World War II, was elected to the East German parliament (Volkskammer) in 1949, and became a member of the SED Politburo in 1958. He was responsible for security, and instigated the building of the Berlin Wall in 1961 and the infamous *Schiessbefehl* (shoot-to-kill order) against would-be escapees. During the 1960s he served as a secretary of the National Defence Council before being appointed first secretary of the SED in 1971. After Walter ◊Ulbricht's death in

1973, Honecker became leader of East Germany. He permitted only limited economic reform and cultural liberalization during the 1970s and 1980s, but did foster closer relations with West Germany.

Mikhail ◊Gorbachev's *glasnost* and *perestroika* initiatives in the Soviet Union, combined with the loss of Moscow's backing, resulted in large-scale civil disturbances in 1989, and Honecker was replaced by his protégé Egon Krenz. Three weeks after his overthrow as Communist Party leader, the Berlin Wall was opened and the process of German reunification began. Within a year the two Germanys were reunited.

Honecker was placed under house arrest in 1990 and charged with high treason, misuse of office, and corruption. In 1991 he was transferred from a Soviet military hospital to Moscow, but the German government demanded his return to face manslaughter charges in connection with the killing of those illegally crossing the Berlin Wall 1961–89. He returned to Germany in 1992, but the courts ruled that he was too ill to stand trial.

FURTHER READING

Childs, D (ed) *Honecker's Germany* 1985
Lippmann, H *Honecker and the New Politics of Europe* 1973

relief work. After a period as secretary of commerce 1938–40, he was appointed supervisor of the lend-lease programme in 1941, and undertook missions to the UK and the USSR during World War II.

Hopkins was born in Sioux City, Iowa, and educated at Grinnell College, Iowa, In 1932 President F D Roosevelt appointed him director of the New York State Temporary Emergency Relief Administration. He later became one the leading administrators of the New Deal.

Hore-Belisha, (Isaac) Leslie, 1st Baron Hore-Belisha (1893–1957)

British politician. A National Liberal, he was minister of transport 1934–37, introducing Belisha beacons to mark pedestrian crossings. He was war minister from 1937, until removed by Neville Chamberlain in 1940 on grounds of temperament, and introduced peacetime conscription in 1939.

Horkheimer, Max (1895–1973)

German social theorist. He rejected empiricism and positivism and believed technology posed a threat to culture and civilization because the physical sciences upon which it is based ignored human values.

Horkheimer was director of the Institut für Sozialforschung (Institute for Social Research) in Frankfurt from 1930. When the Nazis came to power, he moved with the institute to Columbia University, New York, and later to California. He returned to Frankfurt in 1949 and became rector of the university there in 1951.

In his seminal papers of the 1930s, collected under the title *Kritische Theorie/Critical Theory: Selected Essays* (1968), he argues that only a radical transformation in social theory and practice will cure modern civilization of its sickness. 'Critical theory' has to discover and describe the social origins of knowledge in order to emancipate human beings.

He collaborated with, among others, Theodor W ◊Adorno on *Dialectic of Enlightenment* (1947).

Horn, Gyula (1932–   )

Hungarian economist and politician, president of the Hungarian Socialist Party (HSP) from 1990 and prime minister 1994–98. Under his leadership the ex-communist HSP enjoyed a resurgence, capturing an absolute majority in the July 1994 assembly elections. Despite opposition to the ongoing economic restructuring programme, Horn, as a trained economist, recognized the need to press on with reforms and formed a coalition with the centrist Free Democrats. He pursued a free-market economic programme, which, by attracting foreign inward investment, brought economic recovery. However, Horn lost power after the May 1998 general elections, following a collapse in support for his coalition partners, the Free Democrats, and was replaced by László Kovásc.

Horn worked in the international department of the Hungarian Socialist Workers' Party (HSWP) 1969–85 and, during the period of one-party communist rule, was undersecretary and then minister for foreign affairs 1985–90. In anticipation of the introduction of multiparty politics, the HSWP transformed itself into the HSP in 1989, and the pragmatic Horn was chosen as its new president in 1990. He is the author of several books on East–West relations.

Horn was born in Budapest and educated at the Don-Rostov College of Economics and Finance, graduating in 1954.

FURTHER READING
Horn, Gyula *Cölöpök* 1991

Horthy, Miklós Horthy de Nagybánya (1868–1957)

Hungarian politician and admiral. Leader of the counter-revolutionary White government, he became regent in 1920 on the overthrow of the communist Bela ◊Kun regime by Romanian and Czechoslovak intervention. He represented the conservative and military class, and retained power until World War II, trying (although allied to Hitler) to retain independence of action. In 1944 he tried to negotiate a surrender to the USSR but Hungary was taken over by the Nazis and he was deported to Germany. He was released from German captivity the same year by the Western Allies. He was not tried at Nürnberg, however, but instead was allowed to go to Portugal, where he died.

Horthy's relations with Germany were somewhat ambivalent. He ordered Hungarian forces to invade Yugoslavia in August 1941 in support of Hitler's aims in the region and the following month formally declared an anti-Soviet alliance with Germany. In November 1940 he joined the Tripartite Pact. In April 1941 Hungarian forces took part in the German attack on Yugoslavia. Horthy declared war with the USSR in June 1941, and with the USA in December 1941. However, he refused to send more troops to the Eastern Front in May 1943 and went further in 1944, demanding the return of Hungarian troops from Germany and an end to the use of Hungary as a supply base, and attempting to halt the deportation of Hungarian Jews. He backed down on all these points when Hitler threatened to occupy Hungary and from then on began trying to remove Hungary from the war.

FURTHER READING
Sakmyster, Thomas L *Hungary's Admiral on Horseback: Miklós Horthy, 1918–1994* 1994
Szinai, Miklós, and Szucs, László (eds) *The Confidential Papers of Admiral Horthy* 1965

Hosokawa, Morishiro (1938–   )

Japanese politician. He was elected to the house of councillors in 1971 as a Liberal Democrat and was appointed governor of Kumamoto in 1983. His government's main achievement was to push through reform of the Japanese political system, but he was forced to resign in April 1994 after questions were asked about his political finances.

Born in Tokyo, he was educated at the Sophia University and after graduating took up a career in journalism with the *Daily Asahi Shimbun*.

House, Edward Mandell (1858–1938)

US politician and diplomat. He was instrumental in obtaining the presidential nomination for Woodrow Wilson in 1912 and later served as Wilson's closest adviser. During World War I, House served as US liaison with the UK and was an important behind-the-scenes participant in the 1919 Versailles Peace Conference.

House was born in Houston, Texas, attended Cornell University, and, after working for many years on his family's holdings, became active in state Democratic politics. As personal adviser to a succession of Texas governors 1892–1904, he was awarded the honorary title of colonel.

Howard, Ebenezer (1850–1928)

English town planner. Aiming to halt the unregulated growth of industrial cities, he pioneered the ideal of the garden city through his book *Tomorrow* (1898; republished as *Garden Cities of Tomorrow* in 1902). He also inspired and took an active part in building the garden cities of Letchworth and Welwyn.

His ideas were influenced by the US writers Walt Whitman, Ralph Waldo Emerson, and in particular by the Utopian novel *Looking Backward* (1888) by Edward Bellamy (1850–1898). Every house was to have its own plot of land; land usage was to be arranged zonally with civic amenities at the centre and factories on the edge of the city; and the whole city was to be surrounded by a 'green belt'.

Howard, John Winston (1939–)

Australian politician, prime minister from 1996. Firmly on the conservative wing of the Liberal party, after entering the federal parliament in 1974, Howard served in the governments of Malcolm Fraser 1975–83, and then held senior opposition posts. He has the unusual distinction of being leader of his party on two separate occasions.

Howard won the party leadership from Andrew Peacock in 1985 then, following the general election defeat in 1987, lost it to Peacock. He tried to regain it in 1993 but was beaten by John Hewson who, in turn, was replaced by Andrew Downer in 1994. Howard chose not to contest the party leadership again when Downer resigned in January 1995, but was elected unopposed at a party caucus meeting. Generally regarded as a 'safe pair of hands', his elevation to prime minister in February 1996 presented the country with a stark contrast to his predecessor, the abrasive leader of the Labor party, Paul Keating, and took Australia into a quieter, less combative, period of politics.

Educated at Sydney University, where he studied

◆ HOUPHOUËT-BOIGNY, FÉLIX (1905–1993) ◆

Côte d'Ivoire right-wing politician, president 1960–93. He held posts in French ministries, and became president of the Republic of Côte d'Ivoire on independence in 1960, maintaining close links with France, which helped to boost an already thriving economy and encourage political stability. Pro-Western and opposed to communist intervention in Africa, Houphouët-Boigny was strongly criticized for maintaining diplomatic relations with South Africa. He was re-elected for a seventh term in 1990 in multiparty elections, amid allegations of ballot rigging and political pressure.

He was Africa's longest-serving head of state, having begun his political career as a left-wing nationalist under French colonial rule, and became the first president of the independent Côte d'Ivoire, with closer links with France than any other African state. Under his guidance his country became one of the most stable and prosperous states in the continent, and he became known in Paris as 'the grand old man of Africa'.

After 30 years of one-man, one-party rule, he conceded in 1990 to demands for free elections, which he and his party won with ease.

Born Félix Houphouët, in a prosperous land-owning family, he later added Boigny, meaning 'ram', to his name, apparently to indicate the force of his ambitions. After training as a doctor in Dakar, he returned in 1925 to practise medicine, earning a reputation for care of the underprivileged. He left medicine in 1940 to look after his family's estates, and then moved into politics, being elected an overseas deputy in the French Assembly. His first political associations were with the communists; he later aligned himself with the socialists, becoming a close friend of François Mitterrand. He was the first African to be given a seat in a French cabinet and was later an adviser to General Charles ◊de Gaulle. His links with France assisted his presidency and Côte d'Ivoire prospered under his firm, paternalistic leadership.

law, Howard became a partner in a prominent firm of Sydney solicitors before embarking on a full-time political career.

Howard, Michael (1941–)

British Conservative politician, home secretary 1993–97. On the right of the Conservative Party, he championed the restoration of law and order as a key electoral issue, but encountered stiff opposition to his proposals for changes to the criminal-justice system and for increased police powers, as embodied in the 1994 Criminal Justice and Public Order Bill. A new crime bill, focusing on tougher sentencing, was announced by Howard at the 1995 Conservative Party conference, and immediately condemned by the Lord Chief Justice.

Howard was born in Gorseinon, south Wales. After a successful legal career, he entered the House of Commons 1983 and, under Margaret Thatcher, made rapid ministerial progress through the departments of trade and industry, environment, and employment, until being appointed home secretary by John Major in 1993. His populist approach to law and order won him the plaudits of grass-roots party members, but he was forced to retreat on a number of key points, including that of police restructuring, in the face of criticism from senior Conservative figures as well as members of the judiciary.

His position as home secretary was seriously threatened in October 1995 following allegations that he had unduly interfered in the operations of the prison service. After the Conservative Party's election defeat in May 1997, he unsuccessfully contested for the party's vacant leadership, but allegations by former colleague Ann Widdecombe about his conduct as home secretary undermined his challenge.

Howe, (Richard Edward) Geoffrey, Baron Howe of Aberavon (1926–)

British Conservative politician, member of Parliament for Surrey East. As chancellor of the Exchequer 1979–83 under Margaret Thatcher, he put into practice the monetarist policy that reduced inflation at the cost of a rise in unemployment. In 1983 he became foreign secretary, and in 1989 deputy prime minister and leader of the House of Commons. On 1 November 1990 he resigned in protest at Thatcher's continued opposition to the UK's greater integration in Europe.

Howe was born in Port Talbot, Glamorgan, and educated at Westminster School and Trinity Hall, Cambridge. Many of the ideas proposed by Howe in the early 1960s were subsequently taken up by the Thatcher government. Under Edward Heath he was solicitor general 1970–72 and minister for trade 1972–74.

A barrister, Howe was elected Conservative member of Parliament for Bebington in 1964, but was defeated in 1966. In 1970 he was elected for Reigate and became member of Parliament for East Surrey in 1972. He was an opposition spokesperson on labour and social services in 1965–66 and became solicitor general in

---

Inflation is a great moral evil. Nations which lose confidence in their currency lose confidence in themselves.

GEOFFREY HOWE *The Times* July 1982

1970, when he was knighted, as is customary on appointment to the post. Sir Geoffrey was one of the ministers responsible for drafting and guiding the Conservatives' Industrial Relations Act through Parliament. He was opposition spokesperson on the social services from 1974. He published his memoirs, *Conflict of Loyalty*, in 1994.

FURTHER READING

Hillman, J, and Clarke, P *Geoffrey Howe: A Quiet Revolutionary* 1988

Hoxha, Enver (1908–1985)

Albanian communist politician, the country's leader 1954–85. He founded the Albanian Communist Party in 1941, and headed the liberation movement 1939–44. He was prime minister 1944–54, also handling foreign affairs 1946–53, and from 1954 was first secretary of the Albanian Party of Labour. In policy he was a Stalinist and independent of both Chinese and Soviet communism.

Following World War II, in November 1945 Hoxha's government obtained Allied recognition on condition that free elections were held. On 2 December 1945 a communist-controlled assembly was elected, and Albania was declared a republic on 11 January 1946.

FURTHER READING

Hoxha, Enver *Speeches, Conversations, and Articles* 1977, *Imperialism and the Revolution* 1979, *Laying the Foundations of the New Albania: Memoirs and Historical Notes* 1984

Hoxha, Enver, and Halliday, John (ed) *The Artful Albanian Memoirs of Enver Hoxha* 1986

O'Donnell, James *A Coming of Age: Albania under Enver Hoxha* 1998

Hoyte, (Hugh) Desmond (1929–)

Guyanese politician and president 1985–92. He held a number of ministerial posts before becoming prime minister under Forbes Burnham. On Burnham's death in 1985 he succeeded him as president.

Hoyte was born in Georgetown and studied at London University and the Middle Temple, taught in a boys' school in Grenada 1955–57, and then practised as a lawyer in Guyana. He joined the socialist People's National Congress (PNC) and in 1968, two years after

Guyana achieved full independence, was elected to the National Assembly.

Hrawi, Elias (1930–)

Lebanese Maronite Christian politician, president 1989–98. He implemented the 1989 Taif peace agreement, which he had helped to draw up, ending Lebanon's 14-year civil war, and which reduced the president's executive powers. His position was strengthened in 1990 when the Syrians, with whom he enjoyed good relations, put down a rebellion by the Christian militia leader General Michel ◊Aoun. In 1991 a treaty was signed with Syria. In 1995 the term of the presidency (six years) was extended by a further three years to allow Hrawi to continue and provide stability while Prime Minister Rafiq al- ◊Hariri pressed ahead with economic reconstruction.

A Maronite Christian, he was born in Zahle in the Bekaa Valley, into an old landholding family. He established the country's first agricultural cooperative and, after success as an agricultural entrepreneur, was elected in 1972 as a deputy to the National Assembly. As public works minister 1980–82, he oversaw an ambitious road-building programme. In November 1989 he was elected by the parliament to succeed René Mouawad as president under the Lebanese constitutional arrangement of 1943 that provides for a Maronite Christian president and Sunni Muslim prime minister. Mouawad was assassinated after only 17 days in office.

Hrushevsky, Mikhail Sergeevich (1866–1934)

Ukrainian historian and politician. After the February Revolution of 1917, he joined the party of Ukrainian Socialist Revolutionaries and was president of the short-lived Ukrainian Central Council. He emigrated in 1918, but returned to Kiev, Ukraine, in 1924, and became a member of the Ukrainian Academy of Sciences, and in 1929 of the USSR Academy of Sciences. In 1930 he was arrested and deported from Kiev.

Hrushevsky was educated at Kiev University. From 1894 he was professor at Lvov University, and from 1897 he was president of the Shevchenko Scientific Society at the same institution. This was, at the time, the main centre of Ukrainian intellectual life. In his works – the ten-volume *History of the Ukraine-Russia* (1898–1936), *Outline History of the Ukrainian People* (1904), and the five-volume *History of Ukrainian Literature* (1923–26) – Hrushevsky laid the foundations of the nationalist school of Ukrainian historiography based on the idea that Kievan Russia was a specifically Ukrainian state, and not a state belonging to all the Russian peoples (namely Great Russians, Ukrainians, and Belorussians).

FURTHER READING
Prymak, Th M *Mykhailo Hrushevsky: The Politics of National Culture* 1987

Hua Guofeng or *Hua Kuofeng* (1920–)

Chinese communist politician, leader of the Chinese Communist Party 1976–81 and premier 1976–80.

Born near Tiayuan, in Shanxi province in northern China, Hua was the illegitimate son of a rich landlord's daughter who, after being disowned by her family, later married a communist underground labour organizer. Brought up in Shaanxi province, Hua joined the Chinese Communist Party (CCP) in 1938 and fought under ◊Zhu De, the Red Army leader, during the liberation struggle and civil war of 1937–49, serving as a political commissar and propagandist. After the establishment of the People's Republic in 1949, Hua began a steady climb up the CCP administrative ladder, working in Hunan, Mao Zedong's home province, where he specialized in agriculture and education. He entered the CCP Central Committee in 1969, was made party leader in Hunan in 1970, and joined the CCP Politburo in 1973.

In January 1975 Hua was appointed public security minister, an important post at a time of intense political in-fighting, and also became the country's sixth-ranking vice premier in January 1975. On the death, in January 1976, of the popular Zhou Enlai, he became prime minister and eight months later, on Mao's death, was elected party leader. With his relative inexperience, Hua was a surprising choice and was a compromise candidate. He was an orthodox, loyal Maoist, who opposed the leftist excesses of Jiang Qing's Gang of Four, whom he had arrested in October 1976.

However, he also pragmatically accepted the need for economic modernization, but without structural reform, and for improved relations with the West. Hua briefly dominated politics during 1976–77, but, with the rehabilitation in July 1977 of Deng Xiaoping he was

---

We will resolutely uphold whatever policy decisions Chairman Mao made, and unswervingly follow whatever instructions Chairman Mao made.

HUA GUOFENG Slogan devised by Hua Guofeng after the death of Mao Zedong in September 1976, which was derided by 'Dengist' opponents as the 'Two Whatevers' policy

---

soon eclipsed. He was replaced in September 1980 as prime minister by Zhao Ziyang and in June 1981 as CCP chair by Hu Yaobang. He was finally ousted from the CCP Politburo in September 1982, but was to remain a member of the CCP Central Committee, although he had effectively become 'politically invisible'. See photograph on page 83

FURTHER READING
Wang, Ting *Chairman Hua: The Leader of the Chinese Communists* 1980

Huerta, Victoriano (1854–1916)

Mexican soldier and political leader, president 1913–14. As provisional president, he established a military dictatorship in 1913. Military pressure from insurgents, notably Venustiano ◊Carranza, Francisco ◊Villa, and Emiliano ◊Zapata, forced him to resign in July 1914 and flee to Europe.

Born in Jalisco state and educated at an army college, he joined the military and became a brigadier general under President Porfirio ◊Díaz in 1902. After the 1911 revolution of Francisco ◊Madero, he became commander of the federal forces, but in February 1913 plotted to ensure Madero's removal, followed by his death. His dictatorship as president resulted in corruption, imprisonment, and assassinations of opponents, and clashed with hostile US forces at Tampico.

He moved from exile in Europe to the USA, where he was arrested twice for conspiring to incite a new Mexican revolution, and died in El Paso, Texas, an alcoholic.

Hughes, (James) Langston (1902–1967)

US poet, novelist, and playwright. A leading black writer of his time, he published several collections of poetry, including *The Weary Blues* (1926); the novel *Not Without Laughter* (1930) and plays, including *Mulatto* (1935).

Other works include a study of music for children, *The First Book of Jazz* (1955), and folklore, *The Book of Negro Folklore* (1958).

Hughes often commented on the realities of black life through the figure of Jess B Simple, originally created for a newspaper column but also the hero of a series of books.

Further Reading

Barksdale, R *Langston Hughes* 1977
Berry, Faith *Langston Hughes* 1983
Hughes, Langston *The Big Sea* 1940, 1993
Rampersad, Arnold *The Life of Langston Hughes* 1986–88

Hughes, Billy (William Morris) (1862–1952)

Australian politician, prime minister 1915–23; originally Labor, he headed a national cabinet. After resigning as prime minister in 1923, he helped Joseph ◊Lyons form the United Australia Party in 1931 and held many other cabinet posts 1934–41. He joined the Liberal Party in 1944.

Born in London, the son of a Welsh carpenter, he emigrated to Australia in 1884. He became founding president of the Waterside Workers Federation and in 1894 was elected to the New South Wales assembly, representing the Labor Party. He entered the federal parliament in 1901, as a free trader, and – being a barrister – was attorney general 1908–09, 1910–13, and 1914–21. He was expelled from the Labor Party in 1917 for refusing to abandon his pro-conscription stance and his championing of imperial interests. He repre-sented Australia in the Versailles peace conference after World War I.

Further Reading

Fitzhardinge, L F *William Morris Hughes: A Political Biography* (2 vols) 1964–79
Hudson, W J *Billy Hughes in Paris: The Birth of Australian Diplomacy* 1978

Hull, Cordell (1871–1955)

US Democratic politician. As F D Roosevelt's secretary of state 1933–44, he was a vigorous champion of free trade, and opposed German and Japanese aggression. He was identified with the 'Good Neighbor' policy of nonintervention in Latin America. An advocate of collective security after World War II, he was called by Roosevelt 'the father of the United Nations'. He was awarded the Nobel Peace Prize in 1945.

Hull was a member of Congress 1907–33. After December 1941 foreign policy was handled more directly by Roosevelt, but Hull was active in reaching agreements with Vichy France, though these were largely cancelled by the rising influence of General Charles ◊de Gaulle.

Hull was born in Olympus, Tennessee, graduated from Cumberland University, and became a lawyer. He served as a captain in the Spanish–American War in 1898. He was a member of the Tennessee House of Representatives 1893–97, then a judge in Tennessee 1903–07. He was a leading figure in the Pan-American conference at Montevideo in 1933. Like Roosevelt, he showed, as early as 1933, that he belonged emphatically to the internationalist, as opposed to the isolationist, school of thought.

Hume, John (1937–)

Northern Ireland politician, leader of the Social Democratic and Labour Party (SDLP) from 1979. Hume was a founder member of the Credit Union Party, which later became the SDLP. A member of Parliament since 1969 and a member of the European Parliament, he has been one of the chief architects of the peace process in Northern Ireland. In 1998 he shared the Nobel Peace Prize with David ◊Trimble in recognition of their efforts to further the peace process.

In 1993 he held talks with the Sinn Féin leader, Gerry Adams, on the possibility of securing peace in Northern Ireland. This prompted a joint Anglo-Irish peace initiative, which in turn led to a general cease-fire 1994–96. Despite the collapse of the cease-fire, Hume continued in his efforts to broker a settlement. This was achieved in the 1998 Good Friday Agreement and the SDLP polled strongly in the subsequent June 1998 elections to the new Northern Ireland assembly.

Further Reading

Drower, G M F *John Hume: Man of Peace* 1996, *John Hume: Peacemaker* 1995

Hume, J *Personal Views: Politics, Peace and Reconciliation in Ireland* 1996

Murray, G *John Hume and the SDLP: Impact and Survival in Northern Ireland* 1998

Routledge, P *John Hume: A Biography* 1998

Humphrey, Hubert (Horatio) (1911–1978)

US political leader, vice president 1965–69. He was elected to the US Senate in 1948, serving for three terms, and distinguished himself an eloquent and effective promoter of key legislation.

He was an unsuccessful candidate for his party's nomination for president in 1960. Serving as vice president under L B Johnson, he made an unsuccessful run for the presidency in 1968, and further unsuccessful attempts for the Democratic nomination in 1972 and 1976. He was re-elected to the Senate in 1970 and 1976.

Humphrey was born in Wallace, South Dakota, and trained as a pharmacist. Settling in Minnesota, he became active in Democratic party politics and was elected mayor of Minneapolis in 1945. He strongly supported the 1964 Civil Rights Act.

Hun Sen (1950–)

Cambodian political leader, prime minister 1985–93, deputy prime minister from 1993, and single effective leader from July 1997. His leadership was characterized by the promotion of economic liberalization and a thawing in relations with exiled non-Khmer opposition forces as a prelude to a compromise political settlement. After the defeat of his Cambodian People's Party (CCP) in the 1993 elections, Hun Sen agreed to participate in a power-sharing arrangement as second premier. In July 1997 he launched a successful coup to oust first deputy prime minister, Prince Norodom Ranariddh, and secure full effective control over Cambodia. In February 1998 he accepted a Japanese-brokered peace plan to allow for Ranariddh's return, after he was found guilty in a March 1998 show trial and then pardoned by his father, King Norodom Sihanouk.

Born into a peasant family in the eastern province of Kampang-Cham, Hun Sen joined the Khmer Rouge in 1970. He rose to become a regiment commander, but, disillusioned, defected to the Vietnam-based anti-Khmer Cambodian forces in 1977. On his return to Cambodia after the Vietnamese-backed communist takeover, he served as foreign minister in 1979 before taking over as prime minister in 1985. From 1991 until the United Nations-administered elections in 1993, he ruled the country in conjunction with the UN Transitional Authority in Cambodia and representatives of the warring factions. See photograph on page 395.

Hurd, Douglas (Richard), Baron Hurd of Westwell (1930–)

British Conservative politician, home secretary 1985–89 and foreign secretary 1989–95. In November 1990 he was an unsuccessful candidate in the Tory leadership contest following Margaret Thatcher's unexpected resignation.

Hurd was born in Marlborough, Wiltshire, and entered the House of Commons in 1974, representing Witney in Oxfordshire from 1983. He was made a junior minister by Margaret Thatcher, and the sudden resignation of Leon Brittan projected him into the home secretary's post. He was appointed foreign secretary in 1989 in the reshuffle that followed Nigel Lawson's resignation as chancellor of the Exchequer, and retained his post in Prime Minister John Major's new cabinet, formed after the 1992 general election. He was replaced as foreign secretary in the reshuffle that followed Major's re-election as party leader in July 1995, having earlier announced his intention to retire from Parliament at the 1997 election. He was created a Baron in 1997.

Hurd was in the diplomatic service 1952–66, serving in Beijing and at the United Nations in New York and Rome. He then joined the Conservative research department and became a secretary to the party leader Edward Heath. As a hobby, he writes thrillers.

Husák, Gustáv (1913–1991)

Czechoslovak politician, leader of the Communist Party of Czechoslovakia (CCP) 1969–87 and president 1975–89. After the 1968 Prague Spring of liberalization, his task was to restore control, purge the CCP, and oversee the implementation of a new, federalist constitution. He was deposed in the popular uprising of November–December 1989 and expelled from the CCP in February 1990.

Husák, a lawyer, was active in the Resistance movement during World War II, and afterwards in the Slovak Communist Party (SCP), and was imprisoned on political grounds 1951–60. Rehabilitated, he was appointed first secretary of the SCP in 1968 and CCP leader 1969–87. As titular state president he pursued a policy of cautious reform. He stepped down as party leader in 1987, and was replaced as state president by Václav ◊Havel in December 1989 following the 'velvet revolution'.

FURTHER READING

Husák, Gustáv *Gustáv Husák, President of Czechoslovakia: Speeches and Writings* 1986

Hu Shi or *Hu Shih* (1891–1962)

Chinese liberal scholar and reformer. He wrote extensively on Chinese philosophy, but is best known for his championing of *bai hua*, the new Chinese vernacular that would make literature accessible to the masses. An opponent of communism, he served the Nationalist government as ambassador to the USA 1938–42 and United Nations in 1957, and was president of the Academia Sinica of Taiwan 1958–62.

◊Lawrence persuaded him, in 1916, to join the Arab Revolt against Turkish rule, when he was proclaimed the independent king of the Hejaz region of Arabia. In 1919 he proclaimed himself king of all the Arab countries. This led to conflict with ◊Ibn Saud of the neighbouring emirate of Nejd. Hussein accepted the caliphate in 1924, but was forced to abdicate in 1924 by Ibn Saud. He took refuge in Cyprus and died in Ammam, Jordan.

One of his sons, ◊Ali ibn Hussein, succeeded him as ruler, but was deposed within a year by Ibn Saud, who proclaimed himself king of Hejaz. Another son, Abdullah ibn Hussein, became king of Jordan, while another, ◊Faisal I, became king of Iraq. Hussein was the great-grandfather of King ◊Hussein ibn Talal of Jordan.

FURTHER READING

Alangari, H *The Struggle for Power in Arabia: Ibn Saud, Hussein and Great Britain, 1914–1924* 1997

Hussein ibn Ali (1856–1931)

King of the Hejaz 1916–24 and founder of the modern Hashemite dynasty. Emir (grand sherif) of the Muslim holy city of Mecca 1908–16, at the start of World War I he sided with the Turks and Germany. However, T E

Hussein ibn Talal (1935–1999)

King of Jordan 1952–99. By 1967 he had lost all his kingdom west of the River Jordan in the Arab-Israeli Wars, and in 1970 suppressed the Palestine Liberation Organization (PLO) acting as a guerrilla force against his rule on the remaining East Bank territories. Subsequently, he became a moderating force in Middle Eastern politics, and in 1994 signed a peace agreement

◆ HUSSEIN, SADDAM (1937–) ◆

Iraqi politician, in power from 1968, president from 1979. He presided over the Iran–Iraq war 1980–88, and harshly repressed Kurdish rebels in northern Iraq. He annexed Kuwait in 1990 but was driven out by a US-dominated coalition army in February 1991. Defeat in the Gulf War led to unrest, and both the Kurds in the north and Shi'ites in the south rebelled. His savage repression of both revolts led to charges of genocide. In 1995, to counter evidence of rifts among his closest supporters, he called a presidential election, in which he was elected (unopposed) with 99.6% of the vote. In September 1996 his involvement in Kurdish faction fighting in northern Iraq provoked air retaliation by US forces.

Hussein joined the Arab Ba'ath Socialist Party as a young man and soon became involved in revolutionary activities. In 1959 he was sentenced to death and took refuge in Egypt, but a coup in 1963 made his return possible, although in the following year he was imprisoned for plotting to overthrow the regime he had helped to install. After his release he took a leading part in the 1968 revolution, removing the civilian government and establishing a Revolutionary Command Council (RCC). At first discreetly, and then more openly, Hussein strengthened his position and in 1979 became RCC chair and state president, progressively eliminating real or imagined opposition factions as he gained increasing dictatorial control.

In 1977 Saddam Hussein al-Tikriti abolished the use of surnames in Iraq to conceal the fact that a large number of people in the government and ruling party all came from his home village of Tikrit and therefore bore the same surname. Ruthless in the pursuit of his objectives, he fought a bitter war against Iran 1980–88, with US economic aid, and opposed Kurdish rebels

with Israel, ending a 46-year-old state of war between the two countries.

A great-grandson of ◊Hussein ibn Ali, he became king following the mental incapacitation of his father, Talal. After Iraq's annexation of Kuwait in 1990 he attempted to mediate between the opposing sides, at the risk of damaging his relations with both sides. In 1993 he publicly distanced himself from the Iraqi leader Saddam ◊Hussein. He dismissed his brother as heir-apparent the month before his death and was succeeded by his eldest son Abdullah ibn Hussein.

FURTHER READING
Dallas, R *King Hussein: A Life on the Edge* 1998
Dann, U *Hussein and the Challenge of Arab Radicalism,* 1989, *King Hussein's Strategy of Survival* 1992
Hussein, King *Uneasy Lies the Head* 1962
Lunt, J *Hussein of Jordan: A Political Biography* 1990

Hu Yaobang (1915–1989)

Chinese communist politician, reformist leader of the Chinese Communist Party (CCP) 1981–87.

Born into a poor peasant family in Hunan province, Hu left home at the age of 15 to join the communists as a child soldier. He became involved in propaganda and organization and was a political commissar during the 1934–35 Long March. In 1941 he served under Deng Xiaoping and became his trusted and loyal protégé. He followed his patron to provincial administration in southwestern China 1949–51 and then moved to Beijing, in 1952, to become head of the Communist Youth League and in 1956 gained entry to the CCP Central Committee. Hu was purged as a 'capitalist roader' at the start of the 1966–69 Cultural Revolution. He was dismissed from his post as CCP leader in Shaanxi province and sent into the countryside for 're-education', working on a dairy farm. He was rehabilitated in 1972 but disgraced again when Deng fell from prominence in 1976.

In December 1978, with Deng established in power, Hu was inducted into the CCP Politburo and became head (general secretary) of the revived policy-making CCP Secretariat in February 1980 and CCP chair in June 1981, replacing Hua Guofeng. Working in tandem with Prime Minister Zhao Ziyang, he presided over a radical overhaul of the party structure and personnel and attempted to quicken reaction against the ideology of Mao Zedong. Lacking a formal education, he was a more direct and earthy speaker than the urbane Zhao, but was equally flexible and liberal in his policy outlook. He was also the first CCP leader publicly to wear a Western business suit. However, in January 1987 he was dismissed for his relaxed handling of a wave of student unrest in December 1986, which had been allowed to get out of control. Hu's death, in April 1989, ignited the prodemocracy movement, which was eventually crushed in Tiananmen Square in June 1989. Depicted as the 'soul of China', he acted as a unifying symbol who had combined traditional socialist virtues with awareness of the necessity of Western-influenced modernizing reform.

FURTHER READING
Pang, Pang *The Death of Hu Yaobang* 1989
Yang, Zhong Mei *Hu Yao Bang: A Chinese Biography* 1988

---

seeking independence, using chemical weapons against civilian populations. The 1990 Kuwait annexation followed a long-running border dispute and was prompted by the need for more oil resources after the expensive war against Iran. Saddam, who had enjoyed US support for being the enemy of Iran and had used poison gas against his own people in Kurdistan without any falling-off in trade with the West, suddenly found himself almost universally condemned.

Iraq's defeat in the ensuing Gulf War undermined Saddam's position as the country's leader; when the Kurds rebelled again after the war, he sent the remainder of his army to crush them, bringing international charges of genocide against him and causing hundreds of thousands of Kurds to flee their homes in northern Iraq. His continued indiscriminate bombardment of Shi'ites in southern Iraq led the United Nations (UN) to impose a 'no-fly zone' in the area in August 1992. Another potential confrontation with the West was averted in 1994. However, in September 1996 the USA retaliated against Hussein's encroachment into UN protected territories in northern Iraq, carrying out missile attacks on Iraqi military bases in the area.

His refusal to comply with a UN resolution to provide access to his suspected stores of weapons of mass destruction resulted in strong economic sanctions and then, in late 1998, to US-led air strikes on military and strategic targets throughout the country.

Saddam's son, Uday, was crippled in an assassination attempt in January 1997. The attack was carried out as part of a feud by the family of a senior Iraqi general (Uday's uncle) killed by the Iraqi leader for criticism of his regime seven years earlier.

FURTHER READING
Bullock, John, and Morris, Harvey *Saddam's War* 1991
Henderson, Simon *Instant Empire: Saddam Hussein's Ambition for Iraq* 1991
Karsh, E, and Rantsi, I *Saddam Hussein* 1991

Huysmans, Camille (1871–1968)

Belgian politician. He entered parliament as a Socialist in 1910. From 1905 to 1921 he was secretary of the Second International, and between the world wars held several posts in the Belgian cabinet. He served as burgomaster of Antwerp 1933–40, but escaped to England during World War II; he was reinstated as burgomaster in 1944. He was prime minister in a postwar coalition government 1946–47 and subsequently minister of education 1947–49. Huysmans was born in Bilsen, and was educated in Liège, Belgium.

Hyde, Douglas (1860–1949)

Irish writer, scholar, and propagandist, president of Ireland 1938–45. He became president of the Gaelic League in 1893. His translations of Irish poetry and prose developed an English style that reflected Gaelic idiom and syntax, and had considerable influence on the younger writers of the Irish literary revival. However, he attempted to resist the politicization of the Gaelic League, and resigned as its president in 1915. He was a member of the Senate from 1925, and was chosen as president of Ireland by agreement between the parties in 1938.

Hyde was professor of Irish at University College Dublin 1909–32. His published works include *Love Songs of Connacht* (1893), his *Literary History of Ireland* (1899) and *The Religious Songs of Connacht* (1906). He wrote *Casadh ant Sugáin* (1901), the first modern play in Irish.

Born in County Sligo, Hyde studied law at Trinity College, Dublin. His 1892 inaugural address as president of the National Literary Society was a rallying cry for those who wished to arrest the decline in the use of the Irish language. It has been seen as a key moment in that Gaelic element in reinvigorated national sentiment around the turn of the century.

Hymans, Paul (1865–1941)

Belgian statesman and diplomat. He entered parliament as a Liberal in 1900. In 1914, after the German invasion of Belgium, he travelled to the USA on a mission to President Woodrow Wilson. He was Belgian minister in London, England, 1915–17, minister of economic affairs in 1917, and minister of foreign affairs 1918–20, 1924–25, 1927–34, and 1934–35. Hymans attended the conference at Versailles in 1918, and represented Belgium at the Peace Conference in 1919. Hymans was born in Ixelles, Belgium, and was educated at Brussels University.

Hyndman, Henry Mayers (1842–1921)

British socialist. The first important British-born Marxist, he founded the Democratic Federation in 1881 (renamed the Social Democratic Federation (SDF) in 1884) and devoted his life to revolutionary propaganda and agitation.

Hyndman was born in London to upper-middle-class parents. After leaving Cambridge, he played cricket for the Sussex county eleven and worked for the *Pall Mall Gazette*. In 1881 he published *England For All*, which presented Marxist theories in popular form. Hyndman did not acknowledge Marx as the book's inspiration, arguing, with a typical chauvinism, that British workers would have been put off by foreign names. But he failed to convince Marx and Engels, who refused to speak to him again.

Hyndman edited the SDF newspaper *Justice*, but his superior manner tended to sharpen divisions in the movement. The SDF concentrated on propaganda rather than trade-union activity, although several 'new unionists' such as Tom Mann, Ben Tillett, and Will Thorne were SDF members. In 1884 the Socialist League broke away from the SDF and Hyndman's influence was further weakened by the rise of the Independent Labour Party after 1893. Mobilizing support among the unemployed, he was tried and acquitted for his part in the West End riots of 1886.

Hyndman stood for Parliament four times in Burnley without success. Attempts at cooperation with the Labour Party failed, and the SDF remained a small fringe group on the left of British politics. In 1911 it merged into the British Socialist Party, which opposed British involvement in World War I. Hyndman supported the war and formed a rival National Socialist Party in 1916. During the war he was a Labour representative on the consumer council of the ministry of food.

Ibáñez del Campo, Carlos (1877–1960)

Chilean military dictator and president 1927–31 and 1952–58. His administration instituted programmes of public works and educational and labour reform, but the effects of global economic depression in 1931 resulted in civil unrest and he was forced into exile. During his second term in office, opposition in congress and his own frailty hampered his aims to curb inflation and to reform bureaucratic governmental structures. On his exit from office, Chile's economic condition was critical.

Ibáñez del Campo served as minister of war 1925–27 and vice president in 1927, later becoming president upon the forced resignation of President Emiliano Figueroa.

He returned from exile in 1939 and after several attempts to regain power during the period 1937–1942, he gained election to the senate in 1949, and a second presidential term in 1952.

Ibarruri, Dolores, known as *La Pasionaria* ('the passion flower') (1895–1989)

Spanish Basque politician, journalist, and orator; she was first elected to the Cortes (Spanish parliament) in 1936. She helped to establish the Popular Front government and was a Loyalist leader in the Civil War. When General Franco came to power in 1939 she left Spain for the USSR, where she was active in the Communist Party. She returned to Spain in 1977 after Franco's death and was re-elected to the Cortes (at the age of 81) in the first parliamentary elections for 40 years.

She joined the Spanish Socialist Party in 1917 and wrote for a workers' newspaper under the pen name La Pasionaria.

Ibn Saud, Abdul Aziz al-Saud (1880–1953)

See page 210.

Icaza, Jorge (1906–1978)

Ecuadorian author and novelist His play *El Dictador*, scripted in 1933, gained widespread criticism and evoked censorship by the government. His first novel, *Huasipungo* (1934), was openly critical of government apathy towards the treatment of native Indian peoples. He was a diplomat in Russia and Eastern Europe during the period 1973–77.

Ichikawa, Fusaye (1893–1981)

Japanese feminist and politician. In 1924 she formed the Women's Suffrage League in Japan. Following World War II she became head of the New Japan Women's League, which secured the vote for women in 1945, and went on to fight for their wider rights. She campaigned against legalized prostitution and served in the Japanese Diet (parliament) 1953–71, where she continued to press for an end to bureaucratic corruption. After defeat in 1971 she was returned to parliament in 1974 and 1980.

Starting her working life as a teacher, she moved to Tokyo as a young woman and became involved in politics and feminism. She helped to found the New Women's Association in about 1920, which successfully fought for the right of women to attend political meetings. During her time in the USA 1921–24 she was impressed by the US suffrage movement.

Ickes, Harold LeClair (1874–1952)

US public official. A liberal Republican, he was appointed secretary of the interior by F D Roosevelt in 1933. As director of the Public Works Administration (PWA, established in 1935), he administered Roosevelt's New Deal development projects. He served briefly under President Harry Truman, but resigned from the cabinet in 1946.

Born in Blair County, Pennsylvania, Ickes was educated at the University of Chicago and was admitted to the bar in 1907. After resigning from his political post, he wrote a newspaper column and published several autobiographical works. *The Secret Diary of Harold L Ickes* appeared in 1953.

Idris I or *Mohammed Idris al-Mahdi* (1889–1983)

Libyan head of the Sanusiya order and king 1951–69. He played a major role in both the struggle for independence from the Italians and the preservation of his country's unity and integrity. His pro-Western attitude, especially towards the presence of US and British military bases, was a source of friction between him and President Gamal ◊Nasser of Egypt.

Idris came to be criticized for his lack of enthusiasm regarding the Arab cause and his reign was to be challenged particularly by young educated Libyans, most of them devotees of Nasser ideals. He was overthrown in a bloodless military coup in 1969 and died in Egypt.

Iglesias, Pablo (1850–1925)

Spanish politician, founder of the Spanish Socialist Party (Partido Socialista Obrero Español, PSOE) in 1879. In 1911 he became the first socialist deputy to be elected to the Cortes (Spanish parliament).

Ikeda, Hayato (1899–1965)

Japanese politician and economist, prime minister 1960–64. He introduced an 'income doubling policy' of economic growth and higher living standards. He was a supporter of the US–Japan Security Treaty of 1960, and developed a low-key style in international relations during the postwar recovery period.

Educated in Kyoto, he became finance minister of the Liberal (Conservative) Party in 1949.

Iliescu, Ion (1930–)

Romanian president 1990–96. A former member of the Romanian Communist Party (PCR) and of Nicolae Ceauşescu's government, Iliescu swept into power on Ceauşescu's fall as head of the National Salvation Front.

Iliescu was elected a member of the PCR central committee in 1968 and became its propaganda secretary in 1971. Conflict over the launching of a 'cultural revolution' and the growth of Ceauşescu's personality cult led to Iliescu's removal from national politics: he was sent to Timişoara as chief of party propaganda. At the outbreak of the 'Christmas revolution' in 1989, Iliescu was one of the first leaders to emerge, becoming president of the Provisional Council of National Unity in February 1990. He won an overwhelming victory in the presidential elections in May 1990, despite earlier controversy over his hard line. He was defeated in the second ballot run-off race for the presidency in November 1996.

Iliescu was educated at the Bucharest Polytechnic Institute and the Institute for Energetics in Moscow.

FURTHER READING
Iliescu, Ion *Revolutia traita* 1995

Illia, Arturo (1900–1983)

Argentine politician and president 1963–66. His administration inherited a nation with severe econ-

---

◆ IBN SAUD, ABDUL AZIZ AL-SAUD (1880–1953) ◆

First king of Saudi Arabia, 1932–53. His personal hostility to ◊Hussein ibn Ali, the British-supported political and religious leader of the Al Hijaz (Hejaz) region of western Arabia, meant that he stood back from the Arab Revolt of World War I, organized by T E ◊Lawrence and in which ◊Abdullah ibn Hussein and ◊Faisal I of Iraq participated. However, after the war, supported by the Wahhabi-inspired Ikhwan (Brethren), Ibn Saud extended his dominions to the Red Sea coast, capturing Jedda and the Muslim holy cities of Mecca and Medina (with their lucrative pilgrimage revenue). By 1921, all central Arabia had been brought under his rule, and in 1924 he successfully invaded the Hejaz, defeating Hussein ibn Ali, who, in 1919, had proclaimed himself king of all the Arab countries. In January 1926, at Mecca, he was proclaimed king of Hejaz and Nejd and in 1932 the territories were unified, under the title 'Kingdom of Saudi Arabia'. In 1934 Saudi forces attacked Yemen and captured further territories in the south, including the towns of Najran and Jizan.

Oil was discovered in 1938, with oil concessions being leased to US and British companies, and exports began in 1946. Between 1947 and 1952, during the 'first oil boom', the country was transformed from a poor pastoral kingdom into an affluent modernizing state, as annual oil revenues increased from $10 million to $212 million. During World War II, Ibn Saud remained neutral, but sympathetic towards the UK and the USA. In 1945 he founded the Arab League to encourage Arab unity.

His father was the son of Faisal, the sultan of Nejd (Najd), in central Arabia, at whose capital, Riyadh, Ibn Saud was born. The al-Saud family had dominated central Arabian politics since the mid-18th century, when it had established itself as the standard bearer of the Wahabi fundamentalist Islamic sect. In 1891 a rival north Arabian dynasty, the Rashidis, seized Riyadh, and Ibn Saud went into exile with his father, who resigned his claim to the throne in favour of his son, who was brought up in Kuwait. In 1902, following a Bedouin (nomadic Arab tribe) revolt, Ibn Saud recaptured Riyadh and recovered the kingdom. By 1914 he controlled much of the former Turkish possessions along the Persian Gulf, and in 1915 Britain recognized him as emir of Hasa (eastern Arabia) and Nejd.

Ibn Saud was a Arab tribal warrior of the classic mould, matching his military prowess with a large number of wives and children. He ruled in a personal and idiosyncratic manner and ran the country as a family state, being assisted by some of his 43 sons. His eldest son, Saud, was made crown prince in 1933, and became king on Fahd's death in November 1953. Another of Ibn's elder sons, Faisal, served as his foreign minister.

FURTHER READING
Hoden, D, and Johns, R *The House of Saud* 1981
Howarth, D A *The Desert King* 1964

omic problems. Although economic restructuring had brought about some improvements, Illia was unable to deal effectively in restoring stable economic conditions. His attempts to disunite the Peronist camp failed, and led to a Peronist-supported coup in 1966 that deposed Illia from power and resulted in General Juan Carlos ◊Ongania taking up office.

A physician by profession, Illia entered political life in the 1930s. During the period 1948–52, he was a minority political figure in the Peronist-dominated national legislature. In the 1963 elections, Illia, the candidate for the People's Radical Civic Union, gained presidential office, but with only 25% of the vote.

Illich, Ivan (1926–)

US radical philosopher and activist, born in Austria. His works, which include *Deschooling Society* (1971), *Towards a History of Need* (1978), and *Gender* (1983), are a critique of contemporary economic development, especially in the Third World.

Illich was born in Vienna and has lived in the USA and Latin America. He believes that modern technology and bureaucratic institutions are destroying peasant skills and self-sufficiency and creating a new

Abdul Aziz al-Saud Ibn Saud, 1911. *AKG London*

In a consumer society there are inevitably two kinds of slaves: the prisoners of addiction and the prisoners of envy.

IVAN ILLICH *Tools for Conviviality* chap 3

---

form of dependency: on experts, professionals, and material goods. True liberation, he believes, can only be achieved by abolishing the institutions on which authority rests, such as schools and hospitals.

Inácio da Silva, Luiz, popularly known as *Lula* (1945–)

Brazilian politician and trade-union activist. In 1980 he founded the Partido de Trabalhadores (PT; Worker's Party), the first independent labour party associated with the *autêntico* branch of the trade-union movement. By the 1990s it was the the largest left-wing opposition party in the country.

Lula became renowned in Brazil for his strong trade-union links, which originated from his early days as a trade-union activist in a car factory in São Paulo. In 1986, Lula's election as federal deputy enabled him to expand his political career, representing the PT in congress. The growth of the party continued, with coalitions being formed between other parties. By 1988, the party had majorities in many urban areas, including São Paulo, Vitória, and Porto Alegre.

The appeal of the party ultimately allowed Lula to stand for the 1989 presidency elections, but he lost to Fernando Collor de Mello by a margin of 6%. His attempt to become president in 1994 also failed when Fernando Henrique Cardoso was elected.

FURTHER READING
Branford, Sue, and Kucinski, Bernardo *Brazil Carnival of the Oppressed: Lula and the Brazilian Worker's Party* 1995

Indritz, Phineas (1916–1997)

US attorney and women's rights activist. Described as 'an unsung hero of the movement for social justice and equal treatment under law', Indritz authored the Pregnancy Disability Act of 1978 and additional Maryland legislation prohibiting discrimination against women. He worked with Catherine East, Mary Eastwood, and others to motivate the founding of the National Organization of Women (NOW) and authored much of the civil-rights legislation that later became law.

Born in Silver Spring, Maryland, Indritz became a respected attorney in Washington, DC, and gave generously of his time and talents in writing appellate court briefs in women's rights cases. He was presented with a pro bono award in 1993 from the NAACP Legal Defense and Education Fund.

Ingraham, Hubert A (1947–)

Bahamian politician, prime minister from 1992. A minister of housing and social services in Lynden ◊Pindling's Progressive Liberal Party (PLP) administration, he was dismissed from the cabinet in 1984 and from the PLP in 1986 after speaking out against corruption. He was elected as an independent in 1987, and became leader of the Free National Movement (FNM) in 1990. Campaigning on an anti-corruption platform, Ingraham led the FNM to a stunning victory in 1992, ending 25 years of rule by Pindling. His government was successful in attracting inward foreign investment, promoted political decentralization, and introduced a minimum wage. It secured re-election in 1997.

Ingraham trained and worked as a lawyer and joined the ruling PLP in the 1970s, being elected to the House of Assembly in 1977, and appointed minister in 1982.

Inönü, Ismet (1884–1973)

Turkish politician and soldier, president 1938–50, and prime minister 1923–38 and 1961–65. He continued the modernization and westernization of Turkey begun by the republic's founder Kemal Atatürk, and kept his country out of World War II. After 1945 he attempted to establish democratic institutions.

He was born in Smyrna, in Asia Minor, and pursued a career as an army officer before and during World War I. During the Turkish War of Independence 1919–22 he was Atatürk's chief of army staff, and stopped the Greek advance in Anatolia at the first and second battles of Inönü in 1921 (from which he later took his name). Representing Turkey at the peace conference, he signed the Treaty of Lausanne in 1923. He was the first prime minister of Turkey and was elected president after the death of Atatürk in 1938. Despite the efforts of the British prime minister Winston Churchill to bring Turkey into World War II, Inönü managed to keep the country neutral until 1945. Although a supporter of one-party rule between 1939 and 1946, he later became a champion of democracy. Losing power to Adnan Menderes in the first free elections in 1950, Inönü was leader of the opposition until he became prime minister in 1961 after the military coup of 1960 and execution of Menderes in 1961. He lost power to the pro-Western Suleyman Demirel in 1965.

Inouye, Daniel Ken (1924–)

US Democrat politician, senator from Hawaii. From 1962 he represented Hawaii in the US Senate on behalf of the Democratic Party. During the early 1970s, he served on the Senate committee that investigated the Watergate scandal, which led to the resignation of President Richard ◊Nixon.

Born in Honolulu, Inouye studied law at the University of Hawaii and George Washington University Law School. He fought bravely in World War II, losing his right arm in action, and returned to Hawaii, where he became an assistant public prosecutor in 1953. In 1959, after Hawaii became the 50th state of the Union, he became its representative and the first Japanese-American member in the US Congress.

Inukai, Tsuyoshi (1855–1932)

Japanese politician, prime minister 1931–32. He first achieved a ministerial position in 1898 and after a long political career eventually became prime minister. His policies angered the military and he was assassinated in an attempted coup in May 1932.

Initially a journalist, he was involved in politics from 1882 and was elected to the Diet (parliament) in Japan's first general election in 1890.

Irigoyen, or *Yrigoyen*, Hipólito (1850–1933)

Argentine politician and president 1916–22 and 1928–30. He became leader of the Radical Civic Union Party (bourgeois reformist group) in 1896 and worked for electoral reform, which, when it came in 1912, brought him to power as the first radical president, replacing the landowning oligarchy. He maintained Argentine neutrality during World War I.

During his second term his administration was plagued by severe economic depression and he was deposed by a military coup.

Isaacs, Rufus Daniel, 1st Marquess of Reading (1860–1935)

British Liberal lawyer and politician. As Lord Chief Justice he tried the Irish nationalist Roger Casement in 1916. He was viceroy of India 1921–26, and foreign secretary in 1931.

Itagaki, Taisuke (1837–1919)

Japanese military and political leader. Involved in the overthrow of the Tokugawa shogunate and the ◊Meiji restoration of 1868, Itagaki became leader of the people's rights movement. He was the founder of Japan's first political party, the Jiyūtō (Liberal Party), in 1881.

After his ennoblement in 1887 he retained the leadership of the party and cooperated with ◊Itō Hirobumi in the establishment of parliamentary government in the 1890s.

Itō, Hirobumi (1841–1909)

Japanese politician, prime minister 1885–88, 1892–96, 1898, and 1900–01. He was a key figure in the modernization of Japan and was involved in the ◊Meiji restoration of 1868 and in official missions to study forms of government in the USA and Europe in the 1870s and 1880s. He played a major role in drafting the Meiji constitution of 1889.

Itō was a samurai from Chōshū, a feudal domain that rebelled against the shogunate in the 1850s–60s. In 1863 he became one of the first Japanese to study in the UK, and in 1871–73 he was a member of the Iwakura mission to Europe and the USA. Given responsibility for drafting the constitution, he went abroad again 1882–83 to study European models. Following a spell as resident general in Korea 1906–09, he was assassinated by a Korean nationalist – an event that led to Japan's annexation of that country.

Politically Itō was a moderate, favouring negotiation and compromise.

Izetbegović, Alija (1925–)

Bosnia-Herzegovinan politician, president from 1990. A lifelong opponent of communism, he founded the Party of Democratic Action (PDA) in 1990, ousting the communists in the multiparty elections that year. Adopting a moderate stance during the civil war in Bosnia-Herzegovina, he sought an honourable peace for his country in the face of ambitious demands from Serb and Croat political leaders, and signed the Dayton peace accord in November 1995. He was re-elected president of a three-member collective presidency in September 1996 (with Serb nationalist Momcil Krajisnik and Croat Kresimir Zubak) and September 1998 (when Nikola Poplasen outpolled the pragmatic Western-backed Biljana Plavsic to become president of the Serb Republic).

Born in Bosarski Šamac, Bosnia, Izetbegović was educated at Sarajevo University. A former legal adviser, he was imprisoned for 'pan-Islamic activity' 1946–48 and 1983–88.

FURTHER READING

Izetbegović, Alija *The Islamic Declaration: A Programme for the Islamization of Muslims and the Muslim Peoples* 1990, *Islam Between East and West* 1993

Jackson, George (died 1971)

US revolutionary. Convicted of a $70 robbery and sent to San Quentin prison, Jackson became a best-selling writer (with his book *Blood in My Eye* 1990) and a 'revolutionary hero' of the civil-rights movement. On 21 August 1971, he led the infamous San Quentin massacre, which resulted in his death and the deaths of five others. Two months later, Stephen Bingham was indicted for murder and conspiracy for allegedly smuggling the gun to Jackson.

FURTHER READING

Jackson, George, et al *Soledad Brother: The Prison Letters of George Jackson* 1994

Jackson, Glenda (1936–)

British actress and politician, Labour member of Parliament from 1992, and parliamentary undersecretary for transport from 1997. Among her films are the Oscar-winning *Women in Love* (1969), *Sunday Bloody Sunday* (1971), and *A Touch of Class* (1973). On television she played Queen Elizabeth I in *Elizabeth R* (1971).

In 1990 she was chosen by the Labour Party as a candidate for Parliament and was elected member for Hampstead and Highgate in North London in April 1992.

Jackson, Jesse Louis (1941–)

US Democratic politician, a cleric and campaigner for minority rights. He contested his party's 1984 and 1988 presidential nominations in an effort to increase voter registration and to put black issues on the national agenda. He is an eloquent public speaker, and in 1998 emerged as a spiritual adviser to President Bill Clinton.

We've removed the ceiling above our dreams. There are no more impossible dreams.

JESSE JACKSON *Independent* 9 June 1988

Born in North Carolina and educated in Chicago, Jackson became a powerful Baptist preacher and black activist politician, working first with the civil-rights leader Martin Luther King, Jr, then on building the political machine that gave Chicago a black mayor in 1983. Jackson sought to construct what he called a rainbow coalition of ethnic-minority and socially deprived groups. He took the lead in successfully campaigning for US disinvestment in South Africa in 1986.

Jagan, Cheddi Berret (1918–1997)

Guyanese left-wing politician, president from 1992. He led the People's Progressive Party (PPA) from 1950, and was the first prime minister of British Guyana 1961–64. As presidential candidate in August 1992, he opposed privatization as leading to 'recolonization'. The PPA won a decisive victory, and Jagan became president (succeeding Desmond Hoyte). Vice president Samuel Hinds succeeded to the presidency on Jagan's death.

FURTHER READING

Cheddi, Jagan *Forbidden Freedom: The Story of British Guiana* 1954

Jagan, Janet (1920–)

Guyanese left-wing politician, president from 1997. With her husband, Cheddi ◊Jagan, she cofounded the left-wing People's Progressive Party (PPP) in 1950 and was its general secretary until 1970. When Cheddi won the presidency in 1992 she became Guyana's first lady and ambassador at large. On his death in March 1997 she became interim prime minister and then, after the December 1997 general election, president in her own right. The results of the election were disputed by the opposition and in January 1998 it was agreed that they would be independently audited.

Born in Chicago, USA, she met and married Cheddi Jagan in 1943 while she was studying in the USA. She is Guyana's first female and first white head of state.

Jakeš, Miloš (1922–)

Czech communist politician, a member of the Politburo from 1981 and party leader 1987–89. A conservative, he supported the Soviet invasion of Czechoslovakia in 1968. He was forced to resign in November 1989 following a series of prodemocracy mass rallies.

Jakeš, an electrical engineer, joined the Communist Party of Czechoslovakia (CCP) in 1945 and studied in Moscow 1955–58. As head of the CCP's central control commission, he oversaw the purge of reformist personnel after the suppression of the 1968 Prague Spring. In December 1987 he replaced Gustáv Husák as CCP leader.

Although he enjoyed close relations with the Soviet leader Mikhail Gorbachev, Jakeš was a cautious reformer who was unpopular with the people.

James, Edison C (1943–)

Dominican left-of-centre politician, prime minister from 1995. He formed the United Workers' Party (UWP) in 1988, leading it in 1990 to become the main opposition to Eugenia ◊Charles's Dominica Freedom Party (DFP), ahead of the long-established Dominica Labour Party (DLP). The UWP narrowly won the 1995 general election and James became prime minister, also holding the foreign affairs, labour, and legal affairs portfolios.

James was born in Marigot, northeast Dominica, and trained as an agronomist at UK universities 1969–76. On his return he worked as a farm improvement officer and in agricultural management, and was general manager of the Dominica Banana Marketing Corporation from 1980 to 1987.

Jameson, Leander Starr (1853–1917)

British colonial administrator, born in Edinburgh, Scotland. In South Africa, early in 1896, he led the Jameson Raid from Mafeking into the Transvaal to support the non-Boer colonists there, in an attempt to overthrow the government (for which he served some months in prison). Returning to South Africa, he succeeded Cecil Rhodes as leader of the Progressive Party of Cape Colony, where he was prime minister 1904–08. He was created 1st Baronet in 1911.

Jaruzelski, Wojciech Witold (1923–)

Polish army general, appointed first secretary of the Polish United Workers Party (PUWP) in 1981. He was responsible for the imposition of martial law in Poland in December 1981. He was prime minister 1981–85 and president 1985–90. During martial law he attempted to suppress the Solidarity trade union, interning its leaders and political dissidents. In 1989 he approved the 'Round Table' talks with the opposition that led to partially free parliamentary elections and to the appointment of a coalition government under a non-communist prime minister, Tadeusz ◊Mazowiecki.

Jaruzelski was deported to the USSR during World War II. In 1943 he joined the Polish Kościuszko Division formed in the USSR. In 1947 he became a member of the Polish Workers Party (PWP). From 1968 he was minister of defence and entered the central committee of the party in 1971. He remained a professional soldier throughout his career, simultaneously holding party functions. In 1987 he introduced a four-point plan for the demilitarization of Central Europe – the so-called Jaruzelski Plan. In December 1990 he resigned from all official posts.

FURTHER READING
Labedz, Leopold *Poland under Jaruzelski: A Comprehensive Source Book on Poland During and After Martial Law* 1984

Jaurès, (Auguste Marie Joseph) Jean (Léon) (1859–1914)

French socialist politician. He was considered a commanding intellectual presence within the socialist movement in France, through his writings (which included a magisterial social history of the French revolution), his oratory, and his journalism. In the decade leading up to the outbreak of World War I, Jaurès's impassioned opposition to the rising tide of militarism in Europe brought him centre stage within the Second International.

Born in southwestern France into a middle-class family with commercial and military connections, Jaurès trained at the Ecole Normale Supérieure and became a philosophy teacher and university lecturer in Toulouse before being elected to parliament 1885–89. A series of bitter strikes by miners and glassworkers in his native Tarn *département* in the 1890s helped shift his strongly republican convictions decisively leftwards. As a leader writer on the newspaper *La Petite République*, Jaurès took up Emile Zola's campaign to establish the innocence of the Jewish military captain Alfred Dreyfus, falsely convicted of treason. In parliament again as a deputy 1892–88 and 1902–14, he supported the participation of socialists in government and in 1902 helped create the first quasi-formal alliance between Radicals and socialists. This *bloc des gauches*, under Emile Combes's premiership, secured the separation of church and state. Founder of *L'Humanité* in 1904, and its editor until his death, Jaurès joined with Jules Guesde and Edouard Vaillant to unify France's hitherto organizationally fragmented socialist movement in 1905. Within the newly constituted French Section of the Second International (SFIO), Jaurès advocated a working partnership with the syndicalist General Confederation of Labour (CGT) that would respect the latter's organizational and political autonomy. He was assassinated in Paris by a young right-wing nationalist on 31 July 1914.

Javits, Jacob K(oppel) (1904–1986)

US senator. A liberal Republican, he served a district of New York City in the US House of Representatives 1947–54, as New York state attorney general 1954–57, and in the US Senate 1957–81. Although initially a supporter of the Vietnam War, he introduced the legislation that became the War Powers Act, restricting the president's power to commit troops abroad.

He was born in New York City.

Jawara, Dawda Kairaba (1924–)

Gambian politician, prime minister 1965–70 and president 1970–94. After entering politics in 1960 he progressed rapidly, becoming minister of education and then premier in 1962. Following full independence within the Commonwealth in 1965 he became prime minister and, with the adoption of republican status in 1970, he assumed the presidency. An abortive coup against him in 1981 was thwarted by Senegalese troops bringing the two countries closer together into the Senegambia confederation of 1982–89. He lost power in 1994 following a military coup.

Jawara had been re-elected in 1972, 1977, 1982, and 1987, but the coup in July 1994, staged by junior army officers, established a military council to oversee the activities of the civilian government. Jawara fled the country and Yahya Jammeh was named as his replacement.

Jay, Douglas Patrick Thomas, Baron Jay of Battersea (1907–1996)

British Labour politician. Elected member of Parliament for Battersea North in a 1946 by-election, he held the seat (known from 1974 as the Battersea division of Wandsworth) until 1983. Jay was financial secretary to the Treasury 1947–50 and shadow spokesperson on trade and treasury affairs 1951–62. Under Harold Wilson, Jay was president of the Board of Trade from 1964 until being sacked in 1967. Jay stood out as an opponent of the UK's entry into the European Economic Community (he campaigned for a 'no' vote in the 1975 referendum).

Jay emerged at the close of the 1930s as one of a generation of bright Labour economists, such as Hugh Gaitskell and Evan Durbin. He worked for *The Times* 1929–33, *The Economist* 1933–37, and the *Daily Herald* 1937–41. He worked at the Board of Trade from 1943 and was personal assistant to Prime Minister Clement Attlee after 1945.

Jay published various works, notably *The Socialist Case* (1937) and *Socialism in the New Society* (1962). In 1980 he published his memoirs, *Change and Fortune*. He was created Baron in 1987.

Jay, Margaret Ann, Baroness of Paddington in the City of Westminster (1939–)

British Labour minister for women and deputy leader of the House of Lords from 1997. Jay, created a life peer in 1992, was principal opposition spokesperson on health in the House of Lords 1995–97 and minister of state for health during part of 1997. She was appointed minister for women in the cabinet reshuffle in 1997. As leader of the House of Lords, she had the task in late 1998 of steering through a reluctant chamber the government's plans to scrap the right of hereditary peers to sit and vote in the House of Lords.

The daughter of former prime minister Jim Callaghan, Jay initially pursued a career in television journalism. In the mid-1980s she worked on one of the first TV programmes on AIDS, and as a result she was invited to become a trustee of the National AIDS Foundation which, in turn, led to her job as director of the National AIDS Trust 1988–92. Her involvement in the Trust widened her knowledge and interest in health issues, which became the focus of her political career during the mid-1990s. In her post as minister for women, Jay began working on the Labour government's future agenda for women, due to be launched early in 1999.

Jayawardene, Junius Richard (1906–1996)

Sri Lankan politician. Leader of the United Nationalist Party from 1973, he became prime minister in 1977 and the country's first president 1978–88. Jayawardene embarked on a free-market economic strategy, but was confronted with increasing Tamil–Sinhalese ethnic unrest, forcing the imposition of a state of emergency in 1983. In 1987 he signed the Colombo Accord, with the Indian prime minister Rajiv Gandhi, in an attempt to solve the Tamil dispute, but the employment of Indian troops to enforce the accord fanned unrest among the Sinhala community. Protest riots erupted and Jayawardene was targeted for assassination. He stepped down in 1988 and was succeeded by Ranasinghe Premadasa.

Jenkins, (David) Clive (1926–)

Welsh trade union leader. Jenkins was well known as a militant negotiator and a fluent controversialist, and as an advocate of British withdrawal from the European Economic Community. He was a member of the Trades Union Congress (TUC) General Council from 1974. He was a Metropolitan borough councillor 1954–60, editor of *Trade Union Affairs*, and author of several publications including *The Kind of Laws the Unions Ought to Want* (1968), which he co-authored with J Mortimer.

Jenkins was born in Port Talbot, Wales, where he was educated before going on to Swansea Technical College. He started work in a metallurgical test house in 1940. In 1946 he was branch secretary and area treasurer for the Association of Scientific Workers; in 1947 he was assistant Midlands divisional officer for ASSET (Association of Supervisory Staffs, Executives and Technicians). He became transport industrial officer in 1949, and national officer in 1954. He then served as general secretary of ASSET (1961–68) and, from 1970, as general secretary of the Association of Scientific, Technical, and Managerial Staffs.

Jenkins, Roy Harris, Baron Jenkins of Hillhead (1920–)

British politician, born in Monmouthshire, Wales. He became a Labour minister in 1964, was home secretary 1965–67 and 1974–76, and chancellor of the Exchequer 1967–70. He was president of the European Commission 1977–81. In 1981 he became one of the founders of the Social Democratic Party (SDP) and was elected as an SDP member of Parliament in 1982, but lost his seat in 1987. In the same year, he was elected chancellor of Oxford University and made a life peer. In 1997 he was appointed head of a commission, set up by the Labour government, to recommend, in 1998, a new voting system for elections to Parliament.

Jenkins was educated at Abersychan Grammar School and Balliol College, Oxford, where he became a close friend of the future Labour leader Hugh Gaitskell. He served in World War II, and became Labour MP for Southend 1948–50 and for Birmingham Stechford 1950–76. He was minister of aviation 1964–65, then home secretary and chancellor of the Exchequer under Harold Wilson. As chancellor he pursued policies that resulted in a record balance of payments surplus. In 1970 he became deputy leader of the Labour Party, but resigned in 1972 because of his disagreement with Wilson on the issue of UK entry to the European Community (now the European Union). Jenkins was a leading member of the pro-European supporters in the referendum campaign of 1975. He unsuccessfully contested the Labour leadership in 1976.

FURTHER READING
Campbell, John *Roy Jenkins: A Biography* 1983

Jiang Jie Shi or *Chiang Kai-shek* (1887–1975)

Chinese nationalist Kuomintang (Guomindang) general and politician, president of China 1928–31 and 1943–49, and of Taiwan 1949–75.

Born in Fenghua, in Zhejiang province, Jiang, a Christian, trained in military academies in China and in Japan, where he met Sun Zhong Shan (Sun Yat-sen), a Chinese republican, and joined the United Revolutionary League. Jiang returned to Shanghai to take part in the Republican Revolution of 1911 that overthrew the Qing dynasty of the Manchus and took a leading role in the Nationalists' 1915–16 military campaign against the northern warlord Yüan Shikai.

After visiting Russia in 1923 to study Soviet military systems, Jiang returned to China in 1924 to become head of the Whampoa Military Academy, which trained the new Kuomintang nationalist army. On the death, in 1925, of Sun Zhong Shan, the Kuomintang leader, Jiang became commander in chief of the nationalist armies in southern China and in 1926–27 joined with the Chinese Communist Party (CCP) to launch a successful 'Northern Expedition' against the northern warlords. However, in 1927 Jiang ended collaboration with the communists and sought their liquidation. He largely unified China in the mid-1930s, by pushing the communists northwards, in the 'Long March' of 1934–35.

Cooperation with the CCP was resumed in 1936 after the Xi'an Incident, in which Jiang was kidnapped by the Nationalist general Zhang Xueliang, since China needed to pool military strength in the struggle against the Japanese invaders of World War II. During the

> *We shall not talk lightly about sacrifice until we are driven to the last extremity which makes sacrifice inevitable.*
>
> JIANG JIE SHI Speech to Fifth Congress of the Guomindang

period of Chinese occupation, Jiang set up capital in Chongqing, in Sichuan province, in southwest China, and organized resistance. He was made supreme commander of the Allied forces in China from 1942. After the Japanese surrender in 1945, civil war between the Nationalists and communists erupted, and, after defeat in the Battle of Huaihai in 1948–49, the Nationalist forces' resistance collapsed. In December 1949 Jiang and his followers were forced to take refuge on the island of Taiwan, maintaining a large army in the hope of reclaiming the mainland. His authoritarian right-wing regime, which claimed to remain the legitimate rulers of mainland China, enjoyed US support until his death, in April 1975, and promoted rapid economic advance. His son Jiang Qing-guo (Chiang Ching-kuo) then became president.

Jiang married into the wealthy Western-educated Soong family in 1927 and his wife's elder sister was Sung Quingling, the widow of Sun Zhong Shan.

FURTHER READING
Crozier, B, and Chou, E *The Man Who Lost China* 1976
Foruya, K *Chiang Kai-shek: His Life and Times* 1981
Loh, P P Y *The Early Chiang Kai-shek: His Personality and Politics, 1887–1924* 1971
Miller, M *Chiang Kai-shek* 1988
Morwood, W *Duel for the Middle Kingdom: The Struggle Between Chiang Kai-Shek and Mao Tse-Tung for Control of China* 1979

Jiang Qing or *Chiang Ching* (1914–1991)

Chinese communist politician, third wife of Mao Zedong and leader of the ultra-leftist 'Gang of Four', which played a key role in the 1966–69 Cultural Revolution.

Born Li Yun-ho, the daughter of a brutal Shandong province carpenter, she began her career as a university librarian and briefly married in her teens, before becoming, from 1933, a Shanghai film actress, with the adopted name Lan Ping. She joined the Chinese Communist Party (CCP) in 1937 and, after meeting the CCP leader Mao Zedong at the CCP headquarters in Yan'an, became his wife in 1939. She emerged as a radical, egalitarian Maoist, although enjoying a great personal love of material luxuries, and, after the establishment of the People's Republic in 1949, became head of the film office of the Propaganda Department.

In 1960 she became minister for culture and revolutionized the Beijing opera, replacing traditional works with a repertoire of Maoist works. Jiang played a key role in the 1966–69 Cultural Revolution as the leading member of the ultra-leftist Shanghai-based 'Gang of Four', which also included Wang Hongwen, Yao Wenyuan, and Zhang Chunqiao.

Whomever he [Mao Zedong] told me to bite, I bit.

JIANG QING Jiang's statement, in defence of her subversive actions, made during the November 1980 trial of the 'Gang of Four'

Her influence waned during the early 1970s and her relationship with Mao became embittered. On Mao's death, in September 1976, the 'Gang of Four', with Jiang as a leading figure, sought to seize power by organizing military coups in Shanghai and Beijing. They were arrested for treason by Mao's successor, Hua Guofeng, and tried in November 1980–January 1981. The Gang was blamed for the excesses of the Cultural Revolution, but Jiang asserted during her trial that she had only followed Mao's orders as an obedient wife. This was rejected, and Jiang received a death sentence, with a two-year reprieve. This was commuted in March 1983 to life imprisonment. She reportedly committed suicide, while in prison, in May 1991.

FURTHER READING

Bonavia, D *Verdict in Beijing: The Trial of the Gang of Four* 1984

Terrill, R *The White Boned Demon: A Biography of Madame Mao Zedong* 1984

Witke, R *Comrade Chiang Ch'ing* 1977

Jiang Qing-guo or *Chiang Ching-kuo* (1910–1988)

Taiwanese politician, eldest son of Jiang Jie Shi (Chiang Kai-shek), prime minister 1972–78, president 1978–88. After Jiang Jie Shi's Kuomintang (Guomindang, nationalist) forces fled to Taiwan in 1949, in the wake of the communist takeover of the Chinese mainland, Jiang Qing-guo worked to strengthen the security and intelligence forces and established a youth wing for the ruling Kuomintang. He became Taiwan's prime minister in 1972 and, after the death of his father in April 1975, he became Kuomintang leader and, from 1978, head of state.

Jiang introduced modernizing economic, social, and political reforms and during his tenure the country enjoyed rapid economic development as an export-oriented 'Tiger economy'. Gradual democratization was permitted, along with 'Taiwanization' of the Kuomintang, which had hitherto been dominated by Chinese 'mainlanders' who had accompanied Jiang Ji Shi to Taiwan in 1949. An opposition political party, the Democratic Progressive Party (DPP), was permitted, for the first time, to participate in parliamentary elections in 1986; martial law, which had been in force since 1949, was lifted in 1987; and he allowed travel to the communist-controlled mainland for family reunions. The pace of political liberalization accelerated under Jian's successor, the Taiwan-born Lee Teng-hui.

Jiang studied for 12 years in the Soviet Union before returning to China in 1937, where he worked assisting his father.

Jiang Zemin (1926–)

Chinese communist politician, leader of the Chinese Communist Party (CCP) from 1989, and state president from 1993.

Born in Yangzhou, near Shanghai, Jiang was the son-in-law of ◊Li Xiannian. He joined the CCP in 1946, after studying engineering at university, and underwent practical training as an electrical engineer at the Stalin Automobile Factory in Moscow. On his return to China, Jiang held a succession of posts in the machine and electronics industry ministries in the new People's Republic. His career was temporarily derailed by the Cultural Revolution of 1966–69, but with his educational attainments, fluency in Russian and English, and enthusiasm for economic reform, he was subsequently earmarked for promotion by ◊Deng Xiaoping.

Jiang was brought into the CCP Central Committee in 1982 and served in the Moscow embassy and as mayor of Shanghai from 1985, before being inducted into the CCP Politburo in November 1987. During the May–June 1989 student protests, he secured a peaceful end to the demonstrations in Shanghai, where he was party chief. This was done while loyally supporting the Dengist line. Indeed, in May 1989 Jiang was the first provincial leader to send a message to Prime Minister Li Peng supporting the imposition of martial law. Jiang's record as an economic manager had been less impressive during his four years in Shanghai. This led to his acquiring the unflattering nickname of 'flowerstand', someone who was pleasant to look at, but was of no substance. Nevertheless, Jiang was rewarded for his 'soundness' during 1989 by replacing ◊Zhao Ziyang as CCP general secretary on 24 June. He subsequently succeeded his patron Deng Xiaoping as head of the influential Central Military Commission, in November 1989, and replaced ◊Yang Shangkun as state president in March 1993.

A conciliatory figure, Jiang sought to curb the widening income differences in China as economic growth gathered pace in the coastal cities, and promoted the idea of 'spiritual civilization', involving national pride and high moral standards. The death of 'paramount leader' Deng Xiaoping in February 1997 left Jiang as 'first among equals' within a collective leadership. He was re-elected state president in March 1998 by China's parliament, the National People's Congress, and continued to press on with a combination of market-centred economic reform, coupled with unswerving adherence to the CCP's political line. He also launched a campaign against official corruption, which saw the dismissal, in April 1995, of the mayor of Beijing, Chen Xitong, and placed allies from his Shanghai power-base in leading government positions.

Jiménez Oreamuno, Ricardo (1859–1945)

Costa Rican liberal politician, president on three occasions, 1910–14, 1924–28, and 1932–36. During his presidencies, 'Don Ricardo' promoted political reforms, including a switch to direct presidential elections, in his first term, and social and economic reforms, including land distribution to the landless and the creation of a National Bank of Insurance, during his final term.

He was admired for his moral rectitude and modesty, insisting, for example, that his portrait not be displayed in government offices. Before becoming president, he was a legislator and judge.

Jinnah, Muhammad Ali (1876–1948)

Indian politician, Pakistan's first governor general from 1947. He was president of the Muslim League 1916 and 1934–48, and by 1940 was advocating the need for a separate state of Pakistan. At the 1946 conferences in London he insisted on the partition of British India into Hindu and Muslim states.

FURTHER READING

Bolitho, H *Jinnah* 1954

McDonagh, S *Mohammed Ali Jinnah, Maker of Modern Pakistan* 1971

John, Patrick (1937–)

Dominican centre-left politician, chief minister 1974–78 and prime minister 1978–80. Having succeeded Edward Le Blanc as chief minister, John led the Dominica Labour Party (DLP) to victory in 1975, and became the country's first prime minister after independence within the British Commonwealth was secured in 1978. His increasingly authoritarian style of government, which included attempts to restrict trade-union and media freedoms, led to violent demonstrations, and in 1980 he was obliged to resign. In 1985 he was found guilty of complicity in a plot to overthrow Prime Minister Eugenia ◊Charles in 1981, and sentenced to 12-years' imprisonment.

John XXIII, born Angelo Giuseppe Roncalli (1881–1963)

Pope from 1958. An army chaplain in World War I, he served successively as apostolic delegate to Bulgaria, Greece, and Turkey 1925–44, and as papal nuncio in France following the Liberation in 1944. He was Cardinal and Patriarch of Venice 1953–58. His pontificate was remarkable above all for the calling of the Second Vatican Council, which was wholly unexpected and due to his own personal initiative. This was responsible for a revolutionary transformation of the social teaching, liturgy, and organization of the Roman Catholic Church. He also initiated official Catholic participation in the ecumenical movement.

FURTHER READING

Hebblethwaite, P *John XXIII* 1984

John Paul II, born Karol Józef Wojtyła (1920–)

Polish priest, pope from 1978, the first non-Italian pope since 1522. He was associated with a conservative, pietist, and anti-reformist trend in the Catholic Church, upholding the doctrine of papal infallibility and opposing all forms of contraception. At the same time, he used his authority to open up a dialogue with other Christian denominations, notably with the Eastern Orthodox Church and with the Jewish community.

His tenure was marked by orthodoxy in matters relating to the church's role but also a strong involvement in moral and political matters. While condemning priests for their involvement in politics in Central America, notably in the 'Theology of Liberation', and disciplining liberal clergy, John Paul II took a high-profile part in facilitating political rapprochement in various trouble spots around the world. He assisted negotiations between the Polish government and the Solidarity trade union. More recently, he visited Cuba, thus breaking the US policy of isolation. He campaigned against economic deprivation and arms manufacture. In the Far East he condemned birth-control programmes.

His frequent and well-publicized visits to Catholic communities around the world raised the profile of the Catholic Church. By the mid-1990s ill health had forced him to scale down his travels.

Born in Wadowice, near Kraków, Poland, Wojtyła was conscripted in 1939 for forced labour in Germany. After the war he taught ethics and theology at the universities of Kraków and Lublin. In 1978 he was made a cardinal. An attempt on his life was made in Rome in 1981.

FURTHER READING

Buttiglione, Rocco *Karol Wojtyła: The Thought of the Man who Became Pope John Paul* 1997

Johnson, Paul *Pope John Paul II and the Catholic Restoration* 1982

Kwitny, Jonathan *Man of the Century: The Life and Times of Pope John Paul II* 1997

Thomas, Gordon, and Morgan-Witts, Max *Pontiff* 1983

Williams, G H *The Mind of John Paul II* 1981

Johnson, Hiram Warren (1866–1945)

US politician. He was the 'Bull Moose' party candidate for vice president in Theodore Roosevelt's unsuccessful bid to regain the presidency in 1912. Elected to the Senate in 1917, Johnson served there until his death. He was an unyielding isolationist, opposing US involvement in World War I as well as membership in the League of Nations and World Court.

Born in Sacramento, California, Johnson attended the University of California and was admitted to the bar in 1888. In 1902 he established a law practice in San Francisco before entering politics and serving as governor of California 1911–17.

Johnson, James Weldon (1871–1938)

US writer, lawyer, diplomat, and social critic. He was a strong supporter of President Theodore Roosevelt and served him and President William Taft as US consul in Venezuela and Nicaragua 1906–12. He was editor of *New York Age* 1912–22 and was active in the National Association for the Advancement of Colored People (NAACP). As a poet and anthropologist, he became one of the chief figures of the Harlem Renaissance of the 1920s. His major work, *Autobiography of an Ex-Colored Man*, was published anonymously in 1912 and republished under his own name in 1927. *The Book of the American Negro Poetry* (1922) edited by Johnson, was the first anthology of black American poetry. His autobiography, *Along This Way*, was published in 1933.

Born in Jacksonville, Florida, and educated at Atlanta University, Johnson became the first black American admitted to the Florida bar in 1897.

Johnson, Lyndon Baines (1908–1973)

36th president of the USA 1963–69, a Democrat. He was a member of Congress 1937–49 and the Senate 1949–60. Born in Texas, he brought critical Southern support as J F Kennedy's vice-presidential running mate in 1960, and became president on Kennedy's assassination.

After Kennedy's assassination, Johnson successfully won congressional support for many of Kennedy's New Frontier proposals, most conspicuously in the area of civil rights. He moved beyond the New Frontier to declare 'war on poverty' supported by Great Society

---

I'd rather give my life than be afraid to give it.

LYNDON BAINES JOHNSON On his decision to walk in President J F Kennedy's funeral procession 25 November 1963

---

legislation (civil rights, education, alleviation of poverty). His foreign policy met with considerably less success. After the Tonkin Gulf Incident, which escalated US involvement in the Vietnam War, support won

by Johnson's domestic reforms dissipated, and he declined to run for re-election in 1968.

Johnson was born in Stonewall, Texas, and trained as a teacher and lawyer. While working as secretary to a Texan congressman, he attracted the attention of Franklin D Roosevelt, who in 1936 appointed him director of the National Youth Administration in Texas. During World War II he went to Australia and New Zealand as President Roosevelt's special emissary.

FURTHER READING

Dallek, Robert *Lone Star Rising: Lyndon Johnson and His Times* 1991, *Flawed Giant: Lyndon B Johnson and His Times, 1961–1973* 1998

Divine, R A *The Johnson Years* 1987

Heath, J F *Decade of Disillusionment: The Kennedy–Johnson Years* 1975

Johnson, Lyndon Baines *The Vantage Point* 1971

Miller, Merle *Lyndon: An Oral Biography* 1980

Johnson, Yormie (1959–)

Liberian military veteran and rebel leader. He was educated at the Army Officers' School, Monrovia, and at Fort Jackson, South Carolina, USA. He joined the army in 1971 and was commander of the Liberian military police 1976–77. He broke away from Charles Taylor's National Patriotic Front of Liberia and in 1991 formed his own organization, the Independent National Patriotic Front of Liberia (INPFL).

Jonathan, Chief (Joseph) Leabua (1914–1987)

Lesotho politician. A leader in the drive for independence, Jonathan became prime minister of Lesotho in 1965. His rule was ended by a coup in 1986.

As prime minister, Jonathan played a pragmatic role, allying himself in turn with the South African government and the Organization of African Unity.

Jones, Mary ('Mother Jones'), born Harris (1830–1930)

Irish-born US labour leader who, beginning in the 1890s, organized coalminers and strikes for the United Mine Workers in Virginia, West Virginia, and Colorado. Known for her bold tactics, she fought on for decades; at the age of 89 she joined in a major steel walkout, earning a prison term.

She was born near Cork. Emigrating to Canada and then the USA as a child, she was widowed in 1867 when her husband, and four children, died of yellow fever. She lost her home in the Chicago fire of 1871. She resumed earlier work as a dressmaker, and worked with the Knights of Labor as an organizer. In the 1960s a socially conscious periodical, *Mother Jones Magazine*, was named after her.

Jones, Thomas (1870–1955)

Welsh administrator and political adviser. He gave up an academic career (professor of economics at Queen's

University, Belfast, in 1909) to become a political adviser. He acted first for David Lloyd George, as assistant secretary of the War Cabinet in 1916, and then successively for Andrew Bonar Law, Stanley Baldwin, and Ramsay MacDonald. He was also highly successful as a fundraiser.

Jong, Erica Mann (1942–)

US novelist and poet. She won a reputation as a feminist poet with her first collection *Fruits & Vegetables* (1971).

Her novel *Fear of Flying* (1973) depicted a liberated woman's intense sexual adventures and became an

---

In every woman's heart there is a god of the woods, and this god is not available for marriage or for home improvement or for parenthood.

ERICA JONG *Fear of Fifty*

---

instant best seller. It was followed by two sequels, *How To Save Your Own Life* (1977) and *Parachutes and Kisses* (1984).

Joseph, Helen, born Fennell (1905–1992)

British-born South African teacher and anti-racist campaigner. A fearless fighter for racial tolerance and equality, she became a close friend of leading figures in the African National Congress (ANC), including Nelson ◊Mandela and Walter ◊Sisulu. For her work with the ANC, she was awarded its highest honour, Isithwalandwe-Seaparankoe.

Born in Sussex, she left in the 1920s to teach in India. She settled in South Africa in the early 1930s, returning to the UK during World War II to serve in the Women's Auxiliary Air Force (WAAF). At the end of hostilities she returned to South Africa, mixing with the affluent white and Indian communities but quietly retaining her belief in the equality of humanity, irrespective of race or colour. Living in Durban, she met and married a dentist, Billy Joseph, but the marriage was short-lived. She then moved to Johannesburg and became progressively active in trade-union affairs and politics. Her abhorrence of apartheid and her campaigning for its removal earned her the respect of black African leaders and the contempt of the white minority government as she threw herself into the movement against apartheid and, especially, the promotion of the rights of black women. She was the first South African woman to be placed under house arrest by the government. Despite being diagnosed as having cancer in 1971, and eventually confined to a wheelchair, she continued her fight against oppression.

Joseph, Keith Sinjohn, Baron Joseph (1918–1994)

British Conservative politician. A barrister, he entered Parliament in 1956. He held ministerial posts 1962–64,

1970–74, 1979–81, and was secretary of state for education and science 1981–86. He was made a life peer in 1987.

He served in the governments of Harold Macmillan, Alec Douglas-Home, and Edward Heath during the 1960s and 1970s, but it was not until Margaret Thatcher came to office in 1979 that he found a prime minister truly receptive to his views and willing to translate them into policies. With her, he founded the right-wing Centre for Policy Studies, which sought to discover and apply the secrets of the successful market economies of West Germany and Japan.

Born in London, Joseph was educated at Harrow public school and Magdalen College, Oxford, and was elected a fellow of All Souls. After war service, he studied to become a barrister, then immersed himself in Conservative politics, first at local level and then in Parliament, entering the House of Commons in 1956. After holding various junior offices he was minister of housing and local government from 1962 to 1964. In 1970 he became secretary of state for social services, a post he held until the Conservatives' defeat in 1974.

He enjoyed more success as a theoretician than as a practical minister; his political legacy is not so much what he did as what others did at his inspiration. He was the principal author of the Conservative Party's 'New Right' ideology, which became the seedbed of Thatcherism.

Jospin, Lionel (1937–)

French socialist politician, first secretary of the Socialist Party (PS)1981–88 and 1995–97, then prime minister, under President Jacques ◊Chirac, from June 1997, heading a 'pluralist left' coalition with communist, green, and left radical parties.

Trained at the Ecole Nationale d'Administration and from a Protestant background, Jospin was a career civil servant in the Foreign Affairs Ministry when he joined François Mitterrand's leadership circle in the PS in 1972. A deputy for a Paris suburb 1981–93 and respected for his integrity and modesty, as first secretary Jospin promoted his party's realignment with a more pragmatic social-democratic stance. He was minister of education in the government of Michel Rocard 1988–91, and emerged as the PS presidential front-runner in 1995 only after Jacques ◊Delors declined to stand, polling a respectable 47% against Chirac on the second ballot. As premier, he enjoyed considerable popularity into 1998, despite failing to act on such campaign commitments as halting privatization and repealing recent immigration laws, and despite facing protests over continuing high levels of unemployment.

Jouhaux, Léon Henri (1879–1954)

French trade unionist, the most prominent non-communist trade-union leader in France in the 20th century. Jouhaux served as secretary general of the General Confederation of Labour (CGT) 1909–47 and played a key role in the negotiations with Léon ◊ Blum's Popular Front government that gave French workers paid holidays and the 40-hour week.

Active in the Matchworkers' Union and influenced by the anarcho-syndicalist thinking then predominant amongst militant workers in France, Jouhaux had by 1914 come to reject its central tenets – advocacy of the general strike to achieve social revolution and anti-militarism. After World War I, he succeeded in retaining most of the CGT's membership under his reformist leadership, only a small minority going into the communist-led breakaway. However, following the communist unions' reunification with the CGT in 1935, Jouhaux led a non-communist minority out of the CGT in 1947 at the onset of the Cold War. He then served as president of Workers' Power (FO) from 1948 until his death.

As a leading trade unionist Jouhaux was interned by the Vichy authorities during World War II.

Juan Carlos (1938–)

King of Spain from 1975. The son of Don Juan, pretender to the Spanish throne, he married Princess Sofia, eldest daughter of King Paul of Greece, in 1962. In 1969 he was nominated by Francisco ◊ Franco to succeed on the restoration of the monarchy intended to follow Franco's death; his father was excluded because of his known liberal views. Juan Carlos became king in 1975, and played a vital role in the smooth transition to democratic stability. He was instrumental in the defeat of an attempted military coup in 1981.

Jumblatt, Walid (1949–)

Lebanese Druze Muslim politician. His charismatic father, Kamal, was founder of the Progressive Socialist Party (PSP) in 1949, and he became PSP leader in March 1977 after Kamal's assassination and subsequently played an important role in Lebanese politics. He made strategic alliances with Syria and with the moderate Shia Amal militia of Nabih Berri in defence of the semi-autonomous Druze enclave against encroaching Maronite Christian forces.

In 1983, following the withdrawal of Israeli forces from the Shuf (Chouf), east of Beirut, Jumblatt organized an onslaught of Druze militia against Maronite Christian militias in the Shuf. This was successful and was followed, in 1984–85, by further expansion of the enclave southwards and westwards. In 1984 and 1989 Jumblatt served as a minister in broad-based Lebanese governments, but in 1987 the Druze militia were involved in fierce clashes with Amal.

Jumblatt was born into a family that has been the traditional head of the Druze community, a Muslim sect dating back to the Middle Ages and based in the Shuf mountains. He studied at universities in Beirut

and France. He broke Druze traditional by marrying a non-Druze Jordanian. With his liking for motorbikes and leather jackets, he is an unconventional figure and, politically, he has been unpredictable in his alliances.

Juppé, Alain Marie (1945–)

French neo-Gaullist politician, foreign minister 1993–95 and prime minister 1995–97. In 1976, as a close lieutenant of Jacques Chirac, he helped to found the right-of-centre Rally for the Republic (RPR) party, of which he later became secretary general, then president. He was appointed premier by the newly-elected President Chirac in May 1995 but, within months, found his position under threat as a result of a housing scandal. Opposition to his government's economic programme, particularly welfare cuts, provoked a general strike in November 1995.

The son of a Gascony farmer, Juppé was educated at the prestigious Ecole d'Administration and his early career was as a 'fast-track' civil servant. He was first elected to the French National Assembly, for a Paris constituency, in 1983. Nicknamed 'Amstrad' for his lightning intellect, he became a budget minister in the 1986–88 Chirac administration and was an outstanding foreign minister in Edouard Balladur's government of 1993–95. A pro-European technocrat, he became prime minister when Chirac was elected president in May 1995. Juppé was re-elected mayor of Bordeaux in June 1995, and elected president of the RPR in October 1995. He resigned as prime minister after the right of coalition was defeated by the Socialist Party in the June 1997 National Assembly elections.

In August 1998 Juppé came under investigation for alleged payroll abuses in Paris when he was the city's finance director, and Jacques Chirac, France's current president, was the mayor of Paris.

Justo, Agustin Pedro (1876–1943)

Argentine military leader and president 1932–38. During his administration, economic and political problems, left over from the previous administrations, were rife. He was instrumental – along with his foreign minister, Carlos Saavedra Lamas – in ending the Chaco War between Bolivia and Paraguay 1932–35.

During World War II, Justo was openly critical of former president Ramón Castillo's policy of neutrality and sought to support the Allied cause by declaring war on the Axis powers.

Justo was born in Concepción del Uruguay and educated at several military schools. He had an active career teaching military science before entering into political life. As an army general, he became prominent as a war minister in 1922, under Marcelo Torcuato de Alvear. He also served as a minister of agriculture and public works. He took part in the conservative overthrow of President Hipólito Irigoyen in 1930, and later went on to become the victorious presidential candidate in the 1931 elections.

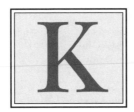

K

Kabila, Laurent-Desiré (1939–)

Congolese soldier and politician, president of the Democratic Republic of Congo (formerly Zaire) from 1997. Opposed to the oppressive regime of President Sese Seko Mobutu, his Tutsi-led uprising was supported by the presidents of neighbouring Angola, Rwanda, and Uganda, becoming the Alliance of Democratic Forces for the Liberation of Congo (ADFL) from November 1996. The ADFL, led by Kabila, made rapid advances westwards from the Great Lakes region, reaching the outskirts of the capital, Kinshasa, in May 1997. After President Nelson Mandela of South Africa failed to broker a political agreement Mobutu fled the country, and Kabila declared himself president. In August 1998 Rwanda and Uganda supported the launch of the Congolese Assembly for Democracy (RCD), a rebel offensive against Kabila, but Angola and Zimbabwe maintained their backing for the president.

Kabua, Amata (1928–1996)

Marshall Islands politician, president 1979–96. He campaigned for separation from Micronesia from the early 1970s, and helped draft the new separatist constitution of 1979. He was elected executive president in 1979 and was re-elected four times between 1983–95. He steered the country to independence, which was achieved when the USA's United Nations trusteeship was terminated in December 1990, and sought to promote tourism and economic diversification.

Born on Jabor Island, Jaluit Atoll, Kabua worked as a schoolteacher before becoming active in politics. He was a member of the Marshall Islands Congress 1958–63 and was a senator representing the Marshall Islands in the Congress of Micronesia 1963–78.

On his death, in December 1996, he was succeeded as president by his cousin Imata Kabua, who was head of the Kabua family and Iroijlaplap (paramount chief) of the Marshall Islands.

Kádár, János (1912–1989)

Hungarian communist leader, in power 1956–88, after suppressing the national uprising. As leader of the Hungarian Socialist Workers' Party (HSWP) and prime minister 1956–58 and 1961–65, Kádár introduced a series of market-socialist economic reforms, while retaining cordial political relations with the USSR.

Kádár was a mechanic before joining the outlawed Communist Party and working as an underground resistance organizer in World War II. After the war he was elected to the National Assembly, served as minister for internal affairs 1948–50, and became a prominent member of the Hungarian Workers' Party (HSP). Imprisoned 1951–53 for deviation from Stalinism, Kádár was rehabilitated in 1955, becoming party leader in Budapest, and in November 1956, at the height of the Hungarian national rising, he was appointed head of the new HSWP. With the help of Soviet troops, he suppressed the revolt. He was ousted as party general secretary in May 1988, and forced into retirement in May 1989.

FURTHER READING

Kádár, János *Socialism and Democracy in Hungary: Speeches, Articles, Interviews 1957–82* 1984
Molnar, Miklós *From Béla Kun to János Kádár* 1990
Rooke, Margaret *The Hungarian Revolt of 1956: Janos Kadar – Traitor or Saviour?* 1986

Kaganovich, Lazar Moiseevich (1893–1991)

Soviet politician who was in charge of the enforced collectivization of agriculture 1929–34, and played a prominent role in the purges of the Communist Party carried out under Joseph Stalin in the 1930s. He was minister of transport 1935–44, and the Moscow metro underground system was built under his direction.

Before entering politics, Kaganovich was a leatherworker and union organizer. He joined the Bolshevik party in 1911, and during the October revolution, led the seizure of power by the Bolsheviks in Gomel, Belarus. In 1924 he became secretary of the party's Central Committee and then headed the party in the Ukraine 1925–28. He held the post of deputy prime minister 1938–39. After serving on the State Defence Committee during World War II, he resumed control in the Ukraine 1947–48. In this role he became a political rival of Nikita Khrushchev, who later, as premier after Stalin's death, dismissed Kaganovich from all his government and party positions. In 1961 he was expelled from the party, along with Vyacheslav Molotov, and thereafter lived in obscurity as manager of a cement factory in Siberia.

Kaifu, Toshiki (1932–)

Japanese conservative politician, prime minister 1989–91. A protégé of former premier Takeo Miki, he was selected as a compromise choice as Liberal Democratic Party (LDP) president and prime minister in August 1989, following the resignation of Sosuke ◊Uno. Kaifu resigned in November 1991, having lost the support of important factional leaders in the LDP, and was replaced by Kiichi Miyazawa. During 1994–95, Kaifu was leader of the Shinshinto (New Frontier Party) opposition coalition.

Kaifu entered politics in 1961, was deputy chief secretary 1974–76 in the Miki cabinet, and was education minister under Yasuhiro Nakasone. He is a member of the minor Komoto faction. In 1987 he received what he claimed were legitimate political donations amounting to £40,000 from a company later accused of bribing a number of LDP politicians. His popularity as prime minister was dented by the unconstitutional proposal, defeated in the Diet (parliament), to contribute Japanese forces to the UN coalition army in the Persian Gulf area after Iraq's annexation of Kuwait in 1990. His lack of power led to his replacement as prime minister in 1991.

Kalinin, Mikhail Ivanovich (1875–1946)

Soviet politician, founder of the newspaper *Pravda*. He was prominent in the 1917 October Revolution, and in 1919 became head of state (president of the Central Executive Committee of the Soviet government) until 1937, then president of the Presidium of the Supreme Soviet until 1946.

Kallio, Kyosti (1873–1940)

Finnish politician, president of Finland 1937–40. After serving several terms of office as prime minister, he was elected president and led his country's defence against the USSR's invasion in the Winter War of 1939–40. Kallio was forced by ill-health to step down in November 1940, and died shortly afterwards.

Kaltenbrunner, Ernst (1903–1946)

Austrian Nazi leader. After the annexation of Austria in 1938 he joined police chief Heinrich Himmler's staff, and as head of the Security Police (SD) from 1943 was responsible for the murder of millions of Jews and Allied soldiers in World War II. After the war, he was tried at Nürnberg for war crimes and hanged in October 1946.

Kamenev, Lev Borisovich, born Rosenfeld (1883–1936)

Russian leader of the Bolshevik movement after 1917 who, with Joseph Stalin and Grigory Zinoviev, formed a ruling triumvirate in the USSR after Lenin's death in 1924. His alignment with the Trotskyists led to his dismissal from office and from the Communist Party by Stalin in 1926. Arrested in 1934 after Sergei Kirov's assassination, Kamenev was secretly tried and sentenced, then retried, condemned, and shot in 1936 for allegedly plotting to murder Stalin.

Kane, Sheikh Hamidou (1928–)

Senegalese novelist, writing in French. His first novel, *L'Aventure ambiguë/Ambiguous Adventure* (1961), is an autobiographical account of a young African alienated from the simple faith of his childhood and initiated into an alien Islamic mysticism, before being immersed in materialist French culture.

He studied law and philosophy in France before returning to Senegal as a French civil servant.

Kang Keqing or *K'ang K'o-ch'ing* (1911–)

Chinese political leader. In 1957 she was elected to the committee of the Chinese Democratic Women's Federation, becoming its president in 1978, then honorary president in 1988. Since her election in 1977 to the 11th Central Committee, she has held influential political posts, including membership of the Praesidium of the National People's Congress since 1980.

Born in Wan'an, Jiangxi (Kiangsi) province, she studied at Jinggangshan Red Army College, and the Anti-Japan Military and Political Academy. She joined the Chinese Youth League in 1927, and organized Red Army guerrilla units. After her marriage in 1929 to General ◊Zhu De, she became commander of the Red Army's Women's Department, and was one of the few women on the Long March of 1934–35.

Kang Sheng or *K'ang Sheng* (1899–1975)

Chinese politician. A prominent member of the Communist Party during the 1960s, he exercised considerable influence behind the scenes in his capacity as head of party security. During the Cultural Revolution he was associated with the radical left group led by Mao Zedong's wife, ◊Jiang Qing. Since Mao's death in 1976, Kang's role in the persecution of party members and intellectuals during the Cultural Revolution has been condemned.

Karadžić, Radovan (1945–)

Montenegrin-born leader of the Bosnian Serbs, leader of the community's unofficial government 1992–96. He cofounded the Serbian Democratic Party of Bosnia-Herzegovina (SDS-BH) in 1990 and launched the siege of Sarajevo in 1992, plunging the country into a prolonged and bloody civil war. A succession of peace initiatives for the region failed due to his ambitious demands for Serbian territory, and he was subsequently implicated in war crimes allegedly committed in Bosnia-Herzegovina. In the autumn of 1995, in the wake of a sustained NATO bombardment of Bosnian Serb positions around Sarajevo, Karadžić agreed to enter peace negotiations; in November he signed the US-sponsored Dayton peace accord, under the terms of which he was forced to step down as the Bosnian Serb prime minister. The accord divided Bosnia into separate Muslim, Croat, and Serb areas, and although this seemingly excluded him from further power, he remained a dominant backstage force. He was charged with genocide and crimes against humanity at the Yugoslav War Crimes Tribunal in The Hague, the Netherlands, in November 1995 but subsequently defied NATO orders to arrest him on sight by continuing to travel openly about the region. He stepped down as party leader in July 1996. His position was further weakened when, in January 1998, the moderate Milorad Dodik became prime minister of the Bosnian Serb Republic.

Distrusted in the West and viewed as an intransigent figure, he is nevertheless viewed as moderate by many Bosnian Serbs.

Karamanlis, Konstantinos (1907–1998)
Greek politician of the New Democracy Party. A lawyer and an anticommunist, he was prime minister 1955–58, 1958–61, and 1961–63 (when he went into self-imposed exile because of a military coup). He was recalled as prime minister on the fall of the regime of the 'colonels' in July 1974, and was president 1980–85.

Karami, Rashid (1921–1987)
Lebanese politician, prime minister of Lebanon 1955–56, 1958–60, 1961–64, and five times subsequently between 1965 and 1976. His final term of office began in 1984. Karami was a member of the predominantly Muslim National Front, but tried to ensure stability for Lebanon by sharing power with representatives of the Maronite Christian community. To this end, he headed a coalition government formed by the Christian president Amin ◊Gemayel in 1984, which it was hoped would end the country's bitter civil war, but was assassinated three years later.

Karami was born at Miriata, Tripoli, and trained as a lawyer at Fuad I University, Cairo, Egypt.

Karimov, Islam (1938–   )
Uzbek politician, president from 1990. A member of the Communist Party of the Soviet Union (CPSU) from 1964, he became Uzbekistan's communist party leader in 1989. Faced with rising nationalist sentiment, he declared the republic's sovereignty in June 1990 and independence in August 1991. Directly elected president in December 1991, his mandate was extended until 2000 by a March 1995 plebiscite. His authoritarian administration promoted gradual, market-centred economic reform, but harassed and banned opposition groups, particularly Islamic militants.

Born in Samarkand, he worked initially in an aviation construction factory and then as a technocrat economic planner and minister. In August 1991, when there was an attempted coup in Moscow against

Mikhail Gorbachev by conservative communists, Karimov initially failed to condemn it. After independence, he promoted closer links with Turkey, but ties with Russia remained strong, and an economic, military, and social union was formed with neighbouring Kazakhstan and Kyrgyzstan.

Karmal, Babrak (1929–1996)
Afghani communist politician, president 1979–86. In 1965 he formed the People's Democratic Party of Afghanistan (PDPA). As president, with Soviet backing, he sought to broaden the appeal of the PDPA but encountered wide resistance from the Mujaheddin (Muslim guerrillas).

Karmal was imprisoned for anti-government activity in the early 1950s. He was a member of the government 1957–62 and of the national assembly 1965–72. In December 1979 he returned from brief exile in Eastern Europe with Soviet support to overthrow President Hafizullah Amin and was installed as the new head of state. Karmal was persuaded to step down as president and PDPA leader in May 1986 as the USSR began to search for a compromise settlement with opposition groupings and to withdraw troops. In July 1991 he returned to Afghanistan from exile in Moscow.

Kasavubu, Joseph (1910–1969)
Congolese politician, first president of the Republic of Congo 1960–65. After winning a power struggle with Prime Minister Patrice ◊Lumumba when the Congo gained independence from Belgium, he fought off a challenge from Sese Seko ◊Mobutu in the ensuing civil war. However, he was later ousted by Mobutu in a coup in November 1965.

Kasavubu began to train as a priest at mission schools and seminaries, but abandoned this to become a teacher and then a civil servant. Entering politics, he became mayor of Léopoldville (now Kinshasa) in 1957, but was arrested by the Belgians in 1959 for nationalist agitation. In the turmoil following the Belgian withdrawal from the Congo, Kasavubu came to power in June 1960, aided by UN forces sent to restore law and order.

Katayama, Sen (1859–1933)
Japanese labour and political organizer. Imprisoned in 1912, he went into permanent exile in 1914. After the October Revolution he joined the Communist Party. From 1922 he lived in the USSR, working for the Comintern, and when he died in 1933 he was buried in the Kremlin wall.

Coming from a peasant background, Katayama went to the USA in 1884, worked in a succession of menial jobs, and eventually gained a higher education. In 1896 he returned to Japan and, in the face of government repression, tried unsuccessfully to organize trade unions and a socialist party.

Katayama, Tetsu (1887–1978)

Japanese politician. He headed a coalition government 1947–48, becoming the country's first socialist prime minister. His government created a new ministry of labour, enacted an anti-monopoly law, and presided over the dissolution of the prewar financial combines (zaibatsu), but became increasingly unpopular when economic crisis forced it to impose price and wage controls. After his resignation in 1948 he became identified with the party's right wing, and later, in 1950, helped to form the moderate Democratic Socialist Party, which supported the 1951 Security Treaty with the USA.

A Christian socialist, he helped form the Socialist People's Party (Shakai Minshuto) in 1926, one of a number of 'proletarian parties' founded during the 1920s. In 1945 he emerged as leader of the newly created Japan Socialist Party, which achieved a plurality of votes in the first elections held under the 1947 Peace Constitution.

Katō, Taka-akira (1860–1926)

Japanese politician, prime minister 1924–26. After a long political career with several terms as foreign minister, Katō led probably the most democratic and liberal regime of the Japanese empire.

Katsura, Tarō (1847–1913)

Prince of Japan, army officer, politician, and prime minister 1901–06, 1908–11, and 1912–13. He was responsible for the Anglo-Japanese treaty of 1902 (an alliance against Russia), the successful prosecution of the Russo-Japanese war 1904–05, and the annexation of Korea in 1910.

Having assisted in the Meiji restoration 1866–68, Katsura became increasingly involved in politics. His support for rearmament, distaste for political parties, and oligarchic rule created unrest; his third ministry December 1912–January 1913 lasted only seven weeks.

Kaunda, Kenneth David (1924–)

Zambian politician, president 1964–91. Imprisoned 1958–60 as founder of the Zambia African National Congress, in 1964 he became the first prime minister of Northern Rhodesia, then the first president of independent Zambia. In 1973 he introduced one-party rule. He supported the nationalist movement in Southern Rhodesia, now Zimbabwe, and survived a coup attempt in 1980 thought to have been promoted by South Africa. He was elected chair of the Organization of African Unity in 1970 and 1987. In November 1991 he lost the first multiparty elections to Frederick Chiluba.

In July 1995 he was elected president of the United National Independence Party (UNIP) and announced his return to active politics, though his decision was not widely applauded. In May 1996 the Zambian constitution was controversially amended, making it impossible for non-second-generation Zambians to stand for the presidency, thereby effectively debarring Kaunda from future contests. The move was criticized

> *The inability of those in power to still the voices of their own consciences is the great force leading to change.*
>
> KENNETH KAUNDA *Observer* July 1965

by Commonwealth observers. In 1998, while under house arrest, he was charged with concealing knowledge of an abortive coup in October 1997. In June 1998 he was freed, after five-months' detention.

FURTHER READING
Kaunda, Kenneth *The Riddle of Violence* (memoirs) 1981
MacPherson, Fergus *Kaunda of Zambia* 1975

Kautsky, Karl Johann (1854–1938)

German socialist theoretician who opposed the reformist ideas of Edouard ◊Bernstein from within the Social Democratic Party. In spite of his Marxist ideas, he remained in the party when its left wing broke away to form the German Communist Party (KPD).

Kawakami, Hajime (1879–1946)

Japanese Marxist academic. As an economics professor at Kyoto University, Kawakami was the author of the best-selling *Tale of Poverty* (1916). He moved towards Marxism after the October Revolution and joined the underground Communist Party in 1932. Arrested in 1933, he was imprisoned until 1937. On his release he lived in seclusion until his death.

Kazan, Elia, born Elia Kazanjoglous (1909–)

Turkish-born US stage and film director, producer, and writer. A founding member of the Actors' Studio, he directed *A Streetcar Named Desire* (1947), *Death of a Salesman* (1949), and *Cat on a Hot Tin Roof* (1955). Many of Kazan's films have a social or political theme. His Oscar-winning film *On the Waterfront* (1954) is based on Budd Schulberg's account of New York City harbour unions. The theme of conflicting loyalties had parallels to Kazan's own life; he had given a testimony in 1952 to the House Committee on Un-American Activities and admitted past membership in the Communist party, naming others from his group.

FURTHER READING
Kazan, Elia *Elia Kazan: A Life* 1997

Keating, Paul John (1944–)

Australian politician, Labor Party (ALP) leader and prime minister 1991–96. He was treasurer and deputy leader of the ALP 1983–91. In 1993 he announced plans for Australia to become a federal republic by the year 2001, which incited a mixed reaction among Australians. He and his party lost the February 1996 general election to John ◊Howard, leader of the Liberal Party.

Keating was active in ALP politics from the age of 15 and, an admirer of Jack ◊Lang, stood at the party's right wing. He entered the federal parliament in 1969 and held several posts in Labor's shadow ministry 1976–83. As finance minister 1983–91 under Bob ◊Hawke, Keating was unpopular with the public for his deregulatory economic policies at a time of economic recession. He successfully challenged Hawke for the ALP party leadership in December 1991 and his premiership was confirmed by the March 1993 general election victory of the ALP, for an unprecedented fifth term of office, at a time of high unemployment. He offended many with his arrogance and acerbic tongue.

FURTHER READING
Carew, Edna *Paul Keating: Prime Minister* 1992

Kefauver, (Carey) Estes (1903–1963)

US Democratic politician. He served in the House of Representatives 1939–49 and in the Senate 1949 until his death. He was an unsuccessful candidate for the Democratic presidential nomination in 1952 and 1956, losing to Adlai Stevenson both times.

Born near Madisonville, Tennessee, Kefauver was educated at the University of Tennessee. He received a law degree from Yale in 1927 and established a private law practice in Chattanooga, Tennessee. As chair of the Senate Judiciary Committee, he held televised hearings on organized crime 1950–51. In 1956 he was Stevenson's vice-presidential running mate.

Keïta, Modibo (1915–1977)

Mali politician, president of the Independent Republic of Mali 1960–68. A pan-Africanist radical who was influenced by the Ghanaian leader Kwame ◊Nkrumah, he was deposed in a military coup led by Moussa Traoré and imprisoned until his death.

Keïta was educated at the William-Ponty Lycée in Dakar, Senegal. In 1946, he was a founder member of the Rassemblement Démocratique Africaine (RDA), a cross-national African political party that sent representatives to the French National Assembly. Keïta represented Sudan 1956–58. In 1958 he was elected president of the Constituent Assembly at Dakar, and in the following year president of the Council of the Mali Federation.

Kekkonen, Urho Kaleva (1900–1986)

Finnish politician, prime minister of Finland four times in the early 1950s and president 1956–81. An advocate of détente, he was the prime mover behind the Helsinki Conference on European security in 1975, an important superpower summit.

Kekkonen gained ministerial office as a representative of the Agrarian Party in the 1930s and 1940s. As president, he adopted a policy of cautious friendship with the USSR. He was due to remain in office until 1984, but ill-health forced him to resign the presidency in 1981.

Kellogg, Frank Billings (1856–1937)

US politician and diplomat. Elected to the Senate in 1916, he was appointed ambassador to the UK by President Warren Harding in 1922 and secretary of state under Calvin Coolidge 1925–29. He formulated the Kellogg–Briand Pact in 1927, the international antiwar resolution, for which he was awarded the Nobel Peace Prize in 1929.

Kellogg was born in Potsdam, New York, studied law in Minnesota, and qualified as a barrister in 1877. He was a prosecutor of federal antitrust cases before serving in the Senate 1917–23. From 1930 to 1935 he served as a judge on the World Court (the forerunner of the International Court of Justice).

Kelly, Petra (1947–1992)

See page 228.

Kemp, Jack French (1935–   )

US congressman and secretary of housing and urban development 1989–93, under President George Bush. A conservative Republican, Kemp championed supply-side economics and urban enterprise zones, co-authored the 1981 Kemp–Roth tax-cut bill, and ran unsuccessfully for the 1988 Republican presidential nomination.

Born in Los Angeles, California, he was a professional football quarterback for 13 seasons 1957–69, primarily with the San Diego Chargers and the Buffalo Bills. He was elected as a representative from the state of New York in 1970.

FURTHER READING
Kemp, Jack *American Renaissance* 1979

Kenilorea, Peter (Kauona Keninarais'Ona) (1943–   )

Solomon Islands right-of-centre politician, chief minister 1976–78 and prime minister 1978–82 and 1984–86. He abolished the five provincial ministries that had been established by the preceding administration of Solomon ◊Mamaloni. Facing allegations that he had secretly accepted $47,000 of French aid to repair cyclone damage to his home village, and a looming no-confidence vote, he resigned the premiership in December 1986. However, Kenilorea remained as natural resources minister and, from February 1988, as joint foreign minister and deputy premier, under Prime Minister Ezekiel ◊Alebua, until the right-of-centre Solomon Islands United Party (SIUPA) coalition was defeated in the 1989 general election. He served as foreign minister in the 'national unity' government of Solomon Mamaloni 1990–93.

Kenilorea was born in Takataka, on Malaita Island. After training in New Zealand, he worked as a teacher before entering the Solomon Islands' civil service in 1971. He then moved into politics, eventually leading the SIUPA. He became chief minister in June 1976 and prime minister after independence in July 1978. His opposition to decentralization led to his departure in 1981, but he returned in 1984, leading a coalition government.

Kennedy, Anthony (1936–)

US jurist, appointed associate justice of the US Supreme Court in 1988. A conservative, he wrote the majority opinion in *Washington v Harper* (1990) that the administration of medication for mentally ill prisoners, without the prisoner's consent, is permissible.

Kennedy was born in Sacramento, California, and attended Stanford University (spending his fourth year at the London School of Economics) and the Harvard Law School. He established a private law practice in California 1962–75. He taught constitutional law at McGeorge School of Law of the University of the Pacific 1965–88 and was appointed judge of the US Court of Appeals for the Seventh Circuit in 1976. He was appointed to the Supreme Court by President Ronald Reagan.

He supported the majority opinion in the 1989 case, *Texas v Johnson*, which ruled that the burning of the US flag in protest was protected by the First Amendment. In *Saffle v Parks* (1990) he wrote the opinion that a writ of habeas corpus may be obtained only according to the laws in force at the time of a prisoner's conviction.

Kennedy, Edward Moore ('Ted') (1932–)

US Democratic politician. He aided his brothers John and Robert Kennedy in their presidential campaigns of 1960 and 1968 respectively, and entered politics as a senator for Massachusetts in 1962. He failed to gain the presidential nomination in 1980, largely because of questions about his delay in reporting a car crash at Chappaquiddick Island, near Cape Cod, Massachusetts, in 1969, in which his passenger, Mary Jo Kopechne, was drowned.

Kennedy, John F(itzgerald) ('Jack') (1917–1963)

See page 230.

Kennedy, Joseph (Patrick) (1888–1969)

US industrialist and diplomat. As ambassador to the UK 1937–40, he was a strong advocate of appeasement of Nazi Germany. He groomed each of his sons – Joseph Patrick Kennedy, Jr (1915–1944), John F ◊Kennedy, Robert ◊Kennedy, and Edward ◊Kennedy – for a career in politics.

> *When the going gets tough, the tough get going.*
>
> JOSEPH KENNEDY
> J H Cutler *Honey Fitz*

A self-made millionaire, Kennedy ventured into the film industry, then set up the Securities and Exchange Commission (SEC) for F D Roosevelt. His eldest son, Joseph, was killed in action with the naval air force in World War II.

Kennedy, Robert Francis (1925–1968)

US Democratic politician and lawyer. He was presidential campaign manager for his brother John F ◊Kennedy in 1960, and as attorney general 1961–64 pursued a racket-busting policy and worked to enforce federal law in support of civil rights. He was assassin-

---

◆ K ELLY , P ETRA (1947–1992) ◆

German politician and activist. She was a vigorous campaigner against nuclear power and other environmental issues and founded the German Green Party in 1972. She was a member of the Bundestag (parliament) 1983–90, but then fell out with her party.

Born in Germany, Kelly was brought up in the USA and was influenced by the civil-rights movement there. She worked briefly in the office of lawyer and politician Robert Kennedy and, returning to Germany, she joined the European Economic Community as a civil servant in 1972. Her goal, to see the ecological movement as a global organization, became increasingly frustrated by the provincialism of the German Green Party. She died at the hands of her lover, the former general Gert Bastian, who then committed suicide.

Deeply concerned with radioactivity in the environment, having seen the early death of her half-sister from leukaemia, she carried out pioneering ecological work in her position with the European Economic Community. With her fluency in English, she emerged as the German Green Party's most prominent early spokesperson, and the leader of its pragmatic ('realo') wing as the party split into its increasingly bitter divisions. She was Green member of the German parliament 1983–90, and was one of the first Green MPs in the world.

Questions regarding the exact circumstances of Kelly's tragic death, and whether there had been a suicide pact between her and Gert, remain unanswered.

ated during his campaign for the 1968 Democratic presidential nomination.

He was also a key aide to his brother. When John F Kennedy's successor, Lyndon Johnson, preferred Hubert H Humphrey for the 1964 vice-presidential nomination, Kennedy resigned as attorney general and was elected senator for New York. When running for president, he advocated social justice at home and an end to the Vietnam War. During a campaign stop in California, he was shot by Sirhan Bissara Sirhan.

Kennedy was educated at Harvard and the University of Virginia Law School. He was an attorney at the Criminal Division of the Department of Justice 1951–52; chief counsel of the Senate Permanent Subcommittee on Investigations 1954–61; and chief counsel of the Senate Select Committee on Improper Activities in the Labor and Management Field 1957–61.

> *The free way of life proposes ends, but it does not prescribe means.*
>
> ROBERT KENNEDY *The Pursuit of Justice* part 5

His publications include *The Enemy Within* (1960), *Just Friends and Brave Enemies* (1962), and *The Pursuit of Justice* (1965).

FURTHER READING

Guthman, Edwin, and Shulman, Jeffrey *Robert Kennedy: In His Own Words* 1988

Newfield, Jack *Robert Kennedy: A Memoir* 1969

Schlesinger, Arthur *Robert Kennedy and his Times* 1978

Shannon, William *The Heir Apparent* 1967

Kent, Bruce (1929–)

English peace campaigner who was general secretary of the Campaign for Nuclear Disarmament (CND) 1980–85. He has published numerous articles on disarmament, Christianity, and peace. He was a Catholic priest until 1987.

Kent stood as the Labour party candidate for Oxford West and Abingdon in 1992 and organized a pressure group for tactical voting.

Kenyatta, Jomo (c.1894–1978)

See page 232.

Kerekou, Mathieu Ahmed (1933–)

Benin socialist politician and soldier, president 1980–91 and from 1996. In 1972, while deputy head of the Dahomey army, he led a coup to oust the ruling president and establish his own military government. He embarked on a programme of 'scientific socialism', changing his country's name to Benin to mark this change of direction. In 1987 he resigned from the army and confirmed a civilian administration. He was reelected president in 1989, but lost to Nicéphore Soglo in the 1991 presidential elections. He surprisingly won the March 1996 presidential elections despite claims of fraud.

Petra Kelly, leader of the German Green Party, talks to party supporters in Bonn, 1983. *Rex*

Kerensky, Alexandr Feodorovich (1881–1970)

Russian revolutionary politician, prime minister of the second provisional government before its collapse in November 1917, during the Russian Revolution. He was overthrown by the Bolshevik revolution and fled to France in 1918 and to the USA in 1940.

Kerouac, Jack (Jean Louis) (1922–1969)

US novelist. He named and epitomized the Beat Generation of the 1950s. The first of his autobiographical, myth-making books, *The Town and the City* (1950), was followed by the rhapsodic *On the Road* (1957). Other works written with similar free-wheeling energy and inspired by his interests in jazz and Buddhism include *The Dharma Bums* (1958), *Doctor Sax* (1959), and *Desolation Angels* (1965). His major contribution to poetry was *Mexico City Blues* (1959).

Kerouac became a legendary symbol of youthful rebellion from the late 1950s, but before his early death from alcoholism he had become a semi-recluse, unable to cope with his fame.

FURTHER READING

Charters, A *Kerouac: A Biography* 1973, 1994

Gifford, Barry, and Lee, Lawrence *Jack's Book: An Oral History of Jack Kerouac* 1978

Nicosia, Gerald *Memory Babe* 1983

Kerr, John Robert (1914–1990)

Australian lawyer who as governor general 1974–77

controversially dismissed Prime Minister Gough ◊Whitlam and his government in 1975.

He was the son of a Sydney boilermaker. After graduating from the University of Sydney, where he studied law, Kerr embarked on a legal career on the New South Wales circuit, becoming a judge of the Australian Supreme Court 1966–72 and chief justice of the Supreme Court of New South Wales 1972–74. He was appointed governor general in 1974 and achieved notoriety with the events of the following year. His dismissal of the Whitlam Labor government in November 1975, after the Senate had blocked the budget, divided the country. The government had suffered a defeat in the Senate, but retained a majority in the House of Representatives. Kerr called upon the leader of the opposition, Malcolm Fraser, to form an administration. Continuing widespread controversy over the correctness of his actions was a factor in Kerr's retirement in 1977.

FURTHER READING
Kerr, John *Matters for Judgment* 1978

Keynes, John Maynard, 1st Baron Keynes (1883–1946)

English economist. His *General Theory of Employment, Interest, and Money* (1936) proposed the prevention of financial crises and unemployment by adjusting demand through government control of credit and currency. He is responsible for that part of economics that studies whole economies, now known as macroeconomics.

Keynes's intellect was the sharpest and clearest that I have ever known. When I argued with him I felt that I took my life in my hands …
BERTRAND RUSSELL On John Maynard Keynes, in *Autobiography*

Keynes led the British delegation at the Bretton Woods Conference in 1944, which set up the International Monetary Fund.

His theories were widely accepted in the aftermath of World War II, and he was one of the most influential economists of the 20th century. His ideas are today

◆ KENNEDY, JOHN F(ITZGERALD) ('JACK') (1917–1963) ◆

35th president of the USA 1961–63, a Democrat; the first Roman Catholic and the youngest person to be elected US president. In foreign policy he carried through the unsuccessful Bay of Pigs invasion of Cuba, and secured the withdrawal of Soviet missiles from the island in 1962. His programme for reforms at home, called the New Frontier, was posthumously executed by Lyndon Johnson. Kennedy was assassinated while on a visit to Dallas, Texas, on 22 November 1963. Lee Harvey Oswald (1939–1963), who was shot dead within a few days by Jack Ruby (1911–1967), was named as the assassin.

The son of industrialist and diplomat Joseph Kennedy, he was born in Brookline, Massachusetts, educated at Harvard and briefly at the London School of Economics, and served in the navy in the Pacific during World War II, winning the Purple Heart and the Navy and Marine Corps medal.

After a brief career in journalism he was elected to the House of Representatives in 1946. At this point he was mainly concerned with domestic politics and showed few signs of the internationalism for which he later became famous. In 1952 he was elected to the Senate from Massachusetts, defeating Republican Henry Cabot Lodge, Jr, one of Dwight D Eisenhower's leading supporters. In 1953 he married socialite Jacqueline Lee Bouvier (1929–1995).

Kennedy made his name as a supporter of civil-rights legislation and as a prominent

internationalist, but his youth and his Roman Catholicism were considered serious barriers to the White House. His victory in all seven primaries that he entered, however, assured his place as Democratic candidate for the presidency in 1960. His programme was a radical one, covering promises to deal with both civil rights and social reform. On television Kennedy debated well against the Republican candidate Richard ◊Nixon, yet went on to win the presidency by one of the narrowest margins ever recorded.

Those who make peaceful revolution impossible will make violent revolution inevitable.
JOHN F KENNEDY Speech at White House
13 March 1962

Critics suggest style was more important than substance in the Kennedy White House, but he inspired a generation of idealists and created an aura of positive activism. He brought academics and intellectuals to Washington, DC, as advisers, and his wit and charisma combined with political shrewdness disarmed many critics. His inaugural address, with its emphasis on the New Frontier, was reminiscent of Franklin D Roosevelt. In fact Kennedy did not succeed in carrying through any major domestic legislation, though, with the aid of his brother Robert ◊Kennedy, who was attorney

often contrasted with monetarism, the theory that economic policy should be based on control of the money supply.

Keynes was a fellow of King's College, Cambridge. He worked at the Treasury during World War I, and took part in the peace conference as chief Treasury representative, but resigned in protest against the financial terms of the treaty. He justified his action in *The Economic Consequences of the Peace* (1919). He was created Baron in 1942.

Khaddhafi, Moamer al (1942–)

See page 234.

Khalaf, Salah, also known as *Abu Iyad* (1933–1991)

Palestinian nationalist leader. He became a refugee in 1948 when Israel became independent, and was one of the four founder members – with Yassir Arafat – of the Palestine Liberation Organization (PLO) in the 1960s. One of its most senior members, he was involved with the Black September group, and is believed to have orchestrated their campaign of terrorist attacks such as the 1972 killing of 11 Israeli athletes at the Munich Olympics. He later argued for a diplomatic as well as a terrorist campaign. He was assassinated by an Arab dissident follower of Abu Nidal.

Khalid, ibn Abdul Aziz al-Saud (1913–1982)

King of Saudi Arabia 1975–82. A cautious and unassuming traditionalist leader, he maintained close ties with Bedouin tribesmen, who shared his interests in falconry and hunting. Suffering from a deteriorating heart condition, he relied on his half-brother, the more liberal and westernized Crown Prince ◊Fahd, to oversee day-to-day government. However, Khalid used his influence to bring a halt to the Lebanese civil war 1975–76 and to persuade fellow members of the Organization of Petroleum-Exporting Countries (OPEC) to moderate their price increases. However, Saudi Arabia refused to support the Israel–Egypt Camp David peace accords of 1978 and from 1980 Khalid gave backing to Iraq in its war against Iran. This was motivated by fears of the potentially destabilizing influence of the fundamentalist Shi'ite Muslim revolution in Islam, which had led to Saudi Shi'ite demon-

---

general, desegregation continued and the Civil Rights Bill was introduced. He created the Peace Corps – volunteers who give various types of health, agricultural, and educational aid overseas – and he proposed the Alliance for Progress for aid to Latin America.

There is something very 18th century about this young man. He is always on his toes during our discussions. But in the evening there will be music and wine and pretty women.

HAROLD MACMILLAN On John F Kennedy. Quoted in the *New York Journal*, 1962

It was in foreign affairs that Kennedy's presidency was most notable. Early in 1961 came the fiasco of the Bay of Pigs, which, though partially carried over from the previous administration, was undoubtedly Kennedy's responsibility. This was redeemed by his masterly handling of the Cuban missile crisis of 1962, where his calm and firm approach had a prolonged effect on US–Soviet relations. The Nuclear Test Ban Treaty of 1963 achieved a further lessening of tension. Kennedy's internationalism won him a popular European reputation not attained by any of his predecessors. He visited Western Europe in 1961 and 1963, and was tumultuously received on each occasion. The US involvement in the Vietnam War began during Kennedy's administration.

On 22 November, while on a tour of Texas,

Kennedy was shot while being driven through Dallas and died shortly afterwards. His presumed assassin, Lee Harvey Oswald, was himself shot on 24 November while under arrest. Kennedy's death caused worldwide grief and his funeral was attended by heads of state and their representatives from all over the world. He was buried in Arlington National Cemetery.

In the 30 years following his assassination, more than 2,000 books were published about his death and a number of conspiracy theories put forward, mostly involving the KGB, FBI, or CIA. The case was investigated by a special commission headed by Chief Justice Earl ◊Warren. The commission determined that Oswald acted alone, although a later congressional committee re-examined the evidence and determined that Kennedy 'was probably assassinated as a result of a conspiracy'. Oswald was an ex-marine who had gone to live in the USSR in 1959 and returned when he could not become a Soviet citizen. Ruby was a Dallas nightclub owner, associated with the underworld and the police. See photograph on page 232.

FURTHER READING

Gadney, R *Kennedy* 1983

Lane, Mark *Rush to Judgement: A Critique of the Warren Commission Enquiry* 1966

Longford, Lord *Kennedy* 1976

Manchester, William *Death of a President* 1967

Schlesinger, Arthur M, Jr *A Thousand Days: John F Kennedy in the White House* 1965

Sorenson, Theodore *Kennedy* 1965

White, T H *The Making of the President 1960* 1961

John F Kennedy, 1963. *AKG London*

was assassinated. With annual oil revenues exceeding $22 billion in 1974, Saudi Arabia had become, by this time, the most influential country in the Arab world. Oil revenues were distributed to support generous welfare provision to Saudi citizens, who, in return, accepted autocratic rule by the al-Saud family.

Khalifa, Sheikh Isa bin Sulman al- (1933–)

Emir of Bahrain from 1961. Using the country's oil wealth, he improved transportation, housing, and education. His younger brother, Sheikh Khalifa bin Salman al-Khalifa (1935–), became prime minister in 1970. However, despite a short-lived attempt 1973–75 at a popularly elected National Assembly, the al-Khalifa family proved wary of sharing power. During the 1990–91 Gulf War, Bahrain supported the UN-sponsored military action against Iraq, which had invaded Kuwait. However, in 1994–95 the moderate pro-Western al-Khalifa monarchy was shaken by violent Shi'ite Muslim demonstrations in the capital, Manama, calling for the restoration of the National Assembly. Shi'ite opposition to the regime has been growing since the 1979 Iranian Revolution.

Educated at the royal court by British and Arab tutors, Sheikh Isa was born into the Sunni Muslim al-Khalifa family that had dominated Bahrain since the late 18th century, enjoying British protection since 1820. He became heir apparent in 1958 and succeeded his father, Sheikkh Sulman, as head of state in November 1961. The title emir was assumed in August 1971, after Bahrain was established as an independent state, in the wake of the collapse of a short-lived federation with Qatar and the Trucial States (forerunners of the United Arab Emirates).

Khama, Seretse (1921–1980)

Botswanan politician, prime minister of Bechuana-

strations in Hasa 1979–80, and to a two-week protest by Wahabi extremists, in the Grand Mosque in Mecca, against the Saudi regime's alleged deviation from the true path of Islam.

The fourth son of King Abdul Aziz ◊Ibn Saud, the founder of the Saudi dynasty, he succeeded to the throne in 1975 when his half-brother, King ◊Faisal,

---

◆ KENYATTA, JOMO (C. 1894–1978) ASSUMED NAME OF KAMAU NGENGI ◆

Kenyan nationalist politician, prime minister from 1963, as well as the first president of Kenya from 1964, until his death. He led the Kenya African Union from 1947 (KANU from 1963) and was active in liberating Kenya from British rule.

A member of the Kikuyu ethnic group, Kenyatta was born near Fort Hall, son of a farmer. Brought up at a Church of Scotland mission, he joined the Kikuyu Central Association (KCA), devoted to recovery of Kikuyu lands from white settlers, and became its president. He spent some years in the UK, returning to Kenya in 1946. He became president of the Kenya African Union (successor to the banned KCA in 1947). In 1953 he was

sentenced to seven years' imprisonment for his management of the guerrilla organization Mau Mau, though some doubt has been cast on his complicity. Released to exile in northern Kenya in 1958, he was allowed to return to Kikuyuland in 1961 and became prime minister in 1963 (also president from 1964) of independent Kenya. His slogans were *'Uhuru na moja'* (Freedom and unity) and *'Harambee'* (Let's get going).

FURTHER READING
Gertzel, C *The Politics of Independent Kenya* 1970
Kenyatta, Jomo *Suffering Without Bitterness* (memoirs) 1968
Murray-Brown, Jeremy *Kenyatta* 1973

land in 1965, and first president of Botswana 1966–80. He founded the Bechuanaland Democratic Party in 1962 and led his country to independence in 1966. Botswana prospered under his leadership, both economically and politically, and he won every post-independence election until his death in July 1980. He was knighted in 1966.

Son of the Bamangwato chief Sekoma II (died 1925), Khama studied law in the UK and married an Englishwoman, Ruth Williams. This marriage was strongly condemned by his uncle Tshekedi Khama, who had been regent during his minority, as contrary to tribal custom. Despite this opposition, Seretse Khama was publicly appointed the *kgosi* (king) of the Bangwato in June 1949. The British government refused to recognize his title and forced him to live in exile in England in 1950. Seretse and Ruth Khama were allowed to return to Bechuanaland in 1956 on condition that he renounced his claim to chieftaincy.

Khamenei, Ayatollah Said Ali (1939–   )

Iranian Muslim cleric and politician, president of Iran 1981–89 and Supreme Spiritual Leader from 1989. From the early 1960s Khamenei founded the Council of Militant Clerics and was an active supporter of Ayatollah Ruhollah ◊Khomeini's movement against Shah Reza Pahlavi. He was arrested in 1963 and detained in prison 1967–69 and 1974–75, before being exiled in 1977. After the revolution in 1979, Khamenei founded the Islamic Republican Party (IRP), which became the ruling party, and served as a Majlis (parliament) deputy, commander of the Revolutionary Guard, and deputy defence minister. Wounded in an assassination attempt in June 1981, four months later he was elected state president. He was re-elected in August 1985, defeating two opponents, but on Khomeini's death in June 1989, resigned to become the country's Supreme Spiritual Leader and was given the religious title of Ayatollah. Somewhat less extreme than his predecessor, Ayatollah Khamenei sought to 'unfreeze' relations with the USA and to improve an economy that had been shattered by the 1980–88 Iran–Iraq War.

Born in Mashhad, in Khorasan province in northeast Iran, into a family of Islamic clerics, Khameini studied Islamic theology in An Naja, in Iraq, and at Qom, in Iran (studying under Khomeini).

Khan, Habibullah (1872–1919)

Afghan politician, emir of Afghanistan 1901–19. He renewed the arrangement with Britain by which the control of foreign relations was delegated to the British government. He also supported Britain during World War I. He was assassinated.

He was the son of Abd-er-Rahman.

Jomo Kenyatta. *Rex*

Khan, Ra'ana Liaquat Ali, born R'ana Pant (1905–1990)

Pakistani politician. In 1933 she married Nawabzada ◊Liaquat Ali Khan, who became prime minister on partition in 1947, and she was one of the first to organize assistance for refugees during the mass transit. In 1952 she was appointed a United Nations delegate, and between 1954 and 1966 represented her country as the first woman ambassador to the Netherlands, Italy, and Tunisia. In 1973 she became the first woman governor of Sind and was given the 1979 Hunan Rights Award.

Born in Almor, North India, she studied economics from Lucknow University before becoming lecturer in economics at Indraprashtha College for Women in New Delhi.

Khasbulatov, Ruslan (1943–   )

Russian politician, chair of the Supreme Soviet 1991–93. As Russian first vice president, he was a strong supporter of Boris ◊Yeltsin, but from 1991 relations between the two deteriorated and Khasbulatov repeatedly tried to block the Russian leader's economic and political reforms. His critics accused him of shifting his ideological ground to pursue his personal ambitions. In September 1993 he was arrested and imprisoned after leading a rebellion

Moamer al Khaddhafi, 1982. *Rex*

against Yeltsin, but was granted an amnesty and released in February 1994. He subsequently announced his retirement from national politics, but in December 1995 contested the leadership elections in his native Chechnya.

Khashoggi, Adnan (1935–)

Saudi entrepreneur and arms dealer who built up a large property company, Triad, based in Switzerland, and through ownership of banks, hotels, and real estate became a millionaire. In 1975 he was accused by the USA of receiving bribes to secure military contracts in Arab countries, and in 1986 he was financially disadvantaged by the slump in oil prices and political problems in Sudan. In April 1989 he was arrested in connection with illegal property deals. He successfully weathered all three setbacks.

Khatabi, Abdelkrim Mohamed al- (1882–1963)

Moroccan resistance leader. He led the uprising in the Rif Mountains 1920–26 and extended his resistance to include Spanish- and French-occupied territories. His struggle to maintain his short-lived Rif republic was to serve as a source of inspiration to the emerging nationalist movement in its fight for independence. It was only after a joint French and Spanish military campaign that he surrendered and was made prisoner. Exiled to the French colony of Réunion, he escaped to Egypt in 1947 and died there.

Khatami, Sayed Muhammad (1943–)

Iranian Islamic-reformist political leader, president since 1997. Backed by the Servants of Iran's Construction Party (popularly known as G-16), the urban middle classes, and left-wing groups, he was elected president in May 1997, with nearly 70% of the popular vote, comprehensively defeating the conservative speaker of the Majlis (assembly), Ali Akbar Nateq-Nuri. He formally replaced Ali Akbar Hashemi ◊Rafsanjani as Iran's fifth president in August 1997.

As president, Khatami, who is effective head of government, sought a rapprochement with the West, as a means of improving the economy. In October 1998 it was announced that the Iranian regime would not continue to pursue the arrest and punishment of the British author Salman Rushdie, whose *Satanic Verses* (1988) had offended many Muslims. However, Khatami faced continuing opposition from Islamic conservatives, grouped around Iran's spiritual leader,

---

◆ KHADDHAFI, MOAMER AL (1942–) OR GADDAFI OR QADDAFI ◆

Libyan revolutionary leader. Overthrowing King Idris in 1969, he became virtual president of a republic, although he nominally gave up all except an ideological role in 1974. He favours territorial expansion in North Africa reaching as far as the Democratic Republic of Congo (formerly Zaire), has supported rebels in Chad, and has proposed mergers with a number of countries. During the Gulf War, however, he advocated diplomacy rather than war. Imbued with Nasserism, he was to develop afterwards his own theories (*Green Book*), based on what he called 'natural socialism' of an egalitarian nature.

Khaddhafi's alleged complicity in international terrorism led to his country's diplomatic isolation during the 1980s and in 1992 United Nations sanctions were imposed against Libya after his refusal to allow extradiction of two suspects in the Lockerbie and Union de Transports Aériens bombings.

In 1995 Khaddhafi faced an escalating campaign of violence by militant Islamicists, the strongest challenge to his regime to date.

Ayatollah Ali ◊Khamenei. This was evident in April 1998 when Khatami's reformist ally, Gholamhossain Karbaschi, the popular mayor of Tehran, was briefly arrested as part of a corruption investigation.

Born in Ardakan, Khatami was a graduate of the religious science centre in Qom and also studied theology and philosophy in Hamburg, Germany. During the 1970s, he was active in resistance to the westernizing shah of Iran, Reza Pahlavi, though he acquired a reputation for religious tolerance and political liberalism. He returned to Iran after the Islamic Revolution of 1979 and was elected a Majlis (parliamentary) deputy in 1980. From 1982, as minister of culture, he eased censorship, allowing more foreign publications into Iran. This provoked conservative attacks, culminating in his resignation in July 1992, after being accused of excessive leniency towards westernized intellectuals.

Khomeini, Ayatollah Ruhollah, born Ruholla Hendi (1900–1989)

Iranian Shi'ite Muslim leader. An active critic of the pro-Western Pahlavi dynasty, he was exiled to Turkey and Iraq in 1964 and to France in 1978. He returned when the shah left the country in 1979, and established a fundamentalist Islamic Republic.

Born in Khomein, Iraq, he was a religious scholar and leader. He became a virtual head of state after the collapse of the Pahlavi regime and presided over the turbulent Islamic Revolution which aimed at stripping the country of all Western influences. In 1989 he called a *fatwa* demanding the death of the controversial writer Salman Rushdie, author of *Satanic Verses* (1988). His rule was marked by political instability, a protracted war with Iraq, economic difficulties, and a fierce suppression of opposition within Iran, including executions of thousands of opponents.

FURTHER READING
Bakhash, S *The Reign of the Ayatollahs* 1986
Keddie, N R *Religion and Politics in Iran* 1983
Montazzam, M A A *The Life and Times of Ayatollah Khomeini* 1994

Khrushchev, Nikita Sergeyevich (1894–1971)

Soviet politician, secretary general of the Communist Party 1953–64, and premier 1958–64. He emerged as leader from the power struggle following Joseph Stalin's death and was the first official to denounce Stalin, in 1956. His de-Stalinization programme gave rise to revolts in Poland and Hungary in 1956. Because of problems with the economy and foreign affairs (a breach with China in 1960, conflict with the USA in the Cuban missile crisis of 1962), he was ousted by Leonid Brezhnev and Alexei Kosygin.

Born near Kursk, the son of a miner, Khrushchev fought in the post-Revolutionary civil war 1917–20, and in World War II organized the guerrilla defence of his native Ukraine. He denounced Stalinism in a secret session of the party in February 1956.

Many victims of the purges of the 1930s were either released or posthumously rehabilitated, but when Hungary revolted in October 1956 against Soviet domination, there was immediate Soviet intervention. In 1958 Khrushchev succeeded Nikolai Bulganin as chair of the council of ministers (prime minister). His policy of competition with capitalism was successful in the space programme, which launched the world's first satellite (*Sputnik*). Because of the Cuban crisis and the personal feud with Mao Zedong that led to the Sino-Soviet split, he was compelled to resign in 1964, although by 1965 his reputation was to some extent officially restored. In April 1989 his 'secret speech' against Stalin in February 1956 was officially published for the first time. See photograph on page 82.

We are in favour of a détente, but if anybody thinks that for this reason we shall forget about Marx, Engels, and Lenin, he is mistaken. This will happen when shrimps learn to whistle.
NIKITA KHRUSHCHEV At Geneva conference
July 1955

FURTHER READING
Ebon, Martin *Nikita Khrushchev* 1986
Khrushchev, Nikita *Khrushchev Remembers* (memoirs) translation 1970–74
Medvedev, Roy A *Khrushchev* 1982

Kiesinger, Kurt Georg (1904–1988)

West German Christian Democrat politician. He succeeded Ludwig ◊Erhard as chancellor in 1966, heading a 'grand coalition' of the Christian Democrats (CDU) and the Social Democrats (SPD) until 1969, when Willy ◊Brandt took over as chancellor.

Kiesinger was born in Ebingen and trained as a lawyer. He joined the Nazi party in 1933 and worked in the German Foreign Office during World War II. After a period of internment after the war, he was exonerated by a German court in 1948 and was elected to the lower house of the West German legislature (Bundestag) in 1949. In 1958 he became minister president of Baden Württemberg, serving in this capacity until 1966, when an economic crisis led to the resignation of Erhard. He was also president of the Bundesrat (the upper house of the German legislature) 1962–63.

Kilmuir, David Patrick Maxwell Fyfe, 1st Earl of Kilmuir (1900–1967)

British lawyer and Conservative politician, born in Aberdeen, Scotland. He was solicitor general 1942–45 and attorney general in 1945 during the governments of Winston Churchill. He was home secretary 1951–54 and Lord Chancellor 1954–62.

Kim Dae Jung (1924–)

South Korean social-democratic politician, president from 1998. As a committed opponent of the regime of

General Park Chung Hee, he suffered imprisonment and exile.

A Roman Catholic, born in the poor southwestern province of Cholla, Kim was imprisoned by communist troops during the Korean War. He rose to prominence as an opponent of Park and was only narrowly defeated when he challenged Park for the presidency in 1971. He was imprisoned 1976–78 and 1980–82 for alleged 'anti-government activities' and lived in the USA 1982–85. On his return to South Korea he spearheaded a fragmented opposition campaign for democratization, but, being one of several opposition candidates, was defeated by the government nominee, Roh Tae-woo, in the presidential election of December 1987.

A political firebrand, Kim enjoyed strong support among blue-collar workers and fellow Chollans, but was feared and distrusted by the country's business and military elite. He was again defeated in the presidential elections in 1992. However, assisted by divisions on the right, he was eventually elected president in December 1997 and started in office in 1998, facing a serious economic crisis in the country and the entire region. He granted amnesty to 2,304 prisoners in March 1998, and introduced new labour laws, ending the right to lifelong employment, which provoked a series of strikes.

Kim Il Sung (1912–1994)

North Korean communist politician and marshal. He became prime minister in 1948 and led North Korea in the Korean War 1950–53. He became president in 1972, retaining the presidency of the Communist Workers' party. He liked to be known as the 'Great Leader' and campaigned constantly for the reunification of Korea. His son Kim Jong Il succeeded him.

Kim Jong Il (1942–)

North Korean communist politician, national leader from 1994, when he succeeded his father, ◊Kim Il Sung in what was the first dynastic succession in the communist world. Despite his official designation 'Dear Leader', he lacked his father's charisma and did not automatically inherit the public adulation accorded to him. In October 1997 he formally became general secretary of the ruling communist party amid famine in North Korea.

Kim Jong Il held a succession of senior party posts from the early 1960s. He was a member of the politburo from 1974 and its controlling inner presidium from 1980 and, although he had received no military training, was made commander in chief of the armed forces in 1991. The belief that he masterminded terrorist activities in the 1970s and 1980s made the West apprehensive about the succession.

Kim Young Sam (1927–)

South Korean democratic politician, president 1993–98. In 1990 he merged the National Democratic Party (NNP) with the ruling party to form the Democratic Liberal Party (DLP), now known as the New Korean Party. In the December 1992 presidential election he captured 42% of the national vote, assuming office in February 1993. As president, he encouraged greater political openness, some deregulation of the economy, and a globalization (segyehwa) initiative.

A member of the National Assembly from 1954 and president of the NDP from 1974, he lost his seat and was later placed under house arrest because of his opposition to President Park Chung Hee. In 1983 he led a prodemocracy hunger strike but in 1987 failed to defeat Roh Tae-woo in the presidential election.

As president, in 1996 he was instrumental in placing on trial the former presidents Roh Tae-woo and Chun Doo-hwan on sedition charges. In 1997 his reputation was tarnished by a financial scandal related to the failed Hanbo conglomerate, and in October 1997 his son Kim Hyum Chul was fined $1.5 million and jailed for three years for bribery and tax evasion. He was replaced as president by the veteran opposition leader ◊Kim Dae Jung, following elections which he was unable to contest as a result of Korea's term-limit rules.

King, Billie Jean, born Moffitt (1943–)

US tennis player. She won a record 20 Wimbledon titles 1961–79 and 39 Grand Slam titles, and fought for equal treatment and equal pay for women tennis players. In 1973 she formed the Women's Tennis Association and the Players' Union. In 1974, with Olympic swimmer Donna de Varona and others, she created the Women's Sports Foundation to support and promote women in sport. That same year, in front of a worldwide audience, she beat Bobby Riggs, a self-confessed chauvinist and critic of women in sport.

FURTHER READING
King, Billie Jean *The Autobiography of Billie Jean King*
Sanford, William R, and Green, Carl R *Billie Jean King* 1993

King, W(illiam) L(yon) Mackenzie (1874–1950)

See page 238.

Kinnock, Neil Gordon (1942–)

British Labour politician, party leader 1983–92. Born and educated in Wales, he was elected to represent a Welsh constituency in Parliament in 1970 (Islwyn from

---

If Margaret Thatcher wins on Thursday, I warn you not to be ordinary, I warn you not to be young, I warn you not to fall ill, and I warn you not to grow old.

NEIL KINNOCK Speech at Bridgend 7 June 1983

1983). He was further left than prime ministers Harold Wilson and James Callaghan, but as party leader (in succession to Michael Foot) adopted a moderate position, initiating a major policy review 1988–89. He resigned as party leader after Labour's defeat in the 1992 general election. In 1994 he left Parliament to become a European commissioner and was given the transport portfolio.

FURTHER READING
Harris, Robert *The Making of Neil Kinnock* 1984
Jones, Eileen *Neil Kinnock* 1994

Kiriyenko, Sergei Maksimovich (1963–)

Russian politician, prime minister March–August 1997.

Kiriyenko was the youngest, and shortest-lived, Russian prime minister to date. A banker and oil-refinery executive who rose with Boris Nemtsov, the radical governor of Nizhniy-Novgorod, he was brought to Moscow by Nemtsov when the latter was first deputy prime minister, to take up the post of deputy energy minister in 1997. But when, in March 1998, President Boris ◊Yeltsin wanted to send a message that he was swinging his support behind another bout of radical reform, Kiriyenko was plucked from obscurity to lead the government. Impressing even sceptics with his grasp of detail before a parliament that only reluctantly confirmed him in the third round of voting, he was, however, overwhelmed by the economic storm. He could not get his emergency programme past parliament and announced, on 17 August, default on domestic and foreign debt and a devaluation of the rouble. He was fired later that month and replaced – albeit briefly – by the man he had replaced, Viktor ◊Chernomyrdin.

Kirk, Norman Eric (1923–1974)

New Zealand Labour centre-left politician, prime minister 1972–74. He withdrew New Zealand troops from the Vietnam War, attempted to block French nuclear tests in the Pacific, and developed closer ties with Australia, as a counterbalance to UK's entry to the European Economic Community (EEC; now the European Union). He died in office and was succeeded as prime minister by his finance minister, Wallace ◊Rowling.

After working as an engine driver, he entered parliament in 1957, representing the Labour Party. He became party president in 1964 and was leader of the opposition in the House of Representatives until victory in the 1972 general election ended 12 years of National Party government.

Kirkland-Casgrain, Marie-Claire (1924–)

Canadian Liberal politician who was the first woman to be elected to the Legislative Assembly of Quebec

---

◆ KING, MARTIN LUTHER, JR (1929–1968) ◆

US civil-rights campaigner, black leader, and Baptist minister. He first came to national attention as leader of the Montgomery, Alabama, bus boycott in 1955, and was one of the organizers of the march of 200,000 people on Washington, DC, in 1963 to demand racial equality. An advocate of nonviolence, he was awarded the Nobel Peace Prize in 1964. On 4 April 1968 he was assassinated in Memphis, Tennessee, by James Earl Ray (1928–).

King was a founder of the Southern Christian Leadership Conference in 1957. A brilliant and moving speaker, he was the symbol of, and a leading figure in, the campaign for integration and equal rights in the late 1950s and early 1960s. In the mid-1960s his moderate approach was criticized by black militants. He was the target of

---

I want to be the white man's brother, not his brother-in-law.

MARTIN LUTHER KING *New York Journal-American*
10 September 1962

---

intensive investigation by the federal authorities, chiefly the FBI under J Edgar ◊Hoover. His personal life was scrutinized and criticized by those opposed to his policies.

King's birthday (15 January) is observed on the third Monday in January as a public holiday in the USA.

The son of a Baptist minister, King was born in Atlanta, Georgia, educated at Morehouse College and Boston University, and ordained to the ministry in Atlanta in 1947. He became a pastor in Montgomery, but moved back to his father's church in Atlanta in 1956. He wrote *Stride Toward Freedom* (1958), *Why We Can't Wait* (1964), and *Where Do We Go From Here: Chaos or Community* (1967).

Amidst speculations surrounding his death, the US attorney general Janet Reno announced in 1998 that a new review into the assassination would be opened. See photograph on page 239.

FURTHER READING
Fairclough, A *To Redeem the Soul of America* 1987
Lewis, D L *Martin Luther King: A Critical Biography* 1970
Oates, S B *Let the Trumpet Sound: A Life of Martin Luther King Jr* 1982

1961–73 and also the first woman appointed as a cabinet minister. She played a significant role in the promotion of women's issues, culminating in the passing of three bills (1964, 1969, and 1973), which protected the civil rights of married women in particular.

Born in Palmer, Massachusetts, USA, Kirkland-Casgrain trained as a lawyer and was keen to follow her father, Charles-Aimé, into politics. In the 1960s, she became an adviser to the Young Liberals and was president of the Mariana B Jodoin Club's Constitution Committee and the Fédération des Femmes Libérales du Québec. She was a minister without portfolio from 1962–64, and minister of transportation and communications 1964–66. In 1970 she moved to the department of tourism, game, and fishing. She left politics in 1973 and, from 1980, worked as a judge until her retirement in 1991.

Kirkpatrick, Jeane Duane Jordan (1926–)

US politician and professor of political science. She served as US ambassador to the United Nations 1981–85. Originally a Democrat, she often spoke out against communism and left-wing causes. She joined the Republican Party in 1985.

Born in Duncan, Oklahoma, she graduated from Barnard College and Columbia University. She taught at Georgetown University 1967–81 and helped to form the Coalition for a Democratic Majority in 1972.

Kirov, Sergei Mironovich (1886–1934)

Russian Bolshevik leader who joined the party in 1904 and played a prominent part in the 1918–20 civil war. As one of Joseph ◊Stalin's closest associates, he became first secretary of the Leningrad Communist Party. His assassination, possibly engineered by Stalin, led to the political trials held during the next four years as part of the purge.

Kishi, Nobusuke (1896–1987)

Japanese right-wing politician and prime minister 1957–60. A government minister during World War II and imprisoned in 1945, he was never put on trial and returned to politics in 1953. During his premiership, Japan began a substantial rearmament programme and signed a security treaty with the USA that gave rise to massive protests both in the Diet (parliament) and on the streets.

Kissinger, Henry (Alfred) (1923–)

See page 240.

Kita, Ikki (1883–1937)

Japanese political activist whose convictions were a mixture of socialism, anti-Westernism. and nationalism. These ideas influenced the young officers who attempted an unsuccessful coup against the government in February 1936. In the subsequent repression, Kita was arrested and executed.

◆ KING, W(ILLIAM) L(YON) MACKENZIE (1874–1950) ◆

Canadian Liberal prime minister 1921–26, 1926–30, and 1935–48. He maintained the unity of the English- and French-speaking populations, and was instrumental in establishing equal status for Canada with the UK.

In 1925 King's request to Governor General Julian Byng to dissolve parliament was initially refused. As a result, after his re-election in 1926 King insisted that the governor general should represent only the British crown and not the British government. This was eventually incorporated in the Statute of Westminster of 1931, which defined dominion status.

When Britain declared war on Germany in 1939, King, by postponing Canada's declaration for a week, affirmed Canada's independence in foreign affairs. When the Conservative opposition criticized Canada's war efforts as inadequate, King sought re-election and gained it decisively, the real issue being conscription, which he consistently opposed.

King was born in Berlin (now Kitchener), Ontario, and educated at Toronto University. He became deputy minister of labour and editor of

the *Labour Gazette* in 1900, and chaired several royal commissions on labour and immigration problems. In 1906 and 1908 he represented Canada in negotiations with the UK regarding immigration, and in 1908 became a member of the Dominion of Canada parliament. Beaten in the Liberal overthrow of 1911, he spent the years 1914–18 with the Rockefeller Foundation in the USA.

He was re-elected to parliament in 1919 and became leader of the Liberal Party in August that year, succeeding Wilfrid Laurier, and in 1921 became prime minister in succession to Arthur Meighen. In July 1930 the elections went against King, and he was succeeded by the Conservative Richard Bennett. In 1935, however, the Liberals won the most sweeping victory in the history of Canadian politics, winning 174 seats out of 250, and King became premier again. In August 1940 he negotiated with US president Franklin D Roosevelt the setting-up of a permanent Joint Defence Committee for the defence of the western hemisphere. King resigned as prime minister in 1948, and was succeeded by Louis S St Laurent.

Kitchener, Horatio (Herbert), 1st Earl Kitchener of Khartoum (1850–1916)

British soldier and administrator. He defeated the Sudanese at the Battle of Omdurman in 1898 and reoccupied Khartoum. In South Africa, he was commander in chief 1900–02 during the Boer War, and he commanded the forces in India 1902–09. Appointed war minister on the outbreak of World War I, he was successful in his campaign calling for voluntary recruitment.

Kitchener was born in County Kerry, Ireland. He was commissioned in 1871, and transferred to the Egyptian army in 1882. Promoted to commander in chief in 1892, he forced a French expedition to withdraw from the Sudan in the Fashoda Incident. During the Boer War he acted first as Lord Roberts's chief of staff and then as commander in chief. He conducted war by a scorched-earth policy and created the earliest concentration camps for civilians. Subsequently he commanded the forces in India and acted as British agent in Egypt, and in 1914 received an earldom. As British secretary of state for war from 1914, he modernized the British forces. He was one of the first to realize that the war would not be 'over by Christmas', and planned for an entrenched three-year war, for which he began raising new armies. He bears some responsibility for the failure of the Gallipoli campaign, having initially refused any troops for the venture, and from then on his influence declined. He drowned when his ship struck a German mine on the way to Russia.

FURTHER READING
Cassar, G H *Kitchener: Architect of Victory* 1977
Royle, T *The Kitchener Enigma* 1985
Warner, Phillip *Kitchener: The Man Behind the Legend* 1986

Klaus, Václav (1941–)

Czech politician and economist, prime minister of the Czech Republic 1993–97. Before the break-up of Czechoslovakia, he served in the government of Václav Havel and was chair of Civic Forum from 1990, breaking away to form the right-of-centre Civic Democratic Party (CDP) in 1991. The architect of Eastern Europe's initially most successful economic reform programme, he was a keen promoter of membership of the European Union.

Klaus was born and educated in Prague and went on to hold a number of academic posts 1971–87. He became politically active in the events that led to the 'velvet revolution' of November 1989. He was federal finance minister in the government of Václav Havel 1991–92 and was then elected chair of Civic Forum in October 1990. Moving to the right of the political spectrum, he established the CDP in 1991 as deputy prime minister. When the new independent republic

Martin Luther King. *Rex*

was created, in January 1993, Klaus became its first prime minister. Market-centred reforms were swiftly introduced and met with success, but after elections in 1996, Kalus headed an increasingly divided minority coalition and faced problems of slowing economic growth driving levels of corruption. He resigned in November 1997 after a scandal over party financing, which led to a serious split in the CDP in 1998 and to the formation of a breakaway Freedom Union party.

FURTHER READING
Klaus, Václav *The Ten Commandments of Systemic Reform* 1993, *Dopocítávání do jedné* 1995, *Renaissance: The Rebirth of Liberty in the Heart of Europe* 1997

Knowland, William Fife (1908–)

US politician. He was a Republican senator 1945–59 and leader of the Senate 1953–59. In 1964 he promoted the presidential candidature of Barry ◊Goldwater.

Koch, Ed(ward Irving) (1924–)

US politician, mayor of the city of New York 1979–89. A Democrat, he was a member of Congress 1969–79. As mayor, he faced a budget deficit and the deterioration of the inner city. He handled these problems skilfully and saved the city from bankruptcy. Defeated as a mayoral candidate in 1989, he returned to his law practice.

Koch was born in New York City, the son of Polish Jewish immigrants. He practised as a lawyer 1949–69, helping to found a Wall Street law firm, before being elected to the House of Representatives, serving five terms. His books include *His Eminence and Hizzoner* (1989), *All the Best, Letters from a Feisty Mayor* (1990), *Citizen Koch* (1992), and *Ed Koch on Everything* (1994).

Kocharian, Robert (1954–)

Armenian politician, founder of the Karabakh movement, prime minister of Armenia from 1997. He proclaimed the Nagorno-Karabakh region a republic within Azerbaijan on 2 September 1991. In the referendum of 10 December 1991 he was elected to the Supreme Council of the Nagorno-Karabakh Republic in Azerbaijan. He became chair of the State Committee for Defence and the leader of the republic from 1992 to 1994. He served as the first president of the Nagorno-Karabakh Republic in Azerbaijan, when he was elected by the Supreme Council in 1994. He became the prime minister of Armenia in March 1997.

Born in Stepanakert, he was educated at the Yerevan Polytechnic Institute and trained as an engineer, work-

ing at the Karabakh Silk Production Factory 1981–87 and serving as the secretary of the factory's Communist Party 1987–89. In 1989 he left the Communist Party and became a deputy of the Armenian Supreme Council 1989–94. In May 1998 he lifted the ban on the centre-left Armenian Revolutionary Federation (ARF) and brought two of its members into his cabinet.

Kohl, Helmut (1930–)

German conservative politician, leader of the Christian Democratic Union (CDU) from 1976, West German chancellor (prime minister) 1982–90, and German chancellor 1990–98. He oversaw the reunification of East and West Germany 1989–90 and in 1990 won a resounding victory to become the first chancellor of a reunited Germany. His miscalculation of the true costs of reunification and their subsequent effects on the German economy led to a dramatic fall in his popularity, but as the economy recovered, so did his public esteem, enabling him to achieve a historic fourth electoral victory in 1994. In November 1996 Kohl entered his 15th year as chancellor, overtaking the record previously held by Konrad Adenauer, Kohl's political mentor. His close working relationship with President François Mitterrand of France was the foundation for accelerating progress towards closer European integration, and Kohl was a strong backer of the project of a single European currency. His popu-

◆ KISSINGER, HENRY (ALFRED) (1923–) ◆

German-born US diplomat. After a brilliant academic career at Harvard University, he was appointed national security adviser in 1969 by President Richard Nixon, and was secretary of state 1973–77. His missions to the USSR and China improved US relations with both countries, and he took part in negotiating US withdrawal from Vietnam in 1973 and in Arab-Israeli peace negotiations 1973–75.

There cannot be a crisis next week. My schedule is already full.

HENRY KISSINGER *New York Times Magazine* 1 June 1969

His secret trips to Beijing and Moscow led to Nixon's visits to both countries and a general détente. In 1973 he shared the Nobel Peace Prize with Le Duc Tho, the North Vietnamese Politburo member, for his part in the Vietnamese peace negotiations, and in 1976 he was involved in the negotiations in Africa arising from the Angola and

Rhodesia crises. In 1983 President Ronald Reagan appointed him to head a bipartisan commission on Central America. He was widely regarded as the most powerful member of Nixon's administration.

Born at Furth in Bavaria, Kissinger emigrated to the USA in 1938. After work in Germany for army counter-intelligence, he won a scholarship to Harvard, and subsequently became a government consultant. With his book *Nuclear Weapons and Foreign Policy* (1956), he emerged as an authority on foreign affairs, advising presidents J F Kennedy and Lyndon Johnson. Kissinger was professor of government at Harvard 1962–69. His other publications include *The Necessity for Choice* (1961), *The Troubled Partnership* (1965), *American Foreign Policy*, and his autobiography *World Restored* (1973).

FURTHER READING

Isaacson, Walter *Kissinger: A Biography* 1992
Kissinger, Henry *White House Years* (memoirs) 1979, *Years of Upheaval* (memoirs) 1982
Starr, H *Henry Kissinger* 1984

larity slipped as a result of record levels of unemployment, which reached 12.6% in January 1998, and he lost office following his defeat by Gerhard Schroeder in the elections of September 1998.

Kohl studied law and history before entering the chemical industry. Elected to the Rhineland-Palatinate *Land* (state) parliament in 1959, he became state premier in 1969. After the 1976 Bundestag (federal parliament) elections Kohl led the CDU in opposition. He became federal chancellor in 1982, when the Free Democratic Party (FDP) withdrew support from the socialist government of Helmut Schmidt, and was elected at the head of a new coalition that included the FDP. From 1984 Kohl was implicated in the Flick bribes scandal over the illegal business funding of political parties, but he was cleared of all charges in 1986, and was re-elected chancellor in January 1987, December 1990, and October 1994.

FURTHER READING
Abromeit, H, and Padgett, S (eds) *Adenauer to Kohl: The Development of the German Chancellorship* 1994
Clemens, C, and Patterson, W E (eds) *The Kohl Chancellorship* 1998
Pruys, K H *Kohl: Genius of the Present* 1996

Koivisto, Mauno Henrik (1923–)
Finnish politician, prime minister 1968–70 and 1979–82, and president 1982–94. He was finance minister 1966–67 and led a Social Democratic Party coalition as prime minister 1968–70. He became interim president in 1981 after the resignation of Urho Kekkonen, and was elected president the following year. As president he shared power with Centre Party prime minister Esko Aho in Finland's unusual 'dual executive'.

Kok, Wim (1938–)
Dutch trade unionist and politician, leader of the Labour Party (PvdA) and prime minister from 1994. After an inconclusive general election in May 1994, Kok eventually succeeded in forming a broad-based three-party coalition of the PvdA with the People's Party of Freedom and Democracy (VVD) and Democrats 66, both centrist parties.

Kok spent over 20 years in the trade-union movement before winning a parliamentary seat for the PvdA in 1986. He became its leader and served as deputy prime minister 1989–94 in the centre-left coalition of Ruud Lubbers, before accepting the challenge of succeeding him.

Kollontai, Alexandra Mikhailovna, born Domontovich (1872–1952)
Russian revolutionary, politician, and writer. In 1905 she published *On the Question of the Class Struggle*, and, as commissar for public welfare, was the only female member of the first Bolshevik government. She campaigned for domestic reforms such as acceptance of free love, simplification of divorce laws, and collective child care.

In 1896, while on a tour of a large textile factory, she saw the appalling conditions endured by factory workers in Russia. Thereafter she devoted herself to improving conditions for working women. She was harassed by the police for her views and went into exile in Germany in 1914. On her return to the USSR in 1917 she joined the Bolsheviks. She was sent abroad by Stalin, first as trade minister, then as ambassador to Sweden in 1943.

Kollontai took part in the armistice negotiations ending the Soviet-Finnish War in 1944. She toured the USA to argue against its involvement in World War I and organized the first all-Russian Congress of Working and Peasant Women in 1918. In 1923 she published *The Love of Worker Bees*, a collection of short stories.

FURTHER READING
Clements, Barbara *Bolshevik Feminist* 1979
Kollontai, Alexandra *Autobiography of a Sexually Emancipated Woman* translation 1972
Porter, C *Alexandra Kollontai* 1981

Komura, Jutaro (1855–1911)
Japanese politician and diplomat. Komura was foreign minister at the time of the Russo-Japanese War (1904–05), which broke out over control of the northern Chinese province of Manchuria. Before the war, he had taken an uncompromising position toward Russia, and, when Japan emerged victorious, secured sole Japanese control over the important South Manchuria Railway.

Komura was born in Miyazaki on the island of Kyushu. He went abroad to study in the USA, graduating from Harvard University in 1877. He was appointed minister of foreign affairs in 1901. He later negotiated new, favourable commercial treaties with Japan's trading partners.

Kondyles, George (1879–1936)
Greek general and politician. A royalist supporter, Kondyles led a number of military interventions in Greek political life, most notably to restore King George II to the throne in 1935.

After fighting the Bulgarians in the Second Balkan War in 1913, Kondyles was made a colonel during World War I. During the 1920s, he divided his time between the military and politics, serving as minister of the interior 1923–25. In 1926 he led a coup against a republican government, briefly assumed the premiership in order to secure fair elections, and then resigned. He returned to political life in 1932 as war minister, and crushed an uprising by supporters of Eleuthérios ◊Venizelos in March 1935. Acting as regent, Kondyles succeeded in re-establishing George II as monarch in November 1935.

Konoe, Fumimaro, Prince (1891–1945)

Japanese politician and prime minister 1937–39 and 1940–41. He helped to engineer the fall of the ◊Tōjō government in 1944 but committed suicide after being suspected of war crimes.

He entered politics in the 1920s and was active in trying to curb the power of the army in government.

Koo, Vi Kyuin Wellington (1888–1985)

Chinese Nationalist politician, and diplomat. Born in Shanghai, as Ku Wei-chun, he studied in the USA, at Columbia University. At the conclusion of World War I, Koo represented Republican China at the 1919 Paris Peace Conference and during the interwar years served as foreign minister 1922–24 and 1931–32, and as finance minister 1926–27. Thereafter, as the Kuomintang (Guomindang, nationalist) regime which he supported was forced on the retreat, by the twin challenges of the communists and the Japanese, Koo concentrated on a diplomatic career.

He represented the Republic of China at the League of Nations 1932–34 and was ambassador to France 1932–41, the UK 1941–46, and the USA 1946–56. After the communist takeover of the mainland in 1949, he followed the Kuomintang Jiang Jie Shi (Chiang Kai-shek) to Taiwan and remained a senior official adviser to President Jiang until 1974.

Koresh, David, adopted name of Vernon Wayne Howell (1959–1993)

US Christian religious leader of the Branch Davidians, an offshoot of the Seventh-Day Adventist Church that believes in the literal apocalyptic end of history, as described in the biblical Book of Revelation, prior to the second coming of Christ. With a number of coreligionists, he died in a fire at the cult's headquarters in Waco, Texas, as a result of military intervention.

Koresh, born in Houston, Texas, began as a Seventh-Day Adventist. He is said to have memorized the New Testament by the time he was 12, and as a teenager he would pray for hours. But he was expelled from the Adventists as a 'bad influence on the young', and joined the Branch Davidians in 1981, rising to become their leader. Identifying with his own understanding of Christ as a vengeful messiah, he stressed sacrifice and martyrdom and meted out corporal punishment to children who disobeyed. He married a 14-year-old girl, Rachel Jones, in 1983 and considered it his right to have sexual relations with any woman in the group or their children.

The practices of the sect became increasingly repressive under Koresh's leadership, which led eventually to the siege of the Branch Davidians' camp in Waco by the Federal Bureau of Investigation in 1993. Their strong-arm military tactics fuelled the paranoia of the cult members, many of whom died when a fire broke out at the culmination of the siege.

Koroma, Alhaji Abdul Karim (1945–)

Sierra Leonean diplomat and lawyer, permanent representative to the United Nations (UN) from 1993, and permanent delegate to UNESCO. He was first elected to parliament in 1977, subsequently becoming minister of education, and remaining in the post until 1982. In 1985 he was promoted to foreign minister. In 1994 he became a judge in the International Court of Justice. He was ambassador to Ethiopia and to the Organization of African Unity (OAU) in 1988.

He received his higher education in England, where he gained a postgraduate degree in international relations. He is a former ambassador to the European Economic Community (now the European Union).

Kostov, Ivan (1949–)

Bulgarian politician, prime minister from 1997. A trained economist, he was elected to the National Assembly in 1991, representing the right-of-centre Union of Democratic Forces (UDF). Appointed finance minister, he introduced market-centred economic reforms. These provoked a wave of strikes, which brought down the government in 1992. However, in April 1997 he led the UDF to a decisive electoral victory over the Socialist Party, which had been undermined by a new economic crisis. His administration pledged to battle against corruption and organized crime and seek early membership of NATO and the European Union.

A forceful leader, Kostov transformed the UDF from a disparate body comprising 15 groups into a single party, which united with a number of smaller parties to fight the 1997 election. He inherited a near-bankrupt and lawless economy, and embarked on an ambitious privatization programme, with serious consequences to the unemployment level.

Kosygin, Alexei Nikolaievich (1904–1980)

Soviet politician, prime minister 1964–80. He was elected to the Supreme Soviet in 1938, became a member of the Politburo in 1946, deputy prime minister in 1960, and succeeded Nikita Khrushchev as premier (while Leonid Brezhnev succeeded him as party secretary). In the late 1960s Kosygin's influence declined.

Kotoku, Shusui (1871–1911)

Japanese journalist and political activist. A prolific writer, Kotoku moved from social democracy to pacifism to anarchist communism. In 1903, just before the Russo–Japanese War of 1904–05, he launched the antiwar *Heimin Shinbun* (*Common People's Newspaper*). First imprisoned in 1905, he was arrested again in 1910 in the infamous High Treason Incident and was executed in 1911.

Koundouriotis, Paul (1855–1935)

Greek admiral and president 1924–29. He acted as regent on the death of King Alexander in 1920 and again on the departure of King George II in 1923, and was proclaimed president in 1924. He successfully commanded the navy in the Balkan Wars of 1912–13, and was minister of marine in 1915 and 1917–19.

In April 1924 he was proclaimed president; he resigned in March 1926 after General Theodoros Pangalos assumed dictatorial powers, but a further military coup restored him to office on 25 August. Re-elected on 3 June 1929, he resigned on 9 December the same year.

Kovac, Michal (1930–)

Slovak politician, president 1993–98, when Czechoslovakia split in two to become the Czech and Slovak republics. He was known to favour some confederal arrangement with the Czech Republic and, in consequence, his election was welcomed by the Czech government.

Born in Lubiša in eastern Slovakia, Kovac was educated at the Commercial Academy at the Bratislava University of Economics. After a career as an academic economist and banker, he served as Slovak minister of finance in the post-communist administration between 1989 and 1991. A member of the centre-left nationalist Movement for a Democratic Slovakia (HZDS), he was the speaker of Czechoslovakia's federal assembly from 1992 and, after the 'velvet divorce' of January 1993, became the Slovak Republic's first president. From 1995 Kovac's relations with his prime minister, Vladimír ◊Meciar, became strained over allegations of Meciar's intent to oust him. Kovac's presidential powers went to Meciar after he stepped down at the end of his term in March 1998, after repeated failures to elect a successor. In August 1998 the presidency was taken over by the national council chair, Ivan Gasparovic.

Immediately after his election as president Kovac said he would resign his membership of the HZDS 'as a signal that we are ready to put the general interests of the country above partisan interests'.

Kozyrev, Andrei Vladimirovich (1951–)

Russian politician, foreign minister 1991–95. Appointed by Boris ◊Yeltsin as Russia's foreign minister while it still had no official foreign policy as part of the USSR, Kozyrev inherited in January 1991 a ministry that had been headed by Andrei ◊Gromyko and, under Mikhail Gorbachev, Eduard ◊Shevardnadze.

Like his economic colleagues, he was forced to change track and develop a policy that sought to emphasize Russia's dominant role among former Soviet states and was increasingly critical of Western, especially US, policies, particularly in the Balkans. He was, however, unable to stop or even to disguise convincingly the rapid decline of Russia's power in the world; under him – though not because of him – Russia sank from being at least formally the second superpower to being an ailing giant. He never succeeded in elaborating a foreign policy, largely because all policies were overtaken by the speed and scale of Russia's collapse.

Krasin, Leonid Borisovich (1870–1926)

Russian Bolshevik politician and diplomat. An early confederate of ◊Lenin, he played a leading role in the Russian Revolution of 1905. Following the success of the 1917 October Revolution, he held various official appointments within the new Soviet Union, and helped normalize its relations with other countries.

When still a student, Krasin joined one of the first social democratic organizations in Russia in 1890, and was expelled from St Petersburg Technical Institute. He finally graduated in 1900, and for the next 15 years combined working as an engineer with radical political activity. In 1904–05 he opposed Lenin's dictatorial methods within the Bolshevik Party and had him banished from the Central Committee. Despite this and further rifts with Lenin, however, he was made chair of the Council for Army Supply in 1918, and helped negotiate the Treaty of Brest-Litovsk, by which the Bolsheviks ended the war with Germany. He then held the posts of People's Commissar for Trade and Industry and for Transportation, before being made responsible for generating foreign trade. From 1922 to 1926 he was twice ambassador to Britain and once to France. Krasin's outstanding technical ability and business acumen enabled him to bring some order to the chaotic postwar Russian economy, and to persuade many foreign technical specialists to bring their expertise to the aid of the Soviet Union.

Kravchuk, Leonid Makarovych (1934–)

Ukrainian politician, president 1990–94. Formerly a member of the Ukrainian Communist Party (UCP), he became its ideology chief in the 1980s. After the suspension of the UCP in August 1991, Kravchuk became an advocate of independence and market-centred economic reform. Faced with a rapidly deteriorating economic situation in 1993, he assumed direct control of government, eliminating the post of prime minister. He was, however, defeated by former prime minister Leonid Kuchma in the July 1994 presidential elections.

Born in Velykyi Zhytyn, Kravchuk was educated at the Kiev State University and the Academy of Social Sciences in Moscow. He was directly elected to the presidency in 1991 at the same time as a referendum voted overwhelmingly in favour of independence from the USSR.

FURTHER READING
Kravchuk, Leonid Makarovych *Ie taka derzhava – Ukraïna* 1992

Mikhal'chenko, Nikolay Ivanovych *Belovezh'e, Kravchuk, Ukraïna, 1991–95* 1996

Kreisky, Bruno (1911–1990)

Austrian Social Democrat politician and diplomat, chancellor of Austria 1970–83. He headed Austria's first Socialist government since the war, and consolidated his position when the 1975 general election gave his party an absolute majority. He stepped down after being defeated in elections in 1983.

A lawyer by training, Kreisky joined the Social Democratic Party and was imprisoned 1935–37. He fled abroad when Hitler incorporated Austria into the Nazi Third Reich (the *Anschluss*), and lived in Sweden 1938–45. He worked as a diplomat at the Austrian embassy in Stockholm 1946–51. In 1959 he was appointed foreign minister, and negotiated Austria's entry into the European Free Trade Association (EFTA). Though himself of Jewish extraction, Kreisky took a pro-Arab line on Middle Eastern affairs, and received both the Palestine Liberation Organization leader Yassir Arafat and the Libyan leader Colonel Khaddhafi on state visits.

Krenz, Egon (1937–   )

East German communist politician. A member of the East German Socialist Unity Party (SED) from 1955, he joined its politburo in 1983 and was a hardline protégé of Erich ◊Honecker, succeeding him as party leader and head of state in 1989 after widespread prodemocracy demonstrations. Pledging a 'new course', Krenz opened the country's western border and promised more open elections, but his conversion to pluralism proved weak in the face of popular protest and he resigned in December 1989 after only a few weeks as party general secretary and head of state. In 1997 a Berlin court found Krenz guilty of manslaughter in connection with the deaths of East Germans who had attempted to flee to the West during the period of communist rule, and sentenced him to six and a half years' imprisonment.

Krishna Menon, Vengalil Krishnan (1897–1974)

Indian politician who was a leading light in the Indian nationalist movement. He represented India at the United Nations 1952–62 and was defence minister 1957–62, when he was dismissed by Jawaharlal Nehru following China's invasion of northern India.

He was a barrister of the Middle Temple in London, and a Labour member of St Pancras Borough Council 1934–47. He was secretary of the India League in the UK from 1929, and in 1947 was appointed Indian high commissioner in London. He became a member of the Indian parliament in 1953, and minister without portfolio in 1956. He was dismissed by Nehru in 1962 when China invaded India after Menon's assurances to the contrary.

FURTHER READING
Brecher, M *India and World Politics: Krishna Menon's View of the World* 1968
George, T J S *Krishna Menon* 1964

Kroger, Helen, adopted name of Leoninta Cohen (1913–1992)

US communist sympathizer and Soviet spy. Convicted in the UK of espionage in 1961, with her husband Morris Cohen, she was imprisoned and then released eight years later in a spy-swap deal, allowing her and her husband to settle in Moscow.

Born in Brooklyn, New York City, Kroger married Morris Cohen, whom she dominated, and instilled in him her deeply felt belief in the rightness of communism. Together they became active in the Soviet spy network in the USA and were suspected of involvement in the Rosenberg atomic espionage ring. When Julius Rosenberg was arrested in 1950 the Cohens disappeared. They moved to England, via Vienna, having acquired New Zealand passports and the names of Peter and Helen Kroger. From a modest bungalow in Ruislip, Middlesex, where Peter supposedly ran a small antiquarian book business, they operated a sophisticated radio station, passing vital defence information to Moscow. They were arrested, charged with espionage, and sentenced to 20 years' imprisonment at the Old Bailey in March 1961. They were released in 1969 in exchange for the British university lecturer Gerald Brooke, who had been imprisoned for spying in Moscow. At the time it was a major *cause célèbre* and provoked Hugh Whitemore to write the play *A Pack of Lies* (1983), which enjoyed success in the UK and the USA.

Kropotkin, Peter Alexeivich, Prince Kropotkin (1842–1921)

Russian anarchist. Imprisoned for revolutionary activities in 1874, he escaped to the UK in 1876 and later moved to Switzerland. Expelled from Switzerland in 1881, he went to France, where he was imprisoned 1883–86. He lived in Britain until 1917, when he returned to Moscow. Among his works are *Memoirs of a Revolutionist* (1899), *Mutual Aid* (1902), and *Modern Science and Anarchism* (1903).

Kropotkin was a noted geologist and geographer. In 1879 he launched an anarchist journal, *Le Révolté*. Unsympathetic to the Bolsheviks, he retired from politics after the Russian Revolution.

Krueger, Walter (1881–1967)

US general. After building his reputation as a trainer, he took command of the 6th US Army in Australia 1943, under General Douglas ◊MacArthur. He soon made it into a highly efficient force that served in New Guinea, New Britain, and the Admiralty Islands. He invaded the Philippines in October 1944, finally taking Manila after a month of house-to-house fighting.

Krylenko, Nikolai Vasilievich (1885–1940)

Russian Bolshevik politician. A military commander in the immediate aftermath of the revolution of 1917, he helped suppress White forces during the Russian Civil War of 1918–21. Later he was appointed a public prosecutor in revolutionary tribunals, and conducted several show trials of alleged counter-revolutionaries. However, he himself disappeared during Josef Stalin's purges of the Communist Party in the 1930s.

After taking part in the revolution of 1905 as a Bolshevik, Krylenko became an anarcho-syndicalist, but later rejoined his former party. He was active in the Bolshevik seizure of power in the October Revolution of 1917, and was appointed commissar for war in the first Soviet government. By 1936 he had risen to the position of principal commissar of justice of the USSR, but was never seen again after 1937, and was presumed murdered or deported to a forced labour camp, where he met his end.

Krzaklewski, Marian (1950–   )

Polish politician and trade-union leader, leader of the Solidarity trade union from 1991 and Solidarity Electoral Action (AWS) from 1996. A member of the anti-communist Solidarity since its inception in 1980, he revived the body as a political force from the mid-1990s. Its right-of-centre offshoot, the AWS, was able to form a coalition government after the September 1997 general election. However, expecting to put in a bid for the presidency in 2000, Krzaklewski chose not to become prime minister, preferring to exert behind-the-scenes influence over the new prime minister, Jerzy Buzek, his former economic adviser.

Krzaklewski was a scientific worker at the Polish Academy of Sciences and Silesian Polytechnic 1976–90. He formed the AWS as an electoral grouping of over 30 right-of-centre and Christian bodies. In 1997 it successfully fought on a platform of faster privatization, 'Catholic values', decentralization, reform of pensions, and early membership of the European Union.

Kubitschek, Juscelino (1902–1976)

Brazilian president 1956–61. His term as president saw political peace, civil liberty, and rapid economic growth at the cost of high inflation and corruption. He had a strong commitment to public works and the construction of Brasília as the nation's capital.

Kubitschek entered congress in 1934, remaining there until its dissolution in 1937 (he re-entered in 1946). He was mayor of Belo Horizone, Minas Gerais state, from 1939 and governor of Minas Gerais

1951–55, pursuing an active policy of road building, electrification, and industrial development.

He was born in Diamantia, Minas Gerais, and studied medicine at Minas Gerais University, later practising in Europe and Brazil, until 1933 and again 1937–39.

Kučan, Milan (1941–   )

Slovene politician, president of Slovenia from 1990. He served as chair of the parliament 1978–86 and became chair of the Communist Party 1986–89. He became president of Slovenia in April 1990.

Born in Krizevci, Slovenia, he was educated at Ljubljana University. He joined the Federation of Communists of Slovenia in 1958, rising to the position of chair of the Central Committee in 1968.

Kuchma, Leonid (1938–   )

Ukrainian politician, prime minister 1992–93, and president from 1994. A traditional Soviet technocrat, he worked his way up the hierarchy of the Communist Party (CPSU) and, when the USSR was dissolved and Ukraine gained independence in 1991, was well placed to assume a senior position within the Ukrainian administration. As prime minister, he established himself as a moderate reformer and in July 1994 defeated the incumbent Leonid Kravchuk to become president. Once in power, his programme for reform followed a considerably more pro-Western course than originally pledged. However, the large communist-party presence in Ukraine's parliament resulted in the blocking of radical market-centred reforms.

Kuchma campaigned for closer ties with Russia, negotiating a treaty in May 1997, and received around 90% of the vote in Russian-speaking regions of eastern Ukraine and in Crimea.

FURTHER READING
Kuzio, Taras *Ukraine under Kuchma: Political Reform, Economic Transformation, and Security Policy in Independent Ukraine* 1997
Wilson, Andrew, and Burakovsky, Igor *Ukrainian Economy under Kuchma* 1996

Kumaratunga, Chandrika Bandaranaike (1945–   )

Sri Lankan politician, president from 1994. After becoming head of state, she sought to end the long-running civil war with the separatist Tamil Tigers through a radical devolution plan. This was rejected by the Tigers, resulting in the government waging all-out war from 1995. The daughter of former prime ministers Solomon ◊Bandaranaike, the founder of the left-of-centre Sri Lanka Freedom Party (SLFP), and Sirimavo ◊Bandaranaike, she won the 1994 parliamentary and presidential elections in alliance with her mother, who became prime minister. Both her father, in 1959, and her husband, Vijaya Kumaratunga, in 1988, were assassinated.

Kun, Béla (1886–1937)

Hungarian politician. He created a Soviet republic in Hungary in March 1919, which was overthrown in August 1919 by a Western blockade and Romanian military actions. The succeeding regime under Admiral Miklós ◊Horthy effectively liquidated both socialism and liberalism in Hungary. Kun was assassinated in 1937.

Kunaev, Dimmukhamed Akhmedovich (1912–1993)

Kazakh politician. He worked his way up the Kazakh party ladder in the 1940s and 1950s, coming into close contact with Leonid Brezhnev and being made first secretary in 1960. He was demoted by Nikita Khrushchev in 1962, but was reappointed in 1964 by Brezhnev, who also brought him into full membership of the Politburo. His dismissal by Mikhail Gorbachev in 1986 led to riots in Alma Ata, but these were countered by charges of extensive corruption.

K'ung, H H or K'ung Hsiang-hsi (1881–1967)

Chinese politician and banker. As governor of the Bank of China and minister of finance 1933–44, he attempted to increase the government's financial control of the modern sector. Through control of the four major banks, the government floated more bond issues to finance its military projects. K'ung's abandonment of the silver standard in favour of a managed paper currency in 1935 was to lead ultimately to hyperinflation in the 1940s.

He came from a family of traditional bankers and received a missionary education in China before studying in the USA 1901–07. Through marriage, he developed close ties with both Sun Zhong Shan (Sun Yat-sen) and Jiang Jie Shi (Chiang Kai-shek) (their wives were sisters), joining the Guomindang (Kuomintang) in 1924 and becoming minister of industry and commerce of the new Nationalist government in 1928.

During the war against Japan, he was instrumental in obtaining US loans and was China's representative at the United Nations Bretton Woods Conference in 1944. He moved to the USA permanently in 1948.

Kuntsler, William (1919–1995)

US civil-rights attorney. He represented both the American Civil Liberties Union (ACLU) and Martin Luther King during the civil-rights struggles of the 1960s. He also represented several native American activists and prisoners after the 1971 rebellion in the Attica Correctional Facility. His most famous case was in defence of the Chicago Seven – a group charged with conspiracy to incite rioting at the 1968 Chicago Con-

vention. Kunstler won the acquittal of all of the defendants for conspiracy, although five of the defendants were convicted of lesser charges. For his role in the proceedings Judge Julius J Hoffmann sentenced Kunstler to over four years in prison for contempt of court. All convictions, including Kunstler's, were overturned on appeal; however, the appeals process hindered the activities of many left-wing leaders in the late 1960s for several years.

Kunstler began practising law in the late 1940s. After starting in lucrative law practice, he became radicalized by the mid-1950s. In his later years Kunstler appeared on popular TV shows such as *Law and Order*.

FURTHER READING
Kunstler, William M *Hints and Allegations : The World in Poetry and Prose According to William M Kuntsler* 1985

Kuti, Fela Anikulapo (1938–1997)

Nigerian musician and political activist, a strong proponent of African nationalism and critic of neocolonialism and military rule. After graduating from the Trinity College of Music in 1962 he formed the Kuola Lobitos and returned to Nigeria. He developed Afro-beat, a fusion of jazz and African rhythms with lyrics in Yoruba or pidgin English, during the late 1960s. Whilst in the USA during 1969 he became involved with the Black Panthers and the pan-Africanist movement, which gave a sharper political edge to his music. He had his first Nigerian hit in 1971 and released increasingly critical protest songs on the corruption of the Nigerian authorities. In 1974 he was arrested but later released and his commune was attacked and ransacked in 1977.

In 1979 Kuti formed Movement of the People (MOP) and put himself up for election; however, MOP was not recognized as a political party. He continued to record profusely and was arrested and imprisoned 1984–86.

Kuti was born in Abeokuta, and was the son of the politician and women's rights activist Funmilayo ◊Ransome-Kuti.

Kuusinen, Otto Vilhelm (1881–1964)

Finnish-born Soviet politician. Founder of the Finnish Communist Party in 1918, he went to Russia in 1930, returning to his home country after it had been invaded by the USSR 1939–40. He was installed by the Soviets as head of the territory seized from Finland (the 'Finno-Karelian Republic') 1940–56.

Kuusinen began his political career as a Social Democrat in Finland, but, inspired by Bolshevism in Russia, took an active role in the 1905 and 1917 revolutions there. After the Communist Party was outlawed in Finland, he settled in the USSR and became a leading figure in the Comintern. In 1957 he was appointed by Nikita Khrushchev to the Politburo.

Kwaśniewski, Aleksander (1954–)

Polish reform-communist politician, leader of the Democratic Left Alliance (SLD), president from 1995.

In 1990 Kwaśniewski became chair of the post-communist Social Democratic Party (SdRP). He led the party to electoral success in November 1993, forming a government with the Peasant Alliance (PSL). He became chair of the Parliamentary Constitutional Committee that drafted the first postwar constitution. In 1995 Kwaśniewski defeated Lech ◊ Wałęsa in presidential elections. As president, he steered Poland towards joining NATO and the European Union. He also tried to improve Poland's standing in Europe by holding negotiations with the Russian Federation and talks with the Belorussian and Ukrainian governments.

After completing an economics degree at Gdańsk university he became a full-time official of the Polish United Workers Party (PUWP). He held senior posts in the youth wing of the party, and from 1987 to 1989 was minister with special responsibilities for youth affairs in the government of Mieczysław Rakowski. He participated in the 'Round Table' talks that led to the emergence of the first democratic post-communist government.

In spite of accusations that he and other SdRP leaders had in the past acted as Soviet spies, he proved to be a skilful and popular mediator and conciliator, especially after the electoral victory in 1997 of the right-of-centre Solidarity Electoral Action.

Kyprianou, Spyros (1932–)

Cypriot politician, president 1977–88. Foreign minister 1961–72, he founded the federalist, centre-left Democratic Front in 1976.

Educated in Cyprus and the UK, he became a barrister in the UK in 1954. He became secretary to Archbishop Makarios in London in 1952 and returned with him to Cyprus in 1959. On the death of Makarios in 1977 he became acting president and was then elected. He was defeated in the 1988 presidential elections.

Lacalle, Luis Alberto (1941–)

Uruguayan politician and president 1989–94. His period of office promoted the continuation of democratic political and human-rights practices that his predecessor Jose Mariá Sanguinetti had initiated, after over a decade of military dictatorship (1971–84). Huge foreign debts, however, were a major constraint to the success of Lacalle's administration.

A member of the Herrista faction of the conservative Blanco party, Lacalle became president with a relatively peaceful transition of power from the former Colorado-aligned administration of Sanguinetti. His election marked a 23-year period since the last Blanco candidate gained office.

La Follette, Robert Marion (1855–1925)

US political leader. A senator 1906–25, he was a leader of the national progressive reform movement and unsuccessfully ran for president on the Progressive ticket in 1924. He was popularly known as 'Fighting Bob'.

La Follette was born in Primrose, Wisconsin, educated at the state university, and became a barrister in 1880. Entering politics, he served as district attorney 1880–94 and as a member of the House of Representatives 1885–91. He was defeated in his bid for re-election to Congress in 1890 but was governor of Wisconsin 1901–06. He ran unsuccessfully for the Republican presidential nomination three times: in 1912, 1916, and 1920.

In 1912 he helped to found the Progressive Party, bitterly attacking President William Taft for signing the Payne–Aldrich Tariff Bill, which revised the tariff upwards. In 1924 he formed a new Progressive Party, and was nominated for president, but obtained only the electoral votes of his own state.

His *Autobiography, A Personal Narrative of Political Experiences* appeared in 1913.

Lafontaine, Oskar (1943–)

German socialist politician, federal deputy chair of the Social Democrat Party (SPD) from 1987 and chair from 1995. Leader of the Saar regional branch of the SPD from 1977 and former mayor of Saarbrucken, he was nicknamed 'Red Oskar' because of his radical views on military and environmental issues. His attitude became more conservative once he had become minister-president of Saarland in 1985.

He was the SPD's unsuccessful candidate for chancellor in the first all-German general election in 1990, surviving a serious knife attack during the campaign, in which he warned of the economic cost of unification. In November 1995 he toppled Rudolph Scharping at the SPD conference to become party leader. He opposed the Maastricht Treaty on European union, viewing it as insufficiently federalist, but supported early German participation in the European single currency, and indicated that he may seek to construct an SPD–Green–Reformed Communist 'broad centre-left' coalition to replace the dominant Christian Democrats. However, his policy prescription received setbacks in March 1996 and September 1997 as support for the SPD slumped in state polls.

La Guardia, Fiorello (Henry) (1882–1947)

US Republican politician. He was mayor of New York 1933–45. Elected against the opposition of the powerful Tammany Hall Democratic Party organization, he improved the administration of the city, suppressed racketeering, and organized unemployment relief, slum-clearance schemes, and social services. Although nominally a Republican, he supported the Democratic president Franklin D Roosevelt's New Deal.

La Guardia was born in New York and educated at New York University. He was deputy attorney general of New York 1915–17, and a congressman 1917–19 and 1923–33. In World War I he commanded the Eighth Centre Aviation School and the American Flying Force on the Italian front. From 1940 he chaired the US section of the Canada–US Defense Board and he was director of US civil defence 1941–42. In 1946 he was director general of the United Nations Relief and Reconstruction Agency (UNRRA), an organization helping European recovery after World War II.

La Guardia Airport in New York is named after him.

FURTHER READING
Heckscher, A, and Robinson, P *When La Guardia was Mayor: New York's Legendary Years* 1978
Kessner, Thomas *Fiorello H La Guardia and the Making of Modern New York* 1989

Lahoud, or *Lahud*, Emile

Lebanese Maronite Christian politician, president from 1998. A career army officer, Lahoud was appointed commander of the Lebanese army in November 1989, and with the backing of Syria's president Hafez Assad, was elected president in October 1998. As president, Lahoud's task was to reconcile Christians to a new political order in which the Sunni Muslim prime minister and Shi'a Muslim speaker of the parliament had increased powers. However, within months of his election, Rafik Hariri resigned as prime minister, to be replaced by Salim al-Hoss.

Lahoud had become commander of the Lebanese army after the dismissal of General Michel Aoun by President Elias Hrawi. He established greater unity among an armed force drawn from all of the country's 18 fractious religious sects.

Lajpat Rai, Lala (1865–1928)

Indian politician and writer. His published articles advocated technical education and industrial self-help and criticized the Congress as being a gathering of English-educated elites. Arguing that Congress should openly and boldly base itself on the Hindus alone, he led a wave of nationalism in Punjab 1904–07. The Congress split in the Surat session in 1907 and he formed the 'extremist' trio of Lal, Pal, and Bal, with Bal Gangadhar Tilak (1856–1920) and Bipin Chandra ◊ Pal. Deported on charges of inciting the peasants, he led the noncooperation movement in Punjab in 1921.

Lajpat Rai was a follower of the militant Hindu sect the Arya Samaj (Society of Nobles) and when, in 1893, it split, he and Hans Raj led the moderate 'college faction', which concentrated on building up a chain of 'Dayanand Anglo-Vedic colleges'. He also developed a sustained involvement in Swadeshi movement enterprises, including a boycott of foreign-made goods, initiated in protest against the partition of Bengal.

FURTHER READING

Bakshi, S R *Lajpat Rai: Socio-Political Ideology* 1990
Kaushik, K *Russian Revolution & Indian Nationalism: Studies of Lajpat Rai, Subhas Chandra Bose & Rammanohar Lohia* 1984
Lajpat Rai, L *Perspectives on Indian National Movement: Selected Correspondence of Lala Lajpat Rai* 1998
Shahi, S *Lala Lajpat Rai, His Life and Thought* 1986

Lake, (William) Anthony (Kirsopp) (1939–1996)

US government official, national security adviser 1993–96. He helped to shape President Bill Clinton's foreign policy of support for the new market-based democracies in Eastern Europe and elsewhere.

Having joined the foreign service, Lake was sent to South Vietnam in 1963. As special assistant to Henry Kissinger, President Richard Nixon's national security adviser, 1969–70, Lake tried to persuade Kissinger to urge Nixon to withdraw US troops from Southeast Asia. He resigned in 1970 after the US invasion of Cambodia. Under President Jimmy Carter he was director of policy planning for Secretary of State Cyrus Vance 1976–80. In 1997 he was initially nominated to become the new director of the Central Intelligence Agency (CIA), but withdrew after facing difficult Senate confirmation hearings.

Lake became a professor of international relations at Mount Holyoke College in 1981 after Carter's defeat in the presidential election. His books include *Our Own Worst Enemy: The Unmaking of American Foreign Policy* (1984) and *Somoza Falling* (1989).

Lamizana, Sangoulé (1916–   )

Politician and army officer, second president of independent Upper Volta (now Burkina Faso), 1966–80. He came to power in a coup, and ruled autocratically; although he allowed political activity to resume in 1970, he returned the country to army rule in 1974. He himself was ousted by the military in 1980.

After embarking on a career in the French army, Lamizana saw action in World War II and in the French colonial conflict in Indochina (Vietnam), winning the *légion d'honneur* for bravery. In 1961 he was promoted to the rank of major, and in 1963–64 was appointed chief of staff and a lieutenant-colonel in the army of Upper Volta. On 3 January 1966 he led the military coup that finally overthrew President Yaméogo, and became president of the Republic and president of the Council.

Lamont, Norman Stewart Hughson (1942–   )

British Conservative politician, chief secretary of the Treasury 1989–90, chancellor of the Exchequer 1990–93. In September 1992, despite earlier assurances to the contrary, he was forced to suspend the UK's membership of the European Community (now the European Union) Exchange Rate Mechanism (ERM). He was replaced as chancellor by Kenneth Clarke in May 1993, after which he became a fierce right-wing critic of John Major's administration. He lost his House of Commons seat in the May 1997 general election.

Born in the Shetland Islands and educated at Cambridge University, Lamont was elected to Parliament in 1972 as member for Kingston upon Thames. He masterminded John Major's leadership campaign. As chancellor of the Exchequer, he firmly backed the UK's membership of the ERM and, despite signs that the pound was in trouble, specifically ruled out devaluation on 10 September 1992. A week later, in the face of mounting international pressure on the pound, he was forced to devalue and withdraw from the ERM, inciting fierce criticism and calls for his resignation.

Landon, Alf(red Mossman) (1887–1987)

US politician. A popular liberal Republican, he ran for president against the incumbent Franklin D Roosevelt in 1936 but was overwhelmingly defeated. He later accepted a presidential appointment as US delegate to the 1938 Pan-American Conference.

Landon, born in West Middlesex, Pennsylvania, was raised in Kansas and received a law degree from the University of Kansas in 1908. After a successful career in business, he entered politics and was elected governor of Kansas in 1932. After World War II, Landon became a voice for the elimination of trade barriers and for international development.

Landsbergis, Vytautas (1932–)

Lithuanian politician, president 1990–93. He became active in nationalist politics in the 1980s, founding and eventually chairing the anticommunist Sajudis independence movement in 1988. When Sajudis swept to victory in the republic's elections in March 1990, Landsbergis chaired the Supreme Council of Lithuania, becoming, in effect, president. He immediately drafted the republic's declaration of independence from the USSR, which, after initial Soviet resistance, was recognized in September 1991. In October 1996, after a general election, he took the chair of the new parliament.

Born in Kaunas, Landsbergis was educated at the Vilnius Conservatoire where he later taught, and is a recognized composer and musicologist. He served as the leader of the Council of the Baltic States 1990–92. He then formed the Homeland Union in 1993, a right-of-centre conservative force to replace Sajudis, which went on to win the 1996 general election.

FURTHER READING

Landsbergis, Vytautas *Laisves byla, 1990–91: kalbos, pranesimai, uzrasai, laiskai, pokalbiai, interviu, ivarius dokumentai* 1992

Landsbergis, Vytautas, Packer, Anthony, and Sova, Eimutis *Lithuania – Independent Again: Autobiography of Vytautas Landsbergis* 1998

Lane, William (1861–1917)

Australian radical political journalist and union activist, born in England, who established New Australia in Paraguay in 1893. His writings include the novel *The Workingman's Paradise* (1892).

Lang, Jack (John Thomas) (1876–1975)

Australian Labor politician, premier of New South Wales 1925–27 and 1930–32. His first government introduced social reforms such as child endowment, widows' pensions, and reduced working hours. His second term of government was at the height of the depression. At this time the New South Wales Labor Party split from the national Labor Party and Lang was instrumental in the fall of James ◊Scullin's government. Lang's Keynesian plan for combating the economic problems of the time by boosting public works and non-payment or reduction of interest on loans led to his dismissal in May 1932 by the governor, Sir Philip Game, and his defeat at the subsequent election. He remained a powerful figure in Australian politics with an electoral following despite his rejection by the federal Labor Party and his propensity for faction fighting. Finally expelled from the New South Wales Labor Party in 1942 for opposing conscription, he entered federal parliament in 1946 representing his own 'non-communist' Labor Party but lost the seat three years later. His turbulent career had seen him move from the far left to the far right of the Australian Labor movement. He was readmitted to the Labor Party in 1971 as a result of the efforts of Paul ◊Keating, his firm admirer.

FURTHER READING

Lang, Jack *The Turbulent Years* 1970

Nairn, Bede *Big Fella: Jack Lang and the Australian Labor Party 1891–1949* 1986

lang, k(athryn) d(awn) (1961–)

Canadian singer and songwriter. Her mellifluous voice and androgynous image have gained her a wide following beyond the country-music field where she first established herself. Lang, a lesbian icon, has been prominent in the support of animal rights since 1981 and caused controversy while supporting a protest against meat in 1990. She also has promoted the work of AIDS charities through benefit concerts.

Lange, Christian Louis (1869–1938)

Norwegian pacifist and historian. He was active in fostering international understanding, especially through his work with the Interparliamentary Union, forerunner of the League of Nations. Jointly with Karl Branting, he was awarded the Nobel Peace Prize in 1921. His major publication was *History of International Relations from 1814* (1919).

Lange was secretary of the Nobel Commission of the Storting (the Norwegian parliament) 1900–09, and also a member of the Nobel Prize committee. In 1907 he was Norwegian delegate to the International Peace Conference in The Hague, the Netherlands.

Lange, David Russell (1942–)

New Zealand Labour centre-left politician, prime minister 1983–89. A skilled parliamentary debater, he became Labour's deputy leader in 1979, and in 1983 replaced Wallace ◊Rowling as party leader. Taking advantage of economic difficulties and a changing public mood, Lange led Labour to a decisive win in the 1984 general election, replacing Robert ◊Muldoon of the National Party as prime minister. The centrepiece of his policy programme was non-nuclear military policy. This was put into effect, despite criticism from the USA, becoming law in 1987. It prevented US nuclear-armed or nuclear-powered ships visiting New Zealand's ports and resulted in the USA suspending its defence obligations to New Zealand under the ANZUS treaty. Lange's government also introduced a free-market economic policy, which was a significant and controversial departure for Labour, and improved Maori rights and the position of women. His government was re-elected in 1987, but in August 1989 Lange unexpectedly resigned, as a result of health problems but also pressure being exerted by supporters of the right-wing former finance minister Roger Douglas. Lange, who had become a critic of Douglas's liberalizing policies, had dismissed Douglas in 1988. Lange was replaced as prime minister by Geoffrey ◊Palmer and served under him as attorney general until 1990.

Born near Auckland, he trained and worked as a barrister, specializing in representing the underprivileged. A member of the Labour Party, he was first elected to the House of Representatives in 1977, for Mangere district, a working-class suburb of Auckland.

FURTHER READING
Lange, David Russell *Nuclear Free – The New Zealand Way* 1990
McQueen, H *The Ninth Floor: Inside the Prime Minister's Office, a Political Experience* 1991
Wright, V *David Lange, PM: A Profile* 1984

Lange, Oskar Ryszard (1904–1965)

Polish economist and politician. He was Polish ambassador to the USA 1945–47, and delegate to the United Nations (UN) Security Council. From 1957 to 1959 he was chair of the UN Economic Commission for Europe, in addition to holding various state positions in Poland.

After studying in Poznań and Kraków, Lange became active in the left wing of the Polish Socialist Party. In 1938 he settled in the USA. During World War II he confounded the Polish government in exile by his public advocacy of Polish–Soviet cooperation and his visit to the USSR in 1944, with the unofficial support of the US government. In 1948 he was elected to the Central Committee of the Polish United Workers Party (PUWP). His excellent international contacts brought him to prominence after 1956. In 1957 he was appointed deputy chair of the Council of State (the Polish collective presidency at the time). Before World War II he published various works arguing the compatibility of market mechanisms with socialism, and after 1945 he wrote on statistics, econometrics, and cybernetic approaches to economic planning.

FURTHER READING
Baran, P A (ed) *On Political Economy and Econometrics: Essays in Honour of Oskar Lange* 1965
Lange, Oskar *On the Economic Theory of Socialism*

Lansbury, George (1859–1940)

British Labour politician, leader in the Commons 1931–35. He was a member of Parliament for Bow from 1910–12 – when he resigned to force a by-election on the issue of votes for women, which he lost – and again 1922–40. In 1921, while mayor of the London borough of Poplar, he went to prison with most of the council rather than modify their policy of more generous unemployment relief.

Lansbury founded the *Daily Herald* in 1912 and edited it until 1922, carrying it on as a weekly throughout World War I. He was the leader of the parliamentary Labour party 1931–35, but resigned (as a pacifist) in opposition to the party's militant response to the Italian invasion of Abyssinia (present-day Ethiopia).

FURTHER READING
Holman, Robert *George Lansbury* 1990
Lansbury, George *Looking Backwards – And Forwards* (autobiography) 1935
Postgate, R *The Life of George Lansbury* 1951

Lansdowne, Henry Charles Keith Petty-Fitzmaurice, 5th Marquis of Lansdowne (1845–1927)

British Liberal Unionist politician, governor general of Canada 1883–88, viceroy of India 1888–93, war minister 1895–1900, and foreign secretary 1900–06. While at the Foreign Office he abandoned Britain's isolationist policy by forming an alliance with Japan and an entente cordiale with France. His letter of 1917 suggesting an offer of peace to Germany created a controversy. He was created Marquess in 1866.

Lansing, Robert (1864–1928)

US politician and lawyer. In 1915 he succeeded William J Bryan as secretary of state. He was one of the five delegates to represent the USA at the Inter-Allied Peace Conference in Paris in 1919. He published *The Peace Negotiations* (1921) and *The Big Four and Others of the Peace Conference* (1921). His war memoirs appeared in 1935 and *The Lansing Papers 1914–20* in 1939–40.

FURTHER READING
Beers, B F *Vain Endeavor: Robert Lansing's Attempts to End the American-Japanese Rivalry* 1962
Smith, D M *Robert Lansing and American Neutrality, 1914–1917* 1958

Largo Caballero, Francisco (1869–1946)

Spanish politician, leader of the Spanish Socialist Party (PSOE), and prime minister 1936–37. He became prime minister of the Popular Front government elected in February 1936 and remained in office for the first ten months of the Civil War before being replaced in May 1937 by Juan Negrin (1887–1956).

Larkin, James (1876–1947)

Irish labour leader. He founded the Irish Transport and General Workers' Union (ITGWU) in 1909. Depressed by his failure in the 1913 Dublin lockout, he went to the USA in 1914. He returned to Ireland in 1923, only to be embroiled in a bitter dispute with William O'Brien, who had built up the ITGWU in his absence. Larkin eventually joined the Labour Party, and was elected to the Dáil (parliament) in 1943.

Born of Irish parents in Liverpool, Larkin became a convinced trade unionist and socialist. He was sent to Belfast in 1907 to attempt the unionization of the Belfast docks, where he was confronted by the city's intense sectarianism. In 1912 he persuaded the Irish Trade Union Congress to set up a congress-based Labour Party. During his stay in the USA he attended the founding convention of the American Communist Party and was sentenced to three years' imprisonment for 'criminal anarchy'.

FURTHER READING
Larkin, J *The American Trial of Big Jim Larkin, 1920* 1976
Larkin, E J *James Larkin: Irish Labour Leader, 1876–1947* 1989

Laski, Harold Joseph (1893–1950)

English political theorist. Professor of political science at the London School of Economics from 1926, he taught a modified Marxism and was active in the Socialist League during the 1930s. He published *A Grammar of Politics* (1925), a central text of Fabian political science, and *The American Presidency* (1940). He was chair of the Labour Party 1944–45.

> *The meek do not inherit the Earth unless they are prepared to fight for their meekness.*
> HAROLD LASKI Attributed remark

FURTHER READING
Newman, M *Harold Laski, A Political Biography* 1993

Laugerud Garcia, Kjell Eugenio (1930–)

Guatemalan soldier and right-wing politician, president 1974–78. Standing as the candidate of the right-wing, army-backed Movement of National Liberation (MLN), he was elected president in 1974 in a rigged contest, defeating General Efraín ◊Ríos Montt of the National Opposition Front (FNO) coalition. He held power during a period of heightened political violence, as the army brutally cracked down against left-wing guerrillas and political opponents.

He was succeeded as president, in 1978, by General Fernando Romeo Lucas García, also of the MLN, and his former defence minister.

Born in Guatemala City, Laugerud Garcia followed a military career and between 1970 and 1974 served as defence minister and army chief of staff, under President Carlos ◊Araña Osorio.

Laurier, Wilfrid (1841–1919)

Canadian politician, leader of the Liberal Party 1887–1919 and prime minister 1896–1911. The first French-Canadian to hold the office, he encouraged immigration into Canada from Europe and the USA, established a separate Canadian navy, and sent troops to help the UK in the Boer War. He was awarded the GCMG in 1897.

Laurier was born at St Lin, near Montréal, and educated at McGill University. He practised law for a time in Montréal, then moved to Québec. In 1871 he was elected to the provincial legislature for Drummond and Arthabaska counties, and from 1874 represented the same constituency in the Dominion parliament, though later he represented Québec East. He was minister for inland revenue in the cabinet of Alexander MacKenzie 1877–78, and succeeded Edward Blake as Liberal leader in 1887. Laurier always favoured free trade, and in 1896 won the election and became prime minister.

His sending of troops to aid the British in South Africa was not approved by his native province, which was better pleased by his resistance, at the Imperial Conference in 1902, to Joseph Chamberlain's scheme of unified empire defence. He carried the general elections of 1900 and 1908, despite being hotly opposed by the nationalists for 'supporting British jingoism'. His once-popular policy of reciprocity with the USA was defeated at the elections of 1911. During World War I he was invited by Robert ◊Borden to form a coalition, but declined.

> *Whether splendidly isolated or dangerously isolated – this isolation of England comes from her superiority.*
> WILFRID LAURIER Speech in the Canadian House of Commons 5 February 1896

FURTHER READING
Schull, J *Laurier: The First Canadian* 1965

Laval, Pierre (1883–1945)

French extreme right-wing politician. He gravitated between the wars from socialism through the centre ground (serving as prime minister and foreign secretary 1931–32 and again 1935–36) to the extreme right. As head of the Vichy government and foreign minister 1942–44, he was responsible for the deportation of Jews and for requisitioning French labour to Germany.

Born near Vichy and elected as a socialist deputy in 1914, Laval had trained as a lawyer and acquired considerable wealth from his legal practice. In his second term as premier he negotiated the Hoare–Laval Pact in 1935, providing concessions to Italy in Abyssinia (now Ethiopia). In July 1940 he was instrumental in securing the voting of full powers to Marshal Philippe ◊Pétain and served as his vice premier until December 1940. At Hitler's insistence Laval was reinstated as head of government from April 1942, reducing Pétain to the role of figurehead. He fled the country in 1944 but was captured in Austria, tried for treason in France in October 1945, and was executed by firing squad, after trying to poison himself.

FURTHER READING

Cole, H *Laval: A Biography* 1963

Kupferman, F *Laval* 1987

Law, Andrew Bonar (1858–1923)

British Conservative politician, born in New Brunswick, Canada, of Scottish descent. He succeeded Arthur Balfour as leader of the opposition in 1911, became colonial secretary in H H Asquith's coalition government 1915–16, chancellor of the Exchequer 1916–19, and Lord Privy Seal 1919–21 in David Lloyd George's coalition. He formed a Conservative cabinet in 1922, but resigned on health grounds.

> *If I am a Great man, then a good many of the great men in history are frauds.*
>
> ANDREW BONAR LAW Quoted in Lord Beaverbrook, *Politicians and the War*

Law made a fortune in Scotland as a banker and iron-merchant before entering Parliament in 1900.

FURTHER READING

Adams, R J Q *Bonar Law* 1999

Blake, R *The Unknown Prime Minister, Life and Times of Andrew Bonar Law* 1955

Lawrence, T(homas) E(dward), known as *Lawrence of Arabia* (1888–1935)

British soldier, scholar, and translator. Appointed to the military intelligence department in Cairo, Egypt, during World War I, he took part in negotiations for an Arab revolt against the Ottoman Turks, and in 1916 attached himself to the emir Faisal. He became a guerrilla leader of genius, combining raids on Turkish communications with the organization of a joint Arab revolt, described in his book *The Seven Pillars of Wisdom* (1926).

Lawrence was born in Wales, studied at Oxford, and during 1910–14 took part in archaeological expeditions to Syria and Mesopotamia. On the outbreak of war he was recalled to the UK and was employed producing maps of the Arab regions. When the sheriff of Mecca revolted against the Turks in 1916 Lawrence was given the rank of colonel and went with the British mission to King Hussein. There he reorganized the Arab army, which he practically commanded, and conducted guerrilla operations on the flank of the British Army 1916–18. In 1918 he led his successful Arabs into Damascus. At the end of the war he was awarded the DSO for his services, and became adviser to the Foreign Office on Arab affairs. Disappointed by the Paris Peace Conference's failure to establish Arab independence, he joined the Royal Air Force in 1922 as

> *It's the most amateurish, Buffalo-Billy sort of performance, and the only people who do it well are the Bedouin.*
>
> T E LAWRENCE Letter 1917, describing an attack on a Turkish train

an aircraftman under the name Ross, transferring to the tank corps under the name T E Shaw in 1923 when his identity became known. In 1935 he was killed in a motorcycle accident.

FURTHER READING

Clements, F *T E Lawrence: A Reader's Guide* 1973

James, L *The Golden Warrior* 1990

Lawrence, T E *The Mint* 1955

Stewart, D *T E Lawrence* 1977

Tabachnick, S *The T E Lawrence Puzzle* 1984

Wilson, J *Lawrence of Arabia: The Authorized Biography* 1989

Yardley, M *Backing into the Limelight: A Biography of T E Lawrence* 1985

Lawson, Nigel, Baron Lawson of Blaby (1932–)

British Conservative politician. A former financial journalist, he was financial secretary to the Treasury 1979–81, secretary of state for energy 1981–83, and chancellor of the Exchequer 1983–89. He resigned as chancellor after criticism by government adviser Alan Walters, supported by Prime Minister Margaret Thatcher, over his policy of British membership of the European Monetary System.

Lawson was educated at Westminster School and Christ Church, Oxford. He was a member of the editorial staff of the *Financial Times* 1956–60, and was the City editor for the *Sunday Telegraph* 1961–63. He wrote for the *Financial Times* in 1965, for the *Sunday Times* 1970–71, for *The Times* 1971–72, and was editor of the *Spectator* 1966–70. His publications include *The View from No 11: Memoirs of a Tory Radical* (1992).

Leadbelly, stage name of Huddie William Ledbetter (1889–1949)

US blues and folk singer, songwriter, and guitarist. He was a source of inspiration for the urban folk movement of the 1950s. He was 'discovered' in prison by folklorists John Lomax (1875–1948) and Alan Lomax (1915–), who helped him begin a professional concert and recording career in 1934. Within a year he became a favourite among left-leaning folk singers. He performed at rallies and union halls in support of left-wing causes with contemporaries Woody ◊Guthrie and Pete ◊Seeger. His songs 'Bourgeois Blues' and 'Scottsboro Boys' carried strong political messages.

FURTHER READING
Garvin, Richard M *The Midnight Special: The Legend of Leadbelly* 1971
Wolfe, Charles, and Lornell, Kip *The Life and Legend of Leadbelly* 1994

Leahy, William D (1875–1959)

US admiral and diplomat during World War II. After two difficult years as ambassador to the Vichy government of France 1940–42, he was recalled by President F D Roosevelt to become his chief of staff 1942–49. In this position he exerted considerable influence on the operations of US forces during World War II.

Leahy was born in Hampton, Iowa, and entered the US Naval Academy in 1897. He was made rear admiral in 1930. As chief of naval operations 1937–39, he had the task of strengthening the US navy after the Japanese denunciation of the limits imposed by the Washington and London Naval Treaties. He was governor of Puerto Rico 1939–40.

Leakey, Richard Erskine Frere (1944–)

Kenyan palaeoanthropologist. In 1972 he discovered at Lake Turkana, Kenya, an apelike skull estimated to be about 2.9 million years old. In 1984 his team found an almost complete skeleton of *Homo erectus* some 1.6 million years old.

He was appointed director of the Kenyan Wildlife Service in 1988, waging a successful war against poachers and the ivory trade, but was forced to resign in 1994 in the face of political interference. He was reappointed to the post in 1998. In 1995 he cofounded the Kenyan political party Safina (Swahili for Noah's Ark), which aimed to clean up Kenya. The party was accused of racism and colonialism by President Daniel arap Moi.

Leary, Timothy (1920–1996)

US writer and psychologist. Controversial and influential, he was a guiding iconic figure of the counterculture of the 1960s and 1970s. He helped develop the theory of transactional analysis and conducted a series of psychedelic experiments at Harvard University that helped pave the way for an era of cultural and psychosocial upheaval. His book *The Interpersonal Diagnosis of Personality* 1950 enjoys wide-ranging praise and influence.

Born in Springfield, Massachusetts, he studied at Holy Cross College, West Point, and the University of Alabama. He earned a doctorate in psychology from the University of California at Berkeley in 1950. By the mid-1950s Leary was teaching at Berkeley and had been appointed director of psychological research at the Kaiser Foundation, in Oakland, California.

FURTHER READING
Horowitz, M *An Annotated Bibliography of Timothy Leary* 1988
Leary, Timothy, et al *Chaos and Cyber Culture* 1994
Leary, T F *Design for Dying* 1997

Lebed, Aleksandr Ivanovich (1950–)

Russian soldier and politician. He was briefly national security adviser in 1996 and successfully negotiated a peace settlement that ended the 1994–96 civil war in Chechnya. He was sacked by President Boris ◊Yeltsin in 1997. In May 1998 he was elected governor of Krasnoyarsk region, which made him a serious contender for the Russian presidency in 2000.

An Afghan War veteran, Lebed sided with Yeltsin's supporters during the coup attempt in 1991, putting his tanks at the service of the defence of the Russian parliament. He was rewarded with the command of the 14th army based in the eastern region of Moldova; when Moldova became an independent state, Lebed remained in place, and was credited with a successful intervention in the fighting between Moldovans and the largely Russian and Ukrainian population of the TransDniestr region. He was dismissed from the Russian army by Yeltsin in June 1995.

After challenging Yeltsin for the Russian presidency in June 1996, Lebed was appointed national security adviser as a reward for transferring his support to the president. In spite of his peace plan for Chechnya and his public popularity, Lebed was sacked by Yeltsin in October 1996 amid accusations by interior minister Anatoly Kulikov that he was planning a 'creeping coup'. In March 1997 he formed his own political party, the Russian People's Republican Party, to act as a 'third force' political alternative to President Yeltsin.

Lebed was born in Novocherkassk, southern Russia, and educated at the Ryazan Airborne Command School. During the Afghan War, Lebed served in the elite airborne troops, rising to command the Tula Airborne Division.

FURTHER READING
Elletson, H *The General Against the Kremlin: Alexander Lebed, Power and Illusion* 1998
Lambeth, B S *The Warrior who Would Rule Russia: A Profile of Aleksandr Lebed* 1997

Lebrun, Albert (1871–1950)

French politician. He became president of the senate in 1931 and in 1932 was chosen as president of the republic. In 1940 he handed his powers over to Marshal Philippe Pétain.

Le Duc Anh (1920–)

Vietnamese soldier and communist politician, president 1992–97. A member of the politburo's military faction, he is regarded as a conservative, anxious to maintain tight party control over domestic policies.

A long-standing member of the Vietnamese Communist Party, he led Vietcong combat units during the Vietnam War. Later, as a politburo member, he held a succession of government posts, including internal security, foreign policy, and defence, before being elected to the new post of state president, replacing a collective presidency, in September 1992. He stepped down as president at the October 1997 communist party congress and was replaced by Tran Duc Luong.

Le Duc Tho (1911–1990)

North Vietnamese diplomat who was joint winner (with US secretary of state Henry Kissinger) of the 1973 Nobel Peace Prize for his part in the negotiations to end the Vietnam War. He indefinitely postponed receiving the award.

Lee, Jennie (Janet), Baroness Lee of Asheridge (1904–1988)

British socialist politician. She became a member of Parliament for the Independent Labour Party representing North Lanark at the age of 24, and in 1934 married Aneurin ◊Bevan. Representing Cannock 1945–70, she was on the left wing of the Labour Party. She was on its National Executive Committee 1958–70, became a privy councillor from 1966, and was minister of education 1967–70, during which time she was responsible for founding the Open University in 1969. She was made a baroness in 1970.

Her publications include *Tomorrow is a New Day* (1939) and *My Life with Nye* (1980).

FURTHER READING
Hollis, P *Jennie Lee, A Life* 1997

Lee, Spike, born Shelton Jackson Lee (1957–)

US film director, actor, and writer. His work presents the bitter realities of contemporary black American life in an aggressive, often controversial manner. His films, in which he sometimes appears, include *She's Gotta Have It* (1986), *Do The Right Thing* (1989), *Jungle Fever* (1991), *Malcolm X* (1992), *Clockers* (1995), and *He Got Game* (1998). His more recent projects include *Get on the Bus*, about the Million Man March on Washington, DC, and a film about Jackie Robinson.

FURTHER READING
Hardy, James Earl, et al *Spike Lee: Filmmaker* 1995
Haskins, James *Spike Lee: By Any Means Necessary* 1997

Lee Kuan Yew (1923–)

Singaporean politician, prime minister 1959–90. Lee founded the anticommunist Socialist People's Action Party in 1954 and entered the Singapore legislative assembly in 1955. He was elected the country's first prime minister in 1959, and took Singapore out of the Malaysian federation in 1965. He remained in power until his resignation in 1990, and was succeeded by

Goh Chok Tong. He held on to the party leadership until 1992.

FURTHER READING
George, T J S *Lee Kuan Yew's Singapore* 1973
Josey, A *Lee Kuan Yew: The Struggle for Singapore* 1974
Minchin, J *No Man Is an Island: A Portrait of Singapore's Lee Kuan Yew* 1990

Lee Teng-hui (1923–)

Taiwanese right-wing politician, vice president 1984–88, president and Kuomintang (Guomindang) party leader from 1988. The country's first island-born leader, he was viewed as a reforming technocrat. He was directly elected president in March 1996, defying Chinese opposition to the democratic contest.

Born in Tamsui, Lee taught for two decades as professor of economics at the National Taiwan University before becoming mayor of Taipei in 1979. A member of the Kuomintang party and a protégé of Jiang Qing-guo (Chiang Ching-kuo), he became vice president of Taiwan in 1984 and succeeded to both the state presidency and Kuomintang leadership on Jiang's death in January 1988. He significantly accelerated the pace of liberalization and Taiwanization in the political sphere.

Leguía, Agusto Bernardino (1863–1932)

Peruvian politician and president 1908–12 and 1919–30. During his first term, he actively embarked on a programme of fiscal, social, and public infrastructural reform. He participated in the negotiations that ultimately resolved the territorial boundary disputes between his own country, Brazil, and Bolivia. His second term in office was marked by his severance of ties with the old Peruvian oligarchy. In 1920 he promulgated a new constitution, and ruled dictatorially, vigorously suppressing all opposition.

His modernization of the country and the capital, Lima, produced vast national debts. The Tacna-Arica controversy with Chile, initiated in 1883, was resolved under Leguía, though his acceptance of a compromise caused contention. Growing economic depression and the oppressive nature of his administration ultimately brought about the termination of his office; in 1930, Leguía was removed from power in a coup. He was later found guilty of embezzlement and imprisoned.

Leguía was born in Lambayeque, a descendant of a prominent family of the Peruvian oligarchy. Before entering into political life, Leguía had successfully established his own company, in 1896. During the period 1903–1908, his main government positions were as finance minister and prime minister.

Lehman, Herbert Henry (1878–1963)

US Democratic politician. In 1932 he became governor of New York, and his subsequent support of F D Roosevelt's reform policies earned his own administration the name 'Little New Deal'. In 1942 Lehman was appointed director of the federal Office of Foreign Relief and Rehabilitation. He served in the Senate 1949–57.

Lemass, Sean Francis (1899–1971)

Irish nationalist politician. A longtime associate of Eámon ◊de Valera in the Fianna Fáil party, he was the chief architect of the republic's economic programmes and served as prime minister 1959–66.

Having been his deputy since 1945, Lemass was the natural successor to de Valera as prime minister in 1959. He displayed a more outward-looking approach and sought Irish membership of the European Economic Community (EEC; now the European Union). As a preliminary to this, he re-established free trade with the UK.

Lemass was born in Ballybrack, County Dublin, and educated at the O'Connell Schools in Dublin. At the age of 15 he joined the nationalist paramilitaries, the Irish Volunteers. The captain of his company was de Valera, of whom Lemass was to prove a loyal follower. He fought at the General Post Office in Dublin during the Easter Rising of 1916, but escaped deportation and returned to school. After working in his father's drapery shop for a short time, he joined the newly formed Irish Republican Army (IRA) as an officer to continue

fighting the British. He was interned for a year 1920–21.

Like de Valera, Lemass rejected the Anglo-Irish Treaty of 1921, which established the Irish Free State within the British Empire. He fought on the Republican side in the civil war as a member of the headquarters staff of the IRA 'Irregulars' until captured and imprisoned 1922–23.

Elected to the Dáil Éireann (lower house of the Irish parliament) in 1924, like other Republicans he refused to take his seat until 1926, when he became a founder member of de Valera's Fianna Fáil party. He served as Teachta Dála (member of parliament) for a Dublin constituency for the following 43 years. When de Valera became prime minister in 1932, he appointed Lemass his minister for industry and commerce. He held this post for all but eight of the next 27 years, and was only out of office when Fianna Fáil was out of government 1948–51 and 1954–57. He helped build up Irish industry behind a wall of high tariffs, and created state boards to provide Ireland with a national shipping company and airline. In 1965 he paid a visit to Belfast and met with the prime minister of Northern Ireland. Ill health prompted his resignation in 1966.

FURTHER READING

Bew, P *Seán Lemass and the Making of Modern Ireland, 1945–66* 1982

◆ LENIN, VLADIMIR ILYICH, ADOPTED NAME OF VLADIMIR ILYICH ULYANOV (1870–1924) ◆

Russian revolutionary, first leader of the USSR, and communist theoretician. Active in the 1905 Revolution, Lenin had to leave Russia when it failed, settling in Switzerland in 1914. He returned to Russia after the February revolution of 1917. He led the Bolshevik revolution of November 1917 and became leader of a Soviet government, concluded peace with Germany, and

---

Communism is Soviet power plus the electrification of the whole country.

VLADIMIR LENIN Report to 8th Congress of the Communist Party 1920

---

organized a successful resistance to White Russian (pro-tsarist) uprisings and foreign intervention 1918–20. His modification of traditional Marxist doctrine to fit conditions prevailing in Russia became known as **Marxism-Leninism**, the basis of communist ideology.

Lenin was born on 22 April 1870 in Simbirsk (now renamed Ulyanovsk), on the River Volga, and became a lawyer in St Petersburg. His brother

was executed in 1887 for attempting to assassinate Tsar Alexander III. A Marxist from 1889, Lenin was sent to Siberia for spreading revolutionary propaganda 1895–1900. He then edited the political paper *Iskra* ('The Spark') from abroad, and visited London several times. In *What is to be Done?* (1902), he advocated that a professional core of Social Democratic Party activists should spearhead the revolution in Russia, a suggestion accepted by the majority (*bolsheviki*) at the London party congress 1903. From Switzerland he attacked socialist support for World War I as aiding an 'imperialist' struggle, and wrote *Imperialism* (1917).

After the renewed outbreak of revolution February–March 1917, he was smuggled back into Russia in April by the Germans so that he could take up his revolutionary activities and remove Russia from the war, allowing Germany to concentrate the war effort on the Western Front. On arriving in Russia, Lenin established himself at the head of the Bolsheviks, against the provisional government of Kerensky. A complicated power struggle ensued, but eventually Lenin triumphed on 8 November 1917;

Farrell, B *Séan Lemass* 1983
Horgan, J *Séan Lemass: The Enigmatic Patriot* 1997
Murphy, G *Towards a Corporate State?: Séan Lemass and the Realignment of Interest Groups in the Policy Process, 1948–1964* 1997

Leone, Giovanni (1928–)

Italian Christian Democrat politician, president of Italy 1971–78. Before his election as president, he had been prime minister of two caretaker ministries, June–December 1963 and June–November 1968.

Leoni, Raúl (1905–1972)

Venezuelan politician and president 1964–69. His administration was relatively uneventful, although some guerrilla activity required government action. The wealth generated by the oil industry at this period assisted considerably in the generation of economic growth and development.

Leoni was a member of the ruling Acción Democrática party (AD; Democratic Action Party). The lack of an outright constitutional majority during the 1964 elections meant that his government formed a coalition.

Leoni was fortunate politically, as he came to office at a time when the national economy was vibrant and politically stable. With the retirement of President Romulo Betancourt from office, the nation had just

a Bolshevik government was formed, and peace negotiations with Germany were begun, leading to the signing of the Treaty of Brest Litovsk on 3 March 1918.

From the overthrow of the provisional government in November 1917 until his death, Lenin effectively controlled the USSR, although an assassination attempt in 1918 injured his health. He founded the Third (Communist) International in 1919. With communism proving inadequate to put the country on its feet, he introduced the private-enterprise New Economic Policy in 1921.

In 1898 he married Nadezhda Konstantinova Krupskaya (1869–1939), who shared his work and wrote *Memories of Lenin*.

Lenin's embalmed body is in a mausoleum in Red Square, Moscow. See photograph on page 258.

FURTHER READING
Conquest, Robert *Lenin* 1972
Hill, Christopher *Lenin and the Russian Revolution* 1978
Schapiro, Leonard, and Reddaway, Peter (eds) *Lenin* 1987
Shub, D *Lenin* 1966
Ulam, Adam *Lenin and the Bolsheviks* 1965
Volkogonov, Dmitri *Lenin: Life and Legacy* translation 1994

experienced, for the first time in a century, an extended period of relative stability and democratic rule.

Leopold III (1901–1983)

King of the Belgians 1934–51. He was educated at Eton, England, and at Ghent University. Against the prime minister's advice he surrendered to the German army in World War II in 1940. Postwar charges against his conduct led to a regency by his brother Charles and the establishment of a commission to investigate his actions. This found no fault, and a referendum in 1950 produced a small majority in favour of his return, but he was persuaded to abdicate in 1951 in favour of his son Baudouin.

Le Pen, Jean-Marie (1928–)

French extreme right-wing politician, founder of the National Front (FN) in 1972. His talents as a public speaker, his demagogic mixing of nationalism with law-and-order populism – calling for immigrant repatriation, stricter nationality laws, and the restoration of capital punishment – and his hostility to the European Union attracted a wide swathe of electoral support, the FN winning 14% of the national vote in the 1986 National Assembly elections and 15% in 1997. Le Pen's 1988 and 1995 presidential bids attracted similar support on the first ballot, concentrated particularly amongst the unemployed, small-business owners, and young white males. He was elected to the European Parliament as head of the FN list in 1984, 1989, and 1994 but in early 1998 was debarred from voting or holding elective office for two years, following his conviction for assaulting a socialist woman candidate during the 1997 election campaign.

Le Pen had served as a paratrooper in French Indochina and Algeria during the 1950s. He was elected to the National Assembly in 1956 on Pierre ◊Poujade's party list. In the 1960s he actively supported General ◊Salan's Organisation de l'Armée Secrète (OAS), devoted to perpetuating French rule in Algeria.

FURTHER READING
Marcus, J *The National Front and French Politics: The Resistible Rise of Jean-Marie Le Pen* 1995
Simmons, H G *The French National Front: The Extremist Challenge to Democracy* 1996

Lescot, Elie (1883–1974)

Haitian politician, dictator–president 1941–46. After replacing Sténio ◊Vincent in 1941, he quickly established a tyrannical and corrupt dictatorship, surviving through his close ties with the USA, which secured military and economic aid, and his support for the Allies in World War II. Having declared war on the Axis powers in 1941, Lescot suspended the constitution and assumed 'emergency powers'. In 1944 he extended his presidential term from five years to seven, but after the

Lenin in disguise, August 1917. *Mary Evans Picture Library*

and creative issues appeared in *O Taste and See* (1964) and *The Poet in the World* (1973). Her 22nd collection, *Sands of the Well*, was published in 1998.

Lévesque, René (1922–1987)

French-Canadian politician, premier of Québec 1976–85. In 1968 he founded the Parti Québecois, with the aim of an independent Québec, but a referendum rejected the proposal in 1980.

Lewis, (Harry) Sinclair (1885–1951)

US satirical novelist who, in 1930, became the first US writer to receive the Nobel Prize for Literature. With the appearance of *Main Street* (1920), Lewis was recognized as a new force in US literature, a satirist of the first order who saw his country with clear eyes. His best-selling *Main Street* was followed by *Babbitt* (1922), the story of a self-satisfied US businessman. *Martin Arrowsmith* (1925) satirizes the medical profession, and *Elmer Gantry* (1927) paints a savage picture of the professional religious revivalists. *Dodsworth* (1929) was the fruit of numerous trips to Europe.

He was born in Sauk Center, Minnesota. Graduating from Yale University in 1907, he worked for a time as a newspaper reporter and then in various editorial capacities with US publishing firms.

FURTHER READING

Hutchisson, James M *The Rise of Sinclair Lewis, 1920–1930* 1996

Lundquist, James *Sinclair Lewis* 1973

Schorer, Mark *Sinclair Lewis: An American Life* 1961

Lewis, John L(lewellyn) (1880–1969)

US labour leader. President of the United Mine Workers (UMW) 1920–60, he was largely responsible for the adoption of national mining safety standards in the USA. His militancy and the miners' strikes during and after World War II led to President Harry Truman's nationalization of the mines in 1946.

He helped found the American Federation of Labor's offshoot, the Congress of Industrial Organizations (CIO), in 1935, which unionized workers in mass-production industries.

Born in Lucas, Iowa, Lewis worked in the coal mines from an early age. He became a regional officer of the UMW and served as its liaison with the American Federation of Labor in 1911. In the presidential elec-

war his attempts to muzzle the opposition press sparked student-led demonstrations. A military coup in 1946, led by Major Paul Eugène Magloire, forced Lescot to flee to the USA, although he later returned to Haiti.

It was alleged that Rafael ◊Trujillo Molina, dictator of the Dominican Republic and an ally of Lescot, provided him with funds to bribe members of the Haitian Assembly to secure his election in 1941. During his government, political opponents were arbitrarily arrested and foreign assets appropriated for his family's enrichment.

Lescot was drawn from the mulatto (mixed ethnic) social and political elite. After studying in Canada, where he secured a doctorate, he had a varied career in business, as a diplomat, and as a cabinet minister.

Levertov, Denise (1923–1997)

English-born US poet. She published her first volume of poetry, *The Double Image*, in 1946, after which she moved to the USA. In the 1950s she was associated with the Black Mountain poets, and in the 1960s campaigned for civil rights. Poetry collections include *Here and Now* (1957), *Candles in Babylon* (1982), and *A Door in the Hive* (1993). Her essays on political, feminist,

tion of 1940 he urged US labour to support Wendell ◊Willkie, believing that F D Roosevelt was leading the country into war. The result was that he split the ranks of the CIO, and ensured Roosevelt's return in triumph. Lewis accordingly resigned from the presidency of the CIO, but continued to exercise a strong influence on US labour.

Ley, Robert (1890–1945)

German Nazi administrator. He was responsible for directing Germany's labour needs both before and during World War II. On 16 May 1945 he was captured by US troops. He was eventually tried at Nuremberg as a war criminal, but committed suicide.

He was born in Niederbreidenbach, Hesse. He joined the National Socialist party in 1924 and represented it in the Reichstag in 1932. When Hitler came to power, Ley was given the task of abolishing the trade unions and setting up a new labour organisation with himself at its head.

FURTHER READING
Smelser, R M *Robert Ley: Hitler's Labor Front Leader* 1988

Leye, Jean-Marie (1933–)

Vanuatuan Francophone politician, president from 1994. In November 1997, after two years of political instability and deadlock, he intervened controversially to dissolve parliament and call fresh elections.

Born on Aneityum Island, he was educated at French-speaking schools and had a successful career in the private sector, becoming a director of Air Vanuatu. In 1957 he was elected president of his island's local council and helped draft the new constitution that provided for the New Hebrides' independence, in 1980, as the Republic of Vanuatu. In 1983 Leye was elected to the Vanuatu parliament, as vice president of the Francophone Union of Moderate Parties (UMP), which remained in opposition to the Anglophone Vanuaaku Pati (VP) until 1991.

Liao Zhongkai or *Liao Chung-k'ai* (1878–1925)

Chinese politician. Born in the USA, he studied in Japan before becoming the leading financial expert of the Kuomintang (Guomindang) after 1912. Associated with the left wing of the party, he supported the United Front with the communists in 1923, advocating a planned economy along socialist lines. In 1924 he played an important role in setting up both the workers' and peasants' departments under Kuomintang auspices as part of its new strategy of mass mobilization.

As the leading Kuomintang representative at the Whampoa Military Academy, he also laid the basis for the political commissar system that was to be used throughout the National Revolutionary Army. He aroused opposition from right-wing members of the Kuomintang who opposed the United Front, and who may have been involved in his assassination.

Liaquat Ali Khan, Nawabzada (1895–1951)

Indian politician, deputy leader of the Muslim League 1940–47, first prime minister of Pakistan 1947–51. He was assassinated by objectors to his peace policy with India.

Liberia-Peters, Maria (1942–)

Netherlands Antilles centre-right politician, prime minister 1984–85 and 1988–93. Representing the National People's Party (PNP), she became the Netherlands Antilles' first woman minister-president (prime minister) in 1984. Heading a coalition government, she faced the economic problems posed by Shell's closure of its oil refinery on Curaçao. Her second coalition, from 1988, was reformed after the 1990 general election, but she resigned in 1993 after a referendum on Curaçao supported the continuation of the island's existing status in the Antillean Federation.

The premiership between her two periods of office, 1985–88, was held by Don Martina of the socialist New Antilles Movement (MAN).

Liberia-Peters had a university education in the Netherlands, and returned to the Netherlands Antilles in 1962 to work initially as a kindergarten teacher and school administrator. She entered the Curaçao legislature in 1976.

Li Dazhao or *Li Ta-chao* (1888–1927)

Chinese revolutionary. He was one of the founders of the Chinese Communist Party, and his interpretation of Marxism as applied to China had a profound influence on ◊Mao Zedong. In 1927, when the Manchurian military leader Zhang Zuolin (Chang Tsolin), then occupying Beijing (Peking), raided the Soviet Embassy, Li was captured and executed.

Appointed head librarian of Beijing University in 1918 and professor of history in 1920, he had the young Mao as a library assistant, and founded one of the first of the communist study circles that, in 1921, were to form the Communist Party.

FURTHER READING
Meisner, M J *Li Ta-Chao and the Origins of Chinese Marxism* 1967

Lie, Trygve Halvdan (1896–1968)

Norwegian Labour politician and diplomat. He became secretary of the Labour Party in 1926. During the German occupation of Norway in World War II he was foreign minister in the exiled government 1941–46, when he helped retain the Norwegian fleet for the Allies. He became the first secretary general of the United Nations 1946–53, but resigned over Soviet opposition to his handling of the Korean War.

FURTHER READING

Barros, J *Trygve Lie and the Cold War: The UN Secretary-General Pursues Peace, 1946–1953* 1989

Liebknecht, Karl (1871–1919)

German socialist, son of Wilhelm Liebknecht. A founder of the German Communist Party, originally known as the Spartacus League, in 1918, he was one of the few socialists who refused to support World War I. He led an unsuccessful revolt with Rosa Luxemburg in Berlin in 1919 and both were murdered by army officers.

Liebknecht practised as a barrister in Berlin and did his military service in the Prussian Guard, but turned to socialism while defending a group of agitators in Königsberg in 1904. Imprisoned for sedition in 1907, he was eventually elected to the Reichstag (parliament) in 1912 but was expelled in 1916 and again imprisoned.

Liem Sioe Liong, Indonesian name *Sudono Salim* (1916–)

Chinese-born Indonesian billionaire businessman. By the 1990s he controlled Indonesia's largest corporate group (Indocement, Indofood); was the major shareholder in the Bank of Central Asia, the country's largest private bank; and had huge businesses in the Philippines, Thailand, Hong Kong, and China.

Born in Fujian province, China, Liem Sioe Liong emigrated to Java in 1938 and began building his business empire. He was the main supplier of provisions for the rebel army fighting for Indonesian independence during the 1940s and developed close ties to President Thojib ◊Suharto.

Ligachev, Egor Kuzmich (1920–)

Soviet politician. He joined the Communist Party of the Soviet Union (CPSU) in 1944, and became a member of the Politburo in 1985. He was replaced as the party ideologist in 1988 by Vadim Medvedev.

Ligachev was regarded as the chief conservative ideologist, and the leader of conservative opposition to President Mikhail ◊Gorbachev. In July 1990 he failed to secure election to the CPSU Politburo or Central Committee and also failed in his bid to become elected as party deputy general secretary.

FURTHER READING

Ligachev, E K *Inside Gorbachev's Kremlin: The Memoirs of Yegor Ligachev* 1996
March, L *Egor Ligachev: A Conservative Reformer in the Gorbachev Period* 1997

Li Lisan (1899–1867)

Chinese communist politician, party leader 1927–30. He became a leading figure in the Chinese Communist Party (CCP) and a key proponent of the conventional Leninist and Russian-supported line of seeking to foment a proletarian revolution in China's cities and among its industrial workforce.

He was active in Shanghai from 1924 and in the Nanchang uprising of 1927, when he replaced Chen Duxiu as effective leader of the CCP. By the early 1930s, faced with the suppression of the CCP's urban cells by the Kuomintang (Guomindang, nationalist) leader Jiang Jie Shi (Chiang Kai-shek), it was clear that the 'Li Lisan line' had failed. A new rural-based, revolutionary approach, devised by ◊Mao Zedong, now gained the upper hand. Li Lisan fled to Moscow in 1931 and was imprisoned there as a Trotskyist in 1936. He returned to China in 1945. Following the establishment of the People's Republic in 1949, he became a minister of labour, until 1954. Thereafter, Li held minor party posts in north China until his death in December 1967.

Born in Liling county of Hunan province, the son of a schoolteacher, Li studied in France in the early 1920s where, along with ◊Deng Xiaoping and ◊Zhou Enlai, he helped found the French branch of the CCP in 1922.

Lin Biao or *Lin Piao* (1908–1971)

Chinese communist soldier and politician, deputy leader of the Chinese Communist Party (CCP) 1969–71.

Born Lin Yu-yung, in Wuhan, Hubei province, he was the son of a factory owner. Lin trained at the Whampoa Military Academy, graduating in 1926, and joined the CCP in 1927. He became a commander of Mao Zedong's Red Army in the struggle against Kuomintang (Guomindang) nationalists and was involved in the 1934–35 'Long March'. Lin had considerable success during the 1937–45 military struggle with the Japanese and, in the civil war of 1945–49, led the Northeast People's Liberation Army, routing the Kuomintang forces at Mukden in October 1948.

After the establishment of the People's Republic in 1949, Lin commanded the Chinese 'volunteer army' in North Korea 1950–52 and, after recovering from tuberculosis, was made a marshall in 1955 and defence minister in 1959. An ascetic radical who favoured the promotion of world revolution through China's sponsorship of Third World guerrilla wars, Lin's position advanced during the leftist Cultural Revolution 1966–69. He was made vice chair of the party in April 1969 and was termed Mao's 'designated successor'. However, in 1971, with his health deteriorating and fearing an imminent purge, Lin, along with Chen Boda and a number of People's Liberation Army (PLA) colleagues, formulated 'Project 571' with the aim of assassinating CCP chairman Mao Zedong during a Shanghai–Beijing train journey and seize power in a coup. However, this plot was uncovered and Lin was killed in an aeroplane crash in Outer Mongolia on 17 September 1971, while fleeing to the USSR. His co-conspirators were later tried and found guilty, in January 1981.

FURTHER READING

Ginneken, J van *The Rise and Fall of Lin Piao* 1976

Murphy, Ch J V *Who Killed Lin Piao?* 1973

Teiwes, F C *The Tragedy of Lin Biao: Riding the Tiger During the Cultural Revolution, 1966–1971* 1996

Wu, Tien-wei *Lin Biao and the Gang of Four: Contra-Confucianism in Historical and Intellectual Perspective* 1983

Yao, M *The Conspiracy and Death of Lin Biao* 1983

Lindsay, John (Vliet) (1921–)

US politician. He was mayor of New York 1965–73, during which time he abandoned the Republican Party for the Democrats.

Lindsay was educated at Yale University and became a lawyer in 1949. He was elected to the House of Representatives as a Republican in 1959, and was noted for his liberal attitudes on issues such as civil rights. In November 1965 he became New York's first Republican mayor in 20 years (since Fiorello La Guardia), defeating both a Democrat and a right-wing Republican to achieve this. Later re-elected as a Liberal, he became a Democrat in 1971.

Lini, Walter Hadye (1942–1999)

Vanuatuan centre-left politician and priest, chief minister 1979–80 and prime minister 1980–91. A member of the New Hebrides National Party, later named the Vanuaaku Pati (VP), he campaigned for the return of land to the aboriginal Melanesian population. He became chief minister in 1979 and, on independence in 1980, prime minister of the new Republic of Vanuatu. On the basis of a controversial non-aligned foreign policy and a 'Melanesian socialist' domestic pro-gramme, he was re-elected in 1983 and 1987, and survived an unconstitutional challenge to his leader-ship in 1988, engineered by President Ati ◊Sokomanu, who was later imprisoned. The VP split in 1991 and was defeated in elections that year, when a coalition government was formed. Lini, who had been replaced as VP leader by Donald Kalpokas, formed, in 1991, the breakaway National United Party (NUP), which later split in 1993. Lini returned to government in late 1996 as justice and culture minister in a coalition govern-ment led by Serge Vohor, and after the March 1998 general election he became deputy prime minister and justice and interior minister in a coalition led by Kalpokas.

Born on Pentecost Island, Lini trained for the Anglican priesthood in the Solomon Islands and New Zealand, being ordained in 1980.

FURTHER READING

Lini, Walter Hadye *Beyond Pandemonium* 1980

Li Peng (1928–)

Chinese communist politician, prime minister 1987–98.

Born in Chengdu, in Sichuan province, the son of the writer Li Shouxun (who took part in the Nanchang communist rising in 1927 and was executed in 1930), Li was adopted, from 1939, by the leading communist ◊Zhou Enlai. He studied at the Chinese Communist Party (CCP) headquarters in Yan'an from 1941 and trained as a hydroelectric engineer at the Moscow Power Institute from 1948. Helped by Zhou's patron-age, Li survived the violent pro-Maoist 1966–69 Cul-tural Revolution and by 1981 had become minister of the electric power industry. In 1983 he was made a vice premier, with responsibility for education, energy, and transportation, and in 1986 was inducted into the CCP Poliburo. When Zhao Ziyang resigned in November 1987 to concentrate on his new role as CCP leader, Li became prime minister.

He emerged as more conservative than his prede-cessor, launching, with the support of 'paramount leader' Deng Xiaoping and President Yang Shangkun, the crackdown on prodemocracy demonstrators in Beijing that led to the June 1989 massacre of 2,000 students in Tiananmen Square. The demonstrators had campaigned, unsuccessfully, for his resignation. Li sought improved relations with the USSR, before its demise in 1991, and, more hardline than Jiang Zemin, who became CCP leader in June 1989, advocated maintaining firm central and party control over the economy. In March 1998 Li stpped down as prime minister, being replaced by the more reformist ◊Zhu Rongji. He was elected chair of the National People's Congress (China's parliament), although an un-precedented 200 of the 2,950 delegates voted against his nomination.

Lippmann, Walter (1889–1974)

US liberal political commentator. From 1921 he was the chief editorial writer for the *New York World* and from 1931 wrote the daily column 'Today and Tomor-row', which was widely syndicated through the *New York Herald Tribune*. Among his books are *A Preface to Morals* (1929), *The Good Society* (1937), and *The Public Philosophy* (1955).

The final test of a leader is that he leaves behind him in other men the conviction and the will to carry on.

WALTER LIPPMANN *New York Herald Tribune* 14 April 1945

Lippmann was born in New York and educated at Harvard. He was one of the founders of the *New Republic* magazine in 1914. After service in army intelligence during World War I, he became an adviser to President Woodrow Wilson at the Versailles peace conference.

Litvinov, Maxim, adopted name of Meir Walach (1876–1951)

Soviet politician, commissioner for foreign affairs

under Stalin from January 1931 until his removal from office in May 1939.

Litvinov believed in cooperation with the West and obtained US recognition of the USSR in 1934. In the League of Nations he advocated action against the Axis (the alliance of Nazi Germany and Fascist Italy), and as a result was dismissed just before the signing of the Hitler–Stalin nonaggression pact of 1939. After the German invasion of the USSR, he was ambassador to the USA 1941–43.

> *Peace is indivisible.*
> MAXIM LITVINOV Speech to League of Nations July 1936

FURTHER READING

Phillips, H D *Between the Revolution and the West: A Political Biography of Maxim M Litvinov* 1992, *Maxim M Litvinov and Soviet-American Relations, 1918–1946* 1996

Liu Shaoqi or *Liu Shao-chi* (1898–1969)

Chinese communist politician, president 1960–65, and the most prominent victim of the 1966–69 leftist Cultural Revolution. A Moscow-trained labour organizer, he was a firm proponent of the Soviet style of government based around disciplined one-party control, the use of incentive gradings, and priority for industry over agriculture. This was opposed by ◊Mao Zedong, but began to be implemented by Liu while he was state president. He was brought down during the Cultural Revolution.

The son of a Hunan peasant farmer, Liu attended the same Changsha school as Mao Zedong. Interested in radical politics, he visited the USSR in 1920 to study communism and returned to China to join the Chinese Communist Party (CCP) in Shanghai in 1921. Liu became a trade-union organizer and, after joining Mao at his Jiangxi soviet (people's republic), participated in the 'Long March' of 1934–35. During the mid-1930s he was the CCP's main theoretician, with his writings better known than Mao's. After the establishment of the People's Republic in 1949, he rapidly rose to become second-ranking vice chair of the CCP and in 1960 succeeded Mao as chairman (president) of the republic.

After the failure of the 1958–61 Maoist 'Great Leap Forward' experiment with agricultural communes, Liu, working closely with Deng Xiaoping, implemented his ideas in a recovery programme. Communes were broken up, the use of communal dormitories and mess halls ended, and rural markets and private subsidiary farming plots were re-introduced. This programme was successful, but, with widening income differentials, was seen as a return to capitalism. The leftist 'Cultural Revolution' was directed against Liu and his 'capitalist roader' supporters. In October 1968 he was denounced by the CCP's Central Committee as a 'scab, renegade, and traitor' and in April 1969 he was formally stripped of his post and expelled from the CCP. He was banished to Kaifeng, in Henan province, where he died of pneumonia in November 1969 after being locked in a disused bank vault.

> *A great Marxist, proletarian statesman and theorist ... who is loved by the party, the army and the people even today.*
> JIANG ZEMIN Eulogy in November 1998, during a special ceremony to mark the centenary of Liu Shaoqi's birth.

Liu was rehabilitated posthumously in 1980, after the accession to power of Deng Xiaoping. He received eulogies from President Jiang Zemin in November 1998, on the centenary of his birth.

FURTHER READING

Dittmer, L *Liu Shaoqi and the Chinese Cultural Revolution* 1974, *Liu Shaoqi and the Chinese Cultural Revolution* 1998

Kent, A E *Indictment Without Trial: The Case of Liu Shao Ch'i* 1969

Livingstone, Ken(neth) (1945–)

British left-wing Labour politician, leader of the Greater London Council (GLC) 1981–86, and member of Parliament for Brent East from 1987. He stood as a candidate for the Labour Party leadership elections in 1992 and declared himself a candidate for the mayorship of London in 1998, although he lacked backing from the Labour Party's leadership.

> *Part of the problem is that many MPs never see the London that exists beyond the wine bars and brothels of Westminster.*
> KEN LIVINGSTONE Quoted in *Observer* 22 February 1987

Livingstone was born in London and educated at Tulse Hill Comprehensive and Phillipa Fawcett College of Education. He joined the Labour Party in 1968, and was active in London politics from 1971, serving as a local councillor for Lambeth 1971–78 and for Camden 1978–82. As leader of the GLC until its abolition in 1986, he displayed the latest unemployment figures outside GLC headquarters so that they were clearly visible to MPs in the Palace of Westminster across the River Thames.

FURTHER READING

Livingstone, K *If Voting Changed Anything, They'd Abolish It* 1987

Carvel, J *Citizen Ken* 1987

Li Xiannian (1909–1992)

Chinese communist politician, president 1983–88.

Born into a poor peasant family in Hubei province, Li trained as a carpenter and joined the Kuomintang (Guomindang, nationalist) forces during the 'Northern Expedition' of 1926–27. He joined the Chinese Communist Party (CCP) later in 1927 and became a leading figure in the rural soviet (workers' republic) set up at Oyuwan on the borders of Hubei, Henan, and Anhui provinces 1931–33. During the 'Long March' of 1934–35, northwards to Yanan, in Shaanxi province, and the Liberation War of 1937–49, Li served as a political commissar. He was made commander of the Central China military region in 1944 and governor of Hubei in 1949.

During the 1950s and early 1960s Li was vice premier to the State Council and minister for finance and was inducted into the CCP Politburo and Secretariat in 1956 and 1958 respectively. He fell from favour during the 1966–69 Cultural Revolution, but was rehabilitated as finance minister in 1973, by ◊Zhou Enlai, and proceeded to implement cautious economic reform. He was elected to the Politburo's controlling Standing Committee in 1977, where he was to remain until 1987, and he was state president in June 1983. As part of a general move to retire the CCP's ageing 'old guard', Li stepped down as president in April 1988 and became chair of the Chinese People's Political Consultative Conference, a broad-based discussion forum. The father-in-law of ◊Jiang Zemin, Li remained influential as a party elder until his death in 1992, establishing himself as a critic of destabilizing liberalization.

Lleras Camargo, Alberto (1906–1990)

Colombian politician and president 1945–46 and 1958–62. His first term in office was very brief, but during his second term Lleras temporarily succeeded in stabilizing the economy, though unemployment, difficulties in the coffee industry, and increased reliance on foreign aid brought about economic stagnation towards the end of his administration.

Lleras entered into politics as a Liberal party member. He occupied many important government positions during the 1930s and 1940s, leading up to a limited presidential term 1945–46. He served as the director of the Pan-American Union 1947–48 and also as secretary general of the Organization of American States 1948–54.

Lleras was instrumental in formulating a constitutional arrangement for a Frente Nacional (National Front) government – a coalition of conservatives and liberals. This facilitated a unique agreement enabling bipartisan power sharing between the two main parties over a 12-year period (subsequently extended to 16 years). The amendment was embodied in the 'Declaration of Sitges' of December 1957 and ended over a decade of political instability that had cost in excess of 200,000 lives. In the 1958 elections the failure of the

Conservatives to select a candidate resulted in Lleras's selection to hold the presidential seat.

Lloyd George, David, 1st Earl Lloyd-George of Dwyfor (1863–1945)

See page 264.

Lloyd George, Lady Megan (1902–1966)

English politician. The younger daughter of the former prime minister, the 1st Earl Lloyd George, she became Liberal member of Parliament for Anglesey in 1929. She retained the seat until her defeat at the general election in 1951. A pronounced Radical in her views, in 1955 she joined the Labour Party, re-entering Parliament as a Labour MP in 1957.

She was born in Criccieth, Wales, and was educated at Banstead and in Paris.

FURTHER READING
Jones, M *A Radical Life: The Biography of Megan Lloyd George, 1902–66* 1991

Loach, Ken(neth) (1936–)

English film and television director. Loach became known for his trenchantly realistic treatment of social issues with television dramas such as *Up the Junction* (1965) and *Cathy Come Home* (1966), concerning the plight of homeless people.

His films include *Kes* (1971), dealing with working-class life in the north of England; *Hidden Agenda* (1990), about the Northern Ireland troubles; the comedy *Riff Raff* (1991); and *Tierra y libertad/Land and Freedom* (1995), a period piece set in the Spanish Civil War.

Lodge, Henry Cabot (1850–1924)

US Republican politician. He was senator from Massachusetts 1893–1924 and chair of the Senate Foreign Relations Committee after World War I. He supported conservative economic legislation at home but expansionist policies abroad. Nevertheless, he influenced the USA to stay out of the League of Nations in 1920, arguing that it posed a threat to US sovereignty.

Lodge was born in Boston, Massachusetts. He was a Republican member of the House of Representatives 1887–93. As an advocate of US pursuit of empire, he joined President Theodore ◊Roosevelt in calling for war against Spain in 1898. He insisted on modifications to the Treaty of Versailles with its provisions for the League of Nations. President Woodrow Wilson refused to accede and the Senate became deadlocked, finally refusing to ratify the treaty.

Lodge, Henry Cabot, II (1902–1985)

US diplomat. He served as the US representative at the United Nations 1953–60. He was the Republican Party's unsuccessful candidate for vice president in

1960. During the Vietnam War he was ambassador to South Vietnam 1963–64 and 1965–67, and President Richard Nixon's negotiator in the peace talks of 1969.

Born in Nahant, Massachusetts, he was a grandson of Henry Cabot Lodge. He was educated at Harvard, and worked as a journalist. Serving in the Senate 1937–44, he was re-elected in 1947 but defeated by J F Kennedy in 1952. He was also Dwight D Eisenhower's presidential campaign manager in 1952. In the Vietnam peace talks of 1969, he replaced Averell Harriman.

Lombardo Toledano, Vicente (1894–1968)

Mexican labour leader. In 1923 he joined the Mexican Regional Confederation of Workers (CROM) and, in 1933, established the Confederation of Mexican Workers (CTM). Under Lombardo's leadership, the CTM became influential, founding a workers' university and promoting labour and welfare reforms, some of which were accepted by Lázaro ◊Cárdenas, who was Mexican president 1934–40. However, Lombardo and the CTM faced repression under the conservative regime of Manuel ◊Ávila Camacho 1940–46.

Born in Puebla state, into a middle-class family of Italian origin, Lombardo worked initially as a Marxist-influenced journalist and lawyer and, in 1920, became governor of his home state. He left the CTM to form the Popular (Socialist) Party in 1948 and unsuccessfully contested for the presidency in 1952. In 1949 he established the Latin American Confederation of Labor (CTAL).

FURTHER READING

Millon, R P *Mexican Marxist, Vicente Lombardo Toledano* 1966

Long, Huey (Pierce) ('the Kingfish') (1893–1935)

US Democratic politician. As governor of Louisiana 1928–32 and senator for Louisiana 1932–35, he became legendary for his political rhetoric. He was popular with poor white voters for his programme of social and economic reform, which he called the 'Share Our Wealth' programme. It represented a significant challenge to F D Roosevelt's New Deal economic programme.

Long's scheme called for a massive redistribution of wealth through high inheritance taxes and confiscatory taxes on high incomes. His own extravagance – including the state capitol building at Baton Rouge, built of bronze and marble – was widely criticized. Although he became a virtual dictator in the state, his slogan was 'Every man a king, but no man wears a crown'. He was assassinated.

Born in Winnfield, Louisiana, he graduated from Tulane University with a law degree. He was fatally shot at the capitol in Baton Rouge, one month after announcing his intention to run for the presidency.

◆ LLOYD GEORGE, DAVID 1ST EARL LLOYD-GEORGE OF DWYFOR (1863–1945) ◆

British Liberal politician, prime minister 1916–22, and chancellor of the Exchequer 1908–1915.

Lloyd George was born of Welsh parents in Manchester, became a solicitor, and was member of Parliament for Caernarvon Boroughs 1890–1945. During the Boer War he was prominent in opposing the war, though neither a pacifist or anti-imperialist. He also opposed Arthur Balfour's

---

Four spectres haunt the poor – old age, accident, sickness and unemployment. We are going to exorcise them. We are going to drive hunger from the hearth. We mean to banish the workhouse from the horizon of every workman in the land.

DAVID LLOYD GEORGE Speech, 1910

1902 Education Act, though not anxious to cast himself as a non-conformist. In Henry Campbell-Bannerman's government he was president of the Board of Trade. A radical pioneer of social reform and the welfare state, as chancellor he introduced old-age pensions in 1908 and health and unemployment insurance in 1911. His 1909 budget (with graduated direct taxes and taxes on land values) provoked the Lords to reject it, and resulted in the Act of 1911 limiting their powers. In the coalition of May 1915, Lloyd George took the post of minister of munitions and succeeded Horatio Kitchener a year later. In December 1916 there was an open breach between Lloyd George and prime minister H H Asquith, and he became prime minister of a coalition government, bringing energy and a renewed determination to win the war. Securing a unified Allied command, he enabled the Allies to withstand the last German offensive and achieve victory. After World War I he had a major role in the Versailles peace treaty. In Britain he promised 'homes fit for heroes'. In the 1918 election (the so-called 'coupon' election in which the prime minister endorsed certain coalition candidates) he achieved a huge majority over Labour, non-coalition Tories, and Asquith's followers.

High unemployment, industrial discontent, intervention in the Russian Civil War, and the use

David Lloyd George, 1929. *AKG London*

FURTHER READING
Liebling, A J *The Earl of Louisiana* 1961
Sindler, A P *Huey Long's Louisiana* 1972
Williams, T Harry *Huey Long* 1969

Longford, Frank (Francis Aungier) Pakenham, 7th Earl of Longford (1905–   )

British Labour politician. He was brought up a Protestant but became a leading Catholic and an advocate of penal reform. He worked in the Conservative Party Economic Research Department 1930–32, yet became a member of the Labour Party and held ministerial posts 1948–51 and 1964–68. He became Earl in 1961.

Longo, Luigi (1900–   )

Italian Communist politician and wartime resistance member. He became the Italian Communist Party secretary-general in 1964.

He joined the Communist Party while a student. He was imprisoned for political activities 1923–24, and later left Italy. Longo was in Moscow 1932–34, and was then inspector general of the International Brigade in Spain 1936–39. He settled in France. He was imprisoned there 1939–41, and returned to Italy to work with Communist resistance groups. In 1945 he became deputy secretary general of the Italian Communist Party, and entered parliament in 1946. He succeeded Palmiro Togliatti as secretary general of the party.

of the military police force, the Black and Tans, in Ireland divided the coalition and eroded Lloyd George's support as prime minister. The creation of the Irish Free State in 1921 and (immediately) his pro-Greek policy against the Turks caused the collapse of the government. At a Carlton Club meeting in October 1922, with a notable contribution from Stanley Baldwin, Conservative backbenchers brought the coalition down. Within the Liberal Party, he had become largely distrusted, though he resumed its leadership after Asquith in 1926. Though a wily political operator, armed in the later 1920s with a bold Keynesian package to counter unemployment, Lloyd George never regained office. In 1944 he moved to Llanystumdwy in north Wales, and was made an Earl in 1945.

FURTHER READING
Campbell, J *Lloyd George: The Goat in the Wilderness* 1977
Constantine, Stephen *Lloyd George* 1992
Grigg, John *Lloyd George*, 3 volumes: *The Young Lloyd George* 1973, *The People's Champion 1902–1911* 1978, *From Peace to War 1912–1916* 1985
Pugh, M *Lloyd George* 1988
Woodward, David *Lloyd George and the Generals* 1983

López Arellano, Oswaldo (1922–   )

Honduran soldier and right-wing political leader, president 1963–71 and 1972–75. In October 1963, as army chief of staff, López removed President Ramón ◊Villeda Morales in a violent coup and subsequently headed the junta before, in 1965, being made president by the constituent assembly. López reversed some of Villeda's liberal economic policies, but faced workers' unrest and agitation for agrarian reform. His decision to repatriate Salvadorian immigrants, in an effort to reduce population pressure, precipitated a five-day war with El Salvador in 1969 and, as a result, Honduras pulled out of the Central American Common Market.

A career soldier, López joined the airforce in 1942, became defence minister in 1956, and was a member of the ruling military junta that overthrew President Julio Lozano Díaz in October 1956 and handed over power to President Villeda in December 1957.

Under a national unity plan, Ramón Cruz of the right-wing National Party was elected president in 1971, heading a coalition with the Liberals. López remained influential as commander of the armed forces and, in December 1972, replaced Cruz as president in a bloodless coup. After implication in a bribery scandal, López was himself ousted in 1975.

López Mateos, Adolfo (1910–1969)

Mexican political leader, president 1958–64. Representing the Institutional Revolutionary Party (PRI), as president he promoted agrarian reform and foreign inward investment, nationalized the power industry, and introduced profit-sharing for workers. He also reached agreement with the USA, in 1963, for the return to Mexico of El Chamizal, a long-disputed 177 ha/437 acre area along the Texas border.

A lawyer, he became active in the governing National Revolutionary Party, later known as the Institutional Revolutionary Party, and served in the senate 1946–52. Under President ◊Ruiz Cortinez, he was a particularly active labour minister 1952–58, settling more than 10,000 disputes.

López Portillo y Pacheco, José (1920–   )

Mexican right-wing politician, president 1976–82. He halted land redistribution, sought to develop Mexico's oil reserves, and helped mediate several Pan-American disputes. However, Mexico faced mounting financial difficulties after 1980 when oil prices fell and, as the country became threatened with potential international bankruptcy, he dramatically nationalized the banking system in September 1982. The administration was accused of corruption and constrained its successors through its legacy of debt.

Born in Mexico City and educated at the University of Mexico, he was a lawyer and university professor before becoming finance minister 1973–75, under President Luis ◊Echeverría, and overseeing important reforms to the tax system. In 1976, standing as the candidate of the ruling Institutional Revolutionary Party (PRI), he was elected president.

López Portillo is also the author of books on political theory and novels.

Loubet, Emile François (1838–1929)

French politician. He was president of the French Republic 1899–1906, succeeding Faure. During his presidency the Dreyfus case was finally settled. The separation of Church and State was also approved in the Chamber of Deputies, and the French ambassador was subsequently recalled from the Vatican.

Loubet was born in Marsanne, Drome. He entered politics in 1876, and supported the Gambetta and Ferry ministries. In 1885 he became a senator, and two years later was appointed minister of public works. In 1892 he became minister of the interior, and in 1895 president of the Senate.

Louisy, Allan

St Lucian centre-left politician, prime minister 1979–81. The leader of the St Lucian Labour Party (SLP) from 1974, he led the SLP to victory soon after independence in 1979, ending 15 years in opposition to John ◊Compton's United Workers' Party (UWP). As prime minister, he promoted development of the agricultural sector and closer economic ties with other English-speaking Caribbean states. Forced to resign in 1981 when the government's budget was defeated, the SLP subsequently split, with the left-wing deputy prime minister George Odlum leaving to form the breakaway Progressive Labour Party (PLP).

Louisy initially practised as a barrister, and worked from 1946 to 1974 as a crown attorney or magistrate in different states in the Caribbean.

Low, David Alexander Cecil (1891–1963)

New Zealand-born British political cartoonist, creator (in newspapers such as the *London Evening Standard*) of the characters Colonel Blimp and the TUC Carthorse.

Low's work is remarkably free from the conventional devices of the professional cartoonist, and in his drawings of celebrities in various walks of life, which appeared in the *New Statesman*, he showed a gift for genially humorous portraiture. During the 1930s and 1940s, his appeals to national sentiment were founded on an understanding of the principal political figures of the period, from Winston Churchill, Stanley Baldwin, and Neville Chamberlain to Mussolini, Hitler and Hermann Goering. He was particularly critical of British Conservative supporters of appeasement.

Born in Dunedin, New Zealand, he worked for various New Zealand papers until 1911, when he joined the staff of the *Bulletin* in Sydney, New South Wales, Australia. He went to London in 1919 to work on the *Star*, at the suggestion of the novelist Arnold Bennett, and became celebrated for his portraits of David Lloyd George. He left the *Star* for the *Evening Standard* in 1927, and moved to the *Daily Herald* in 1950. In 1953 he became political cartoonist of the *Manchester Guardian* (now the *Guardian*), where he remained until his death. He published collections of his cartoons, including *The New Rake's Progress* (1934), *Years of Wrath* (1949), *Low's Company* (1952), and *The Fearful Fifties* (1960). He was Knighted in 1962.

FURTHER READING
Low, David *Low's Autobiography* 1956
Seymour-Ure, C, and Scheff, J *David Low* 1985

Lowell, Abbott Lawrence (1857–1943)

US historian. In 1896 his *Government and Parties in Continental Europe* attracted wide notice. In 1900 he was apppointed professor of the science of government at Harvard; in 1909 he became president of the university. He had an enormous influence on educational methods at Harvard.

He was born in Boston, and was a brother of the poet Amy Lowell. He was educated at Harvard and in Germany, and practised as a barrister 1880–97.

His other publications include *The Government of England* (1908), *Public Opinion and Popular Govern-*

ment (1913), and *What a College President Has Learned* (1938).

Lowell, Robert Traill Spence, Jr (1917–1977)

US poet. His brutal yet tender verse stressed the importance of individualism, especially during times of war. During World War II he was imprisoned for five

---

If we see light at the end of the tunnel, / It's the light of the oncoming train.

ROBERT LOWELL 'Since 1939'

---

months for conscientious objection. Several of his poems, notably *Memories of West Street and Lepke*, reflect on this experience. In the 1960s he was again a war protester and also a civil-rights activist. His works include *Lord Weary's Castle* (1946, Pulitzer prize), *Life Studies* (1959), and *For the Union Dead* (1964).

FURTHER READING
Axelrod, S G *Robert Lowell: Life and Art* 1978
Hobsbaum, P *A Reader's Guide to Robert Lowell* 1988
Mazzaro, J *The Poetic Themes of Robert Lowell* 1965

Lubbers, Rudolph Franz Marie (Ruud) (1939–)

Dutch politician, prime minister of the Netherlands 1982–94. Leader of the right-of-centre Christian Democratic Appeal (CDA), he became minister for economic affairs in 1973.

Lubke, Heinrich (1894–1972)

German politician. He was president of the German Federal Republic l959–69, after serving as minister of food and agriculture 1953–59. He was a member of the Christian Democratic Union. He had been a member of the prewar Prussian Landtag 1931–33, but was stripped of all offices and imprisoned 1933–35.

Lucas, Robert (1937–)

US economist, leader of the University of Chicago school of 'new classical' macroeconomics, which contends that wage and price adjustment is almost instantaneous and that the level of unemployment at any time must be the natural rate (it cannot be reduced by government action except in the short term and at the cost of increasing inflation).

FURTHER READING
Sinn, H-W *Inflation and Welfare: Comment on Robert Lucas* 1999
Vercelli, A *Methodological Foundations of Macroeconomics: Keynes and Lucas* 1991

Luce, (Ann) Clare Boothe (1903–1987)

US journalist, playwright, and politician. She was managing editor of *Vanity Fair* magazine 1933–34, and

wrote several successful plays, including *The Women* (1936) and *Margin for Error* (1940), both of which were

---

There's nothing like a good dose of another woman to make a man appreciate his wife.

CLARE BOOTHE LUCE Quoted in L and M Cown *Wit of Women*

---

made into films. She served as a Republican member of Congress 1943–47 and as ambassador to Italy 1953–57.

Lucinschi, Petru (1940–)

Moldovan politician, president from 1996. He was a member of the Communist Party of the Soviet Union (CPSU) 1964–91. He became a member of the central committee of the CPSU in 1989 and served as secretary 1990–91. He was also a member of the CPSU Politburo 1990–91. He served as the Moldovan ambassador to Russia 1992–93, becoming the chair of the Moldovan parliament from 1993. He became president in November 1996.

Born at Floreşti, he was educated at Chişinău (Kishinev) University and at the CPSU Central Committee Higher Party School in Moscow. He served in the Soviet Army 1962–63, and undertook Komsomol work for the central committee of the Moldovan Communist Party 1963–71. He held a number of posts in the CPSU, rising to the post of deputy head of the central committee's propaganda department 1978–86.

Luckock, Margarette Rae Morrison (1893–1972)

Canadian politician. Luckock joined the Cooperative Commonwealth Federation (CCF) when it was formed in 1932, serving as its education critic, and focusing on funding for university scholarships, free university education, and improving rural education. She also promoted equal pay for equal work and paying homemakers for work done in the home. It was not until 1943, however, that she became involved in provincial politics, winning election to the Ontario legislative assembly. Luckock and Agnes Macphail were the first women elected to the Ontario legislature. In 1948, she was one of a number of suspected communists within the CCF who were expelled from the party.

Luckock grew up on the family farm in Arthur, Ontario. Her father, James J Morrison, was one of the founders of the United Farmers of Ontario party in 1914; his political activism influenced the young Luckock. Shortly after a peace visit to China in 1956 she was diagnosed with Parkinson's disease. She spent the last 14 years of her life in hospital.

Ludendorff, Erich von (1865–1937)

German general, chief of staff to Paul ◊Hindenburg in World War I, and responsible for the eastern-front victory at the Battle of Tannenberg in 1914. After

Hindenburg's appointment as chief of general staff and Ludendorff's as quartermaster general in 1916, the two men effectively directed Germany's war effort 1916–18. With Walther Rathenau, Ludendorff organized the mobilization of national resources for war. After the war he propagated the myth of the 'stab in the back', according to which the army had been betrayed by the politicians in 1918. A right-wing Nationalist, he participated in the Nazis' Munich rising of 1923. He also wrote influentially on the lessons of wartime government, for example in his book *Kriegs-führung und Politik/The Conduct of War and Politics*.

Lukács, Georg (1885–1971)

Hungarian philosopher and literary critic, one of the founders of 'Western' or 'Hegelian' Marxism, a philosophy opposed to the Marxism of the official communist movement. He also wrote on aesthetics and the sociology of literature.

In *History and Class Consciousness* (1923) he discussed the process of reification, reintroducing alienation as a central concept, and argued that bourgeois thought was 'false consciousness'. Rejected by official socialist literati, he was also an outsider to the dominant literary movements of the West. He argued for realism in literature and opposed modernism, particularly the work of James Joyce and Franz Kafka.

Lukács joined the Hungarian Communist Party in 1918 and was deputy minister of education during the short-lived Hungarian Soviet Republic in 1919. When the Hungarian communist uprising was put down in 1919, he emigrated first to Germany and then, in 1930, to the USSR. His Marxist views were considered unorthodox by the Soviet leaders and he had to make a humiliating public retraction of his 'errors' in Moscow in 1930. He consistently protested against demands that literature should support Stalin's policies and misdeeds. In 1945 Lukács returned to Hungary. He was a member of the short-lived Hungarian revolutionary government of 1956 and was briefly imprisoned when it was ended with the arrival of Soviet tanks.

Influenced by the German sociologists Georg Simmel and Max Weber, Lukács wrote two of his best books on literature, *Soul and Form* (1910) and *The Theory of the Novel* (1916), before he became a communist.

Fᴜʀᴛʜᴇʀ Rᴇᴀᴅɪɴɢ

Corredor, Eva L *Lukács after Communism: Interviews with Contemporary Intellectuals* 1997
Joos, Ernest *George Lukács and His World: A Reassessment* 1988
Kadarkay, Arpad *Georg Lukács: Life, Thought, and Politics* 1991, *The Lukács Reader* 1995
Lichtheim, George *Lukács* 1970
Lukács, György *The Meaning of Contemporary Realism* 1979, *The Destruction of Reason* 1980, *Ontology of Social Being* 1980–82, *The Process of Democratization* 1992.

Marcus, Judith, and Tarr, Zoltan *Georg Lukács: Theory, Culture, and Politics* 1989
Parkinson, George *Georg Lukács: The Man, His Works, and His Ideas* 1970
Redner, Harry *Malign Masters Gentile, Heidegger, Lukács, Wittgenstein: Philosophy and Politics in the Twentieth Century* 1997
Sim, Stuart *Georg Lukács* 1994

Lukashenko, Aleksandr Grigorevich (1954–)

Belarussian politician, president from 1994. A former collective farm chief, he became chair of the Belarus parliament's anti-corruption commission in 1993 and was unexpectedly elected president in July 1994. He campaigned on a populist and anti-corruption platform, which included the pledge of a 'job and home' for all citizens, price controls, and a Slav union with Russia. However, his rule became increasingly autocratic; Lukashenko used plebiscites 1995–96 to increase his power in relation to that of parliament, to extend his term to 2001, and to integrate more closely with Russia.

In April 1995 he sent in troops to storm the parliament, where nationalist-minded opposition deputies were on hunger strike against his pro-Russian policies. A year later, following a plebiscite, the legislature was disbanded and media freedoms were curtailed. Under Lukashenko, economic conditions in Belarus deteriorated, with very little foreign investment or privatization.

Lumumba, Patrice Emergy (1925–1961)

Congolese politician, prime minister of the Republic of the Congo (now the Democratic Republic of Congo) in 1960. Founder of the National Congolese Movement in 1958, he led his party to victory in the elections following independence in 1960. However, the country collapsed into civil war, and Lumumba was ousted in a coup led by Sese Seko Mobutu in September 1960, and murdered a few months later.

Fᴜʀᴛʜᴇʀ Rᴇᴀᴅɪɴɢ

Kanza, T R *The Rise and Fall of Patrice Lumumba: Conflict in the Congo* 1978
Orwa, D K *The Congo Betrayal: The UN–US and Lumumba* 1985
Reshetnyak, N *Patrice Lumumba* 1990

Lunacharski, Anatoli Vasilievich (1873–1933)

Russian politician and literary critic. From the October Revolution until 1929, he was people's commissar for education in the Russian Federal Republic. Modernistic experimentation in schools ended with his removal from the ministry. Later, liberal Soviet literary critics referred to Lunacharski's views to support an easing of cultural policy.

From early youth he belonged to Marxist circles, later joining the Social Democratic party and its

Bolshevik faction. In 1904–05 he supported Lenin against the Bolshevik Central Committee. In 1909 he broke with Lenin. With Bogdanov and Gorki, he formed the left-wing Bolshevik sub-faction 'Forward'. During World War I he was an internationalist. After the February Revolution in 1917 he returned to Russia from emigration and soon rejoined the Bolshevik party. Himself a Bogdanovist, Lunacharski was largely responsible for the flourishing of Bogdanovism in the 1920s. In 1933 he was appointed ambassador to Spain, but died in Paris on the way there.

Lusinchi, Jaime (1924–)

Venezuelan politician and president 1984–88. The austere policies he followed in an effort to solve his country's economic problems proved unpopular and he lost the 1988 election to his Democratic Action Party (AD) rival, Carlos Andres Perez.

Lusinchi was born in Clarines, Anzoategui state. He joined the AD while a medical student but was exiled during the repressive regime of General Marlos Pérez Jiménez, spending time in Argentina, Chile, and the USA 1952–58. The revival of democratic government saw his return and he became politically active again, entering parliament and eventually becoming AD leader. In 1984 he succeeded Christian Social Party (COPEI) leader Luis Herrera as president.

Luthuli, or Lutuli, Albert John (c. 1898–1967)

South African politician, president of the African National Congress (ANC) 1952–67. A Zulu tribal chief, he preached nonviolence and multiracialism.

Arrested in 1956, he was never actually tried for treason, although he suffered certain restrictions from 1959. He was under suspended sentence for burning his pass (an identity document required of non-white South Africans) when awarded the 1960 Nobel Peace Prize.

Luxemburg, Rosa (1870–1919)

Polish-born German communist. She helped found the Polish Social Democratic Party in the 1890s, the forerunner of the Polish Communist Party. She was a leader of the left wing of the German Social Democratic Party from 1898 where she collaborated with Karl ◊Liebknecht in founding the Spartacus League in 1918. Imprisoned during World War I for opposing the continuation of the war, she was also critical of the decision to launch an uprising in November 1918. She disagreed with leading Polish left-wing ideologists on the issue of Polish nationalism. Luxemburg was also the author of a Marxist critique of capitalist imperialism, *The Accumulation of Capital* (1913). She was murdered, together with Liebknecht, in January 1919 by the Frei Corps who put down the Spartacist uprising.

FURTHER READING
Abraham, R *Rosa Luxemburg: A Life for the International* 1989
Bronner, S E *Rosa Luxemburg: A Revolutionary for Our Times* 1997
Ettinger, E *Rosa Luxemburg: A Life* 1986
Frölich, Paul *Rosa Luxemburg* translation 1970
Nettl, J P *Rosa Luxemburg: A Biography* 1966, 1969

Luzhkov, Yuri Mikhailovich (1937–)

Russian politician, mayor of Moscow from 1992. He came to prominence in the mid-1990s, when he came to be seen to be providing an alternative administration in Moscow to Boris Yeltsin's presidency, with – moreover – an increasingly open ambition to replace the president.

Yeltsin, while Communist Party first secretary for Moscow, brought Luzhkov into his administration to replace officials he saw as corrupt and slothful; Luzhkov took charge of the city's cooperatives, established himself as a radical under the intellectual mayor Gavril Popov, and took over when Popov found the job too burdensome in 1992. His command of the city became absolute; little could be done without his personal approval. He opposed the government's privatization programme, and dared to set himself up against Anatoly ◊Chubais, the powerful privatization minister – and got Yeltsin's grudging backing for his own, much slower, programme. He flatly denied any allegations of corruption, but commanded a wealth large enough to fuel his presidential ambitions: the relative wealth of the capital, into which nearly all foreign investment came and where some 90% of the banking capital was concentrated, was held by him to be an excellent advertisement for attracting support from the rest of the country. He added flavour to his reputation for efficiency with a sharper edge of Russian nationalism.

Lynch, Jack (John Mary) (1917–)

Irish politician, Taoiseach (prime minister) 1966–73 and 1977–79, and leader of Fianna Fáil 1966–79.

Lynch entered the Dáil (lower chamber of the Irish parliament) in 1948 and served in various ministerial capacities before emerging as the surprise winner of the contest to succeed Sean Lemass as Fianna Fáil leader in 1966. Lynch continued the conciliatory policies of his predecessor towards Northern Ireland, visiting Terence O'Neill in Belfast in December 1967, and receiving the Northern Irish premier in Dublin the following month. The renewed violence in the North, however, destabilized Lynch's government, and its internal conflicts burst into the public arena in May 1970 when Lynch sacked his finance minister, Charles Haughey, and his minister of agriculture and fisheries, Neil Blaney, for allegedly using government money to import arms for the Irish Republican Army (IRA).

There was also a political aspect to the affair, since both Haughey and Blaney harboured leadership aspirations, and hoped to reveal Lynch's weakness on the Northern Ireland issue. Lynch narrowly lost the election of 1973, but regained power in 1977. However, serious economic mismanagement by his government, and the re-emergence of personal and political tensions within the party led to Lynch's sudden decision to resign in 1979.

Lyons, Joseph Aloysius (1879–1939)

Australian politician, founder of the United Australia (now Liberal) Party in 1931, prime minister 1931–39. Lyons followed the economic orthodoxy of the time, drastically cutting federal spending. He also cracked down on communism and introduced tough censorship laws.

He was born in Tasmania and worked initially as a school teacher before being selected, as a Labor Party deputy, to the state assembly in 1909. He became deputy party leader and state education minister in 1914 and state premier 1916–19 and 1923–28, before switching to federal politics in 1929, being elected to the House of Representatives. His early social reformism gave way to conservatism from the 1920s, and in 1931 he defected from the Labor Party, left the federal cabinet, and formed the United Australia Party. His wife Enid Muriel Lyons (1897–1981) was, in 1943, the first woman member of the House of Representatives and, in 1949, of the federal cabinet. She became a GBE in 1937.

FURTHER READING
Lyons, E M *So We Take Comfort* 1966
White, Kate *Political Love Story: Joe and Enid Lyons* 1987

Lytton, Victor Alexander George Robert Bulwer Lytton, 2nd Earl (1876–1947)

British administrator, statesman, and author. He was briefly viceroy of India while Lord Reading was absent on leave. He is best remembered for his sustained work for international goodwill and understanding with the League of Nations after World War I, and with the United Nations after World War II.

Lytton was born in Simla, India. He was educated at Eton and Trinity College, Cambridge. He began his public career in 1901 as private secretary to George Wyndham, chief secretary for Ireland. He was civil lord of the Admiralty in 1916, and again in 1919. He was British commissioner for propaganda, France, in 1918, and parliamentary undersecretary of state for India, under Edwin Montagu, in 1920. He was appointed to an India Office committee on the political claims of Burma (Myanmar), and earned a reputation for sympathy with Indian aspirations. He was governor of Bengal from 1922 to 1926. He was the son of the 1st Earl of Lytton, whom he succeeded in 1891.

McAdoo, William Gibbs (1863–1941)

US Democratic politician. As secretary to the Treasury 1913–19, he was responsible for far-reaching financial reforms, such as the Federal Reserve Banking Act and the introduction of the Liberty Loans system, which provided for the huge US war expenditure.

McAdoo was born in Georgia. He rose to become a prominent figure in the Democratic Party, and in 1924 he came close to capturing the Democratic presidential nomination. He was senator from California 1933–39.

McAleese, Mary Patricia (1951–   )

Irish lawyer and academic, president from 1997. When President Mary Robinson announced her resignation, McAleese was nominated by the ruling Fianna Fáil and Progressive Democrats as their candidate in preference to former prime minister Albert Reynolds. She asserted her opposition to violence and secured a clear victory over the Fine Gael nominated candidate Mary Bannotti.

After completing her legal studies at Queen's University, Belfast, and the Inn of Court of Northern Ireland, she held academic posts at Trinity College, Dublin, 1975–87 before becoming Pro-Vice-Chancellor 1994–97 at Queen's University, Belfast.

Macapagal, Diosdado (1911–1997)

Filipino centrist politician, president 1962–65. Representing the centrist Liberal Party, he launched a fight against poverty, unemployment, and corruption, but was constrained because the Liberals lacked an assembly majority. He was defeated in the 1965 presidential election by Ferdinand ◊Marcos. From the late 1970s, as the Marcos regime became increasingly dictatorial, Macapagal developed the National Union for Liberation as an anti-Marcos opposition force.

He worked as a lawyer and diplomat before being elected to serve in the Philippines' house of representatives 1949–56. He represented the Liberal Party and, in 1951, led the Philippines' delegation to the United Nations. A charismatic orator, Macapagal was elected vice president in 1957, serving under Carlos Garcia, who was a political opponent. In 1961 Macapagal defeated Garcia to become president.

His daughter, Gloria Macapagal-Arroyo, was elected Philippines' vice president in May 1998.

MacArthur, Douglas (1880–1964)

US general in World War II, commander of US forces in the Far East and, from March 1942, of the Allied forces in the southwestern Pacific. After the surrender of Japan he commanded the Allied occupation forces there. During 1950 he commanded the United Nations (UN) forces in Korea, but in April 1951, after expressing views contrary to US and UN policy, he was relieved of all his commands by President Harry Truman.

Like the old soldier of the ballad, I now close my military career and just fade away, an old soldier who tried to do his duty as God gave him the light to see that duty. Goodbye.
DOUGLAS MACARTHUR Speech to Congress, April 1955

Born in Arkansas, Macarthur was the son of an army officer. He graduated from West Point in 1903, distinguished himself in World War I, and rose to become chief of staff 1930–35. He defended the Philippines against the Japanese forces 1941–42 and escaped to Australia, where he based his headquarters. He was responsible for the reconquest of New Guinea 1942–45 and of the Philippines 1944–45, being appointed general of the army in 1944. As commander of the UN forces in the Korean War, he invaded the North in 1950 until beaten back by Chinese troops; his threats to bomb China were seen as liable to start World War III and he was removed from command, but received a hero's welcome on his return to the USA.

FURTHER READING
Clayton, J D *The Years of MacArthur* 1970–85
Manchester, W *American Caesar: Douglas MacArthur, 1880–1964* 1978

Macaulay, Herbert Samuel Heelas (1864– 1946)

Nigerian surveyor and leader of Nigeria's first political party. In 1893 he joined the colonial service, experiencing injustice at first hand when he was paid less than his British counterparts. Resigning from the service in 1899, he launched a campaign against colonial rule. In 1912 he was imprisoned for alleged embezzlement of public funds. In 1920 he helped Chief Oluwa obtain adequate compensation for land acquired by the government. In 1922 he founded the Nigerian National Democratic Party, Nigeria's first political party. In 1944 he became the first national president of the National Council for Nigeria and the Cameroons. He died on a campaign tour in 1946.

He was the first Nigerian to be sponsored by the colonial government to study abroad.

MacBride, Seán (1904–1988)

Irish revolutionary, politician, and peace campaigner. He became chief of staff of the Irish Republican Army (IRA) in 1936 but left the movement after the 1937 constitution, and broke with it completely over its 1939 bombing campaign. He won a reputation as a barrister for his defence of IRA suspects during the war years and founded Clann na Poblachta ('Children of the Republic') in 1946. He took his party into coalition as part of the interparty government 1948–51, in which he was minister for external affairs, and split the second interparty government in 1957 over its handling of the IRA's border campaign.

MacBride left politics in 1961 and began a new career in human rights. He was secretary general of the International Commission of Jurists 1963–70, and chair of Amnesty International 1961–74. He was co-author of the United Nations Declaration of Human Rights. He was awarded the Nobel Peace Prize in 1974 and the Lenin Peace Prize in 1977.

Born in Paris, MacBride studied there and at University College, Dublin. He joined the IRA during the Anglo–Irish war and opposed the 1921 Treaty.

McCarran, Patrick (1876–1954)

US Democrat politician. He became senator for Nevada in 1932, and as an isolationist strongly opposed lend-lease during World War II. He sponsored the McCarran–Walter Immigration and Nationality Act of 1952, which severely restricted entry and immigration to the USA; the act was amended in 1965.

McCarthy, Eugene Joseph (1916–)

US politician. He was elected to the House of Representatives in 1948 and to the Senate in 1958. An early opponent of the Vietnam War, he ran for president in 1968. Although his upset victory in the New Hampshire primary forced incumbent Lyndon Johnson out of the race, McCarthy lost the Democratic nomination to Hubert Humphrey.

Born in Watkins, Minnesota, McCarthy received a master's degree in economics from the University of Minnesota and became active in the Democratic-Farmer-Labor party. After another unsuccessful bid for the presidency in 1972, he returned to private life, concentrating on writing and lecturing.

McCarthy, Joe (Joseph Raymond) (1908–1957)

US right-wing Republican politician. His unsubstantiated claim in 1950 that the State Department had been infiltrated by communists started a wave of anticommunist hysteria, wild accusations, and blacklists, which continued until he was discredited in 1954. He was censured by the Senate for misconduct.

McCarthyism is Americanism with its sleeves rolled.

JOE MCCARTHY
Speech in Wisconsin
1952

A lawyer, McCarthy became senator for his native Wisconsin in 1947, and in February 1950 caused a sensation by claiming to hold a list of about 200 Communist Party members working in the State Department. This was in part inspired by the Alger ◊Hiss case. McCarthy continued a witch-hunting campaign against, among others, members of the Harry Truman administration. When he turned his attention to the army, and it was shown that he and his aides had been falsifying evidence, President Dwight D Eisenhower denounced his tactics. By this time, however, many people in public life and the arts had been unofficially blacklisted as suspected communists or fellow travellers (communist sympathizers). McCarthyism came to represent the practice of using innuendo and unsubstantiated accusations against political adversaries.

Born at Grand Chute, Wisconsin, McCarthy graduated from Marquette University in 1935 and practised law in Wisconsin, becoming a circuit judge in 1939. He served in the US marines 1942–45.

FURTHER READING

Landis, M *Joseph McCarthy* 1987
Oshinsky, D M *A Conspiracy So Immense: The World of Joe McCarthy* 1983
Reeves, T C *The Life and Times of Joe McCarthy* 1981

McCone, John Alex (1902–1991)

US industrialist, head of the Central Intelligence Agency (CIA) 1961–65. A devout Catholic and a fervent opponent of communism, he declined to use extreme measures to secure some of the political ends his political masters sought.

Early successes in the steel and construction industries made McCone a multimillionaire on the strength of winning several government contracts. He was chair of the US Atomic Energy Commission 1958–60, and was chosen by President J F Kennedy to succeed Allen Dulles as director of the CIA in 1960. It was while at the CIA that he made the discovery of Cuban-bound Soviet arms that led to the Cuban missile crisis. He was eventually removed from his post by President Lyndon Johnson, and returned to his business career as a director of the International Telephone and Telegraph Corporation (ITT).

MacDiarmid, Hugh, pen name of Christopher Murray Grieve (1892–1978)

Scottish poet. A nationalist and Marxist, he was one of the founders in 1928 of the National Party of Scotland. His works include 'A Drunk Man Looks at the Thistle' (1926) and the collections *First Hymn to Lenin* (1931) and *Second Hymn to Lenin* (1935), in which poetry is made relevant to politics. He developed a form of modern poetic Scots, based on an amalgam of Middle and Modern Scots, and was the leader of the Scottish literary renaissance of the 1920s and 1930s.

MacDonald, (James) Ramsay (1866–1937)

See page 274.

McEwen, Jack (John) (1900–1980)

Australian Country Party politician, prime minister 1967–68. He entered the federal parliament in 1934 and was minister for commerce and agriculture in coalition governments after 1949. In 1956 he reorganized his portfolio into the department of trade and, a fierce protectionist, used it as a powerful base from which to influence government policy on primary and secondary industries. From 1958 he was leader of the Country Party and deputy prime minister. After the death of Harold ◊Holt in 1967 he was caretaker prime minister for three weeks until the Liberal Party chose a new leader. He influenced this choice by vetoing deputy Liberal leader William ◊McMahon as a candidate. He retired in 1971 and was knighted the same year.

Born in Victoria, he was orphaned at seven and brought up by his grandmother. He left school at 13 and became a dairy farmer, after joining the army briefly in 1918.

McFarlane, Robert (1937–)

US national security adviser to Ronald Reagan 1983–87. He became well known as a champion of the MX nuclear missile programme. In 1984 he initiated the review of US policy towards Iran that led directly to an arms deal with Iran and he also supervised early National Security Council efforts to support the Contras in Nicaragua. Shortly after the Irangate (Iran–Contra) scandal was revealed in early 1987, McFarlane took a drugs overdose in an unsuccessful attempt on his own life. He pleaded guilty to four misdemeanours and was sentenced to two years' probation, 200 hours of community service, and fined $20,000 for his role in the scandal.

FURTHER READING

McFarlane, Robert C, and Smardz, Zofia *Special Trust: Inside the Reagan White House* 1994

McGovern, George (Stanley) (1922–)

US Democratic politician. He was elected to the US House of Representatives in 1956, served as an adviser to the J F Kennedy administration, and was a senator

Ramsay MacDonald, 1931. *AKG London*

1963–81. A strong opponent of the Vietnam War, he won the Democratic presidential nomination in 1972, but was soundly defeated by the incumbent, Richard Nixon.

McGovern was born in Avon, South Dakota, served as a combat pilot during World War II, and received a PhD in history from Northwestern University in 1953. He became director of the Food for Peace programme and special assistant to Kennedy in 1961. In 1968 he was defeated by Hubert Humphrey for the Democratic presidential nomination. McGovern was defeated for re-election to the Senate in 1980, made an unsuccessful run for the Democratic presidential nomination in 1984, and retired to a career of lecturing and writing.

Machado y Morales, Gerardo (1871–1939)

Cuban Liberal Party politician and revolutionary, dictator-president 1925–33. The leader of the centrist Liberal Party from 1920, he defeated Mario ◊Menocal in the 1924 presidential election. Increasingly dictatorial, he amended the constitution in 1928 to extend his term to six years. Economic depression after 1929 focused opposition under the leadership of Ramón ◊Grau San Martín, and government repression prompted US diplomatic intervention in 1933. Following a general strike, Machado was ousted by a military coup in August 1933, led by Fulgencio ◊Batista. He died in exile in Florida.

Backed by the incumbent Alfredo ◊Zayas, Machado fought the 1924 election on a nationalist and anti-corruption platform, and his early government imposed taxes on US inward investments, promoted the development of tourism, industries, and mining, and constructed a central highway. However, increasing economic and political instability sparked an abortive opposition revolt in 1931, and students and secret societies of middle-class professionals rebelled with Grau. In 1933 the US envoy, Sumner Welles (1892–1961), attempted to resolve the crisis, but Machado was deposed soon afterwards, Carlos Manuel de ◊Céspedes being installed as provisional president.

Machado fought as a general during the revolution of 1895–98 against Spanish rule, and later became a successful businessman. After independence, he served as mayor of Santa Clara and held posts in the cabinet of José Miguel Gómez, president from 1909 to 1913.

Machel, Samora Moises (1933–1986)

Mozambique nationalist leader, president 1975–86. Machel was active in the liberation front Frelimo from its conception in 1962, fighting for independence from Portugal. He became Frelimo leader in 1966, and Mozambique's first president from independence in

1975 until his death in a plane crash near the South African border.

Mackay of Clashfern, James Peter Hymers Mackay, Baron Mackay of Clashfern (1927–)

British lawyer and Conservative politician, born in Scotland. He became Lord Chancellor in 1987 and in 1989 announced a reform package to end legal restrictive practices.

In 1965 he became a Queen's Counsel (QC) and in 1979 was unexpectedly made Lord Advocate for Scotland and a life peer. His reform package included ending the barristers' monopoly of advocacy in the higher courts; promoting the combination of the work of barristers and solicitors in 'mixed' practices; and allowing building societies and banks to do property conveyancing, formerly limited to solicitors. The plans met with fierce opposition.

McKell, William John (1891–1985)

Australian Labor politician, premier of New South Wales 1941–47, governor general of Australia 1947–53. He was an official of the Boilermakers' Union before entering the New South Wales legislative assembly in 1917, representing the Labor Party. He held several portfolios up to 1932, also studying law and practising at the bar. In 1939 he defeated his longtime rival Jack ◊Lang for the leadership of the Labor Party and, after leading the party to its first electoral victory since the

---

◆ MacDonald, (James) Ramsay (1866–1937) ◆

British politician; first Labour prime minister January–October 1924 and 1929–31 and prime minister of the National Government 1931–35.

MacDonald was born in Scotland, the illegitimate son of a labourer. He was a member of the Fabian Society and the Independent Labour Party in the 1890s and a leading exponent and theoretician of gradual and ethical socialism. With Keir Hardie he was responsible for the establishment of the Labour Representation Committee in 1900 and served as its first secretary. He was finally elected to Parliament (after several attempts) as member for Leicester in 1906. He was leader of the Labour Party from 1906 until 1914 when, in opposition to the war (and Labour's support for it), he resigned. During the war he was active in the Union of Democratic Control, which campaigned for peace with Germany. MacDonald lost his seat in 1918 and only returned as member of Parliament for Aberavon in 1922. By then he was the dominant figure in the movement, earning the support of many members for his principled opposition to

the war and their sympathy for the barrage of press attacks this earned him. The newspaper *John Bull* published his birth certificate to make his illegitimacy public. He won the leadership from John Robert Clynes in 1922.

The nine-month minority government of 1924, in which MacDonald doubled as foreign secretary, achieved little other than proving Labour was 'fit to govern'. The 1929 administration was beset by an economic downturn and rising unemployment, and, in August 1931, a sterling crisis brought the government to breaking point. Only a small

---

MacDonald owes his pre-eminence largely to the fact that he is the only artist, the only aristocrat by temperament and talent in a party of plebeians and plain men.

Beatrice Webb On Ramsay MacDonald, *Diary*, May 1930

---

majority (including Chancellor Phillip Snowden) of the cabinet agreed with MacDonald that a cut in public expenditure and unemployment benefit

depression in 1929, became premier in 1941. In government he combined a vigorous programme of social reform with the war effort, his moderate, popular style laying the groundwork for the Labor governments that held power in New South Wales up to 1965. He was appointed governor general on the recommendation of Prime Minister Ben ◊Chifley. He was awarded a GCMG in 1951.

FURTHER READING
Easson, Michael (ed) *McKell: The Achievements of Sir William McKell* 1988

McLaughlin, Audrey (1936–)

Canadian politician who was the first woman leader of a federal political party in Canada. She entered the House of Commons in 1987 as a member of parliament for Yukon, after a by-election victory. In 1988 she became chair of the New Democratic Party (NDP) and chair of the party caucus, and year later was elected leader of the party. In the 1993 election she retained her seat, but the NDP lost its official party status with only nine seats. McLaughlin announced in April 1994 her decision to step down as party leader but remained leader until 1995, when her successor, Alexa McDonough, was chosen.

McLaughlin was born in Dutton, Ontario. Before her career as a politician, she worked for the Children's Aid Society of Metropolitan Toronto, was a teacher in Ghana, and was executive director of the Metro

was the solution. MacDonald left to form a National Government (and push through the cuts) with the Liberals and Conservatives, which decimated the Labour Party at the 1931 election. He was expelled from Labour party membership. Little more than a figurehead for the overwhelmingly Conservative National Government, he resigned the premiership in 1935.

MacDonald was then transformed from hero to villain in the eyes of the Labour movement. Others referred to the social climbing, the 'aristocratic embrace', to which he had finally succumbed in 1931. Yet whatever the ultimate tragedy or disgrace of his political life, his contribution to the early years of the Labour Party was second to none. In the 1920s he was aptly described by one German commentator as the 'focus for the mute hopes of a whole class'. See photograph on page 273.

FURTHER READING
Marquand, David *Ramsay MacDonald* 1977
Morgan, A *James Ramsay MacDonald* 1987
Sacks, B *Ramsay MacDonald in Thought and Action* 1952

Toronto Branch of the Canadian Mental Health Association. In 1979 she started her own consulting company, which dealt with issues such as child welfare, land claims, and aboriginal self-government.

Maclean, Donald Duart (1913–1983)

English spy who worked for the USSR while in the UK civil service. He defected to the USSR in 1951 together with Guy ◊Burgess.

Maclean, brought up in a strict Presbyterian family, was educated at Cambridge University, where he was recruited by the Soviet KGB. He worked for the Foreign Office in Washington, DC, in 1944 and then in Cairo in 1948 before returning to London, becoming head of the US department at the Foreign Office in 1950.

Maclean, Fitzroy Hew (1911–1996)

Scottish writer, diplomat, and politician whose travels in the USSR and Central Asia inspired his books *Eastern Approaches* (1949) and *A Person from England* (1958).

During 1943–45 he commanded a unit giving aid to partisans in Yugoslavia and advised that Allied support be switched from the Chetniks to the communist partisans under Tito.

Maclean joined the army at the beginning of World War II after six years of diplomatic service in Paris and Moscow. In 1942 he moved to the Special Air Service. He was a member of Parliament 1941–74 and parliamentary undersecretary of state at the War Office 1954–57. Between 1964 and 1974 he chaired a military committee of the United Nations delegation to the North Atlantic Assembly. He was created a Baronet in 1957.

MacLennan, Robert (Adam Ross) (1936–)

British centrist politician, born in Glasgow, Scotland; member of Parliament for Caithness and Sutherland from 1966. He left the Labour Party for the Social Democrats (SDP) in 1981, and was SDP leader in 1988 during merger negotiations with the Liberals. He then became a member of the new Social and Liberal Democrats.

MacLennan was educated in Scotland, England, and the USA, and was called to the English Bar in 1962. When David Owen resigned the SDP leadership in 1988, MacLennan took over until the merger with the Liberal Party had been completed. He took a leading part in the negotiations.

Macleod, Iain Norman (1913–1970)

British Conservative politician. As colonial secretary 1959–61, he forwarded the independence of former British territories in Africa. He died in office as chancellor of the Exchequer.

McLuhan, (Herbert) Marshall (1911–1980)

Canadian theorist of communication who emphasized

the effects of technology on modern society. He coined the phrase 'the medium is the message', meaning that

---

The car has become the carapace, the protective and aggressive shell, of urban and suburban man.

MARSHALL MᴄLᴜʜᴀɴ *Understanding Media* chap 22

---

the form rather than the content of information has become crucial. His works include *The Gutenberg Galaxy* (1962) – in which he coined the phrase 'the global village' for the worldwide electronic society then emerging; *Understanding Media* (1964); and *The Medium is the Massage* (sic, 1967).

FURTHER READING

Miller, Jonathan *Marshall McLuhan* 1971
Theall, Donald *The Medium is the Rear View Mirror: Understanding McLuhan* 1971

McMahon, William (1908–1988)

Australian Liberal politician, prime minister 1971–72. Elected to the House of Representatives in 1949, he held a number of portfolios including navy and labour, becoming deputy leader of the Liberal Party and treasurer in 1966. He gained a reputation as a hardworking and well-prepared minister. After the death of Prime Minister Harold Holt in 1967, Country Party leader John ◊McEwen vetoed McMahon as coalition leader and he continued as treasurer up to 1969 and minister for external affairs 1969–71 under John ◊Gor-

ton. In 1971 the Country Party lifted its embargo on McMahon and he replaced Gorton as prime minister. However, he was no match for opposition leader Gough ◊Whitlam and lost the election of 1972. He was immediately replaced as Liberal Party leader by Billy Snedden, but remained as backbencher until 1982.

McMahon was born in Sydney. He graduated in law and economics from Sydney University and was a socially prominent solicitor before military service in World War II, when he reached the rank of major. He was made a GCMG in 1977.

McNaughton, Andrew George Latta (1887–1966)

Canadian soldier and administrator. On the outbreak of World War II in 1939, he commanded the 1st Division Canadian Overseas Force. He commanded the Canadian Corps 1940–42 and was commander in chief 1942–44. He was minister of defence 1945, during a crisis over the voluntary system for overseas service.

McNaughton was born in Moosomin, Saskatchewan, and educated in engineering at McGill University. Having entered the army in 1910, he served throughout World War I. He was army chief of staff 1929–35, with the rank of major general. He retired from the army in 1944, with the rank of general. He was permanent Canadian delegate to the United Nations, president of the Canadian Atomic Energy Control Board 1946–48, and chair of the Canadian section of the International Joint Commission 1950–62.

◆ MACMILLAN, (MAURICE) HAROLD, FIRST EARL OF STOCKTON (1894–1986) ◆

British Conservative politician, prime minister 1957–63.

A member of a publishing family, he was a scholar at Eton and exhibitioner at Balliol College, Oxford, where he graduated with first-class honours. He served with the Grenadier Guards in World War I and was Conservative

---

As usual the Liberals offer a mixture of sound and original ideas. Unfortunately none of the sound ideas is original and none of the original ideas is sound.

HAROLD MACMILLAN Speech to London Conservatives
7 March 1962

---

member of Parliament for Stockton-on-Tees 1924–29 and 1931–45, and for Bromley 1945–64. As a backbencher he was critical of the Conservative government's foreign policy of appeasement towards Germany. He was

appointed parliamentary undersecretary at the ministry of supply and for a time undersecretary for the colonies 1940–42. From 1942 to 1945 he was minister resident in northwest Africa at allied headquarters.

When the Conservatives returned to power in 1951 Macmillan was appointed minister of housing and local government, and he achieved his target of 300,000 houses built in a year. He was minister of defence 1954–55 and was appointed foreign secretary in April 1955 when Anthony Eden became prime minister. In December 1955 he was appointed chancellor of the Exchequer. His first budget in 1956 introduced premium savings bonds.

Macmillan became prime minister on 12 January 1957 following the resignation of Eden, being selected in preference to the more senior R A Butler. As prime minister Macmillan developed his role as a world statesman, making well publicized trips to the Commonwealth countries, Moscow, and Washington, DC. He restored

MacNeill, John (Eoin) (1885–1945)

Irish scholar and politician. He was minister of finance in the first Dáil (parliament) in 1919 and minister for industries 1919–21. He supported the Anglo-Irish Treaty partitioning Ireland, and was minister of education in the first Executive Council of the Irish Free State 1922–25. He was Free State delegate to the Boundary Commission 1924–25, which shattered nationalist hopes of a revision of the border with Northern Ireland, and MacNeill resigned rather than accept its verdict.

In 1913 he inspired and led the Irish Volunteers, but the organization was taken over by John Redmond, who persuaded most of its members to support the Allies in 1914. He was unaware of the existence of the Military Council of the Irish Republican Brotherhood (IRB), and IRB manipulation steered the remaining Volunteers towards rebellion in 1916, without MacNeill's knowledge. He reluctantly accepted the insurrection, but countermanded it when it became clear that German aid would fail.

Born in Glenarm, Co Antrim, and educated at St Malachy's College, Belfast, MacNeill was an authority on Old Irish. He was professor of Early Irish history at University College, Dublin, 1908–45, and his pioneer work in Irish history asserted the strength of its legal and cultural civilization.

Macphail, Agnes (1890–1954)

Canadian politician. The first female member of the

Harold Macmillan, c. 1960. *AKG London*

cordial relations with the USA, which had been damaged by the Suez crisis.

In the UK, tax reductions and industrial expansion fuelled an economic recovery that swept the Conservative Party to victory in the general election of October 1959. The economic recovery was short-lived and in 1961 the government introduced a 'pay pause' to control wages and prices. However, inflation continued to rise.

In 1960 in Cape Town, Macmillan acknowledged the need for the UK to grant independence to African colonies in his 'winds of change' speech. French rejection of the UK's application for membership of the European Economic Community (EEC) further undermined British influence on the world stage.

At home Macmillan dismissed seven Cabinet ministers following by-election setbacks in 1962.

The Vassall spy case of 1962 and the Profumo scandal of 1963 caused a crisis within the government and Macmillan resigned through ill health in October 1963. Following the October 1964 general election he retired from politics.

Macmillan published six volumes of memoirs, *Winds of Change* (1966), *The Blast of War* (1967), *Tides of Fortune* (1969), *Riding the Storm* (1971), *Pointing the Way* (1972), and *At the End of the Day* (1972). On his 90th birthday in 1984 he became an Earl.

FURTHER READING

Fisher, Nigel *Harold Macmillan: A Biography* 1982

Horne, Alistair *Macmillan, 1894–1956* 1988, *Macmillan, 1957–1986* 1989

Sampson, Anthony *Macmillan: A Study in Ambiguity* 1967

Canadian parliament, she championed the rights of farmers and worked hard for social and prison reform. Defeated at the polls after 19 years in Ottawa, she ran provincially and was twice elected in Ontario as member of the provincial parliament. She continued to champion the poor and underprivileged until her death.

FURTHER READING
Pennington, Doris *Agnes MacPhail: Reformer* 1989

MacSwiney, Terence (1879–1920)

Irish writer and revolutionary. In March 1920 he was elected Lord Mayor of Cork, following the murder of his predecessor by the police. In August he was arrested for possession of a Royal Irish Constabulary cipher and sentenced to two years' imprisonment. He immediately began a hunger strike, demanding his unconditional release. He died in Brixton Prison, London, after a fast of 74 days, which heightened tension in Ireland, and attracted worldwide attention.

He was instrumental in the creation of the Cork Volunteers in 1913, but obeyed Eoin MacNeill's countermand of the order for a rebellion in 1916. He was elected Sinn Féin member of parliament for West Cork in 1918 and helped organize the Dáil's arbitration courts, while continuing his efforts as recruiter and organizer for the Volunteers.

MacSwiney was born in Cork where he trained as an accountant. He was also, however, a nationalist playwright, cofounding the Cork Dramatic Society in 1908.

Madani, Abassi (1931–)

Algerian academic and politician. In 1989 he formed the Front Islamique du Salut (FIS), which was outlawed in the aftermath of the cancellation of the 1991 legislative elections. Accused of sedition, he was sentenced to 12 years' imprisonment in 1992. He was placed under house arrest in 1997.

He joined the Front de Libération Nationale (FLN) in 1955. Arrested by the colonial administration, he was released in 1962. He remained a militant of the FLN party until the end of the 1970s. After that, the rupture with the FLN was to be concomitant with his increasing involvement in the Islamist movement where he virulently attacked the political establishment and championed the application of Islamic law (Shari'a).

Madero, Francisco Indalecio (1873–1913)

Mexican liberal politician, president 1911–13. He took over the presidency from Porfirio ◊Díaz after his resignation following political unrest. However, internal divisions and the continuing civil war paralysed the government. In February 1913, Victoriano ◊Huerta, the commander of the government forces, plotted with rebels in Mexico City and assassinated Madero's brother. He then imprisoned Madero on charges of treason, and usurped power. Madero was murdered on 22 February 1923, after he had allegedly sought to escape.

Díaz imprisoned Madero in June 1910 and was re-elected as president, but in November 1910, on his release, Madero fled to Texas and, in the Plan of San Luis Potosi, called for a revolutionary uprising against Díaz. He returned to Mexico in February 1911 and attracted armed support from rebels in the north, including Francisco ◊Villa. On 9 May 1911 the rebels' capture of Ciudad Juárez severely shook the government's self-confidence and, with rebels also active in the south, under the leadership of Emiliano ◊Zapata, President Díaz resigned on 25 May 1911. Madero was elected as his successor and assumed office in November 1911.

Born in Coahuila state, into an influential landowning family, he studied economics in France and agriculture at the University of California, Berkeley, USA, and returned to Mexico to put into practice this new knowledge. Influenced by theosophy and spiritism, he championed democracy and social reform, setting up welfare institutions to improve the quality of life of the labourers on his family estates. In 1908 he published *La sucesión presidencial en 1910/The Presidential Succession in 1910*, which was critical of the dictatorial regime of Porfirio Díaz. In 1910, as the Anti-Re-electionist Party's presidential candidate, Madero campaigned for a more pluralist political system.

FURTHER READING
Ross, S R *Francisco I Madero: Apostle of Mexican Democracy* 1955

Magsaysay, Ramón (1907–1957)

Filipino politician, president 1953–57. He was elected to the Philippine congress in 1946 and put forward a plan to subdue the communist Hukbalahap (Huk) guerrillas, which persuaded Elpidio ◊Quirino, president from 1948, to appoint him defence secretary in 1950. In this post, he oversaw reform of the army, the capture of leading communists, and the combination of firm military action and land resettlement to counter the leftist Hukbalahap movement. After a dispute with Quirino, he resigned and defected from the ruling Liberal party to join the right-wing Nationalist party and was elected president in 1953, defeating Quirino by a substantial margin. His presidential term saw the maintenance of close ties with the USA and the promotion of land reform.

A guerrilla leader during the Japanese occupation of the Philippines 1941–45, he was appointed military governor of Zambales province by General Douglas ◊MacArthur in 1945.

Magsaysay died in an aeroplane crash in 1957, shortly before presidential elections which he had been expected to win.

Mahathir bin Mohamed (1925–)

Malaysian politician, prime minister from 1981. Leader of the New United Malays' National Organization (UMNO Baru), his 'look east' economic policy, which emulated Japanese industrialization, met with considerable success, but faced its first serious challenge in 1997 when the Malaysian currency came under attack from international speculators. This forced austerity measures in 1998, including the repatriation of many foreign workers.

Mahathir bin Mohamed was elected to the house of representatives in 1964 and gained the support of the radical youth wing of the then dominant United Malays' National Organization (UMNO) as an advocate of economic help to bumiputras (ethnic Malays) and as a proponent of a more Islamic social policy. Mahathir held a number of ministerial posts from 1974 before being appointed prime minister and UMNO leader in 1981. He was re-elected in 1986, but alienated sections of UMNO by his authoritarian leadership and from 1988 led a reconstituted UMNO Baru (New UMNO). In 1994 he temporarily suspended all forthcoming trade deals with the UK after allegations in the British press that aid for Malaysia's Pergau dam had been given in exchange for an arms contract in 1988. In the 1995 elections, his UMNO-Baru-led coalition achieved a landslide victory.

Mahgoub, Muhammad Ahmed (1908–)

Sudanese lawyer and politician. He led the opposition 1954–56, and was foreign minister 1956–58 and 1964–65, before becoming prime minister 1965–66 and 1967–69. His government was overthrown in the coup led by Col Gaafar Mohammed al-Numeiry. He published *Democracy on Trial* (1974) as well as several volumes of Arabic poetry.

He was educated at Gordon College, Khartoum, and Khartoum School of Law. He qualified both as an architect and a lawyer. He was a member of the legislative assembly 1948–54, and of the Umma party.

Mahomed, Ismail (1931–)

South African lawyer, appointed the country's first non-white judge in 1991. As legal adviser to the South-West Africa People's Organization (SWAPO), he was the author of Namibia's constitution, which abolished capital punishment. He defended many anti-apartheid activists in political trials.

Mahomed, born in Pretoria, became a barrister in 1957. Classified as Indian under the apartheid system, he was hampered by restrictions on his movements, but went on to become president of Lesotho's Court of Appeal and a member of Swaziland's Appellate Division, and as a member of the Namibian Supreme Court he ruled corporal punishment unconstitutional. He is an eloquent speaker.

Mahuad Witt, Jamil (1949–)

Ecuadorian politician and president from 1998. Politically aligned to the centre-left Popular Democracy Party (DP), he was elected following the presidency of Abdalá Ortiz Bucaram. Although the Ecuadorian economy stabilized considerably in the 1990s, Mahuad's administration was faced with the need to reduce foreign debts in order to maintain the economic improvements initiated by its predecessors.

Mailer, Norman Kingsley (1923–)

US writer and journalist. One of the most prominent figures of postwar US literature, he gained wide attention with his first, bestselling book *The Naked and the Dead* (1948), a naturalistic war novel. His later works, which use sexual and scatological material, show his personal engagement with history, politics, and psychology. Always a pugnacious and controversial writer, his polemics on the theory and practice of violence-as-sex brought him into direct conflict with feminist Kate Millet in a series of celebrated debates during the 1970s.

> *A modern democracy is a tyranny whose borders are undefined; one discovers how far one can go only by traveling in a straight line until one is stopped.*
>
> NORMAN MAILER *The Presidential Papers*, Preface

His other books include his dark thriller of sex and power *An American Dream* (1965), the fictionalized antiwar journalism of *The Armies of the Night* (1968, Pulitzer prize), and *The Executioner's Song* (1979, Pulitzer prize), about convicted murderer Gary Gilmore. A combative public figure, Mailer cofounded the magazine *Village Voice* in the 1950s, edited *Dissent*, and in 1969 ran for mayor of New York City.

FURTHER READING
Manso, Peter *Mailer: His Life and Times* 1985
Mills, Hilary *Mailer: A Biography* 1982
Poirier, Richard *Norman Mailer* 1972

Maizière, Lothar de (1940–)

German conservative politician, see ◊de Maizière.

Major, John (1943–)

British Conservative politician, prime minister 1990–97. He was foreign secretary in 1989 and chancellor of the Exchequer 1989–90. As prime minister, his initially positive approach to European Community matters was hindered from 1991 by divisions within the Conservative Party. Despite continuing public dissatisfaction with the poll tax, the National Health Service, and the recession, Major was returned to power in the April 1992 general election. His subsequent handling of a series of domestic crises called into question his ability to govern the country effectively, but he won backing for his launch of a joint UK–Irish peace initiative on Northern Ireland in 1993, which led to a general cease-fire in 1994. On the domestic front, local and European election defeats and continuing divisions within the Conservative Party led to his dramatic and unexpected resignation of the party leadership in June 1995 in a desperate bid for party unity. He was narrowly re-elected to the post the following month. Criticized for weak leadership of his divided party, he resigned as leader of the Conservative Party after a crushing defeat in the 1997 general election.

John Major was born in Merton, southwest London. Formerly a banker, he became member of Parliament for Huntingdonshire in 1979 and deputy to chancellor of the Exchequer Nigel Lawson in 1987. Within the space of six months in 1989, he was appointed foreign secretary and, after Lawson's resignation, chancellor. As chancellor he led the UK into the European Exchange Rate Mechanism (ERM) in October 1990. The following month he became prime minister on winning the Conservative Party leadership election in a contest with Michael Heseltine and Douglas Hurd, after the resignation of Margaret Thatcher. Although victorious in the 1992 general election, he subsequently faced mounting public dissatisfaction over a range of issues, including the sudden withdrawal of the pound from the ERM, a drastic pit-closure programme, and past sales of arms to Iraq. In addition, Major had to deal with 'Eurosceptics' within his own party who fiercely opposed any moves that they saw as ceding national sovereignty to Brussels. His success in negotiating a Northern Ireland cease-fire in 1994 did much to improve his standing, but delays in the progress of peace talks resulted in criticism of his cautious approach.

> *I am my own man.*
>
> JOHN MAJOR On succeeding Margaret Thatcher as prime minister October 1990

FURTHER READING
Anderson, Bruce *John Major* 1991
Junor, Penny *The Major Enigma* 1993

Makarios III, born Mikhail Christodoulou Mouskos (1913–1977)

Cypriot politician and Greek Orthodox archbishop 1950–77. A leader of the Greek-Cypriot resistance organization EOKA, he was exiled by the British to the Seychelles 1956–57 for supporting armed action to achieve union with Greece (*enosis*). He was president of the republic of Cyprus 1960–77 (briefly deposed by a Greek military coup July–Dec 1974).

Makeba, Miriam Zenzile (1932–   )

South African singer. In political exile 1960–90, she was one of the first world-music performers to make a name in the West, and is particularly associated with 'The Click Song', which features the glottal clicking sound of her Xhosa language. She was a vocal opponent to apartheid, and South Africa banned her records.

Malan, Daniel François (1874–1959)

South African right-wing politician, prime minister 1948–54. He founded the Purified National Party in 1934. His policy of apartheid was implemented in a series of acts of parliament including the Group Areas Act, the Mixed Marriages Act, and the Immorality Act.

Elected to parliament in 1919, he joined the government as minister of the interior in 1924. When he became prime minister in 1948, as well as minister of external affairs, he formed an exclusively Afrikaner government.

Born near Riebeeck West, Cape Province, Malan was a neighbour and school friend of Jan Smuts, who was to precede him as prime minister. Malan studied in the Netherlands and became a minister of the Dutch Reformed Church. He helped to launch the Nationalist Party in the Cape in 1915, and started the first official newspaper of the party, *Die Burger*, in 1915, working as editor until 1924.

Malcolm X, adopted name of Malcolm Little (1926–1965)

US black nationalist leader. While serving a prison sentence for burglary 1946–53, he joined the Black Muslims sect. On his release he campaigned for black separatism, condoning violence in self-defence, but in 1964 modified his views to found the Islamic socialist Organization of Afro-American Unity, preaching racial solidarity. He was assassinated.

> *You can't separate peace from freedom because no one can be at peace unless he has his freedom.*
>
> MALCOLM X Speech, New York City, 7 January 1965

Malcolm Little was born in Omaha, Nebraska, but grew up in foster homes in Michigan, Massachusetts, and New York. Convicted of burglery in 1946, he spent seven years in prison, becoming a follower of Black Muslim leader Elijah Muhammad and converting to Islam. In 1952 he officially changed his name to Malcolm X to signify his rootlessness in a racist society. Having become an influential national and international leader, he publicly broke with the Black Muslims in 1964. A year later he was assassinated by Nation of Islam opponents while addressing a rally in Harlem, New York City. His *Autobiography of*

Malcolm X, written with Alex Haley, was published in 1964.

FURTHER READING
Goldman, Peter *The Life and Death of Malcolm X* 1979
Green, Cheryll Y (ed) *Malcolm X: Make it Plain* 1994
Wolfenstein, Victor *The Victims of Democracy* 1981

Malenkov, Georgi Maximilianovich (1902–1988)

Soviet prime minister 1953–55, Stalin's designated successor but abruptly ousted as Communist Party secretary within two weeks of Stalin's death by Nikita ◊Khrushchev, and forced out as prime minister in 1955 by Nikolai ◊Bulganin.

Malenkov subsequently occupied minor party posts. He was expelled from the Central Committee in 1957 and from the Communist Party in 1961.

Malik, Yakob Alexandrovich (1906–1980)

Soviet diplomat. He was permanent representative at the United Nations (UN) 1948–53 and 1968–76, and it was his walkout from the Security Council in January 1950 that allowed the authorization of UN intervention in Korea.

Malinovsky, Rodion Yakovlevich (1898–1967)

Russian soldier and politician. In World War II he fought at Stalingrad, commanded in the Ukraine, and led the Soviet advance through the Balkans to capture Budapest in 1945 before going east to lead the invasion of Manchuria. He was minister of defence 1957–67.

Malraux, André (Georges) (1901–1976)

French writer, art critic, and Gaullist politician. Under Charles ◊de Gaulle's Fifth Republic he was given charge of a new ministry of cultural affairs 1960–69. Malraux gained international renown for his novel *La Condition humaine/Man's Estate* (1933), set during the nationalist communist revolution in China in the 1920s, and for *L'Espoir/Days of Hope* (1937), set in Civil War Spain, and made an important contribution to aesthetics with *La Psychologie de l'art/Psychology of Art* (1947–49), revised as *Les Voix du silence/The Voices of Silence* (1951). He also published several volumes of autobiography, including *Antimémoires/Anti-Memoirs* (1967).

An active anti-fascist, Malraux volunteered as a bomber pilot for the International Brigade in the Spanish Civil War, but rejected communism and during World War II supported the Gaullist resistance, becoming de Gaulle's minister of information in the provisional government 1945–46.

FURTHER READING
Hewitt, James *André Malraux* 1978
Lewis, R W B (ed) *Malraux: A Collection of Critical Essays* 1964
Madsen, A *Malraux* 1977
Righter, William *The Rhetorical Hero* 1964

◆ MAMALONI, SOLOMON SUNAONE (1943–) ◆

Solomon Islands centre-left politician, chief minister 1974–76, and prime minister 1981–84, 1989–93 and 1994–97. He was first elected to the Solomon Islands assembly in 1970 and, leading the newly formed centre-left People's Progress Party (PPP), became the country's first chief minister in August 1974. He was replaced as chief minister in June 1976 by Peter ◊Kenilorea, who went on to lead the country to independence in 1978. Mamaloni, now leading the People's Alliance Party (PAP), returned to power in 1981, after Kenilorea was defeated in a no-confidence motion. He formed a coalition government, which embarked on a programme of decentralization, creating five provincial ministries, but the centralist Kenilorea returned to power after the October 1984 general election and reversed this initiative.

At the February 1989 general election, the PAP re-established itself as the dominant party and Mamaloni was able to form the country's first single-party government. He pledged to reduce the influence of 'foreign aid personnel' and establish a republic, but with the economy deteriorating, Mamaloni resigned as PAP leader and, in October 1990, formed a 'government of national unity', which included Kenilorea as foreign minister. This caused splits in the PAP, persuading Mamaloni to form the new Group for National Unity and Reconciliation (GNUR) to contest the June 1993 general election. Although the GNUR was the largest single party in the new parliament, Mamaloni lost power to Francis Billy ◊Hilly until November 1994, when he was re-elected as prime minister. His new government came under criticism for allowing unrestrained logging activity and for corruption within the bureaucracy. He stepped down as GNUR leader before the August 1997 general election, which was won by the Alliance for Change, led by Bartholomew ◊Ulufa'alu.

Born in Rumahui Village, in Arosi, West Makira, he was educated in the Solomon Islands and New Zealand, before joining the British Colonial Administrative Service in 1966.

Mandela, Winnie Madikizela (Nomzamo) (1934–)

South African civil-rights activist, former wife of Nelson ◊Mandela. A leading spokesperson for the African National Congress (ANC) during Nelson Mandela's imprisonment 1964–90, in 1991 she received a six-year prison sentence for her role in the kidnapping and assault of four youths. Her sentence was later waived and in May 1994, following the ANC's victory in the country's first universal-suffrage elections, she was given a deputy ministerial post in the new government. In 1995 she was dismissed from her cabinet post, following allegations of dereliction of duty.

Actively involved in promoting the ANC's cause during her husband's long imprisonment, Winnie Mandela was jailed for a year and put under house arrest several times. In 1989 she was involved in the abduction of four youths, one of whom, Stompie Seipei, was later murdered. She was convicted of kidnapping and assault, and given a six-year jail sentence in May 1991, with the right to appeal. In April 1992 she and Nelson Mandela separated after 33 years of marriage. In the same year she resigned from her ANC posts, including her seat on the ANC National Executive Committee. Her sentence was waived by South Africa's highest court in 1993, and she was later nominated an ANC candidate for the April 1994 elections. She was appointed minister for arts, culture, science, and technology in May 1994, but after allegations of corruption, including the handing out of government contracts in return for kickbacks, she was relieved of her post. In March 1996 her husband was granted a divorce.

Public hearings before the Truth and Reconciliation Commission into Winnie Mandela's alleged involvement in at least six murders in the late 1980s were held in early December 1997. Despite damning evidence provided by many and varied witnesses, Mandela denied all the allegations and shifted the blame to the media and her political opponents. Although it became obvious during the hearings that most of the charges against her would not stand up in court, and she did not admit responsibility for any of the crimes she was charged with, the special public hearings did have a negative effect on her political standing. Four days after the end of the hearings ANC sources claimed that the Women's League had withdrawn its nomination of Mrs Mandela for the deputy presidency.

◆ MANDELA, NELSON (ROLIHLAHLA) (1918–) ◆

South African politician and lawyer, president from 1994. He was president of the African National Congress (ANC) 1991–97. Imprisoned from 1964, as organizer of the then banned ANC, he became a symbol of unity for the worldwide anti-apartheid movement. In February 1990 he was released, the ban on the ANC having been lifted, and entered into negotiations with the

> *Never, never and never again shall it be that this beautiful land will again experience the oppression of one by another.*
>
> NELSON MANDELA Inaugural speech as president of South Africa, May 1994

government about a multiracial future for South Africa. In May 1994 he was sworn in as South Africa's first post-apartheid president after the ANC won 62.65% of the vote in universal-suffrage elections. He shared the Nobel Prize for Peace in 1993 with South African president F W de Klerk.

Mandela was born near Umbata, south of Lesotho, the son of a local chief. In a trial of several ANC leaders, he was acquitted of treason in 1961, but was once more arrested in 1964 and given a life sentence on charges of sabotage and plotting to overthrow the government. In February 1990 he was released from prison on the orders of state president F W de Klerk and in July 1991 was elected, unopposed, to the presidency of the ANC. In December 1991 the ANC began constitutional negotiations with the government and in February 1993 Mandela and President de Klerk agreed to the formation of a government of national unity after free, nonracial elections (that took place in 1994). Relations between Mandela and de Klerk deteriorated when former members of de Klerk's security forces were prosecuted in March 1996. He stepped down as ANC president in December 1997 and was replaced by his former deputy Thabo Mbeki.

Mandela married the South African civil-rights activist Winnie Mandela in 1955. They separated in 1992 and were divorced in 1996. His autobiography, *Long Walk to Freedom* (1994), was widely acclaimed, and his state visit to Britain in July 1996 was a resounding success.

FURTHER READING
Benson, M *Nelson Mandela* 1986
Meer, F *Higher than Hope* 1990
Meredith, Martin *Nelson Mandela* 1998

Nelson Mandela as leader of the ANC, 1992. *Rex*

Mandelson, Peter (Benjamin) (1953–)

British Labour politician. As minister without portfolio 1997–98, and secretary of state for trade and industry in 1998, he worked closely on the Millennium Dome project at Greenwich. He entered the House of Commons in 1992, representing Hartlepool. Before that he had been an influential backroom figure within the Labour Party as director of campaigns and communications 1985–90. His organizational talents were demonstrated in Labour's victory campaign in the 1997 general election. He resigned in late 1998 after it emerged that he had borrowed £370,000 from his cabinet colleague Geoffrey Robinson, who also resigned as paymaster general.

A close confidant of Prime Minister Tony Blair and an expert at media management, he was promoted to the position of secretary of state for trade and industry in the July 1998 cabinet reshuffle. However, Mandelson had many critics on Labour's backbenches, and also among cabinet colleagues.

Born in London, after graduating from Oxford he worked in the TUC's economic department 1977–78,

and then, after serving on Lambeth borough council 1979–82, he was a television producer 1982–85 and an industrial consultant 1990–92. His vision of his party's future is summarized in the book he co-wrote, *The Blair Revolution: Can New Labour Deliver?* (1996).

With a strong political background, his maternal grandfather being the well-known Labour politician, Herbert, later Lord, Morrison, who had served in the cabinets of Winston Churchill and Clement Attlee, he was drawn into the political arena. See photograph on page 284.

Manley, Michael (Norman) (1924–1997)

Jamaican centre-left politician, leader of the socialist People's National Party from 1969, and prime minister 1972–80 and 1989–92. A charismatic orator, he was the son of Norman ◊Manley, founder of the socialist People's National Party (PNP), and became leader of the PNP on his father's death in 1969. After a landslide victory in 1972, his 'democratic socialist' programme was beset by economic depression, losing him the election in 1980. He was re-elected on a more moderate

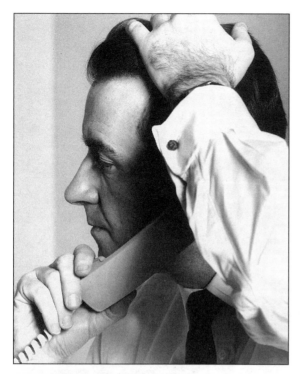

Peter Mandelson, 1996. *Rex*

manifesto in 1989, but ill health forced his resignation as prime minister in March 1992 and retirement from politics. He was succeeded as premier by Percival ◊Patterson.

As prime minister 1972–80, he nationalized the country's bauxite mines and encouraged economic self-reliance. In his foreign policy he attacked 'US imperialism', entered into closer relations with communist Cuba, and founded the Caribbean Community (CARICOM) in 1973. He also advocated political non-alignment and the creation of a new global economic order, benefiting less developed nations. The PNP were re-elected in 1976 but the pro-free-market Jamaican Labour Party (JLP), led by Edward ◊Seaga, gained power in 1980. The more moderate centrist programme of his second premiership included support for economic deregulation and foreign inward investment.

Manley was born in Kingston. He served in the Royal Canadian Airforce, studied at the London School of Economics, and worked as a journalist before returning to Jamaica to become a leader of the National Workers' Union during the 1950s. He was appointed to the Jamaican senate in 1962 and elected to its house of representatives in 1967.

Manley, Norman Washington (1893–1969)

Jamaican centre-left politician, chief minister 1955–59 and prime minister 1959–62. With his cousin Alexander ◊Bustamante, he dominated Jamaican politics

until his death. Manley formed the democratic-socialist People's National Party (PNP), the country's first political party, in 1938. As chief minister he helped create the Federation of the West Indies in 1958. After internal self-government was achieved in 1959, he embarked on a programme of economic development, promoting the tourist and bauxite industries, and land reform.

His son, Michael ◊Manley, succeeded him as PNP leader on his death, and was a future prime minister.

Manley was of mixed Irish and African descent. He studied at Oxford University, returning to Jamaica to become a successful barrister and Queen's Counsel (QC) before entering politics.

Mann, Tom (1856–1941)

English labour leader. One of the leaders of a dock strike in 1889, he was president of the International Ship, Dock, and River Workers 1892–96, and general secretary of the Amalgamated Engineering Union 1919–21. He was secretary of the Independent Labour Party 1894–96 and a founder member of the British Communist Party in 1920.

Mann was born at Foleshill, Warwickshire. He worked from the age of nine on farms and in the mines, served an apprenticeship in engineering for seven years in Birmingham, settled in London in 1876, joined the Amalgamated Society of Engineers in 1881, and became a socialist in 1885.

He was first secretary of the London Reform Union and of the National Democratic Union; he stood as a parliamentary candidate on three occasions. After living 1902–10 in Australia, where he was imprisoned for socialist agitation, he visited South Africa and returned to the UK, where he became leader of the syndicalist movement and in 1912 was imprisoned for inciting the troops to mutiny.

FURTHER READING

Tsuzuki, C *Tom Mann, The Challenge of Labour 1856–1941* 1991

White, J *Tom Mann* 1991

Mannerheim, Carl Gustav Emil von (1867–1951)

Finnish general and politician, leader of the conservative forces in the civil war 1917–18 and regent 1918–19. He commanded the Finnish army 1939–40 and 1941–44, and was president of Finland 1944–46.

After the Russian Revolution of 1917, a Red (socialist) militia was formed in Finland with Russian backing, and independence was declared in December. The Red forces were opposed by a White (counter-revolutionary) army led by Mannerheim, who in 1918 crushed the socialists with German assistance. He was recalled from retirement in 1939 to defend Finland against Soviet invasion, and gave the Soviets a hard fight before yielding. In 1941 Finland allied itself with Germany against the USSR but by 1944 it was obvious the Germans were losing. After leading the defence against Soviet invasion in two wars, he negotiated the peace settlement with the USSR and became president.

Mannheim, Karl (1893–1947)

Hungarian sociologist who settled in the UK in 1933. In *Ideology and Utopia* (1929) he argued that all knowledge, except in mathematics and physics, is ideological, a reflection of class interests and values; that there is therefore no such thing as objective knowledge or absolute truth.

Mannheim distinguished between ruling-class ideologies and those of utopian or revolutionary groups, arguing that knowledge is created by a continual power struggle between rival groups and ideas. Later works such as *Man and Society* (1940) analysed contemporary mass society in terms of its fragmentation and susceptibility to extremist ideas and totalitarian governments.

Manning, Ernest Charles (1908–)

Canadian politician, founder member of the Social Credit Party. He was premier of Alberta 1943–69; he also held the posts of provincial secretary 1944–55 and minister of mines and minerals in 1952.

Manning was born in Cardiff, Saskatchewan, and educated at Rosetown. A follower of William ◊Aberhart, he helped found the Social Credit Party, and in 1935 was elected to the provincial government. On Aberhart's death, he became premier of Alberta.

Manning, Patrick Augustus Mervyn (1946–)

Trinidadian centrist politician, prime minister 1991–95. Manning took over leadership of the People's National Movement (PNM) after corruption scandals and a crushing electoral defeat in 1986 ended the party's 30 years in power, and led the party to victory in 1991. After suffering a mid-term dip in popularity, as unemployment and crime levels increased, the economy improved and Manning called a snap election in 1995. However, he failed to gain a majority, enabling the United National Congress (UNC), led by Basdeo ◊Panday, to form a new coalition government with the Tobago-based National Alliance for Reconstruction (NAR).

During his early political career, Manning served under prime ministers Eric ◊Williams and George ◊Chambers in a range of cabinet posts between 1978 and 1986, including that of energy minister 1981–86.

At the disastrous election of 1986 the PNM lost all but three seats in the house of representatives, Chambers being among those defeated. Winning the 1991 election with 22 seats, the PNM maintained the largest share of the popular vote in 1995, but fell two seats short of an absolute majority.

Manning studied at the University of the West Indies, and originally worked as an oil refinery operator before entering politics.

Mantanzima, Kaiser (1915–)

South African politician. He is chief minister of the Transkei, which became independent in 1976. He believes in separate black development, and has advocated a confederation of black states to form a single supra-national independent state in South Africa.

He graduated from Fort Hare University, where he actively engaged in youth politics in the African National Congress.

Mao Dun or *Mao Tun,* pseudonym of Shen Yanbing or Shen Yen-ping (1896–1981)

Chinese writer. He wrote a trilogy of novellas, published as *Shi* (*Eclipse*) (1930); a bestselling novel, *Ziye* (*Midnight*) (1932), about financial exploiters in the decadent Shanghai of the time; and a collection of short stories. In 1930 he helped to organize the influential League of Left-Wing Writers. After the Communists came to power in 1949 he was China's first minister of culture 1949–65, and founder editor of the literary journal *People's Literature* 1949–53. During the Cultural Revolution he was kept under house arrest in Beijing (Peking) 1966–78.

Mao Zedong or *Mao Tse-tung* (1893–1976)
See page 286.

Mara, Ratu Kamisese (1920–)

Fijian politician, prime minister 1970–92, and president from 1994. He founded the moderate nationalist Alliance Party in 1960 and, as its leader, led the Fijian delegation to a constitutional conference in London in 1965. The outcome of this conference was greater autonomy, which led to Mara becoming chief minister in 1967, before independence was achieved, within the British Commonwealth, in 1970. On independence, Mara became prime minister and also served as foreign affairs minister from 1977. He remained in power until the April 1987 general election, which was won by the multiracial Fijian Labour Party (FLP), led by Timoci ◊Bavadra.

In December 1987 Mara was restored to office, following a series of coups by Major General Sitiveni ◊Rabuka, and proceeded to introduce controversial changes to the constitution that were designed to entrench in power the ethnic Fijian community. Mara also promoted an ambitious programme for economic growth. He stepped down at the 1992 general election and became deputy president. He was appointed president by the Great Council of Chiefs in January 1994, following the death of Sir Penaia ◊Ganilau. He remained head of state from 1997 under a new, nonracial constitution.

Born into a noble family, Mara was educated in Fiji,

New Zealand, and at Oxford University and the London School of Economics, England. He entered the colonial administrative service in 1950 and became a member of the Fiji legislative council (later the house of representatives) in 1953 and of the executive council in 1959.

Marchais, Georges (1920–1997)

French communist politician. As general secretary of the French Communist Party (PCF) 1972–94, he presided over his party's decline, its vote dropping in parliamentary elections from 21% in 1973 to 10% in 1986, and in presidential elections to under 8% in 1988.

◆ MAO ZEDONG OR MAO TSE-TUNG (1893–1976) ◆

Chinese communist politician and theoretician, leader of the Chinese Communist Party (CCP) 1935–76. Mao was a founder of the CCP in 1921, and became its leader in 1935. He organized the Long March 1934–35 and the war of liberation 1937–49, following which he established a People's Republic and communist rule in China. He was state president until 1959, and headed the CCP until his death. His influence diminished with the failure of his 1958–60 Great Leap Forward, but he emerged dominant again during the 1966–69 Cultural Revolution, which he launched in order to promote his own anti-bureaucratic line and to purge the party of 'revisionism'.

Letting a hundred flowers blossom and a hundred schools of thought contend is the policy for promoting progress in the arts and the sciences and a flourishing socialist culture in our land.

MAO ZEDONG Speech, Beijing, 27 February 1957

Mao adapted communism to Chinese conditions, as set out in the *Little Red Book* (1960), in which he stressed the need for rural rather than urban-based revolutions in Asia; for reducing rural–urban differences; and for perpetual revolution to prevent the emergence of new elites. He advocated a 'mass line' form of leadership, involving the broad mobilization of the people in economic, social, and political movements. He was also an advocate of a non-aligned Third World strategy, and helped to precipitate the Sino-Soviet split of 1960, which arose when the USSR withdrew military and technical support from China. His writings and thoughts dominated the functioning of the People's Republic 1949–76, and some 740 million copies of his *Quotations* have been printed to date, while his works as a whole total over 2,000 publications.

Mao was the son of a peasant farmer, and was born in the village of Shaoshan in Hunan province. He had an elementary classical

education in his youth, but specialized in modern subjects at Changsha First Normal School, where he was later headteacher. He served briefly in the Nationalist army during the 1911 Revolution against the Manchu Qing dynasty and was a library assistant at Beijing University 1918–19, before working for the CCP in Hunan province 1921–27. In June 1923 he was elected to the CCP Central Committee, and in January 1924 he became chief of CCP propaganda under the Kuomintang (Guomindang nationalist) leader ◊Sun Zhong Shan (Sun Yat-sen), but was later dismissed by Sun's successor, Jiang Jie Shi (Chiang Kai-shek).

In 1927 Mao organized a peasant uprising against Jiang Jie Shi's nationalist forces in Hunan, and when it failed, led the remnants of his army to Jiangxi province in southeast China. He became chair of the Council of the People's Commissars (Chinese Soviet Republic) in 1931, and in 1931–34 set up a communist people's republic (soviet) in Jiangxi. In an effort to evade the Kuomintang's suppressive tactics, he led the Red Army, together with ◊Zhu De, on the Long March north to Yan'an, in Shaanxi, 1934–35. In Yan'an, Mao built up a second people's republic 1936–47. He gained peasant support to the communist cause by reducing land rents and introducing fair taxes. Mao, whose first wife had been shot by the nationalists and who had divorced his second wife, married ◊Jiang Qing in Yan'an in 1939. From this base, he organized the war of liberation against the Japanese occupying forces, setting up an alliance with the Kuomintang in 1936. After 1945 and the defeat of Japan, the war was continued against the Kuomintang, with the CCP Red Army successfully employing mobile, rural-based guerrilla tactics. They took Beijing on 31 January 1949, and afterwards met little resistance on their march south. After the defeat of the Kuomintang forces at Nanjing in 1949, Jiang Ji Shi fled to Taiwan with his government and 1.5–2 million supporters, and a People's Republic was subsequently established in Beijing on 2 October 1949, with Mao as the elected chair of the republic.

After Liberation, Mao initially followed a traditional Soviet-programme of land redistribution and heavy industrialization and was

Marchais had worked his way up the party organization despite joining relatively late, in 1947. The preceding years, when he was conscripted to work in the Messerschmidt armaments factory in Germany, were to remain clouded by some obscurity. As party leader, he committed the PCF to a 'democratic transition to socialism' before returning to a more orthodox pro-Moscow line from 1978. He negotiated union of the left with the Socialist Party (PS) in 1973, but broke this off in 1977. Having stood as the PCF's 1981 presidential candidate against François Mitterrand, he agreed to communist participation in government from June

re-elected chair of the CCP by the first National People's Congress in 1954. However, from 1956, after the Soviet condemnation of Stalin, he launched a 'let a hundred flowers bloom' campaign in which criticisms were raised of the power of the new bureaucracy and he began to reject the emphasis on development through

> *Communism is not love. Communism is a hammer which we use to crush the enemy.*
> MAO ZEDONG *Time* 18 December 1950

heavy industries. In 1958–62 Mao introduced a series of sweeping economic changes under his second five-year plan. The aim of this programme, known as the Great Leap Forward, was to restructure the economy and polity along communist lines, and to this end Mao created large new agro-industrial communes, which were also designed to end the traditional divide between town and country and act as local political units. The Great Leap Forward eventually collapsed, chiefly because of poor planning, and effectively led to the deaths of over 20 million people from famine, as well as to Mao's own resignation as state president in 1959 and his replacement by the more moderate ◊Liu Shaoqi.

In 1966 Mao dramatically launched the Cultural Revolution. With the assistance of the radical 'Gang of Four', led by Jiang Qing, he mobilized millions of students to smash the existing political organizations and parts of the state apparatus. Various warring factions of Red Guards appeared, and 'liberal revisionist' officials at high and middle levels, including Liu Shaoqi, were denounced as 'capitalist roaders' and removed from their posts. When sections of the Red Guards began to develop independently of the Maoist centre, Mao collaborated with the defence minister ◊Lin Biao to intervene with military force. Finally it was the People's Liberation Army (PLA) which suppressed the Red Guards and ended the Cultural Revolution, and the army's victory was crowned at the 9th Party Congress in April 1969, with the formal designation of Lin as Mao's successor.

At the beginning of the 1970s a new struggle between Mao and Lin broke out, leading to a reported attempt by Lin to seize power in September 1971. Lin's coup attempt was forestalled by Mao with the help of his prime minister ◊Zhou Enlai, who subsequently worked alongside Mao in the reconstruction of China after the damage wrought by the Cultural Revolution. The Mao–Zhou alliance also made an important change in China's foreign policy after 1971 by moving towards reconciliation with the USA and Japan, and the trend towards rapprochement with the USA was further strengthened after the 10th Congress of the CCP in August 1973. In 1973–75 Mao also launched various radical campaigns against Confucianism, 'bourgeois rights', and 'capitulationism'.

After his death in September 1976, Mao was succeeded as chair of the CCP by the more moderate ◊Hua Guofeng and the 'Gang of Four' were arrested. In 1978 the leadership of China effectively passed to ◊Deng Xiaoping, a victim of the 'Cultural Revolution' and former ally of Liu Shaoqi. Deng criticized the policy excesses of Maoism and devised a pragmatic new communist philosophy which sought to combine the use of the market (to encourage increased production and prosperity) with continuing tight CCP control over political activities. In July 1981 the CCP Central Committee published an authoritative official verdict on Mao Zedong and the last 20 years of his life. It assessed Mao as '70 per cent good and 30 per cent bad', praising his contribution to the building of the CCP, PLA, and People's Republic, but criticized him for becoming tyrannical and obsessed with a misguided leftist line from the mid-1950s, culminating in the disastrous Cultural Revolution. Today, Maoism is viewed as just one of the many contributions to Chinese communist thinking. See photograph on page 288.

FURTHER READING

Fitzgerald, C P *Mao Tse-tung and China* 1977
Garfinkel, B *Mao Tse-tung* 1985
Hollingsworth, Clare *Mao and the Men Against Him* 1985
Li, Zhisui *The Private Life of Chairman Mao* 1994
Poole, F K *Mao* 1984
Rule, P *Mao Zedong* 1984
Salisbury, H *The Long March* 1984
Terrill, R *Mao: A Biography* 1980
Wilson, D *Mao, the People's Emperor* 1979

Mao Zedong, 1968. *Rex*

1981 but withdrew in 1984. Marchais's doctrinal and tactical manoeuvring eventually catalysed successive waves of dissidence, challenging the party's internal monolithism. He was succeeded on his resignation by Robert Hue.

Marcos, Imelda Romualdez (1930–   )

Filipino politician and socialite, wife of the dictator-president Ferdinand ◊Marcos, and known as the 'Iron Butterfly'.

Born into poverty, Imelda began her career as a singer and, with her striking looks, won the title of Miss Manila in 1953. A year later, she married Ferdinand Marcos, who was then a member of the Philippines house of representatives. When he was elected president in 1965, she became an unusually politically active first lady. She took a leading role in prestige cultural projects and served as governor of the National Capital Region from 1975 and as minister of human settlements and ecology from 1978. Her influence increased during the 1980s, as her husband's health deteriorated, but she became accused of using her public position improperly to amass private wealth. Following her husband's overthrow as president in February 1986, the couple lived in exile, and

---

◆ MARCOS, FERDINAND EDRALIN (1917–1989) ◆

Filipino right-wing politician, dictator-president 1965–86, when he was forced into exile in Hawaii by a popular front led by Corazon ◊Aquino.

Born in Sarrat, Marcos was convicted, while a law student in 1939, of murdering a political opponent of his father, but eventually secured his own acquittal. In World War II he was a guerrilla fighter against the Japanese invaders, and survived the Japanese prison camps. He worked as a special assistant to President Manuel Roxas during the 1940s and was a member of the house of representatives 1949–59 and senate 1959–61, representing the Liberal Party until 1964, before becoming president in 1965. He was elected as the candidate of the right-wing Nationalist Party, defeating Diosdado ◊Macapagal.

During his first term, Marcos launched military campaigns against communist insurgents and Muslim rebels on Mindanao, and made a reputation as a reformer. He was re-elected in 1969, but, with civil strife increasing, declared martial law in 1972. The Marcos regime became increasingly repressive, with secret pro-Marcos groups terrorizing, arresting, and executing opponents and press censorship being imposed.

The new 1973 constitution made Marcos a virtual dictator. With corruption, nepotism, and electoral fraud rife, Marcos was finally overthrown and exiled in February 1986, following a nonviolent 'people's power' movement, led by Corazon Aquino, the widow of a murdered opposition leader, which obtained international and army support. Marcos was backed by the USA when in power, but in 1988 US authorities indicted him and his wife, Imelda ◊Marcos, for racketeering and embezzlement.

A US grand jury investigating Marcos and his wife alleged that they had embezzled over $100 million from the government of the Philippines, received bribes, and defrauded US banks. Marcos was too ill to stand trial and died in exile in Honolulu, Hawaii, in September 1989. His body was later returned to the Philippines in 1993 and was kept in cold storage, while his widow, Imelda, campaigned for a proper state burial.

FURTHER READING

Bresnan, J *Crisis in the Philippines: The Marcos Era and Beyond* 1986

Youngblood, Robert L *Marcos Against the Church* 1990

Ferdinand and Imelda Marcos at the Manila Cadet Training Academy, 1985. *Rex*

her enormous collection of shoes, clothes, and art was put on display in the Malacanang Palace.

After her husband's death in 1989, Imelda Marcos stood trial in New York in answer to charges of concealing ownership of US property and other goods, purchased with stolen Philippine-government funds. She was acquitted, her lawyer claiming the responsibility had lain solely with her husband. In 1991 the government of the Philippines lifted its ban on Imelda Marcos returning to her homeland in the hope of recouping an estimated $350 million from frozen Marcos accounts in Swiss banks. She returned to Manila in November 1991 and was an unsuccessful candidate in the 1992 presidential elections. In 1993 she was convicted of corruption and sentenced to 18–24 years' imprisonment, but remained free on bail pending an appeal. This succeeded, in October 1998.

In May 1995 she was elected to the Phillipines house of representatives by a landslide majority in her home province of Leyte.

Marcuse, Herbert (1898–1979)

German political philosopher, in the USA from 1934; his theories combining Marxism and Freudianism influenced radical thought in the 1960s. His books include *One-Dimensional Man* (1964).

Marcuse preached the overthrow of the existing social order by using the system's very tolerance to ensure its defeat; he was not an advocate of violent revolution. A refugee from Hitler's Germany, he became professor at the University of California at San Diego in 1965.

Margai, Milton A S (1895–1964)

Sierra Leone nationalist leader and politician, prime minister 1961–64. Appointed a member of the protectorate assembly in 1940, he was elected to Legco in 1951, when he helped found the Sierra Leone People's Party (SLPP) and played a major role in pressing for independence. He was chief minister 1954–58, and became prime minister on full independence in 1961. On his death he was succeeded as party leader and prime minister by his half-brother Albert Margai (1910–1980).

Milton Margai was educated in Roman Catholic mission schools, at Fourah Bay College, and in the UK, where he qualified as a doctor.

Margrethe II (1940–)

Queen of Denmark from 1972, when she succeeded her father Frederick IX. In 1967 she married the French diplomat Count Henri de Laborde de Monpezat, who took the title Prince Hendrik. Her heir is Crown Prince Frederick (1968–).

Mariátegui, José Carlos (1895–1930)

Peruvian politician and writer. He was the first Peruvian intellectual to apply Marxist principles to Peruvian problems and founded the Socialist party in 1928.

In 1923 Mariátegui embarked on a radical programme of political upheaval along with his radical counterpart, Victor Rául Haya de la Torre. The founding of the American Popular Revolutionary Alliance party (APRA; Aprista Party) in 1924 by the exiled Victor Rául Haya de la Torre enabled Mariátegui to become the leading APRA activist in Peru until 1927. The APRA doctrine actively advocated socialist reform.

His book *Siete ensayos de interpretación de la realidad peruana/Seven Interpretive Essays on Peruvian Reality* (1928) is a seminal work of social analysis and has influenced many other Peruvian writers. His *Obras completas/Complete Works* were published in 1959.

Mariátegui was born in Lima and rose to prominence as a self-taught journalist. Educated in Italy, he developed strong ideological ties and became a confirmed Marxist.

Markievicz, Constance Georgina, Countess Markievicz (born Gore Booth) (1868–1927)

Irish revolutionary and politician who married the Polish count Casimir Markievicz in 1900. Her death sentence for taking part in the Easter Rising of 1916 was commuted, and she was released from prison in 1917. She was elected to the Westminster Parliament as a Sinn Féin candidate in 1918 (technically the first British woman member of Parliament), but did not take her seat.

Born in London and educated privately, she married Count Markievicz in 1900, from whom she later separated amicably. She joined Sinn Féin in 1908, launched the republican youth organization Fianna Éireann in 1909, and was active in the women's movement Inghinidhe na hÉireann. She was later president of the overtly militaristic women's organization Cumann na mBan. Markievicz also worked closely with James Connolly during the 1913 Dublin lockout, was an officer in the Citizen Army, and fought in the Easter Rising. She was indignant to learn that her death sentence had been commuted because of her gender. In 1918 she became the first woman ever to be elected to the British Parliament, but she did not take her seat, instead serving as minister of labour in the first Dáil (lower house of the Irish parliament). Markievicz opposed the 1921 Treaty with the British and supported the republicans in the civil war. She joined Fianna Fáil shortly before her death in the public ward of a Dublin hospital.

Marsh, Richard William (1928–)

English Labour politician. He became member of Parliament for Greenwich in 1959. He was minister of power 1966–68 and minister of transport 1968–69. He resigned as an MP in 1971 on his appointment as chair of British Rail, a post which he held until 1976.

He was educated at Jennings School, Swindon, Woolwich Polytechnic, and Ruskin College, Oxford. He was knighted in 1976.

Marshall, David Saul (1908–)

Singapore politician. As leader of the Labour front, he campaigned for radical constitutional reform in Singapore. In 1955 he became chief minister, and visited London regarding proposed changes in Singapore's constitutional status. In 1956 the London conference ended without agreement and Marshall resigned.

Marshall was educated at Raffles Institution and London University. He was succeeded by Lim Yew Hock, and himself subsequently formed a new left-wing group in Singapore.

Marshall, George Catlett (1880–1959)

US general and diplomat. He was army chief of staff in World War II, secretary of state 1947–49, and secretary of defence September 1950–September 1951. He initiated the Marshall Plan for European economic recovery in 1947 and received the Nobel Peace Prize in 1953.

Marshall, born in Uniontown, Pennsylvania, was commissioned in 1901, served in World War I, and in 1939 became chief of staff with the rank of general. Franklin D ◊Roosevelt promoted him to the newly created rank of general of the army.

Following Marshall's retirement from the army, President Harry Truman recalled him to serve as a special envoy to China in November 1945. He attempted to secure a coalition between the Nationalist and Communist forces against Japan. As defence secretary (a post not normally held by a soldier), he backed Truman's recall of General Douglas ◊MacArthur from Korea.

Marshall, John Ross (1912–1988)

New Zealand National Party politician, prime minister in 1972.

He was deputy to Keith ◊Holyoake as prime minister and succeeded him February–November 1972. He was notable for his negotiations of a free-trade agreement with Australia. He was replaced as National Party leader in 1974 by the more assertive Robert ◊Muldoon. He was created GBE in 1974.

Martens, Wilfried (1936–)

Belgian politician, prime minister 1979–92. He was president of the Dutch-speaking Social Christian Party (CVP) 1972–79 and, as prime minister, headed several coalition governments in the period 1979–92, when he was replaced by Jean-Luc ◊Dehaene heading a new coalition.

Martin, (Basil) Kingsley (1897–1969)

English journalist who edited the *New Statesman* magazine 1931–60 and made it the voice of controversy on the left.

He worked for the *Manchester Guardian* newspaper 1927–30 and founded the *Political Quarterly*. He was a conscientious objector during World War I.

FURTHER READING
Rolph, C H *The Life, Letters and Diaries of Kingsley Martin* 1973

Martov, Yuly Osipovich, adopted name of Yuly Osipovich Tsederbaum (1873–1923)

Russian revolutionary. He was a member of the Social Democratic Party from 1892 and leader of the Mensheviks. He cooperated with Lenin at first, but broke with him in 1903. After the October Revolution he became official leader of the Menshevik party.

After the February Revolution in 1917 he was in opposition to the majority of Mensheviks, maintaining an internationalist position against their 'revolutionary defencism'. Martov left Russia in 1920 as head of a Menshevik delegation and remained in Berlin, where he edited the monthly *Socialist Courier*.

Masaryk, Jan Garrigue (1886–1948)

Czechoslovak politician, son of Tomáš ◊Masaryk. He was foreign minister from 1940, when the Czechoslovak government was exiled in London in World War II. He returned in 1945, retaining the post, but as a result of political pressure by the communists committed suicide.

FURTHER READING
Jan Masaryk *Volá Londýn* 1990
Zelman, Zbynek *The Masaryks: The Making of Czechoslovakia* 1976

Masaryk, Tomáš Garrigue (1850–1937)

Czechoslovak nationalist politician. He directed the revolutionary movement against the Austrian Empire, founding with Edvard ◊Beneš and Milan ◊Stefanik the Czechoslovak National Council. In 1918 he was elected first president of the newly formed Czechoslovak Republic. Three times re-elected, he resigned in 1935 in favour of Beneš.

After the communist coup in 1948, Masaryk was systematically removed from public memory in order to reverse his semi-mythological status as the forger of the Czechoslovak nation.

FURTHER READING
Hanak, Harry *T G Masaryk, 1850–1937: Statesman and Cultural Force* 1990
Masaryk, Tomáš Garrigue *Masaryk on Thought and Life: Conversations with Karel Čapek* 1944
Masaryk, Tomáš Garrigue, and Čapek Karel, *Talks with T G Masaryk* 1995

◆ MARSHALL, THURGOOD (1908–1993) ◆

US jurist and civil-rights leader. As US Supreme Court justice from 1967, he frequently presided over landmark civil-rights cases such as *Brown* v *Board of Education* (1954). The first black associate justice, he was a strong voice for civil and individual rights throughout his career.

Marshall was named director of the National Association for the Advancement of Colored People (NAACP) Legal Defense and Education Fund in 1940. He was named to the US Court of Appeals in 1961 and served as solicitor general 1965–67. In 1967 President Lyndon Johnson appointed him to the US Supreme Court.

Marshall was born in Baltimore, Maryland, and received a law degree from Howard University in 1933. In 1936 he worked for the NAACP to remove the barriers set up for black people by the 1896 ruling that states could provide 'separate but equal' facilities for racial minorities. He also persuaded the Supreme Court to force the Maryland Law School to admit nonwhites (Marshall himself had been excluded because of his colour). Other universities were forced to admit and desegregate black students. Finally, in 1954, he led the Supreme Court to abandon the 'separate but equal' doctrine and forbid states from establishing separate schooling for black and white pupils.

Between 1944 and 1960, Marshall took 32 cases to the Supreme Court and won 28 of them, convincing it to ban the 'whites only' rule affecting train waiting rooms, restaurants, and seating on buses. He also overturned covenants preventing the sale of properties to minorities.

When Marshall became a Court of Appeals judge, none of his 112 opinions was reversed by the Supreme Court. He supported freedom of speech, passionately opposed the death penalty, and advocated affirmative action to cancel out the effects of racial prejudice. He ended the use of 'whites only' juries. As the court's liberal majority declined, Marshall found himself in the minority in over a fifth of cases during his last court term.

Masaryk, Tomáš Garrigue, and Kovtun, George J *The Spirit of Thomas G Masaryk (1850–1937): An Anthology* 1990

Pynsent, R B *T G Masaryk, 1850–1937: Thinker and Critic* 1989

Skilling, H Gordon *T G Masaryk: Against the Current* 1994

Szporluk, Roman *The Political Thought of Thomas G Masaryk* 1981

Winters, Stanley B *T G Masaryk: Thinker and Politician* 1990 (v. 1)

Zelman, Zbynek *The Masaryks: The Making of Czechoslovakia* 1976

Masire, Quett Ketumile Joni (1925–)

Botswanan politician, president 1980–98. In 1962, with Seretse ◊Khama, he founded the Botswana Democratic Party (BDP) and in 1965 was made deputy prime minister. After independence in 1966, he became vice president and, on Khama's death in 1980, president, continuing a policy of nonalignment. He retired in March 1998 and was succeeded by Festus Mogae of the BDP.

Masire was a journalist before entering politics, sitting in the Bangwaketse tribal council and then the legislative council before cofounding the BDP. A centrist, he helped Botswana become one of the most stable states in Africa.

Massey, (Charles) Vincent (1887–1967)

Canadian Liberal Party politician. He was the first Canadian to become governor general of Canada 1952–59.

He helped to establish the Massey Foundation in 1918, which funded the building of Massey College and the University of Toronto.

Massey was educated at Toronto University and Balliol College, Oxford. He was a lecturer in modern history at Toronto University 1913–15, and was appointed minister without portfolio in the Dominion cabinet after World War I. He was honorary Canadian minister to the USA 1926–30, president of the National Liberal Federation of Canada 1932–53, and high commissioner for Canada in the UK 1935–46. In his last year of office he was made a Companion of Honour. From 1947 to 1950 he was chancellor of the University of Toronto.

Massey, William Ferguson (1856–1925)

New Zealand right-of-centre politician, prime minister 1912–25. He concentrated initially on controlling militant unions and the newly formed Federation of Labour. He drew upon fellow farmers, 'Massey Cossacks', to act as special constabulary strike breakers in the goldfields and Wellington docks. He also led the country through World War I, supporting the UK war effort, although he was intellectually an isolationist. He attended the Paris Peace Conference at the war's conclusion and was re-elected with a large majority in December 1919. He died in office, and remains today New Zealand's longest-serving prime minister.

Born in Country Derry, Ireland, into a staunch Ulster Protestant family, he emigrated to North Island, New Zealand, in 1870. His father became a dairy farmer and William Massey also worked as a farmer before being elected to the house of representatives in 1894. He emerged as a spokesperson for the agrarian community and, from 1903, became leader of the Reform Party, which he had founded as an offshoot of the Conservative Party. After a decade in opposition, in July 1912 Massey became prime minister.

FURTHER READING
Scholefied, H *The Rt Hon W F Massey* 1925

Mata Hari, stage name of Margaretha Geertruida Zelle (1876–1917)

Dutch courtesan, dancer, and probable spy. In World War I she had affairs with highly placed military and government officials on both sides and told Allied secrets to the Germans. She may have been a double agent, in the pay of both France and Germany. She was shot by the French on espionage charges.

FURTHER READING
Howe, Russell Warren *Mata Hari: The True Story* 1986

Waagenaar, Sam *The Murder of Mata Hari* 1964

Matsudaira, Tsuneo (1877–1949)

Japanese diplomat and politician who became the first chair of the Japanese Diet (parliament) after World War II. He negotiated for Japan at the London Naval Conference of 1930 and acted as imperial household minister 1936–45, advising the emperor, but was unsuccessful in keeping Japan out of a war with the Western powers.

Matsuoka, Yosuke (1880–1946)

Japanese politician, foreign minister 1940–41. A fervent nationalist, Matsuoka led Japan out of the League of Nations in 1933 when it condemned Japan for the seizure of Manchuria. As foreign minister, he allied Japan with Germany and Italy. At the end of World War II, he was arrested as a war criminal but died before his trial was concluded.

Matteotti, Giacomo (1885–1924)

Italian socialist politician. After Mussolini gained power in 1922, Matteotti was an outspoken opponent of the Fascist regime. He was, consequently, murdered in June 1924.

He was born in Fratta Polesine, Rovigo.

Maudling, Reginald (1917–1979)

British Conservative politician, chancellor of the Exchequer 1962–64, contender for the party leadership in 1965, and home secretary 1970–72.

Born in London and educated at Merchant Taylors' and Merton College, Oxford, he became a barrister in 1940. After holding junior office he became minister of supply 1955–57. He was member of Parliament for Barnet 1958–74 and for Chipping Barnet from 1974. He was paymaster general 1957–59, president of the Board of Trade 1959–61, colonial secretary 1961–62, and chancellor of the Exchequer 1962–64. In 1965 Maudling was a candidate for the leadership of the Conservative Party, but was defeated by Edward Heath. Subsequently he became deputy leader of the party.

He resigned his office as home secretary when referred to during the bankruptcy proceedings of the architect John Poulson, since (as home secretary) he would have been in charge of the Metropolitan Police investigating the case. In July 1977 Maudling, together with two other MPs, was censured for conduct inconsistent with the standards of the House of Commons in a report of a select committee in relation to the Poulson affair, but the House subsequently overwhelmingly defeated a motion to suspend him. Maudling was the Conservative spokesperson for foreign affairs 1975–76. His memoirs were published in 1978.

There comes a time in every man's life when he must make way for older men.

REGINALD MAUDLING *Guardian* 20 November 1976. Remark made by Maudling in the Smoking Room of the House of Commons on being replaced in the Shadow Cabinet by John Davies, his elder by four years

---

Mauroy, Pierre (1928–   )

French socialist politician, prime minister 1981–84. He oversaw the introduction of a radical reflationary programme. He was first secretary (leader) of the Socialist Party 1988–92.

Mauroy worked for the FEN teachers' trade union and served as national secretary for the Young Socialists during the 1950s, rising in the ranks of the Socialist Party in the northeastern region. He entered the National Assembly in 1973 and was prime minister in François Mitterand's government of 1981, but was replaced by Laurent Fabius in July 1984.

Maurras, Charles Marie Photius (1868–1952)

French writer and extreme right-wing politician. The leading journalist and polemicist of France's nationalist and counter-revolutionary right, in 1899 Maurras cofounded Action Française and its associated leagues, the Camelots du Roi. He was imprisoned for life in 1945 for collaborating with the German occupying forces in World War II.

Born into a middle-class Provençal family, Maurras developed his intransigeant critique of the Third Republic in response to the Dreyfus affair. Before World War I he had won over much of the far right to his brand of monarchical 'integral nationalism'. His vitriolic anti-Semitism led to a nine-month prison sentence 1936–37, when he was convicted of incitement to murder. A prolific journalist for his movement's daily newspaper, Maurras's published works included literary criticism, prose tales, and poetry, as well as his autobiographical *Au Signe de Flore* (1931) and *Mes Idées Politiques/My Political Ideas* (1937). He was elected to the Académie Française in June 1938.

Maxton, James (1885–1946)

Scottish politician, chair of the Independent Labour Party 1926–40, and member of Parliament for Glasgow Bridgeton from 1922 until his death. One of the most turbulent 'Red Clydesiders', he was expelled from the House of Commons in 1923 for calling a minister a murderer. As chair of the Independent Labour Party, he led its secession for the Labour Party in 1932, and became increasingly isolated from mainstream Labour politics. His extreme views won few supporters, but his sincerity won the respect of many.

A man of strong convictions, he was a staunch pacifist, and suffered imprisonment for attempting to foment a strike of shipyard workers during World War I, in which he was a conscientious objector. In 1928 he produced, with A J ◊ Cook, the Cook–Maxton manifesto which criticized the Labour Party for abandoning the socialism of the party's pioneers.

Born in Glasgow, he was educated at the university there and became a teacher in the east end of the city, where the poverty he witnessed converted him to socialism.

Maxwell, (Ian) Robert (1923–1991)

See page 294.

Mayhew, Patrick (Barnabas Burke), Baron of Kilndown (1929–   )

British lawyer and Conservative politician, Northern Ireland secretary 1992–97. He was appointed solicitor general in 1983 and four years later attorney general, becoming the government's chief legal adviser. His appointment as Northern Ireland secretary came at a propitious time and within two years he had witnessed the voluntary cessation of violence by both Republicans and Loyalists, but allegations of unnecessary delays in the peace process led to the resumption of Irish Republican Army (IRA) violence in February 1996.

Mayhew was born in Cookham, Berkshire, and educated at Tonbridge School and Balliol College, Oxford. After embarking on a successful legal career, he entered the House of Commons in 1974, winning the safe seat of Royal Tunbridge Wells, and five years later began his ministerial ascent in the department of employment. He retired from Parliament in 1997 and was created Baron the same year.

Mazowiecki, Tadeusz (1927–)

Polish politician, adviser to the Solidarity trade-union movement, and Poland's first postwar non-communist prime minister 1989–90. In the presidential elections of November 1990 he lost to Lech ◊Wałęsa. In April 1994 he formed the Freedom Union (UW). In the late 1990s he moved away from direct involvement in Polish internal politics. In 1992 he was appointed special reporter to the United Nations (UN) over conflicts in the former Yugoslavia.

A lawyer by profession, closely linked to a number of Catholic organizations under communist rule, Mazowiecki was associated with, in particular, the PAX group and the Catholic monthly *Więź*. In 1961–70 he was a member of the Polish parliament, the Sejm, and belonged to the Catholic parliamentary group ZNAK. During the Gdańsk dockyard strikes in August 1980 he acted as adviser to the Solidarity trade union in talks with government representatives. He was interned during martial law. After 1990 his links with the Solidarity movement weakened following a break-up with Wałęsa. He was greatly respected for his involvement in investigating war crimes in the former Yugoslavia.

Mazumdar, Charu (1915–1972)

Indian Communist revolutionary, leader of the Naxal-bari movement. In 1965, in opposition to the leadership of the Communist Party of India-Marxist (CPM), Mazumdar began advocating a revolutionary position along Maoist lines. He called for the destruction of existing state power and the creation of a new political order achieved through social revolution. This led to the organization and armed uprising of 15,000 to 20,000 landless peasants, tea plantation workers, and tribal people near the village of Naxalbari in the northern part of West Bengal in March and April 1967. Mazumdar was arrested in Calcutta in July 1972 and died in police custody. After his death the revolutionary movement in India collapsed.

Mbeki, Thabo (1942–)

South African politician, first executive deputy president from 1994. As chair of the African National Congress (ANC) from 1989, he played an important role in the constitutional talks with the government of F W de Klerk that eventually led to the adoption of a nonracial political system. In December 1997 he replaced Nelson Mandela as ANC president.

An active member of the ANC from an early age, Mbeki led its student and, later, youth branches, and was, in consequence, detained for six weeks by the South African authorities in 1962. After his release he worked for the ANC in their London offices 1967–70

◆ Maxwell, (Ian) Robert, born Jan Ludvik Hoch (1923–1991) ◆

Czech-born British publishing and newspaper proprietor. He owned several UK national newspapers, including the *Daily Mirror* and the Macmillan Publishing Company, and the New York *Daily News*. At the time of his death the Maxwell domain carried debts of about $3.9 billion.

In late 1991 Maxwell, last seen on his yacht off the Canary Islands, was found dead at sea. His sons Kevin and Ian were named as his successors. After his death it was revealed that he had been involved in fraudulent practices for much of his career. In 1991 the Serious Fraud Office started an

---

When I pass a belt I cannot resist hitting below it.

Robert Maxwell Quoted in *New York Times* March 1991

---

investigation into pension-fund losses following reports of transfers of over £400 million from the Maxwell pension funds to the private Maxwell firms, to offset mounting company losses, affecting more than 30,000 current and future pensioners. Kevin and Ian Maxwell were arrested,

but in January 1996 were cleared of all charges to defraud the Maxwell pension funds, following an eight-month trial that cost £25 million. Kevin and Ian went on to form, in March 1997, a television media and investment company, Telemonde Holdings. The Department of Trade and Industry inquiry remained pending, but since it was set up no-one has been found guilty of criminal charges.

Maxwell, as he would become, was born in Czechoslovakia, but in 1939 escaped the Nazis first to Romania and later to Britain. His father was shot and his mother and other members of his family died in Auschwitz. As a young man, he had a distinguished wartime army career.

Maxwell was Labour member of Parliament for Buckingham 1964–70. Acquiring the Mirror Group of newspapers from Reed International in 1984, he introduced colour and made it profitable. In 1990 he bought the US book publisher Macmillan and in 1991 the New York *Daily News*, which was on the verge of closure after a bitter labour dispute.

He founded two major organizations: the family-owned Liechtenstein-based Maxwell Foundation, which owns 51% of Mirror Group Newspapers;

Robert Maxwell (right) with his sons Ian and Kevin. *Rex*

and subsequently underwent several months' military training in the USSR. As a leading member of the ANC, he represented it in Swaziland 1975–76 and Nigeria 1976–78.

He was director of information and publicity 1984–89 and then national chair. He is seen as a possible successor to Nelson Mandela as president.

Mboya, Tom (Thomas Joseph) (1930–1969)

Kenyan politician and trade unionist. He helped found the Kenya African National Union (KANU) in 1960, becoming its secretary general. A prominent pan-Africanist, he was elected chair of the All-African People's Conference in Ghana during 1958. He served as minister of labour prior to independence in 1963, and became minister of economic affairs from 1964 until his assassination.

Mboya also founded and led the Kenya Local Government Workers' Union in 1952, and the Kenya Federation of Labour (KFL).

and Maxwell Communication Corporation, 67% owned by the Maxwell family, which has shares in publishing, electronics, and information companies.

He was also the publisher of the English edition of *Moscow News* from 1988, and had private interests (not connected with the Maxwell Corporation) in the Hungarian newspapers *Esti Hirlap* and *Magyar Hirlap* (he owned 40% of the latter from 1989), the German Berliner Verlag company, and the Israeli *Maariv*.

In the UK the national newspapers owned by the Maxwell Foundation 1984–91 were the tabloids the *Daily Mirror*, *Sunday Mirror*, and *People* (all of which supported the Labour Party); in 1990 the weekly *European* was launched.

FURTHER READING

Bower, Tim *Maxwell* 1992, *Maxwell: The Final Verdict* 1995

Greenslade, Roy *Maxwell* 1992

Haines, Joe *Maxwell* 1988

McKenna, Reginald (1863–1943)

English statesman and financier. He was home secretary 1911–15 and chancellor of the Exchequer 1915–16. Through a series of new loans, import duties, and taxes he managed to meet the rising cost of the war. In 1919 he became chair of the London City and Midland Bank, retaining the post until his death.

He was born in London. He was Liberal member of Parliament for North Monmouthshire 1895–1918. After serving as president of the Board of Education 1907–08, he was First Lord of the Admiralty 1908–11, and at the Home Office, where he attempted to deal with the suffragette problem by the 'Cat and Mouse Act' of 1913. As a member of the Macmillan Committee on Finance and Industry he signed the report which appeared in 1931 just before the abandonment of the gold standard.

McManus, Francis Patrick Vincent (1905–)

Australian politician. He was deputy leader of the Australian Labor party in the Senate 1956–57, before founding the left-wing Democratic Labor (DLP) party in 1957. McManus was a DLP senator in Victoria 1957–62 and 1965–73.

He was born in Melbourne, Victoria. Before he entered politics he was a teacher. He was elected to the Victorian Senate in 1955, defeated in 1961, and re-elected in 1964. The Democratic Labor party gained few parliamentary seats, but attracted enough support to lessen the chances of Labor winning federal office.

Means, Russell (1939–)

US Oglala Sioux activist. In 1970 he founded the second chapter of the American Indian Movement (AIM) in Cleveland, Ohio. His flair for guerrilla theatre, including the seizure of the *Mayflower II* on Thanksgiving in 1970 and the Trail of Broken Treaties in 1972, helped bring AIM to national attention. In response to clashes between police and AIM supporters in South Dakota, he and 200 followers seized control of Wounded Knee in 1973 for 71 days.

Means was born in Pine Ridge, South Dakota. In 1974 he was defeated in a runoff election by Richard Wilson for the Sioux Tribal Council presidency; although two federal probes sustained charges of threats, bribery, and ballot-stuffing, the Bureau of Indian Affairs failed to order a new election. He continued his calls for action at places such as the Black Hills and the Custer Battlefield National Monument. In 1992 he appeared in the film *The Last of the Mohicans*.

Meany, George (1894–1980)

US labour leader. Active first in the plumbers' union, then in the New York state federation of labour, he was elected secretary-treasurer of the American Federation of Labor (AFL) in 1939 and its president in 1952. He then became president of the AFL-CIO (Congress of Industrial Organizations) coalition (1955–80). Meany was born in New York City.

Meciar, Vladimír (1942–)

Slovak politician, prime minister of the Slovak Republic January 1993–March 1994 and again October 1994–September 1998. He held a number of posts under the Czechoslovak communist regime until, as a dissident, he was expelled from the party in 1970. He joined the Public Against Violence (PAV) movement in 1989, campaigning for a free Czechoslovakia, then, as leader of the Movement for a Democratic Slovakia (HZDS) from 1990, sought an independent Slovak state. Under the federal system, Meciar became prime minister of the Slovak Republic in 1990 and the new state's first prime minister in January 1993. He resigned in March 1994 after a no-confidence vote in parliament, but was returned as premier in October 1994 following a general election victory.

Born at Zvolen, he was edicated at the Komenský University, Bratislava. With his Czech counterparts, Meciar played an important role in ensuring that the 'velvet revolution' of 1989 was translated into a similarly bloodless 'velvet divorce'. His resignation from the post of premier of the new Slovak Republic in March 1994 followed a confrontation with President Michal Kovac over Meciar's handling of the privatization programme. The HZDS's election victory in October 1994 returned Meciar to power.

A nationalist populist, he pledged to halt voucher privatization and to curb the growing influence of the republic's ethnic-Hungarian minority, clashing with President ◊Kovac in the process. In March 1998, after parliament failed to agree on a successor to Kovac,

presidential power passed to Meciar. In September he stepped down as prime minister after his ruling coalition lost its parliamentary majority in the general election. In early November 1998 a new left–right coalition government was formed under Mikulas Dzurinda, a Christian Democrat.

FURTHER READING

Meciar, Vladimír, and Javorský, Frantisek (ed) *Dialógy Vladimíra Meciara o státnosti* 1992

Petrásová, Eva *Kto ste, Pán Meciar?* 1991

Médici, Emilio Garrastazú (1905–1986)

Brazilian dictator-president 1969–74. He was elected to presidential office by a military junta in 1969, succeeding President Artur da Costa e Silva. His reign was marked by strong oppression and dictatorial powers, but his administration governed the nation successfully and brought about economic vibrancy. He was replaced in 1974 by his own appointed successor, Ernesto Giesel.

Médici was an army general and head of the Brazilian intelligence service before his election.

Medvedev, Vadim Andreyevich (1925–)

Soviet communist politician. He was deputy chief of propaganda 1970–78, was in charge of party relations with communist countries 1986–88, and in 1988 was appointed by the Soviet leader Mikhail Gorbachev to succeed the conservative Egor Ligachev as head of ideology. He adhered to a firm Leninist line.

Meese, Edwin, III (1931–)

US attorney general 1985–88 who was among President Ronald Reagan's most important advisors. As chair of the Domestic Policy Council and the National Drug Policy Board, and as a member of the National Security Council (NSC), Meese played a key role in the development and execution of US domestic and foreign policy in the 1980s. As a conservative deputy district attorney 1958–67 and California legal affairs secretary 1967–74, he prosecuted antiwar students on behalf of Governor Ronald Reagan. He became Reagan's presidential counsel 1981–85 and later, as attorney general, was accused of impeding the Iran–Contra investigation by allowing conspirators to destroy evidence.

Meese was born in Oakland, California. He was educated at Yale University and the University of California at Berkeley. In the 1970s, he was director of the Center for Criminal Justice Policy and Management 1977–80 and a law professor at the University of San Diego.

FURTHER READING

Meese, Edwin *With Reagan: The Inside Story* 1992

Mehta, Pherozeshah Merwanji (1845–1915)

Indian politician. He was the leader of the moderate Congress Party in western India and one of the founders of the Indian National Congress (now the Congress Party), becoming its president in 1890.

He was the first Parsi to become a barrister in England, in 1868.

Meighen, Arthur (1874–1960)

Canadian Conservative politician. He was prime minister 1920–21 and 1926–27. Between 1913 and 1920 he successively held the posts of solicitor general, secretary of state, and minister of the interior.

In 1920 he succeeded Robert Borden as Conservative leader and premier, but lost the 1921 general election to Mackenzie King and the Liberals, and also lost his seat. King formed a coalition with the Progressives that lasted until June 1926. Meighen then accepted a commission from the governor general to form a government; this developed into a constitutional crisis, leading to Meighen's defeat. Richard Bennett succeeded him as Conservative leader in 1927. In 1942 Meighen resigned his senatorship to resume the leadership of the Conservative Party, but failed to win a seat.

Meighen was born in Anderson, Perth County, Ontario. He studied at the University of Toronto, went west to Portage la Prairie to practise law in 1903, and entered politics. He was elected member of parliament for Portage in 1908. In the conscription crisis of 1917 (during World War I), he earned the hatred of Québec for his part in the Military Service Act, which was strongly opposed in that province. In 1918 he attended the Imperial Conference.

Meiji, Mutsuhito (1852–1912)

Emperor of Japan from 1867, under the regnal era name Meiji ('enlightened'). During his reign Japan became a world industrial and naval power. His ministers abolished the feudal system and discrimination against the lowest caste, established state schools, reformed the civil service, and introduced conscription, the Western calendar, and other measures to modernize Japan, including a constitution in 1889.

He took the personal name Mutsuhito when he became crown prince in 1860. He was the son of Emperor Kōmei (reigned 1846–67), who was a titular ruler in the last years of the Tokugawa shogunate.

Meir, Golda, born Mabovitch, later Myerson (1898–1978)

Israeli Labour politician, foreign minister 1956–66, and prime minister 1969–74. Criticism of the Israelis' lack of preparation for the 1973 Arab-Israeli War led to election losses for Labour and, unable to form a government, she resigned.

Born in Russia, she emigrated to the USA in 1906, and in 1921 went to Palestine.

Mellon, Andrew William (1855–1937)

US financier. He was secretary of the Treasury 1921–32, pursuing tax-cutting policies. In 1937 he donated his art collection to found the National Gallery of Art, Washington, DC.

Born in Pittsburgh, Mellon attended the Western University of Pennsylvania and entered the family banking firm. Through far-sighted investments and loans to the expanding steel and oil industries of Pennsylvania, Mellon became one of the wealthiest people in the USA. He founded the Mellon National Bank in 1902. In 1911 he founded the Mellon Institute of Industrial Research at Pittsburgh. He was appointed secretary of the Treasury by President Warren Harding in 1921 and held the post until 1932, under presidents Calvin Coolidge and Herbert Hoover.

Menchú Túm, Rigoberta (1959–)

Guatemalan campaigner for the rights of indigenous peoples. She was awarded the Nobel Peace Prize in 1992 for her efforts to promote intercultural peace, and returned from exile to live and campaign in Guatemala.

Her book I, Rigoberta Menchú (1982) won international acclaim for its stark and moving depiction of the plight of the native peoples of Guatemala.

Born into a Quiché farming family in northwest Guatemala, she began work at the age of eight as a migrant agricultural labourer. From her teens, she became an active campaigner against human-rights abuses and was forced into exile, in Mexico, by the military regime.

Menderes, Adnan (1899–1961)

Turkish politician. In 1945 he became one of the leaders of the new Democratic Party and was made prime minister when it came to power in 1950. Re-elected in 1954 and 1957, he was deposed in 1960 and superseded by General Cemal Gursel following an army coup. He was put on trial and hanged.

Menderes was born near Aydin and, though trained as a lawyer, he initially became a farmer. He entered politics in 1932, at first as member of the opposition and later with the party in power under Kemal Atatürk.

Mendes, Chico (Filho Francisco) (1944–1988)

Brazilian environmentalist and labour leader. Opposed to the destruction of Brazil's rainforests, he organized itinerant rubber tappers into the Workers' Party (PT) and was assassinated by Darci Alves, a cattle rancher's son. Of 488 similar murders in land conflicts in Brazil 1985–89, his was the first to come to trial.

Born in the northwestern Amazonian state of Acre, Mendes became an outspoken opponent of the destruction of rainforests for cattle-ranching purposes (rubber-tapping is a sustainable activity), and received death threats from ranchers. He was awarded the United Nations' Global 500 Ecology Prize in 1987.

FURTHER READING

Burch, Joann J *Chico Mendes: Defender of the Rainforest* 1994

Revkin, Andrew C *The Burning Season: The Murder of Chico Mendes and the Fight for the Amazon Forest* 1994

Mendès-France, Pierre Isaac Isadore (1907–1982)

French centre-left politician. His premiership, July 1954–February 1955, secured France's negotiated withdrawal from Indochina in August 1954, the granting of political autonomy to France's Tunisian protectorate, and a major package of economic reforms, introducing a regional dimension to economic planning and also a value-added tax. Such controversial policies combined with his Jewish background to make him the target of anti-Semitic attacks from the far right (paralleling Léon ◊Blum's experience in the 1930s).

A long-serving radical member of the French parliament 1932–40 and 1945–58, Mendès-France had served in the Free French Airforce 1942–43 before being appointed minister of finance in Charles ◊de Gaulle's provisional government of May 1944–May 1945. He opposed de Gaulle's return to government in 1958, campaigning against the constitution of his new Republic. A founding member of the new-left Unified Socialist Party (PSU) in 1960, he was fleetingly drawn into the political foreground when he addressed a mass meeting of students and striking workers in Charlety stadium during the events of May 1968.

In the 1950s Mendès-France sought to 'break the mould' of governmental instability, using radio and the press to appeal over the heads of the parties and win public support for modernizing France's economy and its republican institutions. But he was only to serve once as prime minister under the Fourth Republic, for just seven months and seven days.

Méndez Montenegro, Julio César (1915–)

Guatemalan politician, president 1966–70, member of the leftist Revolutionary Party. He launched a five-year plan of social and economic reform and offered the communist guerrillas an amnesty.

When the amnesty was rejected, Colonel Carlos ◊Araña Osorio was placed in charge of a concerted anti-guerrilla campaign, in which government forces were supported by right-wing and peasant paramilitaries, but which led to spiralling urban and rural violence. Arana, who had been dismissed for excesses in 1968, replaced Méndez as president in 1970.

Formerly a law professor, following the assassination of his brother, Méndez was elected president in 1966 at a time of intense guerrilla activity.

Menem, Carlos (Saul) (1930–)

Argentine politician, president from 1989; leader of the Peronist Justicialist Party. As president, he introduced sweeping privatization and cuts in public spending to address Argentina's economic crisis and stimulate the free market; released hundreds of political prisoners

jailed under the regime of Raúl Alfonsín Foulkes; and sent two warships to the Gulf to assist the USA against Iraq in the 1992 Gulf War (the only Latin American country to offer support to the USA). He also improved relations with the UK.

The son of Syrian immigrants to La Rioja province in the 1920s, Menem joined the Justicialist Party while training to be a lawyer. In 1963 he was elected president of the party in La Rioja and served as governor there 1973–76 and 1983–84. He was imprisoned 1976–81 during the military coup. In 1989 he defeated the Radical Civic Union Party candidate and became president of Argentina. Despite anti-British speeches during the election campaign, President Menem soon declared a wish to resume normal diplomatic relations with the UK and to discuss the future of the Falkland Islands in a spirit of compromise. He was re-elected in 1995.

He was born in Anillaco, La Rioja Province. He was educated at Universidad de Córdoba, graduating in 1955. He founded the Juventud Peronista (Peronist youth organization) and in 1956 became legal adviser to the General Confederation of Labour.

Mengistu Haile Mariam (1937–)

Ethiopian soldier and socialist politician, head of state 1977–91 (president 1987–91). He seized power in a coup, and instituted a regime of terror to stamp out any effective opposition. Confronted with severe problems of drought and secessionist uprisings, he survived with help from the USSR and the West until his violent overthrow by rebel forces.

As an officer in the Ethiopian army, Mengistu took part in the overthrow in 1974 of Emperor ◊Haile Selassie and in 1977 led another coup, becoming head of state. In 1987 civilian rule was formally reintroduced, but with the Marxist-Leninist Workers' Party of Ethiopia the only legally permitted party. In May 1991, two secessionist forces closed in on the capital, Addis Ababa, and Mengistu fled the country. He was eventually granted asylum in Zimbabwe. In 1995 he was tried in absentia on charges of mass murder, relating to the assassination of Emperor Selassie and the deaths of thousands of his political opponents during the period known as the 'Red Terror' 1977–79. He survived an assassination attempt in November 1995.

Menocal, Mario García (1866–1941)

Cuban Conservative Party politician and revolutionary, president 1913–21. His reformist 'businessman government' was seen as corrupt, and his re-election in 1916, amid charges of electoral fraud, provoked an abortive revolt led by José Miguel Gómez. However, rising sugar prices during World War I and US support brought prosperity and stability. Menocal supported Alfredo ◊Zayas as president in 1920, and remained influential until his defeat by Gerardo ◊Machado in the 1924 presidential contest.

After leading an unsuccessful revolt against Machado in 1931, he lived in exile in the USA. He returned to Cuba after Machado's removal in 1934 and ran unsuccessfully for president in 1936.

As a revolutionary, he was a general in the struggle against Spanish control from 1895. He secured positions in the US military government, which held power after the Spanish–American War of 1898, and became a leading figure within the right-of-centre Conservative Party, as well as a sugar plantation manager. An early presidential bid in 1908 proved unsuccessful.

Menocal was mainly educated in the USA, where he studied engineering at Cornell University. His family had been forced to leave Cuba during the Ten Years' War for independence from Spain 1868–78.

Mercouri, Melina, professional name of Maria Amalia Mercouris (1925–1994)

Greek actress and politician. A vocal opponent of the colonels' regime, she was elected to parliament in 1977 and served as minister of culture 1981–89 and 1993–94. She was a tireless campaigner for the arts both at home and within the European Community (now the European Union), and in particular sought for the return of the Elgin Marbles (or Parthenon Marbles) from the UK to Greece.

Meri, Lennart (1929–)

Estonian politician, president from 1992. He was active in the independence movement in the 1980s and became the founder and director of the Estonian Institute in 1989. He served as minister for foreign affairs 1990–92.

Born in Tallinn, Meri was deported to Siberia together with his family 1941–46. Educated at Tartu University, he worked for Estonian Radio and as a scriptwriter. He is a director of Tallinnfilm and has served as the secretary of the Estonian Writers' Association.

Messali, Hadj (1898–1974)

Algerian nationalist leader. He was one of the most prominent figures in the Algerian nationalist movement. An activist within the Etoile Nord-Africaine, which he led in France in the 1920s, he returned to Algeria and created the Parti du Peuple Algérien in 1937 advocating independence via direct revolutionary action. He was imprisoned following the demonstrations of 8 May 1945, and after his release his outlawed party was resurrected under a new name, Mouvement pour le Triomphe des Libertés Démocratiques (MTLD). When his leadership was challenged from within his own organization, he founded a new party, Mouvement National Algérien, and left for France.

Metaxas, Ioannis (1870–1941)

Greek general and politician, born in Ithaca. He restored ◊George II as king of Greece, under whom he established a dictatorship as prime minister from 1936, and introduced several necessary economic and military reforms. He led resistance to the Italian invasion of Greece in 1941, refusing to abandon Greece's neutral position.

Michels, Robert (1876–1936)

German social and political theorist. In *Political Parties*

◆ MENZIES, ROBERT GORDON (1894–1978) ◆

Australian conservative politician, leader of the United Australia (now Liberal) Party and prime minister 1939–41 and 1949–66.

A Melbourne lawyer, he entered politics in 1928 as a Nationalist in the Victoria parliament, was

---

I did but see her passing by, and yet I love her till I die.

ROBERT GORDON MENZIES Greetings to the Queen during her 1963 royal tour

---

attorney general in the federal parliament 1934–39, and in 1939 succeeded Joseph ◊Lyons as prime minister and leader of the United Australia Party, resigning in 1941 when colleagues were dissatisfied with his leadership of Australia's war effort. In 1949 he became prime minister of a

Liberal–Country Party coalition government, and, exploiting divisions in a divided Labor Party opposition, was re-elected in 1951, 1954, 1955, 1958, 1961, and 1963; he followed the USA's lead in committing Australia to the Vietnam War and retired soon after, in 1966. A conservative and an ardent royalist, who unsuccessfully tried to ban the Communist Party in 1950, he was viewed by critics as a 'frozen Edwardian'. They argued that he did not show enough interest in Asia, and supported the USA and white African regimes too uncritically. His defenders argued that he provided stability in domestic policy and national security.

Born in Victoria, the son of a Presbyterian storekeeper and conservative politician, he studied law at Melbourne University and became a successful barrister. He was created a KT in 1963.

(1911), he propounded the 'iron law of oligarchy', arguing that in any organization or society, even a democracy, there is a tendency towards rule by the few in the interests of the few, and that ideologies such as socialism and communism are merely propaganda to control the masses.

Originally a radical, he became a critic of socialism and Marxism, and in his last years supported the dictators Hitler and Mussolini. Michels believed that the rise of totalitarian governments – both fascist and communist – in the 1930s confirmed his analysis and proved that the masses were incapable of asserting their own interests.

Mihailovič, Draza (Dragoljub) (1893–1946)

Yugoslav soldier, leader of the guerrilla Chetniks of World War II, a nationalist resistance movement against the German occupation. His feud with Tito's communists led to the withdrawal of Allied support and that of his own exiled government from 1943. He turned for help to the Italians and Germans, and was eventually shot for treason.

FURTHER READING

Acin-Kosta, Milos *The First Guerrillas of Europe: The True Stories of General Mihailovič's Warriors* 1964

Karchmar, Lucien *Draza Mihailovič and the Cetnik Movement, 1941–42* 1987

Trew, Simon *Britain, Mihailovič, and the Chetniks, 1941–42* 1998

Vukovic-Bircanin, Momcilo *General Dragoljub-Draza Mihailovič, 1893–1946* 1976

Mikoyan, Anastas Ivanovich (1895–1978)

Armenian communist politician. He was Soviet minister of trade under Stalin and one of only nine members of the State Defence Committee during World War II (the country's supreme body at that time). He supported Nikita Khruschev after Stalin's death and was a first deputy prime minister of the USSR 1955–64 and chair of the Presidium of the Supreme Soviet (president of the USSR) 1964–65.

Mikoyan joined the Communist Party in 1915, and worked in Tiflis (modern Tbilisi, Georgia) and Baku (Azerbaijan). In 1921 he became head of the party organization in Nizhniy-Novgorod, and from 1922 to 1926 in the northern Caucasus. He was made a member of the Party's Central Committee in 1923. He supported Stalin in the inner-party struggle after Lenin's death and was made candidate member of the Politburo in 1926 and a full member in 1935. He was in charge of trade, both foreign and internal, from 1926, and of food industries from 1934 to 1938. In 1937 he was made a Soviet deputy prime minister.

After Georgi Malenkov's resignation as prime minister in 1955 Mikoyan became one of the most promi-

nent members of the 'collective leadership'. He supported Khrushchev as the latter built up his personal dominance, and was frequently used for important missions abroad. He finally retired on grounds of ill-health.

Miller, Arthur (1915–)

US dramatist. His plays deal with family relationships and contemporary American values, and include *Death of a Salesman* (1949, Pulitzer prize) and *The Crucible* (1953), based on the Salem witch trials and reflecting the communist witch-hunts of Senator Joe ◊ McCarthy. He was married 1956–61 to the film star Marilyn Monroe, for whom he wrote the film *The Misfits* (1960).

FURTHER READING

Carson, Neil *Arthur Miller* 1989

Hogan, Robert *Arthur Miller* 1967

Miller, Arthur *Timebends: A Life* 1987

Roudane, M C *Conversations with Arthur Miller* 1987

Schlueter, J and Flanagan, J K *Arthur Miller* 1987

Millerand, Alexandre (1859–1943)

French prime minister in 1920 and president 1920–24. He formed a coalition government, the Bloc National, and supported Poland against the Russian invasion in 1920. He faced opposition from the Radical socialist majority, which, under Edouard Herriot, triumphed in the 1924 elections, and shortly afterwards was forced to resign.

Millerand was born in Paris and became a journalist, later working under Georges Clemenceau on the daily paper *La Justice*. He was minister of commerce in Pierre Waldeck-Rousseau's cabinet 1899–1902, and was expelled from his party in 1904.

Millett, Kate (1934–)

US radical feminist lecturer, writer, and sculptor whose book *Sexual Politics* (1970) was a landmark in feminist thinking. She was a founding member of the National Organization of Women (NOW).

Milner, Alfred, 1st Viscount Milner (1854–1925)

British colonial administrator. As governor of Cape Colony 1897–1901, he negotiated with Paul Kruger but did little to prevent the second South African War

---

If we believe a thing to be bad, and if we have a right to prevent it, it is our duty to try to prevent it, and to damn the consequences.

ALFRED, VISCOUNT MILNER Speech Glasgow 26 November 1909 on the House of Lords and the budget

---

(Boer War); as governor of the Transvaal and Orange River colonies 1902–05 after their annexation, he reorganized their administration. In 1916 he became a member of David Lloyd George's war cabinet. He was created a KCB in 1895, Baron 1901, and Viscount in 1902.

He opposed the 'People's Budget' in 1909 and the reform of the House of Lords. As secretary for war 1918–19 he was largely responsible for creating a unified Allied command under Ferdinand Foch. He emphasized the 'organic union' of the Empire, rather than the need for independence for its members, and he negotiated with Egyptian Nationalist leaders to bring about the Anglo-Egyptian Settlement of 1922, which reduced British political control in the region but defended the Empire's strategic interests. His publications include *The Nation and the Empire* (1913).

FURTHER READING
Gollin, A M *Proconsul in Politics: A Study of Lord Milner in Opposition and Power* 1964

Miłosz, Czesław (1911–)

Polish-born US writer. He became a diplomat before defecting and becoming a US citizen. His poetry in English translation, classical in style, includes *Selected Poems* (1973) and *Bells in Winter* (1978). He was awarded the Nobel Prize for Literature in 1980.

His collection of essays *The Captive Mind* (1953) concerns the impact of communism on Polish intellectuals. Among his novels are *The Seizure of Power* (1955), *The Issa Valley* (1981), and *The Land of Ulro* (1984).

Mindszenty, József, born József Pehm (1892–1975)

Roman Catholic primate of Hungary. He was imprisoned by the communist government in 1949, but escaped in 1956 to take refuge in the US legation. The Pope persuaded him to go into exile in Austria in 1971, and he was 'retired' when Hungary's relations with the Vatican improved in 1974. His remains were returned to Hungary from Austria and reinterred at Esztergom in 1991.

FURTHER READING
Houston, Joseph J *Cardinal Mindszenty* 1979
Közi-Horvath, József *Cardinal Mindszenty: Confessor and Martyr of Our Time* 1979

◆ MILOŠEVIĆ, SLOBODAN (1941–) ◆

Serbian communist politician; party chief and president of Serbia 1986–97, and president of Yugoslavia from 1997. Milošević wielded considerable influence over the Serb-dominated Yugoslav federal army during the 1991–92 civil war and continued to back Serbian militia in Bosnia-Herzegovina 1992–94, although publicly disclaiming any intention to 'carve up' the newly independent republic. Widely believed to be the instigator of the conflict, Milošević changed tactics from 1993, adopting the public persona of peacemaker and putting pressure on his allies, the Bosnian Serbs, to accept negotiated peace terms; this contributed to the Dayton peace accord for Bosnia-Herzegovina in November 1995.

One of his first acts as president of Serbia in 1989 was to repeal the autonomy enjoyed by the province of Kosovo since 1974. In 1998 he faced international condemnation again for Serbian forces' brutal treatment of ethnic Albanians in the province. After the failure of peace talks aimed at giving Kosovo greater autonomy, NATO began air strikes against the Serbs in March 1999.

Milošević was educated at Belgrade University and rapidly rose through the ranks of the Yugoslavian Communist Party (LCY) in his home republic of Serbia, helped by his close political and business links to Ivan Stambolic, his predecessor as local party leader. He won popular support within Serbia for his assertive nationalist stance, encouraging street demonstrations in favour of the reintegration of Kosovo and Vojvodina autonomous provinces into a 'greater Serbia'. Serbia's formal annexation of Kosovo in September 1990 gave him a landslide majority in multiparty elections in December 1990, but in March 1991 there were 30,000-strong riots in Belgrade, calling for his resignation. Despite this, in December 1992 he won a 55% share of the vote in a direct presidential election, defeating the Serbian-born US businessman Milan Panic. In October 1994 Milošević imposed a border blockade of the Bosnian Serbs, as a result of which international sanctions against Yugoslavia were eased. In November 1996 Milošević's Socialist Party of Serbia (SPS) retained a majority in the Yugoslav parliament after new elections. However, in 1997 Milošević faced popular protests in Belgrade against ballot-rigging in municipal elections, which were later conceded to the opposition. Debarred by the constitution from standing for a further term as Serbian president, he became president of Yugoslavia in July 1997. His wife, Mira Markovic, is leader of the communist Yugoslav United Left party. See photograph on page 302.

FURTHER READING
Transcripts from the Interview of Mr Slobodan Milošević, President of the Republic of Serbia, Given to the Sky Network on August 7 1991 1991

Slobodan Milošević, 1997. *Rex*

Minto, Gilbert John Murray Kynynmond, 4th Earl of (1845–1914)

British colonial administrator who succeeded George Curzon as viceroy of India, 1905–10. With John Morley, secretary of state for India, he co-sponsored the Morley–Minto reforms of 1909. The reforms increased Indian representation in government at provincial level, but also created separate Muslim and Hindu electorates which, it was believed, helped the British Raj in the policy of divide and rule. He was created Earl in 1891.

Mintoff, Dom(inic) (1916–   )

Maltese Labour politician; prime minister of Malta 1955–58 and 1971–84. He negotiated the removal of British and other foreign military bases 1971–79 and made treaties with Libya.

Mitchell, Juliet (1940–   )

New-Zealand born British psychoanalyst and writer. Her article in *New Left Review* (1966) entitled 'Women: The Longest Revolution' was one of the first attempts to combine socialism and feminism, using Marxist theory to explain the reasons behind women's oppression. She published *Women's Estate* in 1971 and *Psychoanalysis and Feminism* in 1974.

Other books (with Ann Oakley) include *The Rights and Wrongs of Women* (1976) and (as editor) *What is Feminism?* (1986).

Mitchell, Keith Claudius (1946–   )

Grenadian centrist politician, prime minister from 1995. He succeeded Herbert ◊Blaize as leader of the New National Party (NNP) in 1989, but the NNP, weakened by the breakaway of the National Party

faction led by Ben Jones, met with defeat in 1991. Returned to power in 1995, Mitchell became prime minister and held the finance, trade and industry, foreign affairs, and national security and information portfolios. His government was criticized for lack of consultation and faced a united opposition from 1997.

Mitchell first entered the Grenada parliament in 1984, shortly after the US invasion of the country. Representing the newly formed centrist NNP, he served as minister of communications and public utilities until 1989.

He was born in St George's, and played cricket for Grenada in the 1960s. Having secured a PhD in mathematics and statistics, through studies at universities in the West Indies and the USA, he was appointed professor of mathematics at Howard University, in the USA, from 1977 to 1983.

Mitchell, Sonny (James FitzAllen) (1931–   )

St Vincent and the Grenadines centrist politician, prime minister 1972–74 and from 1984. Initially a St Vincent Labour Party (SVLP) representative, he became premier as an independent in 1972. He founded the centrist New Democratic Party (NDP) in 1975, and led it to power in 1984. As prime minister, he supported moves to integrate with Dominica, Grenada, and St Lucia into a Windward Islands Federation, encouraged agricultural diversification away from banana production, and promoted tourism and the 'offshore banking' sector, but was criticized for his failure to deal with money laundering and drug trafficking.

In the 1980s Mitchell opposed US attempts to increase militarization in the region. On his re-election in 1989, the NDP won all 15 elected house of assembly seats. He had planned to retire before the 1994 general election, but stayed on in the 'national interest'. He received a knighthood in 1995.

Mitchell trained and worked as an agronomist and teacher in Trinidad, Canada, and England from 1958, and then bought and managed a hotel on his home island of Bequia in 1965. He entered politics through the SVLP, representing the Grenadines constituency in the house of assembly in 1966. In the pre-independence period he served in the government of Milton ◊Cato as minister of trade, production, labour, and tourism between 1967 and 1972.

Mitchison, Naomi Mary Margaret, born Haldane (1897–1999)

Scottish writer. She wrote more than 70 books, including *The Conquered* (1923), *The Corn King and the Spring Queen* (1931), and *The Blood of the Martyrs* (1939), novels evoking ancient Greece and Rome. A socialist activist, she also campaigned for birth control.

Mitford sisters

The six daughters of British aristocrat 2nd Lord Redesdale, including: **Nancy** (1904–1973), author of the semi-autobiographical *The Pursuit of Love* (1945) and *Love in a Cold Climate* (1949), and editor and part author of the satirical essays collected in *Noblesse Oblige* (1956) elucidating 'U' (upper-class) and 'non-U' behaviour; **Diana** (1910–), who married British fascist Oswald ◊Mosley; **Unity** (1914–1948), who became an admirer of Hitler; and **Jessica** (1917–), author of the autobiographical *Hons and Rebels* (1960) and *The American Way of Death* (1963).

FURTHER READING
Acton, H *Nancy Mitford: A Memoir* 1975
Hastings, S *Nancy Mitford* 1985

Mitsotakis, Constantine (1918–)

Greek politician, leader of the conservative New Democracy Party (ND) 1984–93, prime minister 1990–93. Minister for economic coordination in 1965 (a post he held again 1978–80), he was arrested by the military junta in 1967, but escaped from house arrest and lived in exile until 1974. In 1980–81 he was foreign minister. He resigned the leadership of the ND after its 1993 election defeat; in January 1996 proposed corruption charges against him were dropped.

Mitterrand, François (1916–1996)

French socialist politician, president 1981–95. After a successful ministerial career under the Fourth Republic, holding posts in 11 governments 1947–58, Mitterrand joined the new Socialist Party (PS) in 1971, establishing it as the most popular party in France before winning two successive terms as president, 1981–88 and 1988–95. From 1982 his administrations reverted from redistributive and reflationary policies to economic orthodoxy and maintenance of the 'strong franc' (linked to the Deutschmark), despite the high levels of unemployment this entailed, and vigorously pursued further European integration.

Mitterrand studied law and politics in Paris. During World War II he came to prominence in the resistance after initially working in Marshal Philippe ◊Pétain's Vichy adminstration. In 1945 he was elected as deputy for Nièvre, as the member of a small centre-left Resistance-based party. Opposed to General Charles ◊de Gaulle's creation of the Fifth Republic in 1958, he formed a Federation of the Left and as its candidate challenged de Gaulle unsuccessfully for the presidency in 1965. In 1971, as leader of the PS, he negotiated an electoral pact and Common Programme of Government with the Communist Party, 1972–77, but again

François Mitterrand during the 1981 presidential election campaign. *Rex*

failed to win the presidency in 1974, this time against Valéry ◊Giscard d'Estaing. He was finally elected president in 1981.

His ambitious programme of social, economic, and institutional reforms was hampered by deteriorating economic conditions after 1983. When the socialists lost their majority in March 1986, he was compelled to work with the Gaullist Jacques ◊Chirac as prime minister, and grew in popularity, defeating Chirac's bid for the presidency in May 1988. In 1993 he entered a second term of 'cohabitation' with the conservative prime minister Edouard ◊Balladur. Towards the end of his presidency his failing health weakened his hold on power. Whereas he was able to enhance his reputation when 'cohabiting' with Chirac, the successful elements of Balladur's premiership contrasted with Mitterrand's waning popularity and weakened influence.

Miyamoto, Kenji (1908–)

Japanese politician. He was leader of the Communist Party from 1958 until Tetsuzo Fuwa took over in 1982. Elected to the upper house of the Diet (house of councillors) in 1977, he remained a councillor until 1989.

Miyamoto joined the underground Communist Party in 1931. Arrested in 1933, he remained in prison until 1945.

Miyazawa, Kiichi (1920–)

Japanese conservative politician, prime minister 1991–93. After holding a number of key government posts, he became leader of the ruling Liberal Democratic Party (LDP) and prime minister in November 1991. Defeated in June 1993 on a vote of confidence (triggered by demand for electoral reform), he called a general election for July. He resigned after the LDP failed to hold its majority (the party's first defeat in 38 years).

Mkapa, Benjamin William (1938–)

Tanzanian politician and diplomat, president from 1995. He became press secretary to President Julius Nyerere in 1974 and went on to hold a number of posts in government. As foreign affairs minister 1977–80, he was active in the negotiations leading to Zimbabwean independence. He was elected to the central committee of the ruling Revolutionary Party of Tanzania (CCM) in 1987, becoming its successful presidential candidate in 1995.

After founding the Tanzania News Agency in 1976, Mkapa was appointed high commissioner to Nigeria until 1977. He served as high commissioner to Canada 1982–83 and then ambassador to the USA, resuming the foreign affairs portfolio 1984–91 and winning a parliamentary seat in 1985. He won the CCM's nomination for the presidency with the support of Mwalimi Nyerere, succeeding Ali Hassan Mwinyi in the first free presidential elections.

Mkapa was born in Ndanda and educated at Makerere University College and Columbia University before joining the foreign ministry and also embarking on a career in journalism.

Mladenov, Petar (1936–)

Bulgarian Communist politician, secretary general of the Bulgarian Communist Party from November 1989, after the resignation of Todor ◊Zhivkov, until February 1990. He was elected state president in April 1990 but was replaced four months later.

Mladic, Ratko (1943–)

Bosnian Serb general, leader of the Bosnian Serb army 1992–96. His ruthless conduct in the civil war in Bosnia, including the widespread maltreatment of prisoners and the disappearance of many more, led to his being indicted for war crimes by the United Nations War Crimes Commission in 1995.

Mladic was born in Kalnovik, Herzegovina. He graduated from a military academy and joined the Yugoslav Communist Party in 1965. He started his military career as a general in the former Yugoslav Federal Army, but when Yugoslavia broke up he became one of the leaders of the Serbian population in Bosnia, and was appointed military commander of the Republika Srbska by its president Radovan ◊Karadžić

in 1992. He led the Bosnian Serb armed forces until the Dayton Agreement brought peace in 1995. In November 1996 he was dismissed as arms chief by Biljana Plavsic, president of the Bosnian Serb Republic; supporters of Mladic sought unsuccessfully to overturn the decision.

FURTHER READING
Bulatović, Ljiljana *General Mladic* 1996

Mobutu, Sese Seko Kuku Ngbeandu Wa Za Banga (1930–1997)

President of Zaire (now the Democratic Republic of Congo) 1965–97. He assumed the presidency in a coup, and created a unitary state under a centralized government. The harshness of some of his policies and charges of corruption attracted widespread international criticism. In 1991 opposition leaders forced Mobutu to agree formally to give up some of his powers, but the president continued to oppose constitutional reform initiated by his prime minister, Etienne Tshisekedi. Despite his opposition, a new transitional constitution was adopted in 1994. In October 1996 Zaire and Rwanda were on the brink of war following mass killings of Hutus by Tutsis. Mobutu was criticized by international observers for his absence abroad during the crisis (for cancer treatment in Europe), which was narrowly averted when thousands of Hutus were allowed to return to Zaire. Meanwhile, the Alliance of Democratic Forces for the Liberation of Zaire–Congo (ADFL), led by Laurent ◊Kabila, made significant advances against government forces and threatened Mobutu's regime. In May 1997, with Kabila's rebels poised to take the capital Kinshasa, government officials announced that President Mobutu was giving up his powers. Kabila claimed victory and the presidency, and renamed Zaire the Democratic Republic of Congo – the country's name from 1964 until Mobutu renamed it in 1971. Mobutu died in Rabat, Morocco, in September 1997.

Mobutu abolished secret voting in elections in 1976 in favour of a system of acclamation at mass rallies. His personal wealth is estimated at $3–4 billion, and more money was spent on the presidency than on the entire social-services budget.

Mohamed V (1909–1961)

Moroccan sultan and king 1956–61. Espousing the nationalist movement's aspirations, he was to become the symbol of resistance to French occupation. His forced exile to Madagascar in 1953 and his replacement by his brother Mulay Ben Arfa only contributed to enhancing his popularity as a leader of the struggle for independence. He returned to his country in 1955 and assumed power as first king of independent Morocco in 1956.

He succeeded the throne on his father's death in 1927. It was not until after World War II that he

President Mobutu with Chinese Foreign Affairs Minister Huang Hua. *Rex*

showed a sense of independent leadership away from French control.

Mohammad, Murtala Ramat (1938–1976)

Nigerian army officer and politician. He succeeded Gen Yakubu Gowon as head of state in July 1975, but was assassinated in February 1976 in an abortive·and irrational coup led by Lt-Col Dimka.

Mohammad was born in Kano. He joined the Nigerian army as a cadet officer in 1958 and in 1959 attended the Royal Military Academy, Sandhurst, England. He returned to Nigeria in 1961, and served with the United Nations peace-keeping force in the Congo. In 1964 he was promoted to captain and placed in charge of the army's first signal squadron in Lagos. During the Nigerian Civil War he was general officer commanding the Second Infantry Division, and was involved in the recapture of the midwest capital, Benin. He was promoted to brigadier in 1971, and in 1974 became federal commissioner for communications.

Moi, Daniel arap (1924–　)

Kenyan politician, president from 1978. Leader of the Kenya African National Union (KANU), he became minister of home affairs in 1964, vice president in 1967, and succeeded Jomo Kenyatta as president. He enjoyed the support of Western governments but was widely criticized for Kenya's poor human-rights record. His administration, first challenged by a coup attempt in 1982, became increasingly authoritarian. In 1991, in the face of widespread criticism, he promised the eventual introduction of multiparty politics. In 1992 he was elected president in the first free elections amid widespread accusations of vote rigging.

Moi was first nominated to the legislative council in 1955. In 1960 he became chair of the Kenya Africa Democratic Union (KADU) and opposition leader after independence in 1963. KADU merged with the ruling KANU party in 1964, and he was appointed vice president of the party in 1966. He became president of the country following Kenyatta's death in 1978.

Mola Vidal, Emilio (1887–1937)

Spanish general and co-leader of the military rising against the Second Republic which initiated the Civil War of 1936–39. Anti-Falangist and anti-monarchist in his sympathies, he posed a problem to General Franco in the early days of the Civil War and when he died in an aircraft crash suspicions of sabotage were voiced, but never substantiated.

Molina Barraza, Arturo Armando (1928–　)

El Salvadorean soldier and politician, member of the conservative-reformist National Conciliation Party (PCN), president 1972–77. His administration promoted agrarian reform and improvements in housing and health provision.

He was chosen as the candidate of the government-backed PCN for the 1972 presidential election. He won a plurality of the vote, defeating the left-wing mayor of San Salvador, José Napoleón ◊Duarte.

Trained at El Salvador's Military College, Molina, as a professional soldier, he became a colonel and secretary under President Fidel ◊Sánchez Hernández.

Mollet, Guy Alcide (1905–1975)

French socialist politician, postwar leader of the Section Française de l'Internationale Ouvrière (SFIO) 1946–69 and prime minister 1956–57. He launched the Anglo-French Suez expedition with British prime minister Anthony ◊Eden, and in Algeria succumbed to settler pressures to remove the liberal governor general Georges Catroux.

A supporter of the Atlantic Alliance and European integration, the class-struggle rhetoric Mollet deployed in party and electoral arenas contrasted with his opportunist policies in government. He retained the party leadership through his control of the party's large departmental federation of Pas-de-Calais, where he served as mayor of Arras and then deputy 1945–75. Mollet supported General Charles ◊de Gaulle's return to government in 1958, serving in his transitional government 1958–59.

Molotov, Vyacheslav Mikhailovich, assumed name of Vyacheslav Mikhailovich Skriabin (1890–1986)

Soviet communist politician. He was chair of the Council of People's Commissars (prime minister) 1930–41 and foreign minister 1939–49 and 1953–56. He negotiated the 1939 nonaggression treaty with Germany (the Ribbentrop–Molotov pact), and, after the German invasion in 1941, the Soviet partnership with the Allies. His postwar stance prolonged the Cold War and in 1957 he was expelled from the government for Stalinist activities.

To Soviet patriots the homeland and communism become fused in one inseparable whole.

VYACHESLAV MOLOTOV Speech to the Supreme Soviet
6 November 1939

Molyneaux, Jim (James Henry), Baron Molyneaux of Killead (1920–)

Northern Ireland Unionist politician, leader of the Official Ulster Unionist Party (the largest Northern Ireland party) 1979–95. A member of the House of Commons from 1970, he temporarily relinquished his seat 1983–85 in protest at the Anglo-Irish Agreement. He resigned as party leader in 1995 and retired from Parliament in 1997. Although a fervent supporter of the union between Britain and Northern Ireland, he was regarded as one of the more moderate Loyalists.

Molyneaux served in the Royal Air Force 1941–46. He was member of Parliament for Antrim South 1970–83 and for Lagan Valley 1983–97. He was knighted in 1996 and given a life peerage in 1997.

Momoh, Joseph Saidu (1937–)

Sierra Leone soldier and politician, president 1985–92. An army officer who became commander in 1983, with the rank of major general, he succeeded Siaka Stevens as president when he retired; Momoh was endorsed by Sierra Leone's one political party, the All-People's Congress. He dissociated himself from the policies of his predecessor, pledging to fight corruption and improve the economy. In April 1992 he fled to neighbouring Guinea after a military takeover.

Mondale, Walter Frederick (1928–)

US Democrat politician, unsuccessful presidential candidate in 1984. He was a senator 1965–77 for his home state of Minnesota, and vice president to Jimmy Carter 1977–81. After losing the 1984 presidential election to Ronald Reagan, Mondale retired from national politics to resume his law practice.

Mondlane, Eduardo (1920–1969)

Mozambican nationalist, first president of Frelimo 1962–69, the group aiming to achieve independence for Mozambique from the Portuguese. He was assassinated by unknown assailants.

As a student at Witwatersrand University in Johannesburg, South Africa, he helped to organize a Mozambican Students' Association and was deported back to Mozambique where he came to the notice of the

---

◆ MONNET, JEAN (1888–1979) ◆

French national and international economic strategist. Monnet's durable contributions were to be the economic planning machinery he established in France in 1946 and the process of European economic and political integration that he set in train, as the author of the 1950 Schuman Plan.

Rooted in the provincial France of family-owned businesses and traditional products, Monnet left school at 16 but was sent to the City of London for two years to improve his English before travelling extensively as the international salesman for his family's cognac business in Picardy. He was rejected on health grounds for military service in World War I, but his involvement in developing economic policy coordination between the Allies was to be a formative experience, as was the period he spent after the war as deputy secretary general of the League of Nations until 1923. Monnet then embarked on a career in international investment

banking. After the fall of France, he worked for the British Supply Council in Washington, DC, but joined General Charles de Gaulle in Algiers and won his support for establishing a new General Planning Commissariat after the war. Headed by Monnet, this brought together leading industrialists and civil servants to set targets for economic growth and modernization. The early success of his Monnet Plan 1946–53, backed by Marshall Funds from 1948, established a framework for 30 years of *dirigiste* industrial policy-making in France.

With the Cold War refocusing attention on Franco-German relations, Monnet drafted an innovative plan for West European states to pool their coal and iron resources and production, ceding sovereignty in these sectors to a supranational High Authority. What came to be termed 'the Monnet method' was thus launched, using a sectoral economic project as a first building block in constructing a politically unified Europe. Monnet chaired the 1951 Paris

Jean Monnet. *Rex*

Portuguese police. He continued his studies in the USA and was employed as a research officer in the United Nations (UN) Department of Trusteeship. Returning to Mozambique in 1961 he left the UN and involved himself with the incipient resistance movements which he later welded into Frelimo.

Monge Alvárez, Luis Alberto (1925–)

Costa Rican social-democratic politician, president 1982–86. He concentrated on making economies in government spending and maintaining good relations with the USA, but refused to join it in an anti-Sandinista alliance to overthrow Nicaragua's new Marxist government.

In 1951 he helped found the social-democratic National Liberation Party (PLN) and was elected to the legislative assembly in 1958, but briefly withdrew from politics in the mid-1960s as a result of concern over the PLN's rightward shift. He became PLN secretary general in 1966 and was president of the legislative assembly 1970–74, and became Costa Rica's president (at the second attempt) in 1982.

Educated at the universities of Costa Rica and Geneva, Monge began his career as a trade-union

conference at which six states, France, Belgium, Germany, the Netherlands, Luxemburg, and Italy, agreed to establish the European Coal and Steel Community (ECSC), and was appointed president of its High Authority 1952–55. Monnet persuaded French premier René Pleven to back a second proposal for a European Defence Community in 1950, but this foundered when the French parliament failed to ratify the treaty in 1954. His third proposal, for a European Atomic Energy Community, was taken up by the Belgian foreign minister Paul-Henri Spaak and adopted at the June 1955 Messina Conference of 'the Six', along with a more ambitious scheme for a Common Market. The treaties founding these two communities were signed in Rome in March 1957.

Monnet also sought to build a wider basis of support for European political union through his Action Committee for the United States of Europe, with leaders of the major parties, unions, and business organizations in these six states meeting together under his chairmanship 1955–75. He published his *Mémoires/Memoirs* in 1976.

activist during the 1940s and supported José ◊Figueres Ferrer during the 1948 civil war.

Montagu, (Montague Francis) Ashley, born Ehrenburg (1905–)

British-born US anthropologist. As a critic of theories of racial determinism, he was a forceful defender of human rights and wrote such important works as *Man's Most Dangerous Myth: The Fallacy of Race* (1942). In 1950 he helped draft the definitive UNESCO 'Statement on Race'.

Born in London, Montagu was educated at the University of London, Columbia University, and the University of Florence. He received his PhD from Columbia under Franz Boas in 1937. He became well known for popularizing social issues, such as 'psychosclerosis', the so-called hardening of the psyche, in *Growing Young* (1981).

Montes, Ismael (1861–1933)

Bolivian liberal politician and president 1904–09 and 1913–17. His first term in office was marked by administrative reform and a rise in the success of, and support for, the Liberal Party. After serving as president, Montes was active in the diplomatic service and in 1913 stood for a second term in office. In his second term, Montes instituted a major capital-investment programme to improve the nation's railway infrastructure. In 1914 a two-party system was conceived, and a new party formed – the liberal-aligned Republican Party.

Monte fought in the War of the Pacific in 1879. He served as war minister in 1900, during which time he was involved in resolving the territorial dispute with

Brazil over Acre state with the Treaty of Petrópolis of 1903. His election as president in 1904 coincided with the signing of the peace treaty that ended the War of the Pacific.

On leaving office in 1917, Montes left Bolivia for France and remained there until 1928.

Montgomery, Bernard Law, 1st Viscount Montgomery of Alamein (1887–1976)

British field marshal. In World War II he commanded the 8th Army in North Africa in the Second Battle of El Alamein in 1942. As commander of British troops in northern Europe from 1944, he received the German surrender in 1945.

At the start of World War II, Montgomery commanded part of the British Expeditionary Force in France 1939–40 and took part in the evacuation from Dunkirk. In August 1942 he took command of the 8th Army, then barring the German advance on Cairo. The victory of El Alamein in October turned the tide in North Africa; it was followed by the expulsion of Field Marshal Erwin Rommel from Egypt and rapid Allied advance into Tunisia. In February 1943 Montgomery's forces came under US general Dwight D Eisenhower's command, and they took part in the conquest of Tunisia and Sicily and the invasion of Italy. Montgomery was promoted to field marshal in 1944. In 1948 he became permanent military chair of the Commanders-in-Chief Committee for Western European defence, and 1951–58 was deputy Supreme Commander Europe. He was created 1st Viscount Montgomery of Alamein in 1946.

Moore, Mike (Michael Kenneth) (1949–   )

New Zealand Labour centre-left politician, prime minister in 1990. He was in power for only 60 days – the second shortest time in office (behind F H Dillon ◊Bell) in the 20th century – being replaced by Jim ◊Bolger, after the National Party won the October 1990 general election. Moore also led the Labour Party to defeat in the November 1993 general election and was then replaced as party leader by Helen Clark.

He worked as a social worker and in a meat-processing plant before being elected to the New Zealand parliament in 1972, at the age of 22, representing the Labour Party. In the 1980s he served in the Labour governments of David ◊Lange and Geoffrey ◊Palmer and took over as prime minister after the unpopular Palmer lost a confidence vote in September 1990.

Morgan, John Pierpont, Jr (1867–1943)

US banker and philanthropist. In World War I he organized a New York bankers' syndicate to underwrite a massive loan to the Allies. He acted for the British and French governments as agent for the purchase of supplies in the USA, and also for the US government when it entered the war in 1917. In his lifetime he gave $36 million to charitable and public institutions, including $9 million to the Metropolitan Museum of Art, New York.

Morley, John, 1st Viscount Morley of Blackburn (1838–1923)

British Liberal politician and writer. He entered Parliament in 1883, and was secretary for Ireland in 1886 and 1892–95. As secretary for India 1905–10, he prepared the way (with Viceroy Gilbert ◊Minto) for more representative government.

He was Lord President of the Council 1910–14, but resigned in protest against the declaration of war. He published lives of the philosophers Voltaire and Rousseau and the politicians Burke and Gladstone. He was knighted in 1908.

Moro, Aldo (1916–1978)

Italian Christian Democrat politician. Prime minister 1963–68 and 1974–76, he was expected to become Italy's president, but he was kidnapped and shot by Red Brigade urban guerrillas.

Morrison, Herbert Stanley, Baron Morrison of Lambeth (1888–1965)

British Labour politician. He was a founder member and later secretary of the London Labour Party 1915–45, and a member of the London County Council 1922–45. He entered Parliament in 1923, representing South Hackney 1923, 1929–31, and 1935–45, and East Lewisham 1945–59. He organized the Labour Party's general election victory in 1945. He was twice defeated in the contest for leadership of the party, once by Clement Attlee in 1932, and then by Hugh Gaitskell in 1955. A skilful organizer, he lacked the ability to unite the party.

Morrison was born in Brixton, London. He was minister of transport 1929–31, home secretary 1940–45, Lord President of the Council and leader of the House of Commons 1945–51, and foreign secretary March–October 1951, and was instrumental in Labour's postwar social revolution. He was created Baron in 1959.

FURTHER READING
Donaghue, B, and Jones, G *Herbert Morrison, Portrait of a Politician* 1973

Morrow, Dwight Whitney (1873–1931)

US diplomat and banker. He was ambassador to Mexico 1927–30, and was successful in bringing to an end the tension between Mexico and the USA. Later he was elected to the US Senate as a Republican senator for New Jersey.

Morse, Wayne Lyman (1900–1974)

US politician. He was senator for Oregon 1945–68. Regarded as a political maverick (he began as a Republican senator, was an Independent for a time, and finally became a Democrat), he was a vigorous opponent of the attacks on the left by Senator Joe ◊McCarthy in the 1950s and of US involvement in the Vietnam War in the 1960s.

Morse was born in Madison, Wisconsin, and was educated at the universities of Wisconsin, Minnesota, and Columbia, New York. He was professor of law at the University of Oregon 1931–44. He served on several federal governmental boards up to the time of his election as senator in 1945. He was defeated for re-election to the Senate 1968.

Mosca, Gaetano (1858–1941)

Italian jurist, politician, and political scientist. His best-known work *Elementi di scienza politica* (1896) (translated as *The Ruling Class* in 1939) set out his theory of the political elite. In all regimes, even nominally democratic ones, effective power was always exercised by organized minorities. Unlike his fellow elite theorist Vilfredo ◊Pareto, Mosca never had any sympathy for fascism, and retained his allegiance to the liberal conservatism of his mentor, the former prime minister the Marquis di Rudini.

Moses, Robert (1888–1981)

US public official and urban planner. As parks commissioner for New York State 1924–64 and New York City 1934–60, he oversaw the development of bridges, highways, and public facilities. Serving as New York secretary of state 1927–28, he was the unsuccessful Republican candidate for New York governor in 1934.

Born in New Haven, Connecticut, and educated at Yale and Oxford universities, Moses received his PhD from Columbia University in 1914. Known as a power broker, he held tremendous power in the USA for more than 40 years.

Mosley, Oswald (Ernald) (1896–1980)

British politician, founder of the British Union of Fascists (BUF) in 1932. He was a member of Parliament 1918–31. A Conservative MP for Harrow 1918–22, he joined the Labour Party in 1924 and represented Shetwick 1926–31. He resigned in 1931 and founded the New Party. He then led the BUF until his internment 1940–43 during World War II. In 1946 Mosley was denounced when it became known that Italy had funded his prewar efforts to establish fascism in the UK, but in 1948 he resumed fascist propaganda with his Union Movement, the revived BUF.

Before the organization of the Blackshirt movement free speech did not exist in this country.

OSWALD MOSLEY Selections from *New Statesman This England*

His first marriage was to a daughter of the Conservative politician Lord Curzon, his second to Diana

Freeman-Mitford, one of the ◊Mitford sisters.

FURTHER READING
Skidelsky, R *Oswald Mosley* 1961

Mossadeq, Muhammad (1880–1967)

Iranian prime minister 1951–53. A dispute arose with the Anglo-Iranian Oil Company when he called for the nationalization of Iran's oil production, and when he failed in his attempt to overthrow the shah he was arrested by loyalist forces with support from the USA. From 1956 he was under house arrest.

FURTHER READING
Bill, J A, and Louis, W R (eds) *Mussadiq, Iranian Nationalism and Oil* 1988
Katouzian, H (ed) *Mussadiq's Memoirs* 1988
Zabih, S *The Mussadigh Era* 1982

Moulin, Jean (1899–1943)

French Resistance leader. A government prefect at the outbreak of World War II, he joined General Charles ◊de Gaulle in London in September 1941. He returned to France and, under his code name Max, played a crucial role in securing the French internal resistance's loyalty to de Gaulle's leadership and unifying it under the National Committee of the Resistance in 1943. Captured in June 1943, and interrogated by the Gestapo officer Klaus ◊Barbie at his Lyon headquarters, Moulin died under torture. His body was reinterred in the Panthéon in 1964.

Mounier, Emmanuel (1905–1950)

French Catholic thinker and writer, leading proponent of 'personalism' in the interwar years and founder of the journal *L'Esprit*, which continues today to provide an influential forum for progressive Catholic thought and debate in France. Through personalism he sought to create a doctrinal basis for breaking the traditional identification of French Catholicism with the political right and, more especially, for challenging the ascendancy achieved by Charles ◊Maurras's reactionary and xenophobic nationalism. His ideas also had some impact on the then papal nuncio in Paris, later Pope John XXIII. A supporter of the Spanish republican cause, later imprisoned under the Vichy regime, Mounier was closely associated with the postwar worker-priest movement and the progressive Catholic organizations set up for young farmers, young workers, and students. Two decades after his premature death this younger generation's success in creating the secular, and combatively socialist, French Confederation of Democratic Labour (CFDT) out of the quiescent Catholic union movement, would serve as a lasting testimony to the influence of Mounier's ideas.

Born in Grenoble, a graduate of the Ecole Normale Supérieure in Paris, Mounier was an admirer of the earlier left-wing Catholic novelist and playwright

Charles Péguy. By the late 1920s he had come to advocate decentralized political institutions and cooperative forms of economic management.

Mountbatten, Louis Francis Albert Victor Nicholas, 1st Earl Mountbatten of Burma (1900–1979)

British admiral and administrator, a great-grandson of Queen Victoria. In World War II he became chief of combined operations in 1942 and commander in chief in southeast Asia in 1943. As last viceroy and governor general of India 1947–48, he oversaw that country's transition to independence. He was killed by an Irish Republican Army (IRA) bomb aboard his yacht at Mullaghmore, County Sligo, in the Republic of Ireland. He was created a KCVO in 1922, Viscount in 1945, and Earl in 1947.

Mowlam, Marjorie ('Mo') (1949–   )

British Labour politician, secretary of state for Northern Ireland from 1997. After her appointment, she made an immediate impact on politics in the province. Her willingness to 'take risks' to promote the peace process, including a January 1998 visit to convicted loyalist terrorists in the Maze Prison, helped bring about the 1998 Good Friday Agreement, paving the way for the election of a power-sharing Northern Ireland assembly.

After studying in the UK and the USA, she embarked on an academic career, at Newcastle University and Northern College, Barnsley, before entering the House of Commons, representing Redcar, at the 1987 general election. She joined Labour's shadow cabinet, covering Northern Ireland 1988–89, trade and industry 1989–92, the Citizen's Charter and women's affairs 1992–93, national heritage 1993–94, and Northern Ireland again 1994–97. She became a member of the Labour Party National Executive in 1995.

Following her appointment as secretary of state for Northern Ireland she initiated a non-ministerial dialogue with Sinn Féin, and took positive steps towards avoiding the clashes between Catholics and Protestants during the annual 'marching season'.

Mowlam was born in Coventry and educated at Coundon Court Comprehensive School, the University of Durham, and Iowa University, where she obtained her doctorate. She cut short a promising academic career to enter full-time politics.

Moynihan, Daniel Patrick (1927–   )

US Democrat politician and diplomat. A senator for New York from 1977, he became chair of the Senate Finance Committee in January 1993. In 1995 he led the opposition to Republican attempts to cut back on welfare spending. He concerned himself with the problem of poverty among urban black families, and was one of the authors of *The Negro Family: A Case for*

National Action (1965), which came to be known as the Moynihan Report.

Moynihan was ambassador to India 1973–75 and to the United Nations 1975–76. He served on the Senate Finance Committee from 1977. In 1996 he was critical of President Bill Clinton's abolition of automatic welfare payments to poor families.

Moynihan was born in Tulsa, Oklahoma. He embarked on an academic career before his appointment to the department of labour in 1961.

He was a member of the Joint Center for Urban Studies of the Massachusetts Institute of Technology and Harvard 1960–65 and its director 1966–69. Assistant to the president for urban affairs 1969–73, he was the architect of President Richard Nixon's family-assistance programme, which was rejected by Congress. In *Family and Nation* (1985) he lays out a taxation policy to encourage two-parent families, in an attempt to check the emergence of an underclass. His *Pandemonium: Ethnicity in International Politics* was published in 1993.

Mubarak, Hosni (1928–   )

Egyptian politician, president from 1981. Vice president to Anwar ◊Sadat from 1975, Mubarak succeeded him on his assassination. He continued to pursue Sadat's moderate policies, and significantly increased the freedom of the press and of political association, while trying to repress the growing Islamic fundamentalist movement. He was re-elected (uncontested) in 1987 and 1993. He survived an assassination attempt in 1995.

Mubarak commanded the air force 1972–75 and was responsible for the initial victories in the Egyptian campaign of 1973 against Israel. He led Egypt's opposition to Iraq's invasion of Kuwait in 1990 and played an instrumental role in arranging the Middle East peace conference in November 1991.

Mugabe, Robert (Gabriel) (1925–   )

Zimbabwean politician, prime minister from 1980 and president from 1987. He was in detention in Rhodesia for nationalist activities 1964–74, then carried on guerrilla warfare from Mozambique. As leader of the Zimbabwe African National Union (ZANU) he was in an uneasy alliance with Joshua ◊Nkomo of the Zimbabwe African People's Union (ZAPU) from 1976.

Mugabe is a member of the Shona people, and was educated at Fort Hare University, South Africa. In 1985 he postponed the introduction of a multiparty state for five years. His failure to anticipate and respond to the 1991–92 drought in southern Africa adversely affected his popularity, but he was re-elected, unchallenged, in February 1996. In May 1998 he faced student demonstrations against alleged government corruption.

Muhammed, Murtala Ramat (1938–1976)

Nigerian military ruler. He enlisted in the Nigerian army and was trained at the Sandhurst Royal Academy in the UK, later serving with the United Nations Peacekeeping Force in the Congo. One of the main leaders in Nigeria's coup of July 1966, he played an active role in the new administration under General Yakubu ◊Gowon. In 1974 he was appointed head of state following the coup against Gowon. He introduced a number of radical anti-corruption measures, drafted a new constitution, and moved the capital to Abuja. Muhammed was a popular leader and a devout Muslim. He was killed by army dissidents in 1976.

Muhoho, George Kamau (1938–   )

Kenyan theologian and administrator. He was director of the National Environment Secretariat and director of information for the United Nations Environment Programme until 1987, and was appointed minister of tourism and wildlife 1987–89 and minister of research, science, and technology 1989–93.

He attended the Morogoro Philosophical and Theological College 1957–63 and the Urbanium University in Rome in 1970.

Muir, John Ramsay Brice (1872–1941)

British historian and politician. He was a Liberal member of Parliament for Rochdale 1923–24, and chair 1931–33, then president 1933–36, of the National Liberal Federation. His chief historical work was *Short History of the British Commonwealth* (two volumes 1920–22).

Muir was educated at University College, Liverpool, and Balliol College, Oxford. He was professor of modern history at Liverpool 1906–13 and at Manchester 1914–21. He was vice president of the Liberal Party organization 1936–41.

Mukhtar, Said Omar al- (1862–1931)

Libyan resistance leader. A loyal representative of the Sanusiya order, he came to symbolize the resistance to, and the struggle against, Italian occupation. He led the insurrection in the Jabal al-Akhdar region of Cyrenaica 1922–31. He was captured and hanged in 1931 once he was cut off from his support base along the border with Egypt. His death marked the end of early Libyan resistance.

Muldoon, Robert David (1921–1992)

New Zealand National Party right-of-centre politician, prime minister 1975–84. He pursued austere economic policies such as a wage-and-price policy to control inflation, sought to introduce curbs on trade unions, was a vigorous supporter of the Western alliance, and was a proponent of reform of the international monetary system. A traditionalist and somewhat authoritarian conservative, Muldoon sought to maintain close links with the UK and the USA, gave state assistance to farmers and industrialists, and promoted traditional social values. He came into conflict with feminists, Maori-rights campaigners, and anti-nuclear campaigners, who sought to prevent US nuclear-powered and nuclear-armed ships visiting New Zealand harbours. With the economy deteriorating, he was defeated in the general election of 1984 by the Labour Party, led by David ◊Lange. He stood down as National Party leader in 1984 and was knighted, but was to remain shadow foreign affairs spokesperson.

Born in Auckland, Muldoon fought in World War II as an infantry soldier in the Pacific and Italy, and worked after the war as a cost accountant. He joined the conservative National Party in 1947 and was first elected to the house of representatives in 1960, for Tamaki district. He served as finance minister in the National Party government of Keith ◊Holyoake 1967–72. In 1974 he became leader of the National Party, replacing John ◊Marshall, who had been criticized for being insufficiently aggressive in opposition. Muldoon led the party to a decisive electoral victory in 1975 and was re-elected, with smaller majorities, in 1978 and 1981.

Müller, Hermann (1876–1931)

German Socialist politician, chancellor for a few months in 1920 and again 1928–30, when he formed a Grand Coalition. He was previously foreign minister in the cabinet of Gustav Bauer in 1919 and signed the Treaty of Versailles at the end of World War I.

Mulroney, Brian (1939–   )

Canadian politician, Progressive Conservative Party leader 1983–93, prime minister 1984–93. He achieved a landslide victory in the 1984 election, and won the 1988 election on a platform of free trade with the USA, but with a reduced majority. Opposition within Canada to the 1987 Meech Lake Agreement, a prerequisite to signing the 1982 Constitution, continued to plague Mulroney in his second term. A revised reform package in October 1992 failed to gain voters' approval, and in February 1993 he was forced to resign the leadership of the Conservative Party, though he remained prime minister until Kim Campbell was appointed his successor in June.

Muluzi, Bakili (1943–   )

Malawi politician, president from 1994. He formed the United Democratic Front (UDF) in 1992 when President Hastings ◊Banda agreed to end one-party rule, and went on to win almost half of the presidential votes. After taking office, he applied his business experience to the task of liberalizing trade and reviving the economy.

Born in Machinga, southern Malawi, he used his entrepreneurial skills to become a wealthy businessman. Entering politics, he became close to President Banda and served in his government as well as being secretary general of the ruling Malawi Congress Party (MCP). In 1982 a rift developed when he was accused of stealing party funds and replaced as secretary general. He then joined the underground opposition and when, in 1992, the president conceded to demands for an end to one-party rule, Muluzi formed the UDF to fight the impending presidential and assembly elections. In May 1994 the UDF won 84 of the 175 assembly seats and Muluzi took 47% of the votes for the presidency.

Banda accepted that his rival was a 'clear winner' and promised to work with him in 'building a better democratic Malawi'.

Murayama, Tomiichi (1924–)

Japanese trade unionist and politician, leader of the Social Democratic Party (SDPJ) 1993–96, prime minister 1994–96. At the age of 70, Murayama, who had held no previous political office, became Japan's first socialist prime minister for more than 40 years. His emergence as a major figure followed months of virtual chaos in Japanese politics, during which two prime ministers resigned. Despite losses for the SDPJ in upper-house elections in 1995, his administration survived until January 1996; he resigned from the SDPJ leadership in September 1996.

A student of economics, Murayama joined the SDPJ immediately on graduating. In September 1993 he succeeded Sadao Yamahana as leader of the SDPJ. In April 1994 Premier Morohiro Hosokawa resigned, charged with financial misconduct, and was succeeded by Tsutomu Hata, heading a seven-party coalition backed by the SDPJ. Murayama's withdrawal of his party's support, which occurred within hours of the new government taking office, forced Hata's eventual resignation. Murayama succeeded him in June.

Murdani or Moerdioni, Leonardus Benjamin ('Benny') (1932–)

Indonesian soldier and politician, head of the Centre for Strategic and International Studies (CSIS), the intelligence branch of the Indonesia Armed Forces (ABRI).

Murdani was a hero in the war for independence and led the invasions of Irian Jaya in 1962 and East Timor in August 1975. He was commander of ABRI 1983–88 and defence minister 1988–96. As head of ABRI, Murdani – a Catholic – was also responsible for the wave of Muslim unrest that spread throughout Indonesia in 1984 after soldiers opened fire on a crowd of Muslim demonstrators near Jakarta.

Murdoch, (Keith) Rupert (1931–)

Australian-born US media magnate with worldwide interests. His UK newspapers, generally right-wing,

include the *Sun*, the *News of the World*, and *The Times*; in the USA, he has a 50% share of 20th Century Fox, six Metromedia TV stations, and newspaper and magazine publishing companies. He purchased a 50% stake in a Hungarian tabloid, *Reform*, in 1989.

His newspapers (which also include *The Sunday Times*) and 50% of Sky Television, the UK's first satellite television service, are controlled by News International, a wholly owned subsidiary of the Australian-based News Corporation. In November 1990 Sky Television and its rival company British Satellite Broadcasting merged to form British Sky Broadcasting (BSkyB). Over 70% of newspapers sold in Australia are controlled by Murdoch.

FURTHER READING
Kiernan, Thomas *Citizen Murdoch* 1986
Leapman, Michael *Barefaced Cheek: The Apotheosis of Rupert Murdoch* 1984
Munster, George *Rupert Murdoch: A Paper Prince* 1985
Regan, Simon *Murdoch* 1976
Shawcross, William *Rupert Murdoch: Ringmaster of the Information Circus* 1992

Murray, (John) Hubert (Plunkett) (1861–1940)

Australian administrator in Papua New Guinea, lieutenant governor 1908–40.

Educated at Sydney University and Oxford University, England, Murray trained as a barrister in London before returning to Australia in the late 1880s. During the 1890s he worked as a crown prosecutor and fought in the Boer War. He became chief judicial officer in New Guinea in 1904 and first lieutenant governor in 1908, when New Guinea was renamed Papua and possession transferred from the UK to Australia. He remained governor until his death. Murray was popular among Papuans for his respect of local traditions, but had been, in the main, frustrated in his aim of developing Papua by European enterprise. He was created a KCMG in 1925.

FURTHER READING
Murray, J H P *Papua of Today* 1925

Murray, Archibald James (1860–1945)

British general. At the start of World War I, he went to France as chief of staff but returned to the UK in October 1915 to become chief of the imperial general staff. He was appointed to command the Mediterranean Expeditionary Force and went to Egypt where he organized the country's defences. He led the British advance into Palestine but failed.

He returned to the UK in 1917 to take over the prestigious Aldershot command, which he retained until 1919.

Murray, Philip (1886–1952)

Scottish-born labour leader. Although he was a strong proponent of labour's cooperation with the govern-

Benito Mussolini, c. 1944. AKG London

ment during World War II and the Korean War, he never abandoned the struggle to improve the situation of labourers. His tact and personal skills kept the Congress of Industrial Organizations (CIO) together during the difficult war years.

Murray was born in New Glasgow, Scotland. A coal miner from the age of 10, he emigrated to the USA in 1902. He held numerous offices within the United Mine Workers Union, climaxing with that of vice president 1920–42. He and John L ◊Lewis founded the CIO in 1935. He was president of the Steel Workers Organizing Committee in 1936 and succeeded Lewis as president of the CIO 1940–52.

Murtopo or *Moertupo*, Ali (died 1994)

Indonesian soldier and politician, a close aide of President Thojib ◊Suharto. During the 1960s he headed OPSUS, Indonesia's intelligence agency. Subsequently he ran the political side of Indonesia's campaign against West Irian (now Irian Jaya) and East Timor. He was also one of the architects of the Association of South East Asian Nations (ASEAN).

Museveni, Yoweri Kaguta (1945–)

Ugandan general and politician, president from 1986. He led the opposition to Idi Amin's regime 1971–78, and became minister of defence 1979–80. Unhappy with Milton Obote's autocratic leadership, he formed the National Resistance Army (NRA). When Obote was ousted in a coup in 1985, Museveni entered into a brief power-sharing agreement with his successor, Tito Okello, before taking over as president. Museveni led a broad-based coalition government, and in 1993 reinstated the country's four tribal monarchies.

Until Amin's removal Museveni led the anti-Amin Front for National Salvation, and he supported the invasion of Uganda by the Tanzanian army in 1979. In the 1980 elections he led the Uganda Patriotic Movement and subsequently the NRA, which helped to remove Obote from power.

Museveni was educated in Uganda and at the University of Dar es Salaam, Tanzania.

Muskie, Edmund S(ixtus) (1914–1996)

US Democrat politician. A moderate by ideology and nature, he was a senator from Maine 1959–81 and secretary of state 1980–81. As a senator he concentrated on the environment, specializing in legislation on clean air and water. In the 1968 presidential election he was Hubert Humphrey's vice-presidential candidate. In 1972 he failed in his bid to win the Democratic nomination for president. He became a member of the US Supreme Court in 1981.

Muskie was born in Rumford, Maine, and practised as a lawyer. He entered the state legislature in 1947, and was governor of Maine 1955–59.

Mutesa II, Edward Frederick William Wulugembe Mutebi (1924–1969)

Ugandan ruler, president 1963–66. He became *kabaka* (king) of Buganda in 1939 and was crowned in 1942. In a dispute with the British government he was deposed in 1953, but reinstated two years later. In 1963 he became commander in chief and president of Uganda when the country became a republic. He was forcibly replaced by Milton Obote in February 1966 and escaped to exile in England.

Muzorewa, Abel (Tendekayi) (1925–)

Zimbabwean politician and Methodist bishop. He was president of the African National Council 1971–85 and prime minister of Rhodesia/Zimbabwe 1979–80. He was detained for a year 1983–84. Muzorewa was leader of the minority United Africa National Council, which merged with the Zimbabwe Unity Movement (ZUM) in 1994. He pulled out of the 1996 presidential election contest at the last minute, claiming the electoral process was unfairly tilted in President Robert Mugabe's favour.

Muzorewa was educated at Methodist colleges in Rhodesia and Nashville, Tennessee, USA.

Mwinyi, Ali Hassan (1925–)

Tanzanian socialist politician, succeeding Julius Nyerere as president 1985–95. He began a revival of private

◆ MUSSOLINI, BENITO AMILCARE ANDREA (1883–1945) ◆

Italian dictator 1925–43. As founder of the Fascist movement in 1919 and prime minister from 1922, he became known as *Il Duce* ('the leader'). He invaded Ethiopia 1935–36, intervened in the Spanish Civil War 1936–39 in support of General Francisco Franco, and conquered Albania in 1939. In June 1940 Italy entered World War II supporting Adolf Hitler. Forced by military and domestic setbacks to resign in 1943, Mussolini established a breakaway government in northern Italy 1944–45, but was killed trying to flee the country.

Mussolini was born in the Romagna, the son of a blacksmith, and worked in early life as a teacher and journalist. He became active in the socialist movement, notably as editor of the party newspaper *Avanti* 1912–14. He was expelled in 1914 for advocating Italian intervention in World War I. He served in the army 1915–17, and in 1919 founded the Fascist movement, whose programme combined violent nationalism with demagogic republican and anticapitalist slogans, and launched a campaign of terrorism against the socialists. Though anti-capitalist in origin, the movement was backed by agrarian and industrial elites in the context of postwar popular unrest. In October 1922 Mussolini came to power by semi-constitutional means as prime minister at the head of a coalition government. In 1925 he assumed dictatorial powers, and in 1926 all opposition parties were banned. During the years that followed, the political, legal, and education systems were remodelled on fascist lines. Fascism prefigured other 'totalitarian' regimes, in that it aspired to be an all-embracing ideology, but Mussolini faced constraints on his power – from monarch, church, and industrial elites – which had no real parallel in Hitler's Germany.

Mussolini's Blackshirt followers were the forerunners of Hitler's Brownshirts, and his career of conquest drew him into close cooperation with Nazi Germany. Italy and Germany formed the Axis alliance in 1936. During World War II Italian defeats in North Africa and Greece, the Allied invasion of Sicily, and discontent at home destroyed Mussolini's prestige, and in July 1943 he was compelled to resign by his own Fascist Grand Council. He was released from prison by German parachutists in September 1943 and set up a 'Republican Fascist' government in northern Italy. In April 1945 he and his mistress, Clara Petacci, were captured by partisans at Lake Como while heading for the Swiss border, and shot. Their bodies were taken to Milan and hung upside down in a public square. See photograph on page 313.

FURTHER READING
Collier, Richard *Duce!* 1971
Fermin, Laura *Mussolini* 1961
Kirkpatrick, I *Mussolini: A Study in Power* 1964
Smith, Denis M *Mussolini* 1981

enterprise and control of state involvement and spending, and also instituted a multiparty political system in 1995. However, in October he lost the first free presidential elections, and was succeeded by Benjamin Mkapa.

Educated in Zanzibar and in the UK, Mwinyi qualified as a schoolteacher and later joined the civil service. He entered the Tanzanian cabinet in 1970 as minister of state, resigning in 1977 after a political scandal. After rejoining the cabinet in 1982, he was appointed vice president in 1984. He was confirmed as president after Nyerere resigned in 1985.

Nader, Ralph (1934–   )

US lawyer and consumer advocate. Called the 'scourge of corporate morality', he led many major consumer campaigns. His book *Unsafe at Any Speed* (1965) led to US car-safety legislation. In 1996 he was nominated for president of the Green Party at the organization's first-ever political convention in the USA.

Nadir Shah, (Khan) Mohammed (c. 1880–1933)

King of Afghanistan 1929–33. He played a key role in the 1919 Afghan War, but was subsequently forced into exile in France. He returned to Kabul in 1929 to seize the throne and embarked on an ambitious modernization programme. This alienated the Muslim clergy and in 1933 he was assassinated by fundamentalists. His successor as king was his son ◊Zahir Shah.

Nagy, Imre (1895–1958)

Hungarian politician, prime minister 1953–55 and in 1956. He led the Hungarian revolt against Soviet domination in 1956, for which he was executed.

Nagy, an Austro-Hungarian prisoner of war in Siberia during World War I, became a Soviet citizen after the Russian Revolution, and lived in the USSR 1930–44. In 1953, after Stalin's death, he became prime minister, introducing liberal measures such as encouraging the production of consumer goods, but was dismissed in 1955 by hardline Stalinist premier Matyas Rákosi. Reappointed in October 1956 during the Hungarian uprising, he began taking liberalization further than the Soviets wanted; for example, announcing Hungarian withdrawal from the Warsaw Pact. Soviet troops entered Budapest, and Nagy was dismissed in November 1956. He was captured by the KGB and shot. In 1989 the Hungarian Supreme Court recognized his leadership of a legitimate government and quashed his conviction for treachery.

FURTHER READING

Dornbach, Alajos (ed) *The Secret Trial of Imre Nagy* 1994

Nahas, Mustafa al- (1897–1965)

Egyptian nationalist and politician, leader of the Wafd party. He was instrumental in the process leading to the establishment of the Arab League, one of his major achievements. The military failure in 1948 and the subsequent burning of Cairo in 1952 brought discredit to the whole political establishment, including the Wafd leaders. The 1952 military coup ended his political career.

A close collaborator with Saad Zaghlul, he succeeded him as leader of the Wafd party 1927–52. He led the negotiations on the Anglo-Egyptian treaty in 1936 and favoured cooperation with the British while being almost constantly in struggle with the palace.

Nahayan, Sheikh Sultan bin Zayed al- (1918–   )

Emir of Abu Dhabi from 1969, when he deposed his brother, Sheik Shakhbut. He was elected president of the supreme council of the United Arab Emirates (UAE) in 1971. In 1991 he was implicated, through his majority ownership, in the international financial scandals associated with the Bank of Commerce and Credit International (BCCI), and in 1994 approved a payment by Abu Dhabi of $1.8 billion to BCCI creditors.

Before 1969 Sheik Nahayan was governor of the eastern province of Abu Dhabi, one of seven Trucial States in the Persian Gulf and Gulf of Oman, then under British protection. An absolute ruler, he was unanimously re-elected emir in 1986 by other UAE sheiks, among whom he enjoyed considerable popularity.

Naidu, Sarojini, born Chattopadhyay, known as *the Nightingale of India* (1879–1949)

Indian feminist and poet. She published three volumes of lyric verse: *The Golden Threshold* (1905), *The Bird of Time* (1912), and *The Broken Wing* (1915). She organized flood relief in Hyderabad in 1908 and lectured and campaigned on feminist issues, such as the abolition of purdah. Associated with Mahatma Gandhi, she was the first Indian woman to be president of the India National Congress in 1925. In 1947 she was appointed governor of United Provinces (Uttar Pradesh).

Born in Hyderabad, she was educated at Madras, India, and London and Cambridge, England. She was imprisoned several times for civil disobedience, and took part in the negotiations leading to independence.

Najibullah, Ahmadzai (1947–1996)

Afghan communist politician, leader of the People's Democratic Party of Afghanistan (PDPA) from 1986, and state president 1986–92. Although his government initially survived the withdrawal of Soviet troops in February 1989, continuing pressure from the Mujaheddin forces resulted in his eventual overthrow. He was executed in September 1996 by the Talibaan (Islamic student army), who had seized control of most of Afghanistan.

A Pathan, Najibullah joined the communist PDPA in 1965, allying with its gradualist Parcham (banner) faction, and was twice imprisoned for anti-government political activities during the 1960s and 1970s. After the Soviet invasion in December 1979, Najibullah became head of the KHAD secret police and entered the PDPA Politburo in 1981. He replaced Babrak Karmal as leader of the PDPA, and thus the nation, in May 1986. His attempts to broaden the support of the PDPA regime had little success, and his hold on power became imperilled in 1989 following the withdrawal of the Soviet military forces. The Mujaheddin continued to demand his resignation and resisted any settlement under his regime. In the spring of 1992 he was captured while attempting to flee the country and placed under United Nations protection, pending trial by an Islamic court. In September 1996 he was executed, with his brother, by the Talibaan government. His body was strung up for public display.

Nakamura, Kuniwo (1943–)

Paluan politician, president from 1992. He became vice president of Palau in 1989, and was faced with a crisis caused by an intractable anti-nuclear clause in the constitution that had prevented Palau moving from the status of a US trust territory to independence, within a Compact of Free Association that guaranteed US financial aid. The solution he recommended was to lower the threshold needed to change the constitution by referendum. In November 1992 Nakamura was narrowly elected president, with 50.7% of the vote, and in October 1994 independence was achieved. He was re-elected in November 1996 with an increased majority, benefiting from an economic upturn resulting from growth in the tourist industry and US aid.

Born in Peleliu state, Nakamura studied economics and business administration at the University of Hawaii and later worked as a teacher and economics adviser to the US trust territory administration of Palau. He entered politics in 1975, being elected to the Congress of Micronesia, and from the late 1970s sat in the Palau and Koror state legislatures.

Nakasone, Yasuhiro (1917–)

Japanese conservative politician, leader of the Liberal Democratic Party (LDP) and prime minister 1982–87. He increased military spending and Japanese participation in international affairs, with closer ties to the USA. He was forced to resign his party post in May 1989 as a result of having profited from insider trading in the Recruit scandal. After serving a two-year period of atonement, he rejoined the LDP in April 1991.

Nakasone was educated at Tokyo University. He held ministerial posts from 1967 and established his own faction within the conservative LDP. In 1982 he was elected president of the LDP and prime minister. He encouraged a less paternalistic approach to economic management. Although embarrassed by the conviction of one of his supporters in the 1983 Lockheed corruption scandal, he was re-elected in 1986 by a landslide.

Namaliu, Rabbie Langanai (1947–)

Papua New Guinea centre-left politician, prime minister 1988–92. He was a founder member of the centre-left Pangu Pati (PP; Papua New Guinea Party) in 1967 and worked as an adviser to Chief Minister Michael ◊ Somare 1974–75. His government introduced IMF-backed austerity measures and, facing growing violence, reintroduced the death penalty. He also used force, initially, to deal with an escalating secessionist conflict on mineral-rich Bougainville island, before seeking, through his foreign minister Michael Somare, a negotiated solution. After the June 1992 general election, Namaliu was replaced as prime minister by Paias ◊ Wingti.

He stepped down as PP leader for family reasons, but remained politically active. From 1994 he was speaker of the national parliament and during 1997 he served as senior minister of state in the coalition government led by Bill ◊ Skate of the People's National Congress (PNC).

Born in Kokopo, East New Britain District, Namaliu studied history at the University of Papua New Guinea and Victoria University, in Canada, before becoming a lecturer in history. After being elected to the house of assembly in 1982, he served under Somare as foreign affairs and trade minister 1982–84 and industry minister 1984–85. He replaced Somare as PP leader in May 1988 and two months later became prime minister, after defeating Paias Wingti on a vote of no confidence.

Namboodiripad, Elamkulam Manakkal Sankaran (EMS) (1909–1998)

Indian politician, leader of the Communist Party of India-Marxist (CPM) 1978–92. In 1934 he helped found the Congress Socialist Party (CSP). When it became the Communist Party of India in 1940 he remained a member of its politburo until it split in 1964. Namboodiripad headed the first communist government ever elected in Asia when he was elected chief minister of Kerala in 1957. He became chief minister a second time 1967–69, leading a seven-party coalition headed by the CPM. In his later years he was a columnist for the Communist Party of India-Marxist weekly *Deshabhimani*.

Nano, Fatos Thanas (1952–)

Albanian politician, prime minister 1991–92 and 1997–98. His political and economic reforms as Albania's last communist-era prime minister came too late to prevent the communists' overthrow in December 1991 by a pro-democracy movement spearheaded by the right-of-centre Democratic Party (DP). Imprisoned in April 1994 on politically motivated corruption charges, he was released in March 1997 and officially pardoned. Four months later, after his Socialist Party had secured electoral victory, he became prime minister again. Taking charge of a country devastated by recent civil strife, he pledged to restore 'stability and normality', but exerted weak authority in the DP-leaning north. In September 1998 Nano accused former president Sali Berisha of trying to form a coup. Civil unrest followed and Nano was forced to resign. He was replaced by 30-year-old Pandeli Majko.

Born in Tirana and educated at Tirana University, he was founder and chair of the Socialist Party of Albania.

Nansen, Fridtjof (1861–1930)

Norwegian explorer and scientist. Born in Store-Froen in Norway, he was educated at Christiania University (now Oslo University) and in Naples, Italy, and led important Arctic expeditions. He became high commissioner of the League of Nations 1921–30 and was particularly concerned with the treatment of refugees. He was responsible for the creation of the so-called Nansen passport, a travel document issued to stateless persons. He won the Nobel Peace Prize in 1922.

Naoroji, Dadabhai (1825–1917)

Indian-born British politician and Indian nationalist. A founder member of the Indian National Congress, he served as its president in 1886, 1893, and 1906. He left India in 1886 to seek a seat in Parliament, which he achieved as Liberal member for Finsbury Central in 1892, the first Indian British MP. Naoroji argued that high taxes and other charges were draining India's wealth and that India's poverty was caused by British exploitation of its resources.

A Parsee, he was a teacher of mathematics in Bombay prior to leaving for the UK.

Narayan, Jaya Prakash (1902–1979)

Indian politician. A veteran socialist, he was an associate of Vinobha Bham in the Bhoodan movement for rural reforms that took place during the last years of British rule. He was prominent in the protest movement against Indira Gandhi's emergency regime 1975–77, and acted as umpire in the Janata party leadership contest that followed Indira Gandhi's defeat in 1977.

Narayanan, Kocheril Raman (1920–)

Indian politician and public servant, president from 1997. A *dalit* ('untouchable') from the southern state of Kerala, after a career chiefly as a diplomat, he became vice president in 1992 and in July 1997 was indirectly elected, with cross-party support, as the country's first ever *dalit* president.

Narayanan was educated in India and England, and joined the Indian Foreign Service in 1949. He worked in Myanmar, Japan, Australia, and the UK, and was appointed ambassador to Thailand 1967–69, Turkey 1973–75, China 1976–78, and the USA 1980–84. After being elected in 1984 to the Lok Sabha, the lower house of parliament, as Kerala constituency representative, he held ministerial positions 1985–88, including minister of state for external affairs and minister of science and technology during the administration of Prime Minister Rajiv Gandhi.

Nash, Walter (1882–1968)

New Zealand Labour centre-left politician, prime minister 1957–60. He became Labour Party leader in 1950, succeeding Peter ◊Fraser, when the party was in opposition. He led Labour to a narrow victory, by one seat, in the 1957 general election to become prime minister. A moderate Christian Socialist, his premiership marked a period of consolidation rather than innovation. Although Labour was defeated in the 1960 general election, Nash remained the party's leader until 1963.

Born in Kidderminster, England, he emigrated to New Zealand in 1909. He was elected to parliament in 1929 and held ministerial posts 1935–49, including finance minister, in the Labour governments of Michael ◊Savage and Peter Fraser. During World War II, he was deputy prime minister and led a special mission to the USA 1942–44. He was created a GCMG in 1965.

FURTHER READING
Nash, Walter *New Zealand: A Working Democracy* 1943

Nasrin, Taslima (1962–)

Bangladeshi writer and feminist, in exile from 1994. Accused of blasphemy, and charged with insulting religious sentiments, she was subjected to death threats and mass demonstrations after the publication in 1993 of her novel *Lajja/Shame*, dealing with Muslim–Hindu conflict. In 1993–94 fatwa calls for her death were issued, and a price was put on her head. She has also criticized Shari'a law.

Born in Myrmensingh, she trained as an anaesthetist, and began writing a syndicated newspaper column in 1990 about religious intolerance and the oppression of women. She has also published several volumes of poetry.

Nasser, Gamal Abdel (1918–1970)

Egyptian politician, prime minister 1954–56, and from 1956 president of Egypt (officially the United Arab Republic 1958–71). In 1952 he was the driving power behind the coup led by Mohammed Neguib, which ended the monarchy. His nationalization of the Suez Canal in 1956 led to an Anglo-French invasion and the Suez Crisis, and his ambitions for an Egyptian-led union of Arab states led to disquiet in the Middle East (and in the West). Nasser was also an early and influential leader of the nonaligned movement.

Nasser entered the army from Cairo Military Academy, and was wounded in the Palestine War of 1948–49. Initially unpopular after the 1952 coup, he took advantage of demands for change by initiating land reform and depoliticizing the army. His position was secured by an unsuccessful assassination attempt in 1954 and his handling of the Suez Crisis in 1956.

Nasution, A(bdul) H(aris) (1918–)

Indonesian army general. In 1959 he became Indonesia's minister of defence. After a failed kidnap and assassination attempt in September 1965 he led attacks against members of the Indonesian Communist Party (PKI) in which nearly 300,000 were killed.

Nasution led guerrilla actions against the Dutch in Java during Indonesia's struggle for independence 1948–49. In March 1957 he convinced President Achmed ◊Sukarno to declare martial law, ending parliamentary democracy in Indonesia. In December 1957 he ordered the army to take control of enterprises seized from the Dutch for their failure to negotiate a settlement over West Irian (now Irian Jaya), thereby consolidating political, military, administrative, and economic power in army hands.

Natsir, Mohammad (1908–1993)

Indonesian politician, a moderate nationalist; prime minister 1950–51. A prominent cabinet minister involved in negotiations with the Dutch for independence after World War II, Natsir became the prime minister of the unitary Republic of Indonesia. His failure to include the Partai Nasional Indonesia (PNI), the second most important party in the country, in his cabinet, forced him to resign after seven months. He subsequently became chair of the Masjumi, a major political party and vehicle for modern Islamic ideas, and in 1958 vice president of the PRRI, the Revolutionary Government of the Republic of Indonesia opposed to Achmed ◊Sukarno.

Naumann, Friedrich (1860–1919)

German politician and writer. He was a founding member of the Democratic party and its first chair in 1919. His influential book *Mitteleuropa/Central Europe* (1915) urged a union of Germany and Austria-Hungary and a new, more humane and democratic organization of industry after World War I.

Naumann was born in Stormthal near Leipzig. A Lutheran pastor, he soon became active in the Christian-Social movement and worked to broaden the base of Wilhelmine Germany through cooperation between the workers and the established classes. In 1896 he founded a National-Social Union (which had nothing to do with the later Nazis). He was a member of the Reichstag (parliament) from 1907, sitting for the Progressive party.

Nawaz Sharif, Mohammed (1949–)

Pakistani politician, prime minister 1990–93 and from 1997. Formerly an industrialist, he moved into politics, with the right-of-centre Pakistan Muslim League (PML), and in 1985 became chief minister in his native Punjab. In 1990 he became Pakistan's first prime minister not be drawn from the country's landholding elite. He embarked on a free-market economic reform programme, but was removed by the president in April 1993 on the grounds of 'maladministration, nepotism and corruption'. After his great rival Benazir ◊Bhutto of the centre-left Pakistan People's Party (PPP) was removed on similar grounds, he returned to power in February 1997, after a landslide electoral victory.

His first political post was as finance minister in Punjab 1981–85, during the military dictatorship of General Zia ul Haq. During his second term as prime minister he remained in dispute with the judiciary over powers to choose supreme court judges, and launched a corruption investigation against Benazir Bhutto.

In May 1998 he responded to India's testings of nuclear weapons by sanctioning Pakistan's first ever tests, despite international condemnation.

Nazarbayev, Nursultan (1940–)

Kazakh politician, president of Kazakhstan from 1990. In the Soviet period he was prime minister of the republic 1984–89 and leader of the Kazakh Communist Party 1989–91, which established itself as the independent Socialist Party of Kazakhstan in September 1991. He was an advocate of free-market policies, and yet also enjoyed the support of the environmentalist lobby.

FURTHER READING
Kumar, Narendra *President Nazarbaev of Kazakhstan: A Political Biography* 1997

Nazimuddin, Khwaja (1894–1964)

Second governor general of Pakistan 1948–51, successor to Muhammad Ali Jinnah. He resigned in 1951 in order to become prime minister after the assassination of Nawabzada Liaquat Ali Khan. His advocacy of the Urdu language, though he was himself a Bengali, and his pro-religious role in the anti-Ahmadi riots in 1952 forced his resignation in 1953.

He was previously an influential collaborator with Jinnah in the Muslim League, where he was minister of education 1929–34, home minister 1937–41, chief minister 1943–45 in the then Bengal government, and, after the creation of Pakistan, premier of East Bengal.

Neave, Airey Middleton Sheffield (1916–1979)

British intelligence officer and Conservative member of Parliament 1953–79. He was a close adviser to Conservative Party leader (later prime minister) Margaret Thatcher. During World War II he escaped from Colditz, a German high-security prison camp. As shadow undersecretary of state for Northern Ireland from 1975, he became a target for extremist groups and was assassinated by an Irish terrorist bomb.

Neguib, Mohammed (1901–1984)

Egyptian army general and politician. He instigated and carried out along with other army officers the coup that ended King Farouk's reign in 1952 and abolished the monarchical system in 1953. Prime minister and then president of the newly emerged republic, he was deposed and succeeded by Gamal Abdel ◊Nasser.

Nehru, Jawaharlal (1889–1964)

Indian nationalist politician, prime minister 1947–64. Before the partition (the division of British India into India and Pakistan), he led the socialist wing of the nationalist Congress Party, and was second in influence only to Mahatma Gandhi. He was imprisoned nine times by the British 1921–45 for political activities. As prime minister from the creation of the dominion (later republic) of India in August 1947, he originated the idea of nonalignment (neutrality towards major powers). His daughter was Prime Minister Indira ◊Gandhi. His sister, Vijaya Lakshmi ◊Pandit, was the UN General Assembly's first female president 1953–54.

FURTHER READING

Ali, Tariq Nehru and the Gandhis 1985
Gopal, Sarvepalli Jawaharlal Nehru: A Biography 1975
Gorev, A Jawaharlal Nehru 1982
Nanda, B The Nehrus 1962
Walpert, Stanley Nehru: A Tryst With Destiny 1996

Nehru, Motilal (1861–1931)

Indian nationalist leader, lawyer, and journalist. He became a follower of Mahatma Gandhi in 1919, founded Allahabad's Independent newspaper, and became the first president of the reconstructed Indian National Congress. In the 1920s he co-headed the Swarajiya party (with Chitta Ranjan ◊Das) in which members of the Congress entered the legislatures, and wrote a report as a basis for Indian constitutional development and the resolution of political differences between Hindus and Muslims. The report was not,

however, acceptable to members of the All-India Muslim League, led by Muhammad Ali Jinnah.

He was the father of Jawaharlal ◊Nehru.

Nena, Jacob (1941–)

Micronesian politician, president from 1997. In May 1991 he became vice president of the Federated States of Micronesia (FSM) and took over as acting president in November 1996, after President Bailey ◊Olter had suffered a stroke. He formally became president in May 1997.

Born in Lelu, in Kosrae state, Nena studied public administration and business management at the University of Hawaii. His early political career was in his home state of Kosrae, of which he became governor on independence in 1979.

Nenni, Pietro (1891–1980)

Italian Socialist politician. He was secretary general of the Italian Socialist party 1944–63 and in 1947 became leader of the main body of the party which refused to participate in the Christian Democrat prime minister Alcide De Gasperi's government. After the Soviet invasion of Hungary in 1956, Nenni broke with the Italian Communists and in 1964 supported the government formed by Aldo Moro. This led to a further split within the party, and in the elections of 1968 Nenni's faction lost votes heavily.

Neruda, Pablo, pen name of Neftalí Ricardo Reyes y Basoalto (1904–1973)

Chilean poet and diplomat. His work includes lyrics and the epic poem of the American continent Canto General (1950). He was awarded the 1971 Nobel Prize for Literature. He served as consul and ambassador to many countries during the period 1927–44.

After World War II Neruda entered political life in Chile as a communist, and was a senator 1945–48. He went into exile in 1948 but returned in 1952; he later became ambassador to France 1971–72.

FURTHER READING

Bizzarro, Salvatore) Pablo Neruda: All Poets the Poet 1979
Bloom, Harold (ed) Pablo Neruda 1989
Costa, Rene de The Poetry of Pablo Neruda 1979
Durán, Manuel Earth Tones: the Poetry of Pablo Neruda 1981

Netanyahu, Binjamin ('Bibi') (1949–)

Israeli right-wing politician and diplomat, leader of the Likud (Consolidation Party) from 1993, and prime minister from 1996. A hard-line politician, he succeeded Yitzak ◊Shamir to the Likud leadership in March 1993 following the party's 1992 electoral defeat. He is Israel's first directly elected prime minister.

He served in the Israeli embassy in Washington, DC, 1982–84 and was a principal representative at the United Nations in New York 1984–88. As deputy foreign minister in the Likud-led government of Shamir, he was the chief Israeli spokesperson in the 1991–92 Middle East peace talks. His elevation to the post of prime minister in 1996 raised doubts about the continuing viability of the Middle East peace process. However, in late 1998 he was signatory to the Wye Accord, signed in the USA, that resulted from peace talks between the Israeli government and the Palestinians.

Neto, (Antonio) Agostinho (1922–1979)

Angolan nationalist and politician, president 1974–79. A member of the Popular Movement for the Liberation of Angola (MPLA), he was imprisoned several times between 1952 and 1962, but escaped to the Congo where he became president and leader of the MPLA in the guerrilla war against Portuguese colonialism. His close ties with Fidel Castro gave him Cuban and Soviet backing, and enabled him to prevail in the civil war following the Portuguese withdrawal. In 1974 he became the first president of Angola, holding the post until his death.

Neto was the son of a Methodist missionary, and was educated in a Methodist school in Luanda before studying medicine in Portugal. He returned to Angola to work in the colonial medical service and joined the MPLA.

Neves, Tancredo de Almeida (1910–1985)

Brazilian politician. He was elected Brazil's first civilian president in 21 years in 1985 but died before his inauguration.

Neves was an ex-minister of justice and a member of the Movimento Democrático Brasileiro (MDB; Brazilian Democratic Movement). He was a skilled politician who managed to create an alliance with dissidents from the military's own party. This enabled the reform of political life by allowing direct elections. In January 1985, military rule came to an end, with the proclamation of the new republic and Neves was elected president. Following the his death, his vice president, José Sarney, assumed office as president.

Ne Win, adopted name of Maung Shu Maung ('Brilliant Sun') (1911–)

Myanmar (Burmese) politician, prime minister 1958–60, ruler 1962–74, president 1974–81, and chair until 1988 of the ruling Burma Socialist Programme Party (BSPP). His domestic 'Burmese Way to Socialism' policy programme brought the economy into serious decline.

Active in the nationalist movement during the 1930s, Ne Win joined the Allied forces in the war against Japan in 1945 and held senior military posts before becoming prime minister in 1958. After leading a coup in 1962, he ruled the country as chair of the revolutionary council until 1974, when he became state president. Although he stepped down as president in 1981, he continued to dominate political affairs, but was forced to resign as BSPP leader in 1988 after riots in Rangoon (now Yangon).

Newton, Huey P (1942–1989)

US civil-rights activist who cofounded the Black Panther Party. In 1967 Newton was accused of killing an Oakland police officer. His trial attracted crowds of demonstrators chanting Panther slogans and demanding his release. Newton was convicted of voluntary manslaughter and sent to the California Men's Colony, but his conviction was later overturned by the California court of appeals. By the 1970s the Black Panther Party had become a potent political force in California, but Newton was once again in serious trouble. He was charged with shooting a prostitute, after which the charges were dropped. He was retried and convicted for the 1969 death of the police officer. The conviction was later reversed.

Newton was born in Monroe, Louisiana. At Oakland City College he founded the Afro-American Society, and in 1966, at San Francisco Law School, Newton and friend Bobby Seale established the Black Panther Party for Self-Defense. In 1980 Newton gained a PhD at the University of California. In the late 1980s he was charged with embezzling state and federal funds from an educational and nutritional programme he headed in 1985, and in 1987 he was convicted of illegal possession of guns. In 1989 he was fatally shot.

FURTHER READING

Morrison, Toni (ed) *To Die for the People: The Writings of Huey Newton* 1995
Newton, Huey P, et al *The Black Panther Leaders Speak* 1976

Ngo Dinh Diem (1901–1963)

Vietnamese politician, president of South Vietnam 1955–63. He became minister of the interior in 1933. He refused to support ◊Ho Chi Minh and Bao Dai (1913–1997), then emperor of Annam, and was forced into exile in 1950. He returned to South Vietnam as prime minister in 1954, masterminded Bao's fall from power, and succeeded him as president in 1955. After causing unrest by embarking on a campaign against militant Buddhists, he was murdered by dissident army officers.

Born in Annam, he was the son of a mandarin and was himself a Roman Catholic. Although almost wholly dependent on US support for his country's economic survival and with hostilities with the North mounting, as president he refused to be counselled by the USA on his handling of the war.

Ngugi Wa Thiong'o, adopted name of James Ngugi (1938–)

Kenyan writer. His work includes essays, plays, short stories, and novels. Imprisoned after the performance of the play *Ngaahika Ndeenda/I Will Marry When I Want* in 1977, he has lived in exile since 1982.

Born in the White Highlands, Ngugi completed his early education in mission and government schools. Some of his family members were involved in the Mau Mau agitation during the 1950s, a period he later recalled in his writings. He attended Makerere University in Uganda 1959–64 where he wrote his first two novels, *Weep Not Child* (1964) and *The River Between* (1965). After postgraduate study at Leeds University, Ngugi was appointed the first African member of the department of English at University College, Nairobi, in 1967. He resigned in 1969 in protest against violations of academic freedom, but returned in 1971. His fourth novel, *Petals of Blood* (1977), portrayed corruption in post-independent Kenyan politics. In 1980 Ngugi published *Caitaani Matharaba-ini* and stated that he would no longer write novels in English. However, his works have continued to be translated.

In exile, Ngugi has campaigned on Kenyan political and human-rights issues. In 1987 he became president of UMOJA, an organization of Kenyan dissident groups.

Nguyen Thi Binh (1927–)

Vietnamese patriot and politician. In 1979 she was appointed minister of education in the United Government and she was vice president of Vietnam from 1992. When the provisional government was formed in 1969, she was appointed foreign minister and in 1973, as representative of the National Liberation Front, she signed the treaty that ended the war.

Born in South Vietnam into a family of nationalists, she dedicated herself at an early age to carrying on the work of her father and grandfather. In 1951 she was imprisoned for her political activities until French rule ended in 1954. Resuming the fight for independence, she fought against ◊Ngo Dinh Diem and later the USA.

Nguyen Van Linh (1914–1998)

Vietnamese communist politician, member of the Politburo 1976–81 and 1985–98, and leader of the Communist Party of Vietnam (CPV) 1986–91. He began economic liberalization and troop withdrawal from Cambodia and Laos.

Nguyen, born in North Vietnam, joined the anticolonial Thanh Nien, a forerunner of the current CPV, in Haiphong in 1929. He spent much of his subsequent party career in the South as a pragmatic reformer. He was a member of CPV's Politburo and secretariat 1976–81, suffered a temporary setback when party conservatives gained the ascendancy, and re-entered the Politburo in 1985, becoming CPV leader in December 1986 and resigning from the post in June 1991.

Nguyen Van Thieu (1923–)

Vietnamese soldier and political leader. In 1963, as chief of staff of the armed forces of the Republic of Vietnam (South Vietnam), he was a leader in the coup against ◊Ngo Dinh Diem. He became deputy premier and minister of defence in 1964, and head of state in 1965. In 1967, as the war against the Vietcong escalated, he became president of the Republic of Vietnam, and in early 1973 was a signatory to the peace treaty that formally ended hostilities. Fighting between North and South continued until the communist victory in 1975 with the fall of Saigon (now Ho Chi Minh City), when Thieu took refuge first in Taiwan, and then in the UK.

Born in Ninh Thuan, he was educated at a Catholic school and at the national military academy in Hue. His military career began in the late 1940s.

Nicholas II (1868–1918)

Tsar of Russia 1894–1917. He was dominated by his wife, Tsarina Alexandra, who was under the influence of the religious charlatan ◊Rasputin. His mismanagement of the Russo-Japanese War and of internal affairs led to the revolution of 1905, which he suppressed, although he was forced to grant limited constitutional reforms. He took Russia into World War I in 1914, was forced to abdicate in 1917 after the Russian Revolution, and was executed with his family.

I shall maintain the principle of autocracy just as firmly and unflinchingly as it was upheld by my ... father.

NICHOLAS II Declaration to representatives of the Zemstvo of Tver, 17 January 1896

In 1995 US and Russian scientists accounced that, by DNA testing, they had determined conclusively that bones found in Russia in 1991 were those of the tsar and his family. The remains were buried in 1998 in St Petersburg.

FURTHER READING
Cowles, V *The Last Tsar* 1977
Grey, I *The Romanovs* 1970
Massie, R *Nicholas and Alexandra* 1967
Vogt, G *Nicholas II* 1987

Nicolson, Harold George (1886–1968)

English author and diplomat. His works include biographies and studies such as *Monarchy* (1962), as well as the 'Diaries and Letters' (1930–62) for which he is best known. He married the poet and novelist Vita Sackville-West in 1913.

Son of Lord Carnock, he entered the foreign service, held embassy appointments, and served on the British delegation to the Paris peace conference of 1919. Briefly associated with British fascist Oswald ◊Mosley, he was a National Labour member of Parliament 1935–45, and in 1947 joined the Labour Party. He was created a KCVO in 1953.

Niebuhr, Reinhold (1892–1971)

US Protestant theologian, a Lutheran minister. His *Moral Man and Immoral Society* (1932) attacked depersonalized modern industrial society but denied the possibility of fulfilling religious and political utopian aspirations, a position that came to be known as Christian Realism. He was a pacifist, activist, and socialist but advocated war to stop totalitarianism in the 1940s.

Man's capacity for justice makes democracy possible, but man's inclination to injustice makes democracy necessary.

Reinhold Niebuhr *The Children of Light and the Children of Darkness*

Niebuhr taught for more than 30 years at the Union Theological Seminary in New York City. Originally a strong exponent of Christian socialism, he became increasingly pessimistic about the possibility of achieving it, given humanity's irreducible egoistic pride, which he identified with original sin. He came to believe that liberal democracy must be sustained not because it can bring about human perfection but as a way of avoiding the systematic cruelty that comes with unrestrained power. From 1945 he founded Americans for Democratic Action and became an adviser to the State Department.

Further Reading

Fox, Richard *Reinhold Niebuhr* 1987
Harland, G *The Thought of Reinhold Niebuhr* 1960
Kegley, C W, and Bretall, R W *Reinhold Niebuhr: His Religious, Social and Political Thought* 1984
Scott, Nathan (ed) *The Legacy of Reinhold Niebuhr* 1975

Niemöller, (Friedrich Gustav Emil) Martin (1892–1984)

German Christian Protestant pastor. He was imprisoned in a concentration camp 1938–45 for campaigning against Nazism in the German church. He was president of the World Council of Churches 1961–68.

Nitti, Francesco Saverio (1868–1953)

Italian politician and economist. He was prime minis-

◆ Nixon, Richard M(ilhous) (1913–1994) ◆

37th president of the USA 1969–74, a Republican. He attracted attention as a member of the House Un-American Activities Committee in 1948, and was vice president to Dwight D Eisenhower 1953–61. As president he was responsible for US withdrawal from Vietnam and the normalization of relations with communist China, but at home his culpability in the cover-up of the Watergate scandal and the existence of a 'slush fund' for political machinations during his re-election campaign of 1972 led him to resign in 1974 when threatened with impeachment.

There can be no whitewash at the White House.

Richard Nixon On Watergate, television speech 30 April 1973

Nixon, a Californian, entered Congress in 1947, and rose to prominence during the McCarthyite era of the 1950s. As a member of the House Un-American Activities Committee, he pressed for the investigation of Alger ◊Hiss, accused of being a spy. Nixon was senator for California from 1951 until elected vice president. He played a more extensive role in government than previous vice presidents, in part because of the poor health of President Eisenhower. He narrowly lost the 1960 presidential election to John F Kennedy, partly because televised electoral debates put him at a disadvantage.

He did not seek presidential nomination in 1964, but in a 'law and order' campaign defeated Vice President Hubert Humphrey in 1968. Facing a Democratic Congress, Nixon sought to extricate the USA from the war in Vietnam. He formulated the Nixon Doctrine in 1969, abandoning close involvement with Asian countries, but escalated the war in Cambodia by massive bombing, although the USA was not officially at war with neutral Cambodia.

Nixon was re-elected in 1972 in a landslide victory over George McGovern, and immediately faced allegations of irregularities and illegalities conducted on his behalf in his re-election campaign and within the White House. Despite his success in extricating the USA from Vietnam, congressional and judicial investigations, along with press exposures of the Watergate affair, undermined public support. He resigned in 1974,

ter and minister of the interior 1919–20, during a time of economic and political crisis following World War I. He introduced proportional representation but failed to create a stable coalition government.

A liberal, he lacked the drive to make his basic principles sufficiently felt, and in a sense his indecisive government paved the way for Mussolini, whom Nitti strongly opposed.

Nitti lived in France throughout the dictatorship of Mussolini, and was held prisoner by the Germans 1943–45; after World War II he returned as a leader of the National Democratic Union, but had by then ceased to exercise much political influence. In 1947 he tried and failed to form a government, and subsequently retired from politics.

Niyazov, Saparmurad (1940–)

Turkmen politician, president from 1990. A member of the Communist Party of the Soviet Union (CPSU) from 1962, he became party leader and prime minister in the Turkmenistan Republic in 1985 and entered the CPSU Politburo in 1990. He led the republic's breakaway from the USSR, after a pro-independence referendum in October 1991, and subsequently ruled in an autocratic manner, developing a personality cult and repressing opposition. Elected unopposed as president

in June 1992, his term was extended to 2002 by a referendum in January 1994.

Born in Ashgabat, he later trained in St Petersburg, Russia, and worked in a variety of party positions in Turkmenistan from the 1960s. He initially supported the attempted coup by conservative communists against Mikhail Gorbachev in August 1991. After independence, he promoted secular values and cautious economic reform, and encouraged foreign investment to develop the country's huge natural gas and oil reserves. He adopted the title 'Turkmenbashi' ('leader of the Turkmen').

Nkomo, Joshua (1917–)

Zimbabwean politician, vice president from 1988. As president of the Zimbabwe African People's Union (ZAPU) from 1961, he was a leader of the black nationalist movement against the white Rhodesian regime. He was a member of Robert ◊Mugabe's cabinet 1980–82 and from 1987.

After completing his education in South Africa, Nkomo became a welfare officer on Rhodesian Railways and later organizing secretary of the Rhodesian African Railway Workers' Union. He entered politics in 1950, and was president of the African National

---

the first and only US president to do so, under threat of impeachment on three counts: obstruction of the administration of justice in the investigation of Watergate; violation of constitutional rights of citizens – for example, attempting to use the Internal Revenue Service, Federal Bureau of Investigation, and Central Intelligence Agency as weapons against political opponents; and failure to produce 'papers and things' as ordered by the Judiciary Committee.

He was granted a pardon in 1974 by President Gerald Ford and turned to lecturing and writing.

Nixon was born in Yorba Linda, California, of a lower-middle-class Quaker family that had migrated from the Midwest; he grew up in Whittier, California, and studied at Whittier College and Duke University Law School. He practised law 1937–42, then served in the navy 1942–46, rising to the rank of lieutenant commander.

Nixon's career was characterized by both ruthless ambition and an insecurity stemming from his feeling of social inferiority. He tasted bitter defeat in the 1960 US presidential and 1962 California governorship elections, but fought back, adopting a less rigid public image, dubbed the 'New Nixon'. Bridging the new-right 'Main Street' and liberal 'Wall Street' wings of Republican philosophy, as president he pursued a

course of cautious conservatism. Stymied at home by a hostile, Democrat-controlled Congress, Nixon turned to the diplomatic arena, achieving rapprochement with Maoist China and negotiating a nuclear-arms limitation treaty with the USSR.

These achievements will for ever be overshadowed by Watergate – the bungling Republican-sponsored break-in of the Democrats' headquarters in 1972 and the sleazy cover-up that followed. The action, though unnecessary, was symptomatic of increasing paranoia in an inward-looking administration. Unlike his closest aides, Nixon – the only president ever to resign his office – escaped imprisonment, being pardoned by President Ford. By the 1980s he had established himself in some quarters as an elder statesman. See photograph on page 324.

FURTHER READING
Aitken, Jonathan *Nixon: A Life* 1993
Ambrose, S *Nixon* 1987
McGinnis, J *The Selling of the President* 1988
Parmet, Herbert S *Nixon and His America* 1990
Sulzberger, C L *The World and Richard Nixon* 1987
Woodward, Bob, and Bernstein, Carl *All the President's Men* 1975, *The Final Days* 1987

Richard Nixon as vice president, 1958. *AKG London*

Born in Panama City, he studied at the university there. After training at a military academy in Peru, Noriega was commissioned in the National Guard in 1962, and received US counterintelligence training. An ally of the military strongman Omar ◊Torrijos Herrera, he became intelligence chief in 1970 and chief of staff in 1982. He wielded considerable political power behind the scenes, which led to his enlistment by the CIA, and he was seen as an ally against Nicaragua until the Irangate scandal limited US covert action there. In the 1984 and 1989 presidential elections, Noriega claimed a fraudulent victory for his candidate. Bribes accepted by Noriega for tacitly permitting money laundering and the transshipment of cocaine are estimated at $15 million, but after 1985 he cooperated with the US Drug Enforcement Administration. However, relations between Panama and the USA deteriorated and in December 1989 President George Bush ordered an invasion of the country by 24,000 US troops. Noriega was seized and taken to the USA for trial. In April 1992 he was given a 40-year prison sentence for drug trafficking and racketeering.

Congress (ANC) in southern Rhodesia 1957–59. In 1961 he created ZAPU, of which he was president.

Arrested along with other black African politicians, he was kept in detention 1963–74. After his release he joined forces with Robert Mugabe as a joint leader of the Patriotic Front in 1976, opposing the white-dominated regime of Ian Smith. Nkomo took part in the Lancaster House Conference, which led to Rhodesia's independence as the new state of Zimbabwe, and became a cabinet minister and vice president.

Noel-Baker, Philip John, Baron Noel-Baker (1889–1982)

British Labour politician. He was involved in drafting the charters of both the League of Nations and the United Nations. He published *The Arms Race* (1958), and was awarded the 1959 Nobel Peace Prize. He was created Baron in 1977.

Noriega Morena, Manuel (Antonio) (1940–)

Panamanian soldier and politician, effective ruler of Panama from 1983, as head of the National Guard, until deposed by the USA in 1989. An informer for the US Central Intelligence Agency (CIA) from the late 1960s, he was known to be involved in drug trafficking as early as 1972.

He enjoyed US support until 1987. In the December 1989 US invasion of Panama, he was forcibly taken to the USA. He was tried and convicted of cocaine trafficking and money laundering in 1992.

North, Oliver (1943–)

US Marine lieutenant colonel. In 1981 he joined the staff of the National Security Council (NSC), where he supervised the mining of Nicaraguan harbours in 1983, an air-force bombing raid on Libya in 1986, and an arms-for-hostages deal with Iran in 1985, which, when uncovered in 1986 (Irangate), forced his dismissal and trial.

North was born in San Antonio, Texas, into a military family, and was a graduate of the US Naval Academy. He led a Marine platoon in the Vietnam War 1968–69. After working as a Marine instructor, as well as participating in a number of overseas secret missions, he became the NSC deputy director for political military affairs.

After Irangate, North was convicted on felony charges of obstructing Congress, mutilating government documents, and taking an illegal gratuity. In September 1991 all charges against him were dropped on the grounds that, since his evidence before Congressional committees in July 1987 had been widely televised, it was impossible to give him a fair trial. He was unsuccessful as Virginia's Republican candidate for the Senate in the 1994 midterm elections.

Northcliffe, Alfred Charles William Harmsworth, 1st Viscount Northcliffe (1865–1922)

British newspaper proprietor, born in Dublin. Founding the *Daily Mail* in 1896, he revolutionized popular journalism, and with the *Daily Mirror* in 1903 originated the picture paper. In 1908 he also obtained control of *The Times*.

Northcliffe left school at the age of 16 and liked to be known as 'The Napoleon of Fleet Street'. He supported the removal of H H Asquith as prime minister in 1916 and David Lloyd George appointed him head of the British War Mission in the USA in 1917, and director of propaganda in enemy countries in 1918. He was created Baron in 1905 and Viscount in 1917.

His brother Harold Sidney Harmsworth, 1st Viscount Rothermere (1868–1940), was associated with him in many of his newspapers. He was created Baron in 1914 and Viscount in 1919.

FURTHER READING

Ferris, Paul *The House of Northcliffe* 1972

Greenwall, H J *Northcliffe: Napoleon of Fleet Street* 1957

Pound, Reginald, and Harmsworth, Geoffrey *Northcliffe* 1959

Nosaka, Sanzo (1892–1993)

Japanese Communist Party leader. He was first elected to the lower house of the Diet (parliament) in 1946 and to the upper house in 1956. At the very end of his life in 1992 he was expelled from the Communist Party on the grounds that documents released in the former USSR revealed that he had betrayed the Japanese Communist Party in the past.

Nosaka joined the underground Communist Party in 1922. Arrested in 1923 and again in 1928, he was released from prison in 1930 due to ill health and went

Kwame Nkrumah with the Guinean president Sékou Touré (wearing hat), 1959. *AKG London*

into exile the following year until 1946. During his years abroad he worked for the Comintern in the USA, USSR, and China. He became a leading member of the legalized Communist Party in postwar Japan.

Nott William Frederick, John (1932–)

British Conservative politician, minister for defence 1981–83 during the Falkland Islands conflict with Argentina. He was created a KCB in 1983.

Nu, U (Thakin) (1907–1995)

See page 326.

◆ NKRUMAH, KWAME (1909–1972) ◆

Ghanaian nationalist politician, prime minister of the Gold Coast (Ghana's former name) 1952–57 and of newly independent Ghana 1957–60. He became Ghana's first president in 1960 but was overthrown in a coup in 1966. His policy of 'African socialism' led to links with the communist bloc.

Originally a teacher, he studied later in both the UK and the USA, and on returning to Africa formed the Convention People's Party (CPP) in 1949 with the aim of immediate self-government. He was imprisoned in 1950 for inciting illegal strikes, but was released the same year. As president he established an authoritarian regime and made Ghana a one-party (CPP) state in 1964. He then dropped his stance of nonalignment and

drew closer to the USSR and other communist countries. Deposed from the presidency while on a visit to Beijing (Peking), China, in 1966, he remained in exile in Guinea, where he was made a co-head of state until his death, but was posthumously 'rehabilitated' in 1973.

FURTHER READING

Bretton, Henry *The Rise and Fall of Kwame Nkrumah* 1967

Davidson, Basil *Black Star: A View of the Life and Times of Kwame Nkrumah* 1973

Kellner, Douglas *Nkrumah* 1987

Nkrumah, Kwame *Ghana: The Autobiography of Kwame Nkrumah* 1957

Nujoma, Sam (1929–)

Namibian left-wing politician, founder and leader of the South West Africa People's Organization (SWAPO) from 1959, president from 1990. He was exiled in 1960, and controlled SWAPO's armed struggle against South Africa from Angolan bases in 1966. When the first free elections were held in 1989 under the United Nations (UN) peace plan, he returned to lead his party to victory, taking office in March 1990.

Nujoma was exiled after SWAPO appointed him to present the case for Namibian independence before the UN in 1960. He set up SWAPO provisional headquarters in Tanzania in 1961 and, apart from a brief return home in 1966 when he was arrested, he remained in exile until 1989. SWAPO was recognized as the legitimate authority by the Organization of African Unity in 1968 and the UN in 1973, but South African opposition delayed the implementation of the UN peace plan.

Nujoma was born near the Angolan border, had little formal schooling, and joined the state railways before entering politics.

Nye, Gerald P(rentice) (1892–1971)

US senator. Originally appointed and then elected to the US Senate (as a progressive Republican from North Dakota 1925–45), he chaired a special committee 1934–37 investigating arms sales in World War I. The findings reinforced the US belief that the USA should remain neutral in World War II.

FURTHER READING
Cole, Wayne S *Senator Gerald P Nye and American Foreign Relations* 1980

Nyerere, Julius Kambarage (1922–)

Tanzanian socialist politician, president 1964–85. He devoted himself from 1954 to the formation of the Tanganyika African National Union and subsequent campaigning for independence. He became chief minister in 1960, was prime minister of Tanganyika 1961–62, president of the newly formed Tanganyika Republic 1962–64, and first president of Tanzania 1964–85. He became head of the Organization of African Unity in 1984.

Nyerere was educated at Makerere University College and in Edinburgh, Scotland and was a teacher before entering politics.

Nyers, Rezso (1923–)

Hungarian socialist leader. A member of the politburo

◆ NU, U (THAKIN) (1907–1995) ◆

Myanmar politician, prime minister of Burma (now Myanmar) for most of the period from 1947 to the military coup of 1962. He was the country's first democratically elected prime minister. Exiled from 1966, U Nu returned to the country in 1980 and in 1988 helped found the National League for Democracy opposition movement.

U Nu was born in Wakema in the Irrawaddy delta, and studied at the new University of Rangoon, leading a nationwide student strike against the British colonial government in 1936. He joined the Dobhama Asiayone ('Our Burma') nationalist organization during the 1930s and was imprisoned by the British authorities at the start of World War II.

He was released in 1942, following Japan's invasion of Burma, and appointed foreign minister in the Ba Maw government. In 1946 Nu was elected vice president of the Anti-Fascist People's Freedom League (AFPFL), the major nationalist front, which had fought since 1945 against Japanese occupation, and in June 1947 he became speaker of the constituent assembly, which had the task of drafting a new constitution. After the assassination of his longtime friend Aung San, a founder of AFPFL, he became Burma's first prime minister in August 1947.

U Nu oversaw the transition to independence in 1948, and sought to promote democracy and preserve unity in a nation faced by insurgencies by the Burmese Communist Party and the separatist Karen community. A devout Buddhist who took vows of celibacy and teetotalism in 1948, he sought to govern as a *rajarsi* (ruler-sage) and promoted Theravāda Buddhism, sponsoring the construction of the Kaba-Aye peace pagoda. Despite leading the fractious AFPFL to successive electoral victories in 1952, 1956, and 1960, U Nu stepped down as prime minister temporarily 1956–57 and 1958–60.

He was overthrown in March 1962 by a military coup led by General ◊Ne Win. He was placed under house arrest for five years, before living in exile in Thailand and India, where he resided near a Buddhist monastery.

On his return to Myanmar in 1980, he abandoned politics and concentrated on translating classic Buddhist texts from Burmese to English. However, moved by the prodemocracy uprising of 1988, he formed the National League for Democracy and declared himself prime minister. He was placed under house arrest in November 1988 by the new military junta that had recently seized power, and in 1991 his party was outlawed. U Nu remained under detention until April 1992.

from 1966 and the architect of Hungary's liberalizing economic reforms in 1968, he was ousted from power by hardliners in 1974. In 1988 he was brought back into the politburo, and was head of the newly formed Hungarian Socialist Party 1989–90.

Obasanjo, Olusegun (1937–)

Nigerian politician and soldier; head of state 1976–79. When Murtala Mohammed's brief military rule of 1975–76 ended in his death during a coup, Obasanjo succeeded as head of state, and oversaw the transfer of control back to civilian rule. After that, he played an important role on the international stage, especially within the Commonwealth and as founder and leader of the African Leadership Forum. In 1998 he announced that he would be a candidate in the Nigerian presidential elections.

Obasanjo joined the Nigerian army in 1958, training in both the UK and India and specializing in engineering. He served with the Nigerian unit in the United Nations Congo operations and was military commander of the federal forces during the Biafran civil war 1967–70. In 1975 he was made federal commissioner of works and housing, and Chief of Staff.

He was educated at Abeokuta Baptist High School and Mons Officers' School. His publications include the autobiographical *My Command* (1980) and the *Challenge of Agricultural Production and Food Security in Africa* (1992).

Obote, (Apollo) Milton (1924–)

Ugandan politician, prime minister 1962–66, and president 1966–71 and 1980–85. After forming the Uganda People's Congress (UPC) in 1959, he led the independence movement from 1961. As prime minister his rule became increasingly authoritarian, and in 1966 he suspended the constitution and declared himself president. He was ousted by Idi ◊Amin in 1971, fleeing to exile in Tanzania. Returning in 1979 after the collapse of the Amin regime, he was re-elected president in 1980 but failed to restore order and was deposed by Lieutenant General Tito Okello in 1985.

Obote was elected to the legislative council in 1958, and a UPC alliance with the royalist Kaboka Yekka ('King Alone') party enabled him to win the 1962 elections. After being overthrown by Amin, he supported a guerrilla movement against Amin in 1971 while exiled in Tanzania. He was reinstalled as president in 1980 after the UPC claimed a majority of the votes, although the result was contested by other parties.

Obregón, Álvaro (1880–1928)

Mexican soldier and Constitutionalist politician, president 1920–24. His anti-clerical measures prompted church opposition and Victoriano ◊Huerta led a revolt against him 1923–24. This was crushed, and Plutárco Elías ◊Calles, Obregón's chosen candidate, became president in 1924. Obregón was chosen president again in 1928, but was assassinated by a Roman Catholic fanatic before taking up office.

Born in Sonora state, he followed the family tradition of farming and, in 1911, supported Francisco ◊Madero in the revolution against Porfirio ◊Díaz. Obregón formed his own army, partly comprising Mayo Indians, which, in 1913 to 1914, worked with his fellow Constitutionalist, Venustiano ◊Carranza, to overthrow Victoriano Huerta, who had usurped the presidency from Madero. Obregón remained allied to Carranza after the latter became president in 1914, and fought against Carranza's opponents, including Francisco ◊Villa, whom he defeated on several occasions. Between 1917 and 1919 Obregón returned to Sonora to run his estate. However, when Carranza sought to avoid an agreed transfer of power in 1920, Obregón led a revolt to overthrow Carranza. After an interim administration by Adolfo de la Huerta, Obregón became president and pushed through agrarian, education, and labour reforms, which Carranza had shelved.

FURTHER READING
Obregón, Álvaro *Ocho mil kilómetros en campaña* 1917

Obuchi, Keizo (1937–)

Japanese politician, prime minister from 1998. Obuchi was first elected to the Diet (parliament) in 1963 on the conservative Liberal Democratic Party (LDP) ticket. He was leader of the LDP's largest faction in 1992 and became president of the LDP and prime minister in 1998.

Ochs, Phil(ip) (1940–1976)

US folk singer and songwriter. His song 'The Cuban Invasion' in 1962 established his credentials as one of the leading political commentators of the folk music scene, and he was considered the main rival to Bob Dylan. His album *All the News That's Fit to Sing* (1964) included such songs as 'Talking Vietnam' and 'Talking

Cuban Crisis', as well as songs about the murders of civil-rights workers Medgar, ◊Evers, and Marsh. Ochs's anthem for the anti-Vietnam movement, 'I Ain't Marching Anymore', established him as an important protest singer of the period, but led to a rift with Dylan, who criticized his overt politicking.

FURTHER READING
Schumacher, Michael and Mathew A *There But For Fortune: The Life of Phil Ochs* 1996

O'Connor, Sandra Day (1930–)

US jurist and the first female associate justice of the US Supreme Court, from 1981. Considered a moderate conservative, she dissented in *Texas* v *Johnson* (1990), a decision that ruled that the legality of burning the US flag in protest was protected by the First Amendment.

Ó Dálaigh, Cearbhall (1911–1978)

Irish politician, president 1974–76. He was a distinguished judge of the European Court of Justice 1973–74 and was nominated as president of the republic following the sudden death of Erskine Childers. In October 1976, Ó Dálaigh resigned the presidency following an intemperate attack upon him by the defence minister Patrick Donegan, after the president had referred the government's Emergency Powers Bill to the Supreme Court.

Born in Bray, County Wicklow, Ó Dálaigh studied law at University College and King's Inns, Dublin. He served as Fianna Fáil attorney general 1946–48 and 1951–54, and as chief justice and president of the Supreme Court 1961–73.

Oddsson, David (1948–)

Icelandic politician, prime minister from 1991. A member of the right-of-centre Independence Party, he was made vice chair of the party in 1989 and chair in 1991, when he succeeded Thorsteinn Pálsson as premier.

Oddsson began his career in local politics, becoming mayor of Reykjavík in 1982. Outside politics, he has an established reputation as a stage and TV dramatist.

Odets, Clifford (1906–1963)

US playwright and communist who was the most renowned of the social-protest dramatists of the Depression era. He was one of the original acting members of the experimental Group Theater directed by Harold Clurman, Lee Strasberg, and Cheryl Crawford, which was committed to producing only native US drama. Through his writing for the Group Theater and other workers' theatre groups, he attacked the capitalist system and the spread of fascism in the USA of the 1930s.

His best-known play, *Waiting for Lefty* (1935), is based on the New York taxi drivers strike of 1934, and the experimental, one-act play was a call to arms for labour unionism. Within a year of its first production *Waiting For Lefty* gained an international reputation and was performed in workers' theatres across the USA and Western Europe. Odets also wrote the anti-Nazi play *Till the Day I Die* (1935). In the late 1930s he went to Hollywood and became a successful film writer and director, though he continued to write plays.

FURTHER READING
Brenman-Gibson, Margaret *Clifford Odets: A Biography* 1981
Cantor, Harold *Clifford Odets: Playwright–Poet* 1978
Miller, Gabriel *Clifford Odets* 1988

Odría Amoretti, Manuel Apolinário (1897–1974)

Peruvian politician and president 1948–56. He assumed power after a coup but was formally elected in 1950. He assumed dictatorial powers and imposed a repressive regime on the opposition parties. He proposed and implemented measures to bring about economic reform and political stability to the nation, though they were ineffective. Towards the end of his term in office, economic problems and rampant inflation were endemic and opposition to his regime resulted in widespread riots and social disturbances.

In 1956 Odría was compelled to permit elections and when succeeded by Manuel Prado, he went into voluntary exile in the USA. In 1962 Odría ran again for the presidency, but was unsuccessful.

A general, and army chief of staff in 1946, he also served as interior minister under President José Bustamante. In October 1948 he was responsible for leading a military coup that ousted Bustamante from office. Following the coup, he took up presidential office.

Ojukwu, (Chukwuemeka) Odumegwu (1933–)

Nigerian politician and soldier. Appointed military governor of the mainly Ibo-speaking Eastern Region of Nigeria following the 1966 coup, he proclaimed the Eastern Region the independent Republic of Biafra in May 1967, precipitating the Biafran civil war. After acting as head of government and supreme commander for three years, his forces were finally defeated in 1970, and he fled to the Côte d'Ivoire. He returned to Nigeria in 1982, but an attempt to return to politics led to two years' imprisonment, and he was banned from standing for president in the 1993 elections.

Ojukwu was educated in church schools in Lagos and at Oxford University, England. He joined the Nigerian army in 1957 and, after attending military college in the UK, served in the Nigerian force in the United Nations Congo operations.

Okuma, Shigenobu (1838–1922)

Japanese politician and prime minister in 1898 and 1914–16. He presided over Japanese pressure for territorial concessions in China, before retiring in 1916.

Holding a series of ministerial appointments after the ◊Meiji restoration of 1868, Okuma specialized in fiscal and constitutional reform.

Olney, Richard (1835–1917)

US Democratic politician. In 1895 he became secretary of state in Grover Cleveland's cabinet. That year he drafted a message insisting that the UK must submit to arbitration over the long-standing dispute between Venezuela and British Guiana.

Olter, Bailey (1932–   )

Micronesian politician, president 1991–97. In 1979 he became vice president of the senate in the first congress of the Federated States of Micronesia (FSM) and in May 1991, standing as a 'senator at large' for Pohnpei, was elected executive president of the FSM. He was unanimously re-elected by the congress in May 1995, but suffered a stroke in July 1996. The vice president, Jacob ◊Nena, took over as acting president in November 1996 while Olter convalesced, and in May 1997 Olter formally stepped down as president.

Born in Mwoakilloa, in Pohnpei state, Olter studied at the University of Hawaii and became a teacher of science and mathematics. His political career began in Pohnpei, where he became treasurer and president of the local legislature.

O'Malley, King (c. 1858–1953)

Australian politician. He claimed to have been born in Québec, Canada, but was in fact probably born in Kansas, USA, and educated there. He migrated in the 1880s and entered the South Australian parliament in 1896, to which membership was restricted to British citizens (hence the Canadian claim). He was elected to the federal house of representatives in 1901 as an

---

The king reigns in theory. In practice he is as utilitarian as the comb of a cock rooster.

KING O'MALLEY Remark on coronation of George V of Great Britain

---

independent but supporting Labor. He was an opponent of conscription and supporter of women's suffrage, but opposed to enfranchising Aborigines. He was minister for home affairs 1910–13 and 1915–16, and was instrumental in founding the Commonwealth Bank and in securing land for the federal capital.

Onassis, Jacqueline (Jackie Lee), born Bouvier (1929–1994)

French-born socialite, US first lady 1961–63. She was the wife of President John F ◊Kennedy. She married the shipping billionaire Aristotle Onassis in 1968. After

his death in 1975, she worked as an editor at the New York publishers Viking and Doubleday.

As a photographer for the *Times Herald*, Bouvier met and captivated Senator John Kennedy; they married in 1953 and had two children, Caroline and John. She shone as first lady when Kennedy became president in 1961. In the redecorated White House, she hosted

---

The one thing I do not want to be called is First Lady. It sounds like a saddle horse.

JACQUELINE ONASSIS Quoted in P Collier and D Horowitz *The Kennedys*

---

parties attended by prominent intellectuals and artists, and charmed world leaders. Her televised tour of the presidential home broke new ground. All this came to an abrupt end with her husband's assassination in 1963.

O'Neill, Terence, Baron O'Neill of the Maine (1914–1990)

Northern Ireland Unionist politician. In the Ulster government he was minister of finance 1956–63, then prime minister 1963–69. He resigned when opposed by his party on measures to extend rights to Roman Catholics, including a universal franchise.

O'Neill was born in London into an Irish family. He was sent to Eton public school, then entered the Irish Guards and war service. He was elected to the House of Commons in 1946, and was created a life peer as Baron in 1970.

O'Neill, Tip (Thomas Philip) (1912–1994)

US Democratic politician, speaker of the House of Representatives 1977–86. An Irish-American 'New Deal' liberal, he was the last Democratic leader from the old school of machine politics. He entered the Massachusetts state legislature in 1936, and the US House of Representatives in 1952.

O'Neill was born in a working-class district in Cambridge, Massachusetts; his political thinking was conditioned by the Great Depression. He entered the Massachusetts state legislature in 1936 and the US House of Representatives in 1952, taking over a seat vacated by John F Kennedy. Through a mixture of stalwart partisanship, legislative shrewdness, and skilful alliance building, O'Neill ascended the Democrat Capitol Hill hierarchy. As speaker from 1977, he took charge of a House that was becoming more atomistic and difficult to control. From 1981 he worked with Republican president Ronald Reagan. O'Neill abhorred Reagan's 'New Right' policies and described him as 'the least knowledgeable president' he had ever met. On retirement from Congress in 1986, O'Neill became something of a media celebrity, writing a best-selling autobiography and being paid handsomely for advertising endorsements.

Ongania, Juan Carlos (1914–1995)

Argentine military leader and president 1966–70. He became president following the establishment of the military junta that ousted President Arturo Illia in 1966. His authoritarian administration, marked by the abolition of democratic parties and the integration of military rule into government, initiated widespread resentment and opposition.

Ongania's failure to follow appropriate economic policy led to further economic decline, rising inflation, and labour conflict. His indecisiveness over the direction of economic reform policies to improve conditions further fuelled opposition to the administration in 1969, leading to social unrest in many cities. In June 1970 Ongania was ousted from government by a military junta, and General Roberto Levingston took control.

Orlando, Vittorio Emanuele (1860–1952)

Italian politician, prime minister 1917–19. He attended the Paris peace conference after World War I, but dissatisfaction with his handling of the Adriatic settlement led to his resignation.

Ortega Saavedra, Daniel (1945–)

Nicaraguan socialist politician, head of state 1979–90. He was a member of the Marxist Sandinista Liberation Front (FSLN), which overthrew the regime of Anastasio ◊Somoza Debayle in 1979, later becoming its secretary general. US-sponsored Contra guerrillas opposed his government from 1982.

Ortega left law studies at the Central American University in Managua at the age of 18 to join the FSLN, and soon became head of the underground urban resistance activities against the Somoza regime. He was imprisoned and tortured several times, and was temporarily exiled to Cuba in 1974. He became a member of the national directorate of the FSLN and fought in the two-year campaign for the Nicaraguan Revolution. Ortega became a member of the junta of national reconstruction, and its coordinator two years later. The FSLN won the free 1984 elections and Ortega became president, but in February 1990, with the economy in tatters, Ortega lost the presidency to US-backed Violeta ◊Barrios de Chamorro. Despite repackaging himself as a more moderate democratic socialist, he was also defeated in the 1996 presidential election, by Arnoldo ◊Alemán.

Ortega y Gasset, José (1883–1955)

Spanish philosopher and critic. Born in Madrid, he was educated at Bilbao and Madrid, and subsequently at German universities. He was professor of metaphysics at the Central University of Madrid 1910–36. In *The Revolt of the Masses* (1929) he depicted 20th-century society as dominated by the mediocrity of the masses, and argued for the vital role of intellectual elites in averting the slide into barbarism. His *Towards a Philosophy of History* (1941) contains philosophical reflections on the state and an interpretation of the meaning of human history.

A republican in politics, he was exiled during the Spanish Civil War, but returned in 1848 and founded the Institute of Humanities in Madrid.

Orwell, George, pen name of Eric Arthur Blair (1903–1950)

English writer. His books include the satirical fable *Animal Farm* (1945), an attack on the Soviet Union and its leader, Stalin, which includes such slogans as 'All animals are equal, but some are more equal than others'; and the prophetic *Nineteen Eighty-Four* (1949), targeting Cold War politics, which portrays the catastrophic excesses of state control over the individual. He also wrote numerous essays. Orwell was distrustful of all political parties and ideologies, and a deep sense of social conscience and antipathy towards political dictatorship characterize his work.

Orwell was born in Motihari, Bengal, India, and educated in England at Eton. He served in Burma (now Myanmar) with the Indian Imperial Police from 1922–27, an experience reflected in the novel *Burmese Days* (1934). In horrified retreat from imperialism, he moved towards socialism and even anarchism. A

George Orwell, c. 1945. *AKG London*

period of poverty, during which he was successively tutor, teacher, dishwasher, tramp, and bookshop assistant, is described in *Down and Out in Paris and London* (1933), and also provided him with material for *The Road to Wigan Pier* (1937) and *Keep the Aspidistra Flying* (1936). In 1936 he fought on the Republican side in the Spanish Civil War and was wounded; these experiences are related in *Homage to Catalonia* (1938). Orwell reacted strongly against his exposure to the brutally practical politics of the communists in Spain. He was forced to flee the country, and the experience made him an active opponent both of communism and fascism. During World War II, Orwell worked for the BBC, writing and monitoring propaganda.

FURTHER READING
Crick, B *George Orwell: A Life* 1980
Hammond, J R *A George Orwell Companion* 1982
Ingle, S *George Orwell: A Political Life* 1993
Stansky, P, and Abrahams, W *The Unknown Orwell* 1972, *Orwell: Transformations* 1980
Williams, R *Orwell* 1970
Woodcock, G *The Crystal Spirit* 1966

Osmeña, Sergio (1878–1961)
Filipino independence leader and politician, president of the Philippines government in exile 1944–46. In 1942, when the Philippines were occupied by Japan, he fled with President Manuel Quezon and became president of the government in exile when Quezon died in 1944. Osmeña returned to the Philippines with the US invasion forces in October 1944, but was defeated by Manuel Roxas in the first presidential elections, in 1946, in the independent Philippines.

Born on Cebu island, Osmeña trained as a lawyer and served as provincial governor of Cebu and the first speaker 1907–16 of the Philippine assembly. He later served in the Philippines senate 1922–35, representing Cebu. He campaigned for the Philippines' independence, leading missions to the USA.

Osorio, Oscar (1910–1969)
El Salvadorean soldier and politician, member of the Revolutionary Party of Democratic Unification (PRUD), president 1950–56. He introduced centre-left reforms, including the legalization of labour unions and collective bargaining, the introduction of social security, and promotion of tourism and light industrial development, through the Salvadorean Institute for Development of Production.

Meanwhile, communist opponents of the regime were rounded up and elections were rigged, leading to an opposition boycott of the 1956 presidential contest, which was won by interior minister José María Lémus.

A professional soldier, educated at the Military Polytechnic, Osorio was exiled to Mexico in 1945, after being implicated in a conspiracy. He returned to El Salvador in 1948, after the overthrow of President Salvador Castañeda Castro, and became head of the ruling military junta, which formed the PRUD party.

Osugi, Sakae (1885–1923)
Japanese anarchist political activist. Despite several spells of imprisonment, Osugi remained faithful to anarchism during the years of repression (known as the 'winter period') following the High Treason Incident of 1910. After the October Revolution, Osugi remained an anarchist, unlike many of his former comrades who joined the Communist Party.

Coming from a military family, Osugi was attracted to the socialist movement while a student in Tokyo and, under Shusui ◊Kotoku's influence, became an anarchist in 1906. He was murdered by the military police in 1923 during the chaos following the Great Kanto Earthquake.

Ould Daddah, Moktar (1924–)
Mauritanian politician. He became vice president of the Government Council on 20 May 1957 and president of the Provisional Government on 28 November 1958. He was appointed prime minister on 28 June 1959 and, on 20 August 1961, the first president of the Islamic Republic of Mauritania. He was re-elected for further five-year terms on 7 August 1966, 8 August 1971, and 8 August 1976.

Ould Daddah was born in Boutilimit, Mauritania. He was educated first at Blanchot, Mauritania, and then at Saint-Louis, Senegal, and finally at the University of Paris in France. He qualified as a lawyer, as well as being awarded a diploma in modern oriental languages. He entered the legal profession as a probationary lawyer in Dakar, Senegal.

Oumarou, Ide (1937–)
Niger diplomat, politician, and administrator, secretary general of the Organization of African Unity (OAU) 1985–89.

He was editor of the country's main daily newspaper *Le Niger* 1961–63, becoming commissioner general of information in 1972. Between 1972 and 1974 he was director general of the office of posts and telecommunications. After Seyni Kountche seized power in 1974, Oumarou, a trusted friend, became the most influential civil servant in the country. In 1979 he was appointed Niger's permanent representative to the United Nations and in 1983 became minister of foreign affairs and cooperation.

As OAU secretary general, Oumarou had the reputation of being an efficient administrator, introducing internal reforms to reduce costs. He was also concerned about the problem of apartheid in South Africa. In 1989 he stood for re-election but was defeated by

Tanzania's deputy prime minister, Salim Ahmed Salim.

In 1987 he was awarded the Grand Prix Littéraire de l'Afrique for his novel *Gros Plan*.

Oviedo, Lino César

Paraguayan military leader and politician. He was elected as presidential candidate for the Asociación Nacional Republicana (ANR; Colorado Party) in the 1998 elections but was forced to withdraw mid-campaign when imprisoned for ten years for refusing to obey former president Juan Carlos ◊Wasmosy's order to resign as head of the army in 1996, after he was accused of attempting to lead a coup against the Wasmosy government. He was accused of assassinating Vice President Luis Maria Argaña in March 1999 and fled to Argentina.

Owen, David Anthony Llewellyn, Baron Owen of the City of Plymouth (1938–)

British politician, Labour foreign secretary 1977–79. In 1981 he was one of the founders of the Social Democratic Party (SDP), and became its leader in 1983. Opposed to the decision of the majority of the party to merge with the Liberals in 1987, Owen stood down but emerged in 1988 as leader of a rump SDP, which was eventually disbanded in 1990.

Owen was born in Plymouth and trained as a doctor before entering Parliament in 1966. In 1992 he replaced Lord Carrington as European Community (now European Union) mediator in the peace talks on Bosnia-Herzegovina. He resigned from the post in 1995, and retired from active politics. He received a life peerage in 1992.

FURTHER READING
Harris, Kenneth *David Owen* 1987

Owens, Jesse (James Cleveland) (1913–1980)

US track and field athlete who excelled in the sprints, hurdles, and the long jump. At the 1936 Berlin Olympics he won four gold medals. The Nazi leader Adolf Hitler is said to have stormed out of the stadium in disgust at the black man's triumph.

FURTHER READING
Baker, William J *Jesse Owens: An American Life* 1986

Oz, Amos, adopted name of Amos Klausner (1939–)

Israeli writer. His poetic novels and short stories document events in Israeli and kibbutz life; for example, the novel *My Michael* (1972), set in Jerusalem in the 1950s. He is a spokesperson for liberal Israelis who oppose Jewish extremism towards the Palestinians. His first novel, *Elsewhere, Perhaps* (1966), depicts life on a kibbutz near the Syrian border. *Touch the Water, Touch the Wind* (1973) is set against the background of the history of Israel between World War II and the Six-Day War. His nonfiction works include *In the Land of Israel* (1983), *Israel, Palestine, and Peace* (1994), and *Under this Blazing Light: Essays* (1995).

Özal, Turgut (1927–1993)

Turkish Islamic right-wing politician, prime minister 1983–89, and president 1989–93. He was responsible for improving his country's relations with Greece, but his prime objective was to strengthen Turkey's alliance with the USA.

Özal worked for the World Bank 1971–79. In 1980 he was deputy to Prime Minister Bülent Ulusu under the military regime of Kenan Evren, and, when political pluralism returned in 1983, he founded the Islamic, right-of-centre Motherland Party (ANAP) and led it to victory in the elections of that year. In the 1987 general election he retained his majority and in November 1989 replaced Evren as Turkey's first civilian president for 30 years. He died in office and was succeeded by Süleiman Demirel.

Born in Malayta and educated at Istanbul Technical University, Özal entered government service and became undersecretary for state planning in 1967. As president, Özal's reputation was greater abroad than at home; he was largely responsible for Turkey's involvement in the 1991 Desert Storm campaign against Saddam Hussein. He campaigned vigorously for the rights of Bosnian Muslims and Azerbaijanis and, less overtly, for the Kurds on his country's remote southeast borders.

P

Pacheco Areco, Jorge (1920–)

Uruguayan politician and president 1966–71. He was an authoritarian politician who governed during a particularly turbulent period in the nation's history. Against a background of economic crisis, he banned left-wing parties and sought to suppress the media. During his administration, the country entered into a dictatorship, moving ever closer to a military dictatorship.

Problems with insurgency arose during his administration, and the guerrilla group the Movimento de Liberación Nacional (also known as the Tuparamos) went on the offensive. The military were called upon to oppose the group's activities.

Pacheco Areco was vice president to Oscar ◊Gestido and entered presidential office after Gestido's untimely death.

Paderewski, Ignacy Jan (1860–1941)

Polish pianist, composer, and politician; prime minister of Poland in 1919. After his debut in Vienna in 1887, he became celebrated in Europe and the USA as an interpreter of Frédéric Chopin's piano music and as the composer of the *Polish Fantasy* for piano and orchestra (1893) and symphony *Polonia* (1903–09).

During World War I Paderewski helped organize the Polish army in France. In 1919, for a short time, he was prime minister of the newly independent Poland, which he had represented at the Versailles peace conference. After the fall of Poland in 1939 he briefly became president of the Polish National Council formed by the government in exile in Paris. Ill health reduced his involvement in wartime politics.

FURTHER READING
Paderewski, Ignacy Jan, and Lawton, Mary *The Paderewski Memoirs* 1939

Paeniu, Bikenibeu (1956–)

Tuvaluan politician, prime minister 1989–93 and from 1996. In October 1989, after a general election had led to a swing in support away from Prime Minister Tomasi ◊Puapua, he became prime minister at the age of 33. He took personal control over foreign affairs and economic planning and sought to reduce the country's dependence on foreign economic aid. The September 1993 general election resulted in a hung parliament, in which no single candidate could attract sufficient support to become prime minister. A new election in November 1993 saw Paeniu's replacement as prime minister by Kamuta Laatasi, but Paeniu returned to power in December 1996 after Laatasi was defeated in a no-confidence vote. In February 1997 his government restored the country's traditional flag and in March 1998 Paeniu was re-elected prime minister.

Born in Bikenibeu, Tarawa, on the island of Nukulalae, Paeniu studied at universities in Fiji and Hawaii and then worked as an economist with the South Pacific Commission in Noumea, New Caledonia. He returned to Tuvalu in 1988.

His 1998 election followed a campaign in which Paeniu and Laatasi had traded lurid allegations of sexual and financial misconduct.

Page, Earle Christmas Grafton (1880–1961)

Australian politician, cofounder and leader of the Country Party 1920–39 and briefly prime minister in April 1939. He represented Australia in the British war cabinet 1941–42 and was minister of health 1949–55.

Born in New South Wales, he was educated at Sydney University and worked as a surgeon before winning the federal seat of Cowper in 1919. In 1922 he became deputy prime minister in a coalition government led by Stanley Bruce's Nationalist Party and was commerce minister in the 1934–39 Joseph ◊Lyons government. He was created a GCMG in 1938.

FURTHER READING
Page, Earl *Truant Surgeon* 1963

Paglia, Camille (1947–)

US writer and academic. An opponent of women's studies, she believes that the great accomplishments of Western civilization have been achieved by men as a result of the male determination to conquer nature. This is set out in *Sexual Personae: Art and Decadence from Nefertiti to Emily Dickinson* (1990). She became professor of humanities at the University of Arts, Philadelphia, in 1984.

She was born in Endicott, New York. Self-assertive, combatively verbose, and combining paeans to rock stars with an erudite surface dazzle, Paglia quickly became popular with the media. She celebrates the glamour of women and their difference from men in such books as *Sex, Art, and American Culture* (1992) and *Vamps and Tramps* (1995).

Pahlavi, Muhammad Reza (1919–1980)

Shah of Iran 1941–79. He succeeded on the abdication of his father, Shah Reza ◊Pahlavi, and soon embarked on a major programme of social reform. However, his plans were frustrated by the poor state of the economy. He was opposed by religious fundamentalists and in 1953 briefly left the country but was returned to the throne with the backing of the USA. With oil revenues improving, Iran became a major force in the Middle East, but religious fundamentalists, led by Ayatollah Ruhollah ◊Khomeini, continued to oppose him and in 1979 he fled the country and was given refuge in Egypt where he spent the rest of his life.

FURTHER READING
Pahlavi, Muhammad Reza *Answer to History* 1980
Wilber, D *Reza Shah Pahlavi* 1975

Pahlavi, Reza (1877–1944)

Shah of Iran 1925–41. In 1923 he became prime minister and two years later was elected shah. He embarked on a programme of social and economic modernization. During World War II the Allies suspected that he had sympathies with the Axis powers and in 1941 they forced him to abdicate in favour of his son ◊Muhammad Reza Shah.

As a youth he joined the Iranian army, rising to the rank of colonel. At the time, his country was largely controlled by Soviet forces and after a rising led by Pahlavi succeeded in expelling them and deposing the ruling regime, he became minister of war and commander in chief of the armed forces.

Paisley, Ian (Richard Kyle) (1926–)

See page 336.

Pal, Bipin Chandra (1858–1932)

Indian nationalist and freedom fighter. He entered politics in 1877 and his association with the reformist Brahma Samâj leader Keshub Chunder Sen (1838–1884) drew him into this movement in 1880. He was also greatly influenced by Bal Gangadhar Tilak (1856–1920), Lala ◊Lajpat Rai (with whom he formed the famous Congress trio 'Lal, Pal, and Bal'), and the religious writer and leader ◊Aurobindo Ghose. In 1902 he launched a weekly journal, *Young India*, through which he championed the cause of Indian freedom.

Though born into an orthodox Zamindar family in Sylhet (in Bangladesh), he opposed traditional orthodoxy and religious practices. He campaigned for the boycott of British goods and also advocated a policy of passive resistance and noncooperation. He spent the years between 1908 and 1911 in the UK, where he worked for India's freedom and published the newspaper *Swaraj*. In the later stages of the freedom

movement, he withdrew from political life, although he continued to write on national matters.

Paley, Grace (1922–)

US short-story writer, critic, and political activist. Her stories express Jewish and feminist domestic experience with highly ironic humour, as in *The Little Disturbances of Man* (1960) and *Later the Same Day* (1985). Her *Collected Stories* appeared in 1994.

Palme, (Sven) Olof Joachim (1927–1986)

Swedish social-democratic politician, prime minister 1969–76 and 1982–86. As prime minister he carried out constitutional reforms, turning the Riksdag into a single-chamber parliament and stripping the monarch of power, and was widely respected for his support of Third World countries. He was assassinated in February 1986.

Palme, educated in Sweden and the USA, joined the Social Democratic Labour Party (SAP) in 1949 and became secretary to the prime minister in 1954. He led the SAP youth movement 1955–61. In 1963 he entered government and held several posts before becoming leader of the SAP in 1969. Palme was shot by an unknown assassin in the centre of Stockholm while walking home with his wife after an evening visit to a cinema.

Palmer, A(lexander) Mitchell (1872–1936)

US public official. He held office in the US House of Representatives 1909–15. A Quaker, he declined an appointment as secretary of war under President Woodrow Wilson, and served instead as custodian of alien property during World War I. As US attorney general 1919–21, he led the controversial 'Palmer raids' against alleged political radicals during the Red Scare.

Palmer, Geoffrey Winston Russell (1942–)

New Zealand Labour centre-left politician, prime minister 1989–90. From 1984 he served as deputy prime minister and attorney general in the Labour government of David ◊Lange and on Lange's resignation in 1989, he became prime minister. With the economy depressed, Palmer soon became unpopular and he was forced to resign in September 1990, after facing a confidence vote. He was succeeded by Michael ◊Moore one month before the 1990 general election, which was won by the National Party, led by Jim ◊Bolger.

A graduate of Victoria University, Wellington, Palmer was a law lecturer in the USA and New Zealand before entering politics, becoming Labour member for Christchurch in the house of representatives in 1979.

Panchen Lama, 11th incarnation (1995–)

Tibetan spiritual leader, second in importance to the ◊Dalai Lama. China installed the present Panchen Lama, seven-year-old Gyantsen Norpo, in December 1995, after rejecting the Dalai Lama's choice, another seven-year-old boy, Gedhun Choekyo Nyima.

Most Tibetans still silently recognize Gedhun Choe-

Ian Paisley, 1971. *Rex*

kyo Nyima, who has been living in the custody of the Chinese since 1995, as the 'true' Panchem Lama. The Dalai Lama has called him the 'world's youngest political prisoner'.

The previous Panchen Lama (1935–1989) was deputed by the Chinese to take over when the Dalai Lama left Tibet in 1959, but was stripped of power in 1964 for refusing to denounce the Dalai Lama. He did not appear in public again until 1978.

Panday, Basdeo (1933–)

Trinidad and Tobago left-of-centre politician, prime minister from 1995. In 1975 he formed the union-backed United Labour Front (ULF), which merged into the centre-left National Alliance for Reconstruction (NAR) in 1984. Expelled from the NAR after disagreements with Prime Minister Arthur ◊Robinson, he formed the left-of-centre United National Congress (UNC) in 1989, a party oriented towards the Indian community. In the hung parliament of 1995, he headed a UNC minority government, which depended on tacit backing from the Tobago-based NAR; as a result, his government proposed greater autonomy for Tobago island.

Panday first gained prominence as a leader of the opposition, and was appointed foreign minister and deputy prime minister in 1986 until dismissed in 1988. As leader of the UNC he became the country's first prime minister of Indian descent; Trinidad and Tobago's Indian community comprises around 40% of the country's population.

He studied economics at London University before returning to Trinidad to become head of the main sugar-workers' union, the All Trinidad Sugar and General Workers' Trade Union, between 1973 and 1995.

◆ PAISLEY, IAN (RICHARD KYLE) (1926–) ◆

Northern Ireland politician, cleric, and leader of the Democratic Unionist Party (DUP) from 1971. An imposing and deeply influential member of the Protestant community, he was staunchly committed to the union with Britain. His political career was one of high drama, marked by protests, resignations, fierce oratory, and a pugnacious and forthright manner.

I would rather be British than just.

IAN PAISLEY *The Sunday Times* 12 December 1971

Paisley was born in Armagh, the son of a Baptist minister, and was educated at the South Wales Bible College and the Reformed Presbyterian Theological College in Belfast. He preached his first sermon at the age of 16, and in 1951 established the Free Presbyterian Church in Belfast. When Catholic civil-rights agitation began

to flourish in the 1960s, Paisley organized numerous marches and speeches in opposition, which led to his imprisonment for six weeks in 1968 for unlawful assembly. In April 1970, one year into 'the Troubles' in Northern Ireland, Paisley won the seat for Bannside in Northern Ireland's Stormont assembly, and he went on to win the North Antrim seat two months later. The following year he established the DUP as a more hardline rival to the ruling dominant Ulster Unionist Party. He was influential in the actions of the Ulster Workers' Council and their general strike, which destroyed the Sunningdale Power Sharing Initiative in 1974. Paisley's powerful speeches and image of strength won him great support within the Protestant community and he scored overwhelming victories in both the 1979 and 1984 European elections, polling around one-third of the first-preference votes each time.

Throughout the 1980s Paisley stuck rigidly to

Pandit, Vijaya Lakshmi (1900–1990)

Indian politician, member of parliament 1964–68. She was involved, with her brother Jawaharlal ◊Nehru, in the struggle for India's independence and was imprisoned three times by the British. She was the first woman to serve as president of the United Nations General Assembly, 1953–54, and held a number of political and diplomatic posts until her retirement in 1968.

After her brother became the first prime minister of India in 1947, Pandit was Indian ambassador to the USSR 1947–49 and to the USA 1949–52, and high commissioner to the UK 1954–61. In 1962 she became governor of the state of Maharashta and after her brother's death in 1964 she took over his constituency, with a large majority. She resigned in 1968, saying that she felt 'out of tune' with the new parliament. During the 1970s she became alarmed by the increasingly authoritarian regime of her niece Indira Gandhi, and became a staunch critic of her government.

Panetta, Leon E(dward) (1938–)

US Democrat politician, White House Chief of Staff 1995–96. An advocate of spending cuts and tax increases in order to deal with the budget deficit, he was director of the Office of Management and Budget 1993–94.

Panetta was born in Monterey, California. He was civil-rights officer of the department of health, education, and welfare under President Richard Nixon, concerned with the desegregation of schools, but resigned in 1970. He was a member of the House of Representatives 1977–93. As chair of the budget com-

his 'no surrender' policies, resigning his seat in 1985 in protest at the Anglo-Irish Agreement. He re-entered Parliament early the following year. His Presbyterian beliefs were inextricably bound up with his political aims, and in 1988 he was ejected from the European Parliament for interrupting an address by Pope John Paul II. Paisley was deeply sceptical of the various initiatives to solve the problems of Northern Ireland, particularly those involving any 'sellout', in his view, to the Dublin government or Sinn Féin and the Irish Republican Army (IRA).

He opposed the 1998 Good Friday Agreement on power-sharing in Northern Ireland and in the May 1998 referendum his North Antrim constituency was the only one of Northern Ireland's 18 seats in which there was a majority against the accord. He went on to lead the opposition to the agreement within the new Northern Ireland Assembly.

mittee 1989–93, he was a leading architect of President George Bush's tax-raising budget of 1990.

Pankhurst, Christabel (1880–1958)

English campaigner for women's suffrage. She was the daughter of the English suffragette Emmeline Pankhurst. After 1918 she devoted herself to a religious movement.

Pankhurst, Emmeline, born Goulden (1858–1928)

English suffragette. Founder of the Women's Social and Political Union (WSPU) in 1903, she launched the militant suffragette campaign in 1905. In 1926 she joined the Conservative Party and was a prospective Parliamentary candidate for Whitechapel.

Is not a woman's life, is not her health, are not her limbs more valuable than panes of glass? There is no doubt of that, but most important of all, does not the breaking of glass produce more effect upon the Government?
EMMELINE PANKHURST Speech 16 February 1912

Mrs Pankhurst was born in Manchester, the daughter of Robert Goulden, a calico-printer and early advocate of women's suffrage. In 1879 she married Richard Marsden Pankhurst (died 1898), a lawyer, and they served together on the committee that promoted the Married Women's Property Act. From 1906, as a militant, she was frequently arrested and in 1913 was sentenced to three years' penal servitude in connection with the blowing up of David Lloyd George's house at Walton.

She was supported by her daughters Christabel ◊Pankhurst, political leader of the movement, and Sylvia ◊Pankhurst. The latter was imprisoned nine times under the 'Cat and Mouse Act', and was a pacifist in World War I.

When World War I broke out Mrs Pankhurst called off the suffrage campaign and went recruiting in the USA. She visited Russia in 1917. She died only a month before Stanley Baldwin's Representation of the People Act gave women full equality in the franchise.

Her autobiography, *The Life of Emmeline Pankhurst*, was published in 1935.

FURTHER READING
Hoy, Linda *Emmeline Pankhurst* 1985
Pankhurst, Emmeline *My Own Story* 1914, reprinted 1970

Pankhurst, Sylvia Estelle (1882–1960)

English campaigner for women's suffrage. She was the daughter of the English suffragette Emmeline Pankhurst. She became a pacifist in 1914 and in 1921 was imprisoned for six months for seditious publications. After the Italian invasion of Ethiopia in 1935, she devoted her life to that country's independence, settling there permanently in 1956. Her works include *The Suffrage Movement* (1931) and a biography of her mother, published in 1935.

FURTHER READING

Castle, Barbara *Sylvia and Christabel Pankhurst* 1987

Pankhurst, Richard *Sylvia Pankhurst: Artist and Crusader* 1979

Romero, Patricia *E Sylvia Pankhurst: Portrait of a Radical* 1987

Papandreou, Andreas (1919–1996)

Greek socialist politician, founder of the Pan-Hellenic Socialist Movement (PASOK); prime minister 1981–89 and again 1993–96. He lost the 1989 election after being implicated in an alleged embezzlement scandal, involving the diversion of funds to the Greek government from the Bank of Crete, headed by George Koskotas. In January 1992 a trial cleared Papandreou of all corruption charges.

Son of a former prime minister, he studied law in Athens and at Harvard. He was director of the Centre for Economic Research in Athens 1961–64, and economic adviser to the Bank of Greece.

He was imprisoned April–December 1967 for his political activities, after which he founded PASOK. After another spell in overseas universities, he returned to Greece in 1974. He was leader of the opposition 1977–81, and became Greece's first socialist prime minister. He was re-elected in 1985, but defeated in 1989 after damage to his party and himself from the Koskotas affair. After being acquitted in January 1992, Papandreou's request for a general election was rejected by the government. However, PASOK won the October 1993 general election, and he again became head of government. Following his hospitalization with pneumonia in November 1995, Papandreou resigned the premiership in January 1996; in March he was declared well and released from hospital, but died three months later.

Papandreou, George (1888–1968)

Greek politician, prime minister in 1944 and 1963–65. After escaping from Greece in 1942 during the German occupation, he returned in 1944 to head a coalition government. However, his socialist credentials were suspected by the army, and he held office for only a few weeks. In 1961 he founded the Centre Union Party, and returned as prime minister in 1963 and 1964. A disagreement with King Constantine II in 1965 led to his resignation, and in 1967, when a coup established a military regime, he was placed under house arrest. His son Andreas ◊Papandreou carried forward his political beliefs.

Born in Salonika, George Papandreou became a lawyer and moved into politics in the early 1920s. A left-of-centre republican, he held office in several administrations of the 1920s and 1930s, including the

period when the monarchy was removed in 1923 and reinstated by the army in 1925.

Papen, Franz von (1879–1969)

German right-wing politician. As chancellor in 1932, he negotiated the Nazi–Conservative alliance that made Hitler chancellor in 1933. He was envoy to Austria 1934–38 and ambassador to Turkey 1939–44. Although acquitted at the Nürnberg trials, he was imprisoned by a German denazification court for three years.

Pareto, Vilfredo (1848–1923)

Italian economist and political philosopher. A vigorous opponent of socialism and liberalism, he justified inequality of income and rule by elites as constants irrespective of which particular economic or political system is in force. In some ways a classical liberal, his ideas nevertheless influenced Mussolini, who appointed him senator in 1922.

Park Chung Hee (1917–1979)

South Korean politician, president 1963–79. Under his rule South Korea had one of the world's fastest-growing economies, but recession and his increasing authoritarianism led to his assassination in 1979.

Parkinson, Cecil (Edward), Baron of Carnforth in the County of Lancashire (1931–)

British Conservative politician, chair of the Conservative Party 1981–83 and from 1997. He was a minister for trade and industry, but resigned in October 1984 following the disclosure of an affair with his former secretary Sarah Keyes, which resulted in her pregnancy. In 1987 he rejoined the cabinet as secretary of state for energy, and in 1989 became transport secretary. He left the cabinet when John Major became prime minister in 1990 and later announced his intention to retire from active politics and enter business. He received a life peerage in 1992.

In 1997 at the request of the new Conservative Party leader, William Hague, he returned to politics.

Pastrana Arango, Andres (1955–)

Colombian politician and president from 1998. He focused on the need for peace as a strategy for national economic development and stability.

Pastrana, a member of the Conservative Party (PC), was elected against a rising upsurge in violence. His election pledges stated his desire to make peace with guerrilla groups, such as the Fuerzas Armadas Revolucionarias de Colombia (FARC; Revolutionary Armed Forces) and the Ejército de Liberación Nacional (ELN; National Liberation Army), who threatened the nation's democracy and political stability. He also pledged to end corruption in government following the scandal of his predecessor, Ernesto Samper, concerning the use of drugs money to fund election campaigns.

Pastrana was Conservative mayor of Bogotá, and the son of the former president Misael Prastrana.

Patel, Sardar Vallabhbhai Javerabhai (1875–1950)

Indian political leader. A fervent follower of Mahatma ◊Gandhi and a leader of the Indian National Congress, he was deputy prime minister 1947–50, after independence.

Patel participated in the *satyagraha* (the struggle for Indian independence by nonviolent, noncooperative means) in Kaira in 1918. He was a member of the right wing of the Indian National Congress and supported conservative opposition to the reform of Hindu law as it applied to the lack of rights of Hindu women.

Patten, Chris(topher Francis) (1944–)

British Conservative politician, governor of Hong Kong 1992–97. He was member of Parliament for Bath 1979–92 and Conservative Party chair 1990–92, orchestrating the party's campaign for the 1992 general election, in which he lost his parliamentary seat. He accepted the governorship of Hong Kong for the crucial five years prior to its transfer to China in 1997. He went on to take part in the reform of the Royal Ulster Constabulary.

A former director of the Conservative Party's research department, he held junior ministerial posts under Prime Minister Margaret Thatcher, despite his reputation for being to the left of the party, and eventually joined the cabinet. As environment secretary 1989–90, he was responsible for administering the poll tax. As governor of Hong Kong, Patten's proposals for greater democracy – which resulted in the first fully democratic elections to legislative bodies in 1994 – were welcomed by Hong Kong's legislative council but strongly opposed by the Chinese government. His prodemocracy, anti-Chinese stance won the backing of many Hong Kong residents, but was criticized by members of its business community. He was also criticized in 1995 when he suggested that UK citizenship could be extended to Hong Kong residents who wished to leave the colony after its transfer to China.

Patterson, Percival (1935–)

Jamaican centre-left politician, prime minister from 1992. Vice president of the moderately socialist People's National Party (PNP) in 1969, he held various ministerial positions 1972–80 and 1989–92 under Michael ◊Manley. Losing his seat in the PNP's crushing defeat by the Jamaican Labour Party (JLP) in 1980, he oversaw the PNP's successful reorganization as a moderate centre-left force. Re-elected in 1989, he succeeded Manley as prime minister in 1992. He pursued a moderate, free-market economic strategy and achieved an increased majority for the PNP in

1993, and an unprecedented third consecutive term in 1997.

Patterson joined the PNP in 1958. He was appointed to the Jamaican senate in 1967 and elected to its house of representatives in 1970. His ministerial portfolios included industry and commerce 1972–76, foreign affairs 1976–80, and planning, development, and finance from 1989.

He was born in Kingston, and studied English literature at the University of the West Indies and law at London University, being later admitted to the Jamaican bar.

Paul, Alice (1885–1977)

US social reformer and lawyer. In 1912 she became chair of the congressional committee of the National American Suffrage Association; impatient with its policies, in 1913 she helped to found the more militant Congressional Union for Woman Suffrage, which merged in 1917 to form the National Woman's Party; she would become this party's chair in 1942. After women won the right to vote with the 19th Amendment (1920), she devoted herself to gaining equal rights for women and in 1923 introduced the first equal rights amendment in Congress. She had meanwhile studied the law and broadened her field to the international arena, and although she did not live to see an equal rights amendment to the US Constitution, she did get an equal rights affirmation in the preamble to the United Nations charter.

She was born in Moorestown, New Jersey. Influenced by her Quaker family, she graduated from Swarthmore in 1905 and went on to do graduate work in New York City and England. While in London 1906–09 she worked in a settlement house and was jailed on three occasions for suffragist actions. She took her PhD from the University of Pennsylvania in 1912.

Paul VI, Giovanni Battista Montini (1897–1978)

Pope from 1963. His encyclical *Humanae Vitae/Of Human Life* (1968) reaffirmed the church's traditional teaching on birth control, thus following the minority report of the commission originally appointed by Pope John rather than the majority view.

He was born near Brescia, Italy. He spent more than 25 years in the Secretariat of State under Pius XI and Pius XII before becoming archbishop of Milan in 1954. In 1958 he was created a cardinal by Pope John, and in 1963 he succeeded him as pope, taking the name of Paul as a symbol of ecumenical unity.

Pauling, Linus Carl (1901–1994)

US theoretical chemist and biologist. His ideas on chemical bonding are fundamental to modern theories of molecular structure. He also investigated the properties and uses of vitamin C as related to human health. He won the Nobel Prize for Chemistry in 1954 and the Nobel Peace Prize in 1962, having campaigned for a nuclear-test ban.

During the 1950s he became politically active, his special concern being the long-term genetic damage resulting from atmospheric nuclear-bomb tests. In this, he came into conflict with the US establishment and several of his science colleagues. He was denounced as a pacifist and a communist, his passport was withdrawn 1952–54, and he was obliged to appear before the US Senate Internal Security Committee. One item in his sustained wide-ranging campaign was his book *No More War!* (1958). He presented to the United Nations a petition signed by 11,021 scientists from 49 countries urging an end to nuclear-weapons testing, and during the 1960s spent several years on a study of the problems of war and peace at the Center for the Study of Democratic Institutions in Santa Barbara, California.

FURTHER READING
Moore, Ruth *The Coil of Life* 1961
Serafini, Anthony *Linus Pauling: A Man and His Science* 1989

Pavlov, Valentin (1937–)

Soviet communist politician, prime minister January–August 1991. He served in the finance ministry, the state planning committee (Gosplan), and the state pricing committee before becoming minister of finance in 1989. In January 1991 he replaced Nikolai Ryzhkov as prime minister, with the brief of halting the gathering collapse of the Soviet economy. In August 1991 he was a member of the eight-person junta that led the abortive anti-Gorbachev coup.

In the midst of the coup, he relinquished his position as premier, citing health reasons. He was arrested when the coup was finally thwarted but released under an amnesty in 1994.

Paz Estenssoro, Victor (1907–)

Bolivian president 1952–56, 1960–64, and 1985–89. He founded and led the Movimiento Nacionalista Revolucionario (MNR), which seized power in 1952. His regime extended the vote to Indians, nationalized the country's largest tin mines, embarked on a programme of agrarian reform, and brought inflation under control.

After holding a number of financial posts, Paz Estenssoro entered politics in the 1930s, was elected to the chamber of deputies in 1940, and founded the MNR in 1942. In 1946 he fled to Argentina during one of Bolivia's many periods of military rule, returning in 1951 and becoming president in 1952. He immediately embarked on a programme of political reform, retaining the presidency until 1956 and being re-elected 1960–64 and again in 1985, returning from near-

retirement at the age of 77. During his long career he was Bolivian ambassador to London 1956–59 and a professor at London University in 1966. Following an indecisive presidential contest in 1989, Paz Estenssoro was replaced by Jaime Paz Zamora of the Movement of the Revolutionary Left (MIR).

Paz, Octavio (1914–1998)

Mexican poet, essayist, and political thinker. His works reflect many influences, including Marxism, Surrealism, and Aztec mythology. *El laberinto de la soledad/ The Labyrinth of Solitude* (1980), the book which brought him to world attention, explores Mexico's heritage. He was awarded the Nobel Prize for Literature in 1990.

In 1962 Paz was appointed Mexican ambassador to India, but resigned in 1968 in protest against the Mexican government's killing of 200 student demonstrators on the eve of the Olympic Games. In 1971 he founded the monthly magazine *Plural* (later called *Vuelta*), which he used to analyse socialism and liberalism, urging Mexico to become independent of communist and US influences.

Born in Mexico City, Paz studied at the National University of Mexico, but left in 1936 to set up a school to help poor children in rural Yucatán. In 1937 he fought in the Spanish Civil War, in a Republican brigade commanded by David Siqueiros. After a time as a left-wing journalist and Mexican diplomat 1946–51, he concentrated on writing.

Paz Zamora, Jaime (1939–)

Bolivian president 1989–94. His administration was uneventful and very much a continuation of the policies established by his predecessor Victor ◊Paz Estenssoro.

Paz Zamora was leader of the centre-left Movimento de la Izquierda Revolucionaria (MIR; Revolutionary Left Movement). He became president as a result of the failure of all the contenders in the 1989 elections to gain at least 50% of the vote – as stipulated in the constitution. Subsequently, congress decided to allow the right-wing Nationalist Democratic Action Party (AND) to form a coalition with the MIR. As leader of the MIR, Paz Zamora was elected president on condition that the opposition obtained the most important ministries.

Pearse, Patrick (Henry) (1879–1916)

Irish writer, educationalist, and revolutionary. He was prominent in the Gaelic revival, and a leader of the Easter Rising in 1916. Proclaimed president of the provisional government, he was court-martialled and shot after its suppression.

Pearse was a founding member of the Irish Volunteers, and was inducted into the Irish Republican Brotherhood in 1913. He came to believe that a 'blood sacrifice' was needed to awaken the slumbering Irish nation. In a famous graveside oration in 1915, he declared that 'Ireland unfree shall never be at peace'.

He was commander in chief of the Volunteers during the Easter Rising in 1916, and read the declaration of the Irish Republic. The rebellion that he led emerged as a defining moment in modern Irish history, its authors as founding martyrs of modern Ireland, and the words of the declaration as the sacred text of modern Irish republicanism.

Born in Dublin, Pearse was educated at a Christian Brothers school and the Royal University. He was attracted at an early age to cultural nationalism, and was prominent in the Gaelic League from 1896. He edited its newspaper *An Claidheamh Soluis* 1903–09 and founded St Enda's, a bilingual secondary school in 1908.

FURTHER READING

Dudley Edwards, Ruth *Patrick Pearse: The Triumph of Failure* 1977

Pearson, Lester Bowles (1897–1972)

Canadian politician, leader of the Liberal Party from 1958, prime minister 1963–68. As foreign minister 1948–57, he represented Canada at the United Nations (UN), playing a key role in settling the Suez Crisis of 1956. He was awarded the Nobel Peace Prize in 1957.

Pearson served as president of the UN General Assembly 1952–53 and helped to create the UN Emergency Force (UNEF) that policed Sinai following the Egypt–Israel war of 1956. As prime minister, he led the way to formulating a national medicare (health insurance) law.

The grim fact is that we prepare for war like precocious giants and for peace like retarded pygmies.

LESTER PEARSON News summaries 15 March 1955

He was born in Toronto, and educated at Toronto University and St John's College, Oxford, England. He was assistant professor of modern history at Toronto University 1926–28, then joined Canada's department of external affairs. He was Canadian ambassador to the USA 1945–46, and entered parliament as a Liberal in 1948. After his resignation as prime minister he became chair of the Commission on International Development for the World Bank.

FURTHER READING

Bothwell, R *Pearson: His Life and World* 1978
Pearson, Lester *Memoirs* 1973–75
Thordarson, Bruce *Lester Pearson: Diplomat and Politician* 1974

Peart, (Thomas) Frederick Baron Peart of Workington (1914–1988)

British Labour politician. He was minister of agriculture 1964–68 and then Lord President of the Privy Council and leader of the House of Commons 1968–70. In March 1974 he again became minister of agriculture. He was created a life peer in September 1976, but remained a member of the cabinet as Lord Privy Seal and leader of the House of Lords.

He was educated at Wolsingham Grammar School and Bede College, Durham University. He became a teacher and, after war service, a Labour member of Parliament in 1945. Between 1970 and 1974 he was successively Opposition spokesperson on agriculture and defence.

Peng Dehuai or *Peng Teh-huai* (1898–1974)

Chinese communist military leader and politician. As deputy commander in Zhu De's 8th Route Army, he played a leading role in the liberation war against Japan 1937–45, successfully using guerrilla tactics. He was made defence minister in 1954, but clashed with party leader Mao Zedong in August 1959 over economic policy and military modernization and was replaced by Lin Biao. Peng was later formally purged in December 1966, during the 'Cultural Revolution', and was to spend the remainder of his life in prison.

Born in Hunan province, a peasant's son, Peng trained at a military school. In 1928 he led an uprising against the Kuomintang (Guomindang) nationalist army and joined the Chinese Communist Party (CCP), becoming a commander in Zhu De's army. He was a key military strategist in the Long March of 1934–35, in which the CCP's army escaped northwards away from Jiang Jie Shi's (Chiang Kai-shek's) nationalist army. After the communist victory in the struggle with the Kuomintang party in 1949, Peng was placed in charge of the Chinese 'volunteer' forces during the 1950–53 Korean War.

His demotion from the position of defence minister followed Peng's presentation, at a party meeting in Lushan, of a letter in which he had strongly criticized Mao's rash 'Great Leap Forward' communalization programme and the impending break with the Soviet Union. He was posthumously rehabilitated in December 1978 by the reformist Deng Xiaoping, who, in a special memorial service, praised Peng for his 'ardent love for the Party' and for his courage, honesty, and integrity.

FURTHER READING

Domes, J *Peng Te-huai: The Man and the Image* 1985

Peng Pai or *P'eng P'ai* (1896–1929)

Chinese rural revolutionary. In 1924 at the Guomindang (nationalist party) base in Guangzhou (Canton), he became secretary of the Peasants' Bureau and director of the Peasant Movement Training Institute.

In 1925 he had helped form the Guangdong Provincial Peasant Association, which claimed 200,000 members. During the Northern Expedition of 1926–28 Peng organized China's first rural soviet. In the wake of ◊Jiang Jie Shie's (Chiang Kai-shek's) counter-revolution against the communists, however, Peng's soviet was crushed in 1928. He was captured and executed by the Guomindang.

From a landlord family, he studied in Japan before joining the Chinese Communist Party and organizing rural tenants in his home district of Haifeng in the southern province of Guangdong (Kwangtung). In 1923 he established a peasants' association, which campaigned for lower rents, led anti-landlord boycotts, and organized welfare activities. The association was crushed by a local warlord in 1924.

Peng Zhen (1902–1997)

Chinese communist politician, mayor of Beijing (Peking) 1951–66, who was purged at the start of ◊Mao Zedong's Cultural Revolution.

Born in Shanxi province, into a poor peasant family, Peng joined the Chinese Communist Party (CCP) in 1923, soon after its founding, and was imprisoned between 1929–35 by the Kuomintang (Guomindang) nationalist regime. He then served as a political commissar during the 1937–45 war against Japan and entered the CCP Politburo in 1945. As mayor of the capital, Beijing, from 1951, Peng became an influential figure in the new People's Republic and, during the early 1960s, was singled-out as one of Mao's 'close comrades-in-arms'. However, the two fell out in November 1965, when Peng tried to prevent the release of a critical article by Yao Wenyuan, 'Hai Jui Dismissed from Office', which marked the opening of the Mao-backed Cultural Revolution of 1966–69. By mid-1966, following criticisms of his 'rightist' leanings by the young ultra-leftist Red Guards, Peng became the first Politburo member to be purged; and in December 1966 he was placed on public trial. He did not reappear in public again until January 1979, following the rise to power of the reformist Deng Xiaoping. Peng was fully rehabilitated, being restored to the Politburo (where he remained until 1987) and to his old post in Beijing, and in 1979 he helped draft China's first legal code. He served as chair of the National People's Congress (parliament) standing committee until 1987 and, thereafter, until his death retained behind-the-scenes influence as a party elder.

Peres, Shimon (1923–)

Israeli Labour politician, prime minister 1984–86 and 1995–96. He was prime minister, then foreign minister, under a power-sharing agreement with the leader of the Likud Party, Yitzhak ◊Shamir. From 1989 to 1990 he was finance minister in a Labour–Likud coalition. As foreign minister in Yitzhak Rabin's Labour government from 1992, he negotiated the 1993 peace agreement with the Palestine Liberation Organization (PLO). He was awarded the 1994 Nobel Prize for Peace jointly with Rabin and PLO leader Yassir Arafat.

Following the assassination of Rabin in November 1995, Peres succeeded him as prime minister, and pledged to continue the peace process in which they had both been so closely involved, but in May 1996 he was defeated in Israel's first direct elections for prime minister.

Peres emigrated from Poland to Palestine in 1934, but was educated in the USA. In 1959 he was elected to the Knesset (Israeli parliament). He was leader of the Labour Party 1977–92, when he was replaced by Rabin.

FURTHER READING
Golan, M *Shimon Peres* 1982

Pérez Balladares, Ernesto (1946–)

Panamanian right-wing politician, president from 1994. He promoted a free-market economic programme.

He was a founding member of the right-wing Democratic Revolutionary Party (PRD) in 1979, which was sympathetic to General Omar ◊Torrijos. He served as PRD leader from 1992 and in May 1994 won the presidential election with 33% of the national vote. This was viewed as the country's first completely free and competitive election.

Pérez studied economics at the University of Notre Dame and graduated with a Master of Business Administration (MBA) from the University of Pennsylvania, USA. He then developed a career in business, from which he emerged a millionaire.

Pérez de Cuéllar, Javier (1920–)

Peruvian diplomat, fifth secretary general of the United Nations (UN) 1982–91. He raised the standing of the UN by his successful diplomacy in ending the Iran–Iraq War in 1988 and in securing the independence of Namibia in 1989. He was a candidate in the Peruvian presidential elections of 1995, but was defeated by his opponent Alberto Fujimori.

He was unable to resolve the Gulf conflict resulting from Iraq's invasion of Kuwait in 1990 before combat against Iran by the UN coalition began in January 1991, but later in 1991 he negotiated the release of Western hostages held in Beirut.

A delegate to the first UN General Assembly 1946–47, he subsequently held several ambassadorial posts, including ambassador to Switzerland and the USSR. Between 1971 and 1975 he was Peru's permanent representative to the UN, becoming an undersecretary in 1979.

FURTHER READING
Pérez de Cuellar, J et al *Pilgrimage for Peace: A Secretary-General's Memoir* 1997

Pérez Esquivel, Adolfo (1932–   )

Argentine sculptor and architect. As leader of the Servicio de Paz y Justicia (Peace and Justice Service), a Catholic–Protestant human-rights organization, he was awarded the 1980 Nobel Prize for Peace.

Pérez Jiménez, Marcos (1914–   )

Venezuelan president 1952–58. He led the military junta that overthrew the Acción Democrática government of Rómulo Gallegos in 1948 and was made provisional president in 1952. In 1953 he was approved as constitutional president by congress. His regime had a reputation as the most repressive in Venezuelan history. It also encouraged European immigration and undertook massive public works in the capital, Caracas.

Pérez Rodriguez, Carlos Andrés (1922–   )

Venezuelan politician and president 1974–79 and 1989–93. During his first term, he governed the nation at a time of massive economic growth due to the wealth generated by the export of oil. He embarked on a programme of state nationalization of the iron and steel industries in 1975 and oil in 1976, and actively sought to ameliorate relations with Venezuela's geographic neighbours. His second term in office was more tumultuous, with increasing discontent and public unrest over the government's free-market economic policy ending in his suspension from office on charges of inappropriate practices with public funds. An attempted coup took place in 1992, the leader of which, Hugo Chávez, was elected to the presidency in 1998.

Pérez held the position of leader of the Acción Democrática party (AD; Democratic Action Party). Like his two predecessors, presidents Raúl ◊ Leoni and Rafael ◊ Caldera, his first term enjoyed prosperity and massive increases in national oil revenues due to rising national oil production and the increase in worldwide oil prices as a result of the Arab–Israeli War (when the Arab nations embargoed oil). Massive government spending programmes were initiated, but worldwide recession in the latter half of the 1970s began to threaten the economic stability of the country and Pérez's administration was seen to be weakened.

Perkins, Frances (1882–1965)

US public official. She became the first female cabinet officer when she served as secretary of labour under F D Roosevelt 1933–45. Under Harry Truman she was a member of the federal civil service commission 1946–53.

Perón, (María Estela) Isabel, born Martínez (1931–   )

Argentine president 1974–76, and third wife of Juan ◊ Perón. She succeeded him after he died in office in 1974 (she had been elected vice president in 1973), but labour unrest, inflation, and political violence pushed the country to the brink of chaos. Accused of corruption in 1976, she was held under house arrest for five years. She went into exile in Spain in 1981.

Perón, Evita (María Eva), born Duarte (1919–1952)

Argentine populist leader. A successful radio actress, she became the second wife of Juan ◊ Perón in 1945. When he became president the following year, she became his chief adviser and virtually ran the health and labour ministries, devoting herself to helping the poor, improving education, and achieving women's suffrage. She founded a social welfare organization called the Eva Perón Foundation. She was politically astute and sought the vice presidency in 1951, but was opposed by the army and withdrew.

FURTHER READING

de Elia, Tomas *Evita: An Intimate Portrait of Eva Perón* 1997

Fraser, Nicholas, and Navarro, Marysa *Evita: The Real Lives of Eva Perón* 1996

Ortiz, Alicia Dujorvne et al *Eva Perón* 1997

Perón, Eva D and Page, Joseph *In My Own Words: Evita* 1996

Perón, Juan Domingo (1895–1974)

Argentine politician, dictator 1946–55 and from 1973 until his death. His populist appeal to the poor was enhanced by the charisma and political work of his second wife Evita ◊ Perón. After her death in 1952 his popularity waned and, with increasing economic difficulties and labour unrest, he was deposed in a military coup in 1955. He fled to Paraguay and, in 1960, to Spain. He returned from exile to the presidency in 1973, but died in office in 1974, and was succeeded by his third wife Isabel ◊ Perón.

A professional army officer, Perón took part in the right-wing military coup that toppled Argentina's government in 1943 and his popularity with the *descamisados* ('shirtless ones') – former trades unions that were converted into militant organizations – led to his election as president in 1946.

He instituted social reforms, but encountered economic difficulties. He was instrumental in initiating long-lasting changes in the national political arena, and today Peronism remains a powerful political force.

FURTHER READING

Alexander, Robert Jackson *The Perón Era* 1952

Perot, Ross (1930–   )

US industrialist and independent politician, an unsuccessful presidential candidate in 1992 and 1996, losing to Bill Clinton. Critical of the economic policies of the main political parties, he entered the 1992 presidential contest as a self-financed, independent candidate campaigning on the platform of balancing the federal budget. Despite securing no electoral college votes, Perot had the highest popular vote of any third presidential candidate since Theodore Roosevelt. In September 1995 he established the Reform Party to support his challenge for the 1996 presidential elections, in which he gained 8% of the popular vote, down 11 points on 1992. In November 1997 he announced that he would throw the weight of his party behind the Democrats in the November 1998 congressional election, to punish the Republicans for blocking efforts to reform campaign finance laws.

He was born in a Texas border town and, after service in the US Navy and then with IBM, he established his own company, Electronic Data Systems, quickly becoming a billionaire.

Perry, William James (1927–)

US Democrat politician, defence secretary 1994–96. As a mathematician and head of research at the Defense Department 1977–81, he was involved in the early development of stealth technology.

Before moving to the Defense Department in 1967 as a technical consultant, Perry was director of electronic military laboratories in Mountain View, California, 1954–64. He was professor and co-director of the Center for International Security and Arms Control at Stanford University, California, 1989–93. He retired as defence secretary in 1996 after President Bill Clinton was re-elected for a second term and was replaced by William Cohen.

Persson, Goran (1949–)

Swedish politician, prime minister from 1996. He was elected to parliament in 1979 and made leader of the Social Democratic Labour Party (SAP) in 1996.

Persson was born in Vingaker and educated at Örebro University. Active in the Swedish Democratic Youth League, he entered parliament at the age of 36. After serving for a time as finance minister, he succeeded Ingvar Carlsson as prime minister in March 1996, promising to revive the economy with harsh but realistic policies.

Pétain, (Henri) Philippe Benoni Omer Joseph (1856–1951)

French general and head of state. Voted in as prime minister in June 1940, Pétain signed an armistice with Germany on 22 June before assuming full powers on 16 July. His authoritarian regime, established at Vichy, collaborated with the Germans and proposed a reactionary 'National Revolution' for France under the slogan 'Work, Family, Fatherland'. Convinced in 1940 of Britain's imminent defeat, Pétain accepted Germany's terms for peace, including the occupation of northern France. In December 1940 he dismissed his deputy Pierre ◊Laval, who wanted to side with the Axis

powers, but bowed to German pressures to reinstate him in April 1942. With Germany occupying the whole of France from that November, Pétain found himself head, in name only, of a puppet state. Removed from France by the German army in 1944, he returned voluntarily and was tried and condemned to death for treason in August 1945. He died in prison on the Ile d'Yeu, his sentence having been commuted to life imprisonment.

A career soldier from northern France, Pétain's defence of Verdun in 1916 had made him, at the age of 60, a national hero. Promoted in 1917 to commander in chief, he came under Marshal Ferdinand Foch's supreme command in 1918. Subsequently, as a leading member of the Higher Council for War, his advocacy of a purely defensive military policy culminated in France's reliance on the Maginot Line as protection from German attack.

Peter I (1844–1921)

King of Serbia from 1903. He was the son of Prince ◊Alexander I Karageorgevich and was elected king when the last Obrenovich king was murdered in 1903. He took part in the retreat of the Serbian army in 1915, and in 1918 was proclaimed first king of the Kingdom of Serbs, Croats, and Slovenes (renamed Yugoslavia in 1921).

Peters, Winston (1946–)

New Zealand centrist politician; founder, in 1992, of the Maori-oriented New Zealand First Party (NZFP) and deputy prime minister from 1996. He emerged as a critic of the conventional monetarist economic strategy pursued by his party's leader, Jim ◊Bolger, who was prime minister from 1990, and left the National Party in 1993 to form the NZFP. Under Peters' charismatic leadership, the NZFP, which campaigned for greater state economic intervention and Maori rights, secured 13% of the vote in the October 1996 general election. These elections were held for the first time under a mixed member system of proportional representation and produced an inconclusive result, with the NZFP holding the balance of power. A coalition government was formed after the election, with Bolger as prime minister and Peters as deputy prime minister and treasurer (finance minister). Under the coalition agreement, extra spending was promised on healthcare and other social initiatives and in 1998 a bill was passed giving South Island Maoris compensation for past injustices.

After studying law and politics at university, Peters began his political career in the centre-right National Party. He soon attracted attention as the party's most prominent Maori and as a result of his debating skills.

Phan Boi Chau (1867–1940)

Vietnamese nationalist. Together with ◊Phan Chau

Trinh, he dominated the anti-colonial movement in Vietnam in the early 20th century. In 1912, in China, he was involved in the establishment of the Revival Society (Quang Phuc Hoi), which sought to bring about a democratic republic in Vietnam. Following his arrest in 1925, he was sentenced to life imprisonment. The ensuing public outcry led to his release and he spent the rest of his life in gently guarded retirement at Hue.

Born into a scholarly Confucian family, he was in essence a Confucian revolutionary. In 1905 he went to Japan where he wrote a history of Vietnam's loss of independence to the French, copies of which were then smuggled back to Vietnam. In 1915 he raised forces that launched, from South China, poorly organized attacks on French units.

Phan Chau Trinh (1872–1926)

Vietnamese nationalist. Along with ◊Phan Boi Chau, he was a leading figure in the anti-colonial movement in Vietnam in the early 20th century. In contrast to Phan Boi Chau's commitment to a revolutionary monarchism, Phan Chau Trinh advocated Western-style republicanism. His funeral in 1926 was held in Saigon, provoking unprecedented mass demonstrations and student strikes. This heralded a new phase in the anti-colonial struggle in Vietnam, one that would involve greater popular participation.

Between 1911 and 1925 he was in France, spending some of that time in prison. From France he launched strong attacks on the Vietnamese monarchy.

Philby, Kim (Harold Adrian Russell) (1912–1988)

British intelligence officer from 1940 and Soviet agent from 1933. He was liaison officer in Washington, DC, 1949–51, when he was confirmed to be a double agent and asked to resign. Named in 1963 as having warned Guy Burgess and Donald Maclean (also double agents) that their activities were known, he fled to the USSR and became a Soviet citizen and a general in the KGB. A fourth member of the ring was Anthony Blunt.

> To betray, you must first belong. I never belonged.
> KIM PHILBY *The Sunday Times* 17 December 1967

His autobiography, *My Secret Life*, was published in 1968.

Phomvihane, Kaysone (1920–1992)

Laotian politician. In 1975 he became prime minister of the newly formed People's Democratic Republic of Laos and general secretary of the Lao People's Revolutionary Party. Initially he attempted to follow a radical socialist programme of industrial national-

ization and rural collectivization, but later began a policy of economic and political liberalization.

Born in Savannakhet province and educated at Hanoi University, he fought with the anti-French forces in Vietnam after World War II and joined the exiled Free Lao Front (Neo Lao Issra) nationalist movement in Bangkok in 1945. He later joined the communist Pathet Lao, became, with North Vietnamese backing, its leader in 1955, and successfully directed guerrilla resistance to the incumbent rightist regime.

Pieck, Wilhelm (1876–1960)

German communist politician. He was a leader of the 1919 Spartacist revolt and a founder of the Socialist Unity Party in 1946. He opposed both the Weimar Republic and Nazism. From 1949 he was president of East Germany; the office was abolished on his death.

Pierce, William L

US author and revolutionary. Viewed as an intellectual leader of the US far right, he authored *The Turner Diaries* (1978), which is regarded as the novel that influenced the Oklahoma City bomber Timothy McVeigh. An ultra-right-wing novel, it recounts the experiences of Earl Turner, a leader of an underground guerrilla force (the Organization) that engages in a campaign of terrorism against a 'Jewish-controlled' US government.

Born in Atlanta, Pierce was employed at Oregon State University as an assistant professor of physics 1962–65. After joining a number of other far-right groups, he founded the National Alliance in 1974, an Arlington-based group devoted to promoting the progress of the white race.

Piercy, Marge (1937–)

US poet and novelist. Her fiction takes a passionate look at the fringes of US social life and the world of the liberated woman. Her novels include *Small Changes* (1972), the utopian *Woman on the Edge of Time* (1979), *Fly Away Home* (1984), a war novel *Gone to Soldiers* (1987), and *Summer People* (1989).

FURTHER READING
Shands, Kerstin W *The Repair of the World: The Novels of Marge Piercy* Contributions in Women's Studies, No 145, 1994

Piłsudski, Józef (Klemens) (1867–1935)

Polish nationalist politician, dictator from 1926. Born in Russian Poland, he founded the Polish Socialist Party in 1892 and was twice imprisoned for anti-Russian activities. During World War I he commanded a Polish force to fight for Germany and evicted the Russians from eastern Poland but fell under suspicion of intriguing with the Allies and was imprisoned by the Germans 1917–18. When Poland became independent in 1919, he was elected chief of state, and led a Polish attack on the USSR in 1920, driving the Soviets out of Poland. He retired in 1923, but in 1926 led a military coup that established his dictatorship until his death.

Pindling, Lynden (Oscar) (1930–   )

Bahamian politician, prime minister 1967–92. In the 1960s he became leader of the centrist Progressive Liberal Party (PLP), formed in 1953. Attracting support from the islands' demographically dominant black community, the PLP won the 1967 House of Assembly elections, the first to be held on a full adult voting register, and Pindling became the Bahamas' first black prime minister. He led the country to independence, within the British Commonwealth, in 1973 and successfully expanded the tourist industry, but accusations of government corruption grew in the 1980s and the PLP lost power in 1992. After further electoral defeat in 1997, Pindling retired as PLP leader.

The PLP had been re-elected in 1972, 1977, 1982, and 1987, but allegations of government complicity in drug trafficking and the receipt of 'improper' payments from developers contributed to their defeat in August 1992, with power passing to the Free National Movement (FNM), led by Hubert ◊Ingraham.

Before entering politics as a member of the PNP, Pindling studied law in London, and returned to the Bahamas to work as a lawyer.

Pinochet (Ugarte), Augusto (1915–   )

Chilean military dictator from 1973, when a coup backed by the US Central Intelligence Agency (CIA) ousted and killed President Salvador Allende, until 1989. Pinochet took over the presidency as the result of the coup and governed ruthlessly, crushing all political opposition (including more than 3,000 people who 'vanished' or were killed) but also presiding over the country's economic expansion in the 1980s, stimulated further by free-market reforms. In 1988 he called and lost a plebiscite to ratify him as sole nominee for the presidency. He was voted out of power when general elections were held in December 1989 but remained head of the armed forces until March 1998 when he became senator for life, which gave him instant legal immunity.

Pinochet's attempts to reassert political influence were firmly censured by President Patricio Aylwin in 1990, and by President Eduardo Frei Ruiz-Tagle in 1995.

Pinochet's resignation in 1998 from the post of commander of the country's armed forces ended his 65-year military career that turned him into one of Latin America's longest-lasting dictators. Under the terms of the constitution he wrote himself as president, Pinochet assumed a senate seat in March 1998.

In October 1998 he was arrested in London, where he was undergoing medical treatment, on a warrant from a Spanish judge investigating the crimes of his regime and seeking his extradition.

FURTHER READING
Constable, Pamela, and Val, Arturo *A Nation of Enemies: Chile under Pinochet* 1993

Pius XII (Eugenio Pacelli) (1876–1958)

Pope from 1939. He was conservative in doctrine and politics, and condemned Modernism. In 1950 he proclaimed the dogma of the bodily assumption of the Virgin Mary, and in 1951 restated the doctrine (strongly criticized by many) that the life of an infant must not be sacrificed to save a mother in labour. He was criticized for failing to speak out against atrocities committed by the Germans during World War II and has been accused of collusion with the Nazis.

Plaatje, Solomon Tshekiso (1875–1932)

South African black community leader, the founder and first secretary general of the South African National Congress (SANNC) in 1912. Later the African National Congress (ANC), the SANNC campaigned against the Land Act of 1913. Plaatje led a protest delegation to the UK in 1914, and remained there until 1917, lecturing and writing. In 1919 he joined another unsuccessful SANNC delegation to the Versailles peace conference and later participated in the pan-African congress organized by the US educator and social critic W E B Du Bois. He returned to South Africa in 1923 and continued to write until his death in 1932.

Trained as a schoolteacher, Plaatje became a journalist after the Boer War 1899–1902. He wrote *Native Life in South Africa* while working in the UK after 1914.

Playford, Thomas (1896–1981)

Australian Liberal Country League politician. He was premier of South Australia 1938–65, a record term in Australia and the Commonwealth, during which time his programmes attracted immigration and secondary industry to the state. He retired from politics in 1968.

He was born in Norton Summit, South Australia. His grandfather, Thomas Playford (1837–1915), was twice premier of the state. A paternalist conservative, he entered the state assembly in 1933 and became party leader in 1938.

FURTHER READING
Cockburn, Stewart *Playford: Benevolent Despot* 1982

Plaza Lasso, Galo (1906–1987)

US-born Ecuadorian politician, diplomat, and president 1948–52. A liberal democrat, he was the first constitutionally elected president in 28 years to complete a full term in office. His agricultural expertise had a significant influence on the development of this sector during his administration, and his policies were credited with bringing about record export figures for the country's principal export crops: banana, cacao, and coffee.

Plaza Lasso served as a diplomat to the USA before his election as president in 1948. He later returned to diplomacy, acting as a United Nations mediator in Lebanon in 1958, Congo in 1960, and Cyprus 1964–65. He also served as secretary general of the Organization of American States 1968–75.

Plekhanov, Georgi Valentinovich (1857–1918)

Russian Marxist revolutionary and theorist, founder of the Menshevik party. He led the first populist demonstration in St Petersburg, became a Marxist and, with Lenin, edited the newspaper *Iskra* ('Spark'). In 1903 his opposition to Lenin led to the Bolshevik–Menshevik split.

Pleven, René (1901–1989)

French centrist politician; prime minister 1950–51 and 1951–52, and holding ministerial office for much of the Fourth Republic. In October 1950 he put forward a plan for a European Defence Community (EDC) prepared by Jean ◊Monnet. The proposal caused bitter rifts in France's parties and finally foundered when, under Pierre ◊Mendès-France's premiership, the National Assembly failed to ratify the EDC Treaty in August 1954. After a decade out of government, he served as justice minister under President Georges ◊Pompidou 1969–73.

Socially conservative but a strong early supporter of European integration, he belonged to the same small Resistance-based party as François Mitterrand. With a strong local and regional political base in northeastern Brittany, Pleven was also closely involved in campaigning for regional economic development.

Poincaré, Raymond Nicolas Landry (1860–1934)

French moderate republican politician and president 1913–20. He served as prime minister and foreign minister 1912–13, 1922–24 (when he ordered the occupation of the German Ruhr in lieu of reparations for war damage), and 1926–29 (when he successfully stabilized the franc).

Born in Lorraine where he had lived under German occupation following France's defeat in 1870, Poincaré represented the Meuse as deputy 1887–93, and senator 1903–13 and 1920–29. With a reputation for integrity and hard work, Poincaré had chosen to devote himself to his practice at the Paris Bar after early ministerial success 1893–95, but was called upon to serve his country at the highest levels in successive times of crisis. Poor health forced his retirement from politics in 1929.

Poindexter, John Marlane (1936–)

US rear admiral and Republican government official.

In 1981 he joined the National Security Council (NSC) of Ronald Reagan's administration and became national security adviser in 1985. As a result of the Irangate scandal, Poindexter was forced to resign in 1986, along with his assistant, Oliver North.

Poindexter had sanctioned North's illegal operations to use money from arms sales to Iran to fund the Contra rebels of Nicaragua. In April 1990 he was sentenced to six months in jail for five felony counts of obstructing justice and lying to Congress, but his convictions were overturned on appeal in November 1991.

A doctor in nuclear physics, Poindexter served in the navy, rising to become deputy head of naval educational training 1978–81. From 1983 he worked closely with the NSC head, Robert McFarlane, and took over when McFarlane left in December 1985. Poindexter retired from the navy in December 1987.

FURTHER READING

Allen, Howard W *Poindexter of Washington: A Study in Progressive Politics* 1981

Pol Pot, also known as *Saloth Sar, Tol Saut*, and *Pol Porth* (c. 1925–1998)

Cambodian politician and leader of the Khmer Rouge communist movement that overthrew the government in 1975. After widespread atrocities against the civilian population, his regime was deposed by a Vietnamese invasion in 1979. Pol Pot continued to help lead the Khmer Rouge despite officially resigning from all positions in 1989. He was captured in 1997 but escaped from Cambodia, reportedly to Thailand, in January 1998 to avoid facing an international court for his crimes against humanity. The Cambodian government announced in mid-April 1998 that he had been captured inside Thailand. However, a few days later reports of Pol Pot's death were confirmed. He died following a heart attack, in a Cambodian village near the Thai border.

Pol Pot was a member of the anti-French resistance under Ho Chi Minh in the 1940s. In 1975 he proclaimed Democratic Kampuchea with himself as premier. His policies were to evacuate cities and put people to work in the countryside. The Khmer Rouge also carried out a systematic extermination of the Western-influenced educated and middle classes (1–4 million people).

Pomare, Maui Wiremu Pita Naera (1876–1930)

New Zealand Maori leader. He was elected to the house of representatives in 1911 and served under William ◊Massey as minister of health and of the interior. He helped reorganize New Zealand's mental hospitals and secure two Royal Commissions to deal with Maori land grievances. He advocated the Maoris' acceptance of pakeha (white) ways to survive in modern society.

A member of the Tainui tribe, he was born into a distinguished Maori family. After training as a medical doctor, he became New Zealand's first Maori health officer in 1900 and, with the Tohunga Suppression Act of 1907, helped improve Maori living conditions.

Pompidou, Georges Jean Raymond (1911–1974)

French Gaullist politician and head of state, President Charles ◊de Gaulle's second prime minister 1962–68 and his successor as president 1969–74. As prime minister he played a key role in managing the Gaullist party but his moderate and pragmatic conservativism brought a rift with de Gaulle in May–June 1968, when he negotiated the Grenelle Agreement with employers and unions to end the strike movement. Their political divergences were confirmed when, during his own presidency, he authorized a devaluation of the franc (which de Gaulle had vetoed in 1968), agreed to British entry into the European Community (which de Gaulle had twice vetoed in the 1960s), and approved initial steps towards a European Monetary System. Pompidou died in office before completing his full seven-year presidential term.

A teacher trained at the Ecole Normale Supérieure, and himself the son of a school teacher, Pompidou worked on de Gaulle's personal staff during his premiership 1944–46, then joined Rothschild's Bank, becoming its director general in 1954. As head of de Gaulle's personal staff again in 1958, he was involved in the negotiations surrounding the drafting the new constitution in 1958 and was appointed to the new Constitutional Council in 1959. For a politician of his generation, Pompidou was exceptional in attaining high political office having neither participated in the Resistance nor played any public role in electoral and party politics.

Porritt, Jonathon (1950–)

English environmental campaigner, director of Friends of the Earth 1984–90. He has stood in both British and European elections as a Green (formerly Ecology) Party candidate.

Porter, Michael (1947–)

US management theorist and expert on competitive strategy. His first book, *Competitive Strategy* (1980), set out his theory on strategies for competitive advantage and is regarded by many as the definitive work in the field. He applied the same theory to countries in his *Competitive Advantage of Nations* (1990) to explain why some countries are richer than others.

Portillo, Michael (Denzil Xavier) (1953–)

British Conservative politician, employment secretary 1994–95, and defence secretary 1995–97. Representative of the right wing of the party in John Major's

government, his progress up the ministerial ladder was swift. He lost his House of Commons seat of Enfield Southgate in the 1997 general election.

After a short spell in industry, Portillo joined the research department at Conservative Central Office, where his role as adviser to several government ministers gave him an appetite for active politics. He entered the Commons in 1984 in the London Southgate by-election. His appointment as employment secretary in 1994 made him directly responsible for UK policy on the controversial European Union Social Chapter, the *bête noire* of right-wing Tories. Until 1997 he was viewed by those on the right of the party as a potential leader. He is an avowed Thatcherite, convinced of the supremacy of the market and suspicious of the encroaching powers of the European Union.

Potanin, Vladimir Olegovich (1961–)

Russian financier; deputy prime minister in 1996.

Educated in the elite Moscow State Institute for International relations, Potanin left the path of diplomatic service when it became obvious that the USSR was breaking up and set up a bank named Oneximbank – the foundation stone of his later wealth. By the mid-1990s his interests included oil, nickel, investment banking, engineering, optics, and media holdings, and he entered into a partnership with British Petroleum (BP) to develop fields owned by his company Sidanco.

Second only to Boris ◊Berezovsky in wealth, he was a close associate of Russia's privatization minister Anatoly ◊Chubais and was brought into government in 1996 as deputy prime minister when the former's star was at its height. However, Potanin lost out in an internal power struggle with Berezovsky, and returned to tend his business empire.

Poujade, Pierre-Marie (1920–)

French entrepreneur and right-wing politician. His 'Poujadist' movement made a dramatic entry into French politics in the 1956 parliamentary elections (when the youngest deputy elected on Poujade's ticket was Jean-Marie ◊Le Pen) before fading in 1958. A salesman-turned-wholesaler in the rural department of Lot, Poujade came from a monarchist and anti-republican family. Beginning in 1953 with direct action against tax inspections and organized from 1954 as the Union for the Defence of Tradesmen and Artisans (UDCA), Poujadism came to denote a militant and nationalist protest against France's modernizing state, spreading out from its anti-taxation core to embrace the cause of a French Algeria. He published his political credo in *J'ai choisi le Combat* (1956).

Pouvana'a a Oopa, Marcel (1895–1977)

Tahitian political leader, campaigner for independence. He was elected to the French National Assembly in 1949, representing French Oceania for the Democratic Rally for the Tahitian People (RDPT), which he had formed shortly before. He continued to press for independence and, in 1958, was exiled and imprisoned after being charged with attempting, with supporters, to burn down the capital city, Pape'ete. Pouvana'a was pardoned in 1968 and allowed to return to Tahiti and was elected to the French Senate in 1971.

Born on Huahine island, he served with French forces during World War I. He returned to Tahiti to lead the nationalist struggle and, as a consequence, was exiled by the French to Huahine.

Powell, (John) Enoch (1912–1998)

British Conservative politician. He was minister of health 1960–63, and contested the party leadership in 1965. In 1968 he made a speech against immigration that led to his dismissal from the shadow cabinet. He resigned from the party in 1974, and was Official Unionist Party member for South Down, Northern Ireland, 1974–87.

As I look ahead, I am filled with foreboding. Like the Roman, I seem to see 'the River Tiber foaming with much blood'.

ENOCH POWELL Speech at Conservative Political Centre, Birmingham 20 April 1968

Born in Stechford, Birmingham, he was educated at St Edward's School, Birmingham, studied classics at Trinity College, Cambridge, and became a fellow of that college in 1934. He was professor of Greek at the University of Sydney, Australia, 1937–39, when he resigned to enter the British army, becoming its youngest brigadier in 1944 at the age of 32. At the end of World War II he joined the Conservative Party's research department.

He was a member of Parliament for Wolverhampton from 1950 and subsequently a member of the cabinet. He refused to serve under Alec Douglas-Home, but subsequently, in opposition, became one of the Conservative Party's principal spokesmen. In 1965 he stood as a candidate at the election of a new Conservative leader, but came third to Edward Heath and Reginald Maudling. His radical views on the social services and prices and incomes policy often conflicted with those of the Conservatism of the day and from 1968 his attitude towards immigrants and his repatriation proposals made him a controversial figure. He was dismissed from the shadow cabinet by Edward Heath, following his controversial speech on immigration, and was not offered a post in the Conservative administration of 1970–74. He was an opponent of British membership of the European Economic Community (now the European Union). Declining to stand in the February 1974 election, he attacked the Heath government and resigned.

His publications include *The History of Herodotus* (1939), *The Social Services: Needs and Means* (1952), *Change is Our Ally* (1955), *Saving in a Free Society* (1960), and *The House of Lords in the Middle Ages* (with K Wallis, 1968).

FURTHER READING

Cosgrove, P *The Lives of Enoch Powell* 1989

Powell, Adam Clayton, Jr (1908–1972)

US Democratic politician. A leader of New York's black community, he was elected to the city council in 1941. He was appointed to Congress in 1944, and later became chair of the House Education and Labor Committee. Following charges of corruption, he was denied his seat in Congress in 1967. Re-elected in 1968, he won back his seniority after a decision of the US Supreme Court in 1969.

Powell, Colin (Luther) (1937–)

US general, chair of the Joint Chiefs of Staff from 1989–93 and, as such, responsible for the overall administration of the Allied forces in Saudi Arabia during the Gulf War of 1991. A Vietnam War veteran, he first worked in government in 1972 and was national security adviser 1987–89. Following intense media speculation, in November 1995 Powell announced that he would not seek the Republican party's presidential nomination in 1996, citing family reasons.

Powell was born in New York, the son of Jamaican immigrants; he joined the army in the 1950s, was sent to Vietnam in 1962 and volunteered to return in 1968. He worked for Caspar ◊Weinberger and Frank ◊Carlucci at the Office of Management and Budget in 1972, before being posted to Korea in 1973.

He returned to Washington, DC, as assistant to Carlucci at the Defense Department 1981–83 and as adviser to Weinberger 1983–86 and was promoted to general. After a year in West Germany he was recalled to Washington following the Irangate scandal, first as assistant to Carlucci and then replacing him as national security adviser. In 1989 he was made a four-star general and chair of the Joint Chiefs of Staff, a position from which he retired in 1993. He was the first black American to hold this position.

Powell, Lewis Stanley (1907–)

US jurist. He was associate justice of the US Supreme Court 1971–87 under President Richard Nixon. A conservative, Powell voted to restrict Fifth Amendment guarantees against self-incrimination and for capital punishment. In *United States v Nixon* (1974), he sided with the majority in limiting executive privilege.

Born in Suffolk, Virginia, Powell received his undergraduate and law degrees from Washington and Lee universities and an MA in law from Harvard University. He practised in Virginia, becoming president of the American Bar Association 1964–65 and president of the American College of Trial Lawyers 1968–69. He retired from the Supreme Court in 1987 for health reasons.

Pozsgay, Imre (1933–)

Hungarian socialist politician, presidential candidate for the Hungarian Socialist Party from 1989. Influential in the democratization of Hungary 1988–89, he was rejected by the electorate in the parliamentary elections of March 1990, coming a poor third in his constituency.

Pozsgay joined the ruling Hungarian Socialist Workers' Party (HSWP) in 1950 and was a lecturer in Marxism–Leninism and an ideology chief in Bacs county 1957–70. He was minister of education and culture from 1976 before becoming head of the Patriotic People's Front umbrella organization in 1982. Noted for his reformist social-democratic instincts, he was brought into the HSWP politburo in 1988 as a move towards political pluralism began. Having publicly declared that 'communism does not work', he helped remould the HSWP into the new Hungarian Socialist Party in 1989 and was selected as its candidate for the presidency.

FURTHER READING
Pozsgay, Imre *1989: politikus-pálya a pártállamban és a rendszerváltásban* 1993, *Esélyünk a reform* 1988

Pramoedya Ananta Toer (1925–)

Indonesian novelist. His books, written in everyday Javanese and in a rich prose, depict rural Javanese life and culture under Dutch rule and during the Revolution. In 1962 he joined communist-sponsored cultural groups and during the suppression of communist supporters in 1965 was imprisoned until 1980. During this time he wrote four historical novels, two of which (*Bumi manusia/This Earth of Mankind* (1973) and *Anak semus bangsa/Child of All Nations*) were banned in Indonesia. The remaining two had to be published abroad.

In 1945 he joined the nationalists fighting against Dutch colonial rule, broadcast on Voice of Free Indonesia, and produced an Indonesian-language magazine before being arrested by the Dutch in July 1947. He was jailed for two years during which time he wrote his first novel, *Perburuan/The Fugitive*. After independence he wrote a number of novels and short stories with political themes.

Prasad, Rajendra (1884–1963)

Indian politician. He was president of the Indian National Congress several times between 1934 and 1948 and India's first president after independence 1950–62.

Prasad was trained as a lawyer, and was a loyal follower of Mahatma ◊Gandhi.

Premadasa, Ranasinghe (1924–1993)

Sri Lankan right-wing politician, prime minister 1978–88, president 1988–93, having gained popularity through overseeing a major house-building and poverty-alleviation programme. He sought peace talks with the Tamil Tiger guerrillas. He was assassinated in office by a suicide bomber in the centre of Colombo; the Tamil Tigers denied responsibility.

A member of the lowly hinaya caste, he was born in a poor area of Colombo, but was educated at the prestigious Roman Catholic St Joseph's College. Originally a Labour Party member, after independence in 1948 Premadasa became a municipal councillor and deputy mayor. In 1960 he was elected to parliament as a representative of the conservative United National Party (UNP) and became a protégé of J R ◊Jayawardene, who was prime minister 1977–78 and president 1978–88. After serving as UNP chief whip 1965–68 and 1970–77 and minister of local government, housing, and construction 1968–70, Premadasa became prime minister in 1978 under Jayawardene. He launched an initiative to provide universal housing and alleviate poverty. He also adopted a Sinhalese nationalist stance in 1987 and refused to support the Indo–Sri Lankan Colombo Accord signed by Jayawardene and Indian prime minister Rajiv ◊Gandhi.

As president, Premadasa negotiated the Indian peacekeeping force's withdrawal from the northern Jaffna peninsula, and secured a 15-month cease-fire with the Tamil Tiger separatist forces. He sanctioned harsh action against the southern-based Marxist JVP movement, which cost at least 5,000 lives August–September 1989. These forthright actions brought back political stability and revived Sri Lanka's economy. Alienated by Premadasa's autocratic style, UNP rivals – including former national security minister Lalith Athulathmudali (also assassinated in 1993) and Gamani Dissanayake – left to form the new Democratic United National Front.

Prem Tinsulanonda (1920–)

Thai general and politician, prime minister 1980–88. During the military administration of General Kriangsak Chomanam 1977–80, he served as deputy minister of the interior and, from 1979, as defence minister, before being appointed prime minister in March 1980. Prem formally relinquished his army office and established a series of civilian coalition governments. He withstood coup attempts in 1981 and 1985 and ruled in a cautious, apolitical manner, retaining the confidence of key business and military leaders.

Under his stewardship, Thailand achieved rapid annual economic growth rates in excess of 9%. He retired on 'personal grounds' in 1988.

Educated at the Chulachomklao Royal Military Academy, Bangkok, he began as a sub-lieutenant in 1941 and rose to become commander general of the

2nd Army Area in 1974 and assistant commander in chief of the Royal Thai Army in 1977.

Prescott, John Leslie (1938–)

British Labour politician, deputy leader from 1994, deputy prime minister from 1997. He unsuccessfully contested for the party leadership in 1988 and 1992. After the 1997 Labour victory he was given a key appointment in Tony Blair's new government, combining the role of deputy prime minister with responsibility for transport, the environment, and the regions.

Tony reminds us that we can't be complacent. We can't have any triumphalists. Oh sod it, yes we can!

JOHN PRESCOTT Addressing the Labour Party Conference on 29 September 1997; *Daily Telegraph*, 30 September 1997

Born in Prestatyn, Clwyd, Wales, Prescott became a merchant sailor 1955–63 and trade-union official, and continued his education through Workers' Educational Association correspondence courses and at Ruskin College, Oxford, and Hull University. He was member of Parliament for Kingston upon Hull (East) 1970–83 and for Hull East from 1983. In 1975 he became a member of the European Parliament, despite being opposed to the UK's membership of the European Community (now the European Union). A strong parliamentary debater and television performer, he was sometimes critical of his colleagues, but has shown strong loyalty to the leader.

Préval, René (1943–)

Haitian liberal politician, president from 1996. A protégé of President Jean-Bertrand ◊Aristide, he was appointed prime minister in 1991. He succeeded Aristide as president in the first peaceful handover of power to an elected president since the country's independence in 1804, attracting 87% of the electoral vote. He implemented an IMF-approved structural adjustment programme, but faced opposition from within the Haitian congress.

Préval was born in Port-au-Prince and became an outspoken advocate for democracy. His opposition to the dictatorial ◊Duvalier regimes 1956–86 forced him into ten years of exile in the USA. When Jean-Claude Duvalier was overthrown in 1986, Préval returned as a founding member of the Group for the Defence of the Constitution. He was chair of the committee ('Pa Blie') responsible for investigating the disappearance of persons during the Duvalier regime.

Price, George Cadle (1919–)

Belizean politician, prime minister 1954–84 and 1989–93. In 1950 he founded the country's first political party, the People's United Party (PUP), a left-of-centre grouping that grew out of a smaller group, the People's Committee, and called for the independence of Belize. Partial self-government was achieved in 1954 and Price became prime minister, continuing to lead his country until it achieved full independence in 1981. A charismatic but ascetic politician, he became known as the 'father of the nation'. He unexpectedly returned to power in 1989 and remained there until 1993.

In 1984 the PUP's 30 years of uninterrupted rule ended when the general election was won by the United Democratic Party (UDP), led by Manuel ◊Esquivel, and Price lost his seat.

Primakov, Yevgeny Maksimovich (1928–)

See page 352.

Primo de Rivera, Miguel, Marqués de Estella (1870–1930)

Spanish soldier and politician, dictator from 1923 as well as premier from 1925. He was captain general of Cataluña when he led a coup against the ineffective monarchy and became virtual dictator of Spain with the support of Alfonso XIII. He resigned in 1930.

Prior, James Michael Leathes, Baron Prior (1927–)

British Conservative politician. He held ministerial posts from 1970. As employment secretary he curbed trade-union activity with the Employment Act 1980, and was Northern Ireland secretary 1981–84. After his resignation in 1984 he became chair of the General Electric Company. He was made a peer in 1987.

Pritt, Denis Nowell (1887–1972)

British lawyer, communist, and politician. Initially a Conservative, Pritt joined the Liberals in 1914 and was elected Labour member of Parliament for Hammersmith North in 1935. Expelled from the party in 1940 for his increasingly pro-Soviet stance, Pritt nonetheless held his seat at the 1945 election, but lost it in 1950. Pritt worked on a number of famous political cases, notably defending Jomo ◊Kenyatta in 1952 against charges of colluding with the nationalist activities of the Mau Mau.

Awarded the Lenin Peace Prize in 1954, he retired from the bar in 1960, worked at the university of Ghana in 1965, and published a three-volume autobiography in 1966.

Profumo, John Dennis (1915–)

British Conservative politician, secretary of state for war from 1960 to June 1963. He resigned following the disclosure of his involvement with Christine Keeler, mistress also of a Soviet naval attaché, and admitted he had deceived the House of Commons about the affair. The scandal caused great damage to the government of Harold Macmillan, contributing to its downfall. In 1982 Profumo became administrator of the social and educational settlement Toynbee Hall in London.

◆ PRIMAKOV, YEVGENY MAKSIMOVICH (1928–) ◆

Russian politician, prime minister from 1998. He was appointed to succeed Andrei ◊Kozyrev as foreign minister in 1995 in order to give President Boris ◊Yeltsin some credibility with those who supported the communists and nationalists. He was no more successful than Kozyrev in stopping decline, but his championing of Russia's interests and his willingness to use anti-Western rhetoric restored some of the damage done to injured pride. Still, it was a surprise when Yeltsin, reeling under the shock of economic collapse in the summer of 1998, appointed him prime minister with what seemed almost an anti-reform mandate. Primakov, though far from an old-fashioned communist and relatively subtle in his private diplomacy, still saw the achievement of consensus as more important than reform, and refused to adopt an economic programme that could attract the support of the IMF. The result was that political peace was preserved, at the cost of a disastrously declining economy – though it was clear to no-one what plan could assist Russia's revival.

Previously, Primakov had been head of the reformed KGB, heading the section responsible for secret service work overseas and for counter-espionage. Though he oversaw a dramatic scaling down of its personnel and its activity, he emerged as a sharp critic of Western policy towards Russia, issuing warnings that the Western secret services were infiltrating Russian political and economic life through a variety of aid and other organizations. His anti-Westernism made him popular in a country in which capitalism was working only for the few and democracy was seen by many as a sham.

Primakov had a successful career under every regime he encountered in his adult life. Accepted for the prestigious Institute for Eastern Studies in Stalin's time, he became a leading journalist on *Pravda* – the summit of Soviet journalism – in the 1960s under Nikita Krushchev, then climbed further as a leading theorist and adviser on foreign affairs under Leonid Brezhnev to become, under Mikhail Gorbachev, a close aide, especially on Middle Eastern and African policy. He did not, however, sink with Gorbachev as many of the last Soviet general secretary's aides did.

Puapua, Tomasi (1938–)

Tuvaluan politician, prime minister 1981–89. He was elected prime minister in September 1981, replacing Toaripi Lauti, the first prime minister on Tuvalu's independence in 1978, who had been implicated in an investment scandal. Puapua was re-elected in 1985. A referendum held in 1986, on a switch to republican status, failed to receive national backing and after the September 1989 general election Puapua was replaced as premier by Bikenibeu ◊Paeniu. During his period as prime minister, he was outspoken in his opposition to France's testing of nuclear weapons on Mururoa Atoll, in French Polynesia. In December 1996 Puapua, who was parliamentary speaker, helped bring down the government of Prime Minister Kamuta Laatasi, through withdrawing his support.

P'u-i, Henry or *Pu-Yi* (1906–1967)

Last Manchu Qing emperor of China (as Hsuan Tung) 1908–12 and puppet ruler of Manchuria 1932–45.

He became emperor at the age of two, on the death of Guangxu (1871–1908), who was murdered by the conservative Empress Dowager Zi Xi, after he had attempted modernizing reforms. (The Empress had controlled the government from 1898, and was herself to die a day after Guangxu's murder.) The 'boy king' was deposed in the republican revolution of 1912 and given a pension and summer palace near Beijing (Peking). After his deposition, he chose to be called Henry. He was restored for a week in 1917 until, in 1932, he was made president (and, from 1934, emperor) of the Japanese puppet state of Manchukuo, in Manchuria.

Captured by Soviet troops in 1945, he was imprisoned but then returned to China after the 1949 communist revolution. He was put on trial in the new People's Republic of China in 1950 and 'politically re-educated'. Pardoned by ◊Mao Zedong in 1959, he became a worker in a botanical garden in Beijing.

His life is captured in Bernardo Bertolucci's Oscar-winning film, *The Last Emperor* (1987). His autobiography *From Emperor to Citizen* was published in 1964.

Pyke, Margaret (1893–1966)

British birth-control campaigner. In the early 1930s she became secretary of the National Birth Control Association (later the Family Planning Association, FPA), and campaigned vigorously to get local councils to set up family-planning clinics. She became chair of the FPA in 1954.

Pym, Francis Leslie, Baron Pym (1922–)

British Conservative politician. He was defence secretary 1979–81, and succeeded Lord Carrington as foreign minister in 1982, but was dismissed in the post-election reshuffle of 1983. He was created Baron in 1987.

Qaboos bin Said (1940–)

Sultan of Oman, the 14th descendant of the Albusaid family. Opposed to the conservative views of his father, he overthrew him in 1970 in a bloodless coup and assumed the sultanship. Since then he has followed more liberal and expansionist policies, while maintaining his country's position of international non-alignment.

Qassem, or *Qasim*, Brigadier Abdul Karim al- (1914–1963)

Iraqi soldier and politician, ruler 1958–63. In July 1958 he led a successful coup and proceeded to establish himself as a dictator, appointing himself commander in chief, prime minister, and defence minister. In February 1963 he was overthrown by a combination of nationalist anti-communist military officers and civilian Ba'ath activists. This coup, which resulted in the death of Qassem and close associates, brought Abdul Salam Arif to power.

As ruler, Qassem faced challenges from colleagues, including an attempted coup in March 1959 by Colonel Shawwaf. He drew on support from the communists to suppress this mutiny, but, within months, turned on the communists, who had launched mass demonstrations demanding free elections and legalization of the Communist Party. He introduced a significant measure of land reform in September 1958, but faced internal rebellion by Kurds, as well as both British and Arab opposition to his attempt, in 1961, to take over Kuwait, through military means.

Born in Baghdad, into a lower-middle-class Sunni Muslim family, Qassem was commissioned as an army officer in 1938. He served as a battalion commander during the 1948 Palestine War and from 1956 became head of the self-named 'Free Officers' group, which plotted to overthrow King Faisal II and end Iraq's 'special relationship' with Britain.

Nicknamed 'the Mad Dictator', Qassem was an erratic ruler, who, with a similar background and motivations to Gamal Nasser, lacked the Egyptian leader's charisma and strategic vision.

Qiu Jin or *Ch'iu Chin* (1875–1907)

Chinese feminist and revolutionary. She left her family to study in Japan in 1904, where she became actively involved in radical Chinese student associations calling for the overthrow of the Manchu Qing (Ch'ing) dynasty. Returning to China in 1906, she founded a women's journal in which she argued that the liberation of women was an essential prerequisite for a strong China. In 1907 she was implicated in an abortive anti-Manchu uprising and was executed by the Qing authorities.

Quadros, Jânio da Silva (1917–1992)

Brazilian politician and president in 1961. He was a political independent who gained a huge majority in the 1960 presidential elections. His implementation of economic reforms on taking office encountered unprecedented opposition in congress with the result that he only served a seven-month term as president before resigning and seeking exile. His resignation caused national chaos; he was succeeded by his equally controversial vice president João Goulart.

Quadros eventually returned to his country, was rehabilitated, and became, in 1985, mayor of the state of São Paulo again (he had been mayor once before from 1953 to 1959).

Quayle, (James) Dan(forth) (1947–)

US Republican politician, vice president 1989–93. A congressman for Indiana 1977–81, he became a senator in 1981.

Born into a rich and powerful Indianapolis newspaper-owning family, Quayle was admitted to the Indiana bar in 1974, and was elected to the House of Representatives in 1976 and to the Senate in 1980. When George Bush ran for president in 1988, he selected Quayle as his running mate, admiring his conservative views and believing that Quayle could deliver the youth vote. This choice encountered heavy criticism because of Quayle's limited political experience. As Bush's vice president, Quayle attracted criticism for, among other things, his enlistment in the 1960s in the Indiana National Guard, which meant that he was not sent overseas during the Vietnam War.

Quezon (y Molina), Manuel Luis (1878–1944)

Filipino nationalist politician, president 1935–44. He was elected to the senate in 1916 and was chosen to serve as its president. This was the highest elective office in the country at the time and he remained in this position until 1935. He spoke out against the imperious administration of Governor General Leonard Wood 1921–27 and in 1934 helped secure the passage of the Tydings–McDuffie Bill, which established the Commonwealth of the Philippines and promised full independence in 1946. Queson was elected the first president of the Philippine Commonwealth. He established a highly centralized government, verging on one-man rule, but displayed great courage during the Japanese onslaught on General Douglas ◊ MacArthur's defences in 1941, refusing to evacuate to the USA until appealed to by President Franklin ◊ Roosevelt. He led a government in exile and died in Saranac, USA.

Born in Baler, Luzon, Quezon studied at Manila and, while still a law student, joined Emilio ◊ Aguinaldo's insurrectionary army, which fought US forces 1898–1901. He was briefly imprisoned for his role in the insurrection. In 1903 Quezon was admitted to the bar and in 1905 was elected governor of Tayabas province and 1907–09 served in the first Philippine assembly. In 1909 he went to Washington, DC, as one of the resident Philippine commissioners and began to work for his country's independence. He was instrumental in securing the passage of the Jones Act in 1916, which increased self-government.

The new capital of the Philippines on the island of Luzon is named after him, as was Tayabas province, in 1946.

FURTHER READING
Quezon, Manuel Luis *The Good Fight* 1946

Quirino, Elpidio (1890–1956)

Filipino politician, president 1948–53. After the liberation of the Philippines after World War II, Quirino was elected vice president of the independent Philippines in 1946. He became president when Manuel Roxas died in office in 1948, then won the 1949 presidential election. During his presidency, he faced the communist Hukbalahap insurrection. Despite ailing health, Quirino ran for re-election in 1953, but was defeated by Ramón ◊ Magsaysay.

Born in Vignan, on Luzon, Quirino was admitted to the bar in 1915, but later served for many years as political aide to the independence leader Manuel Quezon. During the interwar period he was a member of the house of representatives 1919–25 and senate 1925–35, before serving in Quezon's government from 1935. After the Japanese invasion in 1942, during World War II, he became a leader in the underground resistance and suffered the loss of his wife and three of his five children.

Quisling, Vidkun Abraham Lauritz Jonsson (1887–1945)

Norwegian politician. Leader from 1933 of the Norwegian Fascist Party, he aided the Nazi invasion of Norway in 1940 by delaying mobilization and urging non-resistance. He was made premier by Hitler in 1942, and was arrested and shot as a traitor by the Norwegians in 1945. His name became a generic term for a traitor who aids an occupying force.

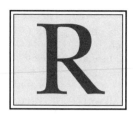

Rabin, Yitzhak (1922–1995)

Israeli Labour politician, prime minister 1974–77 and 1992–95. As a former soldier, he was a national hero in the Arab-Israeli Wars. His policy of favouring Palestinian self-government in the occupied territories contributed to the success of the centre-left party in the 1992 elections. In September 1993 he signed a historic peace agreement with the Palestinian Liberation Organization (PLO), providing for a phased withdrawal of Israeli forces. He was awarded the 1994

The government of Israel has decided to recognize the PLO as the representative of the Palestinian people.

YITZHAK RABIN On signing peace agreement with PLO, September 1993

Nobel Prize for Peace jointly with Israeli foreign minister Shimon Peres and PLO leader Yassir Arafat. He was shot and killed by a young Israeli extremist while attending a peace rally in Tel Aviv in November 1995.

Rabin was minister for defence under the conservative Likud coalition government 1984–90.

FURTHER READING
Horowitz, D (ed) *Rabin: Soldier of Peace* 1996
Kort, Michael G *Yitzhak Rabin: Israel's Soldier Statesman* 1997
Rabin, Yitzhak *Rabin Memoirs* translation 1979
Slater, Robert *Rabin of Israel* 1993

Rabuka, Sitiveni (1948–   )

Fijian soldier and politician, prime minister from 1992. When the April 1987 elections produced a new left-of-centre government, headed by Timoci ◊Bavadra, which was determined to end discrimination against the country's ethnic Indian community, Rabuka staged two successive coups, in May and September 1987. Within months of the second coup he stepped down, allowing a civilian government headed by Kamisese ◊Mara, to take over. In 1992 Rabuka was nominated as the new Fijian premier. He was re-elected to the post in 1994 and, after revising the constitution so as not to discriminate against the

ethnic Indian community, secured Fiji's readmission to the Commonwealth in October 1997.

Born in Nakobo, Rabuka joined the Fijian army at an early age and was trained in New Zealand, Australia, and at the Sandhurst military academy, England. He commanded a unit of the United Nations peacekeeping force in Lebanon 1980–81, for which he was awarded the OBE. In May 1987 Rabuka removed the new ethnically bipartisan Fijian government at gunpoint, leading to inter-ethnic violence, but Governor General Penaia ◊Ganilau regained control within weeks. In July 1987 Rabuka introduced a new constitution that favoured the ethnic Fijian community and in September 1987 he staged a second coup, in which Fiji was proclaimed a republic and withdrew from the British Commonwealth. He gave way to a civilian government in December 1987, but retained behind-the-scenes control as home affairs minister, in charge of the army and security. Rabuka founded the Fijian Political Party (FPP) in 1991, which secured victory in the 1992 general election, enabling him to become prime minister in May 1992.

FURTHER READING
Rabuka, Sitiveni *No Other Way* 1988

Raczyński, Edward (1891–1993)

Polish diplomat and politician of the postwar government in exile in London.

He entered the Polish ministry for foreign affairs in 1919, and his early diplomatic experience included assignments in Copenhagen and London. Between 1932 and 1934 he acted as Polish delegate to the Disarmament Conference. He was Polish ambassador to London 1934–45. During World War II Raczyński was first acting minister for foreign affairs and then, in 1942, prime minister. After the war, when recognition was withdrawn from the exile government, Raczyński acted as Polish representative to a number of foreign office and home office committees dealing with the Polish community in the UK. He became a symbol of continuing Polish presence in the West. From 1979 to 1986 he was president of the Polish government in exile.

FURTHER READING
Raczyński, Edward *In Allied London* 1963

Radhakrishnan, Sarvepalli (1888–1975)

Indian philosopher and politician. In 1946 he was chief Indian delegate to UNESCO, becoming its chair in 1949. A member of the Indian assembly in 1947 he was appointed vice president 1952–62 and president 1962–67.

He was professor at the universities of Mysore, Calcutta, and Oxford, where he became Spalding Professor of Eastern Religions and Ethics in 1936. He also lectured in the USA in 1926 and 1944, and in China in 1944. From 1931 to 1939 he was in Geneva as a member of the Committee of Intellectual Cooperation of the League of Nations. His Hibbert lectures of 1929 were published as *An Idealist View of Life* (1932). He was appointed to the Order of Merit in 1963.

Born in Riruttani, Madras, he was educated at Madras Christian College. His scholarly philosophical works include *Indian Philosophy* (1927) and *Eastern Religions and Western Thought* (1939).

Radić, Stjepan (1871–1928)

Yugoslav nationalist politician, founder of the Croatian Peasant Party in 1904. He led the Croat national movement within the Austro-Hungarian Empire and advocated a federal state with Croatian autonomy. His opposition to Serbian supremacy within Yugoslavia led to his assassination in parliament.

Raeder, Erich (1876–1960)

German admiral. Chief of Staff in World War I, he became head of the navy in 1928, but was punished by Adolf Hitler in 1943 because of his failure to prevent Allied Arctic convoys from reaching the USSR and resigned. Sentenced to life imprisonment at the Nürnberg trials of war criminals, he was released in 1955 on grounds of ill health.

He successfully evaded the restrictions of the Versailles treaty while expanding the navy in 1930s. He was behind the successful U-boat campaign against Britain and launched attacks against the Arctic convoys supplying the USSR. Following the humiliation of the Battle of Barents Sea in December 1942, Hitler threatened to remove big guns from battleships and install them as coastal defence weapons. This was too much for Raeder and he resigned in 1943.

Rafsanjani, Hojatoleslam Ali Akbar Hashemi (1934–)

Iranian politician and cleric, president 1989–97. When his former teacher Ayatollah ◊Khomeini returned after the revolution of 1979–80, Rafsanjani became the speaker of the Iranian parliament and, after Khomeini's death, state president and effective political leader. He was succeeded in 1997 by Seyyed Mohammad Khatami.

Rafsanjani was born near Kerman, southeastern Iran, to a family of farmers. At 14 he went to study Islamic jurisprudence with Khomeini in the Shi'ite holy city of Qom and qualified as an alim (Islamic teacher). During the period 1964–78, he acquired considerable wealth through his construction business but kept in touch with his exiled mentor and was repeatedly imprisoned for fundamentalist political activity. His attitude became more moderate in the 1980s, and as president he normalized relations with the UK in 1990. He was re-elected with a reduced majority in 1993.

Rahman, Sheik Mujibur (1920–1975)

Bangladeshi nationalist politician, president in 1975. He was arrested several times for campaigning for the autonomy of East Pakistan. He won the elections in 1970 as leader of the Awami League but was again arrested when negotiations with the Pakistan government broke down. After the civil war in 1971, he became prime minister of the newly independent Bangladesh. He was presidential dictator January–August 1975, when he was assassinated.

Rahman, Tunku (Prince) Abdul (1903–1990)

Malaysian politician, first prime minister of independent Malaya 1957–63 and of Malaysia 1963–70.

Born at Kuala Keda, the son of the sultan and his sixth wife, a Thai princess, he studied law in the UK. After returning to Malaya he founded the Alliance Party in 1952. The party was successful in the 1955 elections, and he became prime minister of Malaya on gaining independence in 1957, continuing when Malaya became part of Malaysia in 1963. His achievement was to bring together the Malay, Chinese, and Indian peoples within the Alliance Party, but in the 1960s he was accused of showing bias towards Malays. Ethnic riots followed in Kuala Lumpur in 1969 and, after many attempts to restore better relations, he retired in 1970. In his later years he voiced criticism of the authoritarian leadership of Mahathir bin Mohamed.

Rais, Amien (1935–)

Indonesian politician and leader of the 28-million-member Muslim organization Mohammadiyeh. A university lecturer with a doctorate in politics from the University of Chicago, Rais was a leading government critic and in March 1998 demanded President Thojib ◊Suharto's resignation. Although he lacked a well-organized political machine he was considered one of the leading contenders to replace President Bacharuddin ◊Habibie.

Rakhmanov, Imamali, or *Emomali Rakhmonov* (1952–)

Tajik politician; head of state from 1992, initially by virtue of his position as chair of the Tajikistan parliament (Supreme Soviet) and then, from 1994, by direct election. Assisted by Commonwealth of Independent

States (CIS) peacekeeping forces, he brought an end to the 1992–93 civil war and in February 1997 signed a peace agreement with United Tajik Opposition (UTO) Islamic rebels. Directly elected president in November 1994, he ruled in an authoritarian manner, placed tight curbs on opposition and Islamic fundamentalist activities, and developed close links with Russia and Uzbekistan.

Born in Dangara and educated at the Tajik University in Dushanbe, Rakhmanov worked initially as an electrician before becoming a trade-union and communist-party activist and administrator. His support bases were in the Communist Party of Tajikistan (CPT) and the People's Party of Tajikistan (established in 1994).

Ramaphosa, Cyril (1954–)

South African politician, secretary general of the African National Congress (ANC) from 1991. He was a chief negotiator in the constitutional talks with the South African government that led to the first universal suffrage elections in May 1994, and was subsequently elected by parliament to chair the assembly that would write the country's new permanent constitution. He is seen by some as Nelson Mandela's natural successor as president. In July 1996 he announced his resignation from active politics to concentrate on a business career.

Trained as a lawyer, Ramaphosa was a successful organizer of the National Union of Mineworkers from 1981.

Ramgoolam, Navin Chandra (1947–)

Mauritian politician, prime minister from 1995. He became leader of the centrist, Hindu-oriented Mauritius Labour Party (MLP) in 1991, becoming its president soon afterwards. Entering an electoral agreement with the Mauritian Militant Movement (MMM), the MLP and MMM secured a landslide victory and Ramgoolam was appointed prime minister.

Son of Seewoosagur Ramgoolam (1900–), the country's first prime minister, Ramgoolam practised as a doctor and lawyer before entering politics and becoming leader of the MLP.

Ramos, Fidel (Eddie) (1928–)

Filipino centre-right politician, president 1992–98. He launched a commission to consult with Muslim secessionist rebel groups on Mindanao, which produced a peace deal with one of the rebel groups in September 1996. In addition, as part of a government move to end corruption and human-rights abuses, he purged the police force. These and other initiatives won him popular support, and in the May 1995 congressional elections, with the economy booming, his supporters won a sweeping victory. However, from 1997 the economic situation deteriorated, with the peso being devalued in July 1997. Ramos was pre-

vented, by the constitution, from seeking a second term in 1998 and he was succeeded by the former vice president Joseph ◊Estrada.

Drawn from the Philippines' Protestant minority community, Ramos was a graduate of the prestigious West Point US military academy and saw active military service in Korea and Vietnam. In 1981, under President Ferdinand ◊Marcos, who was his second cousin, Ramos was appointed deputy chief of staff of the armed forces. However, in February 1996, along with defence secretary Juan Ponce Enrile, he sided with opposition leader Corazon Aquino in her 'people power' struggle against the Marcos dictatorship. Aquino made Ramos army chief of staff in 1986 and defence secretary in 1988. He remained her staunchest ally, standing by her during a succession of attempted coups, and was rewarded by securing nomination as her successor. Enjoying the backing of the centrist Lakas – National Union of Christian Democrats – Ramos won the May 1992 presidential election, but his share of the national vote was only 24%.

Ramphal, Shridath Surendranath ('Sonny') (1928–)

Guyanese politician. He was minister of foreign affairs and justice 1972–75 and secretary general of the Commonwealth 1975–90.

Randolph, Asa Philip (1889–1979)

US labour and civil-rights leader. Devoting himself to the cause of unionization, especially among black Americans, he was named a vice president of the American Federation of Labor and Congress of Industrial Organizations (AFL-CIO) in 1957. He was one of the organizers of the 1963 civil-rights march on Washington, DC.

He founded the periodical *Messenger* in 1917 and, after successfully organizing railway workers, served as the president of the Brotherhood of Sleeping Car Porters 1925–68.

Ransome-Kuti, Olunfunmilayo (1900–1978)

Nigerian politician and women's rights activist. In 1944 she established the Abeokuta Women's Union (later Nigerian Women's Union) and led campaigns against local administration and colonial taxation. She was appointed as the women's representative in the National Council of Nigeria and Cameroons (NCNC) delegation to London in 1947. Failing to gain the party's nomination in the 1959 elections, Ransome-Kuti put herself forward as an independent candidate but was unsuccessful.

She was born in Abeokuta, and educated at local mission schools and in the UK. After returning to Nigeria in 1923, she worked as a schoolteacher and became an active member of the Nigeria Union of Teachers (NUT); she later established her own primary and secondary schools.

Rao, P(amulaparti) V(enkata) Narasimha (1921–)

Indian politician, prime minister 1991–96 and Congress leader 1991–96. He governed the state of Andhra Pradesh as chief minister 1971–73, and served in the cabinets of Indira and Rajiv Gandhi as minister of external affairs 1980–85 and 1988–90 and of human resources 1985–88. He took over the Congress party leadership after the assassination of Rajiv Gandhi. Elected prime minister the following month, he instituted a market-centred and outward-looking reform of the economy. He survived a vote of no confidence in 1993. After Congress was defeated in national elections in May 1996, Rao resigned as prime minister and dissolved parliament. He resigned as Congress leader in September 1996 as allegations mounted over his alleged involvement in political bribery.

Rapacki, Adam (1909–1970)

Polish minister for foreign affairs 1956–68, architect of the plan for the demilitarization of Central Europe ('Rapacki plan').

An economist by training, he was a member of the Polish Socialist Party (PSP) until it merged with the Polish United Workers Party (PUWP). Until ill health forced him to withdraw from public life, he was a member of the party's central committee. In 1957, anticipating the US decision to site nuclear warheads in the German Federal Republic (West Germany), Rapacki put forward a proposal for Central Europe to become a nuclear-free zone. He suggested that Poland, Czechoslovakia, the Democratic Republic of Germany (East Germany), and the German Federal Republic make a joint commitment to demilitarization. The plan was dismissed as a Soviet attempt to undermine NATO, and in due course nuclear warheads were stationed in the territory of the German Federal Republic.

Rasmussen, Poul Nyrup (1943–)

Danish economist and politician, prime minister from 1993. Leader of the Social Democrats from 1992, he succeeded Poul Schluter as prime minister, heading the first majority coalition government since 1982. He was returned to power in the 1994 general election, and in March 1998 his centre-left coalition with the small centrist Radical Liberal party was returned again, with a one-seat majority.

Following his country's initial rejection of the Maastricht Treaty, he negotiated exemptions from the Treaty's key provisions, including those on defence, and won the nation's backing in a second referendum in May 1993.

Rasputin (Russian 'dissolute'), born Grigory Efimovich Novykh (1871–1916)

Siberian Eastern Orthodox mystic. He acquired influ-ence over the tsarina Alexandra, wife of ◊Nicholas II, and was able to make political and ecclesiastical appointments. His abuse of power and notorious debauchery (reputedly including the tsarina) led to his murder by a group of nobles.

Rasputin, the illiterate son of a peasant, began as a wandering 'holy man'. Through the tsarina's faith in his power to ease her son's suffering from haemophilia, he became a favourite at the court, where he instigated wild parties under the slogan 'Sin that you may obtain forgiveness'. A larger-than-life character, he even proved hard to kill: when poison had no effect, his assassins shot him and dumped him in the River Neva.

Rathbone, Eleanor Florence (1872–1946)

English feminist and social reformer. She made an extensive study of the position of widows under the poor law, and became the leading British advocate for family allowances. A leader in the constitutional movement for female suffrage, she was an independent member of Liverpool city council from 1909, working in the housing campaign between the wars. She was elected as an independent member of Parliament for the Combined English Universities 1929–46.

Born in Liverpool, she read classics at Somerville College, Oxford. She advocated intervention in the Spanish Civil War, and denounced Italian aggression in Ethiopia. She fought to gain the franchise for Indian women, denounced child marriage in India, and was a vigorous worker on behalf of refugees, as a result of which she became a supporter of Zionism.

Her publications include 'The Disinherited Family' (1924), 'The Case for Family Allowances' (1940), *Child Marriage: The Indian Minotaur* (1934), and *War Can Be Averted* (1937), in which she attacked appeasement of Hitler.

Rathenau, Walther (1867–1922)

German politician. He was a leading industrialist and was appointed economic director during World War I, developing a system of economic planning in combination with capitalism. After the war he founded the Democratic Party, and became foreign minister in 1922. The same year he signed the Rapallo Treaty of Friendship with the USSR, cancelling German and Soviet counterclaims for indemnities for World War I, and soon after was assassinated by right-wing fanatics.

Ratushinskaya, Irina (1954–)

Soviet dissident poet. Sentenced in 1983 to seven years in a labour camp plus five years in internal exile for criticism of the Soviet regime, she was released in 1986. Her strongly Christian work includes *Grey is the Colour of Hope* (1988).

Rau, Johannes (1931–)

German socialist politician. The son of a Protestant

pastor, he was state premier of North Rhine–Westphalia 1978–98. In January 1987 he stood for chancellor of West Germany but was defeated by the incumbent conservative coalition. In March 1998 he announced his retirement from the premiership of North Rhine–Westphalia.

Rawlings, Jerry (John) (1947–)

Ghanaian politician, president from 1981. He first took power in a bloodless coup in 1979, and, having returned power to a civilian government, staged another coup in 1981. He then remained in power until 1992, when he was elected president under the new multiparty constitution. He was re-elected for a second term in December 1996.

Rawlings first took power in a military coup in 1979, pledging to root out widespread corruption and promote 'moral reform'. Within four months he had restored civilian government, but threatened a further coup if politicians were to put their own interests before those of the nation. Alleging renewed corruption in government circles, he seized power again in 1981 and, despite promising a speedy return to civilian rule, remained as military leader for more than a decade. Following a referendum supporting multiparty politics in 1992, Rawlings left the air force (in which he had been a flight lieutenant) and successfully contested the presidency as a civilian under the new constitution.

Criticized by many traditional politicians and senior military figures as an opportunist adventurer, he retained his popular appeal and successfully made the transition from military leader to constitutionally elected head of state.

Rayburn, Samuel Taliaferro (1882–1961)

US Democratic politican. Elected to Congress in 1912, he supported President Franklin D Roosevelt's New Deal programme of 1933, and was elected majority leader in 1937 and Speaker of the House in 1940. With the exception of two terms, he served as Speaker until his death.

Born in Roane County, Tennessee, and raised in Texas, Rayburn received a law degree from the University of Texas in 1908. He served in the state legislature 1907–12, serving as its Speaker from 1911. A leader of the Democratic Party, Rayburn chaired the national conventions in 1948, 1952, and 1956. His tenure in the House of Representatives 1912–61 was the longest on record.

Razak, Tun Abdul (1922–1976)

Malaysian politician and civil servant. In 1970 he was appointed as Malaysia's second prime minister after independence, but he died prematurely from cancer six years later.

Razak was educated at Malay College in Kuala Kangsar and Raffles College in Singapore. He then studied law at Lincoln's Inn, London. He joined the civil service, and in 1955 became the chief minister of Pahang. He held the posts of deputy prime minister and minister of defence in 1959 in the newly-formed Federation of Malaya.

Reagan, Ronald (Wilson) (1911–)

See page 360.

Redmond, John Edward (1856–1918)

Irish nationalist politician, leader of the Irish Parliamentary Party (IPP) 1900–18. He rallied his party after Charles Stewart Parnell's imprisonment in 1881, and came close to achieving Home Rule for all Ireland in 1914. However, the pressure of World War I, Unionist intransigence, and the fallout of the 1916 Easter Rising destroyed both his career and his party.

Redmond was born in Ballytrent, County Wexford, the son of a member of Parliament. He was educated at Clongowes Wood College and Trinity College, Dublin, and was elected MP for New Ross in 1881. He quickly established himself as an able speaker and loyal supporter of Parnell, then party leader. He became MP for North Wexford in 1885, and then for Waterford in 1891 until his death. After Parnell's death in 1891, Redmond led the Parnellite minority which had split from the party, until the party reunified under Redmond's leadership in 1900.

In 1910, with the Conservative and Liberals evenly split in terms of seats, Redmond's party held the balance of power. In return for his support for the Liberal government, Redmond secured the passage of the Third Home Rule Bill in May 1914. With the Lords' veto abolished in 1911, it appeared that Home Rule had at long last been achieved. However, two factors counted against it: one was the threat of a civil war between the Irish nationalists and the Ulster Unionists, who were enjoying much sympathy from within the Conservative Party and from the British military; the other was World War I, which crucially delayed the implementation of Home Rule and ultimately fatally split the Liberal Party, upon whom Redmond depended for support. Redmond professed Ireland's loyalty to Britain as a means of keeping Home Rule on track with his Woodenbridge Speech on September 1914, when he called upon Irish volunteers to enlist in the British Army and fight for the empire. This angered radical Irish nationalists and helped to bring together those elements that staged the Easter Rising in 1916. This event caught Redmond completely by surprise, and his condemnation of it as a 'German intrigue' displayed the extent to which he was out of touch with a new generation of Irish nationalists. He later condemned the execution of the rebel leaders, but was ignored by David Lloyd George's coalition and the

British military, who no longer needed him. By 1917 Redmond was being squeezed between a reorganized Sinn Féin, which was gaining mass support for its more extreme republican ethos, and Unionist demands for the partition of Ireland.

FURTHER READING
Bew, Paul *John Redmond* 1996

Redwood, John (1951–)

British Conservative politician. He was Welsh Secretary 1993–95, when he resigned to contest the Conservative leadership following John Major's decision to challenge his critics within the party by forcing a leadership election. Positioned on the far-right wing of the party, Redwood contested the leadership again, unsuccessfully, in 1997.

Although he was defeated, Redwood fought a creditable campaign, increasing his public profile and establishing himself as a serious potential leader from the right of the party. His seemingly unemotional character, which earned him the nickname 'Vulcan', was to some extent dispelled by his performance during the campaign, and even his fiercest critics have had to acknowledge his intellectual ability.

Born in Dover, he graduated from Magdalen College, Oxford, and at the age of 21 was appointed a Fellow of All Souls College. He began his political career as an Oxfordshire county councillor 1973–77, and after an unsuccessful attempt to enter the House of Commons in 1982, he headed Margaret Thatcher's policy unit 1983–85 before winning the Wokingham seat in the 1987 general election. In 1995 he became director of a newly established independent think-tank – the Conservative 2000 Foundation.

Building on his experience as an investment analyst, he has written a number of books in that field as well as a work on privatization. A confirmed Eurosceptic, in his book *The Global Marketplace* (1993) he advocated closer links with the USA in preference to Europe. In domestic politics he has strongly promoted Christian family values.

Rees, Merlyn (1920–)

British Labour politician. From 1972 to 1974 he was opposition spokesperson on Northern Ireland affairs and in March 1974 became secretary of state for Northern Ireland, a post he retained until he was appointed home secretary in September 1976.

He was educated at Harrow Weald Grammar School, Goldsmiths' College, University of London, and the London School of Economics and Political Science. After war service he became a lecturer in economics. In 1963 he succeeded Hugh Gaitskell as Labour member of Parliament for Leeds South. Between 1965 and 1970 he was successively parliamen-

◆ REAGAN, RONALD (WILSON) (1911–) ◆

40th president of the USA 1981–89, a Republican. He was governor of California 1966–74, and a former Hollywood actor. Reagan was a hawkish and popular president. He adopted an aggressive policy in Central America, attempting to

---

Politics is supposed to be the second oldest profession. I have come to realize that it bears a very close resemblance to the first.
RONALD REAGAN At a conference in Los Angeles
2 March 1977

---

overthrow the government of Nicaragua, and invading Grenada in 1983. In 1987, Irangate was investigated by the Tower Commission; Reagan admitted that US–Iranian negotiations had become an 'arms for hostages deal', but denied knowledge of resultant funds being illegally sent to the Contra guerrillas in Nicaragua. He increased military spending (sending the national budget deficit to record levels), cut social programmes, introduced the deregulation of

domestic markets, and cut taxes. His Strategic Defense Initiative, announced in 1983, proved controversial owing to the cost and unfeasibility. He was succeeded by Vice President George Bush.

Reagan was born in Tampico, Illinois, the son of a shoe salesman who was bankrupted during the Depression. He graduated from Eureka College, Illinois, and was a sports announcer in Davenport and Des Moines, Iowa, 1932–37. He became a Hollywood actor in 1937 and appeared in 50 films, including *Bedtime for Bonzo* (1951) and *The Killers* (1964). He is best remembered for the films *Knute Rockne, All American* (1940), where he used the film line 'Win one for the Gipper', and for *Kings Row* (1942).

As president of the Screen Actors' Guild 1947–52, he became a conservative, critical of the bureaucratic stifling of free enterprise, and named names before the House Un-American Activities Committee. He joined the Republican Party in 1962, and his term as governor of California was marked by battles against student protesters.

Having lost the Republican presidential nomination in 1968 and 1976 to Richard Nixon and Gerald Ford respectively, Reagan won it in

tary undersecretary, Ministry of Defence, and parliamentary undersecretary at the Home Office.

Rees-Mogg, Lord William (1928–)

British journalist, editor of *The Times* 1967–81, chair of the Arts Council 1982–89, and from 1988 chair of the Broadcasting Standards Council. In 1993 he challenged the government over its ratification of the Maastricht Treaty, notably the government's right to transfer foreign policy decisions to European Community (now European Union) institutions. His challenge was rejected by the High Court.

Regan, Donald Thomas (1918–)

US Republican political adviser to Ronald ◊Reagan. He was secretary of the Treasury 1981–85 and chief of White House staff 1985–87, when he was forced to resign because of widespread belief in his complicity in the Irangate scandal.

Regan was born in Cambridge, Massachusetts, and graduated from Harvard in 1940. He joined the United States Marine Corps, retiring at the end of World War II as a lieutenant colonel. In January 1981 he became the 66th secretary of the Treasury. Later that year he was elected chair of the Depository Institutions Deregulation Committee, which was created by Congress to phase out interest-rate ceilings on deposits in commercial banks, mutual savings banks, savings and loan associations, and credit unions.

Regan is the author of *A View from the Street* (1972), an analysis of the events on Wall Street during the crisis years of 1969 and 1970.

FURTHER READING

Regan, Donald *For the Record: From Wall Street to Washington* 1988

Rehnquist, William (1924–)

US lawyer, chief justice of the US Supreme Court from 1986. Under his leadership, the Court established a reputation for conservative rulings on such issues as abortion and capital punishment.

Active within the Republican Party, Rehnquist was appointed head of the office of legal counsel by President Richard Nixon in 1969 and controversially defended such measures as pre-trial detention and wiretapping. He became an associate justice of the Supreme Court in 1972. As chief justice, he wrote the majority opinion for such cases as *Morrison* v *Olson* (1988), in which the Court ruled that a special court can appoint special prosecutors to investigate crimes by high-ranking officials, and *Hustler* v *Falwell* (1988), in which the Court ruled that public figures cannot be compensated for stress caused by a parody that cannot possibly be taken seriously. Rehnquist dissented in *Texas* v *Johnson* (1989), in which the Court ruled that the burning of the US flag in protest is protected by individual rights set forth in the First Amendment. In 1990 he dissented on the Court's ruling that it is unconstitutional for states to require a teenager to notify her parents before having an abortion.

As an associate justice, Rehnquist argued in dissent for the death penalty in *Furman* v *Georgia* (1972), and again in dissent against the right to abortion in *Roe* v *Wade* (1973). Writing for the majority, Rehnquist held in *Rostken* v *Goldberg* (1981) that it is constitutional to exclude women for registering for the draft.

Reich, Robert B(ernard) (1946–)

US Democratic politician and political economist, secretary of labour 1993–96. In *Minding America's Business: The Decline and Rise of the American Economy* (1982), he proposed the diversion of government financial incentives away from declining manufacturing industries to those employing new technology.

Reich entered the Justice Department in 1974, became director of policy planning at the Federal Trade Commission in 1976, and a lecturer in political economy at the John F Kennedy School of Government, Harvard University, in 1981. His other books include *New Deals: The Chrysler Revival and the American System* (1979), an analysis of government intervention to bail out the car manufacturer Chrysler; *Tales of a New America* (1987); *The Resurgent Liberal (and Other Unfashionable Prophecies)* (1989); and *The*

1980 and defeated President Jimmy Carter. He was wounded in an assassination attempt in 1981. The invasion of Grenada, following a coup there, generated a revival of national patriotism, and Reagan was re-elected by a landslide in 1984. His insistence on militarizing space through the Strategic Defense Initiative, popularly called Star Wars, prevented a disarmament agreement when he met the Soviet leader Mikhail ◊Gorbachev in 1985 and 1986, but a 4% reduction in nuclear weapons was agreed in 1987. In 1986 he ordered the bombing of Tripoli, Libya, in alleged retaliation for the killing of a US soldier in Berlin by a guerrilla group. Leaving office at the age of 78, he was the oldest president in US history.

The Washington National Airport in Washington, DC, was renamed the Ronald Reagan Washington National Airport in his honour in February 1998.

FURTHER READING

Blumenthal, S, and Edsall, T B *The Reagan Legacy* 1988

Boyarsky, B *Ronald Reagan: His Life and Rise to Presidency* 1981

Palmer, John L (ed) *Perspectives on the Reagan Years* 1986

Wills, Garry *Reagan's America: Innocents at Home* 1987

Work of Nations: Preparing Ourselves for 21st Century Capitalism (1991), where he called for the education of a skilled and flexible workforce, able to adapt to new techniques. His ideas had an influence on the thinking and policy of the 'New Labour' government in the UK, led by Tony Blair from 1997.

Reid, George Houstoun (1845–1918)

Australian politician, born in Scotland; premier of New South Wales 1894–99, and prime minister 1904–05. While premier he brought in reforms in the areas of taxation, public administration, land law, and social legislation. He was an equivocal supporter of federation but entered the first federal parliament in 1901 as leader of the conservative Free Trade Party. In 1904 he was able to form a coalition government but his majority was not secure enough for his government to forward initiatives and he was defeated after ten months. He retired from parliament in 1908.

Reid was the son of a Presbyterian cleric, his family arriving in Australia in 1852. He qualified as a lawyer in 1879 and worked at the Colonial Treasury and Crown Law Office in Sydney before entering the New South Wales parliament in 1880. He was created a KCMG in 1909.

After retirement in 1910 he moved to London to become Australia's high commissioner (until 1916) and a member of the House of Commons from 1916.

FURTHER READING
McMinn, Winston G *George Reid* 1988
Reid, George *My Reminiscences* 1917

Reid, James (Jimmy) (1932–)

Scottish communist trade-union activist. In 1971, when the four shipyards of the publicly owned Upper Clyde Shipbuilders (UCS) consortium were threatened with closure, he led a 'work-in' that ultimately forced the Conservative government of Edward Heath to find a package to keep the yards open.

This success was attributed to the efforts of the shop stewards' committee, led by Reid's tough militancy and media abilities (he described the Heath government as being 'an 007 government with a licence to kill industry').

Born in Clydebank, Reid was initially employed at the Scottish Stock Exchange before becoming an engineering apprentice at the age of 15. He had been successful as national secretary of the Young Communist League in the early 1960s, but less so as secretary of the Scottish Communist Party and had returned to work in the shipyards in 1969.

Reid was elected rector of Glasgow University by its students and stood (unsuccessfully) as a Communist candidate for Clydebank in 1974. He publicly left the Communist Party in 1976.

Reina Idiaquez, Carlos Roberto (1926–)

Honduran centre-right politician, president from 1994. He oversaw an upturn in the economy, although the unemployment rate remained high.

A member of the centre-right Liberal Party of Honduras (PLH), he served in the Honduras National Assembly, the International Court of Justice, and as ambassador to the UK and France, before winning the November 1993 presidential election. He was succeeded as president in January 1998 by Carlos Roberto ◊Flores Facusse, also of the PLH.

Trained in law at the National University of Honduras, Cambridge University, UK, and the Sorbonne in Paris, France, Reina taught as a law professor at the University of Honduras, developing an expertise in international law.

Reith, John Charles Walsham, 1st Baron, Reith of Stonehaven (1889–1971)

First general manager 1922–27 and director general 1927–38 of the British Broadcasting Corporation (BBC). He was enormously influential in the early development of the BBC and established its high-minded principles of public-service broadcasting. He held several ministerial posts in government during World War II, including minister of information in 1940, transport in 1940, and minister of works 1940–42.

Reith was born in Glasgow, Scotland. He was chair of the Colonial Development Corporation 1950–59. His publications include *Into the Wind* (1949).

FURTHER READING
Smart, C *The Reith Diaries* 1975

René, France-Albert (1935–)

Seychelles left-wing politician. He became the country's first prime minister after independence in 1976, and president from 1977 after a coup. He followed a non-nuclear policy of nonalignment. In 1993 René and his party, the People's Progressive Front, won the country's first free elections in 16 years.

In 1964 René founded the left-wing Seychelles People's United Party (SPUP), pressing for complete independence. When this was achieved in 1976, he became prime minister and James Mancham, leader of the Seychelles Democratic Party, became president. René seized the presidency in 1977 and set up a one-party state, but this was replaced by a multiparty constitution adopted in 1993. He was re-elected president in March 1998 and the SPUP won the concurrent assembly elections.

Reno, Janet (1939–)

US lawyer, attorney general under President Bill Clinton. Having been appointed to the post in 1993, she took full responsibility in the same year for the attack by the Federal Bureau of Investigation (FBI) on the compound of the Branch Davidian cult at Waco, Texas, in which 86 people died.

Reno was born in Miami, Florida. As chief prosecutor for Dade County, Florida, 1978–93, she concentrated on helping disadvantaged children to grow into responsible citizens. She is a Democrat and is the first woman to be appointed US attorney general.

Restrepo, Carlos Lleras (1908–1994)

Colombian politician and president 1966–70. His administration was extremely successful, particularly in regard to economic policy. He instituted effective political reforms that significantly reduced inflation, improved the balance of payments deficit, and bolstered national economic growth. He also played a significant role in reducing the reliance on the one-crop coffee economy, through greater economic diversification.

Towards the end of his period in office, Colombia had attained high rates of economic growth, in part attributable to the economic policies formulated and implemented by Lleras.

Lleras was a member of the Liberal party, and served as its head in 1948, following the assassination of Jorge Eliécer Gaitán, and again in 1961.

Reuther, Walter Philip (1907–1970)

US trade-union leader. He was vice chair of the Union of United Automobile, Aircraft, and Agricultural Implement Workers of America 1942–46 and its president from 1946. He was president of the Congress of Industrial Organizations 1952–56 and vice president of the combined American Federation of Labor and Congress of Industrial Organizations 1955–70.

Reuther was educated at Wayne University. From 1927 he worked for various motor companies, and in 1935 began to organize the workers in the motor industry into a union.

Reyes, Rafael Prieto (1850–1921)

Colombian dictator and president 1904–09. After his election he assumed dictatorial powers and vigorously embarked on a programme of national economic reform that strengthened the country's infrastructure.

Although his administration was considered effective, his repression of the opposition and his creation of constitutional changes provoked increasing apprehension. His attempts to conclude a treaty with the USA recognizing Panama's independence ultimately spawned a crisis that led to his resignation.

Reyes entered into politics under the dictator Rafael Núñez. He served as interior secretary, ambassador to France, and as a member of the Pan-American Conference in Mexico 1902–03. He also played an active role in the attempt to secure redress from the USA for its part in the Panamanian Revolution of 1903.

Reyes was born in Santa Rosa, New Granada. For several years from 1874 he and his two brothers explored the Colombian Amazon basin. On his return, Reyes joined up with the conservative military forces.

Reynaud, Paul (1878–1966)

French prime minister in World War II, who succeeded Edouard Daladier in March 1940 but resigned in June after the German breakthrough. He was imprisoned by the Germans until 1945, and again held government offices after the war.

Reynolds, Albert (1932–)

Irish Fianna Fáil politician, Taoiseach (prime minister) 1992–94. He was minister for industry and commerce 1987–88 and minister of finance 1988–92. In December 1993 Reynolds and UK prime minister John Major issued a joint peace initiative for Northern Ireland, the Downing Street Declaration, which led to a cease-fire by both the Irish Republican Army (IRA) and the loyalist paramilitaries the following year.

Reynolds became party leader and prime minister in January 1992, but his government was defeated on a vote of confidence in November 1992. He succeeded in forming a Fianna Fáil–Labour coalition, but resigned as premier and party leader in November 1994 after Labour disputed a judicial appointment he had made and withdrew from the coalition.

Reynolds saw the advantages of European Community membership, and after a referendum in 1992 ratified the Maastricht Treaty for closer union.

Reynolds was born in Rooskey, County Roscommon, and qualified as an accountant by correspondence course. He embarked on a business career, developing a pet-food company with a multi-million-pound turnover, before entering the political arena.

He joined Fianna Fáil in 1977, and held various government posts. In 1992, when Charles ◊Haughey was forced to resign, he was elected president of Fianna Fáil by a majority of 66 votes to 16. As the year progressed, however, Reynolds's sure touch seemed to have deserted him and, after losing a confidence vote in parliament, he sought a personal mandate through a general election. He did not achieve a clear victory and was forced into a coalition with the Labour Party. Now growing in confidence, Reynolds announced a six-year development plan for 'the transformation of Ireland' in October 1993. Seeing closer relations with Britain as a key to unlocking the Northern Ireland problems, he participated in the Downing Street Declaration. But in 1994, after a deep disagreement with its leader Dick ◊Spring, Reynolds lost the support of the Labour Party. The coalition collapsed and he resigned the premiership and gave up the leadership of Fianna Fáil. In March 1998 he announced that he was leaving politics to pursue his international business interests. This followed the failure of his bid to succeed Mary ◊Robinson as Irish president.

Rhee, Syngman (1875–1965)

Korean right-wing politician. A rebel under Chinese and Japanese rule, he became president of South Korea from 1948 until riots forced him to resign and leave the country in 1960. He established a repressive dictatorship and was an embarrassing ally for the USA.

Ribbentrop, Joachim von (1893–1946)

German Nazi politician and diplomat. As foreign minister 1938–45, he negotiated the non-aggression pact between Germany and the USSR (the Ribbentrop–Molotov pact of 1939). He was tried at Nürnberg as a war criminal in 1946 and hanged.

Born in the Rhineland, Ribbentrop was awarded the Iron Cross in World War I, and from 1919 became wealthy as a wine merchant. He joined the Nazi party in 1932 and acted as Hitler's adviser on foreign affairs; he was German ambassador to the UK 1936–38. A political lightweight and social climber, his loyalty was useful to Hitler since he posed no threat, although he was regarded with contempt by his colleagues.

FURTHER READING
The Ribbentrop Diaries 1954

Ribeiro, Darcy (1922–)

Brazilian social anthropologist, politician, and author. His novel *Maíra* (1978; translated into English in 1983) highlights the conflict between native Amazonian peoples and the Europeanized Brazilian society.

Rich, Adrienne (1929–)

US radical feminist poet, writer, and critic. Her poetry is both subjective and political, concerned with female consciousness, peace, and gay rights. Her works include *On Lies, Secrets and Silence* (1979), *The Fact of a Doorframe: Poems, 1950–84* (1984), and *What is Found There: Notebooks on Poetry and Politics* (1994). In 1974, when given the National Book Award, she

---

The connections between and among women are the most feared, the most problematic, and the most potentially transforming force on the planet.

ADRIENNE RICH *Chrysalis* no. 7, 1979

---

declined to accept it as an individual, but, with Alice Walker and Audrey Rich, accepted it on behalf of all women.

FURTHER READING
Yorke, Liz *Adrienne Rich: Passion, Politics, and the Body* 1998

Ridley, Nicholas (1929–1993)

British Conservative politician, cabinet minister 1983–90. After a period in industry he became active as a 'dry' right-winger in the Conservative Party. He served under Harold Macmillan, Edward Heath, and Alec Douglas-Home, but did not become a member of the cabinet until 1983. His apparent disdain for public opinion caused his transfer, in 1989, from the politically sensitive department of the environment to that of trade and industry, and his resignation in July 1990 after criticisms of European colleagues and Germany.

In the autobiographical *My Style of Government* (1991) Ridley claimed Margaret Thatcher's government was wrongly undermined by Nigel Lawson and Geoffrey Howe, who forced her into supporting the European Exchange Rate Mechanism against her better judgement. The memoirs also showed him to be a devoted admirer of Mrs Thatcher.

Ridley was born in Newcastle upon Tyne, and after an education at Eton and Balliol College, Oxford, he spent his early career in industry around Tyneside before entering politics. He entered Parliament as member for Tewkesbury in 1959 and represented it until 1992. He held junior government posts before being made minister of state in the department of trade and industry 1970–72 under Edward Heath. In his mistrust of Brussels bureaucracy, he was ideologically in tune with Margaret Thatcher, who gave him progressively senior portfolios, including transport 1983–86, environment 1986–89, and trade and industry 1989–90. His article denigrating Germany in the *Spectator* (1990) eventually cost him his ministerial post and his political career.

Rifkind, Malcolm Leslie (1946–)

British lawyer and Conservative politician, foreign secretary 1995–97, born in Scotland. As defence secretary 1992–95, his incisive intellect enabled him to manage the 'peace dividend', with its inevitable run-down of parts of the armed forces, more successfully than some of his predecessors. He lost his parliamentary seat of Edinburgh Pentlands in the 1997 general election.

Educated at Edinburgh University, Rifkind initially embarked on an academic career but was called to the Scottish bar in 1975 and in the same year entered politics, winning the Edinburgh Pentland seat. A junior minister in the Scottish Office from 1979, he progressed through the Foreign and Commonwealth Office to become Scottish secretary in 1986 and transport secretary in 1990.

Rimington, Stella (1935–)

British public servant and director general of the counter-intelligence security service (MI5) 1992–96. She was the first head of MI5 to be named publicly, and in July 1993 published a booklet containing hitherto undisclosed details on the service, including its history, organization, and constitutional role.

Rimington joined MI5 in 1969 as a desk officer and progressed to become director of counter-terrorism. She was promoted to senior deputy director general in

1990, and in 1992 became the first woman to hold the top post.

Ríos Montt, Efraín (1927–)

Guatemalan soldier and right-wing politician, president 1982–83. He launched a crackdown against corruption and guerrilla and left-wing activity, with thousands of native Indians being killed by the armed forces. Unpopular because of this repression and his Protestant fundamentalist beliefs, in what is a predominantly Catholic country, Ríos Montt was overthrown and forced into exile by an August 1983 coup led by General Oscar Humberto Mejía Victores.

A professional soldier from 1943, Ríos Montt rose to become a general and army chief of staff. He made an unsuccessful presidential bid in 1974, as candidate of the Christian Democrat-led National Opposition Front (FNO), but secured power in March 1982, after leading, along with younger right-wing army officers, a coup to seize power after a disputed presidential election. Ríos Montt swiftly dissolved the ruling junta and installed himself as president.

He returned to fight the 1990–91 presidential elections, but was debarred since the constitution prevented coup leaders from standing. However, he gave his backing to his protégé Jorge ◊Serrano Elias, who was elected.

Rivera, Fabian Alarcon (1947–)

Ecuadorian politician and president 1997–98 of an interim government.

Rivera was a member of the centre-left Frente Radical Alfarista (FRA; Radical Alfarista Front), and held many public administrative positions, mostly in Quito. Between 1984 and 1988, he was the provincial mayor of Pichincha, and president of the consortium of provincial councils of Ecuador in 1984. He also held important national congress committee positions 1990–94. He was a republican deputy 1990–92 and 1994–96, director of the FRA 1994–96, vice president in 1995, and president of the national congress 1996–97. In 1997 he was elected by congress to be president until August 1998 after President Abdala Bucaram was ousted from power because of 'mental incapacity'.

Rivera was born in Quito, and educated in social sciences and legal studies at the Universidad Católica de Quito.

Rivera, Julio Adalberto (1921–1973)

El Salvadorean soldier and politician, president 1962–67, and founder of the National Conciliation Party (PCN). His government relied on the support of the conservative planter elite, but took action to set minimum wages for agricultural workers and his presidency was marked by economic advance.

An army lieutenant colonel, he led the five-member junta (Civil–Military Directory) that, in January 1961, overthrew a recently established radical junta. Rivera formed the conservative-reformist PCN and was popularly elected president in 1962.

He was succeeded as president by another army officer, Fidel ◊Sánchez Hernández.

Robens, Alfred, Baron Robens of Woldingham (1910–)

English trade unionist and industrialist, chair of the National Coal Board 1961–71. A full-time trade-union officer of the Union of Distributive and Allied Workers, he was elected to Parliament in 1945 and for six months in 1951 was a member of the Cabinet as minister of labour and national service. He was made a life peer in 1961.

Robertson, George Islay MacNeill (1946–)

British Labour politician, secretary of state for defence from 1997. He entered the House of Commons, representing Hamilton, in 1978. After serving as parliamentary private secretary to the secretary of state for social services in the last months of James Callaghan's government in 1979, when Labour went into opposition he became shadow spokesperson on Scotland 1979–80, on defence 1980–81, on foreign and Commonwealth Affairs 1984–93, and on European and community affairs 1985–93. He was shadow Scottish secretary 1993–97.

He was born at Port Ellen, Isle of Islay, Scotland, and educated at the University of Dundee. After graduating he worked for the General and Municipal Workers Union (GMWU) in Scotland 1969–78.

Robertson, Pat (Marion Gordon) (1930–)

US Republican politician and religious broadcaster. A born-again evangelical Christian, he founded the Christian Broadcasting Network (CBN) in 1961. He was the host of its daily talk show, *The 700 Club*, and was a candidate for the Republican presidential nomination in 1988. In 1989 he founded the Christian Coalition political pressure group.

A 'Bible conservative' who believes in 'traditional values', Robertson was born in Lexington, Virginia, studied at the New York Theological Seminary, and was ordained into the Southern Baptist Church in 1961. He launched CBN after buying a run-down television station in Portsmouth, Virginia, and it grew into a large network. He founded CBN University in 1977, and built the CBN Center in Virginia Beach. His books include his autobiography, *Shout It from the Housetops* (1972), and *The New World Order* (1991).

Robeson, Paul Bustill (1898–1976)

See page 366.

Robinson, Mary (1944–)

Irish Labour politician, president 1990–97. She became a professor of law at the age of 25. A strong supporter of women's rights, she campaigned for the liberalization of Ireland's laws prohibiting divorce and abortion.

Robinson won a seat in the Irish senate (Seanad Éireann) in 1969 and held it for 20 years. As a lawyer she achieved an international reputation in the field of human rights. She tried unsuccessfully to enter the Dáil Éireann (lower house of parliament) in 1990, and then surprisingly won the presidency of her country. In 1997 she became the United Nations High Commissioner for Human Rights.

Robinson was born in County Mayo and educated at Trinity College, Dublin, and Harvard University, USA. In 1969 she became the youngest law professor at Trinity College. As a member of the Labour Party, she fought two unsuccessful elections to enter the Dáil Éireann but entered the senate instead.

At the start of the presidential campaign she was the 100–1 underdog, but then the leading contestant, the Fianna Fáil candidate Brian Lenihan (1930–   ), was sacked as deputy prime minister by Charles Haughey following charges of scandal. The first woman to hold the post, Robinson raised the profile of the presidency considerably, campaigning for greater equality for women and holding an outward-looking, pro-European stance.

Robinson, Ray (Arthur Napoleon Raymond) (1915–   )

Trinidad and Tobago centre-left politician, prime minister 1986–92, and president from 1997. Leader of the National Alliance for Reconstruction (NAR), he won a landslide victory in 1986, becoming prime minister with portfolios for the economy and Tobago. However, economic recession caused political instability and in 1990 an attempted coup by Islamic fundamentalists ended in a six-day siege. Defeated in 1991 by the People's National Movement (PNM), led by Patrick ◊Manning, Robinson returned to centre-stage in 1995, as adviser to the coalition government of Basdeo ◊Panday. In 1997 he was elected to the largely titular position of president.

Robinson's political career began as a representative in the Federation of the West Indies 1958–61. He served as finance minister 1961–67, PNM deputy leader 1967–70, and foreign minister 1967–68 under the centrist PNM administration of Eric ◊Williams. After the Black Power riots of 1970 he distanced himself from the PNM, becoming leader of the new Democratic Action Congress 1971–86 and chair of the

◆ ROBESON, PAUL BUSTILL (1898–1976) ◆

US singer, actor, lawyer, and activist. From the 1930s he was a staunch fighter against anti-Semitism and racism against black people, and he was a supporter of the various national liberation movements that came to prominence in Africa after World War II. Robeson appeared in Eugene O'Neill's play *The Emperor Jones* (1924) and the Jerome Kern musical *Show Boat* (1927), in which he sang 'Ol' Man River', and took the title role in *Othello* in 1930.

The son of a preacher who had escaped from slavery, Robeson became deeply politicized by his experiences when he lived and worked in the UK in the 1930s. He graduated from Rutgers University with an assortment of honours for excellence, then studied law at Columbia University. He was the first black law graduate to enter one of New York's most prestigious law firms. Robeson was an outstanding athlete, becoming one of the first black men to play professional American football. In the cinema Robeson was the first black actor to rise to international prominence in film and, through his outspokenness at the stereotyping of black actors, was the first to bring dignity and respect to black characters. His films include *Sanders of the River* (1935) and *King Solomon's Mines* (1937).

Robeson was also a communist and a supporter of the Soviet Union. Before the McCarthy House Un-American Activities Committee he refused to say whether he was a communist or not. But on his return from a visit to the Soviet Union his passport was withdrawn. For eight years he could not act or sing abroad. In 1949, as anti-communist fervour gripped the country, a Robeson concert was attacked at Peekskill just outside New York City. The concert, in aid of the Harlem chapter of the Civil Rights Congress, was abandoned as jeering crowds screamed abuse and pulled concert-goers from their cars. Robeson returned the following week determined that he and his followers would not give in to mob violence.

Robeson spoke over 20 different languages including several different African languages, Chinese, Russian and Arabic. He spent time with several of Africa's future leaders while in London. In later years, Robeson gained the respect and recognition within the USA that he had long had internationally. His last years were spent in the UK, where he continued to fight against prejudice of any kind until his death.

FURTHER READING

Duberman, Martin *Paul Robeson* 1989, 1995
Hamilton, Virginia *Paul Robeson* 1974
Robeson, Paul *Here I Stand* 1958
Robeson, Susan *The Whole World in His Hands* 1981

Paul Robeson singing the national anthem with shipyard workers building US warships, 1942. *AKG London*

assembly in Tobago, which was created in 1980. In 1986 the victory of the NAR, formed in 1985 to bring together a number of left-wing parties, ended 30 years of dominance by the PNM.

With oil prices falling, the economy became depressed, putting a strain on the disparate NAR, which began to fracture. In April 1990 the currency was devalued and IMF financial assistance sought, and in July there was an attempted coup by 120 Islamic fundamentalists, who held parliamentarians and ministers hostage. Robinson was shot in the legs by the extremists, but the siege was lifted after six days.

Before entering politics Robinson studied at Oxford University and trained as a barrister in London.

Rocard, Michel (1930–)

French socialist politician, prime minister 1988–91. Widely popular as the exponent of a moderate and modernizing social democracy, he was leader of the Socialist Party (PS) 1993–94.

Trained at the Ecole Nationale d'Administration (where he attended classes with Jacques ◊Chirac), Rocard joined the new Unified Socialist Party (PSU) led by Pierre ◊Mendès-France and stood as its presi-

dential candidate in 1969 before joining the PS in 1974. He unsuccessfully challenged François Mitterrand for the party's 1981 presidential nomination. He served under Mitterrand as minister of planning and regional development 1981–83 and agriculture 1983–85, but resigned from government protesting at the introduction of proportional representation for the 1986 parliamentary elections. He played a key role in Mitterrand's strategy of 'opening to the centre' in his second presidential term. Tipped to be the party's next presidential candidate, he resigned as leader after its poor performance in the 1994 European elections.

Rocco, Alfredo (1875–1935)

Italian Nationalist theorist and later Fascist politician. An academic lawyer, he achieved prominence within the Italian Nationalist Association on the eve of World War I. The association merged with the Fascists in 1923, and Rocco served as minister of justice from 1925 to 1932. In this capacity he played a major role in constructing the institutional framework of the Fascist state in accordance with his openly elitist and authoritarian ideas.

Rockefeller, Nelson (Aldrich) (1908–1979)

US Republican politician, vice president 1974–77. He was an official in the administrations of Franklin D Roosevelt, Harry Truman, and Dwight D Eisenhower, and governor of New York 1958–73. He gained a reputation as a progressive and activist administrator.

He was a leader of the party's moderate 'Eastern establishment' wing, and an unsuccessful candidate for the Republican presidential nomination in 1960, 1964, and 1968. Although appointed vice president by Gerald ◊Ford, Rockefeller was not retained as Ford's running mate in 1976.

Rockefeller was born in Bar Harbor, Maine, and was educated at Dartmouth College. He was assistant secretary of state for Latin American affairs 1944–45, special assistant for foreign affairs to Eisenhower 1954–55, and chair of the president's Advisory Committee on Government Organization 1953–58. He was coordinator for inter-American affairs 1940–44 and 1969–74. His publications include *The Future of Federalism* (1962).

Rodríguez, Andrés (1923–   )

Paraguayan military leader and president 1991–93. He was responsible for deposing President Alfredo ◊Stroessner in 1989, ending one of the most corrupt and repressive dictatorships the nation had ever known.

Rodríguez gained office as president in the elections held in 1991, as a member of the military-dominated Asociación Nacional Republicana (ANR; Colorado Party). His term in office ended with Juan Carlos ◊Wasmosy gaining the majority result in the 1993 elections.

Röhm, Ernst (1887–1934)

German leader of the Nazi Brownshirts, the SA (Sturmabteilung). On the pretext of an intended SA putsch (uprising) by the Brownshirts, the Nazis had some hundred of them, including Röhm, killed 29–30 June 1934. The event is known as the Night of the Long Knives.

Roh Tae-woo (1932–   )

South Korean right-wing politician and general, president 1988–93. He held ministerial office from 1981 under President Chun Doo-hwan, and became chair of the ruling Democratic Justice Party in 1985. He was elected president in 1988, amid allegations of fraud and despite being connected with the massacre of about 2,000 anti-government demonstrators in 1980. In October 1995 Roh admitted publicly to having secretly amassed £400 million during his term in office, of which he retained £140 million for personal use. He was arrested in November on corruption charges, along with former president Chun, and placed on trial in 1996, on charges of sedition and military rebellion in

1980. He was found guilty in August 1996, heavily fined, and sentenced to 22 years' imprisonment. In December 1996 an appeal court reduced his prison sentence to 17 years.

A Korean Military Academy classmate of Chun Doo-hwan, Roh fought in the Korean War and later, during the 1970s, became commander of the 9th Special Forces Brigade and Capital Security Command. Roh retired as a four-star general in July 1981 and served as minister for national security, foreign affairs, and, later, home affairs.

Rohwedder, Detler (1932–1991)

German Social Democrat politician and business executive. In August 1990 he became chief executive of Treuhand, the body concerned with the privatization or liquidation of some 8,000 East German businesses. His attempt to force market-oriented solutions on Treuhand was controversial, many preferring a more interventionist stance. He was assassinated the following April.

Rojas Pinilla, Gustavo (1900–1975)

Colombian dictator and president 1953–57. His administration was oppressive and highly corrupt, and his attempts at fiscal reforms failed.

Rojas was head of the armed forces that ousted President Laureano Gómez in the 1953 coup – the first such military intervention in the 20th century.

In 1957 he was deposed by a military junta backed by both liberals and conservatives, and was forced into exile. He subsequently organized the Acción Nacional Popular (ANAPO; National Popular Alliance), along with his daughter, María Eugenia Rojas de Moreno (1934–   ), who was a senator. The party gained widespread popular support from the poor. In 1970 he ran unsuccessfully for president, and ill health forced him to retire in 1973.

Roldós Aquilera, Jaime (1940–1981)

Ecuadorian politician and president 1979–81, whose election marked an important milestone in Ecuador's political history – that of democratic rule after decades of dominance by military rule.

Roldós was a social democrat and candidate of the centre-left Concentración de Fuerzas Populares (CPF; Concentration of Popular Forces). He actively sought to improve social conditions in his country. In the period leading up to the 1979 elections, he was involved in committees charged with electoral and legislative change, which were instrumental in the creation of the new 1979 constitution. In 1980 he set up his own political party. His reformist administration ended in 1981, with his death in an air crash. His vice president, Osvaldo Hurtado Larrea, assumed the presidential office.

Romero Barceló, Carlos (1932–)

Puerto Rican politician and advocate of full US statehood, governor 1977–85. He helped to form the New Progressive Party (PNP) in 1967, and became PNP leader in 1973. As governor, he promoted house construction, inward US investment, and privatization. Re-elected in 1980, his advocacy of US statehood fanned terrorist outrages by the Armed Forces for National Liberation (FALN) and, in the wake of a police scandal, he lost his governorship to Rafael ◊Hernández Colón in 1984. After 1993 he became Puerto Rico's resident commissioner in Washington, DC, sitting in the US House of Representatives, but holding restricted voting powers.

Romero established the PNP with Luis Antonio Ferré Aguayo, and in 1968 Ferré was elected governor of Puerto Rico and Romero mayor of San Juan. After a successful two terms as mayor, he replaced Ferré as PNP leader, and was narrowly elected governor in 1976, having campaigned on a programme of economic restructuring. His housing programme was engineered through a Puerto Rico Development Fund.

He was born into a prominent San Juan political family, his grandfather having founded the now defunct Liberal Party and his father being a Supreme Court judge. He studied at Yale University and practised as a lawyer, before entering politics in the mid-1960s as a member of the Statehood Republican Party, which advocated full US statehood for Puerto Rico.

Romero y Galdames, Oscar Arnulfo (1917–1980)

El Salvadorean Roman Catholic prelate, archbishop, and champion of human rights. He courageously spoke out against the military regime's bloody repression of the poor, which had claimed thousands of lives, and was nominated for the Nobel Peace Prize in 1979. He was assassinated in March 1980 by right-wing paramilitaries, while preaching at a San Salvador cathedral.

Born in Ciudad Barrios, in eastern El Salvador, he was ordained in 1942, made a bishop in 1970, and became archbishop of San Salvador in 1977. Hitherto viewed as a conservative traditionalist who favoured only limited social reform, he was radicalized by the upsurge in political violence across El Salvador in the late 1970s, involving the extreme right and left. Public revulsion at his assassination helped to bring the reformist José Napoleon ◊Duarte back to power.

FURTHER READING
Erdozain, P *Archbishop Romero: Martyr of El Salvador* 1981
Romero, Oscar Arnulfo *The Church Is All of You* 1984

Rommel, Erwin Johannes Eugen (1891–1944)

German field marshal. He served in World War I, and in World War II played an important part in the invasions of central Europe and France. He was commander of the North African offensive from 1941 (when he was nicknamed 'Desert Fox') until defeated in the Battle of El Alamein, and was expelled from Africa in March 1943.

Rommel was commander in chief for a short time against the Allies in Europe in 1944 but (as a sympathizer with the ◊Stauffenberg plot against Hitler) was forced to commit suicide.

Romulo, Carlos Pena (1899–1895)

Filipino diplomat and journalist. He represented the Philippines at the United Nations and also served as ambassador to the USA 1952–53 and 1955–62 and as foreign minister 1968–84, in the government of Ferdinand ◊Marcos. He was awarded a Pulitzer prize in 1942.

Born in Manila, after studying at the University of the Philippines and Columbia University, Romulo worked as a newspaper editor and professor of English 1926–30. During World War II he fought with distinction, becoming a brigadier general in the US Far East army, led by General Douglas ◊MacArthur.

FURTHER READING
Romulo, Carlos Pena *My Brother Americans* 1945, *Clarifying the Asian Mystique* 1969

Roosevelt, (Anna) Eleanor (1884–1962)

US social worker, lecturer, and first lady. Her newspaper column 'My Day', started in 1935, was widely syndicated. She influenced New Deal policies, especially those supporting desegregation. She was a delegate to the United Nations (UN) general assembly and chair of the UN commission on human rights 1946–51, and helped to draw up the Declaration of Human Rights at the UN in 1945. She was married to her cousin President Franklin D ◊Roosevelt, and was the niece of Theodore ◊Roosevelt.

> *No one can make you feel inferior without your consent.*
> ELEANOR ROOSEVELT *Catholic Digest*

She was born in New York and educated in Europe. After her husband's death in 1945, she continued to work on civil rights for black Americans and for human rights worldwide. Within the Democratic Party she formed the left-wing Americans for Democratic Action group in 1947.

FURTHER READING
Hershan, Stella *A Woman of Quality* 1970
Lash, Joseph *Eleanor and Franklin* 1971, *Eleanor: The Years Alone* 1972
Roosevelt, Eleanor *Autobiography* 1961
Wiesen Cook, Blanche *Eleanor Roosevelt* 1992

Roosevelt, Theodore (1858–1919)

26th president of the USA 1901–09, a Republican. After serving as governor of New York 1898–1900 he became vice president to William McKinley, whom he succeeded as president on McKinley's assassination in 1901. He campaigned against the great trusts (associations of enterprises that reduce competition), while carrying on a jingoist foreign policy designed to enforce US supremacy over Latin America.

The men with the muck-rakes are often indispensable to the well-being of society; but only if they know when to stop raking the muck.

THEODORE ROOSEVELT Speech in Washington 14 April 1906

As president, Roosevelt became more liberal. He tackled business monopolies, initiated measures for the conservation of national resources, and introduced the Pure Food and Drug Act. In 1904 he announced the Roosevelt Corollary to the Monroe Doctrine, to the effect that the USA would intervene in Latin America in order to prevent European intervention. He won the Nobel Peace Prize in 1906 for his part in ending the Russo-Japanese war. Alienated after his retirement by the conservatism of his successor W H Taft, Roosevelt formed the Progressive or 'Bull Moose' Party. He unsuccessfully ran for the presidency in 1912. During World War I he strongly advocated US intervention.

Roosevelt, born in New York, graduated from Harvard in 1880 and was elected to the state legislature in 1881. He was police commissioner of New York City in 1895, and assistant secretary of the navy 1897–98. During the Spanish–American War of 1898 he commanded a volunteer force of 'rough riders'.

A feature of Roosevelt's presidency was the Hay–Pauncefote Treaty, which made possible the Panama Canal scheme.

A big-game hunter (on one safari he killed over 3,000 animals), he refused in 1902 to shoot a bear cub, and teddy bears are named after him. He wrote historical and other works, including *The Naval War of 1812* (1882) and *The Winning of the West* (1889–96).

FURTHER READING

Burton, David *Theodore Roosevelt* 1973
Collins, Michael *That Damned Cowboy* 1989
Harbaugh, William *The Life and Times of Theodore Roosevelt* 1975
McCullough, David *Mornings on Horseback: The Story of an Extraordinary Family, a Vanished Way of Life, and the Unique Child Who Became Theodore Roosevelt* 1981
Norton, A A *Theodore Roosevelt* 1980
Roosevelt, Theodore *Autobiography* 1913

Root, Elihu (1845–1937)

US Republican politician. He was secretary of war in

◆ ROOSEVELT, FRANKLIN D(ELANO) (1882–1945) ◆

32nd president of the USA 1933–45, a Democrat. He served as governor of New York 1929–33. Becoming president during the Great Depression, he launched the **New Deal** economic and social reform programme, which made him popular with the people. After the outbreak of World War II he introduced lend-lease for the supply of war materials and services to the Allies and drew up the Atlantic Charter of solidarity. Once the USA had entered the war in 1941, he spent much time in meetings with Allied leaders.

Born in Hyde Park, New York, of a wealthy family, Roosevelt was educated in Europe and at Harvard and Columbia universities, and became a lawyer. In 1910 he was elected to the New York state senate. He held the assistant secretaryship of the navy in Woodrow Wilson's administrations 1913–21, and did much to increase the efficiency of the navy during World War I. He suffered from polio from 1921 but returned to politics, winning the governorship of New York State in 1929. When he became president in 1933, Roosevelt inculcated a new spirit of hope by his skilful 'fireside chats' on the radio and his inaugural-address statement: 'The only thing we have to fear is fear itself.' Surrounding himself by a 'Brain Trust' of experts, he immediately launched his reform programme. Banks were reopened, federal credit was restored, the gold standard was abandoned, and the dollar devalued. During the first hundred days of his administration, major legislation to facilitate industrial and agricultural

---

Let me assert my firm belief that the only thing we have to fear is fear itself – nameless, unreasoning, unjustified terror which paralyses needed efforts to convert retreat into advance.

FRANKLIN D ROOSEVELT Inaugural address 4 March 1933

---

recovery was enacted. In 1935 he introduced the Utilities Act, directed against abuses in the large holding companies, and the Social Security Act, providing for disability and retirement insurance. The presidential election of 1936 was won entirely on the record of the New Deal. During 1935–36 Roosevelt was involved in a conflict over the

William McKinley's cabinet 1899–1904, and secretary of state under Theodore Roosevelt 1905–09. A member of the Permanent Court of Arbitration in The Hague, the Netherlands, he won the Nobel Peace Prize in 1912.

Root was born in Clinton, New York, and educated at Hamilton College. He was a peace advocate, and was a senator 1909–15.

Rorty, Richard McKay (1931–)

US philosopher. His main concern has been to trace the personal and social implications of our changing perception of human identity, and his work draws inspiration from the US philosopher John ◊ Dewey and German social theorist Jürgen ◊ Habermas.

In his *Contingency, Irony and Solidarity* (1989), Rorty argues that language, self, and community are determined by history and are not expressions of an essential human nature. When we accept that human identity is not fixed, he argues, we then need to reconcile two seemingly conflicting consequences: at the personal level, the possibility of autonomy and self-creation; and at the public level, the need to create a freer and less cruel society.

Rosebery, Archibald Philip Primrose, 5th Earl of Rosebery (1847–1929)

British Liberal politician. He was foreign secretary in 1886 and 1892–94, when he succeeded William Gladstone as prime minister, but his government survived less than a year. After 1896 his imperialist views gradually placed him further from the mainstream of the Liberal Party. He was created Earl in 1868.

Rosenberg, Julius (1918–1953) and Ethel, born Greenglass (1915–1953)

US married couple, convicted of being leaders of an atomic-espionage ring passing information from Ethel's brother via courier to the USSR. The Rosenbergs were executed after much public controversy and demonstration. They were the only Americans executed for espionage during peacetime.

Both were born in New York City; Julius owned a radio repair shop and was a member of the Communist Party. Despite an offer of clemency from the government, they both maintained their innocence right up to their executions. Other implicated party members received long prison terms. The Cold War atmosphere was one of widespread fear of the Soviet Union, and several major spy scandals had occurred at this time. The death penalty was ruled as justified because of the danger to the USA from their actions. Recently published journals kept by the Soviet leader Nikita Khrushchev further implicate the Rosenbergs.

Rosenberg, Alfred (1893–1946)

German politician, born in Tallinn, Estonia. He became the chief Nazi ideologist and was minister for

composition of the Supreme Court, following its nullification of major New Deal measures as unconstitutional. In 1938 he introduced measures for farm relief and the improvement of working conditions.

In his foreign policy, Roosevelt endeavoured to use his influence to restrain Axis aggression, and to establish 'good neighbour' relations with other countries in the Americas. Soon after the outbreak of war, he launched a vast rearmament programme, introduced conscription, and provided for the supply of armaments to the Allies on a 'cash-and-carry' basis. In spite of strong isolationist opposition, he broke a long-standing precedent in running for a third term; he was re-elected in 1940. He announced that the USA would become the 'arsenal of democracy'. Roosevelt was eager for US entry into the war on behalf of the Allies. In addition to his revulsion for Adolf Hitler, he wanted to establish the USA as a world power, filling the vacuum he expected to be left by the break-up of the British Empire. He was restrained by isolationist forces in Congress.

Public opinion, however, was in favour of staying out of the war, so Roosevelt and the military chiefs deliberately kept back the intelligence reports received from the British and others concerning the imminent Japanese attack on the naval base at Pearl Harbor in Hawaii. The deaths at Pearl Harbor on 7 December 1941 incited public opinion, and the USA entered the war. From this point on, Roosevelt concerned himself solely with the conduct of the war. He participated in the Washington 1942 and Casablanca 1943 conferences to plan the Mediterranean assault, and the conferences in Québec, Cairo, and Tehran in 1943, and Yalta in 1945, at which the final preparations were made for the Allied victory. He was re-elected for a fourth term in 1944, but died in 1945. See photograph on page 408.

FURTHER READING
Alsop, Joseph *The Life and Times of Franklin D Roosevelt* 1982
Burns, James *Roosevelt: The Lion and the Fox* 1956
Freidel, Frank *Franklin D Roosevelt* 1952–73
Heinrich, W *The Threshold of War: Franklin D Roosevelt and the American Entry into World War II* 1988
Lash, Joseph *Eleanor and Franklin* 1971
Leuchtenburg, William *Franklin D Roosevelt and the New Deal* 1963
Schlesinger, Arthur, Jr *The Age of Roosevelt* 1957–1960

eastern occupied territories 1941–44. He was tried at Nürnberg in 1946 as a war criminal and hanged.

Rossoni, Edmondo (1884–1965)

Italian trade unionist and Fascist politician. As head of the Fascist trade unions from 1922, he was the leading advocate of Fascist syndicalism, which aimed to establish worker participation in management and profit-sharing through revolutionary general strike. However, between 1926 and 1928 the Fascist unions were emasculated as an independent force and subjected to state control.

Rossoni began his career as a member of the Socialist party and a revolutionary syndicalist activist. He supported intervention in World War I, volunteered, and subsequently joined the Fascist movement at its foundation.

Rothermere, Vere Harold Esmond Harmsworth, 3rd Viscount Rothermere (1925–1998)

British newspaper proprietor. He became chair of Associated Newspapers in 1971, controlling the right-wing *Daily Mail* (founded by his great-uncle Lord ◊Northcliffe) and *Mail on Sunday* (launched in 1982), the London *Evening Standard*, and a string of regional newspapers.

I don't think the British public are sanctimonious. They love to read humbug, their appetite for it is limitless, but I don't believe they are actually humbugs themselves.

LORD ROTHERMERE Interviewed a month before his death in the *Daily Telegraph*, August 1998.

In that year he closed the *Daily Sketch* and successfully transformed the *Daily Mail* into a tabloid. In 1977 he closed the London *Evening News* with heavy loss of jobs, but obtained a half-share of the more successful *Evening Standard*, and gained control of the remainder in 1985. He became Viscount in 1978.

Rothschild, Nathaniel Mayer Victor, 3rd Baron Rothschild (1910–1990)

English scientist and public servant. After working in military intelligence during World War II he joined the zoology department at Cambridge University 1950–70, at the same time serving as chair of the Agricultural Research Council 1948–58 and Shell Research 1963–70. In 1971 he was asked by Prime Minister Edward Heath to head his new think tank, the Central Policy Review Staff, a post he held until 1974.

Rowbotham, Sheila (1943–)

English socialist, feminist, historian, lecturer, and writer. Her pamphlet *Women's Liberation and the New*

Politics (1970) laid down the fundamental approaches and demands of the emerging women's movement.

Rowbotham taught in schools and then became involved with the Workers' Educational Association. An active socialist from the early 1960s, she contributed to several left-wing journals. Her books include *Hidden from History* and *Women's Consciousness, Man's World* (both 1973), *Beyond the Fragments* (1979), and *The Past is Before Us* (1989).

Rowling, Bill (Wallace Edward) (1927–1995)

New Zealand Labour politician, prime minister 1974–75.

Born in Motueka, South Island, he studied at Canterbury University and then served in the education corps of the New Zealand army before beginning his political career. He was elected to parliament, representing the Labour Party, and served as finance minister in the 1972–74 government of Norman ◊Kirk. He took over as prime minister when Kirk died in office, but lost the 1975 general election to the National Party, led by Robert ◊Muldoon. He then served as ambassador to the USA.

Roxas (y Acuña), Manuel (1892–1948)

Filipino politician, president 1946–48. He served as finance secretary under Manuel Quezon 1938–41. He was captured by the Japanese invasion forces in 1942. He then served in the Japanese puppet government, but supplied intelligence information to the Filipino resistance and was subsequently cleared of collaboration. In 1946 he was elected the first president of the independent Philippines, defeating Sergion ◊Osmeña.

Born in Capiz, in Panay, he studied at the University of Manila and was elected to the Philippines house of representatives in 1921. He served as its speaker 1922–34 and became an ally of Manuel Quezon.

He maintained close political and economic links with the USA and died in office, being succeeded by Elpidio ◊Quirino.

Roy, Manabendra Nath, adopted name of Narendranath Bhattacharya (1887–1954)

Indian politician, founder of the Indian Communist Party. He was exiled to Tashkent in 1920. Expelled from the Comintern in 1929, he returned to India and was imprisoned for five years. A steadfast communist, he finally became disillusioned after World War II and developed his ideas on practical humanism.

Royo Sánchez, Arístides (1940–)

Panamanian politician, president 1978–82. He presided over a deteriorating economy, which forced the imposition of unpopular austerity measures. This, along with increasing opposition from within the military, forced his resignation in 1982.

Formerly education minister, Royo Sánchez was

made president in 1978 by General Omar ◊Torrijos Herrera, who had ruled the country since 1968 as a military dictator. However, Torrijos, using his power as head of the National Guard, remained the de facto ruler of the country until his death in 1981.

Rubin, Jerry (1938–1994)

US activist, financier, and entrepreneur. A radical political activist in the 1960s, he cofounded the US Youth International Party, whose members were known as 'Yippies'. He gained international fame for his disruptive actvities for the anti-Vietnam War protest movement.

Following a visit to Cuba in 1964, Rubin became active in the Free Speech Movement in Berkeley, California. In 1967 he campaigned to have a pig elected president. In 1968, along with Abbie ◊Hoffman and Tom Hayden, he became the media focus in the 'Battle of Chicago', the conflict between the police and protesters around the National Democratic Convention. At the subsequent trial in 1969, he was a member of the 'Chicago Seven', tried for conspiracy and inciting riots, although all seven were later acquitted. He wrote about his activism in a best-selling autobiography, *Do It! Scenarios of the Revolution* (1970).

In the 1980s he renounced his earlier anti-capitalist activities and became a successful Wall Street securities analyst and later an independent entrepreneur, claiming that power 'really comes out of the cheque book'.

Rugova, Ibrahim (1944–)

Albanian politician active in the 1990s in the Serbian region of Kosovo; leader of the Democratic League of Kosovo (LDK). He was instrumental in setting up a system of parallel administration for ethnic Albanians in Kosovo, mirroring Albanian governmental and educational structures, and even football leagues. His 'government' was exiled first to Germany and then to Switzerland, Macedonia, and Albania.

Rugova was elected leader of the LDK, the first non-communist party in Kosovo, after Serb president Slobodan ◊Milošević abolished Kosovo's autonomy in 1989. He developed a strategy of passive resistance against the Serb forces, but his stance appeared to be changing when the 1995 Dayton peace accord did not address tensions in the province and the Kosovo Liberation Army (KLM) was formed. Despite attempts by rival Albanian groups to marginalize Rugova, the support for him has proved enduring.

Rugova studied linguistics at the Sorbonne, Paris, and worked as an academic and writer. A member of the former Communist Party of Yugoslavia, he was expelled for demanding changes to Serbia's constitution.

FURTHER READING
Rugova, Ibrahim *La Question du Kosovo* 1994

Ruiz Cortinez, Adolfo (1891–1973)

Mexican political leader, member of the Institutional Revolutionary Party (PRI), president 1952–58. He promoted administrative honesty and internal colonization to relieve rural poverty. During his presidency, women were given the right to vote and 'civic betterment juntas' were established locally. Strikes by railway workers and teachers were severely repressed in 1958.

Born in Veracruz, Ruiz Cortines held positions in the administrations of presidents Manuel ◊Ávila Camacho and Miguel Alemán 1940–52, including interior minister, and was governor of Veracruz state 1944–48.

Runciman, Walter, 1st Viscount Runciman (1870–1949)

British Liberal politician. He entered Parliament in 1899 and held various ministerial offices between 1908 and 1939. In August 1938 he undertook an abortive mission to Czechoslovakia to persuade the Czech government to make concessions to Nazi Germany. He was created Viscount in 1937.

Rusk, (David) Dean (1909–1994)

US Democrat politician. He was secretary of state to presidents J F Kennedy and L B Johnson 1961–69, and became unpopular through his involvement with the Vietnam War.

He was prominent in Korean War negotiations. Convinced of the need not to appease communist expansionism, he played a key part in the US decision to defend South Korea against invasion by North Korea. However, he advised President Kennedy against the unsuccessful Bay of Pigs invasion of Cuba in 1961.

Rusk was born in Cherokee County, Georgia, the son of a Presbyterian minister, and studied politics at Oxford University, England, as a Rhodes scholar. He taught political science on his return to the USA, before military service during the World War II, where he was involved in intelligence and guerrilla operations in Burma (now Myanmar). He joined the US State Department after the war and progressed to becoming assistant secretary for Far Eastern affairs 1950–51. In 1952, when the Republican general Dwight D Eisenhower was elected president, Rusk left the State Department to become president of the internationalist Rockefeller Foundation.

Despite criticism from peace campaigners, Rusk never wavered in his advocacy of a firm interventionist line in Vietnam in an effort to halt the perceived spread of communism. Having been appointed secretary of state by Kennedy, he continued in that office under Lyndon Johnson, before retiring in 1969 to teach international law at the University of Georgia. Liberal on social issues but hawkish and internationalist on external matters, Rusk was an archetypal 'defence Democrat'.

Russell, Bertrand Arthur William, 3rd Earl Russell (1872–1970)

Welsh philosopher, mathematician, and peace campaigner. He contributed to the development of modern mathematical logic and wrote about social issues. His works include *Principia Mathematica* (1910–13, with A N Whitehead); *The Problems of Philosophy* (1912); and *A History of Western Philosophy* (1946). He was an outspoken liberal pacifist. He was awarded the Nobel Prize for Literature in 1950. He became Earl in 1931.

Russell was born in Monmouthshire, Wales the grandson of Prime Minister John Russell (1792–1878). He studied mathematics and philosophy at Trinity College, Cambridge, where he became a lecturer in 1910. His pacifist attitude in World War I lost him the lectureship, and he was imprisoned for six months for an article he wrote in a pacifist journal. From 1949 he advocated nuclear disarmament and until 1963 was on the Committee of 100, an offshoot of the Campaign for Nuclear Disarmament (CND).

FURTHER READING
Ryan, A *Bertrand Russell, A Political Life* 1988

Russell, Charles Edward (1860–1941)

US journalist and writer. He was managing editor of the *New York American* 1897–99 and publisher of the *Chicago American* 1900–02. A Socialist candidate for the governorship of New York in 1910 and 1912, and for US senator in 1914, he declined the Socialist nomination for the presidency in 1916.

Russell, Dora Winifred, born Black (1894–1986)

English feminist who married Bertrand ◊Russell in 1921. The 'openness' of their marriage (she subsequently had children by another man) was a matter of controversy. She was a founding member of the National Council for Civil Liberties in 1934.

She was educated at Girton College, Cambridge, of which she became a fellow. In 1927 the Russells founded the progressive Beacon Hill School in Hampshire. After World War II she actively supported the Campaign for Nuclear Disarmament.

Rustin, Bayard (1910–1987)

US institute head and civil-rights activist. After many years' involvement in politics and civil rights, Rustin joined the Southern Christian Leadership Conference (SCLC) in 1955 as Martin Luther ◊King's special assistant. In 1964 he became executive director of the

newly founded A Philip Randolph Institute, where he worked to to promote programmes to cure America's social and economic ills. Although an advocate of black political power, he was not in favour of separatism.

Rustin joined the Fellowship of Reconciliation, a nonviolent antiwar group, in 1941. He served several jail terms in the 1940s for conscientious objection during World War II, for demonstrating in the Native American independence movement, and for participating in a North Carolina 'freedom ride' in 1947.

Rutledge, Wiley Blount, Jr (1894–1949)

US jurist and associate justice of the US Supreme Court 1943–49. He was known as a liberal, often dissenting from conservative Court decisions, such as in *Wolf* v *Colorado* (1949), which allowed illegally obtained evidence to be used against a defendant in state courts.

Born in Cloverport, Kentucky, Rutledge studied law at the University of Colorado was admitted to the bar in 1922, and taught law at Colorado, Washington, and Iowa universities 1924–39. In 1939 he was appointed judge of the US Court of Appeals for the District of Columbia.

FURTHER READING
Rutledge, Wiley *A Declaration of Legal Faith*

Rutskoi, Aleksander (1947–)

Russian politician, founder of the reformist Communists for Democracy group, and vice president of the Russian Federation 1991–93. During the abortive August 1991 coup he led the Russian delegation to rescue Soviet leader Mikhail Gorbachev from his forced confinement in the Crimea. In September 1993, with Rusian ◊Khasbulatov, he led the insurrection against the Russian president Boris ◊Yeltsin. Both men were arrested and imprisoned but then released in 1994 on the instructions of the federal assembly. Shortly after his release, Rutskoi, as leader of the Russian Social Democratic People's Party, professed his support for a reconstituted Soviet Union. In August 1996 Rutskoi became a leading member of the communist-led Patriotic Popular Union of Russia. He was elected governor of Kursk in southwestern Russia in October 1996.

A former air officer and highly decorated Afghan War veteran, Rutskoi became increasingly critical of the Yeltsin administration, especially its price liberalization reforms. In 1992 Yeltsin placed Rutskoi in charge of agricultural reform.

Ryzhkov, Nikolai Ivanovich (1929–)

Russian politician. He held governmental and party posts from 1975 before being brought into the Politburo and serving as prime minister 1985–90 under Mikhail Gorbachev. A low-profile technocrat, Ryzhkov was the author of unpopular economic reforms. In August 1996 he became a leading member of the communist-led Patriotic Popular Union of Russia, one of the main left-wing factions in Russia's Duma.

An engineering graduate from the Urals Polytechnic in Ekaterinburg (formerly Sverdlovsk), Ryzhkov rose to become head of the giant Uralmash engineering conglomerate. A member of the Communist Party from 1959, he became deputy minister for heavy engineering in 1975. He then served as first deputy chair of Gosplan (the central planning agency) 1979–82 and Central Committee secretary for economics 1982–85 before becoming prime minister. He was viewed as a more cautious and centralist reformer than Gorbachev. In 1990 he was nearly forced to resign, as a result of the admitted failure of his implementation of the *perestroika* economic reform programme, and he survived only with the support of Gorbachev. He stepped down as Soviet premier following a serious heart attack in December 1990. In June 1991 he unsuccessfully challenged Boris ◊Yeltsin for the presidency of the Russian Federation.

Saadawi, Nawal al- (1931–)

Egyptian novelist and feminist. Her main contention is that the manipulation of Islam by Arab governments contributes to the oppression of women. Because of her opinions she was jailed during the presidency of Anwar ◊Sadat, and after self-exile to the USA she returned to Egypt.

She has to her credit many books dealing with the condition of women in Arab societies. A strong advocate of women's rights, Saadawi has denounced the concept of 'family honour' and its corollary notion of virginity.

Saavedra Lamas, Carlos (1880–1959)

Argentine diplomat. He served as minister of foreign affairs 1932–38 and president of the assembly of the League of Nations in 1936. He was instrumental in drafting an antiwar agreement in 1932, which was subsequently adopted by many South American republics 1933–34. In association with Argentine president Agustín Pedro Justo, Saavedra was successful in bringing to an end the Chaco War in 1935. He was awarded the 1936 Nobel Peace Prize.

He was born in Buenos Aires and graduated from the University of Buenos Aires in 1903. He stayed there to teach political economy and constitutional law.

Sabah, Sheikh Jabir al-Ahmad al-Jabir al- (1928–)

Emir of Kuwait from 1977. He suspended the national assembly in 1986, after mounting parliamentary criticism, ruling in a feudal, paternalistic manner. On the invasion of Kuwait by Iraq in 1990 he fled to Saudi Arabia, returning to Kuwait in March 1991. In 1992 a reconstituted national assembly was elected.

Sacco, (Ferdinando) Nicola (1891–1927)

Italian anarchist. Sacco emigrated to the USA in 1908. In 1920 he was accused, with Bartolomeo ◊Vanzetti, of murdering two men while robbing a shoe factory in Massachusetts. Although the evidence was largely circumstantial, the two men were tried in 1921 and sentenced to death. They were executed in 1927 after a controversial and lengthy appeal. It has been claimed that they were punished for their socialist sympathies, but experts now believe that Sacco was guilty, and Vanzetti innocent.

Sadat, (Muhammad) Anwar (1918–1981)

Egyptian politician, president 1970–81. Succeeding Gamal ◊Nasser as president in 1970, he restored morale by his handling of the Egyptian campaign in the 1973 war against Israel. In 1974 his plan for economic, social, and political reform to transform Egypt was unanimously adopted in a referendum. In 1977 he visited Israel to reconcile the two countries, and shared the Nobel Peace Prize with Israeli prime minister Menachem Begin in 1978. Although feted by the West for pursuing peace with Israel, Sadat was denounced by the Arab world. He was assassinated by Islamic fundamentalists and succeeded by Hosni Mubarak.

Sáenz Peña, Roque (1851–1914)

Argentine politician and president 1910–14. His administration was principally renowned for electoral reform, and Sáenz was instrumental in establishing a statute that enabled the land-owning oligarchy to be replaced by a new party, known as the Radicals (led by Hipólito Irigoyen). Sáenz, however, did not live to see the outcome of his political reforms, dying two years before the official end of his term in office.

Sáenz was born in Buenos Aires, the son of former president Luis Sáenz Peña (1892–95). Sáenz had a varied and active career. In the 1870s, before entering into political life, he travelled throughout Europe. He served as a cabinet minister in the foreign office, and was posted as a diplomat to Spain in 1901 and to Italy in 1907.

Saint Marie, Buffy (1941–)

Canadian singer and songwriter. Born on a Cree Native American reservation in Canada, she was orphaned and then adopted in the USA. Her songwriting talents came to the fore during the folk revival of the 1960s, when she became known as a writer of protest and love songs. Her song 'The Universal Soldier' became one of the major anthems of the 1960s peace movement, but she concentrated on campaigning for the rights of Native Americans and the environment. She retired from recording in 1976.

Saionji, Kinmochi (1849–1940)

Japanese prince and politician, prime minister 1906–08 and 1911–12. He was one of the group of elder statesmen known as Genro. By surviving all the other Genro, Saionji exerted considerable influence behind the scenes at times of political uncertainty in the 1920s and 1930s.

Born into an aristocratic family, he was adopted by the Saionji family. He took part in the Meiji restoration of 1868 and studied in France during much of the 1870s.

Sakharov, Andrei Dmitrievich (1921–1989)

Soviet physicist. He was an outspoken human-rights campaigner, who with Igor Tamm (1895–1971) developed the hydrogen bomb. He later protested against Soviet nuclear tests and was a founder of the Soviet

---

Every day I saw the huge material, intellectual and nervous resources of thousands of people being poured into the creation of a means of total destruction, something capable of annihilating all human civilisation. I noticed that the control levers were in the hands of people who, though talented in their own ways, were cynical.

ANDREI SAKHAROV *Sakharov Speaks* 1974

Human Rights Committee in 1970, winning the Nobel Peace Prize in 1975. For criticizing Soviet action in Afghanistan, he was sent into internal exile 1980–86.

Sakharov was elected to the Congress of the USSR People's Deputies in 1989, where he emerged as leader of its radical reform grouping before his death later the same year.

Sakharov was born and educated in Moscow and did all his research at the P N Lebedev Institute of Physics. In 1948 Sakharov and Tamm outlined a principle for the magnetic isolation of high-temperature plasma, and their subsequent work led directly to the explosion of the first Soviet hydrogen bomb in 1953. But by 1950 they had also formulated the theoretical basis for controlled thermonuclear fusion – which could be used for the generation of electricity and other peaceful ends.

In the early 1960s Sakharov was instrumental in breaking biologist Trofim Lysenko's hold over Soviet science and in giving science some political immunity. Sakharov's scientific papers in the 1960s concerned the structure of the universe. He also began publicly to argue for a reduction of nuclear arms by all nuclear powers, an increase in international cooperation, and the establishment of civil liberties in Russia. Such books as *Sakharov Speaks* (1974), *My Country and the World* (1975), and *Alarm and Hope* (1979) made him an international figure but also brought harassment from the Soviet authorities.

FURTHER READING
Bailey, George *The Making of Andrei Sakharov* 1989
Bonner, Elena *Alone Together* (a memoir by his wife) translation 1986
Lozansky, Edward, and Sakharov, Andrei (eds) *Andrei Sakharov and Peace* 1985
Sakharov, Andrei *Alarm and Hope* translation 1978

Saklatvala, Shapurji (1874–1936)

Indian lawyer and Communist politician, who represented Battersea North as a Labour member of Parliament 1922–23 and as a Communist 1924–29. He was associated with the Indian Trades Union Congress and joined the National Liberal Club in 1905. In 1910 he joined the Independent Labour Party, later the British Socialist Party, and in 1920 helped form the British Communist Party.

Prevented from entering the USA in 1925 on grounds of his revolutionary creed, Saklatvala also served a two-month jail sentence for a speech made on May Day 1926 in Hyde Park.

Born in Bombay, Saklatvala studied law and was a member of Lincoln's Inn. He was not the first Indian to enter Parliament (Dabadhai Naoroji had done so for the Liberals in 1892).

Salan, Raoul Albi Louis (1899–1984)

French general. As commander in chief of France's forces in Algeria 1956–58 he was instrumental in securing Charles ◊de Gaulle's return to government in the crisis of 1958. However, after the failure of his Algiers putsch with General Challe in April 1961, Salan founded the terrorist Organisation de l'Armée Secrète (OAS) from his base in Spain, plotting de Gaulle's assassination. Arrested, tried, and sentenced to life imprisonment in 1962, he was amnestied by President de Gaulle in 1968.

A professional soldier, Salan had been commander in chief in Indochina when the government of Pierre ◊Mendès-France negotiated France's withdrawal following its humiliating defeat at Dien-Bien-Phu. Salan's subsequent hostility to de Gaulle's tactical manoeuvring towards Algerian independence led to his recall to France in late 1958, and to his retirement from the army in 1960.

Salazar, António de Oliveira (1889–1970)

Portuguese prime minister 1932–68 who exercised a virtual dictatorship. During World War II he maintained Portuguese neutrality but fought long colonial wars in Africa (Angola and Mozambique) that impeded his country's economic development as well as that of the colonies.

A corporative constitution on the Italian model was introduced in 1933, and until 1945 Salazar's National Union, founded in 1930, remained the only legal party. Salazar was also foreign minister 1936–47.

FURTHER READING

Gallagher, T *Portugal: A Twentieth-Century Interpretation* 1983

Kay, Hugh *Salazar and Modern Portugal* 1970

Robinson, R *Contemporary Portugal* 1979

Saleh, Ali Abdullah (1942–)

Yemeni politician and soldier, president from 1990. He became president of North Yemen on the assassination of its president (allegedly by South Yemen extremists) in 1978, and was re-elected to the post in 1983 and 1988. In 1990 he was elected president of a reunified Yemen, but within three years differences between north and south had resurfaced and civil war re-erupted in 1994. Saleh's army inflicted a crushing defeat on the southern forces of Vice President al-Baidh, who fled into exile, and a new ruling coalition was formed.

Salim, Salim Ahmed (1942–)

Tanzanian diplomat and secretary general of the Organization of African Unity (OAU) from 1989. His administration took a tough line on countries that have not paid their contributions. In Tanzania he was minister of foreign affairs 1968–69, prime minister 1984–85, and deputy prime minister and minister of defence 1986–89. In 1984 he was a leading candidate to succeed Julius ◊Nyerere as president and, although unsuccessful at the time, was still considered to be a likely contender in the future. He was ambassador to India, China, Korea, Jamaica, Cuba, and also worked extensively for the United Nations (UN).

Salim was born on Pemba Island, Zanzibar, and educated at Lumumba College, the University of Delhi, India, and Columbia University, New York. He began his political career in 1960 as secretary general of the Zanzibar Youth Movement. Between 1961 and 1962 he was deputy chief representative of the Zanzibar office in Havana, Cuba.

Salinas de Gortari, Carlos (1948–)

Mexican politician, president 1988–94, a member of the dominant Institutional Revolutionary Party (PRI). During his presidency he promoted economic reform, including privatization, and signed a North American Free Trade Agreement (NAFTA) with the USA and Canada in December 1992. However, he was also confronted with problems of drug trafficking and violent crime, including the murder of his nominated successor, Luis Donaldo Colosio, in 1994. He went into exile in 1995 after his brother Raúl was implicated in the assassination of another high-ranking PRI official and held in jail. It was later revealed that his brother had amassed more than $84 million in a Swiss bank account.

Educated in Mexico and the USA, where he received a doctorate in political economy at Harvard University, Salinas was a university lecturer before joining the

◆ SAMPER PIZANO, ERNESTO (1950–) ◆

Colombian Liberal politician and president 1994–98.

Samper was born in Bogotá and studied law and economics at the Universidad Javeriana. He worked temporarily in the Universidad Central de Bogotá, but moved on to specialize in the share market within the National Finance Company, in Mexico. He remained in the banking sector for 11 years until 1981, when he entered into political life.

He had a number of important roles in his career, from president of the Asociación Nacional de Instituciones Financieras (ANIF; National Association of Financial Institutions) to United Nations ambassador. He was also founder and director of the Institute of Liberal Studies and secretary general of the Liberal party.

In 1984 he entered into assembly elections in Bogotá and in 1986 became a senator, gaining massive votes superseded only by those for the former political leader Carlos Galán Sarmiento, with whom he had sustained an amicable personal relationship. Samper followed a long, hard campaign to remove structural bureaucracy from the Liberal party, pronouncing a political ideology that had advanced liberal ideas and deep social roots. In 1989, as candidate for the presidency, he survived an assassination attack. Under the government of César Garivia in 1990, Samper was nominated minister of the economy. Between 1991 and 1993, he was an ambassador to Spain, coordinating Colombian participation in the celebrations of the discovery of the Americas, 500 years previously, as well as promoting the role of Colombia in Europe.

In June 1994 he was elected president with one of the highest votes in the history of the country. His new government aimed to create over 1.5 million jobs and implement programmes to incorporate women into wider society, promote peace, and maintain strong policies against drug trafficking. However, the administration was plagued by social and labour unrest and terrorist and guerrilla attacks, threatening the political stability of the country. Despite limited success in peace talks with two guerrilla groups in 1994, those guerrilla groups external to the talks maintained their offensive operations, killing and

government in 1971. He thereafter held a number of posts, mostly in the economic sphere, including financial planning and budget 1982–87 under President Miguel De La Madrid Hurtado. He narrowly won the 1988 presidential election, despite allegations of fraud.

Salisbury, Robert Arthur James Gascoyne-Cecil, 5th Marquess of Salisbury (1893–1972)

British Conservative politician. He was Dominions secretary 1940–42 and 1943–45, colonial secretary 1942, Lord Privy Seal 1942–43 and 1951–52, and Lord President of the Council 1952–57. He became Baron in 1941 and Marquess in 1947.

Salmond, Alex (Alexander Elliott Anderson) (1954–)

Scottish nationalist politician, leader of the Scottish National Party (SNP) from 1990. He entered the House of Commons in 1987 as SNP member of Parliament for Banff and Buchan. He became SNP leader in 1990 and, through his ability to project a moderate image, did much to improve his party's credibility, even though its proposals to make Scotland an independent member of the European Union (EU) went far beyond the limits of what the majority of Scottish electors would support. The SNP won six of Scotland's 72 seats and over one-fifth of the Scottish vote in the 1997 general election. The SNP supported the new Labour government's proposals for Scottish devolution, viewing it as a stepping-stone towards independence, and were expected to poll strongly in the 1999 elections to Scotland's new parliament.

Salote Tupou III, Mafili'o Pilolevu (1900–1965)

Queen of Tonga 1918–65. Her prosperous reign saw the reunion, for which she was mainly responsible, of the Tongan Free Church majority with the Wesleyan Church in 1924. There were also significant improvements in education, health, and agriculture. Education was made mandatory from 1929, a central medical school was established in 1929, and the economy was diversified to lessen dependence on the production of copra.

Educated in Auckland, New Zealand, she married Prince William Tupoulahi Tungi at the age of 15 and succeeded her father, King George Tupou II (who had reigned since 1893), in 1918. She was succeeded on her death by her eldest son, Prince Tungi, who became King ◊Taufa'ahau Tupou IV.

Sampaio, Jorge (1940–)

Portuguese lawyer and politician, president from 1996. A former leader and lifetime member of the Socialist Party (PS), he was mayor of Lisbon before defeating his opponent, former prime minister Cavaco Silva, in the 1996 presidential elections.

Samuel, Herbert Louis, 1st Viscount Samuel of Mount Carmel and Toxteth (1870–1963)

British Liberal politician and administrator. He was leader of the Liberal Party 1931–35, held several ministerial offices, and served as high commissioner of Palestine 1920–25.

A keen social reformer, as undersecretary at the Home Office 1905–09 he was largely responsible for the Children's Act of 1908, which set up juvenile courts and borstals. After entering the cabinet, he was chancellor of the Duchy of Lancaster 1909–10, postmaster general 1910–14 and 1915–16, president of the Local Government Board 1914–15, and home secretary in 1916. When the Liberal Party split in 1916, Samuel sided with Herbert Asquith and went into opposition. He lost his seat in 1918.

Re-elected to Parliament in 1929, Samuel held the Liberal leadership 1931–35, which is to say that he led the main faction of a fragmented and fast-declining party. In 1931, the 'Samuelite' Liberals joined the National Government coalition, in which Samuel served as home secretary for just over a year. A free-trader, he opposed the introduction of protective tariffs and led his followers out of the coalition in September 1932 in protest at the Ottawa Agreements on imperial preference.

maiming people throughout the country.

Economic problems, particularly inflationary pressures, were also of concern. Despite attempts to improve its international image, Colombia's long history of violent terrorist and guerrilla attacks made it exceedingly difficult for the administration, led by Samper, to implement programmes that would attract more foreign investment into the country. Relations with the USA were constrained by US criticism of Colombia's limited and ineffective policies against organized crime in the ongoing drugs war.

Political crisis emerged in 1995, with accusations that Samper had willingly accepted drugs money to fund campaign expenses in return for more lenient custodial sentences for drugs traffickers. Despite his denial of any such wrongdoing, opposition grew to his refusal to resign from office. In 1996, after a 19-month investigation, he was formally accused of electoral fraud and illegal enrichment by the national chief prosecutor, Alfonso Valdivieso. Although this provoked the resignation of many of his cabinet ministers, Samper remained in office as president pending a congressional accusation committees review. In June 1998 he was replaced as president by Andres Pastrana Arango.

Samuel was born in Liverpool. After studying at Oxford, he was a social worker in the East End of London before entering Parliament in 1902.

During his five years as high commissioner of Palestine, he promoted economic development and tried to keep the peace between Jews and Arabs with varying success. On his return to the UK, he chaired the Royal Commission on the Coal Industry 1925–26. Although its recommendations were unacceptable to pit owners and miners alike, Samuel played a part in resolving the General Strike of 1926.

After losing his seat in the 1935 general election, he was given a peerage in 1937 and led the Liberals in the House of Lords 1944–55. As a politician, he was widely regarded as conscientious, reliable, and uninspiring.

Sanchez de Lozada Bustamente, Gonzalo (1930–)

Bolivian president 1993–97. His governance emphasized free-market economic policies, with privatization high on the political agenda, but his economic policies met with some labour unrest, particularly in 1995, with the eruption of violent protests and strikes. Such problems were later superseded by cocaine-related problems in the Chapare region.

Sanchez de Lozada was leader of the centrist Nationalist Revolutionary Movement (MNR). His political appeal among the urban population was bolstered by that of his Aymara vice president Victor Hugo Cárdenas, who had strong appeal among the native Indian peoples.

Sánchez Hernández, Fidel (1917–)

El Salvadorean soldier and politician, president 1967–72, at the time of the 1969 Football War with Honduras.

Sánchez was elected president with the backing of the military-reformist National Conciliation Party (PCN). He appointed a largely civilian cabinet and his reforms, although limited, included establishing a minimum wage. A five-day war (called the 'Football War' as it coincided with a World Cup qualifying match between the two countries) with neighbouring Honduras in July 1969, which Sánchez directed in the field, caused economic problems and raised nationalist feelings.

A professional soldier, he was military attaché in Washington, DC, 1960–62, and then interior minister under PCN leader Julio ◊Rivera, who was president 1962–67. His protégé Colonel Arturo Armando ◊Molina was his successor as president, in 1972.

Sandiford, Erskine Lloyd (1937–)

Barbadian centre-left politician, prime minister 1987–94. As deputy leader of the Democratic Labour Party (DLP), he took over as prime minister after Errol ◊Barrow's sudden death in 1987. Although criticized for his leadership style and economic management, he secured re-election for the DLP in 1991. However the economy deteriorated, and Sandiford resigned as DLP leader shortly before the party was decisively defeated in 1994 by the Barbados Labour Party (BLP), led by Owen ◊Arthur.

He was replaced as DLP leader by his finance minister, David Thompson. His first finance minister, Ritchie Haynes, an early critic of his administration, formed the breakaway National Democratic Party (NDP).

Sandino, Augusto César (1895–1934)

Nicaraguan revolutionary and guerrilla leader. He made the mountains of northern Nicaragua his stronghold and led guerrilla resistance to the US forces occupying the country from 1912. His success in evading them and the Nicaraguan National Guard generated sympathy for his cause, and a great deal of anti-US feeling. After the withdrawal of US marines in 1933, the National Guard leader, Anastasio Somoza, arranged a meeting with him, apparently to discuss peace. This, however, was a ruse, and Sandino was murdered on Somoza's orders near Managua.

Born in Niquinohomo, La Victoria, he worked as a farmer and mining engineer before joining the Liberal revolution of 1926 against the Conservative government of Emilianu Chamorra. A Sandinista National Liberation Front (FSLN) was set up in his name to fight the Somoza dictatorship. The Nicaraguan revolutionaries of 1979 (later known as the Sandinistas), led by Daniel ◊Ortega, regarded him as their principal hero.

FURTHER READING
Selser, G *Sandino* 1981

Sandys, (Edwin) Duncan, Baron Duncan-Sandys (1908–1987)

British Conservative politician. As minister for Commonwealth relations 1960–64, he negotiated the independence of Malaysia in 1963. He was created Baron in 1974.

Sanger, Margaret Louise, born Higgins (1883–1966)

US health reformer and crusader for birth control. In 1914 she founded the National Birth Control League. She founded and presided over the American Birth Control League 1921–28, the organization that later became the Planned Parenthood Federation of America, and the International Planned Parenthood Federation in 1952.

Sanger was born in Corning, New York; she received nursing degrees from White Plains Hospital and the Manhattan Eye and Ear Clinic. As a nurse, she saw the deaths and deformity caused by self-induced abortions and became committed to providing health and birth-control education to the poor. In 1917 she was briefly sent to prison for opening a public birth-control clinic in Brooklyn in 1916. Her *Autobiography* appeared in 1938.

Sanguinetti, Julio Maria (1936–)

Uruguayan politician and president 1985–90 and from 1994. His liberal and progressive government was characterized by the consolidation of democracy, human rights, and economic restructuring, particularly in relation to Latin American integration.

A member of the long-established progressive Colorado Party (PC), which had its origins in the civil war of 1836, he was elected as federal deputy to the assembly in 1963, and appointed minister of labour and industry and minister of education and culture 1969–73. The oppressive regime of Juan Maria Bordaberry 1972–76 was forcibly removed and military rule imposed before democratic government was restored in 1985. The 1966 constitution was restored with some modifications, and Sanguinetti was elected president.

He was born in Montevideo and graduated in law and social sciences from the University of Montevideo in 1961.

Sankara, Thomas (1950–1987)

Burkina Faso politician and soldier, prime minister and head of state 1983–87. While serving as a minister in Saye Zerbo's government, he came to believe that only popular revolution would expunge the effects of French colonialism. Leading a coup in 1983, he became prime minister and head of state and introduced a wide range of progressive policies that made him enemies. Despite his great symbolic popularity among young radicals (outside Burkina Faso as much as inside), he was shot during a military coup led by his close associate Blaise Compaoré in 1987.

After seizing power in 1983 Sankara ruled through a council of ministers; opposition members were arrested, the national assembly was dissolved, and a National Revolutionary Council (CNR) set up. His government strengthened ties with Ghana and established links with Benin and Libya. In 1984 he announced that the country would be known as Burkina Faso ('land of upright men'), symbolizing a break with its colonial past.

Sankara joined the army in Ouagadougou in 1969 and first began to develop radical political ideas while attending the French Parachute Training Centre between 1971 and 1974.

Santer, Jacques (1937–)

Luxembourg politician, prime minister 1984–94. In January 1995 he succeeded Jacques Delors as president of the European Commission.

The manner of his selection as European Com-mission president, as a compromise alternative to the rejected Belgian prime minister, Jean-Luc Dehaene, weakened his standing as a worthy successor to Delors. However, Santer made a personal appeal to the newly elected European Parliament, of which he had been a member 1975–79, claiming that his aspirations for closer European union were at least as strong as those of Dehaene.

San Yu, U (1919–1996)

Myanmar (Burmese) politician, president 1981–88. A member of the revolutionary council that came to power in 1962, he became president in 1981 and was re-elected in 1985. He was forced to resign in July 1988, along with Ne Win, after riots in Yangon (formerly Rangoon).

Sarkis, Elias (1922–)

Lebanese Maronite Christian politician, president 1976–82. His term was marked by the resumption and escalation of the civil war, which had begun in 1975 and had officially ended in October 1976. With militias and the Syrian army gaining the upper hand, central authority weakened and Sarkis, although respected, was unable to make an impact. In June 1982, three months before his presidential term ended, Israeli forces invaded Lebanon.

Born into a lower-middle-class family, Sarkis, after graduating in law, worked as a judge at the audit office, where he impressed Fuad Shihab, who was president 1958–64. Sarkis served as governor of Lebanon's Central Bank 1967–76, at a time of economic difficulties. He narrowly failed, by one vote, to be elected president by parliament in 1970, but in 1976, with Syrian backing, became president, succeeding Suleiman ◊Franjiyeh.

Sarney (Costa), José (1930–)

Brazilian politician, member of the centre-left Democratic Movement (PMDB), president 1985–90, and chair of the senate in 1996.

Sarney was elected vice president in 1985 and within months, on the death of President Tancredo Neves, became head of state. Despite earlier involvement with the repressive military regime, he and his party won a convincing victory in the 1986 general election. His administration was disastrous, partly because Sarney had not chosen his ministerial team and also because he had to contend with a powerful new congress. There were major problems during his term, including corruption and hyperinflation. In December 1989, Ferdinando Collor de Mello of the Party for National Reconstruction was elected to succeed Sarney in March 1990.

Saro-Wiwa, Ken (1931–1995)

See page 382.

Satre, Jean-Paul (1905–1980)

See page 383.

Ken Saro-Wiwa. *Rex*

Sassau-Nguesso, Denis (1943–)

Congolese socialist politician, president 1979–92 and from 1997. He progressively consolidated his position within the ruling left-wing Congolese Labour Party (PCT), at the same time as improving relations with France and the USA. In 1990, in response to public pressure, he agreed that the PCT should abandon Marxism-Leninism and that a multiparty system should be introduced. He returned to power in November 1997.

Sastri, V(alangunian) S(ankarana-Rayana) Srinvasa (1869–1946)

Indian politician. He was secretary of the Madras session of Congress in 1908 and took an active part in drawing up the Lucknow pact between the Congress and Muslim League, which demanded 'responsive government' for India, and was opposed to Mahatma Gandhi's policy of nonviolence and noncooperation. Elected to the Madras Council in 1913, he became a member of the Imperial Legislative Council in 1915 and the Council of State in 1921.

He was a member of the delegation to South Africa that led to the Cape Town agreement, which committed the South African government to shelving its Class Area Bill to segregate Indians. He also struggled for the cause of Indians living in Kenya and British East Africa and was president of the Servants of India Society for some years. In 1945 he strongly opposed Muhammad Ali Jinnah's two-nation proposal.

Satō, Eisaku (1901–1975)

Japanese conservative politician, prime minister 1964–72. He ran against Hayato Ikeda (1899–1965) for the Liberal Democratic Party leadership and succeeded him as prime minister, pledged to a more independent foreign policy. He shared a Nobel Prize for Peace in 1974 for his rejection of nuclear weapons. His brother Nobusuke Kishi (1896–1987) was prime minister of Japan 1957–60.

Saud, ibn Abdul Aziz al-Saud (1902–1969)

King of Saudi Arabia 1953–64. He initially maintained warm relations with Egypt's new ruler Gamal Abdel ◊Nasser, but became concerned at Nasser's growing power in the region from 1956, and thus developed close ties with the UK and the USA, which he visited in

◆ SARO-WIWA, KEN (1931–1995) ◆

Nigerian writer, environmentalist, and political leader of the Ogoni, an ethnic minority occupying Nigeria's oil-rich delta region. In 1991 he founded the Movement for the Survival of the Ogoni People (MOSOP) and began a vigorous international campaign against the environmental damage caused by oil exploitation. Arrested for the murder of four prominent Ogoni activists in May 1994, Saro-Wiwa and eight others were executed by the military leadership in November 1995. Nigeria was suspended from the Commonwealth and condemned by the United Nations in a General Assembly vote as a result of the executions.

After reading English at the University of Ibadan, Saro-Wiwa taught at the universities of Nsukka and Lagos. In 1968, during the Nigerian civil war, he was appointed administrator of the oil port of Bonny and later became a minister in the newly created Rivers State. After he was dropped in 1973, he concentrated on his writing, his works including *On a Darkling Plain* (1987), a book about the Biafran civil war from the perspective of a minority ethnic group, and the script for a popular television comedy series. In 1994 he won the international Right Livelihood Award for his work for the Ogoni.

March 1957. His younger half-brother, ◊Faisal, was crown prince from 1953 and, after Saud's extravagant spending had produced a financial crisis, was made prime minister in 1958. Saud, as an Arab traditionalist, was uneasy with Faisal's advocacy of gradual Westernization, including the education of women. This led to conflicts and Faisal's resignation in 1960. However, he returned as prime minister in November 1962, after Saud fell ill. Faisal immediately published a ten-point reform and development programme that was designed to take the country into the modern age, through using the country's increasing oil wealth to provide social welfare benefits to Saudi citizens. In early 1964 Faisal became regent and in November 1964, after a meeting of a council of the senior members of the al-Saud family, Saud was persuaded to abdicate. Faisal became king and Saud lived the remainder of his life in exile.

The son of King Abdul Aziz ◊Ibn Saud, the founder of the Saudi dynasty, he was made crown prince in 1933 and became prime minister, three months before his father's death, in November 1953.

Relations with Egypt deteriorated to such a degree that it was alleged, by Nasser, that in 1958 Saud had paid a Syrian politician to attempt to assassinate the Egyptian leader. Four years later, Saudi territory was bombed by Egyptian jets who were attacking Yemeni royalist forces.

Sauve, Jeanne (1922–)

Canadian politician. In 1974 she was elected to the House of Commons for Ahuntsic. She was appointed minister for science and technology in 1972, minister of the environment in 1974, and minister of communications in 1975.

Sauve was born in Prud'homme, Saskatchewan, and educated at the universities of Ottawa and Paris. She was a freelance journalist and commentator on Canadian Broadcasting Company radio and television before entering politics.

Savage, Michael Joseph (1872–1940)

New Zealand Labour left-of-centre politician, prime

Jean-Paul Sartre, c. 1950. *AKG London*

minister 1935–40. He introduced much social security legislation and a popular marketing act, which helped Labour secure re-election in October 1938. He was also concurrently minister in charge of broadcasting and relations with the Maori peoples and, as foreign minister, pledged support to the UK during World War II. He died in office and was succeeded as prime minister by Peter ◊Fraser.

Born in Benalla, Victoria, Australia, he emigrated to South Island in 1907 and became a labour union organizer. He was a founding member of the Labour

---

◆ SARTRE, JEAN-PAUL (1905–1980) ◆

French writer and philosopher. From the late 1930s Sartre's espousal of revolutionary values and causes established him as France's leading politically committed intellectual. Initially an exponent of existentialism, from the early 1950s his sensitivity to the social and material constraints on people's actions led Sartre to elaborate a more fully Marxist theoretical position, notably in his *Critique de la raison dialectique/Critique of Dialectical Reason* (1960).

After studying at the Ecole Normale Supérieure Sartre taught philosophy until 1945. During World War II he was imprisoned for nine months and, on his return from Germany, joined the Resistance. He later campaigned actively against France's war in Algeria and against US military intervention in Vietnam in the 1960s, supporting the students' cause in France in May 1968.

Party in 1916 and became a member of Parliament in 1919 and leader of the Labour Party in 1933. His optimism and self-confidence, at a time of economic depression, and his courting of rural interests secured victory for Labour in the November 1935 general election and he became New Zealand's first Labour prime minister.

Savimbi, Jonas Malheiro (1934–)

Angolan soldier and right-wing revolutionary, founder and leader of the National Union for the Total Independence of Angola (UNITA). From 1975 UNITA, under Savimbi's leadership, tried to overthrow the government. A peace agreement was signed in 1994. Savimbi rejected the offer of vice presidency in a coalition government in 1996; however, in 1998, UNITA was demilitarized and accepted as a national political party.

The struggle for independence from Portugal escalated in 1961 into a civil war. In 1966 Savimbi founded the right-wing UNITA, which he led against the left-wing People's Movement for the Liberation of Angola (MPLA), led by Agostinho Neto. Neto, with Soviet and Cuban support, became president when independence was achieved in 1975, while UNITA, assisted by South Africa, continued its fight. A cease-fire was agreed in June 1989, but fighting continued, and the truce was abandoned after two months. A further truce was signed in May 1991. Civil war re-erupted in September 1992 following an election victory for the ruling party, a result which Savimbi disputed. Representatives of UNITA and the government signed a peace agreement in 1994. He was offered the post of vice presidency by President José Dos Santos, but turned it down.

Saw Maung (1929–)

Myanmar (Burmese) soldier and politician. Appointed head of the armed forces in 1985 by ◊Ne Win, he led a coup to remove Ne Win's successor, Maung Maung, in 1988 and became leader of a totalitarian 'emergency government', which remained in office despite being defeated in the May 1990 election. In April 1992 he was replaced as chair of the ruling military junta, prime minister, and commander of the armed forces by Than Shwe.

Sayles, John (1950–)

US film director, screenwriter, actor, producer, and novelist. He is considered one of the most distinctive and adventurous of the USA's independent film directors. Sayles's work is based on both his personal and political beliefs. He has directed a number of low-budget films – examples are *Matewan* (1987), *City of Hope* (1991), and *Lone Star* (1996) – which deal with 'difficult' and complex themes. *Matewan* examines the personal and political dimensions of trade-union activities in the Virginian coal mines of the 1920s.

After having written scripts for Roger Corman films,

such as *Piranha* (1978) and *The Lady in Red* (1979), Sayles went on to become a film director of some renown with the likes of *Secaucus Seven* (1980), *Lianna* (1983), and *Eight Men Out* (1988). Although he is known primarily as a film director, he is also active in other media – writing novels and plays, directing videos, and even acting.

FURTHER READING
Sayles, John, and Smith, Gavin *Sayles on Sayles* 1998

Scalia, Antonin (1936–)

US jurist and associate justice of the US Supreme Court from 1986. He concurred with the majority in *Texas v Johnson* (1989), which ruled constitutional the burning of the US flag in protest. He dissented in *Edwards v Aguillard* (1987), when the Court ruled that states may not mandate the teaching of the theory of creationism to counteract the teaching of the theory of evolution.

Born in Trenton, New Jersey, Scalia graduated from Georgetown University and Harvard University Law School. From 1971 he worked as a lawyer in the executive branch of the federal government, ultimately becoming assistant attorney general in 1974, where he advised the Gerald Ford White House in the Watergate scandal. President Ronald Reagan appointed Scalia to the Supreme Court in 1986.

Scargill, Arthur (1938–)

British trade-union leader. Elected president of the National Union of Miners (NUM) in 1981, he embarked on a collision course with the Conservative government of Margaret Thatcher. The damaging strike of 1984–85 split the miners' movement. In 1995, criticizing what he saw as the Labour Party's lurch to the right, he announced that he would establish a rival party, the independent Socialist Labour Party. This proved to be largely ineffectual, and made little impact in consequent elections. By 1997 membership of the NUM had fallen to 10,000.

Born in Leeds, Scargill became a miner on leaving school and was soon a trade-union and political activist, in the Young Communist League 1955–62, and then in the Labour Party from 1966. President of the Yorkshire miners' union 1973–81, he became a fiery and effective orator. During the 1984–85 miners' strike he was criticized for not seeking an early NUM ballot to support the strike decision. He was a member of the TUC General Council 1986–88 and formed the Socialist Labour Party in 1996.

Scarman, Leslie George, Baron Scarman (1911–)

English judge and legal reformer. A successful barrister, he was a High Court judge 1961–73 and an appeal-court judge 1973–77, prior to becoming a law lord. He was the first chair of the Law Commission for the reform of English law, 1965–73.

He gradually shifted from a traditional position to a more reformist one, calling for liberalization of divorce laws in 1965 and campaigning for a bill of rights in 1974. As chair of the inquiry into the Brixton riots in 1981, he proposed positive discrimination in favour of black people. He campaigned for the release of the Birmingham Six and the Guildford Four. He was knighted in 1961 and created Baron in 1977.

Schacht, Hjalmar Horace Greely (1877–1970)

German financier. As president of the Reichsbank from 1923–29, he founded a new currency that ended the inflation of the Deutschmark. In 1933 he was recalled to the Reichsbank by the Nazis and, as minister of economics, restored Germany's trade balance. Dismissed from the Reichsbank after a dispute with Hitler over expenditure on rearmament, he was charged with high treason and interned; he was later acquitted of crimes against humanity at Nürnberg in 1945 and cleared by the German de-Nazification courts in 1948.

In 1952 Schacht advised Muhammad Mossadeq on Iran's economic problems, and in 1953 he set up his own bank in Düsseldorf.

Scheidemann, Philipp (1865–1939)

German politician and journalist, born in Kassel, Germany. In 1903 he was elected to the Reichstag (parliament), and in 1911 joined the executive committee of the Social-Democratic party. During World War I he was, with Friedrich Ebert, leader of the Majority Social Democrats, who voted for the government's war credits, but nevertheless worked for a peace of reconciliation. When, in 1918, Ebert became chancellor, Scheidemann, on his own initiative, proclaimed Germany a republic. In February 1919 Scheidemann was elected prime minister by the National Assembly at Weimar. A few months later he resigned, following his failure to obtain amendments of the Allies' peace conditions, and his refusal to sign the Treaty of Versailles. When Hitler came to power he left the country, and died in Denmark.

Schleicher, Kurt von (1882–1934)

German soldier and chancellor. A member of the Prussian nobility, he held staff posts throughout World War I, afterwards joining the Reichswehr ministry, where he became the link between the army and politicians. Schleicher engineered the elimination of the Socialists from government in 1930, then played a major role in Heinrich Brüning's fall two years later. He was minister of defence in 1932, and in December of the same year he became chancellor of Germany in succession to Franz von Papen. His government lasted only until 28 January 1933, as a result of the hostility fomented by Adolf Hitler and the Nazis. President Paul Hindenburg refused to authorize him to dissolve the Reichstag (parliament) and appointed Hitler as chancellor, and Schleicher then retired into private life. Together with his wife he was murdered during the Nazi purge of 30 June 1934.

Schlüter, Poul Holmskov (1929–)

Danish right-wing politician, leader of the Conservative People's Party (KF) from 1974, and prime minister 1982–93. His centre-right coalition survived the 1990 election and was reconstituted, with Liberal support. In January 1993 Schlüter resigned, accused of dishonesty over his role in an incident involving Tamil refugees. He was succeeded by Poul Nyrup Rasmussen.

Having joined the KF in his youth, he trained as a lawyer and then entered the Danish parliament (Folketing) in 1964.

Schmidt, Helmut Heinrich Waldemar (1918–)

German socialist politician, member of the Social Democratic Party (SPD), chancellor of West Germany 1974–83. As chancellor, Schmidt introduced social reforms and continued Willy ◊Brandt's policy of Ostpolitik. With the French president Giscard d'Estaing, he instigated annual world and European economic summits. He was a firm supporter of NATO and of the deployment of US nuclear missiles in West Germany during the early 1980s.

Schmidt was elected to the Bundestag (federal parliament) in 1953. He was interior minister for Hamburg 1961–65, defence minister 1969–72, and finance minister 1972–74. He became federal chancellor (prime minister) on Brandt's resignation in 1974. Re-elected in 1980, he was defeated in the Bundestag in 1982 following the switch of allegiance by the SPD's coalition allies, the Free Democratic Party. Schmidt retired from federal politics at the general election of 1983, having encountered growing opposition from the SPD's left wing, who opposed his stance on military and economic issues.

FURTHER READING

Carr, Jonathan *Helmut Schmidt* 1985
Childs, David, and Johnson, Jeffrey *West Germany: Politics and Society* 1981

Schmitt, Carl (1888–1895)

German political theorist and jurist. He created the concept of 'decisionism', which states that any legal order rests ultimately on sovereignty, and that the location of sovereignty depends on who has the power to make emergency decisions. A critic of liberalism and Weimar parliamentary democracy, Schmitt defended the Nazis' seizure of power and was an influential apologist for the new political order of the Third Reich.

From 1928 to 1945 he held a chair at the University of Berlin.

Schneerson, Menachem Mendel (1902–1994)

Ukrainian-born US rabbi, leader from 1950 of the Lubavitch right-wing orthodox Judaic movement. A charismatic figure, he was regarded by some of his followers as a Messiah. Under his guidance, the Lubavitch movement expanded worldwide, and the community's publishing division became the world's largest distributor of Jewish books.

Schneerson was born in Nikolayev, Ukraine, the son of a rabbi. The vicissitudes of the Nazi era took him to Latvia, Poland, Germany, France, and finally, in 1941, to the USA. In addition to his Talmudic and mystical studies, he studied mathematics, physics, and engineering at universities in Berlin and Paris. The Lubavitch movement was founded by Shneur Zalman (1745–1813) of Lyadi, who developed Habad Hasidism; it became a force in US Judaism from its centre in Brooklyn, New York, from 1940. On the death in 1950 of the movement's sixth leader, Joseph Isaac Schneerson, Mendel Schneerson (a distant relation) became Rebbe (Hasidic leader).

The Habad Hasidic Rebbe is regarded as an almost superhuman being who is beyond criticism, and Schneerson was able to sustain this difficult role. Habad Hasidism became an evangelical doctrine, aiming at the return of the whole Jewish people to traditional observance; inspired by the Rebbe, it was especially active in the countries of the communist bloc. Taking on a role in Israeli politics, the Rebbe supported the right-wing policy of not ceding territory, and even opposed the peace treaty with Egypt. Although rejecting a messianic basis for Israeli politics, he saw his evangelical campaign as messianic in intent.

Schroeder, Gerhard (1944–)

German politician, Social Democratic Party (SPD) chancellor from October 1998. Elected premier of Lower Saxony in 1990, his re-election in March 1998, with an increased share of the vote, persuaded the SPD to select him to challenge Helmut Kohl in the September 1998 general election. A moderate, media-skilled, populist politician, Schroeder has been dubbed 'Germany's Tony Blair'. On his election he was regarded as more Eurosceptic than either Kohl or the SPD chair Oskar Lafontaine.

Schumacher, Fritz (Ernst Friedrich) (1911–1977)

German economist who made his career in the UK. He believed that the increasing size of institutions, coupled with unchecked economic growth, creates a range of social and environmental problems. He argued his case in books such as *Small is Beautiful* (1973), and established the Intermediate Technology Development Group.

Schumacher studied at Oxford and held academic posts there and in the USA at Columbia in the 1930s and 1940s. After World War II he was economic adviser to the British Control Commission in Germany 1946–50 and to the UK National Coal Board 1950–70.

He also served as president of the Soil Association and as director of the Scott-Bader Company, which manufactures polymers and is based on common ownership. He advised many governments on problems of rural development.

His book *A Guide for the Perplexed* (1977) deals with philosophy.

Schumacher, Kurt (1895–1952)

German socialist politician. He was arrested in 1933, and spent 11 years in concentration camps. In 1945 he reorganized the German Social Democratic Party (SPD), and in 1949 became leader of the opposition in the West German parliament.

Schumacher was a deputy in the Württemberg parliament 1924–31, and in the Reichstag 1930–33. After World War II he led a sustained but ultimately unsuccessful opposition to Chancellor Konrad Adenauer's campaign for a German contribution to Western defence.

Schuman, Robert Jean-Baptiste Nicolas (1886–1963)

French Christian-Democrat politician, prime minister 1947–48, and foreign minister 1948–55. He was a member of the postwar Mouvement Républicain Populaire (MRP). His Schuman Declaration of May 1950, drafted by Jean Monnet, outlines a scheme for pooling coal and iron-ore resources. The resultant European Coal and Steel Community, established by France, Belgium, Germany, the Netherlands, Italy and Luxembourg under the 1951 Paris Treaty, was the forerunner of the European Community (now the European Union).

Schuschnigg, Kurt von (1897–1977)

Austrian chancellor 1934–38, in succession to Engelbert ◊Dollfuss. He tried in vain to prevent Nazi annexation (*Anschluss*) but in February 1938 he was forced to accept a Nazi minister of the interior, and a month later Austria was occupied and annexed by Germany. He was imprisoned in Germany until 1945, when he went to the USA; he returned to Austria in 1967.

Schwarzkopf, Norman, nicknamed 'Stormin' Norman' (1934–)

US general. He was supreme commander of the Allied forces in the Gulf War of 1991. He planned and executed a blitzkrieg campaign, 'Desert Storm', sustaining remarkably few Allied casualties in the liberation of Kuwait. He was a battalion commander in the Vietnam

War and deputy commander of the US invasion of Grenada in 1983.

Schwarzkopf was born in Trenton, New Jersey. A graduate of the military academy at West Point, he obtained a master's degree in guided-missile engineering. He became an infantry soldier and later a paratrooper, and did two tours of service in Vietnam, as an adviser 1965–66 and in command of an infantry battalion 1969–70. Maintaining the 28-member Arab–Western military coalition against Iraq in 1991 extended his diplomatic skills, and his success in the Gulf War made him a popular hero in the USA. He retired from the army in August 1991.

FURTHER READING
Anderson, Jack, and Van Atta, Dale *Stormin' Norman: An American Hero* 1991
Petre, Peter *It Doesn't Take a Hero: H Norman, General Schwarzkopf* 1993

Scialoja, Vittorio (1856–1935)

Italian jurist and politician. He became minister of justice in the second ministry of Sidney Sonnino (1909–10), minister without portfolio in the Boselli and Orlando cabinets during World War I, and of foreign affairs under Francesco Nitti (1919–20). He was the Italian representative at the peace conference in 1919, and as minister of foreign affairs he assisted in framing the Covenant of the League of Nations. Scialoja was minister of state in 1927. He wrote many works on law, especially Roman law.

Scialoja was born in Turin, Italy. He studied at the University of Rome, and became professor of Roman law at the universities of Camerino in 1879, Siena in 1881, and Rome in 1884.

Scott, C(harles) P(restwich) (1846–1932)

English newspaper editor and Liberal politician. At the age of 26 he was appointed editor of the *Manchester Guardian*, which he developed into a serious liberal rival to *The Times*. It was characterized by independent and often controversial editorial policies, such as opposition to the Boer War, and by high literary standards. He was a Liberal member of Parliament for Leigh 1895–1906.

He was born in Bath and educated at Corpus Christi College, Oxford.

FURTHER READING
Wilson, T *The Political Diaries of C P Scott 1911–28* 1970

Scott, Michael (1907–1983)

English Anglican missionary and social and political activist. Working as a missionary in South Africa from 1943 to 1950, he exposed human-rights violations and took the case of the dispossessed Herero people to the United Nations, becoming *persona non grata* in South Africa and in the Central African Federation (Nyasa-

land and Northern and Southern Rhodesia). In 1958 he was briefly imprisoned for his part in nuclear-disarmament demonstrations, and in 1966 he was expelled from Nagaland in northeast India.

During his time in South Africa he brought to light atrocities in the Bethal farming area and in the Transvaal, and defended the Basutos against wrongful arrest. He founded the London Africa Bureau in 1952. His works include an autobiography, *A Time to Speak* (1958), and *A Search for Peace and Justice* (1980).

Scott was educated at King's College, Taunton, and St Paul's College, Grahamstown, and served in a London East End parish and as chaplain in India 1935–39, where he collaborated with the communists. He was invalided out of the RAF in 1941 and ceased his associations with communists in the 1940s.

Scott, Rose (1847–1925)

Australian social reformer and suffragette. She was a founding member of the Women's Literary Society in 1889, from whose members the Womanhood Suffrage League of New South Wales was formed in 1891. After national suffrage was secured in 1902, she campaigned against prostitution and discrimination in the public service. Her report on conditions at Sydney's Darlinghurst Gaol led to the establishment, in 1906, of a separate prison for women. She was first president of the Women's Political Educational League, and in 1910 was instrumental in raising the age of consent to 16.

Born into an affluent New South Wales pastoralist family, she was educated at home and became a literary socialist after moving to Sydney in the 1880s.

FURTHER READING
Allen, Judith *Rose Scott: Vision and Revision in Feminism* 1994

Scullin, James Henry (1876–1953)

Australian Labor politician, prime minister 1929–32. Scullin entered the House of Representatives in 1910. He lost his seat in 1913 and was re-elected in 1922, becoming Labor leader in 1928. With the electoral victory over the government of Stanley ◊Bruce in 1929 he became prime minister. His period in power was dominated by the economic depression and his government was rendered virtually powerless by a hostile Senate, uncooperative state premiers, and internal divisions. Numerous defections forced him to an election in 1932, at which Labor was defeated by the newly formed United Australia Party under Joseph ◊Lyons. He stepped down as Labor leader in 1935 and retired from parliament in 1949.

Scullin was born in Ballarat, Victoria, and was a devout, teetotal Catholic. He left school at an early age and was earning his own living by the age of 12. He became an active member of the Labor Party in 1903 and an organizer for the Australian Workers' Union.

While out of parliament 1913–22 he took up journalism, editing a Labor daily newspaper in which he propounded his socialist and anti-conscription views. In the House of Representatives he gained a strong reputation as a parliamentarian and an orator.

FURTHER READING
Robertson, J *J H Scullin* 1974

Seaga, Edward Philip George (1930–)

US-born Jamaican centre-right politician, prime minister 1980–89. Leader of the Jamaican Labour Party (JLP) and the opposition from 1974, he defeated Michael ◊Manley's People's National Party (PNP) in 1980. Abandoning his predecessors' socialist and nonaligned stance, he promoted free-enterprise, severed diplomatic ties with communist Cuba in 1981, and developed close US links. In 1983 Seaga's JLP won all 60 seats in the House of Representatives, but lost power to the PNP, led by a more moderate Manley, in 1989; the JLP was defeated again in 1993 and 1997.

Seaga was first elected to the House of Representatives in 1962 and was minister of welfare and development in the 1962–67 government of William ◊Bustamante, and finance minister 1967–72 under Hugh Shearer, before becoming leader of the JLP, and the opposition, in 1974.

Born in Boston, Massachussets, to Jamaican parents of Lebanese descent, Seaga went to school in Kingston, Jamaica, but later studied at Harvard University in the USA. He began his career as a university lecturer in Jamaica, before joining the JLP.

Seale, Bobby (1936–)

US political activist and educator. One of the original Black Panthers, Seale gained notoriety for his vociferous demonstrations during and after the 1968 Chicago convention. Later adopting a moderate political approach, he ran unsuccessfully for mayor of Oakland, California, in 1973 and resigned as Black Panther chair in 1974.

Seddon, Richard John (1845–1906)

New Zealand Liberal Party centrist politician, prime minister 1893–1906. During the 1890s he provided military assistance to the UK during the Boer War in South Africa. In 1901 he secured the transfer of control over the Cook Islands from the UK to New Zealand and introduced state coal-mining; in 1903 he introduced Imperial Preference, to encourage trade within the British Empire. He died at sea, while returning to New Zealand from Australia.

Born in Lancashire, England, he emigrated to Australia in 1863 and then settled in New Zealand in 1866, working initially in the Westland goldfields. He was first elected to the House of Representatives in 1879 and in 1891 became a minister in the Liberal Party government of John Ballance. In 1893 he succeeded

Ballance as prime minister. His long premiership, which lasted until his death in 1906, was notable for its liberal social reforms, including the introduction of old-age pensions, and he gained the nickname, 'King Dick'.

Seeger, Pete (1919–)

US folk singer and songwriter who greatly influenced the development of modern folk music. He wrote antiwar protest songs, such as 'Where Have All the Flowers Gone?' (1956) and 'If I Had a Hammer' (1949). With Woody Guthrie, in the late 1930s, he formed the politically oriented Almanac Singers with several other folk singers to promote unions and condemn fascism. He also cofounded People's Songs and People's Artists. Seeger was a victim of the anti-communist witch-hunt of Senator Joe ◊McCarthy. As a result, his folk group The Weavers (1948–58), which scored massive hits with 'Goodnight Irene' and 'On Top of Old Smokey', lost their record contract and bookings in the late 1950s. Seeger refused to testify before the House Committee on Un-American Activities and was charged with contempt of Congress, but won his case in 1962.

FURTHER READING
Seeger, Pete *Where Have all the Flowers Gone?: A Musical Autobiography* 1996
Seeger, Pete, and Reiser, Bob *Carry it On!: A History in Song and Picture of the Working Men and Women of America* 1985

Segni, Antonio (1891–1965)

Italian politician. A Christian Democrat, he was Italian premier 1955–57 and 1959–60, and foreign secretary 1960–62, when he became president of Italy. He resigned in December 1964 on the grounds of ill-health, shortly after the revelation of a projected coup in which members of the secret service were implicated. Segni was educated at Rome University; he held several law professorships.

Seifert, Jaroslav (1901–1986)

Czech poet. He won state prizes under the communists, but became an original member of the Charter 77 human-rights movement. His works include *Mozart in Prague* (1970), *Umbrella from Piccadilly* (1978), and *The Prague Column* (1979). He was awarded the Nobel Prize for Literature in 1984.

FURTHER READING
Seifert, Jaroslav *The Casting of Bells* 1983, *The Selected Poetry of Jaroslav Seifert* 1986

Seipel, Ignaz (1876–1932)

Austrian politician. A Catholic priest and professor of theology, he became minister of welfare in the last cabinet before the collapse of old Austria in October

1918. From 1921 he led the Christian Socialists, the largest party in the new Austrian parliament, becoming chancellor the following year, and helping the republic to a period of reasonable stability. Surviving an assassination attempt in 1924, he resumed the premiership in 1926 and held it until 1929. Austria's strong man in the 1920s, Seipel nevertheless failed to consolidate its political institutions. He so mistrusted the Social Democrats that he encouraged the paramilitary forces of the Right, especially the Heimwehr, and toyed with the idea of an Anschluss with Germany. Seipel was born in Vienna, Austria.

Selwyn Lloyd, (John) Selwyn Brooke Lloyd, Baron Selwyn Lloyd (1904–1978)

British Conservative politician. He was foreign secretary 1955–60 and chancellor of the Exchequer 1960–62. He was created Baron in 1976.

He was responsible for the creation of the National Economic Development Council, but the unpopularity of his policy of wage restraint in an attempt to defeat inflation forced his resignation. He was Speaker of the House of Commons 1971–76.

Senanayake, Don Stephen (1884–1952)

Sri Lankan politician; first prime minister of independent Sri Lanka (formerly Ceylon) 1948–52. Active in politics from 1915, he became leader of the United National Party and negotiated independence from the UK in 1947. A devout Buddhist, he promoted Sinhalese–Tamil racial harmony and rural development.

Senanayake, Dudley Shelton (1911–1973)

Sri Lankan politician; prime minister 1952–53, 1960, and 1965–70. The son of Don Senanayake, he sought to continue his father's policy of communal reconciliation.

Senghor, Léopold Sédar (1906–)

Senegalese politician and writer. He was the first president of independent Senegal 1960–80. Previously he was Senegalese deputy to the French national assembly 1946–58, and founder of the Senegalese Progressive Union. He was also a well-known poet and a founder of *négritude*, a black literary and philosophical movement.

Senghor studied at the Sorbonne in Paris 1935–39 (the first West African to complete the *agrégation* there), where he was a strong advocate of pride in his native Africa, developing the literary movement known as *négritude*, celebrating black identity, and lamenting the baneful impact of European culture on traditional black culture.

He served in the French army during World War II, and was in a German concentration camp 1940–42; his wartime experience aided him in leading his country, French West Africa, to independence in 1956 as Senegal. His works, written in French, include *Songs of the Shade* (1945), *Ethiopiques* (1956), and *On African Socialism* (1961). He was a founder of the journal *Présence africaine*.

FURTHER READING
Blair, D *African Literature in French* 1976
Hymans, Jacques *Léopold Sédar Senghor* 1971
Peters, J A *A Dance of Masks* 1978

Serrano Elias, Jorge (1945–)

Guatemalan politician, member of the Solidarity Action Movement (MAS), president 1991–93. He restored diplomatic relations with Belize, whose territory had formerly been claimed by Guatemala, and took a firm line against military dissidents. However, he failed in his declared goal of securing a peace settlement with the Guatemalan Revolutionary National Unity (URNG) guerrillas.

Serrano was elected president by a large margin in the January 1991 run-off round. In May 1993, with student and industrial unrest mounting, Serrano partially suspended the constitution and sought to rule by decree. However, the military secured his removal in June 1993 and replacement by Ramiro ◊de León Carpio.

Partly educated abroad, at Stockholm University, Sweden, and Stanford University, USA, Serrano worked as an industrial engineer and property developer before becoming president of the council of state, under Efraín ◊Ríos Montt, who was president 1982–83, and who shared his Protestant fundamentalist beliefs.

Servan-Schreiber, Jean Jacques (1924–)

French publisher and radical politician, founder in 1953 of the magazine *L'Express*, which supported and popularized Pierre ◊Mendès-France's modernizing republicanism in the mid-1950s. He was the author of the widely influential polemic, *Le Défi américain* (1967).

From a publishing and journalistic dynasty, Servan-Schreiber attended the elite Ecole Polytechnique, and worked for a period on *Le Monde* as a foreign affairs correspondent. A critic of Gaullism and Charles ◊de Gaulle's European policies, he backed Gaston ◊Defferre's abortive attempt to reorganize the centre-left in 1964. In *Le Défi américain* he argued that US economic and technological dominance could only be challenged by a united left-wing Europe. As president 1971–75 and 1977–79 of the Radical Party, which had been a major force in government under the Third and Fourth Republics but was now reduced to a rump organization, he took it into Valéry ◊Giscard D'Estaing's centre-right confederation, the Union pour la Démocratie Française (UDF), in 1978.

Seyss-Inquart, Arthur (1892–1946)

Austrian lawyer and politician. He joined the Nazi party in 1928. He was minister of the interior and security in the Schuschnigg Cabinet from February to

March 1938. Seyss-Inquart became governor of Austria in 1938 and deputy governor general of Poland in 1939. As Reich commissioner for the Netherlands he became notorious for his cruelty, and after the war was executed as a war criminal. Seyss-Inquart was born in Moravia.

Sforza, Carlo (1873–1952)

Italian diplomat and politician. In 1919 he became undersecretary of state, and in 1920 foreign minister under Giovanni Giolitti. He was ambassador to France in 1922. After Mussolini's March on Rome, he resigned and returned to Italy, where he was an active opponent of fascism. By 1928 he was forced into exile, first in Belgium, and later in the USA. He returned to Italy in 1943, and made a dramatic re-entry into European diplomacy at the Paris Conference of 1947, once more becoming Italy's foreign minister. His efforts to restore Italian influence in world politics and to bring Italy into the Western alliance occupied the last years of his life. By the time he resigned, owing to ill-health, in 1951, he had seen his policies brought to a successful fruition.

Sforza was born in Montignoso, near Massa, Italy. He had a distinguished diplomatic career in Constantinople (Istanbul), Peking (Beijing), Paris, Madrid, and London. Among his publications are *Fifty Years of War and Diplomacy in the Balkans* (1941), *Machiavelli: Latin and Italian* (1942), *The Real Italians* (1942), *Totalitarian War and After* (1942), *Contemporary Italy: Its Intellectual and Moral Origins* (1946), and *Italy and the Italians* (1948).

Shagari, (Alhaji) Shehu (Usman Aliyu) (1925–)

Nigerian politician, president 1979–83. An experienced minister prior to the 1966 coup, he became both state commissioner for education in Sokoto province and federal commissioner for economic development and reconstruction 1968–70, and then commissioner for finance 1971–75. He was a member of the constituent assembly that drew up the constitution for the Second Republic, and in 1979 was the successful presidential candidate for the National Party of Nigeria. He was overthrown in a military coup in 1983.

Shagari began his political career as a member of the federal parliament 1954–58. He was minister of economic development 1959–60, minister of establishments 1960–62, minister of internal affairs 1962–65, and minister of works 1965–66.

He was educated in northern Nigeria, and became a schoolteacher before entering politics. In 1981 he published his collected speeches, entitled *My Vision of Nigeria*.

Shamir, Yitzhak Yernitsky (1915–)

Polish-born Israeli right-wing politician; prime minister 1983–84 and 1986–92; leader of the Likud (Consolidation Party) until 1993. He was foreign minister under Menachem Begin 1980–83, and again foreign minister in Shimon ◊Peres's unity government 1984–86.

In October 1986, he and Peres exchanged positions, Shamir becoming prime minister and Peres taking over as foreign minister. Shamir was re-elected in 1989 and formed a new coalition government with Peres; this broke up in 1990 and Shamir then formed a government without Labour membership and with religious support. He was a leader of the Stern Gang of guerrillas 1940–48 during the British mandate rule of Palestine.

> *Our image has undergone a change from David fighting Goliath to being Goliath.*
>
> YITZHAK SHAMIR On Israel, *Observer* January 1989

Sharett, Moshe (1894–1965)

Israeli Labour politician, prime minister 1954–55. He was responsible for the volunteering of Palestinian Jews into the British army during World War II, and following the establishment of the state of Israel in 1948, Sharett became foreign minister and a Knesset (parliament) deputy, gaining a reputation as a moderate. In January 1954 he replaced David Ben-Gurion as prime minister, and remained foreign minister. He was replaced as prime minister in November 1955, when, following parliamentary elections, Ben-Gurion was returned to power.

As prime minister, Sharett sought to promote peace with Egypt, but faced opposition from army chief of staff Moshe Dayan. After 1955 Sharett remained foreign minister a further year and privately opposed Ben-Gurion's military plans and the Sinai Campaign. This led to his dismissal in June 1956.

Born in Russia, with the surname Shertok, his family emigrated to Palestine in 1906. Sharett fought for the Turkish army during World War I. After the war, he studied at the London School of Economics and returned to Israel, in 1925, to become a journalist and politician. In 1930 he joined the Labour Party (Mapai) and, from 1933, served as 'foreign minister' of the Yishuv and the Zionist movement, ranking second to David Ben-Gurion.

FURTHER READING

Sheffer, Gabriel *Moshe Sharett: Biography of a Political Moderate* 1996

Shariadmatari, Muhammad Kazem (1899–1986)

Iranian religious leader, head of the Shi'ite community in Iran 1970–79. He advocated the creation of a modern and democratic Islamic state, which was tolerant of its minorities, at ease with new technologies and moderate towards the West. Consequently, he was critical of the excesses of the fundamentalist Islamic Revolution of 1979, including Ayatollah ◊Khomeini's use of the messianic title of Imam and the capture of

US hostages. In late 1979 he gave his blessing to the formation of the Muslim People's Republican Party (MPRP), a broad anti-Khomeini coalition that spearheaded a revolt in Tabriz, where Shariatmadari commanded a large following, particularly among ethnic Azerbaijanis. This attempted counter-revolution was crushed by the Khomeini regime and Shariatmadari was persuaded to order closure of the MPRP. Two years later, after being implicated in another coup attempt, he was placed under house arrest.

Born in Tabriz, Shariatmadari studied Islamic law and philosophy at Qom, where he was a classmate of Ruhulla Khomeini. In the 1930s he carried out further studies in Najaf, Iraq, and then taught in Tabriz and Qom. During the 1960s he vied with Khomeini, who was exiled from 1963 for his anti-modernization views, for leadership of Iran's Shi'ite establishment and in 1970, on the death of Ayatollah Muhsin Hakim, he became head of the Shi'ite community within Iran, but Khomeini was its leader in exile.

Sharon, Ariel (1928–)

Israeli soldier and right-wing politician. Initially a soldier, he left the army in 1973 to help found the right-wing Likud party, with Menachem ◊Begin, and was elected to the Knesset (Israeli parliament). He soon established himself as a leading figure within the strongly nationalist 'new right'. As agriculture minister 1977–81, during the Begin administration, Sharon encouraged new Jewish settlements in recently occupied territories. He then served as defence minister and oversaw Israel's invasion of Lebanon, but was forced to resign in 1983 after the scandal aroused by massacres in Sabra and Chatila. Sharon returned in 1984, as trade and industry minister in a Likud–Labour national unity government. However, his opposition in 1990 to Middle East peace proposals drawn up by US secretary of state James ◊Baker helped bring an end to this coalition. Sharon was housing minister in Yitzhak ◊Shamir's 1990–92 Likud administration.

Born on a moshav (agricultural settlement), Sharon made his name as a fearless and ruthless soldier. In the early 1950s he founded and led the counter-insurgency Unit 101; in 1956 he led paratroops during the Suez war; in the 1967 war he was a divisional commander in Sinai; and in the 1973 Arab–Israeli War he had success in the Suez Canal region.

Shastri, Lal Bahadur (1904–1966)

Indian politician, prime minister 1964–66. He campaigned for national integration, and secured a declaration of peace with Pakistan at the Tashkent peace conference in 1966.

Before independence, he was imprisoned several times for civil disobedience. Because of his small stature, he was known as 'the Sparrow'.

Shaw, George Bernard (1856–1950)

Irish dramatist. He was also a critic and novelist, and an early member of the socialist Fabian Society, although he resigned in 1911. His plays combine comedy with political, philosophical, and polemic aspects, aiming to make an impact on his audience's social conscience as well as their emotions. They include *Arms and the Man* (1894), *Devil's Disciple* (1897), *Man and Superman* (1903), *Pygmalion* (1913), and *St Joan* (1923). He was awarded the Nobel Prize for Literature in 1925.

FURTHER READING
Ganz, A *George Bernard Shaw* 1983
Gibbs, A M *The Art and Mind of Shaw* 1983
Holroyd, M *George Bernard Shaw* 1988–91

Anarchism is a game at which the Police can beat you.
GEORGE BERNARD SHAW
Misalliance

Shawcross, Hartley William Shawcross, Baron Shawcross (1902–)

British jurist. After service in World War II, he was attorney general 1945–51 and president of the Board of Trade in 1951 in the Labour government. He established an international legal reputation for himself as chief British prosecutor at the Nürnberg trials 1945–46, led the investigations of the Lynskey Tribunal in 1948, and was prosecutor in the Klaus Fuchs atom spy case in 1950. Finding the narrow opposition tactics

George Bernard Shaw, 1944. *AKG London*

of the Labour Party irksome, he resigned his parliamentary seat in 1958.

He was born in Giessen, Germany, and was educated at Dulwich College, London. He was called to the bar at Gray's Inn in 1925 and was senior lecturer in law at Liverpool 1927–34. He was created a life peer in 1959 and published *Life Sentence* in 1995.

Shephard, Gillian Patricia (1940–)

British Conservative politician, education and employment secretary 1995–97. She became education secretary in 1994 at a time when relations between the government and the teaching profession were particularly fraught.

Shephard was born in Norfolk and educated at Oxford University. After a career in education as an extra-mural lecturer, education officer, and schools' inspector, Shephard entered politics in her mid-forties, winning the South-West Norfolk seat in 1987. She made steady progress through ministerial ranks, entering the cabinet as secretary of state for employment in 1992, and then moved rapidly through agriculture to education. Her open conciliatory approach did much initially to alleviate the situation, although teachers' patience rapidly dissipated in the face of ongoing cuts in education budgets. In the cabinet reshuffle that followed Prime Minister John Major's successful re-election bid for the party leadership in July 1995, she was also given responsiblity for employment.

Shevardnadze, Edvard Amvrosievich (1928–)

Georgian politician, Soviet foreign minister 1985–91, and head of the state of Georgia from 1992. A supporter of Mikhail ◊Gorbachev, he was first secretary of the Georgian Communist Party from 1972 and an advocate of economic reform. In 1985 he became a member of the Politburo, working for détente and disarmament. In July 1991 he resigned from the Communist Party of the Soviet Union (CPSU) and, along with other reformers and leading democrats, established the Democratic Reform Movement. In March 1992 he was chosen as chair of Georgia's ruling military council, and in October was elected speaker of parliament (equivalent to president). He survived assassination attempts in 1995 and in February 1998.

On 20 December 1990 he dramatically resigned as foreign minister in protest against what he viewed as the onset of a dictatorship in the USSR, as reactionary forces, particularly within the military, regained the ascendancy. Following the abortive anti-Gorbachev coup in August 1991 (in which he stood alongside Boris ◊Yeltsin) and the dissolution of the CPSU, his Democratic Reform Party stood out as a key force in the 'new politics' of Russia and the USSR. Shevardnadze turned down an offer from President Gorbachev to join the post-coup security council, but subsequently agreed to join Gorbachev's advisory council. In March 1992,

Soviet Foreign Minister Edvard Shevardnadze with American vice president George Bush, 1988. *Rex*

following the ousting of President Zviad ◊Gamsakhurdia, he was chosen as chair of Georgia's ruling State Council, and in the first parliamentary elections in October was elected speaker of parliament, with 90% of the vote.

Shevardnadze inherited a nation affected by a continuing civil war and secessionist movement in Abkhazia. Reluctantly, he turned to Russia for military aid to crush the insurgencies and attempted to disband private militias. He was directly elected executive president in November 1995.

He was born in Mamati Lanchkhutsky region, Georgia, and educated at the Party School of the Central Committee of the Communist Party of Georgia and at the Kutaisi Pedagogical Institute.

FURTHER READING

Ekedahl, Carolyn McGiffert, and Goodman, Melvin *The Wars of Eduard Shevardnadze* 1997
Shevardnadze, Edvard *The Future Belongs to Freedom* 1991

Shidehara, Kijuro (1872–1951)

Japanese politician and diplomat, prime minister 1945–46. As foreign minister 1924–27 and 1929–31, he promoted conciliation with China, and economic rather than military expansion. After a brief period as prime minister, he became speaker of the Japanese Diet (parliament) 1949–51.

Shilts, Randy Martin (1951–1994)

US journalist and writer. As a reporter on the *San Francisco Chronicle* from 1981, he pioneered awareness of the AIDS epidemic in the USA. *The Mayor of Castro Street: The Life and Times of Harvey Milk* (1982) is his biography of a local gay politician murdered in 1978 as well as an analysis of prejudice against homosexuals in US politics.

Shilts was one of the first openly gay reporters in the USA, writing for the *Advocate* magazine in the 1970s. In *And the Band Played On: Politics, People, and the AIDS Epidemic* (1987) he exposed Ronald Reagan's administration's inadequate handling of the AIDS crisis. His last book was *Conduct Unbecoming: Lesbians and Gays in the US Military* (1993).

Shinwell, Emmanuel ('Manny'), Baron Shinwell (1884–1986)

British Labour politician. In 1935 he defeated Ramsay MacDonald at Seaham Harbour, Durham, in one of the most bitterly contested British election battles of modern times. From 1942 he was chair of the Labour Party committee which drafted the manifesto 'Let us face the future', on which Labour won the 1945 election. As minister of fuel and power he nationalized the mines in 1946.

In 1947, when he was said to be a scapegoat for the February fuel crisis, he became secretary of state for war. From 1950 to 1951 he was minister of defence. He was parliamentary Labour Party chair from 1964 to 1967.

Born in Spitalfields, London, he began work as an errand boy in Glasgow at the age of 12. An early student of public-library and street-corner socialism, he was elected to the Glasgow Trades Council in 1911 and, as one of the 'Red Crusaders', served a five-month prison sentence for incitement to riot in 1919.

He entered Parliament in 1922 as member for Linlithgow and was appointed secretary to the department of mines in 1924 and 1930–31. Shinwell's considerable administrative ability outshone his prickly party-political belligerence and earned him the respect of Winston Churchill and Bernard Montgomery. In his later years he mellowed into a backbench 'elder statesman'. He was created a Companion of Honour in 1965 and was awarded a life peerage in 1970.

His autobiographical works include *Conflict without Malice* (1955), *I've Lived Through It All* (1973), and *Lead with the Left* (1981).

FURTHER READING
Slowe, Peter M *Manny Shinwell: An Authorized Biography* 1993

Shipley, Jenny (1952–)

New Zealand right-of-centre politician, prime minister from 1997. She joined the conservative National Party at the age of 23 and, after a spell as a local councillor, was elected to the House of Representatives in 1987. When the National Party came to power in 1990, Shipley entered Jim ◊Bolger's government as minister of social welfare and women's affairs 1990–93, health and women's affairs 1993–94, and minister of transport and state services 1996–97. She provoked controversy through benefit-cutting and introducing an internal market into the health service.

On the right wing of the National Party, Shipley became increasingly disillusioned with Bolger's cautious policy approach and began to challenge his leadership in 1997. During Bolger's absence at the Commonwealth heads of government conference in the UK, in November 1997, she consolidated her position and on his return warned him that she had enough support within the parliamentary party to force his resignation. This persuaded Bolger to resign as party leader and she was elected as his replacement and became, in December 1997, New Zealand's first female prime minister. She headed a coalition with the New Zealand First Party, led by Winston ◊Peters.

Born in Gore, on the southern tip of South Island, Shipley, who was brought up in Wellington and Blenheim, was the daughter of a Presbyterian minister who died while she was in her teens. She began her career as a teacher and then, after marriage, became a farmer.

Shore, Peter David, Baron Shore of Stepney (1924–)

British Labour politican. Member of Parliament for Stepney 1964–97, he was parliamentary private secretary to Harold Wilson, and held several government posts, including secretary of state for economic affairs 1967–69, for trade 1974–76, and for the environment 1976–79. After holding various opposition posts, he became shadow leader of the Commons 1984–87. A persistent critic of European economic union, he launched a 'No to Maastricht' campaign in 1992.

Shore was educated at Cambridge and joined the Labour Party in 1948, heading its research department for five years before becoming MP for Stepney. He was a member of the Fabian Society and an unsuccessful candidate in the Labour Party leadership elections of 1983. He published *Leading the Left* in 1993 and was awarded a life peerage in 1997.

Short, Clare (1946–)

British Labour politician, secretary of state for international development from 1997. Formerly a civil servant in the Home Office 1970–75, she became the director of community organizations concerned with race and urban deprivation in Birmingham 1976–77 and youth aid 1979–83. She was then elected member of Parliament for her home constituency, Birmingham Ladywood, in 1983. In the House of Commons she was opposition spokesperson on employment 1985–88, social security 1989–91, environmental protection 1992–93, women 1993–95, transport 1995–96, and shadow minister for overseas development 1996–97.

She was born in Ladywood, Birmingham, and educated at Keele and Leeds universities. She faced criticism in 1997 for her handling of the crisis in Montserrat following a volcanic eruption.

Shriver, (Robert) Sargent, Jr (1915–)

US Democratic politician. He played an important role in the successful presidential campaign of John F Kennedy in 1960. He was director of the Peace Corps 1961–66, and director of the Office of Economic Opportunity 1964–68; he also served as special assistant to President Lyndon Johnson 1964–68.

Shriver was born in Westminster, Maryland, and educated at Yale University. Initially a lawyer and journalist, he became general manager of the Chicago Merchandise Mart 1948–60.

He was ambassador to France 1968–70, and was the unsuccessful Democratic vice-presidential candidate in 1972. He remained active in national politics, and was an unsuccessful candidate for the Democratic presidential nomination in 1976.

Shultz, George Pratt (1920–)

US Republican politician, economics adviser to President Ronald ◊Reagan 1980–82, and secretary of state 1982–89. Shultz taught as a labour economist at the University of Chicago before serving in the 1968–74 Richard ◊Nixon administration. His posts included secretary of labour 1969–70 and secretary of the Treasury 1972–74.

Shushkevich, Stanislav (1934–)

Belarussian politician, president 1991–94. He was elected to parliament as a nationalist 'reform communist' in 1990 and played a key role in the creation of the Commonwealth of Independent States (CIS) as the successor to the USSR. A supporter of free-market reforms, he opposed the alignment of Belarus's economic and foreign policy with that of neighbouring Russia.

Shushkevich, the son of a poet who died in the gulag, was educated at the University of Belarus in Minsk and gained a doctorate in technical education; he was deputy rector for science at the Lenin State University in Minsk. He entered politics as a result of his concern at the Soviet cover-up of the Chernobyl disaster in 1986.

Shuttlesworth, Fred

US preacher and black civil-rights activist. Possibly the most courageous of the black ministers who led the civil-rights movement, Shuttlesworth, a Baptist and founder of the Alabama Christian Movement for Human Rights, became known principally for his involvement with Martin Luther ◊King and his campaign for desegregation in the early 1960s. Shuttlesworth's personal courage and unwavering commitment were evident early on during attacks on black churches by Ku Klux Klan chapters and later while he was imprisoned with Martin Luther King prior to the Children's March in Birmingham, Alabama, in 1963. Shuttlesworth's conviction that the march should go ahead, despite opposition from the local community and the arrest of over 900 children, persuaded Martin Luther King, who wanted to abandon the march, and focused the nation's attention on racial inequality in the South. He also helped found the Southern Christian Leadership Conference.

Siad Barre, Mohamed (1921–1995)

Somalian soldier and politician, president of Somalia 1969–91. Seizing power in a bloodless coup, with promises to solve clan rivalries and regenerate his country through a policy of 'scientific socialism', he exploited those rivalries to promote his own regime and presided over a socialist government that degenerated into an autocracy based on a ruthless personality cult.

Born in the Ogaden region, a member of the Marehan clan, Siad Barre, despite only a rudimentary education, rose from the rank of ordinary police officer in Italian-controlled Somalia to become brigadier general of police when his country achieved independence in 1960, and commander in chief of the armed forces five years later. When the Somalian president died in 1969, Siad Barre, with 20 fellow army officers and five police officers, seized power, suspended the constitution, and began to rule by decree. His repressive regime became increasingly discredited and in January 1991 his opponents forced him out of office.

He left the capital, Mogadishu, to return to his own clan area, from where he hoped to rally support and return to power. In April 1992 he went into exile in Kenya, where he became a source of embarrassment to the government of President Daniel arap Moi, who eventually persuaded him to accept the protection of Nigeria, where he died.

Sidky, Ismail (1875–1950)

Egyptian politician. He joined Saad Zaghlul and the Wafd in the struggle for Egyptian independence. With Zaghlul and others he was deported by the British to Malta, but released at Edmund Allenby's insistence in April 1919. Subsequently Sidky broke with Zaghlul, and, with the British, soon became the Wafd's most formidable enemy. In 1924 he was appointed prime minister. He held ruthless sway for three years, but in January 1933 became seriously ill. After his recovery, in 1936, he joined the national delegation which negotiated the Anglo-Egyptian treaty with the British. He opposed every suggestion that Egypt should declare

Norodom Sihanouk (left) with Cambodian prime minister Hun Sen, 1987. *Rex*

war on the Axis, and in the period of World War II shed the last remnants of his reputation as a British puppet. He was recalled to office again in 1946.

Sidky was educated at the Collège des Frères in Cairo, Egypt, and at the Khedival Law School.

Sikandar Hayat Khan (1892–1942)

Indian politician. He was elected to the Punjab legislative council in 1921, and was appointed chair of the Punjab Reforms Committee to work with the Somon Commission. Elected chief minister of the Punjab at the start of World War II, he launched rural reconstruction programmes, extended irrigation facilities, laid new roads, and established and strengthened the roles of panchayats (local councils). After his death the Punjab was plunged into political turmoil.

From a rich landed family, he was educated in Aligarh and at University College, London. In World War I he was appointed an honorary recruiting officer and was granted a commission. During the third of the Afghan Wars he acted as a company commander in 1919. He was knighted in 1933 and appointed governor of the Reserve Bank in 1935.

Sikorski, Władysław Eugeniusz (1881–1943)

Polish general and politician; prime minister 1922–23,

◆ SIHANOUK, NORODOM (1922–   ) ◆

Cambodian politician, king 1941–55 and from 1993. He was prime minister 1955–70, when his government was overthrown in a military coup led by Lon Nol. With ◊Pol Pot's resistance front, he overthrew Lon Nol in 1975 and again became prime minister 1975–76, when he was forced to resign by the Khmer Rouge. He returned from exile in November 1991 under the auspices of a United Nations-brokered peace settlement to head a coalition intended to comprise all Cambodia's warring factions (the Khmer Rouge, however, continued fighting). He was re-elected king after the 1993 elections, in which the royalist party won a majority; in 1996, however, it was announced that he was suffering from a brain tumour and might abdicate. In October 1997, three months after a successful coup by communists, he left for China and his return was uncertain. In March 1998 he pardoned his son, Prince Norodom Ranariddh, who had been sentenced to 30 years' imprisonment for smuggling arms and colluding with the Khmer Rouge.

Educated in Vietnam and Paris, he was elected king of Cambodia in 1941. He abdicated in 1955 in favour of his father, founded the Popular Socialist Community, and governed as prime minister 1955–70.

After he was deposed in 1970, Sihanouk established a government in exile in Beijing and formed a joint resistance front with Pol Pot. This movement succeeded in overthrowing Lon Nol in April 1975 and Sihanouk was reappointed head of state, but was forced to resign in April 1976 by the communist Khmer Rouge leadership. Based in North Korea, he became the recognized head of the Democratic Kampuchea government in exile in 1982, leading a coalition of three groups opposing the Vietnamese-installed government. International peace conferences aimed at negotiating a settlement repeatedly broke down, fighting intensified, and the Khmer Rouge succeeded in taking some important provincial capitals.

A peace agreement was eventually signed in Paris on 23 October 1991. On his return from exile, Sihanouk called for an international trial of the leaders of the Khmer Rouge on charges of genocide. His son, Prince Norodom Ranariddh, became prime minister in July 1993. In October 1993 Sihanouk was crowned king under a new constitution providing for an elected monarch with limited powers. During 1994 there were a number of attempted coups against him, led by his close relatives.

and 1939–43 in the Polish government in exile in London during World War II. He was killed in an aeroplane crash near Gibraltar in controversial circumstances.

Together with Józef ◊Piłsudski he fought for the restoration of an independent Poland during World War I. As a result of his opposition to the military coup of 1926 he was denied a military appointment. Instead, he concentrated on studying military strategy and wrote a number of books based on his analysis of the French wartime experiences. In September 1939 he left Poland for Paris where, after a bitter contest with supporters of the prewar regime, he formed a government in exile committed to close military cooperation with France and the UK. After the fall of France he moved to London. In July 1941, strongly supported by the UK prime minister Winston Churchill, he signed a controversial agreement for military cooperation with the USSR, which evoked strong opposition from within the Polish army in the UK and in the USSR. Following Sikorski's death, the Polish government in exile lost its sense of direction and its influence declined.

Siles Zuazo, Hernán (1914–1996)

Bolivian president 1956–60 and 1982–85, conservative politician, and lawyer. He founded the National Revolutionary Movement (MNR) and led the bloody revolt that brought the MNR into power in 1952. He was vice president to Victor Paz Estenssoro 1952–56, succeeding him as president in 1956. His administration continued with the reform programmes initiated by his predecessor. He also implemented a successful programme to improve the nation's economy. Labour disputes, high inflation, and monetary devaluation marred his second term in office.

In 1960 Paz Estenssoro returned to power. Siles went into exile after 1964, remaining politically active with the formation of a breakaway group of the MNR – the Movimento de la Izquierda Revolucionaria (MIR; Revolutionary Left Movement). He returned to Bolivia and became president again in 1982.

Silverman, (Samuel) Sidney (1896–1968)

British lawyer and Labour politician. He was Labour member of Parliament for Nelson and Colne 1935–68. He served as chair of the British section of the World Jewish Congress and argued strongly after the war for unlimited access to Palestine for all Jewish refugees. Overlooked for a post in the postwar Labour administration, Silverman was increasingly a voice on the left of the party. His support for the Campaign for Nuclear Disarmament (CND) led to his expulsion from the party.

Silverman was also a powerful campaigner on behalf of the abolition of the death penalty, building a powerful lobby through the 1950s for legislation that had to wait for Labour's return to office in 1964.

Born in Liverpool to a Jewish family and educated at Liverpool University, Silverman registered as a conscientious objector in 1916 and this limited his chances of career advancement after the war. He qualified as a lawyer and by 1927 was representing the poor in criminal cases and cases against landlords.

Simitis, Costas (Constantine) (1936–)

Greek politician, prime minister from 1996. Entering parliament in 1985, he served under Andreas Papandreou as minister of agriculture 1981–85, minister of national economy 1985–89, minister of education 1989–93, and was responsible for industry, energy, technology, and commerce from 1993. In 1996 he was chosen by the ruling Panhellenic Socialist Movement (PASOK) to replace Papandreou on the latter's resignation in 1996.

Simitis was born in Athens and educated at the University of Marburg and the London School of Economics. Initially combining an academic career with an involvement in politics, he was a member of the National Council of the Panhellenic Liberation Movement while the country was under military control 1967–74, and a member of PASOK from 1974.

Simmonds, Kennedy Alphonse (1936–)

St Kitts centre-right politician, prime minister 1980–95. He helped form the centre-right People's Action Movement (PAM) in 1965 and became its leader in 1976, challenging the dominant St Kitts Labour Party (SKLP). In 1980 he became prime minister over a PAM-led coalition with the Nevis Reformation Party (NRP). After defusing secessionist demands on Nevis Island by establishing a federation in 1982, he led the country through independence in 1983, and sought to promote tourism and diversification of agriculture. In 1995 he lost power to the SKLP, led by Denzil ◊Douglas.

In 1979 Simmons was the first non-SKLP candidate to be elected to the national assembly from St Kitts since 1952. His government was re-elected in 1984, 1989, and 1993.

He was born in the capital, Basseterre, and studied medicine at the University of West Indies, in Jamaica, and in the USA, before later working as a doctor.

Simon, John Allsebrook, 1st Viscount Simon (1873–1954)

British Liberal politician. He was home secretary 1915–16, but resigned over the issue of conscription. He was foreign secretary 1931–35, home secretary again 1935–37, chancellor of the Exchequer 1937–40, and lord chancellor 1940–45. He was knighted in 1910 and created Viscount in 1940.

Sinclair, Upton Beall (1878–1968)

US novelist. His polemical concern for social reform was reflected in his prolific output of documentary novels. His most famous novel, *The Jungle* (1906), is an important example of naturalistic writing, which exposed the horrors of the Chicago meat-packing industry and led to a change in food-processing laws. His later novels include *King Coal* (1917), *Oil!* (1927), and his 11-volume Lanny Budd series (1940–53), including *Dragon's Teeth* (1942), which won a Pulitzer prize.

FURTHER READING
Bloodworth, William A, Jr *Upton Sinclair* 1977
Sinclair, Upton *The Autobiography of Upton Sinclair* 1962

Singh, Karan (1931–)

Indian politician and author. In 1949 his father, Maharaja Hari, appointed him regent of Jammu and Kashmir. In November 1952 he was elected head of state of Jammu and Kashmir and was re-elected in 1957 and 1962, and elected governor in 1965 and 1967. Singh also held several ministerial positions and was India's ambassador to the USA 1989–91. In 1967, at the age of 36, he became the youngest person to become a central cabinet minister in India when he joined Indira ◊Gandhi's cabinet.

Singh founded the International Centre for Science, Culture, and Consciousness, wrote a number of books on political science, and was associated with many cultural and academic institutions. In the 1990s he was chair of the Jammu and Kashmir Autonomy Committee.

Singh, Vishwanath Pratap (1931–)

Indian politician, prime minister 1989–90. As a member of the Congress (I) Party, he held ministerial posts under Indira Gandhi and Rajiv Gandhi, and from 1984 led an anti-corruption drive. When he unearthed an arms-sales scandal in 1988, he was ousted from the government and party and formed a broad-based opposition alliance, the Janata Dal, which won the November 1989 election. Mounting caste and communal conflict split the Janata Dal and forced him out of office in November 1990.

Singh was born in Allahabad, the son of a local raja. He was minister of commerce 1976–77 and in 1983, Uttar Pradesh chief minister 1980–82, minister of finance 1984–86, and minister of defence 1986–87, when he revealed the embarrassing Bofors scandal. Respected for his probity and sense of principle, Singh emerged as one of the most popular politicians in India.

Singleton, John Daniel (1968–)

US film director. Singleton's debut film, *Boyz N the Hood*, dealt with the issues around black youth in south-central Los Angeles and their gang-based lives. Singleton became the youngest individual and the first black American ever nominated for an Academy Award for best director for the film. His *Rosewood* (1997) dealt with the burning of a small prosperous black town in Idaho, which was burnt to the ground by the white population of a neighbouring town, called Sumner.

Sinyavski, Andrei Donatovich (1925–1997)

Russian literary critic and prose writer, in exile in France from 1973. His early works were published in the West under the pseudonym of Avram Tertz, and included two short novels, *Liubimov* and *Sud idyot/The Trial Begins* (1960), and a critique of Socialist Realism. Together with Yuli Daniel, he was tried in 1966 for anti-Soviet activities. His later writings include unconventional studies of major Russian writers.

A thinker who was committed to the undermining of ideology, accepted ideas, and any form of determinism, Sinyavski was sentenced to seven years' hard labour in 1966. His and Daniel's trial marked the end of the cultural thaw that had begun under Nikita Khrushchev. When Sinyavski was allowed to leave the USSR in 1973, he settled in Paris, teaching Russian literature at the Sorbonne and editing the influential journal *Sintaksis*.

Siqueiros, David Alfaro (1896–1974)

Mexican painter and graphic artist, labour organizer, and revolutionary. He was a prominent Social Realist and an outstanding member of the Mexican muralist movement of the 1930s. A lifelong political activist, who served as captain with the revolutionary army of Venustiano ◊Carranza before 1919, his work championed his revolutionary ideals, as in *Portrait of the Bourgeoisie* (1939, Electrical Workers' Union, Mexico City). He was imprisoned 1960–64 for organizing a student riot.

He was an active labour organizer 1925–30. Exiled to the USA in 1932, in 1936 he fought as a lieutenant colonel in the Republican Army in Spain. He was implicated in the 1940 assassination in Mexico of the Russian revolutionary Leon ◊Trotsky, and lived in exile in Argentina and Cuba 1941–43.

Sisulu, Walter Max Ulyate (1912–)

South African civil-rights activist, deputy president of the African National Congress (ANC) from 1991. In 1964 he became, with Nelson Mandela, one of the first full-time secretaries general of the ANC. He was imprisoned following the 1964 Rivonia Trial for opposition to the apartheid system and released in 1989, at the age of 77, as a gesture of reform by President F W ◊de Klerk. In 1991, when Mandela became ANC president, Sisulu became his deputy.

Sithole, Ndabaningi (1920–)

Zimbabwean politician. With Robert ◊Mugabe he founded the Zimbabwe African National Union

(ZANU) in 1963, the members of which originally formed the core of the Rhodesian guerrilla movement. In 1964 he was arrested for alleged incitement to violence and was later accused of plotting political assassinations. In 1974 he was conditionally released in order to participate in talks about Rhodesia's (modern-day Zimbabwe) future. In 1975 he sought refuge abroad, returning in July 1977 to help bring about a Rhodesian settlement.

He studied in the USA and was a pastor of the Methodist Church. In 1959 he published *African Nationalism*.

Sjahrir, Sutar (1909–1966)

Indonesian politician, prime minister 1945–47. He negotiated the Linggadjati Agreement whereby the Dutch acknowledged Indonesia's authority in Java and Sumatra, but his conciliatory policies forced him to resign in 1947. The following year he formed the anti-communist Partai Sosialis Indonesia (Indonesian Socialist Party). President Achmed ◊Sukarno banned it in 1960 and in January 1962 Sjahrir was arrested on charges of conspiracy but died before being tried.

Educated in law at the University of Leiden, Sjahrir established the socialist party Pendidikan Nasional Indonesia in 1931 in opposition to Sukarno's Partai Nasional Indonesia (Indonesian Nationalist Party). Exiled by the Dutch in 1934, he returned in 1942 and pushed Indonesia to declare independence.

Skate, Bill (William Jack) (1953–)

Papua New Guinea politician; prime minister from 1997, heading a five-party coalition government, which included his People's National Congress (PNC). His government negotiated a permanent cease-fire in January 1998 to end the eight-year-old Bougainville conflict, and announced plans to extend education. However, Skate's position was weakened in November 1997 when a videotape, shown on Australian television, suggested that he had connections with Port Moresby's notorious 'raskol' criminal gangs and that he had authorized bribes. Skate claimed that he had been drunk at the time of the filming and dismissed the demand, made by opposition leader Michael ◊Somare, for his resignation.

Born in Ara'ara village, Baimuru, in the Gulf province, Skate studied accountancy at university and during the 1980s had a successful career in management and business. His political career began in 1992 when he was elected to the national parliament and he swiftly became its speaker. In August 1994 he resigned as speaker to challenge Julius ◊Chan, unsuccessfully, for the premiership. He later stepped down from parliament in mid-1995 to become governor of the National Capital District (Port Moresby).

Skate challenged Chan for the premiership once again in March 1997, following a scandal over the government's hiring of 60 foreign mercenaries to assist the government's war effort against secessionists on

◆ SLOVO, JOE (1926–1995) ◆

South African lawyer and politician, general secretary of the South African Communist Party 1987–91; chief of staff of Umkhonto we Sizwe (Spear of the Nation), the armed wing of the African National Congress (ANC) 1985–87; and minister of housing in President Nelson Mandela's government 1994–95. He was one of the most influential figures in the ANC, and spent 27 years in exile.

Born in Lithuania, Slovo emigrated to South Africa as a child with his parents, who had originally intended to settle in Argentina. Forced by poverty to leave school to take manual work before finishing his formal education, he soon became an industrial shop steward, where he secured benefits for white workers but, to his dismay, not for blacks. Despite his restricted education, he won a place to read law at Witwatersrand University, where he graduated with high honours. His early involvement with the South African Communist Party was consolidated

when, in 1949, he married Ruth First, the daughter of the party's treasurer. As a partnership, they became a legend and their home a meeting place for radicals. In 1982 Ruth First was killed by a terrorist bomb in Mozambique.

After Mandela and F W de Klerk, Slovo was perhaps the most significant figure in South Africa's recent history in that he was white and yet respected and trusted by the ANC and able to persuade Mandela that the ANC could embrace all shades of opinion and all races and colours. During his exile from South Africa, Slovo travelled widely from his base in Mozambique, preparing for a guerrilla war, which, he was convinced, was the only way of removing the hated system of apartheid and the regime that had installed it. A believer in the fundamental tenets of communism from an early age, he admitted in the 1980s that his uncritical support of the undemocratic Soviet regimes had been misguided.

Joe Slovo. *Rex*

Bougainville island. He eventually became prime minister after the June 1997 general election.

Smith, Al(fred Emanuel) (1873–1944)

US political leader who served four terms as governor of New York. The first Roman Catholic to receive a presidential nomination, he unsuccessfully fought for the 1924 presidency as a Democrat, on a platform of liberalizing Prohibition. In his lively, yet unsuccessful, campaign against Herbert Hoover he was called the 'Happy Warrior'. His defeat nonetheless forged a breakthrough for the Democrats, re-establishing support in the larger cities and attracting support from the farm states of the West.

Born in New York of Irish Catholic extraction, Smith left school in his teens and became involved in local Democratic politics. After serving in the New York state assembly 1905–15, he became New York County sheriff 1915–17.

In 1918 he was elected governor of New York. He was defeated for re-election in 1920 but was victorious in 1922, 1924, and 1926.

FURTHER READING

Neal, Donn C *The World Beyond the Hudson: Alfred E Smith and National Politics, 1918–1928* 1983

Pringle, Henry S *Alfred E Smith: A Critical Study* 1927

Smith, Arnold Cantwell (1915–)

Canadian diplomat. He was ambassador to the United Arab Republic 1958–61 and to the USSR 1961–63. From 1965 to 1975 he was secretary general of the newly formed Commonwealth Secretariat.

Smith was educated at Toronto, Canada; Grenoble, France; and Oxford, England, and in law at Gray's Inn, London. He joined the Canadian diplomatic service in 1939. In 1975 he went to Carleton University, Ottawa, as professor of international affairs.

Smith, Christopher Robert (Chris) (1951–)

British Labour politician, secretary of state for culture, media, and the arts from 1997. He entered the House of Commons in 1983, representing Islington South and Finsbury. He was shadow Treasury minister 1987–92, shadow secretary of state for the environment 1992–94, for national heritage 1994–95, for social security 1995–96, and for health 1996–97.

He was born in Hertfordshire and educated at George Watson's College, Edinburgh, Pembroke College, Cambridge, where he was president of the Union in 1972, and Harvard University, USA, where he was a

Kennedy scholar. Having unsuccessfully contested Epsom and Ewell in 1979, he was elected member of Parliament for Islington South and Finsbury from 1983. Before that Smith worked in the field of housing: with the Housing Corporation 1976–77, the Shaftesbury Society Housing Association 1977–80, and the Society for Cooperative Dwellings 1980–83. During this time he also served on Islington Borough Council.

Smith, Herbert (1862–1938)

English miners' leader. He became president of the Yorkshire Miners Association in 1906 and was president of the Miners Federation of Great Britain 1922–29. During the mining strike of 1926, he was particularly concerned with ensuring the survival of the federation.

Adopted from the workhouse, Smith became a miner at the age of ten. He always had a keen interest in safety issues and rescue efforts, not only in the UK, but also in Europe. He was president of Castleford Trades Council from 1896 to 1904, a councillor in the West Riding of Yorkshire from 1903, and mayor of Barnsley in 1932.

Smith, Ian (Douglas) (1919–)

Rhodesian politician. He was a founder of the Rhodesian Front in 1962 and prime minister 1964–79. In 1965 he made a unilateral declaration of Rhodesia's independence and, despite United Nations sanctions, maintained his regime with tenacity.

In 1979 he was suc-

> *I don't believe in black majority rule ever in Rhodesia ... not in a thousand years.*
>
> IAN SMITH Speech 1976

ceeded as prime minister by Bishop Abel Muzorewa, when the country was renamed Zimbabwe. He was suspended from the Zimbabwe parliament in April 1987 and resigned in May as head of the white opposition party. In 1992 he helped found a new opposition party, the United Front.

Smith, John (1938–1994)

British Labour politician, party leader 1992–94, born on the Scottish island of Islay. He was trade and industry secretary 1978–79 and from 1979 held various shadow cabinet posts, culminating in that of shadow chancellor 1987–92. When Neil Kinnock resigned the leadership after losing the 1992 general election, Smith was readily elected as his successor. During his two years as leader, building on Kinnock's efforts, he drew together the two wings of the Labour Party to make it a highly electable proposition. He won the trust and support of colleagues of all shades of opinion, and built a formidable front-bench team. His sudden death from a heart attack shocked British politicians of all parties.

The son of a primary-school headteacher, Smith graduated in history at Glasgow University. He turned to law and became an advocate at the Scottish bar in 1967 and Queen's Counsel (QC) in 1983. However, forsaking a promising legal career for politics, he entered the House of Commons in 1970. His talents were recognized by prime ministers Harold Wilson and James Callaghan and, after holding several junior posts, he became trade and industry secretary in 1978. During Labour's years of opposition from 1979 he was a key front-bench member. Positioned at the centre-right of the party, as shadow chancellor he advocated a cautious, prudent economic programme funded by tax increases aimed at high earners. As leader of the opposition, he won a reputation as a man of transparent honesty and a formidable parliamentarian.

Smith, Tommie (1944–   )

US athlete. Smith won the 200-metres gold medal in a world-record time at the 1968 Olympic Games in Mexico City, but is remembered for his actions after the victory. After accepting his medal, he, and John Carlos (the bronze-medal winner and fellow black American), raised a black-gloved fist as the US national anthem was played. The pair were immediately expelled from the Games and sent home. Their non-violent protest on the rostrum in Mexico city attracted attention to the fight for civil rights in the USA. Not only did they make the black power salute, but they were also barefoot and wore black scarves – symbols of poverty and lynchings.

Their protest had not been worked out in advance, however the philosophy behind it had. Smith and Carlos, like many US athletes, were members of a group called the Olympic Project for Human Rights. Back in the USA they received a cool reception and had

difficulty settling into a 'normal' life. Eventually, in 1972, Smith gained a position as track coach at Oberlin College, Ohio, and later moved on to coach at Santa Monica College, California.

Smuts, Jan Christian (1870–1950)

South African politician and soldier; prime minister 1919–24 and 1939–48. He supported the Allies in both world wars and was a member of the British imperial war cabinet 1917–18.

During the Second South African War (Boer War) 1899–1902, Smuts commanded the Boer forces in his native Cape Colony. He subsequently worked for reconciliation between the Boers and the British. On the establishment of the Union of South Africa, he became minister of the interior 1910–12 and defence

---

Perhaps it is God's will to lead the people of South Africa through defeat and humiliation to a better future and a brighter day.

JAN SMUTS Referring to the end of the Boer War, speech May 1902

---

minister 1910–20. During World War I he commanded the South African forces in East Africa 1916–17. He was prime minister 1919–24 and minister of justice 1933–39; on the outbreak of World War II he succeeded General James Hertzog as premier. He was made a field marshal in 1941.

Smuts received the Order of Merit in 1947. Although more of an internationalist than his contemporaries, he was a segregationalist, voting in favour of legislation that took away black rights and land ownership.

FURTHER READING
Hancock, William Keith *Smuts* 1962–68
Smuts, J C *Jan Christian Smuts* (a biography by his son) 1952
Williams, Basil *Botha, Smuts and South Africa* 1946

Snegur, Mircea (1940–   )

Moldovan politician, chair of the Party of Resurrection, president of Moldova 1990–96 and leader of the opposition from 1996.

He was a member of the Communist Party of the Soviet Union (CPSU) 1964–90. He worked as an agronomist and manager of state collective farms 1967–71 and then for the ministry of agriculture 1971–78. He rose through the ranks of the Communist Party of Moldova to become secretary of its central committee 1985–89. He became chair of the Supreme Soviet of Moldova in 1990.

Snowden, Philip, 1st Viscount Snowden (1864–1937)

British right-wing Labour politician, chancellor of the Exchequer in 1924 and 1929–31. He was member of

Parliament for Blackburn 1906–31 and entered the coalition National Government in 1931 as Lord Privy Seal, but resigned in 1932. He was created Viscount in 1931.

FURTHER READING
Laybourn, K, and James, D *Philip Snowden, First Labour Chancellor of the Exchequer* 1987

Soames, (Arthur) Christopher (John), Baron Soames (1920–1987)

British Conservative politician. He held ministerial posts 1958–64, was vice president of the European Commission 1973–77, and served as governor of (Southern) Rhodesia during its transition to independence as Zimbabwe December 1979–April 1980.

He was educated at Eton and Sandhurst and married a daughter of Sir Winston Churchill. Soames entered Parliament as a Conservative in 1950, and after holding junior office was minister of war 1958–60, and minister of agriculture 1960–64. He lost his parliamentary seat at the 1966 general election. Between 1968 and 1972 he was British ambassador to France. From 1973 to 1977 he was a commissioner of the European Economic Community, one of the first two to be nominated by the UK following its entry into the Community. He was knighted in 1972 and made a life peer in 1978.

Soares, Mario Alberto Nobre Lopes (1924–)

Portuguese socialist politician, president 1986–96. Exiled in 1970, he returned to Portugal in 1974, and, as leader of the Portuguese Socialist Party, was prime minister 1976–78. He resigned as party leader in 1980, but in 1986 he was elected Portugal's first socialist president.

Sobchak, Anatoly (1937–)

Soviet centrist politician, mayor of St Petersburg 1990–96, cofounder of the Democratic Reform Movement (with former foreign minister Edvard ◊Shevardnadze), and member of the Soviet parliament 1989–91. He prominently resisted the abortive anti-Gorbachev coup of August 1991.

Sobchak was born in Siberia, studied law at the University of Leningrad, and became professor of economic law there in 1983. He was elected to parliament in the semi-free poll of March 1989, chaired the congressional commission into the massacre of Georgian nationalists, and became a leading figure in the radical Interregional Group of deputies.

He left the Communist Party in 1990 after only two years' membership and in May 1991 was elected mayor of Leningrad (renamed St Petersburg later the same year). When tanks advanced on the city during the coup attempt in August, Sobchak negotiated an agreement to ensure that they remained outside the city, and upheld the democratic cause. In May 1996 he was defeated in the mayoral elections by his former deputy Vladimir Yakovlev.

Sobhuza I (1889–1982)

Swazi king and the world's longest serving monarch at the time of his death. He was one of the few traditional rulers to have retained political power in post-colonial Africa. His main achievements lay in bringing Swaziland to independence in 1968, in regaining land ceded to Europeans, and in creating a flourishing economy. Despite his autocratic rule he was a popular and respected leader.

Sobhuza was proclaimed king of the Swazi nation upon the death of his father, King Bhunu, soon after his birth. His grandmother Gwamile acted as regent until his coronation in 1921. He was also known as Ngwnyama ('the Lion').

Sobukwe, Robert (1924–1977)

South African nationalist leader. Originally a member of the African National Congress (ANC) Youth League, he was dismissed from his teaching post in 1952 because of his participation in the defiance campaign, and in 1959 helped found the Pan-Africanist Congress (PAC), being elected its president. The PAC was banned in 1960 and he was imprisoned until 1969.

Sobukwe was educated at Fort Hare College, and became president of the Students' Representative Council in 1949; he later taught at Fort Hare from 1952 to 1959.

Soglo, Nicéphore (1934–)

Benin politician, prime minister 1990–91, and president 1991–96. He first became prominent as inspector general of finances at the Benin finance ministry and as a governor of the International Monetary Fund. As leader of the Benin Renaissance Party, he was prime minister of a transitional national executive council after a civilian coup in 1990, and became president in a coalition government from 1991 to October 1996.

Soglo was born in Lomé, Togo, and educated at the Sorbonne in Paris.

Sokomanu, Ati George (1937–)

Vanuatuan politician, president 1980–88. Upon becoming president, he caused a constitutional crisis in December 1988 when he dismissed Walter ◊Lini, the prime minister since 1980; dissolved parliament; and appointed his nephew, Barak Sope, who had been expelled from parliament in July 1988, as head of an interim administration. The Vanuatu Supreme Court ruled that these actions had been unconstitutional and Sokomanu and Sope were arrested by security forces loyal to Lini, who was restored to office. Sokomanu was replaced as president by Fred ◊Timakata and in March 1989 Sokomanu was sentenced to six years' imprisonment. However, the Court of Appeal quashed this sentence and Sokomanu was released in April 1989. He served as secretary general of the South Pacific Commission 1992–95, and was a deputy prime minister and home affairs minister in the government of Maxime ◊ Carlot Korman, leader of the Francophone Union of Moderate Parties (UMP), 1994–95.

Prior to independence, in 1980, Sokomanu served as a deputy chief minister and interior minister, when Vanuatu was known as the New Hebrides.

Somare, Michael Thomas (1936–)

Papua New Guinea centre-left politician, chief minister 1972–75, and prime minister 1975–80 and 1982–85. He founded the pro-independence centre-left Pangu Pati (PP; Papua New Guinea Party) in 1967. After independence in 1975, Somare became prime minister, heading a coalition government. He was forced to resign in March 1980 in the wake of a government corruption scandal, but returned as prime minister after the June 1982 general election, heading a new coalition government. This coalition fell apart in 1985, after the deputy prime minister, Paias ◊ Wingti, resigned to join forces with the opposition, and Somare's tax-raising budget strategy came under attack. In November 1985 Somare was defeated on a no-confidence vote and Wingti became prime minister. In 1988 Somare stepped down as PP leader and became foreign minister in the government of Rabbie ◊ Namaliu, and remained in this post until 1992. He resigned from the PP in 1993 and later formed the National Alliance (NA) to campaign against corruption. The NA polled strongly in the June 1997 general election, but Somare failed in his bid to challenge Bill ◊ Skate, leader of the People's National Congress (PNC), for the premiership. He was knighted in 1990.

Born in Rabaul, in East New Britain Province, the son of a police sergeant, Somare was educated at Sogeri High School. He worked initially as a teacher 1956–62 and then a journalist 1966–68. He was elected to the house of assembly a year later and in 1972 became chief minister.

Somoza Debayle, Anastasio (1925–1980)

Nicaraguan soldier and politician, president 1967–72 and 1974–79. The second son of Anastasio ◊ Somoza García, he followed in the footsteps of his brother Luis ◊ Somoza Debayle as president of Nicaragua in 1967, to head an even more oppressive and corrupt regime, characterized by tightened press censorship and rising popular discontent as the economic situation deteriorated. He was removed by Sandinista guerrillas in 1979 and assassinated in Paraguay in 1980.

Trained at the US military academy West Point, he joined the Nicaraguan national guard (which combined military and police power), becoming its commander from 1955.

Somoza Debayle, Luis (1923–1967)

Nicaraguan nationalist liberal politician, president 1956–63. He took over the presidency on the assassination of his father, Anastasio ◊ Somoza Garcia. He introduced a number of social reforms, including low-cost housing and land reform, and reduced the level of political repression, but remained a staunch anti-Communist, supporting the USA in its 1961 Bay of Pigs invasion of Cuba.

As he had promised, Somoza Debayle did not seek re-election at the end of his presidential term in 1963. However, his successor, René Schick Gutiérrez, was his close associate. Somoza Debayle subsequently served in the senate, leading the Liberal Party, until his sudden death in April 1967 from a heart attack.

The oldest and most liberal son of the dictator Anastasio ◊ Somoza García, he studied at universities and military academies in the USA before returning to Nicaragua to become a colonel in the national guard. In 1950 he entered the Nicaraguan congress as a nationalist liberal.

Somoza García, Anastasio (1896–1956)

Nicaraguan soldier and politician, president 1937–47 and 1950–56. A protégé of the USA, who wanted a reliable ally to protect their interests in Central America, he was virtual dictator of Nicaragua from 1937 until his assassination in 1956. He exiled most of his political opponents and amassed a considerable fortune in land and businesses. Members of his family retained control of the country until 1979, when they were overthrown by popular forces.

Song Jiaoren or *Sung Chiao-jen* (1882–1913)

Chinese revolutionary and champion of parliamentary government. Song was the principal spokesperson of the Kuomintang (Guomindang; nationalist party) in the elections of 1912, carrying out a vigorous western-style electioneering campaign which called for a figurehead presidency, a responsible cabinet system, and local autonomy. The Kuomintang won the elections and Song was widely tipped to become prime minister. His programme, however, was a direct challenge to the hegemonic ambitions of the president, ◊ Yuan Shikai, and he was assassinated at Shanghai railway station by Yuan's henchmen.

Before 1911 Song was one of the leading members of ◊ Sun Zhong Shan's (Sun Yat-sen's) revolutionary anti-Manchu organization, the Tongmenghui (T'ungmenghui, Alliance League), helping to set up a branch in central China. On the establishment of a republic in 1912, the Tongmenghui was transformed into the Kuomintang.

Sonnino, (Giorgio) Sidney, Baron Sonnino (1847–1922)

Italian politician and diplomat, prime minister in 1906 and 1909–10. As foreign minister 1914–20 he was responsible, with Prime Minister Antonio Salandra (1853–1941), for bringing Italy into World War I on the side of the Allies. He later attended the postwar conference in Paris with the Italian delegation.

Sonnino was born in Pisa of an English mother. He entered parliament in 1880 and occupied various ministerial posts during his early career, including that of treasury minister 1894–96.

Soong, T V (Tse-Ven) or *Tzu-Wen Sung* or *Ziwen Song* (1894–1971)

Chinese nationalist financier and politician. He was finance minister of the nationalist government at Guangzhou (Canton) 1925–27 and at Nanjing 1928–33. He westernized Chinese finances, standardized the Chinese currency, and founded the Bank of China in 1936. Soong was foreign minister 1942–45. In 1949, following the Communist revolution, he went to the USA.

Born in Shanghai, he was the son of Charles Jones Soong (died 1927), a successful US-educated trader and Methodist missionary who was the father of Soong Ching-ling (Sung Quingling). He studied at Harvard and Columbia universities, in the USA.

His sister, Soong Mei-ling (Sung Meiling, born 1897), married Jiang Jie Shi (Chiang Kai-shek) in 1927.

Soong Ching-ling or *Sung Qingling* (1890–1981)

Chinese politician, wife of the Kuomintang (Guomindang) nationalist leader ◊Sun Zhong Shan (Sun Yatsen); she remained a prominent figure in Chinese politics after his death, being appointed one of the three non-communist vice chairs of the People's Republic of China in 1950, and serving as acting head of state of communist China 1976–78.

Born in Guangdong province, the second daughter of Charles Jones Soong (died 1927), a successful US-educated trader and Methodist missionary, she studied at the Wesleyan College for Women, in Macon, Georgia, in the USA, securing a degree in 1913. She returned to become Sun Zhong Shan's secretary and the couple were married in 1914. Following Sun's death, in 1925, she lived in Europe between 1927 and 1931 and in 1932 founded the China League for Civil Rights. When Shanghai fell to the Japanese in 1937, Sung went to Hong Kong, where she established the China Defence League to promote resistance. With a reputation for left-wing activism, Sung remained in mainland China after the Communist victory in 1949 and became a bitter opponent of Jiang Jie Shi (Chiang Kai-shek), who was married to her younger sister, Soong Mei-ling.

Souphanouvong, Prince (1902–1995)

Laotian politician, president 1975–86. After an abortive revolt against French rule in 1945, he led the

Soong Ching-ling. *Rex*

guerrilla organization Pathet Lao (Land of the Lao), and in 1975 became the first president of the Republic of Laos.

Souphanouvong was born in Louangphrabang, the youngest of the 22 sons of Prince Boun Khong, the *uparat* (or regent) in the royal house. He became attracted to radical politics while studying civil engineering in Paris. On his return to Laos in 1938, while working as a civil engineer for the French colonial authorities, he opposed the re-establishment of French control after the close of World War II.

He joined the Lao Issara (Free Laos) nationalist movement in 1946 and spent the period to 1949 in exile in Thailand. When moderate elements within the Lao Issara, including his half-brother Prince Souvanna Phouma, made a semi-autonomy agreement with France in 1949, Souphanouvong joined the Vietminh, or Communist Party of Indochina, which was dominated by Vietnamese communists. The Pathet Lao was formed by Souphanouvong in 1950 as a Laotian breakaway.

Assisted by North Vietnam, the Pathet Lao spent much of the next 15 years waging a guerrilla war, first against the French (to 1954) and then, after independence, against the rightist pro-Western regime, which was headed from 1958 by Souvanna Phouma. By contrast with his half-brother, Souphanouvong was dubbed the 'Red Prince'.

In 1975 Souphanouvong, who had briefly held positions in coalition governments formed in 1957–58, 1962, and 1973, became the first president of the communist Lao People's Democratic Republic. This was largely a ceremonial position and the real controlling force in the new state was Kaysone Phomvihane, leader of the Lao People's Revolutionary Party (LPRP). Souphanouvong stepped down in 1986 as head of state, but remained a member of the LPRP's ruling politburo until 1991.

Soustelle, Jacques (1912–)

French scholar and politician. He joined Charles ◊de Gaulle in London, England, during World War II, and became minister for information in 1945. He was the leading Gaullist deputy, and was governor general in Algeria. He played a leading part in the events of 1958 that led to the establishment of the Fifth Republic. He quarrelled with de Gaulle over Algerian policy, and was exiled 1962–68.

Soustelle was born in Montpellier, France. He was educated at the Ecole Normale Superieure. He is an expert on Aztec civilizations.

Souter, David Hackett (1939–)

US jurist, appointed as associate justice of the US Supreme Court by President George Bush in 1990.

Born in Melrose, Massachusetts, Souter graduated from Harvard College, received a Rhodes scholarship to Oxford University, and graduated from the Harvard Law School. After private practice in New Hampshire, Souter served as state assistant and deputy attorney general before being appointed state attorney general in 1976.

He became a judge on the state trial court in 1978 and was named to the state supreme court in 1983. He was appointed by President Bush to the US Court of Appeals for the First Circuit in 1990 and to the Supreme Court later in the same year.

Soyinka, Wole, pen name of Akinwande Oluwole Soyinka (1934–)

Nigerian author and dramatist. His plays explore Yoruba myth, ritual, and culture, with the early *Swamp Dwellers* (1958) and *The Lion and the Jewel* (1959), culminating with *A Dance of the Forests* (1960), written as a tragic vision of Nigerian independence. Tragic

---

◆ SOUSA, HERBERT DE, KNOWN AS 'BETINHO' (1935–1997) ◆

Brazilian sociologist, social activist, and campaigner. Born in Bocaiúva, Minas Gerais state, he became renowned as a leading social commentator and activist against the hunger and misery that Brazil suffered in the 20th century. A militant opponent of the military dictatorships, Sousa transformed his political ideas into concrete actions even after the return of democracy. He actively campaigned for human rights, for agricultural reform, for the control of AIDS, and – most notably – against hunger.

A graduate in sociology and politics from the Federal University of Minais Gerais, Sousa was a cofounder of the left-wing Ação Popular (Popular Action) – a clandestine political organization. From 1964 he was active in the resistance movement against the military regime, until he was forced into exile in Chile in 1970. While in Chile, he advised and also assisted the future president Salvador Allende. With the rise in repression following the 1973 military coup, he left Chile and lived in Canada, Scotland, and Mexico. After an amnesty in 1979, he returned to Brazil and, two years later, helped to cofound the Instituto Brasileiro de Análises Sociais e Econômicas (IBASE; Brazilian Institute for Social and Economic Analysis), a nongovernmental organization that develops awareness campaigns and policies aimed at alleviating socio-economic

deprivation and injustice. He later became its president.

A haemophiliac, Sousa contracted the HIV virus in 1986 through a routine blood transfusion and, in 1988, lost his two brothers (also haemophiliacs), who had also contracted the virus. Sousa, who was president of the Associação Brasileira Interdisciplinar da AIDS (ABIA; Brazilian Interdisciplinary Association of AIDS), actively campaigned for more controls on blood supplies.

Sousa was also responsible for the creation, in 1992, of a national campaign against hunger, Citizens' Action against Poverty and Hunger and for Life (more commonly called the Campaign of Hunger). This campaign involved working with business people, performing artists, politicians, and landowners to gather the necessary financial resources to make his campaign a success.

In recognition of his humanitarian work, under President Fernando Henrique ◊Cardoso he was made a member of the Conselha da Communidade Solidária (Community Solidarity Council). In 1991, he received the United Nations' Global 500 Prize for his role in the struggle for native Indians and his demands for agrarian reform within Brazil. The following year, he was awarded the National Prize for Human Rights. He died in 1997, after a struggle against hepatitis C.

inevitability is the theme of *Madmen and Specialists* (1970) and of *Death and the King's Horseman* (1976), but he has also written sharp satires, from *The Jero Plays* (1960 and 1973) to the indictment of African dictatorship in *A Play of Giants* (1984). In 1986 he was the first African to receive the Nobel Prize for Literature. A volume of poetry, *From Zia with Love*, appeared in 1992.

Soyinka was a political prisoner in Nigeria 1967–69, during the civil war. He was charged with treason by the Nigerian government in March 1997 over a spate of bomb blasts in the country, but the charge was dropped in May 1998 after the death of President Sani Abacha, and Soyinka was allowed to visit Nigeria in September that year.

Spaak, Paul-Henri (1899–1972)

Belgian socialist politician. From 1936 to 1966 he held office almost continuously as foreign minister or prime minister. He was an ardent advocate of international peace.

FURTHER READING

Huizinga, J H *Mr Europe: A Political Biography of Paul-Henri Spaak*
Spaak, Paul-Henri *The Continuing Battle: Memoirs of a European, 1936–1966* 1971

Speer, Albert (1905–1981)

German architect and minister in the Nazi government during World War II. He was appointed Hitler's architect and, like his counterparts in Fascist Italy, chose an overblown Classicism to glorify the state, for example, his plan for the Berlin and Nürnberg Party Congress Grounds in 1934. He built the New Reich Chancellery, Berlin, 1938–39 (now demolished), but his designs for an increasingly megalomaniac series of buildings in a stark Classical style were never realized.

As armaments minister he raised the index of arms production from 100 in January 1942 to 322 by July 1944. In the latter months of the war he concentrated on frustrating Hitler's orders for the destruction of German industry in the face of the advancing Allies. After the war, he was sentenced to 20 years' imprisonment for his employment of slave labour. His memoirs, *Inside the Third Reich* (1969), gave a highly influential account of the period, but in portraying their author as a technocrat they understated his participation in the Nazi project.

FURTHER READING

Sereny, Gitta *Albert Speer: His Battle with Truth* 1995

Spence, William Guthrie (1846–1926)

Australian labour leader and politician, born in Orkney, Scotland. He founded the Australian Workers' Union in 1894, amalgamating the shearers' and rural workers' unions. From 1901 to 1917 he was a Labor member of the House of Representatives and a member of Andrew Fisher's ministry during World War I. After a split over conscription, which he supported, he represented the Nationalist Party 1917–19. His book *Australia's Awakening* (1909) expounded the principle of industrial unionism.

> *Unionism came to the Australian bushman as a religion. It came bringing salvation from years of tyranny.*
> WILLIAM GUTHRIE SPENCE *Australia's Awakening*, 1909

His family migrated to Victoria, Australia, in 1852, and his early work as a shepherd and gold miner and his Presbyterian faith helped him develop a strong social conscience. He founded the Creswick Miners Union in 1878 and the Amalgamated Shearers Union in 1886, and led a shearers' strike in 1891.

Spencer, George Alfred (1873–1957)

Britsh miners' leader and Labour politician. He became president of the Nottinghamshire Miners Association in 1912 and was Labour member of Parliament for Broxtowe 1918–29. He was opposed to the militant line taken by A J ◊Cook, as secretary of the Miners Federation of Great Britain (MFGB), from 1925, and when the mining crisis precipitated the 1926 General Strike, Spencer formed a breakaway union that was supported by coalowners and opposed by the federation.

Spencer's union survived until 1937, when it merged with the old association to become the Nottinghamshire Miners Federated Union. Spencer was its president until 1945.

Spencer was born in Nottinghamshire and entered the mines aged 12. Although left-wing in the immediate aftermath of the war, Spencer believed the Nottinghamshire association might best negotiate its own terms without the Federation. For this, he was described by Herbert Smith in October 1926 as 'a coward'.

Spencer did not wish unions to have political ties and in this he was supported by a minority of others such as the seamen's union leader, Havelock Wilson. Spencer also served on the executive of the MFGB in 1942 and opposed the nationalization of the mines in 1946.

Spinelli, Altiero (1907–1989)

Italian journalist, politician, and proponent of European federalism. An early anti-Fascist activist, he was co-author of the Ventonene manifesto in 1941, the clarion call of the European Federalist Movement, which he founded in 1943. He served as a member of the European Commission 1967–70, the Italian chamber of deputies 1976–79, and the European Parliament

1976–87. His principal achievement was the draft treaty establishing the European Union in 1984.

As a member of the European Parliament he joined the Communist group, although he had long ceased to belong to the Italian Communist Party.

Spring, Dick (Richard) (1950–)

Irish Labour Party leader from 1982. He entered into a coalition with Garret ◊FitzGerald's Fine Gael in 1982 as deputy prime minister (with the posts of minister for the environment 1982–83 and minister for energy 1983–87). In 1993 he became deputy prime minister to Albert ◊Reynolds in a Fianna Fáil–Labour Party coalition, with the post of minister for foreign affairs. He withdrew from the coalition in November 1994 in protest over a judicial appointment made by Reynolds, and the following month formed a new coalition with Fine Gael, with John Bruton as prime minister, in power until 1997.

Springsteen, Bruce (1949–)

US rock singer, songwriter, and guitarist. His music combines melodies in traditional rock idiom and reflective lyrics about working-class life and the pursuit of the American dream on such albums as *Born to Run* (1975), *Born in the USA* (1984), and *Human Touch* (1992). Springsteen's philanthropy is legendary – he donated thousands of dollars to women's groups in the UK in 1983 during the miners' strike, and he headlined Amnesty International's World Tour in 1988.

Born in New Jersey, USA, Springsteen's early life was dominated by his working-class surroundings, his parents regularly out of work or in poorly paid jobs. He learned to play piano and guitar by himself after rejecting formal music lessons and signed to Columbia records in 1972, releasing his first album *Greetings from Asbury Park* later that year. Often compared to Bob Dylan in the early years, he eventually attained superstardom in 1975 with his album *Born to Run*. Regular releases of inspired story-telling and small-town evocation followed.

Although Springsteen had declared himself for the Democrats, the title track from *Born in the USA* was used by the Republican party in the 1984 Presidential election. Ronald Reagan is quoted as having said, 'America's future rests in a thousand dreams inside your heart. It rests in the message of hope in the songs of a man so many young Americans admire, New Jersey's Bruce Springsteen'.

FURTHER READING
Cullen, Jim *Born in the USA* 1997

Starr, Kenneth Winston (1946–)
See page 409.

Stauffenberg, Claus von (1907–1944)

German colonel in World War II who, in a conspiracy to assassinate Hitler (the July Plot), planted a bomb in the dictator's headquarters conference room in the Wolf's Lair at Rastenburg, East Prussia, on 20 July

---

◆ STALIN (RUSSIAN 'STEEL'), JOSEPH, ADOPTED NAME OF JOSEPH VISSARIONOVICH DJUGASHVILI (1879–1953) ◆

Soviet politician. A member of the October Revolution committee of 1917, Stalin became general secretary of the Communist Party in 1922. After Vladimir ◊Lenin's death in 1924, Stalin sought to create 'socialism in one country' and clashed with Leon ◊Trotsky, who denied the possibility of socialism inside Russia until revolution had occurred in Western Europe. Stalin won this ideological struggle by 1927, and a series of five-year plans was launched to collectivize industry and agriculture from 1928. All opposition was eliminated in the Great Purge 1936–38. During World War II, Stalin intervened in the military direction of the campaigns against Nazi Germany. He managed not only to bring the USSR through the war but to help it emerge as a superpower, although only at an immense cost in human suffering to his own people. After the war, Stalin quickly turned Eastern Europe into a series of Soviet satellites and maintained an autocratic

rule domestically. His role was denounced after his death by Nikita Khrushchev and other members of the Soviet regime.

> *It will unmake our work. No greater instrument of counter-revolution and conspiracy can be imagined.*
> JOSEPH STALIN On the telephone, quoted in L D Trotsky *Life of Stalin*

Stalin was born in Georgia, the son of a shoemaker. Educated for the priesthood, he was expelled from his seminary for Marxist propaganda. He became a member of the Social Democratic Party in 1898, and joined Lenin and the Bolsheviks in 1903. He was repeatedly exiled to Siberia 1903–13. He then became a member of the Communist Party's Politburo, and sat on the

1944. Hitler was merely injured, and Stauffenberg and 200 others were later executed by the Nazi regime.

Steel, David Martin Scott (1938–)

British politician, leader of the Liberal Party 1976–88, born in Kirkaldy, Fife, Scotland. He entered into a compact with the Labour government 1977–78, and into an alliance with the Social Democratic Party (SDP) in 1983. Having supported the Liberal–SDP merger (forming the Social and Liberal Democrats), he resigned the leadership in 1988, becoming the party's foreign affairs spokesperson. At the 1994 party conference, he announced that he would not seek re-election to the next parliament. He is the president of Liberal International. He entered the House of Lords in 1997. He was knighted in 1990.

FURTHER READING
Bartram, Peter *David Steel: His Life and Politics* 1981

Stefanik, Milan Ratislav (1884–1919)

Slovakian general. He joined the French army as a private soldier in 1914 and rapidly rose to the rank of general. He went to the Italian front in 1916 and flew several missions to drop propaganda pamphlets on Czech troops in the Austro-Hungarian army. Active in rallying Czech and Slovak troops from all areas, he worked with the Czech legion in Siberia in 1918 and, on the formation of the Czechoslovakian republic in

October Revolution committee. Stalin rapidly consolidated a powerful following (including Vyacheslav Molotov); in 1921 he became commissar for nationalities in the Soviet government, responsible for the decree granting equal rights to all peoples of the Russian Empire, and was appointed general secretary of the Communist Party in 1922. As dictator in the 1930s, he disposed of all real and imagined enemies. His anti-Semitism caused, for example, the execution of 19 Jewish activists in 1952 for a 'Zionist conspiracy'. See photograph on page 408.

FURTHER READING
Jonge, Alex de *Stalin and the Shaping of the Soviet Union* 1986
McNeal, R H *Stalin* 1988
Richards, Michael *Stalin* 1979
Smith, E E *The Young Stalin* 1967
Tucker, R C *Stalin in Power* 1990
Ulam, Adam *Stalin* 1973
Urban, George *Stalinism* 1982

1918, he became commander in chief and war minister. He was killed in a flying accident while on his way to Prague.

Steffens, (Joseph) Lincoln (1866–1936)

US investigative journalist. Intent on exposing corruption and fraud in high places, he initiated the style known as 'muckraking' while working for *McClure's* magazine. He later covered the Mexican Revolution and befriended the Soviet leader Lenin.

> *I have seen the future; and it works.*
> LINCOLN STEFFENS Of the newly formed Soviet Union, in a letter to Marie Howe, 3 April 1919

Steinbeck, John Ernst (1902–1968)

US novelist. His realist novels, such as *In Dubious Battle* (1936), *Of Mice and Men* (1937), and *The Grapes of Wrath* (1939; Pulitzer prize; filmed 1940), portray agricultural life in his native California, where migrant farm labourers from the Oklahoma dust bowl struggled to survive. He was awarded the Nobel Prize for Literature in 1962.

FURTHER READING
Benson, J J *The True Adventures of John Steinbeck, Writer* 1984
Levant, H *The Novels of John Steinbeck: A Critical Study* 1975
Reef, Catherine *John Steinbeck* 1996

Steinem, Gloria (1934–)

US journalist and liberal feminist. She emerged as a leading figure in the US women's movement in the late 1960s. She was also involved in radical protest campaigns against racism and the Vietnam War. She cofounded the Women's Action Alliance in 1970 and *Ms* magazine. In 1983 a collection of her articles was published as *Outrageous Acts and Everyday Rebellions*.

> *We are becoming the men we wanted to marry.*
> GLORIA STEINEM *Ms* July/August 1982

FURTHER READING
Stern, Sydney Ladensohn *Gloria Steinem* 1997

Stettinius, Edward Riley (1900–1949)

US business executive and diplomat. During World War II, President F D Roosevelt appointed him lend-lease administrator. He was made secretary of state in 1944, and was chief adviser to Roosevelt at the Yalta Conference of 1945.

Stettinius was born in Chicago and educated at Virginia University. In 1926 he joined General Motors, becoming vice president of the company in 1931. In 1934 he moved to the US Steel Corporation, and

Stalin with President Franklin D Roosevelt and Prime Minister Winston Churchill at the Tehran Conference, 1943. *Rex*

subsequently became chair of its board of directors. He became undersecretary of state in 1943, before succeeding Cordell Hull as secretary of state the following year. His work at the Inter-American Conference in Mexico City confirmed his abilities as a negotiator, and he was appointed, by President Harry Truman, the first US delegate to the United Nations conference in San Francisco. In 1946 he returned to business.

He wrote *Lease-Lend: Weapon for Victory* (1944), and *Roosevelt and the Russians: The Yalta Conference* (1949).

Stevens, John Paul (1920–)

US jurist and associate justice of the US Supreme Court from 1975, appointed by President Gerald Ford. A moderate whose opinions and dissents were wide-ranging, he opined that the death penalty is not by definition cruel and unusual punishment in *Jurek v Texas* (1976), and that the burning of the US flag in protest is unconstitutional in *Texas v Johnson*.

Stevens, Siaka Probin (1905–1988)

Sierra Leone politician, president 1971–85. He was the leader of the moderate left-wing All People's Congress (APC), from 1978 the country's only legal political party.

Stevens became prime minister in 1968, and in 1971, under a revised constitution, became Sierra Leone's first president. He created a one-party state based on the APC, and remained in power until his retirement at the age of 80.

Born of mixed ethnic origins in the north of the country, he joined the colonial police force in 1923. After leaving the police he became a trade-union activist and was a founder of the Sierra Leone People's Party (SLPP) in 1951. After success in the 1957 elections, Stephens quarrelled with the SLPP leadership and left the government. In 1960 he founded the APC and won the 1967 elections. After his retirement in 1985 he wrote his autobiography, *What Life Has Taught Me*.

Stevenson, Adlai Ewing (1900–1965)

US Democratic politician. As governor of Illinois 1949–53 he campaigned vigorously against corruption in public life, and as Democratic candidate for the presidency in 1952 and 1956 was twice defeated by Dwight D Eisenhower. In 1945 he was chief US delegate at the founding conference of the United Nations.

Stevenson was born in Los Angeles. He was educated

> *I have been thinking that I would make a proposition to my Republican friends ... that if they will stop telling lies about the Democrats, we will stop telling the truth about them.*
>
> ADLAI STEVENSON Speech during 1952 presidential campaign

at Princeton University, and Northwestern University Law School, and went on to be admitted to the bar in 1926.

FURTHER READING
Cochran, Bert *Adlai Stevenson* 1969
Darling, Grace and David *Stevenson* 1977
Sievers, R M *The Last Puritan? Adlai E Stevenson* 1983

Stewart, (Robert) Michael (Maitland), Baron Stewart of Fulham (1906–1990)

British Labour politician, member of Parliament 1945–79. He held ministerial office in the governments of Clement Attlee and Harold Wilson, rising to foreign secretary in 1968.

Stewart was born in Bromley, Kent. He became member of Parliament for Fulham in 1945. He soon entered Clement Attlee's government, rising from a junior whip in 1945 to secretary of state for war in 1951. His quietly spoken, schoolmasterish image disguised a strong political determination, a quality recognized by Harold Wilson, who made him education secretary 1966–67, and then foreign secretary in 1968. He remained in the House of Commons until 1979, when he accepted a life peerage.

Stewart, Potter (1915–1985)

US jurist, appointed associate justice of the US Supreme Court 1958–81 by President Dwight D Eisenhower. Seen as a moderate, he was known for upholding civil rights for minorities and for opinions on criminal procedure. He dissented in both *Escabedo* v *Illinois* (1964) and in *In re Gault* (1967), which gave juveniles due process rights.

Born in Chicago, Illinois, Stevens graduated from Yale University and Yale Law School and entered private practice in New York City and Cincinnati, Ohio. He was appointed judge of the US Court of Appeals for the Sixth Circuit in 1954.

Stilwell, Joseph Warren, known as 'Vinegar Joe' (1883–1946)

US general in World War II. In 1942 he became US military representative in China, when he commanded the Chinese forces cooperating with the British (with whom he quarrelled) in Burma (now Myanmar). He

---

◆ STARR, KENNETH WINSTON (1946–) ◆

US attorney and judge. Starr's role as independent counsel in charge of the Whitewater investigation led to the impeachment of US president Bill ◊Clinton on 19 December 1998, after Starr expanded his investigation in January 1998 to include allegations of an affair between President Clinton and White House intern Monica Lewinsky. His report on the affair was published on the Internet in 1998.

Starr was born in Texas, the youngest of three children, and raised with deep religious convictions. His father was a Baptist minister and Starr planned to follow his father into the ministry but then switched his interest to political science and attended law school at Duke University. At the age of 27, Starr became a clerk to former Supreme Court Justice Warren ◊Burger. Here he gained a reputation as a workaholic and within a decade he was the youngest judge ever appointed to the US Circuit Court of Appeals for the District of Columbia.

Though conservative in his rulings he had an independent streak that pleased civil libertarians. At 37 he was appointed by President Ronald ◊Reagan to the US Court of Appeals. At President George ◊Bush's request, he reluctantly left the bench in 1989 to become solicitor general. In his first tough case Starr ruled against President Bush, which is thought to have been a factor in his being overlooked as Supreme Court Justice in 1990, his life-long ambition. In 1993 he returned to private practice.

Starr accepted the job of independent counsel in the Whitewater investigation after attorney general Janet Reno's choice of Robert Fiske, Jr, was deemed too partisan. The investigation quickly expanded from analysing financial records to include the suicide of White House official Vince Foster, the firing of seven White House Travel Office employees, the alleged misuse of FBI background files and whether the president, first lady Hillary Clinton, or White House aides had lied under oath. Starr, working with an unlimited budget, won several convictions, but the Clintons went unscathed. In February 1997 Starr announced that he would resign as special prosecutor to take a job as a law school dean at California's Pepperdine University but he withdrew his resignation days later, expanding the Whitewater investigation yet again to expose Bill Clinton's affair with Monica Lewinsky.

later commanded all US forces in China, Burma, and India until recalled to the USA in 1944 after differences over nationalist policy with the Kuomintang (Guomindang; nationalist) leader Jiang Jie Shie (Chiang Kaishek). Subsequently he commanded the US 10th Army on the Japanese island of Okinawa.

Born in Palatka, Florida, Stilwell graduated from West Point military academy in 1904. He served in the Philippines 1904–06, and was an instructor at West Point 1906–10. He then served in China, and studied the Chinese language, making him one of the foremost US authorities on Chinese life. In World War I he served in France.

He sought the engagement of 30 divisions of Chinese nationalist troops in battle against the Japanese. Jiang Jie Shie refused, preferring to reserve his forces for use against the Chinese Communists in the anticipated Chinese civil war. At Jiang's insistence, President F D ◊Roosevelt recalled Stilwell, giving him command of the US 10th Army on Okinawa.

Stimson, Henry Lewis (1867–1950)

US politician. He was war secretary in President William Taft's cabinet 1911–13, Herbert Hoover's secretary of state 1929–33, and war secretary 1940–45.

As secretary of state, he formulated the **Stimson Doctrine** of non-recognition of territories and agreements obtained by acts of aggression. He headed the US delegation to the London Naval Conference in 1930, and was a member of the Permanent Court of Arbitration at The Hague in 1938.

Stimson was born in New York City, and educated at Yale and Harvard universities. He became a barrister in New York City in 1891, and was US attorney for the Southern district of New York State 1906–09. During World War I he served in the army. His publications include *Democracy and Nationalism in Europe* (1934), *The Far Eastern Crisis* (1936), and his memoirs, *On Active Service in Peace and War* (with M Bundy) (1948).

Stone, Harlan Fiske (1872–1946)

US jurist. He was associate justice to the US Supreme Court 1925–41 and chief justice 1941–46 under President Franklin D Roosevelt. During World War II he authored opinions favouring federal war powers and the regulation of aliens.

As an associate justice, Stone favoured judicial restraint, the making of decisions on constitutional rather than personal grounds. He dissented from numerous conservative decisions opposing President Roosevelt's New Deal legislation. He supported voting rights and the use of the Constitution's commerce clause to justify federal legislation regulating interstate commerce.

Stone, Oliver (1946–)

US film director, screenwriter, and producer. Although working in Hollywood's mainstream, he has tackled social and political themes, for example in *Born on the Fourth of July* (1989) (war veterans), *Wall Street* (1987) (finance), and the epic-scaled *JFK* (1991) (President Kennedy).

Stone won his first Academy Award for his screenplay for *Midnight Express* (1978). His other film credits include *Scarface* (1983) (screenplay), *Salvador* (1986) (director, screenplay, producer), his trilogy of films on the Vietnam War (*Platoon* (1986), *Born on the Fourth of July*, and *Heaven and Earth* (1993), the biography of a Vietnamese woman), *Reversal of Fortune* (1990) (producer), and *The Doors* (1991) (director, screenplay). *Natural Born Killers* (1994) is an ultraviolent satire on media irresponsibility.

Stonehouse, John Thomson (1925–1988)

British Labour Party politician. An active member of the Cooperative Movement, he entered Parliament in 1957 and held junior posts under Harold Wilson before joining his cabinet in 1967. In 1974 he disappeared in Florida in mysterious circumstances, surfacing in Australia amid suspicions of fraudulent dealings. Extradited to Britain, he was tried and imprisoned for embezzlement. He was released in 1979, but was unable to resume a political career.

Stopes, Marie Charlotte Carmichael (1880–1958)

Scottish birth-control campaigner. With her second husband H V Roe (1878–1949), an aircraft manufacturer, she founded Britain's first birth-control clinic in London in 1921. In her best-selling manual *Married Love* (1918) she urged women to enjoy sexual intercourse within their marriage, a revolutionary view for the time. She also wrote plays and verse.

Her other works include *Wise Parenthood* (1918) and *Radiant Motherhood* (1921).

Stoph, Willi (1914–)

East German politician. The leading economist in the ruling East German party after World War II, he became a member of its central committee in 1950 and of East Germany's Politburo in 1953. He also helped develop the police and the army in the German Democratic Republic, and succeeded Otto Grotewohl as its president in 1964. Stoph's meetings with Willy Brandt in 1970 helped to inaugurate the latter's Ostpolitik. Stoph was born in Berlin, Germany.

Stoutt, Hamilton Lavity (1929–1995)

British Virgin Islands centre-right politician, chief minister 1967–71, 1979–83, and 1986–95. He became leader of the Virgin Islands' Party (VIP) and the territory's first chief minister in 1967, but lost power to the United Party (UP) in 1971. Appointed minister for natural resources and public health in 1975, and re-elected as chief minister in 1979, he was in opposition to Cyril Romney's administration from 1983. He regained office in 1986 and election as chief minister in 1990 and 1995. Stoutt promoted the tourist industry, and introduced tougher regulation of the offshore financial sector 1990–91 to counteract its abuse by drug traffickers.

On Stoutt's unexpected death in May 1995, the deputy chief minister, Ralph O'Neal, took over as chief minister and finance minister.

Stoyanov, Petar (1952–)

Bulgarian politician, member of the Union of Democratic Forces, president from January 1997. In 1992 he became deputy minister of justice, and served as a member of parliament 1994–96.

Educated at Sofia University, he was a former divorce lawyer who only became politically active in 1989, following prodemocratic changes in the country.

Strachey, (Evelyn) John St Loe (1901–1963)

British Labour politician. His controversial period as minister of food 1946–50 included the food crisis of 1947, the unpopular prolongation of rationing, and the abortive Tanganyika groundnuts and Gambia egg schemes 1947–49. As secretary of state for war 1950–51 he had to contend with the Korean War and the communist insurrection in Malaya.

He was born in Guildford, Surrey, and educated at Eton and Magdalen College, Oxford. He was Labour member of Parliament for Aston, Birmingham, from 1929 until 1931, when he resigned from the Labour Party and gave his support to extremist political organizations. He served in the RAF during World War II and in 1945 became Labour undersecretary for air. In 1950 he became member of Parliament for West Dundee.

His publications include *Why You Should Be a Socialist* (1938), *Contemporary Capitalism* (1956), and *End of Empire* (1959).

FURTHER READING
Newman, M *John Strachey* 1989
Thompson, N *John Strachey: An Intellectual Biography* 1993

Strasser, Gregor (1892–1934)

German politician, born in Geisenfeld in Upper Bavaria. He took part in Hitler's putsch of 1923. Later he organized the National Socialist party in the Reichstag (parliament). He lost favour for his radically anticapitalist views. Hitler had him first expelled from the party, then murdered in the 1934 purge.

Strauss, Franz Josef (1915–1988)

German conservative politician, leader of the West German Bavarian Christian Social Union (CSU) party 1961–88, premier of Bavaria 1978–88.

Born and educated in Munich, Strauss, after military service 1939–45, joined the CSU and was elected to the Bundestag (parliament) in 1949. He held ministerial posts during the 1950s and 1960s and became leader of the CSU in 1961. In 1962 he lost his post as minister of defence when he illegally shut down the offices of *Der Spiegel* for a month, after the magazine revealed details of a failed NATO exercise. In the 1970s Strauss opposed Ostpolitik (the policy of reconciliation with the East). He left the Bundestag to become premier of Bavaria in 1978, and was heavily defeated in 1980 as chancellor candidate. From 1982 Strauss sought to force changes in the economic and foreign policy of the coalition under Chancellor Helmut Kohl.

Straw, Jack (1946–)

British Labour lawyer and politician, home secretary from 1997. After graduating in law he qualified as a barrister in 1972. Having unsuccessfully contested the Tonbridge and Malling parliamentary seat in 1972, he became special adviser to the social services secretary, Barbara Castle, 1974–76, and then the environment secretary, Peter Shore, 1976–77. After a short period with Granada Television, he entered the House of Commons, representing Barbara Castle's former constituency of Blackburn. Before this he had served on Islington Borough Council and the Inner London Education Authority (ILEA). He became a member of Labour's front bench team in 1980, and then shadow education secretary 1987–92, shadow environment secretary 1992–94, and shadow home secretary 1994–97.

Born in Buckhurst Hill, Essex, and educated at Leeds University, he first came to public notice as president of the National Union of Students.

Street, Jessie Mary Grey, born Lillingston (1889–1970)

Australian feminist, humanist, peace worker, reformer, and writer. She was involved in the suffragette movement in the UK and later helped to found the Family Planning Association of Australia, and was active in the campaign for equal pay for women. She initiated the movement that resulted in the 1967 referendum that granted citizenship to Australian Aborigines.

Street was born in central India. Her family migrated to Australia in 1896 and she was educated in England and at Sydney University. In 1928 she cofounded the United Association of Women (UAW), a largely middle-class body. In 1945 she successfully lobbied for the United Nations to adopt a charter of women's rights. She stood unsuccessfully for the federal parliament twice, in 1942 and 1949.

Street was married to Kenneth Whistler Street (1890–1970), who was Lieutenant Governor and Chief Justice of New South Wales. Laurence Lillingston

Whistler Street (1926–   ), also Chief Justice of New South Wales, is their son. Her activities were often at odds with the political outlook and social position of her family.

FURTHER READING
Sekuless, P *Jessie Street: A Rewarding but Unrewarding Life* 1978
Street, Jessie *Truth or Repose* 1966

Streicher, Julius (1895–1946)

German politician. After World War I, he began a violent anti-Semitic and nationalistic movement in Nürnberg, Germany. He founded a special weekly paper for 'the struggle for the truth against traitors' entitled *Der Sturmer*, which specialized in Jew-baiting. After Hitler's triumph in 1933 the views of *Der Sturmer* soon prevailed throughout Germany, and when Hitler decided on boycotting Jewish shops, Streicher was made Aktionsführer (riot leader). Later he became governor of Franconia. Streicher was born in Fleinhausen near Augsburg, Germany. He was sentenced to death at the Nürnberg trial in 1946 and executed.

Stresemann, Gustav (1878–1929)

German politician; chancellor in 1923 and foreign minister 1923–29 of the Weimar Republic. During World War I he was a strong nationalist but his views became more moderate under the Weimar Republic. His achievements included reducing the amount of war reparations paid by Germany after the Treaty of Versailles of 1919, negotiating the Locarno Treaties of 1925, and negotiating Germany's admission to the League of Nations. He shared the 1926 Nobel Peace Prize with Aristide Briand.

FURTHER READING
Turner, H A *Stresemann and the Politics of the Weimar Republic* 1963

Strijdom, Johannes Gerhardus (1893–1958)

South African politician. He was prime minister of the Union of South Africa and leader in chief of the National Party 1954–58. Strijdom was member of Parliament for Waterberge 1929–58. He was born in Willowmore, Cape Province, South Africa.

Stroessner, Alfredo (1912–   )

Paraguayan military dictator and president 1954–89. As head of the armed forces from 1951, he seized power from President Federico Chávez in a coup in 1954, sponsored by the right-wing ruling Colorado Party. Accused by his opponents of harsh repression, his regime spent heavily on the military to preserve his authority. Despite criticisms of his government's civil-rights record, he was re-elected seven times and remained in office until ousted in an army-led coup in 1989, after which he gained asylum in Brazil.

FURTHER READING
Americas Watch Staff *Rule by Fear: Paraguay after Thirty Years under Stroessner* 1985
Lewis, Paul H *Paraguay under Stroessner* 1980
Miranda, Carlos R *The Stroessner Era: Authoritarian Rule in Paraguay* 1990

Struve, Petr Berngardovich (1870–1944)

Soviet economist, sociologist, and politician, of German descent. In the 1890s he was the leading Marxist theorist in Russia, and in 1898 drafted the manifesto of the Russian Social Democratic Workers' party.

He soon left Social Democracy and became leader of the constitutional movement of the liberal intelligentsia, editing, in the years 1902–05, its journal, *Liberation*, which was published abroad. In 1905 he returned to Russia and joined the Constitutional Democratic party. In 1907 he became a member of the Second Duma. He took a leading part in the Vekhi movement and advocated the cooperation of liberals with the government. During the Russian Civil War he was minister of foreign affairs in Ferdinand Wrangel's government in the Crimea. Later he emigrated and was prominent in the activities of the moderate Right.

Struve's two main works are the two-volume *Economy and Price* (1913–16) and *Social and Economic History of Russia* (1952).

Sturzo, Luigi (1871–1959)

Italian Catholic political leader and leading opponent of Fascism. Ordained as a priest in 1894, he opposed the church's prohibition on Catholics' participation in Italian electoral politics. He founded the Partito Popolare Italiano (PPI; Italian Popular Party) in 1919 as a mass movement of Catholics devoted to secular reform. Unlike some members of his party, Sturzo opposed collaboration with Fascism, and was declared an enemy of the state in 1923, being forced into exile until 1946. He became a senator in 1952.

Sturzo's exile was spent in London from 1924 to 1940, and in New York between 1940 and 1946.

Suárez González, Adolfo (1932–   )

Spanish politician, prime minister 1976–81. A friend of King Juan Carlos, he was appointed by the king to guide Spain into democracy after the death of the fascist dictator General Francisco Franco.

Suárez became prime minister following a career in the National Movement that spanned 18 years. In 1997 he called and won the first free elections in Spain for more than 40 years as leader of the Union of the Democratic Centre (UCD). He resigned the premiership in 1981, and in the following year founded the Democratic and Social Centre party (CDS).

Suchocka, Hanna (1946–   )

Polish politician, prime minister 1992–93. She was

chosen by President Lech Wałęsa because her una-ligned background won her the support of seven of the eight parties that agreed to join a coalition govern-ment. In 1993 she lost a vote of confidence prior to her centrist coalition being ousted in a general election.

Formerly a lecturer in law, Suchocka served on the legislation committee of the Polish parliament (Sejm), where her abilities brought her to the attention of influential politicians. In 1992 she replaced Prime Minister Waldemar Pawlak, who was unable to form a viable government, but was later, in turn, replaced by Pawlak. She remains an active figure within centre-right politics and is a strong supporter of privatization.

Sudharmono (1927–   )

Indonesian soldier, military lawyer, and politician, vice president 1988–93. Sudharmono was President Thojib ◊Suharto's aide from 1966 and served as sec-retary of state 1973–88 and chair of the government-sponsored Golkar party 1983–88.

Suharto, Thojib I (1921–   )

Indonesian politician and general, president 1967–98. His authoritarian rule met with domestic opposition from the left, but the Indonesian economy enjoyed significant growth until 1997. He was re-elected in 1973, 1978, 1983, 1988, 1993, and, unopposed, in March 1998. This was despite his deteriorating health and the country's economy being weakened by a sharp decline in value of the Indonesian currency, which had provoked student unrest and food riots. After mount-ing civil unrest reached a critical point, on 21 May 1998 he handed over the presidency to the vice president, Bacharuddin Jusuf Habibie. It was reported in late May that Suharto and his children might face pros-ecution for corruption and misuse of power.

Formerly Chief of Staff under Achmed ◊Sukarno, he dealt harshly with a left-wing attempt to unseat his predecessor and then assumed power himself. He ended confrontation with Malaysia, invaded East Timor in 1975, and reached a cooperation agreement with Papua New Guinea in 1979. After being elected to his seventh five-year term in early March 1998, Suharto was granted additional powers to maintain national unity and deal with the economic crisis. He remained opposed to economic reforms demanded by his critics and supported by the International Monetary Fund (IMF) and formed a new 'family cabinet' composed of relatives and close associates.

Suhrawardy, Hussein Shaheed (1893–1963)

Indian and Pakistani politician, prime minister of Pakistan 1956–57. In 1945 he became chief minister of the Muslim League, which argued for the partition of India after the British left. In 1946 he was elected chief minister of Bengal in a landslide victory and was in large part responsible for the deaths in August 1946 of hundreds of Hindu workers by middle-class Muslims in what is known as 'The Great Calcutta Killing'.

Trained in Calcutta and Oxford as a lawyer, Suhra-wardy was elected to the new Bengal assembly in 1937 and held the finance, public health, local self-govern-ment, and labour portfolios. With independence in 1947 he moved to Pakistan and in 1949 formed the Awami League. He was elected president in 1956, but after a subsequent government barred him from politi-cal life and imprisoned him briefly, he became an outspoken advocate of a return to a parliamentary system.

Sukarno, Achmed (1901–1970)

Indonesian nationalist, president 1945–67. During World War II he cooperated in the local administration set up by the Japanese, replacing Dutch rule. After the war he became the first president of the new Indone-sian republic, becoming president-for-life in 1966; he was ousted by Thojib ◊Suharto.

Sukarnoputri, Megawati (1947–   )

Indonesian politician. The daughter of President Achmed ◊Sukarno, she became the leading contender for the leadership of Indonesia after President Thojib ◊Suharto resigned in May 1998.

Sukarnoputri entered politics in 1987. In 1993 she became chair of the Indonesian Democratic Party (PDI), although she was removed in June 1996 in a government-sponsored attempt to prevent her from running for the presidency.

Summerskill, Edith Clara (1901–1980)

British Labour politician. From 1945 she was minister of food, being criticized by the Housewives League for continuing rationing, but achieving a significant breakthrough against tuberculosis with legislation that introduced pasteurized milk. She was a strong campaigner on food standards, medicine, and abortion.

Born in London to radical parents, she qualified as a doctor by 1924 and was active in the Socialist Medical Association. She was Labour member of Parliament for West Fulham 1938–55 and then represented War-rington until being made a peer in 1961. In 1966 she was made a Companion of Honour.

Sun Yat-sen

Wade-Giles transliteration of ◊Sun Zhong Shan.

Sun Zhong Shan or Sun Yat-sen (1867–1925)

Chinese revolutionary leader, provisional president in 1912.

Born in Xiangshan, near Guangzhou (Canton), Sun was the Western-educated son of a Christian-convert peasant farmer. Brought up by his elder brother in

Hawaii, he studied medicine in Hong Kong, and practised as a doctor in Macao and Guangzhou. Convinced of the need to overthrow the Manchu Qing dynasty and establish a modern republican form of government in China, in 1894 he founded the New China Party, in Honolulu, and attempted to foment an anti-Manchu uprising in Guangzhou, in 1895. This failed and Sun was forced to live in exile. Travelling extensively, he built up international support for his cause and in 1905 formed, in Tokyo, the United Revolutionary League, which was based on three principles: nationalism, democracy, and social reform.

Sun returned to China during the 1911 Revolution that saw the defeat of Manchu forces at Wuchang, in October, and the overthrew of the Qing dynasty. In early 1912 he was elected provisional president of the new Republic of China, with its capital in Nanjing. However, in an effort to promote unity, he resigned in 1912 in favour of the northern warlord Yüan Shikai. As a result of Yüan's increasingly dictatorial methods, Sun established an independent republic in southern China based in Guangzhou, in 1916.

He was criticized for lack of organizational ability, but his 'three people's principles' came to be accepted by both the nationalists and the Chinese communists. He also transformed his revolutionary organization into the Kuomintang (Guomindang) nationalist party which was to dominate politics in the Republic of China (today known as Taiwan) and came to be organized on Leninist lines.

Between 1916 and Sun's death in 1925, his southern-based nationalist regime contended for supremacy with northern-based warlords and from the early 1920s received support from the Soviet Union and the new Chinese Communist Party (CCP). He failed in his goal of securing national reunification, which was left to be achieved, briefly, by his successor, Jiang Jie Shi (Chiang Kai-shek).

Suu Kyi, Aung San (1945–)

Myanmar (Burmese) politician and human-rights campaigner, leader of the National League for Democracy (NLD), the main opposition to the military junta. Despite her being placed under house arrest in 1989, the NLD won the 1990 elections, although the junta refused to surrender power. She was awarded the Nobel Prize for Peace in 1991 in recognition of her 'nonviolent struggle for democracy and human rights' in Myanmar. Finally released from house arrest in 1995, she was banned from resuming any leadership post within the NLD by the junta. She is the daughter of former Burmese premier ◊Aung San.

Suzman, Helen Gavronsky (1917–)

South African politician and human-rights activist. A university lecturer concerned about the inhumanity of the apartheid system, she joined the white opposition to the ruling National Party and became a strong advocate of racial equality, respected by black communities inside and outside South Africa. In 1978 she received the United Nations Human Rights Award. She retired from active politics in 1989.

Suzuki, Zenkō (1911–)

Japanese politician. Originally a socialist member of the Diet (parliament) in 1947, he became a conservative (Liberal Democrat) in 1949, and was prime minister 1980–82.

Sverdlov, Yakov Mikhailovich (1885–1919)

Russian politician. He joined the Russian Social Democratic Workers' party in 1901, and worked as a professional revolutionary in the Bolshevik organizations 1902–17, always strictly following Lenin's policy. In 1913 he was co-opted onto the Bolshevik Central Committee. After the February Revolution of 1917, Sverdlov became the party's main organizer. Soon after the seizure of power by the Bolsheviks, he succeeded Lev Kamenev as chair of the All-Russian Central Executive Committee of the Soviets, and was thus titular head of the state. For a time, in 1918–19, Sverdlov, together with Stalin, was Lenin's closest collaborator.

Swan, John William David (1935–)

Bermudian centre-right politician, prime minister 1982–95. Leader of the liberal-conservative United Bermuda Party (UBP), he replaced David Gibbons as prime minister in 1982, and oversaw the continued development of the island as a prosperous centre for tourism and off-shore banking. An advocate of indepen-

Aung San Suu Kyi. *Rex*

dence from British colonial rule, he resigned as prime minister after a 1995 referendum voted decisively against constitutional change, and retired from the assembly in 1997.

A businessman-turned-politician, Swan was first elected to the Bermuda assembly in 1972 and served as home affairs minister 1978–82. Under his leadership, the UBP won the general elections of 1983, 1985, 1989, and 1993.

Sykes, Percy Molesworth (1867–1945)

English explorer, soldier, and administrator who surveyed much of the territory in southwest Asia between Baghdad, the Caspian Sea, and the Hindu Kush during World War I.

In 1894 he was the first British consul to Kerman (now in Iran) and Persian Baluchistan. Later he raised and commanded the South Persian Rifles. His histories of Persia and Afghanistan were published in 1915 and 1940. He was knighted in 1915.

Tabai, Ieremia T (1950–)

Kiribati politician, chief minister 1978–79, and president 1979–91. He was leader of the opposition until February 1978, when he became chief minister, and on independence, in July 1979, he became the country's first executive president. Tabai served concurrently as foreign minister and was re-elected in 1982, 1983, and 1987. From the mid-1980s opposition began to grow to his leadership. Although he had generally pursued a pro-Western foreign policy, Tabai's negotiation of a controversial (and short-lived) fishing agreement with a Soviet state-owned company, Sovrybflot, led to the formation of the country's first political party, the Christian Democratic Party, by opposition leader Harry Tong. Tabai stepped down as president in July 1991 and was replaced by Teatao Teannaki, as the constitution prevented him from seeking a further term.

Educated in New Zealand, Tabai was first elected to the assembly on its creation in May 1974, when Kiribati was known as the Gilbert Islands and was a British colony.

Tafawa Balewa, Alhaji Abubakar (1912–1966)

Nigerian politician, prime minister 1957–66. In September 1957 he was appointed prime minister, a post he retained at Nigerian independence three years later. In 1962 he declared a state of emergency in response to a political crisis in the Western Region. He was assassinated in a coup.

Balewa trained as a schoolteacher and later served as an education officer in the colonial administration. He became a member of the Northern House of Assembly in 1946 and joined the Northern People's Congress in 1951. After entering the House of Representatives in 1952, he became minister of works 1952–54, and minister of transport 1954–57. He was knighted in 1960.

Taft, Robert Alphonso (1889–1953)

US right-wing Republican senator from 1939, and a candidate for the presidential nomination in 1940, 1944, 1948, and 1952. He sponsored the Taft–Hartley Labor Act of 1947, restricting union power. He was the son of President William Taft.

Taft was born in Cincinnati, Ohio, and educated at Harvard and Yale universities. Known as 'Mr Republican', he was the standard-bearer of the conservative wing of the Republican Party, and he was lost in the liberal tide that swept across the USA during the 1930s. He was further isolated by his resistance to US involvement against Nazi Germany, a view he held as late as 1943.

In 1952 his rejection for the Republican presidential nomination, in favour of Dwight D Eisenhower, was interpreted as the end of an era in US Republicanism. After Eisenhower's election Taft became Senate majority leader.

Taft, William Howard (1857–1930)

27th president of the USA 1909–13, a Republican. He was secretary of war 1904–08 in Theodore Roosevelt's administration, but as president his conservatism provoked Roosevelt to stand against him in the 1912 election. Taft served as chief justice of the Supreme Court 1921–30.

Born in Cincinnati, Ohio, Taft graduated from Yale University and Cincinnati Law School. He was appointed US solicitor general in 1890 and became a federal circuit court judge in 1892. His first interest was always the judiciary, although he accepted a post as governor of the Philippines and took responsibility for the construction of the Panama Canal. His single term as president was characterized by struggles against progressives, although he prosecuted more trusts than had his predecessor. As chief justice of the Supreme Court, he supported a minimum wage.

FURTHER READING
Anderson, Judith *William Howard Taft: An Intimate History* 1981
Coletta, P *The Presidency of William Howard Taft* 1973
Steven, B *William Howard Taft: The President Who Became Chief Justice* 1970

Tagore, Rabindranath (1861–1941)

Bengali Indian writer. He translated into English his own verse *Gitanjali/Song Offerings* (1912) and his

The butterfly counts not months but moments, and has time enough.

RABINDRANATH TAGORE *Fireflies*

verse play *Chitra* (1896). He was awarded the Nobel Prize for Literature in 1913.

An ardent nationalist and advocate of social reform, he resigned his knighthood as a gesture of protest against British repression in India.

FURTHER READING
Dutta, Krishna, and Robinson, Andrew *Rabindranath Tagore: The Myriad-Minded Man* 1995
Kripalani, H R *Rabindranath Tagore: A Biography* 1962
Lago, Mary *Rabindranath Tagore* 1976

Takeshita, Noboru (1924–)

Japanese conservative politician. Elected to parliament as a Liberal Democratic Party (LDP) deputy in 1958, he became president of the LDP and prime minister in 1987. He and members of his administration were shown in the Recruit scandal to have been involved in insider-trading and he resigned in 1989.

Tambo, Oliver (1917–1993)

South African nationalist politician, in exile 1960–90, president of the African National Congress (ANC) 1977–91. Because of poor health, he was given the honorary post of national chair in July 1991, and Nelson ◊Mandela resumed the ANC presidency.

Tambo first met Mandela while a student at Fort Hare University, from which he was expelled for organizing a student protest. He joined the ANC in 1944 and, with Mandela, helped to found the ANC Youth League, becoming its vice president; together they also established a law practice in Johannesburg in 1952.

A devout Christian, Tambo applied to join the priesthood, but before he could be accepted as a candidate, received a year's imprisonment for subversive activities in 1956. When the ANC was banned in 1960, as ANC deputy president, he was advised to go into exile and left South Africa to set up an external wing. Before long the organization's main leaders had been imprisoned or killed, and Tambo worked tirelessly from his London base as acting ANC president, becoming president in 1977. His return to South Africa in December 1990 was rapturously received.

Tanaka, Kakuei (1918–1993)

Japanese conservative politician, leader of the dominant Liberal Democratic Party (LDP) and prime minister 1972–74. In 1976 he was charged with corruption and resigned from the LDP but remained a powerful faction leader.

In the Diet (Japanese parliament) from 1947, Tanaka was minister of finance 1962–65 and of international trade and industry 1971–72, before becoming LDP leader. In 1974 he had to resign the premiership because of allegations of corruption and in 1976 he was arrested for accepting bribes from the Lockheed Corporation while premier. He was found guilty in 1983, but remained in the Diet as an independent deputy pending appeal.

The son of a small cattle trader in rural western Japan, Tanaka trained at night school as a quantity surveyor and made his fortune as a building contractor. In 1947 he was elected to Japan's house of representatives. He used his personal wealth and connections to operate a powerful faction within the LDP. Tanaka's meteoric political rise culminated in his becoming postwar Japan's youngest prime minister in 1972. As premier he was initially popular, having charisma and a raffish common touch. The Tanaka political dynasty survived Kakuei's death with his daughter, Makiko, representing his former parliamentary seat from 1993.

Tan Malaka, Ibrahim Datuk (1894–1949)

Indonesian Communist leader. In 1927 he organized the Indonesian Republic Party in an attempt to gain independence from the Netherlands. In 1946 he was involved in a failed coup attempt for which he was imprisoned without trial for two years. After his release, he helped form the Partai Murba (Proletarian Party) and in 1948 made a bid to control the Indonesian revolution proclaiming himself head of Indonesia from the city of Kedri. The Dutch attacked Kedri and although he escaped he was captured by supporters of Achmed ◊Sukarno a few months later and executed.

Tanumafili II, Susuga Malietoa (1913–)

Samoan head of state, constitutional monarch from 1962. On independence, on 1 January 1962, he became joint head of state and in April 1963, when the other joint monarch, Tupua Tamasese Mea'ole, died, he became sole head of state. He will hold his position for life, but future heads of state will be elected by the legislative assembly.

Educated in New Zealand, he succeeded to the title of Malietoa (head of one of the country's four traditional royal families) on his father's death in 1940. In the same year he became a Fautua (adviser) to the New Zealand governor of (Western) Samoa. In 1958 Tanumafili joined the New Zealand delegation to the United Nations and chaired the constitutional convention that paved the way for independence.

Tatchell, Peter (1952–)

Australian-born peace activist and lesbian- and gay-rights campaigner. Following his move to London in 1971, he joined the Gay Liberation Front and the Troops Out Movement, opposing the presence of British troops in Northern Ireland. He also campaigned against nuclear weapons and the 1982 Falklands War. In 1983 he stood unsuccessfully as Labour candidate in the Bermondsey by-election and was subjected to virulent media attacks for his socialism and sexuality.

Since 1990 he has been active in the radical direct-action group Outrage, campaigning for equal rights for lesbians and gay men and exposing prejudice in the military and the church.

Taufa'ahau Tupou IV (Tupouto Tungi) (1918–1999)

King of Tonga from 1965. On succeeding to the throne on his mother's death, he assumed the designation King Taufa'ahau Tupou IV and shared power with his brother, Prince Fatafehi Tu'ipelehake (1922–), who served until 1991 as prime minister and agriculture minister. King Taufa'ahau negotiated the country's independence within the British Commonwealth in 1970, but remained the strongest supporter of the Western powers in the Pacific region. (The Tongan government did not, unlike neighbouring states, con-demn France for resuming nuclear weapons testing in the South Pacific in 1995.) He promoted improvements in education and social services in Tonga, establishing the University of the South Pacific in Suva in 1969, but resisted growing calls to democratize what remains an absolutist political system.

The eldest son of Queen ◊Salote Tupou III, he was the first Tongan monarch to receive a Western edu-cation and the first Tongan to secure a university degree, studying arts and law at Newington College and Sydney University. A keen mathematician and Wesleyan lay preacher, he served successively as min-ister for education in 1943 and health 1944–49, before becoming prime minister (and foreign affairs and agriculture minister) under his mother in 1949.

His heir, Crown Prince Tupouto'a, is defence minis-ter and foreign minister and viewed as politically more liberal.

Tawney, Richard Henry (1880–1962)

English economic historian, social critic, and reformer. He had a great influence on the Labour Party, especially during the 1930s, although he never became a member of Parliament. His *Labour and the Nation* was the party's manifesto for the 1929 general election. His other books include the classic *Religion and the Rise of Capitalism* (1926).

After leaving Oxford University, Tawney taught for the Workers' Educational Association while working on *The Agrarian Problem in the 16th Century* (1912). He helped found the Economic History Society in 1926 and became the joint editor of its journal, the *Econ-omic History Review*.

A committed Christian, Tawney based his socialism on moral values. *Religion and the Rise of Capitalism* examined morals and economic practice in England in the years 1588–1640. One of his most widely read books is *The Acquisitive Society* (published in 1921, and later abridged as *Labour and the Nation*), in which he criticized capitalism because it encourages acquisi-tiveness and so corrupts everyone. In *Equality* (1931)

he argued for urgent improvements in social services to deal with some of the glaring inequities of the class system.

FURTHER READING
Wright, A *R H Tawney* 1987

Taylor, Ann (1947–)

British Labour politician, born in Motherwell, Scot-land; President of the Council and Leader of the House of Commons 1997–98, and chief whip from 1998. She was elected member of Parliament for Bolton West in 1974 and then for Dewsbury. She served as a whip 1977–79 in the government of James Callaghan and, in opposition, as spokesperson on education 1979–81, housing 1981–83, the Home Office 1987–88, and the environment 1988–92. She was shadow secretary of state for education 1992–94, spokesperson on the Citizen's Charter 1994–96, and shadow Leader of the House 1996–97. She is the first woman to hold the post of government chief whip.

She was a member of the Standards in Public Life Select Committee in 1995 and the Standards and Privileges Committee 1995–97.

Taylor, Charles (1948–)

Liberian head of state from 1997. He was leader of the National Patriotic Front of Liberia (NPFL), part of the force that overthrew President Samuel ◊Doe. He played a prominent role in the Doe regime but in 1983 he was accused of embezzlement and fled to the USA. Escaping to Ghana he was detained on suspicion of working for the US Central Intelligence Agency (CIA) but was later granted political asylum. He formed the NPFL with the aim of forcing Doe out of office, and received military support from Libya. In 1987 the NPFL attacked a border town. This escalated into full-scale civil war and caused the collapse of the Liberian government. From 1990 Taylor's forces advanced rapidly across the country. In 1994 Taylor and other factional leaders signed an accord agreeing to a cease-fire.

Tebbit, Norman Beresford, Baron Tebbit (1931–)

British Conservative politician. He was minister for employment 1981–83, minister for trade and industry 1983–85, chancellor of the Duchy of Lancaster 1985–87, and chair of the party 1985–87. As his relations with Margaret Thatcher cooled, he returned to the back benches in 1987.

Created a life peer in 1992, he went on to carve out a new career in business.

Teller, Edward (1908–)

Hungarian-born US physicist known as the father of the hydrogen bomb (H-bomb). He worked on the Manhattan Project developing the fission bomb – the first atomic bomb – 1942–46, and on the fusion, or

Edward Teller, c. 1955. AKG London

hydrogen, bomb 1946–52. Vigorous in his promotion of nuclear weapons and in his opposition to communism, he was, in the 1980s, one of the leading advocates of the Star Wars programme (the Strategic Defense Initiative). He was a key witness against his colleague J Robert Oppenheimer at the security hearings in 1954.

Temple, William (1881–1944)
English church leader, archbishop of Canterbury 1942–44. He was a major ecumenical figure who strove to achieve church unity. His theological writings constantly sought to apply Christian teachings to contemporary social conditions, as in his *Christianity and the Social Order* (1942).

Te Puea, Herangi, Princess (1883–1952)
New Zealand Maori nationalist leader. Born in Waikato, on North Island, into a chiefly family, she became a leading figure, from 1911, within the Maori nationalist movement, the Kingitanga. During the interwar period the Kingitanga became an important instrument for the settlement of Maori grievances against colonial rule and for social and cultural advance.

Ter-Petrossian, Levon Akopovich (1945–)
Armenian politician and philologist, president 1990–98. He pursued a career as an academic and writer before forming, in November 1989, the Armenian Pan-Nationalist Movement (APM) to campaign for independence. As president from May 1990, he led the country to independence in September 1991 and backed the ethnic Armenians in the enclave of Nagorno-Karabakh in their fight to break away from neighbouring Azerbaijan. Although he promoted market-centred economic reforms and was re-elected president in 1991 and 1996, he enjoyed decreasing support for himself and the APM, and stepped down in February 1998 amidst divisions over his policy toward Nagorno-Karabakh. He was replaced by Robert ◊Kocharian.

Born in Aleppo, Syria, into a renowned Armenian literary family, he was educated at the State University of Yerevan in Armenia, gained a doctorate in Armenian–Assyrian studies from the St Petersburg Oriental Institute in Russia, and worked as a researcher before becoming a full-time political activist in the late 1980s. A long-time dissident, he was imprisoned 1988–89 after founding the Armenian Karabakh Committee.

Terra, Gabriel (1873–1942)
Uruguayan politician and president 1931–38. His administration during a period of severe economic decline spurred him to lead a coup in 1933 (supported by Blanco leader, Luis Alberto de Herrera), that suspended congress and abolished the constitution. A new constitution in 1934 restored presidential power and authority to Terra, and the nation was governed dictatorially 1934–38. A revolt in 1935 was suppressed. Terra during the remainder of his term of office continued with the programme – initiated by his predecessor, Batlle y Ordóñez – of socializing the republic.

Early in his career, Terra served as an Asociación Nacional Republicana (ANR; Colorado Party) member under President Batlle, and occupied several diplomatic and political positions. The death of Batlle in 1929 enabled Terra to advance his career by running for the presidency in 1930. He was succeeded by General Alfredo Baldomir.

Thalmann, Ernst (1886–1944)
German Communist politician and associate of Stalin.

He was a member of the Reichstag (parliament) 1924–33, leader of the German Communist party, and stood as Communist candidate for the presidency in 1932. A close associate of Stalin, he maintained a narrowly pro-Soviet stance. After Hitler came to power Thalmann was sent to a concentration camp and was probably executed at Buchenwald in August 1944.

Thani, Sheikh Khalifa bin Hamad al- (1932–)

Qatar political leader, emir (ruler) 1972–95. He utilized the small state's burgeoning oil revenues to modernize the bureaucratic structure, diversify the economy, and develop education and the social services. He also sought to curb the extravagances of the royal family and pursued a pro-Western foreign policy, joining the United Nations-coalition forces in the 1990–91 Gulf War against Iraq. However, although he appointed an advisory council, he continued to rule in an authoritarian manner. In June 1995 he was deposed as emir by his son, Sheikh Hamad bin Khalifa al-Thani (1950–), who had been crown prince and defence minister since 1977.

Born in Ar Rayyn, the fourth son of Hamad, of the ruling al-Thani dynasty, Khalifa received a traditional Arab Islamic education from private tutors. His father died in 1947 while his grandfather Ali bin Abdullah al-Thani, who ruled 1913–49, was still emir. In 1960, when his cousin Sheikh Ahmad bin Ali al-Thani became the new emir, Khalifa became Qatar finance minister and by the mid-1960s was effectively running the country. In 1968 he was made president of the Provisional Federal Council, which brought together the smaller states of the Persian Gulf in preparation for independence after the announced withdrawal of British military forces from the Gulf region. Independence was achieved in 1971. A year later, Khalifa became emir, deposing Ahmad in a bloodless coup while he was out of the country.

Thant, U (1909–1974)

Burmese diplomat, secretary general of the United Nations (UN) 1962–71. He helped to resolve the US–Soviet crisis over the Soviet installation of missiles in Cuba, and he made the controversial decision to withdraw the UN peacekeeping force from the Egypt–Israel border in 1967.

Thomas, (Thomas) George (1909–)

Welsh Labour politician who became Speaker of the House of Commons.

A teacher, he was elected Labour member of Parliament for Cardiff Central 1945 and has been MP for Cardiff West since 1950. From 1951 to 1964 he was a member of the Chairmen's Panel of the House of Commons, and between 1964 and 1968 he was successively parliamentary undersecretary at the Home Office, minister of state at the Welsh Office, and minister of state at the Commonwealth Office. He entered the cabinet in 1968 as secretary of state for Wales, a post he held until Labour's defeat in 1970. In 1974 he became chair of Ways and Means and deputy speaker of the House of Commons, and in 1976 he was only the second Labour MP to become Speaker of the House of Commons.

◆ THATCHER, MARGARET HILDA, born ROBERTS (1925–) ◆

British Conservative politician, prime minister 1979–90, Conservative Party leader 1975–1990.

Margaret Thatcher was born in Grantham in Lincolnshire, daughter of Alderman Alfred Roberts, a grocer, and she was educated at Grantham High School and Somerville College, Oxford, where she read chemistry. She married Denis Thatcher in 1951, was called to the bar in 1953, and was elected Conservative member of Parliament for Finchley in 1959.

There is no such thing as Society. There are individual men and women, and there are families.

MARGARET THATCHER *Woman's Own* 31 October 1987

Thatcher joined the shadow cabinet in 1967. She was secretary of state for education and science 1970–74 and joint shadow chancellor 1974–75. In 1975 she was elected leader of the Conservative Party, the first women to lead a political party in the UK.

In May 1979 the Conservative Party won the general election. Margaret Thatcher became the dominant figure in British politics, leading the party to two further general election victories in 1983 and 1987. Thatcher's political philosophy was strongly influenced by her parliamentary colleague Keith Joseph, who championed the role of individualism and the importance of the market. Her policies were geared to rolling back the influence of the state, freeing individual choice, controlling the power of the trade unions, and attacking the Labour left as socialist extremists. Under Thatcher, Britain moved into a deregulated economy with new service industries becoming more important than the hitherto dominant manufacturing sector.

Thatcher reduced income tax-rates, sold council houses to their tenants, and transformed the public utilities into companies in the private sector (privatization). Her government abolished the Greater London Council and reduced the autonomy of local government by placing a ceiling on their expenditure (rate-capping). Legislation regulating trade unions continued throughout her

He was educated at a state secondary school and the University of Southampton.

Thomas, Clarence (1948–)

US Supreme Court justice from 1991. Born in Savannah, Georgia, he received a law degree from Yale University Law School in 1974. President Ronald Reagan appointed him head of the civil-rights division of the department of education in 1981 and the head of the Equal Employment Opportunities Commission in 1982. Thomas served there until 1990, when President George Bush appointed him a justice on the US Court of Appeals. It was widely believed that his Republican views and opposition to abortion, rather than his legal experience, caused him to be nominated to the Supreme Court the following year, and the nomination was not supported by the National Association for the Advancement of Colored People, which would normally back a black nominee. After extremely bitter and sensational confirmation hearings, in which he was accused of sexual harassment by former colleague Anita Hill, Thomas was confirmed by the Senate by 52 votes to 48, the narrowest margin for any nominee to the Supreme Court in the 20th century, and took his seat on the Court.

Thomas, James Henry (1874–1949)

Welsh Labour politician. He was made secretary of state for the colonies in the first Labour government in 1924.

As an engine-driver he was elected to the Swindon town council, and in 1904 became president of the Amalgamated Society of Railway Servants. Thomas was Labour member of Parliament for Derby from 1910 to 1936. In World War I he was a member of Arthur ◊Balfour's mission to the USA. Thomas was appointed secretary of state for the colonies in the first Labour government, in 1924, and Lord Privy Seal and minister of employment in the second Labour government, 1929–30. In June 1930 he became secretary of state for dominion affairs, being transferred to the Colonial Office in 1935. In 1936 he resigned both from office and from Parliament as a result of the report of a tribunal set up to consider unauthorized disclosures relating to the Budget. Thomas was author of *When Labour Rules* (1920), *The Red Light on Railways* (1921), and *My Story* (1937).

He was born in Newport, Monmouthshire (Gwent), son of a labourer.

Thomas, Lowell Jackson (1892–1981)

US journalist, a radio commentator for the Columbia Broadcasting System (CBS) 1930–76. Travelling to all World War II theatres of combat and to remote areas of the world, he became one of the USA's best-known journalists.

Born in Woodington, Ohio, Thomas was educated at Northern Indiana University and the University of

terms of office, placing serious constraints on union rights.

Thatcher's economic policy was directed towards controlling inflation. But unemployment figures were pushed up to 3 million people in her first term. However, adverse economic conditions were neutralized by Britain's victory in the Falklands conflict with Argentina in 1982 and there was a Conservative victory in the general election of 1983.

The defeat of the miners' strike in 1984–85, Thatcher's decisive conduct of government after the IRA bombing of the Conservative Party conference in October 1984, and her confrontational defence of British interests within the European Economic Community (EEC) established her image as a strong-minded, authoritative leader.

The Conservatives' third general victory under Thatcher in May 1987 made her the first prime minister in 160 years to be elected for a third term of office. Her increasingly autocratic attitude caused problems with her Cabinet colleagues. Michael Heseltine resigned in 1986 during the Westland helicopter affair, and Nigel Lawson resigned as chancellor in 1989 when Thatcher supported her financial adviser, Alan Walters,

against him. Thatcher's disagreement with Geoffrey Howe over the government's approach to the EEC caused Howe to resign as foreign secretary and deputy prime minister. His resignation, combined with growing popular opposition to the poll tax introduced in 1989, forced Thatcher's resignation as party leader and prime minister in 1990.

Thatcher was created a life peer in 1992. After leaving public office, she established the Thatcher Foundation to propagate her political philosophy. Her memoirs, *The Downing Street Years*, were published in 1993. See photograph on page 422.

FURTHER READING
Harris, Kenneth *Thatcher* 1988
Jenkins, Peter *Mrs Thatcher's Revolution* 1987
Minogue, Kenneth, and Biddiss, Michael *Thatcherism: Personality and Politics* 1987
Thatcher, Margaret *The Path to Power* (memoirs) 1995
Young, Hugo *The Iron Lady* 1989, *One of Us* 1991

Margaret Thatcher, 1975. *AKG London*

Denver and joined the staff of the *Chicago Journal* in 1912. After receiving an MA from Princeton in 1915, he served as a special observer for President Woodrow Wilson during World War I. His first-person account of the Arab Revolt was published as *With Lawrence in Arabia* (1924).

Thomas, Norman Mattoon (1884–1968)

US political leader, six times Socialist candidate for president 1928–48. One of the founders of the American Civil Liberties Union in 1920, he also served as a director of the League for Industrial Democracy 1922–37. He was a brilliant speaker and published *A Socialist's Faith* (1951).

Born in Marion, Ohio, Thomas graduated from Princeton University in 1905 and, after studying at the Union Theological Seminary, was ordained a Presbyterian minister in 1911. As pastor of the East Harlem Church he first confronted the problem of urban poverty and joined the Socialist Party in 1918, leaving the ministry for political activism two years later.

Thomson of Dundee, George Morgan Thomson (1921–)

Welsh Labour politician who was influential in negotiating the UK's entry into the European Economic Community (EEC).

He was educated at Grove Academy, Dundee. After service in World War II he became a journalist, and was elected Labour member of Parliament for Dundee East in 1952. Between 1964 and 1967 he held office as minister of state at the Foreign Office and as chancellor of the Duchy of Lancaster. In 1967 he entered the Cabinet as secretary of state for Commonwealth Affairs and then became minister without portfolio in 1968, and chancellor of the Duchy of Lancaster again in 1969. Strongly in favour of British membership of the EEC, he was responsible for negotiations for British entry between 1968 and 1970. In 1972–73 he was chair of the Labour Committee for Europe, and in 1973 he became one of the UK's two nominees on the Commission of the European Communities, with special responsibility for regional policy. His term of office expired in 1977.

Thorez, Maurice (1900–1964)

French communist politician. As leader of the French Communist Party (PCF) 1930–64, he took it into the Popular Front alliance in the 1930s and was one of France's first three communist ministers when he joined General Charles ◊de Gaulle's Provisional Government in November 1945.

In May 1947, faced with a substantial unofficial strike movement, the PCF deputies voted against the government's wage-freeze, and Thorez was dismissed by Paul Ramadier, de Gaulle's successor as prime minister. With the onset of the Cold War, Thorez led his party through its most Stalinist period, adopting a position of unwavering support for the USSR on all questions until 1956, when he refused to accept Nikita ◊Khrushchev's denunciation of ◊Stalin.

Having worked briefly as a coalminer in Pas-de-Calais, Thorez joined the Communist Party at its foundation in 1920. He was made first secretary of the party in 1930, when the earlier generation of leaders fell foul of Stalin. In 1934 he followed Moscow's tactical turn to the 'united front' (promoting this anti-fascist alliance in France as the Popular Front) and sought to embrace progressive Catholics too. From not much more than a sect the PCF mushroomed into a mass membership organization in this period. Thorez, rewarded with the title of general secretary, was to retain undisputed control over the highly disciplined party machine until his death.

Thorez survived the difficult period of the German–Soviet Pact of 1939–41 by deserting from the French army to which he had been conscripted and fleeing to the USSR, where he stayed until amnestied in the run-up to de Gaulle's Moscow visit in November 1944.

Thorpe, (John) Jeremy (1929–)

British Liberal politician, leader of the Liberal Party 1967–76.

From a family of members of Parliament, Thorpe first trained as a barrister, then became a Liberal MP in

1959 and party leader in 1967. A flamboyant campaigner, party fortunes advanced under his leadership, but he was forced to step down in 1976 following allegations that he had had a homosexual affair with Norman Scott, and that he had conspired in the attempted murder of his lover. He was acquitted of all charges in 1979, but lost his parliamentary seat at the general election. See photograph on page 449.

Thurmond, J(ames) Strom (1902–)

US governor and senator, a Democrat. He served as governor of South Carolina 1947–51. Although relatively progressive, especially in matters of education, he was staunchly opposed to the Democrats' civil-rights programme in 1948; at that year's convention he led the walkout of the Southern Democrats and ran as the presidential candidate of the State's Rights Democratic Party or 'Dixiecrats'. The split in the Democratic Party and disruption of the concept of the 'solid South' ultimately benefitted Harry S Truman, who went on to win an unexpected presidential election victory.

Originally appointed as a Democrat to the US Senate in 1954, Thurmond was elected on his own in 1956, switching to the Republican Party in 1964. He continued to be re-elected and became a prominent force in the emergence of a conservative Republican Party in the South.

Thurmond was born in Edgefield, South Carolina. A teacher and superintendent of education before turning to the law, he was judge of the state's circuit court 1938–42, before volunteering for service with the US Army in World War II 1942–45.

FURTHER READING
Cohodas, Nadine *Strom Thurmond and the Politics of Southern Change* 1994

Tikhonov, Nikolai Aleksandrovich (1905–1997)

Soviet politician. He was a close associate of President Leonid Brezhnev, joining the Politburo in 1979, and was prime minister (chair of the Council of Ministers) 1980–85. In April 1989 he was removed from the Central Committee.

Tilak, Bal Gangadhar (1856–1920)

Indian nationalist politician and philosopher who was the leading campaigner for full independence before Mahatma ◊Gandhi. Tilak gathered popular support by linking political action with an appeal to Hindu religious and cultural identity. He was twice imprisoned for anti-British activities, and founded the Home Rule League in 1914. In 1916 he signed the Lucknow Pact with the Muslim leader Mohammed Ali Jinnah, which united the Hindu and Muslim communities in the independence struggle.

Tilak was born into a high-caste family in Ratnagiri. After taking a university degree, he taught mathematics, and joined the Indian National Congress. To promote the nationalist cause and raise cultural awareness, he founded two newspapers in Bombay and sponsored religious festivals.

Tillett, Ben(jamin) (1860–1943)

English trade-union leader and politician. He became general secretary of the powerful Dockers' Union, and was a principal organizer of national strikes that hit Britain's docks in 1889 and 1911. He sat as Labour member of Parliament for North Salford, Lancashire, 1917–24 and 1929–31.

Tillett was born in Bristol, and was employed in a brickworks before joining the Royal Navy. Active in the Trades Union Congress, and serving briefly as its president in 1929, he helped put the general labour unions on an equal footing with the skilled craftsmen's organizations.

Timakata, Fred (1936–)

Vanuatuan centre-left politician, president 1989–94. He served as deputy prime minister and home affairs minister under Walter ◊Lini, who was prime minister 1980–91, before becoming speaker of the parliament 1985–88. His alleged bias towards the dominant, Anglophone, centre-left Vanua'aku Pati (VP) resulted in the Francophone opposition Union of Moderate Parties (UMP) briefly boycotting parliament in 1986. After being appointed health minister in December 1988, Timakata became president in January 1989 after a constitutional crisis, which was caused by the arrest of President George ◊Sokomanu, who had attempted unconstitutionally to oust Prime Minister Lini.

Tindemans, Leo (1922–)

Belgian politician. A regular holder of cabinet posts from 1968, he led the government from 1974 to 1978, and was appointed chair of the Christian People's Party (CVP) in 1979. A prominent role-player in the European Community, he was president of the Group of the European People's Party from 1992, and in 1993 was the first holder of the Jacques Delors chair in Maastricht.

Tindemans studied economics and social sciences at Antwerp, Ghent, and Louvain universities. In 1958 he became secretary to the CVP, entering parliament for Antwerp in 1961.

Tirpitz, Alfred Friedrich von (1849–1930)

German admiral. As secretary for the navy 1897–1916, he created the German navy and planned the World War I U-boat campaign.

Tisza, Istvan, Count Tisza of Borosjeno and Szeged (1861–1918)

Hungarian politician, prime minister of Hungary 1903–05 and 1913–17. The son of Kalman Tisza, Liberal prime minister (and virtual dictator) of Hungary 1875–90, he was a loyal supporter of the Austro-Hungarian Empire, and refused to make any concessions to the demands of Slav and Romanian separatists. Tisza also strongly backed the alliance with Germany in World War I, and was assassinated by soldiers when a nationalist uprising began in Hungary on 31 October 1918.

On the death of the emperor Francis Joseph in 1916, Tisza's influence began to wane. He resigned the following year when faced with the new emperor Charles's policies of conciliation towards the Slavs and extending voting rights.

Tito, Teburoro (1953–)

Kiribati politician, president from 1994. He was first elected to the Kiribati parliament in 1987 and led a Christian Democratic faction of the Maneaban te Mauri (MTM) party opposition to the Gilbertese National Progressive Party governments of Ieremia Tabai 1978–91 and Teatao Teannaki 1991–94. After claims of misconduct by the outgoing government, he was elected president by a landslide margin in September 1994. His government sought to reduce Nauru's dependence on foreign economic aid and, in September 1995, severed diplomatic relations with France in protest against its resumption of nuclear-weapons testing at Mururoa Atoll, in the South Pacific.

Born at Tabiteuea North, he studied science at the University of the South Pacific, in Fiji, where he was also active in student politics. On his return to Kiribati in 1980, Tito worked as senior education officer and chair of the football association.

Todd, (Reginald Stephen) Garfield (1908–1992)

New Zealand-born Rhodesian politician, prime minister of Southern Rhodesia (now Zimbabwe) 1953–58. He founded and led the United Rhodesia Party, but was removed as its leader by opponents of his liberal policies, which were also rejected by an increasingly right-wing White electorate. He was placed under restriction by the Rhodesian Front regime of Ian Smith 1965–76.

Todd was educated at Otago University, New Zealand, and Witwatersrand University, South Africa. He came to Rhodesia to work as a missionary in 1934. After entering politics, he was member of Parliament for Shabani 1946–58. In 1959 he founded the progressive Central African Party, but returned to farming when it lost the general election of 1962. Todd was a friend and political ally of the leader of the black nationalist ZAPU party, Joshua ◊Nkomo.

Todd, Ron(ald) (1927–)

English trade-union leader. He rose from shop steward to general secretary of Britain's largest trade union, the Transport and General Workers' Union, a post he held 1985–92. Although a Labour Party supporter, he criticized its attitude towards nuclear disarmament.

◆ TITO, ADOPTED NAME OF JOSIP BROZ (1892–1980) ◆

Yugoslav communist politician, in effective control of Yugoslavia 1943–80.

Tito (as he would come to be known) was born into a peasant family in Kumrovec in today's Croatia in 1892. His early career as a locksmith in Zagreb was interrupted by World War I. He served as a sergeant in the Austro-Hungarian army on the Serbian and Russian fronts. During his service at the Russian front he was wounded and captured in 1915. He joined a Red Guard unit at Omsk in Siberia in 1917. Following his return to the newly created Yugoslavia in 1920, he joined the Communist Party of Yugoslavia (KPJ) and engaged in the radical trade-union movement.

He allegedly took part in clandestine revolutionary communist terrorist activity in the 1920s, which led to his arrest and imprisonment for the possession of explosives. Upon his release in 1934 he joined the KPJ's Politburo in exile. At this point he assumed the name 'Tito'. Following the purge of the KPJ in 1937, he rose to the rank of general secretary in 1940.

Tito was single-minded in his belief in a federal Yugoslavia, modelled on the Soviet republics. He was uncompromising in his determination not to cooperate with non-communist groups. These two principles also formed the cornerstone of his approach to fighting the Germans during World War II. When Yugoslavia was attacked in April 1941, Tito coexisted uneasily with the German occupation, whilst secretly setting up the KPJ's network and military organization. The German invasion of the USSR gave Tito the final incentive to issue a call to arms, not only in the hope of assisting the USSR but also to take the opportunity afforded by the war to launch an armed revolution.

Tito's wartime strategy was to act independently of the Četniks led by Draza Mihailovič, and of the government in exile in London. His partisans conducted operations of their own, not as part of a coordinated Allied strategy. Tito developed a sophisticated political network at the local level. By 1943 he was recognized as the leader of the Yugoslav resistance by the Western Allies, forcing the government in exile to cooperate with him.

Tito, c. 1950. AKG London

Todt, Fritz (1891–1942)

German engineer who was responsible for building the first autobahns (German motorways) and, in World War II, the Siegfried Line of defence along Germany's western frontier, and the Atlantic Wall.

Todt's success as minister for road construction led the Nazi dictator Hitler to put him in charge of completing the Siegfried Line in 1938. His ***Organization Todt***, formed for this task, continued constructing defences on the Atlantic Coast using forced labour until 1944. He was made minister for arms and munitions in 1940. In 1942, alarmed at the attrition of equipment on the Eastern Front, he advised Hitler to end the war with the USSR. He was killed in an air crash on the way back from this meeting.

Tofilau, Eti Alesana (1924–)

Samoan politician, prime minister 1982–85 and from 1988. He entered the Fono (parliament) in 1957 and was a member of the 1960 constitutional convention that paved the way for independence from New Zealand rule in 1962. He returned to the Fono in 1967 and became deputy prime minister and minister of finance in 1982 and leader of the Human Rights Protection Party (HRPP) – a party based around family and local allegiances – in the same year. In December 1982 Tofilau began his first term as prime minister and remained in office, also serving as foreign minister, after the HRPP polled strongly in the February 1985 general election. However, in December 1985, a split in the HRPP led to his being replaced as prime minister by Va'ai Kolone. Tofilau returned to power in April 1988 and pushed through legislation, in 1990, to

Following the entry of the USSR into Serbia in October 1944, Tito set up headquarters in Belgrade. By May 1945 he had ruthlessly established a communist state in Yugoslavia. Unlike the countries of Eastern Europe that had been occupied by Soviet forces following the war, Yugoslavia was consolidated under Tito, who set a revolution in motion and then expelled non-communists from the government.

Tito's independence prompted the Soviet leadership to plot to overthrow him. Following the 1948 Cominform resolution expelling Yugoslavia from the communist bloc, Western support guaranteed its autonomy during the Stalinist era. Tito was elected president in 1953 under a new constitution. During the 1950s and 1960s he followed a policy of 'positive neutralism': non-alignment in foreign affairs and self-dependence on the domestic front, including defence. Despite reconciliation with Moscow in 1955, Tito spoke out against Soviet oppression in Hungary in 1956 and in Czechoslovakia in 1968. In 1974 his principle of self-management and defiant independence culminated in the adoption of a new constitution that promoted greater decentralization within the country. The constitution, however, failed to address growing internal tension amongst the national and religious populations of the federation, and was, in a way, contradicted by the increasingly anachronistic modus operandi of the ageing leader. The tension, never resolved but merely suppressed, mounted after Tito's death on 4 May 1980, and ultimately led to the disintegration of Yugoslavia and to civil wars in the area.

FURTHER READING
Auty, Phyllis *Tito: A Biography* 1980
Deakin, F W *The Embattled Mountain* 1971
Djilas, Milovan *Tito: The Story from Inside* 1981
Ormcanin, Ivo *Tito* 1984
Ridley, Jasper *Tito: A Biography* 1994
Tito, Josip Broz *The Yugoslav Road* 1983
Vukcevich, Bosko S *Tito: Architect of Yugoslav Disintegration* 1994
West, Richard *Tito and the Rise and Fall of Yugoslavia* 1995

introduce universal adult suffrage (instead of indirect elections by matai, or clan chiefs). The HRPP won the 1991 and 1996 general elections and Tofilau remained prime minister, despite deteriorating health (after heart surgery) and mounting public opposition to political corruption and the government's sensitivity to media criticism.

Born in Vaitogi, in American Samoa, he moved with his Congregational Christian missionary parents to Western Samoa in 1930. He served in the Samoan defence force during World War II and in 1946 received a matai (elected clan chief) title, which allowed him to vote and stand for election. He had a career in business before becoming involved in politics.

Togliatti, Palmiro (1893–1964)

Italian politician who was a founding member of the Italian Communist Party in 1921 and effectively its leader for almost 40 years from 1926 until his death. In exile 1926–44, he returned after the fall of the Fascist dictator Mussolini to become a member of Pietro Badoglio's government and held office until 1946.

Togliatti trained as a lawyer, served in the army, and was wounded during World War I. He was associated with the revolutionary wing of the Italian Socialist Party that left to form the Communist Party in 1921. He edited the newspaper *Il comunista* 1922–24 and became a member of the party's central committee. He was in Moscow when Mussolini outlawed the party, and stayed there to become a leading member of the Comintern, joining the Secretariat in 1935. Returning to Italy after Mussolini's downfall, he advocated coalition politics with other leftist and democratic parties, a policy that came to fruition in the elections of 1948, where the communists won 135 seats.

FURTHER READING
Urban, Joan Barth *Moscow and the Italian Communist Party: From Togliatti to Berlinguer* 1995

Tōjō, Hideki (1884–1948)

Japanese general and premier 1941–44 during World War II. Promoted to chief of staff of Japan's Guangdong army in Manchuria in 1937, he served as minister for war 1940–41 where he was responsible for negotiating the tripartite Axis alliance with Germany and Italy in 1940. He was held responsible for defeats in the Pacific in 1944 and forced to resign. After Japan's defeat, he was hanged as a war criminal.

His main concern was winning the war in China, but both he and the Japanese army felt this was being hampered by the Western powers denying Japan vital resources. He brought Japan into the war to take Allied colonial possessions in the Pacific and Southeast Asia and put Japan in a position of strength in subsequent negotiations. As part of this strategy, he ordered the occupation of Indochina in 1941 and maintained peace negotiations with the USA right up until the attack on Pearl Harbor in 1941.

Tokuda, Kyuichi (1894–1953)

Japanese political communist activist. He became leader of the Communist Party in 1945 and was elected to the Diet (Japanese parliament) in 1946. Forced to go underground by the US-directed 'Red Purge' in 1950, Tokuda fled to China where he died in Beijing in 1953.

He came from a poor Okinawan background and was an early member of the Japanese Communist Party, formed in 1922. He made repeated visits to Moscow during the 1920s. After earlier short spells of imprisonment, he was arrested in 1928 and not released from prison until 1945.

Tolbert, William Richard (1913–1980)

Liberian politician and 19th president of Liberia, 1971–80. He succeeded the long-standing president William V S Tubman, and was the last president to come from the American-African elite that had ruled Liberia for 160 years since its foundation. Tolbert was executed in a coup by African Liberians under Master Sergeant Samuel Doe in 1980.

Tolbert was born at Bensonville and educated at Liberia College (now the University of Liberia, Monrovia), graduating in 1934. After working in the Liberian Treasury 1935–43, he was a member of House of Representatives for the True Whig Party 1943–51, and then Tubman's vice president for 20 years, 1951–71. A devout Baptist, he was also, from 1965, president of the Baptist World Alliance.

Torrijos Herrera, Omar (1929–1981)

Panamanian soldier and political leader, dictator 1968–78. In 1972 he was declared 'maximum leader' for a six-year term by an elected assembly, which granted him full civil and military powers for six years while a civilian figurehead occupied the presidency. In 1977 he negotiated a new Panama Canal treaty with US President Jimmy ◊Carter, providing for the canal's eventual transfer to Panamanian control.

In 1978 he decided not to run for the presidency, enabling Arístides ◊Royo Sánchez to become president. However, he remained leader of the national guard and thus effectively controlled the regime until his death, in a plane crash, in 1981.

Born in Santiago, the son of schoolteachers, he became a professional soldier. As a lieutenant colonel in the national guard, he led the 1968 coup that ousted President Arnulfo ◊Arias, and became the country's effective ruler. Torrijos became a brigadier general in 1969 and, ruling by decree, introduced corporatist economic and social reforms, including land expropriation, and enlarged the public sector. He also banned political parties and imprisoned opponents.

Touré, (Ahmed) Sékou (1922–1984)

Guinean politician, president 1958–84. Initially active as a trade unionist, and a founder member of the Rassemblement Démocratique Africaine (RDA) in 1946, he organized an overwhelming 'non' vote to General Charles de Gaulle's referendum on self-government within a French community in 1958. Guinea was granted its independence immediately, the French removing as much of their possessions as possible. As president he retained his uncompromisingly radical views of domestic and foreign politics, and survived several attempts, supported by outside powers, to overthrow him.

After 1958 Touré made the Democratic Party of Guinea the only political organization and embarked upon a policy of socialist revolution. At first rigidly Marxist, crushing all opposition, he gradually moved towards a mixed economy, with private enterprise becoming legal in 1979. Following a series of unsuccessful coups in the 1960s, Touré put his country into virtual diplomatic isolation, but by 1975 relations with most of his neighbours had eased and he sought closer ties with Western powers, particularly France and the USA. Despite his harsh and authoritarian regime, he was re-elected unopposed in 1980.

Touré was educated in Quran schools and at Conakry from 1936 to 1940. He turned to trade-union activity and attended the Confédération Générale des Travailleurs (CGT) Congress in Paris in 1947, after which he was imprisoned for a brief period. In 1952 he became secretary general of the RDA in 1952, as well as secretary general of the local CGT branch. He was a member of the territorial assembly from 1953, mayor of Conakry in 1955, and a deputy in the French national assembly in 1956. See photograph on page 325.

Toure, Amadou Toumany (1948–)

Malian army officer, head of state and leader of the National Reconciliation Council 1991–92. From 1993 he was the director of the Interstate Group for the Eradication of Guinea Worm.

Tower, John Goodwin (1925–1991)

US Republican politician, a senator for Texas 1961–83. Despite having been a paid arms-industry consultant, he was selected in 1989 by President George Bush to serve as defence secretary, but the Senate refused to approve the appointment because of Tower's previous heavy drinking.

Tower, in 1961 the first Republican to be elected senator for Texas, emerged as a military expert in the Senate, becoming chair of the Armed Services Committee in 1981. After his retirement from the Senate in 1983, he acted as a consultant to arms manufacturers and chaired the 1986–87 Tower Commission, which investigated aspects of the Irangate arms-for-hostages scandal.

Townsend, Francis E(verett) (1867–1960)

US physician and social reformer. Almost destitute as a result of ill health, he conceived of his old-age revolving pension plan for the elderly; its essential feature was that every American over 60 would be given a pension to be financed by a national sales tax. Within two years the so-called *Townsend plan* spawned a social movement with 2.25 million members throughout the USA and its own newspaper (1935). Several bills incorporating the Townsend plan were introduced in Congress 1935–36, but his plans were later discredited by financial scandals

Townsend was born near Fairbury, Illinois. He moved to Belle Fourche, South Dakota, to practise medicine in 1903 and served as a physician in World War I. After an acute attack of peritonitis, he moved to Long Beach, California, with his family in 1919. Appointed assistant health officer of Long Beach, he remained in this position until he was ousted in a local political upheaval in 1933. His health remained a problem and he lost most of his savings during the Great Depression.

Traoré, Moussa (1936–)

Malian army officer and politician who seized power to become president of Mali in 1968 (and prime minister from 1969). He restored civilian government by 1979 and remained as president, but internal unrest continued and he was himself overthrown by the military in 1991. He was sentenced to death in 1993 for human-rights abuses, but the sentence was not carried out.

Traoré was educated at the Military Training College, Fréjus, and served first in the French army before joining the army of newly independent Mali in 1960 and rising through the ranks. On 19 November 1968 he led the coup that overthrew President Modibo Keïta. He established a one-party state in 1976, but violent demonstrations against this in 1991 brought his downfall.

Treurnicht, Andries Petrus (1921–1993)

South African Conservative Party politician. A former minister of the Dutch Reformed Church, he was elected to the South African parliament as a National Party member in 1971 but left it in 1982 to form a new right-wing Conservative Party, opposed to any dilution of the apartheid system.

His party, which sought the establishment of an independent Boer republic, gained ground in the 1987 and 1989 elections but dropped back in 1992. Towards the end of his life Treurnicht softened the party's approach and participated in multiparty constitutional talks.

Born in Piketberg, Treurnicht was a student at Stellenbosch and Cape Town universities, acquiring a doctorate in political philosophy. He was a minister of the Dutch Reformed Church 1946–60, later becoming the editor of its influential journal *Die Kerkbode*. In this capacity he came to the attention of Prime Minister Hendrik ◊Verwoerd, who was seeking some philosophical justification for the policy of apartheid. Treurnicht provided this and, having sampled the fringe of politics, decided to commit himself wholeheartedly, and was elected member of Parliament for Waterbury in 1971.

He occupied a number of governmental posts, including education and training 1976–78, plural relations and development 1978–79, public works, statistics, and tourism 1979–80, and state administration and statistics 1980–82. He broke away from the National Party when it accepted a proposal to create a tricameral parliament in which whites, coloureds, and Indians would be represented in separate chambers.

Trevelyan, George Otto (1838–1928)

British politician and historian, a nephew of the historian Lord Macaulay, whose biography he wrote in 1876. He succeeded to baronetcy in 1886.

Trotsky, Leon, adopted name of Lev Davidovitch Bronstein (1879–1940)

Russian revolutionary. He joined the Bolshevik party and took a leading part in the seizure of power in 1917 and in raising the Red Army that fought the Civil War 1918–20. In the struggle for power that followed Vladimir ◊Lenin's death in 1924, Joseph ◊Stalin defeated Trotsky, and this and other differences with the Communist Party led to his exile in 1929. He settled in Mexico, where he was assassinated at Stalin's instigation. Trotsky believed in world revolution and in permanent revolution, and was an uncompromising, if liberal, idealist.

Trotsky became a Marxist in the 1890s and was imprisoned and exiled for opposition to the tsarist regime. He lived in Western Europe from 1902 until the 1905 revolution, when he was again imprisoned but escaped to live in exile until 1917, when he returned to Russia and joined the Bolsheviks. Although as a

---

Any contemporary of ours who wants peace and comfort before anything has chosen a bad time to be born.

LEON TROTSKY Quoted in *Observer* 26 March 1933

---

young man Trotsky admired Lenin, when he worked with him organizing the revolution of 1917, he objected to Lenin's dictatorial ways. He was second in command until Lenin's death, and was minister for foreign affairs 1917–18 and minister for war 1918–January 1925. In exile in Mexico, he was killed with an ice pick. Official Soviet recognition of responsibility for his assassination through the secret service came in 1989.

Trotsky's later works are critical of the Soviet regime; for example, *The Revolution Betrayed* (1937). His greatest work is his magisterial *History of the Russian Revolution* (1932–33).

◆ TRIMBLE, DAVID (1944–) ◆

Northern Ireland politician, leader of the Ulster Unionist party (or Official Unionist Party, OUP) from 1995 and Northern Ireland's first minister from 1998. Representing the Upper Bann constituency in the House of Commons from 1990, he won the leadership of the OUP in August 1995, when James ◊Molyneaux decided to retire at the age of 75. In 1998 Trimble shared the Nobel Peace Prize with John ◊Hume in recognition of their work to find a peaceful solution to the conflict in Northern Ireland.

Trimble, originally seen as a hardliner and not likely to move easily into Molyneaux's seat, proved to be more flexible and tolerant than had been predicted. Following his election as OUP leader, he sought to give an impetus to the Northern Ireland peace process, meeting UK prime minister John Major, Irish taoiseach John Bruton, and US president Bill Clinton. Still emphasizing the need for the Irish Republican Army (IRA) to decommission its weaponry, he nevertheless suggested a route to all-party talks through elections, although this proposal was opposed by republican spokesmen.

He accepted the 1998 Good Friday Agreement on power-sharing, which was rejected by the more extreme Democratic Unionist Party, led by Ian Paisley, and the United Kingdom Unionist Party, led by Robert McCartney. He was chosen as Northern Ireland's first minister after the newly elected Northern Ireland Assembly met in June 1998, and seemed determined to make the peace agreement work. In the first meeting between Unionist and Republican leaders for several generations he met the president of Sinn Féin, Gerry Adams, at Stormont in September 1998.

Educated at Queen's University Belfast, Trimble qualified as a barrister and lectured in law at Queen's for 22 years before fully committing himself to politics. He represents a new, less dogmatic, breed of Northern Ireland politicians, willing to consider closer links with the province's southern neighbour.

FURTHER READING

Deutscher, Isaac *The Prophet Armed* 1954, *The Prophet Unarmed* 1959, *The Prophet Outcast* 1963

Mandel, Ernest *Trotsky: A Study in the Dynamic of His Thought* 1979

Segal, Ronald *Leon Trotsky: A Biography* 1979

Trotsky, Leon *My Life* translation 1930

Trudeau, Pierre Elliott (1919–)

Canadian Liberal politician. He was prime minister 1968–79 and 1980–84. In 1980, having won again by a landslide on a platform opposing Québec separatism, he helped to defeat the Québec independence movement in a referendum. He repatriated the constitution from the UK in 1982, but by 1984 had so lost support that he resigned.

In Pierre Elliot Trudeau Canada has at last produced a political leader worthy of assassination.

IRVING LAYTON *The Whole Bloody Bird*

Trudeau was born in Montréal. He studied law, political science, and economics, and began to practise law in Montréal in 1951. He was elected to the Canadian parliament in 1965 as a representative of the Federal Liberal Party. In 1966 he became parliamentary secretary to the prime minister, Lester ◊Pearson, and in 1967 became minister of justice and attorney general. Following the resignation of Pearson, Trudeau became leader of the Liberal Party on 6 April 1968.

FURTHER READING

Butson, T *Pierre Trudeau* 1986

Radwanski, George *Trudeau* 1978

Trujillo Molina, Rafael Leónidas (1891–1961)

Dominican Republic right-wing politician, dictator 1930–61, and president 1930–38 and 1942–52. As commander of the Dominican Guard, he seized power from President Horacio ◊Vásquez and was elected president unopposed. He established a ruthless autocracy, aided by a powerful terroristic police force and murder squads, his personal control over much the economy, and his manipulation of 'puppet presidents'. There was economic progress and impressive public works projects, but at the cost of political repression and strained relations with neighbouring states, where he tried to foment right-wing revolutions. He was assassinated by military leaders in May 1961.

During what was an exceptionally tight and personal dictatorship, Trujillo owned all the mass media and the transport and communications systems in the Dominican Republic as well as 80% of the land and the country's banks, services, and utilities. He also owned around 45% of all sources of production, created his own political party, the Dominican Party, and renamed the capital, Santo Domingo, 'Trujillo City'. In 1937 Dominican troops entered Haiti and massacred 10,000 Haitians in a campaign against Haitian infiltration. His regime was censured by the Organization of American States (OAS) and economic sanctions were imposed. Between 1939 and 1941, and from 1953, as foreign minister, he retained political dominance through puppet presidents. After his assassination he was succeeded as army chief by his older son, Rafael Leonidas Trujillo, Jr, for five months.

Trujillo was born in San Cristóbal, into a middle-class family. He worked on a sugar estate before being trained by US Marines during the US military occupation of 1916–24. He rose to become a brigadier general and commander of the Dominican Guard, and served as army chief under Vásquez before ousting him in 1930.

Truman, Harry S (1884–1972)

33rd president of the USA 1945–53, a Democrat. In January 1945 he became vice president to F D Roosevelt, and president when Roosevelt died in April that year. He used the atom bomb against Japan, launched the Marshall Plan to restore Western Europe's economy, and nurtured the European Community (now the European Union) and NATO (including the rearmament of West Germany).

It's a recession when your neighbour loses his job; it's a depression when you lose yours.

HARRY S TRUMAN Quoted in *Observer* 13 April 1958

Born in Lamar, Missouri, he farmed his parents' land near Independence for 12 years. Soon after the USA entered World War I, Truman joined the army and served in France. In 1922 he was elected judge of the Jackson County court. He became a senator in 1934, and was selected as Roosevelt's last vice president. As president, Truman took part in the Potsdam Conference of July 1945. In 1947 he initiated the ***Truman Doctrine***, a policy for helping countries threatened by, or anxious to resist, communism.

In 1948 he was elected as president for a second term in a surprise victory over Thomas Dewey, governor of New York. At home, he had difficulty converting the economy back to peacetime conditions, and failed to prevent witch-hunts on suspected communists such as Alger ◊Hiss. In Korea, he intervened when the South was invaded, but sacked General Douglas ◊MacArthur when the general's policy threatened to start World War III. Truman's decision not to enter Chinese territory, betrayed by the double agent Kim Philby, led to China's entry into the Korean War.

FURTHER READING

Alonzo, L (ed) *Harry S Truman and the Fair Deal* 1974
Ferrell, Robert *Harry S Truman and the Modern American Presidency* 1983
Jenkins, Roy *Truman* 1986
Kirkendall, R (ed) *The Harry S Truman Encyclopedia* 1989
McCoy, D R *The Presidency of Harry S Truman* 1984
Miller, R *Truman: The Rise to Power* 1986

Tubman, William Vacanarat Shadrach (1895–1971)

Liberian politician. The descendant of US slaves, he was a lawyer in the USA. After his election to the presidency of Liberia in 1944 he concentrated on uniting the various ethnic groups. Re-elected several times, he died in office of natural causes, despite frequent assassination attempts.

Tung Chee-hwa (1937–)

Hong Kong business executive and politician, chief executive of the Hong Kong Special Administrative Region (SAR) from 1997. As the SAR chief executive he launched a populist initiative to make housing more affordable, and had to deal with a succession of currency crises. In May 1998 he suffered a setback when prodemocracy opposition candidates polled strongly in elections to the legislative council.

Born into a wealthy household, his father, C Y Tung, a shipping magnate, moved his family from Shanghai, then a French concession, to Hong Kong at the time of the communist revolution in China in 1949. Tung Chee-hwa tudied engineering at Liverpool University in the UK, and worked for General Electric in the USA. When his father died in 1982, he took charge of the family's huge shipping empire, Orient Overseas, and rescued it from collapse, with financial assistance in 1985 from mainland China. A conservative but affable and conciliatory figure, he was effectively selected by the Chinese to be SAR chief executive from July 1997. He was a particular admirer of Lee Kuan Yew, the authoritarian capitalist former prime minister of the city state of Singapore.

◆ TUDJMAN, FRANJO (1922–) ◆

Croatian nationalist leader and historian, president from 1990. As leader of the centre-right Croatian Democratic Union (CDU), he led the fight for Croatian independence. During the 1991–92 civil war, his troops were hampered by lack of arms and the military superiority of the Serb-dominated federal army, but Croatia's independence was recognized following a successful United Nations-negotiated cease-fire in January 1992. Tudjman was re-elected in August 1992 and again in October 1995. Despite suffering from stomach cancer, he was re-elected president in June 1997.

Born in Veliko Trgovisce, Croatia, Tudjman was educated at the Higher Military Academy in Belgrade and studied for a doctorate at the University of Zagreb. During World War II he joined Tito's partisan force and rose to the rank of major general before leaving the army in 1960. He was expelled from the League of Communists of Yugoslavia in 1967 for Croatian nationalist writings and imprisoned for separatist activities 1972–74 and 1981–84. In 1990 he was elected president, having campaigned under a nationalist, anti-Serbia banner. He was criticized for his hesitant conduct during the 1991–92 civil war but, despite many soldiers having opted to fight under the banner of the better-equipped right-wing extremist faction by December 1991, Tudjman retained the vocal support of the majority of Croatians.

In 1993, in violation of the 1992 UN peace accord, Tudjman launched an offensive to recapture Serb-held territory in the disputed Krajina enclave, and further offensives into western Slavonia and Krajina in 1995, which created more than 150,000 Serb refugees and were allegedly accompanied by widespread human-rights violations. In August 1995 Krajina was recaptured from the Serbs, and Serbia subsequently agreed to gradually hand back control over eastern Slavonia. Tudjman called an early election in October 1995, seeking a popular mandate to continue with his militaristic policies, but, although re-elected, his party failed to win the two-thirds majority for which he had hoped.

FURTHER READING

Bosnić, Sava *Franjo Tudjman: Une Carrière ambiguë* 1993
Bulajić, Milan *Tudjman's 'Jasenovac Myth': Genocide Against Serbs, Jews, and Gypsies* 1994
Knezević, Anto *An Analysis of Serbian Propaganda: The Misrepresentation of the Writings of the Historian Franjo Tudjman in Light of the Serbian-Croatian War* 1992
Palić-Kusan, Zdenka (transl) *Croatia on Trial: The Case of the Croatian Historian Dr F Tudjman* 1981
Tudjman, Franjo *Horrors of War: Historical Reality and Philosophy* 1997, *Croatia at the Crossroads* 1991

Franjo Tudjman, 1992. *Rex*

Turner, Ben (1863–1942)

British trade-union leader and politician. After working as the general secretary of the textile workers'
union 1902–22, he was elected president of the Trade
Union Congress (TUC) in 1928. He was a Labour
member of Parliament 1922–24 and 1929–31.

Turner was born in Holmfirth, Yorkshire, and began
work at a textile mill. In 1929 he was appointed
secretary for mines in the Labour government, but
soon resigned to resume his trade-union work. He was
knighted in 1931.

Turner, John Napier (1929–)

Canadian Liberal politician, prime minister in 1984.
He was elected to the House of Commons in 1962 and
served in the cabinet of Pierre Trudeau until his
resignation in 1975. He succeeded Trudeau as party
leader and prime minister in 1984, but lost the 1984
and 1988 elections. Turner resigned as leader in 1989,
and returned to his law practice. He was replaced as
Liberal Party chief by Herbert Gray in February 1990.

Ubico Castañeda, Jorge (1878–1946)

Guatemalan soldier and politician, member of the Progressive Party, dictator-president 1931–44. His rule was characterized by a combination of economic efficiency and political authoritarianism. His government supported business, carried out extensive road construction, increased health and educational provision, and restored the country's finances.

Opposition to his presidency, which mounted as economic conditions deteriorated in World War II, was firmly suppressed and Ubico's presidential term was twice extended by extralegal 'plebiscites'. In June 1944, after a popular revolt in El Salvador that deposed Maximiliano ◊Hernández Martínez, Ubico was overthrown by a general strike and driven into exile, to New Orleans, USA.

Educated partly in the USA, Ubico became a professional soldier, reaching the rank of general. He won the 1930 presidential election with the support of the Liberal Party, and took office in February 1931.

Uddin, Pola Manzila, Baroness Uddin (1959–)

Bangladeshi-born English Labour working peer (created in 1998), one of three Muslim members of the House of Lords. Lady Uddin was elected to Tower Hamlets Borough Council in 1990, the first Bangladeshi-born woman to sit on a local authority in the UK, and became deputy leader of the council. She left Tower Hamlets to become a social services manager for the London Borough of Newham.

Ulbricht, Walter (1893–1973)

East German communist politician, in power 1960–71. He lived in exile in the USSR during Hitler's rule 1933–45. A Stalinist, he became first secretary of the Socialist Unity Party in East Germany in 1950 and (as chair of the Council of State from 1960) was instrumental in the building of the Berlin Wall in 1961. He established East Germany's economy and recognition outside the Eastern European bloc.

Ulmanis, Gauntis (1939–)

Latvian politician, president from 1993. He worked principally as an economist and as a municipal employee of Riga 1963–92 and became a member of the Board of the General Bank of Latvia in 1992. He served as a deputy to the parliament from June 1993 and became president in July 1993.

Born in Riga, Ulmanis was exiled to Russia as a child with his family, returning in 1946. He was educated at the University of Riga and joined the Communist Party of the Soviet Union in 1965; he remained a member until 1989.

FURTHER READING
Ulmanis, Gauntis *Put' presidenta/The Path of the President* 1996

Ulufa'alu, Bartholomew (1950–)

Solomon Islands centre-right politician, prime minister from 1997. He was elected to the national parliament in 1976. He became leader of the National Democratic Party (Nadepa), which he reorganized and renamed (in 1986) the Solomon Islands Liberal Party (SILP), and was finance minister 1980–84, in the government of Solomon ◊Mamaloni. Ulufa'alu was out of parliament for much of the period 1984–97, but was intermittently an economic adviser to Mamaloni and to international development programmes. Re-elected to parliament at the August 1997 general election, Ulufa'alu became prime minister, heading an Alliance for Change coalition, which was centred around his SILP. This government quickly moved to introduce structural economic and administrative reforms, designed to streamline government and stimulate the private sector.

Born in Laulasi, in Malaita province, Ulufa'alu studied economics at the University of Papua New Guinea. On his return to the Solomons in 1975, he set up the Solomon Islands Union of Workers.

Uno, Sōsuke (1922–1998)

Japanese conservative politician, member of the Liberal Democratic Party (LDP). He held various cabinet posts from 1976, and was designated prime minister in June 1989 in an attempt to restore the image of the LDP after several scandals. He resigned after only a month in office when his affair with a prostitute became public knowledge.

Vaea of Houma, Baron (1921–   )

Tongan politician, prime minister from 1991. He worked as an aide to Queen ◊Salote 1954–59, as governor of the Ha'apai island group 1960–68, and as Tonga's high commissioner in the UK 1970–72. He was awarded the title of baron in 1970 by King ◊Taufa'ahau Tupou IV and, after serving as labour and industry minister from 1973, became prime minister in August 1991, following the resignation of the king's brother, Prince Fatafehi Tu'ipelhake, for health reasons.

Born in the capital, Nuku'alofa, he studied at the Wesley College in New Zealand and at Oxford University. He inherited the title Vaea in 1942 and, after military service during World War II with the New Zealand Airforce, worked in the Tongan civil service.

Vajpayee, Atal Behari (1926–   )

Indian politician, prime minister in 1996 and from 1998. Leader of the liberal wing of the Hindu-nationalist Bharatiya Janata Party (BJP), he served as prime minister for 13 days during May 1996 and, heading a minority administration, from March 1998. As prime minister, he called for national 'reconciliation and accord', but also controversially sanctioned India's nuclear tests. This led to international sanctions, and to Pakistan conducting nuclear tests in response.

Born in Gwalior, in north-central India, Vajpayee joined the militant Hindu Rashtriya Swayamsevak Sangh (RSS) in 1941, and was a founder member of the right-wing Bharatiya Jana Sangh in 1951, and the BJP in 1980. A member of the Indian parliament from 1957, he was foreign minister 1977–79 in the Janata party coalition government of Morarji Desai, and opposition leader from 1993.

Vance, Cyrus Roberts (1917–   )

US Democratic politician, secretary of state 1977–80. He was United Nations negotiator in the peace talks on Bosnia-Herzegovina 1992–93, resigning from the post due to ill health. Together with European Community negotiator David Owen, he devised the Vance–Owen peace plan for dividing the republic into ten semi-autonomous provinces. The plan was rejected by the Bosnian Serbs.

Vandenberg, Arthur Hendrick (1884–1951)

US politician. A Republican, he was elected to the US Senate in 1928 and remained there for the next 23 years. Although initially an isolationist, he supported F D Roosevelt's war policies and was a supporter of the United Nations in 1945. He became the Republican party's chief spokesperson on foreign affairs, and was chair of the Senate Foreign Relations Committee 1946–48.

Born in Grand Rapids, Michigan, Vandenberg briefly attended the University of Michigan Law School. He left to join the staff of the *Grand Rapids Herald*, of which he became editor in 1906, and later became active in state politics.

Van Devanter, Willis (1859–1941)

US jurist. He was appointed US Supreme Court justice 1910–37 by President William Taft. Active in Republican politics, he served as assistant US attorney general 1897–1903 and federal circuit judge 1903–10. A staunch conservative, Van Devanter was a bitter opponent of the New Deal until his retirement.

Born in Marion, Indiana, Van Devanter was educated at Asbury University and received a law degree from the University of Cincinnati in 1881. Settling in Cheyenne, Wyoming, he served as city attorney 1887–88 and chief justice of the territorial supreme court 1888–90.

Vansittart, Robert Gilbert, 1st Baron Vansittart (1881–1957)

British diplomat, noted for his anti-German polemic. He was permanent undersecretary of state for foreign affairs 1930–38 and chief diplomatic adviser to the foreign secretary 1938–41. He was created a KCB in 1929 and Baron in 1941.

Vanzetti, Bartolomeo (1888–1927)

Italian anarchist. He emigrated to the USA in 1908, finding work as a fish peddlar. In 1920 he was accused, with Nicola ◊Sacco, of murdering two men while robbing a shoe factory in Massachusetts. Although the evidence was largely circumstantial, the two men were tried in 1921 and sentenced to death. They were executed in 1927 after a controversial and lengthy appeal. It has been claimed that they were punished for their socialist sympathies, but experts now believe that Sacco was guilty, and Vanzetti innocent.

Vargas, Getúlio Dornelles (1883–1954)

Brazilian president 1930–45 and 1951–54. Following his presidential election failure in 1930, he overthrew the republic and in 1937 set up a totalitarian, profascist state known as the Estado Novo. Ousted by a military coup in 1945, he returned as president in 1951 with the support of the labour movement but, amid mounting opposition and political scandal, committed suicide in 1954.

He was born in São Borja and educated in law at Porto Alegre Law School. In 1922 he was elected to congress, becoming a minister of finance in 1926. In 1928 he was elected governor of Rio Grande do Sul state.

Vargas Llosa, (Jorge) Mario (Pedro) (1936–)

Peruvian novelist and politician. He wrote *La ciudad y los perros/The Time of the Hero* (1963) and *La guerra del fin del mundo/The War at the End of the World* (1982). In the course of his political career, Vargos Llosa began as a communist and turned to the right; he ran unsuccessfully for the presidency in 1990, when he was defeated by Alberto Fujimori.

FURTHER READING

Booker, Keith M *Vargas Llosa among the Postmodernists* 1994

Durán, Victor Manuel *A Marxist Reading of Fuetes, Vargas Llosa and Puig* 1994

Sommers, Joseph *Literature and Ideology, Vargas Llosa's Novelistic Evaluation of Militarism* 1975

Vargas Llosa, Alvaro *The Madness of Things Peruvian: Democracy under Siege* 1994

Vásquez, Horacio (1860–1936)

Dominican Republic politician, president in 1899, 1902–03, and 1924–30. He rose to power after the assassination of dictator Ulises Heureaux in 1899, and dominated politics until overthrown by the dictator Rafael ◊Trujillo Molina in 1930. After helping to negotiate US withdrawal from the republic in 1924, he won the US-supervised presidential elections. Ruling with honesty, he promoted reforms instituted by the US regime 1916–24, but in 1928 his presidential term was unconstitutionally extended to six years and he adopted US Republican Charles ◊Dawes's report on fiscal reform. When economic depression intensified from 1929, he was deposed and forced into exile.

During the 1880s and 1890s Vásquez participated in plots to overthrow Heureaux, who was president 1882–84 and 1886–99.

Vassiliou, Georgios Vassos (1931–)

Greek-Cypriot politician and entrepreneur, president

of Cyprus 1988–93. A self-made millionaire, he entered politics as an independent and in 1988 won the presidency, with Communist Party support. He subsequently, with United Nations help, tried to heal the rift between the Greek and Turkish communities, but was unsuccessful. In the February 1993 presidential elections he was narrowly defeated by Glafkos Clerides.

Vega, Suzanne (1959–)

US singer and children's rights campaigner. She was born in California and moved to New York City at the age of two. She attended the High School of Performing Arts, then Barnard College. She was still at Barnard when she began attracting attention at Greenwich Village folk clubs. Her chief works include *Suzanne Vega* (1985) and *Solitude Standing* (1987), which features 'Luka', a song about child abuse that became a surprise hit in 1987. Since then she has worked tirelessly in support of children's rights, addressing meetings and conferences, as well as performing fundraising concerts for Amnesty International amongst others.

Veil, Simone (1927–)

French centrist politician, the first woman to hold a full cabinet post under the Fifth Republic, as Valéry ◊Giscard d'Estaing's minister for health 1974–79. A survivor of Hitler's concentration camps (where she lost both her parents and her brother), she trained for the judiciary and worked in the justice ministry prior to her appointment as a full cabinet minister. She was widely respected and popular as a politician despite the French right's hostility to her legalization of abortion in 1975. Veil chose then to develop her political career at the European level. Elected to the European Parliament (EP) 1979–93, and its first president 1979–82, she presided over the EP liberal-democratic group 1982–93 before returning as French minister for health, urban, and social affairs under Edouard ◊Balladur 1993–95. She was appointed to the Constitutional Council in February 1998.

Velasco Ibarra, José Maria (1893–1979)

Ecuadorian politician; president five times between 1934 and 1968. He dominated political life in Ecuador in the postwar era, gaining presidential election five times (1934–35, 1944–47, 1952–56, 1960–61, and 1968–72). He only completed one full term in office, however. A populist politician among the Ecuadorian peoples, his administration was extremely erratic, often instituting abrupt policy changes, inappropriate economic policy, oppression, and even military intervention.

In his political career, Velasco Ibarra was elected and deposed as president twice before succeeding Galo ◊Plaza Lasso in 1952. His third (and only complete) term in office saw widespread media censorship and infrastructure investment during an economically stable period. In 1960 Velasco Ibarra initiated changes in the nation's socio-economic structures and his governmental style succeeded in creating strong opposition from the two main parties: the liberals and conservatives. In 1961 he was forced to resign by a military junta. The period 1968–72 was marked by mounting hostility and political chaos as economic problems worsened. Many opposition members believed that national economic growth would be considerably impeded, as many of the successful policies established by previous administrations were invariably terminated or reversed by Velasco Ibarra during his terms in office. In June 1970, with riots and public unrest, Velasco Ibarra, with support from the military, established a dictatorship. He was later overthrown by a military junta and General Guillermo Rodriguez Lara became president.

Venizelos, Eleuthérios Kyriakos (1864–1936)

Greek politician born in Crete, leader of the Cretan movement against Turkish rule until the union of the island with Greece in 1905. He later became prime minister of the Greek state on five occasions, 1910–15, 1917–20, 1924, 1928–32, and 1933, before being exiled to France in 1935.

Having led the fight against Turkish rule in Crete, Venizelos became president of the Cretan assembly and declared the union of the island with Greece in 1905. As prime minister of Greece from 1910, he instituted financial, military, and constitutional reforms and took Greece into the Balkan Wars 1912–13. As a result, Greece annexed Macedonia, but attempts by Venizelos to join World War I on the Allied side led to his dismissal by King Constantine. Leading a rebel government in Crete and later in Salonika, he declared war on Bulgaria and Germany and secured the abdication of King Constantine.

As prime minister again from 1917 he attended the Paris Peace Conference in 1919. By provoking a war with Turkey over Anatolia in 1920 he suffered an electoral defeat. On his last return to office in 1933, he was implicated in an uprising by his supporters and fled to France, where he died.

Verwoerd, Hendrik (Frensch) (1901–1966)

South African right-wing Nationalist Party politician, prime minister 1958–66. As minister of native affairs 1950–58, he was the chief promoter of apartheid legislation (segregation by race). He banned the African National Congress (ANC) in 1960 and withdrew South Africa from the Commonwealth in 1961, making the country a republic. He was assassinated in 1966.

Born in the Netherlands, Verwoerd was educated in South Africa, the Netherlands, and Germany. After beginning an academic career in sociology, he became editor of the nationalist *Die Transvaler* in 1937 and

stood as a National Party candidate in the 1948 election. Having failed to gain a seat he was appointed to the Senate, which he led until he was elected to parliament in 1958.

Vicky, pen name of Victor Weisz (1913–1966)

Hungarian cartoonist who settled in the UK from 1935. He worked for a number of British papers but is best known for his contributions to the *New Statesman* magazine from 1954 and the *Evening Standard* from 1958. His satirical cartoons attacked power and privilege, and his serious drawings exposed the plight of the poor and oppressed.

Born in Berlin of Hungarian parents, he first worked for the Berlin *12 Uhr Blatt* and published an anti-Hitler cartoon as early as 1928. He went to the UK in 1935 after the Nazis came to power.

Victor Emmanuel III (1869–1947)

King of Italy from the assassination of his father, Umberto I, in 1900. He acquiesced in the Fascist regime of Mussolini from 1922 and, after the dictator's fall in 1943, relinquished power to his son Umberto II, who cooperated with the Allies. Victor Emmanuel formally abdicated in 1946.

Vidal, Gore, originally Eugene Luther Vidal (1925–)

US writer and critic. Few contemporary writers have generated as much controversy. He shocked America by a frank account of homosexual life in his second book, *The City and the Pillar* (1948), at a time when homosexuality was taboo. He went on to challenge established ideas and concepts throughout his life. Much of his work deals satirically with history and politics and includes the novels *Myra Breckinridge* (1968), *Burr* (1973), and *Empire* (1987); plays and screenplays, including *Suddenly Last Summer* (1958); and essays, such as 'Armageddon?' (1987). His autobiography, *Palimpsest*, appeared in 1995.

FURTHER READING
Parini, Jay (ed) *Gore Vidal: Writer Against the Grain* 1992

Videla, Gabriel Goncález (1898–1980)

Chilean president 1946–52. He was a political reformist and outlawed the Communist Party in Chile in 1948, despite having communist members in his cabinet 1946–48 and sided with the USA in the Cold War. He made little progress in improving Chile's socio-economic problems during his term in office.

Videla was elected president following the death of President Juan Antonio Ríos Morales in 1946. By the end of his term in office, Chileans were apathetic of politicians and widespread disenchantment with the conservative administration under Videla led to Ibáñez del Campo winning the presidency in 1952.

Videla, Jorge Rafael (1925–)

Argentine military leader and president 1976–81. He was the main architect of the 'dirty war' against left-wing elements 1976–83.

In 1975 Videla was appointed commander in chief of the army by President Isabel Perón, under military pressure. From this position he began a reorganization of the military leadership, removing officers sympathetic to Peronism. In the same year, he led an army campaign against the Ejército Revolucionario del Pueblo (ERP; People's Revolutionary Army) in the northern Tucumán province, which resulted in the annihilation of hundreds of leftist guerrillas.

He deposed Isabel Perón on 24 March 1976 to became the de facto president as head of a three-man military junta. Videla then suspended congress and vested legislative powers in a nine-man military commission. He also halted the functioning of the courts, political parties, and labour unions. Military personnel filled all important government posts. Hundreds of persons suspected of being left-wing guerrillas were arrested in the last week of March 1976 alone, and between 10,000 and 30,000 others 'disappeared' over the next few years. Videla retired in 1981 and was succeeded by Roberto Viola.

Videnov, Zhan (Jan) Vassilev (1959–)

Bulgarian politician, prime minister 1995–96. He played a key role in the remodelling of the Bulgarian Communist Party (BKP) as the reformed Bulgarian Socialist Party (BSP), becoming its leader in 1991. He took the party back to power in the 1994 general election, but resigned in December 1996 after a BSP-backed candidate was defeated in the presidential election.

Born in Plovdiv and educated at the Moscow State Institute for International Relations, Videnov climbed the ranks of the ruling BKP and became leader of the new, reform-socialist BSP in December 1991. Pledging to construct a social safety net to cushion the impact of the transition to a market economy and also to improve links with Russia, the BSP was elected to power under Videnov's leadership in December 1994, less than five years after the overthrow of the communist regime. However, Videnov's position was weakened in November 1996 when Petar ◊Stoyanov, of the right-of-centre opposition Union of Democratic Forces (UDF), was elected president.

Villa, Pancho (Francisco), originally Doroteo Arango (1877–1923)

Mexican revolutionary. The Mexican Revolution of 1911 made him famous as a military commander. In a fierce struggle for control of the revolution, he and Emiliano ◊Zapata were defeated in 1915 by Álvaro ◊Obregón and Venustiano ◊Carranza, with whom Villa had earlier allied himself against the dictatorship of General Victoriano ◊Huerta. Both Villa and Zapata withdrew to mountain strongholds in north and central Mexico and continued to carry on guerrilla warfare. In 1916 Villa was responsible for the shooting of a number of US citizens in the town of Santa Isabel, Chihuahua, as well as an attack on the city of Columbus, New Mexico, USA, which precipitated the sending of a US punitive force by President Woodrow ◊Wilson. He eventually made peace with the government in 1920, being pardoned in return for agreeing to retire from politics, but was murdered in Parral.

Born near San Juan del Rio, Durango, the son of a field labourer, Villa had various modest occupations and was a bandit in Chihuahua and Durango. He gave early support to Francisco ◊Madero.

FURTHER READING
Arnold, O *Pancho Villa: The Mexican Century* 1979
Machado, M A *Centaur of the North: Francesco Villa, the Mexican Revolution, and Northern Mexico* 1988

Villeda Morales, Ramón (1908–1971)

Honduran centrist Liberal Party politician, president 1957–63. He launched a centre-left reform programme, involving agrarian reform, a progressive land tax, a new labour code, modernization of the country's infrastructure, increased spending on health and education, new welfare benefits, and a social security law. A treaty was also signed providing for entry into the Central American Common Market. In October 1963, shortly before presidential elections, Villeda was overthrown in an army coup led by Colonel Osvaldo López Arellano and went into exile.

Although Villeda won a plurality of the vote in the 1954 presidential election, Vice President Julío Lozano Díaz usurped the presidency and Villeda was forced into exile. He was made ambassador to the USA by the military junta that overthrew Lozano in October 1956 and, after the Liberals won new elections to the congress, Villeda became president in December 1957.

Trained in Honduras and Europe, he worked as a practising paediatrician during the right-wing National Party dictatorship of Tiburcio ◊Carías Andino, 1933–49. He became leader of the Liberal Party in 1949 and founded the party's newspaper, *El Pueblo*.

Villeda died in New York, in October 1971, soon after becoming head of the Honduran delegation to the United Nations.

FURTHER READING
Baciu, Stefan *Ramón Villeda Morales: Ciudano de America* 1970

Vincent, Sténio (Joseph) (1874–1959)

Haitian politician, president 1930–41. During the US occupation of 1915–34, he was elected president by the national assembly, after Joseph ◊ Bornó stepped down. A shrewd, pragmatic political tactician, he visited Washington, DC, in 1934 to successfully negotiate US withdrawal from the country. He had his term in office extended for five years by a plebiscite in 1935, and sought further extension in 1941, but was persuaded to retire by the USA. He was replaced by Elie ◊ Lescot.

Before his election as president, Vincent served as a senator and secretary of state, and also headed the Nationalist Party, which campaigned for the withdrawal of US troops.

He was drawn from the mulatto (mixed ethnic) social and political elite, and had a successful career as a lawyer and diplomat, representing Haiti, Berlin, and The Hague. He also founded two political journals.

Vinson, Frederick Moore (1890–1953)

US jurist. He held office in the US House of Representatives 1924–28 and 1930–38 and was appointed chief justice of the US Supreme Court 1946–53 by President Harry Truman. He defended federal intervention in social and economic matters, and dissented in *Youngstown Sheet and Tube Co v Sawyer* (1952), revoking presidential nationalization of the steel industry during the Korean War.

Born in Louisa, Kentucky, Vinson received his undergraduate and law degrees from Centre College and became a lawyer active in Democratic politics. He was appointed judge of the US Court of Appeals for the District of Columbia in 1939.

Viola, Roberto Eduardo

Argentine military leader and de facto president March–December 1981. Foreign debts, hyperinflation, and economic collapse as a result of heavy national spending were to render his governance ineffective. He was later imprisoned.

On 29 March 1981 Viola succeeded Jorge Rafael ◊ Videla as de facto president. Nine months later, however, the de facto government announced that Viola was to step down for health reasons, and General Leopoldo Galtieri took the post. Viola was sentenced to 17 years in prison by a civilian court in December 1985. He was released after serving only four years of the sentence as a result of pressures imposed by the military.

Vogel, Hans-Jochen (1926–)

German socialist politician, chair of the Social Democratic Party (SPD) 1987–91. A former leader of the SPD in Bavaria and mayor of Munich, he served in the West German governments of Willy Brandt and Helmut Schmidt in the 1970s as housing and then justice minister and then, briefly, as mayor of West Berlin.

A centrist, compromise figure, Vogel unsuccessfully contested the 1983 federal election as chancellor candidate for the SPD and in 1987 replaced Brandt as party chair; he left that post in 1991 and later in the year stood down as SPD parliamentary leader.

Vohor, Serge (1955–)

Vanuatuan politician, prime minister 1996–98. He was elected to parliament in 1983, representing the Francophone Union of Moderate Parties (UMP). Vohor became UMP deputy leader in 1987, while his rival, Maxime ◊ Carlot Korman, became leader. When Carlot formed a UMP-led coalition government after the December 1991 general election, Vohor became foreign minister and, from 1993, economics and industry minister. Support for the UMP fell in the November 1995 general election, but Vohor managed to become prime minister by aligning his faction of the UMP with the Anglophone Unity Front opposition. In February 1996, faced with certain defeat on a no-confidence motion, Vohor resigned, to be replaced as prime minister by Carlot, whom Vohor had sought to expel from the UMP. However, Vohor was reinstated as prime minister on 30 September 1996. His government survived another year, but was incapacitated by infighting and corruption scandals, which persuaded President Jean-Marie ◊ Leye to dissolve parliament in November 1997 and call a fresh general election for March 1998. The UMP polled poorly in this election and Vohor went into opposition.

Born in Port-Olry, on Santo island, he trained as a medical technician in Mauritius, and returned to Vanuatu in 1983.

Voroshilov, Klement Efremovich (1881–1969)

Marshal of the USSR. He joined the Bolsheviks in 1903 and was arrested many times and exiled, but escaped. He became a Red Army commander in the civil war 1918–20, a member of the central committee in 1921, commissar for war in 1925, member of the Politburo in 1926, and marshal in 1935. He was removed as war commissar in 1940 after defeats on the Finland front and failing to raise the German siege of Leningrad. He was a member of the committee for defence 1941–44 and president of the Presidium of the USSR 1953–60.

Vorster, John, originally Balthazar Johannes (1915–1983)

South African National Party politician, prime minister 1966–78, and president 1978–79. During his term as prime minister some elements of apartheid were allowed to lapse, and attempts were made to improve relations with the outside world. He resigned the presidency because of a financial scandal.

> *As far as criticism is concerned, we don't resent that unless it is absolutely biased, as it is in most cases.*
>
> John Vorster *Observer* November 1969

Vranitzky, Franz (1937–)

Austrian socialist politician, federal chancellor 1986–97. A banker, he entered the political arena through the moderate, left-of-centre Socialist Party of Austria (SPÖ), and became minister of finance in 1984.

He succeeded Fred Sinowatz as federal chancellor in 1986, heading an SPÖ-ÖVP (Austrian People's Party) coalition, which was returned in the October 1994 and December 1995 general elections. He resigned in January 1997.

Vyshinsky, Andrei Yanuaryevich (1883–1954)

Soviet politician. As commissar for justice, he acted as prosecutor at Stalin's treason trials 1936–38. He was foreign minister 1949–53 and often represented the USSR at the United Nations.

Wacha Dinshaw Edulji (1844–1936)

Indian politician. A member of the Bombay legislative council and the imperial legislative council, he worked for the peaceful development of his country through social reform, education, and through participation in politics. A founder member of the Congress party, he was its president in 1901. He criticized the British government's economic and financial policies and freely expressed his nation's viewpoint before the Welby Commission in London.

Waddington, David Charles, Baron Waddington (1929–)

British Conservative politician, home secretary 1989–90. He trained as a barrister, and was member of Parliament for Nelson and Colne 1968–74 and for Clitheroe (Ribble Valley since 1983) 1979–91. A Conservative whip from 1979, Waddington was a junior minister in the department of employment and in the Home Office before becoming chief whip in 1987. In 1990 he was made a life peer and became leader of the House of Lords in John Major's government.

Wagner, Robert (1910–1991)

US Democratic politician, mayor of New York City 1954–65. He demolished slum areas, built public housing, and was instrumental in introducing members of ethnic minorities into City Hall.

Wahid, Abdurrahman (1940–)

Indonesian religious leader; chair, from 1984, of the Nahdlatul Ulama Islamic Group, Indonesia's largest Islamic organization with 34 million followers in 1998. He was a proponent of political liberalization and believed government should be secular. Although health problems, especially poor eyesight, limited his effectiveness, his position placed him in the role of 'kingmaker' after President Thojib ◊Suharto's resignation.

Waite, Terry (Terence Hardy) (1939–)

English religious adviser to the archbishop of Canterbury (then Dr Robert Runcie) 1980–87. As the archbishop's special envoy, Waite disappeared on 20 January 1987 while engaged in secret negotiations to free European hostages in Beirut, Lebanon. He was taken hostage by an Islamic group and released on 18 November 1991.

His kidnapping followed six conversations he held with US agent Oliver ◊North, who appeared to be hoping to ransom US hostages through Waite.

He was awarded a CBE and the Roosevelt Freedom Medal in 1992. His books include *Taken on Trust* (1993) and *Footfalls in Memory* (1995).

Waldheim, Kurt (1918–)

Austrian politician and diplomat, president 1986–92. He was secretary general of the United Nations 1972–81, having been Austria's representative there 1964–68 and 1970–71.

He was elected president in spite of revelations that during World War II he had been an intelligence officer in an army unit responsible for transporting Jews to death camps. His election therefore led to some diplomatic isolation of Austria, and in 1991 he announced that he would not run for re-election.

FURTHER READING
Bassett, Richard *Waldheim and Austria* 1988
Herzstein, R E *Waldheim: The Missing Years* 1988
Waldheim, Kurt *In the Eye of the Storm*
(autobiography) translation 1986

Wałęsa, Lech (1943–)

Polish trade-union leader, president of Poland 1990–95. One of the founding members of the Solidarity free-trade-union movement, which emerged to challenge the communist government during strikes in the Gdańsk shipyards in August 1980, Wałęsa led the movement to become a national force. He was awarded the Nobel Prize for Peace in 1983. After his election as president, he gradually became estranged from Solidarity. In 1997 he formed a Christian Democratic party, which was, however, unlikely to make a significant impact on Polish political life.

A brilliant orator and negotiator, as an electrician at the Lenin Shipyard in Gdańsk, Wałęsa became a trade-union organizer and led a series of strikes in 1970 and 1976. In August 1980 he successfully challenged the government to improve working conditions and grant political concessions. After the imposition of martial law in December 1981 he was interned. A devout Catholic, he obtained the support of the church hierarchy in his negotiations with the authorities.

In 1990 he became president but lost his power base due to his apparent inability to work with the freely elected parliament and conflicts with previous allies and advisers, most notably Tadeusz ◊Mazowiecki. In 1995 he was defeated in the presidential elections by the Social Democrat Aleksander ◊Kwaśniewski. Although he continues to take an active part in Poland's political life, his influence is not significant. The leader of the Solidarity trade union, Marian ◊Krzaklewski, effectively blocked all Wałęsa's efforts to use it as a springboard for further involvement in the country's politics.

FURTHER READING

Boyes, Roger *The Naked President: A Political Biography of Lech Wałęsa* 1994

Craig, Mary *The Crystal Spirit: Lech Wałęsa and his Poland* 1986

Eringer, R *Strike for Freedom* 1982

Reiquam, Steve (ed) *Solidarity in Poland* 1988

Wałęsa, Lech *The Struggle and the Triumph* 1992

Walker, Alice Malsenior (1944–)

US poet, novelist, critic, and essay writer. She has been active in the US civil-rights movement since the 1960s and, as a black woman, wrote about the double burden of racist and sexist oppression, about colonialism, and the quest for political and spiritual recovery. Her novel *The Color Purple* (1982, filmed 1985), told in the form of letters, won a Pulitzer prize. Her other works include *Possessing the Secret of Joy* (1992), which deals passionately with female circumcision.

Walker, Jimmy (James John) (1881–1946)

US public official; mayor of New York City 1925–32. Although he made great improvements to the city's infrastructure and was a popular figure, he was charged with corruption and forced to resign in 1932.

Born in New York, Walker attended St Francis Xavier College and was admitted to the bar in 1912. Becoming active in Democratic party politics, he served in the state assembly 1909–15 and the state senate 1915–25, where he became a protégé of Al Smith.

FURTHER READING

Walsh, George *Gentleman Jimmy Walker, Mayor of the Jazz Age* 1976

Walker, Peter Edward, Baron Walker of Worcester (1932–)

British Conservative politician, energy secretary 1983–87, and secretary of state for Wales 1987–90. He was made a life peer in 1992.

As energy secretary he managed the government's response to the national miners' strike 1984–85, which resulted in the capitulation of the National Union of Miners. He retired from active politics in 1990.

He was educated at Latymer Upper School, London. As a partner in a firm of insurance brokers, he rapidly established himself in a career in the City of London, ultimately becoming deputy chair of Slater, Walker Securities Ltd. He was active in the Young Conservatives during the 1950s, achieving national office, and was elected Conservative member of Parliament for Worcester in 1961.

Between 1964 and 1970 he was an opposition spokesperson in various fields and entered the cabinet as secretary of state for the environment in 1970, a post he held until 1972 when he was appointed secretary of state for trade and industry. He was again an opposition spokesperson after the February election of 1974, but was dropped from the shadow cabinet when Margaret Thatcher became Conservative Party leader in 1975.

Wallace, George Corley (1919–1998)

US politician; governor of Alabama 1963–67, 1971–79, and 1983–87. Wallace opposed the integration of black and white students in the 1960s. He contested the presidency in 1968 as an independent (the American Independent Party) and in 1972 campaigned for the Democratic nomination but was shot at a rally and became partly paralysed.

Wallace was born in Clio, Alabama, and educated at the University of Alabama. He served in the Alabama state legislature 1951–55, and was a judge on the third judicial circuit 1955–63. During the 1963 integration of the University of Alabama, he defied a court order and prevented access to black students; he later complied with the order. His wife served as governor 1967–71 when he was ineligible to run for a third consecutive term. Wallace moderated his staunch anti-integration views and was elected for a fourth term as governor by a populist coalition of blacks and whites 1982. He retired in 1987.

> *Segregation now, segregation tomorrow and segregation forever!*
>
> GEORGE WALLACE
> Inaugural speech as
> governor of Alabama
> January 1963

Wallace, Henry Agard (1888–1965)

US politician and journalist. Appointed secretary to the Treasury by Franklin Roosevelt in 1933, he served as vice president during Roosevelt's third term 1941–45. He later broke with Harry Truman and, after serving as editor of the *New Republic* 1946–47, was the unsuccessful Progressive Party candidate for president in 1948.

Born in Adair County, Iowa, Wallace was educated at Iowa State College and in 1910 joined the staff of the family-owned periodical *Wallace's Farmer*. Although his father was a prominent Republican, the younger Wallace joined the Democratic Party in 1928.

Wallace became secretary of commerce in 1945. In 1946 he attacked the government's attitude to Russia, and resigned. When fighting broke out in Korea in 1950, he announced his support for United Nations action there, and retired from politics shortly afterwards, returning to his farming interests.

> *The century on which we are entering – the century which will come out of this war – can be and must be the century of the common man.*
>
> HENRY WALLACE Speech 8 May 1942

Walter, George Herbert (1928–)

Antiguan politician, prime minister 1971–76. An active trade unionist in the 1950s and 1960s, and founder of the Antigua Workers' Union (AWU), he formed the country's first political party, the left-of-centre Progressive Labour Movement (PLM), in 1968, leading it to victory in 1971. As prime minister, he established a social security system, comprehensive labour legislation, and promoted agricultural diversification after the closure of unprofitable sugar factories. In 1976 the PLM was defeated by the Antigua Labour Party (ALP), led by Vere ◊Bird, although it won the majority of the electoral vote.

During the 1950s Walter joined Bird's Antigua Trade and Labour Union (ATLU) and became its general secretary and chief negotiator. In the 1960s he left the ATLU to form the rival Antigua Workers' Union (AWU), after Bird and his colleagues in government refused to resign from their ATLU positions.

Walters, Alan Arthur (1926–)

British economist and government adviser 1981–89. He became economics adviser to Prime Minister Margaret Thatcher, but his publicly stated differences with the policies of her chancellor Nigel ◊Lawson precipitated, in 1989, Lawson's resignation from the government as well as Walters's own departure.

Walters held the post of economics professor at the London School of Economics 1968–75 and was professor of political economy at the Johns Hopkins University, Baltimore, from 1976. He was also economics adviser to the World Bank 1976–80. He was knighted in 1983.

Wang Zhen (1908–1993)

Chinese communist political leader. He was a veteran of the Long March and vice president of the Chinese Communist Party's (CPP's) Central Advisory Committee from 1988. A hardline Marxist, he strongly supported the Tiananmen Square crackdown against the student-led prodemocracy movement in June 1989.

Born in the south-central province of Hunan, Wang began his career in the labour movement, working initially on the railways. He joined the CCP in 1927, and until the 1950s was an important army commander and political officer. He took part in the Long March 1934–35 when the communists retreated northwards under the attack of the Nationalist forces. Following the communist victory in 1949 Wang directed the forced 'liberation' and Han Chinese colonization of the largely Muslim far-western province of Xinjiang. He became a full member of the CCP's influential central committee in 1956.

An unswerving Marxist, Wang escaped the purge during the ultra-leftist Cultural Revolution 1966–69. He was the only member of the subsequent reformist administration of Deng Xiaoping to do so. He became vice premier in 1975 and joined the CCP's Politburo in 1978. Advancing age forced Wang to retire as vice premier in 1980, but he served as vice chair of the Central Advisory Committee 1985–87, a body set up by Deng to accommodate senior party figures. In his position as a party elder, he worked, via his protégés, to defend 'Mao's revolution'. In 1987 he was influential in securing the ousting of the liberal-minded CCP leader Hu Yaobang.

Wang Dan (1968–)

Chinese prodemocracy activist, imprisoned 1989–93 and 1995–98 for his role in the 1989 prodemocracy campaign. He emerged in mid-April 1989 as one of the young leaders of the student prodemocracy campaign in Beijing, which was to end with the 3–4 June 1989 Red Army massacre in Tiananmen Square. Wang was freed in April 1998 on 'medical parole' and exiled to the USA.

A reserved history student from Beijing University, Wang was the 'thinker' of the inchoate movement and had come into contact with Fang Lizhi through the 'Democracy Salon' seminars, which he had informally organized. Wang escaped Beijing on 27 May 1989, prior to the Tiananmen Square denouement, but appeared on the 'most wanted' list of 21 alleged student ringleaders, which was issued by the Chinese government on 13 June. He was captured in July 1989 and sent to the high-security Qincheng Prison, near Beijing. After spending four years in prison, he was re-arrested in May 1995 and sentenced to a further 11 years' imprisonment, in the northeastern province of Liaoning, for 'subversion'. His release was part of a conciliatory move by the Chinese authorities designed to improve relations with the USA. However, according to Chinese government figures, more than 2,000 dissidents remained in prison for political crimes.

Wang Hongwen (1935–1992)

Chinese communist politician, member of the ultra-leftist Gang of Four, who played a leading role in the destabilizing Cultural Revolution 1966–69, launched against so-called 'bourgeois reactionaries' and 'capitalist roaders' within the Chinese Communist Party (CCP). In October 1976, a month after the death of Mao Zedong, Wang was arrested and expelled from the CCP, along with the other members of the Gang, who had been plotting an armed uprising. The Gang members were tried 1980–81 and found guilty. Wang, who was sentenced to life imprisonment and permanent deprivation of his political rights, died in prison in 1992.

Born in Changchun, in Jilin province in northeastern China, Wang moved to Shanghai where his early career was as a textile mill worker. He became politically active in the left-wing of the local CCP. There he became allied with ◊Jiang Qing, Yao Wenyuan, and Zhang Chunqiao, the other members of the Gang of Four.

In January 1967 Wang and the other members of the Gang overthrew the moderate 'Liuist' Shanghai CCP committee and established a 'People's Commune', influenced by the model of the 1871 Paris Commune. Wang served as vice chair of this 'Revolutionary Committee' and in 1969 was brought into the CCP's influential national Central Committee. He became Shanghai municipality party leader in 1971 and two years later, at the age of 38, was inducted into the CCP Politburo's inner controlling Standing Committee and Mao Zedong made him vice chair of the CCP. This meteoric rise drew strong criticism from party traditionalists who, as believers in gerontocracy, mocked Wang as 'a baby still smelling of milk'. However, Wang's ascendancy was brief.

Wang Jingwei, or *Wang Ching-wei* (1883–1944)

Chinese Nationalist politician, president of the Japanese-backed 'reformed Chinese government'. Wang became leader of the Kuomintang (Guomindang; nationalist) party's left wing after the death of ◊Sun Zhong Shan (Sun Yat-sen). He opposed the right-wing Jiang Jie Shi (Chiang Kai-shek) and between May and December 1931 led an alternative Kuomintang government based in Guangzhou (Canton). A rapprochement with Jiang ended after Wang was seriously injured in an assassination attempt in November 1935. In December 1938, soon after the Japanese invasion of southern China and occupation of Guangzhou, Wang defected and in March 1940 the Japanese declared him the president of a 'reformed Chinese government', centred on Nanjing (Nanking).

By 1943 this puppet government had secured control of Shanghai and had an army of half a million. Wang died in November 1944, before the Japanese were defeated.

FURTHER READING

Bunker, G *The Peace Conspiracy: Wang Ching-wei and the China War* 1972

Wan Li (1916–1996)

Chinese communist politician. Wan was made party leader in Anhui province in 1977 and successfully instituted a programme of market-centred economic reforms that attracted the attention of the new 'paramount leader' Deng Xiaoping. Wan was rewarded, in 1980, with a place in the Chinese Communist Party's (CCP's) Central Committee and was made vice premier, responsible chiefly for agriculture. In 1982 he became a member of the CCP's controlling Politburo and became a particularly close ally of Prime Minister Zhao Ziyang.

Wan's relative political liberalism prevented him from rising further. In November 1987 the conservative power-broker Chen Yun insisted that the more cautious Li Peng should become prime minister rather than Wan, when Zhao Ziyang took over as party leader, and Wan was moved to become chair of the National People's Congress (parliament). During the May–June 1989 political crisis caused by prodemocracy demonstrations in Tiananmen Square in Beijing, Wan's role was equivocal. Away on an official visit when martial law was imposed, he flew back to China, apparently to provide backing to Zhao Ziyang's bid to reach a non-military solution. However, Wan was detained en route in Shanghai by local party leader Jiang Zemin, and was persuaded to lie low and rest for 'health reasons'.

Born in Sichuan province, Wan joined the CCP in 1936 and studied in France before the establishment of the People's Republic in 1949. After Liberation, he became a Communist bureaucrat, gaining a reputation as a liberal reformer. Close to Liu Shaoqi, whom he accompanied on a state visit to Korea in 1963, he was 'purged' in the Cultural Revolution of 1966–69, when he was placed on mass trial and denounced as a 'bourgeois reactionary'. Rehabilitated in 1971, he was briefly purged again in 1976, when Jiang Qing's 'Gang of Four' were in the ascendancy.

Wan's son-in-law, Li Ruihuan (1935–), who established a reputation 1982–89 as a reformist mayor of Tianjin, China's third largest city, rose above Wan in the post-Tiananmen reconstruction of the CCP Politburo. He was promoted to its six-member inner Standing Committee and given charge, within the Secretariat, of the CCP ideology portfolio.

Ward, Barbara, Baronesss Jackson of Lodsworth (1914–1981)

English economist. She became president of the Institute for Environment and Development in 1973. In 1976 she received a life peerage as Baroness Jackson of Lodsworth. Her books include *Policy for the West* (1951), *The Widening Gap* (1971), and her best-known work, *Only One Earth* (with René Dubois) (1972).

Ward, Joseph George (1856–1930)

Australian-born New Zealand centre-right politician, prime minister 1906–12 and 1928–30. He first became prime minister after Richard ◊Seddon's death in 1906 and remained in the post until 1912. During World War I, he served in the 1915–19 coalition government. He was then out of parliament 1919–25, but returned as prime minister in 1928, after leading his United Party to electoral victory. With his physical powers visibly waning, this second administration proved to be a failure and Ward resigned as prime minister in 1930, just six weeks before his death.

Ward's family emigrated from Australia to New Zealand in 1860. He was elected mayor of Cambell-town (Bluff) in 1881 and to New Zealand's parliament in 1887. He sat as a Liberal Party member of Parliament, serving in the government of Richard Seddon, but was forced to resign from parliament in 1897 after he was bankrupted following a financial scandal involving the Colonial Bank. Ward was soon voted back to parliament and, as postmaster general, introduced penny postage in 1901.

Warren, Earl (1891–1974)

US jurist and chief justice of the US Supreme Court 1953–69. He served as governor of California 1943–53. As chief justice, he presided over a moderately liberal court, taking a stand against racial discrimination and ruling that segregation in schools was unconstitutional. From 1963 to 1964 he headed the commission that investigated President J F Kennedy's assassination.

Wasmosy Monti, Juan Carlos (1938–)

Paraguayan politician and president 1993–98. He was successful in making some improvements in national economic conditions during his term in office but came under attack for corrupt business methods.

Wasmosy came into conflict with the military during his administration, in particular with General Lino Cesár ◊Oviedo, the head of the army.

Wasmosy was invited to stand as president in August 1993, by the Asociación Nacional Republicana (ANR; Colorado Party) after he, as a successful businessman, headed the consortium involved in the construction of the world's largest hydroelectric dam – Itaipu, bordering Paraguay and Brazil.

Wasmosy was born in Asunción, and graduated in civil engineering from the National University of Asunción in 1962.

Watson, John Christian (1867–1941)

Australian trade-union leader and Labor politician, prime minister of Australia in 1904. His administration was the first to be formed by the Labor Party (founded in 1891) in the Australian federal parliament.

After an education in New Zealand, Watson settled in New South Wales, Australia, where he became head of the newspaper compositors' trade union. In 1894 he entered the Legislative Assembly and soon afterwards was elected leader of the parliamentary Labor Party. In 1901 he became leader of the federal Labor Party. He retired from politics in 1910 to concentrate on his business interests, mainly in newspaper publishing.

Wavell, Archibald Percival, 1st Earl Wavell (1883–1950)

British field marshal in World War II. As commander in chief in the Middle East, he successfully defended Egypt against Italy in July 1939 and successfully conducted the North African war against Italy 1940–41. He was transferred as commander in chief in India in July 1941, and became Allied Supreme Commander after Japan entered the war. He was unable to prevent Japanese advances in Malaya and Burma and Winston Churchill became disillusioned with him. He was viceroy of India 1943–47. He was created KCB in 1939, Viscount in 1943, and Earl in 1947.

Waverley, John Anderson, 1st Viscount Waverley (1882–1958)

British administrator, born in Scotland. He organized civil defence for World War II, becoming home secretary and minister for home security in 1939. *Anderson shelters*, home outdoor air-raid shelters, were named after him. He was chancellor of the Exchequer 1943–45. He was created a KCB in 1919 and Viscount in 1952.

Webb, (Martha) Beatrice (born Potter) (1858–1943) and Sidney James, 1st Baron Passfield (1859–1947)

English social reformers, writers, and founders of the London School of Economics (LSE) in 1895. They were early members of the socialist Fabian Society, and were married in 1892. They argued for social insurance in their minority report (1909) of the Poor Law Commission, and wrote many influential books, including *The History of Trade Unionism* (1894), *English Local Government* (11 volumes, 1906–29), and *Soviet Communism* (1935). They founded the *New Statesman* magazine in 1913.

> *The inevitability of gradualness.*
> SIDNEY WEBB Of the Fabian Society

Sidney Webb was professor of public administration at the LSE 1912–27. He is credited with drafting Clause Four of the 1918 Labour Party constitution (concerning the common ownership of the means of production). He was a member of the Labour Party executive 1916–25, entered Parliament in 1922, and was president of the Board of Trade in 1924, dominions secretary 1929–30, and colonial secretary 1929–31. He became a baron in 1929.

Beatrice Webb wrote *The Co-operative Movement in Great Britain* (1891), *My Apprenticeship* (1926), and *Our Partnership* (1948). She also worked on Charles Booth's *Life and Labour of the People of London* (1891–1903).

FURTHER READING

MacKenzie, Jeanne *A Victorian Courtship: The Story of Beatrice Potter and Sidney Webb* 1979

Muggeridge, Kitty, and Adam, Ruth *Beatrice Webb: A Life, 1858–1943* 1967

Radice, L *Beatrice and Sidney Webb: Fabian Socialists* 1984

Seymour-Jones, Carole *Beatrice Webb: Woman of Conflicts* 1992

Wei, Jingsheng (1951–)

Chinese prodemocracy activist and essayist, imprisoned 1979–97 for attacking the Chinese communist system. He is regarded as one of China's most important political dissidents.

In 1978 he joined the 'Democracy Salon' movement of reformist dissidents in Beijing and published essays critical of the government in the journal *Explorations*, which he cofounded. Most courageously, he called for 'the Fifth Modernization – Democracy'. In 1979 he was arrested and sentenced to 15 years' imprisonment 'for handing military secrets to foreigners'. He was released in September 1993, but within six months he was re-arrested twice and placed under interrogation by the Chinese authorities. He was re-arrested again in November 1995 on the capital charge of trying to overthrow the government and was sentenced to 14 years' imprisonment. He was released in November 1997, on medical parole, in a move designed to improve Chinese relations with the USA. During a stay in the USA for health reasons, he met President Bill Clinton in 1997, and in 1998 he was in exile in the UK.

The son of a Communist Party official in Anhui province, Wei joined the Red Guards in the Cultural Revolution in 1966 and later became an electrician at Beijing Zoo.

Following his arrest in 1979 he was sent to a labour camp in the remote Qinghai province, where his health deteriorated. This prompted the dissident scientist Fang Lizhi to write an 'open letter' in January 1989 to Deng Xiaoping pleading for Wei's release.

Weinberger, Caspar Willard (1917–)

US Republican politician. He served under presidents Richard Nixon and Gerald Ford, and was Ronald Reagan's defence secretary 1981–87.

In 1992 he was indicted for involvement in the Irangate cover-up, but protested his innocence and was granted immunity from prosecution by President George Bush.

Weizmann, Chaim Azriel (1874–1952)

Zionist leader, the first president of Israel 1948–52. He conducted the negotiations leading up to the Balfour Declaration, by which the UK declared its support for an independent Jewish state.

Born in Russia, he became a naturalized British subject, and as a qualified chemist and director of the Admiralty laboratories 1916–19 discovered a process for manufacturing acetone, a solvent. He became head of the Hebrew University in Jerusalem, then in 1948 became the first president of the new republic of Israel.

Weizsäcker, Richard, Baron von (1920–)

German Christian Democrat politician, president 1984–94. He began his career as a lawyer and was also active in the German Protestant Church and in Christian Democratic Union party politics. He was elected to the West German Bundestag (parliament) in 1969 and served as mayor of West Berlin from 1981, before being elected federal president in 1984.

Welensky, Roy (originally Roland) (1907–1991)

Rhodesian politician. He was instrumental in the creation in 1953 of the Central African Federation, comprising Northern Rhodesia (now Zambia), Southern Rhodesia (now Zimbabwe), and Nyasaland (now Malawi), and was prime minister 1956–63, when the federation was disbanded. His Southern Rhodesian Federal Party was defeated by Ian Smith's Rhodesian Front in 1964. In 1965, following Smith's unilateral declaration of Southern Rhodesian independence from Britain, Welensky left politics. He was knighted in 1953.

Wells, H(erbert) G(eorge) (1866–1946)

English writer. He was a pioneer of science fiction with such novels as *The Time Machine* (1895) and *The War of the Worlds* (1898), which describes a Martian invasion of Earth and brought him nationwide recognition. He was originally a Fabian and later became a Labour party supporter. He was a Labour candidate for London University in 1921 and 1922.

Wells was a prophet of world organization. His theme was the need for humans to impose their mastery upon their own creations and to establish benevolent systems and structures by which to rule themselves, and in pursuing this concept he became a leading advocate of social planning. A number of prophecies described in fictional works such as *The First Men in the Moon* (1901) and *The Shape of Things to Come* (1933), as well as in *The Outline of History* (1920) and other popular nonfiction works, have been ful-

> *Human history becomes more and more a race between education and catastrophe.*
>
> H G WELLS *Outline of History*

filled; among them, the significance of aviation, tank warfare, World War II, and the atomic bomb.

FURTHER READING

Coren, M *The Invisible Man: The Life and Liberties of H G Wells* 1993

Dickson, L *H G Wells: His Turbulent Life and Times* 1969

Foot, M *HG: The History of Mr Wells* 1996

Mackenzie, N and J *The Time Traveller* 1973

West, A *Aspects of a Life* 1984

Wells, H G *Experiment in Autobiography* 1934

Wells or *Wells-Barnett*, Ida Bell (1862–1931)

US journalist and political activist. She joined the staff of *New York Age* in 1891 and embarked on extensive lecture tours. She served as secretary of the National Afro-American Council 1898–1902 and as a Chicago probation officer 1913–16.

Born in Holly Springs, Mississippi, Wells was educated in a segregated school and became a teacher in Memphis, Tennessee. Losing her job in 1891 as the result of a suit she had filed against state segregation laws, she began a career of political activism after moving to New York City. She later married and settled in Chicago in 1895.

Wesker, Arnold (1932–)

English dramatist. His socialist beliefs were reflected in the successful trilogy *Chicken Soup with Barley*, *Roots*, and *I'm Talking About Jerusalem* (1958–60). In 1961 Wesker tried unsuccessfully to establish a working-class theatre with trade-union backing at the Round House in London. His autobiography, *As Much as I Dare*, was published in 1994.

West, Morris Langlo (1916–)

Australian novelist. An abandoned vocation with the Christian Brothers and experience as secretary to a former Australian prime minister, Billy Hughes, and as Vatican correspondent for the *Daily Mail* contributed to the recurring themes of Catholicism in crisis, political power, and moral dilemma in his novels. He first attracted international attention with the award-winning *Devil's Advocate* (1959, filmed 1977).

Born near Melbourne, he was educated at Melbourne University and worked as a school teacher before serving in World War II. He moved to Italy after the war.

West, Rebecca, pen name of Cicily Isabel Fairfield (1892–1983)

English journalist and novelist, an active feminist from 1911. Her novels, of which the semi-autobiographical *The Fountain Overflows* (1956) and *The Birds Fall Down* (1966) are regarded as the best, demonstrate a social and political awareness.

Wheatley, John (1869–1930)

British Labour politician, born in County Waterford, Ireland. He grew up in the former county of Lanarkshire, Scotland, became a Lanarkshire councillor, and was elected member of Parliament for Glasgow Shettleston in 1922, holding the seat until his death. In the 1924 Labour government, Wheatley served as housing minister, introducing an act designed to enable local authorities to build large stocks of council houses at affordable rents.

After 1924 he drifted to the left of the party (with much of the Independent Labour Party) and was not offered a post in the 1929 government.

Wheatley grew up in Lanarkshire in considerable poverty with his ten siblings and he became a coal miner at the age of 11. His initial politics were influenced by his Catholicism and he worked for the *Catholic Herald* newspaper. In 1908 he left the United Irish League to join the Independent Labour Party (ILP) and he did much to win Irish voters to the Labour Party.

White, Edward Douglass, Jr (1845–1921)

US jurist. Elected to the US Senate in 1891, he was nominated by President Stephen Grover Cleveland as associative justice to the US Supreme Court in 1893, and under President William Taft he was nominated as chief justice 1911–21. During his office the Court made important decisions on US economic policy as in *United States v E C Knight and Co* (1895) when he joined the majority in weakening the Sherman Antitrust Act by removing manufacture of goods from its purview.

Born in Lafourche Parish, Louisiana, White attended the Jesuit College in New Orleans and Georgetown University, but left his college studies to serve in the Confederate Army. In 1865, after the American Civil War, he studied law at the University of Louisiana Law School in New Orleans; he was admitted to the bar in 1868. Becoming active in Democratic politics, he was elected to the state senate in 1874 and was a justice of the Louisiana supreme court 1878–80.

White, Patrick Victor Martindale (1912–1990)

Australian writer. He did more than any other to put Australian literature on the international map. His partly allegorical novels explore the lives of early settlers in Australia and often deal with misfits or inarticulate people. They include *The Aunt's Story* (1948), written during his voyage back to Australia, *The Tree of Man* (1955), *Voss* (1957), based on the ill-fated 19th-century explorer Ludwig Leichhardt, and *Riders in the Chariot* (1961), exploring suburban life. He was awarded the Nobel Prize for Literature in 1973. White became a fervent republican after the dismissal of the Gough ◊Whitlam government in 1975, returning his Order of Australia in 1976, and supported conservation causes in his later years.

White, Walter (Francis) (1893–1955)

US civil-rights leader and author. A leading member of the National Association for the Advancement of Colored People (NAACP), he fought against lynching and launched numerous campaigns against segregation in public facilities, white primaries, and the poll taxes, and against educational discrimination. Journalistic research he conducted in Europe, published as *A Rising Wind* (1945), influenced President Harry Truman's decision to desegregate the armed forces. In 1946 he further pressured President Truman to set up the President's Committee on Civil Rights, and this led the Democrats to adopt their divisive civil-rights platform in 1948.

White was born in Atlanta, Georgia. Fair-skinned, blond, and blue-eyed although part black, he could pass for white but chose to champion the cause of the black race after experiencing a race riot in Atlanta, Georgia, in 1906; later, in 1926 he published his novel *Flight*, based on his experiences of 'passing'. One of the most ardent anti-lynching proponents in the USA, he investigated more than 40 lynchings and 8 race riots. As a Guggenheim Fellow he conducted a study of lynching in the USA, which became the basis of his *Rope and Faggot: A Biography of Judge Lynch* (1929).

As an insurance company cashier, he took the lead in establishing a branch of the NAACP in Atlanta in 1916. He was named assistant secretary of the NAACP 1918–31 and NAACP executive secretary 1931–55. Author of several other books and numerous articles, he was awarded the Spingarn Medal in 1937 in recognition of his efforts on behalf of black Americans. Because of his efforts and those of A Philip Randolph, President Franklin Roosevelt prohibited discrimination in the defence industries and established the Fair Employment Practices Commission in 1941. Also concerned with worldwide prejudice, he was less successful on this front and was criticized as an autocrat inside the NAACP. Although he retained his post until his death, from 1949 on his powers were limited.

Whitehead, Edgar (Cuthbert Fremantle) (1905–1971)

Rhodesian politician, leader of the United Rhodesia Party and prime minister of Southern Rhodesia (now Zimbabwe) 1958–62. He gained the premiership when his predecessor Garfield ◊Todd was dropped by his party for his liberal views. However, even Whitehead's more conservative programme was rejected in 1962 by the white electorate in favour of the racist Rhodesian Front.

Whitehead was born in England, and educated at University College, Oxford. He emigrated to Rhodesia in 1928 and was first elected to the legislative assembly in 1939. After war service and a year as Rhodesian High Commissioner in London, he returned to act as minister of finance 1946–53. Following his electoral defeat in 1962, he continued to sit in the assembly, but retired to England when Ian Smith declared unilateral independence (UDI) in 1965.

Whitehouse, Mary (1910–)

British media activist. A founder of the National Viewers' and Listeners' Association, she campaigned to censor radio and television for their treatment of sex and violence.

Whitelaw, William Stephen Ian, 1st Viscount Whitelaw (1918–)

British Conservative politician, born in Scotland. As secretary of state for Northern Ireland 1972–73 he introduced the concept of power sharing. He was chief Conservative whip 1964–70 and leader of the House of Commons 1970–72. He became secretary of state for employment 1973–74, but failed to conciliate the trade unions. He was chair of the Conservative Party in 1974 and home secretary 1979–83, when he was made a peer. He was Lord President of the Council and leader of the House of Lords 1983–87.

Whitelaw was educated at Winchester and Trinity College, Cambridge. He is a farmer and landowner and was elected Conservative member of Parliament for Penrith and Border in 1955. He became a government whip in 1959 and was parliamentary secretary in the ministry of labour 1962–64. From 1964 to 1970 he was opposition chief whip, becoming Lord President of the Council and leader of the House of Commons in 1970. In 1972 he became secretary of state for Northern Ireland, following the imposition of direct rule.

He made strenuous efforts to secure a solution to the problems of Northern Ireland: the 'no-go' areas of Belfast and Londonderry were cleared and a constitutional settlement appeared to have been reached between the Unionist Party and the SDLP at the Sunningdale Conference of 1973, but the agreement was to break down later.

Prior to the miners' strike of 1974 he was appointed secretary of state for employment, but was unable to avert the strike. In 1975 he unsuccessfully contested the Conservative leadership.

He autobiography, *The Whitelaw Memoirs*, was published in 1989.

Whitlam, (Edward) Gough (1916–)

Australian politician, leader of the Labor Party 1967–78 and prime minister 1972–75. He ended conscription and Australia's military commitment in Vietnam, introduced the Medibank national health service, abolished university fees, expanded Aboriginal rights, attempted redistribution of wealth, raised loans to increase national ownership of industry and resources, and recognized mainland China.

When the opposition blocked finance bills in the Senate, following a crisis of confidence, Whitlam refused to call a general election and was dismissed by the governor general, John ◊ Kerr. He was defeated in the subsequent general election by Malcolm ◊ Fraser. He served as ambassador to UNESCO 1982–86.

Born near Melbourne, the son of a senior civil servant, Whitlam studied law at Sydney University after wartime service in the air force. He initially worked as a barrister, before being elected to the federal parliament in 1952, for the Labor Party (ALP), of which he became deputy leader in 1960, promoting reforms opposed by the left-wing 'old guard'.

Whitman, Christine, born Todd (1946–)

US Republican politician, governor of New Jersey from 1994. She was on the left of her party on social issues, but fiscally conservative.

She was born in New Jersey, the daughter of a millionaire, and began her career working for President Richard ◊ Nixon. As governor, she cut state income tax and appointed the first black American to the state's supreme court. She supported feminism and minority rights, and was tipped as a future presidential candidate.

Widgery, John Passmore, Baron Widgery of South Molton (1911–)

English judge, lord chief justice of England 1971–80. He conducted an inquiry into the killing by British paratroops of 13 unarmed protestors during a civil-rights march in Londonderry, Northern Ireland, on Sunday 30 January 1972 ('Bloody Sunday'). The Widgery Report exonerated the soldiers, claiming they had acted in self-defence. In 1997 the Irish government published a dossier of evidence calling into question the verdict of the Widgery Report. As a result, in January 1998 the British prime minister Tony Blair agreed to a fresh inquiry into the shootings.

Widgery was educated at Queen's College, Taunton. He qualified as a solicitor in 1933 and as a barrister (at Lincoln's Inn, London) in 1946. He was made a Queen's Counsel (QC) in 1958, a judge of the High Court of Justice (Queen's Bench Division) in 1961, and was appointed to sit on the Court of Appeal in 1968.

Wiesel, Elie (Eliezer) (1928–)

US academic and human-rights campaigner, born in Romania. He was held in Buchenwald concentration camp during World War II, and assiduously documented wartime atrocities against the Jews in an effort to alert the world to the dangers of racism and violence. He was awarded the Nobel Peace Prize in 1986.

Wigley, Dafydd (1943–)

Welsh politician, president of Plaid Cymru, the Welsh nationalist party, 1981–84 and from 1991. He aimed to see Wales as a self-governing nation within the European Community. He was Plaid Cymru member of Parliament for Caernarfon from February 1974, and sponsored the Disabled Persons Act of 1981.

Wigley worked as an industrial economist 1964–74, and published *An Economic Plan for Wales* (1970).

Wijdensobsch, Jules

Surinamese politician and president from 1996. His administration faced many long-standing economic problems, worsened by the erratic flow of limited Dutch aid during the previous two decades.

Wijdensobsch was a former prime minister under the military dictatorship of Désiré ◊ Bouterse. As no party or coalition gained the necessary two-thirds majority on the May 1996 election date, Wijdensobsch was elected by the United People's Conference – a 51-member assembly of parliamentary representatives, community, and district councils on 5 September 1996.

Wilkins, Roy (1901–1981)

US journalist and civil-rights leader who worked to achieve racial equality without the use of violence and spoke out against both white supremacy and black-American separatism. From 1931 he served as executive assistant secretary of the National Association for the Advancement of Colored People (NAACP) and was editor of the organization's newspaper, *Crisis*, 1934–49. He was named acting secretary of the NAACP in 1949 and was later made executive secretary 1955–77, eventually winning praise from Jesse ◊ Jackson and other younger black US leaders.

Born in St Louis, Missouri, he was reared by an aunt and uncle in St Paul, Minnesota. He was editor of his school newspaper in 1923 and after graduation edited a black-American weekly, the *St Paul Appeal*, before joining the staff of the *Kansas City Call*, another leading black weekly. He went on to join the NAACP and was instrumental in bringing to fruition school desegregation and the 1964 Civil Rights Act.

FURTHER READING

Wilkins, Roy, and Matthews, Tom (contributor) *Standing Fast: The Autobiography of Roy Wilkins* 1994

Wilkinson, Cecily Ellen (1891–1947)

English journalist and Labour politician. Often known as 'Red Ellen', she was an early member of the Independent Labour Party and an active campaigner for women's suffrage and the unemployed. As member of Parliament for Jarrow in 1936, she led the Jarrow March of 200 unemployed shipyard workers from Jarrow to London.

She was Labour MP for Middlesbrough 1924–31 and

for Jarrow 1935–47. She was minister of education 1945–47 under Clement Attlee.

FURTHER READING
Vernon, B D *Ellen Wilkinson* 1982

William II (German *Wilhelm II*) (1859–1941)

Emperor of Germany from 1888, the son of Frederick III and Victoria, daughter of Queen Victoria of Britain. In 1890 he forced Chancellor Otto von Bismarck to resign in an attempt to assert his own political authority. The result was an exacerbation of domestic and international political instability, although his personal influence declined in the 1900s. He was an enthusiastic supporter of Admiral Alfred von ◊Tirpitz's plans for naval expansion. In 1914 he first approved Austria's ultimatum to Serbia and then, when he realized war was inevitable, tried in vain to prevent it. In 1918 he fled to Doorn in the Netherlands after Germany's defeat and his abdication.

FURTHER READING
Balfour, Michael *The Kaiser and His Times* 1972
Palmer, Alan *The Kaiser* 1978
Röhl, J C G *Kaiser Wilhelm II: New Interpretations* 1982,
   The Kaiser and his Court: Wilhelm II and the government of Germany 1994

Williams, Eric (1911–1981)

Trinidad and Tobago centre-left politician and historian, prime minister 1956–81. In 1956 he founded the People's National Movement (PNM). As chief minister, he took Trinidad and Tobago into the Federation of the West Indies in 1958, but seceded in 1961, and achieved full independence within the British Commonwealth in 1962. Economic downturn and increasing authoritarianism led to Black Power riots in 1970, but during the 1970s rising oil prices provided the basis for large-scale industrialization and nationalization by his government. In 1976 Williams oversaw Trinidad and Tobago's shift to republican status.

Williams' centre-left nationalist PNM was the country's first political party, and drew support chiefly from the majority African elements of the population. On joining the Federation of the West Indies, he insisted on a powerfully centralized government, but when this failed to materialize and Jamaica seceded in 1961, he took Trinidad and Tobago out of the union, declaring 'one from ten leaves zero'. In the negotiations towards independence, his slogan was 'Discipline, Production and Tolerance'. His popularity soared until economic and political unrest erupted in April 1970, the violence of the US-inspired Black Power movement leading to an army mutiny, and a state of emergency being briefly imposed. Williams committed suicide in March 1981.

Williams, Shirley Vivien Teresa Brittain, Baroness Williams of Crosby (1930–)

British Liberal Democrat politician. She was Labour minister for prices and consumer protection 1974–76, and education and science 1976–79. She became a founder member of the Social Democrat Party (SDP) in 1981 and its president in 1982, but lost her parliamentary seat in 1983. In 1988 she joined the newly merged Social and Liberal Democratic Party (SLDP). She is the daughter of the socialist writer Vera ◊Brittain. She was made a life peer in 1993.

She was educated at St Paul's Girls' School, Somerville College, Oxford, and Columbia University, New York. She was general secretary of the Fabian Society 1960–64, and was elected Labour member of Parliament for Hitchin in 1964, and was MP for Hertford and Stevenage from 1974. Between 1966 and 1970 she was successively parliamentary secretary at the ministry of labour, minister of state at the department of education and science, and minister of state at the Home Office. From 1970 to 1974 Mrs Williams was an opposition spokesperson on social services, home affairs, and prices and consumer protection.

In March 1974 she entered the cabinet as secretary of state for prices and consumer protection. In addition to this post she was appointed paymaster general and chair of several important cabinet committees by James Callaghan, following his appointment as prime minister in 1976. Later in 1976 Mrs Williams became secretary of state for education and science, still retaining the office of paymaster general.

Willis, Norman David (1933–)

English trade-union leader. A trade-union official since leaving school, he was the general secretary of the Trades Union Congress (TUC) 1984–93 and president of the European TUC 1991–93.

He presided over the TUC at a time of falling union membership, hostile legislation from the Conservative government, and a major review of the role and policies of the Labour Party.

Willis, Ted (1914–1992)

English writer and politician. He created one of British television's most popular characters, Constable Dixon (later Sergeant), the main character in the television series *Dixon of Dock Green*, which ran for 22 years. He was also the author of numerous novels, plays, and scripts for films, radio, and television. He was made a Labour life peer in 1970, one of the first life peers.

His political life began with a resolve to oppose fascism. He became national leader of the Labour Party's League of Youth, but in the late 1930s joined the Communist Party. He spent his war years with the Army Kinematographic Service, producing scripts for documentary films. He became a theatre critic for the communist newspaper the *Daily Worker*, and producer and writer for the left-wing Unity Theatre. He helped found the Writers' Guild and served for many years as its president.

Willkie, Wendell Lewis (1892–1944)

US politician who was the Republican presidential candidate in 1940. After losing to F D Roosevelt, he continued as a leader of the liberal wing of the Republican Party. Becoming committed to the cause of international cooperation, he published *One World* (1942).

Born in Elwood, Indiana, Willkie was educated at Indiana University, and became a barrister in 1916. After service in World War I, he became corporate counsel for a private utility and an outspoken opponent of the economic policies of the New Deal, notably in relation to the Tennessee Valley Authority.

A former Democrat, in 1940 he was the surprise Republican candidate for the US presidency, when Roosevelt was elected for his third term. However, he later served as Roosevelt's personal representative abroad.

Wilson, Cairine Reay Mackay (1885–1962)

Canadian Liberal politician. Wilson was appointed as the country's first woman senator in 1930 by Prime Minister W L MacKenzie King only four months after the ruling in the 'Persons Case', which qualified women to sit in the Senate. As a senator, Wilson worked in the areas of divorce and immigration. She became Canada's first woman delegate to the United Nations General Assembly in 1949 and the first woman to chair a Senate standing committee (on immigration and labour). She was also chair of the Canadian National Committee on Refugees. For her work with refugee children, she was given the honour of Knight of the Legion of Honour (France) in 1950.

Cairine Reay Mackay was born in Montréal. She was steeped in politics: as a child she spent a great deal of time travelling with her Liberal senator father, family friends were politicians, and in 1909 she married a Liberal member of Parliament.

Wilson, Pete (1933–)

US Republican politician, governor of California from 1991. He was senator from California 1983–91, and mayor of San Diego, California, 1971–83.

Wilson was born in Lake Forest, Illinois. He pioneered controlled urban growth in San Diego, encouraging public transport, discouraging the use of private cars, and concentrating development in rural areas. As governor of California (he had defeated Dianne Feinstein in the election), he increased taxes in order to

Prime Minister Harold Wilson with Edward Heath, leader of the Conservative Party, and Jeremy Thorpe, leader of the Liberal Party, September 1974. *Rex*

reduce the large budget deficit. He was re-elected in 1994, but unexpectedly failed to challenge for the Republican Party's 1996 presidential nomination.

Wilson, (Thomas) Woodrow (1856–1924)

28th president of the USA 1913–21, a Democrat. He kept the USA out of World War I until 1917, and in January 1918 issued his 'Fourteen Points' as a basis for a just peace settlement.

At the peace conference in Paris he secured the inclusion of the League of Nations in individual peace treaties, but these were not ratified by Congress, so the USA did not join the League. He was awarded the Nobel Peace Prize in 1919.

Wilson was born in Virginia, and became president of Princeton University in 1902. In 1910 he became governor of New Jersey. Elected president in 1912 against Theodore Roosevelt and William Taft, he initiated anti-trust legislation and secured valuable social reforms in his progressive 'New Freedom' programme. He strove to keep the USA neutral during World War I but the German U-boat campaign forced him to declare war in 1917. In 1919 he suffered a stroke from which he never fully recovered.

Democracy is not so much a form of government as a set of principles.

WOODROW WILSON
Atlantic Monthly
March 1901

After graduating from Princeton, Wilson studied law at the University of Virginia, and practised for a short time in Atlanta. He obtained a PhD from Johns Hopkins University in 1886, and was associate professor of history and political economy at Bryn Mawr College 1886–88, and at Wesleyan University 1888–90. He returned to Princeton in 1890 as professor of jurisprudence and political economy. His publications include *A History of the American People* (five volumes) and *Constitutional Government in the United States* (1908).

FURTHER READING

Bailey, T A *Woodrow Wilson and the Great Betrayal* 1945
Cooper, John *The Warrior and the Priest: Woodrow Wilson and Theodore Roosevelt* 1983
Levin, N G *Woodrow Wilson and World Politics* 1968
Link, Arthur (ed) *Woodrow Wilson: A Profile* 1968

Wingate, Orde Charles (1903–1944)

British soldier. In 1936 he established a reputation for unorthodox tactics in Palestine. In World War II he served in the Middle East and organized guerrilla forces in Ethiopia, and later led the Chindits, the Third Indian Division, in guerrilla operations against the Japanese army in Burma (now Myanmar).

◆ WILSON, (JAMES) HAROLD, BARON WILSON OF RIEVAULX (1916–1995) ◆

British Labour politician, prime minister 1964–70 and 1974–76, Labour Party leader 1963–76.

Wilson was born in Huddersfield, West Yorkshire. He was educated there and in Chesire and at Jesus College, Oxford. In 1943–44 he worked as a civil servant in the ministry of fuel and power. In 1945 he became Labour member of Parliament for Ormskirk and was appointed parliamentary secretary to the ministry of works. In 1947 he became president of the Board of Trade but resigned with Aneurin Bevan in 1951 over health service cuts.

In 1963, on Gaitskell's death, Wilson was elected leader of the Labour Party, and became prime minister in 1964 with a small majority. The 1966 general election victory increased the majority. As prime minister Wilson proved himself an effective television performer, projecting a populist image. The unilateral declaration of independence (UDI) by Rhodesia caused problems for the Wilson government, and Wilson's tacit support for US president Lyndon Johnson's escalation of the Vietnam War drew criticism from the party and the electorate.

Wilson's domestic policies included long-term planning for British industry and incomes policy. They were marred by constant balance of payments problems in the economy. Departments such as the Department of Economic Affairs (DEA), intended to revitalize British industry, were abandoned for more short-term measures.

A week is a long time in politics.

HAROLD WILSON Attributed remark

The white paper on industrial relations, 'In Place of Strife' (1968), intended to implement the recommendations of the Donovan Commission on Trade Unions and Employers' Association, was defeated by opposition from the trade-union movement and within the cabinet. In 1969 an initiative from Wilson resulted in the establishment of the Open University. Despite opposition within the Labour Party, Wilson applied for British entry into the European Economic Community (EEC), but the French

FURTHER READING

Royle, T *Wingate, Imaginative Soldier* 1993
Sykes, C *Orde Wingate* 1959
Tulloch, D *Wingate in Peace and War* 1967

Wingti, Paias (1951–)

Papua New Guinea centrist politician, prime minister 1985–88 and 1992–94. He became prime minister in November 1985 at the head of a five-party coalition. He championed Melanesian interests in both the South Pacific forum and the newly formed Spearhead Group, which also included Vanuatu and the Solomon Islands, but with opposition mounting to his economic strategy and leadership style, he was defeated on a no-confidence motion in July 1988.

Wingti returned as prime minister following the June 1992 general election, heading a three-party coalition government, which included the centre-right People's Democratic Movement party (PDM) and the centre-left Pangu Pati (PP; Papua New Guinea Party). He instituted a drive against political corruption and crime, which had both increased during recent years, but was replaced as prime minister in August 1994 by Julius ◊Chan. This followed a Supreme Court ruling that a snap re-election in June 1993, contrived by Wingti to prolong the government's period of immunity from a vote of no confidence, was invalid.

Born in Moika, in the Western Highlands, Wingti

President, Charles de Gaulle, vetoed British entry for the second time.

Following his return to office in January 1974 (leading a minority government until a second general election in October), Wilson adopted a 'social contract' approach to the trade unions involving incomes policy. Entry to the EEC having taken place in 1973 (achieved by Edward Heath's government 1970–74), there were calls within the Labour Party for withdrawal. A referendum was held on the issue in 1975, in which Wilson took no active part, although he let it be known he favoured Britain remaining in the Community. The referendum returned a decisive majority in favour of continued membership. In 1976 Wilson resigned unexpectedly and he was succeeded by James Callaghan. Wilson was made a life peer in 1983. See photograph on page 449.

FURTHER READING

Haines, Joe *The Politics of Power* 1977
Pimlott, B *Harold Wilson* 1992
Smith, Dudley *Harold Wilson: A Critical Biography* 1964
Wilson, Harold *Memoirs: The Making of a Prime Minister, 1916–64* 1986
Ziegler, Philip *Wilson: The Authorised Life* 1993

studied economics and politics at Port Moresby University. He joined the PP and, after being elected to the House of Assembly in 1977, served as minister of transport and then planning under Prime Minister Michael ◊Somare during the later 1970s and early 1980s. He eventually became deputy prime minister in August 1982, but resigned in March 1985 to form the PDM.

Wolf, Naomi (1962–)

US feminist writer. In *The Beauty Myth: How Images of Beauty are Used Against Women* (1990), she attributes the prevalence of eating disorders to the exaggerated importance given to a woman's appearance.

She argues that the cosmetics and diet industries force women to be preoccupied with attaining an ideal of beauty, thereby lowering their self-esteem. In *Fire with Fire: The New Female Power and How it will Change the Twenty-First Century* (1993), she proposes that women are powerful enough to move on from traditional feminism.

Wolfe, Tom, pen name of Thomas Kennerly Wolfe, Jr (1931–)

US journalist and novelist. In the 1960s he was a founder of the 'New Journalism', which brought fiction's methods to reportage. Wolfe recorded US mores and fashions in pop-style essays in, for example, *The Kandy-Kolored Tangerine-Flake Streamline Baby* (1965). His sharp social eye is applied to the New York of the 1980s in his novel *The Bonfire of the Vanities* (1988, filmed 1990).

Wood, (Howard) Kingsley (1881–1943)

English Conservative politician who served in the governments of Stanley Baldwin and Neville Chamberlain in the 1930s, and was chancellor of the Exchequer 1940–43 in the all-party wartime coalition.

Wood trained as a lawyer but entered politics, being elected Unionist member of Parliament for West Woolwich in 1918. He was appointed postmaster-general in the National Government of 1931–35. He became minister of health in 1935 and secretary of state for air in 1938. As chancellor of the Exchequer, he sought the advice of the economist John Maynard Keynes and introduced the 'pay-as-you-earn' (PAYE) system of income tax, but died before it was announced. He was knighted in 1918.

Woodcock, George (1904–1979)

English trade-union leader. He was a civil servant from 1934 to 1936 before joining the research and economic department of the Trades Union Congress (TUC). He sat on several royal commissions, including the Donovan Commission on Trade Unions and Employers' Associations 1965–68. After retiring from the TUC he was chair of the Commission on Industrial Relations 1969–71.

Born in Walton-Le-Dale, Lancashire, he was educated at the local elementary school and, under trade-union auspices, at Ruskin College and New College, Oxford, where he obtained first-class honours in philosophy and politics.

Woodward, Bob (Robert Upshur) (1943–)

US journalist. He is best known for unmasking, with Carl ◊Bernstein, the Watergate scandal and cover-up. Born in Geneva, Illinois, he was a *Washington Post* reporter 1971–78, and metropolitan editor 1979–81, and assistant managing editor from 1981. Woodward and Bernstein's coverage of the Watergate scandal, the investigative story of the century, won almost every major journalistic prize including a 1973 public-service Pulitzer Prize for the paper. Woodward wrote the controversial 'insider' books such as *The Brethren* (with Scott Armstrong, 1979), *Wired* (1984), and *The Commanders* (1991).

FURTHER READING
Bernstein, Carl, and Woodward, Bob *All the President's Men* 1994

Woolf, (Adeline) Virginia, born Stephen (1882–1941)

English novelist and critic. In novels such as *Mrs Dalloway* (1925), *To the Lighthouse* (1927), and *The Waves* (1931), she used a 'stream of consciousness' technique to render inner experience. In *A Room of One's Own* (1929) (nonfiction), *Orlando* (1928), and *The Years* (1937), she examines the importance of economic independence for women and other feminist principles.

Wootten, George Frederick (1893–1970)

Australian military officer and solicitor. Promoted to major general during World War II, he commanded the 9th Australian Division in the New Guinea and Borneo campaigns and accepted the surrender of the Japanese in Borneo in 1945. He was created a KBE in 1958.

Worner, Manfred (1934–1994)

German politician, North Atlantic Treaty Organization (NATO) secretary general 1988–94. He was elected for the centre-right Christian Democratic Union (CDU) to the West German Bundestag (parliament) in 1965 and, as a specialist in strategic affairs, served as defence minister 1982–88. He was a proponent of closer European military collaboration.

His appointment as defence minister in 1982 by Chancellor Helmut Kohl gave Worner the difficult task of overseeing the deployment of US cruise and Pershing II nuclear missiles on West German soil during the early 1980s in the teeth of opposition from the growing German peace movement. He also sanctioned an extension of military service from 15 to 18 months to compensate for the country's declining birth rate.

In 1988 he succeeded British politician Peter Carrington as secretary general of NATO at a time of fast-changing East–West relations, as communism began to collapse in central and Eastern Europe.

In 1990 an agreement was signed that provided for large cuts in Soviet and NATO conventional (non-nuclear) forces stationed in Europe, and in 1991 NATO was forced to adjust to the disintegration of the USSR and the disbandment of the Warsaw Pact. A North Atlantic Cooperation Council was formed, including all the former Soviet republics, and in 1994 a Partnership for Peace programme was launched, inviting former Warsaw Pact members to participate in military cooperation agreements.

Worrall, Denis John (1935–)

South African politician, member of the white opposition to apartheid. A co-leader of the Democratic Party (DP), he was elected to parliament in 1989.

Worrall, a former academic and journalist, joined the National Party (NP) and was made ambassador to London 1984–87. On his return to South Africa he resigned from the NP and in 1988 established the Independent Party (IP), which later merged with other white opposition parties to form the reformist DP, advocating the dismantling of the apartheid system and universal adult suffrage.

Wright, Louis Tompkins (1891–1952)

US physician, surgeon, and civil-rights leader. He was born in LaGrange, Georgia, and studied at Clark University, Atlanta, and at Harvard Medical School. From 1919 he worked at the Harlem Hospital, New York, rising to director of surgery in 1942 and director of the medical board of Harlem Hospitals in 1948. He was the first black doctor to be appointed to a municipal hospital position in New York City. In 1929 he also became the first black police surgeon in the history of the city. Wright was chair of the board of directors of the National Association for the Advancement of Colored People for 17 years.

Wright, Richard (Nathaniel) (1908–1960)

US writer and poet. He was regarded as an inspiration by black American writers such as James Baldwin. Wright's term 'living the ethics of Jim Crow' encapsulated his bitterness at the establishment. He joined the Communist Party 1934–44. His *Uncle Tom's Children* (1938), a collection of four stories, was highly acclaimed. His masterpiece *Native Son* (1940) features a character called Bigger Thomas, a black man forced to murder, and brought Wright overnight fame. In 1945 he wrote the autobiographical *Black Boy*, which railed against racial injustice.

Born on a plantation near Natchez, Mississippi, the grandson of slaves and son of a sharecropper, Wright went to school in Jackson, Mississippi, though only up to the ninth grade, but got a story published at the age of 16 while working at various jobs in the South. In 1927 he went to Chicago, Illinois, and worked briefly in the post office but was forced onto relief by the Depression. With two more minor works published, he found employment with the Federal Writers Project. In 1937 he moved to New York City, where he was an editor on the Communist newspaper *Daily Worker*.

After living mainly in Mexico 1940–46, he had become so disillusioned with both the Communists and white America that he went to Paris, France, where he lived the rest of his life as an expatriate.

FURTHER READING

Fabre, Michel *The Unfinished Quest of Richard Wright* translation 1973

Felgar, Robert *Richard Wright* 1980

Webb, Constance *Richard Wright: A Biography* 1968

Wright, Peter (1916–1995)

English intelligence agent. His book *Spycatcher* (1987), written after his retirement, caused an international stir when the British government tried unsuccessfully to block its publication anywhere in the world because of its damaging revelations about the secret service.

Wright joined MI5 in 1955 and was a consultant to the director general 1973–76, when he retired. In *Spycatcher* he claimed, among other things, that Roger ◊Hollis, head of MI5 1955–65, had been a Soviet double agent; this was later denied by the KGB.

Wuerkaixi (1968–)

Chinese dissident, one of the leading figures in the May–June 1989 prodemocracy movement that was crushed in Tiananmen Square, Beijing. He was a second-year student at Beijing Normal University when he became caught up in the student-led prodemocracy demonstrations. He left Tiananmen Square on 27 May 1989, but returned on 3 June for the denouement of the crisis. Following the Red Army crackdown, he escaped from Beijing on 4 June, via the 'underground railway' to Hong Kong, and later moved to Paris, France.

Outspoken and brusque when he came into contact with the hard-line communist premier Li Peng, Wuerkaixi was one of the most charismatic and radical of the student leaders.

In Paris, in September 1989, he was elected vice chair of the Federation for a Democratic China, which sought to unite the various exiled prodemocracy bodies. Wuerkaixi later studied at Harvard University, but lost his place and became a teacher in the USA.

He came from the predominantly Muslim autonomous region of Xinjiang Uighur.

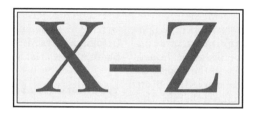

X–Z

Yadin, Yigael (1917–1984)
Israeli archaeologist, soldier, and politician. He directed excavations at Hazor, Megiddo, Masada, and other sites in Israel, and led the exploration of the Judaean desert caves. He was a guerrilla leader at the time of the British mandate in Palestine, and chief of staff with the rank of major general in the Israeli defence forces in 1949 and 1952. In 1977 he formed a political party, the Democratic Movement for Change, which won 14 seats in the Israeli elections that year. The party favoured compromise over the occupied territories and advocated a capitalist economic policy.

Yahya Khan, Agha Muhammad (1917–1980)
Pakistani president 1969–71. His mishandling of the Bangladesh separatist issue led to civil war, and he was forced to resign.

Yahya Khan fought with the British army in the Middle East during World War II, escaping German capture in Italy. Later, as Pakistan's chief of army general staff, he supported General Ayub Khan's 1958 coup and in 1969 became military ruler. Following defeat by India in 1971, he resigned and was under house arrest 1972–75.

Yamagata, Aritomo (1838–1922)
Japanese soldier, politician, and prime minister 1889–91 and 1898–1900. As war minister in 1873 and chief of the imperial general staff in 1878, he was largely responsible for the modernization of the military system. He returned as chief of staff during the Russo-Japanese War 1904–05 and remained an influential political figure as one of the elder statesmen known as Genro.

Yamamoto, Gombei (1852–1933)
Japanese admiral and politician. As prime minister 1913–14, he began Japanese expansion into China and initiated political reforms. He became premier again in 1923 but resigned the following year.

Yamani, Ahmad Zaki al- (1930–   )
Saudi Arabian politician, oil minister 1962–86. An exemplar of a new generation of young Western-trained technocrats who came to serve the ruling al-Saud family, al-Yamani rose to prominence as the government's legal adviser from 1958, and in 1962 became minister of oil and natural resources. He remained in this post until October 1986 and during these years was the most influential figure within the Organization of Petroleum-Exporting Countries (OPEC), the cartel of oil-producing states formed in 1960. He played a key role in orchestrating, through restrictions on output, the surge in world oil prices during the 1970s, which saw Saudi annual oil revenues rise from $2.7 billion in 1972 to $102 billion in 1981. During the early 1980s al-Yamani changed strategy and advocated increased Saudi, and OPEC, oil production, in an effort to maintain the cartel's share of world output. The consequence was a fall in world oil prices, which raised al-Yamani's popularity in the West, but led to his dismissal in 1986.

Educated at Cairo, New York, and at Harvard University, he was a lawyer before entering politics.

Yanayev, Gennady (1937–   )
Soviet communist politician, vice president of the USSR 1990–91. He led the August 1991 attempted coup against Mikhail Gorbachev, after which he was arrested and charged with treason. He was released in 1994 under an amnesty.

Yanayev rose in the ranks as a traditional, conservative-minded communist bureaucrat to become a member of the Politburo and Secretariat, and head of the official Soviet trade-union movement from 1990. In December 1990 he was President Gorbachev's surprise choice for vice president. In August 1991, however, Yanayev became titular head of the eight-member 'emergency committee' that launched the reactionary coup against Gorbachev.

Yang Shangkun (1907–1998)
Chinese communist politician. He held a senior position in the Central Committee of the Communist Party of China (CCP) 1956–66 but was demoted during the Cultural Revolution. He was rehabilitated in 1978, elected to the Politburo in 1982, and served as state president 1988–93.

As president, Yang played a key role, along with Deng Xiaoping, in ordering the June 1989 military crackdown against student prodemocracy demonstrators in Tiananmen Square, Beijing. His nephew, Yang Jianhua, commanded the highly disciplined 27th Group Army, which was brought in from Hebei province to suppress the 'uprising'. By the early 1990s his personal links with so many key commanders in the People's Liberation Army (PLA) were so extensive that some Chinese had begun to dub the PLA 'the Yang Family Army'.

The son of a wealthy Sichuan landlord, Yang joined the CCP in 1926 and studied at the Sun Yat-sen University in Moscow between 1927 and 1930. A veteran of the Long March 1934–35 and the war against Japan 1937–45, Yang rose in the ranks of the CCP before being purged for alleged revisionism in the Cultural Revolution.

Yao Wenyuan (1931–)

Chinese communist politician, member of the ultra-leftist Gang of Four. Yao joined with other members of the Gang to overthrow, in January 1967, the moderate Shanghai Chinese Communist Party (CCP) committee and replace it with a 'People's Commune'. Yao became a vice chair of this 'Revolutionary Committee' and in 1969 a member of the CCP Politiburo. However, in October 1976, after the death of Mao Zedong, the members of the Gang were arrested and in 1980–81 they were tried and found guilty of having contrived an armed uprising in 1976.

Yao was sentenced to 20 years' imprisonment and deprivation of his political rights for five years (the most lenient of the sentences given to a member of the Gang). He was released from prison in October 1996.

Born near Shanghai, Yao became a radical journalist, who developed political links with with ◊Jiang Qing, Wang Hongwen, and Zhang Chunqiao, the other members of the notorious Gang of Four. As editor chief of the *Liberation Daily* in Shanghai, in November 1965 he rose to prominence through publishing an article in which he attacked Wu Han's play, *Hai Jui Dismissed*. This was seen as marking the beginning of the Cultural Revolution of 1966–69, in which so-called 'bourgeois reactionaries' and 'capitalist roaders' within the CCP came under concerted attack by young ultra-leftist Maoists who believed in the theory of 'perpetual revolution'.

Yao Yilin (1915–1994)

Chinese communist politician. During the 1960s he served as commerce minister, but was purged in 1967, during the 'anti-bourgeois' Cultural Revolution of 1966–69, having been branded a 'three-anti-element'. However, he was rehabilitated in 1973 and, with the support of the reformist Deng Xiaoping, was made a vice premier in 1979. As a member of the policy-making Chinese Communist Party (CCP) Secretariat 1980–85 and Politburo from 1985, Yao oversaw economic planning during the 1980s at a time when radical 'market socialist' reforms were being introduced by the prime minister, Zhao Ziyang, transforming the Chinese economy.

Yao was an equivocal supporter of these reforms since he believed in the need to maintain CCP central control so as to correct regional disparities and prevent social unrest. Consequently, he emerged as a conservative figure within the new 'Dengist' leadership and was instrumental in securing the appointment of the more cautious Li Peng as prime minister, when Zhao became party leader in 1987. Yao was also a proponent of closer relations with Russia, signing a trade pact in July 1985. He also supported Deng and Li Peng in the use of force to crush the June 1989 student prodemocracy movement. In October 1992 he retired from the CCP Politburo to make way for a younger echelon of party leaders.

Born in Anhui province, the son of a landlord, Yao was educated at a Christian school and later studied at Qinghua University. He joined the CCP in 1935, while still at university, and served as political commissar in the People's Liberation Army (PLA) during the liberation struggle and civil war of 1937–49. After the communist triumph in 1949, Yao became a party bureaucrat, specializing in economic affairs, where he gained a reputation as a pragmatic economic planner.

Yavlinsky, Grigory Alekseevich (1952–)

Ukrainian-born politician; leader of the Russian political party Yabloko with Y Boldyrev and V Lukin from 1993, and chairman from 1995. An economist, he became an economics minister in one of Boris Yeltsin's governments when Russia was still part of the USSR but refused all posts once the USSR collapsed, concentrating on building up Yabloko (Russian for 'apple'). The party remained the only consistently reformist party in the Duma (lower house), and Yavlinsky continued to be a potentially powerful player on the political stage.

In many ways Yavlinsky was the most successful leading liberal politician in Russia – but one who, at least in Yeltsin's time, never succeeded in achieving power. He was a free marketeer, but a constant and often loud critic of Yegor ◊Gaidar and his successors, claiming that reform had not really started and that corruption had cancelled out all hope of progress under Yeltsin. He ran as a presidential candidate, but received a low vote; many of the liberals disliked him for his criticism of Gaidar while the anti-reformists disliked him for his espousal of reform.

Ydígoras Fuentes, Miguel (1895–)

Guatemalan politician, president 1958–63. He promoted reform but encountered conservative opposition, while falling coffee prices resulted in social disorder to which Ydígoras responded by imposing martial law. He involved Guatemala as a satellite supporter of the USA in the 1961 Bay of Pigs invasion of Cuba. This stirred up left-wing opposition to the government, culminating in an attempted coup in February 1962 by leftist guerrillas, supported by student protesters. In March 1963 Defence Minister Enrique Peralta Azurdia ousted and replaced Ydígoras, forcing him into exile.

Ydígoras served under presidents Jorge ◊ Ubico Castañeda and Juan José ◊ Arévalo and was defeated in the presidential elections of 1950 and 1957.

Yeats, W(illiam) B(utler) (1865–1939)

Irish poet. He was a leader of the Celtic revival and a founder of the Abbey Theatre in Dublin. His early work was romantic and lyrical, as in the poem 'The Lake Isle of Innisfree' and the plays *The Countess Cathleen* (1892) and *The Land of Heart's Desire* (1894). His later books of poetry include *The Wild Swans at Coole* (1917) and *The Winding Stair* (1929). He was a senator of the Irish Free State 1922–28. He was awarded the Nobel Prize for Literature in 1923.

Ye Jianying or *Yeh Chien-ying* (1898–1986)

Chinese communist politician, head of state 1978–83. Ye entered the Chinese Communist Party (CCP) policy-making Secretariat in 1966 and replaced Lin Biao as defence minister in 1971. He played a key role in organizing the September–October 1976 Hua Guofeng coup against the ultra-leftist 'Gang of Four', led by Jiang Qing, and in facilitating the rehabilitation of the reformist Deng Xiaoping. Ye served as chair of the National People's Congress (NPC) Standing Committee 1978–83 and was thus de facto head of state.

He was a member of the CCP Politburo's Standing Committee 1977–85, advocating rapprochement with the USA, and military and economic modernization.

The son of a prosperous Guangzhou (Canton) trader, Ye graduated from the Yunnan Military Academy in 1919 and worked alongside Zhou Enlai as an instructor at the Whampoa Military Academy from 1924 to 1926. He joined the CCP and, in 1927 fled to the Soviet Union to escape the nationalist Kuomintang's (Guomindang's) anti-communist purge. He returned in 1931 and, after taking part in the 'Long March' of 1934–35, served as chief of staff of the Eighth Route Army during the Liberation War of 1937–49. Ye was appointed commander of the Guangdong region, after the People's Republic was established in 1949, and was honoured with the rank of marshal in 1955.

His son, Ye Xuanping (1924–), became governor of Guangdong province and successfully introduced market-centred economic reforms from the 1980s.

Yezhov, Nikolai Ivanovich (1895–1939)

Soviet politician and party functionary. As head of the NKVD (the Soviet secret police) 1936–38, he was a

◆ Yeltsin, Boris Nikolayevich (1931–) ◆

Russian politician, president of the Russian Soviet Federative Socialist Republic (RSFSR) 1990–91, and president of the newly independent Russian Federation from 1991. He directed the Federation's secession from the USSR and the formation of a new, decentralized confederation, the Commonwealth of Independent States (CIS), with himself as the most powerful leader. A referendum in 1993 supported his policies of price deregulation and accelerated privatization, despite severe economic problems and civil unrest. He survived a coup attempt later the same year, but was subsequently forced to compromise on the pace of his reforms after far-right electoral gains, and lost considerable public support. He suffered two heart attacks in October and November 1995, yet still contested the June 1996 presidential elections, in which he secured re-election by defeating Communist Party leader Gennady Zyuganov in the second round run-off.

Born in Sverdlovsk (now Ekaterinburg), Yeltsin began his career in the construction industry. He joined the Communist Party of the Soviet Union (CPSU) in 1961 and became district party leader.

Brought to Moscow by Mikhail Gorbachev and Nikolai Ryzhkov in 1985, he was appointed secretary for construction and then, in December 1985, Moscow party chief. His demotion to the post of first deputy chair of the State Construction Committee in November 1987 was seen as a blow to Gorbachev's *perestroika* initiative and a victory for the conservatives grouped around Yegor Ligachev. Yeltsin was re-elected March 1989 with an 89% share of the vote, defeating an official Communist Party candidate, and was elected to the Supreme Soviet in May 1989. A supporter of the Baltic states in their calls for greater independence, Yeltsin demanded increasingly more radical economic reform. In 1990 he renounced his CPSU membership and was elected president of the RSFSR, the largest republic of the USSR.

Advocating greater autonomy for the constituent republics within a federal USSR, Yeltsin prompted the Russian parliament in June 1990 to pass a decree giving the republic's laws precedence over those passed by the Soviet parliament. In April 1991 he was voted emergency

Boris Yeltsin. *Rex*

major figure in Stalin's ruthless purges of the Communist Party. The bloody suppression of all dissent in this period came to be known after him, as the 'Yezhovshchina', but he himself was arrested 1938–39 and never seen again.

Yezhov emerged from obscurity in 1934 to become chair of the Commission of Party Control, the party's internal intelligence service, whose express task it was to discover and eliminate opponents of Stalin. He was dismissed in 1938 soon after becoming a member of the Politburo, and was succeeded as police chief by Lavrenti ◊ Beria.

Yilmaz, A Mesut (1947–)

Turkish politician, prime minister in 1991, 1996, and from 1997. He rose to power through a number of ministerial posts 1986–90 and became leader of the right-of-centre Motherland Party (ANAP) in 1991.

Yilmaz was born in Istanbul and educated in Ankara, London, and Cologne. He followed a business career before entering politics and joined the Islamic ANAP, founded in 1983 by Turgut Özal.

He was appointed prime minister by President Özal in 1991. However, dissatisfaction with the state of the economy lowered ANAP's popularity and Yilmaz's government was replaced, within a year of his taking office, by a centre-right coalition led by the True Path

powers by congress, enabling him to rule by decree, and two months later was popularly elected president. In the abortive August 1991 coup against Gorbachev, Yeltsin, as head of a democratic 'opposition state' based at the Russian parliament building, played a decisive role, publicly condemning the usurpers and calling for the reinstatement of President Gorbachev.

As the economic situation deteriorated within Russia, Yeltsin's leadership came under increasing challenge. An attempted coup by parliamentary leaders was successfully thwarted September–October 1993, but unexpected far-right gains in assembly elections in December forced him to compromise his economic policies and rely increasingly on the support of the military. From early 1995 he came under criticism for his apparent sanctioning of a full-scale military offensive in the breakaway republic of Chechnya. His hospitalization with a heart condition in July, and again in October and November 1995, raised speculation as to his possible successors. In May 1996, less than three weeks before the elections, he negotiated a peace agreement with the Chechen rebels. Yeltsin, who suffered a third heart attack in June 1996, successfully underwent quintuple heart bypass surgery in November the

same year. In May 1997 a peace treaty was signed with Chechnya and in June 1997 a Union Treaty with Belarus, committing the state to future integration. An active 1997 ended with Yeltsin briefly returning to hospital in December with an acute respiratory viral infection.

In March 1998 Yeltsin astounded both Russia and the West by sacking the entire cabinet, and appointing as prime minister the 35-year-old fuel and energy minister Sergei Kiriyenko. Yeltsin put pressure on the Duma to accept Kiriyenko as prime minister, which finally happened after three rounds of voting in April 1998. Yeltsin was seeking to fulfil his pledge to ensure that Russia was run by a younger, more dynamic and market-oriented generation, but the new government faced a financial crisis as the value of the rouble fell sharply by mid-1998.

FURTHER READING

Morrison, John *Boris Yeltsin: From Bolshevik to Democrat* 1991

Steele, Jonathan *Eternal Russia: Yeltsin, Gorbachev and the Mirage of Democracy* 1994

Solovyov, Vladimir, and Klepikova, Elena *Boris Yeltsin: A Political Biography* 1992

Party (DYP). The DYP coalition collapsed in September 1995 and after five months of negotiation a new coalition was agreed in February 1996, with the premiership rotating between Yilmaz and the DYP leader Tansu Ciller. In May 1996 the DYP withdrew from the coalition and Yilmaz continued as prime minister. In June 1996 Yilmaz's government was replaced by a new coalition of the pro-Islamic Welfare Party (RP) and the DYP, Necmettin Erbakan becoming prime minister. In June 1997 Yilmaz returned to power as prime minister for the third time.

Yoshida, Shigeru (1878–1967)

Japanese diplomat and conservative Liberal politician who served as prime minister for most of the period 1946–54, including much of the US occupation 1945–52. Under Yoshida, Japan signed the San Francisco Peace Treaty with the USA and its allies in 1951.

Young, Andrew (Jackson), Jr (1932–)

US civil-rights activist, protestant minister, and public official. He was an exponent of moderation and reform within the black American community.

Born in New Orleans, Louisiana, as a minister he joined the Southern Christian Leadership Conference (SCLC) in 1960 and came to be one of the closest associates of Martin Luther King, Jr. As the SCLC's executive director 1964–70, he took an active role in working at desegregation. Elected to the US House of Representatives as a Democrat 1973–77, he was the first black American to represent Georgia in Congress since 1871. In 1977 he resigned from Congress to accept an appointment from President Jimmy Carter as US Representative to the United Nations. He was forced to resign in 1979 after it was revealed that he had met secretly with members of the Palestinian Liberation Organization (PLO). He served as mayor of Atlanta, Georgia, 1981–89.

Young, David Ivor, Baron Young of Graffham (1932–)

British Conservative politician, chair of the Manpower Services Commission (MSC) 1982–84, secretary for employment from 1985, and trade and industry secretary 1987–89, when he retired from politics for a new career in business. He was subsequently criticized by a House of Commons select committee over aspects of the privatization of the Rover car company. He was created Baron in 1984.

Young, Neil (1945–)

Canadian rock guitarist, singer, and songwriter. His song-writing is littered with political statements both on the right and the left of politics, most notably 'Ohio' (1972), a song written about the Ohio State University student riots in 1970. In the 1980s he embraced the homespun philosophy of Ronald Reagan with the albums *Hawks and Doves* (1980) and *Old Ways* (1985), both of which bear the influence of conservative, right-wing politics. He returned to his left roots in the late 1980s with *Freedom* (1989) – its track 'Rocking in the Free World' criticized US imperialism and George Bush's presidency, and became the highlight of Nelson Mandela's Freedom concert.

FURTHER READING
Downing, David *A Dreamer of Pictures: Neil Young – The Man and His Music* 1985
Young, Scott, and Buck, Peter (ed) *Neil and Me* 1997

Younger, George Younger, 1st Viscount Younger of Leckie (1851–1929)

Scottish Conservative politician, member of Parliament for Ayr 1906–22. In 1917, he was appointed by Conservative leader Andrew Bonar Law as party chair. In this role, he was largely responsible for the success of the Liberal–Conservative coalition in the so-called Coupon Election of 1918.

George Younger was born into the prominent Younger's brewing dynasty. He was raised to the peerage in 1923.

Youssoufi, Abderrahmane al- (1924–)

Moroccan politician; prime minister from 1998. He joined the Parti de l'Istiqlal (PI) in 1944 and participated in the formation of the left-wing National Union of Popular Forces in 1959 (renamed the Socialist Union of Popular Forces in 1975), which he led from 1992.

Harassed and arrested on several occasions in 1959, 1963, and 1965, he departed for Paris in November 1965. While in exile he was condemned to death during the Marrakesh trials 1969–75. Granted a pardon in 1980, he returned to Morocco and, following the 1997 legislative elections, became prime minister in February 1998.

Yüan Shikai (1859–1916)

Chinese soldier and politician, leader of Republican China 1911–16. He assumed dictatorial powers in 1912, dissolving parliament and suppressing Sun Zhong Shan's (Sun Yat-sen's) Kuomintang (Guomindang, nationalist) party. He died soon after proclaiming himself emperor.

Born in Xiangzheng, in Henan province, Yüan served in the Chinese Imperial Army and became imperial resident in Korea between 1885 and 1894. Although committed to military reform, Yüan betrayed the modernizing emperor Guangxu (ruled 1875–1908) and sided with the ultra-conservative Empress Dowager ◊Zi Xi during the Hundred Days' Reform in 1898. He was rewarded by being appointed governor of Shandong in 1900 and viceroy of Chihli (now Hebei) province 1901–07. He was forced into retirement, however, on Zi Xi's death in 1908. With a power base in northern China, Yüan was appointed prime minister and commander in chief after the 1911 Republican Revolution against the Manchu Qings and became president in February 1912. He soon set up a dictatorship, outlawing Sun Zhong Shan's Kuomintang party and dissolving parliament, but lost credibility after submitting to Japan's demands in 1915, ceding territory to Japan. A rebellion in southern China forced him to resign in April 1916 and he died two months later.

Zaghlul, Saad (1857–1927)

Egyptian nationalist and politician, prime minister in 1924. Leader of the Wafd party, he came to be regarded as the 'father' of an independent Egyptian nation-state. His intransigent, uncompromising attitude to, and open criticism of, the negotiations with the British, costing him deportation to Malta in 1919 and the Seychelles in 1921, made him the symbol and hero of the Egyptian nationalist cause to end the protectorate. He became prime minister of the first elected government in January 1924 and resigned 11 months later in protest against the British ultimatum to his government.

Zahir Shah, Muhammad (1914–   )

King of Afghanistan 1933–73. He was educated in Kabul and Paris, and served in the government 1932–33 before being crowned king. He was overthrown in 1973 by a republican coup and went into exile. He became a symbol of national unity for the Mujaheddin Islamic fundamentalist resistance groups.

In 1991 the Afghan government restored Zahir's citizenship.

Zapata, Emiliano (1879–1919)

Mexican revolutionary leader. He led a revolt against the dictator Porfirio ◊ Díaz from 1910 under the slogan 'Land and Liberty', to repossess for the indigenous Mexicans the land taken by the Spanish. By 1915 he was driven into retreat, and was assassinated in his stronghold, Morelos, by an agent of Venustiano ◊ Carranza.

Initially he was allied with the northern-based revolutionary leader Francesco ◊ Madero, but he dissociated himself from him because of Madero's timidity at land reforms. He also fought against the succeeding regimes of Victoriano ◊ Huerta and Venustiano Carranza, from 1913, recruiting an army of Native Americans from local plantations and estates.

Born in Morelos estate, in south Mexico, Zapata was an illiterate tenant farmer of pure Native American descent. He remains an ideal for Native Americans in southern Mexico, and has inspired the Zapatista revolutionaries active in Chiapas state since the mid-1990s.

Zappa, Frank (Francis Vincent) (1940–1993)

US rock musician, bandleader, and composer. His crudely satirical songs, as in *Joe's Garage* (1980), deliberately bad taste, and complex orchestral and electronic compositions make his work hard to categorize. His group the Mothers of Invention 1965–73 was part of the 1960s avant-garde, and the Mothers' hippie parody *We're Only in It for the Money* (1967) was popular with its target audience. He was a vociferous opponent of US initiatives to censor pop lyrics, pointing out that 'people who make bad laws are more dangerous than songwriters'. In 1989 he visited Czechoslovakia's new president, the long-time Zappa fan Václav ◊ Havel, and advised the Czech government on cultural liaison with the West.

> It isn't necessary to imagine the world ending in fire or ice – there are two other possibilities: one is paperwork, and the other is nostalgia.
>
> FRANK ZAPPA *The Real Frank Zappa Book*
> chap 9

Zayas, Alfredo (1861–1934)

Cuban Liberal politician, president 1921–25. He served as vice president of the centrist Liberal Party under José Miguel Gómez 1909–13, but in 1920 challenged him for the presidency after their relations had become strained. He won with the backing of Mario ◊ Menocal and his Conservative Party, although US intervention was necessary after claims of electoral rigging from Gómez. Beset by financial crisis, caused by a collapse in sugar prices, his government was criticized for indecisiveness and corruption.

In 1924 he left office with his personal wealth greatly increased and backed Gerardo ◊ Machado's successful bid for the presidency.

Zayas first became prominent as vice-presidential candidate of the newly formed Liberal Party in 1905, led by Gómez. Unsuccessful, he supported the 1906 Liberal rebellion that ousted President Tomás ◊ Estrada Palma and resulted in renewed US rule. As Liberal Party candidate in the presidential elections of 1912 and 1916, he was defeated by Menocal.

Zayed, Sheikh bin Sultan al-Nahyan
(1916–)

United Arab Emirates (UAE) political leader, ruler of the emirate of Abu Dhabi from 1966 and president of the UAE from 1971. He used his statesmanlike skills to bring unity among Abu Dhabi's fractious tribes and used its oil wealth to develop the infrastructure and social services. In 1971 he played a key role in persuading the neighbouring small Persian Gulf states to join together and form the United Arab Emirates and became the confederation's president. The moderate, pro-Western Zayed promoted peace in the region, helping to set up the Gulf Cooperation Council in 1981, and mediated during border disputes between Oman and Yemen and during the 1980–88 conflict between Iran and Iraq. During the 1990–91 Gulf War he made bases available for US-led allied forces, but, after Iraq had been driven out of Kuwait, opposed the continuance of United Nations sanctions against Iraq. Sheikh Zayed was financially damaged in 1991 by the sudden collapse of the Bank of Credit and Commerce International (BCCI), in which he had been a major shareholder and investor.

Born into the al-Nahyan family, Sunni Muslim rulers of Abu Dhabi since the 18th century, Zayed had a traditional Arab Islamic education. After serving successfully for two decades as governor of Al 'Ayn province, in 1966 he succeeded his deposed brother, Sheikh Shakhbut, as emir (ruler) of Abu Dhabi.

Zedillo Ponce de León, Ernesto (1951–)

Mexican politician, president from 1994. With the assassination of Eduardo Colosio in March 1994, Zedillo was chosen as the new candidate of the Institutional Revolutionary Party (PRI) and narrowly won the August 1994 presidential election. Taking office as president in December 1994, within weeks he faced an economic crisis as the currency, the peso, fell in value by 40%. The austerity resources introduced in return for US financial aid caused a deep recession. Zedillo proved unexpectedly sympathetic to democratic reforms, and overhauled the corrupt justice system, made the electoral process fairer, and in 1996 signed a peace pact with the Zapatista rebels (based in the southern state of Chiapas).

A member of the PRI, he served as budget and planning minister under President Carlos ◊Salinas de Gortari from 1988, formulating an anti-inflation plan and promoting the free-trade agreement with the USA and Canada, and as education minister from 1992. In 1993 he resigned to manage the campaign of Luis Eduardo Colosio, Salinas's hand-picked successor.

Born in Mexicali, in the north, he studied at the National Polytechnic Institute and earned a doctorate in economics at Yale, USA, in 1981. He went to work at the Banco de Mexico (the country's central bank) and helped to devise a successful programme to manage Mexico's enormous foreign debt.

Zelaya, José Santos (1853–1919)

Nicaraguan politician, leader of the Liberal Party, president 1893–1909. He ended 30 years of political dominance by the Conservatives and established an effective dictatorship. In 1894 Zelaya seized the Mosquito Coast, in the northwest, by force from the UK.

He promoted extended railway and steamer transportation, coffee planting, and modernization of the army. Influenced by his earlier studies in France, he also sought greater separation of church and state and secularization and expansion of education, but his regime was also characterized by corruption. He also attempted to re-establish a Central American Federation and to install in power sympathetic regimes in neighbouring states. These efforts were opposed by the USA and by Manuel ◊Estrada Cabrera, Guatemala's dictatorial ruler 1898–1920. In 1909 Zelaya was overthrown in a revolution supported from the USA, and was forced into exile.

Zenawi, Meles (1955–)

Ethiopian politician and former guerrilla fighter, prime minister from 1995. He was the leader of the Ethiopian People's Revolutionary Democratic Front (EPRDF) which overthrew the regime of Mengistu Haile Mariam in 1991, and was president of the interim administration 1991–95. It was under Zenawi that Eritrea was allowed to opt for independence.

Zenawi was born in Adua in the north of the country to a Tigrean father and an Eritrean mother.

Zeroual, Lamine (1941–)

Algerian politican and soldier, president from 1994. He was brought into government in 1993 as defence minister, and the following year became commander-in-chief of the armed forces. Appointed president at a time of increasing civil strife, he initially attempted dialogue and reconciliation with imprisoned Islamic fundamentalist leaders. After this failed, Zeroual increasingly resorted to military tactics to counter the unrest. Following his victory in a direct presidential election in November 1995, he attempted to reopen dialogue with the outlawed Islamic Salvation Front (FIS), and in September 1996 announced plans for constitutional changes allowing for multiparty politics. During 1997 the weekly civilian death toll from the civil war approached 200.

Zhang Chunqiao (1917–1992)

Chinese communist politician, member of the ultra-leftist Gang of Four. Zhang was elected to the Chinese Communist Party (CCP) Politburo in 1969, became Shanghai party leader in 1971, and in 1975 became vice premier and chief political commissar of the

People's Liberation Army (PLA). He began organizing a 'people's militia' with a view to seizing national power and installing himself as premier and ◊Jiang Qing as party leader on the death of Mao Zedong. This plot was crushed in October 1976, when Zhang and the rest of the Gang were arrested by forces loyal to Hua Guofeng.

Zhang was sentenced to death in January 1981, but this was commuted, in March 1983, to life imprisonment.

Born in Shandong province, Zhang joined the CCP in 1940 and fought against the Japanese in northeast China 1942–43. After the establishment of the People's Republic in 1949, he became a party propagandist and radical writer, based in Shanghai from the late 1950s. In January 1967 in Shanghai, with Jiang Qing and other members of the Gang of Four, he seized control of the Shanghai Chinese Communist Party (CCP) machine and established a 'People's Commune' on the model of the 1871 Paris Commune.

Zhang Xueliang or *Chang Hsüeh-liang* (1901–)

Chinese nationalist soldier who kidnapped ◊Jiang Jie Shi (Chiang Kai-shek) in the Xi'an Incident of 1936. Convinced of the need for a united nationalist–communist front to fight against the Japanese threat, Zhang held Jiang under house arrest at Xi'an, in Shaanxi, for 13 days while he persuaded him to accept reconciliation with the communists. Zhang was later arrested by Jiang and remained in confinement, in Taiwan, until the 1960s.

Known as the 'Young Marshal', Zhang succeeded his father, ◊Zhang Zuolin, the 'Old Marshal', as military ruler of Manchuria when the latter was assassinated by Japanese military agents in June 1928. Before the Xi'an Incident, in 1930 he assisted Jiang Jie Shi in expelling the warlord Feng Yu-hsiang from Beijing, and with the Japanese in control of Manchuria from 1931, Zhang continued to assist Jiang Jie Shi in his campaign against the Chinese communists.

Zhang Zuolin or *Chang Tso-lin* (1873–1928)

Chinese warlord, ruler of Manchuria 1917–28. The son of a shepherd, Zhang was born in southern Manchuria and, taking advantage of the instability of his times, became a successful and wealthy plunderer of Russian border forces. He built up his own powerful private army and by 1917 had become de facto ruler of Manchuria. From 1921 he also controlled Inner Mongolia. Zhang profited by selling economic concessions to the Japanese, and at the same time secured recognition of his authority in Manchuria from the USSR. He was assassinated in June 1928 near Mukden, when his train was blown up by Japanese military agents.

Known as the 'Old Marshal', he was succeeded as ruler of Manchuria by his son, ◊Zhang Xueliang, who became known as the 'Young Marshal', but who faced growing pressures from the Japanese and Jiang Jie Shi's (Chiang Kai-shek's) nationalist forces.

FURTHER READING
McCormack, G *Chang Tso-lin in North East China* 1977

Zhao Ziyang (1919–)

Chinese communist politician, prime minister 1980–87, and leader of the Chinese Communist Party (CCP) 1987–89. His reforms included self-management and incentives for workers and factories. He lost his secretaryship and other posts after the Tiananmen Square massacre in Beijing in June 1989.

The son of a wealthy Henan province landlord, Zhao joined the Communist Youth League in 1932 and worked underground as a CCP official during the Liberation War of 1937–49. He rose to prominence in the party in Guangdong from 1951. As a supporter of the reforms of Liu Shaoqi, Zhao was dismissed as Guangdong party leader during the 1966–69 Cultural Revolution, was paraded through Guangzhou (Canton) in a dunce's cap, and in 1971 was assigned to work in Inner Mongolia.

He was rehabilitated by Zhou Enlai in 1973 and sent to China's largest province, Sichuan, as first party secretary in 1975. Here he introduced radical and successful market-oriented rural reforms, which led to

Chinese prime minister Zhao Ziyang speaking on the White House lawn, with US president Ronald Reagan in the background, 1984. *Rex*

rapid increases in output. This impressed Deng Xiaoping, who had him inducted into the Politburo as an alternate member in 1977 and as a full member in 1979. After six months as vice premier, Zhao was appointed prime minister in 1980, succeeding Hua Guofeng, and became CCP general secretary in January 1987, after the dismissal of Deng's apparent protégé, Hu Yaobang, following student prodemocracy demonstrations. Zhao's economic reforms led to rapid economic growth, especially in China's coastal region, but were criticized by party conservatives for causing inflation and social dislocation. He also promoted political reforms, seeking a clearer separation between 'party and government'.

In his immaculately tailored Western-style silk jackets, he became the epitome of the new modernizing China. However, Zhao's liberal views of the student prodemocracy demonstrations during 1989, which culminated in the student occupation of Tiananmen Square, Beijing, in May, were to lead to his downfall. He refused to support the use of military force to suppress the demonstrations and when Deng Xiaoping declared in a crucial 17 May 1989 Politburo meeting 'I have the army behind me', he reportedly retorted, 'But I have the people behind me. You have nothing'. Zhao sought to resign as party leader and on 19 May 1989 made a final, tearful plea to the hunger-strikers in Tiananmen Square to end their fast. After the June 1989 military crackdown he was sacked as CCP leader and replaced by Jiang Zemin. He remained a CCP member, but became 'politically invisible'.

FURTHER READING
Shambaugh, David *The Making of a Premier: Zhao Ziyang's Provincial Career* 1984

Zhdanov, Andrei Aleksandrovich (1896–1948)

Soviet politician. As secretary of the Central Committee of the Communist Party from 1934 onwards, he was largely responsible for formulating the ideology of Stalinism. During World War II he played a leading role in the defence of the besieged city of Leningrad (now St Petersburg), 1941–44.

Zhdanov joined the Bolsheviks in 1915, took part in the October Revolution of 1917, and was appointed head of the party organization in Nizhniy Novgorod 1924–34. In 1939 he became a full member of the Politburo. He imposed Socialist Realism as a rigid doctrine on all writers and artists, and after World War II condemned all Western cultural influences. In 1947 he set up the Cominform organization to liaise between East European communist parties. On his death the Ukrainian Black Sea port of Mariupol was renamed Zhdanov in his honour; it reverted to its former name when communism collapsed in 1989.

Zhelev, Zhelyu (1935–)

Bulgarian politician, president 1990–96. In 1989 he became head of the opposition Union Democratic Forces (UDF) coalition. He was a proponent of market-centred economic reform and social peace.

The son of peasants, born in Veselinovo in the Varna region, he was educated at the St Kliment of Ohrid University and later became professor of philosophy at Sofia University. He was a member of the Bulgarian Communist Party 1961–65, when he was expelled for his criticisms of Lenin. He was made president of Bulgaria in 1990 after the demise of the 'reform communist' regime, and was directly elected to the post in 1992. In June 1996 he was defeated in the UDF's presidential primary by Petar ◊Stoyanov.

FURTHER READING
Zhelev, Zhelu *Relatsionna teoriia za lichnostta* 1993

Zhirinovsky, Vladimir (1946–)

Russian politician, leader of the far-right Liberal Democratic Party of Russia (LDPR) from 1991. His strong, sometimes bizarre views, advocating the use of nuclear weapons and the restoration of the Russian empire, initially cast him as a lightweight politician. However, his ability to win third place out of six candidates in Russia's first free presidential elections in 1991, and the success of his party in winning nearly 23% of the vote and 15% of the seats in the December 1993 federal assembly elections, forced a reassessment. However, in the June 1996 presidential elections his support fell to below 6%.

His complex, unpredictable personality is tellingly revealed in his autobiography *My Struggle: The Explosive Views of Russia's Most Controversial Political Figure* (1996), which has been likened to Hitler's *Mein Kampf*. He has been seen as a threat to democratic progress in Russia.

Zhivkov, Todor Hristo (1911–1998)

Bulgarian Communist Party (BCP) leader 1954–89, prime minister 1962–71, and president 1971–89. His period in office was one of caution and conservatism. In 1990 he was charged with embezzlement during his time in office and in 1992 sentenced to seven years under house arrest. He was released in January 1997.

Zhivkov, a printing worker, joined the BCP in 1932 and was active in the resistance 1941–44. After the war he was elected to the national assembly and soon promoted into the BCP secretariat and politburo. As BCP first secretary, Zhivkov became the dominant political figure in Bulgaria after the death of Vulko Chervenkov in 1956. He was elected to the new post of state president in 1971, serving in that capacity until the Eastern bloc upheavals of 1989.

FURTHER READING
Bell, John D *The Bulgarian Communist Party from Blagoev to Zhivkov* 1986

Zhivkov, Todor *Todor Zhivkov: Statesman and Builder of New Bulgaria* 1985

Zhou Enlai or *Chou En-lai* (1898–1976)
See page 464.

Zhu De or *Chu Teh* (1886–1976)
Chinese communist military leader, 'father' and commander of the Chinese Red Army 1931–54.

The son of a wealthy Sichuan province landlord, Zhu studied at the Yunnan Military Academy and served in the Chinese Imperial Army before supporting Sun Zhong Shan (Sun Yat-sen) in the 1911 revolution. He rose to the rank of brigadier in Sun's Republican Army in 1916, but, suffering from opium addiction, was sent to Germany in 1921 to study engineering. There he became converted to communism, joining the Communist Party in Berlin in 1922, and he remained in Germany and Paris, studying communism, until 1926.

On his return to China, he presented his inherited wealth to the Chinese Communist Party (CCP) and led an army revolt in Nanchang against the Kuomintang (Guomindang, nationalist) regime in 1927. Working closely with Mao Zedong, he organized a communist Red Army, of which he became commander in chief and directed the Red Army's break-out from its base in Jiangxi and its epic 'Long March' northwards to Yanan, in Shaanxi province, 1934–35. Influenced by the ancient popular Chinese texts the *Water Margin* and Sun Tzu's *Art of War*, he devised the tactic of mobile guerrilla warfare, which proved particularly effective when he led the 18th Route Army during the Liberation War of 1937–49. Zhu was made a marshal in 1955.

In the early phase of the Cultural Revolution (1966–69), his house was ransacked by young ultra-leftist Red Guards, after he had defended Liu Shaoqi, and he was dropped from the CCP Politburo Standing Committee in 1969. However, he was restored in 1971 and served as head of state (chair of the Standing Committee of the National People's Congress) from January 1975 until his death in July 1976.

FURTHER READING
Smedley, A *The Great Road: The Life and Times of Chu Teh* 1956

Zhu Rongji (1928–)
Chinese communist politician, vice premier from 1991 and prime minister from 1998. He rose to prominence 1988–91 when, as mayor of Shanghai, he promoted market-centred economic reforms and negotiated a peaceful resolution to the prodemocracy demonstrations in the city in 1989. He became a vice premier in 1991, with a particular interest in economic affairs, and entered the Chinese Communist Party (CCP) Politburo in 1992.

The 1997 party congress designated Zhu the third-ranking figure in the CCP, behind President Jiang Zemin and Li Peng, whom he replaced as prime minister in March 1998. He immediately announced a radical downsizing of the government to meet the needs of a market economy. Fifteen of the 40 ministeries were to be abolished or merged, and half of the 8 million bureaucrats to be made redundant.

Born in Changsha city, in Hunan, the province of Mao Zedong, the university-educated Zhu joined the CCP in 1949. He worked in the State Planning Commission, but in 1957 and 1962, during campaigns by Maoist ultra-leftists, was denounced as a 'rightist capitalist roader' and exiled briefly to the countryside, where he worked as a farm labourer and pig feeder. He was fully rehabilitated from the late 1970s, with Deng Xiaoping in power, and during the 1980s worked as a minister in the state economic commission. Between 1993 and 1995 he served as governor of China's Central Bank and gained the reputation of being a tough and innovative technocrat. Dubbed by the media 'China's Gorbachev', Zhu is a strong opponent of bureaucratic corruption, stating once that he wished that he had 100 bullets '99 for corrupt officials and one for myself'.

Zia, Begum Khaleda (1945–)
Bangladeshi conservative politician, prime minister 1991–96. As leader of the Bangladesh Nationalist Party (BNP) from 1984, she successfully oversaw the transition from presidential to democratic parliamentary government, but faced mounting opposition from 1994.

In 1958 she married Captain Zia ur Rahman who assumed power in a military coup in 1976. He became president in 1977, and was assassinated in 1981. Begum Khaleda Zia then entered opposition politics, becoming leader of the BNP in 1984. In 1990 she helped form a seven-party alliance, whose pressure for a more democratic regime resulted in the toppling of General Hussain ◊Ershad, a long-standing military ruler, during whose regime she had been detained seven times. From December 1994 she faced a mounting campaign against her government, with opposition MPs boycotting parliament and the longest general strike in the country's history being called. The opposition boycotted the February 1996 general elections, and one month later she handed over power to a neutral coalition government to enable fresh elections to be held. The BNP was defeated by its chief rival, the Awami League, in the general election that followed in June 1996, and boycotted the parliament for four months 1997–98.

Zia ul-Haq, Muhammad (1924–1988)
Pakistani general, in power from 1977 until his death, probably an assassination, in an aircraft explosion. He became army chief of staff in 1976, led the military coup against Zulfikar Ali ◊Bhutto in 1977, and became president in 1978. Zia introduced a fundamentalist Islamic regime and restricted political activity.

Zia was a career soldier from a middle-class Punjabi Muslim family. As army chief of staff, his opposition to the Soviet invasion of Afghanistan in 1979 drew support from the USA, but his refusal to commute the death sentence imposed on Bhutto was widely condemned. He lifted martial law in 1985.

Zimmerman, Arthur (1864–1940)

German politician. As foreign secretary 1916–17, he sent the notorious *Zimmermann Telegram* to the German minister in Mexico in January 1917. It contained the terms of an alliance between Mexico and Germany, by which Mexico was to attack the USA with German and Japanese assistance in return for the 'lost' states of New Mexico, Texas, and Arizona. Publication of the message in March 1917 finally brought the hesitant USA into the war against Germany, and Zimmermann 'resigned' shortly afterwards.

Zimmerman was born in East Prussia. After diplomatic service in China, he directed the eastern division of the German foreign office from 1904 until his appointment as foreign secretary in 1916.

Zinn, Howard (1922–)

US historian and social activist. Active in social and political affairs throughout his life and an authority on the history of US civil disobedience, he participated with the Student Nonviolent Coordinating Committee (SNCC) during the civil-rights movement of the 1960s and 1970s. As a prominent protester against US aggression in Vietnam, he helped secure the release of the first three US prisoners of war. His *La Guardia in Congress* received the Beveridge Prize in 1959.

Born in New York City, he received an Air Medal and battle stars for service in the US Army Air Forces 1943–45. He was educated at New York University, gaining a BA in 1951, and Columbia, gaining an MA in 1952 and a PhD in 1958. He taught at Upsala College 1953–56, Spelman College 1956–63, and Boston University 1964–88 (professor emeritus 1988).

He drew upon personal experience to discuss civil rights in *SNCC – The New Abolitionists* (1964) and US militarism in *Vietnam: The Logic of Withdrawal* (1967). His work *A People's History of the United States* (1980) approaches history from the viewpoint of working class and minority groups.

Zinoviev, Grigory Yevseyevich (1883–1936)

Russian communist politician whose name was attached to a forgery, the *Zinoviev letter*, inciting

---

◆ ZHOU ENLAI OR CHOU EN-LAI (1898–1976) ◆

Chinese communist politician, prime minister 1949–76.

Born into a declining mandarin gentry family in Huaian, near Shanghai, Zhou studied at Nankai University, Tianjin, and in Japan and Paris, where he worked in a Renault car factory and became a founder member, with Deng Xiaoping in 1922, of the overseas branch of the Chinese Communist Party (CCP). He adhered, initially, to the Moscow line of urban-based revolution in China and cooperation with the Kuomintang (nationalists), organizing communist cells in Shanghai and heading the political department of Jiang Jie Shi's (Chiang Kai-shek's) Whampoa Military Academy. After the break between the CCP and the Kuomintang, he took part in an abortive uprising in Nanchang in 1927, which marked the founding of the Red Army, and entered the CCP Politburo. In 1935 Zhou supported the election of Mao Zedong as CCP leader and remained a loyal ally during the next 40 years. He took part in the 1934–35 'Long March' north from the Jiangxi soviet to Yanan, in northern Shaanxi, and, based

in Chongqing, in Sichuan province, served as liaison officer 1937–46 between the CCP and Jiang Jie Shi's Kuomintang government. In October 1949 he became the People's Republic's first prime minister, an office he held until his death in January 1976, and was also foreign minister until 1958.

A moderate Maoist, Zhou acted as a bridge between the opposing camps of the reformist Liu Shaoqi, and and the more left-wing Mao Zedong. He restored orderly economic progress after the disruptions caused by the disastrous Great Leap Forward 1958–60 and the excesses of the Cultural Revolution 1966–69, which he weathered despite the fall of close colleagues, such as Chen Yi. At one stage during the Cultural Revolution, he directly confronted a crowd of more than 1 million people. He helped thwart an attempted military coup, in September 1971, by Lin Biao and his support proved crucial in the political survival of many later reformers, including Deng Xiaoping and Zhao Ziyang.

After the Cultural Revolution, Zhao emerged,

Britain's communists to rise, which helped to topple the Labour government in 1924.

A prominent Bolshevik, Zinoviev returned to Russia in 1917 with Lenin and played a leading part in the Revolution. He became head of the Communist International in 1919. As one of the 'Old Bolsheviks', he was seen by Stalin as a threat. He was accused of complicity in the murder of the Bolshevik leader Sergei Kirov in 1934, and was tried and shot.

Zi Xi or *Tz'u-hsi* (c. 1834–1908)

Empress dowager of China, who was effective ruler 1861–89 and 1898–1908.

A nobleman's daughter, she was presented as a concubine, or secondary wife, to Xianfeng (Hsien-Feng), China's emperor from 1850. On his death in 1861, as the mother of his only son Tongzhi (or T'ung-chih) (1856–1875), who was only five years old when he was made emperor, she became regent. He came of age in 1873, but died in 1875 and Zi Xi became regent again by placing her sister's young four-year-old son, Guangxu (or Kuang-hsu) (1871–1908), on the throne. Guangxu came of age in 1889 and sided with Westernizing reformers, but when he launched a Hundred Days' Reform initiative in 1898, the reaction-

ary Zi Xi joined with other conservatives to block the programme. She had the emperor confined to the imperial palace and, despite the Manchus' dynastic custom which forbade women to reign, assumed power again.

In 1900 she instigated the anti-foreigner and anti-Christian Boxer Rebellion, which led to international military reprisals. Her policies helped deny China a peaceful transition to political and economic reform and she had Guangxu murdered a day before her own death. An inveterate intriguer, she acquired the nickname, the 'Old Buddha'.

Zog, Ahmed Bey Zogu (1895–1961)

King of Albania 1928–39. He became prime minister of Albania in 1922, president of the republic in 1925, and proclaimed himself king in 1928. He was driven out by the Italians in 1939 and settled in the UK.

FURTHER READING
Fischer, Bernd *King Zog and the Struggle for Stability in Albania* 1984

Zuckerman, Solly, Baron Zuckerman of Burnham Thorpe (1904–1993)

South African-born British zoologist, educationalist, and establishment figure. He did extensive research on primates, publishing a number of books that became classics in their field, including *The Social Life of Monkeys and Apes* (1932) and *Functional Affinities of Man, Monkeys and Apes* (1933). As chief scientific adviser to the government during Harold Wilson's premiership, he had his own office within the Cabinet Office, with direct access to the prime minister himself. He published his autobiography, *From Apes to Warlords*, in 1978.

Zuganov, Gennadi Andreyevich (1944–)

Russian politician, leader of the Communist Party of the Russian Federation (CPRF) from 1992. During President Mikhail Gorbachev's *glasnost* programme 1988–91, he served as deputy director of the party's ideology department. He failed in his challenge for the presidency against Boris Yeltsin in 1996.

Zyuganov was born near Orel, Russia, and joined the Soviet Communist Party while in his 20s. In December 1992, after the break-up of the Soviet Union, he assumed leadership of the (then-banned) reform-socialist CPRF and oversaw the resurrection of the party's fortunes. In the December 1995 Russian parliamentary elections, the CPRF finished in first place with 22% of the vote. In the July 1996 Russian presidential election Zyuganov attracted 40% of the national vote.

behind Mao, as the country's second most powerful political leader. He was the architect of the Four Modernizations programme in 1975. Involving the modernization of agriculture, industry, science and technology, and national defence, it was the forerunner of later, more radical, reforms by Deng Xiaoping. Abroad, Zhou sought to foster Third World unity at the Bandung Asian–African Conference in 1955, averted an outright border confrontation with the USSR by negotiation with Prime Minister Alexei Kosygin in 1969, and was the principal advocate of détente with the USA during the early 1970s, which saw the signing in 1972 of the Shanghai Communiquint with President Richard Nixon. Zhou's death on 8 January 1976, after a long battle against cancer, was marked by a genuine outpouring of public grief, showing him to have been the most loved of all China's communist leaders.

FURTHER READING
Suyin, Han *Eldest Son: Zhou Enlai and the Making of Modern China* 1994
Wilson, D *The Story of Zhou Enlai, 1878–1984* 1984

Appendices

Argentine Presidents from 1944

Term	Name	Party
1944–46	Edelmiro Farrell	military
1946–55	Juan Perón	Justice Front of Liberation
1955	Eduardo Lonardi	military
1955–58	Pedro Aramburu	military
1958–62	Arturo Frondizi	Civic Radical Union-Intransigent
1962–63	José Guido	acting: independent
1963–66	Arturo Illía	Civic Radical Union of the People
1966–70	Juan Onganía	military
1970–71	Roberto Levingston	military
1971–73	Alejandro Lanusse	military
1973	Héctor Cámpora	Justice Front of Liberation
1973	Raúl Lastiri	acting: independent
1973–74	Juan Perón	Justice Front of Liberation
1974–76	Maria Estela de Perón	Justice Front of Liberation
1976–81	Jorge Videla	military
1981	Roberto Viola	military
1981–82	Leopoldo Galtieri	military
1982	Alfredo Saint-Jean	acting: military
1982–83	Reynaldo Bignone	military
1983–89	Raúl Alfonsín	Civic Radical Union
1989–	Carlos Saúl Menem	Justice Party

Belgian Prime Ministers from 1944

Term	Name	Party
1944–45	Hubert Pierlot	Catholic Party
1945–46	Achille van Acker	Socialist Party
1946	Paul-Henri Spaak	Socialist Party
1946	Achille van Acker	Socialist Party
1946–47	Camille Huysmans	Socialist Party
1947–49	Paul-Henri Spaak	Socialist Party
1949–50	Gaston Eyskens	Christian Social Party
1950	Jean Duvieusart	Christian Social Party
1950–52	Joseph Pholien	Christian Social Party
1952–54	Jean van Houtte	Christian Social Party
1954–58	Achille van Acker	Socialist Party
1958–61	Gaston Eyskens	Christian Social Party
1961–65	Théodore Lefèvre	Christian Social Party
1965–66	Pierre Harmel	Christian Social Party
1966–68	Paul van den Boeynants	Christian Social Party
1968–72	Gaston Eyskens	Christian Social Party
1972–74	Edmond Leburton	Socialist Party
1974–78	Léo Tindemans	Christian Social Party
1978–79	Paul van den Boeynants	Christian Social Party
1979–81	Wilfried Martens	Christian People's Party
1981	Mark Eyskens	Christian People's Party
1981–92	Wilfried Martens	Christian People's Party
1992–	Jean-Luc Dehaene	Christian People's Party

Australian Prime Ministers from 1901

Term	Name	Party
1901–03	Edmund Barton	Protectionist
1903–04	Alfred Deakin	Protectionist
1904	John Watson	Labor
1904–05	George Reid	Free Trade–Protectionist coalition
1905–08	Alfred Deakin	Protectionist
1908–09	Andrew Fisher	Labor
1909–10	Alfred Deakin	Fusion
1910–13	Andrew Fisher	Labor
1913–14	Joseph Cook	Liberal
1914–15	Andrew Fisher	Labor
1915–23	William Hughes	Labor (National Labor from 1917)
1923–29	Stanley Bruce	National–Country Coalition
1929–32	James Scullin	Labor
1932–39	Joseph Lyons	United Australia–Country coalition
1939	Earle Page	United Australia–Country coalition
1939–41	Robert Menzies	United Australia
1941	Arthur Fadden	Country–United Australia coalition
1941–45	John Curtin	Labor
1945	Francis Forde	Labor
1945–49	Joseph Chifley	Labor
1949–66	Robert Menzies	Liberal–Country coalition
1966–67	Harold Holt	Liberal–Country coalition
1967–68	John McEwen	Liberal–Country coalition
1968–71	John Gorton	Liberal–Country coalition
1971–72	William McMahon	Liberal–Country coalition
1972–75	Gough Whitlam	Labor
1975–83	Malcolm Fraser	Liberal–National coalition
1983–91	Robert Hawke	Labor
1991–96	Paul Keating	Labor
1996–	John Howard	Liberal–National coalition

Belgian Monarchs from 1831

Reign	Name
1831–65	Leopold I
1865–1909	Leopold II
1909–14	Albert I
1914–18	German occupation
1918–34	Albert I
1934–40	Leopold III
1940–44	German occupation
1944–50	Prince Charles (regent)
1950–51	Leopold III
1951–93	Baudouin
1993–	Albert II

Brazilian Presidents from 1945

Term	Name	Party
1945–46	José Linhares	independent
1946–51	Eurico Dutra	Social Democratic Party
1951–54	Getúlio Vargas	Brazil Labour Party
1954–55	João Café	Social Progressive Party
1955	Carlos da Luz	independent
1955–56	Nereu Ramos	independent
1956–61	Juscelino Kubitschek	Social Democratic Party
1961	Jânio Quadros	Christian Democratic Party/Democratic National Union
1961–64	João Goulart	Brazil Labour Party
1964	Ranieri Mazzili	independent
1964–67	Humberto Branco	military
1967–69	Arthur da Costa e Silva	military
1969–74	Emilio Medici	military
1974–79	Ernesto Geisel	military
1979–85	João Figueiredo	military
1985–89	José Sarney	Social Democratic Party
1989–92	Fernando Collor de Mello	National Reconstruction Party
1992–94	Itamar Franco	National Reconstruction Party
1995–	Fernando Henrique Cardoso	Social Democratic Party

Canadian Prime Ministers from 1867

Term	Name	Party
1867–73	John A Macdonald	Conservative
1873–78	Alexander Mackenzie	Liberal
1878–91	John A Macdonald	Conservative
1891–92	John J Abbott	Conservative
1892–94	John S D Thompson	Conservative
1894–96	Mackenzie Bowell	Conservative
1896	Charles Tupper	Conservative
1896–1911	Wilfred Laurier	Liberal
1911–20	Robert L Borden	Conservative
1920–21	Arthur Meighen	Conservative
1921–26	William L M King	Liberal
1926	Arthur Meighen	Conservative
1926–30	William L M King	Liberal
1930–35	Richard B Bennett	Conservative
1935–48	William L M King	Liberal
1948–57	Louis S St Laurent	Liberal
1957–63	John G Diefenbaker	Conservative
1963–68	Lester B Pearson	Liberal
1968–79	Pierre E Trudeau	Liberal
1979–80	Joseph Clark	Progressive Conservative
1980–84	Pierre E Trudeau	Liberal
1984	John Turner	Liberal
1984–93	Brian Mulroney	Progressive Conservative
1993	Kim Campbell	Progressive Conservative
1993–	Jean Chretien	Liberal

Chinese Prime Ministers and Communist Party Leaders

Term	Name	Term	Name
Prime Ministers		Communist Party Leaders	
1949–76	Zhou Enlai	1935–76	Mao Zedong
1976–80	Hua Guofeng	1976–81	Hua Guofeng
1980–87	Zhao Ziyang	1981–87	Hu Yaobang
1987–98	Li Peng	1987–89	Zhao Ziyang
1998–	Zhu Rongji	1989–	Jiang Zemin

Danish Monarchs from 1848

Reign	Name
House of Oldenburg	
1848–63	Frederick VII
Line of Glücksburg	
1863–1906	Christian IX
1906–12	Frederick VIII
1912–47	Christian X
1947–72	Frederick IX
1972–	Margrethe II

Danish Prime Ministers from 1945

Term	Name	Party
1945	Vilhelm Buhl	Social Democratic Party
1945–47	Knud Kristensen	Agrarian Party
1947–50	Hans Hedtoft	Social Democratic Party
1950–53	Erik Eriksen	Agrarian Party
1953–55	Hans Hedtoft	Social Democratic Party
1955–60	Hans Hansen	Social Democratic Party
1960–62	Viggo Kampmann	Social Democratic Party
1962–68	Jens-Otto Krag	Social Democratic Party
1968–71	Hilmar Baunsgaard	Radical Party
1971–72	Jens-Otto Krag	Social Democratic Party
1972–73	Anker Jørgensen	Social Democratic Party
1973–75	Poul Hartling	Liberal Party
1975–82	Anker Jørgensen	Social Democratic Party
1982–93	Poul Schlüter	Conservative Party
1993–	Poul Nyrup Rasmussen	Social Democratic Party

English Sovereigns From 899

Reign	Name	Relationship
West Saxon Kings		
899–924	Edward the Elder	son of Alfred the Great
924–39	Athelstan	son of Edward the Elder
939–46	Edmund	half-brother of Athelstan
946–55	Edred	brother of Edmund
955–59	Edwy	son of Edmund
959–75	Edgar	brother of Edwy
975–78	Edward the Martyr	son of Edgar
978–1016	Ethelred (II) the Unready	son of Edgar
1016	Edmund Ironside	son of Ethelred (II) the Unready
Danish Kings		
1016–35	Canute	son of Sweyn I of Denmark who conquered England in 1013
1035–40	Harold I	son of Canute
1040–42	Hardicanute	son of Canute
West Saxon Kings (restored)		
1042–66	Edward the Confessor	son of Ethelred (II) the Unready
1066	Harold II	son of Godwin
Norman Kings		
1066–87	William I	illegitimate son of Duke Robert the Devil
1087–1100	William II	son of William I
1100–35	Henry I	son of William I
1135–54	Stephen	grandson of William II
House of Plantagenet		
1154–89	Henry II	son of Matilda (daughter of Henry I)
1189–99	Richard I	son of Henry II
1199–1216	John	son of Henry II
1216–72	Henry III	son of John
1272–1307	Edward I	son of Henry III
1307–27	Edward II	son of Edward I
1327–77	Edward III	son of Edward II
1377–99	Richard II	son of the Black Prince
House of Lancaster		
1399–1413	Henry IV	son of John of Gaunt
1413–22	Henry V	son of Henry IV
1422–61, 1470–71	Henry VI	son of Henry V
House of York		
1461–70, 1471–83	Edward IV	son of Richard, Duke of York
1483	Edward V	son of Edward IV
1483–85	Richard III	brother of Edward IV
House of Tudor		
1485–1509	Henry VII	son of Edmund Tudor, Earl of Richmond
1509–47	Henry VIII	son of Henry VII
1547–53	Edward VI	son of Henry VIII
1553–58	Mary I	daughter of Henry VIII
1558–1603	Elizabeth I	daughter of Henry VIII
House of Stuart		
1603–25	James I	great-grandson of Margaret (daughter of Henry VII)
1625–49	Charles I	son of James I
1649–60	the Commonwealth	
House of Stuart (restored)		
1660–85	Charles II	son of Charles I
1685–88	James II	son of Charles I
1689–1702	William III and Mary	son of Mary (daughter of Charles I); daughter of James II
1702–14	Anne	daughter of James II
House of Hanover		
1714–27	George I	son of Sophia (granddaughter of James I)
1727–60	George II	son of George I
1760–1820	George III	son of Frederick (son of George II)
1820–30	George IV (regent 1811–20)	son of George III
1830–37	William IV	son of George III
1837–1901	Victoria	daughter of Edward (son of George III)
House of Saxe-Coburg		
1901–10	Edward VII	son of Victoria
House of Windsor		
1910–36	George V	son of Edward VII
1936	Edward VIII	son of George V
1936–52	George VI	son of George V
1952–	Elizabeth II	daughter of George VI

French Rulers 751–1958

Date of accession	Title of ruler	Name	Date of accession	Title of ruler	Name
751	King	Pepin III/Childerich III	1574	King	Henri IV
752		Pepin III	1610		Louis XIII
768		Charlemagne/Carloman	1643		Louis XIV
814		Louis I	1715		Louis XV
840		Lothair I	1774		Louis XVI
843		Charles (II) the Bald	1792	National Convention	
877		Louis II	1795	Directory (five members)	
879		Louis III	1799	First Consul	Napoléon Bonaparte
884		Charles (III) the Fat	1804	Emperor	Napoléon I
888		Odo	1814	King	Louis XVIII
893		Charles (III) the Simple	1815	Emperor	Napoléon I
922		Robert I	1815	King	Louis XVIII
923		Rudolf	1824		Charles X
936		Louis IV	1830		Louis XIX
954		Lothair II	1830		Henri V
986		Louis V	1830		Louis-Philippe
987		Hugues Capet	1848	President of the National Assembly	Philippe Buchez
996		Robert II			
1031		Henri I	1848	Minister of War	Louis Cavaignac
1060		Philippe I	1848	President	Louis Napoléon Bonaparte
1108		Louis VI			
1137		Louis VII	1852	Emperor	Napoléon III
1180		Philippe II	1871	President	Adolphe Thiers
1223		Louis VIII	1873		Patrice MacMahon
1226		Louis IX	1879		Jules Grevy
1270		Philippe III	1887		François Sadui-Carnot
1285		Philippe IV	1894		Jean Casimir-Périer
1314		Louis X	1895		François Faure
1316		Jean I	1899		Emile Loubet
1328		Philippe V	1913		Armand Fallières
1322		Charles IV	1913		Raymond Poincaré
1328		Philippe VI	1920		Paul Deschanel
1350		Jean II	1920		Alexandre Millerand
1356		Charles V	1924		Gaston Doumergue
1380		Charles VI	1931		Paul Doumer
1422		Charles VII	1932		Albert Le Brun
1461		Louis XI	1940	Vichy government	Philippe Pétain
1483		Charles VIII	1944	provisional government	
1498		Louis XII	1947	President	Vincent Auriol
1515		François I	1954		René Coty
1547		Henri II			
1559		François II			
1560		Charles IX			
1574		Henri III			

French Presidents and Prime Ministers from 1959 (the Fifth Republic)

Term	Name	Party
Presidents		
1959–69	General Charles de Gaulle	Gaullist
1969–74	Georges Pompidou	Gaullist
1974–81	Valéry Giscard d'Estaing	Republican/Union of French Democracy
1981–95	François Mitterand	Socialist
1995–	Jacques Chirac	Neo-Gaullist RPR
Prime Ministers		
1959–62	Michel Debré	Gaullist
1962–68	Georges Pompidou	Gaullist
1968–69	Maurice Couve de Murville	Gaullist
1969–72	Jacques Chaban-Delmas	Gaullist
1972–74	Pierre Messmer	Gaullist
1974–76	Jacques Chirac	Gaullist
1976–81	Raymond Barre	Union of French Democracy
1981–84	Pierre Mauroy	Socialist
1984–86	Laurent Fabius	Socialist
1986–88	Jacques Chirac	Neo-Gaullist RPR
1988–91	Michel Rocard	Socialist
1991–92	Edith Cresson	Socialist
1992–93	Pierre Bérégovoy	Socialist
1993–95	Edouard Balladur	Neo-Gaullist RPR
1995–97	Alain Juppé	Neo-Gaullist RPR
1997–	Lionel Jospin	Socialist

German Political Leaders from 1949

Term	Name	Party
Federal Republic		
Chancellors		
1949–63	Konrad Adenauer	Christian Democrat
1963–66	Ludwig Erhard	Christian Democrat
1966–69	Kurt Kiesinger	Christian Democrat
1969–74	Willy Brandt	Social Democrat
1974–82	Helmut Schmidt	Social Democrat
1982–98[1]	Helmut Kohl	Christian Democrat
Germany		
Chancellors		
1998–	Gerhard Schröder	Social Democrat
Democratic Republic		
Communist Party leaders		
1949–50	Wilhelm Pieck	
1950–71	Walter Ulbricht	
1971–89	Erich Honecker	
1989	Egon Krenz	
Prime Ministers		
1989–90	Hans Modrow	
1990–91	Lothar de Maizière	

[1] The official reunification of the two countries, with Kohl as chancellor, took place in 1990.

Indian Prime Ministers

Term	Name	Party
1947–64	Jawaharlal Nehru	Congress
1964–66	Lal Bahadur Shastri	Congress
1966–77	Indira Gandhi	Congress (I)
1977–79	Morarji Desai	Janata
1979–80	Charan Singh	Janata/Lok Dal
1980–84	Indira Gandhi	Congress (I)
1984–89	Rajiv Gandhi	Congress (I)
1989–90	Viswanath Pratap Singh	Janata Dal
1990–91	Chandra Shekhar	Janata Dal (Socialist)
1991–96	P V Narasimha Rao	Congress (I)
1996	Atal Behari Vaj Payee	Bharatiya Janata Party
1996–97	H D Deve Gowda	Janata Dal
1997–98	Inder Kumar Gujral	Janata Dal
1998–	Atal Bihari Vaijpayee	Bharatiya Janata Party

Irish Prime Ministers from 1922

Term	Name	Party
1922	Michael Collins	Sinn Féin
1922–32	William T Cosgrave	Fine Gael
1932–48	Eamon de Valera	Fianna Fáil
1948–51	John A Costello	Fine Gael
1951–54	Eamon de Valera	Fianna Fáil
1954–57	John A Costello	Fine Gael
1957–59	Eamon de Valera	Fianna Fáil
1959–66	Sean Lemass	Fianna Fáil
1966–73	Jack Lynch	Fianna Fáil
1973–77	Liam Cosgrave	Fine Gael
1977–79	Jack Lynch	Fianna Fáil
1979–81	Charles Haughey	Fianna Fáil
1981–82	Garrett Fitzgerald	Fine Gael
1982	Charles Haughey	Fianna Fáil
1982–87	Garrett Fitzgerald	Fine Gael
1987–92	Charles Haughey	Fianna Fáil
1992–94	Albert Reynolds	Fianna Fáil
1994–97	John Bruton	Fine Gael
1997–	Patrick 'Bertie' Ahern	Fianna Fáil

Israeli Prime Ministers from 1948

Term	Name	Party
1948–53	David Ben-Gurion	Mapai
1953–55	M Sharett	Mapai
1955–63	David Ben-Gurion	Mapai
1963–69	Levi Eshkol	Mapai/Labour
1969–74	Golda Meir	Labour
1974–77	Yitzhak Rabin	Labour
1977–83	Menachem Begin	Likud
1983–84	Yitzhak Shamir	Likud
1984–86	Shimon Peres	Labour
1986–92	Yitzhak Shamir	Likud
1992–95	Yitzhak Rabin	Labour
1995–96	Shimon Peres	Labour
1996–	Binyamin Netanyahu	Likud

Italian Prime Ministers from 1945

Term	Name	Party
1945–53	Alcide de Gasperi	Christian Democratic Party
1953–54	Giuseppe Pella	Christian Democratic Party
1954	Amintore Fanfani	Christian Democratic Party
1954–55	Mario Scelba	Christian Democratic Party
1955–57	Antonio Segni	Christian Democratic Party
1957–58	Adone Zoli	Christian Democratic Party
1958–59	Amintore Fanfani	Christian Democratic Party
1959–60	Antonio Segni	Christian Democratic Party
1960	Fernando Tambroni	Christian Democratic Party
1960–63	Amintore Fanfani	Christian Democratic Party
1963	Giovanni Leone	Christian Democratic Party
1963–68	Aldo Moro	Christian Democratic Party
1968	Giovanni Leone	Christian Democratic Party
1968–70	Mariano Rumor	Christian Democratic Party
1970–72	Emilio Colombo	Christian Democratic Party
1972–73	Giulio Andreotti	Christian Democratic Party
1973–74	Mariano Rumor	Christian Democratic Party
1974–76	Aldo Moro	Christian Democratic Party
1976–79	Giulio Andreotti	Christian Democratic Party
1979–80	Francesco Cossiga	Christian Democratic Party
1980–81	Arnaldo Forlani	Christian Democratic Party
1981–82	Giovanni Spadolini	Republican Party
1982–83	Amintore Fanfani	Christian Democratic Party
1983–87	Benedetto (Bettino) Craxi	Socialist Party
1987	Amintore Fanfani	Christian Democratic Party
1987–88	Giovanni Goria	Christian Democratic Party
1988–89	Ciriaco de Mita	Christian Democratic Party
1989–92	Giulio Andreotti	Christian Democratic Party
1992–93	Giuliano Amato	Socialist Party
1993–94	Carlo Azeglio Ciampi	Christian Democratic Party
1994–95	Silvio Berlusconi	Freedom Alliance
1995–96	Lamberto Dini	independent
1996–98	Romano Prodi	Olive Tree Alliance
1998–	Massimo D'Alema	Democrats of the Left

Japanese Prime Ministers from 1945

Term	Name	Party
1945–46	Kijurō Shidehara	coalition
1946–47	Shigeru Yoshida	Liberal
1947–48	Tetsu Katayama	coalition
1948	Hitoshi Ashida	Democratic
1948–54	Shigeru Yoshida	Liberal
1954–56	Ichirō Hatoyama	Liberal[1]
1956–57	Tanzan Ishibashi	LDP
1957–60	Nobusuke Kishi	LDP
1960–64	Hayato Ikeda	LDP
1964–72	Eisaku Satō	LDP
1972–74	Kakuei Tanaka	LDP
1974–76	Takeo Miki	LDP
1976–78	Takeo Fukuda	LDP
1978–80	Masayoshi Ohira	LDP
1980–82	Zenkō Suzuki	LDP
1982–87	Yasuhiro Nakasone	LDP
1987–89	Noboru Takeshita	LDP
1989	Sōsuke Uno	LDP
1989–91	Toshiki Kaifu	LDP
1991–93	Kiichi Miyazawa	LDP
1993–94	Morohiro Hosokawa	JNP-led coalition
1994	Tsutoma Hata	Shinseito-led coalition
1994–96	Tomiichi Murayama	SDPJ-led coalition
1996–98	Ryutaro Hashimoto	LDP
1998–	Keizo Obuchi	LDP

[1] The conservative parties merged in 1955 to form the Liberal Democratic Party (LDP, Jiyū-Minshūtō).

Kenyan Presidents from 1963

Term	Name	Party
1963–78	Jomo Kenyatta	Kenya African National Union (KANU)
1978–	Daniel arap Moi	KANU

Italian Kings from 1861

Reign	Name
1861–78	Victor Emmanuel II
1878–1900	Umberto I
1900–46	Victor Emmanuel III
1946	Umberto II (abdicated)

Japanese Emperors

Japanese chronology does not always match the emperor's reign dates. Rather, it is marked by occurrences, such as significant political events, military gains, and natural disasters.

(Date in parentheses = date of enthronement, when later than date of accession.)

Reign dates[1]		Name	Reign dates[1]		Name
Probable	Traditional		Probable	Traditional	
Legendary and Yamato Period 40 BC–592 AD			Heian Period 794–1192		
40–10 BC	660–585 BC	Jimmu	781–806		Kammu
10 BC–AD 20	581–49 BC	Suizei	806–09		Heizei
20–50	549–11 BC	Annei	809–23		Saga
50–80	510–477 BC	Itoku	823–33		Junna
80–110	475–393 BC	Kōshō	833–50		Nimmyō
110–40	392–291 BC	Kōan	850–58		Montoku
140–70	290–15 BC	Kōrei	858–76		Seiwa
170–200	214–158 BC	Kōgen	876–84		Yōzei
200–30	157–98 BC	Kaika	884–87		Kōkō
230–58	97–30 BC	Sujin	887–97		Uda
259–90	29 BC–70 AD	Suinin	897–930		Daigo
291–323	71–130	Keikō	930–46		Suzaku
323–56	131–90	Seimu	946–67		Murakami
356–62	192–200	Chūai	967–69		Reizei
363–80	201–269	Jingū Kōgō (regent)	969–84		En'yū
380–95	270–310	Ōjin	984–86		Kazan
395–428	313–99	Nintoku	986–1011		Ichijō
428–33	400–05	Richū	1011–16		Sanjō
433–38	406–10	Hanzei	1016–36		Go-Ichijō
438–55	412–53	Ingyō	1036–45		Go-Suzaku
455–57	454–56	Ankō	1045–68		Go-Reizei
457–90	457–79	Yūryaku	1068–73		Go-Sanjō
490–95	480–84	Seinei	1073–87		Shirakawa (1086–1129
495–98	485–87	Kenzō			cloistered rule)
498–504	488–98	Ninken	1087–1107		Horikawa
504–10	499–506	Buretsu	1107–23	(1108)	Toba (1129–56 cloistered
510–34	507–31	Keitai			rule)
534–36	531–35	Ankan	1123–42		Sutoku
536–39	535–39	Senka	1142–55		Konoe
539–71		Kimmei	1155–58		Go-Shirakawa (1158–92
572–85		Bidatsu			cloistered rule)
585–87		Yomei	1158–65	(1159)	Nijō
587–92		Sushun	1165–68		Rokujō
Asuka Period 592–710			1168–80		Takakura
593–628		Suiko (empress)	1180–85		Antoku
629–41		Jomei	Kamakura Period 1192–1333		
642–45		Kōgyoku (empress)	1183–98	(1184)	Go-Toba
645–54		Kōtoku	1198–1210		Tsuchimikado
655–61		Saimei (empress)	1210–21	(1211)	Juntoku
661–72	(668)	Tenji	1221		Chūkyō
672		Kōbun	1221–32	(1222)	Go-Horikawa
672–86	(673)	Temmu	1232–42	(1233)	Shijō
686–97	(690)	Jitō (empress)	1242–46		Go-Saga
697–707		Mommu	1246–60		Go-Fukakusa
Nara Period 710–794			1260–74		Kameyama
707–15		Gemmei (empress)	1274–87		Go-Uda
715–24		Genshō (empress)	1287–98		Fushimi
724–49		Shōmu	1298–1301		Go-Fushimi
749–58		Kōken (empress)	1301–08		Go-Nijo
758–64		Junnin	1308–18		Hanazono
764–70		Shōtoku (empress)	Edo Period 1603–1867		
770–81		Kōnin	1586–1611	(1587)	Go-Yōzei
Namboku Period 1334–92[2]			1611–29		Go-Mizunoo
The Southern Court			1629–43	(1630)	Meishō (empress)
1318–39		Go-Daigo			
1339–68		Go-Murakami			

Reign dates[1]		Name	Reign dates[1]		Name
Probable	Traditional		Probable	Traditional	
1368–83		Chōkei	1643–54		Go-Kōmyō
1383–92		Go-Kameyama	1655–63	(1656)	Gosai
The Northern Court			1663–87		Reigen
1331–33	(1332)	Kōgon	1687–1709		Higashiyama
1336–48	(1338)	Kōmyō	1709–35	(1710)	Nakamikado
1348–51	(1350)	Sukō	1735–47		Sakuramachi
1351–71	(1354)	Go-Kōgon	1747–62		Momozono
1371–82	(1375)	Go-En'yū	1762–71	(1763)	Go-Sakuramachi
Muromachi Period 1392–1573[3]					(empress)
1382–1412	(1392)	Go-Komatsu	1771–79		Go-Momozono
1412–28	(1415)	Shōkō	1780–1817		Kōkaku
1428–64	(1430)	Go-Hanazono	1817–46		Ninkō
1464–1500	(1466)	Go-Tsuchimikado	1846–67	(1847)	Kōmei
1500–26	(1521)	Go-Kashiwabara	Meiji Period 1868–1912		
1526–57	(1536)	Go-Nara	1867–1912	(1868)	Meiji (Mutsuhito)
Momoyama Period 1573–1603			Taisho Period 1912–26		
1557–86	(1560)	Ōgimachi	1912–26	(1915)	Taisho (Yoshihito)
			Showa Period 1926–89		
			1926–89	(1928)	Showa (Hirohito)
			1989–		Heisei Akihito

[1] Reign dates for the first 28 emperors are the subject of some doubt and speculation. The traditional view, upon which the National Calendar is based, places the accession of Jimmu at 660 BC. Modern research approximates the date to be much later at c. 40 BC. Both probable and traditional dates are given until 539.

[2] Although the Southern Court was set up in exile, it retained the imperial regalia and is considered to be the legitimate line.

[3] The Muromachi Period begins with the unification of the Southern and Northern Courts in 1392.

Longest Reigning Monarchs

As of 1998

Rank	Name	Country	Reign	Years
1	King Mihti	Arakan (Myanmar)	c. 1279–1374	95[1]
2	Pharaoh Phiops (Pepi) II	Egypt (Neferkare)	c. 2269–2175 BC	94[1]
3	King Louis XIV	France	1643–1715	72
4	Prince Johannes II	Liechtenstein	1858–1929	71
5	King Harald I	Norway	c. 870–940	70
6	Emperor Franz Josef	Austria	1848–1916	68
7	Queen Victoria	Great Britain	1837–1901	63
8	Emperor Hirohito (Showa)	Japan	1926–89	62
9	Emperor Kangxi	China	1661–1722	61
10	Emperor Qianlong	China	1735–96	60
11=	King George III	Great Britain	1760–1820	59
11=	King Louis XV	France	1715–74	59
11=	King Christian IV	Denmark	1588–1648	59
11=	Prince Honore III	Monaco	1733–93	59
15=	Emperor Pedro II	Brazil	1831–89	58
15=	Queen Wilhelmina	Netherlands	1890–1948	58
17	King Henry III	England	1216–72	56
18	King Sisavang Vong	Laos (Luang Prabang)	1904–59	55
19	Sultan Shaikh Isa bin Ali al-Khalifa	Bahrain	1869–1923	54
20	King Eric III	Norway	1389–1442	53
21=	King Boleslaw V	Poland	1227–79	52
21=	Shah Tahmasp I	Iran (Persia)	1524–76	52
21=	King Bhumibol Adulyadej (Rama IX)	Thailand	1946–	52
24	Shogun Ienari Tokugawa	Japan	1787–1838	51
25=	King Georgios I	Greece	1863–1913	50
25=	Sultan Said bin Sultan	Oman	1806–1856	50

[1] The historical evidence to authenticate the length of these reigns is fragmented.

Mexican Presidents from 1946

Term	Name	Party
1946–52	Miguel Alemán Valdés	Institutional Revolutionary Party
1952–58	Adolfo Ruiz Cortines	Institutional Revolutionary Party
1958–64	Adolfo López Mateos	Institutional Revolutionary Party
1964–70	Gustavo Díaz Ordaz	Institutional Revolutionary Party
1970–76	Luís Echeverría Alvarez	Institutional Revolutionary Party
1976–82	José López Portillo y Pacheco	Institutional Revolutionary Party
1982–88	Miguel de la Madrid Hurtado	Institutional Revolutionary Party
1988–94	Carlos Salinas de Gortari	Institutional Revolutionary Party
1994–	Ernesto Zedillo Ponce de Léon	Institutional Revolutionary Party

Dutch Monarchs from 1806

Reign	Name
1806–10	Lodewijk I
1810	Lodewijk II
1810–13	French annexation
1813–15	Provisional government
1815–40	Willem I
1840–49	Willem II
1849–90	Willem III
1890–1940	Wilhelmina
1940–45	German occupation
1945–48	Wilhelmina
1948–80	Juliana
1980–	Beatrix

Dutch Prime Ministers from 1945

Term	Name	Party
1945	Pieter Gerbrandy	Anti-Revolutionary Party
1945–46	Willem Schermerhorn	Socialist Party
1946–48	Louis Beel	Catholic Party
1948–58	Willem Drees	Socialist Party
1958–59	Louis Beel	Catholic Party
1959–63	Jan de Quay	Catholic Party
1963–65	Victor Marijnen	Catholic Party
1965–66	Joseph Cals	Catholic Party
1966–67	Jelle Zijlstra	Anti-Revolutionary Party
1967–71	Petrus de Jong	Catholic Party
1971–73	Barend Biesheuvel	Anti-Revolutionary Party
1973–77	Johannes (Joop) den Uyl	Labour Party
1977–82	Andreas van Agt	Christian Democratic Appeal Party
1982–94	Rudolphus (Ruud) Lubbers	Christian Democratic Appeal Party
1994–	Wim Kok	Labour Party

New Zealand Prime Ministers from 1891

Term	Name	Party
1891–93	John Ballance	Liberal
1893–1906	Richard Seddon	Liberal
1906	William Hall-Jones	Liberal
1906–12	Joseph Ward	Liberal
1912	Thomas MacKenzie	Liberal
1912–25	William Massey	Reform
1925–28	Joseph Coates	Reform
1928–30	Joseph Ward	United
1930–35	George Forbes	United
1935–40	Michael Savage	Labour
1940–49	Peter Fraser	Labour
1949–57	Sidney Holland	National
1957	Keith Holyoake	National
1957–60	Walter Nash	Labour
1960–72	Keith Holyoake	National
1972	John Marshall	National
1972–74	Norman Kirk	Labour
1974–75	Wallace Rowling	Labour
1975–84	Robert Muldoon	National
1984–89	David Lange	Labour
1989–90	Geoffrey Palmer	Labour
1990–97	Jim Bolger	National
1997–	Jenny Shipley	National

Nigerian Leaders from 1960

Term	Name	Party
Governor-Generals		
1960	James Robertson	independent
1960–63	Nnamdi Azikiwe	Nigerian National Democratic Party
Presidents[1]		
1963–66	Nnamdi Azikiwe	Nigerian National Democratic Party
1966	Johnson Aguiyi-Ironsi	military
1966–75	Colonel Yakubu Gowon	military
1975–76	Murtala Mohammed	military
1976–79	General Olusegun Obasanjo	military
1979–83	Shehu Shagari	National Party of Nigeria
1983–85	Major General Mohammed Buhari	military
1985–93	Major General Ibrahim Babangida	military
1993	Ernest Shonekan	independent
1993–98	General Sani Abacha	military
1998–99	General Abdusalam Abubakar	military
1999–	Olusegun Obasanjo	People's Democratic Party

[1] Heads of state from January 1966 until October 1979 and from December 1983 did not officially use the title of president.

Norwegian Monarchs from 1905

Reign	Name
1905–40	Haakon VII (exiled)
1940–45	German occupation
1945–57	Haakon VII (restored)
1957–91	Olaf V
1991–	Harald V

Norwegian Prime Ministers from 1945

Term	Name	Party
1945–51	Einar Gerhardsen	Labour Party
1951–55	Oscar Torp	Labour Party
1955–63	Einar Gerhardsen	Labour Party
1963	John Lyng	Conservative Party
1963–65	Einar Gerhardsen	Labour Party
1965–71	Per Borten	Centre Party
1971–72	Trygve Bratteli	Labour Party
1972–73	Lars Korvald	Christian People's Party
1973–76	Trygve Bratteli	Labour Party
1976–81	Odvar Nordli	Labour Party
1981	Gro Harlem Brundtland	Labour Party
1981–86	Kaare Willoch	Conservative Party
1986–89	Gro Harlem Brundtland	Labour Party
1989–90	Jan Syse	Conservative Party
1990–96	Gro Harlem Brundtland	Labour Party
1996–97	Thorbjoern Jagland	Labour Party
1997–	Kjell Magne Bondevik	Christian People's Party

Polish Political Leaders from 1945

Term	Name	Party
Communist Party Leaders[1]		
1945–48	Władysław Gomułka	
1948–56	Bolesław Bierut	
1956	Edward Ochab	
1956–70	Władysław Gomułka	
1970–80	Edward Gierek	
1980–81	Stanisław Kania	
1981–89	Wojciech Jaruzelski	
Presidents		
1990–95	Lech Wałęsa	Solidarity/independent
1995–	Aleksander Kwaśniewski	Democratic Left Alliance

[1]From 1945–90 the political leaders were the Communist Party leaders.

Longest Serving Political Leaders

As of 1998

Rank	Name	Position	Country	Term(s)	Years
1	Jiang Jie Shi	general and president	China and Taiwan	1928–75	47[1]
2	Kim Il Sung	Communist leader	North Korea	1948–94	46
3	Ibrahim Didi	prime minister	Maldives	1883–1925	42
4	Enver Hoxha	Communist leader	Albania	1954–85	40
5	Fidel Castro Ruz	Communist leader	Cuba	1959–	39
6=	Francisco Franco Bahamonde	dictator	Spain	1939–75	36
6=	Antonio de Oliveira Salazar	dictator	Portugal	1932–68	36
6=	Marshal Tito	Communist leader	Yugoslavia	1943–80	36
9=	Todor Zhivkov	Communist leader	Bulgaria	1954–89	35
9=	Alfredo Stroessner	dictator	Paraguay	1954–89	35
11	Omar Bongo	president	Gabon	1964–	34
12	Felix Houphouet-Boigny	president	Côte d'Ivoire	1960–93	33
13	Mobuto Sese Seko	president	Zaire	1965–97	32
14=	Suharto	president	Indonesia	1967–98	31
14=	Habib Bourguiba	president	Tunisia	1956–87	31
14=	Lee Kuan Yew	prime minister	Singapore	1959–90	31
14=	Josef Stalin	Communist leader	Soviet Union (Russia)	1922–53	31
18	John Compton	prime minister	St Lucia	1964–79 and 1982–	30
19=	Vere Bird	prime minister	Antigua and Barbuda	1960–71 and 1976–94	29
19=	Moamer al Khaddhafi	revolutionary leader	Libya	1969–	29
21	Sheikh Khalifa bin-Sulman al-Khalifa	prime minister	Bahrain	1970–	28
22=	William Tubman	president	Liberia	1944–71	27
22=	Kenneth Kaunda	president	Zambia	1964–91	27
22=	Mao Zedong	Communist leader	China	1949–76	27
22=	Klemens von Metternich	chancellor	Austria	1821–48	27

[1]During the late 1930s and 1940s, Jiang was leader in only a small nationalist stronghold portion of China.

South African Prime Ministers and Presidents from 1910

Term	Name
Prime Ministers	
1910–19	L Botha
1919–24	Jan Smuts
1924–39	James Hertzog
1939–48	Jan Smuts
1948–54	Daniel Malan
1954–58	J Strijdon
1958–66	Hendrik Verwoerd
1966–78	Balthazar Johannes Vorster
1978–84	Pieter Botha
Presidents[1]	
1984–89	Pieter Botha
1989–94	F W de Klerk
1994–	Nelson Mandela

[1] The post of prime minister was abolished in 1984 and combined with that of president.

Spanish Rulers 1516–1931

Reign	Name
House of Habsburg	
1516–56	Charles I
1556–98	Philip II
1598–1621	Philip III
1621–65	Philip IV
1665–1700	Charles II
House of Bourbon	
1700–46	Philip V
1746–59	Ferdinand VI
1759–88	Charles III
1788–1808	Charles IV
1808	Ferdinand VII (deposed)
1808–13	Joseph Napoleon[1]
1813–33	Ferdinand VII (restored)
1833–68	Isabel II
1868–70	provisional government
1870–73	Amadeus I[2] (abdicated)
1873–74	first republic
1874–86	Alfonso XII
1886–1931	Alfonso XIII (deposed)

[1] House of Bonaparte.

[2] House of Savoy.

Spanish Presidents, Chiefs of State, and Prime Ministers from 1931

Term	Name	Party	Term	Name	Party
Presidents			1935–36	Manuel Portela	
1931–36	Niceto Alcala Zamora	Liberal Republicans		Valladares	Radical Republican Party
1936	Diego Martinez y Barro	Radical Party	1936	Manuel Azaña y Diéz	Left Republican Party
1936–39	Manuel Azaña y Diéz	Left Republican Party	1936	Santiago Cásares	
Chiefs of State				Quiroga	Left Republican Party
1939–75	Francisco Franco y	National Movement/	1936	José Giral y Pereira	Left Republican Party
	Bahamonde	Falange	1936–37	Francisco Largo	
Prime Ministers				Caballero	Socialist Party
1931–33	Manuel Azaña y Diéz	Left Republican Party	1937–39	Juan Negrin	Socialist Party
1933	Alejandro Lerroux y		1939–73	Francisco Franco	
	García	Radical Republican Party		Bahamonde	National Movement
1933	Diego Martínez y Barro	Radical Republican Party	1973	Luis Carrero Blanco	National Movement
1933–34	Alejandro Lerroux y		1973–74	Torcuato Fernández	
	García	Radical Republican Party		Miranda	National Movement
1934	Ricardo Samper Ibañez	Radical Republican	1974–76	Carlos Arias Navarro	National Movement
		Party–Valencian branch	1976–81	Adolfo Suárez González	Union of the Democratic
1934–35	Alejandro Lerroux y				Centre
	García	Radical Republican Party	1981–82	Leopoldo Calvo-Sotelo	Union of the Democratic
1935	Joaquín Chapaprieta y			y Bustelo	Centre
	Terragosa	independent	1982–96	Felipe González	
				Márquez	Socialist Workers' Party
			1996–	José María Aznar	Popular Party

Swedish Monarchs from 950

Period	Name	Period	Name
950–95	Erik VIII	1464–65	Carl VIII Knutsson
995–1022	Olof	1465–67	Interregnum
1022–50	Anund Jakob	1467–70	Carl VIII Knutsson
1050–60	Edmund	1470–97	Sten Sture the Elder (regent)
1060–80	Stenkil	1497–1501	Johan II
1080–1110	Inge I/Halsten	1501–03	Sten Sture the Elder (regent)
1110–18	Filip	1503–12	Svante Sture (regent)
1118–22	Inge II	1512–20	Sten Sture the Younger (regent)
1130–56	Sverker I	1520–23	Christian II
1150–60	Erik IX Jerdvardsson	1523–60	Gustaf I
1161–67	Carl VII Sverkersson	1560–68	Erik XIV
1167–96	Knut I Eriksson	1568–92	Johan III
1196–1208	Sverker II Carlsson	1592–99	Sigismund
1208–16	Erik X Eriksson	1604–1611	Carl IX
1216–22	Johan I Sverkersson	1611–32	Gustaf II Adolf
1222–29	Erik XI Eriksson	1632–54	Christina
1229–34	Knut II	1654–60	Carl X Gustaf
1234–50	Erik XI Eriksson	1660–97	Carl XI
1250–75	Valdemar	1697–1718	Carl XII
1275–90	Magnus I Laduläs	1718–20	Ulrica Eleonora
1290–1318	Birgir Magnusson	1720–51	Fredrik
1319–56	Magnus II Eriksson	1751–71	Adolf Fredrik
1356–59	Magnus II Eriksson/Eric XII	1771–92	Gustaf III
1359–62	Magnus II Eriksson	1792–1809	Gustaf IV Adolf
1362–63	Magnus II Eriksson/Haakon	1809–18	Carl XIII
1364–89	Albrekt	1818–44	Carl XIV Johan
1389–97	Margrethe	1844–59	Oscar I
1397–1434	Erik XIII	1859–72	Carl XV
1434–36	Regent: Engelbrekt Engelbrektsson	1872–1907	Oscar II
1436–40	Regent: Carl Knutsson	1907–50	Gustaf V
1441–48	Christoffer	1950–73	Gustaf VI Adolf
1448–57	Carl VIII Knutsson	1973–	Carl XVI Gustaf
1457–64	Christian I		

Soviet and Russian Presidents and Communist Party Leaders

Term	Name	Term	Name
USSR			
Communist Party Leaders		1964–65	Anastas Mikoyan
1917–22	Vladimir Ilich Lenin	1965–77	Nikolai Podgorny
1922–53	Joseph Stalin	1977–82	Leonid Brezhnev
1953–64	Nikita Khrushchev	1982–83	Valery Kuznetsov (acting)
1964–82	Leonid Brezhnev	1983–84	Yuri Andropov
1982–84	Yuri Andropov	1984	Valery Kuznetsov (acting)
1984–85	Konstantin Chernenko	1984–85	Konstantin Chernenko
1985–91	Mikhail Gorbachev	1985	Valery Kuznetsov (acting)
Presidents		1985–88	Andrei Gromyko
1917–22	Vladimir Ilich Lenin[1]	1988–91	Mikhail Gorbachev
1919–46	Mikhail Kalinin[2]		
1946–53	Nikolai Shvernik	Russia	
1953–60	Marshal Kliment Voroshilov	Presidents	
1960–64	Leonid Brezhnev	1991–	Boris Yeltsin

[1] In 1917 Lenin was elected chairman of the Council of People's Commisars, that is, head of government. He held that post until 1922.

[2] In 1919, Kalinin became head of state (president of the Central Executive Committee of the Soviet government until 1937; president of the Presidium of the Supreme Soviet until 1946.)

Swedish Prime Ministers from 1946

Term	Name	Party
1946–69	Tage Erlander	Social Democratic Labour Party
1969–76	Olof Palme	Social Democratic Labour Party
1976–78	Thorbjörn Fälldin	Centre Party
1978–79	Ola Ullsten	Liberal Party
1979–82	Thorbjörn Fälldin	Centre Party
1982–86	Olof Palme	Social Democratic Labour Party
1986–91	Ingvar Carlsson	Social Democratic Labour Party
1991–94	Carl Bildt	Moderate Party
1994–96	Ingvar Carlsson	Social Democratic Labour Party
1996–	Göran Persson	Social Democratic Labour Party

United Kingdom Prime Ministers from 1721

Term	Name	Party	Term	Name	Party
1721–42	Sir Robert Walpole	Whig	1868	Benjamin Disraeli	Conservative
1742–43	Earl of Wilmington	Whig	1868–74	W E Gladstone	Liberal
1743–54	Henry Pelham	Whig	1874–80	Benjamin Disraeli	Conservative
1754–56	Duke of Newcastle	Whig	1880–85	W E Gladstone	Liberal
1756–57	Duke of Devonshire	Whig	1885–86	Marquess of Salisbury	Conservative
1757–62	Duke of Newcastle	Whig	1886	W E Gladstone	Liberal
1762–63	Earl of Bute	Tory	1886–92	Marquess of Salisbury	Conservative
1763–65	George Grenville	Whig	1892–94	W E Gladstone	Liberal
1765–66	Marquess of Rockingham	Whig	1894–95	Earl of Rosebery	Liberal
1767–70	Duke of Grafton	Whig	1895–1902	Marquess of Salisbury	Conservative
1770–82	Lord North	Tory	1902–05	Arthur James Balfour	Conservative
1782	Marquess of Rockingham	Whig	1905–08	Sir H Campbell-Bannerman	Liberal
1782–83	Earl of Shelburne	Whig	1908–15	H H Asquith	Liberal
1783	Duke of Portland	coalition	1915–16	H H Asquith	coalition
1783–1801	William Pitt the Younger	Tory	1916–22	David Lloyd George	coalition
1801–04	Henry Addington	Tory	1922–23	Andrew Bonar Law	Conservative
1804–06	William Pitt the Younger	Tory	1923–24	Stanley Baldwin	Conservative
1806–07	Lord Grenville	coalition	1924	Ramsay MacDonald	Labour
1807–09	Duke of Portland	Tory	1924–29	Stanley Baldwin	Conservative
1809–12	Spencer Perceval	Tory	1929–31	Ramsay MacDonald	Labour
1812–27	Earl of Liverpool	Tory	1931–35	Ramsay MacDonald	national coalition
1827	George Canning	coalition	1935–37	Stanley Baldwin	national coalition
1827–28	Viscount Goderich	Tory	1937–40	Neville Chamberlain	national coalition
1828–30	Duke of Wellington	Tory	1940–45	Sir Winston Churchill	coalition
1830–34	Earl Grey	Tory	1945–51	Clement Attlee	Labour
1834	Viscount Melbourne	Whig	1951–55	Sir Winston Churchill	Conservative
1834–35	Sir Robert Peel	Whig	1955–57	Sir Anthony Eden	Conservative
1835–41	Viscount Melbourne	Whig	1957–63	Harold Macmillan	Conservative
1841–46	Sir Robert Peel	Conservative	1963–64	Sir Alec Douglas-Home	Conservative
1846–52	Lord Russell	Liberal	1964–70	Harold Wilson	Labour
1852	Earl of Derby	Conservative	1970–74	Edward Heath	Conservative
1852–55	Lord Aberdeen	Peelite	1974–76	Harold Wilson	Labour
1855–58	Viscount Palmerston	Liberal	1976–79	James Callaghan	Labour
1858–59	Earl of Derby	Conservative	1979–90	Margaret Thatcher	Conservative
1859–65	Viscount Palmerston	Liberal	1990–97	John Major	Conservative
1865–66	Lord Russell	Liberal	1997–	Tony Blair	Labour
1866–68	Earl of Derby	Conservative			

Chronological Index

1868
Alain
Alessandri Palma, Arturo
Alvear, Marcelo Torcuato de
Bourassa, Henri
Constantine I
Du Bois, W(illiam) E(dward) B(urghardt)
Fuad I
Garner, John Nance
Horthy, Miklós Horthy de Nagybánya
Markievicz, Constance Georgina, Countess
    Markievicz
Maurras, Charles Marie Photius
Nicholas II
Nitti, Francesco Saverio

1869
Aguinaldo, Emilio
Carmona, Antonio
Chamberlain, (Arthur) Neville
Clynes, John Robert
Forbes, George William
Gandhi, Mahatma
Goldman, Emma
Goldstein, Vida Jane Mary
Hamilton, Alice
Haywood, William Dudley
Lange, Christian Louis
Largo Caballero, Francisco
Sastri, V(alangunian) S(ankarana-Rayana) Srinvasa
Victor Emmanuel III
Wheatley, John

1870
Baruch, Bernard Mannes
Belloc, (Joseph) Hilaire (René Pierre)
Bennett, Richard Bedford
Cardozo, Benjamin Nathan
Childers, (Robert) Erskine
Connolly, James
Das, Chitta Ranjan
Hamaguchi, Osachi
Jones, Thomas
Krasin, Leonid Borisovich
Lenin, Vladimir Ilyich
Luxemburg, Rosa
Metaxas, Ioannis
Primo de Rivera, Miguel, Marqués de Estella
Runciman, Walter, 1st Viscount Runciman
Samuel, Herbert Louis
Smuts, Jan Christian
Struve, Petr Berngardovich

1871
Badoglio, Pietro
Baker, Newton Diehl
Browder, Earl Russell
Céspedes, Carlos Manuel de
Chamorro Vargas, Emiliano

Craig, James, 1st Viscount Craigavon
Ebert, Friedrich
Hull, Cordell
Huysmans, Camille
Johnson, James Weldon
Kotoku, Shusui
Lebrun, Albert
Liebknecht, Karl
Machado y Morales, Gerardo
Radić, Stjepan
Rasputin
Sturzo, Luigi

1872
Hill, Joe
Aurobindo Ghose
Birkenhead, F(rederick) E(dwin) Smith
Blum, Léon
Coolidge, (John) Calvin
Davison, Emily Wilding
Griffith, Arthur
Haakon VII
Hacha, Emil
Hailsham, Douglas McGarel Hogg, 1st Viscount and
    Baron
Hand, Learned Billings
Herriot, Edouard
Khan, Habibullah
Kollontai, Alexandra Mikhailovna
Muir, John Ramsay Brice
Palmer, A(lexander) Mitchell
Phan Chau Trinh
Rathbone, Eleanor Florence
Russell, Bertrand Arthur William
Savage, Michael Joseph
Shidehara, Kijuro
Stone, Harlan Fiske

1873
Ali, Maulana Shaukat
Amery, Leo(pold Charles Maurice Stennett)
Bondfield, Margaret Grace
Bonomi, Ivanoe
Chernov, Viktor Mikhailovich
Green, William
Haq, Fazlul
Kallio, Kyosti
Lunacharski, Anatoli Vasilievich
Madero, Francisco Indalecio
Martov, Yuly Osipovich
Morrow, Dwight Whitney
Sforza, Carlo
Simon, John Allsebrook, 1st Viscount Simon
Smith, Al(fred Emanuel)
Spencer, George Alfred
Terra, Gabriel
Zhang Zuolin

Hiratsuka, Raicho
Kirov, Sergei Mironovich
Kun, Béla
Masaryk, Jan Garrigue
Murray, Philip
Nicolson, Harold George
Schuman, Robert Jean-Baptiste Nicolas
Thalmann, Ernst
Zhu De

1887

Bonham-Carter, (Helen) Violet
Canaris, Wilhelm Franz
Chiang Kai-shek
Citrine, Walter McLennan Citrine, 1st Baron
Dalton, (Edward) Hugh (John Neale)
Gálvez, Juan Manuel
Garvey, Marcus (Moziah)
Grau San Martín, Ramón
Hillman, Sidney
Jiang Jie Shi
Katayama, Tetsu
Landon, Alf(red Mossman)
McNaughton, Andrew George Latta
Massey, (Charles) Vincent
Mola Vidal, Emilio
Montgomery, Bernard Law
Pritt, Denis Nowell
Quisling, Vidkun Abraham Lauritz Jonsson
Röhm, Ernst
Roy, Manabendra Nath

1888

Alexander I, Karageorgevich (of Yugoslavia)
Azad, Maulana Abul Kalam
Brookeborough, Basil Stanlake Brooke, Viscount
   Brookeborough
Bukharin, Nikolai Ivanovich
Dulles, John Foster
Es-Sa'id, Nuri
Homma, Masaharu
Kennedy, Joseph (Patrick)
Koo, Vi Kyuin Wellington
Lawrence, T(homas) E(dward)
Li Dazhao
Monnet, Jean
Morrison, Herbert Stanley
Moses, Robert
Papandreou, George
Radhakrishnan
Schmitt, Carl
Vanzetti, Bartolomeo
Wallace, Henry Agard

1889

Akhmatova, Anna
Chaplin, Charlie (Charles Spencer)
Cole, G(eorge) D(ouglas) H(oward)
Cripps, (Richard) Stafford

Freyberg, Bernard Cyril
Hitler, Adolf
Idris I
Leadbelly (Ledbetter, Huddie William)
Lippmann, Walter
Nehru, Jawaharlal
Noel-Baker, Philip John, Baron Noel-Baker
Randolph, Asa Philip
Reith, John Charles Walsham, 1st Baron
Salazar, António de Oliveira
Sobhuza I
Street, Jessie Mary Grey
Taft, Robert Alphonso

1890

Callaghan, Daniel J
Casey, Richard Gardiner
Collins, Michael
Cooper, (Alfred) Duff
Deakin, Arthur
de Gaulle, Charles André Joseph Marie
Douglas, Marjory Stoneman
Eisenhower, Dwight David ('Ike')
Flynn, Elizabeth Gurley
Forde, Frank (Francis Michael)
George II (of Greece)
Griffiths, James
Herbert, A(lan) P(atrick)
Ho Chi Minh
Hopkins, Harry Lloyd
Ley, Robert
Macphail, Agnes
Molotov, Vyacheslav Mikhailovich
Quirino, Elpidio
Soong Ching-ling
Vinson, Frederick Moore

1891

Albizu Campos, Pedro
Costello, John
Dönitz, Karl
Gramsci, Antonio
Harriman, (William) Averell
Hu Shi
Konoe, Fumimaro, Prince
Low, David Alexander Cecil
McKell, William John
Nenni, Pietro
Raczyński, Edward
Rommel, Erwin Johannes Eugen
Ruiz Cortinez, Adolfo
Sacco, (Ferdinando) Nicola
Segni, Antonio
Todt, Fritz
Trujillo Molina, Rafael Leónidas
Warren, Earl
Wilkinson, Cecily Ellen
Wright, Louis Tompkins

Ward, Barbara
Willis, Ted
Zahir Shah, Muhammad

1915
Cato, (Robert) Milton
Dayan, Moshe
Dellinger, David
Eban, Abba
Echandi Jiménez, Mario
Greenglass, Ethel
Hu Yaobang
Keïta, Modibo
Mantanzima, Kaiser
Mazumdar, Charu
Méndez Montenegro, Julio César
Miller, Arthur
Pinochet (Ugarte), Augusto
Profumo, John Dennis
Robinson, Ray (Arthur Napoleon Raymond)
Shamir, Yitzhak Yernitsky
Shriver, (Robert) Sargent, Jr
Smith, Arnold Cantwell
Stewart, Potter
Strauss, Franz Josef
Vorster, John
Yao Yilin

1916
Aung San
Bandaranaike, Sirimavo
Ben Bella, Mohammed Ahmed
Botha, P(ieter) W(illem)
Bradshaw, Robert Llewellyn
Caldera Rodriguez, Rafael
East, Catherine
Heath, Edward (Richard George)
Indritz, Phineas
Lamizana, Sangoulé
Liem Sioe Liong
McCarthy, Eugene Joseph
Mintoff, Dom(inic)
Mitterrand, François
Moro, Aldo
Neave, Airey Middleton Sheffield
Wan Li
West, Morris Langlo
Whitlam, (Edward) Gough
Wilson, (James) Harold
Wright, Peter
Zayed, Sheikh bin Sultan al-Nahyan

1917
Gandhi, Indira Priyadarshani
Gligorov, Kiro
Hardy, Frank (Francis Joseph)
Healey, Denis Winston
Kennedy, John F(itzgerald) ('Jack')
Lowell, Robert Traill Spence, Jr

Lynch, Jack (John Mary)
Marcos, Ferdinand Edralin
Maudling, Reginald
Nakasone, Yasuhiro
Nkomo, Joshua
Park Chung Hee
Quadros, Jânio da Silva
Romero Y Galdames, Oscar Arnulfo
Sánchez Hernández, Fidel
Suzman, Helen Gavronsky
Tambo, Oliver
Vance, Cyrus Roberts
Weinberger, Caspar Willard
Yadin, Yigael
Yahya Khan, Agha Muhammad
Zhang Chunqiao

1918
Agnew, Spiro (Theodore)
Araña Osorio, Carlos
Blaize, Herbert Augustus
Ceauşescu, Nicolae
Crosland, (Charles) Anthony (Raven)
Figueiredo, João Baptista de Oliveiro
Ganilau, Ratu Penaia
Goulart, João
Hamer, Fannie Lou
Herzog, Chaim
Jagan, Cheddi Berret
Joseph, Keith Sinjohn
Mandela, Nelson (Rolihlahla)
Mitsotakis, Constantine
Nahayan, Sheik Sultan bin Zayed al-
Nasser, Gamal Abdel
Nasution, A(bdul) H(aris)
Regan, Donald Thomas
Rosenberg, Julius
Sadat, (Muhammad) Anwar
Schmidt, Helmut Heinrich Waldemar
Tanaka, Kakuei
Taufa'ahau Tupou IV
Waldheim, Kurt
Whitelaw, William Stephen Ian

1919
Andreotti, Giulio
Aylwin, (Azòcar) Patricio
Barrientos Ortuño, René
Boudiaf, Mohamed
Bundy, McGeorge
Carrington, Peter Alexander Rupert
Charles, (Mary) Eugenia
Clerides, Glafkos John
Den Uyl, Joop
Dobrynin, Anatoly Fedorovich
Kuntsler, William
Pahlavi, Muhammad Reza
Papandreou, Andreas

Perón, Evita (María Eva)
Price, George Cadle
San Yu, U
Seeger, Pete
Smith, Ian (Douglas)
Trudeau, Pierre Elliott
Wallace, George Corley
Zhao Ziyang

1920
Abzug, Bella Savitsky
Barber, Anthony Perrinott Lysberg
Barrow, Errol Walton
Ben Barka, Mehdi
Cosgrave, Liam
Farmer, James Leonard
Farouk
Hua Guofeng
Jagan, Janet
Jenkins, Roy Harris
Leary, Timothy
Le Duc Anh
Ligachev, Egor Kuzmich
López Portillo y Pacheco, José
Mara, Ratu Kamisese
Marchais, Georges
Miyazawa, Kiichi
Molyneaux, Jim (James Henry)
Mondlane, Eduardo
Narayanan, Kocheril Raman
Pacheco Areco, Jorge
Pérez de Cuéllar, Javier
Phomvihane, Kaysone
Poujade, Pierre-Marie
Prem Tinsulanonda
Rahman, Sheik Mujibur
Rees, Merlyn
Shultz, George Pratt
Sithole, Ndabaningi
Soames, (Arthur) Christopher (John)
Stevens, John Paul
Weizsäcker, Richard, Baron von
Wojtyła, Karol Józef

1921
Barco Vargas, Virgilio
Bentsen, Lloyd Millard
Bokassa, Jean-Bédel
Dubček, Alexander
Faulkner, (Arthur) Brian (Deane)
Friedan, Betty (Elizabeth, born Goldstein)
Gimbutas, Marija
Glenn, John Herschel, Jr
Helms, Jesse
Karami, Rashid
Khama, Seretse
Lindsay, John (Vliet)

Muldoon, Robert David
Rao, P(amulaparti) V(enkata) Narasimha
Rivera, Julio Adalberto
Sakharov, Andrei Dmitrievich
Siad Barre, Mohamed
Suharto, Thojib I
Thomson of Dundee, George Morgan Thomson
Treurnicht, Andries Petrus
Vaea of Houma

1922
Anderson, John
Ashley, Jack
Belkacem, Krim
Berlinguer, Enrico
Blake, George
Boutros-Ghali, Boutros
Braine, John (Gerard)
Choonhavan, Chatichai
Diop, Cheikh Anta
Durán Bellén, Sixto
Echeverría Alvarez, Luis
Ennals, David Hedley
Evers, (James) Charles
Gairy, Eric Matthew
Göncz, Árpád
Heffer, Eric Samuel
Jakeš, Miloš
Kerouac, Jack (Jean Louis)
Lévesque, René
López Arellano, Oswaldo
McGovern, George (Stanley)
Neto, (Antonio) Agostinho
Nyerere, Julius Kambarage
Paley, Grace
Pérez Rodriguez, Carlos Andrés
Pym, Francis Leslie, Baron Pym
Rabin, Yitzhak
Razak, Tun Abdul
Ribeiro, Darcy
Sarkis, Elias
Sauve, Jeanne
Sihanouk, Norodom
Tindemans, Leo
Touré, (Ahmed) Sékou
Tudjman, Franjo
Uno, Sōsuke
Zinn, Howard

1923
Abdel Meguid, Ahmed Esmat
Aidit, D N
Aliyev, Geidar Alirza
Betancur Cuartas, Belisario
Bonner, Yelena
Burnham, (Linden) Forbes (Sampson)
De Roburt, Hammer

Carabillo, Toni
Compton, John George Melvin
Dean, John
Elizabeth II
Fitt, Gerry (Gerard)
FitzGerald, Garret Michael
Foucault, Michel Paul
Galtieri, Leopoldo Fortunato
Ginsberg, (Irwin) Allen
Giscard d'Estaing, Valéry
Haldeman, H(arry) R(obbins)
Howe, (Richard Edward) Geoffrey
Illich, Ivan
Jenkins, (David) Clive
Jiang Zemin
Kirkpatrick, Jeane Duane Jordan
Malcolm X
Paisley, Ian (Richard Kyle)
Reina Idiaquez, Carlos Roberto
Slovo, Joe
Vajpayee, Atal Behari
Vogel, Hans-Jochen
Walters, Alan Arthur

1927

Alfonsín Foulkes, Raúl Ricardo
Armstrong, Robert Temple
Azcona del Hoyo, José Simon
Batt, Philip
Belafonte, Harry
Bhumibol Adulyadej
Boumaza, Bachir
Castro (Ruz), Fidel
Chavez, Cesar Estrada
Cohn, Roy M (Marcus)
Dinkins, David
Genscher, Hans-Dietrich
Gibson, Althea
Kim Young Sam
Mackay of Clashfern, James Peter Hymers Mackay,
   Baron Mackay of Clashfern
Mazowiecki, Tadeusz
Moynihan, Daniel Patrick
Nguyen Thi Binh
Özal, Turgut
Palme, (Sven) Olof Joachim
Perry, William James
Prior, James Michael Leathes, Baron Prior
Ríos Montt, Efraín
Rowling, Bill (Wallace Edward)
Sudharmono
Todd, Ron(ald)
Veil, Simone

1928

Andrade, Mario Pinto de
Angelou, Maya
Badinter, Robert
Belaid, Abdessalem

Bhutto, Zulfikar Ali
Boross, Peter
Brzezinski, Zbigniew
Bulatović, Momir
Buthelezi, Chief Mangosuthu Gatsha
Chomsky, (Avram) Noam
De Mita, Luigi Ciriaco
Fuentes, Carlos
Guevara, Che (Ernesto)
Harrington, Michael
Kabua, Amata
Kane, Sheikh Hamidou
Leone, Giovanni
Le Pen, Jean-Marie
Li Peng
Marsh, Richard William
Mauroy, Pierre
Molina Barraza, Arturo Armando
Mondale, Walter Frederick
Mubarak, Hosni
Primakov, Yevgeny Maksimovich
Ramos, Fidel (Eddie)
Ramphal, Shridath Surendranath ('Sonny')
Rees-Mogg, Lord William
Sabah, Sheik Jabir al-Ahmad al-Jabir al-
Sharon, Ariel
Shevardnadze, Edvard Amvrosievich
Walter, George Herbert
Wiesel, Elie (Eliezer)
Zhu Rongji

1929

Arafat, Yassir
Balladur, Edouard
Bedjaoui, Mohamed
Boothroyd, Betty
Braithwaite, Nicholas
Chadli, Benjedid
Diallo, Boubacar Telli
Doi, Takako
Eisner, Thomas
Ewing, Winnie (Winnifred Margaret)
Foley, Thomas S(tephen)
French, Marilyn
Habermas, Jürgen
Hassan II
Hawke, Bob (Robert James Lee)
Hoyte, (Hugh) Desmond
Karmal, Babrak
Kent, Bruce
King, Martin Luther, Jr
Mayhew, Patrick (Barnabas Burke)
Meri, Lennart
Nujoma, Sam
Onassis, Jacqueline (Jackie Lee)
Rich, Adrienne
Ridley, Nicholas (politician)
Ryzhkov, Nikolai Ivanovich

Saw Maung
Schlüter, Poul Holmskov
Stoutt, Hamilton Lavity
Thorpe, (John) Jeremy
Torrijos Herrera, Omar
Turner, John Napier
Waddington, David Charles

1930
Habré, Hissène
Achebe, Chinua (Albert Chinualumogo)
Assad, Hafez al
Baker, James Addison III
Barayi, Elijah
Berrios Martínez, Rubén
Biffen, (William) John
Carlucci, Frank Charles
Chambers, George Michael
Ershad, Hussain Muhammad
Fraser, (John) Malcolm
Garbus, Martin
Hrawi, Elias
Hurd, Douglas (Richard)
Iliescu, Ion
Kohl, Helmut
Kovac, Michal
Laugerud Garcia, Kjell Eugenio
Marcos, Imelda Romualdez
Mboya, Tom (Thomas Joseph)
Menem, Carlos (Saul)
Mobutu, Sese Seko Kuku Ngbeandu Wa Za Banga
O'Connor, Sandra Day
Perot, Ross
Pindling, Lynden (Oscar)
Robertson, Pat (Marion Gordon)
Rocard, Michel
Sanchez de Lozada Bustamente, Gonzalo
Sarney (Costa), José
Seaga, Edward Philip George
Williams, Shirley Vivien Teresa Brittain
Yamani, Ahmad Zaki al-

1931
Acheampong, Ignatius Kutu
Adams, Tom (John Michael)
Cabral, Luiz
Cardoso, Fernando Henrique
Chun Doo-hwan
Flosse, Gaston
Franco, Itamar
Gorbachev, Mikhail Sergeyevich
Gorman, Teresa
Madani, Abassi
Mahomed, Ismail
Meese, Edwin, III
Mitchell, Sonny (James FitzAllen)
Murdoch, (Keith) Rupert
Parkinson, Cecil (Edward)
Perón, (María Estela) Isabel

Rau, Johannes
Rorty, Richard McKay
Saadawi, Nawal al-
Saro-Wiwa, Ken
Singh, Karan
Singh, Vishwanath Pratap
Tebbit, Norman Beresford
Vassiliou, Georgios Vassos
Wolfe, Tom
Yao Wenyuan
Yeltsin, Boris Nikolayevich

1932
Antall, József
Banks, Dennis
Chirac, Jacques René
Cuomo, Mario Matthew
Dini, Lamberto
Falkender, Marcia Matilda
Hattersley, Roy Sydney George
Horn, Gyula
Kaifu, Toshiki
Kennedy, Edward Moore ('Ted')
Kyprianou, Spyros
Landsbergis, Vytautas
Lawson, Nigel
Makeba, Miriam Zenzile
Murdani, Leonardus Benjamin ('Benny')
Nott William Frederick, John
Olter, Bailey
Pérez Esquivel, Adolfo
Reid, James (Jimmy)
Reynolds, Albert
Roh Tae-woo
Rohwedder, Detler
Romero Barceló, Carlos
Suárez González, Adolfo
Thani, Sheikh Khalifa bin Hamad al-
Walker, Peter Edward
Wesker, Arnold
Young, Andrew (Jackson), Jr
Young, David Ivor

1933
Anyaoku, Eleazar Chukwuemeka (Emeka)
Aquino, (Maria) Corazon ('Cory')
Bani-Sadr, Abu'l-Hassan
Biya, Paul
Dukakis, Michael Stanley
Farrakhan, Louis
Feinstein, Dianne
Ginsburg, Ruth Joan Bader
Gowda, H D Deve
Hayden, Bill (William George)
Heseltine, Michael (Ray Dibdin)
Kerekou, Mathieu Ahmed
Khalaf, Salah
Khalifa, Sheikh Isa bin Sulman al-
Leye, Jean-Marie

Momoh, Joseph Saidu
Obasanjo, Olusegun
Obuchi, Keizo
Oumarou, Ide
Pavlov, Valentin
Piercy, Marge
Powell, Colin (Luther)
Sandiford, Erskine Lloyd
Santer, Jacques
Sobchak, Anatoly
Sokomanu, Ati George
Tung Chee-hwa
Vranitzky, Franz
Yanayev, Gennady

1938

Annan, Kofi
Beatrix, (Wilhelmina Armgard)
Bird, Lester B
Buchanan, Pat(rick Joseph)
Chernomyrdin, Viktor Stepanovich
Chuan Leekpai
Claes, Willy
Fowler, (Peter) Norman
Fujimori, Alberto
George, Eddie
Hosokawa, Morishiro
Juan Carlos
Karimov, Islam
Kok, Wim
Kuchma, Leonid
Kuti, Fela Anikulapo
Mkapa, Benjamin William
Muhammed, Murtala Ramat
Muhoho, George Kamau
Ngugi Wa Thiong'o
Owen, David Anthony Llewellyn
Panetta, Leon E(dward)
Prescott, John Leslie
Puapua, Tomasi
Rubin, Jerry
Scargill, Arthur
Smith, John (politician)
Steel, David Martin Scott
Wasmosy Monti, Juan Carlos

1939

Barrios de Chamorro, Violeta
Ahtisaari, Maarti
Atwood, Margaret Eleanor
Berri, Nabih
Brittan, Leon
Brundtland, Gro Harlem
Cavaco Silva, Anibal
Chan, Julius
Chissano, Joaquim
Clark, Joe (Charles Joseph)
Connerly, Ward(ell)
Constantinescu, Emil

Cunningham, John A ('Jack')
Fairbairn, Joyce
Gamsakhurdia, Zviad
Gould, Bryan Charles
Greer, Germaine
Gummer, John Selwyn
Hayden, Tom
Howard, John Winston
Jay, Margaret Ann
Kabila, Laurent-Desiré
Khamenei, Ayatollah Said Ali
Lake, (William) Anthony (Kirsopp)
Lubbers, Rudolph Franz Marie (Ruud)
Means, Russell
Mulroney, Brian
Oz, Amos
Paz Zamora, Jaime
Reno, Janet
Souter, David Hackett
Ulmanis, Gauntis
Waite, Terry (Terence Hardy)

1940

Abbey, Joseph Leo Seko
Archer, Jeffrey Howard
Arias Sanchez, Oscar
Buzek, Jerzy Karol
Clarke, Kenneth Harry
Dehaene, Jean-Luc
de Maizière, Lothar
Dobson, Frank
Esquivel, Manuel
Lucinschi, Petru
Maizière, Lothar de
Margrethe II
Mitchell, Juliet
Nazarbayev, Nursultan
Niyazov, Saparmurad
Noriega Morena, Manuel (Antonio)
Ochs, Phil(ip)
Qaboos bin Said
Roldós Aquilera, Jaime
Royo Sánchez, Arístides
Sampaio, Jorge
Shephard, Gillian Patricia
Snegur, Mircea
Wahid, Abdurrahman
Zappa, Frank (Francis Vincent)

1941

Ashdown, Paddy (Jeremy John Durham)
Babangida, Ibrahim
Baez, Joan
Berisha, Sali
Bossi, Umberto
Brown, (Ronald Harmon) Ron
Carmichael, Stokely

Debray, Régis
Dylan, Bob
Geingob, Hage Gottfried
Gephardt, Richard Andrew
Ghannouchi, Rachid
Goh Chok Tong
Holbrooke, Richard
Howard, Michael
Jackson, Jesse Louis
Klaus, Václav
Kučan, Milan
Lacalle, Luis Alberto
Milošević, Slobodan
Nena, Jacob
Saint Marie, Buffy
Zeroual, Lamine

1942
Ali, Muhammad
Brenton, Howard
Buhari, Muhammadu
Carlot Korman, Maxime
Cerezo Arévalo, Mario Vinicio
de León Carpio, Ramiro
Dos Santos, José Eduardo
Frei Ruiz-Tagle, Eduardo
Gemayel, Amin
González Márquez, Felipe
Gramm, Phil
Hani, Chris (Martin Thembisile)
Jong, Erica Mann
Khaddhafi, Moamer al
Kim Jong Il
Kinnock, Neil Gordon
Lamont, Norman Stewart Hughson
Lange, David Russell
Liberia-Peters, Maria
Lini, Walter Hadye
Mbeki, Thabo
Meciar, Vladimír
Newton, Huey P
Palmer, Geoffrey Winston Russell
Saleh, Ali Abdullah
Salim, Salim Ahmed

1943
Abacha, Sani
Ali, Tariq
Ashe, Arthur (Robert, Jr)
Baader, Andreas
Beckett, Margaret
Callejas Romero, Rafael Leonardo
Chiluba, Frederick
Cubas Grau, Raúl
Gingrich, Newt (Newton Leroy)
Goria, Giovanni
James, Edison C
Kenilorea, Peter (Kauona Keninarais'Ona)
Khasbulatov, Ruslan

Khatami, Sayed Muhammad
King, Billie Jean
Lafontaine, Oskar
Major, John
Mamaloni, Solomon Sunaone
Mladic, Ratko
Muluzi, Bakili
Nakamura, Kuniwo
North, Oliver
Préval, René
Rasmussen, Poul Nyrup
Rowbotham, Sheila
Sassau-Nguesso, Denis
Wałęsa, Lech
Wigley, Dafydd
Woodward, Bob

1944
Akayev, Askar
Bashir, Omar Hassan Ahmad al-
Bernstein, Carl
Bishop, Maurice
Davis, Angela Yvonne
Gambari, Ibrahim Agboola
Gandhi, Rajiv
Giuliani, Rudolph W
Hariri, Rafik al-
Keating, Paul John
Leakey, Richard Erskine Frere
Mendes, Chico (Filho Francisco)
Patten, Chris(topher Francis)
Robinson, Mary
Rugova, Ibrahim
Schroeder, Gerhard
Smith, Tommie
Trimble, David
Walker, Alice Malsenior
Zyuganov, Gennadi Andreyevich

1945
Birendra, Bir Bikram Shah Dev
Carlos, John
Clodumar, Kinza
Cohn-Bendit, Daniel
Firestone, Shulamith
Garang, John
Inácio da Silva, Luiz
Juppé, Alain Marie
Karadžić, Radovan
Koroma, Alhaji Abdul Karim
Kumaratunga, Chandrika Bandaranaike
Livingstone, Ken(neth)
Museveni, Yoweri Kaguta
Ortega Saavedra, Daniel
Serrano Elias, Jorge
Suu Kyi, Aung San
Ter-Petrossian, Levon Akopovich
Young, Neil
Zia, Begum Khaleda

Index by Country

Individuals appear under the current name of the country with which they were mainly associated.

Fadden, Artie (Arthur William)
Fisher, Andrew
Forde, Frank (Francis Michael)
Forrest, John
Franklin, (Stella Marian Sarah) Miles
Fraser, (John) Malcolm
Gair, Vinc(ent) Clair
Goldstein, Vida Jane Mary
Gorton, John Grey
Greer, Germaine
Hardy, Frank (Francis Joseph)
Hawke, Bob (Robert James Lee)
Hayden, Bill (William George)
Henry, Alice
Holt, Harold Edward
Howard, John Winston
Hughes, Billy (William Morris)
Keating, Paul John
Kerr, John Robert
Lane, William
Lang, Jack (John Thomas)
Lyons, Joseph Aloysius
McEwen, Jack (John)
McKell, William John
McMahon, William
McManus, Francis Patrick Vincent
Menzies, Robert Gordon
Murdoch, (Keith) Rupert
Murray, (John) Hubert (Plunkett)
O'Malley, King
Page, Earle Christmas Grafton
Playford, Thomas
Reid, George Houstoun
Scott, Rose
Scullin, James Henry
Spence, William Guthrie
Street, Jessie Mary Grey
Watson, John Christian
West, Morris Langlo
Whitlam, (Edward) Gough
Wootten, George Frederick

Austria

Aehrenthal, Count Aloys von
Conrad, Franz Xaver Josef
Dollfuss, Engelbert
Eichmann, (Karl) Adolf
Herzl, Theodor
Illich, Ivan
Kaltenbrunner, Ernst
Kreisky, Bruno
Schuschnigg, Kurt von
Seipel, Ignaz
Seyss-Inquart, Arthur
Vranitzky, Franz
Waldheim, Kurt

Azerbaijan

Aliyev, Geidar Alirza

Bahamas

Ingraham, Hubert A
Pindling, Lynden (Oscar)

Bahrain

Khalifa, Sheikh Isa bin Sulman al-

Bangladesh

Ershad, Hussain Muhammad
Hasina Wazed, Sheika
Nasrin, Taslima
Rahman, Sheik Mujibur
Zia, Begum Khaleda

Barbados

Adams, Grantley Herbert
Adams, Tom (John Michael)
Arthur, Owen S
Barrow, Errol Walton
Sandiford, Erskine Lloyd

Belaruss

Lukashenko, Aleksandr Grigorevich
Shushkevich, Stanislav

Belgium

Claes, Willy
Dehaene, Jean-Luc
Huysmans, Camille
Hymans, Paul
Leopold III
Martens, Wilfried
Spaak, Paul-Henri
Tindemans, Leo

Belize

Esquivel, Manuel
Price, George Cadle

Benin

Kerekou, Mathieu Ahmed
Soglo, Nicéphore

Bermuda

Swan, John William David

Bolivia

Banzer Suárez, Hugo
Barrientos Ortuño, René
Montes, Ismael
Paz, (Estenssoro) Victor
Paz Zamora, Jaime

Ríos Montt, Efraín
Serrano Elias, Jorge
Ubico Castañeda, Jorge
Ydígoras Fuentes, Miguel

Guinea
Cabral, Amilcar
Cabral, Luiz
Diallo, Boubacar Telli
Touré, (Ahmed) Sékou

Guyana
Burnham, (Linden) Forbes (Sampson)
Hoyte, (Hugh) Desmond
Jagan, Cheddi Berret
Jagan, Janet
Ramphal, Shridath Surendranath ('Sonny')

Haiti
Aristide, Jean-Bertrand
Bornó, (Joseph) Louis
Duvalier, François
Duvalier, Jean-Claude
Estimé, Dumarsais
Lescot, Élie
Préval, René
Vincent, Sténio (Joseph)

Honduras
Azcona del Hoyo, José Simon
Callejas Romero, Rafael Leonardo
Carías Andino, Tiburcio
Flores Facussé, Carlos Roberto
Gálvez, Juan Manuel
López Arellano, Oswaldo
Reina Idiaquez, Carlos Roberto
Villeda Morales, Ramón

Hungary
Antall, József
Boross, Peter
Göncz, Árpád
Horn, Gyula
Horthy, Miklós Horthy de Nagybánya
Kádár, János
Kun, Béla
Lukács, Georg
Mannheim, Karl
Mindszenty, József
Nagy, Imre
Nyers, Rezso
Pozsgay, Imre
Teller, Edward
Tisza, Istvan

Iceland
Oddsson, David

India
Abdullah, Sheik Muhammad

Aga Khan III
Ali, Maulana Muhammad
Ali, Maulana Shaukat
Aurobindo Ghose
Azad, Maulana Abul Kalam
Basu, Jyoti
Bhindranwale, Sant Jarnail Singh
Bose, Subhas Chandra
Das, Chitta Ranjan
Desai, Morarji Ranchhodji
Fateh Singh, Sant
Gandhi, Indira Priyadarshani
Gandhi, Mahatma
Gandhi, Rajiv
Gokhale, Gopal Krishna
Golwalkar, Madhavrao Sadashivrao
Gowda, H D Deve
Haq, Fazlul
Krishna Menon, Vengalil Krishnan
Lajpat Rai, Lala
Mazumdar, Charu
Mehta, Pherozeshah Merwanji
Naidu, Sarojini
Namboodiripad, Elamkulam Manakkal Sankaran (EMS)
Narayan, Jaya Prakash
Narayanan, Kocheril Raman
Nehru, Jawaharlal
Nehru, Motilal
Pal, Bipin Chandra
Pandit, Vijaya Lakshmi
Patel, Sardar Vallabhbhai Javerabhai
Prasad, Rajendra
Radhakrishnan
Rao, P(amulaparti) V(enkata) Narasimha
Roy, Manabendra Nath
Sastri, V(alangunian) S(ankarana-Rayana) Srinvasa
Shastri, Lal Bahadur
Sikandar Hayat Khan
Singh, Karan
Singh, Vishwanath Pratap
Tagore, Rabindranath
Tilak, Bal Gangadhar
Vajpayee, Atal Behari
Wacha Dinshaw Edulji

Indonesia
Aidit, D N
Habibie, Bacharuddin Jusuf
Hasan, Mohammad ('Bob')
Hatta, Mohammad
Liem Sioe Liong
Murdani, Leonardus Benjamin ('Benny')
Murtopo, Ali
Nasution, A(bdul) H(aris)
Natsir, Mohammad
Pramoedya Ananta Toer

Grandi, Dino, Count
John XXIII
Leone, Giovanni
Longo, Luigi
Matteotti, Giacomo
Moro, Aldo
Mosca, Gaetano
Mussolini, Benito Amilcare Andrea
Nenni, Pietro
Nitti, Francesco Saverio
Orlando, Vittorio Emanuele
Pareto, Vilfredo
Paul VI, Giovanni Battista Montini
Pius XII
Rocco, Alfredo
Rossoni, Edmondo
Scialoja, Vittorio
Segni, Antonio
Sforza, Carlo
Sonnino, (Giorgio) Sidney, Baron Sonnino
Spinelli, Altiero
Sturzo, Luigi
Togliatti, Palmiro
Victor Emmanuel III

Jamaica
Bustamante, (William) Alexander
Garvey, Marcus (Moziah)
Manley, Michael (Norman)
Manley, Norman Washington
Patterson, Percival
Seaga, Edward Philip George

Japan
Anami, Korechika
Asanuma, Inejiro
Doi, Takako
Fukuda, Takeo
Hamaguchi, Osachi
Hara, Kei
Hashimoto, Ryutaro
Hatoyama, Ichiro
Hiratsuka, Raicho
Hirohito
Homma, Masaharu
Hosokawa, Morishiro
Ichikawa, Fusaye
Ikeda, Hayato
Inukai, Tsuyoshi
Itagaki, Taisuke
Itō, Hirobumi
Kaifu, Toshiki
Katayama, Sen
Katayama, Tetsu
Katō, Taka-akira
Katsura, Tarō
Kawakami, Hajime
Kishi, Nobusuke

Kita, Ikki
Komura, Jutaro
Konoe, Fumimaro, Prince
Kotoku, Shusui
Matsudaira, Tsuneo
Matsuoka, Yosuke
Meiji, Mutsuhito
Miyamoto, Kenji
Miyazawa, Kiichi
Murayama, Tomiichi
Nakasone, Yasuhiro
Nosaka, Sanzo
Obuchi, Keizo
Okuma, Shigenobu
Osugi, Sakae
Saionji, Kinmochi
Satō, Eisaku
Shidehara, Kijuro
Suzuki, Zenkō
Takeshita, Noboru
Tanaka, Kakuei
Tōjō, Hideki
Tokuda, Kyuichi
Uno, Sōsuke
Yamagata, Aritomo
Yamamoto, Gombei
Yoshida, Shigeru

Jordan
Abdullah ibn Hussein
Hussein ibn Talal

Kazakhstan
Kunaev, Dimmukhamed Akhmedovich
Nazarbayev, Nursultan

Kenya
Kenyatta, Jomo
Leakey, Richard Erskine Frere
Mboya, Tom (Thomas Joseph)
Moi, Daniel arap
Muhoho, George Kamau
Ngugi Wa Thiong'o

Kiribati
Tabai, Ieremia T
Tito, Teburoro

Korea
Kim Il Sung
Kim Jong Il
Chun Doo-hwan
Kim Dae Jung
Kim Young Sam
Park Chung Hee
Rhee, Syngman
Roh Tae-woo

Kuwait
Sabah, Sheik Jabir al-Ahmad al-Jabir al-

Atassi, Hashem al-
Bitar, Salah Eddin

Taiwan
Jiang Qing-guo
Lee Teng-hui

Tajikistan
Rakhmanov, Imamali

Tanzania
Mkapa, Benjamin William
Mwinyi, Ali Hassan
Nyerere, Julius Kambarage
Salim, Salim Ahmed

Thailand
Bhumibol Adulyadej
Choonhavan, Chatichai
Chuan Leekpai
Chulalongkorn
Prem Tinsulanonda

Togo
Eyadema, Etienne Gnassingbé

Tonga
Salote Tupou III, Mafili'o Pilolevu
Taufa'ahau Tupou IV
Vaea of Houma

Trinidad and Tobago
Carmichael, Stokely
Chambers, George Michael
Manning, Patrick Augustus Mervyn
Panday, Basdeo
Robinson, Ray (Arthur Napoleon Raymond)
Williams, Eric

Tunisia
Achour, Habib
Ben Ali, Zine el Abidine
Ben Salah, Ahmed
Ben Youssef, Salah
Bourguiba, Habib ben Ali
Ghannouchi, Rachid
Hachad, Farhat

Turkey
Abd al-Hamid II
Atatürk, Mustafa Kemal. Name assumed 1934 by
    Mustafa Kemal Pasha
Bayer, Mahmud Jelâl
Ciller, Tansu
Demirel, Süleyman
Ecevit, Bülent
Enver Pasha
Gursel, Cemal
Inönü, Ismet
Menderes, Adnan
Özal, Turgut
Yilmaz, A Mesut

Turkmenistan
Niyazov, Saparmurad

Tuvalu
Paeniu, Bikenibeu
Puapua, Tomasi

Uganda
Amin (Dada), Idi
Museveni, Yoweri Kaguta
Mutesa II, Edward Frederick William Wulugembe
    Mutebi
Obote, (Apollo) Milton

Ukraine
Bandera, Stepan
Hrushevsky, Mikhail Sergeevich
Kravchuk, Leonid Makarovych
Kuchma, Leonid

United Arab Emirates
Nahayan, Sheik Sultan bin Zayed al-
Zayed, Sheikh bin Sultan al-Nahyan

United Kingdom
Adams, Gerry (Gerard)
Alexander of Hillsborough, Albert Victor Alexander
Ali, Tariq
Amery, Leo(pold Charles Maurice Stennett)
Archer, Jeffrey Howard
Armstrong, Robert Temple
Ashdown, Paddy (Jeremy John Durham)
Ashley, Jack
Asquith, Herbert Henry
Astor, Nancy
Attlee, Clement (Richard)
Auden, W(ystan) H(ugh)
Baker, Kenneth Wilfrid
Baldwin, Stanley
Balfour, Arthur James
Barber, Anthony Perrinott Lysberg
Barnes, George Nicoll
Beaverbrook, (William) Max(well) Aitken, 1st Baron
    Beaverbrook
Beckett, Margaret
Belloc, (Joseph) Hilaire (René Pierre)
Benn, Tony (Anthony Neil Wedgwood)
Berlin, Isaiah
Besant, Annie, born Wood
Besant, Walter
Bevan, Aneurin (Nye)
Beveridge, William Henry
Bevin, Ernest
Biffen, (William) John
Birkenhead, F(rederick) E(dwin) Smith
Blair, Tony (Anthony Charles Lynton)
Blake, George (spy)